MW00610675

Several years ago, a friend gave me a bound copy of Dr. Daniel's notes on the history of Calvinism and the doctrines of grace. I've kept it nearby ever since. It's one of the most useful and informative resources in my entire library—well written, crystal clear, and thorough without being ponderous. I'm delighted to see this expanded edition in print.

John MacArthur, Senior Pastor, Grace Community Church, Sun Valley, California, President of the Master's Seminary and the Master's University

This invaluable volume is a virtual goldmine containing the rich history and theology of the Reformed truths known as Calvinism. The beauty of this book is its comprehensive breadth and accessible readability that surveys the vast landscape of this immense subject matter. Ever since these pages first appeared years ago, it has been a trusted guide to me to navigate my journey through the many pivotal individuals, strategic movements, and doctrinal issues of biblical Calvinism. No serious student of church history or systematic theology can afford to be without this work in your personal library.

Steven J. Lawson, President, OnePassion Ministries, Dallas, TX

Curt is a proven scholar and a personal devotee of the doctrines to which he gives such careful attention in this book. It does not merely go over the well-known history already present in many volumes (though it does not ignore that) but gives both substance and perspective that is needed today in a time when there is growing renewed interest in these doctrines. I personally hope that you will pursue the opportunity to publish this substantial volume which interacts so thoroughly with Calvinism in its various nuances and denominational expressions.

Tom Nettles, Professor of Church History, The Southern Baptist Theological Seminary, Louisville, Kentucky

There is no doubt that Calvinism (even though John Calvin would abhor the term) has played a critical role in the history of the Christian faith. Amazingly, though, there have been very few studies that have sought to provide a comprehensive overview of both its history and theology. Dr Daniel's survey of the narrative and thought of this influential worldview does just that and does it magisterially. This textbook (for that is what it truly is) is thus very welcome and will be enormously helpful for all who are interested in this tremendous Christian movement.

Michael A. G. Haykin, Chair & professor of Church History, The Southern Baptist Theological Seminary, Louisville, Kentucky

It would be pretty hard to overstate how helpful Curt Daniel's notes on Calvinism have been in my study of historical theology and the Protestant Reformation. He has an uncanny knack for untangling hard theological knots and deftly sweeping away confusion and misunderstanding. I have gained more insight from this volume than from any other book on systematic theology or church history, and yet this is a resource I can (and regularly do) recommend to lay people—even those who are just beginning to study theology seriously. It's rare and refreshing to find a treatise on theology that is so comprehensive and yet so easy to read. This is that book. Get a copy. I promise you will thank me for the recommendation.

Phil Johnson, Executive Director, Grace to You

The History and Theology of Calvinism is a fascinating, tortuous, compelling drama. Curt Daniel, through a lifetime of study, deftly and insightfully sketches the course and essential content of that drama. Daniel understands the variegated nature of Calvinism and ably guides us through the highs and lows of the drama, never failing to engage us with the often-maligned characters and often misunderstood theology that constitute historic Calvinism. This is a book that is vast in its sweep and deep in its analysis. I highly recommend it.

Ian Hamilton, Professor of Systematic Theology, Edinburgh Theological Seminary, Edinburgh, Scotland; and editor, Banner of Truth magazine

Curt Daniel has done extensive research into the history and theology of Calvinism and has written one of the most helpful and readable treatments of Calvinism in print. The comments are fair and irenic, and the book attempts to cover the entire sweep of Calvinism (including much information on Puritanism and other Reformed groups, past and present). It is worth its weight in gold!

Lance Quinn, Senior Pastor, Bethany Bible Church, Thousand Oaks, California

The History and Theology of Calvinism

The History and Theology of Calvinism

Curt Daniel

EP BOOKS

(Evangelical Press) Registered Office: 140 Coniscliffe
Road, Darlington, Co Durham DL3 7RT

www.epbooks.org
admin@epbooks.org

EP Books are distributed in the USA by:

JPL Books
www.jplbooks.com
orders@jplbooks.com

and

100fThose Ltd
www.100fthose.com
sales.us@100fthose.com

British Library Cataloguing in Publication Data

ISBN 978-1-78397-282-1

Printed by Bell and Bain Ltd, Glasgow

Contents
with Brief Summaries

The History of Calvinism

The Theology of Calvinism

The Sovereignty of God

The Five Points of Calvinism

Total Depravity

Foreword by Joel Beeke

You and I are living in a unique time. Relativism and religious tolerance have won the day in our culture. Truth, the world tells us, is whatever you make it out to be. Men and women are encouraged to determine their own identity, their own moral standards, and their own beliefs about God, history, and the afterlife. A god may exist, but that is up to you to decide. Sadly, many professing Christians have been swept away by this tide of postmodern madness.

Yet there is something remarkable happening against this dismal backdrop. By God's grace, we are witnessing a substantial revival of Calvinism in Christ's church around the world. Christians living in this relativistic, "wishy-washy" age are in search of strong, transcendent truths worth living and dying for. And multitudes are discovering such hearty, soul-satisfying truths in Reformed theology.

This revival of Calvinism — though in many places only partial and by no means without shortfalls — is cause for rejoicing and for prayer that God will multiply, purify, and mature it. For the sovereign, gracious God of Reformed theology is nothing more and nothing less than the God of the Bible. He is the true and living God who created and rules over you and me. And when many are coming to see and savor Him in His majestic splendor and beauty, we ought to rejoice!

I trust, in God's providence, that such rejoicing will be the result of Christians reading this helpful work by my good friend, Curt Daniel. *The History and Theology of Calvinism* is a gold mine for those wanting to know more about Calvinistic thought. The great value of this work lies in its wedding together of history and theology in an accessible, pastoral, and theocentric manner. Dr. Daniel argues that central to Calvinism is its God-centeredness, and his work exemplifies this throughout. He is captivated by the glory of the Triune God and zealous for us to see this God more accurately and worshipfully. If your intentions in picking up this book are merely academic, you have come to the wrong place. The author is certainly after your mind, but only that thereby you might be impelled to holiness and doxology. He wants you to catch a vision of the grandeur of God that changes you.

If you know next to nothing about church history, do not be intimidated by the size of this work. Curt's sketch of the history of Calvinism is concise and easily understandable. And even if you are quite knowledgeable about the history of the church, there is something here for you. Readers may be surprised to find that the history of Calvinism does not begin with a German monk and 95 theses in 1517 but reaches back into the ancient and medieval church. Tracing the unity and diversity of the movement, we are given a historical picture of Calvinism in all its developments and declines. This is vital for Christians to understand, for far too many of us are impoverished and vulnerable due to a lack of insight into the origins of our rich theological heritage.

Theologically, this book focuses on those doctrines that are peculiar to Calvinism, especially the doctrines of grace (i.e., the five points of Calvinism). He argues convincingly that these truths are not forced onto the Bible but are actually drawn out of the Bible. He is also not afraid to wrestle with difficult matters such as the free offer of the gospel, the problem of evil, and the salvation of dying infants. But he does so in a user-friendly way, with the Scriptures as his authority.

There is an evident polemical thrust to this work. It does not shy away from confronting unorthodox theology, providing fair analysis and sound critique of Arminianism, Hyper-Calvinism, and Neo-Orthodoxy. Along with this, it would appear that no stone has been left unturned when it comes to responding to objections concerning Calvinism. The reader will find every conceivable complaint against such Word-based, God-centered, Calvinistic truth being set forth in this book with gracious, biblical responses. Curt's dealing with these various objections is alone worth the price of the book and will prove invaluable for pastors and others who have questions or doubts about Reformed doctrine.

While this work is profoundly historical, theological, and polemical, readers will also encounter a pastoral warmth and wisdom. This is evidenced in chapter titles such as "Prayer and the Sovereignty of God," "Practical Implications of Election," and "The Practical Application of Calvinism." Practical insights are not limited to these chapters, however, but are skillfully woven throughout. Curt shows us the life-transforming relevance of the Reformed faith. There is no room here for ivory tower theologians. Truly, Calvinism is doctrine for all of life.

Curt Daniel has done the twenty-first-century church a great service in writing *The History and Theology of Calvinism*. Whether you are a new Calvinist, an old Calvinist, or no Calvinist at all, there is much benefit to be derived from these pages. One does not need to agree with every detail of this large book to appreciate and mine the riches of historical and biblical truth it offers. Here indeed are truths worth living and dying for.

May God be pleased to use this book to spread the cause of biblical, confessional, experiential, pastoral, practical Calvinism far and wide, for His glory and for the good of His people.

Joel R. Beeke

Foreword by John MacArthur

Charles Spurgeon famously wrote,

> I have my own private opinion that there is no such thing as preaching Christ and Him crucified, unless we preach what nowadays is called Calvinism. It is a nickname to call it Calvinism; Calvinism is the gospel, and nothing else. I do not believe we can preach the gospel, if we do not preach justification by faith, without works.[1]

Those three sentences have been subjected to lots of misunderstanding, misapplication, and controversy by Calvinism's allies and opponents alike. But taken in context and understood as Spurgeon intended it, the point he makes is exactly right — and it is an important one.

Consider the easy part of Spurgeon's statement first: "It is a nickname..." "Calvinism" is actually something of a misnomer. Although we normally use the term to designate those key articles of faith that are often grouped together under the acronym TULIP and collectively called "the five points of Calvinism," I generally prefer to speak of "the doctrines of grace." Those five doctrines have a long pedigree that goes back through Augustine to the apostles, who learned them from Jesus himself. And our Lord was not introducing new ideas either. Every one of the five points is taught in the Old Testament.

It was a group of Dutch Remonstrants (the original Arminians) who singled out those five points in order to dispute them. They tied them forever to Calvin's name. Calvin himself never outlined his doctrine in five points.

Furthermore, the notion that Calvin was proposing a new or distinctive system of theology was repugnant to him. His most famous doctrinal treatise, *Institutes of the Christian Religion*, is well-salted with quotations from patristic sources dating back to the earliest days of the church age. And in a prefatory address at the beginning of the work, speaking of his Roman Catholic critics, he wrote,

> They unjustly set the ancient fathers against us (I mean the ancient writers of a better age of the church) as if in them they had supporters of their own impiety. If the contest were to be determined by patristic

---

1 Susannah Spurgeon and Joseph Harrald, *The Autobiography of Charles H. Spurgeon: Compiled from His Diary, Letters, and Records*, 4 vols. (London: Passmore & Alabaster, 1899), 1:172.

authority, the tide of victory would turn to our side. Now, these fathers have written many wise and excellent things. Still, these so-called pious children of theirs, with all their sharpness of wit and judgment and spirit, worship only the faults and errors of the fathers. The good things that these fathers have written they either do not notice, or misrepresent or pervert. You might say that their only care is to gather dung amid gold. Then, with a frightful to-do, they overwhelm us as despisers and adversaries of the fathers! But we do not despise the fathers; in fact, if it were to our present purpose, I could with no trouble at all prove that the greater part of what we are saying today meets [the Church Fathers'] approval.[2]

Calvin was clearly convinced of the antiquity and the biblical foundation of every doctrine he ever confessed. He said, "By calling it 'new' they do great wrong to God, whose Sacred Word does not deserve to be accused of novelty."[3] He abominated the notion that what he taught was original or unique to him. Had he known that the doctrines of grace would eventually gain a nickname implying that he was their inventor or discoverer, I am quite sure he would have strenuously objected.

For the sake of argument, however, and as a convenient way of speaking in shorthand, we adopt and accept the nickname "Calvinism." In doing so, we are not professing fidelity to a man — or even to his complete system of doctrine. Of course, there are countless Baptists who embrace the so-called five points of Calvinism. Every one of them would differ strongly with Calvin's view of the sacraments. I do not know of a single credible theologian or popular teacher who slavishly follows John Calvin as if the Reformer's writings had ex cathedra authority. "Calvinism" is simply a convenient and generally well understood label for the five articles of doctrine Arminians commonly dispute.

But what did Spurgeon mean when he wrote, "Calvinism is the gospel"? He was not suggesting, of course, that the gospel is a message about John Calvin. Nor was he saying there are no true believers except those who have mastered and embraced Calvinism as a system. Spurgeon himself had numerous Arminian friends whom he counted as dear brethren in Christ and spiritual allies in his battle against modernism. He could not have been suggesting that saving faith entails wholehearted embrace of the five points. In fact, later in that same piece, Spurgeon said this:

---

2 Ford Lewis Battles, trans., John Calvin, *Institutes of the Christian Religion*, 2 vols. (Grand Rapids: Eerdmans, 1960), 1:18.
3 Ibid., 1:15.

There is no soul living who holds more firmly to the doctrines of grace than I do, and if any man asks me whether I am ashamed to be called a Calvinist, I answer — I wish to be called nothing but a Christian; but if you ask me, do I hold the doctrinal views which were held by John Calvin, I reply, I do in the main hold them, and rejoice to avow it. But far be it from me even to imagine that Zion contains none but Calvinistic Christians within her walls, or that there are none saved who do not hold our views.[4]

So why did he write, "Calvinism is the gospel"? Spurgeon was making a simple but profound point — namely, that the core of all gospel truth is the same principle that lies at the root of Calvinism. And it is this: Salvation is the Lord's work, not the sinner's.

Indeed, Spurgeon's meaning is made crystal clear in the immediate context of those controversial three sentences. At the beginning of that same paragraph, he quotes Jonah 2:9 and comments on the truth of it:

> "Salvation is of the Lord." That is just an epitome of Calvinism; it is the sum and substance of it. If anyone should ask me what I mean by a Calvinist, I should reply, "He is one who says, Salvation is of the Lord." I cannot find in Scripture any other doctrine than this. It is the essence of the Bible. "He only is my rock and my salvation." Tell me anything contrary to this truth, and it will be a heresy; tell me a heresy, and I shall find its essence here, that it has departed from this great, this fundamental, this rock-truth, "God is my rock and my salvation."[5]

That truth is the very essence of the gospel, and it is also the heart and the linchpin of Calvinist doctrine. It is why I am convinced that more than any other doctrinal study we might ever undertake, a sound and faithful understanding of the doctrines of grace will instruct and help anyone who is seeking to articulate the gospel with clarity and accuracy.

For years I have used and appreciated Curt Daniel's notes on the history and doctrines of Calvinism as a key resource for learning and teaching about the doctrines of grace and the long history of Calvinism's influence. My first exposure to Daniel's work came sometime in the 1990s, when his notes existed only as a thick sheaf (nearly five hundred pages) of typed, photocopied notes on letter-size sheets of paper. But it has been the single most useful resource

---

4 Spurgeon and Harrald, Ibid., 1:176.
5 Ibid., 1:172.

on my shelf of historical theology volumes. I along with others had urged him for years to publish the work in book form. So I am thrilled to see it in this revised and expanded, quality-bound edition. I know many others will treasure it as I have.

Dr. Daniel has read and studied primary resources (perhaps more thoroughly than anyone else I know) on the history of Calvinism, Hyper-Calvinism, Arminianism, and the many debates and theological nuances that arise from these topics. He earned his PhD from the University of Edinburgh with a massive dissertation on John Gill and Hyper-Calvinism. And he is as adept at teaching as he is as an academic. This current book originally grew from notes he wrote and distributed to classes of lay people. It is both comprehensive and comprehensible — easily readable, informative, and full of biblical as well as historical insight. He spent years meticulously reviewing, refining, and expanding those original notes, and the result is well worth the wait.

If you want a fuller understanding of what Spurgeon meant when he said, "Calvinism is the gospel," I know of no better or more thorough answer than this book. Keep your copy handy. It is a resource I know you will turn to again and again.

John MacArthur

Preface

A preface should be short. This one is.

I wish to thank Phil Johnson, director of Grace to You, for his valuable editorial counsel. Thanks also to Joel Beeke, David Lachman, and others for help in theological or historical areas in which they are more knowledgeable than I am. I am grateful to Gary Catherwood, Albert Crocker, Steve Lawson, and Lance Quinn for their regular encouragement to "get it published." I owe many thanks to elders Steve and Will Andras and members of Faith Bible Church, Springfield, Illinois, for their prayers and the privilege of being their pastor. Thanks also goes to Believers Chapel, Dallas, Texas, where the messages that formed the basis for this volume were first delivered from 1987–89. All errors herein are my own.

Research for this project was done at numerous seminary and university libraries, especially the matchless Speer Library of Princeton Theological Seminary. Many thanks go to head librarians Stephen Crocco and Donald Vorp and research librarian Kate Skrebutenas. I am grateful to Westminster Theological Seminary (and the late Grace Mullen), Calvin Theological Seminary (especially the H. Henry Meeter Center for Calvin Studies), Dallas Theological Seminary, Southwestern Baptist Theological Seminary, Puritan Reformed Theological Seminary, Concordia Seminary (St. Louis, Missouri), Covenant Theological Seminary, Saint Louis University, and others. The foundation for my studies in Calvinism reaches back to my doctoral studies at New College, The University of Edinburgh, 1976–83. I made extensive use of The British Library, The Evangelical Library, and Dr. Williams' Library, all in London.

Let me offer my heartfelt thanks to the editorial staff of my publisher. Many thanks also go to Liz Smith for preparing the manuscript for publication. Without her expert editorial assistance and advice, this Herculean project could never have been finished.

All biblical quotations are from the New King James Version except where indicated.

I dedicate this book to the loving memory of my late parents, Guy and Doris Daniel.

Introduction

The volume you are holding is a middle-level handbook, a sort of "Calvinism 202" textbook that bridges the gap between the many short introductions (Steele-Thomas-Quinn, Palmer, etc.) and the more advanced scholarly works (Heppe, Muller, Turretin, etc.). It is rather like Loraine Boettner's classic, *The Reformed Doctrine of Predestination*, which served its generation well but is now somewhat outdated.

It should be used for what it is and not judged for what it does not claim to be. It is not a systematic theology, theological dictionary, or Bible commentary. Some readers will wish I employed more biblical exegesis. Others will wish that I had devoted more space to their favorite persons (like John Owen) or topics (such as union with Christ). I cannot say everything, but I can say something. If the Lord wills, I plan to write a much more extensive and scholarly history of Reformed theology as well as in-depth treatments of limited atonement and Hyper-Calvinism.

This work is based on an unpublished syllabus consisting of seventy-five weekly handouts prepared to accompany public messages delivered from 1987–89.[1] Many persons have requested that I revise, correct, and update that syllabus. This is that. The syllabus should be retired and not quoted; it has many errors in it and was meant only for private distribution and not publication. Furthermore, no one has my permission to put it on the internet (some have done so, even for profit). In Christian charity and fairness, I ask that those who have pirated it remove it from their websites.

I have included hundreds of illustrative quotations from Calvinist writers. This is to illustrate what I wish to say in the way that preachers quote other preachers or writers. That is, they are illustrations not authorities. Scripture alone is our authority. The quotes will introduce readers to writers worth reading. The large bibliography will direct interested students to further studies, often of a more detailed nature. I have especially quoted Augustine because of his enormous influence, Jonathan Edwards because he is my favorite theologian, and John Calvin for obvious reasons. When I document a quote from Calvin's *Institutes*, I use the standard method of book, chapter, and section, but I add page numbers

---

1 The audio messages, now partially outdated, may be heard on Sermonaudio.com. I do not object that other websites have put them online, so long as they are not accessible for profit.

from the standard McNeill-Battles edition for those readers unaccustomed to the accepted manner of citation. I also use Arabic numbers rather than Roman numerals, which is becoming increasingly popular, just as modern theological writers quote Scripture as "John 3:16" rather than "John III:16."

One may ask at the outset, *What is Calvinism?* In one sense, it is simply the theology of John Calvin. In another sense, it is the theology that he shared with the other Swiss Reformers or that which was taught by his theological successors who amplified or modified his teaching on certain subjects. Some define Calvinism in terms of the consensus of the great Reformed confessions. Abraham Kuyper once wisely commented that "a system is not known in what it has in common with other preceding systems; but that it is distinguished by that which it differs from those preceding systems."[2] Calvinism shares many things in common with historic Lutheranism, Arminianism, Anabaptism, and even Roman Catholicism, but I concentrate on where Calvinists differ from them.[3] Calvinists agree with other truly evangelical Protestants on the five *sola* doctrines (*sola Scriptura, sola gratia, sola fide, solus Christus, soli Deo gloria*)[4] and the five fundamentals (verbal inspiration, virgin birth, vicarious atonement, victorious resurrection, visible return of Christ). But it seems to me the five points of Calvinism are not held by any other evangelical theology, though Luther came close, as did several of the pre-Calvinists such as Augustine, Gottschalk, Bradwardine, and Wycliffe.

If historic Lutheranism has emphasized *sola fide*, Calvinism has emphasized *soli Deo gloria*. This comes as close as any other doctrine to being the "central dogma" of Reformed theology. Some writers have nominated union with Christ, the covenant, the Holy Spirit, or other subjects to that position. In my opinion, the distinctives of Calvinism are best seen in its view of divine sovereignty and the doctrines of grace, better known as the *five points of Calvinism*.[5] This is usually the case in the popular mind. Only Calvinists hold to these

---

2 Abraham Kuyper, *Lectures on Calvinism* (Grand Rapids: Eerdmans, 1931/70), 100.

3 So, for example, Edward A. Engelbrecht, ed., *The Lutheran Difference: An Explanation & Comparison of Christian Beliefs* (St. Louis: Concordia, 2010).

4 For Reformed expositions of the five *solas*, see: Terry L. Johnson, *The Case for Traditional Protestantism: The Solas of the Reformation* (Edinburgh: Banner of Truth, 2004); James Montgomery Boice, *Whatever Happened to the Gospel of Grace?* (Wheaton: Crossway, 2001); and R. C. Sproul Jr., ed., *After Darkness, Light* (Phillipsburg, NJ: P&R, 2003).

5 Kenneth J. Stewart suggests that the acronym TULIP can be traced no earlier than 1913. See *Ten Myths about Calvinism* (Downers Grove, IL: IVP Academic, 2011), 79, 291–92. The Canons of the Synod of Dort presented five "heads" of doctrine but not in the same order or enumeration as the popular TULIP.

truths. Calvinism is certainly more than the five points, but it is also not less. I would not be doing justice to the subject if I concentrated on where it agrees with others and ignored or minimized where it is unique. That I do not have discussions on, say, the resurrection of Christ or the Christian family certainly does not mean that we Calvinists do not believe in them. I will, however, show where we stand distinctively on a few subjects other than the five points.

Though there are fine points of difference between the terms *Calvinism* and *Reformed theology*, I will basically use both synonymously.[6] Calvin did not approve of the term *Calvinist* (or *Calvinian*, as was first used in his day), but he did once say, "We are reformed Christians."[7] As we shall see, *Reformed* refers to the Swiss branch of the Reformation going back to Zwingli, in contradistinction to the Lutheran *evangelische* branch or the Anabaptist branch. Some today use the term *Truly Reformed* to differentiate themselves from modified or pseudo-Reformed teachings. Point taken. Others use the term *sovereign grace*.[8] Some prefer *the doctrines of grace* to *the five points of Calvinism*. In any river of thought, there are currents and backwashes but also a mainstream — hence, *mainstream Calvinism* refers to the majority report. There is truth in all these observations.

Non-Reformed Christians sometimes object: "But the word *Calvinism* is not even in the Bible. Let's just stick with Scriptural terms." They forget that they themselves use extra-biblical words like *Trinity* or *rapture*. Others decry the use of labels, but I would remind them that labels are useful on bottles of medicine. All disciplines use labels, and in theology we speak of Lutheranism, dispensationalism, Arminianism, and the like. Even the word *Christianity* is a label not strictly found in the Bible, though the word *Christian* is used three times, evidently coined by non-Christians (Acts 11:26; 26:28; 1 Peter 4:16). Spurgeon wisely commented:

> Let it not be misunderstood, we only use the term for shortness. That doctrine which is called "Calvinism" did not spring from Calvin; we believe that it sprang from the great founder of all truth. Perhaps Calvin himself derived it mainly from the writings of Augustine. Augustine obtained

---

6 For instance, the Baptist writer Kenneth Good wrote *Are Baptists Calvinists?* (Oberlin: Regular Baptist Heritage Fellowship, 1975) and answered yes then later said no to the title of his book *Are Baptists Reformed?* (Lorain, Ohio: Regular Baptist Heritage Fellowship, 1986). To many Baptists, the term *Calvinist* mainly means the five points, while *Reformed* includes infant baptism and Presbyterian ecclesiology.

7 John Calvin, *Sermons on Acts 1–7* (Edinburgh: Banner of Truth, 2008), 579.

8 E.g., the Sovereign Grace Baptists, but also the charismatic Sovereign Grace Ministries movement.

his views, without doubt, through the Spirit of God, from the diligent study of the writings of Paul and Paul received them of the Holy Ghost, from Jesus Christ the great founder of the Christian dispensation. We use the term then, not because we impute any extraordinary importance to Calvin's having taught these doctrines. We would be just as willing to call them by any other name, if we could find one which would be better understood, and which on the whole would be as consistent with fact. And then again, this afternoon, we shall have very likely to speak of Arminians, and by that, we would not for a moment insinuate that all who are in membership with the Arminian body, hold those particular views. There are Calvinists in connection with the Calvinistic Churches, who are not Calvinistic, bearing the name but discarding the system.[9]

Likewise, Jonathan Edwards said:

However the term "Calvinist" is in these days, among most, a term of greater reproach than the term "Arminian"; yet I should not take it at all amiss, to be called a Calvinist, for distinction's sake; though I utterly disclaim dependence on Calvin, or believing the doctrines I hold, because he believed and taught them; and cannot justly be charged with believing in everything just as he taught.[10]

George Whitefield confessed, "I embrace the Calvinistic scheme, not because Calvin but Jesus Christ taught it to me."[11] Both James Montgomery Boice[12] and Steven Lawson[13] have chapters on "Christ the Calvinist," which is not really an anachronism when properly understood. I like the term *Biblical Calvinism*; I wrote a short booklet on the five points with that title. Martyn Lloyd-Jones professed to believe in "Bible Calvinism" rather than "system Calvinism."[14] His point is good and avoids the tendency of some to imply, "I am of Calvin," à la 1 Corinthians 1:12. The system of doctrine known as Calvinism is drawn *from* the Bible, not forced *on* the Bible.

---

9 Charles Haddon Spurgeon, *Metropolitan Tabernacle Pulpit* (Pasadena, TX: Pilgrim Publications, 1981), 7:298. See also *New Park Street Pulpit* (Pasadena, TX: Pilgrim Publications, 1981), 6:136.

10 Jonathan Edwards, *The Works of Jonathan Edwards* (New Haven: Yale University Press, 1957), 1:131.

11 Quoted in Arnold Dallimore, *George Whitefield* (London: Banner of Truth, 1970), 1:406.

12 James Montgomery Boice, *The Gospel of John* (Grand Rapids: Zondervan, 1977), 1:128–34.

13 Steven J. Lawson, *A Long Line of Godly Men* (Orlando: Reformation Trust, 2006), 1:241.

14 Quoted in Christopher Catherwood, *Martyn Lloyd-Jones: His Life and Relevance for the 21st Century* (Wheaton: Crossway, 2015), 31.

Contrary to what many Hyper-Calvinists believe, one does not have to be a Calvinist to be a Christian. The five points do not constitute the non-negotiable essentials of the gospel. There are many godly evangelical Arminians (such as A. W. Tozer), Lutherans (such as Luther), and others. Calvin once wryly commented that some people jokingly said that "the path to paradise passes through Geneva."[15] Some Lutherans would say Wittenberg. The real path passes through Calvary.

I invite our non-Calvinist friends and opponents to see exactly what we teach and not follow unfounded rumors or misunderstandings. More importantly, let us all test these teachings by Scripture.[16] If they are weighed in the balance and found wanting, disregard them. But if they are indeed biblical, we must believe them.

Here, then, is my survey of the history and theology of Calvinism.

---

15 John Calvin, *Faith Unfeigned* (Edinburgh: Banner of Truth, 2010), 65.
16 "Test all things; hold fast to what is good" (1 Thessalonians 5:21). Cf. Acts 17:11; 1 John 4:1; Isaiah 8:20.

The History of Calvinism

Chapter 1
Pre-Calvinism

John Calvin did not invent the theology of Calvinism any more than Christopher Columbus invented America. Both merely discovered what was already there. Augustine and others had previously explored the landscape of grace, even as the Inuit and Amerindians had already lived in North America.

Like all true Christians, Calvinists believe that their theology is based on the Bible. But what about the fifteen hundred years between the New Testament and the Reformation? Let us do a brief survey to see how the theology of sovereign grace declined and occasionally reappeared in various forms of what I call "pre-Calvinism." It would be the backdrop for the major rediscovery in the time of Calvin.[1]

The Early Church

After the New Testament period ended around the year AD 100, the church went through several waves of persecution. Christians went to the lions and the flames singing praises to God. Some responded with preaching and writing in defense of the faith against pagan assaults and pseudo-Christian heresies such as Gnosticism.

The earliest theologians were more interested in apologetics and Christology than in the doctrines of grace, atonement, and predestination. When they did mention these topics, their views were generally a diluted version of biblical teaching. It was similar to what would later be called Semi-Pelagianism or synergism. Their theology may be summarized as follows: Man is sinful from birth and in need of salvation. God gives regeneration through baptism.[2] Sinners

---

1 Two useful histories of the doctrines of grace and predestination before the Reformation are Steven Lawson, *A Long Line of Godly Men* (Orlando: Reformation Trust, 2011); and Guido Stucco, *God's Eternal Gift: A History of the Catholic Idea of Predestination from Augustine to the Renaissance* (Bloomington, Ind.: XLibris, 2009). Lawson is an evangelical Protestant, while Stucco is an emphatic Catholic Augustinian sympathetic to Gottschalk.
2 Everett Ferguson and others have argued that there is no proof of infant baptism before around AD 200 and that it arose out of concern for the salvation of dying infants. However, unlike evangelical Calvinists, Ferguson holds to baptismal regeneration. *Baptism in the Early Church* (Grand Rapids: Eerdmans, 2009).

are called on to believe, but the biblical teaching on justification by faith and the imputation of Christ's righteousness almost completely disappeared shortly after the New Testament. The seeds of the theology of merit were planted.

If election was mentioned at all, it was usually seen as based on foreseen faith or obedience. Little was said about the atonement. The main view of atonement seems to have been the "*Christus Victor*" theory in which Christ defeated Satan. Some writers proposed the "mousetrap" or "fishhook" theory in which God caught Satan by means of the cross.

The earliest Christians tended to react against Gnostic and astrological determinism by emphasizing human free will. This was especially the case with Origen (c. 185–c. 254) and all subsequent writers in the Greek-speaking Eastern church. But there were hints at a higher view of divine sovereignty and grace in the Latin-speaking western church, such as in Cyprian (c. 200–58) and Ambrose (c. 339–97).[3]

Constantine the Emperor professed conversion in 312 and put an end to the persecution of Christians in 313. Christian leaders were then free to discuss theology more openly, and theology began to blossom in the fourth century. The Trinity and full deity of Christ were defended at the councils of Nicea and Constantinople. By the end of the century, it was time to reopen the debate on the doctrines of grace.

Augustine

The major breakthrough came through a North African named Aurelius Augustinus (354–430).[4] Raised by a pagan father and a Christian mother, young Augustine forsook Christianity as a teenager and lived the life of a wanton prodigal for the next fifteen or so years. He fathered an illegitimate son with his mistress but found no peace for his soul.[5] He began to study philosophy, especially the offspring of Gnosticism known as Manichaeism.

---

3 Augustine appealed to Cyprian and Ambrose as holding similar views to his own but offered only isolated and somewhat vague quotations. John Gill and others have attempted to prove that some pre-Augustine writers held to the higher form of grace, but their proof is unconvincing to me.

4 The standard biography is Peter Brown, *Augustine of Hippo: A Biography,* 2nd ed. (Berkeley: University of California Press, 2000). The best compact reference work in English is Allan D. Fitzgerald, ed., *Augustine Through the Ages* (Grand Rapids: Eerdmans, 1999). The fullest reference work in English is Karla Pollman, ed. *The Oxford Guide to the Historical Reception of Augustine* (Oxford: Oxford University Press, 2013).

5 Later Augustine penned the famous words, "You have made us and drawn us to yourself, and

One day Augustine overheard some children sing a little song with the words "Take up and read." He took up a copy of the New Testament and read at random Romans 13:14: "Put on the Lord Jesus Christ, and make no provision for the flesh, to fulfill its lusts." He was soundly converted at age thirty-two. Before long, his gifts were recognized, and he was ordained a priest and later bishop of Hippo.

It is no exaggeration to say that Augustine has been the most influential Christian theologian in history following the New Testament. His impact on both Catholicism and Protestantism has been enormous. More books have been written about him than any other post-biblical figure. He wrote more than most theologians — and before printing and electricity! Among his many books were *The Trinity*, *Christian Doctrine*, *Enchiridion*; expositions of Genesis, Psalms, the Sermon on the Mount, and John; treatises against the Manichaeans, the Pelagians, and the Donatists; hundreds of letters and sermons; and his masterpiece, *The City of God*.[6] By far his most popular work was a spiritual autobiography written in midlife, *The Confessions*. It contained a short prayer that signaled his shift from his previous synergism to a fuller view of divine grace: "Give what you command and command what you will."[7]

The Pelagian Controversy

A British monk named Pelagius (c. 355–c. 418) read that prayer and was infuriated. He thought that it encouraged moral laxity. He traveled to Rome, North Africa, and Palestine preaching against the new view of grace taught by Augustine. This became the leading controversy for some twenty years. Some theologians and popes sided with Pelagius. Others, such as Jerome (c. 345–420), opposed Pelagius without fully supporting Augustine. We have very few of Pelagius' writings.[8] Most of what we know comes from his three closest

---

our heart is unquiet until it rests in you." *Confessions* I:1; *The Works of Saint Augustine* (Hyde Park: New City, 1997), I/1:39.

6 The best and only complete edition in English is *The Works of Saint Augustine*, to be completed in fifty volumes (Hyde Park: New City, 1990–). The set in the Post-Nicene Fathers series, often reprinted, has all his major works but contains less than half of his writings. I will generally quote from the New City Press edition.

7 Augustine, *Confessions*, 10:29:40, in *The Works of Saint Augustine*, I/1:263. Also: "When what you command is done, it is by your gift." *Confessions*, 10:31:45; in *Works*, I/1:267.

8 See B. R. Rees, *Pelagius: Life and Letters* (Woodbridge: Boydell, 1998). Of his commentaries on Paul's epistles, the one on Romans is most important. See Theodore de Bruyn, ed., *Pelagius' Commentary on St. Paul's Epistle to the Romans* (Oxford: Clarendon, 1993).

disciples: Celestius, Rufinus the Syrian, and especially Julian of Eclanum (380–c. 455), as well as lengthy quotations in the anti-Pelagian writings of Augustine.

Pelagius went beyond the synergism of the previous era. His was a monergism of man, not of God. He denied all forms of original sin. Man, he said, is born as sinless as Adam was when he was first created. Adam was created mortal and would have died even if he had never sinned. We sin by choosing to imitate other sinners. We are thus sinners by choice, not by nature. Indeed, said Pelagius, a few people in the Bible never sinned: Abel, Enoch, Job, Joseph, Daniel, and others. It is still theoretically possible to live a sinless life. For those who have already sinned, grace might help but it is always resistible. Man is basically saved by moral obedience to the commands of God. Grace only illumines us to what to believe and do. Christ is mainly the example to follow.

Further, argued Pelagius, baptism only helps us, not regenerates us. Above all, he emphasized that man has free will. He is equally able to sin or not sin. If he ought to do good, then he can do good. Responsibility requires ability. Moreover, God is just and never interferes with the human will nor commands the impossible. He commands obedience, and it is up to man to obey — contrary to Augustine's prayer. God foreknew who would use free will to believe and obey, and so He chose them to salvation. But all our good works, faith, salvation, and grace can eventually be lost if man does not continue to exert his free will. Thus taught Pelagius.

Augustine's Reply

Augustine replied to Pelagius and his disciples in several treatises, sermons, and letters.[9] First, he reaffirmed the doctrine of original sin even stronger than previous theologians had done. He based some of his views on the Latin of Romans 5:12, "Therefore, just as through one man sin entered the world, and death through sin, and thus death spread to all men, *in whom all sinned*" (emphasis added).[10] All humanity was seminally in Adam; therefore, men are born with a sinful nature that affects our whole being. We are guilty and morally unable to obey God. We are spiritually dead, said Augustine, not alive and well as Pelagius said.

Like most Christians of his day and before, Augustine taught the baptismal regeneration of infants as the cure for original sin. Unbaptized dying infants

---

9 The treatises are in *The Works of Saint Augustine*, vols. I/23–26.

10 Augustine wrote in Latin and used the Old Latin and Vulgate versions. He knew very little Greek and even less Hebrew.

go to Hell. Reversing his previous views, Augustine strongly asserted that God freely and sovereignly predestined some persons to salvation, not on the basis of foreseen faith or obedience. In a few places, he even taught double predestination — that is, the predestination of some sinners to Hell. The elect would persevere to the end. In a curious twist, however, he said that some non-elect persons experience salvation, but do not persevere because they were not predestined.

One key element in his teaching was the principle of operative grace. God effectually moves the fallen will of some sinners so that they always respond with faith, which is a divine gift. The glory goes to God, for "God crowns his own gifts, not your merits."[11] In keeping with the prevalent theology of the day, he taught justification through infused righteousness rather than by imputation. He taught relatively little about atonement, though in a few places he seems to have taught that redemption was limited to the elect.

Given his situation in theological history, this was a major breakthrough. In other areas he taught doctrines that would be developed in mainstream Roman Catholicism, especially in ecclesiology. But it would be incorrect to reject Augustine's view of sovereign grace because of those errors.[12] Should we reject his doctrine of the Trinity because of his faulty view of baptism? It would take hundreds of years of debate until the Protestant Reformers would rectify the weaknesses of Augustine's theology.

Semi-Pelagianism

The views of Pelagius and his followers were eventually condemned at the councils of Carthage (417) and Ephesus (431) and the Synod of Arles (473).[13] Pelagius himself drifted into obscurity. Very few persons would later adhere to outright Pelagianism for over a thousand years. But another system arose which closely resembled the pre-Augustinian synergism, a theology that would later be named *Semi-Pelagianism*.[14]

---

11 Augustine, *The Works of Saint Augustine*, I/26:81.

12 Dave Hunt and others use the faulty "guilt by association" argument to discredit Augustine and Calvinism. See *What Love is This?* 3rd ed. (Bend, OR: Berean Call, 2006), 51–66.

13 Henry Bettenson and Chris Maunder, eds., *Documents of the Christian Church*, 4th ed. (Oxford: Oxford University Press, 2011), 62–64.

14 The term was coined by either Theodore Beza or the Lutherans who produced the Book of Concord in the late sixteenth century to counter certain anti-Augustinian Anabaptists. It has become the accepted name for the fifth-century system, though challenged by some. Augustine and his followers usually referred to them as *Massilians*.

Several ascetic monks in Marseilles in southern Gaul (modern France) rejected Pelagianism but felt that Augustine had gone too far. The main Semi-Pelagians were John Cassian (c. 360–435), Vincent of Lerins (?–c. 450), and Faustus of Riez (c. 405–c. 490). They taught a modified view of original sin and a weakened view of free will. Man is sick, not well or dead. He inherits the tendency to sin, not the necessity to sin or the guilt of Adam. He is half good and half bad. He cannot save himself; he needs grace. God infuses grace and righteousness through infant baptismal regeneration. God chose to salvation those whom He foresaw would use this grace by faith and obedience and did not predestine anyone to Hell, for God wills that all men be saved. The main point is that man must take the first step toward God, and only then will God help him. Grace is not irresistible, and it can be lost. Asceticism is the best course of life to develop personal salvation.

This approach would naturally be opposed by the now elderly Augustine and his followers, especially Prosper of Aquitaine, Gaul (c. 390–c. 463); Paul of Orosius, Spain (c. 385–c. 420); and later Caesarius of Arles, Gaul (470–542). The Second Council of Orange (579) and the Council of Valence (530) rejected but did not outright condemn Semi-Pelagianism. Orange in particular favored Augustine but modified his theology by rejecting double predestination and any idea of God predestining sin.[15]

If Augustinianism was basically pre-Calvinism, then Calvinism is also a perfected Augustinianism. Likewise, Semi-Pelagianism was a kind of pre-Arminianism, and Arminianism is a modified version of Semi-Pelagianism. These two views would serve as the poles of debate for the next fifteen hundred years.

The Dark Ages

In the following centuries there would be some notable Augustinians and semi-Augustinians. Fulgentius of Ruspe (468–533) was an emphatic supporter of Augustine as was Isidore of Seville, Spain (c. 560–630). Pope Gregory the Great (c. 540–604) was more or less semi-Augustinian as was the Venerable Bede in Britannia (c. 673–735).

But forms of Semi-Pelagianism continued as well. Virtually all Eastern Orthodox theologians promoted the synergistic Semi-Pelagianism of Origen,

---

15 The pertinent documents of the Council of Orange are in Bettenson and Maunder, eds. *Documents of the Christian Church*, 64–66.

such as John of Damascus (c. 675–c. 749). It was time for another major debate on grace, and it arose in northern Europe in the ninth century.

Gottschalk

Gottschalk of Orbais (c. 804–c. 869) was a German monk and poet and the most outspoken advocate of the Augustinian view of grace to date.[16] He was defended by Ratramnus of Corbie (?–c. 868), who wrote a significant work on predestination, and also Prudentius of Troyes (?–861). Servatus Lupus (c. 805–62) defended Gottschalk's views in a rather anonymous way.

Gottschalk reaffirmed Augustine's theology of grace and expanded it. He taught predestination by sovereign grace and not by foreseen faith and even explicitly taught double predestination. He repeated Augustine's doctrine of original sin and inherent depravity but also his views on baptismal regeneration and justification by infused righteousness. Saving grace, said Gottschalk, is always effectual, and those who receive it always persevere to the end. Moreover, Gottschalk explicitly taught that Christ redeemed the elect alone at the cross. Thus, Gottschalk was the most explicit and emphatic pre-Calvinist between Paul and the Reformation.

But he had his antagonists, such as Bishop Rabanus Maurus (c. 780–856), Hincmar of Reims (806–62), and the controversial and erratic philosopher-theologian John Scotus Eriugena of Ireland (810–77), author of a unique Semi-Pelagian treatise on predestination. The Catholic hierarchy came down hard on Gottschalk. Following several trials, it condemned him at the synods of Mainz (848) and Quiercy (849). Gottschalk refused to recant. His writings were burned, though a few survived. He was flogged and imprisoned for the rest of his life in a monastery dungeon. After twenty years of such mistreatment, he had a breakdown, but he died without denying his belief in sovereign grace.

Medieval Debates

The discussion continued for the next six hundred years among leading scholastic theologians. During this period, Catholic theology blossomed but also hardened. More was written then than at any previous time in church history, and of course, everyone had to interact with Augustine. The papacy strengthened its power. Catholics went on Crusades to protect the Holy Land

---

16 The standard work in English is Victor Genke and Francis X. Gumerlock, eds., *Gottschalk and a Medieval Predestinarian Controversy* (Milwaukee, WI.: Marquette University Press, 2010), which includes his major writings and a useful history.

from Muslims. Sacramentalism and merit theology became more pronounced. Pelagianism was dead, but the leading theologians basically fell into three camps in the issue of grace.

First, there were the semi-Augustinians who taught a modified view of Augustine's view of grace. These included Anselm of Canterbury (c. 1033–1109), Bernard of Clairvaux (1090–1153), Peter Lombard (c. 1100–1160), and Thomas Aquinas (1225–74). Their views were less Augustinian than the earlier followers of Augustine and certainly less than Gottschalk, but they were closer to Augustine than many later Calvinists realize.[17] But they were all still infected with the disease of merit theology and baptismal regeneration.

Second, there were those who more or less fell into the category of Semi-Pelagianism and synergism. The first was the liberal Peter Abelard (1079–1142), then John Duns Scotus (c. 1265–1308) and William of Ockham (c. 1285–1347). All three incurred official disapproval from the Catholic establishment hierarchy, but only Ockham was formally excommunicated. This approach was especially popular among the Franciscan order in contrast to those in the Dominican order such as Aquinas.

Third, there were the outright Augustinians in the Augustinian order, such as Gregory of Rimini, Italy (c. 1300–1358) and Giles of Rome (c. 1243–1316). Ockham and other Englishmen at Oxford were castigated severely by the great English philosopher and mathematician Thomas Bradwardine (1295–1349). His large volume *De Causa Dei Contra Pelagium* (The Cause of God Against the Pelagians) argued that the views of Duns Scotus and Ockham opened the door to the old Pelagian heresy. He briefly served as the Archbishop of Canterbury before his death. He was the most outspoken Augustinian since Gottschalk.[18]

Bradwardine greatly influenced another Englishman named John Wycliffe (c. 1330–84), who is mainly known for being the first to translate the whole Bible into English, howbeit from Latin, helped by the Lollards. Wycliffe's emphatic Augustinian view of grace paved the way for the Reformation. He downplayed Catholic sacramentalism and merit theology and argued in favor of pure sovereign grace. In turn, Wycliffe influenced Jan Hus of Bohemia (1372–1415), who also taught the high view of grace. Hus paid for it with his life.

---

17 This refers to their view of grace and predestination and not to justification.
18 The Reformers would have appealed to Bradwardine except for the fact that his *De Causa Dei* was not published until 1618. One of the editors was William Twisse, who later served as Prolocutor of the Westminster Assembly. There is a vital need for an English translation of this significant work.

Conclusion

The stage was set for a return not only to Augustine's doctrine of grace but to a fuller grasp of forensic justification by faith alone based on the imputed righteousness of Christ. The big breakthrough would come in the Protestant Reformation through Martin Luther and still more through John Calvin.

Chapter 2
The Reformation

The Protestant Reformation of the sixteenth century was the greatest revival in the history of Christianity. It was also the greatest rediscovery of the doctrines of grace, surpassing even that of Augustinianism. It was truly a "back to the Bible" movement that sought to reform the deformed theology, worship, and practice of the apostate Roman Catholic Church. It began in Germany, spread throughout Europe, and continues to affect Christians around the world.[1]

Martin Luther

The door had been opened by pre-Reformers such as Wycliffe and Hus, but it was the German Augustinian monk named Martin Luther (1483–1546) who walked through that door and fathered the Reformation.[2] After becoming a Doctor of Theology, Luther had his "tower experience" around 1515 through reading Augustine, Johann Tauler, the *Theologia Germanica,* and especially the Bible, particularly Romans. Romans 1:17 was his life verse: "The just shall live by faith." He was personally influenced by Johann von Staupitz (1460–1524), who called for reform but did not go as far as Luther.

The birthday of the Reformation was All Hallows Eve, October 31, 1517, when Luther nailed his *Ninety-five Theses* to the door of the castle church in Wittenberg. This was a challenge to debate the sale of indulgences, including Pope Julian's participation and approval. Luther attacked the very heart of Catholic theology. The pope excommunicated him, but that did not stop him. Luther called the papacy the Antichrist. While in hiding he translated the whole Bible into German in 1534. He married Katharine Von Bora in 1525. Aided by Philip Melanchthon (1497–1560), he led thousands out of Roman darkness into biblical light.

Luther was a prolific writer.[3] In addition to expositions of the Bible (especially Genesis, Romans, and Galatians), he wrote treatises, letters, sermons, catechisms,

1 Of the many surveys of the Reformation, a good introduction is Matthew Barrett, ed. *Reformation Theology* (Wheaton, IL: Crossway, 2017).
2 The standard biography of Luther is Roland Bainton, *Here I Stand* (Nashville: Abingdon, 1950).
3 The standard English translation of most of his writings is *Luther's Works* in sixty-two-

and hymns such as "A Mighty Fortress is Our God."[4] His informal chats were transcribed by hearers and published as the colorful *Tabletalk*. He always considered *The Bondage of the Will*[5] to be his most important book. He wrote it against the eminent Catholic theologian Desiderius Erasmus (c. 1466–1536). It was thoroughly Augustinian against Erasmus' rather Semi-Pelagian position.

Luther taught that fallen man is spiritually dead and in bondage to sin and Satan. He can do no good or offer any merit to God. God begins to save a sinner by regenerating him through infant baptism, then pronounces him just when he believes in Jesus Christ. Justification is a legal pronouncement, not an experiential process of being made holy. This was a radical challenge to all previous Roman Catholic theology. The righteousness of Christ is imputed to the believer. It is all monergistic — by God alone. God foreordained all, chose some sinners to be saved, rejected others, effectually calls the elect, gives them saving faith, and glorifies them in the end.

Like Augustine, Luther taught that unbaptized infants who die go to Hell. He rejected the Catholic dogma of transubstantiation in the Mass and replaced it with a doctrine called *consubstantiation*. That is, the Communion elements do not change physically, but the spiritual presence of Christ is present in, with, and under the bread and wine. Luther also undermined the authority of Romanism by appealing to the Bible alone as spiritual authority. This is often called "The Formal Principle of the Reformation." The "Material Principle" would be justification by faith alone.

Lutheranism

Philip Melanchthon was Luther's closest associate. His most important work was the *Loci Communes* (*Common Places*), the first Protestant systematic theology. But he watered down Luther's strong monergism and advocated a synergism that came close to Semi-Pelagianism. He also modified Luther's strong views on the bondage of the will and sought for reunion with Rome if possible (it was not). Curiously, most later historic Lutherans have been closer to Melanchthon than to Luther on the topics covered in *The Bondage of the Will*.

---

plus volumes (St. Louis: Concordia; and Minneapolis: Augsburg). He was perhaps the most prolific writer of the German language, certainly of German theology.

4 Historians generally now tend to deny that Luther himself wrote the Christmas hymn "Away in a Manger."

5 It is contained in *Luther's Works*, but many readers prefer the English translation by J. I. Packer and O. R. Johnston (Cambridge: James Clarke, 1957).

Martin Chemnitz (1522–86), "The Second Martin," was Melanchthon's main disciple and theological successor. He wrote a large systematic theology entitled *Loci Theologici* (*Theological Places*) and a large refutation of the Catholic Church's Council of Trent, called to refute the Reformation. He was the leading theologian of the "Golden Age of Lutheran Orthodoxy" (1550–1600). In the "Silver Age of Lutheran Orthodoxy" (1600–1700), the leading theologians were Johann Gerhard (1582–1637) and Johann Andreas Quenstedt (1617–88). Both wrote enormous systematic theologies. All were strongly opposed to Calvinism. Historic Lutheranism found credal expression in the Augsburg Confession (1530), Luther's Short and Large Catechisms (1529), the Smalkald Articles (1537), and the Formula of Concord (1577). They were collected in *The Book of Concord* (1580).

Later Lutheran orthodoxy became spiritually cold and dry. This gave rise to a reaction called Pietism late in the seventeenth century. Sadly, the eighteenth-century Enlightenment deeply infected Lutheranism, and then nineteenth-century theological liberalism decimated most Lutheranism in Germany. In America, historic Lutheranism continues today mainly in the Lutheran Church-Missouri Synod and the Wisconsin Synod Lutheran Church.

The Anabaptists

Shortly after the Lutheran Reformation began, another branch developed along somewhat different lines. The popular name for the movement is *Anabaptism*,[6] though church historians often prefer the term the *Radical Reformation*. It began in Switzerland, then spread throughout Europe, especially in the Netherlands. Early leaders included Conrad Grebel (1498–1526), Balthasar Hubmeier (1485–1528), and Menno Simons (1496–1561).

The movement was very diverse. Most Anabaptists were pacifists, but some were violent revolutionaries, such as Thomas Muntzer (c. 1490–1525) and his followers. Most were Trinitarians, but some like Michael Servetus (1511–53) and Lelio (1525–62) and Faustus (1539–1604) Socinus (Sozzini) denied both the Trinity and the deity of Christ. Some were mystics. Few were trained theologians. While they agreed with the Lutherans that Roman Catholicism was corrupt and apostate, they felt that Luther and the Lutherans did not come out of Rome far enough. While they generally agreed with the five *sola* doctrines, they usually preferred a Semi-Pelagian synergism to Augustinian monergism.

---

6 The standard work is George Hunston Williams, *The Radical Reformation*, 3rd ed. (Kirksville, MO.: Sixteenth Century Journal, 1999).

Their main emphases revolved around three points. First, they rejected all infant baptism, even that of the Reformers who rejected baptismal regeneration. Second, they taught that only true believers are part of the true church (something that Wycliffe and Hus had taught); a person must give a valid testimony in word and life to become a member of a local church. Third, they rejected all notions of a state church. The true church is a separate and spiritual organism. Today, historic Anabaptism is found mainly among the Mennonites (named for Menno Simons), various Brethren churches, and the Amish.

The Swiss Reformation

The third branch of the Reformation also began in Switzerland. Huldrych Zwingli (1484–1531) developed his views independently of Luther but with remarkable similarity on many points.[7] At first he tolerated the Anabaptists, then dramatically opposed them. His closest associate was Johannes Oecolampadius (1482–1531). Zwingli taught that the Lord's Supper was mainly a symbolic memorial without the "real presence" of consubstantiation. Zwingli and Oecolampadius debated Luther and Melanchthon on the subject at the Colloquy of Marburg (1529). Exasperated, Luther wrote the words, *"Hoc est corpus meum"* (Latin for "This is my body"), threw down the chalk, opposed the Swiss as heretics, and stormed out of the room. Zwingli and Oecolampadius died in 1531 as military chaplains in the Swiss civil war between the Protestants and Roman Catholics.

Zwingli lived and ministered in Zürich, the center of German-speaking Switzerland. His immediate successor was Heinrich Bullinger (1504–75). More systematic and scholarly than Zwingli, he was also less innovative. He wrote a large New Testament commentary, a history of the Swiss Reformation, and an influential systematic theology consisting of fifty sermons entitled *The Decades*.[8] He was the main author of the First and Second Helvetic Confessions and with Calvin wrote the *Consenus Tigurinus* confession that forged a kind of theological unity among the various branches of the Swiss Reformed.

A fourth leader in the German Swiss Reformation was Wolfgang Musculus (1497–1563) who followed Bullinger in most areas. He wrote a large exposition of Romans and an important systematic theology. Later Thomas Erastus (1524–

---

7 Some older writers used the spelling *Ulrich*. Two popular studies are: G. R. Potter, *Zwingli* (Cambridge: Cambridge University Press, 1976) and W. P. Stevens, *The Theology of Huldrych Zwingli* (Oxford: Clarendon Press, 1986).
8 Translated into English and recently reprinted by Reformation Heritage Books (Grand Rapids).

83), a medical doctor, would develop Bullinger's ecclesiology into Erastianism. That theory said that the civil state and magistrate may exercise discipline and authority in the church.

The Swiss Reformation also spread to areas where French was the main language, mainly in the southwestern region. Geneva became the central hub. The first French Swiss Reformer was Guillaume (William) Farel (1489–1565). More able as a preacher than as a theologian, the fiery redheaded preacher built on Zwingli's foundation and thundered the gospel as he led the Swiss Reformation in a slightly different direction than the German Swiss. Another significant French Swiss Reformer was Pierre Viret (1511–71). He was an exceptionally eloquent and profound preacher and writer, such as in his *Christian Instruction*. Less bombastic and more irenic than Luther or Farel, he was an exponent of what may be termed *Swiss Reformed ecumenism*.

The Swiss branch of the Reformation, then, was distinct enough from the other two branches to deserve the title *Reformed Theology* in contradistinction with Lutheran *evangelische theologie* (evangelical theology).

The German Reformed Reformation

In the buffer zone between the staunch Lutheranism in central and northern Germany and German-speaking Switzerland arose a sub-branch of the Reformation. It shared most of its theology with the Swiss but offered some distinctive contributions of its own. The movement came to be known as the German Reformed Church. It revolved around Heidelberg and Strasbourg on the German-French border. It had some parallels with the Reformed movement up in northern Germany in Emden and Brandenberg. Some say it took the best of Lutheranism and Swiss Reformed while avoiding the errors of both.

The first undisputed leader was Martin Bucer (1491–1551). Brought into the Reformation by reading Luther, he was friendly with the Zwinglian Swiss Reformation, much more so than was Luther. Like Melanchthon and Viret, he hoped for a reunion of the Germans and the Swiss. It was he who organized the failed Colloquy of Marburg. He wrote extensively, including massive expositions of John, Romans, and Ephesians. He taught that theology must be primarily biblical rather than scholastic.[9]

---

9 Very few of Bucer's many writings have been put into English. A good selection is compiled in *The Common Places of Martin Bucer*, ed. David F. Wright (Appleford: Sutton Courtenay, 1972). Older German writers sometimes preferred the spelling *Butzer*.

Bucer's main contribution had to do with the controversial subject of the Lord's Supper. He presented a position somewhat between the consubstantiation view of the Lutherans and the symbolic memorial view of Zwingli and Oecolampadius. It is sometimes called the *Word and Spirit* view. The sacrament without the Word and Holy Spirit is nothing. Even the Word is a dead letter without the Spirit. The Spirit never works in a special way without the Word (that would be mysticism). This also applies to salvation, sanctification, and the sacraments. Bucer's view was taken over in large part by Calvin and has been the mainstream Reformed view ever since. It may correctly be called the *Reformed View of Communion*.

It must be added that Bucer, like Bullinger and Calvin, exercised much influence around Europe, especially in England. Late in life Bucer moved to England and advised bishops and monarchs. He taught for a while at Cambridge University. Six years after his death, during the persecutions under Mary Tudor, his corpse was exhumed and publicly burned.

Peter Martyr Vermigli (c. 1500–62) may be considered another leader in the German Reformed branch but also in the Swiss Reformed. An Italian by birth, he took refuge north of the Alps and lived in Switzerland, Germany, and England. He continued and developed Bucer's view of Communion. For example, he emphasized that personal spiritual communion with Christ as the Christian hears and believes the Word when he eats and drinks the elements is at the heart of the sacrament. Vermigli (some older writers preferred to call him simply Peter Martyr) wrote large expositions of Judges and Romans and many treatises. Excerpts were collected into a massive systematic theology.[10]

Conclusion

Luther towered over all the Lutherans in Germany. But in the Swiss and German Reformed movement, as in Anabaptism, there were several leaders who were more or less considered equal in influence. Zwingli came first and set the theological trajectory. But there was still another leader who has become the most famous of all — John Calvin. He deserves a chapter by himself.

---

10 Many of his works were translated into English but not reprinted for centuries. A recent translation series in entitled *The Peter Martyr Library* (Kirksville, MO: Truman State University Press, 1994–).

Chapter 3
John Calvin

When Gerard Cauvin and his wife, Jeanne, became parents of a little boy in 1509, they could not have known that he was destined — or should we say predestined — to become one of the truly great men of all time. They named him Jean. In French, his name is Jean Cauvin. In Latin, Johannes Calvinus. But we know him as John Calvin.

Biography

Calvin was born July 10, 1509, in Noyon in Picardy, about sixty miles northeast of Paris.[1] Upon reaching his teenage years, he began formal studies toward becoming a Roman Catholic priest. He studied theology at Paris from 1523 to 1528. During this time, he was influenced by Jacques Lefèvre d'Étaples (1455–1536) and Nicholas Cop (1501–40). Disillusioned with Catholicism, he switched to studying law and transferred to Orleans and Bourges with a view to becoming a lawyer. Soon after finishing his studies, he published his first book, a detailed commentary on Seneca's *De Clementia*.

Like young Augustine, Calvin's heart was restless until it found its rest in God through conversion in 1533. He left Roman Catholicism forever. But those were dangerous days for ex-Catholics early in the Reformation. He decided to leave France for Basel, Switzerland, to take up the life of a private scholar. It was never to be. Passing through Geneva, he met Guillaume Farel, who was so impressed with the young man that he warned him that God would curse him if he did not stay and help the Reformed cause in Geneva. Calvin stayed.

He published the first edition of his masterpiece, *The Institutes of the Christian Religion*, in 1536. It was immediately hailed as the finest Protestant systematic theology to date. Calvin and Farel set to work to help reform the church in Geneva and French-speaking Switzerland. They proposed that all citizens take an oath of faith. Many Genevans accepted it; some did not and strongly opposed them. In 1538, Calvin called for the church to have authority to fence

---

1 See the bibliography for biographies of Calvin. That by T. H. L. Parker is generally considered the best short biography. Alexander Ganoczy's work is best for Calvin's youth.

the Lord's Table and exclude anyone living in flagrant sin. Opponents ran Calvin and Farel out of town.

Calvin went to Strasbourg on the French-German border and pastored a French-speaking congregation and lectured in the theological academy. He became a close friend of Martin Bucer. He always considered those three years to be a time of peace and growth. The Geneva city council then recalled Calvin and Farel. Calvin took up preaching from the same text he left off three years earlier. But it would be another twenty years until the church had the formal authority to excommunicate all those citizens living in open sin.

It was in Strasbourg that Calvin met his wife. Idelette de Bure was the widow of an Anabaptist with two children. She and Calvin had only one child together, and he died as an infant. She too died in 1549, after only nine years of marriage. Calvin never remarried and was in continual bad health.

Calvin worked toward a godly society in Geneva in several ways. In addition to preaching and teaching, he helped develop a system of charity for the poor and elderly, a public sewer system, and more. He is often credited for helping develop what is known as free enterprise economics, or capitalism, to succeed the medieval feudal system. Max Weber popularized the view that this "Protestant Work Ethic" revolutionized European society as much as Protestant theology had done.[2] To Calvin, it was simply the logical and biblical application of the principle that the carpenter in his shop glorifies God through honest work as much as the monk in the monastery.

In 1555, Geneva welcomed many refugees from England and Scotland. Their leaders studied with Calvin and brought his teaching with them back home when persecution subsided. Calvin also helped found the Geneva Academy to train pastors; it later became the University of Geneva. The Reformed church in Geneva sent out hundreds of pastors as evangelists in France but also sent a group of missionaries to Brazil. This gives the lie to the canard that Calvinism stultifies evangelism and missions.

The Servetus Incident

Calvin was involved in several controversies with opponents, such as Sebastian Castellio (1515–63) and Jerome Bolsec (?–1584). But it was the incident with Servetus that was most controversial of all. Michael Servetus (1511–53) was an Anabaptist physician from Spain and a notorious heretic. He combined

---

2 Max Weber, *The Protestant Ethic and the Spirit of Protestantism* (New York: Scribner, 1958).

astrology, pantheism, Neo-Platonism, and Semi-Pelagianism with Socinianism. He denied both the Trinity and deity of Christ. The Roman Catholic Inquisition had condemned him to death, but he escaped and fled to Geneva hoping for sanctuary. Calvin heard of it and warned him to stay away or face the consequences. Perhaps Servetus hoped to foster a revolution with the help of the local libertines who opposed Calvin and the city council.

Servetus was recognized in a church service and arrested and put on trial for blasphemy as per Leviticus 24:16, "Whoever blasphemes the name of the Lord shall surely be put to death." Calvin was a witness for the prosecution but was not the judge nor prosecutor, as modern anti-Calvinists sometimes suppose. Servetus was adamant and unrepentant. He was found guilty and sentenced to be burned at the stake. Calvin pleaded for a painless execution by beheading instead, which was denied. So on October 27, 1553, Servetus was executed by burning. Many, perhaps most, Protestants and Catholics around Europe agreed with the sentence. Indeed, Servetus would probably have incurred the same treatment almost everywhere else.

The debate has raged for centuries as to the justice of this incident. Very few have defended the execution. Some say that Servetus should have been imprisoned or simply exiled. Others say that the city council should have granted full religious liberty and not arrested him at all. An "expiatory monument" was erected in 1903 on the site of the execution as a public apology. Some historians suggest that Servetus seems to have had a death wish to become a martyr. In any case, we must remember that there was no absolute freedom of religion anywhere in Europe at that time, and Geneva was more lenient than most nations, certainly more than the Roman Catholic countries where the Inquisition still flourished.

Modern opponents of Reformed theology use the Servetus incident to discredit Calvinism.[3] This is illogical. Should we also deny the Trinity because Calvin taught trinitarianism and Servetus did not? Should we deny justification by faith also? One wonders if such anti-Calvinists sympathize with Servetus too much. It was certainly an unfortunate incident that should have been handled differently. My own opinion is that Servetus should have simply been exiled from Geneva to keep pure the godly society that Calvin and Farel had worked so hard to maintain. Great men make great mistakes, and it is too easy for armchair critics to jump to hasty conclusions without studying the *sitz in leben* and the issues in a dispassionate manner. All told, the incident

---

3 E.g., Dave Hunt, *What Love Is This?* 3rd ed. (Bend, OR: Berean Call, 2006), 79–83.

was unfortunate but did not undermine the great contribution of Calvin and Reformed theology.

Calvin's Writings

Calvin wrote more per year than most Christians today read in a year, and he did it without a computer or electricity. He wrote a large commentary on almost the entire Bible that is still widely used and praised today.[4] He produced numerous theological treatises on reforming the church, sacraments, and worship as well as on predestination, sin, and life after death. He authored the French Confession of Faith, a catechism, at least one poem, some hymns, paraphrases of the Psalms, and more.

He preached at least five times a week and lectured in theology almost every day. His sermons are masterpieces of expository preaching.[5] Some preachers' sermons are timely; Calvin's were timeless and have stood the test of time for their value. Most are still in print in English: 200 on Deuteronomy, 159 on Job, 134 on the Pastoral Epistles, 43 on 2 Samuel, 97 on Genesis, 44 on Acts, 22 on Psalm 119, 28 on Micah, 48 on Ephesians, 44 on Galatians, and many more. Sadly, the unpublished manuscripts of hundreds more were thrown out early in the nineteenth century when Geneva forsook its godly heritage.

Calvin also wrote more than 4,000 letters, often giving advice to persecuted Christians outside of Switzerland. Some were to foreign monarchs. Many were to fellow theologians. Some 1,686 are still in print in English.[6] It is hoped that more will be translated in the future.

The Institutes

Calvin's *magnum opus* was *The Institutes of the Christian Religion*. The first edition was in Latin and was expanded in several subsequent editions until the

---

4 Hunt casually dismisses Calvin's commentaries with the remark, "The wide praise heaped upon Calvin as a great exegete is badly misplaced." (Hunt, *What Love Is This?*, 38.) This is an astounding charge in light of the almost universal praise of Calvin's commentaries by even many non-Calvinists.

5 See Leroy Nixon, *John Calvin, Expository Preacher* (Grand Rapids: Eerdmans, 1950) and T. H. L. Parker, *Calvin's Preaching* (Louisville: Westminster/John Knox, 1992). Most of the sermons are published by Banner of Truth.

6 Many were translated in *Tracts and Letters* (Banner of Truth) and *Selected Works of John Calvin* (Baker Book House) in seven volumes.

final definitive edition of 1559.[7] He also produced several versions in French.[8] There have been numerous abridgements as well.

It is basically a systematic theology centered around the theme of the knowledge of God. He discusses salvation, the Christian life, ecclesiology, the sacraments, the Lord's Prayer, the Ten Commandments, the Apostles' Creed, church-state relations, and more. There is a delightful devotional section that has often been republished separately as *The Golden Booklet of the True Christian Life*.

Calvin's Theology

If justification by faith alone was the key to Luther's theology, then the doctrine of God was the center of Calvin's theology. The first paragraph of the *Institutes* was on the knowledge of God. Truly Calvin was a "God-intoxicated man." This includes his emphasis (but not overemphasis) on the sovereignty of God. God rules over all in predestination and providence as well as salvation.

His theology was evangelical and Protestant. He accepted the Apostles' Creed, the Nicene Creed, and the five *sola* doctrines of the Reformation. It was Bible-based, for we must not forget Calvin's lengthy commentaries and expository sermons. He accepted the infallibility and inerrancy of Scripture and was one of the first to teach the internal testimony of the Holy Spirit to authenticate the inspiration of the Bible.

He went beyond even Luther in describing human depravity but also higher than all before him in exalting the majesty of God. He built on Augustine's theology of grace and modified some of its weaknesses. He laid the foundation for the Presbyterian form of government. (His overall theology is explained in more detail in the second part of this volume.)

Conclusion

Calvin died on May 27, 1564, at the age of fifty-five in the arms of his successor, Theodore Beza. As per his request, there was no grave marker (though later Genevans included a statue of him in the famous Reformation Memorial). Though often ill, it might be more accurate to say that he worked himself to

---

7 The best edition is the two-volume edition edited by John T. McNeill and translated by Ford Lewis Battles, *The Institutes of the Christian Religion* (Philadelphia: Westminster Press, 1960).
8 The first French edition has been translated more than once, e.g., by Robert White, *Institutes of the Christian Religion* (Edinburgh: Banner of Truth, 2014).

death in the service of God. The greatest theologian since the apostles was once mocked because his only son died. He replied: "God gave me a little son and took him away. But I have myriads of children in the whole Christian world." How true.

Chapter 4
The Spread of Calvinism

The first phase of the Reformation stretched from 1517 to about 1560. This covered the lives of the major Reformers. The second phase lasted from 1560 to 1600. Lutheranism spread mainly in Germany and Scandinavia, while the Reformed branch spread to France, the Netherlands, England, Scotland, and a little in what is now Hungary and Romania.[1]

Theodore Beza

Theodore Beza (1519–1605) was born in Burgundy, France, and like Calvin studied law, then wanted to be a private scholar.[2] In 1548 he renounced Roman Catholicism and cast in his lot with the Reformation. The next year he became professor of Greek at Lausanne, Switzerland, and later professor and principal of the Geneva Academy from 1558 to his death in 1605.

As one of Calvin's closest associates, Beza was the obvious successor and key leader in the generation following Calvin's death. He wrote an important biography of Calvin and was moderator of the Company of Pastors in Geneva for many years. Beza was a kind of Renaissance man in Reformed apparel, a multi-talented man who excelled in several areas. He was active in several conferences to unify the Swiss and German branches of the Reformation as well as had dialogues with Rome. He assisted the French Reformation in various ways. In his book *De Jure Magistratu* (*The Law of the Magistrate*), he was one of the first to say that Christians may resist and even overthrow tyrannical rulers.

Beza translated the New Testament into Latin and edited nine editions of the Greek New Testament. The last edition was used for the King James Version. He discovered the famous Greek-Latin manuscript that bears his name, *Codex Bezae*, which he donated to Cambridge University. He wrote a commentary

---

1 A good survey is John T. McNeill, *The History and Character of Calvinism* (New York: Oxford University Press, 1954), 237–350. See also Menna Prestwich, ed., *International Calvinism 1541–1715* (Oxford: Clarendon, 1985).
2 Shawn D. Wright has written two useful works on Beza: *Our Sovereign Refuge: The Pastoral Theology of Theodore Beza* (Carlisle: Paternoster, 2004) and *Theodore Beza: The Man and the Myth* (Fearn: Christian Focus, 2015).

on the entire New Testament, essays on church-state relations, and dozens of theological treatises.

Beza was more scholastic than Calvin, employing some of the methods of the medieval Catholic theologians who were heavily influenced by Aristotle. He was one of the earliest Reformers to teach the supralapsarian view of election and was an early exponent of limited atonement. He is frequently cited as departing from Calvin in method, emphasis, and possibly content in certain "high" areas that later produced High and Hyper-Calvinism. Otherwise, he was remarkably close to Calvin and the other Swiss Reformed theologians. He is often unfairly given a bad press by critics, but he deserves more credit as a scholar, upholder of Reformed orthodoxy, and the leading Calvinist theologian in the last generation of the sixteenth century.

The German Reformed Church

Reformed theology took root in Germany mainly in the Palatinate area in the south, centered in Heidelberg and its famous university. The crowning achievement of the movement at this time was the great Heidelberg Catechism. It was co-written by two young theologians named Zacharias Ursinus (1534–83) and Caspar Olevianus (1536–87) in 1563. It has taught the minds and warmed the hearts of millions over the centuries and has perhaps been the most widely used Reformed statement of faith.

One lovely feature is the personal touch. Questions are asked by the teacher in the form of *you* or *your* and answered *I*, *me*, or *mine*. The first two are timeless examples:

Q.1: What is your only comfort in life and in death?

A. That I belong — body and soul, in life and in death — not to myself but to my faithful Savior, Jesus Christ, who at the cost of his own blood has fully paid for all my sins and completely freed me from the dominion of the devil; that he protects me so well that without the will of my Father in heaven not a hair can fall from my head; indeed, that everything must fit his purpose for my salvation. Therefore, by his Holy Spirit, he also assures me of eternal life, and makes me wholeheartedly willing and ready from now on to live for him.

Q.2: How many things must you know that you may live and die in the blessedness of this comfort?

A. Three. First, the greatness of my sin and wretchedness. Second, how I am freed from all my sins and the wretched consequences. Third, what gratitude I owe to God for such redemption.

Jerome Zanchius (1516–90) was also influential at this time.[3] Like Vermigli, he was Italian by birth and Augustinian by theology when he joined the Reformation. Historians often credit Beza, Vermigli, and Zanchius with laying the foundation for Reformed scholasticism, even as Bullinger, Ursinus, and Olevianus took a slightly different approach in presenting covenant theology. Though he wrote much, little is available in English. His short *Absolute Predestination* has been reprinted many times.[4]

David Pareus (1548–1622) was the leading disciple and successor of Ursinus. He attempted a kind of rapprochement with the Lutherans in several areas. Johannes Piscator (1546–1625) disagreed with most Reformed theologians by teaching that only the passive obedience of Christ (His death) is imputed to believers in justification. Jacobus Kimedoncius (c. 1550–96) wrote an early defense of modified limited atonement called *The Redemption of Mankind*.

The French Reformed Church

Jacques Lefèvre d'Étaples (1455–1536) was to Calvin what Johann Von Staupitz was to Luther — a kind of pre-Reformer who never left Romanism or joined the Reformation. Peter Ramus, or Pierre de la Ramée (1515–72), attacked the prevailing influence of Aristotle in theology and offered a much simpler method often called *Ramism*. It is based on two main principles. First, all truths can be divided into two parts (dichotomism). Every truth can be contrasted with its opposite. Second, he taught the use of the simple syllogism over the complicated accretions of Aristotelean logic. He influenced many of the early Puritans such as William Ames.

The French Protestants were known as Huguenots.[5] They were overwhelmingly

---

3 The name Jerome Zanchius is generally most popular but less accurate than Hieronymus (Latin) or Girolamo (Italian) Zanchi.

4 It was translated in the eighteenth century by Augustus Toplady, but the reader should note that Toplady added some material of his own, even a reference to Arminius(!). A fresh translation is desired. A better source of his theology is the Latin-English *De religione christiana fides—Confession of Christian Religion*, edited by Luca Baschers and Christian Moser (Leiden: Brill, 2007).

5 There is still disagreement as to the source and meaning of the word *Huguenot*. Beza wrote an important history of the French Reformation, which unfortunately has never been translated into English.

Reformed (Calvinist) in theology and practice. Their holy lives were in stark contrast to the decadent lifestyles and tyranny of the French monarchy and aristocracy. But they were severely persecuted. Opposition reached its zenith in the Saint Bartholomew's Day Massacre (August 24, 1572). The Catholic majority slaughtered thousands of Huguenots, including Peter Ramus.

Philippe Duplessis-Mornay (1549–1623) was the leading Huguenot of the time. The French Calvinists followed his lead in resisting the persecution. This led to the several Wars of Religion. Some historians consider him to have been the anonymous author of the highly controversial book *Vindiciae Contra Tyrannos* (*A Vindication Against Tyrants*) which went beyond Beza and outright advocated righteous civil revolution. Eventually the wars ended in a kind of stalemate. The Edict of Nantes (1598) put an end to the wars and granted limited freedom to the Huguenots.

The Netherlands

Holland and the Low Countries had always been a haven for out-of-the-mainstream Catholics such as the Friends of God and other late-medieval mystical movements. Erasmus lived in Rotterdam. Many Anabaptists settled in the area because of the relative freedom granted them.

Calvin helped spread the influence of the Reformed movement there in several ways. One was his tract *A Short Treatise Showing What a Faithful Man Knowing the Truth of the Gospel Ought to Do When He Is Among the Papists.* At first, the Reformed were in the minority, but often occupied influential places in the government and education. Guido de Bres (1522–67) authored the popular Belgic Confession (1561), which is still widely used in Dutch Reformed circles today.

Threatened by Catholic Spain, the Dutch Reformed took the lead in resisting Spanish imperialism. William I of Orange, also know as William the Silent (1533–84), renounced Catholicism for the Dutch Reformed cause and led the fight for Dutch independence from Spain. He helped lay the foundation for the great Dutch Republic and blossoming of Dutch Reformed theology in the next century.

England

Thomas Bradwardine (1295–1349) and John Wycliffe (c. 1330–84) were pre-Reformers who paved the way for sixteenth-century Reformers like William

Tyndale (1494–1536) to reform England. All three were strongly Augustinian. Wycliffe and Tyndale exercised much influence by translating the Bible into English.

Lutheranism was the main influence in the early stages of the English Reformation through Robert Barnes (1495–1540) and others. But soon the main influence came from the Swiss and German Reformed, including Bucer, Bullinger, Vermigli, and John à Lasco of Poland (1499–1560).[6] King Henry VIII was certainly no Protestant Reformer, but he wanted a male heir, which his queen was not able to provide, and the pope would not give him a dispensation to divorce her. So he pulled the English church out of Roman Catholicism in order to obtain another wife and a possible heir. After several wives, he eventually got a son, Edward VI (1537–53), who was quite favorable to the Reformation.

Soon great leaders arose to further the English Reformation, such as Archbishop Thomas Cranmer (1489–1556), Hugh Latimer (1485–1555), Nicholas Ridley (1500–1555), John Bradford (1510–55), John Hooper (1495–1555), Archbishop Matthew Parker (1504–75), Archbishop Edmund Grindal (1519–83), Archbishop John Whitgift (1544–1600), and John Jewell (1522–71).

When Edward VI died young, he was succeeded by his Catholic sister Mary Tudor (1516–58). She worked fast and furiously to crush Protestantism. She had hundreds of Protestants burned at the stake. The great John Foxe (1516–87) recorded these martyrdoms in the multi-volumed *Acts and Monuments of Matters Happening in the Church*. The abridged version has been generally known as *Foxe's Book of Martyrs*. It has been one of the most-read books in the English language for centuries.

Many English Protestants fled to the continent for refuge. Many went to Geneva and studied with Calvin. Some of them translated the Bible into English and added helpful footnotes — *The Geneva Bible*. When "Bloody Mary" died, they returned fully armed with Reformed theology to continue the English Reformation. Calvinism in an English dress can be seen in the important Thirty-Nine Articles of the Church of England, less so in the *Book of Common Prayer*. Then during the reign of Elizabeth I (1533–1603), the Calvinists pushed for further reforms to "purify" the Church of England from leftover Romanist doctrines and practices. They were nicknamed "Puritans." The Elizabethan Settlement was a halfway compromise along the lines of the

---

6 More properly, Jan Laski. Alas, very little of his writings are available in English.

moderate Protestantism of Richard Hooker (1554–1600). That compromise produced mainline Anglicanism, which has continued to the present time.

Scotland

In the sixteenth century, England and Scotland were still separate countries occasionally united by the same monarch. They had often been at war with each other. The Reformation started earlier in England but solidified further in Scotland. Several exiles went to Geneva. Edinburgh became the center of the Scottish Reformation.

John Knox (1514–72) was the most influential leader.[7] He was particularly known as a fiery uncompromising preacher against Romanism in the mold of Luther and Farel. Knox was in frequent conflict with a series of monarchs named Mary (Tudor, Guise, and Stuart), which gave occasion to his short treatise *The First Blast of the Trumpet Against the Monstrous Regiment of Women*. He argued that it was a judgment of God to have female rulers (Isaiah 3:12).

The Scottish Reformers imitated Calvin's ecclesiology and established Presbyterianism in the Scottish churches. Knox was the main author of the Scots Confession (1560). Other great Reformers were Patrick Hamilton (1504–28), the first Scottish martyr in the Reformation; George Wishart (1513–46), also a martyr; John Craig (1512–1600), who wrote a popular catechism; Andrew Melville (1534–1622); Christopher Goodman (c. 1521–1603); and Robert Rollock (1555–99).

Eastern Europe

Eastern Europe was dominated by the Eastern Orthodox churches (Greek, Russian, etc.), but Calvinism made some headway in several places. John à Lasco (1499–1560) was Polish but ministered in several other countries. The Socinians brought their heresy to Poland. Some areas were influenced by neighboring German Lutheranism, but Poland has remained predominantly Roman Catholic to this day.

Reformed churches were planted in Romania, Hungary, and Bohemia and produced some important confessions of faith. Their churches are a small but lively remnant today, having suffered the ravages of the Catholic Inquisition, Nazism, and Communism.

---

7 His *History of the Reformation of Religion Within the Realm of Scotland* (Edinburgh: Banner of Truth, 1982) is still considered the best source of eyewitness material.

Conclusion

The Reformed faith spread quickly in the sixteenth century but faced challenges as it developed its own theology distinct from Catholicism, Lutheranism, and Anabaptism.

Chapter 5
The Synod of Dort

During the 1600s, the Dutch Republic was at the height of its fame and influence in culture, art, literature, foreign exploration, and theology. The "tulip craze" of 1633–37 was a strange fad in which tulip bulbs skyrocketed in price, then plummeted.[1] In the first decades of the century there was another tulip controversy, not of flowers but of theology, concerning the five points of Calvinism, later labeled "TULIP": Total depravity, Unconditional election, Limited atonement, Irresistible grace, and Perseverance of the saints.

Jacob Arminius

Not all early Protestants accepted the Augustinian view of grace. Most Anabaptists were like the fifth-century Semi-Pelagians. In Holland, Dirck Coornhert (1522–90) expressed dissatisfaction with Reformed theology. But the main protestor was Jacob Arminius (1560–1609).[2] He studied theology at the University of Leyden, then under Beza in Geneva, and then under Franciscus Gomarus back at Leyden. He taught theology there from 1603 to his death in 1609.

Originally a Calvinist, Arminius began to have doubts about the doctrine of total depravity. He felt that Romans 7:14–25 described unregenerate man, not the Christian. A fallen sinner can thus will good toward God. He inherits the bent toward sin from his parents and Adam but not the necessity or the guilt. His will, therefore, is sick — not dead.

Then Arminius reinterpreted Romans 8:29–30 to mean that God predestined some sinners to salvation by foreseeing that they would believe. Coming to Romans 9, he denied the Reformed view of reprobation. He was especially offended by the supralapsarianism of Beza and William Perkins but also rejected the mainline Reformed infralapsarian view. Since the Dutch Reformed

---

1 Mike Dash, *Tulipmania* (London: Gollanz, 1999). The term might wryly be applied to Hyper-Calvinists who overemphasize the TULIP doctrines and make them of the essence of the gospel.
2 More accurately, Jacob Harmanzoon. Less accurately, James. Jacobus would be the Latin form. The standard biography is Carl Bangs, *Arminius: A Study in the Dutch Reformation* (Nashville: Abingdon Press, 1971).

Church adhered to the very Reformed Belgic Confession and the Heidelberg Catechism, he called for a revision so that he could remain a teacher in good standing.

Arminius denied being Pelagian and claimed to be Reformed. But his theology was remarkably similar to the old Semi-Pelagianism of the Massilians, certain medieval schoolmen, and the more recent Jesuit theologian Luis de Molina (1535–1600).

The Arminians

Arminius died in 1609 but lit the fuse of controversy for his followers to continue, several of whom went further from mainstream Reformed theology than Arminius had. Simon Episcopius (1583–1643) succeeded Gomarus as professor of theology at Leyden and continued the views of Arminius. Some "Arminians," as they were sometimes called, were too friendly with the Socinians, who denied the Trinity and deity of Christ.[3] Others were strong Trinitarians. Episcopius and others taught a form of subordinationism, in which Christ was God but less so than the Father. That error has always been anathema to Reformed theologians. Many have argued that Arminianism has the tendency not only to Semi-Pelagianism but various forms of liberalism.

Conrad Vorstius (1569–1622), another teacher at Leyden, also was friendly with Socinianism and was more anti-Calvinist than Arminius had been. Gerard Vossius (1577–1649) argued that their position was well-represented by pre-Augustinian church fathers and that the Augustinian-Calvinist view was the intruder into historical orthodoxy, not the Semi-Pelagian and Arminian theologies. Johannes Uytenbogaert (1557–1644) also studied under Beza at Geneva and befriended Arminius there. Later he served as chaplain to Maurice of Orange.

The most well-known Arminian at that time was Hugo Grotius (1583–1645). Even his opponents recognized his genius: entered university at twelve, became the "father of international law," was a forerunner of modern critical approaches to interpreting Scripture, and was a prolific writer. He is often credited with the so-called Governmental Theory of the atonement, which fit in well with Arminius' rejection of limited atonement. Grotius rejected the Anselmian theory of satisfaction but strenuously opposed the Socinian view of example.

---

3 See Martin Mulsow and Jan Rohls, eds., *Socinianism and Arminianism: Antitrinitarians, Calvinists, and Cultural Exchange in Seventeenth-Century Europe* (Leiden: Brill, 2005).

The Remonstrance

The Arminians rallied around a five-point document drawn up by Uytenbogaert known as the *Remonstrance*, or "The Protest."[4] They were often known as *Remonstrants* — that is, protestors. Here is a brief summary:

1. God decreed to save believers who persevere to the end and to leave unbelievers to go to Hell. This implied that election is based on foreseen faith.

2. Christ died equally for all men, but only believers benefit from its efficacy.

3. Fallen man is not able of himself to do any good without God's assistance. This implies that God assists all men, a view developed at length later.

4. God's saving grace is resistible.

5. Unless a believer perseveres to the end, he will not finally be saved, though it is not certain from Scripture whether all who believe will in fact persevere to the end.

The Anti-Remonstrants

Several notable Calvinists resisted the Remonstrance. The most notable was Franciscus Gomarus (1563–1641). He taught with Arminius at Leyden for six controversial years and resigned in protest when Vorstius was chosen to succeed Arminius. Gomarus upheld the mainline Reformed interpretation of Romans 7–9, except that like Beza he was supralapsarian.

The anti-Remonstrants (Calvinists) stood with Maurice of Orange, the son of Prince William of Orange. The Remonstrants sided with John van Oldenbarneveldt, the Advocate-General of Holland and Friesland. The Remonstrants called for less governmental interference in religion and for more tolerance for non-Calvinists, including the Anabaptists. The anti-Remonstrants wanted to uphold firm bulwarks against Arminianism and Socinianism. They believed that a united Netherlands would be safer against the return of Roman Catholicism from Spain and the southern (Belgic) regions.

The Synod of Dort

The Estates-General called a synod to meet at Dort (or Dordt, short for Dordrecht). Eighty-four delegates were chosen: fifty-eight from Holland,

---

4 In James T. Dennison Jr., ed., *Reformed Confessions of the 16th and 17th Centuries in English Translation* (Grand Rapids: Reformation Heritage Books, 2012), 4:41–44.

eighteen secular commissioners, and the rest from England, Switzerland, France, the German Palatinate, and others. The French delegates were not allowed by the French government to attend, but some of them wrote extensive books and tracts on the issues under debate. The Synod of Dort would be the largest international gathering of Reformed theologians to date and one of the most prestigious and influential in history.

The five English delegates, including bishops John Davenant (1576–1641) and Joseph Hall (1574–1656), together with the German delegates, were more moderate than others. One of the most extreme delegates was the controversial Johannes Maccovius of Poland (1588–1644) who was officially rebuked by the Synod for his extreme scholasticism and unguarded language. William Ames (1576–1633) and John Robinson (1575–1625) of England were influential but unofficial observers. The great Gisbertus Voetius (1589–1676) was, with Gomarus, the most influential divine present. Giovanni Diodati (1576–1649), Beza's successor at the Geneva Academy, was a Swiss delegate. He translated the entire Bible into both Italian and French and wrote a popular commentary on the Bible. Jacobus Trigland (1583–1654) was an important Dutch delegate, as was Johannes Bogerman (1576–1637), the president of the Synod.

The Synod met for 154 sessions from November 13, 1618, to May 9, 1619. Since delegates were chosen by the churches, the Remonstrants were not delegates but defendants and were in the small minority. The Synod considered the suggestion to revise the Belgic Confession and the Heidelberg Catechism if necessary. It also approved a new translation of the Bible into Dutch — the *Statenvertaling* (*States Bible*), which would serve as the major Dutch version for centuries, like Luther's in Germany or the King James Version in Britain and America. A large Bible commentary was also commissioned.[5] But the main purpose of the Synod was to answer the Remonstrance and the Remonstrants.

The Canons of Dort

The Synod produced its decisions in a series of canons. They do not form a full confession of faith like the Belgic Confession or the Heidelberg Catechism, but no serious study of Reformed theology is complete without them. They are grouped under five "heads" answering the five Remonstrance points, with both positive affirmations and negative rejections. It is worth remembering that

---

5 Theodore Haak, *The Dutch Annotations Upon the Whole Bible* (London, 1657. Reprinted Leerdam: Gereformeerde Bijbelstichting, 2002).

these "five points of Calvinism" were prepared as an answer to what may be termed the "five points of Arminianism," not vice versa.[6]

The first head confessed that election and reprobation are both taught in the Bible, though election is more prominent. Election is by sovereign grace, not foreseen faith. The number of the elect and reprobate cannot be increased or diminished, nor can anyone change from one to the other. A person can know he is elect, and this leads to holy living and not licentiousness. Reprobation does not make God the author of sin. Godly parents should not doubt their dying children's election. Though some delegates were supralapsarian (Gomarus, Voetius, Maccovius, et al plus Ames), the canons are usually interpreted as being infralapsarian without outright condemning supralapsarianism.

The second head confessed that Christ died a substitutionary death and is to be preached to all. The atonement has infinite value and is sufficient for all men, but only the elect are actually redeemed. This allowed for moderates such as Davenant, Hall, and the German Matthias Martinus (1572–1630) to affirm the canons. Thus, it taught limited atonement while allowing some kind of universal dimension — neither strictly particular nor universal but primarily for the elect.

The third and fourth heads are combined and deal with man's sin and God's grace. They upheld the traditional Augustinian and Reformed doctrines of original sin, total depravity, and inability of the will. There is no free will, though a common grace enables sinners to do outward acts of religion and social good. Conscience alerts all men to the existence of a holy God and the difference between right and wrong. The law cannot save. There is an external call of the gospel to all men but also a special call by the Spirit to the elect alone, which is always efficacious and irresistible. Regeneration precedes faith and repentance. God is not obligated to give these to anyone, and He gives them to the elect alone.

The fifth head upholds the preservation and perseverance of the saints. Once regenerated, a person will always be so. He may fall into occasional sin, but God does not allow him to stay in it, for the Spirit continues to supply him with grace and faith.

---

6 English translations may be found in several sources, e.g., Dennison Jr., *Reformed Confessions*, 4:120–53. Some editions unfortunately omit the Rejection of Errors.

The Aftermath

The Remonstrants were dismissed on a point of order for protesting too much. Those preachers who would not consent to the canons would be dismissed from their churches. Many such as Grotius would be exiled or imprisoned. A few, such as Oldenbarneveldt, would be executed for treason because of the political ramifications and not for heresy per se. This was relaxed after Maurice died in 1625. Arminians were then allowed a measure of liberty. The Remonstrant Church has continued for hundreds of years down to the present day.

Post-Dortian Arminians tended to go much further than Arminius and the Remonstrants. Philip Limborch (1633–1712) was such a one. The New Testament textual critic J. J. Wettstein (1693–1754) was another. Some went into outright Socinianism. A more conservative and evangelical Arminianism was developed in the eighteenth century under John and Charles Wesley in England.

Conclusion

What Alan P. F. Sell has called the "Great Debate"[7] has continued ever since. The five points of both sides find defenders today. The debate is basically that of the Semi-Pelagians and Arminians on one side and the Augustinians and Calvinists on the other. With some justification it could be said to come down between free will and free grace.

---

7 Alan P. F. Sell, *The Great Debate* (Grand Rapids: Baker, 1983).

Chapter 6
Seventeenth-Century Calvinism

By the year 1600, Calvinism had spread far and wide in Europe. But in the new century it underwent new developments and controversies. We have seen the debate over Arminianism; the debates over Amyraldism and antinomianism would follow. But several others bear mentioning, including two outside Protestantism.

Reformed Scholasticism

About the year 1000, Catholic theologians developed what has been called *scholasticism*, the theological method of the schools. They rediscovered the ancient Greek philosophers — especially Aristotle — and incorporated them into their theology and methods. Thomas Aquinas was the leading Catholic scholastic. In sum, it was the merging of theology and philosophy.

The first-generation Reformers rejected this approach. Luther called this philosophy "the Devil's whore." Though Calvin at times employed a few scholastic features, by and large he was not favorable to the system. The Reformers much preferred Augustine to Aristotle and relied on Scripture far more than medieval scholastics had done. *Sola Scriptura* prevailed not only over the fathers and the Catholic magisterium but over the philosophers. But a Protestant scholasticism began to develop in the post-Reformation era. Johann Gerhard (1582–1637) and Johann Andreas Quenstedt (1617–88) produced massive Lutheran dogmatics in this mold.

The roots of Reformed scholasticism are usually traced to Beza, Vermigli, and Zanchius.[1] Three phases may be delineated. In the first (1560–1600), the main representatives were Lambert Daneau (c. 1530–95), Benedict Aretius (1505–74), Lucas Trelcatius (1542–1602), William Perkins (1558–1602), and Gulielmus Bucanus (?–1603). In the second period (1600–1650), it reached its zenith with Amandus Polanus (1561–1610), Johannes Wollebius (1586–1629), Johannes Piscator (1546–1625), Bartholomew Keckermann (1571–1609), Johann Heinrich Alsted (1588–1638), William Ames (1576–1633), Johannes Maccovius

---

1 See the several works of Richard Muller, especially *Post-Reformation Reformed Dogmatics*, 2nd ed. (Grand Rapids: Baker Academic, 2003).

(1588–1644), and Gisbertus Voetius (1589–1676). In the third period (1650–1700) were Samuel Maresius (1599–1673), Franciscus Burmannus (1628–79), Petrus van Mastricht (1630–1706), Salomon Van Til (1643–1713), John Owen (1616–83), Johann Heinrich Heidegger (1633–98), and Benedict Pictet (1655–1724). A few, such as John Gill (1697–1771), would carry the torch in the next century.

The high point was best seen in two large systematic theologies: *Institutes of Elenctic Theology* by Francis Turretin (1623–87)[2] and *Synopsis Purioris Theologiae* by Johannes Polyander (1568–1646), Andreas Rivetus (1572–1651), Antonius Walaeus (1573–1639), and Antonius Thysius (1545–1640).[3] Most of the divines were Dutch or Swiss. It concentrated on precise systematic theology but sometimes discussed "cases of conscience" by applying theological principles to specific ethical cases (e.g., Perkins, Ames, and Richard Baxter).

Scholasticism is not easy to define and is unfortunately sometimes used in a derogatory manner. Richard Muller offers a good summary:

> Scholasticism is a methodological approach to theological system which achieves precision of definition through the analysis of doctrinal loci in terms of scripture, previous definition (the traditio), and contemporary debate.[4]

It uses the logic and categories of Aristotle in forming systematic as opposed to biblical or historical theology. It tended to be more cerebral than experimental, more speculative than devotional, and employed deduction after deduction from other truths.[5] Peter Ramus had rejected Aristoteleanism's complicated system, but scholasticism reveled in it.

Occasionally, it could be pedantic and nitpicking on extremely fine points of little concern to the average Christian or pastor. Sometimes resembling the medieval debates on how many angels can dance on the head of a pin, it was charged with quibbling over genealogies (1 Timothy 1:4) or straining out a gnat (Matthew 23:24). One feature was discussing "the state of the question" in such a way as one can affirm or deny it. It was primarily a method, but sometimes

---

2 Francis Turretin, *Institutes of Elenctic Theology*, ed. by James T. Dennison Jr. (Phillipsburg, NJ: P&R, 1992).

3 Dolf te Velde, ed. *Synopsis Purioris Theologiae: Synopsis of a Purer Theology* (Leiden: Brill, 2015).

4 Richard Muller, *Christ and the Decree: Christology and Predestination in Reformed Theology from Calvin to Perkins*, (Durham, NC: Labyrinth, 1986), 11.

5 E.g., Westminster Confession, 1:6, "expressly set down in Scripture, or by good and necessary consequence may be deduced from Scripture."

it seems to have affected the content. Many scholastics were supralapsarian. It often employed formal logic, cause-and-effect chain links, and multiple syllogisms in a kind of Christian Rationalism. But the movement had its strengths. It ably defined and defended Reformed theology, provided useful textbooks, and went deeper into the theological mine than the Reformers had done.

Critics ask, "If the scholastic method is so good, why do we not find it in the Bible?" There is a major methodological difference between the inspired writers and the Greek philosophers, who originated the scholastic method. Do not Colossians 2:8 and 1 Corinthians 1 warn against philosophy? Do we really want to go back to the complicated systems of Aquinas and Duns Scotus? Is not the biblical method of Luther and Calvin far better? A change of method often brings a change in doctrine. Scholasticism without biblical spirituality can produce pride (1 Corinthians 8:1) and a cold, dry orthodoxy that usually produces a negative overreaction into heresy, as history shows. There is debate as to Calvin and medieval Catholic scholasticism and subsequent Reformed orthodoxy scholasticism. There is no doubt that Calvin frequently castigated medieval scholasticism in strong terms. For example: "scholastic theology might well be described as a species of secret magic."[6] "Such corruption has prevailed for far too long among the papists, for what else does all their Scholastic theology amount to except a fearful ruin and an abyss of empty, futile speculation?"[7] He was speaking of method as well as content. He only rarely used the categories of causation of Aristotle and Aquinas.[8] He rarely employed explicit syllogisms or technical hair-splittings. My opinion is that Calvin detested Catholic scholasticism, for when he refers to the medieval scholastics it is usually to disagree with them. He would have had reservations but not outright condemnation of the scholasticism of later Reformed orthodoxy. His theological method is best described as biblicist rather than scholastic, humanist, or experimental. Remember his frequent cautions against prying into God's secrets.

The Dutch Further Reformation

The *Nadere Reformatie* (Further or Second Reformation) began at the end of the sixteenth century along as similar lines to Puritanism in England and

---

6 *Selected Works of John Calvin* (Grand Rapids: Baker Book House, 1983), 1:40.

7 *Sermons on First Timothy* (Edinburgh: Banner of Truth, 2018), xxii.

8 For example, *The Epistles of Paul the Apostle to the Galatians, Ephesians, Philippians and Colossians* (Grand Rapids: Eerdmans, 1980), 126–28.

Pietism in Germany.[9] Some call it Dutch Puritanism[10] or Reformed Pietism.[11] It could be compared to the late-medieval devotional Dutch mysticism that reacted against Catholic scholasticism.

Jean Taffin (c. 1529–1602) and Willem Teelinck (1579–1629) were the first leaders, followed by Gisbertus Voetius (1589–1676) in the next century. In the last phase of its golden age, Herman Witsius (1636–1708), Petrus van Mastricht (1630–1706), and Wilhelmus à Brakel (1635–1711) were most prominent. The high point was reached in two experimental systematic theologies: van Mastricht's *Theoretica-Practica Theologia*[12] and Brakel's *The Christian's Reasonable Service.*[13]

The heart of this theology is that theology is for the heart, not just the head and hand. It was more devotional and spiritual than scholasticism. But adherents faced challenges. Some misused it and became legalistic. Some overemphasized self-examination to the extent of weakening personal assurance. To some, holy affections so outweighed right doctrine that orthodoxy was minimized — a similar weakness in Pietism. A parallel tendency was seen in the French Calvinist Pierre Poiret (1646–1719), whose *The Divine Economy* took Calvinism beyond heart religion into mysticism.

But overall the movement was an excellent development and a good safeguard against the tendency of Reformed scholasticism to become too abstract and speculative. High orthodoxy can become dry orthodoxy. In the recent rediscovery of historic Calvinism, there has arisen a Reformed scholasticism that is balanced by the rediscovery of the *Nadere Reformatie*. Richard Muller is the best representative of the former, Joel Beeke of the latter.

Covenant Theology

A third form of Calvinism developed during this time. I will discuss covenant theology in more detail later, but a few observations are in order here. Its roots go back to Zwingli, Bullinger, and Olevianus, but it matured in the seventeenth century. Its two main proponents were Johannes Cocceius (1603–69)[14] and

---

9 An excellent concise survey is in Joel R. Beeke, *The Quest for Full Assurance* (Edinburgh: Banner of Truth, 1999), 286–309.

10 E.g., Keith L. Sprunger, *Dutch Puritanism* (Leiden: Brill: 1982).

11 E.g., F. Ernest Stoeffler, *The Rise of Evangelical Pietism* (Leiden: Brill, 1971).

12 Petrus van Mastricht, *Theoretical and Practical Theology*, trans. Todd Rester, ed. Joel R. Beeke (Grand Rapids: Reformation Heritage Books, 2018).

13 Wilhelmus à Brakel, *The Christian's Reasonable Service*, trans. Bartel Elshout (Ligonier: Soli Deo Gloria, 1992).

14 Johannes Cocceius, *The Doctrine of the Covenant and Testament of God*, (Grand Rapids:

Herman Witsius (1636–1708).[15] Cocceius strongly opposed scholasticism, even though he himself produced a systematic theology. There were lengthy and sometimes bitter debates between the followers of Cocceius (the Cocceians) and of Voetius (the Voetians). The former were accused of weakening the Sabbath and being too favorable to the new philosophy of René Descartes called *Rationalism*. The Cocceians replied that Reformed scholasticism did not have sufficient exegetical grounds.

The three movements overlapped and were not at complete loggerheads. Voetius was in both the scholastic and *Nadere Reformatie* camps. Witsius was both covenant theology and *Nadere Reformatie*. Each movement had its own contribution that helped keep Reformed theology in balance. The best contribution of covenant theology was its insistence on biblical exegesis. It is often seen as the father of *biblical theology* — theology discussed exegetically in biblical chronology rather than logical categories. The three are complementary, not contradictory. The rejection of any one or overemphasis of another will produce an imbalance in theology and personal spirituality. For example, without the dogmatism of scholasticism, Reformed Pietism can become legalistic or mystical. Without covenant theology, scholasticism drifts into philosophical speculation. A threefold cord should not be broken (Ecclesiastes 4:12). Seminaries and churches need to teach and preach systematic theology, biblical exegesis, and true spirituality.

Jansenism

The sixteenth-century Council of Trent came down hard on the Reformation, and subsequent Catholic theology tried to close the door to a revival of the Augustinian theology of grace in its midst. Michael Baius (1513–89) taught a post-Reformation Augustinianism without the Protestant *sola* doctrines but was stopped. Luis de Molina (1535–1600), a Spanish Jesuit, revived a kind of Semi-Pelagianism and the theory of *Middle Knowledge*.[16] He taught God elects sinners by foreseeing how they would respond in a given situation. Arminius would propose a similar theory.

Going beyond Baius, Cornelius Jansen (1585–1638) answered Molina and the Jesuits by his posthumously published *Augustinus*, subtitled *The Doctrines of St.*

Reformation Heritage Books, 2016).

15 Herman Witsius, *The Economy of the Covenants Between God and Man*, (Escondido: The den Dulk Christian Foundation, 1990).

16 Luis de Molina, *On Divine Foreknowledge*, ed. Alfred J. Freddoso (Ithaca: Cornell University Press, 1988).

Augustine on the Health, the Sickness and the Cure of Human Nature Against the Pelagians and Those of Marseilles. He prepared for this massive tome by reading the entirety of Augustine's works ten times and his anti-Pelagian works thirty times. It remains one of the largest studies of Augustine's theology of grace ever written. We long to see it translated into English.[17]

Fellow leaders in this movement included Jean Duvegier de Hauranna (also known as St. Cyran, 1581–1643); Antoine Arnauld (1612–94); and Pasquier Quesnel (1634–1719). The most well known was the brilliant scientist-mathematician-philosopher Blaise Pascal (1623–62), whose *Provincial Letters* sarcastically mocked Jesuit Semi-Pelagianism. The heart of Jansenism was the convent at Port-Royal near Paris. It has been estimated that more than ten thousand books and tracts were written during the controversy.

Jansenism taught a thoroughly Augustinian view of original sin; human corruption and inability to do any good without grace; the necessity of effectual (operative) grace; election by grace and not foresight; full divine omniscience and not the limited omniscience of Middle Knowledge; limited atonement; and other truths. It sounded remarkably like Calvinism — and it was! One could call it "Catholic Calvinism." It drew a condemnation from Pope Innocent X in 1653, though the Jansenists argued that the condemnation was against the supposed deductions drawn from Augustine rather than Augustine himself or themselves — a fine point that did not win the day. The Jesuits succeeded, and eventually the Port-Royal convent was razed to the ground in 1710–13. Remnants continued in the Old Catholic Church in Utrecht, Netherlands. Ever since then, the Jesuits have been the leading Catholic order and have quashed any return to a Catholic kind of Augustinian theology of grace, though of course all Catholic theologians revere Augustine. The door was sealed shut, for if Jansenism was right, then some of the "faithful" might leave Rome for Protestantism. One wonders what would happen if the case against Jansen was reopened. What if Catholics discovered that he was right about Augustine and the Bible after all? Why, they might deduce that Luther and Calvin were also right. One can hope.

Cyril Lucaris

The Greek Orthodox Church, together with other Eastern churches, split from the Roman Catholic Church in 1054 but had long since departed from any

---

17 Guido Stucco has translated the detailed table of contents in *The Catholic Doctrine of Predestination from Luther to Jansenius* (Bloomington, Ind.: XLibris, 2014), 220–54.

semblance of the biblical and Augustinian view of grace. The ghost of Origen still haunted them, and the doctrines of free will reigned. Many of their number taught universal salvation.

But after the Reformation, one Cyril Lucaris (1570–1638),[18] Patriarch of Constantinople, showed considerable sympathy for Protestantism in general and Calvinism in particular.[19] Like the Jansenists, he strictly opposed the Jesuits and their Semi-Pelagianism. He was especially influenced by the Swiss, Dutch, and English Reformers. He approved a new translation of the Bible that was flavored with Calvinism like the Geneva Bible had been. And he showed his appreciation to the English Puritans by donating the ancient *Codex Alexandrinus* manuscript of the Bible to King Charles I of England with the help of the Puritan Archbishop of Canterbury George Abbot (1562–1633).

In 1629, Lucaris published his *Confession of Faith*[20] in Geneva. It was remarkably Reformed in tone and content. He affirmed that the church is subject to Scripture, the elect are eternally and unconditionally predestined by grace alone, sinners are justified by faith alone, the Lord's Supper and baptism are the only two sacraments, and so forth. The Reformed faith had made very little headway into Greece, but this was "Greek Calvinism" par excellence.

Unfortunately, the Greek Orthodox hierarchy did not at all agree. They reacted vehemently and violently to Lucaris. He was formally condemned and defrocked by several synods. There were rumors that he was assassinated. His influence quickly waned, and the door shut tight against anything further resembling Augustinianism or Calvinism in Orthodox churches. As with Jansenism, one wishes that the so-called Orthodox churches would reopen the case and see that the noble Cyril Lucaris was right after all.

Calvin and Calvinism

Ever since the mid-nineteenth century, there has been a debate among Reformed theologians and historians as to whether mainline Reformed theology after Calvin legitimately carried on his legacy or seriously departed from it. Of course, participants in the debate agree that Calvin was not the all-towering

---

18 I have seen at least ten different spellings of his name, as both the first and last names can be spelled in a variety of ways.
19 A useful study is George A. Hadjiantoniou, *Protestant Patriarch: The Life of Cyril Lucaris (1572–1638), Patriarch of Constantinople* (Richmond: John Knox, 1961).
20 Translated in James T. Dennison Jr., ed., *Reformed Confessions of the 16th and 17th Centuries in English Translation* (Grand Rapids: Reformation Heritage Books, 2014), 4:154–63.

figure over Reformed theology as Luther had been with Lutheranism. But the controversy has centered on Calvin and seventeenth-century Calvinists. It is sometimes referred to as the "Calvin versus the Calvinists" debate.[21]

On one side, Barthians have long argued that Barthianism is the true heir of Calvin's theology, not the Dort-Westminster axis. I shall refute this view in chapter 16, "Neo-Orthodoxy." More evangelical writers have argued that the post-Reformation "Calvinists" departed from Calvin on several key issues. These include Holmes Rolston III,[22] Jack Rogers, Brian Armstrong,[23] Alan Clifford,[24] and R. T. Kendall, whose *Calvin and English Calvinism to 1649*[25] is the most popular presentation of their case. Arminians, members of the "Free Grace" movement (Zane Hodges, et al) and others also have chimed in, often with little or no actual knowledge of the source material.

On the other side, Richard Muller, Paul Helm,[26] Joel Beeke, and many others argue for basic continuity between Calvin and the sixteenth-century Reformed theologians and the mainstream seventeenth-century divines and confessions. Some non-Reformed writers also agree.

The issues are as follows. Some say Calvin was more humanist (a la liberal arts of the Renaissance) rather than scholastic in methodology. Others argue that Beza made predestination the "Central-Dogma" around which all Reformed theology is formed, as opposed to Calvin's theology (some argue that his was Christ-centered, or based on union with Christ or other doctrines). A central point in the debate is whether Calvin taught limited atonement. Others debate whether assurance is of the essence of faith, the order of the decrees, the Sabbath, and other issues.

In many cases, one can detect that participants are trying to claim Calvin for their own position and perhaps squeeze him into their particular viewpoint to score points. One does not usually hear of someone saying Calvin taught such-and-such wrongly in contradistinction to, say, the Puritans. Another more

---

21 Basil Hall reopened the debate with his essay, "Calvin Against the Calvinists." In G. E. Duffield, ed., *John Calvin* (Grand Rapids: Eerdmans, 1966), 19–37.

22 Holmes Rolston III, *John Calvin Versus the Westminster Assembly* (Richmond: John Knox, 1972).

23 Brian G. Armstrong, *Calvinism and the Amyraut Heresy* (Madison: University of Wisconsin Press, 1969).

24 Alan C. Clifford, *Atonement and Justification: English Evangelical Theology 1640–1790—An Evaluation* (Oxford: Clarendon Press, 1990) and other publications.

25 Oxford: Oxford University Press, 1979.

26 He answered Kendall in *Calvin and the Calvinists* (Edinburgh: Banner of Truth, 1982).

cautious approach argues that Calvin and other sixteenth-century Reformed theologians simply did not address certain issues, such as the extent of the atonement, so the debate is rather futile and anachronistic.

My own view is that there are some good points made on both sides, but in general there was basic continuity rather than discontinuity. I tend to agree that Calvin taught universal atonement (or at least an atonement with more universal aspects than strict limitarians such as John Owen). Likewise, I think his method was not as scholastic as Beza and others. Many have shown that Calvin and the continental Reformed taught a less strict view of the Sabbath than the English Puritans and most of the *Nadere Reformatie* divines. While Calvin addressed the biblical covenants, I agree with most who have studied the history of covenant theology in saying that covenant theology proper was rooted in the German-speaking Reformed (Zwingli, Bullinger, Olevianus, et al) rather than the French-speaking (Calvin, Viret, and Beza).

Having said that, I believe there is more basic continuity than some want to admit. Whether Calvin was infralapsarian or supralapsarian, he certainly taught the mainline Reformed view of election as opposed to the Lutheran, Anabaptist, Arminian, or Barthian views. Contrary to Jack Rogers and Donald McKim, Calvin most certainly did teach biblical inerrancy. It was not invented later by Francis Turretin and other seventeenth-century scholastics. Predestination per se may not have been his "Central-Dogma," but if there was one, it would have been his insistence that all theology must be God-centered, which includes his emphasis on the absolute sovereignty of God. Richard Muller has conclusively shown that this includes, not excludes, a Christocentric emphasis.[27]

When one studies Reformed theology from Zwingli to the present, one sees both unity and diversity. The mainstream included Calvin, Beza, Dort, the Puritans, the *Nadere Reformatie*, covenant theology, with Amyraldism on the left and Hyper-Calvinism on the right. But Arminianism, Barthianism, "Free Grace" theology, and other theologies are non-Reformed and even pseudo-Reformed in content.

Conclusion

Reformed theology was at its high-water mark in the seventeenth century. Subsequent chapters will examine further developments and controversies.

---

27 Richard Muller, *Christ and the Decree: Christology and Predestination in Reformed Theology from Calvin to Perkins* (Durham, NC: Labyrinth, 1986).

Chapter 7
The Puritans

To some, the Puritans were superstitious and ignorant witch-burners. To others, they were revolutionary fanatics who overthrew the English monarchy and grabbed all the power they could get. To still others, the Puritans were unsmiling legalists who carried their religion too far. Or they were just religious hypocrites.

All those opinions are wrong. In truth, the Puritans were among the leading intellectuals and godliest Christians in England from 1570 to 1700. They had various ecclesiastical views and differed on other issues. But they were all evangelical, Bible-believing Calvinists and as such are worthy of our study, respect, and imitation.

Origins of Puritanism

After King Henry VIII died, Edward VI became "the boy king" and was favorable to the Reformation and Calvinism in particular. He was succeeded by his sister Mary Tudor, who reestablished the Roman Catholic Church and viciously persecuted Protestants. Some eight hundred Protestant leaders sought refuge from "Bloody Mary" in Europe, especially in Geneva. Others went underground. About three hundred were martyred, such as Thomas Cranmer, Hugh Latimer, Nicholas Ridley, John Bradford, and John Hooper.

In 1558, Elizabeth I became queen and reestablished the Church of England as the state religion. Parliament passed the first Act of Uniformity requiring all preachers subscribe to the Thirty-Nine Articles of Religion and the Book of Common Prayer and other injunctions. The Elizabethan Settlement was a compromise between Catholicism and Calvinism. Many Anglicans, especially those who studied under Calvin while in exile, wanted to "purify" the Church of England of leftover Catholic doctrines and practices like kneeling at Communion, clerical vestments, and the sign of the cross. They were nicknamed *Puritans*.[1]

The heart of the movement began at the White Horse Inn and Cambridge

---

[1] There have been several suggestions as to the origin and meaning of the terms *Puritan* and *Puritanism*, but this one is accepted by many historians.

University, where Martin Bucer and Peter Martyr Vermigli had taught and planted the seeds of Reformed theology. The early leaders might be called "Cambridge Calvinists," but the movement spread far and wide. They wanted to duplicate what their Swiss and Scottish brethren had achieved in church and society. In 1603, some one thousand protestors presented the Millenary Petition to King James I. This led to the Hampton Court Conference of 1604, in which the king heard arguments from traditional bishops and Puritan leaders. Few changes were made, but it led to the commissioning of the Authorized Version of the Bible known as the King James Version of 1611. It eventually became more popular than the more Reformed Geneva Bible.

The Anglican Puritans

Many of the Puritans, especially in the first generation, accepted the official Episcopalian ecclesiology of the Church of England. Some bishops and archbishops like Edmund Grindal (1519–83) and George Abbot (1562–1633) advocated a kind of Episcopalian Reformed ecclesiology, or Anglican Calvinism. There have been many like them ever since. Undoubtedly, the most prominent Anglican Puritan of the era was the great William Perkins (1558–1602) of Cambridge. He was read by more Puritans than even Calvin.[2] His most influential work was *A Golden Chain*, based on Romans 8:29–30, in which he linked salvation from eternal election through temporal salvation to future glorification. It included an oft-reprinted chart.

Perkins' closest disciple was William Ames (1576–1633). He originally ministered at Cambridge but moved to the Netherlands and served as advisor at the Synod of Dort. His book *The Marrow of Theology* became the standard Puritan systematic theology for decades. He also wrote important books on worship and ethics. The Anglican Calvinism tradition continued through Paul Baynes (or Bayne, 1560–1617) and Richard Sibbes (1577–1635), who especially developed Puritan "experimentalism" for the heart. This was the hallmark of Puritan theology, perhaps best exemplified in Ames' famous definition of theology as "the doctrine or teaching of living to God."[3]

Other major Anglican Puritans included John Rainolds of Oxford (1549–1607), a leader at Hampton Court and a translator of the King James Version;

---

2 This can be gauged from the fact that more editions of Perkins' books were published in the Puritan era than those of Calvin. Reformation Heritage Books is currently producing a new edition, *The Works of William Perkins* (2014–).

3 William Ames, *The Marrow of Theology* (Boston: Pilgrim Press, 1968), 77.

Edward Reynolds (1599–1676), bishop and dean of Christ College, Oxford; John Preston of Cambridge (1587–1628); and Joseph Mede (1586–1638), author of a premillennial commentary on Revelation.

Several Anglican Puritans were sent as delegates to the Synod of Dort: bishop John Davenant (1576–1641), bishop Joseph Hall (1574–1656), George Carleton (1559–1628), and Samuel Ward (1572–1643).

Archbishop James Ussher (or Usher, 1581–1656) was perhaps their most able scholar. He served as archbishop of the Church of Ireland, which was in communion with the Church of England, and wrote prolifically: *A Body of Divinity*, a seminal work on Gottschalk, a lengthy study of Bible chronology, and more.[4] He was coauthor of the Irish Articles, which served as the basis for the Westminster Confession of Faith. He was later invited to be a member of the Westminster Assembly but declined out of deference to the king.

Another great Anglican Puritan scholar was William Twisse (1578–1646). He helped edit the publication of Thomas Bradwardine's *De Causa Dei*, served as the first prolocutor (moderator) of the Westminster Assembly, and wrote large theological tomes, such as *The Riches of God's Love unto the Vessels of Mercy*. He leaned toward Presbyterianism.

John Trapp (1601–69) wrote a very popular commentary on the whole Bible. Thomas Adams (1612–53), "The Puritan Shakespeare," was an eloquent preacher and writer of devotional books and a large exposition of 2 Peter. William Gurnall (1617–79) wrote the classic *The Christian in Complete Armour* based on Ephesians 6. Isaac Ambrose (1604–62) was renowned for his personal holiness and writing *Looking Unto Jesus*. It was reported that he spent a whole month each year in private prayer and meditation. Ezekiel Hopkins (1634–90) published expositions of the Decalogue, the Lord's Prayer, and others. Edward Leigh (1602–71) authored one of the earliest Hebrew-Greek-English lexicons and *A Systeme or Body of Divinity*, probably the largest Puritan systematic theology in English. Thomas Gataker (1574–1654) was a major opponent of antinomianism and a leading contributor to the *Westminster Annotations* commentary. Matthew Mead (1629–99) authored the challenging *The Almost Christian Discovered*.

George (1560–1634) and his brother John (1571–1652) Downame wrote several helpful volumes, as did William Pemble (1591–1623), Henry Scudder (c. 1585–1652), and Edward Polhill (1622–94). The venerable John Selden (1584–1654) was

---

4 Ussher popularized the "young earth" date of 4004 BC for creation, which was printed in the margins of many editions of the Bible for centuries.

an important layman delegate to the Westminster Assembly and member of Parliament.

Several Anglican Puritans leaned toward Presbyterian polity, such as Matthew Poole (1624–79), author of an immensely popular Bible commentary in English and a massive scholarly commentary in Latin.[5] John Lightfoot (1602–75), like Selden, was a leading advocate of Erastianism — the view that says the state is over the church and may exercise disciplinary authority in it. Lightfoot was a leading scholar of Hebrew and Jewish writings and customs and a major divine at the Westminster Assembly. Some consider him a Presbyterian.

Then there was Richard Baxter (1615–91), another Anglican friendly to Presbyterianism. By far the most prolific of all Puritan writers, his practical works are classics: *The Reformed Pastor*, the best-selling *A Call to the Unconverted*, the enormous *The Christian Directory*, *The Saints' Everlasting Rest* on Heaven, and dozens of others. One wonders when he ever slept. He was a model pastor that transformed lukewarm Kidderminster into a town filled with godliness. On the other hand, his theology was questionable in several areas. His *Aphorisms of Justification* and others bordered on advocating justification by both imputed and infused righteousness together with our cooperating works. This led to the Neonomian Controversy at the end of the century.[6] In *Catholick Theologie*, he sought a theological compromise between Calvinism, Arminianism, and Lutheranism. In *The Universal Redemption of Mankind*, he promoted a British form of hypothetical universalism resembling that of Moyse Amyraut. His largest work, *Methodus Theologiae Christianae*, was a huge systematic theology never translated from Latin.

Brief mention must be made of the famous and controversial poet John Milton (1608–74), author of *Paradise Lost* and many others. He began as an Anglican Puritan, then turned Presbyterian, then Independent, as he gradually went blind and moved from Calvinism to Arminianism to Arianism. His tragic life and spiritual apostasy are symbolized in his epic poem *Samson Agonistes*. Puritans often pointed to Milton as an example of what can happen when one pulls up the Reformed anchor and makes shipwreck of his faith.

The beloved John Howe (1630–1705) exemplified the best and sweetest of Puritan preaching. He sought peace without doctrinal compromise among various factions at the end of the Puritan era and witnessed the demise of

---

5 Currently being translated by Steven Dilday as *Exegetical Labors of the Reverend Matthew Poole* (Culpeper: Master Poole Publishing, 2007–).
6 I will discuss this later in chapter 10, "Hyper-Calvinism."

Anglican Puritanism around 1700. John Edwards (1637–1716) would be the last in the line of great Anglican Puritans.

The Presbyterian Puritans

Many Puritans believed that the church should be led by elders and not bishops, which they saw as left over from Catholicism. They also denied that the monarchy and the state have authority in or over the church. Further, they objected to the "High Church" liturgicalism of the Anglican system.

Thomas Cartwright (1535–1603) was the first major Presbyterian Puritan. He was expelled from teaching at Cambridge and imprisoned several times for his beliefs. Another student of Beza, Walter Travers (1548–1635), wrote the influential *A Directory of Church Government*. Robert Bolton (1572–1631) was a noted author: *A Treatise on Comforting Afflicted Consciences* and *General Directions for a Comfortable Walking with God*. John Ball (1585–1640) popularized covenant theology in *A Treatise on the Covenant of Grace*. Samuel Bolton (1606–54) became vice-chancellor of Cambridge and wrote *The True Bounds of Christian Liberty* against antinomianism. Joseph Alleine (1634–68) wrote the extremely popular evangelistic book *Alarm to the Unconverted*. His brother Richard (1611–81) wrote *Heaven Opened, Instructions about Heartwork*, and other experimental treatises.

By the time of the mid-century Commonwealth, the Presbyterians had taken the lead from the Anglicans in promoting Puritanism. They were the predominant faction at the Westminster Assembly, whose confession and catechisms teach Presbyterianism. William Gouge (1575–1653) took over from Twisse as prolocutor of the Assembly and was one of its most influential divines. He wrote a large exposition of Hebrews and was a major contributor to the *Westminster Annotations* Bible commentary. Edmund Calamy (1600–1666) was another Westminster divine; he later helped recall Charles II. His grandson of the same name wrote an important history of the Great Ejection of 1662.

Thomas Manton (1620–77) was one of the three official scribes of the Assembly. One of the most popular preachers of the day, he published a large number of sermons, including useful expositions of James and Jude. Stephen Charnock (1628–80) wrote what many have considered to be the best book on God ever penned, *The Existence and Attributes of God*. Thomas Watson (1620–86) was another famous preacher and writer: *A Body of Divinity, The Lord's Prayer, The Ten Commandments, The Beatitudes, A Divine Cordial*, and others. They have a sweet and very readable style.

Stephen Marshall (1594–1655), another Westminster divine, preached before Parliament and the Assembly more than any other preacher. He was one of the few premillennial Puritans. Other notable Westminster Presbyterians were Obadiah Sedgwick (1600–1658), Lazarus Seaman (c. 1610–75), and Anthony Tuckney (1599–1670), who was especially helpful in writing the confession and catechisms. Christopher Love (1618–51) wrote several books that still feed hungry souls, such as *Grace, The Penitent Pardoned, The Soul's Dejected Cure,* and *The Mortified Christian.* A Welshman, he was tried for treason and executed for supporting efforts to return Charles II to the throne.

At the end of the century, several Presbyterians stayed true to Puritanism. John Flavel (c. 1630–91) wrote the classics *The Method of Grace, The Fountain of Life,* and *The Mystery of Providence.* Robert Traill (1642–1716) was from Scotland but ministered in England. He authored *The Throne of Grace* and opposed the Neonomianism of his fellow Presbyterian Daniel Williams (1643–1716). The latter left a large sum of money with his books to start the important Dr. Williams' Library in London, where scholars still go to do serious research in Puritanism. Last but certainly not least, Matthew Henry (1662–1714) closed the Puritan era on a high note by writing an extremely popular commentary on the Bible (completed by others from his notes after his death). His father Philip Henry (1631–96) was another notable Puritan.

The Independent Puritans

The third group were the Independents, also known as Congregationalists in America. Though only a small group at the beginning of the seventeenth century, they came to be the largest faction at the end of the century. There were several subgroups, but all held to congregational church polity. They usually accepted elder-leadership within the local church but held back from formally-binding superstructures beyond the local congregation. They were even more against "High Church" ideas than were the Presbyterians.

The first subgroup was the Separatists. Their early leader was Robert Browne (c. 1553–1633) of Cambridge. More influential as a preacher than a writer, he became less and less Reformed in his beliefs. Henry Barrow (1550–93) suffered imprisonment for his congregational views. Henry Ainsworth (1571–1622), another "Brownist," moved to the Netherlands with other Separatists and wrote a much-respected commentary on the Pentateuch, the Psalms, and the Song of Songs.

The next subgroup was more well known and less separatist. They were led by two of the greatest of all Puritans. The first was the eminent John Owen (1616–83). He served as one of Cromwell's army chaplains, pastored in London, and became vice-chancellor of Oxford during the Commonwealth. He was not a Westminster divine but often preached before Parliament. Owen's scholarship was second to none, though his literary style has often been described as prolix. Someone has commented that it was because his writing style was more like Latin than English. His masterpiece was his large commentary on Hebrews. His two-volume work on the Holy Spirit is often considered the best on the subject. *The Death of Death in the Death of Christ* is perhaps the most influential defense of limited atonement. He wrote on other controversies, such as in *A Display of Arminianism*, and was in frequent debate with Baxter on justification. Though sometimes castigated for his Aristotelianism, he was also a major proponent of Puritan experimental divinity, as seen in *The Mortification of Sin, Communion with God, The Grace and Duty of Being Spiritually Minded*, and others.

The other leading Independent was Thomas Goodwin (1600–1680), London pastor and president of Magdalene College, Cambridge University, and a leading Westminster divine. With Owen he coauthored the Savoy Confession, which was the Independents' revision of the Westminster Confession. Among his many works were *The Holy Spirit, The Object and Acts of Justifying Faith, Christ the Mediator*, and a large work on congregational polity. He was a major proponent of supralapsarianism in *A Discourse of Election*. He also taught that assurance comes through the sealing of the Holy Spirit as a kind of second work of grace. He was also evidently premillennial.

In a way, the most influential of all Independents was neither a preacher nor a theologian, but a statesman and military leader. Oliver Cromwell (1599–1658) represented Cambridge in Parliament and was one of the leaders in the revolution that overthrew King Charles I and Archbishop William Laud. He organized the New Model Army to win the English Civil War. He commissioned many great Puritan preachers to serve as military chaplains. A powerful and charismatic leader, Cromwell could be both severe (as in the harsh treatment of the Irish) and tolerant (many sects were allowed liberty). He reluctantly agreed to the execution of Charles I and Laud but refused the offer of the crown and preferred the title *Lord Protector*. He was buried in Westminster Abbey, but at the Restoration his corpse was exhumed and publicly hanged by the Royalists.

Sir Henry Vane Jr. (1613–62) was another Independent statesman. He was governor of Massachusetts for two years, supported Mrs. Anne Hutchinson in the antinomian controversy, returned to England, and served in Parliament.

Though the Independents were a minority at the Westminster Assembly, they included several of its most influential divines, such as Goodwin. Jeremiah Burroughs (1599–1646) was another but is more well known for writing *The Rare Jewel of Christian Contentment*, a large exposition of Hosea, and many others. He too was premillennial. Joseph Caryl (1602–73) succeeded Owen as pastor and wrote a massive twelve-volume exposition of Job. William Bridge (1600–1670), still another premillennial Puritan, wrote the popular *A Lifting Up of the Downcast*. William Greenhill (1591–1671) penned a large exposition of Ezekiel and other works.

Thomas Brooks (1608–80) was one of the most readable and quotable of Puritan writers, as in *Precious Remedies Against Satan's Devices, The Mute Christian under the Smarting Rod, Apples of Gold,* and others. David Clarkson (1622–86) also followed Owen in London. Thomas Vincent (1634–78) wrote the delightful little book *The True Christian's Love to the Unseen Christ* and others. Elisha Coles (1608–88) produced an oft-reprinted defense of Calvinism entitled *A Practical Discourse of God's Sovereignty*. Christopher Ness (1621–1705) also wrote such a defense, *An Antidote Against Arminianism,* and a Bible commentary. Walter Marshall (1628–79) was an Anglican turned Independent and was known mainly for his excellent *The Gospel-Mystery of Sanctification*.

Another subgroup of Independents will be discussed in a later chapter — the Separatists who fled England and went to North America. These Puritans are more popularly known as the Pilgrim Fathers.

The Baptist Puritans

The Baptists had much in common with the Independents; they said they came out of Roman Catholicism the furthest. Initially they resembled the continental Anabaptists in their Arminianism but gradually became more Reformed in doctrine. Research, however, has shown that they arose from the English separatist movement and not primarily from the European Anabaptists. John Smyth (1554–1612) was the first English Baptist per se. Like Browne, he became decreasingly Calvinistic in doctrine. The Baptist triumvirate of Hanserd Knollys (1599–1691), William Kiffin (1616–1701), and Benjamin Keach (1640–1704) were "the Three K's" who led the Baptists in the Puritan era. Their influence can be seen in the two great London Baptist confessions of 1644 and 1689. The latter, also known as the Baptist Confession of 1689, is a slight revision of the Westminster Confession and is still much used today by Reformed Baptists.

The greatest Baptist Puritan, however, is probably the most well known and most read of all the Puritans: John Bunyan (1628–88). After serving on the Parliamentary side in the Civil War, he was later imprisoned for twelve years during the Restoration for refusing to conform to the reestablished Church of England. *The Pilgrim's Progress* is probably the best-selling book ever written in English and is one of the three best-selling Christian books of all time (together with Augustine's *Confessions* and Thomas a Kempis' *The Imitation of Christ*). *The Holy War* is another popular allegory of the Christian life. Bunyan wrote many other devotional, theological, controversial, and autobiographical works, such as *Grace Abounding to the Chief of Sinners*. He was buried with many other great Puritans in Bunhill Fields, London.[7]

The Scottish Puritans

Technically speaking, Puritanism was an English phenomenon, but seventeenth-century Scottish Calvinism shared most of its doctrines and goals and can be considered Scottish Puritanism. After the English and Scottish monarchies were united, the Scottish Presbyterians were increasingly pressured to accept Episcopalian ecclesiology and theological compromise.

The Scottish reaction led to two main documents. First, the National Covenant (1638) reaffirmed the Reformed faith, rejected Catholicism, and defended Presbyterian polity in Scotland. Some three hundred Scots subscribed to it. Second, the Solemn League and Covenant (1643) formed a covenantal union of England and Scotland, approved by Parliament and the Westminster Assembly, acknowledged Presbyterianism in Scotland, and promised to reform the Church of England along Calvinistic Presbyterial lines.

During the Puritan era, there were many great Scottish Calvinists. Robert Bruce (1554–1631, not to be confused with Robert the Bruce of an earlier era) wrote popular sermons on the Lord's Supper. Alexander Henderson (1583–1646), co-author of the aforementioned covenants, and George Gillespie (1613–48) were the foremost advocates of Presbyterianism at the Westminster Assembly, together with Robert Baillie (1602–62).

The most beloved Scot of all was Samuel Rutherford (1600–1661), another commissioner to the Assembly. He defended revolution against ungodly tyrants in his popular and controversial *Lex Rex* and opposed antinomianism in *A Survey of the Spiritual Antichrist*. He warmed hearts in *The Trial and Triumph of Faith, Christ Dying and Drawing Sinners to Himself*, and others. He expounded

---

7 Also buried there are John Owen, Isaac Watts, Thomas Goodwin, John Gill, and many other "Dissenters" (non-Anglican preachers).

covenant theology in *The Covenant of Life Opened*. But his greatest legacy is the collection of his letters to his parishioners while he was under house arrest for resisting Episcopalianism. They breathe an air of sweet love for Christ and His people.

David Dickson (1583–1663) wrote expositions of several books of the Bible and is often coupled with James Durham (1622–58) as two of the most influential writers in Scotland. William Guthrie (1620–65) penned *The Christian's Great Interest*, a classic on assurance of salvation. Henry Scougal (1650–78) produced the classic *The Life of God in the Soul of Man*, which greatly influenced George Whitefield. Curiously, Scougal was an Episcopalian, not Presbyterian. Likewise, Robert Leighton (1611–84), born in London, was another Scottish Episcopalian and author of a popular exposition of 1 Peter. Hugh Binning (1627–53) died young but touched many. James Fraser of Brea (1638–98) advocated a kind of Scottish hypothetical universalism (akin to Amyraldism).

Further History

Puritanism reached its height around 1650. But there was a severe backlash. Arminians such as Henry Hammond (1605–60), John Goodwin (1594–1665), and Jeremy Taylor (1613–67) taught an evangelical/devotional Arminianism. Daniel Whitby (1638–1726), author of a popular New Testament commentary and a defense of the Remonstrance, drifted into Arianism, as did William Whiston (1667–1752), successor of Sir Isaac Newton and translator of the works of Josephus. They confirmed the Puritans' warnings that unchecked Arminianism leads to either popery or Arianism.

The so-called Cambridge Platonists and Latitudinarians harkened back to the lukewarm Anglicanism of the Elizabethan Settlement and Richard Hooker. By the end of the century, mainstream Anglicanism was in the grip of the insipid moralism of John Tillotson (1630–94) and Edward Stillingfleet (1635–99). Archbishop of Canterbury William Laud (1573–1645) was a tireless opponent of Puritanism and was suspected of Catholic sympathies.

Charles I (1600–1649) became king in 1625 and worked with Laud to halt Puritanism in both the churches and the government. One of their measures was *The Declaration on Sports* (1637), more popularly known as "The Book of Sports." It was directly aimed at opposing the high Puritan view of the Sabbath by listing many activities which were allowable on Sunday.

As the tension increased, Charles summoned the Long Parliament in 1640 for aid, but the Puritans held the upper hand and turned down his proposals. Soon Civil War broke out between the Royalists and the Roundheads, who were mostly Puritans, led by Cromwell, John Pym (1583–1643), Thomas Fairfax (1612–71), and others. Most but not all Puritans supported Parliament in the war. The Scots were caught in the middle, as it were, for they clung to the covenants in order to reestablish Presbyterianism but were theologically more in agreement with the Puritans.

The Parliamentary side eventually won the war. Cromwell called, dismissed, and recalled Parliament several times, for there was not unanimity as to which way to proceed. For fifteen years or so, England under the Puritan Commonwealth had one of the godliest societies in history, on a larger scale than even Geneva in the time of Calvin or Germany in the time of Luther. Together with the heavily Calvinist Dutch Republic at this time, many consider this to be the high point in the history of Calvinism. The effects extended into Scotland and even the American colonies.

The Puritans allowed the Jews to return to England. The Church of England was permitted to continue but was no longer the established state church. Presbyterianism never became the state church as such in England. The Independents and Baptists grew, as did various cults like the Quakers, the Muggletonians, Ranters, Levellers, and Fifth-Monarchy Men. Puritans regularly preached in Parliament. Biblical law was enforced in society to a large measure. It was truly the Golden Age of Puritanism (1645–60).

Then the tide turned. Cromwell died in 1658. Parliament continued to disagree on many measures. Cromwell's son Richard was an ineffectual successor. Royalist forces succeeded in recalling Charles II (1630–85) to the throne in 1660. This led to the restoration of the monarchy and reestablishment of the Church of England. The Act of Uniformity of 1662 required all pastors to subscribe. Two thousand Puritan pastors did not, so they were put out of their churches by force in the Great Ejection.

Up in Scotland, the tables were also turned on the noble Scots who refused to recant the two covenants. These Covenanters were hounded and persecuted; many were even executed during the "killing times."

Then it began to mellow in 1688 when William of Orange (the Netherlands) was called to become king of England after Charles died. With his queen, Mary, the Glorious Revolution succeeded without bloodshed and allowed much tolerance for the Puritans. The Act of Toleration (1688) overturned the

Act of Uniformity (1662). Preachers returned to their pulpits. The Church of England was still the state church and Non-Conformists, as they were now called, were considered second-class citizens.

Puritanism survived but in a weakened form. Most of the great leaders had gone to their heavenly reward. Anglican Puritanism diminished rapidly. Unexpectedly, English Presbyterianism veered into Arianism in the 1700s. Historic Reformed theology was mainly in the hands of Independents and Baptists, many of whom united in "The Happy Union" to survive.

Conclusion

With the rediscovery of historic Calvinism in the mid-twentieth century came a renewed interest in the Puritans. Many of their books have been reprinted. *The Pilgrim's Progress* still sells well today. Those who are dead yet speaketh today. The dream lives on.

Chapter 8
The Westminster Assembly

What many theologians consider to have been the largest gathering of spiritual giants since the days of the apostles met from 1643 to 1648 in the Jerusalem Chamber of Westminster Abbey in London. The documents they produced also rank among the theologically richest in all church history. No study of Calvinism is complete without a look at the Westminster Assembly, its participants, and its documents.

History

King Charles I and Archbishop of Canterbury William Laud were no friends of the Reformation or the Puritans. They attempted to force the new Anglican prayer book on the state churches of England and Scotland in order to curtail Puritanism, but it backfired on them. On July 23, 1637, the Bishop of Edinburgh, Scotland, began to read from it in a service in St. Giles Cathedral — the High Kirk of the Church of Scotland. Legend has it that one Jenny Geddes, a local vegetable-seller and dedicated Calvinist, objected vociferously by throwing at the bishop the little stool on which she was sitting and crying out, "Villain! Do you say Mass at my lug?!" (an old Scottish word for *ear*). A riot broke out. Someone has commented that the tossing of the stool led to the fall of the English throne.

Then in 1638 the noble Scots signed the National Covenant and pledged to uphold the Reformed faith in the churches of Scotland and resist all Romanizing innovations. They claimed scriptural support for such covenants from Joshua 24:25, 2 Kings 11:17, and Isaiah 44:5. They further agreed with the Solemn League and Covenant of 1643. Meanwhile, England turned to Civil War between the Royalist and Parliamentary forces, which were predominantly Puritan. Parliament passed the following resolution on June 12, 1643, setting up the Westminster Assembly: "An Ordinance of the Lords and Commons in Parliament, for the Calling of an Assembly of Divines and others, to be Consulted with by the Parliament for the Settling of the Government and Liturgy of the Church of England, and Clearing of the Doctrine of said Church from false Superstitions and Interpretations."

The Assembly met in 1,163 sessions from July 1, 1643, to February 22, 1648. It was never formally dissolved. Of the 151 members, 121 were "divines" (theologians and preachers) and 30 were "lay assessors" (20 from the House of Commons and 10 from the House of Lords). William Twisse (1578–1646) was the first prolocutor (moderator), followed by William Gouge and Cornelius Burgess. Most of the members were Presbyterians. Five were Independents. A few were Anglicans, but other Anglicans declined out of respect to the king. There were no Baptists. The Church of Scotland sent five "Commissioners," including Samuel Rutherford, George Gillespie, and Alexander Henderson. The Independents and the Scots exercised more influence than their numbers indicate. There were no Arminians present, though the Arminian Anglican Henry Hammond (1605–60) was respectfully invited. Obviously, there were no Roman Catholics, Quakers, or even Lutherans.

Daily attendance averaged about seventy. There were occasionally days of prayer and fasting. None of the members were ejected for heresy, though one was removed for divulging the proceedings to a non-member. Every member took the following vow which was read aloud every Monday morning:

> I do solemnly promise and vow, in the presence of Almighty God, that in this Assembly whereof I am a member, I will maintain nothing in point of doctrine but what I believe to be most agreeable to the Word of God; nor in point of discipline, but what may make most for God's glory and the peace and good of His church.

Important and influential divines included John Arrowsmith, Thomas Goodwin, Thomas Gataker, Anthony Tuckney, William Gouge, Anthony Burgess, Jeremiah Burroughs, Edward Reynolds, and Thomas Manton. John Lightfoot (1602–75) was evidently the only member to attend every session and kept detailed notes. The minutes and other papers have recently been published in full.[1]

The Westminster Standards

The Assembly issued several documents, three of which stand out.[2] First, the

---

1 Chad Van Dixhoorn, ed. *The Minutes and Papers of the Westminster Assembly* (Oxford: Oxford University Press, 2012).

2 The best handy edition is *The Confession of Faith: The Confession of Faith, The Larger and Shorter Catechisms, The Directory for the Public Worship of God, With Associated Historical Documents* (Edinburgh: Banner of Truth, 2018). Various denominations have published their own revised editions. The Confession and catechisms are also in James T. Dennison Jr., ed.,

Westminster Confession of Faith (1646) was written after the Assembly chose not to revise the Anglican Thirty-Nine Articles of Religion. It was based on the Irish Articles (1615), of which James Ussher was the main author. It was initially composed by a committee of twenty-five, of whom Gouge, Gataker, Tuckney, Goodwin, and the Scots were most influential. The Assembly debated and finally approved it, then sent it to Parliament for legal approval. Parliament sent it back with the stipulation that Scripture proofs be added. Thus added, it was formally approved by Parliament and soon after by the Church of Scotland.

The Westminster Confession is often deservedly called "The Queen of Confessions." Longer than most Reformed confessions and more thorough than the Canons of the Synod of Dort, it has stood the test of time. Later the Independents met at Savoy and revised it as the Savoy Confession (1658) to reflect congregational polity.[3] The Baptists also revised it in 1677, though not published until 1688/89 as the Second London Confession of Faith (also known as the Baptist Confession of 1689) to reflect Baptist ecclesiology.[4]

Several chapters stand out. Chapter 1 has one of the finest sections on Scripture ever composed. It teaches biblical infallibility, *sola Scriptura*, and the internal testimony of the Holy Spirit. It includes a section teaching that the whole counsel of God is either expressly set down in Scripture or by "good and necessary consequence" may be deduced from Scripture.

Chapter 3 teaches that God foreordained "whatever comes to pass," including election and reprobation. It implies infralapsarianism. Chapter 7 explicitly teaches covenant theology. Chapter 8 is one of the few confessions to teach the threefold offices of Christ as prophet, priest, and king. Paragraph 8 implies limited atonement. Chapter 19 teaches the three parts of God's law: ceremonial, civil and moral. Chapter 21 says that Sunday is the Christian Sabbath, a major emphasis among the Puritans. Chapter 23 teaches the Reformed "Two Kingdoms" view, thus avoiding both Erastianism and Anabaptist theories. Chapter 25 teaches the difference between the visible and invisible church and that the papacy is the Antichrist (some later revisions omit this).

The Shorter Catechism has 107 questions and answers and was meant for the instruction of children.[5] It covers the Ten Commandments, the Lord's

---

Reformed Confessions of the 16th and 17th Centuries in English Translation, Vol. 4 (Grand Rapids: Reformation Heritage Books, 2014).

3 Dennison Jr., *Reformed Confessions*, 4:457–95.

4 Dennison Jr., 4:531–71.

5 Numerous systematic theologies have been expositions of the Shorter Catechism, e.g.,

Prayer, and important heads of doctrine. All the answers embody the question in the wording, making it a valuable learning device. Four answers are especially popular: "Man's chief end is to glorify God and to enjoy him forever" (1); "God is a Spirit, infinite, eternal, and unchangeable, in his being, wisdom, power, holiness, justice, goodness, and truth" (40); "Sin is any want of conformity unto, or transgression of, the Law of God" (14); and "Justification is an act of God's free grace, wherein he pardoneth all our sins, and accepteth us as righteous in his sight, only for the righteousness of Christ imputed to us, and received by faith alone" (33).

The Larger Catechism has 196 questions and much fuller answers. One interesting answer includes the following principle concerning God's law:

> That as, where a duty is commanded, the contrary sin is forbidden; and, when a sin is forbidden, the contrary duty is commanded; so, where a promise is annexed, the contrary threatening is included; and, where a threatening is annexed, the contrary promise is included (99, paragraph 4).

Related Documents

David Dickson and James Durham, both of Scotland, authored *The Sum of Saving Knowledge* (1650). It has been more popular in Scotland than in England or America. The longest section is "The Practical Use of Saving Knowledge." It applies the basic truths of the *Sum* to evangelism and assurance and gives five "Evidences of True Faith" and four "Warrants to Believe."

The Form of Presbyterial Church-Government (1645) was based on the Solemn League and Covenant and provides a constitution for the church, officers, individual congregations, presbyteries and synods, examinations, and ordination.

The Directory for the Public Worship of God (1645) was not a prayer book as such. It was meant to replace the Anglican *Book of Common Prayer* and was officially accepted by both the English Parliament and the Church of Scotland. *The Directory for Family Worship* (1647) was a devotional manual for use in family worship. It was produced by the Church of Scotland but has often been published with the Westminster Standards, together with the National Covenant and the Solemn League and Covenant.

The Westminster Annotations (1647) was a large Bible commentary unofficially produced by John Ley, William Gouge, Thomas Gataker, Daniel Featley, and

---

Thomas Watson, *A Body of Divinity* (Edinburgh: Banner of Truth, 1974).

others, all anonymous. It deserves to be reprinted today. It serves as a useful index to how the divines generally understood the Scripture proofs in the Confession and catechisms.

The Metrical Psalter was another by-product of the Westminster Assembly. There were other such psalters before and after, but this one has perhaps been the most popular and beloved, especially in Scotland where it is still used by many. Its rendering of Psalm 23 is especially heart-warming.

Conclusion

Parliament won the Civil Wars. Laud and Charles I were executed for treason. Cromwell led the Puritan Commonwealth during the Golden Age of English Puritanism, but it collapsed by 1660 when Charles II was made king. The Restoration and reestablishment of the Church of England undid much of what the Puritans accomplished. But perhaps the greatest legacy of the Puritans is the Westminster Confession and Shorter Catechism, which have instructed and encouraged millions of Christians for centuries.

Chapter 9
Amyraldism

In this chapter, we will briefly look at a subgroup of Reformed theology that has variously been called hypothetical universalism, Low Calvinism, four-point Calvinism, Moderate Calvinism, or more precisely, Amyraldism (or Amyraldianism). There have been variations within this general theology, but I will concentrate on the seventeenth-century controversy surrounding Moyse Amyraut (1596–1664).

Roots of the Controversy

When the Edict of Nantes (1598) ended the Wars of Religion in France between the Catholics and the Protestants, the French Calvinists known as Huguenots prepared for the future. Philippe Duplessis de Mornay (1549–1623) helped found the Theological Academy at Saumur to train pastors. Previously most French Reformed pastors had been trained at the academy in Geneva.

John Cameron (1579–1625) was a Scotsman who taught there for a short time. He approved of the Canons of Dort but disagreed with the High Calvinism of certain theologians who seemed to follow Beza more than Calvin. He certainly did not approve of Arminianism. He promoted what may be termed "Low Calvinism" and influenced several younger men in that direction.

Moyse Amyraut

Moyse Amyraut[1] taught at Saumur from 1633–64. He greatly influenced the French Reformed Church through over a hundred publications, such as his six-volume *Christian Ethics* (over 4,600 pages). But his most controversial work was *A Brief Treatise on Predestination*.[2] While retaining a kind of scholastic method in some of his works, Amyraut was displeased with the tendency of the "higher" Reformed Scholastics and, like Cameron, wanted a return to the more

---

1 Moyse, Moise, or Moses; Amyraut, Amyrauld, or Amyraldus, depending upon the Latin, French, or English.
2 Matthew Harding, *Amyraut on Predestination* (Attleborough: Charenton Reformed Publishing, 2017).

biblically-balanced approach of Calvin, while remaining true to the Canons of Dort.

Amyraut was also concerned that Lutheranism — under the influence of Melanchthon, Chemnitz, and Gerhard — was becoming more synergistic. Indeed, it bore a resemblance to Arminianism and Semi-Pelagianism. He dreamed of a theological reunion of the Swiss and German branches of the Reformation as originally seen in the theology of grace of Luther and Calvin. Such a reunion would help further the Reformation and resist Catholicism better. He also hoped it would successfully draw some Catholics to the Reformation cause.

Other Amyraldians

Others at Saumur sided with Amyraut such as David Blondel (1590–1655), Paul Testard (1599–1650), and Josue de la Place (or Placeus, 1596–1655). Louis Cappel (1585–1658) was a Hebrew scholar who taught the then-controversial but now widely accepted view that only the Hebrew consonants and not the Masoretic vowel points were inspired by God. Jean Daille (1594–1670) was a popular Huguenot preacher and noted scholar.[3] He collected a large mass of quotations from church fathers, medieval theologians, and Protestant Reformers to show that Amyraldism had a good ancestry, though he warned against making the fathers our authority as Catholics had done. Claude Pajon (1626–85) later took the movement much further than what Cameron or Amyraut envisaged.

A somewhat similar movement was developing in Britain at this time. The original English Reformers were moderate and not given to extremes, but some Puritans became too scholastic and supralapsarian. In the seventeenth century, many notable English Puritans rejected "High Calvinism" and preferred the more moderate "Low" approach of the English Reformers and Calvin. These included James Ussher, the English delegates to the Synod of Dort (John Davenant, Joseph Hall, George Carleton, and Samuel Ward), John Preston, Edward Polhill, Lazarus Seaman, John Arrowsmith, Stephen Marshall, Richard Vines, and Richard Baxter. James Fraser of Brea (1638–98) had a similar view in Scotland. Several of the delegates to Dort from the German Palatinate were also of this general persuasion, such as Matthias Martinus (1572–1630). It should be noted that they had differences among themselves as well as with

---

3 Charles Haddon Spurgeon praised his sermons: "Written in a deliciously florid style. Very sweet and evangelical; after the French manner." *Commenting and Commentaries* (London: Banner of Truth, 1969), 179.

the French Amyraldians, but a general sympathy among them can be seen. It is still debated whether British Low Calvinism was Amyraldian or mainstream Moderate Calvinism.

The Anti-Amyraldians

Naturally the movement incurred strong opposition. In France, Pierre du Moulin (1568–1658) and Andreas Rivet (or Rivetus, 1572–1651) wrote thousands of pages of refutation. In Switzerland, Francis Turretin, Friedrich Spanheim (1600–1649), and Johann Heinrich Heidegger (1633–98) joined the fray. The issues were debated at the Westminster Assembly, both for and against. But most of the controversy was between the French and the Swiss, centered around the academies in Saumur and Geneva.

The Issues

The controversy revolved around several issues. One was original sin. Many Amyraldians believed in a traducian or realist theory, in which all mankind was physically and spiritually in Adam. Original sin, therefore, is transmitted mediately to all mankind.

Highly controversial was Amyraut's theory of what has been called *hypothetical universalism*, which the English did not necessarily accept. He argued that out of a general benevolence to all men, God foreordained a conditional (hence, hypothetical) decree of salvation for all men, conditioned on faith. But since men would be totally depraved and unable to believe, God then made an unconditional decree of election and reprobation and would give faith to the elect.

This system of salvation would be developed in history through three covenants. First, God made a covenant of nature with Adam, in which He commanded obedience to the law as revealed in nature. Second, there was the covenant of law made with Israel, demanding full obedience to the written law of Moses. Third, the covenant of grace through Christ included a conditional part between God and all mankind based on universal grace and an unconditional part between God and the elect based on special grace. Amyraut suggested that because of the universal saving will, grace, and natural revelation, it is hypothetically possible for the heathen to be saved without hearing or believing the gospel. But he seems to have denied that any heathen actually have been saved.

Next, Amyraut taught that Christ died *equally* for all men in order to provide for the universal aspect of the covenant of grace. The atonement was unlimited, but its application was limited to the elect. The English, however, tended to shy back from a fully universal atonement and preferred to say that Christ died *especially* for the elect, not *only* for the elect or *equally* for everyone. Amyraut, Daille, and Davenant argued that Calvin taught universal redemption rather than limited atonement. This was an early stage of the "Calvin versus Calvinism" debate.

The Response

The anti-Amyraldians responded as follows. First, many of them taught a federal view of the transmission of original sin. Adam was our legal representative as Christ was for the elect, and we were not physically in either one nor spiritually in them acting good or bad. Sin is passed down immediately, not mediately. Next, they denied that any of the divine decrees were in any way conditional. They may presuppose previous decrees (such as the debate between the infralapsarians and the supralapsarians), but that is not the same thing. Likewise, there was a universal benevolence in God, but that is in the realm of the revealed will of God in the gospel rather than the secret will of predestination. All decrees are unconditional, period.

Some taught that the decree of election logically preceded the decree of atonement. Redemption therefore is limited to the elect alone. Some, such as Turretin and Owen, taught a strictly limited atonement, but others did allow for a universal aspect of redemption, though some said it had nothing to do with salvation. The anti-Amyraldians generally denied that Calvin taught universal redemption.

They replied to Amyraut's covenantalism in several ways. Mainstream covenant theology was not uniform, so their replies varied. Some adhered to Cocceius' system. Others added further covenants. Some had only two covenants. Still others shied back from covenant theology and relied on Reformed scholasticism to counter Amyraut.

Lastly, they strongly recoiled from Amyraut's idea of hypothetical salvation of heathen who never hear the gospel. They stressed that special revelation, not natural revelation, presents the gospel and gives special grace. It is dangerous to suggest that those who never hear might somehow believe.[4]

---

4 See chapter 51, "The Destiny of the Unevangelized."

Further History

Amyraut appeared before several French synods to answer charges against him. The National Synod of Alencon (1637) admonished him but did not condemn him. The Synod of Charenton (1645) cleared him, as did the Synod of Loudon (1659).[5] The Saumur faculty produced a massive two-volume summary of their theology, *Theses Theologicae Salmurienses* (1664–65).

Du Moulin and others kept the printing presses working overtime in producing large tomes to refute Amyraut and others. It came to a head in Switzerland when Turretin, Heidegger, and Lucas Gernler authored the Formula Consensus Helvetica (1675).[6] This important document was not a full confession of faith nor one officially approved by a church to be binding on its members. Rather, like the Canons of Dort, it was meant to provide an answer to what was perceived as a non-Reformed theology that had intruded into the Reformed churches. Among other things, it condemned Cappel's view of the Hebrew vowel points.

Sadly, orthodoxy in both circles rapidly degenerated toward the end of the seventeenth century and throughout the eighteenth century, even in Geneva. The Edict of Nantes was revoked in 1685. Many Huguenots fled France for religious freedom in England, Holland, and America. The two opposing sides were never fully reconciled.

Conclusion

The issues have continued to be debated over the centuries. *Amyraldism* has come to be used rather loosely in some quarters. Often all it means is "four-point Calvinism," in which a person rejects limited atonement but does not necessarily accept the other four points. Others have a better understanding of Amyraut and have defended him, such as Brian Armstrong and Alan Clifford.[7] Roger Nicole was perhaps the foremost authority on the subject. P. F. Van Stam's *The Controversy Over the Theology of Saumur (1635–1650)*[8] is the fullest work in English. Jonathan Moore's fine *English Hypothetical Universalism*:

---

5 John Quick, ed., *Synodicon in Gallia Reformata: or, the Acts, Decisions, Decrees, and Canons of the Those Famous National Councils of the Reformed Churches in France* (London: T. Parkhurst and J. Robinson, 1692). No serious study of the controversy is complete without this grand source, but many popular studies are not even aware of it.

6 Translated in James T. Dennison Jr, ed., *Reformed Confessions of the 16th and 17th Centuries in English Translation* (Grand Rapids: Reformation Heritage Books, 2012), 4:516–30.

7 See Bibliography.

8 Amsterdam: Holland University Press, 1988.

John Preston and the Softening of Reformed Theology[9] is the definitive study on the English debates. Davenant's *Dissertation on the Death of Christ* has been reprinted.[10]

Some see a hint of Amyraldism in the writings of Thomas Boston and the "Marrowmen" in the eighteenth-century controversy surrounding the book *The Marrow of Modern Divinity*. This is unlikely. The charge sometimes comes from Hyper-Calvinists who would level the accusation against mainline Calvinists. A closer similarity can be detected in the "Low Calvinism" of the nineteenth-century Scottish theologians John M'Leod Campbell, Ralph Wardlaw, John Brown of Haddington, and James Morison. Parallel to that in some ways was the "Consistent Calvinism" of nineteenth-century New England Calvinism. In the twentieth century, several leading American dispensationalist theologians such as Lewis Sperry Chafer have advocated a theology akin to Amyraldism. Others such as Norman Geisler have defended what they consider "Moderate Calvinism" but in reality is more similar to Arminianism.

However one labels this general approach, favorably or otherwise, it has been a part of the Reformed tradition for over three hundred years and likely will continue to be so well into the future.

---

9 Grand Rapids: Eerdmans, 2007.
10 Weston Rhyn: Quinta Press, 2006.

Chapter 10
Hyper-Calvinism

Hyper-Calvinism is an often-misunderstood term.[1] Some misapply it to anyone who accepts the five points of Calvinism. Others deny that there is such a thing as Hyper-Calvinism. But in fact, there is such a subgroup within the Reformed tradition that goes beyond Calvin and mainstream Calvinism and has legitimately been described as Hyper-Calvinism.[2]

Background

The roots go back to the post-Reformation era (1560–1600). Beza, Perkins, and others developed *supralapsarianism* — the view that says God elected men from an unfallen mass rather than a sinful mass of humanity, as in the *infralapsarian* view of the Reformers. This approach has sometimes been called *High Calvinism*.[3] It has always been a minority report, but it included some leading seventeenth-century men such as Gisbertus Voetius, Samuel Rutherford, William Twisse, and Thomas Goodwin.

In the 1630s arose a still higher form that is sometimes denominated *antinomianism*.[4] Leading figures included John Eaton (c. 1575–c. 1631), Tobias Crisp (1600–1643), John Saltmarsh (?–1647), and William Dell (?–1664). It would appear they were all supralapsarians, but so were some of their critics such as Rutherford. Twisse, on the other hand, considered them within the circle of orthodoxy. They did not actually deny the general Reformed view of the law, and so the epithet is misleading. Rather, they downplayed the law in several ways. Nor were they guilty of licentious living. They did, however, often use

---

1 See my "Hyper-Calvinism and John Gill" PhD dissertation, The University of Edinburgh, 1983. I hope to publish a book based on it.
2 *Hyper* comes from the Greek word *huper*, which can mean "above." Hyper-Calvinism goes above and beyond mainline Calvinism.
3 As Peter Toon, *The Emergence of Hyper-Calvinism in English Nonconformity, 1689–1765* (London: Olive Tree, 1967).
4 Gertrude Huehns, *Antinomianism in English History* (London: Cresset, 1951); David R. Como, *Blown by the Spirit: Puritanism and the Emergence of an Antinomian Underground in Pre-Civil War England* (Stanford: Stanford University Pres, 2004); Theodore Dwight Bozeman, *The Precisionist Strain: Disciplinary Religion & Antinomian Backlash in Puritanism to 1638* (Chapel Hill: University of North Carolina Press, 2004).

unguarded language and implied that God sees no sin in the life of a believer, sin does no harm to a Christian, the elect were justified in eternity, and so on. But they often defined these assertions in an orthodox manner. What they did was upset the balance of divine sovereignty and human responsibility so as to overemphasize the former and weaken the latter. For example, they taught that faith is a gift and not a condition of justification and that justification precedes and not follows faith in the order of salvation.

The debate calmed down when most of their leaders had died by 1650, but it was renewed when Crisp's works were reprinted in the 1690s. A coterie of "anti-Antinomians" opposed what they saw as a rebirth of antinomianism. They were led by Richard Baxter (1615–91) and Daniel Williams (1643–1716). Their system was termed *Neonomianism*. They argued that the law still continues and the gospel is a new law which commands faith and obedience, with the result that God justifies a sinner on the twin basis of imputed and infused righteousness as well as one's own righteousness.

The anti-Antinomians were in turn opposed by the "anti-Neonomians" such as Isaac Chauncey (1632–1712) and Robert Traill (1642–1716). They did not defend the so-called Antinomians, but they generally were supralapsarian and tended to overemphasize divine sovereignty. Herman Witsius of the Netherlands and John Howe attempted in vain to negotiate a peaceful settlement.

Eighteenth-Century Hyper-Calvinism

Richard Davis (1658–1714) was a Welsh Independent pastor in Northamptonshire, England, who caused no small stir by defending Crisp. Another Independent evangelist in the area was Joseph Hussey (1659–1726). He too defended Crisp. Like Davis, he was involved in evangelism, as seen in his evangelistic book *The Gospel-Feast Opened* (1692). Then he did an about-face and renounced the book and his evangelistic methods. He wrote a massive (and almost incomprehensible) tome entitled *The Glory of Christ Unveiled, Or The Excellency of Christ Vindicated* (1706). This was the first time that a Calvinist rejected the doctrine and practice of the free offer of the gospel. He developed this further with *God's Operation of Grace, But No Offers of Grace* (1707).[5] Soon Davis also rejected free offers, and Hyper-Calvinism was born.

John Skepp (1675–1721) was one of Hussey's disciples and promoted the

---

5 An abridgement has been published by Primitive Baptist Publications (Elon College, 1973) thus establishing a modern link between the English Hyper-Calvinists and the Primitive Baptists.

non-offer view in *Divine Energy*. He is notable for transferring the leadership baton from the paedobaptist Independents to the Baptists. For the next three hundred years, most Hyper-Calvinists have been Baptists. A small number have been Independents, Anglicans, or Dutch Reformed, though very few have been Presbyterians. Skepp was succeeded in his church by John Brine (1703–65), who also rejected the free offer and other doctrines and practices held by mainstream Calvinists.

But it was the eminent Baptist pastor John Gill (1697–1771) who became the most influential Hyper-Calvinist theologian. During his fifty-one-year pastorate in London he reigned as undisputed leader among both the Baptists and Hyper-Calvinists. The church had previously been pastored by Benjamin Keach (1640–1704) and would later be pastored by Charles Haddon Spurgeon (1834–92), both of whom firmly believed in the free offer.

Gill was no theological sophomore. He wrote an enormous commentary on almost the whole Bible — perhaps the largest ever written by a single man. He penned a respected *Body of Divinity* systematic theology, numerous theological treatises, and several volumes of sermons. *The Cause of God and Truth* is a careful discussion of Bible texts appealed to by both Calvinists and Arminians. Most of these books are still in print today. But sadly, English Baptists tended to stultify in the eighteenth century. Historic Calvinism was also in general decline, but Hyper-Calvinism did not help rectify the trend.

Toward the end of the century, five pro-offer English Particular Baptists came to the rescue: Andrew Fuller (1754–1815), William Carey (1761–1834), John Rippon (1751–1836), John Ryland Jr. (1753–1825), and Samuel Pearce (1766–99). Fuller's *The Gospel Worthy of All Acceptation* defended free offers and Duty Faith, which the Hypers had denied. His friend William Carey produced what many consider the mandate for the Great Missionary Movement, *An Inquiry into the Obligations of Christians to Use Means for the Conversion of the Heathens*. They were much influenced by Jonathan Edwards and the Great Awakening in America and the Evangelical Awakening in England, which the Hyper-Calvinists usually ignored or opposed.

Nineteenth-Century Hyper-Calvinism

William Huntington (1745–1813) was a rather eccentric uneducated London paedobaptist Independent pastor and the leading Hyper-Calvinist from 1790 to 1813. Like Hussey and Gill, he admired Crisp, but unlike them he developed a form of doctrinal antinomianism as well as promoted the non-offer perspective.

He argued that the law was basically part of the old covenant and has passed away and been replaced by the gospel and the new covenant. A believer relies on Christ and the Spirit, not the law. Gill certainly taught the historic Reformed view of the law.

Huntington's views, sans the paedobaptism, were carried on by the Gospel Standard Strict and Particular Baptists. This group revered Gill, Brine, Crisp, and Huntington and vehemently opposed Fuller and the Missionary Movement. William Gadsby (1773–1844) of Manchester and the ex-Anglican Joseph Charles Philpot (1802–69) were its primary leaders. Other influential preachers included John Warburton (1776–1857), John Gadsby (1808–93), and John Kershaw (1792–1870). This group continues down to the present as the leading defenders of Hyper-Calvinism. Recent notables include B. A. Ramsbottom and Frank Gosden. Though a paedobaptist, George Ella moves in Gospel Standard circles.

It should be pointed out that not all Strict and Particular Baptists were of this persuasion. Abraham Booth (1734–1806) upheld the free offer and Duty Faith. But there was another Strict Baptist group that was Hyperist, the so-called Earthen Vessels (named for their magazine). John Stevens of London (1776–1847) was their leading light. He emphatically denied the antinomianism of Huntington and the Gospel Standard Baptists. On the other hand, he accepted Hussey's strange theory of Pre-Existerianism — namely, that Christ took on a human soul in the eternal covenant of redemption long before the actual Incarnation in time. Isaac Watts also taught that view.

The controversial James Wells (1803–72) pastored the Surrey Tabernacle, not far from the Metropolitan Tabernacle pastored by Spurgeon. He was basically in the Earthen Vessel camp and incited no small furor when he publicly defended Rahab for lying (Joshua 2:4–6). He said that her lie illustrates how God Himself stretches the truth in pronouncing sinners just when they are not. John Hazelton (1822–88) was another Earthen Vessel, as was W. J. Styles (1842–1914), who in some ways was the most extreme English Hyper-Calvinist of all. But this faction gradually petered out in the twentieth century.

During nineteenth-century England, there were still a few Independents such as Joseph Irons (1785–1852) and Anglicans such as Robert Hawker (1753–1827) and William Parks (1810–67) who taught Hyper-Calvinism. But by the turn of the century, English Hyperism was almost completely in the hands of Baptists.

In America, a slightly different form of Hyper-Calvinism was born among the Primitive Baptists. Like the Gospel Standard Baptists, with whom they had little direct contact, they opposed the Missionary Movement. Most rejected the doctrine of the free offer. Their distinctive tenet was the theory of immediate regeneration — that is, God regenerates the elect directly and not through what they sometimes derisively call "gospel regeneration." That being so, foreign missions, evangelism, and even Sunday schools are unnecessary and should not be employed. Their early leaders were Cushing (1809–80) and Sylvester Hassell (1842–1928), R. H. Pittman (1870–1941), and Gilbert Beebe (1800–81). One spinoff of this group was the now-defunct tiny group called the Two-Seed-in-the-Spirit Baptists led by Daniel Parker (1781–1844). This strange theory, based on an unusual interpretation of Genesis 3:15, said that regeneration is somehow biologically and spiritually planted in the elect from birth. The Primitive Baptists are still around today. Most still adhere to the theory of immediate regeneration and do not support missions. Many also deny the free offer doctrine. Prominent twentieth-century preachers have included W. J. Berry (1908–86), Laserre Bradley Jr., and R. V. Sarrells, author of one of the very few Primitive Baptist systematic theologies.

Twentieth-Century Hyper-Calvinism

In 1920s America, the Christian Reformed Church was influenced by the doctrine of common grace as taught by Abraham Kuyper back in the Netherlands. Louis Berkhof and others formulated the official "Three Points of Common Grace" in 1924. This was vehemently opposed by Herman Hoeksema (1886–1965), Henry Danhof, George Ophoff, and other CRC pastors. They were tried and expelled from the CRC and formed the Protestant Reformed Church based in Grand Rapids, Michigan. They not only denied common grace but also the free offer doctrine. They employed many of the same arguments as Gill, the Gospel Standards, and others. Hoeksema was a very able theologian. He wrote a useful *Reformed Dogmatics*, a large exposition of the Heidelberg Catechism called *The Triple Knowledge*, and numerous other books and pamphlets.

The Protestant Reformed Church survived a split in the 1950s when some of their people returned to the Christian Reformed Church. Subsequent PRC leaders have included Homer Hoeksema (son of Herman) and David Engelsma. Engelsma wrote *Hyper-Calvinism and the Call of the Gospel* in which he curiously rejected free offers but denied being Hyper-Calvinist. The PRC continues to be the main Hyper-Calvinist body in America today and one of the few paedobaptist churches to be Hyperist.

Henry Atherton (1875–1933) was the prominent Hyper-Calvinist pastor of Grove Chapel, London, and one of the last Independent Hyper-Calvinists. He was also a leader of the Sovereign Grace Union, many of whose members were of this view.

There have been a few non-offer Calvinists in Australia and the Netherlands. Arthur W. Pink (1886–1952) occasionally denied free offers, such as in *The Atonement*, but overall usually opposed Hyperism. In their latter years, the American Presbyterians Gordon H. Clark (1902–85) and John H. Gerstner (1914–96) seemed to question the validity of free offers but died before they elaborated their opinions on the subject. Others promote the non-offer view on the internet. Most current Hyper-Calvinists look to Gill and Hoeksema for inspiration.

The Issues

The controversy revolves around four main issues. First, all Hyper-Calvinists reject the idea of the free offer (of the gospel, grace, and/or Christ). All Calvinists before 1700 and the vast majority since then have accepted the free offer. Hyperists sometimes claim Calvin for their cause, but the evidence is heavily against them. This is the main distinctive tenet of Hyper-Calvinism and has been identified as such by mainline Reformed writers for centuries.

Hyper-Calvinists argue that free offers are Arminian and contradict Reformed teaching on total depravity, limited atonement, and unconditional election as well as other teachings. They say we can preach but not offer. The Gospel Standard Baptists say that we can invite only "sensible sinners" who have been convicted of sin to come to Christ. The word *offer* is never used in the Bible of preaching the gospel, they say, and the practice implies that salvation is for sale and is not free. They often say free offers make salvation conditional upon man rather than God. Some agree that the Latin word *offero* was used by Calvin and others as well as the English word *offer* by the Puritans and others, but then say that the word underwent a change and came to mean something different, so it should not be used today.

Mainline Calvinists respond as follows. First, the teaching of the free offer is indeed biblical. The word *offer* is used in several reputable translations of 1 Corinthians 9:18 (e.g., the NIV and NASB). We offer by presenting and setting forth the gospel to lost sinners in general with the call for them to repent and believe in Christ. We invite all lost sinners, not just 'sensible' sinners. The offer is free. God both offers and gives; the two are not contradictory. Lost sinners are unable to accept the offer, but this in no way contradicts either election or particular redemption. There has been no substantial change in the meaning of the words *offero* or *offer*. By far most leading Reformed theologians and preachers have believed in free offers — Calvin and all the Reformers, the Puritans, the Reformed Scholastics, the *Nadere Reformatie* divines, Jonathan Edwards, the Princetonians, Spurgeon, and thousands of others. It is the non-offer men who are out of step with historic Calvinism, not those who believe it.

Second, John Murray and Ned B. Stonehouse wisely noted: "It would appear that the real point in connection with the free offer of the gospel is whether it can properly be said that God desires the salvation of all men."[6] Mainline Calvinists almost unanimously say yes; all Hyper-Calvinists say no. The free offer expresses a universal saving desire in God as part of His revealed will. It is well-meant and sincere. This does not nullify or contradict the secret will, for as Calvin said, it concerns the will of God in the gospel and not that of predestination.[7] Calvin certainly taught the universal saving desire of God. For example: "God declares that he wills the conversion of all, and he directs exhortations to all in common."[8]

Hyper-Calvinists deny that God desires all men to be saved, for that would include the reprobate and would contradict the doctrine of election. But mainline Calvinists argue that Scripture portrays God as holding out His hands all day long to sinners in general (Romans 10:21; Isaiah 65:2; Proverbs 1:14). He takes no pleasure in the death of the lost sinner but rather desires that he repent and be saved (Ezekiel 18:23, 32; 33:11). Paul echoes this in Romans 10:1: "My heart's desire and prayer to God for Israel is that they may be saved" (see also Acts 26:29). God commands faith unto salvation (Acts 16:31), and that certainly indicates a well-meant desire. The eternal decrees never fail, but the revealed will of law and gospel are usually rejected by sinners. Lastly, historic Calvinists differ on the interpretation of 1 Timothy 2:4 and 2 Peter 3:9. Some apply both to predestination, others to the gospel. But even so, the vast majority of historic Calvinists believe in the universal saving will of God. In this the Hyper-Calvinists are in the tiny minority and go beyond biblical truth.

The third issue is *Duty Faith*. The English Hypers usually reject it, but it appears that the PRC tends to accept it in some form. The state of the question,

---

6 John Murray, *The Free Offer of the Gospel* (Edinburgh: Banner of Truth, 2001), 3.

7 John Calvin, *The Epistle of Paul to the Hebrews and the First and Second Epistles of St. Peter* (Grand Rapids: Eerdmans, 1980), 364 (on 2 Peter 3:9).

8 John Calvin, *Institutes of the Christian Religion*, ed. John T. McNeill, trans. Ford Lewis Battles (Philadelphia: Westminster Press, 1960), 3:3:21, (p. 615).

known as the Modern Question, is this: "In the preaching of the gospel, do all lost sinners have the duty to savingly believe in Jesus Christ?" Gill and Brine said that sinners have only the duty to believe the report of the gospel, not the duty to savingly believe personally in Christ. Faith is a gift, they contended, and therefore not a duty. 'Duty faith' implies that sinners are able to believe, for responsibility assumes ability.

Historic Calvinists have replied that saving faith is both a duty and a gift. Spiritual inability does not negate one's responsibility. Sinners are commanded to both believe the report of the gospel (Mark 1:15) and savingly believe in Christ (Acts 16:31). First John 3:23 clearly states, "And this is His commandment: that we should believe on the name of His Son Jesus Christ." A commandment is a duty on us. Christ commanded saving faith in John 12:36, 14:1, and 20:27, as did John the Baptist (Acts 19:4). God commands all men to believe (Isaiah 45:22). Paul commanded that we obey the gospel in "the obedience of faith" (Romans 1:5; 6:17; 10:16; 16:26). The same goes for *duty repentance* — which is both a duty and a gift (see Acts 2:38; 3:19; 17:30). Failure to repent and believe is a great sin (Mark 16:16; John 3:18, 36; 5:38; 16:8–9; Romans 14:23; 1 John 5:10; Hebrews 3:12). Unbelief would not be a sin if faith were not a duty, contrary to Styles' extreme notion. Therefore, the Hyper-Calvinists who deny Duty Faith are both unbiblical and out of the mainstream of Reformed teaching.

The fourth point in dispute is common grace. Hoeksema and the Protestant Reformed Church utterly reject it, but some others such as Gill accept a modified form of it. Mainstream Calvinists before and after Kuyper have taught that, yes, God does indeed have a general love, mercy, and favor for all men (e.g., Psalm 145:8–9), including the reprobate. Out of this general love, God gives good gifts to all men (Acts 14:17; James 1:17), even to the reprobate who end up in Hell (Luke 16:25). Christ, the perfect revelation of God, had compassion on the multitudes of thousands, not all of whom were elect (Matthew 14:14). This was not just in His humanity, as argued by some Hyper-Calvinists, for His holy humanity was in perfect harmony with His deity. He "loved" the lost rich young ruler (Mark 10:21). God commands us to imitate Him by loving all men in general, even our enemies (Matthew 5:43–48; Luke 6:35–36).

Contrary to Hoeksema's contention, historic Calvinists have taught the Three Points of 1924, namely: (1) out of general mercy God restrains sinners (Genesis 20:6); (2) God enables the unconverted (including the reprobate) to do outwardly good things such as giving good gifts to their children (Matthew 7:11); and (3) God has a general love for mankind and provides for the development of culture, science, medicine, government, and the family (Acts 14:17). Out of this common grace there is a delay of judgment, as it were — anything short of Hell is a mercy. Referring to these and other verses, Louis Berkhof commented: "If such passages do not testify to a favorable disposition in God, it would seem that language has lost its meaning, and that God's revelation is not dependable on this subject."[9]

Those such as Herman Hoeksema are well out of the mainstream of the Reformed tradition to deny that God has any love, grace, mercy, kindness, or favor of any kind on all men in general, including the reprobate. Some Hyperists say that God is only fattening the reprobate up for the slaughter and has no remorse whatsoever for their lost state. That is supralapsarianism with a vengeance. It implies that the reprobate are never under grace but only wrath, and conversely, the elect are always under grace and never under wrath (contrary to Ephesians 2:3).

Conclusion

To give them their due, Hyper-Calvinists are firmly evangelical, even if not very evangelistic. They are sound on the five *sola* doctrines, the five "fundamentals," and the five points. They would sooner die than deny biblical infallibility, the Trinity, the deity and resurrection of Christ, and other vital truths. They are to be applauded for upholding traditional biblical ethics as well. Notwithstanding our disagreements on lesser issues, we thank God for them and consider them beloved brethren in Christ. They worship the same God and love the same Christ as do all true Christians.[10]

Not all supralapsarians have been Hyper-Calvinists. Not all "supras" are "Hypers," but all "Hypers" are "supras." There is a connection. Hyper-Calvinism upsets the beautiful balance of divine sovereignty and human responsibility, minimizes or opposes evangelism and missions, usually denies that Arminians are saved, and has been a thorn in the side of mainline Calvinism. If Low Calvinism might be described as "left-wing" Calvinism, then Hyper-Calvinism may be described as "right-wing" Calvinism. Both are in the Reformed family but not in the mainstream. Fortunately, some of their number have reevaluated their views and reentered the mainstream.

---

9 Louis Berkhof, *Systematic Theology* (Grand Rapids: Eerdmans, 1988), 446.

10 Spurgeon rightly said: "A man may be so extreme in his Calvinism that he becomes a fatalist, and so falls into the errors of another sort; but, certainly, never will he give up Evangelical truth because he preaches the doctrines of grace." *C. H. Spurgeon's Forgotten College Addresses*, ed. Terence Peter Crosby (Leominster: Day One, 2016), 165–66.

Chapter 11
Eighteenth-Century Calvinism

The eighteenth century is sometimes mistakenly called the "graveyard of Calvinism," following the heyday of Reformed theology in the previous century. True, Puritanism declined enormously, denominations split, and orthodoxy waned in many places. But in other ways, Calvinism reached new heights under leaders who were among the giants of Reformed history.

The Dutch Reformed Church

Though the southern region of the Low Countries known as Belgium was overwhelmingly Catholic, the northern part was predominantly Protestant. Calvinism was the largest faction. Religious tolerance allowed for the Remonstrants, Anabaptists, Lutherans, Catholics, and others. The Dutch Republic continued to flourish.

Unfortunately, the Enlightenment from neighboring Germany began to spread its nefarious influence around Europe, including the Netherlands. Most of the Dutch Reformed had been able to fend off earlier challenges of secular philosophy under René Descartes and Benedict Spinoza. A few, such as Herman Venema (1697–1787), showed signs of compromise. On the other hand, there were still orthodox theologians such as Johannes Marckius (1656–1731), Melchior Leydecker (1642–1721), and Campegius Vitringa (1659–1722).

But the leading divine was not even Dutch but Scottish. Alexander Comrie (1706–74)[1] has often been compared to and contrasted with Wilhelmus à Brakel (1635–1711) in several areas. Comrie was a supralapsarian; Brakel was infralapsarian. Comrie held to eternal justification before faith; Brakel did not.[2] Comrie was less a part of the *Nadere Reformatie* tradition than Brakel. Others worth naming include Johannes Vander Kemp (1664–1718), Abraham Hellenbroek (1658–1731), and Theodorus Vander Groe (1705–84). The *Nadere Reformatie* kept the heart of Dutch Calvinism alive, but in other areas there were signs of stagnation.

---

1 His delightful book *The ABC of Faith* (Ossett: Zoar Publications, 1978) is one of the few of his writings available in English.
2 See G. C. Berkouwer, *Faith and Justification* (Grand Rapids: Eerdmans, 1954), 152–56.

Elsewhere on the Continent

In France, the Huguenots had their liberty stripped from them when the Edict of Nantes was revoked in 1685. Many fled to England, America, and Holland. Their leaders included Pierre Jurieu (1637–1713) and Antoine Court (1696–1760). The exiled French Reformed Church was sometimes called "The Church in the Desert" (Cf. Acts 7:38). It would suffer under the French Revolution later in the century but would survive.

The German Reformed Church continued but became somewhat less than distinctively Reformed as it was increasingly influenced by the Enlightenment's Christian Wolff and Immanuel Kant. But a remnant remained true, including Friedrich Adolph Lampe (1683–1729), who held the kind of German Reformed Pietism situated between Lutheran Pietism and the Dutch *Nadere Reformatie*. He also continued the tradition of the covenant theology of Cocceius, who also had been German and Reformed.

The Swiss Reformed Church went downhill fast in the eighteenth century. Benedict Pictet (1655–1724), nephew of Francis Turretin, was the last great orthodox Calvinist at the Geneva Academy, but was unable to stem the tide of apostasy. Jean Le Clerc (1657–1736) forsook Calvinism for liberal Arminianism. Jacob Vernet (1698–1789) also departed from orthodoxy and led others with him. Jean-Alphonse Turretin (1671–1737), son of Francis Turretin, especially led the downgrade at the Geneva Academy. The Formula Consensus Helvetica was disavowed, and previous confessions were ignored, weakened, or abandoned. Rationalism and the Enlightenment took a heavy toll, though there were a few pockets of a kind of Swiss Pietism to be found. A few moderate Calvinists remained such as Johann Friedrich Stapfer (1708–75) and Johann Frederick Osterwald (1663–1747).

The Reformed faith in Eastern Europe had always been a minority report and continued as such through the eighteenth century. Yet it survived with rather less devastating effects than their brethren in western Europe. But neither did they make any great strides.

Scotland

The Scots experienced several controversies affecting the Church of Scotland. The first was the Marrow Controversy.[3] Thomas Boston (1676–1732) was a

---

3 The definitive study is David C. Lachman, *The Marrow Controversy 1718–1723* (Edinburgh: Rutherford House, 1988). See also William VanDoodewaard, *The Marrow Controversy and*

popular preacher and writer in the best tradition of previous Scottish Calvinism. He discovered a little seventeenth-century book entitled *The Marrow of Modern Divinity* by one "E. F." (evidently Edward Fisher). It presented Puritan covenant theology in dialogue form with dozens of quotations from the Reformers and Puritans. Boston had it reprinted and later added notes to explain its more controversial sections.

The book sold well and awakened many, but there was a backlash. The defenders were known as the Marrow Brethren (later more popularly called the Marrowmen). They included James Hog (1658–1734) and the brothers Ebenezer (1680–1754) and Ralph (1685–1752) Erskine. James Hadow (1670–1747) led the opposition. *The Marrow* was suspected of teaching antinomianism and Amyraldism, while the opposition was accused of dry orthodoxy and something akin to Hyper-Calvinism and even Neonomianism. Issues included the nature of biblical covenants, the conditions of salvation, preparationism, assurance of faith, and the extent of the atonement. *The Marrow* was condemned by the General Assembly. Many of the Marrow Brethren left and formed the Secession Church.

The remaining establishment came to be dominated by the Moderate Party, exemplified by Hugh Blair (1718–1800) and George Hill (1750–1819). Other minor splits ensued. One involved John Glas (1695–1773) and his son-in-law Robert Sandeman (1718–71). The *Glasites*, or *Sandemanians*, taught that saving faith involved only mental assent to the gospel, not heartfelt trust or surrender. The great English scientist Michael Faraday (1791–1867) would later align himself with the Sandemanian church.

The Scottish Enlightenment's leading philosopher was the skeptic David Hume (1711–76). The Moderate Thomas Reid (1710–96) answered with a Reformed apologetic known as Scottish Common Sense Realism. Later exponents were less Reformed, such as Dugald Stewart (1753–1828) and Sir William Hamilton (1788–1856). John Witherspoon (1723–94) was a Scots-Irish Presbyterian pastor who took this apologetic with him to America where it became part of the Princeton Theology in the next century.

English Calvinism

After the decline of Puritanism at the turn of the century, English

---

Seceder Tradition (Grand Rapids: Reformation Heritage Books, 2011). A more popular-level work is Sinclair B. Ferguson, *The Whole Christ: Legalism, Antinomianism, and Gospel Assurance—Why the Marrow Controversy Still Matters* (Wheaton: Crossway, 2016).

Presbyterianism frequently fell into Arianism. Orthodox Presbyterianism almost disappeared. Thomas Ridgley (1667–1734) was basically orthodox, but in his *A Body of Divinity* (based on the Westminster Larger Catechism), he denied the eternal generation of the Son. That is, he said that though Jesus was eternally divine as the second person of the Trinity, He was not "begotten" as Son until the Incarnation.

The Independents continued but saw challenges as well. Isaac Watts (1674–1748) was the undisputed leader. He pastored the London church that had previously been pastored by John Owen, Joseph Caryl, and Isaac Chauncy. He wrote over six hundred hymns, many of which became classics, such as "When I Survey the Wondrous Cross"; "O God, Our Help in Ages Past"; "Alas, and Did My Saviour Bleed"; "We're Marching to Zion"; and "Joy to the World." Up to this time most Calvinists sang only the psalms. But Watts and the Wesley brothers revolutionized and popularized hymns in what is sometimes called "The Golden Age of Hymnody." Watts had a confused doctrine of the Trinity and the person of Christ. While resisting Arianism, of which he was accused, he taught a theory similar to Sabellianism in the Pre-Existerianism of Joseph Hussey. It does not seem that he actually denied the Trinity or deity of Christ, but his theory revealed the conflicting tendency of many in the Reformed community at that time.

A similar view was held by another great Independent hymn writer, Philip Doddridge (1702–51). He composed "O Happy Day" and other classics as well as the excellent *The Rise and Progress of Religion in the Soul.* He was the headmaster at the Northampton Academy that taught hundreds of Independent pastors. But Doddridge taught in a non-dogmatic way that encouraged students to read unorthodox theology and decide for themselves. Unfortunately, a large number of them went liberal, which contributed to the overall decline of Calvinist orthodoxy in England.

Anglican Puritanism was virtually dead by the year 1700. John Edwards (1637–1716), rather unknown today,[4] was the last important Anglican Puritan. The renowned Augustus Montague Toplady (1740–78) wrote at length to prove that the Church of England had strong Reformed roots and a Calvinist creed in the Thirty-Nine Articles, but the Arminians and Latitudinarians did not care. Before he died young, he wrote some great hymns such as "Rock of Ages." He also had a running debate with John Wesley.

---

4 One of the few studies is the recent one by Jeongmo Yoo, *John Edwards (1637–1716) on Human Free Choice and Divine Necessity* (Gottingen: Vandenhoeck and Ruprecht, 2013).

Two other great Anglican Calvinist hymn writers deserve mention. John Newton (1725–1807) had been a degenerate slave-trading sea captain before being dramatically converted. He became a pastor and wrote many great hymns, including "Amazing Grace," which has become possibly the most beloved hymn of all time. The grace of which that hymn speaks is the electing and irresistible grace of Newton's Calvinism.

Newton was pastor and friend of William Cowper (1731–1800). A lifelong sufferer of chronic depression, Cowper (pronounced "Cooper") was in and out of mental asylums and often thought he had committed the unpardonable sin. The rope broke in a suicide attempt, which led to his writing the hymn "God Works in a Mysterious Way." He is still studied today as a leading English poet but is more beloved for his hundreds of wonderful hymns, such as "There Is a Fountain Filled with Blood" and "O for a Closer Walk with God." Perhaps he could rise to such spiritual heights because he knew such deep emotional lows.

Other notable eighteenth-century Anglican Calvinists were James Hervey (1714–58), John Berridge (1716–93), William Grimshaw (1708–63), and William Romaine (1714–95).

The Evangelical Awakening

Amid the decline of not only Reformed but even Arminian theology and overall cultural decadence (much due to the proliferation of gin), God heard the prayers of His people and sent revival. Actually, the Great Awakening in the American colonies began first but spread its influence back to England through a group of young Oxford students. John (1703–91) and Charles (1707–88) Wesley formed the Holy Club there with George Whitefield (1714–70) and others. None of them were as yet converted. When they were all saved within a short period of time, they soon began preaching enthusiastically and powerfully all over England and Scotland.

The churches could not contain the huge crowds, so they took to preaching out of doors in fields and meadows. Whitefield often preached to as many as fifty thousand listeners — and without a public address system! His favorite text was "You must be born again" (John 3:7). What a workhorse he was: He usually preached several times a day, often at two hours per sermon, for a total of over eighteen thousand sermons, frequently with tears on both sides of the pulpit. His *Journals* make exciting spiritual reading. He traveled seven times to America where he met Jonathan Edwards and preached to large crowds in the Great Awakening.

Now Whitefield was a convinced Calvinist, but the Wesleys were outspoken Arminians. This led to a temporary parting of the ways which was never fully healed. The Wesleys started the Methodist Church, while Whitefield helped found the Welsh Calvinistic Methodist Church with Howell Harris (1714–73) and Daniel Rowland (c. 1711–90).[5] Later the great Welsh hymn writer William Williams of Pantycelyn (1717–91) was another leader. The church thrived in the nineteenth century as the Presbyterian Church of Wales, but sadly declined into liberalism in the twentieth century.

Whitefield is a sterling example of Calvinist evangelism. He disproved the canard that "Calvinism is against evangelism." No, it is Hyper-Calvinism that avoided evangelism, not mainstream Calvinism. There was also another eighteenth-century English Calvinist movement that produced still more evangelism — the Great Missionary Movement.

The Great Missionary Movement

Several young English Baptist Calvinists were influenced by Edwards and, to a lesser extent, Whitefield. They were Andrew Fuller (1754–1815), William Carey (1761–1834), John Rippon (1751–1836), John Ryland Jr. (1753–1825), and Samuel Pearce (1766–99). They started the Baptist Missionary Society, and their vision for missions spread like fire through the churches. Soon missionaries were sent out from many kinds of evangelical churches — Baptist, Anglican, Presbyterian, Independents, and others. This utterly disproves the lie "Calvinism kills missions." Quite the opposite! Hyper-Calvinism opposed missions, but mainline Calvinism took the lead in producing the greatest missionary endeavor the church has ever seen. It continues today.

Conclusion

Even in the dark days of eighteenth-century England, God still had His people and was not through with His cause. The Evangelical Awakening and its twin the Great Awakening were second only to the Reformation as the greatest revivals in history. And Calvinists were at the forefront of all three.

---

5 Most historians, especially the Welsh, prefer the spelling *Rowland* to *Rowlands*.

Chapter 12
New England Theology

Calvinism in America first took root in New England during the Puritan era of the seventeenth century. New England Theology reached its zenith in the eighteenth century with Jonathan Edwards, then it gradually went downhill after Edwards until it virtually disappeared by the year 1900. It was a major force in American Calvinism and is still of much interest today.

The Puritan Pilgrims

It began in early seventeenth-century England with a group of Separatists, the more extreme branch of the Independents (later called Congregationalists in America). Under the influence of Robert Browne (c. 1553–1633) they believed in the independency of the local church as opposed to Episcopalian or Presbyterian church polity. Browne was basically Arminian in doctrine, but this group and others became strongly Calvinistic. England was dominated by the Church of England, and thus the Separatists endured various forms of persecution, so many of them left for refuge in the Netherlands.

The pastor of one particular church was John Robinson (1575–1625). It was he who uttered the famous words, "The Lord has more truth yet to break forth from His Holy Word."[1] In context, he meant that Christians may appreciate previous preachers such as Luther and Calvin but should be prepared to go further than them as God reveals more light on such things as ecclesiology.

After a few years, the church felt uneasy in the Netherlands and decided to embark for America, which at that time had only a few trading outposts and few permanent settlements. They would truly be pilgrims on a "journey into the wilderness." In due time they left on the Mayflower with some non-Puritan passengers. Robinson and a few others stayed behind in the Netherlands. Robinson himself became an observer at the Synod of Dort and wrote in its defense, which testifies to the strong Calvinist sentiments of his flock.

During the trip abroad, the church wrote the Mayflower Compact, a form of Pilgrim covenant, as an adjunct to their official charter to form a colony.

---

1 Quoted in John T. McNeill, *The History and Character of Calvinism* (New York: Oxford University Press, 1954), 336.

The Mayflower reached Plymouth Bay in November 1620 and landed where they decided to settle on December 26. The first governor was John Carver (1576–1621), a Puritan. The first year was rough — about half of the settlers died. When God answered their prayers, they showed their gratitude at the first Thanksgiving feast in October of 1621.

The nearby Massachusetts Bay Colony was formed along similar lines. The governors were decidedly Puritan in outlook: William Bradford (1590–1657) and John Winthrop (1588–1649). The Pilgrim Fathers set up a semi-theocracy similar to that in Geneva in the days of Calvin but without the Presbyterian ecclesiology. The Puritan Pilgrims saw themselves as a covenantal community akin to Old Testament Israel and referred to their colony as "a city on a hill" (Matthew 5:14). As more immigrants arrived, the main issue was how to accommodate them into the Puritan community without compromising doctrine or practice. Curiously, immigration from England almost ceased in the 1640s during the Puritan Commonwealth period. If the Pilgrims had stayed in England, they would have felt quite at home in that society. But very few returned.

The First Theologians and Controversies

The first major theologian in New England was the great John Cotton (1584–1652). He had already made a name for himself back in England before coming to America in 1633. Another great preacher was Thomas Hooker (1586–1647). Like Cotton, he declined an invitation to be a delegate at the Westminster Assembly, realizing that the Independents were in the tiny minority there. He became a cofounder of Connecticut. An influential preacher, he particularly emphasized Experimental Calvinism regarding how the unconverted may be "prepared to seek the Lord" in salvation (referring to such verses as 2 Chronicles 12:14 and 19:3). What became known as *preparationism* was developed in works such as *The Soul's Preparation for Christ* and *The Poor Doubting Christian Drawn to Christ*. The third member of the Puritan triumvirate was Thomas Shepard (1604–49), whose book of sermons *The Parable of the Ten Virgins* influenced many.

Two major controversies tested the Puritan Pilgrims' view of ecclesiology and preparationism. First, Roger Williams (1603–83) challenged the restrictions placed on the members of the community. Moderately Calvinist, perhaps more Arminian, his Baptist convictions on separation of church and state led to his banishment from Massachusetts and settlement in Rhode Island.

The other important controversy involved Mrs. Anne Hutchinson (1591–1643). She had been a member of John Cotton's church back in England and followed him to the New World. She taught a women's home Bible study and propagated controversial views. For one, she was not comfortable with preparationism. She also challenged the prevailing view that one may deduce his election and salvation by self-examination and discovery of practical evidences in one's life. Instead, she emphasized the inner testimony of the Holy Spirit, even outside Holy Scripture. She issued prophecies and denied that faith was a "condition" of salvation, calling it a "blessing" instead. Further, she greatly downplayed the use of the law in conviction, conversion, and sanctification. At first John Cotton supported her but then opposed her for her antinomian mysticism. Hooker was moderator at her trial for heresy that disrupted the peace of the covenant community. Upon her conviction she was banished, and she settled in Rhode Island. She would later be killed by Indians.

Mention must be made of the first missionary to the American Indians, John Eliot (1604–90). He was the first to translate the Bible into an American Indian language. He also translated the famous *Bay Psalm Book*.

The Next Generation

As still more immigrants arrived, and children were born to the settlers, the problem then arose as to how to discern who were true Christians, who would thus be entitled to full covenantal privileges and citizenship. Initially the prevailing practice was that membership was limited to visible saints — namely, those who could testify to the true gospel and back it up with a personal testimony of conversion and godly life. Their children could be baptized but not admitted to the Lord's Supper until they too could provide a valid testimony. By the second generation, relatively few baptized children could testify to a personal conversion.

This led to the Cambridge Platform[2] and the Halfway Covenant.[3] The decision was made that adherents who could not testify to personal conversion would be allowed to have their children baptized, as long as the parents lived moral lives, affirmed correct doctrine, and submitted to the church leadership. However, they could not take Communion. Children were thus seen as halfway members. Only about 10 percent of the community enjoyed full membership

---

2 Williston Walker, *The Creeds and Platforms of Congregationalism* (New York: Pilgrim Press, 1991), 194–237.

3 Walker, *Creeds and Platforms*, 238–339.

and citizenship. Obviously, this was a significant compromise with the views of the original Puritan Pilgrims. Not all New England preachers were fully satisfied with the compromise, such as John Davenport (1597–1670).

Leading theologians of this period included Samuel Willard (1640–1707), author of the first systematic theology in America, entitled *A Compleat Body of Divinity*, based on the Westminster Shorter Catechism. Then there was Increase Mather (1639–1723), who served as president of Harvard College, which had been founded in 1636 to train pastors. He supported the Halfway Covenant and preparationism. He was also known for his "jeremiad" sermons that echoed the warnings of biblical prophets who rebuked God's people for their sins and told them God sent disasters to warn them of judgment.

His son Cotton Mather (1663–1728) was even more influential. Named for his grandfather John Cotton, he was the intellectual leader for a whole generation. He wrote more than 450 publications in science, theology, history, and ethics, including a large Bible commentary. His *Magnalia Christiana Americana* (later published as *The Great Works of Christ in America*) remains a definitive source of historical data for early New England. Mather slightly modified the prevailing Calvinism, such as preparationism. His main weakness was in participating in the Salem Witch Trials of 1692, for which he later apologized.

Then there was Solomon Stoddard (1643–1729), often considered the Pope of Massachusetts. He pastored in Northampton from 1672 to 1729 and witnessed five seasons of "harvests" of spiritual revival. A major advocate of preparationism, he further modified the Halfway Covenant to admit baptized adherents to the Lord's Supper even though they could not provide a testimony of a work of grace in their lives, so long as they professed proper doctrine, were free from outwardly gross sins, and submitted to the church leadership. Indeed, he even called Communion "a converting ordinance."

Back in England, Puritanism declined after the Restoration of 1662 and was nearly extinct after 1700. Calvinism was beginning to stagnate in New England as well. Arminianism began to grow, mainly through the Anglican settlers. Moralism and reason were the bywords during this period influenced by the European movement known as the Enlightenment. The Calvinist society that was vibrant in the time of the Pilgrims became shallow. Nominal religion was widespread. It was against this period that those such as Nathaniel Hawthorne leveled accusations of religious hypocrisy — and some of those charges were true. Those evangelical Calvinists who were true to their heritage cried out to God, who heard their prayers.

Jonathan Edwards

There was a man sent from God, and his name was Jonathan Edwards (1703–58). Both his father and grandfather were preachers. The only son among eleven children, young Jonathan was a child prodigy even before conversion. He studied Latin, Greek, and Hebrew before entering Yale College at thirteen. He experienced salvation there, then served as tutor at Yale and a short pastorate in New York. Then he assisted his grandfather, Solomon Stoddard, at the Northampton church before becoming full pastor upon Stoddard's death. While still young he fell in love with a godly young woman named Sarah Pierpont (1710–58). He sent her a famous love letter,[4] and after their wedding they were blessed with twelve children. Sarah herself was a model of spirituality. She had always loved Christ, but in middle age she fell in love with Christ in an experience of deep spirituality.[5]

While still a young Christian, Edwards showed not only great potential as a preacher and theologian but also as a spiritual giant. For example, he composed a series of "Resolutions," promises of self-examination and dedication to God. Here are some examples:

- "Resolved, never to do any manner of thing, whether in soul or body, less or more, but what tends to the glory of God; nor be, nor suffer it, if I can avoid it."

- "Resolved, never to do anything, which I should be afraid to do, if it were the last hour of my life."

- "Resolved, that I will live so as I shall wish I had done when I come to die."

- "Resolved, whenever I do any conspicuously evil action, to trace it back, till I come to the original cause; and then both carefully endeavor to do so no more, and to fight and pray with all my might against the original of it."

- "Resolved, to examine carefully, and constantly, what that one thing in me is, which causes me in the least to doubt the love of God; and the direct of all my forces against it."[6]

---

4 Johnathan Edwards, *The Works of Jonathan Edwards* (New Haven: Yale University Press, 1998), 16:789–90.

5 Jennifer Adams, ed., *In Love with Christ: The Narrative of Sarah Edwards* (Forest, VA: Corner Pillar, 2010).

6 Edwards, *Works*, 16:253–59.

The Great Awakening

There were some unexpected deaths in 1734 which caused many to contemplate their own mortality. Edwards then preached a series of sermons on justification by faith and directly challenged his hearers to believe in Christ, even though they were baptized members of the church and took Communion. God blessed these messages and sent the revival that came to be known as the Great Awakening. There had previously been seasons of harvest under Solomon Stoddard as well as down in New Jersey under the preaching of the Dutch Reformed pastor Theodorus Frelinghuysen (1691–1747). But those paled in comparison with the Great Awakening. It spread like a brushfire throughout New England and then south through other colonies. Presbyterians such as Samuel Davies (1723–61) and William Tennent (1673–1746) and his four preacher sons were also much used in the revival.

It reached a still higher level when George Whitefield (1714–70) came over from England, where he was involved in a similar revival known as the Evangelical Awakening. He attracted huge crowds all over the colonies, but it was Edwards who was the theologian of the revival. When Whitefield preached in the Northampton church, Edwards sat on the platform weeping.

The high point of the Awakening occurred on July 8, 1741, when Edwards preached the famous sermon "Sinners in the Hands of an Angry God" in Enfield, Connecticut. He had preached it previously in his own church with only moderate effect, but it really exploded in Enfield. Hearers cried out to God, held onto the pillars for fear they would slide into Hell, and even fell on the floor in repentance. The sermon became the most-published sermon in history. Edwards frequently preached on hellfire but also an equal amount on the glories of Heaven, such as his warm and profound sermon "Heaven a World of Love."

Edwards wrote several defenses of the revival to answer critics such as Charles Chauncey (1705–87) and other "Old Light" Calvinists. The Awakening also influenced several young men to become missionaries to the American Indians, of which David Brainerd (1718–47) was the most notable. When he became terminally ill, Edwards and his family cared for him in their home. After his death at age twenty-nine, Edwards published Brainerd's diary, a moving testimony of his spiritual dedication to God. Probably more than any other single book, the diary would inspire hundreds of other Christians to be missionaries in the next century.

The Aftermath of the Awakening

After the revival subsided, Edwards seemed to have second thoughts about it. He increasingly challenged his hearers to examine themselves to make sure they were truly converted. Many had gone back to their old ways and had shown little lasting spiritual fruit. The church became tense. Then there was the embarrassing "Bad Book" incident, in which several young men were caught and rebuked for misusing a midwife's handbook. Edwards then wrote what many have considered his masterpiece, *A Treatise on Religious Affections*. In it he explained what the evidences of true spiritual conversion are. Internal godly attitudes were more important than outward confirmations, and the greatest spiritual virtue was love for God. Elsewhere he expressed one of his most profound observations: "If holiness in God consists chiefly in love to himself, holiness in the creature must chiefly consist in love to him."[7] Edwards frequently displayed a deep love for God and waxed eloquent especially when preaching on the love and loveliness of Christ.

The tension reached its height when Edwards came to disagree with the Halfway Covenant as unbiblical and dangerous to the spiritual state of lost sinners. He began to restrict Communion to those alone who could give visible testimony of a godly life and internal holy affections. The church reacted against this by firing the very man God used to bring them revival. If Edwards could be fired from a church, any preacher could be dismissed then or today. Edwards stayed on briefly to fill the pulpit after the dismissal in 1750, and though many later changed their minds and apologized, he sadly left his beloved Northampton flock. Interestingly, at that time Edwards showed a leaning to Presbyterian polity, for that would have given him a fairer hearing and possible exoneration.

From there he moved with his family to Stockbridge in western Massachusetts to be a preacher to the soldiers and Indians. It was during this time that he wrote some of his greatest works. In *The Freedom of the Will* Edwards demolished the Arminian and Deist idea that the human will is self-determining and neutral. In *The Doctrine of Original Sin* he demonstrated the historic Calvinist view that not only Adam's sin but its guilt was passed down to all humans, as shown in the universality of sin, the death of infants, and other proofs. Perhaps his most profound work was *A Dissertation on the End for Which God Created the World*. He showed that the ultimate purpose of foreordination, creation, and redemption is a display of the glory of God.

---

7 John Piper, *God's Passion for His Glory* (Wheaton: Crossway, 1998), 173.

In 1758, Edwards accepted the call to become president of the College of New Jersey, which later became Princeton University. Sadly, he died of a smallpox inoculation after only a few weeks. His wife, Sarah, and several children died shortly thereafter. He never wrote his masterpiece, a large theology that would discuss biblical doctrines chronologically rather than topically. He did leave a series of published sermons entitled *The History of Redemption* that would have been the basic framework for it. He also left notebooks of "Miscellanies," hundreds of miscellaneous theological thoughts that would be used for his unfinished masterpiece. They contain some of his most profound and moving thoughts.

Edwards published a few sermons in his lifetime, but more followed posthumously. He left over a thousand manuscripts, many just fragments. Many of these and his other major works are included in the definitive twenty-six-volume set published by Yale University Press, which contains at least twice as much material as the popular reprint of the two-volume 1834 set. Moreover, there is at least as much unpublished material that has been transcribed by the Yale committee as in the entire Yale published series.[8]

Jonathan Edwards left a good and godly legacy. He should be considered one of the three or four greatest Calvinist theologians of all time. Historians have often called him the greatest preacher-theologian-philosopher ever to grace the American landscape. He towered as the Mount Everest of American theologians, who like King Solomon surpassed all who preceded and followed him (1 Kings 3:12). No study of Reformed theology is complete without studying Edwards.

Decline of New England Theology

After the death of Jonathan Edwards, New England Theology began a slow decline. The modified theology would be known as New England Theology proper, Consistent Calvinism, or the New Divinity. With some justification it might be called American Amyraldism. Arminianism began to spread. The Enlightenment helped foster the spread of American Socinianism known as Unitarianism, which denied miracles, the deity of Christ, the Trinity, revelation, and other orthodox doctrines. Parallel with this was the rise of universalism that denied the existence of Hell and said everyone would be saved.

The initial decline of Edwardsean theology can be traced to three of his

---

8 These may be read on the website of The Jonathan Edwards Center at Yale University at http://edwards.yale.edu.

associates. Joseph Bellamy (1719–90) was a protégé who studied under Edwards and preached in the Great Awakening. Edwards wrote a recommendatory preface to his main work *True Religion Delineated*. Unlike Edwards, Bellamy explicitly taught universal atonement in a way that resembled the old Arminian "Governmental Theory" of Hugo Grotius. He also weakened the Reformed doctrine of total depravity by emphasizing natural ability more than Edwards had. His mentor had taught that man has natural ability to read the Bible, examine himself, and determine what sins were keeping him from repentance and faith. This was Edwards' view of "seeking" that resembled the earlier preparationism of Hooker and Shepard. However, he counterbalanced natural ability with moral inability. Natural man lacks all moral ability to repent, believe, and obey God. Bellamy gave more weight to the former and modified the latter. He also wrote a defense of divine sovereignty in *The Wisdom of God in the Permission of Evil*.

Samuel Hopkins (1721–1803) was another student of Edwards. He went somewhat further than Bellamy regarding human nature. He saw self-love as the primary essence of sin, and consequently the greatest virtue was "disinterested benevolence." From this he propounded the highly controversial idea that one should be willing to be damned for the glory of God, loosely based on Romans 9:3. He weakened the doctrine of original sin also. His theology was incorporated into his large *System of Doctrines* and came to be called *Hopkinsianism*. One major proponent of it would be Nathaniel Emmons (1745–1840). Emmons said that man is active and not merely passive in regeneration, which is another way of saying that faith precedes regeneration. He accepted a modified view of original sin but denied that guilt is passed on.

The third modifier of New England Theology was Edwards' own son Jonathan Edwards Jr. (1745–1801), often called "Doctor Edwards" to differentiate him from his father, "President Edwards." He opposed Unitarianism and universalism, but like Bellamy, Hopkins, and later Emmons, he weakened the doctrine of total depravity and raised fallen man's ability. This set the trajectory for New England Theology for the next one hundred years. The main idea of discussion and compromise would be the nature of human depravity and the extent of moral inability. Increasingly more power was given to natural ability and then to moral ability. The difference with Edwards and traditional Calvinism was becoming pronounced.

The Second Great Awakening

Around 1790, a new revival began that is usually called the Second Great Awakening. Perhaps because America was much larger — the United States had won the Revolutionary War and began to spread westward — it affected more people than the first Great Awakening and lasted longer. However, while the first one was led almost entirely by Calvinists, the second was led in part by Arminians such as Peter Cartwright (1785–1872) and Barton Stone (1772–1844).

The Awakening hit Yale College, and a third of the students professed conversion. The president of Yale at that time was Timothy Dwight (1752–1817), a grandson of Jonathan Edwards and preacher in his own right. He published a series of theological sermons called *Theology, Defined and Defended* in which he continued the modification of the older Calvinism.

It was Dwight's prized student Nathaniel William Taylor (1786–1858) who more than anyone else led the radical turn in New England Theology. He was the first professor at the new Yale Divinity School, from which came the so-called New Haven Theology. He argued that man is a sinner because he sins, not the other way around as historical Calvinists had argued. More importantly, he said that responsibility requires ability. He proposed the idea of "power to the contrary" as a necessary ingredient of the human will. It more resembled Arminianism than the views of Edwards. The die was cast for further changes.

Remember that New England Theology was almost entirely congregational in ecclesiology. One partial exception was Lyman Beecher (1775–1863), who began as a Presbyterian and changed to Congregationalism during his involvement in the Second Great Awakening. Most Presbyterians at that time followed the Princeton Theology and had reservations about the Awakening. But other Presbyterians were involved and modified their Calvinism to fit the new flavor of the revival. Beecher applied his modified Calvinism to ethical issues such as slavery, gambling, liquor, and dueling. Two of Beecher's children went substantially further in rejecting Calvinism: Henry Ward Beecher (1813–87), who denied the existence of Hell, and Harriet Beecher Stowe (1811–96), author of *Uncle Tom's Cabin*.

There were still adherents to the traditional Calvinist orthodoxy among New England theologians involved in the Awakening at this time, such as the great Asahel Nettleton (1783–1844). He was a popular and well-traveled preacher who avoided and warned against the encroachment of Arminianism, the emotionalism of the Cane Ridge revival, and evangelistic gimmickry.

This leads us to Charles Grandison Finney (1792–1875). Originally a Presbyterian, he switched to Congregationalism and was a leading revivalist for decades. He had been a lawyer, so he used legal arguments in his evangelism and applied legal principles to his theology. For instance, he vehemently opposed the Reformed doctrines of original sin and total depravity/inability as being intrinsically unjust. He further minimalized, if not outright denied, penal substitutionary atonement, imputed righteousness in justification, and other evangelical and Reformed dogmas. Likewise, he argued, God never interferes with the human will. Finney promoted these and other extreme views in his *Lectures on Revival* and *Lectures on Systematic Theology*. The abridged edition of the latter omits some of his more dangerous views. He also popularized the "anxious bench," now known as the "altar call" or "going forward," which Nettleton opposed. He also advocated a form of sinless perfection. In later years he became president of Oberlin College in Ohio, from which proceded the Oberlin Theology of Finney as well as Asa Mahan (1799–1889). Much of Finney's supposed evangelistic success was in upstate New York, but within a few years this became known as the Burned-over District. The thousands of converts seemed to disappear, leaving behind them skepticism and cults like Mormonism and the Oneida sect. Oddly, some historians consider Finney a modified Calvinist, when in truth he was closer to outright Pelagianism than even Arminianism.

After the Civil War, New England Theology fizzled out. Edwards Amasa Park (1808–1900), curiously named for Jonathan Edwards, was professor of theology at Andover Seminary, which had been founded to halt the growing apostasy at Harvard and Yale. Park reluctantly rejected Edwardsean Calvinism and the modified Calvinism of his successors. The nadir was reached perhaps with Horace Bushnell (1802–76). He stringently rejected historic Calvinism as well as evangelical theology in favor of the growing influence of European liberalism. Strongly moralistic in doctrine, he preached that man needs education, not conversion. He denied penal substitutionary atonement in *The Vicarious Sacrifice* and was the last representative of any kind of New England Theology.

Conclusion

New England Calvinism had good roots and a great flower but wilted gradually in the nineteenth century. The same pattern is seen in other areas of Reformed theology, such as eighteenth-century Swiss theology. The Congregationalists handed the torch of orthodox Calvinist leadership to the Princetonian

Presbyterians. Sadly, liberalism took over most of Congregationalism. That became evident in the twentieth century when it merged into the ultra-liberal United Church of Christ, and many joined the even more liberal Unitarian-Universalist church.

But the story is not over. With the revival of historic Calvinism in the twentieth century came a rediscovery of Jonathan Edwards and the American Puritans. These new Calvinists should learn the lessons of the past as charted in this chapter to hold to the truths of orthodox New England Theology and avoid the pitfalls of modifications and departures from it.

Chapter 13
The Princeton Theology

The first Presbyterians in America were Scots-Irish who settled mainly in Virginia and the Carolinas. They brought with them orthodox Reformed theology, a dedicated work ethic, a desire to raise godly families, and a determination to worship God in all of life. This reached its theological high point in the Princeton Theology of nineteenth-century America.

Origins

In 1735 William Tennent (1673–1746) built a log cabin for the purpose of instructing his four sons to be preachers. Soon other young preachers were included as students. Eventually other courses were added. It moved twice before settling in 1756 in Princeton, New Jersey, and assumed the name the College of New Jersey. Jonathan Dickinson (1688–1747), Aaron Burr Sr. (1716–57), Jonathan Edwards (1703–58), and Samuel Davies (1723–61) were the first presidents.

John Witherspoon (1723–94) was president from 1768–94 during the American Revolution and founding of the United States. He was the only preacher to sign the Declaration of Independence and was also a delegate to the Continental Congress. He personally taught and influenced many members of Congress, governors, educators, and preachers. As the school grew, it became less a preachers' college and more a general university, so the Presbyterian Church felt the need for a seminary like the old Log College. The General Assembly voted in 1812 to approve a new institution closely aligned with the College of New Jersey, which would be renamed Princeton University, in 1896. The seminary would be called Princeton Theological Seminary.

Seminary Faculty

Archibald Alexander (1772–1851) was selected as the first president and taught there for thirty-nine years. His vision, as seen in his important book *Thoughts on Religious Experience*, was that ministerial training should be threefold: an uncompromising orthodox theology, careful first-class scholarship, and true heartfelt spirituality. Two of his sons also taught at the seminary: James W.

Alexander (1804–59) and Joseph Addison Alexander (1809–60), a noted Old Testament scholar who was proficient in twenty languages. Samuel Miller (1769–1850) was the second teacher chosen. Later, William Henry Green (1825–1900) was an outstanding Old Testament teacher.

The most well-known teacher of all was Charles Hodge (1797–1878). He instructed over three thousand students during his fifty-six-year career at the seminary, many of whom became leading preachers, theologians, and missionaries. He edited several journals and was involved in numerous theological controversies of the day. If Jonathan Edwards was the greatest American Calvinist genius, Hodge was the greatest organizer of theology. His large three-volume *Systematic Theology* has been a standard textbook up until this day. Like Witherspoon and James McCosh (1811–94) over at the University, Hodge employed Scottish Common Sense Realism in his apologetic method. He produced several useful Bible commentaries (the one on Romans has been especially significant) and other works. He was followed by his son Archibald Alexander Hodge (1823–86). Caspar Wistar Hodge (1830–91) was another son who taught there as well as grandson Caspar Wistar Hodge Jr. (1870–1937). The Alexander-Hodge dynasty solidified the Princeton Theology for over a century.

The Twentieth Century

The most outstanding teacher at the turn of the century was the great Benjamin Breckinridge Warfield (1851–1921), who taught there from 1887 to 1921. He is still revered today for his heroic and stalwart defense of full biblical infallibility and inerrancy in a time when many others were compromising. He wrote on a wide variety of theological subjects: New Testament exegesis, textual criticism, church history, apologetics, and systematic theology, all at the highest level of scholarship without compromising orthodox integrity. Roger Nicole once commented that Warfield was the greatest genius in the Reformed family. One weakness, however, was that he accepted a modified form of the theory of theistic evolution.

Francis Patton (1843–1932) was seminary president until it and the university formally separated into distinct institutions. His book *Fundamental Christianity* was influential in the Fundamentalist-Modernist controversy. Geerhardus Vos (1862–1949) was a Dutch-American who taught biblical theology for many years. Robert Dick Wilson (1856–1930) succeeded Green in Old Testament and taught alongside John D. Davis (1854–1926), editor of a popular Bible dictionary.

William Park Armstrong (1874–1944) taught New Testament; John DeWitt (1842–1923), church history; Charles Erdman (1866–1960), practical theology.

The Fundamentalist-Modernist controversy raged from 1910 to 1930. Orthodox denominations, seminaries, and mission boards were experiencing challenges, compromise, and division across the theological landscape. It affected Princeton after Warfield's death. More and more liberals in the Presbyterian Church were being appointed to the institutional boards, including the seminary's board of directors. President Joseph Ross Stevenson (1866–1939) was relatively conservative and tried to contain the first signs of liberalism at the seminary. Erdman tried to accommodate liberalism, though not a liberal himself. Others, such as the popular preacher Clarence Macartney (1879–1957), were insistent that liberalism should not be tolerated.

J. Gresham Machen (1881–1937) was the most outspoken conservative of all. He taught New Testament from 1906 to 1929 and continued the "Old School" tradition of Alexander, Hodge, and Warfield. His classic book *Christianity and Liberalism* argued that liberalism was not just another form of Christianity but was a fundamentally different religion. Sadly, the denomination voted for a reorganization of the seminary that would allow liberalism into what was once the bastion of conservative evangelical Calvinism.

Westminster Theological Seminary

Machen left Princeton in 1929 with Robert Dick Wilson, Oswald T. Allis (1878–1973), and a very young Cornelius Van Til (1895–1987) to start a new seminary to continue the Old Princeton tradition. It was in nearby Philadelphia and named Westminster Theological Seminary. John Murray (1898–1975) came over from Princeton a year later. Erdman, Vos, Armstrong, and a few others stayed at Princeton, but things were never the same.

Machen continued to stand for the truth in the Presbyterian Church as liberalism spread in other areas, such as missions. The case of liberal missionary Pearl Buck brought things to a head. Evangelicals such as Machen called for a housecleaning, but it was in vain. Machen was charged with schism for helping to found the Independent Board for Presbyterian Missions in 1933. He left and helped form what became the Orthodox Presbyterian Church, which has always had a close relationship with Westminster Seminary. Machen never married but influenced many young preachers to hold to traditional Reformed theology. His influence continues today in conservative Presbyterian circles.

John Murray, a Scotsman, taught New Testament and theology for thirty-six years and produced numerous theology books, of which his commentary on Romans was his crowning achievement. Cornelius Van Til was a Dutch-American who built on the foundation of Abraham Kuyper to produce the apologetic system known as presuppositionalism. He wrote many books and pamphlets, of which *The Defense of the Faith* is probably the best summary of his views. Oswald T. Allis retired while relatively young (he was independently wealthy) but continued to write. His *Prophecy and the Church* was an important refutation of dispensationalism, which was beginning to appear in American Presbyterian churches. Edward John Young (1907–68) in Old Testament and Ned B. Stonehouse (1902–62) in New Testament kept the scholarship level high. R. B. Kuiper (1886–1966), who also taught at Calvin Theological Seminary, Paul Woolley (1902–84), and John Skilton (1906–98) were also part of Westminster's faculty during its golden era.

Later, Jay Adams revolutionized Christian counseling by advocating a *sola Scriptura* approach called *Nouthetic Counseling*. Richard Gaffin, Vern Poythress, Sinclair Ferguson, Meredith Kline, Carl Trueman, and others carried the baton for years. There was a brief but intense controversy in the 1970s over the teaching of Murray's successor, Norman Shepherd, who was accused of straying from the traditional Reformed view of justification by faith.

Westminster Theological Seminary in California was begun at that time to expand its reach. John Frame (1939–) carried on Van Til's legacy before moving to Reformed Theological Seminary in Orlando, Florida. He has produced many important works, including a four-volume work on the knowledge of God and a large *Systematic Theology*. Michael Horton has developed covenant theology in a number of books under the influence of Meredith Kline and Geerhardus Vos. Robert Godfrey has been president for many years. J. V. Fesko and David VanDrunnen have also made useful contributions to Reformed scholarship. The so-called Escondido Theology of "Westminster West" has certain features somewhat different than the eastern school. Both schools more or less continue the tradition of Old Princeton but, like other seminaries, have had to "redig the wells of their father Abraham" (Genesis 26:18) in order to maintain doctrinal purity in the face of contemporary challenges.

The Princeton-Westminster Theology

The theology of this great tradition revolves around historic Reformed theology that has maintained the mainstream since the Swiss Reformation. It embodied Scottish-American Old School Presbyterianism and incorporated Scottish Common Sense Realism. While its earlier teachers respected Jonathan Edwards, they increasingly differed with his successors in New England Theology. For example, the Princetonians were not as involved in the Second Great Awakening, mainly because of differences with the New School Presbyterians and Congregationalists over such things as Finney's invitation system. But while the New England Theology declined in orthodoxy, Princeton stood firm.

The Princeton Theology was historic Calvinism at its best in that century. Thousands of students learned theology from Charles Hodge as he had them read Turretin's *Institutes of Elenctic Theology* in Latin or the handwritten translation of George Musgrave Giger. Some critics such as Jack Rogers have contended that this accounts for Princeton's supposed aberrant form of Calvinism as opposed to Calvin's pure theology. For instance, Rogers charged that Calvin did not hold to biblical inerrancy as taught by Turretin, Hodge, and Warfield.[1] This has been shown to be a serious misinterpretation of Calvin.[2] Princeton held to Calvin's basic theology, including Scripture, while those such as Rogers represent the post-Reformed ideology that infected historic Calvinism in Switzerland, Holland, France, Scotland, and England over the centuries — namely, liberalism. It was that error that helped bring about the demise of Old Princeton and challenges its descendants today.

The Princeton Theology wisely avoided the "Consistent Calvinism" of New England Theology on the one hand and Hyper-Calvinism on the other. One reason is that it firmly held to the Westminster Confession and catechisms. The Princeton-Westminster tradition has generally been faithful to the original threefold foundation envisaged by Alexander over two hundred years ago.

Conclusion

Princeton and then Westminster seminaries were the most influential evangelical and Reformed seminaries in America for decades. But if Old Princeton could depart from evangelical orthodoxy, anyone could. We would all do well to learn from history.

---

1 Jack B. Rogers and Donald K. McKim, *The Authority and Interpretation of the Bible* (San Francisco: Harper and Row, 1979).

2 John D. Woodbridge, *Biblical Authority: A Critique of the Rogers/McKim Proposal* (Grand Rapids: Zondervan, 1982).

Chapter 14
Nineteenth-Century American Calvinism

The United States began to spread westward in the nineteenth century and endured the costliest war in its history — the Civil War. American Calvinism also grew and diversified as it experienced and survived several theological wars.

Old and New School Presbyterianism

As the baton of Calvinistic leadership passed from the Congregationalists to the Presbyterians during the Second Great Awakening, new challenges arose. Not all Calvinists had supported the earlier Great Awakening. Those who did were known as New Lights; those who did not, Old Lights. But they were all basically one in their Reformed theology.

But there were more Arminians, such as Finney, involved in the Second Great Awakening. Other issues arose, such as slavery. Those Presbyterians who supported the revival tended to be influenced by Lyman Beecher (1775–1863) and others in a modified Calvinism. Certain Presbyterians, such as Albert Barnes (1798–1870), taught something similar to New England Theology. For example, Barnes rejected the historic Reformed view of particular redemption.

This gave rise to a major controversy in the Presbyterian Church. On the one side were the Old School traditionalists, such as the Princetonians and Ashbel Green (1762–1848). On the other side, the New School innovators such as Barnes. Barnes was convicted of theological error, which led to the split of the denomination in 1837. He lived long enough to see it reunited in 1864 and 1869.

The North-South Division

The Old School was in the majority during the interval, but another division occurred later. Most Presbyterians in the northern states agreed with the New School that slavery was unbiblical and should be abolished. Some, such as Charles Hodge, argued that slavery per se is not wrong, for it was allowed in the Old Testament. Some thought it was still allowable, while others said that in any case what was practiced in the United States did not match Old Testament standards.

Most Presbyterians in the southern states disagreed. They usually argued that slavery was still biblically allowable, though there were excesses at that time, and it should not be abolished but improved. This overlaps with other arguments in favor of states' rights. After much heated debate, the Presbyterian Church split into the so-called Northern and Southern Presbyterian Churches along the same lines as the Union and the Confederacy.

Samuel Davies (1723–61) is often considered the father of Presbyterianism in the American South. But the leader in the new Southern Presbyterian Church was undoubtedly James Henley Thornwell (1812–62). He considered it inappropriate for the church's General Assembly to adjudicate on the southerners' involvement in slavery. He also disagreed with Hodge's view that the local presbytery should only include teaching elders (pastors) and not all ruling elders.

The leading Southern Presbyterian theologian was Robert Lewis Dabney (1820–98), the southern counterpart of Charles Hodge. His *Lectures in Systematic Theology* was smaller than Hodge's but was every much as scholarly and traditionally Reformed. He wrote in defense of the Confederacy, slavery, and other issues.[1] There were other "Gentlemen Theologians," as E. Brooks Holifield has called them.[2] John Lafayette Girardeau (1825–98) wrote *Calvinism and Evangelical Arminianism*. He was pro-slavery but pastored a black church for eight years and evangelized African-Americans widely before and after the Civil War.

William S. Plumer (1802–80) was from the North but ministered in the South and produced a number of fine commentaries and other volumes. Benjamin Morgan Palmer of New Orleans (1818–1902) was the first moderator of the Southern Presbyterian Church. He wrote a biography of Thornwell, and in turn, his biography was written by Thomas Cary Johnson (1859–1936), who also wrote a biography of Dabney. Other major Southern Presbyterian theologians

---

1 Dabney's controversial defense of the Confederacy and slavery are in his *Discussions, Volume 4* (Harrisonburg: Sprinkle, 1979). These were omitted in the Banner of Truth edition which combines selected material from the original volumes 3 and 4. See also his *Defence of Virginia* (Harrisonburg: Sprinkle, 1977).

2 E. Brooks Holifield, *The Gentlemen Theologians: American Theology in Southern Culture 1795–1860* (Durham: Duke University Press, 1978).

included Thomas Peck (1822–93), Daniel Baker (1791–1857), and Moses Hoge (1818–99).

The Southern Presbyterian Church was officially known as the Presbyterian Church in the United States.[3] The Northern church later united with another church and became the United Presbyterian Church in the United States of America. The two eventually reunited in 1983, by which time there were very few evangelicals and even fewer traditional Calvinists left.

The Briggs Case

Another significant controversy bears mention because of its implications for what was happening in other areas. German liberalism was slowly seeping into American churches across the board, including some Presbyterians. Charles Augustus Briggs (1841–1913) was a leading Presbyterian scholar at Union Theological Seminary, New York. He came to reject the infallibility of the Bible and imbibed various liberal views such as the historical-critical method of hermeneutics. He was opposed by the traditionally staunch Presbyterians Benjamin Breckinridge Warfield, A. A. Hodge, and William G. T. Shedd (1820–94).[4] When he was convicted of heterodoxy and dismissed by the church, Union pulled out of the denomination and professed itself an independent institution. Briggs became an Episcopalian.

Shedd was a highly able and respected Northern Presbyterian theologian who had once been a Congregationalist. His *Dogmatic Theology* ranks with the best Reformed systematic theologies ever written. He also produced a two-volume *History of Christian Doctrine*, a commentary on Romans, a defense of the evangelical doctrine of Hell (*The Doctrine of Endless Punishment*), and others. When the moderates and liberals called for a major revision of the Westminster Confession in a liberal direction, he penned *Calvinism: Pure and Mixed* to defend historic Calvinism.

The Mercersburg Theology

The Reformed Church in the United States, popularly known as the German Reformed Church, also experienced upheaval in the nineteenth century. This body traced its ancestry back to Martin Bucer, Zacharias Ursinus, and Caspar Olevianus in sixteenth-century Germany. Philip Otterbein (1726–1813) was the first major American leader. He held to traditional German Reformed

---

3 This is the denomination in which I was raised in New Orleans.
4 Archibald A. Hodge and Benjamin B. Warfield, *Inspiration* (Grand Rapids: Baker, 1979).

theology but, unlike others, leaned toward the Pietist movement of August Herman Franke and Phillipp Jakob Spener. Lewis Mayer (1783–1849) was not so Pietistically inclined.

Early Reformed theology greatly modified the sacramentalism of Roman Catholicism, even more than the Lutherans did. The view of Calvin, Bucer, and Vermigli became the majority Reformed position on Communion rather than the symbolic theory of Zwingli. All these greatly modified the baptismal regenerationist view of infant baptism as well. But the German Reformed Church in America took a step backward on these issues and advocated a kind of "Reformed Sacramentalism." In some ways it was similar to the High Church movement of the Church of England at that time. Indeed, the new emphasis on the sacraments sounded more Lutheran or Anglican than Reformed. It taught more than the "Word and Spirit" view; it taught the "real presence" view. Calvinist Anglicans had held to that, but most other Calvinists rejected it. These new advocates also explicitly taught baptismal regeneration.

The controversy centered around Mercersburg College in southeast Pennsylvania. John Williamson Nevin (1803–86) had studied under Charles Hodge at Princeton and reacted more vehemently to Finney's "New Measures" than Hodge did. He did not oppose the Second Great Awakening merely because of its Arminian influences but because it was too evangelical and not sacramental enough. He also reacted adversely to Pietism, Puritanism, and Edwardseanism.

He was joined on the faculty by a young German Swiss immigrant named Philip Schaff (1819–93) in 1844. Schaff called for a renewed interest in church history and a somewhat different view of historical theology than, say, Shedd used. It sometimes resembled the Roman Catholic view of developing theology, such as propounded by John Henry Cardinal Newman, though Schaff was not leading a "Back to Rome" movement like the Tractarian Movement over in England was doing at that time. Schaff would become the leading church historian in America for a generation and is still respected today. He wrote a large *History of the Christian Church* (eight volumes), edited *The Creeds of Christendom* (three volumes), edited the translation of Johann Peter Lange's huge Bible commentary, coedited the *Schaff-Herzog Encyclopedia of Religious Knowledge*, and coordinated the translation of many church fathers, among other efforts. He helped lay the foundation for the modern ecumenical movement, was involved in the World Parliament of Religions (1893), and later taught at Union Theological Seminary with Briggs.

More traditional German Reformed men resisted Nevin and Schaff, such as Henry Harbach (1817–67), Emmanuel V. Gerhart (1817–1904), and James I. Good (1850–1924). The traditionalists won the "Battle of Mercersburg," but soon the denomination began to drift into theological liberalism in the next century.

The Dutch-American Reformed

The earliest Dutch Reformed in America centered around New York and New Jersey. Theodorus Jacobus Frelinghuysen (1691–1747) was a precursor of the Great Awakening, which got him in trouble with the majority of the church leadership.

The several divisions of the Dutch Reformed Church back in the Netherlands had an impact on the churches in America. Immigrants tended to be conservative and traditional in lifestyle and theology. Many came from the Christian Reformed Church of the 1834 division. Leaders included Hendrik Peter Scholte (1805–68) and Albertus Van Raalte (1811–76). Others from Kuyper's Doleantie followed. Often the churches and the community were rather insulated from American culture at large, mainly because many continued to speak Dutch. Most of them tenaciously held to the Belgic Confession, the Heidelberg Catechism, and the Canons of the Synod of Dort. As America spread westward, more Dutch Reformed communities grew in Western Michigan and Iowa.

Baptist Calvinists

The Baptists and Methodists were especially energetic in their evangelism and church-planting in the nineteenth century. Earlier Baptists such as Roger Williams (1603–83) were very moderate in their Calvinism, mainly because they remembered the Reformed persecution of Anabaptists in Europe in the sixteenth century. Williams seemed to have bordered on Arminianism at times. Others were explicitly Calvinistic, like the English Baptists such as Bunyan, Keach, Kiffin, and Hanserd Knollys, who immigrated to America and back to England. Isaac Backus (1724–1806) helped found Brown University and was the first major outspoken Calvinistic Baptist in America.

Baptists in America were relatively untouched by the English Hyper-Calvinism of Gill and Brine until the Primitive Baptist movement arose in the nineteenth century. Otherwise, most American Baptists were very Calvinistic in their theology (without infant baptism, of course). This can be seen, for example, in the Philadelphia Confession of 1742, which was a revision of the

Second London Confession (also known as the Baptist Confession of 1689), which itself was the Baptist revision of the Westminster Confession of Faith. The New Hampshire Confession (1833) was also Calvinistic, though less explicitly so.

Just as the Presbyterians divided over slavery, states' rights, and denominational interference in local churches, so the Baptists split north and south in 1845. The northern Baptists were still evangelical but slowly watered down their Calvinism. The southern Baptists, however, remained more evangelical and predominantly and explicitly Calvinistic. Most if not all of the founders of the Southern Baptist Convention were staunch Calvinists,[5] such as: W. B. Johnson (1782–1862), first president of the Southern Baptist Convention; Patrick H. Mell (1814–88), president for seventeen years; John L. Dagg (1794–1884), the first major Southern Baptist theologian; Basil Manly Sr. (1798–1868) and Jr. (1825–92); John Broadus (1827–95), author of Bible commentaries and a standard textbook on preaching; and later B. H. Carroll (1843–1914), founder of Southwestern Baptist Theological Seminary. Most explicitly Calvinist of all was the Princeton-trained James Petigru Boyce (1827–88). He served as president of the SBC, founded the flagship Southern Baptist Theological Seminary (Louisville, Kentucky), and wrote the classic *Abstract of Systematic Theology*.

One group spun off from the Southern Baptists while originally retaining its Calvinistic theology. These were the so-called Landmark Baptists, led by James R. Graves (1820–93) and James M. Pendleton (1811–91). They taught that there has always been a continuous chain-link of Baptist churches since the New Testament, which alone are the only true churches.

Conclusion

Though there were a few Episcopalians and Congregationalists that shared core Calvinistic convictions in this period, the main upholders of historic Reformed theology in nineteenth-century America were primarily the Presbyterians, Dutch Reformed, some German Reformed, and most Baptists (with obvious modifications in ecclesiology). The voices of their leaders still echo today in the hearts of their theological descendants.

---

5 Thomas J. Nettles, *By His Grace and For His Glory*, revised edition (Cape Coral, FL: Founders, 2006).

Chapter 15
Nineteenth-Century
European Calvinism

If the eighteenth century saw major changes in the Reformed community, there would be still more in the nineteenth. The center of geography for Christianity at large was shifting from Europe to America, and the same was true with Calvinism.

German Reformed

Two Germans named *Friedrich* stood out as representing two different directions in the German Reformed Church. The first was Friedrich Schleiermacher (1768–1834). He came from a Pietist background but pulled up his orthodox anchor after rejecting the Rationalism of the Enlightenment and founded a theology that combined philosophical Romanticism and Protestant theology. Often considered "The Father of Liberal Theology," he emphasized that religion is mainly feelings and not dogma, theology is anthropology, and faith is a sense of dependence on the "Other." His rejection of the historical evangelical and Reformed doctrines of substitutionary atonement (especially limited atonement) and eternal Hell led to his drastic reformulation of theology, as seen in his unfinished *The Christian Faith*. The movement diversified across Europe and infected Lutheranism as well for the rest of the century. Schleiermacher led many people out of both evangelical Christianity and historic Calvinism.

By contrast, Friedrich Krummacher (1796–1868) sought to retain the best of historic German Reformed theology and Pietism. He was the most popular German preacher of his day and a best-selling author, several of whose books have been translated into English (*The Suffering Savior*, books on David, Solomon, Elijah, Elisha, and others). He resisted the direction of Schleiermacher but was not very influential in scholarly circles. His Calvinism was more implicit than explicit.

Other conservative German Reformed theologians of the time were Adolf Zahn (1834–1900), Johann Peter Lange (1802–84), August Lang (1867–1945), and Johannes Ebrard (1818–88). Heinrich Heppe (1820–79) was more liberal but wrote at length about Pietism and composed the eminently useful *Reformed Dogmatics: Set Out and Illustrated from the Sources.* He collected hundreds of quotations from early Reformed writers, especially the scholastics, but did not necessarily agree with them.

Mention must be made of Edouard Reuss (1804–91) who with others edited the standard *Opera Calvini* collection of Calvin's works in Latin and French (fifty-nine volumes of the *Corpus Reformatorum*), which is only now being superseded. But he did not adhere to the historic Reformed faith. Based in Strasbourg, he ministered in both the French Reformed and German Reformed churches and published at length in both French and German.

The Lutheran and Reformed churches formally united in 1817, but each continued to maintain certain distinctives of their respective heritages. Sadly, both were dragged into theological liberalism and spread the disease worldwide.

Swiss Reformed

Calvinism in Switzerland was almost dead at the start of the nineteenth century. Wilhelm DeWette at Basel and David Strauss at Zürich had no resemblance whatsoever to Calvin or Zwingli. The library at Geneva threw out whole boxes of Calvin's unpublished sermon manuscripts as trash.

But Calvinism got a shot in the arm through the evangelical movement known as *Le Reveil* (The Revival). The brothers Robert (1764–1842) and James (1768–1851) Haldane were evangelical Scottish Baptist Calvinists who visited Europe in 1810 and ignited revival fires in Switzerland, then in France and the Netherlands. The movement opposed both the Enlightenment and the new liberalism. It breathed life into parts of the Swiss Reformed Church.

Orthodox Swiss leaders in *Le Reveil* included Cesar Malan (1787–1864); J. H. Merle d'Aubigne (1794–1872), who wrote many useful books on church history; and Louis Gaussen (1790–1863), whose book *Theopneustia* has been one of the best defenses of the high evangelical doctrine of biblical inspiration. Frederic Godet (1812–1900) was very moderate in his Calvinism (some consider him more Arminian) but was strongly evangelical in his exegetical commentaries on Luke, John, Romans, and 1 Corinthians.

Alexandre Vinet (1797–1847) was another popular but moderate Calvinist writer. He was somewhat influenced by Schleiermacher, however, in his more mystical approach to spirituality, a kind of Swiss Reformed Pietism. The Monod brothers Frederic (1794–1863) and Adolphe (1802–56) were more traditionally

Reformed and ministered mainly in France. The French Reformed Church suffered greatly first under Catholicism after the revocation of the Edict of Nantes (1685), then under the French Revolution, and then again under the Enlightenment and liberalism. But it still survived.

The Dutch Reformed

The southern region of the Netherlands known as Belgium was predominantly Catholic and was granted independence in 1830. The University of Leiden (formerly spelled *Leyden*), where the Arminian controversy broke out, became the center of nineteenth-century Dutch liberalism, especially through Jan Hendrik Scholten (1811–85) and Abraham Kuenen (1828–91), who first formulated the Documentary Hypothesis of the Pentateuch later popularized by Julius Wellhausen of Germany. The Groningen School also cashed in its orthodox Dutch Reformed heritage. Petrus Hofsted de Groot (1802–86) and others minimized dogma and held to a weak view of sin and conversion. This approach claimed to be Christocentric — the church is primarily an educational institution to help us imitate Christ's example of love and toleration to promote a good society. This was Dutch post-Reformed liberalism.

But there were good signs as well. Isaac Da Costa (1798–1860) was a converted Jew who helped spread *Le Reveil* in the Netherlands. There were also still remnants of the *Nadere Reformatie* in Friesland and other out-of-the-way places. The conservatives eventually reacted to the growing liberalism and were led by Hendrik de Cock (1801–42) out of the state church in the Secession of 1834. This group took the name Christian Reformed Church in 1869. Later, others left the Dutch Reformed Church in the Doleantie of 1886. Groen Van Prinsterer (1801–76) was a lawyer statesman affected by *Le Reveil*. He called for a reformation of society and its laws to reflect the true Dutch Reformed theology.

The most important Dutch Calvinist of all time was the great Abraham Kuyper (1837–1920). A pastor's son, he drifted into liberalism in his youth, but his faith was restored by contact with simple godly adherents of the *Nadere Reformatie*. He soon rose to prominence in many areas. He edited several Christian newspapers (for which he wrote thousands of editorials), formed the Anti-Revolutionary Party with Groen Van Prinsterer to counteract the anti-Christian revolutionary specter of atheism and liberalism, was elected to the Estates-General in 1874, formed a conservative political-social alliance with Catholics in 1878, and was prime minister from 1900 to 1905. Moreover, he led the Doleantie Secession in 1880, helped it merge with the Christian Reformed Church in 1892 to form the Reformed Church in the Netherlands, and started the Free University of Amsterdam. He was an extremely prolific writer as well, with large sets such as *Common Grace, Pro Rege, The Encyclopedia of Sacred Theology, E Voto Dordraceno* (an exposition of the Heidelberg Catechism), a large systematic theology, plus volumes on the Holy Spirit, particular grace, short devotionals, and many others. He gave the famous Stone Lectures on Calvinism at Princeton on 1898. Kuyper was a workhorse who accomplished as much as ten men in a lifetime.

Kuyper was a genius innovator like Calvin and Edwards rather than a mere organizer like Turretin or Hodge. His supralapsarianism taught eternal justification a la Comrie in the previous century. He interpreted Scripture and the Canons of Dort to teach the error of presumptive regeneration — godly parents should presume that their baptized children are not only elect but regenerate until they give evidence they are not. But his main contribution was in the twin theories of common grace and sphere sovereignty. All creation belongs to God, and Christians should strive to bring it all under the rule of Christ. God gives common grace to restrain sin and promote good in science, medicine, education, technology, and other different but overlapping "spheres." Christians have a worldview that is antithetical to non-Christianity, and Kuyper's theology laid the foundation for the later apologetic system known as presuppositionalism. All subsequent Dutch Calvinists are "Sons of Abraham" in one way or another.[1]

English Calvinism

Long after the effects of the eighteenth-century Evangelical Awakening subsided, England survived the threat of the French Revolution and its anti-Christian outlook. But there were godly Christians who helped save England as much as the Duke of Wellington or Admiral Nelson. For example, there were the eminently popular preachers Rowland Hill (1744–1833) and Charles Simeon of Cambridge (1759–1836). Thomas Scott (1747–1821), the pastoral successor of John Newton, wrote an enormously popular commentary on the whole Bible. He also wrote *Remarks on the Refutation of Calvinism* to echo Toplady's earlier defense of the Calvinistic foundation of the Church of England.

---

1 His theology is often called "Neo-Calvinism," occasionally "Kuyper-Calvinism" as a play on the word *Hyper-Calvinism*. Though he was supralapsarian and believed in eternal justification before faith, I have not found any evidence that he was Hyper-Calvinist.

Other worthies followed, such as William Jay (1769–1853), John Angell James (1785–1859), E. A. Litton (1813–97), and Octavius Winslow (1808–78), who ministered also in New York. Probably the most beloved evangelical and Reformed preacher in the Church of England in that century was the great J. C. Ryle (1816–1900), later bishop of Liverpool. His books *Holiness* and *Expository Thoughts on the Gospels* remain classics beloved by Christians around the world.

Among such great lights, one English Calvinist outshone them all — Charles Haddon Spurgeon (1834–92). If Calvin was the greatest Reformed theologian and Whitefield the greatest Reformed evangelist, then Spurgeon was certainly the greatest Reformed preacher of them all, the "Prince of Preachers." Anyone who says that "Baptist Calvinism" is a contradiction in terms must explain Spurgeon or admit defeat.[2] Converted and baptized as a teenager of Methodist stock, he became pastor at age nineteen of the church formerly pastored by Benjamin Keach, John Gill, and John Rippon, later renamed Metropolitan Tabernacle. Attendance soon rose to over five thousand, making it not only the largest church in the world but perhaps the largest church in history up until then. Some 3,561 of his sermons were published in the largest-ever collection of sermons.[3] He wrote many other books, such as *Lectures to My Students*, a large posthumous autobiography, the best-selling *All of Grace*, and his magnum opus *The Treasury of David*, a seven-volume exposition of Psalms. He started an orphanage, a pastors' college, and a colportage association for distributing Christian literature. He supported missions and other endeavors even through numerous physical afflictions. One wonders if there was more than one C. H. Spurgeon.

In 1864 he preached a sermon against baptismal regeneration as taught by the Book of Common Prayer of the Church of England. He called for evangelical Anglicans to secede. A few did, but the backlash was intense. Then there was the Downgrade Controversy in his own Baptist Union denomination which his predecessor John Rippon helped to found. It was once evangelical and Calvinistic, but by 1887, liberalism began to creep in. Spurgeon raised the alarm,

---

2 See Thomas J. Nettles, *By His Grace and For His Glory*, Rev. ed. (Cape Coral, FL: Founders, 2006) and *Living by Revealed Truth: The Life and Pastoral Theology of Charles Haddon Spurgeon* (Fearn: Mentor, 2013).

3 The sixty-three volumes consist of six volumes of *The New Park Street Pulpit* and fifty-seven volumes of *The Metropolitan Tabernacle Pulpit*, reprinted by Pilgrim Publications. Day One Publications has added four further volumes of sermons, and B&H Publishers plans to publish a set of still more previously unpublished sermons in a critical edition.

but very few heeded him. So he left and warned that history would vindicate him within a hundred years. He was right. We need to learn such lessons in our own day.

Scottish Calvinism

Scottish Calvinism continued amid several disputes that produced denominations of varying degrees of Calvinism. One beloved Scotsman early in the century was Robert Murray M'Cheyne (1813–43). Often in ill health, his fervent preaching, warm heart, godly prayers, and holy life showed how revival can come to a local church or individual person. His friend Andrew Bonar (1810–92) edited the classic *Memoir and Remains of Robert Murray M'Cheyne* that has encouraged multitudes.

John Dick (1764–1833), a pastor in the Secession Church, wrote a large *Lectures in Theology*. John Eadie (1810–72) ministered in the Secession and United Presbyterian Church and wrote several exegetical commentaries that are still used today.

Around 1820 a form of Low Calvinism developed that was similar to Amyraldism of seventeenth-century France and nineteenth-century New England Theology. Edward Irving (1792–1834) was the most controversial member of this loose school. He began as assistant to Thomas Chalmers at the influential Tron Church in Glasgow, then assumed the pastorate of a Church of Scotland congregation in London. He rubbed shoulders with famous writers such as Samuel Taylor Coleridge, Henry Drummond, and his childhood friend, Thomas Carlyle. With his tall, dark, and handsome appearance, eloquent oratory, and flair for controversy, he became the talk of the town. But his eccentricities led to his downfall. First, he taught that Christ was born with a sinful nature like Adam's after the Fall, though He never sinned. Second, he preached that the Second Coming was near. Irving was premillennial and one of the first at that time to teach what has come to be known as the *pretribulation rapture* theory. Irving evidently got his views from an obscure Spanish book called *The Coming of Messiah in Glory and Majesty* by one "Juan Josaphat Ben-Ezra" who claimed to be a converted Jew but was in fact the Jesuit Diaz Y Lacunza. Irving translated the book and wrote a large introduction. Some have speculated whether this was the source of the theory. Third, Irving thought that another Pentecost would occur shortly before the Second Coming, so he welcomed speaking in tongues and prophesying in his church. All this led to his defrocking in 1833. Some eight hundred members left with him to start a new church associated with the Catholic Apostolic Church sect. Soon Irving died, despite a "prophecy" that he would be miraculously healed. Unfortunately, there has been much interest and appreciation of Irving by Thomas Torrance and others.

James Morison (1816–93) also rejected limited atonement and, unlike Irving, drifted into Arminianism, for which he was ejected from the United Secession Church to form the Evangelical Union in 1843. He wrote several very popular Bible commentaries. Ralph Wardlaw (1779–1853) was another Low Calvinist at that time. His large three-volume *Systematic Theology* was based on his lectures. W. Lindsey Alexander (1808–84) and John Brown of Haddington (1722–87) also taught a similar Low Calvinism.

Then there was John M'Leod Campbell (1800–1872). He taught universal atonement (but not universal salvation) in a way that resembled the old Moral Influence Theory as opposed to the Anselmian or penal substitutionary theory of mainstream Calvinism. He also promoted the rather bizarre theory of "vicarious repentance" as part of his view that Christ was the perfect vicarious person. His unorthodox opinions are mainly in *The Nature of the Atonement*, which led to his expulsion in 1831. He is hailed today as a major theologian by less than orthodox ex-Calvinists.

The Disruption

During the Ten Years Conflict (1834–43) occurred the biggest division in the history of the Church of Scotland, but it produced the cream of nineteenth-century Reformed theologians in Europe. The Evangelical Party opposed the Moderate Party over the patronage system whereby the wealthy aristocracy had the deciding vote on the selection of pastors in the local church.

On May 18, 1843, Thomas Chalmers (1780–1847) led some 200 ministers out of the General Assembly to form the Free Church of Scotland, with Chalmers as the first moderator. Eventually a total of 474 preachers would leave or be ejected to join the Free Church. A few evangelicals stayed in, but later their numbers dwindled.

The Church of Scotland eventually abolished the patronage system, but its orthodoxy declined. The Free Church suffered several divisions as well. Some members returned to the Church of Scotland. Others founded the Free Presbyterian Church. Many of these churches sang only psalms in worship. Most were very conservative historic Calvinists.

Another product of the Disruption was the founding of New College, with Chalmers as the first principal. Located near the historic Edinburgh Castle, it was a bastion of Reformed theology like Princeton. Later, with a partially reunited Church of Scotland, the state courts deeded it over to the Church of Scotland. As expected, New College followed the gradual decline of its owner. It is now part of the University of Edinburgh. I received my PhD in theology there in 1983.

Nevertheless, the period of 1840–1900 saw a host of great Scottish preachers and theologians, mainly in the Free Church and at New College. Some consider this the Golden Age of Scottish Calvinism. Chalmers pastored the Tron Church, Glasgow. He was a popular preacher, author, and organizer of relief for the poor. He was followed at New College by William Cunningham (1805–61), the Scottish counterpart to Charles Hodge. His *Historical Theology* is still being read today. Robert Candlish (1806–73) was pastor of St. George's Kirk, Edinburgh, but left to join the Free Church. James Buchanan (1804–70) wrote the highly respected book *The Doctrine of Justification* and others. John "Rabbi" Duncan (1796–1870) was not Jewish but served as missionary to Jews in Budapest and taught Hebrew at New College.

Next to Chalmers, Thomas Guthrie (1803–73) was Scotland's most renown preacher. Horatius Bonar (1808–89) was another Disruption leader, historic premillennialist, and author of over six hundred hymns. Patrick Fairbairn (1805–74) wrote the useful *Imperial Bible Dictionary*, *The Revelation of Law in Scripture*, and *The Typology of Scripture*. David Brown (1803–97) commented on the four Gospels and defended postmillennialism. James (1807–68) and his son Douglas (1842–1903) Bannerman both wrote at length on Presbyterian ecclesiology. John Kennedy (1819–84) and James Begg (1808–83) were also major exponents of conservative Presbyterian polity. A. Moody Stuart (1809–98), George Smeaton (1814–89), and Alexander Whyte (1836–1921) were other notable Free Church worthies.

But, as elsewhere, compromise began to seep into the Free Church after the first generation. A. B. Davidson (1831–1902) taught Hebrew at New College and showed hints of the influence of German liberal theories. His best student, William Robertson Smith (1846–94), went still further and imported the Kuenen-Graf-Wellhausen Documentary Theory, which together with other unorthodox opinions in his *The Religion of the Semites*, led to his trial and dismissal. His successor, George Adam Smith (1856–1942), taught much the same but survived a heresy trial. In New Testament studies, A. B. Bruce (1831–

99), Marcus Dods (1834–1909), and James Denney (1856–1917) combined a very moderate Calvinism with some liberal views, and this influenced many of their students leftward. James Orr (1844–1913) in the United Presbyterian Church was also moderate and slightly liberal, though the *International Standard Bible Encyclopedia* which he edited is mostly evangelical. Peter Taylor Forsyth (1848–1921) was a Scottish Independent pastor in London and popular writer. Like the above, he was very moderate in what little Calvinism he professed.

Conclusion

The nineteenth century showed what happens when the anchor of evangelical Reformed orthodoxy is pulled up. Churches, seminaries, and individuals make shipwreck of their faith. But God continued to raise up new ships with stalwart captains and crews.

Chapter 16
Neo-Orthodoxy

A new theology arose early in the twentieth century that claimed to rediscover Calvin and historic Reformed theology. Many have said that Karl Barth was a great Reformed theologian.[1] The theology goes by the name *Neo-Orthodoxy*. Is it really Reformed, as some say, or non-Reformed and less than evangelical? Let us see.

Roots

The roots of this system go back to the proto-Existentialist Danish philosopher Søren Kierkegaard (1813–55) and his dislike for traditional dogma. Others see the roots in Schleiermacher, for though Barth frequently disagreed with him, he also praised him. Barth also said he was influenced by Herman Friedrich Kohlbrugge (1803–75). He was born in Germany but also ministered in the Netherlands. His son-in-law Eduard Boehl (1836–1903) also attempted to adapt Reformed theology to contemporary alternatives.

There were hints in certain moderates in Scotland at the turn of the century, especially Peter Taylor Forsyth (1848–1921) in London. He has been called "a Barthian before Barth." What all these had in common was a growing distaste for traditional Reformed theology, especially Reformed scholasticism, and tried to modernize it to accommodate contemporary liberalism while still claiming to be Reformed.

Karl Barth

Both the son and father of theologians, Karl Barth (1886–1968) was born in Basel, Switzerland. He pastored briefly in the old Swiss Reformed Church within the general German Reformed tradition but spent most of his long career teaching. He taught at Göttingen, Münster, and Bonn, Germany, then was expelled by the Nazis in 1935 for helping lead the Confessing Church and coauthoring the Barmen Declaration that opposed Nazism. He returned to teach at Basel, Switzerland, from 1935 to 1962.

---

1 E.g., F. F. Bruce: "Barth stood squarely within the Reformation tradition." *Answers to Questions* (Grand Rapids: Zondervan, 1973), 155.

While still a pastor, Barth wrote his popular commentary on Romans (1919). It was not an exegetical commentary but a theological exposition. It is more a commentary on Barth than on Paul. It has been called a bombshell that fell on the playground of liberal theology. He went on to write many other books, such as *The Word of God and the Word of Man*, *The Humanity of God*, and several summaries of his theology: *Credo, Dogmatics in Outline, The Kingdom of God and the Service of God*, and *Evangelical Theology*. But his masterpiece was the *Church Dogmatics* in fourteen large volumes of small print. It is the largest systematic theology ever written in any language from any perspective. Begun in 1932 to replace his unfinished *Christian Dogmatics*, it would occupy his attention for the rest of his life and was never completed. It is very difficult to read. My seminary professor, Geoffrey Bromiley, the translator, confirmed the rumor that some Germans preferred to read the English translation rather than the original German. Though it is filled with references to previous Protestant and Catholic theologians, he rarely refers to British or American evangelical writers. He interacted with the early Reformed Scholastics, often to disagree with them. It has been suggested that he relied mainly on Heppe's *Reformed Dogmatics* for this material, for which he wrote a foreword in the twentieth-century edition. He practically ignores the Puritans, Jonathan Edwards, the Princetonians, and other orthodox Reformed divines.

After World War II, Barth rejected infant baptism. He reasoned: "How could so many so-called "Christians" in Europe bring about the worst war in history?" His answer: Most were Christian in name only because they had been baptized as infants (an echo of Kierkegaard). He had always claimed to reject the old nineteenth-century German liberalism, but as we shall see, he fathered a new form of liberalism, just as Schleiermacher formed a new liberalism to follow the liberalism of Rationalism and the Enlightenment. This is the true lineage of Neo-Orthodoxy, for it is not a new orthodoxy after all, but another heterodoxy that was no more Calvinist than Arminianism was.

Barth on Scripture

The early Barth advocated *dialectical theology* which emphasized paradox and downplayed propositional revelation. This became *crisis theology* in which God is known existentially in moments of spiritual encounter. Historic evangelicals suspected he was using Hegelian dialectics to form a new synthesis out of the thesis of orthodoxy and the antithesis of liberalism.

He claimed to have a high regard for the Bible but said that Scripture points to, contains, or becomes the word of God rather than *is* the word by its very nature. Christ alone is *the* Word, he argued. Scripture is basically human words that God uses to affect us, though human language is really inadequate for revelation. He rejected the historic Reformed view of verbal plenary inspiration.

Further, he explicitly denied the infallibility and inerrancy of the Bible. To say it is inerrant, he claimed, is to make it a paper pope and deny its humanity, which is comparable to the heresy of Docetism. Scripture has many contradictions (e.g., law and gospel, Paul and James, the four Gospels, etc.). The writers erred in both theological and historical areas. What's more, the Bible contains many myths, such as most of Genesis 1–11, including Adam and Eve, the Serpent, and the Fall. Those are only "sagas," that is, useful legends with very little basis in historical fact. God speaks and acts in religious history known as *Geschichte*, not factual observable history. While disagreeing with Bultmann over much of this, it is obvious that Barth believed in the old liberal view of Scripture rather than the historical Reformed orthodox view.

Barth on God

The old liberalism emphasized divine immanence — God is near. Barth emphasized divine transcendence — God is out there, "wholly other" with no resemblance to man. God has total freedom, even to be His opposite, whatever that means. God is known only in Christ, not in nature. Theology begins with Christ, not God. In Christ, God is both totally hidden and totally revealed. Barth's emphasis on Christ is sometimes called *Christomonism*, which at times almost resembles Sabellianism except that Barth professed belief in the Trinity. Unlike many old liberals, Barth believed in the virgin birth, sinless humanity, and deity of Christ. Thus, his theology proper and Christology is an improvement on the old liberalism but is still not fully orthodox Calvinism.

Barth on Salvation

Barth said that the doctrine of election is the sum of the gospel, but he had a radically different theory than Calvin and historic Calvinism. He denied absolute foreordination and the twofold will of God. The only will of God is that which is in Christ. He called the idea of an inter-trinitarian covenant of redemption "tri-theistic mythology" — strange, because for Barth it can be useful to believe in myths. Also, he said there is only one covenant and one decree — that of Jesus Christ.

He put forth a "purified supralapsarianism," or "Super-supralapsarianism," centered on Christ, who is the only person who is elected.[2] But he added that every person is both elected and reprobated in Christ. The election of grace wins out in the triumph of grace over sin in the end. The work of Christ on the cross was not limited to the elect nor is it penal substitutionary satisfaction like Calvin or even Arminius proposed.

This strongly implies that Barth believed in ultimate universal salvation. But he neither asserted nor denied it as such. Some think he taught that there is a Hell (but nobody is in it) or that preaching on Hell is only a useful ruse to move people to a crisis of faith. Christ will be Judge to restore order in the universe, not necessarily to consign lost sinners to Hell. In sum, he taught a radically different soteriology than historic Calvinism.

Emil Brunner

Emil Brunner (1889–1966) was also German Swiss from a diluted Reformed background. He taught at Zürich from 1924 to 1953, then at the International Christian University in Tokyo from 1953 to 1956. His theology is summed up in his three-volume *Dogmatics* and briefly in *Our Faith*. He wrote many others: *The Mediator, The Divine Imperative, Man in Revolt, Revelation and Reason, The Divine-Human Encounter, The Theology of Crisis*, and many more. He had an earlier impact in Britain and America than Barth because more of his works were translated into English first, but eventually Barth overshadowed him. There are still many "Barthians" today but very few "Brunnerians."

He was more liberal than Barth in several ways, such as in rejecting the virgin birth. He sometimes implied that unrepentant sinners will be annihilated, but he usually taught universal salvation. Like Barth and Arminius, he said there is only one will in God. People are already saved but do not know it.

In 1934 Brunner wrote *Nature and Grace: A Discussion with Karl Barth* to defend the doctrine of natural revelation. Barth replied with a short publication, *Nein!* The two theologians separated and went their own ways. To Brunner, the worst error in the history of the church is equating the Bible with the Word of God. Verbal plenary inspiration is leftover Jewish legalism and is the letter that kills and does not give life. The old Reformed view was "bibliolatry." Following Martin Buber, the Jewish philosopher (not Martin Bucer the Reformer), he denied that propositional revelation is possible. Revelation occurs in an "I-Thou"

---

2 See chapter 48, "Order of the Decrees," and Christian van Driel, *Incarnation Anyway: Arguments for Supralapsarian Christology* (Oxford: Oxford University Press, 2008).

divine-human encounter. The Bible only points to this revelation but is not the revelation itself.

Like his Swiss rival, Brunner denied and scorned the idea of biblical inerrancy. He denied the Pauline authorship of the Pastoral Epistles. To him, 2 Timothy 3:16 teaches a paper pope. Scripture has myths and contradictions. Adam and Eve were non-historical myths. Moses did not write the Pentateuch, which was compiled by scribes centuries after the prophets wrote their books. Isaiah was written by two later editors. The Gospels contain myths, such as Luke's record of a Roman census and Matthew's star of the Wise Men. Even the Gospel accounts of the Resurrection appearances are contradictory.

Thus said Emil Brunner. Any resemblance between his theology and historic Reformed theology is only coincidental. Yet some still think he was Reformed.

Scottish Neo-Orthodoxy

After World War II, a form of Neo-Orthodoxy began to appear in the Church of Scotland and New College. Much of it was presented in the *Scottish Journal of Theology*. The exponents called for "A New Reformation," not a call to remember the Protestant Reformation. They disliked the Westminster Confession and preferred the Scots Confession, which they interpreted along Barthian lines. They argue that Calvin's true theology was grossly distorted by later Calvinists such as the Puritans and that John M'Leod Campbell and Edward Irving better understood Calvin and presented a true Calvinism.

This was pioneered first by Hugh Ross Mackintosh (1870–1936)[3] and the brothers John (1886–1960) and Donald (1887–1954) Baillie, then by J. K. S. Reid (1910–2002),[4] Harold Knight, G. T. Thompson,[5] and A. M. Hunter (1906–91).

But by far the major leaders were of the Torrance theological dynasty, primarily Thomas F. Torrance (1913–2007). "TFT" studied under Barth at Basel, taught at New College, edited the *Scottish Journal of Theology*, served as moderator of the Church of Scotland, was awarded the prestigious Templeton Prize in Religion, and coedited the English translation of Barth's *Church Dogmatics*. In a way he was the most prestigious British theologian of the twentieth century. He wrote two books on Barth's theology: *Karl Barth: An Introduction to His Early*

---

3 He was one of the editors of the English translation of Schleiermacher's *The Christian Faith*.
4 Reid was the external examiner for my doctoral dissertation at New College on the subject of Hyper-Calvinism, which he curiously approved with flying colors.
5 He translated volume 1 of Barth's *Church Dogmatics*, which was later retranslated by Geoffrey Bromiley. He also translated Heppe's *Reformed Dogmatics*.

Theology, 1910–1931 and *Karl Barth: Biblical and Evangelical Theologian*. He was the main promoter of Barth's theology in Britain, though he did not like to be called a Barthian. He was strongly trinitarian and favored the Greek Orthodox perspective. He taught John M'Leod Campbell's "Vicarious Humanity of Christ" idea and Edward Irving's "Fallen Nature of Christ" error. He strongly opposed Reformed scholasticism, especially limited atonement and particular election.

It was in the area of theological science that Torrance is most well known. He attempted a rapprochement between science and theology by combining the insights of James Clerk Maxwell, Albert Einstein, and Michael Polanyi with his form of post-Reformed Neo-Orthodoxy. His literary style is extremely prolix and has the appearance of profundity, but he rarely stated his views in simple language. His trumpet did not have a distinct sound (1 Corinthians 14:7–8), which has been a common feature with Neo-Orthodox writers. He could write whole chapters without referring to the Bible. And naturally, he denied biblical infallibility and verbal plenary inspiration. But he liked Calvin. He wrote several books on Calvin and coedited the new translation of his New Testament commentaries. At times he was closer to historic Reformed orthodoxy than Barth was.

This general approach was also shared by his brothers James B. (1923–2003)[6] and David (1924–?), his son Iain (1949–), and his nephew Alan (1956–). It was also popularized by Colin Gunton (1941–2003) and a small group that advertises itself as "Evangelical Calvinism,"[7] which is in actuality neither evangelical nor Calvinism. It denies scholastic Calvinism, resents the Westminster Confession, scorns covenant theology, rejects the five points (especially limited atonement), advocates the "vicarious humanity of Christ" theme, and stresses that Christ alone is the Elect One. Alastair I. C. Heron and Alan Lewis were sympathetic to this view.[8] Ronald S. Wallace was slightly favorable as well but was more historically orthodox.

American Neo-Orthodoxy

Reinhold (1892–1971) and Richard (1894–1962) Niebuhr came out of what was

---

6 "J. B." was my first doctoral advisor at New College. He published relatively little, except a certain article against traditional Calvinism and covenant theology that he republished about ten times in various journals and books.

7 Myk Habets and Bobby Grow, eds., *Evangelical Calvinism* (Eugene, OR: Pickwick, 2012).

8 Heron and Lewis were my doctoral advisors at New College after James B. Torrance moved to Aberdeen.

left of the old German Reformed Church in America and developed what some consider an American form of Neo-Orthodoxy. They interacted very little with previous Calvinists and were as far from the Reformed mainstream as their European counterparts.

Most of this loose school was in liberal Presbyterian circles, primarily through Princeton Seminary following the division of 1929. Presidents John A. MacKay (1889–1983) and James I. McCord (1919–90) promoted Barth and Barthianism for decades, as did Edward A. Dowey Jr. (1918–2003), coauthor of the Confession of 1967. Princeton Seminary houses a Barth Center and hosts frequent conferences on Barth.

Others who shared this general approach were George Hendry (1904–93), Arthur C. Cochrane, and to a lesser extent John Leith (1919–2002) and Brian Gerrish (1931–). Shades of Neo-Orthodoxy can be seen occasionally in the works of Canadian John T. McNeill (1885–1975), who edited and annotated the definitive English translation of Calvin's *Institutes* and wrote *The History and Character of Calvinism*.

Evangelicals resisted Neo-Orthodoxy for decades, but some eventually capitulated and claimed to be both evangelical and semi-Barthian. Such was the case with the Englishman Geoffrey Bromiley, the main translator of Barth's *Church Dogmatics*, Donald Bloesch (1928–2010), Bernard Ramm (1916–?), Donald McKim (1950–), and others. Paul King Jewett (1920–91) was originally a conservative Baptist who opposed Brunner but later came to praise him, even though he wrote useful books on election and baptism. This trend was exemplified in the volume *How Karl Barth Changed My Mind*.[9] There has also been a shift in this direction in certain Dutch-American quarters through the influence of G. C. Berkouwer, which I will mention later.

Appraisal

Neo-Orthodoxy may be considered one of Calvinism's two errant and illegitimate children (the other is Arminianism). Both arose as reactions to and rejection of true Calvinism and resemble each other more than either wishes to acknowledge (e.g., their mutual rejection of the TULIP doctrines and insistence on God's universal dealing with man). But at least Arminius and Wesley were evangelical, which Neo-Orthodoxy is not. Nor is Neo-Orthodoxy

---

9 Ed. by Donald K. McKim (Grand Rapids: Eerdmans, 1986).

another form of Amyraldism, which may not have been in the mainstream but at least was in the true Reformed family.

As we saw earlier, many in traditional Reformed churches went liberal beginning in the eighteenth century as they tried to accommodate the Enlightenment, then Romanticism, and then German liberalism. So here. Just belonging to a church with a Presbyterian or Reformed background does not make one Reformed, any more than belonging to a Lutheran church makes one a true Lutheran. Most are not. Many in this movement take the "Calvin against the Calvinists" debate to an extreme and go on a biased quest for the historical Calvin. They devise a Calvin remade in the image of Barth, like the old comment of a German liberal looking into a well for Christ and seeing his own reflection. In fact, there is very little resemblance between the theologies of Calvin and Barth or the others, between historic Calvinism and Neo-Orthodoxy, or between Barthianism and evangelical Christianity.

The Neo-Orthodox are usually united in their opposition to Reformed scholasticism, the Puritans, covenant theology, both Dort and Westminster, and Princeton Theology. They ignore or oppose the truest representatives of Reformed theology, such as John Owen, Jonathan Edwards, and Charles Spurgeon as well as more contemporary Calvinists such as D. Martyn Lloyd-Jones, James I. Packer, R. C. Sproul, and John MacArthur.

Neo-Orthodoxy in general and Barthianism in particular rejects many of the essential distinctives of both Calvin and Calvinism. It denies biblical infallibility and accepts the historical-critical hermeneutic. It generally rejects absolute foreordination and scorns it as "decretal theology."[10] It distorts the Reformed doctrines of election, denies reprobation, and opposes the TULIP. Louis Berkhof was right about Barth's doctrine of election: "It is not even distantly related to that of Augustine and Calvin" and is "neither Scriptural nor historical."[11]

Moreover, the Neo-Orthodox often deny the very areas where the three branches of the Reformation (Lutheran, Anabaptist, and Reformed) agreed, and even where Roman Catholicism was right (such as eternal Hell and biblical infallibility). They have been at the forefront of the ecumenical movement, which the Reformers would have abhorred, especially the pan-religious ecumenism that would even include Islam. Further, the movement usually accepts liberal

---

10 The term is often used derisively, sounds like *decrepit*, and conjures up images of a rickety old wagon with loose wheels.

11 Louis Berkhof, *Systematic Theology* (Grand Rapids: Eerdmans, 1988), III, 101.

ethics on abortion, homosexuality, and female ordination. Historic Calvinists would have opposed Neo-Orthodoxy without a second thought.

Cornelius Van Til wrote over one thousand pages of close analysis of this theology. Here is a summary:

> Nothing could be more untrue to history than to say that the theology of Barth and Brunner is basically similar to that of Luther and Calvin. Dialecticism is a basic reconstruction of the whole of the Reformation theology along critical lines. A Calvinist should not object to the Lutheranism in Barth; there is no Lutheranism there. A Lutheran should not object to the Calvinism of Barth's doctrine of election; there is no Calvinism in it. A Calvinist should not object to the Arminianism in Barth's universalism; there is no Arminianism in it. [. . .] There is no more Christianity and no more theism in Brunner than there is in Barth. [. . .] If evangelical Christianity in general ought to recognize in the Theology of Crisis a mortal enemy, this is doubly true with respect to those who hold to the Reformed faith. [. . .] The Theology of Crisis is a friend of Modernism and a foe of historic Christianity.[12]

Conclusion

Van Til was right. Neo-Orthodoxy is neither another form of Calvinism nor of true Christianity but is the "New Modernism" and pseudo-Christianity. It is not even as evangelical as the Arminianism of John Wesley, for at least Wesley believed in the fundamentals of the gospel. In sum, Neo-Orthodoxy is a bastardized theology that wrongly claims to be Reformed. It is well to be warned.

---

12 Cornelius Van Til, *The New Modernism* (Philadelphia: Presbyterian and Reformed, 1946), 366, 376, 378.

Chapter 17
Twentieth-Century American Calvinism

The day of spiritual giants was not past as American Calvinism entered the twentieth century following the controversies of the previous centuries. It would experience a decline in mid-century but would bounce back with a rediscovery of historical Calvinism later. It was mainly in three constituencies: Presbyterian, Dutch Reformed, and Baptist.

The Presbyterian Denominations

The Presbyterian Church experienced two main splits in the nineteenth century: the Old/New School division of 1837 (reunited in 1864/69) and the North/South division that was not healed until 1983.[1] Shortly after several conservatives left Princeton Seminary in 1929 to form Westminster Seminary, J. Gresham Machen left the Northern Presbyterian Church to help found what became the Orthodox Presbyterian Church (OPC).[2] But it too underwent a split when the "Calvinistic Fundamentalists" left, including Carl McIntire (1906–2002), Allen A. MacRae (1902–97), J. Oliver Buswell Jr. (1895–1977), and others. They disagreed with Machen's group over premillennialism, the use of tobacco and alcohol, and separation from worldliness. They then formed the Bible Presbyterian Church and Faith Theological Seminary. McIntire quickly became the dominant and controversial leader. In 1941 he founded the American Council of Christian Churches to oppose the liberal National Council of Churches as well as the International Council of Christian Churches to counter the liberal World Council of Churches.

Later, in 1956, a majority of the Bible Presbyterian Church seceded in

---

1 A detailed and controversial history of twentieth-century Presbyterian disputes is Gary North, *Crossed Fingers: How the Liberals Captured the Presbyterian Church* (Tyler: Institute for Christian Economics, 1996). A useful chart of the various splits and reunions is in James H. Smylie, *American Presbyterians: A Pictorial History* (Philadelphia: Presbyterian Historical Society, 1985), 250.

2 Charles G. Dennison and Richard C. Gamble, eds. *Pressing Towards the Mark: Essays Commemorating Fifty Years of the Orthodox Presbyterian Church* (Philadelphia: The Committee for the Historian of the Orthodox Presbyterian Church, 1986).

protest to McIntire's leadership. They formed the Evangelical Presbyterian Church, which later united with another to become the Reformed Presbyterian Evangelical Synod. They started Covenant Theological Seminary and Covenant College, where notable theologians such as Buswell, R. Laird Harris, Robert Reyburn, Gordon Clark, and J. Barton Payne taught. The Bible Presbyterian Church underwent still further divisions, one of which led to the founding of Biblical Theological Seminary.

In 1953 the Presbyterian Church in the United States of America (popularly known as the Northern Presbyterian Church) merged with the smaller United Presbyterian Church of North America to form the United Presbyterian Church in the United States of America. Curiously, while the conservatives were dividing, the liberals were uniting to conserve their dwindling numbers. There were still some evangelicals in the liberal-dominated Presbyterian churches, but they were increasingly outnumbered by liberal and Neo-Orthodox clergy and theologians. The Northern Presbyterians produced The Confession of 1967 under the leadership of Edward A. Dowey (1918–2003).[3] This rather Neo-Orthodox document was meant to replace the Westminster Confession, which was ignored by many anyway. The denomination also became increasingly involved in left-wing political and social causes.

Then in 1973 a conservative minority of the Presbyterian Church in the United States (better known as the Southern Presbyterians) withdrew to start the Presbyterian Church in America.[4] A few evangelicals stayed in, though some later left. In 1982 the Reformed Presbyterian Evangelical Synod merged with the Presbyterian Church in America (PCA). The next year the Northern and Southern Presbyterians reunited to form the Presbyterian Church in the United States of America (PCUSA).

There are other small churches, such as the Associate Reformed Presbyterian Church, the Evangelical Presbyterian Church, the Presbyterian Reformed Church, and others. Some of them sing only psalms; some ordain women elders. Most are very conservative and strongly Calvinistic. The Cumberland Presbyterian Church, on the other hand, was founded to be more Arminian and today is sprinkled with liberalism and Neo-Orthodoxy.

---

3 Edward A. Dowey Jr., *A Commentary of the Confession of 1967 and An Introduction to the Book of Confessions* (Philadelphia: Westminster, 1968).
4 Frank J. Smith, *The History of the Presbyterian Church in America*, 2nd ed. (Lawrenceville: Presbyterian Scholars Press, 1999).

Leading Presbyterian Theologians

Loraine Boettner (1901–90) wrote the enormously influential *The Reformed Doctrine of Predestination*, which has been in continuous print since 1932. He also wrote *The Millennium, Roman Catholicism, Studies in Theology,* and *Immortality*. Gordon H. Clark (1902–85) was denied ordination in the OPC due to opposition from Van Til and others over the issue of the incomprehensibility of God, so he taught philosophy at Wheaton College, Butler University, and Covenant College. His more rationalist form of presuppositionalist apologetics was not as popular as Van Til's model, but he greatly impacted moderately Reformed writers such as Edward John Carnell (1919–67), Carl F. H. Henry (1913–2003), and Ronald Nash (1936–2006). His closest disciples have been John Robbins (1948–2008) and Gary Crampton (1943–), who later became a Baptist.

Francis Schaeffer (1912–84)[5] studied at both Westminster and Faith seminaries and became a Bible Presbyterian missionary to post-World War II Switzerland. He became enormously popular in the 1970s with a string of best-selling books that explained his modified presuppositionalist apologetics, such as *The God Who Is There, Escape from Reason, He is There and He is Not Silent,* and *How Should We Then Live?* Toward the end of his life he became involved in the pro-life movement and co-wrote *Whatever Happened to the Human Race?* with C. Everett Koop (1916–2013), who later became Surgeon General of the United States.

Donald Grey Barnhouse (1895–1960) pastored the historic Tenth Presbyterian Church in Philadelphia and resisted calls to leave the Northern Presbyterian Church. A popular radio preacher and writer, he espoused a premillennialism that bordered on dispensationalism. His successor, James Montgomery Boice (1938–2000), later led Tenth into the PCA. He too was premillennial and was a leading defender of biblical inerrancy in "The Battle for the Bible" in the 1970s and 1980s. Many of his expository sermons were published. He was in turn followed at Tenth by Philip Ryken (1966–), who later became president of Wheaton College.

John Gerstner (1914–96) taught church history for decades within the Northern Presbyterian Church before seceding. He was a leading authority on his hero, Jonathan Edwards.[6] Dissatisfied with presuppositionalism, he was a

---

5 Edith Schaeffer, *The Tapestry* (Waco: Word, 1981).
6 His huge magnum opus is *The Rational Biblical Theology of Jonathan Edwards* (Orlando: Ligonier, 1991). Unfortunately, it is often ignored by scholars of Edwards but merits serious

leading proponent of what may be termed "Reformed Rationalism," patterned after Edwards.

Gerstner's main disciple was R. C. Sproul (1939–2017)[7] who became extremely popular in the 1970s and has been perhaps the most well-known popularizer of Reformed theology. He founded Ligonier Ministries and held ministerial credentials in the PCA. He followed the Edwards-Gerstner form of apologetics. He cofounded Reformation Bible College, taught at several seminaries, strongly defended biblical infallibility and the traditional view of justification by faith against the New Perspective on Paul as well as was a leading opponent of the Evangelicals-Catholics Together documents. He coedited *The Reformation Study Bible* and wrote over fifty books, of which his most popular is *The Holiness of God*.

Starting in the 1960s, Christian Reconstruction (also known as *theonomy*) became a major issue in conservative Presbyterian circles.[8] The founder of the movement was Rousas J. Rushdoony (1916–2001), who wrote dozens of books including what may be termed "The Bible of theonomy," *The Institutes of Biblical Law*. His controversial son-in-law, Gary North, and Greg Bahnsen (1948–95) completed the theonomic triumvirate. The movement called for the full use of God's unalterable law in all areas of life, including the civil realm. It combined Van Tilian presuppositionalism with postmillennialism. Others in the movement were David Chilton, James Jordan (1949–), Kenneth Gentry (1950–), Gary DeMar, Mark Rushdoony, and Joseph Morecraft (1944–). The movement has been in decline since the mid-1990s. Some went into the New Perspective on Paul, or the so-called Auburn Avenue Theology, also known as the Federal Vision.

Other notable Presbyterians include Morton Smith (1923–2017), Douglas Kelly (1943–), Ligon Duncan (1960–), and D. James Kennedy (1930–2007). Alan Cairns of Northern Ireland has been the leading preacher and writer in the Free Presbyterian Church based in Northern Ireland.

---

study. Gary Crampton gives a favorable critique in *Interpreting Edwards* (Lakeland: Whitefield Media, 2015).

7 R. C. Sproul Jr., ed., *After Darkness, Light* (Phillipsburg, NJ: P&R, 2003).

8 A recent history is detailed but unfavorable: Michael S. McVicar, *Christian Reconstruction: R. J. Rushdoony and American Religious Conservatism* (Chapel Hill: University of North Carolina Press, 2015).

Dutch-American Calvinists

This family goes all the way back to colonial America and grew with Dutch immigrants to New York, New Jersey, Michigan, and Iowa.[9] The Reformed Church in America was once traditionally Calvinistic but declined dramatically in the twentieth century. This was the denomination of liberals Norman Vincent Peale and Robert Schuller. Yet there were more moderate and traditionally Reformed theologians such as M. Eugene Osterhaven (1915–2004), Donald Bruggink (1929–), John Beardslee III (1914–?), and I. John Hesselink (1928–2018).

The main center of Dutch Reformed theology, however, has been the Christian Reformed Church based in Grand Rapids, Michigan. Its roots go back to the Secession of 1834 back in the Netherlands.[10] It taught thousands of students at Calvin College and Calvin Theological Seminary and was the umbrella, as it were, for a host of publishers such as Eerdmans, Baker, Zondervan, and Kregel. The H. Henry Meeter Center for Calvin Studies, based at Calvin College, is the best research center in the world for Calvin studies. It was founded by Ford Lewis Battles (1915–1979), who translated two editions of Calvin's *Institutes*.

The Christian Reformed Church underwent several controversies in the twentieth century, such as the debate on dispensationalism (Harry Bultema, (1884–1952) and common grace (Herman Hoeksema, 1886–1966). After World War II, the influence of liberalism and Neo-Orthodoxy began to seep in, mainly through G. C. Berkouwer (1903–96) and his American students. This included the Reformed Epistemology group such as Alvin Plantinga (1932–) and Nicholas Wolterstorff (1932–), plus those who were uncomfortable with some parts of the Three Forms of Unity, such as James Daane (1914–83), Lewis B. Smedes (1921–2002), Harry Boer (1913–99), Harold Dekker (1918–2006), Philip Holtrop, Gordon Spykman (1926–?), James Bratt (1949–), and Peter de Klerk (1927–77). Some taught what may be considered a Dutch form of Neo-Orthodoxy. There were also other moderates with less liberalizing tendencies, such as Anthony A. Hoekema (1913–88), Jan Karel Van Baalen (1890–1968), and D. H. Kromminga (1897–1947).

But there were also a host of more conservative evangelicals who defended traditional Calvinism, of whom Louis Berkhof (1873–1957) was chief. His

---

9 Corwin Schmidt, Donald Luidens, James Penning, and Roger Nemeth, *Divided by a Common Heritage* (Grand Rapids: Eerdmans, 2006).

10 Peter de Klerk and Richard De Ridder, eds. *Perspectives on the Christian Reformed Church* (Grand Rapids: Baker, 1983).

Systematic Theology was highly influential even outside Dutch Reformed circles and is one of the best ever written. Another giant was William Hendriksen (1900–82), pastor and teacher of the New Testament. Among his many books was the multi-volume *New Testament Commentary*, completed by Simon Kistemaker (1930–2017). Still another leader was P. Y. DeJong (1915–2005). Mention must be made of Lester DeKoster (1915–2009), William Masselink (1897–1973), and several preachers named *Kuiper* — R. B. (1886–1966), Barend Klaas (1877–1961), and Henry J. (1885–1962). Edwin Palmer (1922–80) was editor of the New International Version of the Bible and wrote the popular *The Five Points of Calvinism*. Earlier in the century were the traditionalists William Heyns (1856–1933), Foppe Ten Hoor (1855–1934), Henry Beets (1869–1947), and Clarence Bouma (1891–1962). At the end of the century and into the next were John Bolt (1947–), Lyle Bierma, and Richard Muller (1948–), the respected authority on post-Reformation Reformed theology. Eventually the tension between the conservative and more liberal factions reached a climax in the 1990s over issues such as biblical infallibility and women's ordination. Many of the conservatives left and founded the United Reformed Church and Mid-America Reformed Seminary. Among its leading lights is Robert Godfrey (1945–), president of Westminster Seminary in California, and Cornelis Venema.

Other Dutch-American denominations in this period tended to be much more traditional and conservative, such as the Protestant Reformed Church under the leadership of Herman Hoeksema and his son Homer, Henry Danhof (1879–1952), and David Engelsma. They strongly oppose the doctrines of common grace and the free offer and are the leading proponents of Hyper-Calvinism in America. The Netherlands Reformed Congregations were led by Gerrit Hendrik Kersten (1882–1948) and underwent a division in the 1990s which produced the Heritage Netherlands Reformed Congregations, whose most prominent leader is Joel R. Beeke (1952–), an extremely prolific writer and the major proponent of Reformed experimental theology following the *Nadere Reformatie* of the 1600s. The Free Reformed Church is another tiny but traditional Dutch-American Reformed church.

Baptist Calvinists

Up until the early 1900s, a large number (perhaps most) of Baptists in America were Calvinistic, differing with Presbyterians and Dutch Reformed mainly on baptism. The Primitive Baptists included many Hyper-Calvinists and argued that evangelism and missions are not necessary because God can regenerate the elect who never hear the gospel. This group has continued down to the present, but many have forsaken its Hyperism and otherwise modified its approach.

By far the largest Baptist denomination in America is the Southern Baptist Convention. As we saw earlier, most of its earliest founders were strongly Calvinistic. This began to change in the 1920s, mainly through the influence of Edgar Young Mullins (1860–1928). By mid-century, Calvinism in the SBC was a tiny minority. Then it began to revive. First there were theologians like Curtis Vaughan (1925–2005) and preachers like Ernest Reisinger (1919–2004). Founders Ministries began to call the SBC back to the Calvinism of its founders. Leaders in the Calvinist resurgence have included Thomas Ascol (1957–), Thomas J. Nettles (1946–), Timothy George (1950–), and Mark Dever. Several noted teachers at the Southern Baptist Theological Seminary (Louisville, Kentucky) are outspoken advocates of Calvinistic Baptist theology, such as president Albert Mohler (1959–), Thomas Schreiner (1954–), Bruce Ware (1953–), and Michael A. G. Haykin (1953–).[11]

The loosely-knit movement known as Sovereign Grace Baptists goes back to the 1920s when Arthur W. Pink ministered in America. It grew in the post-war years through Rolfe Barnard (1904–69), Henry Mahan, and Holmes Moore. Some of its churches are in the Sovereign Grace Baptist Fellowship. These churches combine historic Baptist Calvinism and fundamentalism.

The Reformed Baptists also took root in the 1960s through the leadership of Albert Martin (1934–)[12] and Walter Chantry (1938–) after the initial influence of Ernest Reisinger.[13] It has undergone several splits over issues such as the law, mission boards, and church discipline.[14] One spinoff faction is the New Covenant Baptists. First led by Jon Zens, it combines Reformed theology with the dispensational view of the law that many other Reformed Baptists consider doctrinally antinomian. Fred Zaspel and Tom Wells (1933–2019) are among its leaders today. The Fellowship of Independent Reformed Evangelicals (FIRE) is another subgroup among Reformed Baptists.

Lastly, there have been Calvinistic Baptists in other groups or no groups.

---

11 Gregory A. Wills, *Southern Baptist Theological Seminary 1859–2009* (Oxford: Oxford University Press, 2009).

12 Brian Borgman, *My Heart for Thy Cause: Albert N. Martin's Theology of Preaching* (Fearn: Mentor, 2002).

13 Geoffrey Thomas, *Ernest C. Reisinger* (Edinburgh: Banner of Truth, 2002).

14 Tom Chantry and David D. Dykstra, *Holding Communion Together: The Reformed Baptists, The First Fifty Years—Divided and United* (Birmingham: Solid Ground Christian Books, 2014).

Paul King Jewett (1920–91) wrote the respected *Election and Predestination* and an influential defense of believer's baptism from a modified covenant theology perspective, *Infant Baptism and the Covenant of Grace*. Otherwise he was too liberal to fit into most Calvinistic Baptist circles because he denied biblical infallibility and advocated women's ordination. On the other hand, Roger Nicole (1915–2010) of Switzerland supported women's ordination but strongly defended biblical infallibility while teaching for decades at Gordon-Conwell Theological Seminary. He ministered in the Northern Baptists and was the world's foremost authority on Moyse Amyraut and Amyraldism, which he opposed.

Millard Erickson (1932–) wrote *Christian Theology* and others from a very modified Calvinist perspective. James White (1962–) has written in defense of the five points, inerrancy, and justification by faith in his many apologetic books. Robert Morey (1946–2019) has penned books on the Trinity, inerrancy, the five points, limited atonement, and other issues. Randolph Yeager produced the eighteen-volume *Renaissance New Testament* commentary, a detailed exegesis from the Greek. His denominational affiliation is undetermined.

The "Bible Church" movement is basically Baptist without the label. It more or less began in 1960s. Some of its preachers have been Calvinist, such as S. Lewis Johnson (1915–2004), who taught for decades at Dallas Theological Seminary.[15] Many Bible Church men are moderately Calvinistic. Some belong to the Evangelical Free Church of America. John Feinberg (1946–?) and Donald A. Carson (1946–) have taught the doctrines of grace in less explicit ways than others.

John Piper (1946–) and Wayne Grudem (1948–) have been among the most influential Baptist Calvinists since 1980. Piper promotes what he calls "Christian Hedonism" in *Desiring God* and others and has been a major opponent of the New Perspective on Paul. Grudem's best-selling *Systematic Theology* has taught the doctrines of grace to hundreds of thousands of readers. Both men are staunch defenders of biblical inerrancy and justification by faith and opponents of "evangelical feminism." They have also been influential in the rise of what may be termed "Charismatic Calvinism" starting around 1990. Previously, virtually all Calvinists of any stripe had been non- and even anti-charismatic/Pentecostal, and conversely, almost all charismatics and Pentecostals were Arminian, such as the Assemblies of God.[16] Grudem's controversial views on

---

15 I ministered with him for five years (1987–92) at Believers Chapel, Dallas, Texas.
16 I received my B.A. from the Assemblies of God's Central Bible College, which has since merged with Evangel University.

the gift of prophecy helped open the door for C. Samuel Storms (1951–) and others. Probably the largest grouping of charismatic Calvinists is Sovereign Grace Ministries initially led by C. J. Mahaney (1953–). Similar to this is the Acts 29 Network of churches, first led by the controversial Mark Driscoll (1970–) and later by Matt Chandler. The movement is much involved in the Together for the Gospel conferences.

Charismatic Calvinism has been opposed by more traditional Calvinist Baptists such as John MacArthur (1939–).[17] He combines traditional fundamentalism and dispensationalism with explicit five-point Calvinism. He has written dozens of books, including *The MacArthur Study Bible* and the multi-volume *MacArthur New Testament Commentary*. He is well known for *The Gospel According to Jesus* in which he defends the historic Reformed doctrine of what some call *lordship salvation* — that is, one must believe in Christ as Savior and submit to Him as Lord to become a Christian, as opposed to the opposite view promoted by many dispensationalists such as Zane Hodges. MacArthur is paralleled in this by Steven Lawson, author of *A Long Line of Godly Men* and other studies of great evangelical Calvinists of the past. Paul Washer is another Calvinist Baptist who opposes "easy-believism." Alistair Begg, from Glasgow, Scotland, is still another well-known Calvinist Baptist pastor.

Miscellaneous Calvinists

Reformed theology has appeared from time to time in other traditions. Some Episcopalians have been strongly Calvinist in the tradition of J. C. Ryle. David Wells (1939–) is one. Many in the Reformed Episcopal Church would fit this description as well.

Preachers in the Methodist-Holiness tradition have usually been staunch Arminians and vocal opponents of Calvinism. A small number have been "Calvinism-friendly," shall we say. A. W. Tozer (1897–1963) was a five-point Arminian but had such an exalted view of divine sovereignty that he sometimes seems more Reformed.

There have always been Augustinians in the Catholic Church, but few have fully accepted his theology of grace since the Jansenist controversy of the seventeenth century. Perhaps there will be a revival in the future as Catholics dare to reevaluate Gottschalk, Bradwardine, and Jansen. Guido Stucco is

---

17 Iain H. Murray, *John MacArthur: Servant of the Word and Flock* (Edinburgh: Banner of Truth, 2011).

one such darer. His eminently useful book *God's Eternal Gift* even defends Gottschalk.

There have been a number of Calvinists, however too few, in the African-American community. Among them are Voddie Baucham, Thabiti Anyabwile, and Anthony Carter. The movement is growing. There is a small Reformed movement in the Hispanic, Asian, and Native American communities, but as yet no prominent preachers or theologians have arisen — but who can tell what God will do in these groups in the future?

Toward the end of the century there was a rediscovery of Calvinism among young Christians who were dissatisfied with the shallow man-centered "pop Christianity" of modern evangelicalism. This "Young, Restless, and Reformed" generation draws its numbers from Baptist, Presbyterian, Dutch, charismatic, and other circles. Many will be leaders in the future. Some already are, such as David Platt, Kevin DeYoung, and Matt Chandler.[18]

Many try to maintain historic Calvinism while developing it to address contemporary concerns and methods. Oliver D. Crisp has written numerous books expounding traditional Calvinism but has also stretched the bounds by pushing for what he calls "Deviant Calvinism," in which he attempts several controversial modifications. Others have pushed the boundaries too far, while still others have explored new territory within those bounds to the benefit of the entire Reformed community. Godly wisdom is needed in discerning where the biblical boundaries are, lest we be guilty of moving the ancient landmarks (Proverbs 22:28). Not all that is old is good, and not all that is good is old, but we must have the wisdom to bring forth both old and new treasures (Matthew 13:52). New Calvinists can and should learn from Old Calvinists, and sometimes the old can learn a thing or two from the young men that God is raising up. We need to seek the tried and true paths of our godly Reformed forefathers (Jeremiah 6:16). While on that path that leads to glory, let us not deviate to the right or to the left (Deuteronomy 5:32).

Conclusion

Twentieth-century Calvinism continued its trajectory into the twenty-first century in America and has not reached its peak yet. New challenges arise. The cause goes on.

---

18 Collin Hansen, *Young, Restless, Reformed: A Journalist's Journey with the New Calvinists* (Wheaton: Crossway, 2008).

Chapter 18
Twentieth-Century British Calvinism

As in America, there was a decline in Calvinism early in the twentieth century, but a resurgence in the second half.[1] The rediscovery was due in part to a renewed interest in Calvin, Spurgeon, and especially the Puritans.

The Anglicans

W. H. Griffith Thomas (1861–1924) was one of several "Low Church" Anglicans that carried on the tradition of J. C. Ryle, Charles Simeon, and Thomas Scott. They adhered closely to the Thirty-Nine Articles. Griffith Thomas spent much of his career in Canada and helped found Dallas Theological Seminary late in life. The cofounder Lewis Sperry Chafer led the seminary in a more dispensational direction. One wonders what the influential seminary would have become had Chafer died and Griffith Thomas lived. His *The Principles of Theology* has been used by generations of Anglican Calvinists.

T. H. L. Parker (1916–2016) was for years the world's foremost Calvin scholar. He wrote several books on Calvin and translated several of his commentaries. Philip Edgcumbe Hughes (1915–90) was another Church of England pastor-scholar who ministered in both England and North America. Toward the end of his career he espoused the non-Reformed error of annihilationism, as did the well-known John R. W. Stott (1921–2011). Stott was the most influential evangelical Anglican preacher, writer, and organizer for much of the post-war generation. He was only moderately Reformed, and one wonders if the badge really fit.

The most popular and outspoken Anglican Calvinist of the last hundred years was undoubtedly James I. Packer (1926–). He wrote his Oxford doctoral dissertation on Richard Baxter and has had a lifelong love of the Puritans. He worked with Martyn Lloyd-Jones organizing the Puritan Conference and wrote a popular introduction to John Owen's *The Death of Death*. His small *Evangelism and the Sovereignty of God* popularized the antinomy of divine sovereignty and human responsibility. Packer was also a leading defender of

---

1 John J. Murray, *Catch the Vision: Roots of the Reformed Recovery* (Darlington: Evangelical Press, 2007).

biblical inerrancy, starting with *Fundamentalism and the Word of God*. But by far his most well-known book was *Knowing God*. Echoing the opening section of Calvin's *Institutes*, Packer sets forth the true knowledge of God as more than mere head knowledge, but personal knowledge in the heart. In 1966 he and Stott resisted Lloyd-Jones' call for evangelicals to leave the Church of England, but decades later he did leave it for a more orthodox Episcopalian church. He taught for many years at Regent College in Vancouver, Canada, and raised many eyebrows when he signed the Evangelicals-Catholics Together document.

Other English Calvinists

Peter Toon (1939–2009) wrote several important books on the history and theology of Calvinism that show a general Reformed perspective. He also later taught in the United States. Paul Helm (1940–) taught philosophy at Liverpool, London, Regent College, and elsewhere. His several books on Calvin and Calvinism tend to show his philosophical perspective. He took R. T. Kendall (1935–) to task in the "Calvin and Calvinism" debate of the 1980s. Kendall had published his Oxford dissertation *Calvin and English Calvinism to 1649*, to which Helm replied with *Calvin and the Calvinists*. He also has defended traditional Reformed views of divine foreknowledge and eternity.

Less traditional has been Alan Clifford, who has been a major defender of Amyraut and Amyraldism. Anthony N. S. Lane is a careful scholar of Calvin, particularly his use of the fathers and Bernard of Clairvaux. Alan P. F. Sell (1935–2016) was a prolific writer from a very broad and moderate perspective he once described as "ameliorated Calvinism."[2] He was the most-published voice in the United Reformed Church, which united the declining English Congregationalists and Presbyterians into a body with little sympathy for traditional Calvinism.

Peter Masters has for many years pastored the Metropolitan Tabernacle where Spurgeon pastored a century earlier. The historic church declined in attendance and almost closed midway through the century but bounced back under Masters' leadership. The Strict Baptists declined some but still maintained their stand for historic Calvinism. One notable Strict Baptist was Ernest Kevan (1903–65), whose thorough study *The Grace of Law* examines the Puritans' view of the law as complementary and not contradictory to grace. The more Hyper-Calvinist Gospel Standard Baptists have also continued their distinctive tradition under prominent preachers such as J. K. Popham (1847–1937) and B. A. Ramsbottom.

---

2 Alan P. F. Sell, *The Great Debate* (Grand Rapids: Baker, 1982), 98.

Then there was Arthur W. Pink (1886–1952).[3] He began his ministry in England, moved to the United States, then down to Australia, and ended up in Scotland. Most of the books that bear his name are collections of articles he wrote in his *Studies in the Scriptures* magazine. He did write books as books also. *The Attributes of God* and *The Sovereignty of God* have introduced hundreds of thousands of readers to the Reformed view of God and grace. Always controversial, Pink occasionally bordered on Hyper-Calvinism (he rejected the free offer doctrine in *The Atonement*) but opposed the Hyperism of the Gospel Standard Baptists when he was in Australia. He was Baptist and increasingly became something of a hermit. He had a remarkable talent for putting profound theology into simple language. He wrote on a wide variety of topics and unfortunately has been ignored by the more academic scholars.

Another Briton who has ministered on the international scene has been John Blanchard (1932–) from the Channel Island of Guernsey. He has been a full-time evangelist since 1962 as well as a best-selling author of the evangelistic book *Right with God* and the booklet *Ultimate Questions*. His magnum opus is *Does God Believe in Atheists?* which answered Richard Dawkins and others in the contemporary new atheism.

British Calvinism could be found in several non-Anglican organizations such as the Sovereign Grace Union. The SGU was led for some years by Henry Atherton (1875–1933), pastor of the historic Grove Chapel in London, previously pastored by Joseph Irons and later by Iain Murray. Many but not all in the SGU have been Hyper-Calvinist. It reprinted many older books and published new books along traditional Calvinist lines. Many Calvinist churches have been affiliated with the Fellowship of Independent Evangelical Churches.

The Reformed Baptists have been similar to the Strict Baptists except that most do not practice "baptized members only Communion" and are more evangelistic. Erroll Hulse (1931–2017) from South Africa was perhaps the most influential of their number; his magazine *Reformation Today* is the unofficial organ of the movement.

The Banner of Truth Trust has been the most influential force in the rediscovery of historic Calvinism since the 1950s. It has promoted "Experimental Calvinism" through its magazine, ministers' conferences, and reprints of Puritans, Calvin, and others. It was cofounded by Iain H. Murray (1931–), Lloyd-Jones, and Jack Cullum (1910–1971) and has spread the Word around the world.

---

3 Iain H. Murray, *The Life of Arthur W. Pink*, revised edition (Edinburgh: Banner of Truth, 2004).

Wales

By far the most famous and respected British Calvinist of the last hundred years was D. Martyn Lloyd-Jones (1899–1981) of Wales. "The Doctor" left a promising medical practice to pastor a small church in Wales, then served as assistant to G. Campbell Morgan at the historic Westminster Chapel some two hundred yards from Buckingham Palace. He succeeded him as pastor and continued there for the next thirty-three years. Often considered "The Prince of Twentieth-Century Preachers," Lloyd-Jones exemplified the best of Reformed expository preaching and touched millions, including his one-time assistant Iain Murray, who wrote the standard biography. Most of his many books were transcribed sermons, of which the fourteen-volume set on Romans is the largest, and the two volumes on the Sermon on the Mount are the most popular. His best seller, however, has been *Spiritual Depression*. One of his less popular opinions was the theory that the baptism of the Spirit is a post-conversional experience for assurance of salvation. This resembled the charismatic view. The Doctor had an underlying "Welsh mysticism" approach but was firmly rooted in Scripture. He was not a thorough charismatic, though he did believe that certain gifts might occasionally appear today. Many British "charismatic Calvinists" were influenced by him, such as Terry Virgo, Herbert Carson, and Peter Lewis. Many people do not realize that Lloyd-Jones came to reject infant baptism in favor of believer's baptism.

Welsh Calvinistic Methodism, now officially known as the Presbyterian Church of Wales, long ago departed from its Calvinist and revivalist roots planted by George Whitefield, Howel Harris, and Daniel Rowland. But there remained a traditional witness into the twentieth century in Wales through such preachers as Geoffrey Thomas (1938–), Hywel Jones, and Omri Jenkins. The Evangelical Movement of Wales is the center of gravity for Welsh Calvinism today.

Northern Ireland

The major issue for Christians in Northern Ireland has been the question whether it should stay in the United Kingdom or unite with the Republic of Ireland. Unfortunately, this has produced violence and even terrorism between Roman Catholics and Protestants. The largest Reformed constituency is the evangelical Free Presbyterians. By far their most famous leader was the highly controversial Ian Paisley (1926–2014). As ardent a Unionist as a preacher, he could thunder like Farel or Knox. W. J. Grier and The Christian Bookshop in Belfast introduced many to the Reformed faith in Ulster for many years.

Scotland

The Church of Scotland, once a bastion of historic Calvinism, suffered several divisions and reunions in the nineteenth century and continued its general slide into liberalism in the twentieth. Much of it was due to the Neo-Orthodoxy of New College and the Torrances. But others taught more traditional Reformed theology and history, such as David F. Wright (1937–2008) the church historian. William Still (1911–97), James Phillip, and Eric Alexander were widely-respected preachers in the Crieff Fellowship. Sinclair Ferguson (1948–) has pastored and taught in both Scotland and America. He exemplifies the best of Scottish heartfelt preaching in the style of Robert Murray M'Cheyne. Ronald Wallace (1911–2006) authored several important books on Calvin, but some readers have detected a slightly Neo-Orthodox accent in his theology.

Outside the state church, traditional Calvinism was held to by the Free Church of Scotland, the Free Presbyterian Church, and several smaller groups. Among the more well-known Calvinists were John MacLeod (1872–1948), author of the respected *Scottish Theology*, R. A. Finlayson, G. N. M. Collins, Douglas MacMillan, and Donald MacLeod, around whom a controversy revolved late in the century that led to a split in the Free Church. Many conservative Scots sing psalms only.

There has been a tiny sprinkling of Reformed Baptists in Scotland,[4] such as Jack Seaton and Nicholas Needham. The Banner of Truth moved its offices from London to Edinburgh in the early 1970s. Jack Glass of Glasgow was for some time a fiery opponent of Catholicism in the mold of John Knox or his contemporary Ian Paisley. Calvinism is still alive and well in Scotland.[5]

Conclusion

British Calvinists are still a small minority of the population, but they exert a

---

4 I was a member of a Reformed Baptist church in Edinburgh for seven years while doing doctoral studies, 1976–83.

5 The excellent *Dictionary of Scottish Church History and Theology* edited by Nigel M. de S. Cameron, David F. Wright, David C. Lachman, and Donald E. Meek (Downers Grove, IL: InterVarsity, 1993) is a storehouse of information, including much of twentieth-century Calvinism.

far-reaching influence around the world. They are not likely to disappear in the foreseeable future but may well experience revival and flowering again.

Chapter 19
Twentieth-Century
International Calvinism

For the first fifteen hundred years of its history, Christianity was confined mainly to parts of the Middle East, Northern Africa, and Europe. Starting with the Reformation it began to spread to America, then in the nineteenth-century Missionary Movement it grew slowly around the world. But it really went international in the twentieth century. Wherever Christianity went, Calvinism also went.

The Netherlands

Dutch Calvinism has had a rich heritage but also experienced controversies that diluted pure Reformed doctrine and practice at every stage. This continued in the twentieth century. The nineteenth century ended with Abraham Kuyper as the towering figure. In the following years, he would be succeeded by Herman Bavinck (1854–1921). A pastor's son, he taught at the University of Kampen (1882–1902) and the Free University of Amsterdam (1902–20). His crowning achievement was his large *Reformed Dogmatics*, now finally available in English. Bavinck differed only slightly with Kuyper (e.g., the lapsarian debate, eternal justification, presumptive regeneration), but their methods also differed and produced varying trajectories. Kuyper was like Calvin and Edwards — a genius innovator not afraid of new territory. Bavinck was more like Charles Hodge — a careful organizer with an encyclopedic mind. His last words were: "Now my scholarship avails me nothing, nor my dogmatics. It is only my faith can save me."

He was succeeded at the Free University by Valentine Hepp (1879–1950) from 1922–45. He steered an orthodox course in the tumultuous era between the world wars when liberalism came in like water through a broken dike. Herman Dooyeweerd (1894–1977), also at Amsterdam, followed Kuyper's trajectory to develop presuppositionalism by expanding Sphere Sovereignty and the Antithesis in new areas. Unlike his Dutch-American counterpart Cornelius Van Til, he was more speculative, philosophical, and complicated. He called it "The Philosophy of the Cosmonic Idea," or simply "Calvinistic Philosophy."

D. H. Vollenhoven (1892–1978) and J. M. Spier (1902–1971) also belonged to this school of thought. More orthodox critics said it had little resemblance to true biblical wisdom and rather resembled Greek philosophy.

Certain quasi-Reformed men developed the Historical-Redemptive hermeneutic at this time, such as Seakle Greijdanus (1871–1948), S. D. De Graaf, and Sidney Greidanus. This was an innovative form of covenant theology applied to preaching. On the more conservative side were Herman Ridderbos (1909–2007) and the Dutch-American Geerhardus Vos (1862–1949). One application of this approach led to a somewhat lecturing style of preaching rather than heartfelt spiritual proclamation and application, which was sometimes derided as mere moralism. While the system has its strengths, such as seeing the scriptural context of progressive redemption, some in the movement have strayed from historic orthodoxy.

There were and still are very traditional Calvinists in the old country. For example, Gerrit H. Kersten (1882–1948) helped lead the Netherlands Reformed Congregations along the lines of the *Nadere Reformatie*. Some of their number came to America and continued the tradition. There have also been some generally traditional scholars, such as Willem van Asselt (1946–2015), who have made very important contributions to the study of the history and theology of Calvinism. The Utrecht School, by contrast, has tended to stray from the old paths.[1]

Next to Bavinck, the most significant Dutch Reformed theologian of the twentieth century was Gerrit Cornelius Berkouwer (1903–96). He succeeded Hepp at the Free University in 1945. His major achievement was the fourteen-volume *Studies in Dogmatics*. It was not a systematic theology per se. It was reported that he said that he could not improve on Bavinck's *Reformed Dogmatics* but rather brought it up to date by interacting with contemporary issues.[2] Berkouwer offered many brilliant insights and was well-versed in past and current theology, though he did tend to ignore great heroes of Reformed orthodoxy like Jonathan Edwards, the Puritans, and the Princetonians. He is often praised as upholding traditional Calvinism,[3] but on closer examination another evaluation emerges.

For example, at first he took the historic Reformed view of opposing Roman

---

1 Dolf te Velde, *The Doctrine of God in Reformed Orthodoxy, Karl Barth, and the Utrecht School* (Leiden: Brill, 2013).
2 Warfield supposedly said the same about Hodge's *Systematic Theology*.
3 See the dust jacket blurbs by D. Martyn Lloyd-Jones and Carl F. H. Henry.

Catholicism but reversed it and became an official observer at the Vatican II Council. He became very involved in the ecumenical movement, perhaps under the influence of his fellow Dutchman Hendrik Kraemer (1888–1965), who was only slightly Reformed. He did not oppose theological liberalism as strongly as Kuyper or Bavinck had. Rather, he became increasingly favorable to Neo-Orthodoxy, as seen in *The Triumph of Grace in the Theology of Karl Barth*. More than anyone else, he opened the Dutch door to this aberrant theology.

This was apparent in several areas in which he not only diluted historic Reformed teaching but struck at the very foundations of evangelical Christianity. He greatly modified his early view of election. He denied the idea of an all-encompassing absolute decree, especially the notion of reprobation. He was uncomfortable with the doctrine of the twofold will of God and denied that God has anything at all to do with the origin of sin. He seemed to question the existence of Hell. He modified the "before" of eternal election.[4]

Likewise, he denied biblical inerrancy and began to accept the historical-critical hermeneutic. He argued that God speaks through human error in the Bible, and we cannot dictate to God how He may choose to speak. The theory of inerrancy is a bad by-product of seventeenth-century Reformed scholasticism and should be rejected.[5] Also significant was his theological method. He preferred dialectical dialogue with various views rather than dogmatic statements of faith. One can read whole chapters and know what everyone but Berkouwer believed. He said that all theology must be "preachable," but his lack of dogmatic clarity is anything but preachable to the man in the pew. But when read carefully, his positions become apparent — they were increasingly less than Reformed. Several of his Dutch-American students brought his theology home and led the new direction in the Christian Reformed Church.

Other Dutch theologians went still further afield, such as A. D. R. Polman (1897–1993), H. M. Kuitert (1924–2017), Arnold A. Van Ruler (1908–70), and even the previously stalwart Klaas Runia (1926–2006). Like their Barthian compatriots, they claimed they were only developing Reformed theology in a good direction, when in actuality they were departing from the very foundations of Reformed theology and even the fundamental biblical gospel.[6]

---

4 Alvin Baker, *Berkouwer's Doctrine of Election* (Phillipsburg, NJ: P&R, 1981); Cornelius Van Til, *The Sovereignty of Grace* (Philadelphia: Presbyterian and Reformed, 1969).

5 Jack Rogers, one of his students, was criticized for omitting some of the more unorthodox material in his translation of Berkouwer's *Holy Scripture*.

6 Cornelius Van Til, *The New Synthesis Theology of the Netherlands* (Nutley: Presbyterian and Reformed, 1975).

Meanwhile, there were disputes among the conservative traditionalists. Klaas Schilder (1890–1952) posited a rival view of the covenant to that of the Dutch-American Herman Hoeksema. Both denied Kuyper's doctrine of common grace, which others were distorting and taking to extremes that even Father Abraham would not have imagined or approved of. Another strong conservative was Jakob Van Bruggen (1936–). He emphasized the historic doctrines of *sola Scriptura* and providential preservation to defend the Majority Text of the Greek New Testament.[7] He also advocated a very literal approach to Bible translation.[8] J. van Genderen and W. H. Velema co-wrote a conservative *Concise Reformed Dogmatics*, which has appeared in an English edition.

In 2004 several Dutch denominations united to form the liberal Protestant Church in the Netherlands, which has very little sympathy for traditional Calvinism. It espouses the usual secular liberal ethics such as approving women's ordination, abortion, homosexuality, and same-sex marriage. Kuyper, Bavinck, and even Berkouwer would be horrified at the extreme to which Dutch ex-Reformed churches have gone. The orthodox evangelicals have mourned and cried out to God for revival.

France

Calvinism in the land of Calvin's birth has survived but with bruises. The French Reformed Church has continued as a tiny island in a Catholic ocean which is becoming increasingly secular like the rest of Europe. But there have been some notable Calvinists. Emil Doumergue (1844–1937) produced by far the largest biography and theological study of John Calvin, *Jean Calvin: les Hommes et les Choses de Son Temps* (1899–1917) in five massive volumes. Why has this not been translated into English? Perhaps because some scholars consider it too "hagiographic."

August Lecerf (1872–1943) was influenced by Kuyper and began a large systematic theology, but only completed the prolegomena volume, translated as *An Introduction to Reformed Dogmatics*. Francois Wendel (1905–72) penned the respected *Calvin: The Origins and Development of His Religious Thought*. Pierre Marcel (1910–92) wrote *The Biblical Doctrine of Infant Baptism*. Others could be mentioned. French Calvinism went into retreat but has survived the world wars and theological debates. We pray for another *Le Reveil*.

---

7 Jakob Van Bruggen, *The Ancient Text of the New Testament* (Winnipeg: Premier, 1976).
8 Jakob Van Bruggen, *The Future of the Bible* (Nashville: Thomas Nelson, 1978).

Miscellaneous Europe

The old German Reformed Church, which officially united with the Lutherans in 1817, tried to keep its Reformed heritage, but suffered the devastating toll of liberalism and Neo-Orthodoxy. Those such as Jurgen Moltmann (1928–) are ex-Reformed at best and pseudo-Reformed at worst. Otto Weber (1902–66) was basically Barthian, as can be detected in his *Foundations of Dogmatics*. On the other hand, Wilhelm Niesel (1903–88) and others produced helpful research on Calvin.

As for Switzerland, Calvin's adopted homeland, the Reformed faith would have become almost extinct except for a renewed interest in Calvin. Francis Higman, Irena Backus, and the *Institut d'Histoire de la Reformation* at Geneva are on the cutting edge of contemporary Calvin studies.

Pockets of Calvinism continue in Eastern Europe with foundations going back to the Reformation, especially Hungary. The Reformed faith, small as it is, suffered under and survived Nazism and Communism. But, as almost everywhere else, there was the creeping influence of Barthianism.

There are even fewer outposts of Calvinism in Scandinavia, the Balkans, and the Baltics. There are a few Reformed groups in Italy, mainly due to the remembrance of Peter Martyr Vermigli and the Waldenses, who still survive. There are only tiny Reformed communities in Spain and even fewer in Greece. But since the fall of Communism, Calvinism has slowly grown in Russia and some of the former Soviet nations.

Canada

Canada has always been culturally divided between its British and French heritages and is often overshadowed by the United States. It is heartening to know that not only is evangelical Christianity still very alive there but also Calvinism. Scottish Presbyterians and Dutch Reformed have their own churches, seminaries, and organizations. Some are orthodox, others heterodox. Some Reformed leaders came in from Britain (W. H. Griffith Thomas, J. I. Packer). Conversely some Canadian Calvinists moved south to the United States (D. A. Carson, Michael A. G. Haykin, John T. McNeill).

The Dutch Reformed community grew considerably after World War II and has been involved in inter-church debates between the conservatives and liberals. For example, Klaas Schilder exerted much influence in the Canadian Reformed Church — witness Jelle Faber (1924–2004). On the left have been those associated with the Institute for Christian Studies, Toronto, such as Hendrik Hart and C. T. McIntire, son of Carl. This Dooyeweerdian group has influenced the Christian Reformed Church in both Canada and the United States in its leftward trek.

Several other individuals stand out in other ways. W. Stanford Reid (1913–96) was a respected traditional Presbyterian scholar. Arnold Dallimore (1911–98) was an obscure Baptist pastor who wrote popular biographies of Spurgeon, Edward Irving, Charles Wesley, Susannah Wesley, and the highly acclaimed biography of George Whitefield. T. T. Shields (1873–1955), sometimes called "The Spurgeon of Canada," was a staunch Calvinist Baptist fundamentalist.

Then there was the anthropologist-theologian Arthur Custance (1910–85). Born in England, he worked with the Canadian Defence Research Board and produced a number of fascinating theological works. Many of his essays were collected in *The Doorway Papers* (ten volumes). In these and others such as *Two Men Called Adam*, *Journey Out of Time*, and *The Seed of the Woman*, he discussed theology and made interesting observations about science, often in areas nobody else wrote about. He was the leading defender of the Gap Theory (there was a lengthy gap between Genesis 1:1 and 2) in *Without Form and Void* and wrote a useful middle-level work on Calvinism called *The Sovereignty of Grace*. His main weakness was his toying with accepting the error of annihilationism.

South Africa

Calvinism was brought to South Africa by immigrants and missionaries from the Netherlands and the United Kingdom. The first internationally-known South African Calvinist was Andrew Murray (1828–1917), originally from Scotland. It has been said that he combined Reformed theology and Arminian spirituality.

There have been two main struggles in South African history, and both affected Christians. First was the tug-of-war between the Dutch Afrikaans (Boers) and the British over national sovereignty. The second was the relation between those with European ancestry and those with native African ancestry. This culminated in the bloody debate over apartheid. Historians still argue whether Abraham Kuyper planted the seeds of apartheid in his view of sphere sovereignty, but the Dutch Reformed Church defended apartheid for decades while believing in Calvinism. This paralleled how Southern Presbyterians and Southern Baptists in America could be Calvinist and yet support slavery. The tide eventually turned, and almost all Christians now oppose apartheid.

But sadly, the Reformed faith suffered in the popular arena because so many Calvinists had once supported it.

Several names should be recognized in twentieth-century South African Calvinism. Hendrik G. Stoker (1899–1993) developed a kind of Afrikaans presuppositionalism that paralleled that of Herman Dooyeweerd and Vollenhoven back in Holland. He taught at the Potchefstroom University for Christian Higher Education, which was founded on Kuyperian lines. Later B. J. Van der Walt (1939–) taught at the Institute for the Advancement of Calvinism based there and produced a steady stream of publications in both English and Afrikaans. Like others, he too drifted leftward in time.

Norval Geldenhuys wrote the commentary on Luke in the New International Commentary series. Francis Nigel Lee (1934–2011) was a theonomist author. Erroll Hulse (1931–2017) immigrated to England and became a leader among Reformed Baptists.

Calvinism is still very much alive in South Africa. Like almost everywhere else, there have been conservative traditionalists who hold to the historic Reformed faith and liberal and Neo-Orthodox theologians and clergy who are in Dutch Reformed bodies with only a semblance of Calvinism.

Australia and New Zealand

As in South Africa, Calvinism was brought to these two countries by British and Dutch immigrants and missionaries, especially the Presbyterians and Anglicans. John Dunmore Lang (1799–1878) from Scotland was the first major Presbyterian in Australia (1823). Later Adam Cairns cast a large shadow. Others were Reformed but not quite as outspoken, such as Stuart Barton Babbage, the renown New Testament scholar Leon Morris, and Marcus Loane. Raymond Zorn, Allan Harmon, Rowland S. Ward, and David Broughton Knox were more recognizably Calvinistic. Klaas Runia of the Netherlands taught there for decades. Arthur W. Pink lived there for a short time. A few Australians imbibed Hyper-Calvinism from either the Gospel Standard Baptists (England) or the Protestant Reformed Church (United States).

Over in New Zealand, John MacFarland from Scotland was the first important Presbyterian, followed by David Bruce and Thomas Miller and his sons J. Graham and Robert.

The Far East

There is some Calvinism in Singapore — for example, Timothy Tow and Jeffrey Khoo and the Far Eastern Bible College and Seminary, much influenced by Carl McIntire. There is a small but growing Reformed community in India among the evangelical Anglicans and Presbyterians. There has naturally been a Reformed witness in Indonesia by way of the Dutch, but it has suffered under the increasing Muslim majority — it has more Muslims than any other nation in the world.

Christianity has never grown much in Japan, and so Calvinism has been only a small thing there. Emil Brunner taught at the International Christian University, Tokyo, and Barthians trained in Scotland also imported Neo-Orthodoxy into the small Reformed community. Toyohiko Kagawa (1888–1960) studied at Princeton Seminary and brought a very diluted form of Calvinism with him. Nobuo Watanabe (1960–) and others have produced some useful studies of Calvin and Calvinism. Tokutaro Takakura (1885–1934) is often considered the first significant Japanese Calvinist of note. Masaki Nakaya translated Calvin's *Institutes* into Japanese. Others worth mentioning include Tadakagu Uoki, Masahisa Uemura, Masaichi Takemori, Akira Demura, and Yoshimitsu Akagi. The Japanese Reformed, like Christians in general, have had to face the challenges of Shintoism, Zen Buddhism, and Japanese nationalism as well as material success and how Christians can witness without compromise.

As Communism in China has become increasingly capitalist, more freedom is being granted to Christians. Robert Morrison (1782–1834) and John Livingston Nevius (1829–93) were early Calvinist missionaries. Seeds were planted that survived the horrendous days of Maoist Communism. The underground church has grown dramatically, and there are reports of the spread of Calvinism there. It is very possible that Calvinism will grow still more there in the future.

Last but far from least is the unexpected but wonderful acceptance of evangelical Christianity and historic Calvinism in South Korea, equaling or surpassing any other Reformed revival during the twentieth century. Missionaries had minimal success before the "Korean Pentecost" of 1907, which was evangelical and Reformed, not Pentecostal. John Ross (1842–1915), a Scottish missionary, translated the New Testament into Korean and, like John Nevius in China, emphasized indigenous leadership. Samuel Moffett (1864–1939), Charles Clark (1878–1961), William Reynolds, John Crane, Floyd Hamilton, and Harvie Conn also taught Calvinism in South Korea. But Calvinism grew among the Koreans in a distinct way, not just as followers of the missionaries. Perhaps this is a major reason for its success. The Korean Calvinists faced two main challenges last century. First, conflict with non-Christian forces such as Japanese military aggression, Shintoism, Buddhism, Confucianism, and Chinese Communism. Second, as elsewhere, how to avoid compromise with liberal theology, such as the Minjung Theology. About 25 percent of South Korea is Christian, of which Presbyterianism is the largest sector. Park Hyung Nong, Pak Yune Sun, and many others have been influential leaders.

Conclusion

Calvinism has made some small advancement in Latin America, mainly in Brazil and Mexico. Roman Catholicism dominates Central and South America — but it did in Europe before the Reformation, so who can tell what will happen in the future? There are also slow but steady strides being made in churches in Africa, but as yet there has been no major breakthrough on a large scale such as in South Korea. Christians in general and Calvinists in particular pray for the Holy Spirit to blow across all continents to bring salvation to lost souls everywhere. May it happen in the twenty-first century.

The Theology of Calvinism

Chapter 20
The Sovereignty of God

God is God. He has always been and will always be exactly that — God. He identifies Himself as "I am who I am" (Exodus 3:14). God has a wide variety of attributes in the rainbow of His glory, but there is one that has been given special attention by Calvinists. It is the wonderful divine quality known as the *sovereignty* of God.

The Transcendence of God

God is the self-existent One from eternity. He created the universe to display His glory, but being infinite, He is greater than the universe (1 Kings 8:27). As in the *extra Calvinisticum* regarding the two natures of Christ, we say "The finite cannot contain the infinite." The Lord is the "lofty" God (Isaiah 57:15). All humanity is but a drop in the bucket, mere grasshoppers, nothing, and less than nothing compared with God (Isaiah 40:15, 17, 22; Daniel 4:35).

J. B. Phillips wrote a book entitled *Your God is Too Small*, but Reformed theologians describe a still greater God than Phillips did. God is not only quantitatively bigger, but qualitatively different than man. Yes, we have the image of God (Genesis 1:26).[1] We resemble God in some way. But let us never think that God is simply a big man. He is not a man at all (Numbers 23:19; 1 Samuel 15:29). Psalm 50:21, "You thought that I was altogether like you."[2]

The Deity is "the hidden God" (hence the Latin term *Deus Absconditus*). "Truly You are God, who hide Yourself" (Isaiah 45:15). God has revealed Himself truly but only partially. There is infinitely more concealed than revealed. The unrevealed infinity of God is called the *transcendence* of God. He transcends us like the sky above us (Isaiah 55:9). He is both near and far, both immanent and transcendent (Acts 17:27).

---

1 Barth and other Neo-Orthodox theologians sometimes speak of God as "wholly other." This is true with regard to God's essence, but it tends to overlook the image of God in man whereby he resembles God. See G. C. Berkouwer, *Man: The Image of God* (Grand Rapids, 1972).
2 Luther rightly rebuked Erasmus with the famous words, "Your thoughts of God are too human." *The Bondage of the Will* (Grand Rapids: Fleming H. Revell, 2005), 87. Calvinists give the same rebuke to Arminians.

The Independence of God

Being eternal, self-existent, and infinite, God needs nothing and nobody. He did not create the universe because He needed it, nor does He redeem sinners because He was lonely (Acts 17:25; Job 22:2). This applies to His will also. Before we ask, "Why did God create the world?" we must ask "Why does God do what He does?" Nothing compels Him to do anything. He is totally independent. He alone has totally free will. God therefore does what He does for the simple reason that He chooses to do so. Consider these verses:

- "Our God is in heaven; He does whatever He pleases." (Psalm 115:3)

- "Whatever the Lord pleases He does, in heaven and earth, in the seas and in all the deep places." (Psalm 135:6)

- "And whatever His soul desires, that He does." (Job 23:13)

- "He does according to His will in the army of heaven and among the inhabitants of the earth. No one can restrain His hand or say to him 'What have You done?'" (Daniel 4:35)

This is the mere good pleasure of God (Matthew 11:26). As Arthur W. Pink put it: "God does as He pleases, only as He pleases, always as He pleases."[3] He molds people like clay in any way He so chooses (Romans 9:20–21). We have no right to question how God exercises His sovereign will, for that would be to act as a god, but God alone is God. This is the great lesson that Job had to learn (Job 42:2). Calvinists have learned it; others are in theological kindergarten trying to grasp it with grudging reluctance. Still others veered toward Karl Barth's view that God is free to become His opposite, whatever that means.[4]

Not only does God not have to answer our questions or defend His decisions, He does not need our advice. "Who has become His counselor?" (Romans 11:34; Isaiah 40:13) God is His own counselor, for He "works all things according to the counsel of His will" (Ephesians 1:11). Samuel Rutherford said: "The supreme and absolute Former of all things giveth not an account of any of His matters."[5] The Puritan Thomas Watson warned: "Do not dispute against God's prerogative; let not the clay syllogize with the potter."[6]

---

3 Arthur W. Pink, *The Attributes of God* (Grand Rapids: Baker, 1975), 32. Also in his *The Sovereignty of God* (Grand Rapids: Baker, 1973). 21, 239.
4 E.g., James Daane, *The Freedom of God* (Grand Rapids: Eerdmans, 1973). This is his screed against what he disdains as "decretal theology."
5 Samuel Rutherford, *Letters of Samuel Rutherford* (Edinburgh: Banner of Truth, 1984), 621.
6 Thomas Watson, *The Puritan Pulpit* (Morgan, PA: Soli Deo Gloria, 2004), 79.

Absolute Sovereignty

God repeatedly describes Himself as King, indeed, the King of Kings (Revelation 19:16) and "the only Potentate" (1 Timothy 6:15). He reigns (Psalm 97:1). Only a few nations on earth still have a monarchy, in which king or queen is referred to as "the sovereign." In the United Kingdom, the sovereign reigns but does not rule. Parliament, not the monarch, rules. America won its independence with the slogan, "We serve no sovereign here." That is what unregenerate man selfishly proclaims regarding God. Arminian theology seems to teach something democratic like the Social Contract of John Locke — those that rule do so only with the consent of those who are ruled. But God does not need our permission to rule and reign. He is an absolute monarch, not a president. In fact, the New Testament uses the Greek word *despotes*, from which we get the word *despot*, to describe God (Luke 2:29; Acts 4:24; 2 Timothy 2:21; 2 Peter 2:1; Revelation 6:10). He has total rule; He is a righteous totalitarian ruler. He makes all decrees and laws; He is a benevolent dictator.

Theologians debate whether one attribute of God is superior to the others, or if one is a central quality of God. R. C. Sproul suggested holiness, as many others do. Many Arminians and most liberals say love. John Frame the Calvinist nominates lordship and sovereignty.[7] The Septuagint usually renders the Hebrew proper name *Yahweh* with the Greek word *kurios*, or Lord. The New Testament uses this word more than any other to describe God. Both testaments call him "Lord of Lords" (Deuteronomy 10:17; Revelation 17:14; 19:16). Linguistically at least, Frame may be right. God is described as *Lord* thousands of times more than as holiness, love, or anything else. It is worth pondering. Any idea of God that does not immediately entail Him as Lord is an idol.

In recent decades, evangelicals have debated the lordship salvation controversy — that is, must a sinner submit to the lordship of Christ in order to be saved? Arminians frequently say no, but Calvinists thunder yes! One of the first and central affirmations of faith is the succinct declaration "Jesus is Lord" (1 Corinthians 12:3; Romans 10:9). Lordship is sovereignty. To believe in God is to believe God is Lord. Reformed evangelism proclaims Christ's lordship and demands that every knee bow to Him and confess "Jesus Christ is Lord" (Philippians 2:11). To refuse to do so is rebellious treason deserving the death penalty of eternal damnation.

---

7 John M. Frame, *The Doctrine of God: A Theology of Lordship* (Phillipsburg, NJ: P&R, 2002), 21–46.

Some Arminians think the phrase *Jesus is Lord* only means accepting the deity of Christ, not submitting to His authority. We go much further. One cannot truly believe in Christ's deity without submitting to His total lordship and absolute authority. Not submitting means not believing that He is Lord and God. Thomas the apostle learned this truth when he believed and humbly confessed to Jesus, "My Lord and my God" (John 20:28). To deny the absolute sovereignty of God reveals a deficient view of saving faith. It actually leads to atheism, for if God is not totally sovereign, He is not totally God, and a partial God is no god. But the God of the Bible is both Lord and God and the absolute sovereign of all.

God Is God-Centered

The universe is centered around God. It is a theocentric cosmos. Each of us should be consciously and morally centered around God as well. God Himself is God-centered. The church needs a theological Copernican revolution. Hundreds of years ago, scientists switched from geocentrism to heliocentrism, and we must change from anthropocentrism to theocentrism. For instance, in evangelism we must say, "It's not all about you. It's all about God."[8] We must center on the glory of Christ, not the felt needs of man. In worship we must engage in God-centered praise, not man-centered entertainment. Here is where Reformed theology makes an enormous practical difference. This applies to Christian counseling also, as Michael Horton points out: "Self-esteem, self-image, self-confidence, self-this, and self-that have replaced talk of God's attributes."[9] True biblical counseling helps people by showing them God's principles and promises and putting them back into a God-centered relationship.

The Rights of God

In 1793 the Anglican Calvinist Thomas Scott wrote a profound and delightful little book entitled *The Rights of God* to answer the Deist Thomas Paine's book *The Rights of Man*. Scott expounded Scripture to show that God is the absolute sovereign and has all the rights. God has given to man certain privileges and duties, and men should show fairness and love to each other. But to be sure, man has no rights with God. God has all the rights — period. He has the right to choose whomever He pleases and reject whomever He pleases. Romans 9:15: "I will have mercy on whomever I will have mercy, and I will have compassion on whomever I will have compassion." Matthew Henry commented:

---

8 E.g., R. B. Kuiper, *God-Centered Evangelism* (Edinburgh: Banner of Truth, 1978).

9 Michael Horton, *Putting Amazing Back into Grace* (Grand Rapids: Baker, 1994), 17.

As these great words, I am that I am (Exodus 3:14) do abundantly express the absolute independency of his being, so these words, I will have mercy on whom I will have mercy, do as fully express the absolute prerogative and sovereignty of his will.[10]

In the parable of Matthew 20:15, Jesus has God saying, "Is it not lawful for me to do what I wish with my own things?" Indeed, it is. God has absolute rights over His property — right of possession, right of disposal; the right to bless, the right to punish. This infinitely outweighs any supposed "rights of man." Paine and others (many Arminians, we suspect) project their socio-political notions of democracy upon God.

We dare not quibble or argue with God about rights we presume to have. Romans 9:20: "But indeed, O man, who are you to reply against God?" Daniel 4:35: "No one can restrain His hand or say to Him, 'What have You done?'" Calvin wrote:

Surely we must be out of our minds if we set bounds on God's authority over us in this way, giving more credit to the creature than to the One who created and sustains the heaven and the earth by his Word alone?[11]

God raises up one and brings down another as He pleases (Luke 1:52), which is a hard lesson that Nebuchadnezzar had to learn (Daniel 2:21). He gives power "to whom it seem[s] proper to [Him]" (Jeremiah 27:5). Non-Calvinists echo the popular revolutionary slogan "Power to the people," while Calvinists cry "All power belongs to God!"

Absolute Authority

Being the absolute Lord and King, God has a right to do whatever He pleases to do. He has what may be called a holy and wise arbitrariness. Jonathan Edwards put it like this: "'Tis the glory of God that he is an arbitrary being, that originally he, in all things, acts as being limited and directed in nothing but his own wisdom, tied to no other rules and laws but the directions of his own infinite understanding."[12]

Reformed scholars make a fine point here. Absolute sovereignty is not the

---

10 Matthew Henry, *Commentary on the Whole Bible* (Old Tappan: Fleming H. Revell, n.d.) 6:433 (on Romans 9:15).

11 John Calvin, *Sermons on Galatians* (Edinburgh: Banner of Truth, 1997), 298.

12 Jonathan Edwards, *The Works of Jonathan Edwards* (New Haven: Yale University Press, 2004), 23:202–03.

same as what certain medieval theologians such as Duns Scotus and William of Ockham taught as "absolute power."[13] That error suggests that God is so absolutely free and omnipotent that He can literally will anything at all. It was debated whether God can erase the past, damn an innocent person, justify an unrepentant sinner, make an immoral woman a sinless virgin, or accept something other than the blood and death of Christ as atonement. Calvin rejected all such notions of absolute power,[14] as did John Owen.[15] Rather, historic Reformed theologians accept ordained power. God always wills in perfect accord with His attributes of wisdom, holiness, and so forth. The error of absolute power is not what we mean by "absolute sovereignty." Indeed, the error of voluntarism, as it is usually called, has historically had more in common with Semi-Pelagianism and Neo-Orthodoxy than with Reformed theology.

Calvin likewise rejected the voluntarist[16] notion regarding morality and ethics. It seemed that certain medieval scholastics taught that God could have reversed the commandments to forbid what He commanded and command what He forbade. Calvinists disagree and contend that God's commanding will (the revealed will, as we will see later) is a reflection of His holy nature. True, God gave temporary ceremonial laws to the Jews only, but that is something else. The moral laws are as unchanging as God's own nature and could not be otherwise any more than God could be. This is seen in the command, "Be holy as I the Lord am holy" (1 Peter 1:16). He cannot command lies, for "God cannot lie" (Titus 1:2). God cannot command contrary to His nature, for He cannot deny Himself (2 Timothy 2:13). To suggest otherwise is blasphemy. Sadly, this is sometimes missed by some Hyper-Calvinists. Witness the controversy with James Wells and Rahab's lie. Rutherford and Bradwardine said that God could have accepted a sacrifice other than the death of Christ. Bradwardine should have known better, for he was the main opponent of Duns Scotus and Ockham, whom he charged with Pelagianism. Others have theorized that Arminianism resembles this error in its insistence on free will — man may be fallen, but his will is the determining factor, and he can will contrary to his fallen nature.

When we say, therefore, that the sovereignty of God involves a holy

---

13 For a good survey, see William J. Courtenay, *Capacity and Volition: A History of the Distinction of Absolute and Ordained Power* (Bergamo: Pierluigi Lubrina Editore, 1990).

14 John Calvin, *Institutes of the Christian Religion* (Philadelphia: Westminster, 1960), 3:23:2 (p. 950). On Calvin's views, see David C. Steinmetz, *Calvin in Context* (New York: Oxford University Press, 1995), 40–52.

15 John Owen, *The Works of John Owen* (London: Banner of Truth, 1967), 10:482–604.

16 Voluntarism should not be confused with *voluntaryism*, the nineteenth-century Scottish system opposed to nobility's patronage over a church's selection of a minister.

arbitrariness, we do not mean that it can ever be contrary to His holiness or wisdom. God does not will or act in a willy-nilly manner. Calvin said that absolute power is a "shocking blasphemy," as if God acts by sheer caprice and not by justice.[17] The same goes for His wisdom — neither His decrees nor laws are the result of unwise capriciousness. So also with His omnipotence. Calvin again: "God does not play with us as if we were a ball. Although God is all-powerful, he will not do just anything."[18] And yet again: "For it would be easier to force away the light of the sun from his heat, or his heat from his fire, than to separate the power of God from his justice."[19] His decrees are perfectly wise, for God predestines and commands according to His own counsel and perfect wisdom (Ephesians 1:11).

The Objection

Fallen man does not like the sovereignty of God. He recoils from it and argues against it. Some quibble, "The word *sovereignty* is not even in the Bible." But it depends upon which translation one uses. For instance, the NASB renders Psalm 103:19 as "His sovereignty rules over all." The same goes for the argument that the word *lordship* is not in the Bible. One late anti-lordship theologian actually hinted that the Reformed emphasis on lordship resembles the lost hypocrites on Judgment Day who called Christ "Lord, Lord" (Matthew 7:22). Can such an argument be taken seriously?

A popular objection offers this alternative: "God limits His sovereignty in His dealings with us." This is only partially true, in the sense that God did not foreordain all that He could foreordain — but that itself proves absolute sovereignty, not disproves it. But this alternative idea suggests that just as God does not do all that He is able to do, so He does not choose to know all that He could know. That leads to Open Theism, which I will discuss later. It is ironic that Arminians use the words "God limits His sovereignty" but never say, "God limits His love." But they thereby paint themselves into a corner, for if God does not limit His love, then why not say God saves everyone, including the Devil, as Origen argued? Or to use the *argumentum ad absurdum*, if God does not limit His love, then why not say not only "God loves a sinner but hates the

---

17 John Calvin, *Commentary on the Book of the Prophet Isaiah* (Grand Rapids: Eerdmans, 1955), 2:152.

18 John Calvin, *Sermons on Jeremiah* (Lewiston: Edwin Mellen, 1990), 242.

19 John Calvin, *Calvin's Calvinism* (Grand Rapids: Reformed Free Publishing Assoc., 1991), 195.

sin" but also "God loves both the sin and the sinner?" Such is blasphemy, but fortunately, our opponents do not go that far.

Basically the objection is sin. It is an ethical problem, not just a theological one. The fallen heart of man says, "We will not have an absolutely sovereign God rule over us!" (see Luke 19:14). But God already rules over them! That's the whole point. God is already sovereign, for His sovereignty is not dependent upon our acquiescence. Acknowledging and submitting to His sovereignty does not make Him sovereign, any more than saving faith "makes Jesus Lord." He already is Lord. An attack on the sovereignty of God is an attack on the sovereign God and not just on Calvinists, as Jonathan Edwards put it: "Tis not men, poor Calvinists, but Jehovah that has been trampled on."[20]

D. James Kennedy saw why man objects to the sovereignty of God. Men will not allow God to be sovereign "for a very simple reason — they want to be God themselves."[21] But Calvinists emphasize the opening line of this chapter: "God is God." Man is not nor ever can be God, any more than God can cease being God. We wholeheartedly agree with Luther's battle cry: "Let God be God!"[22] Referring to Romans 9:20, Luther turned the table on the opponents of absolute sovereignty such as Erasmus:

> And he bridles them by commanding them to be silent, and to reserve the majesty of God's power and will, against which we have no rights, which has full rights against us to do what it pleases. No injustice is done to us, for God owes us nothing, He has received nothing from us, and He has promised us nothing but what He pleased and willed.[23]

Like Luther, we Calvinists point our opponents to Romans 9:20: "Who are you, O man, to reply against God?" Denying absolute sovereignty is a serious sin, not just a theological error. In a way, this is the continental divide between Calvinism and Augustinianism on the one side and Pelagianism, Semi-Pelagianism, and Arminianism on the other. Denying or weakening divine sovereignty dishonors God, as Calvin again wrote:

---

20 *The Works of Jonathan Edwards* (New Haven: Yale University Press, 2003), 21:235. It is as if the Lord says to Calvinists as He said to Samuel: "They have not rejected you, but they have rejected Me, that I should reign over them." (1 Samuel 8:7).

21 D. James Kennedy, *Truths That Transform* (Old Tappan: Fleming H. Revell, 1974), 26.

22 See Phillip S. Watson, co-translator of *The Bondage of the Will*, in his book *Let God Be God: An Interpretation of the Theology of Martin Luther* (Philadelphia: Westminster, 1970).

23 Martin Luther, *The Bondage of the Will* (Grand Rapids: Fleming H. Revell, 2005), 215–16. This illustrates Luther's close affinity to Reformed theology. We could call him "Luther the Calvinist." Later Lutherans toned it down.

Let us then remember that God does not receive that honour among men to which he is entitled, if he is not allowed to possess his own inherent sovereignty, and if his glory is obscured by setting up other objects against him with antagonist claims.[24]

Thomas Scott rightly rebuked Paine's Deistic objection that it would be unjust of God to work miracles because that would violate His own laws of nature. But we reply that miracles are not breaking God's moral laws, and He is free to intervene in His creation all that He wishes.

Parallel to this objection, as we shall see repeatedly in this volume, is the argument that it would be unjust of God to intervene in the human will. All this was in the air in the theological and political debates of the 1770s. Scott rightly saw it as indicative of a higher revolution than that of the colonists against the crown of England. Deism was rebellion against God. In a later political context, V. I. Lenin once said that the ultimate question in all politics is "Who whom?" That is, who rules whom? Who has final sovereignty? Theologically it is the same question, and we unabashedly reply: "God rules man."

The Contrast

The Reformed view of divine sovereignty is vastly greater than the shallow view of pop evangelicalism, let alone apostate liberalism. The sovereign God of Calvinism is awesomely and infinitely greater than the toy godling of competing theologies. We like the words of Arthur W. Pink:

The God of the twentieth century is a helpless, effeminate being who commands the respect of no really thoughtful man. The God of the popular man is a creation of a maudlin sentimentality. The God of many a present-day pulpit is an object of pity rather than awe-inspiring reverence.[25]

Hear the words of Charles Haddon Spurgeon on the subject:

There is no attribute more comforting to His children than that of God's Sovereignty. Under the most adverse circumstances, in the most severe trials, they believe that Sovereignty has ordained their afflictions, that Sovereignty overrules them, and that Sovereignty will sanctify them all. There is nothing for which the children ought more earnestly to contend than the doctrine of their Master over all creation — the Kingship of God over all the works of His own hands — the Throne of God and His right

---

24 John Calvin, *Commentary on the Book of Psalms* (Grand Rapids, Eerdmans, 1949), 3:351.
25 Arthur W. Pink, *The Sovereignty of God* (Grand Rapids: Baker, 1973), 24.

to sit upon that Throne. On the other hand, there is no doctrine more hated by worldlings, no truth of which they have made such a football, as the great, stupendous, but yet most certain doctrine of the Sovereignty of the infinite Jehovah. Man will allow God to be everywhere except on His throne. They will allow Him to be in His workshop to fashion worlds and make stars. They will allow Him to be in His almonry to dispense His alms and bestow His bounties. They will allow Him to sustain the earth and bear up the pillars thereof, or light the lamps of heaven, or rule the waves of the ever-moving ocean; but when God ascends His throne, His creatures then gnash their teeth. And we proclaim an enthroned God, and His right to do as He wills with His own, to dispose of His creatures as He thinks well, without consulting them in the matter; then it is that we are hissed and execrated, and then it is that men turn a deaf ear to us, for God on His throne is not the God they love. But it is the God upon the throne that we love to preach. It is God upon His throne whom we trust.[26]

Lastly, reflect upon the thoughts of Jonathan Edwards:

From my childhood up, my mind had been wont to be full of objections against the doctrine of God's sovereignty; in choosing whom he would to eternal life, and rejecting whom he pleased; leaving them eternally to perish, and be everlastingly tormented in hell. It used to appear like a horrible doctrine to me. But I remember the time very well, when I seemed to be convinced, and fully satisfied, as to this sovereignty of God, and his justice in thus eternally disposing of men, according to his sovereign pleasure. But never could give an account, how, or by what means, I was thus convinced; not in the least imagining, in the time of it, nor a long time after, that there was any extraordinary influence of God's Spirit in it: but only that now I saw further, and my reason apprehended the justice and reasonableness of it. However, my mind rested in it; and it put an end to all those cavils and objections, that had till then abode with me, all the preceding part of my life. And there has been a wonderful alteration in my mind, with respect to the doctrine of God's sovereignty, from that day to this; so that I scarce ever found so much as a rising of an objection against God's sovereignty, in the most absolute sense, in showing mercy on whom he will show mercy, and hardening and eternally damning whom he will. God's absolute sovereignty, and justice, with respect to the rest assured of,

---

26 Quoted in Arthur W. Pink, *The Attributes of God* (Grand Rapids, Baker, 1975), 32–33; cf. Charles Spurgeon, *Metropolitan Tabernacle Pulpit* (Pasadena, TX: Pilgrim Publications, 1981), 58:13.

as much as of anything that I see with my eyes; at least it is so at times. But I have oftentimes since that first conviction, had quite another kind of sense of God's sovereignty, than I had then. I have often since, not only had a conviction, but a delightful conviction. The doctrine of God's sovereignty has very often appeared, an exceedingly pleasant, bright and sweet doctrine to me: and absolute sovereignty is what I love to ascribe to God.[27]

Conclusion

This is a summary of the Reformed doctrine of the sovereignty of God. It must be believed at the outset as we discuss other divine attributes as well as the doctrines of grace. This is what we mean when we say that God is sovereign. That is just affirming with high praise and deep adoration *God is God*. Let God be God!

---

27 Edwards, *Works*, 16:791–92.

Chapter 21
Absolute Predestination

The big question is: Why? Why is there something instead of nothing? Why are we here? What is the meaning of life? Whence and whither — where did we come from and where we going? In German there are two words for *why*. *Warum* means "What caused this?" *Wozu* means "What is the purpose or goal of this?" The answer to all these questions is the same: God. Romans 11:36: "For of Him and through Him and to Him are all things, to whom be glory forever. Amen."

What Is Predestination?

Simply put, *predestination* means that God is the source of all things. He not only created everything (Genesis 1:1), but He planned to create everything and has a plan that shall surely come to pass.[1] The best and most well-known brief explanation is in the Westminster Confession:

> God from all eternity did by the most wise and holy counsel of His own will freely and unchangeably ordain whatsoever comes to pass; yet so as thereby neither is God the author of sin, nor is violence offered to the will of the creatures, nor is the liberty or contingency of second causes taken away, but rather established. (3:1)

There are several synonyms. One is *foreordination*. First Corinthians 2:7 refers to "the hidden wisdom which God ordained before the ages for our glory." The words *ordained before* mean "before-ordination," or foreordination. God preordained the universe. The usual Greek word for *world* or *universe* is *kosmos*, order as opposed to chaos (Cf. 1 Corinthians 14:33). Ephesians 2:10 says, "We are His workmanship, created in Christ Jesus unto good works, which God hath before ordained that we should walk in them" (KJV). This "should" is indicative, not imperative. God foreordained that we *shall*, not merely *might*, obey Him (Cf. Ephesians 1:4–5). The words *predestination* and *foreordination* basically mean the same in this sense. They are sometimes confused in the wrong way, as when Mark Twain wryly spoke of "preforeordestination" to make fun of it.[2]

---

1 The standard work in the last one hundred years has been Loraine Boettner, *The Reformed Doctrine of Predestination* (Philadelphia: Presbyterian and Reformed, 1932).
2 Mark Twain, *The Adventures of Huckleberry Finn*, ed. by Victor Fischer and Lin Salamo

Then there is the word *appointment*. "It is appointed for men to die once, but after this the judgment" (Hebrews 9:27). Both our birth days and death days have been appointed by God and shall surely come to pass to the very second. First Peter 2:8 says that the stumbling in disobedience by some people has been appointed by God. Acts 13:48 is especially poignant regarding predestination and election: "And as many as had been appointed to eternal life believed." They were pre-appointed to believe and receive eternal life, and they did so right on schedule. Heinrich Bullinger the Reformer called it "fore-appointment."[3]

Predetermination is not used very much, but it expresses the same idea. God has determined in advance all that will happen. Acts 17:26 links the ideas of predetermination and pre-appointment: "He has [. . .] determined their preappointed times and the boundaries of their dwellings." The word *determinism* refers to the principle accepted by virtually all scientists — all things happen by cause and effect. In philosophy, the system of determinism somewhat resembles Calvinism in that both teach that everything has a cause. But in philosophy it implies that everything happens by blind fate with no free choice at all, whereas Reformed theology says everything happens by God's causation, and humans have responsibility. Martin Bucer observed: "If you require a definition of predetermination, it is assigning of each thing its own purpose, whereby before creating them God destines all things severally from eternity to some final use."[4] Scripture speaks of men "determining" something to do or cause to happen, but it does not always come to pass (1 Samuel 20:7, 9, 33; 25:17; 2 Samuel 13:32; 2 Chronicles 2:1; Esther 7:7; Acts 3:13; 11:29; 15:2, 37; 19:39; 20:16; 25:25; 27:1; 1 Corinthians 2:2; 2 Corinthians 2:1; Titus 3:12). By contrast, God "determines" certain things that He will do or cause to happen (2 Chronicles 25:16; Job 14:5; Isaiah 10:23; 19:17; 28:22; Daniel 9:24, 26, 27). What God determines always comes to pass, "for what has been determined shall be done" (Daniel 11:36). This even refers to the death of Christ being determined by God (Luke 22:22), even by the hands of wicked men: "To do whatever Your hand and Your purpose determined before to be done" (Acts 4:28).

Theoretically, there are only three possibilities to the principle of cosmic cause and effect. First, all is chance. This is not only unbiblical but is literally nonsense. Some scientists, however, admit the existence of chance in the Big

---

(Berkeley: University of California Press, 2001), 147.

3 Heinrich Bullinger, *The Decades of Henry Bullinger* (Grand Rapids: Reformation Heritage Books, 2004), 3:185.

4 Martin Bucer, *Common Places of Martin Bucer*, ed. by David F. Wright (Appleford: Sutton Courtenay, 1972), 97.

Bang. But as one Calvinist pointed out, "In God's empire, there is no chance."[5] Second, there could be an infinite regress of causes in eternity past. Hinduism says something like this to explain cosmic reincarnation of everything. But this too is unbiblical nonsense. Third, there is a unique first cause that is uncaused. And that is what God is — the First Cause and Last End of everything. He alone is self-existent and the uncaused cause of all.

The Word *Predestination*

In English the word *predestination* is a combination of "pre" (before) and "destination" (goal). God has determined the destiny of all things in advance. To use a popular analogy, God is the engineer on the unstoppable train going to its inevitable destination. God follows His own maps and pre-appointed schedule. He is always on time and never fails to arrive at the destination.

The usual Greek word in the New Testament is *proorizo* from *pro* (before) and *orao* (see), thus "to see beforehand." But as we shall see later, it does not mean merely that God foresees all things in advance by omniscience. The word is used six times in a causative way (emphasis added in all verses):

- "To do whatever Your hand and Your purpose *determined* before to be done" (Acts 4:28).

- "For whom He foreknew, He also *predestined*. [. . .] Moreover whom He *predestined*, these He also called" (Romans 8:29–30). This is part of God's "purpose" (v. 28). *Foreknew* here means "fore-loved."

- "The hidden wisdom which God *ordained* before the ages for our glory" (1 Corinthians 2:7). As with Acts 4:28, God predestined all things and not just people. Note the word *before* (*pro*).

- "Having *predestined* us to adoption" (Ephesians 1:5), which is parallel to election (v. 4).

- "Being *predestined* according to the purpose of Him who works all things according to the counsel of His will" (Ephesians 1:11). He predestines according to His own sovereign will, not ours.

The Purpose of God

Before creation, God established a purpose for all things. Scripture speaks of

---

5 William Howard Van Doren, *The Gospel of Luke* (Grand Rapids: Kregel, 1981), 379.

God's ultimate "purpose," as in the well-beloved Romans 8:28. His purpose and counsel are related in Jeremiah 49:20 and 50:45. Psalm 33:11 speaks of this as God's plans: "The counsel of the Lord stands forever, the plans of His heart to all generations." Purpose, counsel, and plans are all intertwined as one. This is illustrated in human activity: "Without counsel, plans go awry, but in the multitude of counselors they are established" (Proverbs 15:22). God's plans are established and never go awry, for they are based in the eternal counsel of the Trinity.

In the New Testament, the Greek word *boule* is often used for God's wise counsel and purpose (emphasis added in all verses):

- "Him, being delivered by the determined *purpose* and foreknowledge of God" (Acts 2:23). Christ's death was purposed (1 Peter 1:20).

- "To do whatever Your hand and Your *purpose* determined before to be done" (Acts 4:28).

- "Who has resisted His *will?*" (Romans 9:19). The non-election of some sinners has been purposed beforehand (v. 18).

- "Being predestined according to the *purpose* of Him who works all things according to the *counsel* of His will; (Ephesians 1:11).

Ephesians 1:11 virtually makes *boule* synonymous with *prothesin*, purpose.

- *Prothesin* is also used in Ephesians 3:11: "According to the eternal *purpose* which he accomplished in Christ Jesus our Lord."

- Ephesians 1:9 uses the verb form: "Having made known to us the mystery of His will, according to His good pleasure that he *purposed* in Himself."

Note that these verses indicate that this purpose is eternal and internal to God. *Prothesin* is used in Romans 8:28: "And we know that all things work together for good to those who love God, to those who are the called according to His *purpose*" (emphasis added). We know for sure because God's purpose is sure.

Prothesin occurs in Romans 9:11 also: "That the *purpose* of God according to election might stand, not of works but of Him who calls" (emphasis added). Paul's point is that the purpose of salvation is sure because it rests on God, not us. His purpose is invincible. Isaiah 46:10: "My counsel shall stand, and I will do all My pleasure." *Prothesin* is also employed in 2 Timothy 1:9: "Who has saved us and called us with a holy calling, not according to our works, but according to His own *purpose* and grace which was given to us in Christ Jesus before time began" (emphasis added). It is an eternal purpose of grace.

The Decree of God

We also speak of predestination as the *decree* of God. The Old Testament describes the decrees of kings as their commands and orders. God is the ultimate king, and He issues both eternal decrees and temporal commands. There is one ultimate decree which involves several individual decrees. Herman Bavinck put it like this:

> The one simple and eternal decree of God unfolds itself before our eyes in time in a vast multiplicity of things and events, a multiplicity that at one and the same time points back to one decree and leads us, humbly speaking, to think of many decrees.[6]

He also says, "The decree is the "womb" of all reality."[7] Johannes Wollebius succinctly defines it for us: "A decree of God is an internal act of the divine will, by which he determines, from eternity, freely, with absolute certainty, those matters which shall happen in time."[8]

Neither the ultimate decree nor the individual decrees must be confused with God's commands or promises. His commands are usually broken but never His decrees. Arthur W. Pink commented: "There is a vast difference between the promises of God and His eternal decrees: Many of the former are conditional, whereas the latter are immutable, depending on nothing for their fulfillment save the omnipotence of God."[9]

The Program and Plan of God

In computer language, we could say that the universe has been preprogrammed by God. His predestination, purpose, and plan are the program for the cosmos. God created everything with a purpose in mind. God does not make it up as He goes along. In Luke 14:28–30, Jesus said a wise builder first counts the cost of his plans before building. Predestination is God's blueprint. In Ezekiel 14:23, God says, "I have done nothing without a cause." He had a reason, purpose, and cause. The world exists "be-cause" God planned. It has been reported that

---

6 Herman Bavinck, *Reformed Dogmatics* (Grand Rapids: Baker, 2004), 2:374.
7 Bavinck, 2:373.
8 In John Beardslee, ed. *Reformed Dogmatics* (New York: Oxford University Press, 1965), 47.
9 Arthur W. Pink, *The Life of David* (Swengel: Reiner, 1976), 1:252.

President Franklin D. Roosevelt once said, "In politics, nothing happens by accident. If it happens, you can bet it was planned that way."[10] So too with God and the universe.

Luke 14:31–32 continues Christ's words. A general first has a battle plan, an overall strategy for winning that involves wise and appropriate tactics. Proverbs 20:18: "Plans are established by counsel; by wise counsel wage war" (cf. 24:6). God's war plan is wise and is always successful. God always wins.

Eternal Predestination

Several of the verses I have quoted tell us that God's predestination is from eternity past. It is predestination, not post-destination. God planned it all in advance "before time began" (2 Timothy 1:9) and "before the foundation of the world" (Ephesians 1:4). The great William Ames explained:

> It is called destination because there is a sure determination of the order of means for the end. Because God determined this order by himself before any actual existence of things, it is called not simply destination but predestination.[11]

It covers everything in time, as Job 14:5 indicates: "Since his days are determined, the number of his months is with You; You have appointed his limits, so that he cannot pass."

And it was all predestined in an eternal moment by God. Gottschalk prayed: "You have foreknown and predestined instantly, that is, without any interval, that is, at one and the same time before the ages, each and every one of your works."[12]

Absolute Predestination

Predestination is absolute and definite, not contingent or merely possible. It is unfrustratable, unstoppable, invincible. Thomas Vincent the Puritan commented:

> Nothing can frustrate God's appointment; God, being so infinite in wisdom, does not appoint anything about which there shall be any reason to alter His determination; and God, being so infinite in power, nothing can hinder the efficacy of what he has determined shall be done.[13]

---

10 Quoted in Gary Allen, *None Dare Call It Conspiracy* (Rossmoor, CA: Concord, 1973), 10.
11 William Ames, *The Marrow of Theology* (Boston: Pilgrim Press, 1968), 152.
12 In Victor Genke and Francis X. Gumerlock, eds. *Gottschalk and a Medieval Predestination Controversy: Texts Translated from the Latin* (Milwaukee: Marquette University Press, 2010), 75.
13 Thomas Vincent, *Christ's Sudden and Certain Appearance to Judgment* (Morgan, PA: Soli

God's purpose is unchangeable. God will not change it, and men cannot change it. It is more irreversible than the laws of the Medes and Persians which cannot be changed (Esther 1:19; 8:8; Daniel 6:8, 12, 15). Like Pilate, God says of His decrees: "What I have written, I have written" (John 19:22). Psalm 148:6, "He has made a decree which shall not pass away." In Hebrews 6:17–18 we are told that God proved "the immutability of His counsel, confirmed it by an oath, that by two immutable things, in which it is impossible for God to lie." Predestination is the ultimate unconditional promise of God. If it fails to come to pass, then God lied (perish the thought!). But God cannot lie (Titus 1:2). Predestination is God's solemn oath to Himself. Men break oaths — God, never.

In time God carries out His unconditional promises and threats (Jeremiah 23:20; 30:24). He does not change His plans in history, according to Isaiah 14:24: "The Lord of hosts has sworn, saying, 'Surely, as I have thought, so it shall come to pass, and as I have promised, so it shall stand.'" That is true not only with temporal promises and threats but with eternal decrees as well. This is where God is different from humans. We plan, but the best laid plans of mice and men often fail. Not so with God. Proverbs 19:21: "There are many plans in a man's heart, nevertheless the Lord's counsel — that will stand." Man proposes, God disposes.

First Samuel 15:29 applies to both eternal plans and temporal promises: "And also the Strength of Israel will not lie nor relent. For He is not a man, that He should relent" (so too Numbers 23:19). God is not fickle like we are. In Jeremiah 4:28, God solemnly said, "Because I have spoken, I have purposed and will not relent, nor will I turn back from it." How many times must God say it before we believe Him? He does not change His predestination ever.

Some Arminians posit that we can frustrate God's plans and predestination. This is to confuse God's precepts with His purposes. No mere man can thwart God's purposes, as Job learned: "I know that You can do everything, and that no purpose of Yours can be withheld from You" (Job 42:2). No one can detour God (2 Chronicles 20:6). Isaiah 14:27: "For the Lord of hosts has purposed, and who will annul it?" The Arminian theory makes predestination merely a good idea that can be prevented. If so, it was faulty and unwise to begin with, which is a slur on the wisdom and omniscience of the Almighty. We emphatically disagree.

Deo Gloria, 1996), 213.

Predestination is unconditional on man. The acts of men in time are not the conditions for the fulfillment of the decrees in eternity, for those very acts themselves were predestined by God.

Predestination of All Means and Ends

Predestination is universal. But here we disagree with Stoicism and Islam. Those systems tend to deny "second causes." We would say God is First Cause, which moves all things as second causes to fulfill His ultimate goal. It is like billiards — the cue ball moves the others in a successful combination shot. God generally works mediately through the things He created, but He sometimes works immediately by miracles. God, then, has predestined all means and ends which He uses in time to enact what He foreordained previously in prehistoric eternity. Some Reformed theologians use Aristotle's fourfold causation scheme to illustrate it. God is a formal cause and uses things as material, efficient, and final causes.[14]

Could God have predestined things differently? In a way, yes. He is independent and did not have to create. Creation is a "free act," not a "necessary act," like the eternal generation of the Son or the eternal procession of the Spirit. On the other hand, contra voluntarism, God's decree of predestination is a revelation of His being and nature, and thus in an unfathomable sense, God's predestination could not have been otherwise. If otherwise, then this way was less than perfect. Abraham Kuyper cautiously comments: "God's being demands this; that is, since God was God, it had to be this way."[15] He then warned against further inquiry into the matter, which we would do well to heed.

A Caution

This will surprise many of our critics, but we agree with Calvin's frequent warnings against undue prying into predestination. For example: "One should not inquire too curiously into it if one does not want to be overwhelmed by glory."[16] Elsewhere he cautioned us of improper curiosity, for God's wise counsel in predestination "surpasses our brains, for the door has been closed to us on that subject. To enter therein by force would be a sacrilege which would

---

14 Peter Martyr Vermigli, *The Peter Martyr Library* (Kirksville, MO: Truman State University Press, 2003), 8:26–27; John Calvin, *The Epistles of Paul the Apostle to the Galatians, Ephesians, Philippians and Colossians* (Grand Rapids: Eerdmans, 1965), 126–27.

15 Abraham Kuyper, *Particular Grace: A Defence of God's Sovereignty in Salvation* (Grandville: Reformed Free Publishing Association, 2001), 268.

16 John Calvin, *The Bondage and Liberation of the Will* (Grand Rapids: Baker, 1996), 199.

not go unpunished!"[17] As the Puritans would say, "Where God has no lips, we should have no ears." And echoing Augustine, Calvin again warned: "But let us note that before God created the world, He appointed hell to put such curious people in."[18] Luther reportedly said that before creation God was climbing a tree to find a strong branch to beat over the heads of fools who ask what God was doing before He made the world.

Deuteronomy 29:29 should be remembered: "The secret things belong to the Lord our God, but those things which are revealed belong to us and our children forever, that we may do all the words of this law." The Westminster Confession wisely cautions us: "The doctrine of this high mystery of predestination is to be handled with special prudence and care" (3:8).

Conclusion

In the next chapter I will address some objections and alternative theories. Some are so silly or blasphemous that they do not deserve an answer, such as the Sikh who thought he was being profound when he wrote: "Man predestines God as much as God predestines Man."[19] Arminianism approaches that in its idea of predestination being contingent upon man rather than God alone.

The alternative to sovereign divine predestination is human tyranny. Rousas J. Rushdoony often observed that if we deny the sovereignty, predestination, and law of God, we are left with only chance and the cruelty of man. Man needs meaning, he noted, and will seek it in an anti-God tyranny, such as absolute Communism. "The mystery of predestination is a great one, but the alternatives are monstrosities"[20] and "It is not predestination in itself which is an offence to man, but predestination by God."[21] One recalls the "Predestinators" and "Social

---

17 John Calvin, *Sermons on Genesis, 1:1–11:4* (Edinburgh: Banner of Truth, 2009), 75, cf. 8. Also: "For there is not a more devilish audacity than to prattle in that fashion about God's secrets further than God has shown them to us by his Word." *Sermons on the Epistle to the Ephesians* (London: Banner of Truth, 1973), 113, cf. 59.

18 John Calvin, *The Deity of Christ and Other Sermons* (Grand Rapids, Eerdmans, 1950), 227.

19 Bhagat Singh Thind, *The House of Happiness* (Salt Lake City, 1931), pagination unknown.

20 Rousas J. Rushdoony, *Salvation and Godly Rule* (Vallecito: Ross House Books, 1983), 129; (cf. 345–49.

21 Rousas J. Rushdoony, *The Mythology of Science* (Nutley: Craig, 1978), 79; (cf. 9–11, 20, 32, 57, 75, 91. This is the central theme of his book *Sovereignty* (Vallecito: Ross House Books, 2007), e.g. p. 459. See also *The Roots of Reconstruction* (Vallecito: Ross House Books, 1991), 60, 594–95, 712, 799–804, 1016; and "Arminian Theology" in Martin G. Selbride et al, *The Great Christian Revolution: The Myths of Paganism and Arminianism* (Vallecito: Ross House Books, 1991), 75–76.

Predestination" of Aldous Huxley's *Brave New World*.[22] Human predestination is a nightmare; God's predestination is paradise.

No man fully understands predestination. Only God does. But He has revealed enough of it in Scripture for us to believe in it. Why? Because God says so.

---

22 Aldous Huxley, *Brave New World* (New York: Modern Library, 1932/46), 11, 37, passim.

Chapter 22
Objections to Predestination

There have been many objections to the Reformed doctrine of absolute predestination. Some come from non-Christians who agree that it is taught in the Bible, but they do not believe in the Bible. Others are Christians who believe the Bible but do not believe that this doctrine is taught there. Here are a few popular objections and Reformed answers.

"Absolute predestination is fatalism."

This popular objection argues that our view is the same as Islamic *kismet* or the words of an old song: "Que sera, sera. Whatever will be, will be." But this misunderstands our view. Would our opponents want to sing, "Whatever will be, will not be?" Islam has a harsh predestination that virtually eliminates second causes and human responsibility. But Calvinists accept both. Nor did we borrow our doctrine from Islam, for Augustine taught it hundreds of years before Muhammad was ever born.

Others say our doctrine came from Stoicism. After all, they say, was not John Calvin's first book on Stoicism?[1] Yes, but he wrote it before his conversion, and even then did not fully approve of Stoicism, let alone afterwards. In his treatise on predestination he wrote this:

> Fate is a term given by the Stoics to their doctrine of necessity, which they had formed out of a labyrinth of contradictory reasonings; a doctrine calculated to call God Himself to order, and to set Him laws whereby to work. Predestination I define to be, according to the Holy Scriptures, that free and unfettered counsel of God by which He rules all mankind, and all men and things, and also all parts and particles of the world by His infinite wisdom and incomprehensible justice. . . . Had you but been willing to look into my books, you would have been convinced at once how offensive to me is the profane term fate.[2]

---

1 John Calvin, *Calvin's Commentary of Seneca's de Clementia*, ed. by Ford Lewis Battles (Leiden: Brill, 1969).

2 John Calvin, *Calvin's Calvinism*, 2nd ed., ed. by Henry Cole and Russell Dykstra (Jennison: Reformed Free Publishing Association, 2009), 234. For a useful denial that Calvinism is Stoic

Stoicism was materialistic, non-supernatural, and pantheistic. Calvinism is none of those. To Stoicism, apathy (*apatheia*) is the chief virtue; to us, love is the chief. Stoics accepted an impersonal blind fate; we teach a personal and seeing God. Loraine Boettner commented: "There is in reality only one point of agreement between the two, which is, that both assume the absolute certainty of all future events. The essential difference between them is that fatalism has no place for a personal God."[3] He goes on to show other differences. Fatalism is non-moral, but only physical necessity; but predestination is from a moral and holy God. Fatalism denies a first cause; there is only an infinite regress of causes. But we affirm that God is the uncaused First Cause. Fatalism denies human responsibility, but we say predestination provides for it. Fatalism leads to skepticism; we say predestination leads to hope.

It is granted that the word *fate* is used in some translations of the Bible (e.g., the NASB of Ecclesiastes 2:14–15; 3:19; 9:2–3). The Hebrew term means "that which happens, an event, a future situation, destiny, destination." In Ecclesiastes, Solomon was speaking of the destiny of death which awaits all men. This is not fatalism, even when Solomon was morose. Rather, he faced the reality that 'it is appointed for men to die once' (Hebrews 9:27). Peter Martyr Vermigli said there is a slight similarity between fatalism and predestination, but since pagan ideas include astrology and exclude God, it is best not to use the word *fate*.[4] Augustine: "We say that nothing happens by fate — for the simple reason that the word "fate" means nothing."[5]

"Things just are."

Deists taught something like this objection. To them, even God is under this higher law. For example, some things are always morally right or wrong because of "the moral nature and fitness of things."[6] This is wrong thinking. There is no principle higher than God. He is the highest. His law is the ultimate canon of

determinism, see John Gill, *The Cause of God and Truth* (Grand Rapids: Baker Book House, 1980), 191–97.

3 Loraine Boettner, *The Reformed Doctrine of Predestination* (Philadelphia: Presbyterian and Reformed, 1932), 205.

4 Peter Martyr Vermigli, *The Peter Martyr Library* (Kirksville: MO: Truman State University Press, 2003), 8:9–10. So too Augustine, *The City of God*, 5:1; *The Fathers of the Church* (New York: Fathers of the Church, 1950), 8:241–42.

5 Augustine, *City of God*, 5:8; *Fathers of the Church*, 8:259.

6 John Gill refuted Deism on this point in *Sermons and Tracts* (Streamwood: Primitive Baptist Library, 1981), 3:463–90.

ethics, and it is based on His holy nature. Things are the way they are because God made them that way, not because they are self-existent. Only God "just is."

"Absolute predestination renders history meaningless."

G. C. Berkouwer[7] and some of his disciples (e.g., James Daane[8]) rejected the historic Reformed doctrine of the absolute decree of predestination and scorned it as "decretal theology."[9] They especially reacted adversely to the Hyper-Calvinist supralapsarian idea of "equal ultimacy" as taught by Herman Hoeksema, but also to the mainstream infralapsarian teaching. Perhaps Hoeksema did tilt the balance of sovereignty and human responsibility too much to the former, with the result that he gave more attention to eternity than to history. But he did not deny the significance of the time-based actions by either God or man. Mainline Calvinism keeps the balance better without swinging the pendulum over to Arminianism or Berkouwer's view. History has meaning precisely because of predestination. If there was no predestination, there would be no meaning, but only chance.

"Predestination is linear, but the universe is cyclical."

This misunderstands both eternity and time. True, predestination occurred "before time began" (2 Timothy 1:9) and "before the foundation of the world" (Ephesians 1:4). As Augustine pointed out, God created time. God existed before time and outside of time as well as fills all time. He is like the ocean that fills and surrounds a submerged cup (Cf. Acts 17:27–28). Berkouwer downplayed the "before" of election contrary to the historic Reformed view.[10] Many Arminians, especially Open Theists, deny that eternity is outside of time. They say that eternity is simply linear time extended into an endless future. We say that it is both endless linear time and infinite "eternal now" non-time. Since predestination is in eternity and not in time, we cannot fully grasp it, for we are time-bound in our thinking. But we dare not deny either eternity or predestination, for both are taught in Scripture.

The Bible does not present the cyclical view of time of Buddhism and

---

7 G. C. Berkouwer, *Divine Election* (Grand Rapids, Eerdmans, 1960).
8 James Daane, *The Freedom of God* (Grand Rapids, Eerdmans, 1973).
9 The rather leftwing theologians of the Christian Reformed Church in the 1970s tended to side with Berkouwer and Daane rather than traditional Calvinism on these points.
10 See Alvin L. Baker, *Berkouwer's Doctrine of Election* (Phillipsburg, NJ: P&R, 1981). On the Reformed doctrine of eternity from a philosophical perspective, see Paul Helm, *Eternal God*, 2nd ed. (Oxford: Oxford University Press, 2010).

Hinduism. Granted, history repeats itself in general patterns (e.g., Ecclesiastes 1:4–11), but that is not the same thing. The Eastern idea is cosmic reincarnation, whereas we deny reincarnation and say that God created the universe in six linear days and will recreate it in the future new heaven and new earth. Meanwhile, history is "His story," which He wrote in advance in predestination.

"God changes His mind."

This objection appeals to the Bible passages in which God is said to "repent" (Genesis 6:6–7; Exodus 32:14; Judges 2:18; 1 Samuel 15:11, 35; 2 Samuel 24:16; 1 Chronicles 21:15; Psalm 106:45; Jeremiah 26:19; Joel 2:13; Amos 7:3, 6; Jonah 3:9–10; 4:2). If He changes His mind, then predestination is not absolute but only tentative.

We reply that one Hebrew and one Greek word for *repent* means "grieve for." God grieved that man sinned (Genesis 6:6–7). In other places, it is spoken "after the manner of man" (Romans 6:19) in what linguists call *anthropopathy* — attributing human emotions to God in a figure of speech (Cf. anthropomorphism). Some of the above references may also refer only to God's give-and-take interaction with men in time rather than denying His eternal predestination. We must not confuse eternal principles with temporal dealings. Some suggest that this is like a battlefield commander who changes tactics while still following the overall strategy of his general. Not a perfect analogy. Better to say that even the appearance of changed tactics is part of the predestined strategy, perhaps like a planned bluff (Cf. Mark 6:48; Luke 24:28).

The above texts must be balanced with others that say, "God is not a man, that He should repent" (Numbers 23:19; 1 Samuel 15:29; Psalm 110:4; Hebrews 7:21). If God could change His mind on such things, what guarantee do we have that He will not repent of His promises as well? Will He revoke the new covenant? Can He decide to release unrepentant sinners from Hell and put them in Heaven or, conversely, throw the elect out of Heaven and into Hell? Arminians cannot consistently deny these possibilities, but Calvinists can.

The Jonah story is an example. The "repenting" does not refer to the eternal decree but to God's reply to the response of the Ninevites to His warning through Jonah. Calvin observed: "When the Lord sent Jonah to the Ninevites, he did not reveal what had been decreed in his secret purpose, but wished to arouse their minds by the preaching of Jonah, that he might have compassion on them."[11] All of this was in perfect accord with God's previous predestination.

The supposed dilemma can also be resolved by pointing out that there are two Greek words for *repent*. *Metamelomai* means to be grieved. *Metanoia* means to change one's mind and direction. Judas had the first (Matthew 27:3), Peter had the second (Luke 22:32; cf. 2 Corinthians 7:9–10). God grieves but does not change His mind or turn from His predestined plan.

"The universe is a game of cosmic chess."

This has occasionally been proposed by Arminians such as Jerry L. Walls and Joseph R. Dongell.[12] It suggests that God and Satan are the players, and humans are the chess pieces. The game has not ended, nor has the finish been predestined. But rest assured, God is a better chess player and will win. He is smarter and can predict how it will end. Besides, He made the first move, and any Grand Master knows that whoever has the first move has the odds in his favor. Also, Satan makes mistakes, but God does not. So says the theory.

This is a dangerous and unbiblical theory. It resembles the Greek gods on Mount Olympus, such as the Fates playing whimsical tricks on men. Worse, it resembles the cosmic dualism of Zoroastrianism, the religion of ancient Persia in which the white god of light and fire opposes the black god of darkness. It sounds like bitheistic polytheism. But, we add, Satan is not a god and certainly is not the equal opposite of God Almighty. God is eternal and infinite; Satan is neither. God predestined that He will win; Satan cannot win. This is not cheating, as the extreme Arminian theory suggests, but reveals the absolute perfection of God. And, as Luther was fond of saying, Satan is "God's Devil" under His ultimate control (Job 1–2).[13] The theory would also give an excuse to sinners: "The Devil made me do it," or worse, "God made me sin." It results in either antinomianism or blasphemy. If other unbiblical theories raise man to God's level, this wicked theory would elevate Satan himself to God's level. Never!

---

11 John Calvin, *Commentary on the Book of the Prophet Isaiah* (Grand Rapids: Eerdmans, 1958), 1:461.
12 Jerry L. Walls and Joseph R. Dongell, *Why I Am Not a Calvinist* (Downers Grove: IL: InterVarsity, 2004), 146; cf. the anonymous booklet *Cosmic Chess* (Burbank, CA: Youth Aflame, c. 1972).
13 I have been unable to find this oft-quoted term in Luther's works.

"History is a battle between God and Satan."

This theory resembles the "cosmic chess" scenario and has a slight basis in Scripture. It was popularized by the ultra-Arminian book, *God's Strategy in Human History,* by Roger T. Forster and V. Paul Marston.[14] They employ the biblical motif of spiritual warfare and allege that God will win because He is stronger and smarter. Unlike cosmic chess, humans are active participants in the battle. When they weaken, God "strengthens" them as He did Pharaoh.

But, the authors argue, the war is not over, and the end has not been predetermined: "There are [Calvinists] whose views amount to a belief that everything happens is God's direct will and the whole conflict is therefore a fake."[15] They admit that God knows the future and is above time, but they also posit that foreknowledge logically precedes foreordination — God destined the end of the conflict because He foresaw that He will win.

We reply that the Bible does indeed portray spiritual warfare between God and the Devil, but we add that the victory is settled in eternal predestination and guaranteed by the cross. Christ is the predestined Lamb slain from the foundation of the world (1 Peter 1:19–20), and His death and resurrection sealed Satan's defeat (Colossians 2:15; Hebrews 2:14; 1 John 3:8). Would Forster and Marston wish to say that the final victory has not been absolutely determined by the cross because we are still fighting? Moreover, if some sinners perish — as they admit — then the theory would have to say that God loses some battles to Satan. If in their scheme God wins all the battles, then the result is universal salvation, which they deny. They cannot have it both ways. Calvinism, however, says that God has predestined not only the final victory but also who will go to Heaven and who will go to Hell. God always wins.

"Predestination leaves no place for chance."

How true! This objection believes in chance rather than predestination. Some who charge Calvin with Stoicism would seem to favor Stoicism's rival, Epicureanism (Acts 17:18). If Stoicism said all is fate, Epicureanism said all is chance. This viewpoint underlies the error of evolution. Further, existentialists and nihilists see the implications. If all is due to chance, then there is no meaning to life nor morality nor hope. It can lead to madness or suicide. This

---

14 Roger T. Forster and V. Paul Marston, *God's Strategy in Human History* (Wheaton: Tyndale House, 1973). They briefly use the chess metaphor on p. 95.
15 Forster and Marston, 26.

vicious objection would kill predestination and the Predestinator, if it could, and replace it with luck, fortune, accidents, and coincidences.

There are pseudo-Christian forms of this objection. They point to verses which contain the word *chance* in some translations, such as 1 Samuel 6:9; 2 Samuel 1:6; Ecclesiastes 9:11; 1 Kings 22:34; and Luke 10:31. History is "open," some contend, and that makes life exciting. God Himself takes risks — and sometimes fails. That makes victories all the more valuable. This is behind the *Risk Theology* that spun off from Open Theism.[16]

We deny that any of this is biblical. The word *chance* in the above texts only refers to events unforeseen by men, not by God. Luke 10:21 uses the Greek word *sunkuria*, literally, "to happen together." A coincidence is not the result of sheer chance but is what happens when two events coincide. Their paths cross; they happen at the same time and place, perhaps not planned by men but definitely planned by God. Indeed, such events illustrate how God carries out predestination by providence.

The notion of chance leads to superstition. Men gullibly believe in good and bad luck. It is often associated with astrology and sometimes gambling. But Calvinists never say, "Good luck" but rather "God bless you." They do not say "If I'm lucky, then XYZ will happen" but rather "If the Lord wills" (James 4:15). Christians should not play "games of chance" for money. It implies a denial of divine sovereignty. Gambling is not only selfish and superstitious but also blasphemous.

Reformed Christians remember Proverbs 16:33: "The lot is cast into the lap, but its every decision is from the Lord." God predestined and controls the outcome of dice, as in Jonah 1:7, Acts 1:24–26, and elsewhere. Curiously, the Arminian John Wesley approved casting lots for guidance, but the Calvinist George Whitefield did not, for it presumes upon God.[17] The only possible legitimate use of lots today might be for the distribution of an inheritance, as in Numbers 26:55. Even so, that assumes divine sovereignty, not chance, does it not?

R. C. Sproul wrote a book entitled *Not a Chance*.[18] Calvin said, "What are thought to be chance occurrences are just so many proofs of heavenly

---

16 John Piper has some good points on this in *The Pleasures of God* (Portland: Multnomah, 1991), 53–58.

17 Cf. Arnold Dallimore, *George Whitefield* (Edinburgh: Banner of Truth, 1980), 2:56–57, 553–54.

18 Grand Rapids: Baker, 1994. See also Vern S. Poythress, *Chance and the Sovereignty of God* (Wheaton: Crossway, 2014).

providence."[19] Luther wrote: "But if God is thus robbed of His power and wisdom in election, what would He be but just that idol, Chance, under whose sway all things happen at random?"[20] If Chance is God, worship him. If the Lord is God, worship Him (Cf. 1 Kings 18:21). Chance is not a god but a satanic idol. God does not believe in chance and neither do Calvinists. Nothing comes to pass by chance, for what is chance to man is choice with God. Augustus Montague Toplady wrote:

> Was I, therefore, to be concerned in drawing up an expurgatory index to language, I would, without mercy, cashier and proscribe such words as chance, fortune, luck, casualty, contingency and mishap. For they are *voces et praetera nihil*. Mere terms without ideas. Absolute expletives which import nothing. Unmeaning cyphers, either proudly invented to hide man's ignorance of real causes, or sacrilegiously designed to rob the Deity of the honours due to His wisdom, providence and power.[21]

Miscellaneous Objections

"Predestination is not democratic." That's right, it's not. God is a king, not a president. We must not impose our political ideals on God.

"But my church does not believe in predestination." Then your church needs to reread the Bible and change its position.

"It won't preach." If it is in the Bible, it can and should be preached. Read Acts 20:27. Jesus, the prophets, and the apostles preached it. So should we.

"It's not practical." The real question should be "Is it biblical?" If it is biblical, then it is practical, for Bible doctrine is the foundation for practical Christian living (2 Timothy 3:16–17). We will later see the practical applications of election and other doctrines of grace.

"I just don't like it." John Blanchard, the Calvinist evangelist, gives this reply: "The obvious answer to those who say they do not like the idea of predestination is that God does."[22]

"It sounds too deep for me." Then study it more. Move from the shallow end

---

19 John Calvin, *Institutes of the Christian Religion* (Philadelphia: Westminster, 1960), 1:4:8 (p. 60).
20 Martin Luther, *The Bondage of the Will* (Grand Rapids: Fleming H. Revell, 2005), 199.
21 Augustus Montague Toplady, preface to *The Doctrine of Absolute Predestination*, by Jerome Zanchius (Grand Rapids: Baker, 1977), 21.
22 John Blanchard, *Sifted Silver* (Darlington: Evangelical Press, 1995), 245.

of the kiddie pool and swim into the depths of good biblical theology. Its depth should cause awe, not abhorrence.

"It's a great idea, but of course, men can overrule it by free will." Some appeal to Luke 7:30: "But the Pharisees and lawyers rejected the will (*boule*, counsel) of God for themselves." They mistakenly think that our free will can thwart divine sovereignty. They thus side with the unbelieving Pharisees in this verse. One can resist but not overthrow predestination, any more than the pagan king could halt the waves of the sea by commanding them to stop.

"Well, nobody can know the truth on these things." We can know because God has told us the truth in Scripture. He has not told us everything, but what He has told us is sufficient.

Conclusion

Other objections will be covered in later chapters. At root, they are all wrong because the Bible emphatically, explicitly, and repeatedly teaches predestination. Luther wryly observed: "All objections to predestination proceed from the wisdom of the flesh."[23] They are not theoretical philosophical objections but sinful rebellions against the sovereign God. God's predestination stands firm.

---

23 Quoted in John Blanchard, *Gathered Gold* (Welwyn: Evangelical Press, 1984), 246.

Chapter 23
Foreknowledge

During the Watergate hearings in the 1970s, one question kept coming up: "What did you know, and when did you know it?" If we ask this of God, the answer would be: "Everything, and from eternity." This leads to another question: What is the relation between foreordination and foreknowledge? This has direct bearing on the Reformed view of the absolute sovereignty of God.[1]

The Omniscience of God

The Bible repeatedly and expressly teaches the omniscience of God. It may be defined as "that perfection of God whereby He, in an entirely unique manner, knows Himself and all things possible and actual in one eternal and most simple act."[2] Observe the following: "The Lord is the God of knowledge" (1 Samuel 2:3). "God [. . .] knows all things" (1 John 3:20). "You know all things" (John 16:30; 21:17). God is "perfect in knowledge" (Job 36:4; 37:16). God knows all our thoughts (1 Chronicles 28:9; Jeremiah 17:10; Hebrews 4:13). Jesus knew what was in all men (John 2:24–25). God knows our secrets (Psalm 90:8; Romans 2:16). He says, "I know the things that come into your mind" (Ezekiel 11:5). David realized that God knew all about him and confessed, "Such knowledge is too wonderful for me; it is high, I cannot attain it" (Psalm 139:6; cf. vv. 1–5). Psalm 147:5 is especially explicit: "His understanding is infinite."

God knows everything past, present, and future, even things which could be but never will be (Matthew 11:21–23; Isaiah 48:18; 2 Kings 13:19). He knows how much a stack of leaves in front of the White House would have weighed if one more leaf fell that did not fall on such-and-such a date. God knows all the details and the relationships between them. He knows immediately and intuitively without research, observation, or syllogizing. God *knows*. What is more, He knows that He knows, and knows that He knows that He knows, and so on eternally.

---

1 I discussed this subject in an article entitled "Beyond Knowledge" in *Tabletalk*, January 2000, pp. 14–15, 58.
2 Louis Berkhof, *Systematic Theology* (Grand Rapids, Eerdmans, 1988), 66.

Absolute Foreknowledge

God never changes. If, then, He now knows all things, then it follows that He has always known all things. We cannot grasp this combination of infinity and eternity. Some theologians use the terms *prescience* (pre-science) and *foresight* as synonyms for foreknowledge. The word *foreknowledge* can be causal (Acts 2:23) or affectionate (Romans 8:29; 1 Peter 1:2), but in this chapter we are discussing foreknowledge as advance omniscience. God sees all now and foresees all beforehand (e.g., Galatians 3:8). God knows what we need before we pray, and He knows what He will give us (Matthew 6:8). Jesus knew that Judas would betray Him (John 6:64).

God has eternal foreknowledge. As Gordon H. Clark noted, "God neither learns nor forgets."[3] God is certain about the future because He has made the future itself to be certain. God never guesses.

This is shown repeatedly in the prophecies of future events. God foretold that something would happen, and it did — always. God never made a false prediction, unlike gamblers and weathermen. He predicted specific things that were at that time unimaginable to the Jews. For example, crucifixion had not even been invented when God foretold that the Messiah would be crucified (Psalm 22:16). These hundreds of prophecies prove that the Lord is God and is different from the non-God idols (Isaiah 40–48, e.g., 41:22–23, 26; 42:9; 44:7–8; 45:21; 48:5–6). He declares the end from the beginning (Isaiah 46:10). "Known to God from eternity are all His works" (Acts 15:18). If God did not know the future, He would not be omniscient and therefore not God. But He does, and He is. His perfect knowledge proves who He is. This also proves the deity of Jesus Christ (John 13:19). Angels are not omniscient (1 Peter 1:12). Satan knows he will go to Hell (Revelation 12:12), as do the demons (Matthew 8:29), but they too are not omniscient. Only an infinite God could be omniscient. It is an incommunicable attribute of God. Even the redeemed elect will never be omniscient in eternal Heaven.

Foreordination and Foreknowledge

In the previous two chapters I showed that God eternally foreordained everything that will ever come to pass in time. He also eternally foreknew everything. But which is logically prior? The answer is explained in the Westminster Confession:

---

3 Gordon H. Clark, *Predestination* (Phillipsburg, NJ: P&R, 1987), 38.

Although God knows whatsoever may or can come to pass upon all supposed conditions, yet hath he not decreed any thing because he foreknew it as future, or as that which would come about upon such conditions (3:2. Paragraph 5 applies this to election.)

God knew that things would most definitely happen. But whence this definiteness? Because He had already predestined them. Things do not just happen. They happen because God foreordained that they would happen. God did not look down the corridors of time and see that something would happen, and then because of that knowledge foreordain it to happen. That would reverse the cause and effect and make future events to be God's teachers. But Scripture says that God predestines on the basis of His own will and counsel (Ephesians 1:11). No one counsels God.

The logical order, then, is that foreordination proceeds foreknowledge. This is not at all to say that there was a time gap between the two or even a sequential order. The order is logical, not chronological. They are so close and inseparable that the word *foreknow* is sometimes used in a causative rather than a cognitive way, as in Acts 2:23. First Peter 1:20 says that Christ was "foreordained before the foundation of the world," and the word is literally *foreknown*. God did not merely foresee the crucifixion — He predestined it (Acts 4:27–28; Luke 22:22).

Dave Hunt, who hunts out Calvinism in several pop theology books, misunderstands Calvinism on this point.[4] He sets up and destroys a straw man. He wrongly thinks that Calvinism denies perfect omniscience and foreknowledge, for he mistakenly thinks we say that God did not know the future until He foreordained it, and therefore God had not foreknown it already. Quite wrong. We say that God's foreordination and foreknowledge were from eternity and not in time. There never was a time when God did not know what He foreordained would be or what He would do.

Middle Knowledge

There are two erroneous theories that seek to evade the absolute foreknowledge and omniscience of God. One can, but does not always, lead to the other. The first is the theory of Middle Knowledge (Latin, *scientia media*). The roots go back to a few Greek philosophers, but it was more precisely formulated by a Jesuit theologian named Luis de Molina (1535–1600).[5] The theory is sometimes

---

4 Dave Hunt, *What Love Is This?* 3rd ed., (Bend, OR: The Berean Call, 2006), 182, 282–83.
5 See his *On Divine Foreknowledge*, ed. Alfred J. Freddoso (Ithaca: Cornell University Press, 1988).

called *Molinism*. He formed his theory to oppose the prevalent orthodox view of Thomas Aquinas and the Dominicans, which was also held by the Protestant Reformers. The Arminians and some Lutherans came to accept a form of it. William Lane Craig is the most well-known proponent of it in recent years.[6] The otherwise forthright Calvinist Bruce Ware has propounded what he considers a kind of Calvinistic Middle Knowledge,[7] a novel theory that has not found acceptance with Reformed theologians.

It can be defined as follows: "a category in the divine knowing according to which God has a conditional or consequent, rather than an absolute and antecedent, foreknowledge of future events."[8] It implies that some things are outside the absolute will or predestination of God. Calvinists deny that anything is outside of God's ultimate will or predestination. Louis Berkhof pinpoints its fundamental error: "It is objectionable, because it makes the divine knowledge dependent on the choice of man, virtually annuls the certainty of the knowledge of future events, and thus explicitly denies the omniscience of God."[9] To put it another way, it denies both absolute foreordination and absolute foreknowledge. It answers the question of the relationship between the two by severely modifying both. Some solution! That would be like trying to resolve the question of the two natures of Christ by making Christ a half God and a half man. But Christ is fully both, and God's foreordination and foreknowledge are both complete and absolute, not partial or relative.

Reformed theologians sometimes add that God knows all possibilities and conditions but knows nothing conditionally. He never says, "Let's wait and see," or "That depends."

The theory of Middle Knowledge misinterprets and misapplies the verses mentioned above. It fails to answer the obvious question, "Where did those alternative possibilities come from anyway?" It assumes "They just are, that's all." It is like the Deist view that "things just are" or the Positivist idea that "the

---

6 William Lane Craig, *The Only Wise God* (Grand Rapids: Baker, 1987). See also Kenneth Keathley, *Salvation and Sovereignty: A Molinist Approach* (Nashville: B&H, 2010) and Kirk R. MacGregor, *A Molinist-Anabaptist Systematic Theology* (Lanham: University of America Press, 2007).

7 "A Modified Calvinist Doctrine of God," in Bruce A. Ware, ed. *Perspectives on the Doctrine of God: Four Views* (Wheaton: Crossway, 2004), 76–120. Paul Helm's response (pp. 121–29) is from the traditional Reformed perspective but uses more philosophical arguments. Alvin Plantinga also proposes a semi-Reformed view of Middle Knowledge.

8 Richard A. Muller, *Dictionary of Latin and Greek Theological Terms, Drawn Principally from Protestant Scholastic Theology*, 2nd ed. (Grand Rapids: Baker Academic, 2017), 326.

9 Berkhof, *Systematic Theology*, 68.

laws of science just exist of themselves and could not have been otherwise." Molinism supposes those possibilities are outside the predestination of God, though not outside of His omniscience. But this is all wrong. God predetermined everything potential as well as actual. He predetermined the theoretical existence of possibilities that will never happen, otherwise they could not have even been possible. These so-called counter-factuals are not "just there," but created by God. They are not uncaused "free acts of men" that are outside the causal dominion of God, for God predestined all our thoughts and actions.

Some advocates of Middle Knowledge apply it to the problem of the destiny of those who never hear the gospel.[10] They argue that all the unevangelized die lost and go to Hell, for God knew by Middle Knowledge that none of them would have believed even if they had heard the gospel. Others turn it around and suggest that some who never hear the gospel are saved, for God knows by Middle Knowledge that they would have believed if they had heard. But this flies square in the face of Matthew 11:21–23. The point that Christ made there was that some persons would have believed had they seen miracles. Why then did God not send miracles to them? Because He did not choose to save them. (I will discuss this later in chapter 51, "The Destiny of the Unevangelized.")

Open Theism

Reformed theology has been the strongest opponent of a theological fad that arose in the 1980s, hit a peak around 2000, and dwindled away thereafter. It is called *Open Theism* or the Openness of God. Actually, it was taught in a similar fashion by Aristotle, Cicero, Marcion, and Origen many centuries ago then was revived by the heretical Socinians at the time of the Reformation. Another form was developed in the Process Theology of Alfred North Whitehead and Charles Hartshorne in the twentieth century.

The theory says that God is in the process of growing in His being and knowledge, therefore God does not have omniscience or perfect foreknowledge. This was a strange but consistent application of the theory of evolution — even God is evolving. In the 1980s, certain extreme Arminians expanded on the theory of Middle Knowledge. Richard Rice, an erstwhile Seventh-Day Adventist, wrote *The Openness of God*, later retitled *God's Foreknowledge and*

---

10 So Donald N. Lake, "He Died for All: The Universal Dimension of the Atonement." In Clark H. Pinnock, ed., *Grace Unlimited* (Minneapolis: Bethany House, 1975), 43; Craig, *The Only Wise God*, 150–51.

Man's Free Will. Clark Pinnock, who claimed to have once been a Calvinist but became an emphatic Arminian, wrote an essay entitled "God Limits His Knowledge."[11] Others followed: Gregory Boyd, John Sanders, David Basinger, William Hasker, and others.

Slightly more moderate Arminians admit to being friendly with Open Theism and do not consider it to be heresy, such as the popular defender of Arminianism Roger Olson.[12] Historic Calvinists took the lead in opposing it as heresy, such as Bruce Ware, Robert Morey, John Frame, Paul Helm, Michael Horton, James White, Justin Taylor, Wayne Grudem, John Piper, and John Feinberg.[13] I do not know of a single Calvinist of any stripe that holds to Open Theism. Open Theists are all Arminians or former Arminians. To be fair, I add that not all Arminians accept this heresy. Many such as Norman Geisler strongly oppose it (Geisler's admitted acceptance of Thomism would set him against the rival school of the Jesuit Molina).

The nineteenth-century Calvinist William Plumer said that the Arminian theologian Adam Clarke taught that just as God does not do all He is able to do, so He does not know all that He is able to know.[14] God willingly chose not to know some things. Certain medieval theologians with Semi-Pelagian tendencies seemed to have taught that God does all that is possible — that is why things are the way they are. They could not have been otherwise, for this is the best of all possible worlds, and there are no undeveloped "potentialities" in God. This was not the same as the Augustinian-Reformed view that, in some sense, God could not have foreordained things differently, as we previously explained.

Fortunately, few Open Theists have used the faulty argument that denies that God has perfect foreknowledge because Christ does not know the date of His Second Coming (Mark 13:32). Jehovah's Witnesses use this to deny the deity of Christ. On a popular level, the orthodox say, "Christ is God" and that He reveals God perfectly, while Karl Barth's Christomonism reverses it and says

---

11 In David and Randall Basinger, eds., *Predestination & Free Will* (Downers Grove, IL: InterVarsity, 1986), 141–62.

12 Roger Olson, *Arminian Theology* (Downers Grove, IL: InterVarsity, 2006), 198–99. So too Joseph Dongell in Jerry L. Walls and Joseph R. Dongell, *Why I Am Not a Calvinist* (Downers Grove, IL: InterVarsity, 2004), 45, 144; and several authors in Clark H. Pinnock, ed., *The Grace of God, The Will of Man* (Grand Rapids: Zondervan, 1989).

13 See bibliography.

14 William Plumer, *Commentary on Romans* (Grand Rapids: Kregel, 1971), 433. I have been unable to find where Clarke discusses this, and Plumer does not document his statement.

something like "God is like Christ." That might imply non-omniscience if not for the fact that Christ had both a divine and human nature. Barth certainly did not accept Open Theism. Jesus Himself said that the Father knows the date of the Second Coming. Christ did not know in His humanity; but in His deity, He did know. (I will touch on this later in chapter 64, "The Two Natures of Christ.")

Open Theism claims to protect the free will of man by saying that God not only does not (or cannot) interfere with the "free acts of men," but He cannot even foreknow them. Those acts are not yet certain until men do them. Therefore, even God cannot know certainly what is not yet certain. This is supposed to be profound, but it is all wrong and strikes at the very nature of God Almighty. The truth is, God foreordained whatever comes to pass and therefore knows with certainty what He has foreordained and what will definitely happen. God knows what He is doing and what He will do.

The theory ignores or twists predictive prophecy by reducing it to mere guesswork — ah, but God is a good guesser, they say. Some even imply that God has sometimes guessed wrong. Some compound their blasphemy (and blasphemy it is) by saying that God "repented" of losing His temper in flooding the world. The whole system is unworthy of the name *theology*. It is mythology. It is Neo-Socinianism. The god of Open Theism is not the God of the Bible.

Conclusion

Calvinism teaches full omniscience and foreknowledge. It alone properly explains the relationship between foreordination and foreknowledge. Rather than tampering with God's truth on the matter, we should humbly bow before His Majesty and confess, "Lord, You know all things" (John 16:30).

Chapter 24
Providence

Who is in charge? God. God rules and guides the entire universe by His invisible hand. We call this the providence of God. The English word *providence* comes from two Latin words that mean "to see over." God is the Overseer of all things. But He not only sees all but guides all. He steers all things to bless His people (Romans 8:28). The sovereign God carries out all the details of His predestination through providence, and without predestination there could be no providence. He planned the work and then worked the plan.

God Provides for the Universe

God alone created the universe (Genesis 1:1), and He alone sustains it. The Creator cares for His creation. He provides all it needs. Hebrews 1:3 says that God upholds all things by the Word of His power (and the power of His Word). He preserves the cosmos. He keeps it in existence. Jonathan Edwards and others erroneously believed in continuous creation — that God creates the universe afresh each moment. Most Reformed theologians believe rather that God ceased creating after day six (Genesis 2:1) and thereafter continues His work in providence (Cf. John 5:17).

He is actively involved in everything. God is not like a clockmaker who winds up the clock and lets it keep time without His interference. That was the error of Deism. God keeps the springs going every second and occasionally interferes with miracles.

God is a God of order, not of confusion (1 Corinthians 14:33). The usual Greek word for *world* is *kosmos*. It is order, not chaos. Colossians 1:17: "In Him all things consist" or hold together. Otherwise it would be chaos, not cosmos. It would be an anarchic multiverse rather than an ordered universe. God is the unifying factor. He uses the laws of science that He created to do this.

God Cares for His Creation

Our Creator has an interest in all life, including the animals. Acts 17:25: "He gives to all life, breath, and all things." Psalm 36:6: "Oh Lord, You preserve man and beast." Nehemiah 9:6: "You preserve them all." Note the present tense in these verses. God feeds the animals (Matthew 6:26; Psalms 104:27; 147:9; Job 39). They are His pets. The animal kingdom is God's menagerie. The garden of Eden was a peaceable walkabout zoo. Robert Murray M'Cheyne once said, "God reigns in a community of ants and ichneumons, as visibly as among living men or mighty seraphim!"[1]

Scripture is replete with examples of how God cares for the waters, trees, mountains, stars, animals, planets, and even the weather. Joseph Hall described it in a lovely way: "Every herb, flower, spire of grass, every twig and leaf, every worm and fly, every scale and feather, every billow and meteor speaks the power and wisdom of their infinite Creator."[2] Jonathan Edwards often meditated on the glory of God in providence as he viewed nature moving and growing.

Take the subject of weather. The Bible does not just say, "It rains." It says that God sends the rain (Matthew 5:45; Psalm 65:10; Job 38:26). It rains because God reigns. It is too bad that weathermen do not acknowledge God in their reports. They prefer to speak of Mother Nature rather than Father God. God uses the rain as part of the water cycle (Ecclesiastes 1:7; Job 36:27–29; 37:11–12). God sometimes withholds rain (James 5:17–18). Christians may pray for rain (or that it would stop) but must never complain about the weather, for that would be to disagree with the wise providence of God. Mark Twain allegedly said, "Everyone talks about the weather but nobody does anything about it." Christians should do something — praise God for it.

Take also lightning and thunder. God controls those as well (Job 36:30–37:5). Parents sometimes calm their frightened children by saying nonsense like, "The clouds are talking to each other," or "The angels are bowling." Rather, they should explain that God is speaking in a non-verbal way to remind us of His power, wrath, and wisdom (Job 36:33; 37:2, 4). God guides every one of the billions of raindrops in each rainfall. He governs the flow of the clouds (Job 37:12–16), sets the thermostat of the temperature, sends ice and snow (Job 37:6–10; 38:22, 29–30), and shows His wisdom and artistry in each and every snowflake, no two being alike. God guides both the rising and the setting of the sun, for He keeps the earth turning every day (Matthew 5:45; Psalm 104:22; Job 38:12). He keeps the world circling the sun and sends rainbows to remind us of His faithfulness (Genesis 8:22; 9:13–16).

---

1 Andrew Bonar, *Memoir and Remains of Robert Murray M'Cheyne* (Edinburgh: Banner of Truth, 1978), 35.

2 Quoted in Philip Benedict, *Christ's Churches Purely Reformed* (New Haven: Yale University Press, 2002), 326.

God takes a special concern for mankind, the crown of creation. He feeds us (Psalm 136:25), heals us (Psalm 103:3), provides pleasure for us (Acts 14:17). John Calvin put it well: "God, effectively, by his own secret power, feeds man, and he does so in accordance with his providence, so that man's life depends entirely on that and not on food and drink."[3] It is God, not autonomous nutrition in food, that gives and sustains life (Acts 17:25). We should thank God for food (1 Timothy 4:3), but we usually do not (Romans 1:21). Every day should be Thanksgiving Day in acknowledgment of the provision of divine providence.

The Laws of Creation

God created the laws of science and uses them in His normal daily providence. He created mathematics, chemistry, physics, astronomy, biology, and zoology and all their laws and principles. If there was no God or providence, there could be no science, only random chaos. God created gravity, light, energy, thermodynamics, quantum physics, and all the rest. They are not self-existent laws but expressions of the hand of God. Scientists above all others should be the first to acknowledge and praise God, but sadly, many question even God's very existence.

Yet many of the great scientists in history have rightly acknowledged the Creator and Provider of all and expressly stated that God is the foundation of all science (Isaac Newton, Blaise Pascal, James Clerk Maxwell, Michael Faraday, et al). Pagan cultures that are pantheist tend to ignore science, and polytheistic cultures have tended to lag behind Western semi-Christian culture because they see nature in chaos because of the conflicting actions of rival gods and goddesses.

Calvinism notes the fixed order of things (Jeremiah 31:35). God sets the limits and boundaries (Psalm 104:9; Acts 17:26). Only on this basis can the scientific method truly operate. When scientists do not acknowledge God, they worship the creation rather than the Creator (Romans 1:25). They show their blind foolishness by pretending things happen by fate or chance (Acts 17:18).

The point is just this: Only an absolutely sovereign God could rule the whole universe. If there was a single autonomous "rogue molecule" in the universe that is outside of God's dominion, we could not employ science or know that

---

3 John Calvin, *The Bondage and Liberation of the Will* (Grand Rapids: Baker, 1996), 33. God is the "secret cultivator" of all things. *Commentary on the Book of Psalms* (Grand Rapids: Eerdmans, 1949), 4:154.

God is Lord.[4] But God sovereignly controls the entire creation, from the largest galaxies to the smallest subatomic particles. He both macromanages and micromanages everything. He controls the big picture and all the tiny interacting details. Calvin said God guides everything "by the bridle of his providence."[5] There are no stray horses in God's herd.

Causality and Concurrence

God is the uncaused First Cause, but He created and uses second causes, third causes, and so forth. The universe is a vast network of means and ends through the created principle of cause and effect. God uses them all. We sing, "This is My Father's World." The Canons of Dort stated: "The almighty operation of God, whereby he prolongs and supports our natural life, does not exclude, but requires, the use of means, by which God of his infinite mercy and goodness hath chosen to exert his influence" (3/4:17). In its grand statement on divine foreordination, the Westminster Confession says, "Nor is the liberty or contingency of second causes taken away, but rather established" (3:1; cf. 5:2).

Every *thing* in creation is a second cause, including the laws of science. To use a popular illustration, God is the master pool player who uses all the balls on the billiard table. The invisible momentum that carries from one ball to another is the secret hand of God. God Himself is the power of the universe. Samuel Rutherford observed that "God's providence has a secret impulse upon all the creatures."[6] Calvin said, "God is leading his creatures in a way we cannot comprehend,"[7] and "God has a strange way of governing the world."[8] It is particularly observable but not ultimately comprehensible. But it is undeniable.

On the one hand, we Calvinists reject Deism's error that says God never interferes, for He is absent. No, we say that God is present everywhere and does interfere (Acts 17:27). On the other hand, we also reject pantheism's claim that God is everything. No, the Creator is not the creation (Romans 1:25). Using the Lutheran formula of Communion, we say that God operates "in, with and under" all things (Acts 17:28). We call this *concurrence*, as Louis Berkhof explains: "Concurrence may be defined as the cooperation of the divine power with all subordinate powers, according to the pre-established laws of operation, causing

---

4 Thanks to R. C. Sproul for popularizing this nice way of putting it.

5 John Calvin, *Institutes of the Christian Religion* (Philadelphia: Westminster, 1960), 1:16:9 (p. 209).

6 Samuel Rutherford, *Fourteen Communion Sermons* (Edinburgh: James Dickson, 1986), 32.

7 John Calvin, *Sermons on Genesis 1:11–11:4* (Edinburgh: Banner of Truth, 2009), 632.

8 Calvin, 709; cf. 827.

them to act and to act precisely as they do."[9] Some use the word *confluence*. We do not mean that God concurs in the sense of agreeing to go along with nature and man. Rather, God acts, and we react. He is the Great Initiator (Cf. 1 John 4:19).

The weakened Arminian view of divine sovereignty has trouble explaining providence, but Reformed theology does not. No one has a higher view of providence than the Calvinist. And though God is the absolute sovereign of providence, He is also the benevolent king of creation. Peter Martyr Vermigli noted, "His government is not tyrannical, but quiet, gentle and fatherly."[10] At the end of the day, we cannot grasp it all, so we must bow in reverent awe and sing with William Cowper, the Calvinist hymn writer, "God works in a mysterious way, His wonders to perform."

Ordinary and Extraordinary Providence

Ordinary providence is the usual way God governs creation through the laws of nature and science. He is at work in all things (Romans 8:28). Ephesians 1:11 says He "works all things according to the counsel of His will." Jesus said, "My Father has been working until now, and I have been working" (John 5:17), which applies to all providence and not just to the miracles they performed together. God rested on the seventh day (Genesis 2:2) but continues in the work of providence (note the context of John 5:17).

As King, "He sends out His command to the earth" (Psalm 147:15), and it always obeys. Creation never sins. Animals never disobey God nor does even the smallest atom. "His kingdom rules over all" (Psalm 103:19). He governs all nations (Job 12:23; Psalm 66:7) and has a special care for His people (Psalm 22:28; Romans 8:28). God even rules in the disobedience of men — sin does not counteract divine providence but is part of it, though man and not God is to blame.[11] God raises up some humans to power and brings others down (Psalm 75:7; 1 Samuel 2:7; Daniel 2:21; Luke 1:52).

There is also extraordinary or special providence. This is His unusual, not usual, way of governing the world. This is when God works miracles. The supernatural hand of God invades the natural realm and supersedes the laws of

---

9 Louis Berkhof, *Systematic Theology* (Grand Rapids: Eerdmans, 1988), 171.
10 Peter Martyr Vermigli, *The Peter Martyr Library* (Kirksville, MO: Truman State University Press, 2003), 8:18.
11 I will discuss this in chapter 30, "The Problem of Evil."

nature. By their very nature miracles are rare. It is inappropriate hyperbole to say, "Everything is a miracle." If everything is a miracle, nothing is a miracle.

Miracles are not undiscovered laws of nature, as some suggest, or chance or blips in the scheme of things. They are supernatural works of God. Only God can perform miracles. They prove that He is God. Jesus worked miracles to prove His deity (John 20:30–31).

God expends no more extra energy in miracles than in ordinary providence. Having infinite power, all things are equally easy to Him. He is never tired or weary (Isaiah 40:28). Historic Reformed theology has a high view of miracles second to none. But non-Reformed theologies sometimes have difficulty explaining how a supposedly limited sovereign can work miracles.

Providence with Purpose

God has an ultimate purpose in providence as well as proximate purposes (Ecclesiastes 3:1, 17). This includes death (Hebrews 9:27; Matthew 10:29). He overrules the sinful deeds of men for higher purposes (Genesis 41:32; 45:8; 50:20). Calvinists can especially take comfort from Romans 8:28. And it all gets back to the absolute sovereignty of God who carries out His eternal predestination. Augustus Montague Toplady deserves to be quoted:

> Providence, in time, is the hand that delivers God's purpose to those beings and events with which that purpose was pregnant from everlasting. [. . .] God's sovereign will is the first link, His unalterable decree is the second, and His all-active providence is the third in the grand chain of causes. [. . .] His will was the adorable spring of all, His decree marked out the channel, and His providence directs the stream.[12]

Conclusion

The Puritan John Flavel wrote a delightful book entitled *The Mystery of Providence*. We should worship God as we read the book of providence around us.[13] The Heidelberg Catechism gives us useful applications:

> What does it profit us to know that God has created and by His providence still upholds all things? We may be patient in adversity, thankful in prosperity, and for what is future have good confidence in our

---

12 Augustus Montague Toplady, preface to *The Doctrine of Absolute Predestination*, by Jerome Zanchius (Grand Rapids: Baker, 1977), 23.
13 But beware of misreading providence by divination!

faithful God and Father that no creature shall separate us from His love, since all creatures are so in His hand that without His will they cannot so much as move (Q. 28).

Amen.

Chapter 25
The Will of God

One cannot understand various theologies without grasping their dichotomies of certain doctrines. With historic Lutherans, it is the difference between law and gospel. For classic Pentecostals, it is salvation and Spirit-baptism as two separate experiences. With Reformed theology there are two. The first is divine sovereignty and human responsibility. The second is like unto it: the twofold will of God. The usual terms are the *secret will* and the *revealed will*. We often refer to Deuteronomy 29:29: "The secret things belong to the Lord our God, but those things which are revealed belong to us and our children forever, that we may do all the words of this law."

The Secret Will

The secret will is God's sovereign purpose of unconditional predestination. It is His eternal decree that foreordains whatever comes to pass in history. John Owen defined it like this: "The secret will of God is his eternal, unchangeable purpose concerning all things which he hath made, to be brought by certain means to their appointed ends."[1] It is secret in that God has not revealed to us all the details. We must not pry into what God has not revealed, as Calvin often warned.[2] Francis Turretin said, "It is called a secret will, not because always concealed from us and never revealed (for frequently God in his word manifests to men certain secrets of his counsel and lays them bare by the event), but because they remain hidden in God (until he reveals them by some sign, as by prophecy, or by the event)."[3]

This will is always carried out, for it is enforced and confirmed by divine omnipotence. It is not like the "Four Spiritual Laws" that can be frustrated. It always comes to pass, period. Jerome Zanchius observed: "God's will is nothing else than God Himself willing; consequently it is omnipotent and

---

1 John Owen, *The Works of John Owen* (London: Banner of Truth, 1967), 10:45.
2 He added the reason why: "Certainly God has no intention of hiding anything from us, except what was superfluous for us to know or too abstruse for our powers of comprehension." *Concerning Scandals* (Grand Rapids: Eerdmans, 1975), 53.
3 Francis Turretin, *Institutes of Elenctic Theology* (Phillipsburg, NJ: P&R, 1992), 1:225.

unfrustratable."[4] It is unconditional upon man, for God fulfills all conditions by His sovereign power in providence. It is not merely a good idea. Among other reasons, this is why mainline Calvinists reject the hypothetical universalism of Moyse Amyraut who postulated that some decrees are contingent rather than absolute. Somewhat related to this is the dichotomy of antecedent and consequent wills as posited by some medieval theologians and a few Reformed theologians.

If we ask why God chose to will what He willed in the secret will, Luther gave a good answer: "What God wills is not right because He ought, or was bound, so to will; on the contrary, what takes place must be right, because He so wills it."[5] This accords well with Reformed acceptance of ordained power rather than absolute power.

Reformed theologians sometimes differentiate two aspects to this will. In the positive or active aspect, God foreordained good. In the negative or passive aspect, He foreordained evil. Some, such as Calvin, rejected this distinction because *permission* sounds too passive, whereas God is always active (Cf. the doctrine of *actus purus*, pure actuality or activity). On the other hand, others think that it implies that God approves of sin and is thereby the author of sin. But with these provisos, mainline Reformed theology holds this bifurcation to maintain God's sovereignty in the absolute will of foreordination without God being the author or approver of sin.[6]

A fine distinction was debated in the Middle Ages. Does God will and do all that He is able to will and do? Some said yes, otherwise there is an inconsistency in God. They said there is no leftover remnant of unaccomplished potential in God. This was sometimes associated with a form of Semi-Pelagianism, such as in the case of Peter Abelard. Others, followed by the Reformers and subsequent Calvinists, countered that God did not actuate all that He is capable of willing, for those possibilities are infinite in the divine mind, but actualized reality is finite. This also relates to the question of absolute versus ordained power. It likewise touches on the relation between God's willing and working and decreeing and doing (Cf. Philippians 2:13; Psalm 135:6). Remigius of Lyons defended Gottschalk and summed up their position: "God does all things that he will, and what he does not, he wills not."[7]

---

4 Jerome Zanchius, *The Doctrine of Absolute Predestination* (Grand Rapids: Baker, 1977), 49.

5 Martin Luther, *The Bondage of the Will* (Grand Rapids: Fleming H. Revell, 2005), 209.

6 E.g., Westminster Confession, 3:1.

7 Quoted in William Lyford, *The Instructed Christian* (Morgan, PA: Soli Deo Gloria, n.d.), 269.

The Revealed Will

The second half of Deuteronomy 29:29 says that God reveals some things so that we may do them. We call this the *revealed will* of God. It is the basis for human responsibility, just as the secret will is based on divine sovereignty. It is our standard for holiness. First Thessalonians 4:3: "For this is the will of God, your sanctification" (Cf. 5:18). Romans 12:2 refers to "what is that good and acceptable and perfect will of God." Jesus called it "the will of My Father" (Matthew 7:21; 12:50); "the will of Him who sent Me" (John 4:34; 6:39); and "His will" (John 7:17). In Gethsemane He submitted His sinless human will to the Father's will when he prayed, "Not my will, but Yours be done" (Luke 22:42; cf. Matthew 26:39; Mark 14:36).

This will has two parts: the law and the gospel. The law also has two parts: the moral law for all men and the ceremonial law which was only for the Jews (some include the civil laws in this category). The first is directly founded on the holiness of God, for God says, "Be holy, for I am holy" (1 Peter 1:16). This law is inscribed internally on the consciences of all people and is revealed to them externally in general revelation in creation (Romans 1–2). It is further revealed verbally in special revelation — the Bible. It also can be dichotomized into positive precepts ("Thou shalt") and negative prohibitions ("Thou shalt not").

Sometimes Reformed theologians say God *necessarily* willed the moral law and *freely* willed the ceremonial law. The first was necessary in that it was directly based on His holiness, while the other was an act of divine freedom and sheer sovereignty. Thus, it is speculated, God could have theoretically willed the ceremonial laws differently without contradicting His holy nature. For instance, He could have commanded the Jews to eat pork and refrain from beef. He could have ordered tattoos and forbidden circumcision. After all, these laws were abolished in the New Testament. Similarly, God could have commanded something other than water baptism and bread and wine as sacraments, for they will not continue into the eternal state. They were therefore willed freely and temporarily. God willed the moral laws necessarily, and they continue forever. He could not have commanded lying, for that would contradict His holiness (Titus 1:2, "God cannot lie"). He could not have forbidden what He commanded nor commanded what He forbade in the Ten Commandments or the two great love commands.

Some Reformed theologians posit a third group between the necessary and free laws, namely, *positive laws*. For instance, God did not have to create humans as sexual beings. They could all have been neuter. Marriage and sexual laws are temporary and do not continue into Heaven (Matthew 22:30). Yet, marriage is a type of Christ and the church (Ephesians 5). God could not have commanded adultery, for that would contradict His immutable faithfulness (1 Thessalonians 5:24; 2 Timothy 2:13).

The Will of God and Salvation

As we will see in the discussion on election, God willed to choose only some sinners to be saved. That is the secret will. The revealed will includes the gospel as well as the law, and in this sense, God wills or desires the salvation of all who hear the gospel. Note the following extracts from John Calvin himself:

- "He wished His coming to be the salvation of all."[8]

- "The heavenly Father does not wish the human race that He loves to perish."[9]

- "The reason he gives why prayers should be offered for all men is that God, in offering the Gospel and Christ as mediator to all men, shows that He wishes all men to be saved."[10]

- "Indeed, God declares that he wills the conversion of all, and he directs exhortations to all in common."[11]

- "We hold, then, that God wills not the death of a sinner, since he calls all equally to repentance, and promises himself prepared to receive them if they only seriously repent. [. . .] God is said not to wish the death of a sinner. How so? since he wishes all to be converted."[12]

- "This is wondrous love towards the human race, that he desires all men to be saved, and is prepared to bring even the perishing to safety. [. . .] No mention is made here [2 Peter 3:9] of the secret decree of God by which the wicked are doomed to their own ruin, but only of His loving-kindness as it is made known to us in the Gospel. There God stretches

---

8 John Calvin, *A Harmony of the Gospels: Matthew, Mark and Luke* (Grand Rapids: Eerdmans, 1979), 2:295.

9 Calvin, *The Gospel According to St. John 1–10* (Grand Rapids: Eerdmans, 1979), 73.

10 Calvin, *The Second Epistle of Paul the Apostle to the Corinthians and the Epistles to Timothy, Titus and Philemon* (Grand Rapids: Eerdmans, 1980), 185.

11 John Calvin, *Institutes of the Christian Religion* (Philadelphia: Westminster, 1960), 3:3:21 (p. 615).

12 John Calvin, *Commentaries on the First Twenty Chapters of the Book of the Prophet Ezekiel* (Grand Rapids: Eerdmans, 1948), 2:246–49.

out His hand to all alike, but He only grasps those (in such a way as to lead to Himself) whom He has chosen before the foundation of the world."[13]

Such comments by Calvin can be multiplied from many of his writings. They surprise both Arminian and Hyper-Calvinists. Similar sentiments have been expressed hundreds of times by mainline Calvinists for centuries. This is neither Arminianism nor Amyraldism but the majority report of mainstream Calvinism. For example, John Murray wrote:

> The will of God to repentance and salvation is universalized and reveals to us, therefore, that there is in God a benevolent lovingkindness towards the repentance and salvation even of those whom he has not decreed to save. This pleasure, will, desire is expressed in the universal call to repentance.[14]

There are several proofs of this. Ezekiel 18:23, 32 and 33:11 expressly say that God has no pleasure in the death of any wicked sinner, but rather that he repents and be saved. Calvin's commentary on those verses is explicit. Next, God commands us to preach the good news to all men everywhere, not just to the elect (Matthew 28:19–20; Mark 16:15–16; Luke 24:47; Acts 1:8). Third, God commands all who hear the gospel to repent and believe (Mark 1:15; Acts 20:21). As John Frame puts it: "If God desires people to repent of sin, then certainly he desires them to be saved, for salvation is the fruit of such repentance."[15] Also, this is more than just a command to believe the report of the gospel, but to savingly believe in Jesus Christ and be saved (John 6:28–29; 12:36; 14:1; Acts 19:4). First John 3:23 is decisive: "And this is His commandment: that we should believe on the name of His Son Jesus Christ." What must a sinner do to be saved? "Believe on the Lord Jesus Christ and you shall be saved" (Acts 16:31). Furthermore, God "commands all men everywhere to repent" (Acts 17:30), which is evangelical repentance and not merely legal repentance (see Acts 2:38; 3:19; 26:20). Failure to repent and believe is a sin that results in damnation (Mark 16:16; Luke 13:3; John 3:18, 36; 5:38; 16:8–9; Romans 14:23; 2 Thessalonians 2:12; Hebrews 3:12; 1 John 5:10). Certainly a command is the expression of a will

---

13 Calvin, *The Epistle of Paul the Apostle to the Hebrews and the First and Second Epistles of St. Peter* (Grand Rapids: Eerdmans, 1980), 364 (on 2 Peter 3:9). He elsewhere paraphrased this verse: "He took pity on humanity, not willing that any should perish" *Sermons on Galatians* (Edinburgh: Banner of Truth, 1997), 23.

14 John Murray, *Collected Writings of John Murray* (Edinburgh: Banner of Truth, 1982), 4:132.

15 John Frame, *The Doctrine of God* (Phillipsburg, NJ: P&R, 2002), 534.

of desire! Therefore, both law and gospel have commands, and together they are the twin elements of the revealed will of God.

1 Timothy 2:4–5 and 2 Peter 3:9

Calvinists have interpreted the key verses of 1 Timothy 2:4–5 and 2 Peter 3:9 in different ways. Some take the first to refer to the revealed will and the second to the secret will (so Thomas Manton[16]); others reverse it; and others, such as Calvin, take both to refer to the revealed will, while yet others take both to refer to the secret will. My own view, and that of many Calvinists, is that 1 Timothy 2:4 refers to the revealed will that literally all who hear the gospel be saved. We should pray for all men (v. 1), for God desires all men to be saved (v. 4). This is reflected in Paul's prayer in Romans 10:1: "Brethren, my heart's desire and prayer to God for Israel is that they may be saved." Paul willed as God willed. He desired their salvation because God desired their salvation. Some take *all* to mean "all types" rather than "all individuals," but this is not how Paul uses the word in the Pastoral Epistles. First Timothy 4:10 differentiates "all men" from believers, viz., "the living God, who is the Savior of all men, especially of those who believe." This concerns the revealed will, not the secret will, as James Henley Thornwell explains: "It is manifestly God's preceptive will as revealed in the offers and invitations of the Gospel which is here meant; there is not a syllable about any purposes or decree to save all men. [. . .] The single distinction of the will of God into preceptive and decretive divests this passage of all its difficulty."[17] Matthew Henry also took this view: "Not that he has decreed the salvation of all, for then all men would be saved; but he has a good will to the salvation of all, and none perish but by their own fault."[18] John Piper well defends this position in *Does God Desire All to Be Saved?*[19]

As for 2 Peter 3:9, many Calvinists interpret this of the secret will because the Greek word *boulomai* is somewhat stronger than the word *thelo* of 1 Timothy 2:4 (see below). This suggests to some interpreters that Peter meant that God

---

16 Thomas Manton, *The Complete Works of Thomas Manton, D.D.* (Worthington: Maranatha, n.d.), 18:227.

17 James Henley Thornwell, *The Collected Writings of James Henley Thornwell* (Edinburgh: Banner of Truth, 1974), 2:168. See especially the eminently useful discussion in Robert Lewis Dabney, *Discussions* (Harrisonburg: Sprinkle, 1982), 1:282–313; and *Systematic Theology* (Edinburgh: Banner of Truth, 1985), 161–64.

18 Matthew Henry, *Commentary on the Whole Bible* (Old Tappan: Fleming H. Revell, n.d.), 6:812 (on 1 Timothy 2:5). Spurgeon took this line often, such as in *Metropolitan Tabernacle Pulpit* (Pasadena, TX: Pilgrim Publications, 1980), 26:49–60.

19 Wheaton: Crossway, 2013.

here wills that only Christians repent and not perish, for God does not give repentance to all men.[20] Thus, this verse speaks of the secret will of election, not the gospel. Some who hold to this interpretation add that other verses speak of the revealed will in the gospel that God desires all men to be saved.

Other Reformed interpreters, such as Calvin quoted above, take 2 Peter 3:9 to refer to the revealed will for all men everywhere, not just the elect. The context uses the illustration of Noah and the ark. It is understood that Noah, a preacher of righteousness, warned his hearers of judgment and invited them onto the ark to be saved, but they rejected the offer. This is seen as a type of our offering Christ as the only way of salvation. Another exegetical point that is often overlooked is the last phrase "and come to repentance." That refers to an unconverted person, not a Christian who has already repented. It would be incongruous to paraphrase this verse as "God is not willing that any Christian perish but that all Christians come to repentance." On the other hand, it would be consistent to interpret it to mean "God does not desire that any lost sinner perish but that they all repent." This interpretation well fits in with similar wording in Ezekiel 18:23, 32 and 33:11. The weight of exegetical evidence favors it.

Further Proofs of a Universal Saving Desire

God is grieved when sinners do not repent and believe. Jesus wept over unrepentant sinners facing damnation (Luke 19:41–42), and so should we.[21] If God had no desire whatsoever for their salvation, Christ's tears were "miswept." God in Christ holds out His arms to lost sinners all day long calling them to Himself (Romans 10:21; Isaiah 65:2; Proverbs 1:24). Surely all these verses prove that God has a will of desire for all men's salvation. It will not do to say that Christ was only doing this in His humanity, not His deity. His sinless perfect humanity revealed the Father to men. To argue otherwise is to promote a distorted view of Christ's hypostatic union.

The Denial of Universal Saving Desire

A minority of Calvinists reject this line of reasoning. A small number inconsistently deny that God desires all men to be saved, yet they still believe in the free offer of the gospel. Others deny both. This is the essence of Hyper-

---

20 KJV and NKJV read "us" according to the Majority text, while ESV, NIV, and others read "you."
21 See especially John Howe, "The Redeemer's Tears Wept over Lost Souls," *The Works of the Rev. John Howe, M.A.* (Ligonier: Soli Deo Gloria, 1990), 2:316–89.

Calvinism. In their masterful paper "The Free Offer of the Gospel," accepted as an official position by the Orthodox Presbyterian Church in 1948, John Murray and Ned B. Stonehouse began with these words: "It would appear that the real point in dispute in connection with the free offer of the gospel is whether it can properly be said that God desires the salvation of all men."[22] They present the overwhelmingly majority Reformed answer, yes. All Hyper-Calvinists say no.[23]

Hyper-Calvinists use various arguments. One is that there can be no contradiction between the two wills of God. Since God does not predestine all men to be saved, they reason, it follows that God does not desire all men to be saved. This involves several logical and theological errors. First, the revealed will can be and usually is broken by sinful men — such as in sinning against the law. But we all know that the secret will cannot be broken. They thus confuse the two wills. To say, "There is never any contradiction between the two wills," invites the question: Does God will that men sin? In the secret will, yes, God has foreordained that men sin. But in the revealed will God emphatically forbids sin. That is an apparent (and only an apparent) contradiction, for it is the paradox and mystery we have already discussed. This undermines the entire Hyper-Calvinist position. The Hyperist makes the reverse error of the Arminians who deny the secret will of salvation for only some because they hold to the revealed will that all be saved. Both commit several logical and exegetical errors. The truth remains that in the secret will God willed only the elect to be saved, while in the revealed will God desires the salvation of all. We must let the divine paradox stand.

The Two Words for *Will*

One popular explanation for the paradox of the twofold will has been adduced. It argues that one word for *will* in Greek is the word *boule* or *boulema*, used some forty-seven times in the New Testament. The verbal form *boulomai* is used some thirty-seven times. They are both used of God and man. Of man: Mark 15:15; Acts 12:4; 25:22; 1 Timothy 2:8; 5:14; 6:9; Titus 3:8, and so forth. Some deal with Christ's will (Matthew 11:27; Luke 10:22), the Holy Spirit's will (1 Corinthians 12:11), and of both God and man (Acts 5:38–39). When used of God, it frequently refers to what we call the secret will of purpose and

---

22 John Murray and Ned B. Stonehouse, *The Free Offer of the Gospel* (Edinburgh: Banner of Truth, 2001), 3. This excellent article can also be found in *Collected Writings of John Murray* (Edinburgh: Banner of Truth, 1982), 4:113–32.

23 See my previous chapter on Hyper-Calvinism as well as my PhD dissertation, "Hyper-Calvinism and John Gill," The University of Edinburgh, 1983.

predestination, as in Acts 2:23; 4:28; Romans 9:19; Ephesians 1:11; and Hebrews 6:17. The word denotes determination and a conscious decision.

The other word is the noun *thelema*, or *thelesis*, used some 63 times, and the verb *thelo* used some 207 times. They are also used of both God and men. When used about God, they frequently, if not usually, refer to what we call the *revealed will*. Linguistically this denotes a wish or desire that would bring about pleasure. Some lexicographers say that *boule* and *thelema* and their cognates are synonyms. Some add that, just as *agape* and *phile* are virtually synonyms, but *agape* is the stronger of the two (especially when both are used together, as in John 21:15–17), so *boule* tends to be stronger than *thelema*. *Boule* tends to refer to God's absolute counsel in predestination, while *thelema* tends to refer to the expressed desire and command of law and gospel. But there is an overlap and not a hard and fast difference. We do not base our theology of the twofold will only on these nuanced variations, but on their contextual uses and theological interpretation. Overall they confirm the Reformed view of the twofold will of God.

Contrast Between the Two Wills

There are a number of differences between the two. The secret will is contained in decrees; the revealed will is expressed in commands and promises. One is the counsel of God; the other the command of God. The first is His intention; the second is His approval. The secret is foreordination and foreknowledge; the revealed is faith and practice.

Some have said that the first is God's own rule for what He will do, while the second is His rule for what we should do. One is eternal and internal within God; the other is temporal and external from God. The secret will is unconditional and always fulfilled; the revealed will is conditional and not always obeyed. One is decree; the other is desire.

The first permits the existence of sin; the second prohibits the commission of sin. In the first, God wills only some to be saved by election, but in the second God desires all men to be saved by evangelism. In the secret will God positively predestines what shall happen and negatively predestines what shall not happen. In the revealed will God positively promises salvation to all who repent and believe in Christ and negatively threatens punishment to all who die in sin. Still other contrasts have been suggested.

One Will or Two?

Arminianism generally says there is only one will in God, what we would call the *revealed will*. Much post-Reformation Lutheranism holds a similar view, as do some Neo-Orthodox. To them, the Reformed idea of two wills is mocked as divine schizophrenia.

Calvin wisely put his finger on the resolution: there is ultimately only one divine will, but God has revealed it to us as two so that we can begin to understand it.[24] This is the appropriate perspective. It is true to Scripture and refrains from denying either in order to explain the paradox. It also draws the line and warns against further prying into God's mysteries.

Some have attempted to draw parallels with other paradoxes that might shed some light on the dichotomy. Some suggest that it is comparable with the two wills of Christ — His human will was always in submission to His divine will, so there really was only one will in Christ (Cf. Matthew 26:39; Luke 22:42; John 5:30; 6:38). Others compare it with the transcendence (secret will) and immanence (revealed will) of God. Conceivably someone might suggest a parallel with general and special revelation, but one wonders what would be meant. One must not search for possible parallel dichotomies too much. In any case, just as there is one decree and many decrees, so there is ultimately only one will in God but two aspects to it. To be sure, it is better described as the twofold will than as the two wills.

The Providential Will

Brief mention must be made of another will that may be the overlap of the two. This has to do with how God reveals His will through providence. On the one hand, this is part of the secret will — predestination produces providence, and providence fulfills predestination. John Gill said, "God's secret will becomes revealed by events in providence."[25] Providence cannot be predicted with

---

24 John Calvin, *Sermons on the Epistle to the Ephesians* (London: Banner of Truth, 1973), 59, 260–61; *A Harmony of the Gospels: Matthew, Mark and Luke, Volume III, and The Epistles of James and Jude* (Grand Rapids: Eerdmans, 1980), 69; *Institutes*, 1:18:3 (p. 234); *Calvin's Calvinism* (Grand Rapids: Reformed Free Publishing Association, 1991), 256; *Commentary on the Twelve Minor Prophets* (Grand Rapids: Eerdmans, 1950), 4:276. He accepted the twofold dichotomy in *The Epistles of Paul the Apostle to the Romans and to the Thessalonians* (Grand Rapids: Eerdmans, 1980), 260.

25 John Gill, *A Complete Body of Doctrinal and Practical Divinity* (Paris, AR: Baptist Standard Bearer, 1984), 71.

certainty except by God alone through prophecy. We must wait on it. We read the book of providence like the Hebrew alphabet — in reverse by looking back.

God occasionally guides us by providence, in which we apply biblical principles to current events in our life. He opens some doors and closes others (Acts 14:27; 1 Corinthians 16:9; 2 Corinthians 2:12; Colossians 4:3). We must be extra careful, however, for an open door may only be there to test us. And we must also beware of testing God by asking for signs (*fleeces*) or using divination to detect them. We need Scripture, as Samuel Rutherford noted: "The book of holy providence is good marginal notes on His revealed will, in His word, and speaks such to us, could we read and understand what he writes, both in the one and in the other."[26] We read the book of providence through the eyeglasses of Scripture, not the other way around.

By the same standard, we must submit our plans to all three. We must not presume upon God's secret will. We must not plan to sin against His revealed will. And we must submit our plans to His providential will with the words "if the Lord wills" (James 4:13–15; Acts 18:21; Romans 1:10; 15:32; 1 Corinthians 4:19). In olden days, Calvinists often wrote the letters *D.V.* on their plans — *Deo volente*, or, God willing.

Conclusion

The secret will is not entirely secret, for it is revealed in part through Scripture and Christ (Ephesians 1:9). We must not pry into it, such as seeking unrevealed prophetic details (Matthew 24:36; Acts 1:7; John 21:22). But we can study it insofar as it is explained in Scripture. Proverbs 25:2 tells us, "It is the glory of God to conceal a matter, but the glory of kings is to search out a matter." Let us study it and be mindful to obey the revealed will.

---

26 Samuel Rutherford, *Letters of Samuel Rutherford* (Edinburgh: Banner of Truth, 1984), 678.

Chapter 26
Divine Sovereignty and Human Responsibility

One of the greatest paradoxes in all theology is the puzzle of divine sovereignty and human responsibility. Some deny or minimize one or the other, but that does not resolve the problem. We must accept both because both are taught in the Bible. What God has joined together, let no man put asunder.

Human Responsibility

Let us limit our discussion to human responsibility, not that of angels (who have it) or animals (who do not have it). It involves the morality of the will. It is the capacity to say, "I will," or "I will not" obey God. God created Adam and Eve with this capacity, and though sin affected their wills, it did not abolish them. All humans ever since, except Jesus, have had sinful wills. Before we address the problem of sinful wills, we must first discuss human wills vis-à-vis divine sovereignty.[1]

Responsibility means accountability. Romans 14:12: "So then each of us shall give account of himself to God." Man is a steward of time, opportunity, and gifts and must give an account to the Master (Matthew 25:14–30). Responsibility also means duty. It is our duty to fear (Ecclesiastes 12:13 KJV) and obey God (Luke 17:10). We have liability — we are liable for reward or punishment. We have obligation and are obliged to obey God — if we do not, God is obliged to punish us. If we are guilty, we have culpability. We have answerability — we must give an answer to God at the Judgment Day.

Human responsibility implies morality and ethics. God has given us a conscience that indicates a certain measure of right and wrong. We have the ethical capacity of virtue and vice. It is the constitutional ability to make moral decisions. This is part of the image of God that is not given to animals or rocks. Morality implies ethical *oughtness*. We ought to obey God.

God has given us the standard of moral responsibility — His law, which is

---

1 I will discuss the paradox of human responsibility and total depravity in chapter 35.

part of His revealed will. Not all men have it equally. Some have more light than others. Some only have conscience (Romans 2:15). Others have only part of the Bible, while still others have the whole Bible and even good preaching from it. Hence, some have more responsibility to God than others. Jesus said, "For everyone to whom much is given, from him much will be required; and to whom much has been committed, of him they will ask the more" (Luke 12:48). More light, more responsibility. More light rejected, more guilt and punishment.

Calvinists hold to human responsibility as much as anyone else. Indeed, as we shall see later, we hold to a far greater doctrine of human guilt than any other theological system. Some Reformed prefer the term *free agency* to *free will*, for the latter may imply a neutral will which we do not have. Others like the term *natural ability*, or *constitutional ability*, that is, the created capacity to will right and wrong. For example, the Westminster Confession says: "God hath endued the will of man with that natural ability, that is neither forced, nor by any absolute necessity of nature determined to do good or evil" (9:1).

Responsibility implies a choice between two options (Deuteronomy 30:15, 19; Joshua 24:15; 1 Kings 18:21). But — and this is crucial — human responsibility does not require equal ability to choose either option. The will is not morally neutral, as some assume. The classic Reformed discussion on this is *The Freedom of the Will* by Jonathan Edwards.[2] He argued that no man is neutral toward Christ, who said, "He that is not with me is against Me" (Matthew 12:30). Nor can man choose both at the same time (Matthew 6:24). Also, as Edwards showed, it is a mistake to suppose that the will is self-determining. God alone is self-determining. Our will always works in conjunction with our nature, as God also does. A good nature produces a good will; a bad nature produces a bad will (Matthew 7:17).[3] Only God has a perfectly free will, but His will is never morally neutral, otherwise God could choose sin. He cannot deny Himself (2 Timothy 2:13). His will is always in perfect harmony with His holy nature. The perfected saints in Heaven have free but not neutral wills, and the damned have bound but not neutral wills in Hell.

God Intervenes in the Human Will

Just as the invisible hand of God's providence regularly guides nature and

---

2 Jonathan Edwards, *The Works of Jonathan Edwards* (New Haven: Yale University Press, 1957), Vol. 1.

3 Later I will discuss the mystery of how the sinless will of Adam sinned.

occasionally intervenes with miracles, so God is legally entitled and able to intervene in the will of morally responsible humans. The Calvinist rejects the popular notion that the human will must be totally free of divine interference to be responsible. In fact, the cry for an independent will is a symptom of a sinful will. A righteous will wants to be free from sin and controlled by God (Cf. Romans 6:16–22; 7:24–25).

The will of man is not off-limits to God. God can go anywhere He pleases. The Arminian notion that God created a will that even He cannot interfere with resembles the philosophical idea of God creating a rock so heavy that He cannot lift it. But no such will or rock has or can exist, for God is omnipotent and sovereign. Does He not have the right to intervene in the hearts of men that He has created?

Proverbs 21:1 says, "The king's heart is in the hand of the Lord, like rivers of water; He turns it wherever He wishes." A river always follows the course of least resistance according to gravity, climate, and other factors. Man's will always follows a course that God sovereignly lays out for it. God invisibly yet irresistibly directs our hearts in such a way that He is sovereign, and we are responsible. Augustine commented: "God works in the hearts of human beings to incline their wills, whether to good actions in accord with His mercy or to evil ones in accord with their merits."[4] He added, "He has in his control the wills of human beings more than they have in their own wills."[5]

God Intervenes for Good Motives

Many verses teach this, such as Ezra 6:22: "The Lord made them joyful, and turned the heart of the king of Assyria toward them." And 7:27: "Blessed is the Lord God of our fathers, who has put such a thing in the king's heart." Note that the king was not righteous. Second Corinthians 8:16: "But thanks be to God who puts the same earnest care for you into the heart of Titus." This sovereign act is cause for thanksgiving, not denial or complaining.

Philippians 2:12–13 is even more explicit: "Work out your own salvation with fear and trembling; for it is God who works in you both to will and to do for His good pleasure." We will because God wills that we should so will. He

---

4 Augustine, *The Works of Saint Augustine* (Hyde Park; New City, 1999), I/26:102. This is from his aptly named treatise *Grace and Free Choice* (21:42).
5 Augustine, I/26:140.

works in us to cause us to do good works.[6] This is according to His sovereign good pleasure and will. Augustine put it like this: "For he has willed that our willing be both his and ours — by his calling and ours by following. He alone bestows, however, what we have willed — that is, the ability to act well and to live blessedly forever."[7] Similarly, Hebrews 13:20–21 says, "Now may the God of peace [. . .] make you complete in every good work to do His will, working in you what is well pleasing in His sight."

God did this with the writers of the Bible. Second Peter 1:21 describes the process of inspiration: "For prophecy never came by the will of man, but holy men of God spoke as they were moved by the Holy Spirit." The Spirit irresistibly overwhelmed them in such a way that what they spoke and wrote was primarily God's words (1 Thessalonians 2:13; 1 Corinthians 14:37) and therefore infallible. Arminian evangelicals fail to see that their theory of non-intervention opens the door to a fallible Bible, for if God cannot interfere with sinful hearts, then they will always sin and create error. But Scripture is inerrant, therefore God does indeed interfere with human wills.

God Works through Sinful Hearts

In Genesis 50:20, Joseph said that his brothers meant evil toward him, but God meant it for good. That is a classic case of human responsibility and divine sovereignty. This does not exonerate them from sin or make God guilty. Luke 22:22 is another such case. Judas betrayed Christ, but this was foreordained by God. He certainly was still guilty. Acts 2:23 and 4:27–28 says the same regarding others involved in Christ's murder.

Revelation 17:17 is especially explicit: "God put it into their hearts to fulfill His purpose, to be of one mind, and to give their kingdom to the beast." Psalm 105:25 is yet another example: "He turned their heart to hate His people." Augustine commented on verses such as these regarding God's ultimate will working through sinful wills:

> By the very fact that they acted against his will, his will was done
> through them. For the great works of the Lord are sought out according
> to all his purposes in order that even what happens against his will should
> in a wonderful and inexplicable way not be done despite his will, since it
> would not happen if he did not permit it, and he does not permit things

---

6 God acts differently in saints and sinners, as well as differently regarding virtue and vice, otherwise God would be the author of sin.

7 Augustine, I/12:193.

unwillingly but willingly; nor would he in his goodness allow anything evil to happen were he not able in his omnipotence even to bring good out of evil. [. . .] But however many wills there are, whether of angels or humans, good or evil, willing the same as God or differently, the will of the Almighty is always undefeated.[8]

The Westminster Confession states that God foreordained all that comes to pass, and adds "yet so as thereby neither is God the author of sin, nor is violence offered to the will of the creatures" (3:1; cf. 9:1). God works through sinful wills but does not force them to sin. God does not push a pistol into men's hands and force them to pull the trigger. Man willingly sins. God does not sin through them. This is what Augustine and Calvin meant when they used the term *free will*. With the rise of Arminianism and its variant meaning, later Calvinists usually abandoned the term and often prefer to use the term *human responsibility*.

The Grand Paradox

Divine sovereignty and human responsibility are both true, but we cannot fully grasp how. They are two sides of the same coin. It is an *antinomy*.[9] Ultimately, they are complementary, not contradictory. In the well-known words of Spurgeon:

> I have often been asked by persons to reconcile the two truths. My only reply is — they need no reconciliation, for they never fell out. Why should I try to reconcile two friends? Prove to me the truths do not agree. [. . .] The two facts are parallel lines; I cannot make them unite, but you cannot make them cross either.[10]

---

8 Augustine, I/8:331–32.

9 J. I. Packer popularized the term in his excellent *Evangelism and the Sovereignty of God* (Downers Grove, IL: InterVarsity, 1961), 18–19. Hendrik G. Stoker, the South African Kuyperian Calvinist, used the rare word *hyperdox*, in E. R. Geehan, ed., *Jerusalem and Athens* (Philadelphia: Presbyterian and Reformed, 1971), 455. I have not found the word used anywhere else.

10 Charles Haddon Spurgeon, *Metropolitan Tabernacle Pulpit* (Pasadena, TX: Pilgrim Publications, 1981), 33:199. See also *New Park Street Pulpit* (Pasadena, TX: Pilgrim Publications, 1981), 4:337–44 and 5:120. Henry Morris — evidently an Arminian — illogically said, "It is like two parallel lines, which finally come together at a distance of infinity." *The Bible Has the Answer* (Grand Rapids: Baker Book House, 1971), 122. By definition, parallel lines never intersect. 4. Spurgeon himself made the same error in *The New Park Street Pulpit*, 4:337. (Pasadena: Pilgrim Publications, 1981).

Man is responsible because God is sovereign, not the other way around.[11] The sovereign God created man to be accountable despite his sin and God's sovereignty. We must not deny or overemphasize either truth nor attempt a hybrid of the two.[12] This is closely related to the twofold will of God: the secret will (divine sovereignty) and the revealed will (the basis for human responsibility). J. I. Packer says that it ultimately gets back to the attributes of God. It is an unexplainable antinomy of God as King and God as Judge.[13]

These two are not equal but opposite spheres. We have seen that God sovereignly intervenes in human responsibility, though human responsibility does not intervene in divine sovereignty. Nor is this synergism: "God does His part, and we do ours." That misunderstands both the paradox and the doctrine of providential concurrence. Synergism arises when those such as the Semi-Pelagians, Philip Melanchthon, and Jacob Arminius so emphasized free will that they weakened divine sovereignty.

Upsetting the grand paradox has bad practical implications. Hyper-Calvinists tend to overemphasize divine sovereignty and weaken human responsibility, with the result that they deny the free offer of the gospel and Duty Faith. For example, the Hyper-Calvinist W. J. Styles wrote, "Since human responsibility and divine sovereignty do not simply involve a paradox but are destructive to each other, one must be untrue."[14] He denied human responsibility and tried to maintain a semblance of human accountability. The outcome was that he not only denied the free offer and Duty Faith but held that lack of saving faith is not a sin.

Arminianism errs on the other side by so stressing human responsibility that it minimizes divine sovereignty. Some Arminian writers claim to believe in both truths, such as in *Divine Sovereignty and Human Freedom* by Samuel Fisk.[15] But upon close examination one discovers that such writers do not accept full and

---

11 "This sovereignty is never limited by human freedom. Rather human freedom is always limited by divine sovereignty." Craig Brown, *The Five Dilemmas of Calvinism* (Orlando: Ligonier Ministries, 2007), 52. Also: "The freedom of the creature is real only because of God's eternal decree, and it is never real except in terms of limitation and responsibility." Rousas J. Rushdoony, *Intellectual Schizophrenia* (Philadelphia: Presbyterian and Reformed, 1961), 116.
12 Compare the Formula of Chalcedon regarding the error of mingling the divine and human natures of Christ rather than keeping them in balance.
13 Packer, *Evangelism and the Sovereignty of God*, 22.
14 W. J. Styles, *A Guide to Church Fellowship* (London, 1902), 86.
15 Neptune, NJ: Loizeaux Brothers, 1973.

absolute divine sovereignty. They may say that God *influences* the will, but they refrain from saying that God *intervenes* in the will.

Conclusion

Both truths must be believed and kept in balance. Preachers must preach both as part of the whole counsel of God (Acts 20:27).[16] When we cannot understand the paradox, let us bow and worship God who does.

---

16 A good example to follow would be Spurgeon's sermon "High Doctrine and Broad Doctrine" on John 6:37, *Metropolitan Tabernacle Pulpit*, 30:49–60.

Chapter 27
Prayer and the Sovereignty of God

A case that illustrates the paradox of divine sovereignty and human responsibility is prayer. If God is sovereign, why pray? What good is prayer if God has already predestined what will happen? Is it presumptuous to pray? Or conversely, if we should pray, does this not imply that God has not foreordained everything or at least that He can change His plans?

What Is Prayer?

The Westminster Shorter Catechism gives a good definition: "Prayer is an offering up of our desires unto God, for things agreeable to his will, in the name of Christ, with confession of our sins, and thankful acknowledgment of his mercies" (Answer 98). God commands us to pray (Luke 18:1; Philippians 4:6; Matthew 7:7; Hebrews 4:16). "Pray without ceasing" (1 Thessalonians 5:17). This is part of the revealed will of God. Not praying is a sin (1 Samuel 12:23). We are given godly examples of "pray-ers" to imitate (James 5:16–18), especially Christ. Prayer is also a privilege. God grants us access to His presence to present our prayers (Hebrews 4:16). God *lets* us pray: "I will also let the house of Israel inquire of Me to do this for them" (Ezekiel 36:37).

In Reformed theology, prayer has been divided into four categories. First, confession of sin. It is our duty to confess our sins with repentance and without excuse (1 John 1:9). We cannot claim "The Devil made me do it," "God foreordained that I would sin," or other blame-shifting excuses like Adam and Eve used (Genesis 3:12–13). Rather, let us imitate David: "I have sinned" (2 Samuel 12:13; Psalm 51). Second, supplication. We ask God to supply our needs (Philippians 4:6). Third, intercession. We ask God for the needs of others (1 Timothy 2:1). Fourth, adoration. We thank God with praise and worship.

Is God Obligated to Answer Prayer?

We offer requests, not demands (Philippians 4:6). We dare not command Almighty God to do anything. Much non-Reformed prayer is highly inappropriate. Rousas J. Rushdoony wrote: "Recently, I heard one evangelical pastor describe much current praying as "giving God His instructions for the day." Such praying is blasphemy."[1] I personally once heard a preacher lead his congregation in prayer with the words, "Lord, we give You permission to do this." That too is blasphemy. God has not given us a blank check that is payable on demand, as in the "Name it, claim it" scheme. No Calvinist would ever dream of such a thing.

Someone might object: "But doesn't Jesus promise to give whatever we ask? What about John 14:13, 15:7, 16:23, and Matthew 21:22?" This misunderstands the privilege of prayer and resembles the presumption of Mark 10:35: "Teacher, we want you to do for us whatever we ask." It overlooks that our prayers must be presented in faith (James 1:6–8). Prayer must not be selfish (James 4:3). Too many people ask God for greeds, not needs. John 9:31 and 1 John 3:22 tell us we must ask in a spirit of obedience. Disobedience blocks prayer (Psalm 66:18; Isaiah 1:15; 1 Peter 3:7). More importantly, God is our king, not our waiter. It also overlooks the sovereign prerogative of God to give whatever He pleases, and He always does so in accordance with His predestination. Note Christ's reply to James and John: "You do not know what you ask. [. . .] To sit on my right hand and my left hand is not Mine to give, but it is for those for whom it is prepared" (Mark 10:38, 40).

On the other hand, God has graciously promised to give certain things we need if we ask in the proper way. First John 5:14–15 tells us that God hears and answers us when we pray according to His will. This is the revealed will, not the secret will. If we pray in Christ's name for things God has commanded us to have, we can know that He will give them to us. For example, we are commanded to be wise (Matthew 10:16 and often in Proverbs). But we are born unwise fools. God promises to give us wisdom when we ask properly (James 1:5). This is indicated in Augustine's famous prayer: "Give what you command and command what you will." Likewise, God commands us to be holy (1 Peter 1:16), but only God can give holiness. He will grant sanctification when we ask properly. It pleases Him to do so.

The problem of unanswered prayer is in us, not in God. It is a matter of misused human responsibility, not divine sovereignty. We should humbly ask, "Lord, teach us to pray" (Luke 11:1). The Holy Spirit helps us in our ignorance and weakness in prayer (Romans 8:26). The main way He does this is through the Holy Bible that He inspired. He illumines our minds to understand what God says about prayer.

---

1   Rousas J. Rushdoony, *The Roots of Reconstruction* (Vallecito: Ross House Books, 1991), 332.

Praying for Lost Sinners

If God has sovereignly chosen only some sinners to be saved, why pray for someone in particular to be saved? To be sure, it would be high presumption, not true acknowledgment of sovereignty, to refuse to pray for someone because of the doctrine of predestination. Nobody believed in predestination more than the apostle Paul (Romans 8–9; Ephesians 1, etc.), yet he prayed fervently for lost Jews to be saved (Romans 10:1). Rather than being a hindrance to prayer, predestination is an incentive. God has predestined some persons to be saved, and He uses prayer for them to carry out His decree. Prayer is one of His *second causes*. We pray that God irresistibly intervene in their hearts and convert them. Augustine said,

> Why, then, do we pray for those who do not will to believe if not in order that God might also produce the will in them? [. . .] After all, our prayer for them is that faith itself may be given to those who do not believe, that is, to those who do not have faith.[2]

It is the Arminian, not the Calvinist, who has problems with prayer. If God never interferes with the human will or gives faith, then why pray? What are they asking God to do? This applies to the Arminian rejection of total depravity also. Peter Martyr Vermigli asked why pray that God save sinners if He has already given them so-called sufficient grace enabling them to believe? Instead, he argued, we pray because God alone is able to open their hearts to believe.[3] We pray for God to give effectual grace, not so-called sufficient grace.

We can pray for anybody, but not everybody. Jesus Himself did not pray for the whole world (John 17:9). God has not chosen everyone to be saved, so we do not pray, "Lord, save each and every person in the world." Yet we do not know who is an unconverted elect, so we can pray for any individual. The prohibition of 1 John 5:16 seems to refer to a sinning Christian, not a lost non-Christian. Nor can we pray that God elects more people. We may not "claim" a person either, for we do not know if he is elect. This has direct application to Christians who sin by marrying unbelievers, presumptuously thinking that God will save their unconverted spouse (1 Corinthians 7:16; cf. 2 Corinthians 6:14). God prohibits what someone has called "missionary marriages." Likewise,

---

2 Augustine, *The Works of Saint Augustine* (Hyde Park: New City, 1999), I/26:162.
3 Peter Martyr Vermigli, *The Peter Martyr Library* (Kirksville, MO: Truman State University Press, 2003), 8:58.

parents should pray for God to save their children and not presumptuously assume they are elect.[4] Remember Jacob and Esau (Romans 9:13).

Calvinists cannot hide behind the doctrine of predestination as an excuse not to pray for the lost. Calvin rightly rebuked such persons: "These words (John 17:9) also serve to expose the perverse stupidity of those who under the excuse of election surrender to laziness, whereas it should rather sharpen us to earnestness and prayer, as Christ teaches us by His example."[5] I would apply this also to the Hyper-Calvinist non-evangelism excuses. Calvin elsewhere exhorted us: "And as we cannot distinguish between the elect and the reprobate, it is our duty to pray for all who trouble us, to desire the salvation of all men, and even to be careful for the welfare of every individual."[6] If, as the Hyper-Calvinist says, God does not desire all men to be saved, then it would be presumption to pray for any man. But He does so desire, and we should have that desire when we pray for lost sinners to be saved (Romans 10:1; 1 Timothy 2:1–4).

Does Prayer Change God's Mind?

"Prayer changes things" is a popular slogan, and it has a molecule of truth to it. But we dare not pray for God to change His mind, for God is not a man that He should repent (Numbers 23:19). Robert Lewis Dabney offered this advice: "Prayer is not intended to produce a change in God, but in us."[7] God changes us, not vice versa. God is our sovereign, not our servant.

We must pray in submission to the sovereignty of God. Jonah 1:14 is an interesting example. The sailors prayed with the realization that "You, O Lord, have done as it pleased you." The sovereignty of God is an incentive to pray, not a hindrance. But what about Jonah 3:10? Did God not change His mind in answer to the prayers of the repentant Ninevites? Let us set the record straight. God gave a conditional warning of judgment if they would not repent (3:4). They did repent, so they were spared. The prophecy was conditional in the revealed will, and the repentance was given according to the secret will. Peter Martyr Vermigli commented: "God also foreknew that the sins of the Ninevites deserved immediate destruction, but he also foreknew that by his mercy he would lead them to repentance and they would be saved."[8] God did not change

---

4 I respectfully disagree with the Canons of Dort on this (1:17).
5 John Calvin, *The Gospel According to St. John 11–21 and the First Epistle of John* (Grand Rapids: Eerdmans, 1979), 141.
6 John Calvin, *Commentary on the Book of Psalms* (Grand Rapids: Eerdmans, 1949), 4:283.
7 Robert Lewis Dabney, *Systematic Theology*, (Edinburgh: Banner of Truth, 1985), 716.
8 Vermigli, *The Peter Martyr Library*, 8:75.

His ultimate mind, but enacted it by warning them, producing repentance in them, and sparing them. What is wrong with that?

Prayer and the Secret Will of God

We must adjust our prayers once we come to grasp the sovereignty of God and the secret will of predestination. For instance, we must not think that God foreordained something because He foreknew that we would pray for it. He did not consult our prayers, for He consulted only within Himself when He foreordained what would happen (Ephesians 1:11). Nobody is God's counselor, even in prayer (Romans 11:34).

We may not pray that God overrule His decrees. He will not do it anyway, and it would be impertinent to ask Him to do so. We may not pray that God save a lost sinner in Hell (let alone Purgatory, which does not exist). Going to Hell confirms that the person was non-elect, and to pray for his salvation would be tantamount to asking God to reverse the decree of reprobation. God will not do that even for Christians who are grieving for their deceased parents or children. I once had to gently remind a Christian friend when he prayed for God to save his deceased mother who died lost and is in Hell. Nor do we pray that God would save someone who has never heard the gospel; we pray that God would bring the gospel to him. And we certainly do not pray that God would save someone without faith and repentance, save him because of his good works, or other such anti-gospel errors.

What about praying that Christ hasten His return to earth? Some persons misapply Revelation 22:20, 2 Peter 3:12, and Song of Solomon 8:14. The date of the Second Coming has already been predestined and is unknown to us (Matthew 24:36). We can pray for God to save elect, and Christ will not return until He has saved all the elect. It is like when God closed the door to Noah's ark when all the animals and Noah's family were on board. We can, however, cheer on the Second Coming and patiently wait for it (Matthew 24:42). Calvin wisely said, "We pray not only that what he has in his own counsel decreed come to pass, but also that, all contumacy being overcome and subdued, he may subject the wills of all to his own and direct them to his obedience."[9]

Thy Will Be Done

This phrase is found in the Lord's Prayer (Matthew 6:10; Luke 11:2). It refers to

---

9 John Calvin, *Calvin: Theological Treatises* (Philadelphia: Westminster, 1954), 125.

the revealed will of God, not the secret will. William Hendriksen commented on it: "It is the ardent desire of the person who sincerely breathes the Lord's Prayer that the Father's will shall be obeyed as completely, heartily and immediately on earth as this is constantly being done by all the inhabitants of heaven."[10]

Thus, it is an act of submission and a request for aid to do God's will. The Westminster Shorter Catechism explains: "We pray that God, by His grace, would make us able and willing to know, obey, and submit to His will in all things, as the angels do in Heaven" (Answer 103). I would add "and the saints." This attitude is essential to the faith (James 1:6) and obedience (1 John 3:22) that is necessary to prayer.

We see it illustrated in our Lord's prayer in Gethsemane (Matthew 26:39, 42; Mark 14:36; Luke 22:42). Some take this to mean that Christ submitted His will to the divine decree that He would be crucified (Acts 2:23; 4:27–28; 1 Peter 1:19–20). He certainly did that, but that is not in view here. Rather, Christ often spoke of obeying the Father's specific will and command to come to earth to die (John 4:34; 5:30; 6:38; 10:18; 17:4; Hebrews 10:7).

John Piper noted: "Sometimes our prayers for God's revealed will to be done will not be done because God has decreed something different to bring about his holy and wise purposes."[11] Christ asked to be relieved of the cross, but His real prayer was to save those the Father gave Him in the covenant of redemption. He was answered (Hebrews 5:7). See Paul's prayer in 2 Corinthians 12:8–9.

Conclusion

God already knows what we need before we ask (Matthew 6:8; Psalm 139:4). He also knows what He has predestined to give us in answer to our prayers.[12] It has been reported that Augustine said, "God does not ask us to tell Him our needs that He may know them, but in order that we may be capable of receiving what He has planned to give us."[13] Why pray? Because God has commanded us to pray. And because God uses our prayers in a mysterious way to carry out what

---

10 William Hendriksen, *New Testament Commentary: Matthew* (Grand Rapids: Baker, 1973), 1:33.

11 John Piper, *A Godward Life: Book Two* (Sisters, OR: Multnomah, 1999), 135.

12 Vermigli: "God's foreknowledge does not call us back from a zeal for praying, for the things both profitable and necessary that God has decreed to give us, he has decreed to give them by means of prayer." *The Peter Martyr Library*, 8:7; cf. pp. 13 and 83.

13 I have been unable to locate this quotation.

He foreordained. We must not wait until we fully understand it, else we will never pray. It is sufficient that God knows.

Chapter 28
The Glory of God

What is the final goal of all things? What is the destination of predestination? The answer is this: the glory of God. "For of Him and through Him and to Him are all things, to whom be glory forever. Amen" (Romans 11:36).[1] God created all things and is worthy of worship (Revelation 4:11). The doctrines of grace could also be called the doctrines of glory. Grace leads to glory. Grace now, glory later (Psalm 84:11).

What Is Glory?

The Hebrew word for glory is *kabod*, which means weight or weightiness. This refers to God's value, like gold's weightiness. The Greek word is *doxa*. It has a wide lexical field, but regarding God it refers to the revelation of God Himself. It is similar to His name, as in the phrase "His glorious name" (1 Chronicles 29:13).

God predestined, created, and guides all things to this great goal. We see His glory indirectly through creation (Romans 1:19–20) and will view it directly in the beatific vision (Matthew 5:8). Divine glory is not something secondary to God, as Thomas Watson explains: "God's glory is such an essential part of His being, that He cannot be God without it."[2] The final revelation of God will be the unveiling of God "as He is" (1 John 3:2).

The glory of God is also the beauty of God. Glory and beauty are closely associated in Exodus 28:2, 40; Job 40:10; and Isaiah 28:5. There is beauty in all of God's attributes, such as "the beauty of holiness." God is pure beauty, ultimate beauty, the essence and zenith of all beauty (Psalm 90:17). Christians will view God in all His beauty one day (Isaiah 33:17). Everything about Christ is lovely and beautiful (Song of Solomon 5:16).

---

1 Most Reformed theologians say all of Romans 11:36 refers to God as God. Abraham Kuyper takes the minority view that it refers to the three persons of the Trinity: All things are of the Father (1 Corinthians 8:6), through the consistency of the Son (Colossians 1:17), to their destiny by the guidance of the Spirit. *The Work of the Holy Spirit* (Grand Rapids: Eerdmans, 1969), 19–20.

2 Thomas Watson, *A Body of Divinity* (Edinburgh: Banner of Truth, 1974), 5. We could define *glory* as "Revealed Godness."

The Revelation of Glory

When we study the many references to the glory of God, we see that they generally fall into two categories which theologians call *glory shown* and *glory received*. The first is the revelation of divine glory; the second is the reflection of glory back to God. God is now invisible to us (1 Timothy 1:17), but one day He will pull back the curtain and reveal His glory fully.

Scripture sometimes speaks of glory as light, such as the Shekinah. Jesus showed His glory as light on the Mount of Transfiguration (Matthew 17:2; John 1:14; 2 Peter 1:17). It was brighter than the sun, for uncreated light is greater than created light. No man can now see God face to face and live, just like we would go blind if we looked directly into the sun for too long. Pure light is white light, and it can be refracted into all the colors of the rainbow when it passes through a prism. Christ is the prism through which the glory of God is revealed as a rainbow (Revelation 4:3).

The members of the Trinity beheld each other's glory from all eternity (John 17:5, 24). God reveals His glory externally to us so that we may return it to Him in worship. This is what it means to glorify and give glory to God (e.g., Romans 4:20). We ascribe to God what He reveals to us about Himself. Psalm 96:8: "Give to the Lord the glory due His name." God already has full glory within Himself. He is "the Father of glory" (Ephesians 1:17); "the glorious Lord" (Isaiah 33:21 KJV); "the God of glory" (Psalm 29:3); and "the Lord of glory" (James 2:1). He created the universe to externally reveal His internal glory.

This is a major theme in Calvin's theology.[3] He called creation "a stupendous theatre whereon to manifest His own glory."[4] "Let us not be ashamed to take pious delight in the works of God open and manifest in this most beautiful theatre."[5] It is "a dazzling theatre,"[6] "this magnificent theatre of heaven and earth,"[7] "an open stage on which God will have his majesty to be seen,"[8] and

---

3 See Susan E. Schreiner, *The Theatre of His Glory: Nature and Natural Order in the Thought of John Calvin* (Durham: Labyrinth, 1991); and Belden C. Lane, *Ravished by Beauty: The Surpassing Legacy of Reformed Spirituality* (New York: Oxford University Press, 2011), 57–96.

4 John Calvin, *Calvin's Calvinism* (Grand Rapids: Reformed Free Publishing Association, 1991), 75.

5 John Calvin, *Institutes of the Christian Religion* (Philadelphia: Westminster, 1960), 1:14:20 (p. 179).

6 Calvin, *Institutes*, 1:5:8 (p. 61).

7 Calvin, *Institutes*, 2:6:1 (p. 341).

8 John Calvin, *Sermons on the Epistle to the Ephesians* (London: Banner of Truth, 1973), 181; cf. p. 258.

"a theatre to contemplate his glory."[9] "This world is like a theatre in which the Lord shows to us a striking spectacle of His glory."[10] "The world was founded for this purpose, that it should be the sphere of divine glory."[11] It is a "beauteous theatre."[12] "The whole world is a theatre for the display of the divine goodness, wisdom, justice, and power, but the Church is the orchestra, as it were — the most conspicuous part of it."[13]

Later, the American Puritan Ebenezer Pemberton said, "God erected the visible world as a monument of His glory, a theatre for the display of His adorable perfections."[14] This emphasis on glory is crucial to Reformed theology and exceeds all others.

Proverbs 16:4 says, "The Lord has made everything for Himself." We were created for His glory and pleasure, not for ourselves. The first question of the Westminster Shorter Catechism is, "What is the chief end of man?" Answer: "Man's chief end is to glorify God and to enjoy Him forever." It is not all about us. It is all about God. To the person who asks, "Why am I here?" we reply, "To glorify God."

Future Glory

Creation now reveals only some of God's glory (Psalm 19:1; Isaiah 6:3), but it is marred by sin. One day it will be renovated to reveal God's glory far more (Revelation 21:1). God has foreordained it, and it shall surely come to pass. Psalm 145:10, "All Your works shall praise You." This is the theology of teleology, the eventual eschaton, the glorious goal, the destination of predestination. God is the First Cause and Last End of all things (Romans 11:36).

The ultimate goal is not salvation but glory. One reason, according to Thomas Watson, is "the glory of God is worth more than the salvation of all men's souls."[15] Not all men will be saved, but all will reflect the glory of God. Sinners

---

9   John Calvin, *Sermons on Genesis 1:1–11:4* (Edinburgh: Banner of Truth, 2009), 6.

10   John Calvin, *The First Epistle of Paul the Apostle to the Corinthians* (Grand Rapids: Eerdmans, 1980), 40.

11   Calvin, *The Epistle of Paul the Apostle to the Hebrews, and the First and Second Epistles of St. Peter* (Grand Rapids: Eerdmans, 1980), 160.

12   John Calvin, *Commentary on the Book of Psalms* (Grand Rapids: Eerdmans, 1949), 4:169.

13   Calvin, *Commentary on the Book of Psalms*, 5:178.

14   Ebenezer Pemberton, *The Puritan Pulpit: The American Puritans* (Orlando: Soli Deo Gloria, 2006), 275.

15   Thomas Watson, *The Beatitudes* (London: Banner of Truth, 1971), 273. Elsewhere he says that God's glory is worth more than heaven or the salvation of souls. *The Lord's Prayer* (Edinburgh:

now steal God's glory but must return it in Hell. If human happiness were the final goal, then Arminians would be right to claim that God's purposes can be frustrated. But that is impossible. The final goal is theocentric, not anthropocentric.

Even in Heaven the final goal is not the happiness of the elect or their holiness. God glorifies saints in joy and sanctification for His own glory. God rejoices and reveals the glory of His joy in what He is doing in the elect. Angels rejoice when a sinner repents (Luke 15:10). How much more does God (Zephaniah 3:17)! We too shall rejoice and give glory to God.

Someone may object: "Doesn't this make God selfish?" In humans it is selfish to be centered around oneself and one's own glory. But it is not wrong for God, for God is God. It is wrong for us for the simple reason that we are not God. The ultimate purpose of man is God. And the ultimate purpose of God is God.[16] Jonathan Edwards added that though God reveals His glory and receives it back in worship, this does not add anything to God. Glory goes to God, the good goes to us.

Christological Glory

Christ is the focal point of all God's dealings with the universe in general and man in particular. Therefore, He reveals His glory superlatively through Christ and for Christ. Philippians 2:5–11 explains it. Christ the God-man laid aside His glory temporarily to suffer and die an inglorious, ignominious death for us. The Father rewarded Him by glorifying Him. It all redounds to the glory of God the Father (v. 11). Edward Pearse, Puritan, put it like this: "God's glory was His greatest end in the dispensation of Christ and our salvation by Him; and also that in and by that He designed the highest revenue of glory to Himself."[17] Colossians 1:16 tells us that all things were created both by and for Christ.

All in Heaven give glory to Jesus Christ in view of His death and resurrection (Revelation 5:12–13). God will reveal His glory through the person of Christ

---

Banner of Truth, 1978), 194. Calvin said that it would be better that the whole world would perish than that the glory of God be destroyed. *Commentary on the Book of the Prophet Isaiah* (Grand Rapids: Eerdmans, 1958), 1:220.

16 See especially J. I. Packer, *Hot Tub Religion* (Wheaton: Tyndale House, 1987), 34–35, 38. Jonathan Edwards has a devastating criticism on Arminianism on this point in *The Works of Jonathan Edwards* (New Haven: Yale University Press, 2002), 20:464.

17 Edwards Pearse, *The Best Match* (Morgan, PA: Soli Deo Gloria, 1994), 137.

fully in Heaven. The glory of God is not just visible light. It is a person — the Lord Jesus Christ. He is the glory of God, "the Lord of Glory" (James 2:1).

Conclusion

If Lutherans emphasize *sola fide*, Calvinists emphasis *soli Deo gloria*. Abraham Kuyper identifies this as "the fundamental principle of the Reformed churches: 'That all things must be measured by the glory of God.'"[18] Calvinists are "*Doxistas*" — "glory-givers."[19] We love to sing, "To God Be the Glory." Arthur C. Custance once said that the chief end of man can be summed up in three words: "to please God."[20] May it be so in our lives. Amen.

---

18 Kuyper, *The Work of the Holy Spirit*, 12.
19 I am deeply indebted to my late friend Maxwell Lathrop, a member of the first team of Wycliffe Bible Translators and a missionary to the Tarascan Indians of southern Mexico, for the word *Doxista*.
20 Arthur C. Custance, *Science and Faith: The Doorway Papers* (Grand Rapids: Zondervan, 1978), 8:186.

Chapter 29
The Origin of Sin

Where did sin come from? If God foreordained it, does that not make Him the author of sin? Reformed theology has the biblical answer. It is not popular with non-Calvinists and is subject to practical misuse. But it is biblical and has good practical implications.

The Problem

The problem can be stated succinctly. How can we harmonize three realities: (1) God is holy, (2) God is omnipotent, and (3) sin exists? Accepting any two of these creates a problem for the third. First, if God is holy, He must desire to prevent sin. If He is omnipotent, He is able to prevent sin. Yet sin exists. Why did God not prevent it? Second, if God is holy and wants to prevent sin and yet sin exists, it would appear that God was not able to prevent it. Yet God is indeed omnipotent and able to prevent it. Third, sin exists. Nothing exists except by the omnipotent creation of God. But that would imply that God is not holy. Yet God is holy.

Gordon H. Clark summed it up like this, assuming the existence of sin: "If God is good and wants to eliminate sin, but cannot, He is not omnipotent; but if God is omnipotent and can eliminate sin, but does not, He is not good. God cannot be both omnipotent and good."[1] This is one of the greatest problems of theology and philosophy. There have been many suggested solutions. Some say there is no answer. Many say that God had nothing whatsoever to do with the origin of sin. Extreme enemies of Christianity say the opposite: God had everything to do with sin because He is evil.

Perhaps the most popular answer among Christians follows Kant's Moral Argument for the existence of God. If there is no God, there would be no such thing as sin, for sin is defined as the breaking of God's law (1 John 3:4). If there is no God, everything is permitted, and there is no problem at all regarding the origin of sin, for there is no sin. The problem, then, actually proves the existence

---

1 Gordon H. Clark, *Religion, Reason, and Revelation* (Jefferson: The Trinity Foundation, 1986), 195.

of God. Calvinists admit that there is some truth in all this as far as it goes, but it does not go far enough.

God Is Not the Author of Sin

To begin, we fully assert that God is not the author of sin. In the words of the Westminster Confession: "God, who, being most holy and righteous, neither is, nor can be, the author or approver of sin" (5:4, cf. 3:1). In 1645 the Westminster Assembly issued "A Declaration of the Assembly Regarding the Abominable and Blasphemous Opinion" that God is the author of evil.[2] Other Reformed confessions and theologians affirm the same in no uncertain terms.

Scripture explicitly and repeatedly asserts the absolute holiness of God.[3] God cannot sin any more than He can lie (Titus 1:2) or die or cease to exist. He is "Holy, holy, holy" (Isaiah 6:3; Revelation 4:8). Far be it from God to do wickedness, and from the Almighty to commit iniquity" (Job 34:10; cf.12). "Shall not the Judge of all the earth do right?" (Genesis 18:25). "For all His ways are justice, a God of truth and without injustice; righteous and upright is He" (Deuteronomy 32:4). "For all that is in the world — the lust of the flesh, the lust of the eyes, and the pride of life — is not of the Father, but is of the world" (1 John 2:16). "God cannot be tempted by evil, nor does He Himself tempt anyone" (James 1:13). "God is not the author of confusion but of peace" (1 Corinthians 14:33).

To make God the author of sin is as great a blasphemy as can be conceived. One atheist philosopher looked around at the world and blasphemously charged, "If God exists, He is the Devil!" The existence of sin is often used by atheists as an argument against theism. But whatever else is true about sin's origin, we know that it did not arise from within God's holy nature. Arthur W. Pink represented Reformed theology here: "God is the Creator of the wicked, not of their wickedness; He is the Author of their being, not the Infuser of their sin."[4] Homer Hoeksema said: "While God is certainly not the author of sin, God has sovereignly determined that man shall be the author and cause of his own sin."[5]

---

2 In Chad Van Dixhoorn, ed. *The Minutes and Papers of the Westminster Assembly 1643–1652* (Oxford: Oxford University Press, 2012), 5:224–27.

3 On the holiness of God from a Reformed perspective, see Stephen Charnock, *The Existence and Attributes of God* (Grand Rapids: Baker, 1979), 2:108–208; R. C. Sproul, *The Holiness of God* (Wheaton: Tyndale House, 1985); and the Reformed systematic theologies.

4 Arthur W. Pink, *The Sovereignty of God* (Grand Rapids: Baker, 1973), 124.

5 Homer Hoeksema, *The Voice of Our Fathers* (Grand Rapids: Reformed Free Publishing

We must not picture God as indifferent to sin. Some seem to do this by misinterpreting Psalm 139:12: "The darkness and the light are both alike to You." That error resembles the atheist Friedrich Nietzsche in his book *Beyond Good and Evil*. By contrast, 1 John 1:5 says, "God is light and in Him is no darkness at all." Nietzsche began by blaming God, then denying God's existence, and ended up a raving lunatic in a Swiss insane asylum for the rest of his life. Accusing God of being the author of sin is insanity as well as blasphemy.

It is strange, then, that so many who use this problem against Christians have a low view of the actual heinousness of sin and the holy wrath of God. Calvinists have a high view of God's holy wrath second to none. We also have a much stronger diagnosis of the evil of evil than all others, as we shall see in chapter 33, "The Depth of Depravity."

Is Satan the Author of Sin?

Some have tried to answer the problem by saying that Satan is the originator and author of sin. He sinned before he tempted Adam and Eve to sin. Romans 5:12 says, "Through one man sin entered the world," which could mean that sin had already existed in the angelic realm. Adam and Eve caught it from the Devil.

The fall of Satan is indicated in 1 John 3:8 and 1 Timothy 3:6. Many theologians see it described or at least typified in Isaiah 14:12–15 and Ezekiel 28:11–19. Some see it in Luke 10:18, Revelation 12:7–12, Jude 6, and 2 Peter 2:4. It is not germane to the question to determine exactly when Satan first sinned (i.e., on which day of Genesis 1). But all this just pushes the problem one step back. God did not create Satan as an evil being any more than He created Adam as a sinner. So where did Satan's sin come from? If he was the first to sin, who tempted him?

God foreordained everything, including the creation and fall of Lucifer who sinned and became Satan. Peter Martyr Vermigli explained: "In this way, neither the wicked, nor the devil himself, nor sins can be excluded from predestination, for God uses all these things according to his will."[6] Calvin commented: "Even

---

Assoc., 1980), 251. Jay Adams: "He has decreed the existence of sin in such a way that men themselves freely [. . .] become the authors of their sin." *The Grand Demonstration* (Santa Barbara: EastGate, 1991), 59.

6 Peter Martyr Vermigli, *The Peter Martyr Library* (Kirksville, MO: Truman State University Press, 2003), 8:15.

the devil himself contributes in some way to the glory of God, though contrary to his wish."[7]

Satan was created a good angel but sinned. He led Adam into sin. But God did not lead either Satan or Adam into sin. In one sense, we can indeed say that Satan is the author of sin, for he was the first to sin. Jesus called him "the father of lies" (John 8:44). He is the greatest instigator of evil. He, not God, is "the Tempter" (James 1:13; Matthew 4:3). But the problem remains as to God's involvement in the origin of sin in the first place.

Foreordination of Sin

We have already seen from many texts that God predestined everything that comes to pass (e.g., Romans 11:36). Sin exists, therefore in some mysterious way it was foreordained by God, howbeit in a way that absolves Him from being its author.

One example sheds light on the puzzle. Acts 2:23 and 4:27–28 tell us that God foreordained the crucifixion of Christ. That was inexcusable murder on the part of the Jewish leaders (Acts 7:52; 1 Thessalonians 2:15). It was the greatest sin in all history, indeed, the worst sin imaginable. Yet it was foreordained by God. If God predestined the worst sin without being blameworthy, it is not inconsistent to say that God foreordained all other sins without being the blameworthy author of sin. This is what is called in logic, the "argument from the greater to the lesser" (an example is in Romans 8:32).

Some refer to Isaiah 45:7: "I form the light and create darkness: I make peace and create evil: I the Lord do all these things" (KJV). The Hebrew word for evil here is *ra*, a common word with several nuances and contextual uses. It sometimes means moral evil, sin, wickedness. But it can also here be rendered *calamity* (NJKV, ESV), *disaster* (NIV), or *woe* (RSV). It could refer to providential calamities, which I will discuss in the following chapter. But it can also refer to moral evil. Note the parallelism between light and peace on the one hand and darkness and evil on the other. *Darkness* in Scripture is often a term for sin (e.g., 1 John 1:5). At the least, this verse could mean that God had something to do with the creation of sin just as He had to do with the creation of darkness, peace, and light (Genesis 1:2–4).

---

7 John Calvin, *Commentary on the Book of the Prophet Isaiah* (Grand Rapids: Eerdmans, 1958), 1:117.

Augustine's Theory

Augustine was one of the first Christian theologians to wrestle with the problem. He put forth a theory that is still popular today, especially with Catholic apologists. He said that all things are good by virtue of creation (Genesis 1:31). Evil is not good, therefore evil is not a thing. It is a "no-thing," nothing. It has no substance. Sin is a negation, a shadow, a moral vacuum. It is a defect, not an effect. It cannot exist on its own, but only as a parasite on moral beings. God is the cause of things but not of sin because sin is not a thing. Sin therefore has no cause as such. Yet Augustine still admitted that whatever sin "is not," God allowed it to come into its unusual non-existence, whatever that means. "He judged it better to bring good out of evil than to allow nothing evil to exist."[8]

God Permitted Sin to Come into Existence

Jonathan Edwards said that in one sense God certainly is not the "author of sin" — that is, the promoter of sin. But in "another way" God is the blameless fore-ordainer and Creator of sin.[9] Others point out that God wills sin in the secret will but not in the revealed will. He willed and "dis-willed" sin (if I can coin a term) in different senses.

Peter Martyr Vermigli explained how God permits sin "in a sense" even in providence: "In one sense, God is said to will sins, either because when he does not prohibit them when he could, or because he does not allow them to burst forth when and how and for what purpose he will, or so that by them he will punish other sins."[10] There is no dispute that God presently allows sin to exist, though without His approval. He either forgives or condemns sinners, but in neither case does He approve of sin. God always hates sin as sin. We can deduce the eternal decree from this. If God now permits sin without approving of it, then He also eternally foreordained to allow it to exist without approving of it. There is deep mystery here. Spurgeon called it "a strange decree that sin should be tolerated; permitted first to enter, and then allowed afterwards to spread its mischievous poison."[11] It could be compared with democracy — we legally permit some things that we do not morally approve of.

---

8 Augustine, *The Works of Saint Augustine* (Hyde Park: New City, 2005), I/8:290. Cf. pp. 278–79.
9 Jonathan Edwards, *The Works of Jonathan Edwards* (New Haven: Yale University Press, 1957), 1:399.
10 Vermigli, *The Peter Martyr Library*, 8:45.
11 Charles H. Spurgeon, *Metropolitan Tabernacle Pulpit* (Pasadena, TX: Pilgrim Publications, 1984), 15:207.

The Paradox of the Problem

This throws us back on the horns of the dilemma of the paradox of the twofold will of God. Clearly God forbids sin in the revealed will but permits it in the secret will. He is not sin's author in one sense, but in another mysterious sense He permitted it to exist. In neither case does God approve or promote sin, for He is holy in all senses and wills.

As shown earlier, the secret will includes two aspects: active (positive) and passive (negative). Some, sounding like Augustine, would describe them as effective and defective. John Gill said sin had a deficient, not an efficient, cause.[12] In the positive, God actively foreordains good with His moral approval and promotion, reflecting His holy nature. In the negative, He passively foreordains sin by permission but with moral disapproval, reflecting His wrath. This touches on wrath as what is sometimes called "His strange work" (Isaiah 28:21 KJV). That is, wrath is a secondary attribute of God, based on the primary attribute of holiness, just as grace is a secondary attribute based on love. Divine wrath is the moral reaction to something outside of and antithetical to God, whereas holiness is a positive reaction to something affectionate to God.

This may be illustrated by the Fall and daily sins. Vermigli again comments: "Although sins are in one sense subject to the will of God, they are not produced by it in the same way as are good deeds."[13] One could say that God created good out of His holiness, but foreordained and created evil by *permissio ex nihilo*, permission out of nothing. The difference is crucial. If God foreordained evil in the exact same sense as He foreordained good, He would indeed be the author of evil. But He did not, nor does He presently allow evil to exist in the same way that He allows good to exist. Stephen Charnock the great Puritan said:

> God wills the permission of sin. He doth not positively will sin, but he positively wills to permit it. And though he doth not approve of sin yet he approves of that act of his will, whereby he permits it. [. . .] God doth not will sin, but he wills the permission of it, and this will to permit is

---

12 John Gill, *The Cause of God and Truth* (Grand Rapids: Baker Book House, 1980), 188.
13 Vermigli, *The Peter Martyr Library*, 8:73. D. A. Carson notes the asymmetry of the dual cause, so God is praised for the good but not blamed for the evil. *Divine Sovereignty and Human Responsibility* (Atlanta: John Knox, 1981), 212. The Bremen Consensus (1595): "However, God does not ordain evil in the same way that He ordains good, that is something pleasing to Him; but rather as something that He hates; though He knowingly and willingly decrees it, permits it to be in the world, and in a wondrous manner uses it for good." In James T. Dennison Jr, ed. *Reformed Confessions of the 16th and 17th Centuries in English Translation* (Grand Rapids: Reformation Heritage Books, 2012), 3:668.

active and positive in God. God is not the cause of sin, but the cause of not hindering sin.[14]

Calvin was uncomfortable with saying that God merely "permits" the existence of sin. Others, especially those of a supralapsarian persuasion, speak too boldly regarding God's active foreordination of sin. The Synod of Dort censured Johannes Maccovius for being too rash in his language and scholastic method on this point. Such persons unwittingly make God the author of sin and incur the disapproval of their fellow Calvinists as well as Arminians and Lutherans and, most of all, God Himself.

Some Provisos

Jay Adams draws a useful parallel with creation: "God decreed water, dry land, mountains, birds of the air, but God is none of the above. Decreeing sin does not make Him a sinner. He decreed the entire creation, but must be distinguished from it."[15] We emphasize that foreordination in eternity is not the same as approval in time, a proviso often overlooked or misunderstood by anti-Calvinists.

Also, God being sovereign was not morally bound not to predestine sin any more than He was bound to predestine good or anything else for that matter. Gordon Clark noted: "There is no law, superior to God, which forbids him to decree sinful acts."[16] Earlier, John Gill put it like this: "We, as creatures, are bound to hinder all the evil we can; but God is under no such obligation."[17] Calvin said, "God willeth righteously those things which men do wickedly."[18] Because of His holiness, God must punish sin. But that is not the same as the self-requirement to prevent sin's existence in the first place. We must be careful, however, to remember that God always wills in perfect harmony with

---

14 Charnock, *The Existence and Attributes of God*, 2:149.

15 Adams, *The Grand Demonstration*, 58.

16 Clark, *Religion, Reason, and Revelation*, 239–40.

17 John Gill, *A Complete Body of Doctrinal and Practical Divinity* (Paris, AR: Baptist Standard Bearer, 1984), 302. Edwards said that there would be an end to all divine law and government if God was obliged to prevent all moral evil and leave it to mere chance. "The Justice of God in the Damnation of Sinners (sermon 357A)," Jonathan Edwards Center at Yale University, accessed February 9, 2018, http://edwards.yale.edu/.

18 John Calvin, *Calvin's Calvinism* (Grand Rapids: Reformed Free Publishing Association, 1991), 202. John Piper: "God does not sin in willing that sin takes place." *Does God Desire All to Be Saved?* (Wheaton: Crossway, 2013), 37. Thomas Watson: "God permits sin but he does not promote it," quoted in John Blanchard, ed., *Sifted Silver* (Darlington: Evangelical Press, 1995), 112.

His holy nature. Those such as Maccovius too closely resembled Duns Scotus and other medieval schoolmen in their voluntarism, whereby God could theoretically decree something directly contrary to His nature. In an ironic way, Duns Scotus also posited a kind of supralapsarianism. Mainline Calvinists have refused to go down that slippery slope. It is no coincidence that infralapsarian Calvinists often accuse supralapsarians of making God the author of sin, but the accusation does not come the other way.

Why Did God Decree to Permit Sin to Exist?

Granted, then, that God foreordained sin to exist, the question then is: Why? The answer is simple: for His own glory. God foreordained everything in order to reveal His glory, including evil. One could say that God reveals and receives more (or different) glory by decreeing sin's existence than by not allowing it to exist at all. William G. T. Shedd observed:

> The reason for the permission of sin was the manifestation of certain Divine attributes which could not have been manifested otherwise. [. . .] The position that sin is necessary to the best possible universe is objectionable, unless by the best possible universe be meant the universe best adapted to manifest the Divine attributes.[19]

Without sin, there could be no grace or wrath, for both presuppose the existence of sin. Grace forgives sin; wrath is angry with sin. It is like Romans 4:15, where it is stated that there is no sin without law. There could be holiness but not wrath without sin. Likewise, there could be love but not grace without sin. God loved the holy angels but never showed them grace. He gave no grace to fallen angels but decreed to give grace to some fallen humans (2 Timothy 1:9).

This sheds light on the principle "where sin abounded, grace abounded still more" (Romans 5:20). This is somewhat displayed in Philemon 15–16: "For perhaps [Onesimus] departed for a while for this purpose, that you might receive him forever, no longer as a slave but more than a slave — a beloved brother." Sin is the black velvet that makes the diamond of God's love sparkle

---

19 William G. T. Shedd, *Dogmatic Theology, 3rd ed.* (Phillipsburg, NJ: P&R, 2003), 328. Edwards said that we would not know about the attribute of mercy without the Fall, for it was not shown to fallen or unfallen angels nor even to Adam before the Fall. "Psalm 136:1 (sermon 413)," Jonathan Edwards Center at Yale University, accessed February 9, 2018, http://edwards. yale.edu/.

more gloriously. God foreordained sin to forgive elect sinners and thereby display super-love, "to the praise of the glory of His grace" (Ephesians 1:6).[20]

The same is true with divine wrath. God revealed holiness to the unfallen angels and to Adam before the Fall. But He then revealed wrath to the fallen angels and humanity once they sinned. Wrath is an extension of holiness, as grace is of love. Wrath is God's angry holiness, His offended purity. It is the violent negative reaction to holiness' opposite. Grace is shown to some of those who deserved wrath (Ephesians 2:3), but God decreed to leave other sinners in sin to display the glory of His wrath (Romans 9:22). Thus, the Reformed doctrines of election and reprobation are crucial to a biblical answer to the question of the origin of sin.

Resembling Augustine, Thomas Watson commented: "God would never permit any evil if he could not bring good out of evil."[21] I would add: He could bring glory out of evil. What depths of wisdom there are in God's foreordination of all things for His glory! (Romans 11:33) This has practical implications, as Calvin pointed out: "Thus, if we ask the question, why did God allow men to fall and become so miserably lost, the answer is that God desired us to lean on his grace alone."[22]

The *Felix Culpa*

The Reformed view is similar in some ways, and yet different in others, to the medieval idea of the *Felix Culpa*, Latin for "the happy fall" or "the fortunate fall."[23] The theory says that Christians can rejoice at the Fall, for it gave them the opportunity of enjoying a greater love of God than if there had been no Fall. This has some truth to it, but it is open to antinomian abuses, such as the excuses "Let us sin that happiness may abound," or "Thank God for sin." Luther was often given to unguarded statements of a similar nature, such as:

> God does not save people who are only fictitious sinners. Be a sinner and sin boldly, but believe and rejoice in Christ more boldly, for he is victorious over sin, death, and the world. As long as we are here we have to sin [. . .] no sin will separate us from the Lamb, even though we commit

---

20 Cf. Theodore Beza, *The Christian Faith* (Lewes: Focus Christian Ministries, 1992), 7.

21 Quoted in Blanchard, *Sifted Silver*, 122.

22 John Calvin, *Sermons on Galatians* (Edinburgh: Banner of Truth, 1997), 329.

23 Alvin Plantinga holds to a form of the *Felix Culpa* in "Supralapsarianism, or "O *Felix Culpa*". In Peter van Inwagen, ed. *Christian Faith and the Problem of Evil* (Grand Rapids: Eerdmans, 2004), 1–25.

fornication and murder a thousand times a day. [. . .] Pray boldly — you too are a mighty sinner.[24]

But it is difficult to see how Christians who love holiness can rejoice at the entrance of sin any more than rejoice over the torture and death of our beloved Jesus. Yet the cross was the means to a greater end, and so was the entrance of sin.

Luke 15:7 says there is more joy in Heaven over the salvation of one sinner who repents than over ninety-nine persons who never sinned. Since all humans (except Jesus) have sinned, this may be a reference to the holy angels (Cf. angels in v. 10). God gets more joy in forgiving elect sinful humans than in keeping holy angels from sinning, who share God's joy in all this.

Similarly, Christ went to the cross "for the joy that was set before Him" (Hebrews 12:2), as if He knew He would have more joy in redeeming and cleansing a sinful bride than an unfallen one. Spurgeon alluded to something similar: "God is more glorified in the person of His Son than He would have been by an unfallen world."[25] But elsewhere he rejected what he calls Augustine's *Beata Culpa* view and added that more of God's love is displayed in Christ than in ten thousand unfallen worlds.[26] Jonathan Edwards accepted the Reformed view of the *Felix Culpa*: "Hence we may learn how vastly higher and more glorious the happiness is that is purchased for the elect by Christ, than that which Adam would have obtained if he had stood."[27] Samuel Rutherford spoke rather unguardedly of "a blessed Fall"[28] and "happy sins (if I may speak so), not of themselves but because they are neighboured with faith and love."[29]

Thomas Manton, Puritan, explicitly accepted the *Felix Culpa* view:

> God is so good, that he would not suffer evil if he could not bring good out of it. In regard of the issue and event of it, sin may be termed (as Gregory said of Adam's fall) Felix Culpa, a happy fall, because it maketh

---

24 *Luther's Works* (Minneapolis: Fortress Press, 1963), 48:282. This was in a letter to Phillip Melanchthon.

25 Quoted in Blanchard, *Sifted Silver*, 170.

26 Spurgeon, *Metropolitan Tabernacle Pulpit*, 41:5.

27 Jonathan Edwards, *The Works of Jonathan Edwards* (New Haven: Yale University Press, 2000), 18:515; cf. 13:307–09. William Farel: "We are restored to a state more noble than what was ever before the sin of Adam in Paradise; not that which is terrestrial, but celestial; not to a life corporeal, corruptible, and that can be lost, but spiritual, without corruption, and which can never be lost." In Dennison Jr., ed., *Reformed Confessions*, 1:57.

28 Samuel Rutherford, *Letters of Samuel Rutherford* (Edinburgh: Banner of Truth, 1984), 657.

29 Rutherford, 600.

way for the glory of God. It is good to note how many attributes are advanced by sin — mercy in pardoning, justice in punishing, wisdom in ordering, power in overruling it; every way doth our good God serve himself of the evils of men.[30]

This does not mean, as some tongue-in-cheek Darwinian theologians say, "Adam fell upward." But it does mean that Adam and elect humanity after him enjoy more divine love than Adam did before the Fall. The elect will experience more joy in the renewed Paradise of Heaven than Adam did in Eden or would have had he passed the probationary test. Surely God's ways are not our ways (Isaiah 55:8).

The *Felix Culpa*, however, must not be equated with the philosophy of utilitarianism, that is, the good/right/true is determined by what brings the most happiness to the most number of people. As we shall see, most Calvinists believe that there will be more lost sinners in Hell than redeemed saints in Heaven.

History is not a Greek tragedy nor a Shakespearean tragedy like Hamlet in which all the leading characters die. History has a happy twist ending for the elect but an ironic poetic justice for the reprobate. We enjoy far more grace than the love that pre-Fall Adam enjoyed. We are also elevated far higher than that from which Adam fell. We would rather be a redeemed sinner than an unfallen angel. We have a song that even the angels cannot sing.

How Did God Allow Adam to Fall?

This has bearing on how God righteously allowed sin to enter in the fall of sinless Adam. This has mystified the greatest minds, Reformed or otherwise. Arminians, of course, usually just deny that God had anything to do with the Fall, which is as unbiblical as saying that God has nothing to do with natural disasters. That will be discussed in the following chapter.

Jonathan Edwards had a controversial theory. He suggested that God created Adam with a holy but peccable nature and that this made it inevitable that he would one day sin.[31] This sounds like "Murphy's Law": If something bad *can* happen, it *will* happen and at the worst possible time. Edwards strongly

---

30 Thomas Manton, *An Exposition of the Epistle of James* (London: Banner of Truth, 1968), 93. He is probably referring to Gregory the Great, though Gregory of Rimini also probably held to a form of the *Felix Culpa*.

31 See John H. Gerstner, *The Rational Biblical Theory of Jonathan Edwards* (Orlando: Ligonier Ministries, 1992), 2:303–22.

opposed the Pelagian error that says that Adam was created morally neutral, a moral *tabula rasa,* and would have died even if he had never sinned. Calvinists universally follow Augustine's view that God created Adam holy, yet not impeccable. He could sin and did sin. In Heaven, of course, redeemed saints will be unable to sin.

Augustine said that God created angels and Adam with the need for God's help to remain sinless.[32] True. If so, then all God had to do was withhold that help, and they would fall. He did, and they did. God was under no obligation to keep Adam from falling, so he cannot be blamed for it.[33] But there is an important adjunct to this observation. God did not force Adam down. He simply withheld support, and Adam fell under his own weight. God dropped Adam, not threw him down. If God had thrown him down, He would have been the author of the first human sin (likewise with Lucifer's previous sin). One could call Adam's constitutional ability to sin even in a sinless state "the law of moral gravity." God created Adam mutable, not immutable, and this opened the door to a possible, if not inevitable, fall. Augustine again said: "What makes such evil possible is the fact that no created nature can be immutable."[34] In Heaven, however, saints will be immutably impeccable, as Augustine accepted. The matter of divine immutability and human mutability is crucial to the Augustinian/Reformed viewpoint.

Alternative Theories

"Evil is an equal but opposite force." This Gnostic theory evolved from Zoroastrianism and lies behind most Eastern religions (Taoism, the yin-yang, etc.). It was in the Manichaeism that Augustine tried and rejected. It is utterly wrong because Satan is not equal to God, nor is evil equal to good. Gnosticism also erred in saying that physical matter is necessarily evil. Genesis 1:31 says that God pronounced all that He made "very good." Christ took on holy flesh (John 1:14).

"Evil is necessary. Sin just is." This is a curious twist on the old Deist argument

---

32 Augustine, *The Works of Saint Augustine,* I/26:131.

33 Vermigli said that God willed the withholding of grace that He was under no obligation to give to Adam. *The Peter Martyr Library,* 8:52.

34 Augustine, *City of God,* 22:1. *The Fathers of the Church* (Washington, D.C.: Catholic University of America Press, 1954), 24:416. The incommunicable attribute of immutability is a major theme in Augustine's doctrine of God. The implications for the Augustinian/Reformed theology are more significant than is usually acknowledged and needs to be explored by further research by Reformed theologians.

against the Reformed doctrine of foreordination, "Things just are." It was sometimes called "the moral nature and fitness of things," which in this case could be mocked as "the immoral nature and unfitness of things." This makes evil an ontological necessity. But God alone is ontologically necessary. He alone is self-existent. *Necessary evil* is a contradiction in terms. If it is necessary, it is not evil, and if it is evil, it is not necessary. The woeful practical implications of this theory are obvious — it gives license to sin.

"Man is the sole author of sin." True, man is to be blamed. Adam wrongly shifted the blame for his sin onto Eve, and Eve shifted the blame to Satan. Both shifted the blame onto God as well. Also, Satan sinned before either of them, so some say that Satan is the first author of sin. This is true insofar as Satan was indeed the first to sin, and he spreads sin as a disease and will one day be punished above all others for it. But this theory does not adequately explain how or why God was involved in the matter.

"Sin itself is a real good." Stoicism suggested something like this. But sin by definition and by nature is not good but non-good. Defending sin as good in disguise does not solve the problem.

"Sin comes from the dark side of God." This blasphemous idea is defended by occultists or used as an accusation against Calvinism. But God did not create evil out of Himself, for "God is light and in Him is no darkness at all" (1 John 1:5). The holiness and wrath of God are not the dark side of God as opposed to His love. There is no more a dark side of God than there is a light side of Satan.

"Is not the Reformed theory like the Jesuit error that 'The end justifies the means?'" Scripture condemns that ethical theory in Romans 3:8, and so do Calvinists. The Jansenist Blaise Pascal rightly mocked the Jesuit theory as licentious. God does no evil when He sovereignly permits others to do it.

"God created man with free will, and He does not interfere, nor *can* He interfere. Thus man was free to fall by himself without any divine assistance." This is the usual theory of Arminianism, for example, as expressed by A. W. Tozer.[35] Adam had a kind of free will in that he had no bondage to sin yet. But he was not free from the overruling sovereign providence of God.

"Nobody knows the answer to the problem of the origin of sin. It is inappropriate to try to answer it." Many throw up their hands at the problem and say, "God only knows." Yes, God alone knows the ultimate answer, but He

---

35 A. W. Tozer, *The Knowledge of the Holy* (London: James Clarker, 1965), 118.

has revealed some of the answer in Scripture. G. C. Berkouwer says that trying to answer the problem is a subtle attempt to shift the blame onto Adam, Satan, or God.[36] He is partly true. But he said this in the context of his un-Reformed view that denies that God foreordained whatsoever comes to pass. We dare not shift the blame, but we should also not deny what God has said about the matter, let alone reject absolute foreordination.

A Caution

We must be doubly humble and repentant in discussing this subject. Some Calvinists have unfortunately not been so circumspect. In their zeal to defend the divine sovereignty, they over-emphasize sovereignty and de-emphasize divine holiness and human responsibility. This was seen in supralapsarians like Maccovius, the so-called Antinomians of the seventeenth century, and some Hyper-Calvinists. This opens them to the charge of making God the author of sin and the father of evil. A reckless attitude is most inappropriate.

We dare not even hint at the excuse "God predestined me to sin." Perhaps the reprobate will attempt such a blasphemous excuse at Judgment Day, but no holy saint entertains such a thought. Rather, we should confess like David, "I have sinned. I am the man" (2 Samuel 12).

Conclusion

John Gill said, "The same decree which permits sin provides for the punishment of it."[37] J. C. Philpot added, "It is sufficient for us to know that sin is, and that it is a blessing to know also there is a cure for it."[38] We should discuss the whole subject only in an attitude of humble repentance and grateful love.

---

36 G. C. Berkouwer, *Sin* (Grand Rapids: Eerdmans, 1971), 1–148.
37 John Gill, *The Cause of God and Truth* (Grand Rapids: Baker, 1980), 194.
38 J. C. Philpot, *Sermons* (Harpenden: Gospel Standard Baptist Fund, 1977), 8:51.

Chapter 30
The Problem of Evil

In this chapter we will look at a problem that is closely related to the problem of the origin of sin. The question can be put like this: How can a loving and holy God allow so much sin and suffering in the world?

Providence and Temptation

First, it is essential to realize that God cannot be blamed for sin or suffering. He is beyond blame, and it is inexcusable blasphemy to blame God. It is also true that God foreordained all things that come to pass, including sin and suffering. And He presently allows them to happen. But providential permission is not the same as uncaring approval.

James 1:12–14 is crucial. Verse 12 says there is a blessing for the person who passes the test of faith. Verse 13 plays on the double meaning of the Greek word *peirazo*. It can mean either to test or to tempt. James then says in verse 13 that God cannot be tempted. He is impeccably holy and cannot sin. Temptations against Him are both ineffectual and impertinent. Sinners attempt to tempt God when they are in the crucible of the test of faith. Some may try to get God to excuse their sin or blame God when they fail the test.

Then we are told that God Himself never tempts anyone. He tests (Genesis 22:1; Hebrews 11:17) but does not tempt. The key is the personal pronoun *Himself*. He never does it directly. He never commands us or forces us to sin. Yet being sovereign, God uses second causes to carry out His purposes. He sovereignly allows others to tempt us — Satan, the demons, other sinners, our own sinful nature. He tests us to show us what is in us and whether we truly love Him (Deuteronomy 8:2).

One example is in 2 Samuel 24:1, "He moved David" to take a census of Israel. Some translations render it "The Lord" or "It," but the subject is clearly *God*. The parallel in 1 Chronicles 21:1 says, "Now Satan stood up against Israel and moved David to number Israel." God Himself did not tempt David directly. He tested David by providentially allowing Satan to tempt him.

Another example is Matthew 4:1: "Then Jesus was led up by the Spirit into the wilderness to be tempted by the Devil." Mark 1:12 says "the Spirit *drove* Him," a forceful word used of casting out demons. The Father tested Jesus by using the Spirit to drive Jesus into the desert to be tempted by the Devil. Satan, not God, was "the Tempter" (Matthew 4:3). Unlike David, the Son of David passed the test. David succumbed to the temptation; Jesus did not. Shortly after this Christ gave us the model prayer: "Do not lead us into temptation but deliver us from the Evil One" (Matthew 6:13). God can lead us into and out of temptation, yet He Himself never tempts anyone. God tests; Satan tempts. God does it for a good reason; Satan for a bad.

Concurrence with Moral Evil

This raises the problem of God's involvement when we fail the test. How does God providentially influence the human will when it sins, yet without forcing it to sin? Calvin agreed with Augustine and noted: "God in a marvelous and secret way wills justly to be done what is done unjustly. [. . .] A man wills with evil will what God wills with a good will."[1] God is the First Cause and uses second causes, such as our will, to guarantee that His ultimate purpose is carried out. Remember the illustration from billiards. God cannot only do a double-combination, two-rail shot, but He can use all fifteen balls and all four rails to pocket whatever ball He wishes. This buffer means that God Himself is not the tempter or the author of our sin. If He drove in the eight ball directly using the pool cue, He would be guilty — but He uses the white cue ball and others to effect the shot. The persons He uses are to blame, not God. Nobody can blame God.

As we have already shown, God foreordained sin in a different way than He foreordained good. In time, God does good directly through us (Philippians 1:6; 2:13), but it cannot be said that God does evil through us. He never sins through us. As in the origin of sin, God simply leaves us to ourselves and thereby permits us to sin by ourselves. We fall by our own weight. Calvin wisely saw this and concluded:

> God is not made the author of evil deeds when he is said to lead the ungodly where he wills and to accomplish and execute his work through them, but rather we shall acknowledge that he is a wonderfully expert craftsman who can use even bad tools as well.[2]

God can use a crooked stick to draw a straight line.

---

1 John Calvin, *Calvin: Theological Treatises* (Philadelphia: Westminster, 1954), 335, 337.
2 John Calvin, *The Bondage and Liberation of the Will* (Grand Rapids: Baker, 1996), 40.

God Restrains Sin and Takes the Restraints Off

God can and does restrain us from sinning: "I withheld you from sinning against Me" (Genesis 20:6). One way is to prevent us from being tempted. Another way is to give us power to resist the temptation by helping us flee it (1 Corinthians 10:13). God is not under any obligation to restrain us. Sometimes He loosens or removes the restraints. He "allowed all nations to walk in their own ways" (Acts 14:16). "I gave them over to their own stubborn heart, to walk in their own counsels" (Psalm 81:12). He "gives them over" to the temptations of the Devil (Acts 7:42; Romans 1:24, 26, 28). Christians should pray that God does not take the restraints off, otherwise there is no sin we would not commit except the unpardonable sin.

Isaiah 10:5–7 is another case in point. Assyria was God's rod to carry out His purpose. Like Joseph's brothers, Assyria meant it for evil, but God meant it for good (Genesis 45:5–8; 50:20). Isaiah 46:11 is similar: "Calling a bird of prey from the east, the man who executes My counsel, from a far country. I indeed have spoken it; I will also bring it to pass. I have purposed it; I will also do it."

This applies to the greatest sin in all history — the murder of the Son of God. God foreordained it (Acts 2:23; 4:27–28; 1 Peter 1:20). In time He took the moral restraints off Judas, the Jewish leaders, and Pontius Pilate. They were guilty. But behind it all was the sovereign hand of God (Isaiah 53:10).

Revelation 17:17 is another example: "God has put it into their hearts to fulfill His purpose, and to be of one mind, and to give their kingdom to the beast until the words of God are fulfilled." They surely sinned; God surely was sovereign. They, not God, were to blame. Edward Polhill the Puritan said, "Wherefore when sin is prevented, God's free grace is to be praised; and when sin is permitted, God's absolute sovereignty is to be adored."[3]

Luther somewhere said that Satan is "God's Devil." We see this in Job 1 and 2. Satan could go no further than God allowed him. God tested Job by allowing Satan to both tempt and afflict Job. This brought about a greater good in the end than at the beginning (Job 42:10), which is what God will do for all the saints. Augustine was right: "To make good use of an evil is so far from being diabolical that God makes good use even of the devil himself."[4] Calvin said, "So that whatever poison Satan produces, God turns it into medicine for his elect."[5]

3 Edward Polhill, *The Works of Edward Polhill* (Morgan, PA: Soli Deo Gloria, 1998), 135.
4 Augustine, *The Works of Saint Augustine* (Hyde Park: New City, 1999), I/25:520.
5 John Calvin, *Commentaries on the First Book of Moses Called Genesis* (Grand Rapids: Eerdmans, 1948), 2:488.

Elsewhere he wrote, "God, by withholding Satan fast bound in obedience to His Providence, turns him whithersoever He will, and this applies to the great enemy's devices and attempts the accomplishments of His own eternal purposes."[6]

This principle applies to God's providential dealings with sin in general. The Lord is never tainted by the sin He providentially permits when He removes moral restraint. Again Calvin:

> For in the same way that the sun shines on carrion and causes it to rot, neither being corrupted nor tainted by it, and by its purity is not the cause of the carrion's stench and infection, God also so truly performs His works through evildoers that His sanctity does not justify them nor does their infection contaminate anything in Him.[7]

The Problem of Natural Evil

The Hebrew word *ra* can mean both moral evil (sin) or natural evil (disaster). How can a good God allow bad things to happen? We can immediately dismiss the suggestion by liberals and many Arminians that God has nothing whatsoever to do with them. This error is also promoted by many Pentecostals who place all involvement on the Devil and say God has nothing to do with suffering or sickness.

Amos 3:6 is explicit: "If there is a calamity in a city, will not the Lord have done it?" We previously mentioned Isaiah 45:7, which some take to refer to moral evil, and others, to natural evil. God permits airplanes to crash, earthquakes to destroy cities, hurricanes to decimate houses, and diseases to strike even children. He allows floods — remember the Flood in Noah's day. He is in charge of all creation and therefore controls all natural disasters.

Creation was not like this at the beginning. There were no earthquakes in the garden of Eden, nor diseases or afflictions of any kind. When Adam and Eve sinned, God pronounced a curse on creation (Genesis 3:17). This applies to the entire universe (Romans 8:20–22). God uses this principle to carry out His overall purpose. He can stop storms if He wishes (Matthew 8:26). He can just as easily bring blessing as destruction. Jeremiah 32:42, "Just as I have brought all

---

6 John Calvin, *Calvin's Calvinism* (Grand Rapids: Reformed Free Publishing Association, 1991), 188. See Calvin's *Sermons on Job* (Edinburgh: Banner of Truth, 1993), and Derek Thomas, *Proclaiming the Incomprehensibility of God: Calvin's Teaching on Job* (Fearn: Mentor, 2004).
7 John Calvin, *Treatises Against the Anabaptists and Against the Libertines* (Grand Rapids: Baker, 1982), 247.

this great calamity on this people, so I will bring on them all the good I have promised them."

A natural evil may or may not be directly due to a specific sin (Luke 13:1–3; John 9:3). Disasters may or may not be punishment for specific sins. Remember Job. But remember also Sodom and Gomorrah. God may use such things to chasten His children and punish His enemies or to drive lost sinners to seek His face. God uses good things to bless bad people (Acts 14:17).

The Problem of Pain

In 1981 Rabbi Harold Kushner wrote the best seller, *When Bad Things Happen to Good People*.[8] He advocated the popular idea that all people are good and do not deserve bad things. Since bad things do happen, he concluded that God, who is good, does not have anything to do with them. He cannot stop bad things from happening to good people. This approach was meant to offer comfort to hurting people.

Calvinists replied that this approach is very wrong and ungodly. We concur that not all bad things are direct punishment for specific sins, and not all natural evil is moral evil. But we add several additional observations. For one, pain can be a good thing. Pain can warn us of harmful things like fire. A surgeon will tell us that sometimes pain can be a good sign that healing is taking place after surgery or a burn.

God sovereignly allows some suffering because of certain sins. God chastens His children (Hebrews 12:5–11). He uses afflictions to humble us, make our hearts pliable, and make us sympathetic to others who suffer (2 Corinthians 1:4–6). God uses such "bad things" to draw us closer to Himself and fill our hearts with love and peace greater than we would know in good times.

But what about the problem of pain on sinful mankind in general? In reality, there is no such problem of pain. Kushner misdiagnosed the problem and therefore gave the wrong antidote. The great Reformed theologian John Gerstner replied with an essay entitled *The Problem of Pleasure*.[9] Gerstner was right; Kushner was wrong. First, Gerstner showed that bad things do in fact happen. Next, God is personally involved in them. Further, and this is the crucial point, there are no good people, only bad sinners who deserve punishment. Punishment involves

---

8 New York: Avon, 1981.
9 Phillipsburg, NJ: Presbyterian and Reformed, 1983. It was later reprinted in his *Primitive Theology* (Morgan, PA: Soli Deo Gloria, 1996), 415–42.

pain, so we guilty sinners deserve pain. We deserve bad things and bad times. We are not getting worse than we deserve; we are getting better than we deserve. Anything less than Hell is a mercy. The worst pain we suffer here will look like paradise compared with Hell.

The real problem is not why there is so much pain, but why there is so much pleasure. Nobody deserves pleasure. Why then does God send pleasure to wretched sinners? Why does God not overwhelm all of us with intense pain every second of every day? Why are we not already in Hell where we belong? Why do the wicked prosper and enjoy so much pleasure while they are still on earth? That is the real problem.

Habakkuk faced it in his day. The evil Assyrians were rampaging through the Middle East and even attacked God's people, Israel. Other prophets such as Jeremiah (indeed, most of the prophets) stated that Israel was getting the punishment it deserved from Assyria and Babylon. Habakkuk wrestled with the converse problem. In 1:13 he cried, "You are of purer eyes than to behold evil, and cannot look on wickedness. Why do You look on those who devour a person more righteous than he?" Why had God not punished the Assyrians, who were worse than Israel who they were attacking? Why did God allow it? It just did not seem fair.

The answer is that God does not punish all sin in this life. Even the pain we suffer in this life is only partial and temporary compared with eternal Hell. All unrepentant sinners will be punished, but not always in this life with natural evil. Sinners deceive themselves when they complain that they do not deserve the bad times they go through, and so they formulate a self-serving "problem of pain" that either blames God or leaves Him out of the world's problems. It thereby exonerates the sinner. In his own blunt way, Gerstner got to the heart of the matter:

> What irony that sinners consider the greatest problem they face in this world the problem of pain. The ultimate insult against God is that man thinks he has a problem of pain. Man, who deserves to be plunged into hell at this moment, and is indescribably fortunate that he is breathing normally, complains about unhappiness. Instead of falling on his knees in the profoundest possible gratitude that God holds back His wrath and infinite fury, the sinner shakes his fist in heaven's face and complains against what he calls "pain." When he receives his due, he will look back on his present condition as paradisaical. What he now calls misery, he will then consider exquisite pleasure. The most severe torment anyone has ever

known in this life will seem like heaven in comparison with one moment of the full fury of the divine Being. The most foolish thing a human being ever says is "the only real Hell there is, is in this world." The truth of that matter is that, for that person, the only heaven there is, is in this world.[10]

There is more. First, God providentially blesses wicked sinners with good things to entice them to repent and turn to God (Romans 2:4). Every day of pleasure on earth is another day in which they may repent. But they do not even thank God for such good things (Romans 1:21). This is the Reformed doctrine of *common grace*, which I will discuss later. But refused common grace becomes damning wrath. God uses all this to fatten up the unrepentant reprobate for the slaughter. They will have nobody to blame but themselves. They will have no excuses on Judgment Day or in Hell. They will know they have refused God's good things, threw them back in His face with ungrateful scorn, and are getting what they truly deserve. The good things they received on earth will redound to their pain in Hell (Luke 16:25).

Theodicy

Gottfried Leibniz, not at all a Calvinist, coined the word *theodicy*.[11] It refers to how we can justify the ways of God to man regarding the existence of both moral and natural evil. Basically his answer is that evil of both kinds must exist to show the glory of the good. For good to be good, there must be bad shown to be bad. This implies that God cannot stop moral or natural evil, for they are just plain necessary in this the best of all possible worlds.

Though there are a few correct points in his theory, by and large, Calvinists reject it. The main point is that we do not have to defend God or His ways; God defends Himself. We only need to give men the words of God in Scripture on these matters. Man, not God, is on trial. God is the judge, not the defendant. Who are we to question the ways of God? (Romans 9:14, 20) Guilty men are tested and condemned by God, not vice versa. God tests us by allowing us to be tempted. But when we test God, we fail the test and provoke His wrath. Read Job. We have no right to question the Almighty's ways. God did not owe an answer to Job and did not give him one except "Trust Me." In the end Job did, and so should we. Furthermore, God does not need bad to prove that He is good.

---

10 Gerstner, *The Problem of Pleasure*, 16–17.
11 G. W. Leibniz, *Theodicy* (London: Routledge and Kegan Paul, 1951)

Wayne Grudem offers a useful analogy.[12] Shakespeare was the author of the play *Macbeth*, in which Macbeth murdered King Duncan. Macbeth was to be blamed, not Shakespeare. Similarly, God is the author of all history but is not the blameworthy "author of evil," whether moral or natural. The analogy is not perfect, but it is adequate.

Conclusion

God owes us nothing. He does not owe us an answer to the problem of evil. He condescends to tell us some of the answer. He gave us the Book of Job, which Job did not have. He humbles us and moves us to trust Him.

The answer involves the following points:

1. God is sovereign and omnipotent. He permits both moral and natural evil to exist.

2. God is holy. He cannot be blamed.

3. Man alone is culpable and cannot shift the blame onto God.

4. God is good. He gives common grace to all and offers special grace to forgive sinners. He even gives comfort to His unrepentant enemies.

5. In the end, God uses both moral and natural evil to punish the reprobate and bless the elect.

6. God will be glorified in all things in the end.

---

12 Wayne Grudem, *Systematic Theology* (Grand Rapids: Zondervan, 1994), 322.

Chapter 31
Original Sin

God's Word teaches that all humans except Jesus Christ inherit a sinful nature from Adam that we call *original sin*. The term is not in the Bible and was probably coined by Augustine.[1] All evangelicals and Roman Catholics believe in it. Pelagius was one of the first to deny it. Semi-Pelagians and Arminians hold to a modified version. Reformed theology has the strongest view of all. To understand the doctrine of total depravity, we must first understand original sin.

The Nature of Original Sin

Ephesians 2:3 says that before their conversion Christians "were by nature children of wrath, just as others." Our very nature is "dead in trespasses and sins" (v. 1) and follows the sinful course of the world and the Devil (v. 2), with sin in our flesh and mind (v. 3). We have a fallen human nature. Sin is what we are, not just what we do. God created Adam holy, not morally neutral as Pelagius held (Genesis 1:31; Ecclesiastes 7:29). Therefore, human nature as such is not necessarily sinful. Christ had a fully human nature but without sin (Hebrews 4:15). Adam sinned and passed his sinful nature on to all his descendants.

We are all born with original sin as a spiritual congenital disease that is passed on to our children and is fatal. No one is exempt, even Mary, contrary to Romanism's doctrine of the Immaculate Conception and impeccable sinlessness of Mary. We are born sons of the Devil (Matthew 13:38; John 8:44; Acts 13:10), not sons of God. We are "young vipers," baby serpents with the fallen nature of the Serpent, as Jonathan Edwards said.[2] This is basically what Paul meant by the word *flesh* — the sinful nature that includes, but is not limited to, our body. Jesus said, "That which is born of the flesh is flesh" (John 3:6; cf. 1:13). That which is born from a sinful parental nature has a sinful familial nature.

It is the sin from which all individual sins proceed. It is the womb of all evil (James 1:15). The Belgic Confession says, "Sin constantly boils forth as though from a contaminated spring" (Article 15). Newborn infants may look innocent,

---

1 See *The Works of Saint Augustine* (Hyde Park: New City, 2008), I/12:179.
2 Jonathan Edwards, *The Works of Jonathan Edwards* (New Haven: Yale University Press, 1972), 4:394.

but that is only because their original sin has not yet shown itself. It will soon blossom. They have it even in the unborn state in the womb. Calvin put it like this: "There is a secret poison lurking in them, and that although they do not show it at first, yet they are like a brood of serpents"[3] (Cf. Matthew 3:7).

Roman Catholic theology tends to say that original sin is simply the negative absence of righteousness. This is not the Pelagian "blank tablet" (*tabula rasa*) error that says we are born morally neutral like Adam was when created. Calvinists go further than Rome. We hold that original sin is both the absence of righteousness and the presence of unrighteousness. It includes the active predisposition to sin. Human nature is never morally neutral. Adam was pro-God before the Fall and anti-God afterwards, as we all are.

Sinful from Conception

To say all this is not to be misanthropic but realistic. It is a biblical diagnosis that fallen man obviously dislikes. It hurts our pride. But a doctor does not hate his patient when he tells him the hard truth that he has terminal cancer. Too often sentimental parents refuse to see that their newborn child is born sinful. When he begins to show it, parents sometimes say, "Isn't that cute?" They should rather mourn that sin is showing itself. They should also mourn that they themselves were the ones who passed original sin onto that child. Just as individual life begins at the moment of conception, so at that very instant original sin is passed on, long before the baby leaves the womb. Calvin said, "Children are already sinners condemned before God while still in their mother's womb."[4] No one has described this so deeply as John Calvin, as in the following:

> Even from infancy we show that we are steeped in the complete infection of sin. Little children coming into the world, though the malice does not appear, do not always fail to be little serpents full of poison, malice and disdain.[5]
>
> So the faithful must realize that their children are cursed, that they are damned, that there is only corruption in them, that there is such disorder in them that hell is prepared for their inheritance. In short, the devil and death dominate them with sin.[6]

---

3 John Calvin, *Sermons on the Epistle to the Ephesians* (London: Banner of Truth, 1973), 143.
4 John Calvin, *John Calvin's Sermons on the Ten Commandments* (Grand Rapids: Baker, 1980), 71.
5 John Calvin, *The Deity of Christ and Other Sermons* (Grand Rapids: Eerdmans, 1950), 62.
6 John Calvin, *Sermons on Genesis 1:1–11:14* (Edinburgh: Banner of Truth, 2009), 493.

We are born with sin, as serpents bring their venom from the womb.[7]

Calvin elsewhere noted the curse of original sin is shown in the fact that even the mother is tainted by sin in bringing forth an infant with original sin, for she was required by the Mosaic law to offer a sacrifice.[8] When parents fail to see sin in their babies, they often later make excuses for their sinful behavior. For example, they presume he is regenerate, even though he shows no evidence thereof but rather much the contrary. Or, they still think their child is saved because she "accepted Jesus into her heart" as a child, even though her lifestyle is blatantly wicked. Babies are just little sinners, just like the elderly are just old sinners. Original sin permeates our nature from womb to tomb.

Biblical Proofs

The first proof is the unity of the human race (Ephesians 2:1–3; Acts 17:26).[9] All humans have sinful humanity in common. If there was no original sin, then there would conceivably be some sinless persons in the world, as Pelagius argued. But there are none. Even regenerate Christians pass it on to their children.

The second proof is the principle of inherited nature. We inherit our humanity from our parents, who got it from their parents, all the way back to Adam and Eve. This includes more than DNA, blood types, and other genetic factors. God created Adam in His image (Genesis 1:26; 5:1–2), but the image was marred when Adam sinned. Adam then passed this marred image onto Cain and Abel, for "Adam [. . .] begat a son in his own likeness, after his image" (Genesis 5:3). We are "little Adams," as it were. If Adam and Eve had produced children before the Fall, the children would be sinless like their parents. But they did not procreate until after the Fall, so it was impossible for Cain and Abel to be born free of sin. The same is true of all humans. Job 14:4 says, "Who can bring a clean thing out of an unclean? No one!" Jesus said, "That which is born of the flesh is flesh" (John 3:6).

The third proof is infant sinfulness. Genesis 8:21: "The imagination of man's heart is evil from his youth." Psalm 58:3: "The wicked are estranged from

---

7 John Calvin, *The Epistles of Paul the Apostle to the Galatians, Ephesians, Philippians and Colossians* (Grand Rapids: Eerdmans, 1980), 141.

8 John Calvin, *A Harmony of the Gospels: Matthew, Mark and Luke* (Grand Rapids: Eerdmans, 1980), 89.

9 I follow Jonathan Edwards' discussion in "Original Sin," in *The Works of Jonathan Edwards*, volume 3 (New Haven: Yale University Press, 1970).

the womb; they go astray as soon as they are born, speaking lies" (Cf. v. 4). Isaiah 48:8: "I knew that you would deal very treacherously, and were called a transgressor from the womb." Proverbs 22:15: "Foolishness is bound up in the heart of a child." If all children have a sinful nature, it follows that they were all born with it.

The fourth proof is infant mortality. Some die in miscarriage, abortion, infanticide, fatal diseases, or sudden infant death syndrome. Most survive birth, but how can we theologically explain infant mortality except, "The wages of sin is death" (Romans 6:23)? If they had no sin, they would not die. Asahel Nettleton issued this challenge:

> Those who deny that infants are sinners, have devolved on them the Herculean task of defending the justice of God in bringing suffering and death upon millions of beings who are perfectly innocent. Those who admit the doctrine of infant depravity, have no difficulty on this subject.[10]

James Jordan commented, "All children deserve to die; it is the mercy of God that he spares some."[11] The death of some proves the guilt of all, unless one puts forth the extremely unlikely and unprovable thesis that only those who die are guilty, and those who live are innocent.

The fifth proof is universal human mortality. All humans die, for all are sinners (Romans 3:23; 5:12; 6:23). We die because of sin (Ezekiel 18:4). First Corinthians 15:22 traces it back to Adam: "In Adam all die." Enoch, Elijah, and Christians living at the Second Coming are exceptions to death but not to sin.

The sixth proof is universal sinfulness. Pelagius wrongly said that some persons in the Bible lived sinless lives, such as Job and Joseph. Someone said the Pelagius denied original sin because he was a bachelor and never saw his young children sin. The Bible repeatedly says that everyone has sinned, even Mary. All sin because they all have a common nature and ancestry. We commit sins because we have sin. Just as rabbits breed rabbits, sinners breed sinners, and sin breeds sin. Pelagius said we sin only by imitation, not by nature. If so, you would

---

10 Asahel Nettleton, *Sermons from the Second Great Awakening* (Ames, IA: International Outreach, 1995), 485.

11 James Jordan, *The Law of the Covenant* (Tyler, TX: Institute for Christian Economics, 1984), 127.

think that there would be at least one person who never followed the universal bad example.[12] But only Christ never sinned, for He alone had no original sin.[13]

How Is Original Sin Transmitted?

The answer involves two questions: where do human souls come from, and how are bodies formed in conception? Biology can answer some of the latter; only theology can answer the former.[14] Original sin is transmitted through the production of human souls via human reproduction. Craig's Catechism (1581) said, "How does sin come to us? [. . .] By natural propagation from our first parents."[15] In Psalm 51:5, David confessed, "Behold, I was brought forth in iniquity, and in sin did my mother conceive me." He was not suggesting that his mother was guilty of adultery, as he had been (note the context of Psalm 51). Nor is he saying, as some Catholics suggest, that sexual intercourse is always sinful.[16] Rather, David confessed his immorality by confessing that he had a sinful nature going back to his conception in his mother's womb.

The Westminster Larger Catechism sums up the Reformed position: "Original Sin is conveyed from our first parents into their posterity by natural generation, so as all that proceed from them in that way are conceived and born in sin" (Q. 26). Since we inherit Adam's sin and not Eve's, though she sinned first and was the mother of their children and all humanity (Genesis 3:20), Calvinists sometimes hold that original sin is propagated through the father and not the mother. He gives whilst she receives and conceives. The virgin birth illustrates this. Jesus had a sinful mother but a sinless Father. Some therefore contend "sin clings to our carnal nature and is transferred by sexual intercourse."[17] Others are more reserved: "We do not believe that it is necessary to search into how sin has

---

12 Canons of Dort, 3/4:2. We more easily imitate the first Adam than the second. Jonathan Edwards wryly asked, if men are born with free will, why is it that every person uses it for sin? Nobody learns it by imitation but by nature. *The Works of Jonathan Edwards*, 3:194. (New Haven: Yale University Press, 1970).

13 Calvinists unanimously affirm the virgin birth of Christ. Many non-Calvinists do not.

14 Ecclesiastes 11:5: "As you do not know what is the way of the wind or how the bones grow in the womb of her who is with child, so you do not know the works of God who makes everything." Some translations render it to refer to the human spirit in the womb.

15 In James T. Dennison Jr, ed., *Reformed Confessions of the 16th and 17th Centuries in English Translation* (Grand Rapids: Reformation Heritage Books, 2012), 3:546.

16 Rome uses this to support their doctrines of the Immaculate Conception and perpetual virginity of Mary. Some Lutherans accept the former but not the latter, while it seems that all Calvinists reject both.

17 The Emden Catechism, question 144, in Dennison Jr., *Reformed Confessions*, 1:619.

been transmitted from one man to his descendants."[18] William Perkins gave an application to his cautionary observation: "But whereas the propagation of sin is as a common fire in a town, men are not so much to search how it came, as to be careful how to extinguish it."[19] Interestingly, Calvin said that because of original sin, women inherit Eve's transgression of sinning against her husband, thus they have the tendency to usurp their husband's authority.[20]

Mediate or Immediate Imputation?

One helpful illustration of the transmission of original sin is fire. A candle's fire can be transmitted to another candle without being extinguished or lessened. Humans transmit a physical nature that is aflame with sin. The popular proverb says, "Where there's smoke, there's fire." Proverbs 26:20 says, "Where there is no wood, the fire goes out." One could say that human nature is the wood, and original sin is the fire. If a man has no children, then he does not pass on original sin. But if he does have children, the sin is passed on like fire spreads through a tree — a family tree.

Does a child inherit guilt together with original sin? Pelagius denied both, and Semi-Pelagians and most Arminians weaken original sin so that infants are said to inherit some kind of sin but no guilt. Calvinism says that infants inherit both sin and guilt, for there cannot be sin without guilt any more than fire without smoke, heat, or light. To deny that original sin brings guilt is in effect to deny original sin, just as to say that a person can sin without incurring guilt.

Calvinists, however, are not agreed on the specific means of the imputation of Adam's sin and guilt. The first theory is *mediate imputation*. This was basically the position of Augustine, the Amyraldians, Jonathan Edwards, William G. T. Shedd, and many others. It is related to the theory of *Traducianism* and is also known as *Realism*. It says that souls come from their parents in the same way that our bodies do, and both are passed down together. We were both physically and spiritually in Adam. When he sinned, we sinned, howbeit unconsciously. Augustine based his view on the Latin of Romans 5:12: "In whom all sinned." Others refer to Hebrews 7:9–10 to show that we are in our parents (especially our fathers) both physically and spiritually. Consequently, our common humanity is the means whereby original sin is mediated to us.

---

18 The Huguenot Confession of La Rochelle (1591), in Dennison Jr., *Reformed Confessions*, 3:311.
19 William Perkins, *A Golden Chaine* (n.p.: Puritan Reprints, 2010), 23.
20 John Calvin, *Sermons on the Epistles to Timothy & Titus* (Edinburgh: Banner of Truth, 1983), 212.

The main alternative to this is known as *immediate imputation*. It is the view of the Westminster Confession, John Murray, Charles Hodge, and others. Scholars still debate whether Calvin held to it. It is sometimes called the *federal headship* view. It says that Adam's sin is transmitted legally and not physically or spiritually, by representation rather than by reproduction. There is no physical means of the transmission of souls, only of bodies. Some add that God creates a new soul at the point of conception. Thus, sin is transmitted by imputation, not infusion. It parallels the imputation of Christ's righteousness, which was certainly by legal representation and not physical union. Proponents appeal to Romans 5:12–21 and say that just as Christ's righteousness is given to us, so Adam's sin was given to all humanity. Yet they admit that in some sense we have a physical relation to Adam.

Likewise, it is argued that our sins were legally but not physically transferred to Christ on the cross. Only a few theologians of questionable orthodoxy (such as Edward Irving and Thomas F. Torrance) suggest that Christ had a sinful nature for Him to make atonement at the cross.

Opponents of immediate imputation may draw a parallel with the error of supralapsarianism. Both errors reverse the order of sin and guilt, thereby making God the author of sin.[21] Immediate imputation sounds like God imputes sin to innocent people who have no active part in the first sin, and then He somehow infuses sin into them to legitimize their imputed guilt and punishment. Those who defend mediate imputation sometimes say that the logical order of transmission is like unto the historic order as reflected in infralapsarianism: We were truly in Adam, whose sinful nature is passed on mediately, with the guilt passed down to us. I favor mediate imputation.

Objections to Original Sin

The most popular objection comes from Arminians when they appeal to Ezekiel 18:20: "The son should not bear the guilt of the father, nor the father bear the guilt of the son" (Cf. Deuteronomy 24:16). It would be high injustice to punish an innocent son for his father's crime or sin. The theory of original sin does just that, they claim. It just is not fair. Some contend that we are trying to shift the blame for our sins onto Adam and our parents.

But this is to misinterpret Ezekiel 18. The Arminians are doing exactly what God, through Ezekiel and Jeremiah, rebuked the Jews for doing. The Jews were then in captivity in Babylon as punishment for their idolatry and other sins.

---

21 I will discuss supralapsarianism in chapter 48, "The Order of the Decrees."

They blamed their forefathers and denied their own guilt — just like those who deny original sin claim babies are innocent, and their parents are the guilty ones. The Jews cried out that they were being treated unfairly. They used the proverb about a father eating sour grapes, and the children's teeth being set on edge (Jeremiah 31:29). God told them not to use that proverb. Ezekiel's point is that the Jews in captivity were no more innocent than their forefathers. Like father, like son. In original sin, we are as guilty as our parents and Adam.

Calvinists take seriously Exodus 20:5, where God says He visits the iniquity of the fathers onto the children for three and four generations "who hate Me." That it is in the Ten Commandments makes it of special significance, such as that it is moral law for all mankind and not just ceremonial law for Israel alone. Sin is passed on; consequently, children inherit hatred for God and guilt. The chain adds new links whenever new children are born. This does not necessarily mean that we inherit the specific sins of our parents and grandparents, otherwise original sin multiplies sins by the million in each generation, and we are far guiltier than Adam.[22] Some specific sins may be passed down and repeated with individual guilt. But the *nature* of original sin is passed on.

Another objection is based on John 9. Our detractors accuse us of the error of the disciples who asked whether the man was born blind because of his sin or that of his parents. If the latter, then original sin is biblical. But, they argue, Christ denied both, so original sin is unbiblical. We reply that they miss the point. Christ did not deny anyone's sin or guilt, any more than He denied the man's blindness. He did deny that the blindness was due to a specific sin of the man or his parents. The Bible nowhere teaches that all afflictions are directly due to specific sins. Remember Job. The disciples in John 9 resembled Job's friends. Christ took the discussion to a higher theological level. He said that God allowed the blindness to show His glory in healing the man, which is exactly what Jesus proceeded to do. This principle applies to the origin of sin and original sin. God sovereignly allowed both to exist for the higher purpose of revealing the glory of His grace in forgiving sin in the elect and revealing the glory of His wrath in punishing sin in the reprobate. Denying original sin impinges on that dual glory.

Another recent objection relates to being born with a certain sexual proclivity. Many homosexuals argue, "I was born this way. God made me gay. Therefore, there is nothing sinful about it any more than being born a certain race." Actually, they are right and wrong — but not in the way they think. In a

22 See *The Works of Saint Augustine*, I/8:302.

way, yes, they were born with a sinful nature that breaks forth in sinful desires and acts, such as homosexuality. But that does not excuse them any more than anyone else with original sin. There is never any excuse for sin or sins. This is not to admit the existence of a "gay gene." Original sin is the source of all kinds of evil (Matthew 15:18–20), including fornication, adultery, and homosexuality. This only serves to condemn them, not excuse them. Their attempt at self-justification is as flimsy and self-defeating as the person who says, "I was born a murderer." Being homosexual is not the same as being born in a certain race. One's racial identity does not involve sin. Sodomy does.

Evil Comes from Evil

One reason why non-Calvinists reject the doctrine of total depravity is because they fail to see its root in original sin. Deny the root, you deny the fruit. But Jesus said that a bad tree brings forth bad fruit (Matthew 7:17). Sinful humans bear sinful children, and a sinful nature bears sinful acts and desires.

Thomas Watson said, "If the water be foul in the well, it cannot be clean in the bucket."[23] Another Puritan, Christopher Love, said, "In that one sin or nature there are many sins contained, all the sins in the world being in the womb of original sin."[24] Later Abraham Kuyper explained the relation of original sin to actual sins:

> That sin is, after all, the fountainhead; your sins are the spray that gushes forth. Your sin is the root; your sins are the distorted blossoms that grow from that root. Or also, your sin is the tainted fountain of blood in you, while your sins are merely like the abscesses and open sores from which that bad blood are produced on your skin![25]

Pelagius and some starry-eyed Arminians would say "There's no such thing as a bad boy." Calvinists reply, "There is no such thing as a good boy."

Conclusion

All humans have this disease. It is a universal terminal illness with disgusting symptoms, and it is passed on to our children. But we can be grateful that there is a cure — and only one cure. Roman Catholicism and some Protestants say

---

23 Thomas Watson, *Discourses on Important and Interesting Subjects* (Ligonier, PA: Soli Deo Gloria, 1990), 1:215.
24 Christopher Love, *The Works of Christopher Love* (Morgan, PA: Soli Deo Gloria, 1995), 1:93.
25 Abraham Kuyper, *Particular Grace: A Defense of God's Sovereignty in Salvation* (Grandville: Reformed Free Publishing Association, 2001), 210.

that original sin is forgiven, though not removed, through baptism. They are wrong. That error is part of the heresy of baptismal regeneration. Others such as the Nazarenes, many "Holiness" churches, and Wesleyans say that original sin may be removed in a post-conversion experience of entire sanctification usually called *perfectionism*. That too is wrong (1 John 1:8; Philippians 3:12). Reformed theology teaches that the guilt of original sin is forgiven in justification, then Christ's holiness is put into us by the sanctification of the Holy Spirit, with the power to resist original sin in part. But original sin remains in us (perhaps specifically in our bodies) as what we call *indwelling sin*. That is why even the best of Christians still sin. It will be in us until the day we die, from birth to earth. But praise God, it is left in the grave and not resurrected to infect us in our new bodies in Heaven, where we will live forever without sin or sins. But lost sinners will continue to have it forever in Hell.

Chapter 32
Total Depravity

Pelagius said man is good. Arminians say man is good and bad. Calvinists say man is bad, very bad. And God is mad, very mad. In this chapter we will explore the Bible's teaching that sin infests all parts of us.

What Total Depravity Is Not

It is not universal sinfulness. Total depravity means more than simply "all men are sinners." It means "all parts of all men are sinful." All evangelicals believe the former, Calvinists alone believe the latter.

It also is not just culpable guilt. Being sinful, we are guilty and deserve punishment. That is the effect of total depravity, not its essence. Calvinists teach that sinful man deserves far more punishment than he realizes, for he is worse than he knows.

Total depravity is also more than extreme cases of sin. We do not say that only gross criminals like Hitler are totally depraved, and the rest of us are not. Some sins are worse than others (John 19:11), and some sinners are worse than others (1 Timothy 3:13). But even the least sinner with the fewest sins is totally depraved. All cups are full, but some cups are larger than others. We are all full of sin.

It is also not animalization. As we shall see in the next chapter, we are still humans. Total depravity does not make us non-moral beings. We do not forfeit the image of God. Some men's consciences are seared (2 Timothy 4:2), but they still know that God exists, and their consciences condemn them (Romans 2:15).

It is also not demonization. Demon-possession is real, and all demoniacs are totally depraved, but not all totally depraved persons are demon-possessed. Very few are. Nor does the doctrine of total depravity mean merely that we cannot save ourselves by good works (Ephesians 2:8–9). Nor is it the same thing as the doctrine of reprobation or hardening of the reprobate. Nor does it mean that some extreme sinners are beyond redemption, and even God cannot save them. Fallen man "has no hope" (Ephesians 2:12) in himself, but there is always hope with God. Lastly, total depravity is not the same thing as the unpardonable sin.

Evil in All Parts

By *total depravity* we mean the very nature of man has been so thoroughly affected by original sin that every part of his being is under the control of sin. Evil totally affects, infects, and defects man. There is not a single part of him that has not been fatally infested. He is infected with the disease of sin from head to toe (Isaiah 1:6), inside and out, top to bottom. James Henley Thornwell said, "He is morally ulcerated from head to foot; he is one universal mass of gangrenous matter."[1]

First Corinthians 5:6 says, "A little leaven leavens the whole lump." Sin is an evil leaven. Abraham Kuyper said that is the nature of evil to spread and multiply: "And from this unholy marsh poisonous gases rise continually throughout our whole nature."[2] Sin spreads like cancer (2 Timothy 2:17).

Robert Murray M'Cheyne observed: "You are all sin, — your entire nature is sin, — your head is sin, — your past life is sin, — your prayers are all sin."[3] We should bless the Lord with "all that is within me" (Psalm 103:1) and love the Lord our God with all our heart, mind, soul, and strength (Mark 12:30). But sin fills all within us, in every nook and cranny of the caverns of our soul. We are filled to overflowing with evil. Our wicked cup runneth over in sins against God and men.

We are not sinners because we sin. We sin because we are sinners. "Wickedness flows from the wicked" (1 Samuel 24:13). Original sin fills the totality of our being and gushes forth in acts of sin. Jesus said, "If you, then, being evil" (Matthew 7:11). We are natural-born sinners. For centuries philosophers and theologians have debated the question: "Is man basically good or bad?" We say he is completely bad with no good whatsoever. He is radically evil, for his *radix* (source) is evil. From the cesspool of his heart spews forth all manner of vice (Matthew 15:19). If the root is bad, the fruit is bad (Matthew 7:16–19; 12:33). We are evil in thought, word, and deed — and in our very nature.

Are there no pockets of good somewhere within us? No, none at all. Romans 7:18: "I know that in me (that is, in my flesh) nothing good dwells." *Nothing* does not mean "a little something." There is not one micro speck of good in even the best of sinners. The best of men are but men at best. When we say

---

1 James Henley Thornwell, *The Collected Writings of James Henley Thornwell* (Edinburgh: Banner of Truth, 1974), 1:402.
2 Abraham Kuyper, *The Work of the Holy Spirit* (Grand Rapids: Eerdmans, 1969), 265.
3 Andrew Bonar, *Memoir and Remains of Robert Murray M'Cheyne* (Edinburgh: Banner of Truth, 1978), 319.

that some sinners are worse than others, we do not mean that some are good or better than others. It only means that some people have committed fewer sins than others. It does not mean that they have done anything good. Augustine said that "Those who are not good are some less evil and others more evil."[4] We are "filled with unrighteousness" (Romans 1:29), not just half full or a mixture of good and bad. Calvin said that we are "rotten through and through"[5] and "full of filth and infection."[6] "While man remains in his natural condition, he is rotten to the core."[7]

Sinful Bodies

When Adam and Eve sinned, they brought in death and the effects of sin in their bodies (Genesis 3:16–19; Romans 5:12). We inherit bodies affected by sin and doomed to death. We begin to die the moment we are conceived. We are on a death march from our mother's womb to the graveyard. Meanwhile, we suffer daily the effects of indwelling sin such as pain, weakness, and disease — none of which Adam and Eve had before the Fall. Sin now affects our bodies so that our members are instruments of unrighteousness (Romans 7:23). Paul calls it "this body of death" (Romans 7:24). In moral theology, the word *concupiscence* refers to the inordinate and selfish effects of sin which cause the senses of our body to succumb to temptation and stir us up to sin. Calvin wrote that "All the parts of our bodies are like kinds of weapons of sin and instruments the devil uses to lead us to hell. Everything — feet and hands, eyes and ears — is depraved and corrupted."[8] Elsewhere he said, "For if our bodies are a pit of abomination and iniquity, our souls are even more so."[9]

Sinful Hearts

The heart of the matter is the matter of the heart. "The heart is deceitful above all things and desperately wicked" (Jeremiah 17:9). Jesus said all manner of sin

---

4 Augustine, *The Works of Saint Augustine* (Hyde Park: New City, 1998), I/24:394.

5 John Calvin, *Sermons on Galatians* (Edinburgh: Banner of Truth, 1992), 607.

6 John Calvin, *Calvin's Sermons on 2 Samuel* (Edinburgh: Banner of Truth, 1992), 264. Also, we are filled with "filth and contagion" and "only contagion and putrefaction." *Sermons on the Acts of the Apostles, Chapters 1–7* (Edinburgh: Banner of Truth, 2000), 96, 268. "There is nothing but corruption and rottenness in us." *Sermons on the Epistles to Timothy & Titus* (Edinburgh: Banner of Truth, 1983), 702.

7 Calvin, *Sermons on Galatians*, 28.

8 John Calvin, *Sermons on Genesis, Chapters 1:1–11:4* (Edinburgh: Banner of Truth, 2009), 97; cf. 210.

9 Calvin, *Sermons on the Acts of the Apostles, Chapters 1–7*, 636.

flows from the heart (Matthew 15:18–19). Our hearts are filled with selfish pride. Aleksandr Solzhenitsyn has been quoted as saying, "Pride grows in the human heart like lard on a pig."[10] He was right. Ecclesiastes 9:3: "Truly the hearts of the sons of men are full of evil; madness is in their hearts while they live." Note the word *full*. To the brim and over the brim.

Hebrews 3:10 says, "They always go astray in their heart" and warns us of "an evil heart of unbelief" (v. 12). We have "cardiac sclerosis" — hardening of the heart. Rather than love God from the heart, our heart hates God. Jonathan Edwards powerfully described it like this: "The heart is a viper, hissing and spitting poison at God."[11] Man's heart is a foul garbage dump, an overflowing sewer, a stinking dung heap, like the hospital containers that collect the foulest refuse and soiled bandages. (I once saw a Scottish hospital container that was labeled "Cin bin" by the manufacturer.)

Edwards also said that the sinner's heart is "a sink of all manner of filthiness and abomination [. . .] a rendezvous of devils [. . .] a grave full of dead men's bones and crawling worms, and all manner of nauseous putrafaction [. . .] a jacques (outdoor toilet) of filthiness and abominable stench."[12] Also, "The devil takes up his abode in the heart [. . .] and fills it with darkness, with loathsome filth and defilement, with the smoke of the bottomless pit, and with the stink of the brimstone of hell."[13] Further: "The heart of man is as destitute of love to God, as a dead, stiff, cold corpse is of vital heat."[14]

Edwards was not diagnosing the hearts of others in a proud pharisaic way, for he elsewhere confessed: "When I look into my heart, and take a view of my wickedness, it looks like an abyss infinitely deeper than hell."[15] Elsewhere he made this earthly analogy: Just as the body carries its own dung in its bowels,

---

10 Quoted in Rousas J. Rushdoony, *The Roots of Reconstruction* (Vallecito: Ross House Books, 1991), 530.

11 Not in the Yale edition, but in Jonathan Edwards, *The Works of President Edwards* (New York: Jonathan Leavitt and John F. Trow, 1843), 4:39. This quotation is sometimes mistakenly cited from *The Freedom of the Will*. It is found in unpublished Sermon #405 from the Jonathan Edwards Center at Yale University website, http://edwards.yale.edu. Calvin said, "In the end they spew venom they have conceived and have kept bottled up inside for so long." *Sermons on Genesis 1:1–11:14* (Edinburgh: Banner of Truth, 2009), 310. Later he said that a child "is already showing he is a little serpent," 562.

12 Jonathan Edwards, *The Works of Jonathan Edwards* (New Haven: Yale University Press, 1992), 10:217.

13 Edwards, 10:573.

14 Jonathan Edwards, *The Works of President Edwards* (New York: Jonathan Leavitt, 1843), 4:40.

15 Edwards, *The Works of Jonathan Edwards*, 16:802.

so the soul carries filthy wickedness in the heart.[16] "There is a beastly, and a devilish nature that reigns in the hearts of natural men."[17] He was not using hyperbole. The depth of wickedness in the heart is beyond exaggeration. Only God who is infinite can know it (Jeremiah 17:10). The heart of man is corrupt and evil. Proverbs 6:14: "Perversity is in his heart. He devises evil continually." James Ussher: "Your heart is a little hell within you."[18] Ezekiel 16:30 gives the awful diagnosis: "How degenerate is your heart!"

Sinful Minds

Original sin affects all our being, including the mind. Calvin wrote, "All our faculties are corrupt, and sin's curse is the only inheritance we bring with us from the womb,"[19] and therefore, "We cannot conceive a single decent idea, as Paul says, until God gives us the ability."[20] Moreover, "Our minds are the best hiding-places! They are deceitful, twisted, and hypocritical beyond belief."[21] The Devil keeps our eyes bandaged by Adam's sin, so our minds cannot truly understand. "We cannot so much as think one good thought, unless God gives it to us."[22]

Is this really what the Bible teaches? Indeed, it is. Proverbs 15:26: "The thoughts of the wicked are an abomination to the Lord." We have broken minds. We are spiritually stupid. Reformed theology calls this the *noetic effects of sin*. Only by God's common grace are we even able to count to a hundred. Titus 1:15: "Even their mind and conscience are defiled." 1 Timothy 6:5 and 2 Timothy 3:8 say we are "men of corrupt minds." Ephesians 4:17–19 describes "the futility of their mind, having their understanding darkened [. . .] because of the ignorance that is in them." Fallen man cannot understand divine truth (1 Corinthians 2:14; Romans 3:11). He mistakenly thinks he is right, but he is on the way to Hell (Proverbs 14:12).

Sinners are adept at devising evil, not good: "They have no understanding. They are wise to do evil, but to do good they have no knowledge" (Jeremiah 4:22). It is an evil science. Men think they are clever, but in reality they are "futile in their thoughts [. . .] Professing to be wise, they become fools. [. . .]

---

16 Edwards, *The Works of Jonathan Edwards*, 11:92, 94.

17 Jonathan Edwards, *The Blessing of God* (Nashville: Broadman and Holman, 2003), 282.

18 James Ussher, *The Puritan Pulpit: The Irish Puritans* (Orlando: Soli Deo Gloria, 2006), 40.

19 John Calvin, *Songs of the Nativity* (Edinburgh: Banner of Truth, 2008), 13.

20 Calvin, 68.

21 Calvin, 203.

22 John Calvin, *Sermons on the Epistle to the Ephesians* (London: Banner of Truth, 1973), 694.

God gave them over to a debased mind" (Romans 1:21–22, 28). The mind is a cesspool of sin. Calvin said, "We know his mind to be a sink and lurking place for every kind of filth."[23] Spiritually speaking, we are all mentally ill.[24]

James Ussher commented that if God said, "Think just one good thought, and for it you shall go to heaven," lost sinners could not do even that.[25] Elsewhere he noted that even our unconscious dreams are affected by sin.[26] We have sinful memories, which tempt us from our own past. Calvin: "We are [. . .] so evil that we do not know how to conceive a single thought that is not at the same time rebellion against God."[27]

Sinful Emotions

We feel both pleasure and pain in both our body and our heart. Sin controls our emotional apparatus so that we have "pleasure in unrighteousness" (2 Thessalonians 2:12). We take pleasure in watching other people sin on television, in the movies, or on the internet (Romans 1:32). We "delight in abominations" (Isaiah 66:3). Arthur W. Pink commented, "The sinner is free to do as he pleases, but his pleasure is sin."[28] Rather than enjoying God (Psalm 34:8), we enjoy evil. We "rejoice in doing evil and delight in the perversity of the wicked" (Proverbs 2:14). "To do evil is like sport to a fool" (Proverbs 10:23), more enjoyable than football or tennis. "Evil is sweet in his mouth" (Job 20:12), more delicious than chocolate. "Fools mock at sin" (Proverbs 14:9), for righteousness and holiness are to them just one big joke for their laughing pleasure.

Scripture warns against lusts and strong desires for sinful pleasure. Some are sexual — sin has corrupted our sex drive. Others are drives for other physical pleasures such as gluttony or drunkenness. There are also mental lusts for pleasure (Matthew 5:28). Ephesians 2:3 calls them "the lusts of the flesh and of the mind." They are "worldly lusts" (Titus 2:12); "deceitful lusts" (Ephesians 4:22); "fleshly lusts" (1 Peter 2:11); and "ungodly lusts" (Jude 18). Rather than

---

23 John Calvin, *Institutes of the Christian Religion* (Philadelphia: Westminster, 1960), 1:14:5, (p. 191).

24 Jay Adams, a Calvinist Christian counselor famous for developing nouthetic biblical counseling, argues that non-organic mental illness is in fact spiritual in nature and needs God's grace applied by biblical principles, not humanist psychology.

25 Ussher, *The Puritan Pulpit: The Irish Puritans*, 35.

26 James Ussher, *A Body of Divinity* (Birmingham: Solid Ground Christian Books, 2007), 133. So also Calvin, *Sermons on Genesis 1:1–11:4*, 562.

27 John Calvin, *The Deity of Christ and Other Sermons* (Grand Rapids: Eerdmans, 1950), 62.

28 Quoted in John Blanchard, *Sifted Silver* (Darlington: Evangelical Press, 1995), 64.

desiring God as the source of holy pleasure, we crave sin as the source of unholy pleasure.

Calvin says we have within us "the lust for iniquity and its envenomed sweetness."[29] Michael Murphy poignantly observed that "the corrupt nature of the emotions causes a man to hate what he should love, or to express joy when he should mourn, and so forth."[30] Augustine said, "He willingly accepts the sweet price of deathly pleasure by which he is being deceived and also delights in contravening the law, since the less it is allowed the more attractive it is [. . .] what is impermissible is ineluctably delightful."[31] Men and women still enjoy the forbidden fruit of sin. Proverbs 21:10: "The soul of the wicked desires evil." Can anything be more explicit or evil?

Sinful Consciences

God gave us an inborn sense of His existence and of right and wrong, but sin has infected it as well. Titus 1:15: "Even their mind and conscience are defiled." We have "an evil conscience" (Hebrews 10:22; cf. 9:14). Some men have a "weak conscience" even after conversion (1 Corinthians 8:12). Others have a conscience seared over with a hot iron — once very sensitive, now almost immune from all feeling (1 Timothy 4:2).

Therefore, fallen man has difficulty discerning right and wrong. He calls good evil and evil good (Isaiah 5:20). He makes excuses for sin, but God says he is "without excuse" (Romans 2:1). Conscience is as full of sin as a fatted calf. Samuel Rutherford: "The wicked man's conscience is like a dung-hill, full of filth."[32] Original sin does not destroy the conscience. It only corrupts it. For instance, pro-abortionist sinners defend baby-killing because they say, "My conscience says it is okay." Even hardened murderers sometimes admit they do not have a guilty conscience in the least. Sinners have forgotten how to blush at sin (Jeremiah 6:15; 8:12). Their conscience is like a broken alarm clock.

Sinful Wills

God gave us all a will, the faculty of moral choice. We should choose God (Joshua 24:15; 1 Kings 18:21), but by nature we choose sin. We do not will to come to Christ (John 5:40). We do not choose life, but death (Deuteronomy

---

29 Calvin, *Institutes*, 2:5:5 (p. 322).

30 Quoted in R. C. Sproul Jr., *After Darkness, Light* (Phillipsburg, NJ: P&R, 2003), 22.

31 Augustine, *The Works of Saint Augustine*, I/12:178.

32 Samuel Rutherford, *Fourteen Communion Sermons* (Edinburgh: James Dickson, 1986), 141.

30:19). Proverbs 21:10: "The soul of the wicked desires evil." We thirst for sin and drink it like water (Job 15:16). Regarding God, the will says, "I will not," and to sin, "I will," like in a wedding vow. This even affects the Christian, who sometimes wills good and sometimes wills sin (Romans 7:15–21). If so with the Christian who has a renewed nature and the Holy Spirit, then how much worse is the will of the unregenerate sinner without the Spirit? All that the natural man wills is sin.

Blind Minds and Hard Hearts

Pelagianism says man sees perfectly well. Arminianism says man needs eyeglasses. Calvinism says man is blind and needs an eye transplant. Jesus healed blind people to illustrate that our minds are as blind as Samson after the Philistines gouged out his eyes (Judges 16:21) Jonathan Edwards said Satan blinds us to make us slaves, like the Philistines did to Samson.[33] We did not go blind; we were like the man in John 9:1 who was born blind. Yet man thinks he sees. An old proverb says, "There are none so blind as those that will not see." Calvin expressed it thusly: "He who attributes any more understanding to himself is all the more blind because he does not recognize his own blindness."[34] See John 9:41.

Man is indeed spiritually blind (Deuteronomy 28:29; Job 5:14; John 3:3; 12:40; Romans 11:7; 2 Corinthians 3:14; 4:4; Ephesians 4:18; 1 John 2:11; Revelation 3:17). Therefore, he walks in darkness (Psalm 82:5; Proverbs 4:19). He is as blind as a bat out of Hell. Jesus called the Pharisees "blind guides" (Matthew 23:16, 24), "fools and blind" (vv. 17, 19), "blind leaders of the blind" who lead people to fall into the ditch of Hell (Matthew 15:14).

We not only suffer from blindness in the eyes but a hardening of the heart. Scripture often describes the hard hearts of fallen humanity (Ezekiel 11:19 and many others). Man is stubborn (Psalm 78:8) and stiff-necked to God (Acts 7:51). He needs a heart transplant as well as an eye transplant, in which God replaces his heart of stone with a heart of flesh (Ezekiel 36:26). In conversion, God breaks the heart by conviction of sin and then melts it by the love of Christ. As strong winds might break large boulders (1 Kings 19:11), so the Holy Spirit must crush our granite hearts.

---

33 Jonathan Edwards, *Knowing the Heart: Jonathan Edwards on True False Conversion* (Ames, IA: International Outreach, 2003), 381.
34 Calvin, *Institutes*, 2:2:21 (p. 281).

Totally Depraved All the Time

Man's total depravity not only extends to the totality of his being, but to the entirety of his lifetime, however short or long. He is always sinful, always thinks sinful thoughts, always wills evil things. Genesis 6:5 is the most explicit verse in the entire Bible on the subject: "Then the Lord saw that the wickedness of man was great in the earth, and that every intent of the thoughts of his heart was only evil continually" (Cf. 8:21). That was the generation before the Flood in Noah's day. Jesus said this will characterize the generation before the Second Coming (Matthew 24:37). Indeed, it describes all human history.

Note three keywords in this diagnostic verse that show us how "great" the heart of sinful man really is. First, *every* intent. Not some, a few, or even most. Second, *only* evil. Not usually, sometimes, or occasionally. Third, *continually*. That means all the time, nonstop from the moment of conception to the moment of death. It is not sporadic, but constant, like an involuntary muscle in the body (the heart or brain muscles, for example). It is not a series of dots, but a continual line.

This verse describes our internal attitude, not just external words or deeds (Cf. Genesis 6:11). This is a hard pill to swallow, for it cuts to the heart of our pride. Some object, "Do you mean that only Christians ever have a good motive? What about Mother Teresa, godly Buddhist monks, and my unbelieving mother? Why, I myself remember having holy attitudes before my conversion." Such emotional reactions are misguided and self-serving. They illustrate the deceitfulness of sin (Hebrews 3:13). Nobody but Jesus Christ ever lived a life that was not only holy all the time, but even part of the time.

According to Jonathan Edwards: "The life of man before repentance is one continual act of sin."[35] Also: "If all that you do is wrong, then nothing that you do can make atonement for any of your sins. It would be a strange way of making satisfaction for sin by committing more sin."[36] Man "always resists the Holy Spirit" (Acts 7:51). Proverbs 6:14 parallels Genesis 6:5: "Perversity is in his heart. He devises evil continually." Christians need the humble boldness to tell lost sinners, "All you have ever done is sin!" Man is a perpetual sin-machine twenty-four hours a day, seven days a week, fifty-two weeks a year for his entire lifetime until he becomes a Christian.

---

35 Edwards, *The Works of Jonathan Edwards*, 10:513.
36 "Romans 3:11–12 (Sermon 389)," Jonathan Edwards Center at Yale University, accessed February 9, 2018, http://edwards.yale.edu/.

Not only our thoughts but all our deeds are unholy before God. Proverbs 15:8 says, "The sacrifice of the wicked is an abomination to the Lord" (cf. Isaiah 1:11). Proverbs 21:4 says that even "the plowing of the wicked" is sin. Even his prayers are sinful (Proverbs 21:27; 28:9). Calvin said the prayers of the unconverted sinners stink and infect the very air.[37] Jonathan Edwards had a powerful sermon, "All That Natural Men Do Is Wrong."[38] Man is enabled by common grace to do outward good deeds, but he does them with bad motives. He does not do them out of love or for the glory of God, therefore they are sin (1 Corinthians 10:31). Jesus indicated this in Matthew 7:11: "You who are evil give good gifts." An unbeliever never does anything at all but sin, for "whatever is not from faith is sin" (Romans 14:23), and by definition, an unbeliever does not have faith.

Is Man as Sinful as He Can Be?

This does not mean that each person commits every sin, as Edwin Palmer explains: "Man does not commit all the sins possible; and those he does commit are not always as bad as possible."[39] Calvin said the same over four centuries earlier: "I grant that not all these wicked traits appear in every man; yet one cannot deny this hydra lurks in the breast of each."[40]

Some Reformed theologians say man is totally but not utterly depraved or absolutely depraved. Not every person commits every sin nor gives in to every temptation. Nor does every internal evil desire break forth in our deeds. The reason is not in man's alleged goodness but in God's common grace that restrains us (Genesis 20:6). If He removed the restraints, there would be no end of our wickedness (Romans 1:24–28). Perhaps this will happen in the last days before the Second Coming (2 Thessalonians 2:6–7).

All of us are capable of committing all sins. Only Christians may not commit the unpardonable sin. It will not do to say, "Well, I am not perfect, but there are some sins I would never do." Remember David and Peter, and take heed lest you fall (Proverbs 16:18; 1 Corinthians 10:12). The worst sins are not always committed by psychotic fiends and deranged sadists but often by upstanding citizens who are otherwise outwardly moral. For example, in *Becoming Evil: How Ordinary People Commit Genocide and Mass Killing*,[41] James Waller shows

---

37 John Calvin, *Sermons on Melchizedek & Abraham* (Willow Street: Old Paths, 2000), 49.
38 Edwards, *The Works of Jonathan Edwards*, 19:525–36.
39 Edwin Palmer, *The Five Points of Calvinism*, Rev. ed. (Grand Rapids: Baker, 1980), 12. Also: "This depravity is extensive rather than intensive (14)."
40 Calvin, *Institutes*, 2:3:2 (p. 291).
41 New York: Oxford University Press, 2002.

how "normal people" have participated in the worst imaginable crimes. Some SS henchmen at Auschwitz went home and sang Christmas carols while hugging their wives and children. Many abortionists are "nice people." Al Capone gave money to the poor and the Catholic Church. Some Calvinists call these *splendid sins*.

John Calvin was absolutely right to say, "All works done before faith, whatever splendor of righteousness may appear in them, were nothing but mere sins, being defiled from their roots, and were offensive to the Lord, whom nothing can please without inward purity of heart."[42] In sum he added, "A world of vices is hidden in the soul of man."[43]

Conclusion

Total depravity refers to the breadth of man's sinfulness. In the next chapter we will discuss its depth. If Calvinism has a far higher view of divine sovereignty than all other theologies, it also has a far lower view of human sinfulness than all others.

---

42 John Calvin, *Commentaries on the First Book of Moses Called Genesis* (Grand Rapids: Eerdmans, 1948), 1:195.
43 Calvin, *Institutes*, 3:7:2 (p. 692).

Chapter 33
The Depth of Depravity

The gap between God and man is not only infinite regarding size and sovereignty but also holiness. Jonathan Edwards said, "Fallen man is infinitely different from God in both these respects; both as little and as filthy."[1] God is infinitely and transcendently holy. Man is abysmally depraved. In this chapter we will explore the depths of his depravity but will not touch the bottom. It is beyond exaggeration or comprehension. But praise the Lord, there is a cure.

Man Is Spiritually Dead

Pelagianism says man is alive and well. Arminianism says man is sick. Calvinism says man is dead. The first two agree that man is alive, which is one reason why Arminianism can easily lead to liberalism and Pelagianism. Reformed theology emphatically states that fallen man has no spiritual life: "If thou art a bad man, certainly thou art a dead man."[2] There may be degrees of health for the living, but there are no degrees of death for the dead. One corpse cannot be deader than another. There is a world of difference between a person who is barely alive and one who is recently deceased. Ecclesiastes 9:4 says, "A living dog is better than a dead lion." As Charles Dickens put it in the opening of *A Christmas Carol*, we are as "dead as a doornail. This must be firmly understood or nothing wonderful can come of the story I'm about to relate." We cannot appreciate God's wonderful grace until we see that we are guilty and terribly sinful.

Scripture clearly states this. Ephesians 2:2: "And you He made alive, who were dead in trespasses and sins" (cf. v. 5). We are "zombies" or living dead, following Satan in a death march to Hell (vv. 2–3): "You have a name that you are alive, but you are dead" (Revelation 3:1). "She who lives in pleasure is dead while she lives" (1 Timothy 5:6). "Let the dead bury their dead" (Matthew 8:22). See also Luke 15:24, 32; Romans 6:13; Ephesians 5:14; and Colossians 2:13.

Arminians and Catholics sometimes say that the sinner is like the beaten

---

1 Jonathan Edwards, *The Works of Jonathan Edwards* (New Haven: Yale University Press, 1989), 8:236.
2 Matthew Henry, *Commentary on the Whole Bible* (Old Tappan: Fleming H. Revell, n.d.), 1:128.

man in Luke 10:30, "half dead" but still alive. One Reformed answer is that our body is physically alive, but our soul is spiritually dead. Jonathan Edwards had a powerfully profound sermon on Matthew 23:27: "For you are like whitewashed tombs which indeed appear beautiful outwardly, but inside are full of dead men's bones and all uncleanness" (cf. Luke 11:44). His thesis: "Wicked men's bodies are as it were the sepulchres of their souls."[3] Abraham Kuyper said that man is like a mummy wrapped in self-righteousness concealing an ugly corpse.[4] Our mouths expel the stench of an open grave (Romans 3:13).

What can a dead body do? Nothing but rot and stink (John 11:39). According to Calvin: "We are by nature rotting in our sins."[5] When a body dies, all of it dies. A sinner is spiritually dead and therefore dead in all his spiritual faculties. A corpse putrefies and decomposes. Jesus raised several people from the dead to illustrate that He gives spiritual life to spiritually dead sinners (John 11:25–26). Just as worms and maggots eat at a cadaver in the grave (Job 19:26; 21:26; 24:20), so sin eats away at all parts of our soul. All corpses are dead, but some have rotted more and longer than others. Hence, some sinners are worse than others, but all are dead.

The sixteenth-century Confession of Tarcal and Torda said, "It is necessary therefore, that grace transform us from rotting and dead stumps into fruitful trees before we produce good fruit."[6] We are "late autumn trees without fruit, twice dead" (Jude 12). We deserve to be cut down and thrown into the flames (Matthew 3:10; 7:19; Luke 13:6–9; John 15:6; Hebrews 6:8). We rot because we are rotten. Job 13:28, "Man decays like a rotten thing, like a garment that is moth-eaten."

Being dead, we have no living virtues toward God. Christopher Love says, "Man's heart by nature is a slaughter-house to holy motions."[7] Arminianism pictures the lost sinner as drowning but still alive, able to cry for help and to grab the lifeline that is thrown to him. Edwin Palmer said that the sinner is

---

3 "Matt. 23:37 (Sermon 425)," Jonathan Edwards Center at Yale University, accessed February 9, 2018, http://edwards.yale.edu/. He says the souls of sinners are in darkness like a corpse in a sepulchre. He then paints a vivid picture of how grotesque a sight it would be to have decaying corpses sitting in church — yet the dead souls of sinners are worse. Lost souls have natural but not spiritual life, and are more miserable than a man who is buried alive.

4 Abraham Kuyper, *The Work of the Holy Spirit* (Grand Rapids: Eerdmans, 1969), 280–81.

5 John Calvin, *Sermons on Galatians* (Edinburgh: Banner of Truth, 1992), 136.

6 In James T. Dennison Jr., ed. *Reformed Confessions of the 16th and 17th Centuries in English Translation*, (Grand Rapids: Reformation Heritage Books, 2010), 2:684.

7 Christopher Love, *The Works of Christopher Love* (Morgan, PA: Soli Deo Gloria, 1995), 1:81.

drowned dead and sunk at the bottom of the Pacific Marianas trench, at thirty-five thousand feet deep the lowest point on earth, with six tons of water over him, being there a thousand years, and the sharks have eaten his heart.[8] He added, in the Fall we are not bruised but are like a man fallen from the Empire State building who is splattered on the pavement. Dead.

The Arminian Dave Hunt fails to see the point that the Bible regularly makes regarding spiritual death. He says that if we are dead, then we could not only not believe and obey God, but we could not even disbelieve and disobey God, for a dead man cannot do anything at all.[9] He thereby casually brushes aside the Bible's whole teaching on spiritual death. But according to the Bible, spiritual death does not mean non-existence or non-activity. It is unbelief, disobedience, and unrighteousness, while spiritual life is faith, obedience, and righteousness. When God says we are spiritually dead, He does not mean we cannot do anything at all — He means that we cannot do anything spiritually *good* at all. A corpse cannot sing, but it can putrefy. A sinner cannot get better, but he can get worse (2 Timothy 3:13). As Spurgeon said, "You will remember while the sinner is dead in sin, he is alive so far as any opposition to God may be concerned."[10] Conversely, a spiritually alive person is dead toward sin (Romans 6:4–13).

Earthy Bible Descriptions

Scripture uses a number of earthy and blunt pictures to describe fallen man — none of them are complimentary! We are like snake venom (Job 20:14; Romans 3:13), putrefying sores oozing pus (Isaiah 1:5–6; Leviticus 15:2), plague (1 Kings 8:38), gangrene and cancer (2 Timothy 2:17), a menstrual cloth (Isaiah 3:22; 64:6), mud and dog's vomit (2 Peter 2:22), scum and filthiness in a boiling pot (Ezekiel 29:11–12), and leprosy (often). Humans are "abominable and filthy" (Job 15:16).

Sinful man is a maggot and a worm that feeds off filth and carrion (Job 25:6). Even David confessed that he was a worm (Psalm 22:6; cf. Isaiah 41:14). Calvin said that man is a "five-foot worm"[11] and "poor earthworms, full of disease and corruption [. . .] no more than earthworms and dung [. . .] poor earthworms

---

8 Edwin Palmer, *The Five Points of Calvinism,* Rev. ed. (Grand Rapids: Baker, 1980), 18.

9 Dave Hunt, *What Love is This?* 3rd ed. (Bend, OR: The Berean Call, 2006), 151, 278.

10 Charles H. Spurgeon, *New Park Street Pulpit* (Pasadena, TX: Pilgrim Publications, 1981), 5:131.

11 John Calvin, *Institutes of the Christian Religion* (Philadelphia: Westminster, 1960), 1:5:4 (p. 56).

and lice."[12] Liberals and Arminians have sometimes censured the Calvinist hymn writer Isaac Watts' famous line, "Would he devote that sacred head for such a worm as I?"[13] Jonathan Edwards said, "We are nothing but worms, yea, less than worms, before God; and not only so, but sinful worms, worms swollen with enmity against God."[14] Also, "They are like a filthy worm that never feeds so sweetly as when feeding on carrion and never has its nature so suited as when crawling in the most abominable filth."[15]

In Philippians 3:8 Paul uses the Greek word *skubalon*, which means refuse, garbage, something thrown away. It was often used of excrement. And he was talking about his best righteousness, not his worst! Thomas Watson said that "Some think sin is an ornament; it is rather an excrement."[16] Calvin often repeated that we are "dung and stench."[17] Watson also described human depravity in terms of a fatal disease:

> Pride is the arrogance of the soul, lust is the fever, error the gangrene, unbelief the plague of the heart, hypocrisy the scurvy, hardness of heart the stone, anger the frenzy, malice the wolf in the breast, covetousness the dropsy, spiritual sloth the green sickness, and apostasy the epilepsy.[18]

Man Is Worse than Animals

God created man higher than the animals and lower than the angels (Genesis 1:28; Leviticus 24:21; Psalm 8:5). We are humans not beasts. Yet in sin, we are worse than any animal. Animals do not sin. We do. Oxen and donkeys know where to be fed from their masters, but men do not gravitate towards God (Isaiah 1:2–3). Chicks run to the mother hen, but sinners do not flee to Christ for safety (Matthew 23:37; Luke 13:34). Sinners often run away from God, not towards Him.

Scripture compares sinful man to beasts in general (Psalms 49:20; 73:22) and hogs in particular — the most unclean animal of all (2 Peter 2:22). Thomas Watson used this earthy illustration: "A sinner is a swine with a man's head."[19]

---

12 Calvin, *Sermons on Galatians*, 374.

13 Isaac Watts, *Alas! And Did My Saviour Bleed?*, 1707–09.

14 Jonathan Edwards, *Sermons on the Lord's Supper* (Orlando: Northampton, 2007), 169.

15 Jonathan Edwards, *The Blessing of God* (Nashville: Broadman and Holman, 2003), 282.

16 Thomas Watson, *The Doctrine of Repentance* (Edinburgh: Banner of Truth, 1999), 108.

17 John Calvin, *Sermons on Psalm 119* (Audubon: Old Paths, 1996), 112, 184.

18 Thomas Watson, *The Puritan Pulpit: Thomas Watson* (Morgan, PA: Soli Deo Gloria, 2004), 156.

19 Watson, *The Doctrine of Repentance*, 41.

God also compares us with dogs (2 Samuel 9:8; Psalm 22:16, 20; Proverbs 26:11; Philippians 3:2; Matthew 7:6; 15:26; 2 Peter 2:22; Revelation 22:15). This especially applies to homosexuals (Deuteronomy 23:18). This does not refer to cute little puppies or pets but "mean, mangy dogs" (Calvin),[20] mad dogs foaming at the mouth with spiritual rabies. Scripture also compares us with wolves (Matthew 7:15; John 10:12).

We are jungle animals, savage beasts, plague-carrying rats, slimy slugs, untamed mustangs, vicious predators. We are hyenas laughing at holiness: "Fools mock at sin" (Proverbs 14:9). Psalm 22:12–16 compares men with bulls, lions, and dogs. Calvin again: "We are born bears and lions and tigers until Christ's Spirit tames us, and out of wild and savage beasts transforms us into a meek flock."[21] We are, he said, "poor vermin and putrid flesh,"[22] indeed worse than "worms, flies, lice and vermin. For there is more worth in all the world's vermin than there is in man."[23] Furthermore, "we are not worthy of being called the most contemptible vermin in the world, for those creatures of God remain in their natural state, and there is only corruption in us."[24] The vilest animal is an angel compared to the best of men.

Thomas Watson said fallen man is "a beast with a man's head,"[25] a kind of half-man, half-beast centaur.[26] George Whitefield popularized the metaphor of man as half-beast and half-devil.[27] Spurgeon referred to Whitefield and commented, "I question whether both beast and devil are not slandered by being compared with man when he is left to himself."[28] Edwards said we are worse than beasts and devils.[29]

---

20 John Calvin, *Songs on the Nativity* (Edinburgh: Banner of Truth, 2008), 13.

21 John Calvin, *The Gospel According to St. John 1–10* (Grand Rapids: Eerdmans, 1970), 261.

22 John Calvin, *John Calvin's Sermons on the Ten Commandments* (Grand Rapids: Baker, 1980), 257.

23 John Calvin, *Sermons on the Epistle to the Ephesians* (London: Banner of Truth, 1973), 133.

24 John Calvin, *Sermons on Genesis, Chapters 11:5–20:7* (Edinburgh: Banner of Truth, 2012), 462.

25 Thomas Watson, *All Things for Good* (Edinburgh: Banner of Truth, 1986), 72–73.

26 Thomas Watson, *A Plea for the Godly* (Pittsburgh: Soli Deo Gloria, 1993), 351.

27 George Whitefield, *The Sermons of George Whitefield*, ed. Lee Gatiss (Wheaton: Crossway, 2012), 1:249. So also J. C. Ryle, *Expository Thoughts on the Gospels: St. Luke* (Cambridge: James Clarke, 1976), 2:442.

28 Charles H. Spurgeon, *Metropolitan Tabernacle Pulpit* (Pasadena, TX: Pilgrim Publications, 1981/87), 22:298; 47:337.

29 Edwards, *The Works of Jonathan Edwards*, 19:720. Sinners are more loathsome to God than dogs, swine, vermin, insects, toads, serpents, and vipers. "Isaiah 53:3b (Sermon 414)," Jonathan Edwards Center at Yale University, accessed February 9, 2018, http://edwards.yale.edu/.

Abraham Kuyper rightly said that in the Fall, man did not cease to be man but became sinful man, a worse creature than the beasts because he uses his constitution and natural ability against God.[30] Watson said we are worse than animals in two ways: (1) Beasts fear fire, but sinners do not fear Hell-fire; (2) a toad or serpent has only what God put in them, but sinners have what the Devil put in them.[31] Edwards said we have a "beastly nature"[32] and "who may as soon infuse the learning of schools and universities into the beasts, as infuse into a natural man this spiritual understanding."[33] To summarize, Calvin said man is a monster.[34] Jonathan Edwards was right: "This hideous, dreadful, most poisonous, loathsome monster clasps us round so close by nature that it has fixed its claws to the very center of our souls."[35]

Children of the Devil

Scripture compares fallen men with snakes (Matthew 3:7; 12:34; 23:33). Our words are snake venom (Psalms 58:4; 140:3; Romans 3:13). Satan is the Great Serpent (Genesis 3:1; 2 Corinthians 11:3; Revelation 12:9, 14, 15; 20:2). Consequently, Christ says to each of us what He said to the Pharisees: "You are of your father the devil, and the desires of your father you want to do" (John 8:44). We are a "brood of vipers" (Matthew 3:7; 12:34; 23:33). We are sons of Belial (Deuteronomy 13:13; 2 Corinthians 6:15), who is Satan. We have more in common with him than with Christ. The pure image of God is distorted, and we now more resemble the Devil than God, said Spurgeon.[36] Samuel Rutherford said we bear "the very image of Satan."[37] If you want to see what Satan looks like, all we have to do is look in the mirror. We are his sons and daughters. There is enough sin in us to make us a second devil.

Though not demon-possessed per se, each sinner belongs to Satan as his

---

30 Kuyper, *The Work of the Holy Spirit*, 224–25.

31 Thomas Watson, *Religion Our True Interest* (Edinburgh: Blue Banner Productions, 1992), 14, 202.

32 Edwards, *The Works of Jonathan Edwards*, 14:83. The Antichrist will be called "The Beast," Revelation 13. Sinners resemble this wicked beast.

33 Edwards, *The Works of Jonathan Edwards*, 14:83.

34 Calvin, *Sermons on the Epistle to the Ephesians*, 406. So too Watson, *All Things for Good*, 72–73.

35 Edwards, *The Works of Jonathan Edwards*, 10:513.

36 Spurgeon, *New Park Street Pulpit*, 5:70.

37 Samuel Rutherford: "Oh, what need is there, then, of Christ's calling, to scour and cleanse, and wash away an ugly, old body of sin, the very image of Satan!" *Letters of Samuel Rutherford* (Edinburgh: Banner of Truth, 1984), 421.

slave. Satan is going to Hell and wants to take his children with him. We have satanic blood in our veins, as it were. Watson said we are "devils in the shape of men"[38] and "devils covered over with flesh."[39] Calvin called us "half devils, so to speak"[40] and rebuked a common error of man's goodness by replying, "To hear us tell it, we are angels, but if someone looks closely, he will find we are worse than devils."[41] Moreover, "There is a conspiracy of men with the Devil to vex God more and more."[42]

Jonathan Edwards said, "Hypocrites are monsters:they have a saint's tongue and the devil's heart."[43] We are, he said, like the Serpent in Eden, "a talking, reasoning beast and an incarnate devil."[44] Christopher Love said, "If there were no devil, yet you would be a devil to yourself and would commit sin."[45] Religion alone does not help, but only makes us hypocrites. Watson again stated that "A moralized man is but a tame devil."[46]

Lovers of Sin, Haters of God

God commands us to love Him (Matthew 22:37) and hate sin (Romans 12:9). But because we are His enemies by nature (Romans 5:10; 8:7; Luke 19:27; 20:43; 1 Corinthians 15:25; Hebrews 1:13; 10:13; Acts 13:10; James 4:4), we love sin and hate God. This goes directly against the feel-good self-image that proud man has of himself. But it is sadly true. We love sin. We delight in abominations (Isaiah 66:3). Men love pleasure, not God (2 Timothy 3:4). We love gold more than God. Man loves sin and drinks it in like water (Job 15:16), and it is "sweet in his mouth" (Job 20:12). Jesus said, "Men loved darkness rather than light"

38 Thomas Watson, *The Beatitudes* (London: Banner of Truth, 1971), 173, 181; cf. *All Things for Good*, 73.

39 Watson, 181.

40 Calvin, *Sermons on Genesis, Chapters 11:5–20:7*, 704.

41 John Calvin, *Sermons on the Acts of the Apostles, Chapters 1–7* (Edinburgh: Banner of Truth, 2008), 580. See also *Sermons on Galatians*, 592.

42 John Calvin, *Sermons on Jeremiah* (Lewiston: Edwin Mellen, 1990), 39.

43 Jonathan Edwards, *The Works of President Edwards* (New York: S. Converse, 1830), 8:344.

44 Edwards, *The Works of Jonathan Edwards*, 24:136. He also said we are worse than devils, for we reject offered grace which was never offered to devils. See John H. Gerstner, *The Rational Biblical Theology of Jonathan Edwards* (Orlando: Ligonier Ministries, 1991), 2:345. Also, a natural man has a heart like the Devil but is restrained by God more than the Devil. "Romans 5:10 (Sermon 405)," Jonathan Edwards Center at Yale University, accessed February 9, 2018, http://edwards.yale.edu/.

45 Christopher Love, *The Works of Christopher Love* (Morgan, PA: Soli Deo Gloria, 1995), 1:152.

46 Thomas Watson, *Discourses on Important and Interesting Subjects* (Ligonier, PA: Soli Deo Gloria, 1990), 1:353.

(John 3:19; cf. v. 20). Psalm 52:3: "You love evil more than good." Man loves evil and hates good (Micah 3:2). Because he loves sin, he does not want to repent and give it up. According to Proverbs 13:19: "It is an abomination to fools to depart from evil."

Edwards preached that as the Gadarenes loved their swine more than Christ, so sinners love filthy sin more than a holy Christ.[47] Elsewhere he said, quoting John 5:43, "The heart of a natural man is as destitute of love to God, as a stiff, cold corpse is of vital heat. [. . .] I know that you do not have the love of God in you."[48]

Conversely, man hates God. And he hates God *as God* precisely because God *is* God. Men are "haters of God" (Psalm 81:15; Romans 1:30). Man is revolted by holiness. He really does hate God (Matthew 6:24; Luke 19:14; John 3:20; 15:18, 23–25; Proverbs 8:36).

Jonathan Edwards frequently said that man would kill God if he could, but his arrows never reach God's heart.[49] Their nails hit Him at Calvary. Robert Murray M'Cheyne said, "If the heart of God were within reach of men, it would be stabbed a million times in one moment."[50] Man hates God with that obsessive compulsion to kill as Captain Ahab had to kill the Great White Whale in *Moby Dick*. Perhaps Melville was alluding to this reality: that man desires the death of God. Man hates even the shadow of God.

Rousas Rushdoony once wrote, "As Cornelius Van Til observed, if Man could press one button which would enable him to step outside God's jurisdiction for a moment, he would keep his finger on that button continuously."[51] Evil men hate their Maker and enter eternity resisting Him. Calvin said that even if God broke the arms of sinners, they would still kick against Him with their legs.[52] Man is inveterately hostile toward God with an insatiable vengeance: "For he stretches out his hand against God, and acts defiantly against the Almighty" (Job 15:25; cf. 36:9).

---

47 "Mark 5:16–17 (Sermon 429)," Jonathan Edwards Center at Yale University, accessed February 9, 2018, http://edwards.yale.edu/.

48 Edwards, *The Works of President Edwards*, 4:40.

49 Conversely, God is aiming His arrow of wrath at sinners, as Edwards described so picturesquely in "Sinners in the Hand of an Angry God." God never misses.

50 Andrew Bonar, *Memoir and Remains of Robert Murray M'Cheyne* (Edinburgh: Banner of Truth, 1978), 441.

51 Rousas J. Rushdoony, *Sovereignty* (Vallecito: Ross House Books, 2007), 380.

52 John Calvin, *Sermons on Deuteronomy* (Edinburgh: Banner of Truth, 1987), 1162.

Men hate God, and the feeling is mutual. Sin incurs divine wrath. Edwards noted that there is a "mutual loathing" between God and man.[53] Calvin said Heaven and earth are ashamed of us.[54] It is, he added, as if God said, "You are stinking to me; your entire life is foul as far as I am concerned."[55] Also, "God loathes us; we are damned and lost before him; the angels abhor us; all creatures curse and detest us, and all things demand vengeance on us, because we defile them."[56] We deserve to have the angels to spit on us.[57]

Calvin also commented that we are so evil and perverse that the earth itself is offended and will vomit us out.[58] Christ Himself vomits out lukewarm pseudo-Christian hypocrites (Revelation 3:16). William Perkins the master Puritan said, "There is no dead carcass so loathsome as man is, the which both argueth the necessity of burial, and how ugly we are in the sight of God by reason of sin."[59] Edwards said we are "nauseous" to God.[60]

Fallen man dares God to punish him, according to Job 15:25, "for he stretches out his hand against God, and acts defiantly against the Almighty." One day the holy fist of an angry God will destroy him like a loathsome bug.

Calvin's Analysis

In all theological literature, no writer has examined the depths of human depravity deeper or more accurately than John Calvin. Here are excerpts from just one book, *Sermons on Genesis, 1:1–11:4* with page numbers in parentheses.[61]

- "For man is only a mass of filth and villainy, a sinking vessel, until he is renewed." (146)

- "As many desires and lusts as are in us, that is how many raging beasts there are still chained up within us, growling and gnashing their teeth or pawing the ground." (162)

---

53 Jonathan Edwards, *The Puritan Pulpit: The American Pulpit* (Morgan, PA: Soli Deo Gloria, 2004), 120–30.

54 Calvin, *Sermons on Galatians*, 314.

55 Calvin, *John Calvin's Sermons on the Ten Commandments*, 170.

56 Calvin, *Sermons on the Epistle to the Ephesians*, 129.

57 John Calvin, *A Harmony of the Gospels: Matthew, Mark and Luke, Volume III and The Epistles of James and Jude* (Grand Rapids: Eerdmans, 1980), 189.

58 Calvin, *Sermons on Genesis, Chapters 11:5–20:7*, 451.

59 William Perkins, *A Golden Chaine* (n.p.: Puritan Reprints, 2010), 115.

60 Edwards, *The Puritan Pulpit: The American Pulpit*, 129.

61 Edinburgh: Banner of Truth, 2009.

- "We are submerged in total stench, for if we were not just on a dung heap, but in the deepest and foulest-smelling privy in the world, we would not be in a more horrendous pit than we are, in this confusion in which we now find ourselves." (239)

- "Subsequently, all our desires and appetites are perverse and filled with iniquity." (244)

- "Everything that comes out of us will be putrid and filthy and can only increase his wrath." (363)

- "We will always find a subtle infection which grows in our hearts." (378)

- "Satan [. . .] drags them about where he wishes and makes them like animals so they fall into such a state of madness they have no scruples about fighting against the living God." (389)

- "If they could spit on God's majesty, they would do it, so carried away are they in their madness." (468)

- "Now a different image followed that one [original image of God], for Adam disfigured himself, as if someone had thrown mud on outstanding image in the world and the world had spat upon it and it had become covered with filth and contagion." (489)

- "There is no vermin in the world that is not worth more than we are." (490)

- "We are born as Satan's slaves under the tyranny of sin, sold into evil, like an animal that one sells and loads and drives where he wishes." (495)

- "But if we are recalcitrant and act like untamable animals, shall not such ingratitude have to be punished more grievously?" (526)

- "There will be enough to condemn hundreds of worlds." (548)

- "It would be like spitting at heaven, but it would not reach God, and we would be splattered with our own spittle." (552)

- "That we have defaced God's image in us and remain contemptuous of him surpasses all the world's murders." (565)

- "The devil takes possession of us and puts us through our paces and makes us trot, not only like wild animals, but like monsters." (634)

- "It is certain that we deserve to be eaten by wild animals, indeed by vermin." (744)

- "All our imaginations are rebellious and perverse, and that all the compartments of man's soul, his reason, his thoughts, all his desires, and all his affections, are workshops for forging weapons to battle against God. That, I say, is what we are by nature." (846)

Calvin's writings contain many such statements.[62] Perhaps his most well known one was: "Man's nature, so to speak, is a perpetual factory of idols."[63] He could be as earthy as the Bible in describing human depravity, but he was not obscene like Luther sometimes was. Unfortunately, Blair Reynolds' translation of Calvin's *Sermons on Micah*[64] repeatedly uses a certain obscene English word. Benjamin Wirt Farley retranslated those sermons in *Sermons on the Book of Micah* with more modest language.[65] Calvin himself warned against obscene language.[66]

Further Descriptions

The Bible often calls us "evil" (e.g., Luke 11:13, 29). Calvin said we are "constantly overflowing with evil"[67] and called us "scum."[68] Psalm 14:3 says we are "corrupt." George Whitefield said that sin has taken God's throne in the temple of our heart, defying God like the Antichrist with the words "we will not have this man to reign over us" (Luke 19:14).[69]

Since we inherit original sin, we are born with this abominable nature, and it shows itself early. Augustine confessed that he sinned greatly in greedily crying for milk as a baby.[70] He also remembered when as a youth he and some other boys stole some pears from a neighbor's tree. They were not starving; they only ate a few and then threw the rest to the pigs. He confessed that they did

---

62 For another such compendium, see *Sermons on the Epistle to the Ephesians*, 37, 129, 133, 156, 179, 278, 293.

63 Calvin, *Institutes*, 1:11:8 (p. 108).

64 Lewiston: Edwin Mellen Press, 1990.

65 Phillipsburg, NJ: P&R, 2003.

66 Calvin, *Sermons on the Epistle to the Ephesians*, 461–467.

67 Calvin, *Sermons on Galatians*, 313.

68 Calvin, *Sermons on Jeremiah*, 83.

69 Whitefield, *The Sermons of George Whitefield*, 1:248.

70 Augustine, *Confessions*, 2:9, in *The Works of Saint Augustine* (Hyde Park: New City, 1997), I/1:67–68.

it simply for the thrill of doing evil.[71] It echoed Adam and Eve stealing the forbidden fruit and the prodigal son eating with the swine. Man is still stealing from God for the sheer pleasure of it.

Ultra-environmentalists, especially earth-worshipers, say that mankind is the chief problem in the world. Some say humanity is a disease on the planet. They are righter than they realize. God cursed the cosmos because of man's sin (Genesis 3:17; Romans 8:20). Earth does not sin. Our continual sin moves creation to want to vomit us out (Leviticus 18:25, 28; 20:22).

Though some sins and sinners are worse than others, there is another sense in which all sins are infinitely wicked, even the so-called smallest sins. As the old Scottish preacher once said, "Nay, laddie, there are no wee sins." A sin is not infinite in duration, nor because any man is infinite. It is infinite because it is committed against God who is infinite in His being and holiness. Calvin called sin "infinite filth."[72]

Jonathan Edwards in particular elaborated on this in an Anselmian way.[73] We all have millions of infinite sins, he argued. Those with more and worse sins will be punished more in Hell than those with fewer or lesser sins (Luke 12:48). But since all sins are infinite, they will be punished to the full duration of infinite time — that is, eternity. God alone is infinite, so God became the God-man to pay the infinite price of the elect's sin and thus accomplish redemption. I would add that if sins were not infinite at all, as some non-Reformed theologians suggest, why did God not send Michael or Gabriel to become an angel-man to die for us? That is quite contrary to Hebrews 2:14–16. So, our view of the depth and degree of sin has direct bearing on our theology of atonement.

Miscellaneous Observations

Sin deserves God's wrath, but man is so in love with sin and in hate with God that he does not care. Thomas Watson observed: "Men sin as if they would spite God and dare him to punish them. Men sin so greedily as if they were afraid hell's gates would be shut up ere they got there."[74] Edwards said they rush to get there first and to get the deepest place in Hell.[75]

---

71 Augustine, *Confessions*, 1:7–11, in *Works*, I/7:43–47.
72 Calvin, *Institutes*, 3:13:3 (p. 765).
73 E.g., *The Works of Jonathan Edwards*, 10:426.
74 Thomas Watson, *The Crown of Righteousness* (Morgan, PA: Soli Deo Gloria, 1996), 54–55.
75 "Hebrews 12:29a (Sermon 257)," Jonathan Edwards Center at Yale University, accessed February 9, 2018, http://edwards.yale.edu/.

Calvinists have always encouraged spiritual self-examination (1 Corinthians 11:28; 2 Corinthians 13:5). First, we must dare to look into the seething cauldron of our heart and see it for what it is, as God sees it. If we are unregenerate, we will not be troubled by what we see, for the unregenerate are morally blind to it anyway. But when the Holy Spirit begins the work of conviction of sin, He awakens us to see our damnable depravity. Jonathan Edwards said, "God turns their hearts as it were inside out to them, and there is no sight so frightful to a sinner [as a sight of his own heart]."[76] By way of analogy, we would all be disgusted to the point of vomiting if we got a good look at the inside of our body — the undigested food in the stomach, bile in the liver, slime in the lungs, waste in the intestines, and bacteria in the saliva. Yet what is in our soul is far more disgusting to God. It should be nauseating to us as well. Ironically, it is a mercy that God does not show us the full depth of our own depravity. We could not take it. We would go insane.

If we are unregenerate, we will defend ourselves and say, "I am not that bad." The very fact that we disagree with God's diagnosis is proof of self-deception. Thomas Watson: "Every man is a dove in his own eye, and therefore does not suspect himself of any disease. He will rather question the Scripture's verity than his own malady."[77] They are like fanatics who deny the Nazi Holocaust despite mountains of verifiable evidence. This is also why many non-Christians defend the atrocity of abortion. They are as spiritually naïve as Anne Frank, later herself a Holocaust victim, when she wrote in her diary, "In spite of everything, I still believe that people are really good at heart."[78] She wrote this just three weeks before she was arrested and shipped off to be killed at a death camp. The Nazi camps were demonstrable proof that people are not really good at heart. Someone has said that the first of the five points of Calvinism is the only one that is universally and empirically verifiable. Fallen man is in denial like an alcoholic or tobacco addict who jokes, "I can quit anytime I want to. Why, I've done it a hundred times." Men will not admit they are hooked on sin but do violently resist efforts to be cured.

It is the very nature of depravity to deceive man. Calvin said, "Men do not know their vices; their hearts are poisoned; their villainy seems good to them, just as a pig does not smell its own stink."[79] We are "accustomed" to our sins

---

76 Edwards, *The Works of Jonathan Edwards*, 14:382.
77 Thomas Watson, *The Puritan Pulpit: The English Puritans* (Morgan, PA: Soli Deo Gloria, 2004), 163.
78 Anne Frank, *The Diary of a Young Girl* (New York: The Modern Library, 1994), 278.
79 Calvin, *Sermons on Jeremiah*, 110.

(Jeremiah 13:23). Luther poignantly said, "The work of Satan is to hold men so they do not recognize their wretchedness, but presume that they can do everything that is stated."[80] He added that the work of God's law is the very opposite. It shows us our wretchedness to drive us to Christ for salvation.

This has implications for evangelism. Much of popular evangelism today says that men are searching for God and that some are even trying to save themselves by good works. The problem, they say, is that sinners do not have enough good works and therefore are lost. It is sometimes pictured that their good deeds get them only halfway across a canyon to God. We Calvinists see it much differently. We say that no one seeks for God (Romans 3:11), but all are running away from God as fast as they can. Good works are only a cover-up to excuse their wicked hearts and fool other sinners and maybe God. Their religious deeds do not take them even one inch closer to God, let alone halfway. Sinners do not have even so much as one truly good work. Rather, they are "workers of lawlessness" (Matthew 7:23). To suggest that we are halfway there is to make us co-saviors and make good works part of salvation. That is a false gospel (Galatians 1:9; 2:16). Fortunately, most Arminians back off from saying that good works have any merit. Calvinists utterly abominate all forms of merit theology, which began with Judaism, was developed in medieval Catholicism, and has seeped into so-called evangelicalism through the "New Perspective on Paul" and other errors. Instead, we contend that sinners merit Hell (Romans 6:23). We deserve eternal punishment.

Extreme Evil

Calvinists also reject the liberal postmodernist view of ethics. Evil is most certainly real and is not relative to personal tastes or cultural mores. Cases of extreme evil shatter the liberal pipe-dream that man is good and there is no absolute standard of right and wrong, much in the way that World War I shattered the old liberal optimism.

Adolf Hitler is usually at the top of public opinion polls of who is the evilest person who has ever lived. He started the worst war in history that resulted in over fifty million dead, including six million Jews during the Holocaust. The SS were not all deranged fiends but were the same kind of persons as the rest of the world.[81] The 9/11 terrorist attacks also revealed "the evil that men do."

---

80 Martin Luther, *The Bondage of the Will* (Grand Rapids: Fleming H. Revell, 2005), 162.
81 See James Waller, *Becoming Evil: How Ordinary People Commit Genocide and Mass Killing* (Oxford: Oxford University Press, 2002). R. J. Rummel has authored several books on

Abortionists murder more babies every day than the number of people who died in the terrorist attacks of 9/11. Abortion in America alone has slaughtered more babies since legalization in 1973 than all who died in World War II. It is still jealously defended by millions of "nice" Americans.[82] The Bible repeatedly condemns homosexuality as a gross abomination, but it too is defended and legalized around the world. Has mankind lost its mind or just its moral compass? The answer is that God is taking the restraints off, and mankind is doing what comes natural.

The Canaanites were a particularly wicked people. In addition to their demon-worship, they practiced human sacrifice (even of infants) and the vilest homosexuality.[83] God destroyed Sodom and Gomorrah as an example of His holy vengeance on sin (Jude 7). Yet Jesus Christ said that the religious hypocrites of His day would be punished even more than the Sodomites for their unbelief (Matthew 11:23–24). Pseudo-Christian hypocrisy is perhaps the worst breed of sin, yet it is widespread and growing. It was religious hypocrites who engineered the worst murder in history. The crucifixion exposed the sin of humanity more than any other. We cannot simply blame the Jews or the Romans. Though we were not personally present, our mutual human nature was present. If we had personally been there, and God removed the restraints, we all would have held the hammer at Calvary. Hebrews 6:6 and 10:29 say that to knowingly reject Jesus Christ is to re-crucify Him, as it were.

Conclusion

Those who oppose the Reformed view of total depravity would do well to heed the exhortation of Anselm as he rebuked Boso's rejection of the Anselmian theory of atonement: "You have not yet considered the exceeding gravity of sin."[84] Calvin echoed this in a rebuke to those who minimize the evil of sin

---

democide, i.e., state-sponsored mass murder. See *Death by Government* (New Brunswick: Transaction, 1994).

82 William Brennan has shown the close parallels between Nazi atrocities and abortion: *The Abortion Holocaust: Today's Final Solution* (St. Louis: Landmark, 1983); and *Medical Holocausts, Volume One* (Boston: Nordland, 1980).

83 Reputable studies show the widespread use of human sacrifice in many ancient religions, including the Amerindians such as the Aztecs. See Nigel Davies, *Human Sacrifice in History and Today* (New York: William Morrow, 1981); Patrick Tierney, *The Highest Altar: The Story of Human Sacrifice* (New York: Viking, 1989); Martin S. Bergmann, *In the Shadow of Moloch: The Sacrifice of Children and Its Impact on Western Religions* (New York: Columbia University Press, 1992).

84 Anselm, *Cur Deus Homo* (Edinburgh: John Grant, 1909), I:21, 50.

and think they can satisfy God themselves: "I say that those who talk such nonsense did not realize what an execrable thing sin is in God's sight."[85] It is not a matter of objectively studying the subject like a high school biology student dissecting a frog. We are the sinners and hence both the *subject* and *object* of self-examination.

Those with sub-biblical opinions of the depth of human depravity reveal their own self-deception. The matter must be studied on our knees with tears of repentance, confessing, "I am the man!" (Cf. 2 Samuel 12:7, 13; Psalm 51).

We dare not deceive ourselves by saying, "Well, I am a sinner, but there are some sins I would never do." Spurgeon wisely warned us: "No man knoweth what villainy he is capable of; he only needs to be placed under certain circumstances and he will develop into a very fiend."[86] Therefore, Christians should daily plead with God to restrain their indwelling sin and not give them over to their inherent depravity.

It was with such a Reformed view of depravity that the Calvinist John Newton described man as a "wretch" in his famous hymn *Amazing Grace*. Paul Washer gives us a useful practical application:

> It is striking that when true believers in Jesus Christ hear a sermon regarding man's depravity, they walk out of church bursting with joy and filled with a new zeal to follow Christ. It is not because they take sin lightly or find some satisfaction in their former state. Rather, the truth fills them with joy unspeakable, because in the greater darkness they see more of Christ! We rob men of a greater vision of God because we will not give them a lower vision of themselves.[87]

---

85 Calvin, *Institutes*, 3:14:13 (p. 780).
86 Edmond Hez Swem, ed., *Spurgeon's Gold* (Morgan, PA: Soli Deo Gloria, 1996), 142. Said Edwards: "Notwithstanding the good opinion that you have of your self, yet a little trial would show you to be a viper." "Romans 5:10 (Sermon 405)," Jonathan Edwards Center at Yale University, accessed February 9, 2018, http://edwards.yale.edu/.
87 Paul Washer, *The Gospel's Power and Message* (Grand Rapids: Reformation Heritage Books, 2012), 80.

Chapter 34
The Bondage of the Will

Do we have free will?

The debate is not new. Augustine wrote *Grace and Free Will*. Martin Luther's most important book was *The Bondage of the Will*. Calvin produced a treatise called *The Bondage and Liberation of the Will*. Perhaps the most important Reformed work has been Jonathan Edwards' *A Careful and Strict Inquiry into the Modern Prevailing Notions of that Freedom of Will, Which is Supposed to Be Essential to Moral Agency, Virtue and Vice, Reward and Punishment, Praise and Blame*, usually shortened to *The Freedom of the Will*. Calvinism is virtually alone in denying that we have free will as popularly understood.

The Bondage of the Will

Our position is well summarized in the Westminster Confession:

> Man, by his fall into a state of sin, hath wholly lost all ability of will to any spiritual good accompanying salvation; so as, a natural man, being altogether averse from that good, and dead in sin, is not able, by his own strength, to convert himself, or to prepare himself thereunto (9:3).

It is not just a question of whether a man can save himself by his own good works or willpower, but whether he is morally able to will anything good at all before he is regenerate.

Pelagianism says we are born totally free. Arminianism says we have a weak but free will. Calvinism says we have a will that is in inescapable bondage to sin until it is freed by Christ in salvation. We do not merely deny that an unregenerate sinner can will to do good but not do good. We assert that he is morally unable even to will good at all. He is unable to be willing and unwilling to be able. The womb of his heart is barren and unable to give birth to any holy thought, word, or deed. He never has holy motives or desires but only sinful affections.

Man's fallen will has a perverse freedom. It can will sin all it wants to but cannot will any good. He can sin more but not less. The will is like a car with an accelerator but not a brake. He cannot cease from sin or even want to. He is like Joseph's brothers who "hated him and could not speak peaceably to him" (Genesis 37:4). Man hates God so much that he is unable to obey Him. He is resolutely determined to go on sinning. "The heart of the sons of men is firmly set in them to do evil" (Ecclesiastes 8:11).

Slaves of Sin

Fallen man is born a slave to sin and lives his whole life as such until freed by Christ. The Bible frequently describes him as a slave, not a free man. Jesus said, "Whoever commits sin is a slave to sin" (John 8:34). Peter warned of false prophets: "While they promise them liberty, they themselves are slaves of corruption; for by whom a person is overcome, by him also he is brought into bondage" (2 Peter 2:19).

Romans 6:16–22 says everyone is a slave, either of sin, uncleanness, and lawlessness or of obedience, righteousness, and holiness. Paul says we are "slaves of sin" (v. 20) before we became "slaves of God" (v. 22). God sets us free (v. 18). And earlier he said in 6:14 that sin does not have dominion over believers, implying that sin *does* have dominion over unbelievers.

Christ said, "The truth shall make you free. [. . .] Therefore if the Son makes you free, you shall be free indeed" (John 8:32, 36). If He sets us free, that means we could not set ourselves free. Acts 8:23 describes Simon Magus as "poisoned by bitterness and bound by iniquity."

All these verses clearly teach that the unbeliever is in slavery to sin. If a slave, then not free. If his will is bound, it is not free will. Augustine asked, "If then they are slaves of sin, why do they boast of free choice?"[1] Zwingli tied it in with original sin: "A slave can beget nothing but a slave."[2]

Slaves of Satan

Worse than that, man is a slave of the Devil. He was born a slave, lives his whole life in satanic bondage, and will die a slave. Sin is the Devil's chain that keeps us in bondage, and each sin we commit is a link we add every time we disobey God. The chain gets longer and stronger every second. Second Timothy 2:26 speaks of "the snare of the devil, having been taken captive by him to do his will." We willingly follow Satan's orders. We follow our leader in the

---

1 Augustine, *The Works of Saint Augustine* (Hyde Park: New City, 1997), I/23:185.
2 In James T. Dennison Jr, ed., *Reformed Confessions of the 16th and 17th Centuries in English Translation* (Grand Rapids: Reformation Heritage Books, 2008), 1:118.

parade of evil that leads to Hell (Ephesians 2:1–3). God transfers us from "the power of Satan" (Acts 26:18) and "the power of darkness" (Colossians 1:13) into His kingdom of light. Fallen man spends his whole life like a blind Samson, grinding corn in the Devil's mill (Judges 16:21).

Calvin says that Satan rides the sinner like a rider on a horse.[3] 1 John 5:19 says "The whole world lies under the sway of the wicked one," which is a twist on the old spiritual, "He's Got the Whole World in His Hand." In Hebrews 2:15 we are told that sinners are "those who through fear of death all their lifetime were subject to bondage" to Satan. Christ became a man to free us from him (v. 14). This is the *Christus Victor* theme in Scripture (Genesis 3:15; 1 John 3:8; Colossians 2:15). Until we are freed by Christ, we remain slaves in the Devil's dungeon.

The sinner loves his chains and kisses every link. Spurgeon: "Men fancy music in the chains with which Satan binds them, and hug the fetters which he hangs upon them."[4] Bondage to Satan is also a just punishment, as Calvin noted: "The sovereignty and tyranny of the devil is a just vengeance of God upon men for their sin."[5] The fact that Christ frees us is proof we were slaves, as Augustine said: "After all, if we hadn't been held in captivity, we wouldn't have needed a deliverer."[6] Calvin put it like this: "Just, then, as the healthy have no need of a doctor, but only those who are ill, so those who are free have no need of a deliverer, but only those who are slaves."[7] Paraphrasing Galatians 2:21, we could ask, "If we were already free, why did Christ die? If we were already free, Christ died in vain." But He died to set us free from the Devil. You see that the whole question of free will has direct bearing on the nature of the atonement. Free will could imply that the atonement was not necessary. But it was.

Each man is either a slave to God or the Evil One. He serves one or the other — not neither and not both. "No one can serve two masters; for either he will hate the one and love the other, or else he will be loyal to the one and despise

---

3 John Calvin, *Institutes of the Christian Religion* (Philadelphia: Westminster, 1960), 2:4:1 (p. 309). So also Samuel Rutherford, *Fourteen Communion Sermons* (Edinburgh: James Dickson, 1986), 244. Calvin: "We see, then, what misery it is when the devil not only enslaves us and drives us to commit all sorts of evil but also sports with us, as if we were apes lacking in discipline and self-control." *Sermons on Titus* (Edinburgh: Banner of Truth, 2015), 244.

4 Charles H. Spurgeon, *Metropolitan Tabernacle Pulpit* (Pasadena, TX: Pilgrim Publications, 1979), 11:77. Also: "Men rattle their chains to show that they are free." *Spurgeon's Proverbs and Sayings with Notes* (Welwyn: Evangelical Press, 1975), 2:17.

5 John Calvin, *Sermons on the Epistle to the Ephesians* (London: Banner of Truth, 1973), 135.

6 Augustine, *The Works of Saint Augustine*, III/2:104.

7 John Calvin, *The Bondage and Liberation of the Will* (Grand Rapids: Baker, 1996), 88.

the other" (Matthew 6:24; Luke 16:13). Fallen man serves, loves, and is loyal to Satan and sin, and he hates and despises God. Redeemed man serves, loves, and is loyal to God, and he hates and despises Satan. Of course, the sinner usually is not conscious of his affections for one and hatred for the other. But if God removed the restraints and allowed Satan to appear to him as he is, the sinner would fall before him in loving worship. He already does that for sin.

This is not an excuse for the sinner. He cannot blame the Devil as Eve did. He is a willing slave. Satan keeps him a blind slave like the Philistines did to Samson.[8] Jonathan Edwards commented, "You can't see that you are under slavery now because of your blindness which is one effect of your servitude."[9]

The Inability of the Will

Fallen man is not only depraved, he is deprived. He lacks the ability to will good. He is "without strength" (Romans 5:6). He cannot change himself, as Jeremiah 13:23 says, "Can the Ethiopian change his skin or the leopard its spots? Then may you also do good who are accustomed to do evil." He is a spiritual eunuch unable to procreate a good will. He can no more will a holy desire than pigs can dance ballet. He is like a man in quicksand — his every effort only makes him sink deeper. Luther said, "'Free-will,' when at its best, is then at its worst, and the more it endeavors, the worse it grows and is."[10]

Man is *unable* in all areas of true spirituality. The world "cannot" receive the Holy Spirit (John 14:17). "You cannot serve the Lord" (Joshua 24:19). Jesus said, "No man can come to Me unless the Father who sent Me draws him," and "No one can come to Me unless it has been granted to him by My Father" (John 6:44, 65). This is spiritual inability to believe. Man lacks "will power" to will anything good but has plenty of "will not power" to will sin. Man is in debt to God and cannot repay Him, nor is he even willing to repay Him. Abraham Kuyper said our will is as "powerless as a chained wheel, unable to turn in the right direction."[11]

---

8 Jonathan Edwards, *Knowing the Heart: Jonathan Edwards on True and False Conversion* (Ames, IA: International Outreach, 2003), 381. Also, it would be better to be a slave to any man on Earth than to the Devil, alluding to 2 Timothy 2:26. "Acts 16:29–30 (Sermon 337)," Jonathan Edwards Center at Yale University, accessed February 9, 2018, http://edwards.yale.edu/. And, lost sinners are Satan's slaves that sleep in his arms. Edwards, "Proverbs 6:22b (Sermon 949)."

9 Quoted by John Gerstner in Thomas R. Schreiner and Bruce A. Ware, eds., *The Grace of God, The Bondage of the Will* (Grand Rapids: Baker, 1995), 2:293.

10 Martin Luther, *The Bondage of the Will* (Grand Rapids: Fleming H. Revell, 2005), 278.

11 Abraham Kuyper, *The Work of the Holy Spirit* (Grand Rapids: Eerdmans, 1969), 493.

Romans 8:7–8 is especially clear: "Because the carnal mind is enmity against God; for it is not subject to the law of God, nor indeed can be. So then, those who are in the flesh cannot please God." Note the words *nor can be* and *cannot*. Parallel to this is Hebrews 11:6: "But without faith it is impossible to please Him."

Moral Inability

Some Reformed theologians, such as Jonathan Edwards[12] and A. W. Pink,[13] differentiate between *natural ability* and *moral ability*. Though this dichotomy was misused in nineteenth-century New England Theology, it has much truth in it. Because man is in the image of God, he has the created natural ability to will good. Animals and rocks do not have this capacity. But — and this is crucial — we do not have the moral ability to will good until freed by Christ.

We have moral inability, or if you will, *immoral ability*. We can and do will sin but cannot and will not will good. The First Helvetic Confession expressed it thus: "We are able to do evil willingly, but we are not able to embrace and follow good."[14] The Second Helvetic Confession was more specific: "Full of all wickedness, distrust, contempt and hatred of God, we are unable to do or even to think anything good of ourselves."[15] The will is in a desperately hopeless condition. The sinner cannot will to be free, let alone obey God's law even for one second. Homer Hoeksema was right: "He will not obey it, cannot obey it, and cannot will to obey it."[16]

Calvinists utterly reject the proverb that some people erroneously think is in the Bible: "God helps those who help themselves." But we cannot help ourselves, nor do we want to be helped by God. In fact, we resist all help. We cannot even start to will to believe or obey. We are therefore without hope (Ephesians 2:12). God alone helps the helpless and hopeless. We are indeed "helpless" (Psalm 10:8, 10, 14). As the hymn puts it, "Help of the helpless, O abide with me."[17] It is no excuse to plead, "I couldn't help sinning." That only compounds our guilt.

---

12 Jonathan Edwards, *The Works of Jonathan Edwards* (New Haven: Yale University Press, 1957), 1:156–62.

13 A. W. Pink, *The Sovereignty of God* (Grand Rapids: Baker, 1973), 177–92.

14 Dennison Jr., ed., *Reformed Confessions*, 1:345.

15 Dennison Jr., ed., 2:820–21.

16 Homer Hoeksema, *The Voice of Our Fathers* (Grand Rapids: Reformed Free Publishing Association, 1980), 469.

17 Henry Francis Lyte, *Abide with Me*, written 1847.

First Corinthians 2:14 also bears on the "cannot" of moral inability: "The natural man does not receive the things of the Spirit of God, for they are foolishness to him; nor can he know them, because they are spiritually discerned." He does not because he cannot. Jesus told the Pharisees, "Why do you not understand My speech? Because you are not able to listen to My word" (John 8:43). This explains why Jesus said in John 5:40, "You are not willing to come to Me that you may have life."

Then in John 15:5, Jesus said, "Without Me you can do nothing." Nothing good, that is. We can do evil but not good. Luther said that "Nothing does not mean a little something."[18] G. C. Berkouwer added: "Christ does not say, 'without me it is more difficult to do this.'"[19] Man both wills not to believe and cannot believe in Christ: "They did not believe in Him. [. . .] They could not believe" (John 12:37, 39). They would not because they could not.

The Sad State of Spiritual Slavery

Edward Pearse the Puritan bewailed this slavery: "As to serve Christ is the greatest liberty, so to serve sin is the cruelest bondage."[20] Calvin said they are "still in bondage, even if they have a noose around their necks" awaiting execution.[21] Also, "The heart of man is a dreadful dungeon."[22]

The unsaved sinner is like Dorian Gray, described by Oscar Wilde in his novel of the same name: "There are moments [. . .] when the passion for sin, or what the world calls sin, so dominates a nature, that every fibre of the body, as every cell of the brain, seems to be instinct with fearful impulses. Men and women at such moments lose the freedom of their will."[23] Wilde was an unrepentant homosexual and did not use these words to repent of his degradation but to defend it. Calvinists say this sordid description is accurate, not only in sporadic passionate moments in some persons but throughout the whole course of all unregenerate sinners.

---

18 Luther, *The Bondage of the Will*, 260–61.
19 G. C. Berkouwer, *Divine Election* (Grand Rapids: Eerdmans, 1960), 30.
20 Edward Pearse, *The Best Match* (Morgan, PA: Soli Deo Gloria, 1994), 124.
21 John Calvin, *Sermons on Galatians* (Edinburgh: Banner of Truth, 1997), 430. See 1 Kings 20:30–31.
22 John Calvin, *The Covenant Enforced: Sermons on Deuteronomy 27 and 28* (Tyler, TX: Institute for Christian Economics, 1990), 54.
23 Quoted in Dewey D. Wallace, *Puritans and Predestination: Grace in English Protestant Theology 1525–1695* (Chapel Hill: University of North Carolina Press, 1982), 195.

The Myth of Free Will

It is no surprise that non-Reformed opponents reject this analysis. Arminianism in particular vehemently defends free will. For instance, some will claim that the Bible itself uses the term *free will* some twenty-six times. We reply that the Hebrew word *nedabah* means "voluntary and not mandatory." It was usually used of offerings. Some offerings were commanded, others were optional. A *freewill offering* was given out of gratitude, more like a birthday present than a financial debt, or more like a contribution to charity than mandatory taxes to the government. But what has that to do with the alleged free will of fallen sinners? Nothing.

Calvinists sometimes prefer the term *free agency* because of the widespread erroneous connotations of the term *free will*, but occasionally they may use the latter to refer to human responsibility. In denying free will we do not at all deny human responsibility, as we shall discuss in the next chapter. Older Reformed writers sometimes used *free will* in the sense of accountability, not Arminian neutrality of will.

Those who defend free will have a vested interest in doing so and resemble the Pharisees in John 8:33 who said, "We are Abraham's descendants and have never been in bondage to anyone." They conveniently overlooked that their ancestors had been slaves in Egypt, Assyria, Babylon, and Persia, and they themselves were at that moment under the dominion of the Roman Empire. Likewise, those who assert they have free will fail to acknowledge their own bondage to sin, even specific sins to which they are obviously addicted. It is not an academic question but an existential one.

Calvin observed: "The idea of free will, also, has been proposed, in order to help us promote ourselves by claiming God's grace does not do everything, but that we need to cooperate with the efforts of our own."[24] That opens the door to self-righteousness and merit theology. Further, "All this is born of the fact that men are so possessed by devilish pride, that they want to 'be someone' in and of themselves."[25] The very assertion of free will is enmity to God. As the proverb says, "Man commits sin to remind himself that he is free." To him, freedom means freedom to sin. Modern America is a good example of this noxious formula. The Pilgrim Fathers were godly Puritans who came here to have freedom of worship, but modern Americans want the worship of freedom. They want laws changed to grant them freedom to sin more without punishment

---

24 John Calvin, *Songs of the Nativity* (Edinburgh: Banner of Truth, 2008), 130.
25 Calvin, *Sermons on Galatians*, 587.

from the state. Witness the legalization of abortion, marijuana, homosexuality, and other vices forbidden by God.

The more sinful a person is, the more he will assert his free will, like a rebellious teenager who insists, "Nobody tells me what to do! I'll do whatever I want to do!" Calvin said, "The greater the mass of vices anyone is buried under, the more fiercely and bombastically does he extol free will."[26] Augustine put forth this paradox: "Thus, a good man, though a slave, is free; but a wicked man, though a king, is a slave. For he serves, not one man alone, but what is worse, as many masters as he has vices."[27] The chain of sin-slavery has many links and locks.

Another self-serving objection is the non-Christian libertarian defense of sin itself:

> If we have free will, then God cannot punish us for using it. That would be like a tyrant punishing a slave who wants freedom. Man must be free to do whatever he freely chooses without any restrictions or punishment. God would be a tyrant to take away his freedom or punish him for using it.

The libertarians applaud the unrighteous Israelites in Judges 21:25: "In those days there was no king in Israel; everyone did what was right in his own eyes." The Arminian defense of free will does not go as far as this, but one can detect the similarities. In truth, the error of free will would give sinners a license to sin.

Conclusion

Before the Fall, man was holy. He had the ability to sin or not to sin. He was not morally neutral, as Pelagius said, but good and willed good. He had free will.

After the Fall, man underwent a drastic change. He lost free will. His will became a slave of sin and Satan. He became able to sin but was not able *not* to sin. This is the state of humanity ever since.

When God regenerates a person, He frees him from the slavery of sin. The regenerate person has a kind of free will but not as free as Adam before the Fall. He still has original sin indwelling him. One could say he has "half-free" will.

---

26 John Calvin, *The Gospel According to St. John 1–10* (Grand Rapids: Eerdmans, 1979), 223. Also: "We must recognize that there is only malice, that we are willful, that what we call wisdom is mere folly and that free will is but abominable slavery to sin." *Sermons on Titus*, 254.
27 Augustine, *The Fathers of the Church* (New York: Fathers of the Church, 1950), 8:194; *City of God*, 4:3. See 1 Corinthians 7:22.

As Calvin put it, "If after regeneration man has only half freedom, what has he in the time of his original carnal generation but total bondage?"[28]

In the fourth stage, we see man in the afterlife. Those who die lost remain in permanent total depravity and slavery to sin and Satan. That is why they will always sin and never repent throughout eternity in Hell. On the other hand, the saints will have a total free will from sin at last in Heaven. They will have it in a greater sense than even Adam before the Fall. Adam was free but peccable — he could sin and did sin. The elect will be perfectly free and impeccable — they cannot and therefore will not sin ever again. As Augustine put it long ago: "The first freedom of the will, then, was the ability not to sin; the final freedom will be much greater, namely, the inability to sin."[29] In this way, they will be like the elect angels and their Lord Jesus Christ.

---

28 Calvin, *The Bondage and Liberation of the Will*, 68.
29 Augustine, *The Works of Saint Augustine*, I/26:132; cf. Calvin, *Institutes*, 2:3:13 (p. 307); and Thomas Boston, *The Fourfold State of Man* (London: Banner of Truth, 1964).

Chapter 35
Total Depravity and Human Responsibility

Earlier we looked at the relation of divine sovereignty and human responsibility. Both are true. Now we look at the relation of total depravity and human responsibility. Both are also true. Yet it is not always easy to explain these sets. But we dare not deny any of these doctrines, for they are all biblical. The state of the question is: If man is totally depraved and morally unable to obey God, then how can he be held accountable to God?

The Arminian Theory

Dave Hunt sums up the Arminian theory: "One cannot be held responsible for what one cannot do."[1] A. W. Tozer also sets it forth with an adjunct: "If man's will is not free to do evil, it is not free to do good! The freedom of human will is necessary to the concept of morality. This is why I have not accepted the doctrine that our Lord Jesus Christ could not have sinned."[2]

By this theory, one must be morally able in order to be responsible to God. Some argue from the very word itself: "response-able"— able to give a response. This gets back to the teaching of Pelagius: "If I ought, I can." To be accountable, one must be equally able to obey or not obey; he must be morally neutral and free to choose good or evil. Hence, neither sin nor God Himself can control the will, else moral accountability is removed. Some grant that sin affects the mind and emotions but deny that it affects the will to the extent of control. Some admit that we have the tendency to sin but not the necessity. Others say we are indeed totally depraved and morally unable but add that God has given *sufficient grace* to all men to enable us to obey, thereby maintaining our responsibility.

New England Theology after Jonathan Edwards drifted away from his strong Calvinistic doctrine of moral inability. Nathaniel William Taylor crossed the Rubicon with his doctrine of "the power to the contrary." The human will,

---

1 Dave Hunt, *What Love Is This?* 3rd ed. (Bend, OR: The Berean Call, 2006), 435.
2 A. W. Tozer, *The Tozer Pulpit* (Harrisburg: Christian Publications, 1978), 7:40.

he contended, must have moral ability to will both good and evil to be held rewardable for virtue and punishable for vice. This is one key difference between Calvinism and Arminianism.

Another objection says that if we are unable to obey, the sinner would be absolved of his guilt. Imagine telling a sinner that he cannot help but sin! A variant says our position is like the "temporary insanity" plea of a murderer. He must be exonerated because he was not in control of his actions. Thus, some critics charge us with actually approving of sin.

Likewise, the objection says our view misrepresents God as a cruel God. It is as if a man tied up the legs of his horse and then whipped it for not running on command. It portrays God as requiring the impossible, like telling a child to draw a square circle. God would then be as unjust as Pharaoh demanding the Jews make bricks without straw. It has God taunting a blind man for not seeing.

In sum, the alternative theory says that human responsibility requires moral ability. Conversely, moral inability negates responsibility. Free will is necessary for human responsibility.

The Myth of Moral Neutrality

Pelagianism and Arminianism presume that one must be morally neutral to be responsible. Proponents often say each of us is at a crossroads and can equally choose either path. But Calvinists reply that Scripture never says anyone is morally neutral. Adam was holy and pro-God before the Fall and unholy and anti-God after the Fall. In neither case was he neutral. Nobody since then has been any different. Even Christ was not morally neutral; He was perfectly holy and pro-God. It was He who said, "He who is not with Me is against Me" (Matthew 12:30). That eliminates all possibility of neutrality.

It is certainly true that moral responsibility involves choices. God offers us life and death, blessing and cursing (Deuteronomy 30:19). We must choose God, not false gods like Satan (Joshua 24:15; 1 Kings 18:21; 1 Thessalonians 1:9). But the choice does not require that we are neutral. If neutral, how could we ever choose? Certainly we must be disposed to choose one or the other. In our sinful state, we are always predisposed to evil. We are not so much at a crossroads as on the wrong road already and must turn around (repent) and get on the right road (Matthew 7:13–14). A sinner will not do that of himself. God must intervene and give him faith and repentance. If moral responsibility requires neutrality, then it could be argued that the person who always chooses one or the other cannot be rewarded or punished, for he was not neutral and therefore not responsible.

Jonathan Edwards decimated the error of moral neutrality in his masterpiece *The Freedom of the Will.*[3] The idea of moral neutrality would eliminate culpability, for that would be damning someone for using the very freedom Arminians insist he must have to be accountable. Arminianism unwittingly agrees with the non-Christian idea of libertarianism and license. Libertarianism is compatible with situation ethics, but Reformed theology is not.

The Arminian theory sometimes appeals to Philippians 1:21–24, in which Paul cannot decide which option he prefers and is therefore neutral. But this is an incorrect interpretation. For one, it is talking about a Christian, not a neutral non-Christian. Also, Paul is not really neutral. He explicitly says he prefers to go to Heaven, not stay on earth. But he submits to God's will in the matter. This resembles Christ's prayer in Gethsemane, "Not My will, but Yours, be done" (Luke 22:42). Neither Paul nor Christ were morally neutral.

The nail in the coffin to this theory is God Himself. He has perfectly free will but certainly is not morally neutral. Would anyone in his right mind suggest that God could as equally choose evil as good? But in fact, medieval voluntarism came close to saying that in the theory that God can freely will anything at all by *absolute power*, suggesting that God can choose contrary to His nature. Thomas Bradwardine charged this with being Pelagian, and later Calvinists alleged that Arminianism sometimes appears to have a similar viewpoint. The very nature of God is at stake, so it is no academic matter.

The Arminian theory also tends to support the usual Arminian acceptance of the peccability of Christ, as seen in the quote by A. W. Tozer above. By contrast, most Reformed theologians accept the impeccability of Christ, with a few exceptions. The mainline Calvinist view is that Christ could be tempted because He was man but could not sin because He was God. So the whole question also has bearing on Christology. All points considered, the contrast between Calvinism and Arminianism becomes evident. We have a higher view of God and a lower view of man than they do. And as we have said before, this confirms the historical tendency of Arminianism toward liberalism.

---

3 Jonathan Edwards, *The Works of Jonathan Edwards*, Volume One (New Haven: Yale University Press, 1957).

Degrees of Responsibility

Earlier we showed that Scripture teaches that there are degrees of responsibility according to the amount of revelation a person has (Luke 12:48). But increased revelation does not increase one's moral ability. One is no more morally able to believe the gospel than he is to obey the law or follow his conscience. This has implications for the question at hand. Arthur Custance explains it:

> If a man's responsibility to obey is to be gauged by his ability to perform, then as his behaviour degenerates and his ability is progressively reduced, he has less duty. The wholly evil man ends up having no responsibility whatsoever, and must be accounted blameless.[4]

Unfortunately, this seems to happen in humanistically guided law courts in which a degenerate criminal is given less punishment, and the victim bears the brunt of the injustice.[5] Reformed jurisprudence would demand that a criminal "who could not help doing it" be punished more, not less. For one thing, he would be more of a future danger than one who did it in a fit of rage and then experienced remorse.

The Law and Human Inability

The next objection runs like this: "The law of God shows what we ought to do. *Oughtness* implies ability. Therefore, the law tells us what we are able to do." We disagree with the minor premise. As John Gill rightly said, "The Law only shows what a man ought to do, not what he can do."[6] Luther said that God's laws "always show, not what [men] can do, or do do, but what they should do."[7] Francis Turretin agreed: "God's commands are not the measure of strength, but a rule of duty. They do not teach what we are now able, but what we are bound to do; what we could formerly do and from how great a height of righteousness we have been precipitated by Adam's fall."[8] Christopher Love added another point: "Commands in Scripture do not show what the creature can do, or what he should do by his own moral power; but such commands in Scripture are charged on the creature to let him know what God will do for His elect."[9]

---

4 Arthur C. Custance, *The Sovereignty of Grace* (Phillipsburg, NJ: P&R, 1979), 117.
5 See Gary North, *Victim's Rights: The Biblical View of Civil Justice* (Tyler, TX: Institutes for Christian Economics, 1990). Rousas J. Rushdoony often addressed this in his many writings.
6 John Gill, *The Cause of God and Truth* (Grand Rapids: Baker, 1980), 25.
7 Martin Luther, *The Bondage of the Will* (Grand Rapids: Fleming H. Revell, 2005), 159.
8 Francis Turretin, *Institutes of Elenctic Theology* (Phillipsburg, NJ: P&R, 1992), 1:677.
9 Christopher Love, *Preacher of God's Word* (Morgan, PA: Soli Deo Gloria, 2000), 91–92.

He also said, "If you have lost ability to obey, God has not lost authority to command."[10]

The law tells us our duty. It shows us that we should obey but cannot obey. In this way it prepares us to believe in Christ (Galatians 3:24). The Puritans called this a *law work*, not to be confused at all with a *work of the Law*. God does the first; we should but cannot do the second. The law was given to show us our wretchedness and inability to obey God and save ourselves, said Calvin.[11] Luther put it like this: "How often do parents thus play with their children, bidding them to come to them, or do this or that, and that they may be compelled to call for help of the parent's hand?"[12] This is illustrated when Christ told the man to stretch forth his withered hand (Mark 3:5), the very thing he was unable to do. But Christ healed him and thus enabled him. As Augustine put it: "God bids us to do what we cannot, that we may know what we ought to seek from Him. [. . .] Let God give what He commands, and command what he will."[13]

Inability Does Not Negate Responsibility

The libertarian theory says that moral inability would nullify personal responsibility. We say it does not. Just as responsibility does not assume a moral ability, so moral inability does not negate moral accountability.[14] Man has fallen into the snare of the Devil (2 Timothy 2:26) and cannot extricate himself. He cannot free himself by his free will. His will is not free; it is a captive. He cannot even want to be free. Sin has a ratchet effect on us — we can get in, but we cannot get out. Unless God frees us, we are locked in and doomed.

A. W. Pink uses two analogies that are popular with Calvinists:

> Inability to pay a debt does not excuse a debtor who has recklessly squandered his estate; nor does drunkenness excuse the mad or violent actions of a drunkard, but rather aggravates his crime. God has not lost his right to command, even though man through his wickedness has lost his power to obey.[15]

---

10 Christopher Love, *The Works of Christopher Love* (Morgan, PA: Soli Deo Gloria, 1995), 1:247.
11 John Calvin, *Institutes of the Christian Religion* (Philadelphia: Westminster, 1960), 2:5:6 (pp. 323–24).
12 Luther, *Bondage of the Will*, 152.
13 Quoted approvingly by Calvin, *Institutes*, 2:5:7 (pp. 324–25).
14 Luther frequently made this point in *The Bondage of the Will*.
15 A. W. Pink, *Gleanings from the Scriptures* (Chicago: Moody, 1974), 86. So also others, such as Christopher Ness, *An Antidote to Arminianism* (Choteau, MT: Old Paths Gospel, n.d.), 53. Calvin: "We are not absolved from our obligation because we cannot pay it; for God holds us

If we cannot repay the loan, God the banker is not under any obligation to forgive the loan. On the Arminian scheme, either we sinners are able to repay God by obedience (which would repeat the error of Catholic merit theology) or else God is unjust to condemn us for not being able to repay Him. Both options are unbiblical. God allows no bankruptcy. Man is more than a debtor. He is an embezzler and a thief. He robbed the bank, not just failed to repay the loan. Is God required to forgive us? Is a bank president morally required not to press charges against a thief who squandered the loot on drugs? If so, then that gives moral and legal license to breakers of both God's and man's laws. Therefore, the Arminian theory, when carried to logical conclusions, actually undermines divine justice and provides a license to sin without penalty. May it never be!

The Heidelberg Catechism addresses the point well: "Q. 9. Is God not unjust in requiring of man in His Law what he cannot do? A. No, for God so created Man that he could do it. But man, upon the instigation of the Devil, by deliberate disobedience, has cheated himself and all his descendants out of these gifts." We have no one to blame but ourselves for our moral inability. Louis Berkhof noted: "We should not forget that the inability under consideration is self-imposed, has a moral origin, and is not due to any limitation which God has put upon man's being."[16] I would add that this point would argue in favor of mediate imputation of original sin.

Calvin further explained that man sins necessarily by reason of a fallen nature. Necessity does not excuse sin or deny punishment, any more than holy necessity of virtue denies reward in man or God.[17] Also, "God is not obliged to conform his demands to our abilities."[18] Jonathan Edwards put his finger on the state of the question: "No man is condemned properly because he is unable but because he is unwilling."[19] The sinner does not will to obey God and is therefore guilty. God does not lower His standard or change the rules. This was pointed out by the opponents of Neonomianism, which suggested that the gospel is a lower standard than the law. God lowered it so that we could believe and be saved. Orthodox Calvinists replied that the gospel fulfills the law, not abolishes it or lowers its standards. Second Peter 2:14 condemns false prophets with "eyes

bound to himself, although we are in every way deficient." *Commentaries on the First Twenty Chapters of the Book of the Prophet Ezekiel* (Grand Rapids: Eerdmans, 1948), 2:263.

16 Louis Berkhof, *Systematic Theology* (Grand Rapids: Eerdmans, 1988), 250.

17 John Calvin, *The Bondage and Liberation of the Will* (Grand Rapids: Baker, 1996), 147.

18 John Calvin, *Sermons on Galatians* (Edinburgh: Banner of Truth, 1997), 262; cf. Arthur C. Custance, *The Sovereignty of Grace*, 117.

19 "Deuteronomy 29:4 (Sermon 794)," Jonathan Edwards Center at Yale University, accessed February 9, 2018, http://edwards.yale.edu/.

full of adultery and that cannot cease from sin." Their being slaves of sin (v. 19) does not let them off the hook; being ceaseless sinning slaves only compounds their guilt.

Addressing the Unconverted

It takes biblical wisdom to address the unconverted in this area. We must tell them that they are commanded to obey God's law. We then tell them they are guilty. Then we tell them they must believe in Jesus Christ to receive salvation. But in none of these do we say that they are actually able to do so at just any time. They are not. We must not mislead them in order to convert them. Bad evangelistic theology makes false converts. We must be honest and leave them to contemplate the utter hopelessness of their sin and moral inability.

Unfortunately, some Hyper-Calvinists overreact to the Arminian system on this very point. The Gospel Standard Baptists have this in their official Articles: "We deny also that there is any capability in man by nature to any spiritual good whatever. So we regret the doctrine that men in a state of nature should be exhorted to believe or turn to God."[20] Their major premise is correct, but their hidden minor premise is not. That error is the same as Arminianism, that is, responsibility requires ability. They reason that since men are not able, then they are not responsible, and therefore we should not preach that they are accountable to believe. This is the debate on Duty Faith. This is closely related to their denial also of the free offer of the gospel, which they think also implies that lost sinners have moral ability. Mainline Calvinists say no such thing. A. W. Pink addressed the Hyper-Calvinists: "If the ungodly are not pointedly and authoritatively called unto repentance of their sins and belief of the Gospel, and if on the contrary they are only told that they are unable to do so, then they are encouraged in their impenitency and unbelief."[21] Spurgeon somewhere said that when the convicted crowds in Acts 2 cried out, "Men and brethren, what shall we do?" Peter did not say, "Do? You are morally unable to do anything." Rather, he commanded them, "Repent" (Acts 2:38). Paul told the Philippian jailer who asked a similar question, "Believe on the Lord Jesus Christ and you shall be saved" (Acts 16:31). We concentrate gospel preaching on their responsibility first and then on their inability second.

---

20 J. H. Gosden, *What Gospel Standard Baptists Believe* (Kingdon Langley: Gospel Standard Societies, 1993), 129.
21 Quoted in Iain H. Murray, *Arthur W. Pink: His Life and Thought*, 1st ed. (Edinburgh: Banner of Truth, 1981), 233. This section has been omitted in the revised edition of 2004.

The Hyper-Calvinist disagrees and cries, "Since the sinner is unable, you may as well be preaching in a cemetery as offer him the gospel and say he has the duty to believe." And they are right. We preach to a world of spiritual zombies who need Christ. Ezekiel was commanded to preach to dead bones (Ezekiel 37), and so are we. We remind our Hyperist friends that God uses the gospel to give life and spiritual ability to the spiritually dead and morally unable elect sinner.

Conclusion

Man is morally responsible to God but morally unable to obey or believe. God is just to punish him. But God is also merciful and grants moral ability to those He has chosen. This leads us to the great biblical doctrine of election.

Chapter 36
Unconditional Election

We now come to the second point of Calvinism. It logically follows from the first. If man is totally depraved and unable to obey God, then he needs salvation. God chose to whom He would give salvation. It also flows from the doctrine of absolute divine sovereignty. God sovereignly and freely elected some sinners to be saved and predestined them to be saved at the right time.

It is clearly and repeatedly taught in Scripture. But some preachers skip over it or misunderstand it. Many Christians have never heard a sermon on it. Others are not interested. They seem to be more interested in political elections than in divine election.

The Biblical Terminology

Psalm 65:4 says, "Blessed is the man You choose, and cause to approach you." This refers to the choice of priests but also to all saints because we are *all* priests. Whatever else election is, it is a great blessing, according to this verse.

Much more is said in the New Testament. Most references involve the Greek word *eklego* and its related forms. The verb is found twenty-two times. Consider the following (emphasis added in all verses):

- "For the elect's sake, whom He *chose*" (Mark 13:20).

- "But God has *chosen* the foolish things of the world to put to shame the wise, and God has *chosen* the weak things of the world to put to shame the things which are mighty; and the base things of the world and the things which are not, to bring to nothing the things that are" (1 Corinthians 1:27–28).

- "He *chose* us in Him before the foundation of the world" (Ephesians 1:4).

- "Has not God *chosen* the poor of this world to be rich in faith and heirs of the kingdom which He promised to those who love him?" (James 2:5).

The noun form is the word *eklektos*, also found twenty-two times, of which seventeen refer to salvation, such as:

- "For the *elect's* sake those days will be shortened" (Matthew 24:22).

- "They will gather together His *elect* from the four winds" (Matthew 24:31).

- "And shall God not avenge His own *elect*" (Luke 18:7).

- "Who shall bring a charge against God's *elect*?" (Romans 8:33).

- "Those who are with Him are called, *chosen* and faithful" (Revelation 17:14).

A related word is *ekloge*, found seven times, such as:

- "That the purpose of God according to *election* might stand" (Romans 9:11).

- "There is a remnant according to the *election* of grace" (Romans 11:5).

- "Knowing, beloved brethren, your *election* by God" (1 Thessalonians 1:4).

- "Therefore, brethren, be ever more diligent to make your call and *election* sure" (2 Peter 1:10).

Proorizo is translated *predestined* in Romans 8:29–30 and Ephesians 1:5 and 11. *Hairgomai* is in 2 Thessalonians 2:13: "God from the beginning *chose* you to salvation" (italics added). The doctrine of election is based on these and other words yet is not dependent merely on specific words but how they and others are used contextually and theologically.

Election in Other Areas

There are instances in which election refers to something other than salvation. For example, God chose certain persons to be civil rulers (Romans 13:1; Isaiah 45:1; Daniel 2:21; 1 Samuel 10:24; Psalm 78:70). God chose some men to be priests (Deuteronomy 18:5) and prophets (Jeremiah 1:5), such as Moses (Exodus 3). God chose the nation of Israel for a special purpose (Deuteronomy 4:37; 7:6–8; 10:15; 14:2; Isaiah 45:4; Psalm 33:12; Acts 13:17).

Jesus chose twelve apostles (John 6:70; Acts 1:2; cf. Matthew 20:23). This was mainly a choice for service and witness and even included Judas (Acts 10:41). God chose Matthias to replace Judas (Acts 1:24). Later God chose Paul to be a unique apostle (Acts 9:15). In all these cases, God did the choosing. The persons chosen did not volunteer or run for office in the election.

Election and Salvation

Some non-Calvinists argue that election is never to salvation, only to service. They overlook three explicit verses in particular:

- "God did not appoint us to wrath, but to obtain salvation through our Lord Jesus Christ" (1 Thessalonians 5:9).

- "God from the beginning chose you for salvation" (2 Thessalonians 2:13).

- "Therefore I endure all things for the sake of the elect, that they also may obtain the salvation which is in Christ Jesus with eternal glory" (2 Timothy 2:10).

Paul dealt with this in Romans 9–11 in addressing the question why some Jews were not saved, and some Gentiles were. His answer is that there is an Israel within Israel (Romans 2:28–29; 9:6).[1] Likewise, there was election to salvation of only some of those chosen to be apostles (John 13:10; 15:16, 19). The "inner Israel," to coin a phrase, was chosen to salvation and not just to external covenantal privileges. And that election typifies how God sovereignly chose some Gentiles to be saved.

The second point of Calvinism deals with this aspect of election. Note that it is election *to* salvation. Election is not salvation itself but the divine plan that prepares salvation for those who are chosen by God. They were chosen in eternity but saved in time. God foreordained both the subjects and method of salvation — indeed, all the details of this holy blessing (2 Thessalonians 2:13; 1 Peter 1:1–2).

Louis Berkhof supplies a good concise definition of election: "That internal act of God whereby He, in His sovereign good pleasure, and on account of no foreseen merit in them, chooses a certain number of men to be the recipients of special grace and eternal salvation."[2]

Election Is Eternal

God elected the elect in eternity, not in time. Consider the following:

- "He chose us in Him before the foundation of the world" (Ephesians 1:4).

- "God chose you from the beginning" (2 Thessalonians 2:13).

---

1 See John Piper, *The Pleasures of God* (Portland: Multnomah, 1991), 134.
2 Louis Berkhof, *Systematic Theology* (Grand Rapids: Eerdmans, 1988), 114.

- "Who has saved us and called us with a holy calling, not according to our works, but according to His own purpose and grace which was given to us in Christ Jesus before time began" (2 Timothy 1:9).

- "Eternal life which God, who cannot lie, promised before time began" (Titus 1:2).

As we saw earlier, back in pre-time eternity, God foreordained everything that comes to pass in time. He predestined everything in history. That is when He elected the elect. It did not happen in time, as some think, such as after the Fall. Election was not a temporal *Plan B* after the Fall nullified *Plan A*. Everything in history happens exactly as God planned it in eternal foreordination, including election.

It is predestination, not post-destination. God did it all before time began, before day one of creation and before we believed. Paul says in Romans 9:11 that it occurred before we did anything good or evil. The verbs for *elect* and *chose* are in the past tense, not the future. They are not in the present tense, as if God is still choosing some persons. What God does in time in salvation is following His eternal decree in eternity. Election therefore is complete and final. He is not choosing anymore. The election is over.

God chose all the elect individually but also all at the same time. He did not choose one person and later another and so on. The entire election happened in one eternal moment.

Some non-Reformed opponents reject this. They argue that since time has no past or future in God but only an *eternal now*, God is still electing persons now. Peter Martyr Vermigli answered this some five centuries ago: "Although in God there is no course of time nor any past or future, that creature whom God foreknows and predestines is not without a beginning; it is not coeternal with God the Creator. It follows of necessity that God predestined it before it was born."[3] He refers to Romans 9:11–12 and Ephesians 1:4. Several of the verses quoted above use the word *before*, so there is a sense in which God elected *before* time. G. C. Berkouwer, once a defender of the historic Reformed view, came to downplay this, if not deny it, in an overreaction to the supralapsarianism of

---

3 Peter Martyr Vermigli, *The Peter Martyr Library* (Kirksville, MO: Truman State University Press, 2003), 8:11.

Herman Hoeksema.[4] Alvin Baker took him to task on it and showed his non-Reformed inconsistencies.[5]

A Definite Number of Elect

The next point to understand is that God elected a specific number of persons. It is a certain and definite number that will not be changed, as the Westminster Confession explains: "Their number is so certain and definite, that it cannot be either increased or decreased" (3:4). God did not select a vague or foggy number of persons. The exact number is not known to us but is known to God alone. Scripture does indicate, however, that it is a very large number (Revelation 7:9).

Theoretically, there were three options. God could have chosen all, none, or some of the entirety of human population. The Bible says He elected only some. If He chose all, then all would be saved — which Scripture everywhere denies. If He chose none, then none would be saved — which Scripture also does not teach. The Bible says that God chose only some, and they alone will be saved. In a later chapter we will discuss whether the elect are in the majority or the minority of humanity.

Spurgeon is alleged to have prayed, "Lord, call in your elect and then elect some more." This sounds apocryphal and contradicts what he said elsewhere. I have never found any documentation for it. God never changes the number for the simple reason that His original choice was perfect. We pray that God call and save those He has already chosen. We tell the gospel to all people, for we do not know who the elect are (2 Timothy 2:10).

Personal Election

Election is individual and personal. When God put their names in the Book of Life, He wrote specific names — not *To whom it may concern* or *Anonymous* or *Mr. X*. For instance, Romans 16:13 says, "Greet Rufus, chosen in the Lord." Paul addresses the Thessalonian believers as personally chosen by God (1 Thessalonians 1:4). It was like the old method of making a person-to-person long distance telephone call. God personally chose some persons to be saved.

God deals with us as persons, not as mere numbers or abstract entities. The Good Shepherd calls His sheep by name (John 10:3). Adam named the animals in Eden (Genesis 2:19–20), and God named all the stars (Psalm 147:4). God

---

4 G. C. Berkouwer, *Divine Election* (Grand Rapids: Eerdmans, 1960).
5 Alvin Baker, *Berkouwer's Doctrine of Election* (Phillipsburg, NJ: P&R, 1981).

Himself named and numbered the persons He chose in election. This occurred before time, somewhat like how some parents choose a name for their unborn baby. Note the personal pronouns in Ephesians 1:4: "He chose us." When He saves us, He gives us a new name (Revelation 2:17), similar to how a bride takes the name of her husband.

There is also a sense in which God chose all the elect together with each other. This is reflected in time. They are not all saved at the same moment just as they had been elected in the same eternal moment, but God saves them and puts them into the same body of Christ. He calls the elect individually and puts them into the same one flock (John 10). The church is "the elect lady and her children" (2 John 1; cf. 1 Peter 5:13). Non-Calvinists sometimes misunderstand this corporate view of election and so propose another. They like to say it is all corporate and not individual, by which they mean that God chose a vague open number and left it up to us to insert our name on the register. Some appeal to Christ's parable of the great feast and the "whosoever will" call. We reply that God has pre-planned name-tags on the chairs in the banquet. Those who were chosen will sit in the right seats, and there will be no empty seats or need for more chairs. Election is God's reservation for specific persons in the Father's house (John 14:2).

No one is more elect than another. Election does not admit of degrees. A person is either elect or not elect. There are degrees of rewards for service but no degrees of salvation. A person may be elect but not yet saved, but there is nobody half-elect, any more than anyone can be half-saved. If he were to die in such a hypothetical situation, would half of him go to Heaven and half to Hell?

Election Is Irrevocable

God will not, and man cannot, change the election. As the Synod of Dort put it: "And as God is most wise, unchangeable, omniscient and omnipotent, so the election made by him can neither be interrupted nor changed, recalled or annulled; neither can the elect be cast away, nor their number diminished" (1:1). All decrees of God are irrevocable including election. God will not change His mind because He is not a man (Numbers 23:19; 1 Samuel 15:29). If He were to change His mind on election, it would be for the better or the worse. But that would indicate a mistake in God. Election is perfect because God is perfect. It could not be any better and certainly not worse. If God could change election in any way, that would be like God changing His mind and casting someone out of Heaven or releasing someone from Hell — both are denied in Luke 16:26.

Some extreme Arminians have theorized that a person can switch from being elect to being non-elect or vice versa. That, too, is biblically incorrect and impossible. Once elect, always elect. Christopher Ness, Puritan, commented: "'Tis unchangeable, because it is written in heaven, and so above the reach of angry men or enraged devils to cancel."[6]

God sealed the decree of election with an oath. He promised to save some persons, and He never breaks a promise. It is an ironclad promise. God never lies (Titus 1:2). Sinful men and demons may demand a recount and challenge the election, but in vain. Indeed, they disagree with the whole subject, but that will not annul divine election. Resistance to divine election is resistance to God who elects.

A Mutual Election

George Whitefield called it "a mutual choice."[7] First, Christ chose His bride in the eternal marriage covenant. Then when He saves us, we choose Him to be our heavenly husband. Richard Sibbes, the great English Puritan, put it like this: "He chose us, loved us, knows us, and therefore we choose, love, and know him."[8] We choose *because* we have been chosen. Or as 1 John 4:19 puts it: "We love Him because He first loved us." The order is vital. Arminianism reverses it.

Spurgeon had a delightful way of thanking God for election:

> I believe the doctrine of election, because I am quite sure that if God had not chosen me I should never have chosen Him; and I am sure He chose me before I was born, or else He never would have chosen me afterwards; or He must have elected me for reasons unknown to me, for I never could find any reason in myself why He should have looked upon me with special love.[9]

That is how all Calvinists look at it. One wonders how the Arminian can thank God when their system proposes that God chose us because He foresaw that we would choose Him. That error almost suggests that God should thank us, not we Him.

---

6 Christopher Ness, *An Antidote to Arminianism* (Choteau, MT: Old Paths Gospel Press, n.d.), 16.
7 George Whitefield, *The Sermons of George Whitefield* (Wheaton: Crossway, 2012), 1:110.
8 Richard Sibbes, *Works of Richard Sibbes* (Edinburgh: Banner of Truth, 1982), 7:295.
9 Charles H. Spurgeon, *Lectures to My Students* (London: Marshall, Morgan and Scott, 1954), 227.

Conclusion

Since God did the electing all by Himself, He met all the conditions. Hence, we call it *unconditional election*. It is unconditional on the elect. Salvation, to be sure, is conditional on faith and repentance, but God gives us those gifts and meets the conditions through us. But since election occurred in eternity past before we were even created, God alone could and did meet all conditions of election.

God did it by the wise counsel of His own will (Ephesians 1:11). Though there was a certain holy and wise arbitrariness to it (as we explained regarding absolute foreordination), it was not willy-nilly happenstance. Sam Storms said that God did not draw names out of a hat by random choice nor flip a coin.[10] We are on holy ground on this matter of why God chose some and not others and how and why He did this. We must not go beyond what is written nor stop short of what is written.

God tells us that He sovereignly chose the elect to display "the glory of His grace" (Ephesians 1:6), and He did it out of sheer sovereign grace. It would be impertinent and futile to seek a reason behind this. Homer Hoeksema spoke for us when he wrote this: "If you go a step further and ask the question why God was pleased to choose them, the answer is: keep silence! God's good pleasure is free, sovereign! Behind that good pleasure of God, you cannot go, and you may not attempt to go."[11] The Westminster Confession urges humble caution and the right holy attitude to election:

> The doctrine of this high mystery of predestination is to be handled with special prudence and care, that men attending the will of God revealed in his word, and yielding obedience thereunto, may, from the certainty of their effectual vocation, be assured of their eternal election. So shall this doctrine afford matter of praise, reverence, and the admiration of God, and of humility, diligence, and abundant consolation, to all that sincerely obey the Gospel (3:8).

Indeed and amen.

---

10 Sam Storms, *Chosen for Life: The Case for Divine Election*, 2nd ed. (Wheaton: Crossway, 2007), 40.

11 Homer Hoeksema, *The Voice of Our Fathers* (Grand Rapids: Reformed Free Publishing Association, 1980), 163.

Chapter 37
The Election of Grace

The Bible not only says that salvation is by grace alone (Ephesians 2:8–9) but that election to salvation is by grace alone. It is "the election of grace" (Romans 11:5). God sovereignly elected some sinners by sheer grace in eternity and saves those same sinners by sheer grace in time. To be sure, both are by sovereign grace.

Sovereign Election

The Reformed doctrine of election can be summed up in three words: "He chose us" (Ephesians 1:4). God did the choosing, not man. It does not say, "We chose Him," or "We chose ourselves." Man does not elect himself any more than a president elects himself (though they usually vote for themselves!). God is the only one who votes in this election. Not even the angels were given a vote. God is the subject; we are the object. God is active; we are passive. It is "your election by God" (1 Thessalonians 1:4). The biblical order is absolutely critical.

Mark 13:20 seems to emphasize this in the words "for the elect's sake, whom He chose." He, not we, did the choosing. Man has no more role in his election than in his creation. Indeed, we were elected even before we were created, so it is completely outside of and before us. Election is the sole prerogative of God. All attempts to deny this would de-throne God from His sovereign majesty. In Great Britain, certain privileges are said to be "the gift of the crown," that is, the sovereign wish of the sitting monarch. Election is the gift of the Sovereign of the universe.

When anyone challenges this, it is no academic matter. It is a proud attempt to take to oneself what belongs only to God. That is rebellion and theft. In effect, such a person wants to play God. We direct such persons to Matthew 20:15: "Is it not lawful for me to do what I wish with my own things? Or is your eye evil (covetous) because I am good?"

The subject-object relation is evident in Christ's words in John 15:16: "You did not choose Me, but I chose you." Nothing could be more explicit. It is a waste of time trying to say that this only refers to His choice of the twelve to serve as apostles. This is a common Arminian misinterpretation. First, Jesus did not address these words to Judas, for he had already left (13:30). Second, it must be interpreted in light of 13:18 when Judas was still there: "I do not speak concerning all of you. I know whom I have chosen." Judas was never chosen to salvation, only to apostleship (cf. 17:12). Third, John 15:19 indicates that Christ is speaking of election to salvation, not to mere apostleship: "I chose you out of the world." This obviously did not include Judas, for he was always "of the world." The others were "not of the world" anymore (John 15:19; 17:14).

He Chose Us

Why do some sinners believe, and others do not? It is because God sovereignly chose some and not others. The chosen will eventually believe; the unchosen will never believe. And this choice was not because of our faith. Augustine explained:

> He says, You have not chosen me, but I have chosen you, for no other reason than that they did not choose him in order that he might choose them, but he chose them in order that they might choose him, for his mercy anticipated them as grace, not at something owed. He, therefore, chose them from the world when he lived here in the flesh, but they had already been chosen in him before the foundation of the world. [. . .] He chose us, not because we believed, but in order that we might believe.[1]

The four Gospels do not record anyone coming to Christ saying, "Please, choose me," or, "I choose You, therefore You must choose me." An old hymn has these words: "'Tis not that I did choose thee, for Lord, that could not be. This heart would still refuse thee, hadst thou not chosen me."[2]

This is shown in time. Galatians 4:9 says, "But now after you have known God, or rather are known by God." We know God because God first knew us, not vice versa as Arminianism says. First John 4:19: "We love Him because He first loved us." Would anyone dare reverse this holy order? First Corinthians 8:3 nicely ties together knowing and loving: "But if anyone loves God, this one is known by Him." This is a loving knowledge. He loved and knew us before we loved and knew Him, therefore it is the "before-knowledge" of love, or what the Bible calls *foreknowledge*. A hymn puts it like this:

---

1 Augustine, *The Works of Saint Augustine* (Hyde Park: New City, 1999), I/26:178, 181. Also: "They chose him because they were chosen; they were not chosen because they chose him," p. 97.

2 Josiah Conder, *Tis Not That I Did Choose Thee*, written 1836.

He loved and chose because He would,
Nor did His choice depend
On creature's works, or bad or good,
But on His sovereign mind.[3]

Election by Grace

God has a general love for all men as His creatures (Psalm 145:9; Matthew 5:45). We will discuss this later in chapter 59, "Common Grace." But God also has a special love only for some persons. Out of His general love God gives good things in providence to all. But out of special love He chose certain sinners to be saved and gives them still other gifts. This special love flows from His sovereign will and good pleasure. It is not based on anything in the recipients. God loves all men with some grace but loves some men with all grace. This is election by *special grace*.

This was illustrated and typified by how God chose Israel to be a special nation. Deuteronomy 7:7–8 tells us that the Lord chose Israel solely because He chose to love them, not because of anything special in them. This is true also with spiritual Israel in salvation as it was with physical Israel in earthly blessings. It is strange that Arminian dispensationalists agree with the former but reject the latter.

Elective grace is given graciously (2 Timothy 1:9). It is free, *gratis*, a gratuitous gift. We should be grateful.

God did not elect on the basis of foreseen faith, for as Calvin put it: "Election is the mother of faith," not its daughter.[4] J. I. Packer commented: "Where the Arminian says, 'I owe my election to my faith,' the Calvinist says, 'I owe my faith to my election.'"[5] The first produces pride and ingratitude; the second produces humility and thanksgiving.

There is spiritual romance in this. Christ chose the elect to be His precious bride. He chose us in eternity and proposed in time, and she accepted. His choice was by sovereign grace, as Spurgeon commented: "It always seems inexplicable to me that those who claim free will so very boldly for man, should

---

3 William Gadsby, *A Selection of Hymns, for Public Worship*, 1838, #530.
4 John Calvin, *Institutes of the Christian Religion* (Philadelphia: Westminster, 1960), 3:22:10 (p. 945).
5 J. I. Packer, *A Quest for Godliness* (Wheaton: Crossway, 1990), 131.

not also allow some free will to God. [...] Why should not Jesus Christ have the right to choose His own bride?"[6]

Let us remember the second point of Calvinism presupposes the first point. We are unlovable depraved sinners. There is nothing at all in us to draw out God's love to us. Indeed, there is everything to attract His wrath. His love sprang solely from within Himself, for "God is love" (1 John 4:8, 16). Nobody deserves to be chosen; we all deserve to be punished. We deserve not to be chosen to go to Heaven but to be reprobated to Hell. God therefore exercised sovereign grace in bestowing His love on worthless wretches like us. Election is by God's sheer sovereignty and sheer grace. Therefore, it is by His sheer sovereign grace. It is *sola gratia*.

Election by Sovereign Grace in Romans 9

In Romans 9, Paul explains why some Jews are saved and not others, and why some Gentiles are saved and not others (vv. 8–10).[7] The reason: "That the purpose of God according to election might stand" (v. 11). God chose Abraham, not Hammurabi; Isaac, not Ishmael; Jacob, not Esau. "Jacob I have loved, but Esau I have hated" (v. 13). Why? Because He chose to, not because Jacob was better than Esau. In fact, a case could be made that Jacob was worse than his twin brother, but even that was not the deciding factor.

Similarly, some descendants of Jacob were chosen to salvation and others were not. Why? Because God said, "'I will have mercy on whomever I will have mercy, and I will have compassion on whomever I will have compassion,' therefore it is not of him who runs, but of God who shows mercy" (vv. 15–16). The election of grace is also the election of mercy and compassion.

The Puritan Edward Polhill observed: "Methinks these words, I will be gracious to whom I will be gracious, import a perfect absoluteness and incausability in God's will; even as that name, 'I am that I am,' imports a perfect absoluteness and incausability in God's essence."[8]

And the purpose of the election of grace? It was "that He might make known the riches of His glory on the vessels of mercy, which He had prepared beforehand for glory" (v. 23), including some Jews and some Gentiles (v. 24). God

---

6 Charles H. Spurgeon, *Metropolitan Tabernacle Pulpit* (Pasadena, TX: Pilgrim Publications, 1979), 13:412.

7 See John Piper, *The Justification of God* (Grand Rapids: Baker, 1993).

8 Edward Polhill, *The Works of Edward Polhill* (Morgan, PA: Soli Deo Gloria, 1998), 121.

is the potter, mankind is the clay. Out of this sinful lump God makes two bowls. One is to hold His wrath (v. 22), the other to contain His mercy (v. 23). Both deserve wrath. One gets wrath, the other gets mercy; neither receive injustice. Romans 9 is full of sovereign grace. As Spurgeon well noted: "As long as that [chapter] remains in the Bible, no man shall be able to prove Arminianism. So long as that is written there, not the most violent contortions of the passage will ever be able to exterminate the doctrine of election from the Scriptures."[9]

Paul would later return to this theme in Romans 11:5–6. Those who are saved are saved because of "the election of grace." There is a sweet note in the *Geneva Bible* (1599 edition) on Romans 11:5: "The election of grace, is not whereby men chose grace, but whereby God chose us of his grace and goodness."

Election by Sovereign Grace in Ephesians 1

Another explicit passage is Ephesians 1. Verse 3 states that God the Father has blessed us in many ways, some of which are mentioned in the following paragraph. Verse 4 says, "He chose us." Translations differ as to the punctuation at the end of the verse. Some put the two words "in love" with verse 4, as in "holy and blameless before Him in love" (KJV, NKJV, ASV, NEB, JB, others). Others put a period after "Him" so that "in love" modifies the verb "predestined" in verse 5, thus: "In love He predestined us to adoption" (NASB, RSV, ESV, NIV, TEV, Phillips, others). If the first is correct, then it says that God chose us to have a relationship of love with Him. If the latter is true, then God predestined us out of love. One speaks of the source, the other of the goal. The difference is slight, and other verses teach each truth. Love is part of both election and predestination.

This includes adoption (v. 5). Romans 8:15–17 says that God adopts us to be His heirs. Couples usually adopt a child because they have so much love to share. The same is true with God. He adopts us as His own children so that He can fill our hearts with His love and give us many treasures as an inheritance.

All this is in keeping with the threefold purpose of God in the grand scheme of Ephesians 1: "to the praise of the glory of His grace" (v. 6); "to the praise of His glory" (v. 12); "to the praise of His glory" (v. 14). God chose us out of grace to display His glory. We get the grace; He gets the glory. If election is not of grace, then God does not get the glory — we do. God shares His glory with no

---

9 Charles H. Spurgeon, *New Park Street Pulpit* (Pasadena, TX: Pilgrim Publications, 1981), 1:315.

one but abundantly showers His grace upon the elect for all eternity (Ephesians 2:7).

The Book of Life

When God graciously chose some sinners to be saved, He wrote their names in the Book of Life. In his excellent short book on the subject, Matthew Mead the Puritan wrote: "The book of life is God's immutable and eternal decree, wherein, as in a book the names of the elect are written."[10] Robert Peterson calls it "the census register of the city of God."[11]

Jesus said in Luke 10:20, "Rejoice because your names are written in heaven." Nothing rejoices the heart more than knowing you are elect. The Bible mentions this book in Philippians 4:3, Hebrews 12:23, and probably Daniel 12:1. Revelation 13:8; 17:8; 20:12, 15; and 21:27 foretell the doom of lost sinners whose names are not written in it. It is called the *Lamb's Book of Life*. It is the directory of the lambs who belong to the Lamb.

There are several erroneous theories regarding this Book of Life. One is that we ourselves write our name in it. Sometimes an overzealous and under-taught evangelist will ask his hearers to "come forward and accept Jesus into your heart. Come and write your name in the Book of Life." But Scripture everywhere says that it is God, not us, that does the writing. It is the register of divine election, not self-election.

A second error is that of the Calvinist Charles Hodge regarding infant baptism: "Do let the little ones have their names written in the Lamb's book of life, even if they afterwards choose to erase them. Being thus enrolled may be the means of their salvation."[12] Surely Hodge knew that the names are not written at the time of baptism, whether of infants or believers, and that the names cannot be erased.

A third error says that God writes a name in it when that sinner believes and is saved. One popular gospel song says, "There's a new name written down in glory."[13] At least this says that it is God that does the writing. But it gets the date wrong.

---

10 Matthew Mead, *A Name in Heaven the Truest Ground of Joy* (Morgan, PA: Soli Deo Gloria, 1996), 16.
11 Robert Peterson, *Election and Free Will* (Phillipsburg, NJ: P&R, 2007), 82.
12 Charles Hodge, *Systematic Theology* (Grand Rapids: Eerdmans, 1979), 3:588.
13 C. Austin Miles, *A New Name in Glory*, written and composed 1910.

Scripture teaches that God wrote the names down "from the foundation of the world" (Revelation 13:8; 17:8), which is the same phrase used for *election* in Ephesians 1:4. One sometimes hears Christians speak of "the Lamb slain from the foundation of the world." While it is true that Christ was foreordained in eternity to be the Lamb of God slain for sinners (1 Peter 1:19–20), this misinterprets Revelation 13:8. Of course, nobody believes that Christ was literally slain in eternity; that happened in time. Revelation 13:8 means that some names were not written in the Book of the slain Lamb and that their names were not there in eternity. This is seen clearly in the parallel in 17:8, which does not mention the slain Lamb. Revelation 13:8 could be paraphrased: "Whose names were not from the foundation of the world written in the Book of Life that belongs to the Lamb who was slain."

The point is that back in eternity past, God chose some sinners to be saved and wrote their names in this book. It is not a literal book but a metaphor. God did not choose other sinners, and so He did not write their names down in it. Later I will discuss this book with regard to those who are not written in it (reprobation), and then again when we look at the objection to the perseverance of the saints that says that names may be erased from it.

Conclusion

Putting all this together, one might wax theologically romantic and put it like this: Out of His infinite love and free grace, the Lord of Love chose a bride to bestow His love on and have her return it to Him in grateful love. When He chose her, He wrote her name down in the Book of Love that belongs to the Lamb of Love.

Chapter 38
Election and Foreknowledge

When one studies the subject of election, sooner or later he faces the question of its relation to foreknowledge. The question is: Did God choose the elect solely by sovereign grace or because He foresaw that they would believe? Calvinists agree with the first; most non-Calvinists accept a form of the second. What saith the Scriptures?

Foreknowledge and Foresight

As we saw in an earlier chapter, the Bible very clearly states that God is omniscient about everything past, present, and future. He does not guess or consult. He knows by certainty, not probability; by absolute omniscience, not by Middle Knowledge. This is proved by His prophesying future events, among other things.

We also saw that God eternally foreordained all means and ends of all that comes to pass in history. He has a definite knowledge of all details and order. He predestined everything by divine sovereignty, not by foresight of what would happen anyway, which is an absurdity. The doctrine of foreordination alone would be enough to substantiate the Reformed doctrine of unconditional election.

Scripture teaches that God foreknew specific things relating to salvation, such as that He would justify Gentiles by faith (Galatians 3:8) and that Christ would rise from the dead (Acts 2:31). Salvation happens exactly as God predetermined it to happen, and God foresaw what He foreordained to do.

There are two Greek words for *foreknow*. One is *proginosko*. It combines *pro* (before) and *ginosko* (know). The other word is *proorao* (or *proorizo*), from *pro* (before) and *orao* (know by seeing). The words are used in three ways: (1) *foresight* (advance factual knowledge); (2) *foreordination* (causal knowledge); and (3) *forelove* (personal affection in advance). Mere etymology does not determine the meaning, however, but rather the use, context, and theology.

Election by Foreknowledge in 1 Peter 1

Peter, in 1 Peter 1:2, is writing to those who are "elect according to the foreknowledge (*prognosin*) of God the Father." Some think this means foresight: God elected them because of their foreseen faith. But Peter does not mention faith. Calvinists take it to mean either *foreordination* or *forelove*.

In 1:20, he says Christ "was foreordained (*proegnosmenou*) before the foundation of the world." Most translations correctly render this as *foreordination* rather than *foresight*. It is causal, not cognitive. God did not merely foresee that Christ would die; He predestined it, as in Acts 2:28 and 4:28. The crucifixion was no accident. It was deliberately foreordained by God. It would be consistent, therefore, to see that Peter used the word in the same way in 1:2. Election there was by divine *foreordination*.

Election by Foreknowledge in Romans 8

William Perkins the Puritan popularized the term "the Golden Chain" to describe Romans 8:29–30. Paul there sets forth salvation in five links: foreknowledge, predestination, calling, justification, and glorification. The chain began in eternity past (links 1 and 2), continues in time (links 3 and 4), and concludes in the future (link 5), so certain that it is spoken of in the past tense. He does not mention other links such as faith because they are not pertinent to his argument. The key phrase is verse 29: "Whom He foreknew (*proegno*) He also predestined (*proorisen*)."

The popular Arminian interpretation is exemplified in *The Living Bible*'s paraphrase: "For from the very beginning God decided that those who came to Him — and all along He knew who would — should become like His Son."[1] This view takes *foreknow* to mean *foresee*. He predestined some persons because He foresaw they would believe.

Another interpretation — fortunately a rare one — inserts the word *some* in each link: "Some of those He foreknew He predestined" and so forth. The links get progressively smaller, and one wonders if anyone is glorified in the end. But Paul did not say "some." *All* is implied. "All whom He foreknew He also predestined."

Context is crucial. Verse 29 begins with the word *for*, which takes us back to verse 28. Everything works out for the good of those who love God *because*

---

1 *The Living Bible* (Wheaton: Tyndale House, 1971), 904.

God foreknew and predestined them to glory. The purpose would be foiled if the chain could be broken. But that is not possible, for Paul begins by saying, "We know."

Arminian exegesis wrongly says that verse 29 means "foresaw their faith." But Paul says God foreknew *them*, not their faith. Faith is not even mentioned. It is *whom*, not *what* in each link. It also hinges on the meaning of the word *foreknew*. Paul would use it again in 11:2 with reference to election in verses 5 and 6. While some Reformed interpreters take Romans 8:29 to mean *foreordination*, by far most take it to mean *forelove*.

Election Is Not by Foreseen Faith

Calvinism has always said that election is not based on foreseen faith. The Canons of Dort said:

> This election was not founded upon foreseen faith, and the obedience of faith, holiness, or any other good quality or disposition in man, as the prerequisite, cause or condition on which it depended; but men are chosen to faith and to the obedience of faith, holiness, etc., therefore election is the foundation of every saving good: from which proceed faith, holiness, and the other gifts of salvation, and finally eternal life itself (1:9).

If election was based on foreseen faith, where did that faith come from? Faith is not something that fallen sinners can generate. It must be given to them. To say that God *foresaw* that He would give them faith, then, is much the same as to say that He *foreordained* that He would give them faith. Calvinists affirm this; Arminians deny it. Calvin said, "God could not foresee what was not in us before he himself put it into us."[2] *The Geneva Bible* note on Ephesians 1:5 is worth quoting: "Neither is faith which God foresaw the cause of predestination, but the effect."

Acts 13:48 also teaches this: "And as many as had been appointed to eternal life believed." This is sometimes misquoted as "Those who believed were appointed to eternal life." God pre-appointed that certain people would believe. *That* is election. It is a question of cause and effect. The cause is God's pre-appointment; the effect is faith. Arminianism reverses the order. Robert Haldane commented: "Faith cannot be the cause of foreknowledge, because foreknowledge is before predestination, and faith is the effect of predestination."[3]

---

2 John Calvin, *Sermons on the Epistle to the Ephesians* (London: Banner of Truth, 1973), 32.
3 Robert Haldane, *The Epistle to the Romans* (London: Banner of Truth, 1966), 397.

Francis Turretin: "If election is from foreseen faith, then God would not have elected man, but man would have elected God, and so predestination should be called postdestination."[4] God is a God of order, not confusion (1 Corinthians 14:33, 40). When we tamper with God's order, theological confusion arises.

We can also dismiss any hint that God chose us based on foreseen holiness or good works. Ephesians 1:4 and 2:10 clearly state that these were predestined by God and therefore cannot be the cause of predestination. God did not choose anyone because He foresaw they were better than others. In point of fact, the elect are often worse than the non-elect. But the degree of one's sinful state has no bearing whatsoever on one's election. Would anyone suggest that God chose someone because he was better — or chose him because he was worse than others? Paul considered himself the chief of sinners yet was elect. The foreseen good character of the regenerated elect was no more the basis of their election than the foreseen bad character of the reprobate was the basis of their non-election. Character has nothing to do with it. Sovereign grace has everything to do with it.

We can also dismiss another Arminian theory. This one that says it is not merely saving faith that was foreseen as the basis of election but persevering faith. Arminianism says that a person can believe and be justified and then later forfeit faith and salvation and die lost. Thus, it says that God had to see that the foreseen believer was one who persevered to the end. But this too gets the cart before the horse. As we shall see later, perseverance is the effect of predestination, not the cause.

We earlier mentioned still another unbiblical theory regarding foreseen faith. It has been argued by some Arminians that God elected to save some persons who will never hear the gospel because He knows by Middle Knowledge that they *would* have believed had they heard the gospel. Others say this explains why God did not elect others who never heard, for He knew by Middle Knowledge that they would not have believed even if they had heard.[5] But this goes directly against Matthew 11:21–23. God does not foreordain anything on the shaky basis of what might happen under certain conditions but based on His own wise counsel (Ephesians 1:11). To say God elected someone because he *might* have believed but did not is like rewarding an injured runner who might have won the race had he not been on the sidelines. Worse, it would be unjust

---

4 Francis Turretin, *Institutes of Elenctic Theology* (Phillipsburg, NJ: P&R, 1992), 1:361.
5 Donald Lake, "He Died for All: The Universal Dimension of the Atonement." In Clark Pinnock, ed., *Grace Unlimited* (Minneapolis: Bethany House, 1975), 43.

of God to reprobate those who never hear the gospel simply because He knew they would not have believed anyway. It would be like punishing a person for something he did not do but would have done if circumstances were otherwise. This whole theory is illogical and reflects badly on the justice of God.

Foreknowledge in Another Sense

Foreknow can also mean *forelove*. In the Bible, *to know* can mean more than to accumulate factual information. It can mean personal affection. In his classic book *Knowing God*,[6] J. I. Packer shows that there is a big difference between knowing about God and knowing God personally. Everyone knows God exists (Romans 1:19–21), but very few know God personally. Many unbelieving theologians know a lot about God but have never known Him personally. An unbeliever does not know God, for knowing God is related to eternal life (John 17:3), and that comes only to those who believe in Jesus Christ (John 3:16). Some have said that it is the difference between head knowledge and heart knowledge. First John 2:3 is similar: "By this we know that we know Him" (cf. 3:6; 4:7–8). This saving knowledge is a personal, heartfelt, experiential knowledge. It comes only through Christ, for to know Christ is to know God (John 8:19, 55; 14:7, 9; Matthew 11:27).

Now we know God because He first knew us (cf. Galatians 4:8–9; 1 John 4:19). God took the initiative in this personal knowledge. And He did it back in eternity when He foreordained to do so in time. That is what is meant by *affectionate foreknowledge*. It is forelove. That is what is meant in Romans 8:29 and perhaps also 1 Peter 1:2. It is not just causative; it is causally affectionate and affectionately causal.

Foreknowledge as Forelove

In John 10:14, Christ said, "I am the good shepherd; and I know My sheep and am known by My own." The order is obvious — they know because they are known by Him. This is not just factual information but personal affection.

Both the Hebrew word *yada* and the Greek word *ginosko* sometimes mean personal and intimate knowledge, even sexual knowledge (Genesis 4:1; Luke 1:34). It is a loving relationship, as in 1 Corinthians 8:3: "If anyone loves God, this one is known by Him." To know God is to love God. To be known by God is to be loved by God. God initiates; we respond.

---

6 Downers Grove, IL: InterVarsity, 1973.

In 2 Timothy 1:12, Paul said that he knows whom he believed. Second Timothy 2:19 says "The Lord knows those who are His." These verses refer to more than mental cognition. They refer to affectionate love.

This is seen several times in the Hebrew Bible. In Hosea 13:5 God says, "I knew you in the wilderness." He personally and lovingly knew them there. In Exodus 33:12 God said to Moses, "I know you by name, and you have found grace in My sight." The knowledge was one of grace. Jeremiah 1:5 spots this knowledge still earlier: "Before I formed you in the womb I knew you." God had a special love for Israel that He did not have for other nations: "You only have I known of all the families of the earth" (Amos 3:2). Obviously God, who is omniscient, knew about all the Gentiles. This clearly means affectionate love. God chose Israel out of this love (Deuteronomy 7:7–8).

This is exactly what happened in election. God predetermined to set special His love on some persons and not others. In doing so, He elected them. This is what is meant by foreknowledge in the affectionate sense. We could paraphrase Romans 8:29 as follows: "For whom God chose to love in a special personal way, He then foreordained that they would be conformed to the image of His Son." It is the same as "the election of grace" (Romans 11:5). To make election based on foreseen faith completely misses the golden truth that it was out of love that God chose the elect and not because of anything good in them, even faith.

This forelove is personal but not universal. At the last judgment, Christ will say to lost sinners, "I never knew you" (Matthew 7:23). Note that He will not say, "You never knew Me," though that is true. This obviously does not mean "I never knew about you," for He knows everything. Nor does it mean "I never knew that you believed." Rather, it means that Christ will reveal that He never set His eternal love upon them in predestination. We shall discuss this later in chapter 44, "The Doctrine of Reprobation."

Conclusion

The answer to the question at the beginning of this chapter is this: God chose the elect solely out of sovereign grace, not because He foresaw that they would believe. He did so because He chose to. And He did it out of love.

Chapter 39
Election in Christ

Election was the work of God alone. Neither angels nor men were involved, for they did not even exist yet and were themselves the object of election. God is a Trinity, and whatever He does He does as a Trinity. Each member has a distinctive yet cooperating role in everything, including election.

The Trinity and Election

Ephesians 1:3–4 teaches us that election was by God the Father: "Blessed be the God and Father of our Lord Jesus Christ. [. . .] He chose us in Him." And 1 Peter 1:2: "[To the] elect according to the foreknowledge of God the Father." The Bible also says that God the Son chose the elect. John 15:16: "You did not choose Me, but I chose you" (cf. 13:18, 15:19). And doubtlessly the Holy Spirit had a role in election, for He also is God.

What each member does externally reflects their respective internal relations with the other members. The Father eternally begets the Son. The Holy Spirit eternally proceeds from the Father and the Son. That is the *ontological Trinity*, Trinity-in-Itself. In time, the Father begot the Son in the womb of Mary by means of the Spirit, but neither the Father nor the Spirit were incarnated. The Son alone died and rose. The Father and the Son sent the Spirit on Pentecost while they remained in Heaven. All three are equal, but the above illustrates the interpersonal order of the Father, Son, and Spirit (Matthew 28:19).

Accordingly, the Father had a certain logical priority initiating election. The Son agreed and is co-elector. The Spirit confirmed and ratified election. When Scripture says "God" elected, it means either the whole Trinity or just God the Father. More will be said on the trinitarian nature of election in the following chapter.

Election in Christ

Three verses teach that election is "in Christ." Romans 16:13 says, "Greet Rufus, chosen in the Lord." In Paul's epistles, *Lord* almost always means the Lord Jesus Christ. Next, 2 Timothy 1:9 says, "Who has saved us and called us with a holy calling, not according to our works, but according to His own purpose and grace, which was given to us in Christ Jesus before time began."

The third and key verse is Ephesians 1:4: "Just as He chose us in Him before the foundation of the world." The phrase *in Christ* is very common in Paul's letters, especially Ephesians. Reformed scholars are not unanimous as to its meaning in this verse. Theodore Beza took it to mean "He chose us to be in Christ."[1] Edward Polhill interpreted it to mean that Christ as God-man "purchased election" for the elect.[2] Franciscus Gomarus and others have taken it in the instrumental sense "through Christ."[3] Martyn Lloyd-Jones says it means "in and through Christ" and is parallel with Christ's prayer in John 17, in which the Father gave the elect to Christ and through the Son gives grace and glory to the elect.[4]

Another popular explanation is that Christ is the Head of the elect and all the members of His body were chosen when He was chosen. Augustine said: "Just as, then, that one was predestined to be our head, so we many have been predestined to be his members."[5] John Gill held this view and added, "Election does not find men in Christ, but puts them there; it gives them a being in Him and union to Him."[6] Still another opinion is that of Francis Turretin: "To be elected in Christ is nothing else than to be destined to salvation to be obtained in Christ or by Him. Therefore Christ is the cause of salvation, not of election."[7] Others say that as God Christ was co-elector, but as the foreordained God-man was the cause of salvation but not of election.

John Calvin interpreted it in keeping with the four Aristotelean links of causation:

> The efficient cause [of salvation] is the good pleasure of the will of God; the material cause is Christ; and the final cause is the praise of His grace. [. . .] The material cause, both of eternal election, and of the love which is now revealed, is Christ, whom he names the Beloved, to tell us that by Him the love of God is poured out to us. [. . .] He now comes to

---

1 Quoted in Charles Hodge, *A Commentary on the Epistle to the Ephesians* (London: Banner of Truth, 1964), 30.

2 Edward Polhill, *The Works of Edward Polhill* (Morgan, PA: Soli Deo Gloria, 1998), 126.

3 G. C. Berkouwer, *Divine Election* (Grand Rapids: Eerdmans, 1960), 143.

4 Martyn Lloyd-Jones, *God's Ultimate Purpose* (Edinburgh: Banner of Truth, 1978), 94–95.

5 Augustine, *The Works of Saint Augustine* (Hyde Park: New City, 1999), I/26:175.

6 John Gill, *A Complete Body of Doctrinal and Practical Divinity* (Paris, AR: Baptist Standard Bearer, 1984), 1:353.

7 Francis Turretin, *The Institutes of Elenctic Theology* (Phillipsburg, NJ: P&R, 1992), 1:353.

the formal cause, the preaching of the Gospel, by which the love of God flows to us.[8]

Elsewhere Calvin explained election in Christ in terms of Christ as the "pattern and mirror of election," that is, "he must have first looked on our Lord Jesus Christ before he could choose us and call us." Christ is also "the true register" of election, for God's promise of election was written down in the Book of Life.[9]

Ephesians 3:11 sheds more light on the subject: "According to the eternal purpose which He accomplished in Christ Jesus our Lord." Interpreters vary as to whether this accomplishment refers to the culmination of election in eternity or the work of Christ on earth. Romans 9:29 also relates Christ to election: "For whom He foreknew, He also predestined to be conformed to the image of His Son, that He might be the firstborn among many brethren." And earlier we showed that God wrote the names of the elect in the Lamb's Book of Life (Revelation 13:8; 17:8).

Election is completely Christ-related. It is in Christ, through Christ, by Christ, for Christ, to be in Christ. There is no election outside of Christ; all election is in Christ. This has bearing on salvation. There is no salvation except by Christ and through faith in Christ (John 14:6; Acts 4:12). This also relates to union with Christ. The elect were united covenantly with Christ in election and then united experimentally with Christ in conversion, with the result that they are now *in Christ*.

This presents a problem to dispensationalists, for they say that "in Christ" is taught only in the New Testament and is therefore a new covenant blessing for the church alone. Old covenant saints were not "in Christ," therefore they did not believe in Christ nor will be raised in Christ. That is dangerously close to saying that they were not saved in and through Christ, but in some other way, contrary to what Peter said to the Jews in Acts 4:12. Reformed theology disagrees most strongly. Salvation has always been only in Christ, received only through faith in Christ by believing the gospel of Christ. Accordingly, all the elect of all dispensations and covenants were elected together in Christ, otherwise there would be election outside of Christ. All the elect — both Jews of the old covenant and Gentiles and Jews in the new covenant — are experientially *in Christ* for they are all united to Him through the indwelling

---

8 John Calvin, *The Epistles of Paul the Apostle to the Galatians, Ephesians, Philippians, and Colossians* (Grand Rapids: Eerdmans, 1980), 126–28.

9 John Calvin, *Sermons on the Epistle to the Ephesians* (London: Banner of Truth, 1973), 32–33.

Spirit. And all believers are in Christ and will be raised from the dead at the Second Coming (1 Thessalonians 4:16).

Arminians sometimes charge that Calvinists teach that election is not in Christ, but their logic is as convoluted as their eisegesis. They suggest that Ephesians 1:4 means Christ alone is elect, not us. We get into Christ when we believe in Him, and it is at that point that we become elect.[10] But the result of this theory is a man-generated election in time rather than a God-generated election in eternity. This directly contradicts Ephesians 1:4. This error illustrates the Arminian tendency to be anthropocentric rather than theocentric.

Others such as Karl Barth say that the historic Reformed view is not Christocentric and is therefore wrong. We reply that election is theocentric and trinitarian, not just Christocentric. Let us not leave the Father and the Spirit out of election! It is Christocentric in the sense that Christ is God, co-elector, and the means and goal of election.

Christ as the Elected One

Christ is not only the subject of election but in a sense is also the object of election. Several verses speak of Him as the "Elect One" or the "Chosen One." Isaiah 42:1: "Behold! My servant whom I uphold, My Elect One in whom My soul delights." This is quoted in Matthew 12:18 as "Behold! My Servant whom I have chosen, My Beloved in whom My soul is well-pleased." This is echoed in Matthew 3:17, 17:5, and Ephesians 1:6.

Psalm 89 is another Messianic prophecy. Verse 3 says, "I have made a covenant with My chosen, I have sworn to My servant David." As in Isaiah 42:1, *chosen* is parallel with *servant*. He is chosen to be the Servant of the Lord. Psalm 89 refers not just to David or his son Solomon, but to David's greatest son, Jesus the Son of David. It is a Messianic title. Verse 19 refers to Him again as "Your holy one [. . .] who is mighty; I have exalted one chosen from the people."

Luke 23:35 records scoffers blaspheming Christ on the cross with the words "Let Him save Himself if He is the Christ, the chosen of God." Some Greek manuscripts and English translations have "My chosen one" in Luke 9:35. Lastly, 1 Peter 2:4 and 6 refers to Jesus as "a living stone, rejected indeed by men, but chosen by God and precious [. . .] a chief cornerstone, elect, precious." This is an allusion to Psalm 118:22 and Isaiah 28:16. Verse 9 refers to Christians as

---

10 For example, Roger T. Forster and V. Paul Marston, *God's Strategy in Human History* (Wheaton: Tyndale House, 1973), 145.

"a chosen generation," hence there is a relation between the Chosen One and the chosen ones. Christopher Love, Puritan, drew a parallel. Christ was elected King, and we are elected as kings and princes in Him in the way the princes are in their father the king.[11]

We can dismiss all theories that Christ's election was the same as ours for two reasons. First, He is God, and we are not. Second, we are sinners, and He is not. God elected us to be saved. God elected Christ to be our Savior.

God chose Moses to lead the people (Psalm 106:23; Exodus 3). He chose Aaron to be high priest (Numbers 16:5; 17:5). He chose David to be king of Israel (Psalm 78:68–72; 1 Samuel 16:7–12). Those were types of Christ's election as Prophet, Priest, and King of His people. He was thus chosen to be their mediator. John Gill explains:

> Out of the vast number of individuals of human nature God determined to create, there was a certain number which he selected for himself, for his own glory and to be eternally happy with him; and out of these he singled out one individuum of human nature, to be united to the eternal Word, the Second Person in the Trinity.[12]

Thus, in this sense at least, Christ was chosen in His foreordained humanity.

Jonathan Edwards took it a step further and related Christ's election to both His natures:

> Christ is the chosen of God both as to his divine and human nature. As to his divine nature he was chosen of God, though not to any addition to his essential glory or real happiness which is infinite, yet to [his] great declarative glory. As he is man, he is chosen of God to the highest degree of real glory and happiness of all creatures. As to both, he is chosen of God to the office and glory of the Mediator between God and man, and the head of all the elect creation. His election as it respects his divine nature was for his worthiness, and excellency, and infinite amiableness in the sight of God; and perfect fitness for that which God chose him to his worthiness, was the ground of his election. But his election as it respects his human nature was free and sovereign, not being for any worthiness, but his election was the foundation of his worthiness. His election as he is God is a manifestation of God's infinite wisdom. The wisdom of any being is discovered by the wise choice he makes. So the infinite wisdom of God

---

11 Christopher Love, *Preacher of God's Word* (Morgan, PA: Soli Deo Gloria, 2000), 155.
12 John Gill, *An Exposition of the Bible* (Grand Rapids: Baker, 1980), 3:227 (on Psalm 89:19).

is manifest in the wisdom of his choice, when he chose his eternal Son —
one so fit upon all accounts for the office of a mediator — when he only
was fit, and when he was perfectly and infinitely fit; and yet his fitness was
so difficultly to be discerned that none but one of infinite wisdom could
ever discover it.[13]

Calvin succinctly put it thus: "Christ was chosen that the whole love of God
might dwell in Him, so as to flow from Him to us as from a full fountain."[14]

The Barthian Theory

Karl Barth's theory is fraught with many inconsistencies and unbiblical errors.
In some ways it is further from historic Calvinism then Arminianism is.
Yet some theologians mistakenly think his theory is not only correct but is
Reformed and even truer to Calvin's than later Calvinists'. By no means! He
himself summed up his position: "The simplest form of the dogma may be
divided at once into two assertations: that Jesus Christ is the electing God, and
that He the elected Man."[15]

At first blush that sounds Reformed. But he denied individual personal
election. He claimed that all men were elected unconditionally in Christ.
Arminianism does not even say this — it may say all men are conditionally
elected in Christ, but they must ratify it by their faith or their election is
nullified.
Barth's theory strongly implies universal salvation, which he neither asserted
nor denied, while evangelical Arminianism strongly denies it. Arminianism is
at least evangelical, while Barthianism is not. Barthianism is fundamentally
liberal.

He also taught that all men are non-elect in Christ, for Christ is both the
Elect One and the Reprobate One. This may sound like the Arminian idea that
Christ died for all men, but it is not. The problem that Barth never explained
is: How can a person be both elect and non-elect? To him it was a paradox.
To historic Calvinists and Arminians, it is a blatant contradiction. Calvinism
teaches that only some persons are elect in Christ. All the rest are non-elect
and not in Christ.

---

13 Jonathan Edwards, *The Works of Jonathan Edwards* (New Haven: Yale University Press,
2000), 18:425; "We are elected in his election." Edwards, 418. His discussion on pp. 414–18 is
theologically scintillating.
14 John Calvin, *Calvin's New Testament Commentaries* (Grand Rapids: Eerdmans, 1979), 4:126.
15 Karl Barth, *Church Dogmatics* (Edinburgh: T. and T. Clark, 1957), II, Part 2, 103.

Conclusion

These are deep waters which we must swim with humility, caution, and wonder. Election is in Christ and related to Christ's election in a mysterious and glorious way. As God He is co-elector. As man — or better, the God-man — He is chosen to be Savior, Mediator, and Head of His people. In fulfilling His predestined office, Christ receives great glory, which in turn redounds to the glory of God the Father (Philippians 2:5–11). Thus Christ has the preeminence in all things (Colossians 1:18), including election.

Chapter 40
The Covenant of Redemption

Many Reformed theologians discuss election in terms of an eternal covenant called the *covenant of redemption* (Latin, *pactum salutis*). It is the first of several covenants that God made. It was made in eternity within the Trinity; the others were made in time with humans. It is the grandest of them all.

What Is the Covenant of Redemption?

Louis Berkhof gives us a good concise definition: "The covenant of redemption may be defined as the agreement between the Father, giving the Son as Head and Redeemer of the elect, and the Son, voluntarily taking the place of those whom the Father has given Him."[1] The seventeenth-century Reformed theologian Johann Heinrich Heidegger gave a more detailed definition:

> The covenant of God the Father with God the Son is a mutual agreement, by which God the Father extracted from the Son perfect obedience to the Law unto the death which He must face on behalf of His chosen seed to be given Him; and promised Him, if He gave the obedience, the seed in question as His own perquisite and inheritance; and in return the Son, in promising this obedience to God the Father and producing it in the literal act, demanded of Him in turn the right to demand this seed for Himself as an inheritance and perquisite.[2]

Not all Reformed theologians accept this concept, and almost all non-Reformed theologians reject it. Dispensationalists tend to reject it or at least downplay it.[3] Karl Barth rejected it as tri-theistic mythology — which is an ironic epithet because Barth himself said that there are myths in the Bible.[4]

---

1 Louis Berkhof, *Systematic Theology* (Grand Rapids: Eerdmans, 1988), 271.
2 Quoted in Heinrich Heppe, *Reformed Dogmatics* (Grand Rapids: Baker, 1978), 376.
3 Lewis Sperry Chafer, the most influential dispensationalist theologian of the twentieth century, gave only one small paragraph to it in his large 8-volume *Systematic Theology*, and even then with reservations. *Systematic Theology* (Dallas: Dallas Theological Seminary Press, 1947), 1:42. John MacArthur, dispensational but considerably more Calvinist, gives a good summary in *The Murder of Jesus* (Nashville: Word, 2000), 77–78.
4 Karl Barth, *Church Dogmatics* (Edinburgh: T&T Clark, 1956), IV, Part 1, 65.

Orthodox Calvinists do not believe there are any myths in Scripture (1 Timothy 1:4; 2 Peter 1:16). This is not mythology or tri-theism but biblical trinitarianism.

Others deny it because they say it is "too commercial" and is an affront to grace.[5] But we reply that the Bible itself uses financial terminology, such as the very word *redemption*. This is the covenant that planned redemption by grace.

Perhaps the major objection is that it is not explicitly stated in Scripture. Some dispensationalists use this argument but forget that the Bible does not explicitly use dispensational terms such as the *dispensation of innocence*. Even the words *rapture* and *Trinity* are extra-biblical in name but not in content. Charles Hodge explains:

> When one person assigns a stipulated work to another person with the promise of a reward upon the condition of the performance of that work, there is a covenant. Nothing can be plainer than that all this is true in relation to the Father and the Son. The Father gave the Son a work to do; He sent Him into the world to perform it, and promised Him a great reward when the work was accomplished. Such is the constant representation of the Scriptures. We have, therefore, the contracting parties, the promise, and the condition. These are the essential elements of a covenant. Such being the representation of Scripture, such must be the truth to which we are bound to adhere. It is not a mere figure, but a real transaction, and should be regarded and treated as such if we would understand aright the plan of salvation.[6]

Scriptural Proof

Psalm 2 is universally acknowledged to be a Messianic psalm. It is quoted in the New Testament and applied to Jesus Christ (such as Hebrews 1:5). It speaks of God's Anointed (v. 2) and the Son (vv. 7 and 12). Verse 8 says: "Ask of Me, and I will give You the nations for Your inheritance, and the ends of the earth for Your possession." The speaker is God the Father.

Psalm 89 is another Messianic psalm. Verse 3 reads, "I have made a covenant with My chosen, I have sworn to My servant David" (see also vv. 28 and 34). God the Father made a covenant with the Messianic Son of David as well as

---

5 This is also a buzzword used against our view of the atonement. *Commercial* conjures up the idea of greedy capitalism and the commercialism of Christmas.

6 Charles Hodge, *Systematic Theology* (Grand Rapids: Eerdmans, 1979), 2:360. This paragraph can also be applied to the covenant of works. Dispensationalists usually reject both.

a lesser one with David. He is the "anointed" one of verse 20 and the special firstborn of the Father (vv. 26–27).

John 17 is sometimes called the High Priestly Prayer of Christ. It contains several indications of the eternal and internal relationship between the Father and the Son. The Son remembers eternity past with the Father (vv. 5, 24). The Father gave the Son authority over all flesh so that the Son would bestow eternal life on some of them (v. 2). The Father sent the Son into the world on a special mission (vv. 3, 8, 18, 21, 23, 25), which is a special theme in John's Gospel (3:17, 34; 5:36–38; 6:29, 38–39, 57; 7:28–29; 8:42; 10:36; 11:42; 20:21). The Father gave the Son a work to do (v. 4; see also 5:36) and will glorify the Son for doing it (v. 22). Of special note is the fact that the Father gave a people to the Son (vv. 2, 6, 9, 24; see 6:37, 39; 10:29). The Son prays for them alone (v. 9). When did the Father give them to the Son? The Father gave them covenantly in eternity, then brought them experientially to the Son in the three-year ministry of Christ and is still doing so. Hebrews 2:13 says that one day Christ will appear before the Father and proclaim, "Here I am and the children God has given Me."

The Father's Part in the Covenant

As the Father eternally generates the Son and initiates election, so He is the initiator of the covenant of redemption. He made promises and stipulations. The Son agreed with the promise and re-stipulations. The Spirit witnessed and sealed the agreement.

The Father not only gave the elect to the Son, but He gave the Son to the elect. Isaiah 42:6: "I will give You as a covenant to the people." It is a covenant that plans redemption, so the Father represents the Trinity as the one to whom the redemption price would be paid. He appointed the Son to pay that ransom. This is the great work mentioned in John's Gospel, especially in chapters 10 and 17. The Father further pledged to prepare a sinless body for the Son (Hebrews 10:5–9, quoting Psalm 40:6–8), for the ransom must be made in a human body and soul. He promised to sustain the Son during His mission (Psalm 89:21) and protect Him from Satan (Psalm 89:22).

The Father promised to appoint the Son as heir of all things (Hebrews 1:2). He thus gave all creation to the Son. John Trapp, the great Puritan Bible commentator, explained the converse of John 3:16: "God so loved his Son that he gave him the world for his possession, Psalm. ii.7; but he so loved the world that he gave his Son for its redemption."[7]

In Luke 22:29, Jesus said, "I bestow (*diatithemai*) on you a kingdom, just as My Father bestowed (*dietheto*) one on Me." The two Greek words are the verbal form of the Greek word *diatheke*, or *covenant*. The Father covenanted with the Son to give Him the Kingdom of God, and the Son covenanted with His people to make them citizens of that kingdom.

The Son's Part in the Covenant

The Son re-stipulated and agreed to the promises and conditions of the Father. He submitted to the Father's will both in the eternal covenant and His specific mission in history. John's Gospel frequently quotes Christ as saying He did not come to do His own will but the will of Him who sent Him. That assumes that the Father expressed His will to the Son before the Incarnation, indeed, before the foundation of the world.

Hebrews 10:5 and 7 refer to Christ's agreement to the mission: "Therefore, when He came into the world, He said: 'Sacrifice and offering You did not desire, but a body You have prepared for me.' [. . .] Then I said, 'Behold, I have come — in the volume of the book it is written of Me — to do Your will, O God.'" Some take this book to be the Old Testament, but others (including myself) refer it to the eternal covenant. It is related to the Book of Life.

In the great eternal covenant, Christ was ordained the great Prophet, Priest, and King for His people. He then exercised these offices when He began His ministry at age thirty. The central part of His covenantal condition was that He would die for His people. He needed a body for this; the Father prepared it through the virgin birth. Hebrews 10:5–6 says that the Father would not be satisfied with mere animal offerings and sacrifices. It would take the Son of God in human form to be the great and only sacrifice. This is a major theme of Hebrews. Hebrews 7:22 says Christ became the "surety" for His people. That has great covenantal significance. He promised to pay for the sins of His people in the covenant of redemption, and He did just that at the cross.

The work of our Savior was no accident. It had all been planned in the covenant of redemption. His atoning death was foreordained from eternity (Luke 22:22; Acts 2:23; 4:28; 1 Peter 1:19–20). Christ obeyed His Father's covenantal commandment to lay down His life for the elect (John 10:18), and

---

7 John Trapp, *A Commentary on the Old and New Testament* (Eureka, CA: Tanski, 1997), 5:731.

His pure blood sealed the covenant once and for all (Hebrews 13:20). As a reward for obeying the conditions of the covenant, Christ the God-man was exalted as Lord (Philippians 2:9–11).

Samuel Rutherford offered the unusual observation that the divine nature of Christ covenanted with His human nature as well.[8] He suggested that Christ's humanity bargained to die for men, while His deity promised to sustain and resurrect His humanity through death. That may be undue speculation, but it is worth pondering. It resembles the theory that Christ in His humanity learned of His deity and messiahship not only from Joseph and Mary, the Spirit, and the Scriptures but also directly from His deity. His deity informed His humanity in some ineffable way.

The Spirit's Part in the Covenant

The Holy Spirit is equally God with the Father and the Son; therefore, it is logical to assume that He had a vital part in the covenant of redemption. Little is written about this by Reformed covenantalists. Scripture itself says very little, but we can deduce His role in several ways. First, just as the Spirit eternally proceeds from the Father and the Son and is sent by both in time (John 15:26), so He is the official witness of the covenant between the Father and the Son. He is sometimes denominated a "witness" (Romans 8:16; John 15:26; Acts 5:32; 20:23; 1 John 5:7–11). Thomas Brooks the Puritan explained:

> The whole compact and agreement between God the Father and our Lord Jesus Christ, about the redemption of poor sinners' souls, was really and solemnly transacted in open court; or, as I may say, and the high court of justice above, in the presence of the great notary of heaven — viz, the Holy Ghost; who being a third person of the glorious Trinity, of the same divine essence, and of equal power and glory, makes up a third legal witness with the Father and the Son.[9]

Brooks alludes to the biblical principle that every testimony must be confirmed by two or three witnesses (2 Corinthians 13:1), hence, the Trinity. On a deeper level, that of the ontological Trinity, the Spirit is the eternal bond of love between the Father and the Son, so it is fitting for Him to be the official witness and enactor of the covenant.

---

8 Samuel Rutherford, *Fourteen Communion Sermons* (Edinburgh: James Dickson, 1986), 252–53. See also *The Covenant of Life Opened* (New Lenox, IL: Puritan Publications, 2005).
9 Thomas Brooks, *The Works of Thomas Brooks* (Edinburgh: Banner of Truth, 1980), 5:397.

We can also deduce what the Spirit promised in the covenant to do from what we know He actually does in time. All three blessed members only do in time what they planned to do back in eternity. As John Gill put it, "There are many things which the Holy Spirit himself undertook and engaged in covenant to do; and nothing more strongly proves this than His doing them; for had He not agreed to do them, they would not have been done by Him."[10]

Among other things, the Spirit was the means of Christ's virgin birth (Luke 1:35), empowerment at His baptism (Matthew 3:16), and helper in His miracles (Matthew 12:28). In a mysterious way He assisted Christ in the atonement (Hebrews 9:14) and resurrection (Romans 8:11). We can deduce by good and necessary consequence that the Spirit pledged to do all these things in the covenant of redemption.

The Covenant of Marriage

Occasionally Reformed writers have spoken of this eternal covenant as a marriage covenant. It follows certain features of Hebrew marriages. Malachi 2:14 refers to marriage as a covenant. A Hebrew father would make a covenant with another father that their son and daughter would be married one day. This could even happen before the children were born. Covenantal gifts were exchanged with oaths and witnesses. Later they gave their children in marriage (see the phrase, "giving in marriage," such as Matthew 24:38; 1 Corinthians 7:38). The son and daughter later consented and were betrothed in an engagement that could only be broken by adultery and divorce. Later, they would be formally married, and the covenant was completed.

In the eternal *covenant of marriage*, God the Father selected a bride for the Son and gave them to each other. The Father is father to her by way of creation, then of redemption. This occurred before she was born and even before the Son was born as a man. The Son agreed first in His deity, then in time in His humanity. The bride agreed when the Spirit drew her to believe in the Son and thereby consented to be His eternal bride (2 Corinthians 11:2; see the type in Genesis 24:58). One day the covenant of marriage will be fully completed when Christ the Groom returns for His bride, and they are married (Matthew 25:1–13; Revelation 19:9; 21:2).

---

10 John Gill, *A Complete Body of Doctrinal and Practical Divinity* (Paris, AR: Baptist Standard Bearer, 1984), 245.

The Covenant of Love

This inter-trinitarian covenant may also be described as the *covenant of love*. Augustine and Jonathan Edwards developed this line of thinking regarding election. "God is love" (1 John 4:8, 16). *Love* is a transitive verb; the subject must have an object. The lover must have a beloved. In eternity there was only God. God loved Himself. This presupposes a plurality in the Godhead. The Father loved the Son (John 5:20; 10:17; Matthew 3:17; 12:18; 17:5; Mark 1:11; 9:7; Luke 9:35; Isaiah 42:1; Proverbs 8:30; Colossians 1:13). The Son loved the Father (John 14:31). The Spirit also loved and was loved by the Father and the Son. Some theologians, following Augustine, say that the Spirit is the bond of love between the Father and the Son (see the phrase, "the love of the Spirit," Romans 15:30). This love-bond among the divine Three is related to the theological idea of *perichoresis* (also called *interpenetration*). That is, the Father is *in* the Son and the Spirit, the Son is *in* the Father and the Spirit, and the Spirit is *in* the Father and the Son.

Just as God decreed to reveal His internal glory externally, so He decreed to reveal His internal love externally. That which is eternal would be manifested in time. Thus, God foreordained to create an outside object for this love. It involved several levels. Angels were created on the highest level. God predestined to show love to some of them by preserving from sinning. God decreed a greater love by giving it to elect men, who were created on a lower level than the angels. Furthermore, this would be super-love, as it were, because, unlike the holy angels, they would fall into sin. This would display greater love than that which was shown to the good angels. The Father chose some humans to receive this redemptive love (John 17:2, 26; Ephesians 1:4). The Son agreed to redeem them in love. The Spirit agreed to apply this redemptive love. This special love is saving grace.

The elect are thus a love gift between the three members of the Trinity. They are not only proofs of the inter-trinitarian love, but the elect are united to God in such a way that they become personal conduits of that great love between them. For example, the Spirit floods their heart with the love of God (Romans 5:5). This is part of the vital union that the elect enjoy in salvation. The elect, then, are a love gift from the Father to the Son and from the Son to the Father and to and from the Spirit. Each member of the Trinity is well pleased to both give and receive this love gift.

The covenant could also be called the *covenant of joy*, for in it the Trinity share their mutual eternal and internal joy with the elect and through the elect with each other. One could say the same with other divine attributes: it is the covenant of wisdom, the covenant of power, and so on. Each attribute of God is shared with one another in a new way through the redeemed elect. The elect are not deified in the Greek Orthodox sense, but their union with the Godhead is part of their glorification. In this wonderful covenant, the divine Trinity is glorified in all His attributes exactly as planned.

The Covenant of Glory

This great covenant provided for redemption, love, and joy but also glory. I call it the *covenant of glory*. God foreordained all things to display His glory (Romans 11:36), so it would be appropriate to theorize that the glorious attributes of God were covenantally decreed to be revealed together in time.

God decreed and covenanted to glorify Himself. Each member of the Trinity covenanted to glorify the others. The Father promised to glorify the Son, and so He did in time (John 17:5). The Son likewise promised to glorify the Father, and so He did. No doubt the Spirit also promised to glorify the Father and the Son (John 16:14), who in turn promised to glorify the Spirit.

From all eternity there was perfect and beautiful glory within the Godhead. For reasons that have not been revealed to us, God chose to reveal this glory externally and temporally — hence, creation. It would be revealed to all creation but especially to the elect (John 17:24). Christ has a special place in this glorious transaction, for He must have preeminence in all things (Colossians 1:18). This included the great joy given to Him as a reward for redeeming the elect as per the covenant (Hebrews 12:2). In the end, the Son presents His covenantal children to the Father so that that glory is returned to the Father through the Son (1 Corinthians 15:24; Philippians 2:11). The bottom line of the covenant of glory is *soli Deo gloria*!

Conclusion

Thomas Goodwin the great English Puritan summed it up well:

> There was never such joy in heaven as upon this happy conclusion in agreement. The whole Trinity rejoiced in it. [. . .] They not only never repented of what they had resolved upon; "He swore and would not repent," Hebrews 7:21; but further, their chiefest delights were taken up with this more than in all their works *ad extra*. God's heart was never taken so much with anything He was able to effect; so as the thoughts

of this business, ever since it was resolved on, became matter of greatest delight upon them.[11]

---

11 Thomas Goodwin, *The Works of Thomas Goodwin* (Eureka, CA: Tanski, 1996), 5:31–32.

Chapter 41
Objections to Election

Some objections to the Reformed doctrine of election are based on misunderstanding and ignorance. Opponents would do well to ponder G. C. Berkouwer's comment: "It is not always easy to differentiate between resistance to the doctrine itself and resistance to the caricatures of it, because more likely than not, reactions to caricatures lead to one-sided formulations."[1] Other objections are based on more serious study. Still others are mainly emotional. Here are some of the main ones with replies.

Objection 1: *"Calvinism kills evangelism."*

Some aim this at the Reformed doctrine of election and say, "If I believed in it, I would never witness to anyone or support missions." Others say, "Calvinists do not evangelize," or, "Any doctrine that hinders evangelism cannot be true," or even, "Evangelism is the main thing, not election."

First, it simply is not true that Calvinism kills evangelism or missions. Consider the great evangelist George Whitefield. The modern Calvinist evangelist John Blanchard has evangelized hundreds of thousands for over fifty years. He authored the best-selling evangelistic book *Right with God* and the booklet *Ultimate Questions*, which has been translated into over fifty languages and has sold more than thirteen million copies. Pastors such as Jonathan Edwards, Andrew Fuller, and C. H. Spurgeon preached the gospel with much success in their churches. The Great Awakening and Great Missionary Movement were both started by five-point Calvinists. John Calvin sent hundreds of missionaries into France and even a team to Brazil. Reformed missionaries have served all around the world for over two hundred years. Only a tiny group of Hyper-Calvinists oppose evangelism and missions.

Election and evangelism complement each other, not contradict each other. Jesus said, "Many are called but few are chosen" (Matthew 22:14). John Blanchard said, "Election is a doctrine I am called upon to believe; evangelism is a command I'm called upon to obey."[2] God ordained evangelism as the means to bring the elect to salvation (2 Timothy 2:10). Election is an incentive to

---

1 G. C. Berkouwer, *Divine Election* (Grand Rapids: Eerdmans, 1960), 9.
2 John Blanchard, *More Gathered Gold* (Welwyn: Evangelical Press, 1986), 87.

evangelism, not a hindrance. Why evangelize if God has not chosen anyone to be saved? We will examine the Reformed view of evangelism later in this volume.

Objection 2: *"Whosoever will may come."*

Some who object to our doctrine simply utter these words without explanation, as if merely saying them ends all argument. The phrase is not actually in the Bible, but is loosely based on Revelation 22:17: "And let him who hears say, 'Come!' And let him who thirsts come. Whoever desires, let him take from the water of life freely." Some refer to John 3:16 also. Historic Calvinists are well aware of these verses and freely invite all lost sinners to come and believe in Jesus Christ. We believe in the free offer and universal invitation.

Revelation 22:17 speaks of our responsibility to believe and God's revealed desire that we come to Christ. It does not say that we are morally able to believe nor deny that God has elected only some to believe. David L. Allen and Steve W. Lemke edited a volume of essays by non-Calvinist Baptists entitled *Whosoever Will* to refute Calvinism.[3] It was answered by a group of Calvinistic Baptists in *Whomever He Wills*, edited by Matthew Barrett and Thomas J. Nettles.[4] The latter has accurate biblical exegesis and mainline Baptist history on their side in the debate. Their book's title alludes to Romans 9:15: "I will have mercy on whomever I will have mercy."

This objection is not well thought out. It wrongly assumes there is a contradiction between election and the free offer. There is not. Jesus extended the offer and invitation in Matthew 11:28 right after mentioning sovereign election in verse 27. He said something similar in John 6:35–40. We may not fully understand how to reconcile the secret will of the election of some with the revealed will of the desire that all will be saved, but both are taught in Scripture, and we dare not deny either.

For what it is worth, Hyper-Calvinism employs the opposite error: It denies the free offer because it cannot reconcile it with election. It commits the same methodological error as Arminianism. If we waited for full understanding before we accepted a paradox, then we would have to deny the Trinity, the two natures of Christ, and many other great truths.

---

3 Nashville: B&H Academic, 2010.
4 Cape Coral, FL: Founders, 2012.

Objection 3: "*Calvinism portrays God turning away sinners because they are not elect.*"

This suggests the following picture. A lost sinner repents and comes to Christ on his hands and knees begging to be saved. He pounds on the door in the snow for Christ to let him in. But the Calvinistic Christ checks the list of the elect and harshly replies, "I'm sorry, you're not on the list," and slams the door on the poor man. Some say that Christ also goes out and drags an unwilling unrepentant believer into the house because he is one of the elect.

The picture is grossly inaccurate and unbiblical. John 6:37 says, "All that the Father gives Me will come to Me, and the one who comes to Me I will by no means cast out." Note who they are who come: those the Father gave to the Son in eternal election. Only they will ever come, and Christ will certainly not refuse them. Verses 44 and 65 say that nobody is even able, let alone willing, to come unless the Father irresistibly draws him. But in doing so, the sinner's will is transformed, and he comes willingly. Christ has never turned away any repentant sinner nor ever will — nor do Calvinists even hint that He will.

Objection 4: "*If election were true, then the non-elect would never have a chance to be saved.*"

In one sense, this is true because there is no such thing as chance. But if it means *opportunity*, it is an ill-founded objection. The gospel call is urgent, sincere, well-meant, and serious. God calls on the lost now to repent (Acts 17:30; see 2 Corinthians 6:2). God holds out His arms all day long, calling to them to come to Him (Romans 10:21).

The objection implies that God stacks the deck of cards against the non-elect and cheats them. This would give the non-elect an excuse on Judgment Day: "I never had a chance!" But this overlooks the plain fact that lost sinners do not want to repent and believe in the first place. God is absolutely fair. He never cheats.

Objection 5: "*God votes for you. Satan votes against you. How you vote decides the election.*"

The only grain of truth in this jingle is that God sincerely calls on unbelievers to believe, Satan tries to stop them, and sinners are responsible to believe. That is not in dispute. The objection suggests that God has chosen everyone, and the election is not over yet. But it *is* over, and God has not chosen everyone — otherwise everyone would be saved.

More seriously the theory posits that God and Satan have equal votes. This parallels the error of cosmic chess that we have already answered. Nor do we have a vote in the election. Our responsibility is to believe, not elect ourselves. It is foolish, to say the least, to imply that the negative votes of Satan and sinners can outweigh God's vote. If one wanted true plurality in election, then the real voters are the Father, the Son, and the Holy Spirit. And they always vote alike.

Objection 6: *"God is no respecter of persons."*

God is impartial (Deuteronomy 10:17; 2 Chronicles 19:7; Acts 10:34; Romans 2:11; Galatians 2:6; Ephesians 6:9; Colossians 3:25; and 1 Peter 1:17). Since God is not partial, neither should we be (James 2:1–9). But the phrase does not mean that God has not chosen anyone to be saved. None of these citations discusses election.

The phrase means something different than what the objection assumes it to mean. It refers to judging a person based on appearance, such as race or other factors. Acts 10:34 is a case in point. Peter followed the popular Jewish error that the Jews had a corner on God's grace because they were special of themselves. The Jewish leaders in his day looked down on Gentiles as hopeless pagans. They forgot their own heritage. God did not choose Israel because they were better (Deuteronomy 7:7–8). Moreover, God chose Israel to be a light to the Gentiles (Isaiah 60:3; 66:19; see Genesis 12:3). N. L. Rice explains its use in Acts 10:34:

> If God had rejected Cornelius, who was truly a pious man, simply because he was a Gentile, whilst he would receive a Jew of the same character, he would have been a respecter of persons. But inasmuch as he accepts all righteous men, of whatever nation, he is not so. A respecter of persons, then, is one who, acting as a judge, decides not according to law and testimony, but is governed by sinister motives; who does not treat those who come before him according to their character; who withholds from some that to which they have a just claim, in order to give to others what is not their due; or who is governed in his treatment of men by prejudice, not by a proper estimate of their real character.[5]

---

5 N. L. Rice, *God Sovereign and Man Free* (Harrisonburg: Sprinkle, 1985), 147. See Calvin's poignant explanation in *Sermons in Galatians* (Edinburgh: Banner of Truth, 1997), 134–35. Elsewhere he said, "And therefore it cannot be said that there is any respecting of person before God, for in choosing those that are unworthy he has respect to his own pure goodness alone." *Sermons on the Epistle to the Ephesians* (London: Banner of Truth, 1973), 30.

Objection 7: *A similar objection says that "Predestination is privilege, and all privilege is wrong."*

The word implies rich parents who lavish luxury on their spoiled children and ignore the under-privileged poor. But this is a false picture. Does God not have the right, like any human parent, to give gifts to His own children? God has generously given much to everyone through common grace. He is not stingy. But nobody deserves anything good from God.

Sometimes Arminians let their emotions govern the reason with this argument, such as when A. W. Tozer wrote, "No one, not even in 1,000 years of jumping up and down on the family Bible, could ever make me believe that God showed anything like partiality."[6] He vehemently rejected the Reformed doctrine of election by confusing it with unfair partiality. He suggests that we Calvinists jump up and down on the family Bible (which would be sacrilege). Rather, we calmly say, "What saith the Scriptures?" The Scriptures say, "He chose us" (Ephesians 1:4).

Objection 8: *"If I am elected, I can live in sin, for God will save me anyway."*

Calvin answered this objection in his day: "Those who claim that God has elected them and that they cannot perish nonetheless yield themselves to every evil; they, I say, show clearly that God has abandoned them and that the devil possesses them."[7] They are unregenerate and very possibly not elect. It bears mentioning that the "easy-believism" and "carnal Christian" errors originated with Arminians and have been propagated by them, not by Calvinists. We believe that God begins to sanctify a person when He saves him and that holy living is a necessary evidence of salvation and election. This will be discussed later in the chapter on the preservation and perseverance of the saints.

Objection 9: *"To deny faith a place in election is like denying faith a place in justification, which is heresy."*

Our answer is that the Bible teaches justification by faith but not election by faith. Election is by God's sovereign grace, not our faith. Arminianism fails to see the gracious nature of election and takes away the final decision from God and gives to it man. This is seen, for example, in the first point of the

---

6 A. W. Tozer, *Christ the Eternal Son* (Camp Hill, PA: Christian Publications, 1991), 143.
7 John Calvin, *Sermons on Genesis, Chapters 11:5–20:7* (Edinburgh: Banner of Truth, 2012), 787–88.

Remonstrance, also known as the *five points of Arminianism*.[8] Arminianism usually says that God elected based on foreseeing our faith. We have already addressed this. But where did that faith come from in the first place? It could not have come from fallen sinners, for they are morally unable to believe. God gives faith to those He chose to save.

A somewhat related objection says, "God chose the plan, not the man." No, God chose both the plan of salvation and the men to be saved.

Objection 10: *"If election were true, then I would be saved if I am elect, whether I believe or not, or I would be damned if not elect, whether I believe or not."*

This was once a popular objection, and one still occasionally hears it. It fails to see that faith is not the deciding factor in election. But faith is a deciding factor in justification. Nobody will be justified without faith. Those who believe were elected to believe. Those who never believe were not elected. God did not choose to give them faith.[9]

Objection 11: *"Election is not practical."*

We will give several practical applications in chapter 43. All biblical truth is practical (2 Timothy 3:16–17).

Objection 12: *"Calvin taught election and burned Servetus at the stake; Augustine taught election and believed in several Catholic heresies such as baptismal regeneration."*

We believe in election because it is taught in the Bible, not because certain men have believed in it. If this objection were valid, then we should also reject the Trinity and biblical infallibility because Calvin and Augustine taught those doctrines.

Objection 13: *"Election is too speculative."*

Election is scriptural, not speculative. Some Calvinists speculate too much on certain aspects of this doctrine, but that does not mean it is a wrong doctrine.

Objection 14: *"Most Christians do not believe in election. My church does not."*

Truth is determined by the Bible alone, not by majority vote among Christians

---

8 Philip Schaff, ed., *Creeds of Christendom* (Grand Rapids: Baker, 1966), 3:545.
9 See Christopher Love, *Preacher of God's Word* (Morgan, PA: Soli Deo Gloria, 2000), 128–29.

or churches. To turn this objection on its head, many church denominations have a history of believing in election in their early confessions and leading theologians (such as Presbyterians, Baptists, Episcopalians, and others). If your church does not believe in election, it needs to reexamine its beliefs in light of the Bible.

Objection 15: *"It sounds like leftover Roman Catholicism."*

Augustine and many Catholic theologians believed in election, but many others did not. Roman Catholicism has not officially endorsed nor condemned election as taught by Augustine and picked up by Calvin. Rome is not always right — or wrong. For example, Rome is wrong on sacramental salvation but right on the Trinity.

Objection 16: *"It sounds too complicated."*

What is complicated about these three words: "He chose us" (Ephesians 1:4)?

Objection 17: *"I heard a well-known preacher warn against election."*

Listen to the Bible itself. Test all the words of preachers with Scripture (Acts 17:11; 1 Thessalonians 5:21; Isaiah 8:20).

Objection 18: *"I have read all the way through the Bible, and I cannot find the doctrine of election anywhere in it."*

Keep reading. Start with Romans 8 and 9 and Ephesians 1. Then look up the dozens of verses mentioned in the chapters in this volume. Check a concordance for the following words: *elect, election, elect's, choose, chosen, predestined, appointed,* and others. Look up these verses, and see for yourself that the Bible mentions the subject many times.

Objection 19: *"I do not believe in election even if it is in the Bible."*

One can expect an outright unbeliever to voice this objection, but fortunately I have never read a professed Christian say it. But I have *heard* at least one professing evangelical Christian say it in person. I suspect many others think it and do not wish to say so.

Some opponents simply do not know the Bible teaches election over and over. They have not studied their own Bible. They can be forgiven for their ignorance. But it is a most serious matter if they do know it is in the Bible and still refuse to believe it. In doing so they are opposing God Himself, not just Calvinism. This must be answered with strong rebuke. The objection calls into question whether the objector is truly a real Christian. To oppose the Word of God is to oppose God of the Word and call Him a liar (1 John 5:10).

This objection parallels the similar objection to the evangelical doctrine of Hell, which has been accepted by all true evangelicals whether Calvinist or Arminian. Some critics who profess to be Christians admit the Bible teaches that Hell is eternal conscious torment, but they go to great lengths to reinterpret the Bible so as to "de-Hell" Hell, as it were. They are left with no Hell at all. But others come right out and deny it while admitting that it is taught by the Bible. Some of the same arguments against election are used against Hell. While one does not have to believe election to be a Christian, the doctrine of Hell is as important as the doctrine of Heaven and salvation. There can be no compromise there.

We must accept any doctrine taught by the Bible whether we understand it or not. We may not pick and choose. We must study the Bible to gain understanding. But the first step is to believe the Bible is God's infallible word and that we must believe whatever it teaches. Then we are open to God to give us light and understanding. Once we believe and begin to understand it, we rejoice in it and love it. We should not take the attitude, "I will believe it, but I do not have to like it." Yes, we *do* have to like it, for God teaches it. Calvinists love it because they love God who teaches it and did the electing.

Objection 20: "*God loves everybody equally, therefore the Reformed doctrine of election is not true.*"

This objection is the theme of Dave Hunt's book *What Love Is This?*[10] He argues that God must love everybody equally, otherwise He does not love anybody at all. He wrongly thinks Calvinism denies that God loves everyone. He overlooks the fact that historic Calvinists have believed in common grace. God has a general love for all people as His creatures. He has a special love for the elect. What kind of love is this electing love? It is a wonderful, God-glorifying love!

Some Arminians say, "Calvinism limits the infinite love of God." Quite the reverse is the case. God's love is as infinite as God Himself, for the love of God is simply God Himself loving. The real issue is how God displays and gives it. He gives some love to all men and all love to some men. He graciously bestows on the elect all the riches of divine love. He also gives lesser love to all persons in various ways (sunshine, happiness, food, and so on). Just because it is lesser love does not mean it is not true and good love. A man has greatest love for his

---

10 Bend, OR: The Berean Call, 2006. 3rd edition.

wife and lesser love for other persons. Humanity is not infinite and is not the bellwether of the infinity of divine love.[11] Even if God elected every person who has ever lived — or a billion times that number — that would still be a finite number and thus not equal to the infinite love of God.

Related to this objection is the sentence, "God has unconditional love for everyone." This is not the way the Bible puts it. It would be truer to say that God's love is undeserved. To say it is unconditional opens the door to liberalism and universal salvation. If God loves everyone unconditionally, then even their sins would not bring them to Hell, for unbelief and non-repentance would be overcome by "the triumph of grace," as taught by Karl Barth.[12] Fortunately, evangelical Arminians do not believe in universal salvation. All evangelicals believe that faith and repentance are the conditions of salvation. "Unconditional" universal love erases all conditions and therefore logically must teach universal salvation. As we showed before, faith is the condition of salvation but not of election. The Bible teaches the unconditional election of some sinners and the undeserved general love of all sinners but not the unconditional love of all sinners resulting in universal salvation. God Himself meets all the conditions of election and even gives faith to the elect, thereby meeting the condition of salvation Himself through them. This better illustrates the greatness of divine love, for the Arminian idea implies that God's greatest love fails when a sinner dies lost.

A variation of this objection is "Election is unloving." To whom? Not to the elect, nor does it deny there is a sense in which God loves all sinners. The objection says that it would be unloving of God not to choose all men when He is able to do so. Norman Geisler uses the following illustration: A farmer comes across some boys swimming in his pond without permission. They get caught in some weeds and begin to drown. The farmer could save all of them but chooses to save only some. That, says Geisler, is unloving.[13]

The illustration is inappropriate and misleading. We are not innocent boys having fun swimming in a pond. We are guilty criminals caught with weapons in our hands. We are not nice little boys but vicious sinners against God. A farmer should try to rescue all drowning boys, but God is under no obligation to pardon God-hating sinners. The boys did not deserve to drown, but sinners

---

11 See William Lyford, *The Instructed Christian* (Morgan, PA: Soli Deo Gloria, n.d.), 192–94.

12 See G. C. Berkouwer, *The Triumph of Grace in the Theology of Karl Barth* (Grand Rapids: Eerdmans, 1956).

13 Norman Geisler, *Chosen But Free*, Rev. ed. (Minneapolis: Bethany House, 1999), 40. Dave Hunt uses a similar illustration in *What Love is This?*, 410–11.

do deserve to go to Hell. A better illustration would be a governor granting a pardon to a criminal on death row while not granting one to others. But even that is inadequate, for Numbers 35 does not allow such a pardon, and no governor can impute perfect righteousness as God can.

If God loves everybody equally, does He love the Devil? If He does, then why did God not elect him? Does God love Satan more or less than humankind? And if God does not love Satan, what love is this?

Objection 21: *"Calvinist election looks like hospital triage. He could not save everyone, so He chose which ones had the best likelihood of being saved."*

This is a gross misunderstanding of the Reformed doctrine. We have already shown that God could have chosen all, none, or some. The choice was His. It had nothing to do with the likelihood or unlikelihood of sinners believing. Without election by sovereign grace, nobody would believe. This objection does not adequately explain why some sinners believe and some do not.

Objection 22: *"It is not fair!"*

This is the basic objection that underlies all others. It is akin to the objections to Hell and other Bible doctrines. With this objection the kid gloves come off, and the objector often becomes very aggressive and defensive — and offensive, too.

We reply as follows. First, God is always absolutely just (Genesis 18:25; Deuteronomy 32:4). Romans 9:14 specifically asserts divine justice in the matter of election. The objection has several flaws. One is that it fails to take into consideration God's just wrath against guilty sinners. Those who are elected and those not elected are all guilty Hell-deserving sinners who do not deserve to be chosen. The second point of Calvinism must be viewed in light of the first point. Calvinists assert the total depravity of sinners far more than all other theological systems.[14] Unless one sees this, he misses the utter graciousness of divine election. It was the Calvinist John Newton who wrote the hymn with the words: "Amazing grace, how sweet the sound, that saved a wretch like me."

If election is not fair, we might ask: "To whom is it not fair?" It certainly is fair to the elect. The non-elect do not deserve to be elected, nor do they want to be, so it is not unfair to them. James Henley Thornwell: "There is no injustice

---

14 See chapter 33, "The Depth of Depravity."

here — no more than there is injustice in my withholding alms from a beggar who despises and calumniates my family."[15]

But more specifically, the objector fails to see the sovereignty of God in the matter. God has the right to choose whomever He pleases. "I will have mercy on whom I will have mercy," says God (Romans 9:15) — and in the very context of answering the charge that election and reprobation are unfair (v. 14). Calvin observed: "God is not bound by any law that should compel Him to show mercy unto all men indiscriminately and alike; but that he is the Lord of His own will, to impart pardon to whom He will and to pass by others as He will."[16]

If God has the right to bestow the natural and temporal blessings of common grace as He pleases, does He not also have the right to bestow spiritual and eternal blessings as He sees fit? Was it unfair of Christ to heal only one beggar at the pool in John 5:1–9? Were Elijah and Elisha unfair in performing beneficial miracles to only some persons (Luke 4:25–27)?

G. C. Berkouwer rightly saw the underlying problem: "The evil eye sees God's generosity, but this projection of generosity only reveals the darkness of man's heart."[17] He explains that this is the point of Christ's parable in Matthew 20:1–16. He is right. See the Reformed commentaries. The clincher is God's words in verse 15: "Is it not lawful for me to do what I wish with my own things? Or is your eye evil (covetous) because I am good?"

As R. C. Sproul has shown, God shows electing mercy to some, withholds mercy from others, but shows injustice to none.[18] When God elected some, there was no injustice to the non-elect.[19]

We must always remember four simple words: "God owes us nothing" (John Calvin).[20] Calvin also said: "He [. . .] owes us nothing and cannot owe us anything."[21] And again: "We ought to note, first, that God is not bound at all to any person. For if we once held that principle, that he owes us the least

---

15 James Henley Thornwell, *The Collected Works of James Henley Thornwell* (Edinburgh: Banner of Truth, 1974), 2:158.

16 John Calvin, *Calvin's Calvinism* (Grand Rapids: Reformed Free Publishing Association, 1991), 252.

17 Berkouwer, *Divine Election*, 75.

18 R. C. Sproul, *Chosen by God* (Wheaton: Tyndale, 1986), 37–38.

19 Non-election will be discussed in the chapters on reprobation, including further objections.

20 John Calvin, *Sermons on Psalm 119* (Audubon: Old Paths, 1996), 154. Note the title of Leszek Kolakowski's book on Blaise Pascal and Jansenism: *God Owes Us Nothing* (Chicago: University of Chicago Press, 1995).

21 Calvin, *Sermons on Genesis, Chapters 11:5–20:7*, 66.

thing in the world, then we call in question his law. [. . .] He on his side has no obligation towards us, but that we owe everything to him while he owes nothing to us."[22]

If one pressed the point, one *could* posit that there is something that God owes us: punishment. That is what we have earned (Romans 6:23). This must be firmly understood while discussing election. Romans 8 and 9 follow Romans 3. This is often ignored by our opponents. Their books usually do not contain words like "God owes us nothing" but rather unbiblical statements like "God loves everyone unconditionally."

The objection actually proves our point. God chose sinners who are His enemies. Opposition to God's election is enmity against God who elects. Paul saw this in Romans 9. Right after plainly teaching election in 8:29–30, he more explicitly taught election and non-election in chapter 9.[23] He answered several objections that, likely, he had already heard. To the basic objection of unfairness, he boldly replied: "But indeed, O man, who are you to reply against God?" (v. 20). It is sin to reply against our holy Maker. The objection is based in rebellion and requires repentance more than further explanation.

Conclusion

Those who offer these and other objections would be well advised to search the Scriptures and humbly set aside their arguments. Jonathan Edwards offered this good advice: "It becomes worms of the dust therefore to subject their understandings to God's and to own that God knows more than they, and not to find fault with what he did from eternal ages in his infinitely wise and holy counsels."[24]

Rather than raising a fist of objection, we should fall on our knees and thank God for election. We should be grateful for it and love it. And we should love God who freely and lovingly elected us poor sinners to be saved.

---

22 Calvin, *Sermons on the Epistle to the Ephesians*, 29.
23 See John Piper, *The Justification of God* (Grand Rapids: Baker, 1993).
24 Jonathan Edwards, *The Works of Jonathan Edwards* (New Haven: Yale University Press, 1997), 14:175.

Chapter 42
The Destiny of the Elect

What is the destination of predestination? God chose the elect in eternity past — what does He have in store for them in eternity future? The subject of Heaven is too vast to cover in depth in one short chapter. The great Puritan Richard Baxter wrote over five hundred pages on it in the classic *The Saints' Everlasting Rest*. I will concentrate on those aspects of Heaven that the Bible associates with predestination and election.

Salvation and Eternal Life

God chose the elect to be saved (2 Thessalonians 2:13) and receive eternal life (Acts 13:48). Both were planned in eternity, secured by Christ at the cross in time, and bestowed on the elect by the Holy Spirit at the appointed time. Faith is the instrument by which the elect receive them (Acts 16:31; John 3:16).

Both are progressively developed in the elect. This does not mean that the process can be stopped. All the elect will pass through all stages. We were saved when we believed, are being saved daily, and will ultimately be saved from this present evil age (see the parallel in 2 Corinthians 1:10). In justification we are saved from the punishment of sin; in sanctification, from its power; and in glorification, from its presence. In regeneration, we receive spiritual life; in sanctification, we grow in that life; in glorification, we continue in perfect eternal life forever.

Holiness

Ephesians 1:4 says, "He chose us in Him before the foundation of the world, that we should be holy and without blame before Him." The *should* is a future indicative (you will) rather than a present imperative (you must). It is a promise, not a command. God is intrinsically holy, and we shall not be holy in that sense any more than we shall be infinite. All our holiness is derivative. God imputes the holiness of Christ to us in justification and then gradually infuses divine holiness into us by the Spirit in sanctification. It will be completed in Heaven.

Like salvation, this has three stages. We were legally set apart from sin positionally in conversion. We are progressively being sanctified daily. We will be perfectly free of all sin when we get to Heaven. But even then our holiness will be derivative. That is why the Holy Spirit will be eternally in us to supply us with divine holiness.

Paul says we will be "without blame" (Ephesians 1:4; see Jude 24). If we are holy, then nobody can blame or accuse us, as Satan now does (Revelation 12:10). God will not accuse His elect, for He is the one who justified them (Romans 8:33). Nor will the angels or other saints accuse us, for they will see us as holy. Nor will we accuse ourselves. Even the memory of past sins will not accuse or condemn us anymore (see 1 John 3:19–20). Our consciences will be perfectly pure.

There will be no sin whatsoever anywhere in Heaven (Revelation 21:27). Ephesians 5:27 says that Christ died to present to Himself a bride that is "holy and without blemish." And He shall do just that at the great heavenly wedding (Revelation 19:7; 21:2). We will be sinlessly "perfect" at last (Hebrews 12:23). All the effects of sin will be erased from our body and soul.

Thomas Boston traced the fall and rise of the elect in his masterful treatise *Human Nature in Its Fourfold State*.[1] Observe the four stages:

1. Innocent Man: Able to sin and able not to sin.

2. Fallen Man: Able to sin and not able not to sin.

3. Redeemed Man: Able to sin and able not to sin.

4. Perfected Man: Able not to sin and not able to sin.

Augustine was perhaps the first to relate these stages regarding our relation to sin: "The first freedom of the will, then, was the ability not to sin; the final freedom will be much greater, namely, the inability to sin."[2] Thomas Watson contrasted our present and future states: "Here it is impossible that we should not sin, in heaven it is impossible that we should."[3] Not only will the very root of original sin be removed, but it will be replaced with the perfect principle of holiness that guarantees impeccability.

To be sure, it is the person of the Holy Spirit that does this, not merely an impersonal principal. He inhabits and sanctifies us now and will continue to

---

1 London: Banner of Truth, 1964.
2 Augustine, *The Works of Saint Augustine* (Hyde Park: New City, 1999), I/26:132.
3 Thomas Watson, *Discourses on Important and Interesting Subjects* (Ligonier, PA: Soli Deo Gloria, 1990), 1:88.

do this in Heaven. There will be no occasion or reason to sin either. There will be no Devil to tempt us nor a second Devil nor forbidden fruit. There will be no temptation from other humans — surely not from the elect nor from the non-elect, for they will be in Hell separated from us by a great gulf (Luke 16:26). We will not even tempt ourselves, as we do now (James 1:14). This will be the fulfillment of the Lord's Prayer: "Thy will be done on Earth as it is in Heaven." God's revealed will shall be done in us perfectly forever. This will see the final coordination of the secret and revealed wills of God.

Unable to sin, we will be unable to die. We will have impeccable souls in immortal bodies. We will be as holy as the angels who never sinned. They willingly and joyfully obey God (Psalm 103:20), and so shall we. This will be perfect freedom at last. It is the freedom to love and worship God. Martin Bucer observed: "We too at the last will enjoy complete liberty when we shall no longer be able to will what is evil and shall necessarily will what is good."[4]

If the Arminian theory of a libertarian will were true, then there is no guarantee that we would not sin again in Heaven. It would be like a celestial Murphy's Law — if we could fall, then we would fall eventually. And so would everyone else. Heaven would then be emptied of all its inhabitants. Arminianism has difficulty accepting eternal impeccability. But God has promised it to the elect, and He cannot lie (Titus 1:2). Like God, we will be incapable of lying or dying. Augustine waxed eloquent in describing this holy freedom:

> The souls in bliss will still possess the freedom of will, though sin will have no power to tempt them. They will be more free than ever — so free, in fact, from all delight in sinning as to find, in not sinning, an unfailing source of joy. By the freedom which was given to the first man, who was constituted in rectitude, he could choose either to sin or not to sin; in eternity, freedom is that more potent freedom which makes all sin impossible.[5]

Just imagine the joy in our hearts when we realize that we will never again sin. It will be heightened by the realization that we will not even be able to sin again. This joy has been predestined by our loving heavenly Father.

---

4 Martin Bucer, *Common Places of Martin Bucer*, ed. by David F. Wright (Appleford: Sutton Courtenay, 1972), 102.
5 Augustine, *City of God*, 22:30; *The Fathers of the Church* (Washington, D.C.: Catholic University of America Press, 1954), 24:507.

Conformity to the Image of Christ

The Golden Chain of Romans 8:29 says, "For whom He foreknew, He predestined to be conformed to the image of His Son." We shall be like Christ when we see Him as He is: pure, without sin, righteous (1 John 3:2–3, 7). The divine Husband will see His reflection in His pure bride.

The image of God was severely marred in the Fall in Eden but will be completely restored in the New Eden. It is now the image of Satan; it will then be a perfect reflection of Christ. We will be a living mirror that shows forth Christ in us. Christ is the ultimate image of God (2 Corinthians 4:4; Colossians 1:15), and we will be perfectly sanctified to be the pure image of the image, surpassing even the holy angels.

Glorification

The last link in the Golden Chain is glorification (Romans 8:30; see vv. 17 and 21). Earlier we discussed the glory of God as the revelation of His beautiful being and attributes. God reveals His glory but does not give it to others (Isaiah 42:8; 48:11). That would be idolatry. Yet He bestows something of His glory on the elect, and we call this *glorification*.

Isaiah 45:25 predicted the day when God will display His glory to His people. Isaiah 49:3 says this glory will be in the Messiah. That means we will be glorified in and through and for Christ, just as we were elected in and through and for Christ. Jesus displayed the glory of God when He was on earth in several ways, such as miracles (John 2:11) and the transfiguration (John 1:14; 2 Peter 1:16–18). We now behold some of that glory by faith (2 Corinthians 3:18). We are partakers of that glory (1 Peter 5:1). We will receive glory, honor, immortality, and peace (Romans 2:7, 10) when Christ returns (1 Peter 1:7; 2 Thessalonians 1:10). Even our bodies will be glorified (Philippians 3:21; 1 Corinthians 15:40–49). Christ died to present Himself a pure bride "in all her glory" (Ephesians 5:27).

As Calvin well said, "If the Lord will share his glory, power and righteousness with the elect — nay will give himself to be enjoyed by them and, what is more excellent, will somehow make them to become one with himself, let us remember that every sort of happiness is included under this benefit."[6] Christ's prayer that we be one with Him in glory will be answered (John 17:21–24).

---

6 John Calvin, *Institutes of the Christian Religion* (Philadelphia: Westminster, 1960), 3:25:10 (p. 1005).

This glorification is not the same as the pagan idea of *apotheosis* or the similar idea of Greek Orthodoxy called *theosis*. It is union with God, but we do not become divine. It is glorification, not deification or divinization. We will remain humans, even as Christ's humanity remained human in the hypostatic union. God will bestow on the elect the fullness of the communicable attributes of God, such as holiness, love, peace, and truth. But He will not bestow the incommunicable attributes of infinity, eternity, aseity, omniscience, omnipresence, or omnipotence. Still, the elect will live in eternity forever, be immutable in holiness, know far more than now (and will go on learning forever), have more power, and visit the entire cosmos. Our present minds cannot conceive what God has in store for us (1 Corinthians 2:9–10). Even His revelation in Scripture is only partial (Deuteronomy 29:29).

The Glory of God's Grace

Ephesians 1:6 says that we were predestined "to the praise of the glory of His grace" (see vv. 12 and 14). God revealed His grace by electing us by sheer grace, then more grace by redeeming us by the cross, and still more irresistible grace by the Spirit. Grace is trinitarian. This sovereign grace reaches its culmination in the elect in their glorification. God will continue to manifest His glorious grace to the elect. God is infinite, and His grace is infinite; therefore, it will take the infinitude of eternity to reveal it in cascading waves of glory upon glory and grace upon grace (John 1:16).

God will especially reveal His glory to the elect in the beatific vision: "They shall see His face" (Revelation 22:4). We will behold in holy wonder and exultant awe God's glory and will continue to respond with delightful worship and reverent praise. We will adore Him with the heartfelt attitude that says, "Thank you for electing me to behold your glory and grace!"

Romans 9:23 says that God elected us "that He might make known the riches of His glory on the vessels of mercy, which He had prepared beforehand for glory." This parallels Ephesians 1:4–5, which says that God predestined the elect to enjoy His love in His presence. Then in Ephesians 2:7 God promises "that in the ages to come He might show the exceeding riches of His grace in His kindness toward us in Christ Jesus." Just as the Spirit pours the love of God into our hearts in irresistible grace (Romans 5:5), He will continue to do so in ever-increasing degrees for eternity. We will be like expanding cups under an increasing waterfall of holy love.

Romans 9:23 and Ephesians 3:10 say that God will do this in the elect to manifest it to others. The angels will behold and rejoice (see Luke 15:10). Even Satan and the demons will see it — but not rejoice in it and instead grumble and curse. The same is true with non-elect sinners in Hell. The elect will behold it in each other and joyfully worship God for pouring out such love to His beloved elect ones.

Heaven Is a World of Love

Jonathan Edwards preached a series of sermons on 1 Corinthians 13:13 on the theme "Heaven Is a World of Love."[7] It has been oft reprinted but never excelled. Here are a few choice excerpts:

> Heaven is the palace, or presence-chamber, of the Supreme Being who is both the cause and the source of all holy love. [. . .] And all this in a garden of love, the Paradise of God, where everything has a cast of holy love, and everything conspires to promote and stir up love, and nothing to interrupt its exercises; where everything is fitted by an all-wise God for the enjoyment of love under the greatest advantages. And all this shall be without any fading of the beauty of the objects beloved, or any decaying of love in the lover, or any satiety in the faculty which enjoys love.[8]

It is truly an ocean of love that has neither shore nor bottom, an ocean in which the elect will swim and bathe forever, loving and being loved by all in the Heaven of Love, including and especially God Himself, who is Love. Such sentiments are common in the letters of Samuel Rutherford and Robert Murray M'Cheyne, who wrote: "It is the world of holy love, where we shall give free, full, unfettered, unwearied expressions to our love forever."[9]

Heaven is a world of love because it is the home of God who is love (1 John 4:8). It is adorned with love, not in the abstract, but in the elect as a manifestation of the inter-trinitarian love of the blessed Three. The elect will freely and exuberantly love God and other saints (and the angels!) thereby fulfilling the two great love commandments. We will know beyond all doubt that God elected us out of love, and we love Him and one another with the pure love that He will continue to reveal in and through us for endless eternity.

---

7 Jonathan Edwards, *The Works of Jonathan Edwards* (New Haven: Yale University Press, 1989), 8:366–97. It is also in *Charity and Its Fruits*, 323–68 (London: Banner of Truth, 1969), and often published as a single sermon by various publishers.

8 Edwards, *The Works of Jonathan Edwards*, 8:369, 385.

9 Andrew Bonar, *Memoir and Remains of Robert Murray M'Cheyne* (Edinburgh: Banner of Truth, 1978), 502.

Conclusion

God chose the elect to salvation, eternal life, holiness, conformity to the image of Christ Jesus, glorification, grace, and love. That is the destination of predestination.

Chapter 43
Practical Implications of Election

To many Christians, the doctrine of election seems too theoretical and irrelevant to their lives. It appears as useless as the medieval debate over how many angels can dance on the head of a pin. They are reluctant to believe in election until they see its practical use.

That is an incorrect way to study theology. Our first question should be: "Is it in the Bible?" not "Is it practical?" If it is truly biblical, it will be truly practical (2 Timothy 3:16–17). Right doctrine (*orthodoxy*) must go before right living (*orthopraxis*). We must be doers of the Word, not just hearers of it (James 1:22–27).

Living to God

In the popular theology textbook *The Marrow of Theology*, the great English Puritan William Ames began by stating, "Theology is the doctrine or teaching of living to God."[1] That applies to the theology of election. Spurgeon commented: "The doctrine is not a dogma to be fought over, as dogs over a bone, but to be rejoiced in, and turned to practical account as an incentive to reverent wonder and affectionate gratitude."[2] The Irish Articles of 1615 gives us a good summary:

> The godly consideration of predestination, and our election in Christ, is full of sweet, pleasant, and unspeakable comfort to godly persons, and such as feel in themselves the working of the Spirit of Christ, mortifying the works of the flesh and their earthly members, and drawing up their minds to high and heavenly things, as well because it greatly confirms and establishes their faith of eternal salvation to be enjoyed through Christ, as because it fervently kindles their love towards God.[3]

R. T. Kendall somewhat derisively refers to Puritan Calvinism as

---

1 William Ames, *The Marrow of Theology* (Boston: Pilgrim Press, 1968), 77.
2 Charles H. Spurgeon, *Metropolitan Tabernacle Pulpit* (Pasadena, TX: Pilgrim Publications, 1970), 14:161.
3 In James T. Dennison Jr., ed., *Reformed Confessions of the 16th and 17th Centuries in English Translation* (Grand Rapids: Reformation Heritage Books, 2014), 4:93.

"experimental predestinarianism,"[4] but he is correct. We modern Puritans believe that predestination touches the heart and not just the head. It causes us to live to God.

Assurance of Election

Contrary to what the Arminian Dave Hunt thinks,[5] the Bible explicitly tells us how we can know if we are elect. Second Peter 1:10 says, "Therefore, brethren, be even more diligent to make your call and election sure." We do not have to wait until we arrive in Heaven to know God chose us. Not every Christian has this assurance, but it is a wonderful blessing to those who have it.

We wait in vain if we expect an angel to fly in the room with a page from the Book of Life and tell us, "See, there is your name. You are one of the elect." A popular error says that Calvinism teaches that material prosperity is evidence of election.[6] We reply that there are many poor elect and many rich non-elect persons (1 Corinthians 1:26–28).

We are to diligently search the Scriptures and apply biblical principles to discern our election. Second Peter 1:10 tells us to first make sure we were called. This is a special call that always results in regeneration, not the general call that invites all sinners to Christ. It is "a holy calling" (2 Timothy 1:9). In other words, discern if you have been born again, and then deduce backward. Heinrich Heppe explains that we know our election "not of course *a priori*, i.e., not by useless poring over the mystery of the divine counsel of grace, but only *a posteriori*, i.e., the moment he is converted and born again."[7]

One cannot know he is elect before he believes in Christ. One cannot know he is non-elect, for he might be elect but not yet a believer. Christopher Love said, "You are bound to make your election sure, but you are not bound to make your reprobation sure."[8] God has not chosen to imprint the words *elect* or *non-elect* on the foreheads of anyone. Yet Reformed theology teaches that

---

4 R. T. Kendall, *Calvin and English Calvinism to 1649* (Oxford: Oxford University Press, 1979), 8 and elsewhere. Experimental means experiential, that which affects the affections of the heart.

5 "There is not a verse in the Bible telling anyone how to be certain that he is among the elect." Dave Hunt, *What Love is This?* 3rd ed. (Bend, OR: The Berean Call, 2006), 484.

6 E.g., Mirian Van Scott, *Encyclopedia of Heaven* (New York: Thomas Dunne Books/St. Martin's, 1998), 95.

7 Heinrich Heppe, *Reformed Dogmatics* (Grand Rapids: Baker, 1978), 176.

8 Christopher Love, *A Treatise on Effectual Calling and Election* (Morgan, PA: Soli Deo Gloria, 1998), 245.

there are certain identifiable spiritual marks we can look for in ourselves that are evidence that we are regenerate and, therefore, called and elect. They do not appear before one is converted. They may be more evident in some Christians than in others, but all have them to some extent.

The Puritans frequently preached and wrote on the subject. In his excellent little book based on 2 Peter 1:10 entitled *A Treatise of Effectual Calling and Election*, Christopher Love had this to say: "Though no man, I say, can enter the bosom of God to know His secret decrees, yet if you can find good Scripture grounds that you are effectually called, you may be sure you are eternally elected and shall hereafter live in glory."[9] In the popular evangelistic book by another Puritan, *An Alarm to the Unconverted*, Joseph Alleine wrote: "Prove your conversion, and then never doubt your election."[10] Thomas Watson said, "O believer, be of good comfort, thou needst not look into the book of God's decree, but look at the book of thy heart, see what is written there: he finds the Bible copied out into his heart."[11]

First, one should discern if he truly believes the true gospel. Nobody is saved who believes a false gospel (Galatians 1:9) or fails to believe the true gospel (Mark 1:15; 16:16). Second Thessalonians 2:13 relates this to election: "God from the beginning chose you for salvation through sanctification of the Spirit and belief in the truth." We have been elected to believe the gospel. Whoever does not believe the gospel cannot know he is elect; he may be non-elect. Saving faith based on the gospel is one evidence of election, as William Perkins put it: "They which truly believe, are elected, (John 6:35), I truly believe [. . .] therefore I am elected."[12] This includes personal faith in Jesus Christ.

Then one looks for evidence in the fruit of spiritual life. By their fruits we shall not only identify false prophets but true believers (Matthew 7:16). First, look for a change in internal attitudes, particularly love for God and hatred for sin. Then see the fruit of the Spirit of Galatians 5:22 and the virtues that Peter alludes to in 2 Peter 1:5–7. Love for other Christians is another such fruit (John 13:35; 1 John 3:14; 4:20). Then there are the evidences of our external lifestyle. A Christian's life is characterized by a general pattern of righteousness and obedience (1 John 2:3–6; 3:6–10). Thomas Watson warned: "So, that till you are holy, you cannot

---

9 Love, *A Treatise of Effectual Calling and Election*, 78.
10 Joseph Alleine, *An Alarm to the Unconverted* (Edinburgh: Banner of Truth, 1978), 30.
11 Thomas Watson, *Discourses on Important and Interesting Subjects* (Ligonier, PA: Soli Deo Gloria, 1990),
12 William Perkins, *A Golden Chaine* (n.p.: Puritan Reprints, 2012), 240.

show any sign of election upon you, but rather the devil's brand-mark."[13] John Calvin: "For the best way to witness to God's having chosen us [. . .] is to be obedient to the voice of his Son, our Lord Jesus Christ."[14]

The third mark is the internal testimony of the Holy Spirit (Romans 8:16; Galatians 4:6; 1 John 3:24; 4:13; 5:10). As Jonathan Edwards put it, "We know that we have the Spirit immediately by feeling that divine, holy, humble, amicable disposition and motion in us, whereby we are assured that we must be God's children."[15]

There is an inseparable relation between present salvation and eternal election in the Golden Chain of Romans 8:29–30. All who are now justified were previously predestined. Therefore, if you know you are justified, you can know you were predestined. This increases our sense of security. We can then look at the future links of the chain and deduce that if we are justified, we shall surely be glorified. A true understanding of election does not breed doubts but sends them packing. The Synod of Dort summed it up:

> The elect in due time, though in various degrees and in different measures, attain the assurance of their eternal and unchangeable election, not by inquisitively prying into the secret and deep things of God, but by observing in themselves with a spiritual joy and holy pleasure, the infallible fruits of election pointed out in the Word of God — such as a true faith in Christ, filial fear, a godly sorrow for sin, a hungering and thirsting after righteousness, etc. (1:12)

Can we know if another person is elect? This is more difficult. We are not infallible, so we must be cautious. Paul knew that the Thessalonian believers were elect (1 Thessalonians 1:4; 2 Thessalonians 2:13), as did Peter with the believers in Asia Minor (1 Peter 1:2). Some reasonable assurance of another person is possible. For example, a Christian may marry only another Christian (2 Corinthians 6:14), which presupposes he can discern if that person is a true believer. This also applies to baptism, church membership, pastoral shepherding, church discipline, counseling, and evangelism. Pastors need special wisdom here.

We should look for true faith in Christ and the true gospel, repentance,

---

13 Thomas Watson, *The Beatitudes* (London: Banner of Truth, 1971), 173.
14 John Calvin, *Sermons on the Book of Micah* (Phillipsburg, NJ: P&R, 2003), 132.
15 Jonathan Edwards, *The Works of Jonathan Edwards* (New Haven: Yale University Press, 2003), 21:488.

internal godly attitudes, and external righteous lives. Detecting the internal testimony of the Spirit can only be done by seeing external fruit, for we cannot listen to what is in a person's heart. Christ said the world can know if we are His disciples if we love one another (John 13:35). If the world can know, believers can know. First John 3:6–10 says a righteous life is an obvious and discernible mark of conversion. So, if we can determine if someone is truly converted, we can deduce that he is elect. Peter Martyr Vermigli: "But we, who do not know or understand God's secret will, can judge only by the effects, that is, those who are cleansed from corrupt doctrine and live godly lives are vessels of honor. [. . .] We can judge others only by some tokens and results."[16] Jerome Zanchius urges this as a needful aid to Christian fellowship.[17]

Caution is needed. An unconverted person may be elect but not yet regenerate. The Second Helvetic Confession wisely advised, "We must hope well of all and not rashly judge any man to be reprobate."[18] Perhaps if we could discern if someone has committed the unpardonable blasphemy against the Holy Spirit we could then know he is reprobate, but that is extremely tenuous.

Spurgeon well preached this assurance's blessings: "I am persuaded that the doctrine of predestination — the blessed truth of providence — is one of the softest pillows upon which the Christian can lay his head, and one of the strongest staffs upon which he may lean in his pilgrimage along the rough road."[19] Such assurance moves us to love Christ more. It helps us to die well.

Humility

It is written: "Therefore, as elect of God, holy and beloved, put on tender mercies, kindness, humility, meekness, longsuffering" (Colossians 3:12). The elect should strive for humility. We must not be proud of our predestination. We are the elect, not the elite. The Synod of Dort tells us, "The sense and certainty of this election afford the children additional matter for daily humiliation before Him" (1:13). We can boast of neither salvation nor election, for both are by God's grace alone (Ephesians 2:8–9; Romans 11:5).

Pride keeps many Christians from believing in election. Nothing humbles a

---

16 Peter Martyr Vermigli, *The Peter Martyr Library* (Kirksville, MO: Truman State University Press, 2003), 8:28.

17 Jerome Zanchius, *The Doctrine of Absolute Predestination* (Grand Rapids: Baker, 1977), 102.

18 Dennison Jr., ed., *Reformed Confessions*, 2:825.

19 Charles H. Spurgeon, *New Park Street Pulpit* (Pasadena, TX: Pilgrim Publications, 1981), 6:455.

person more than knowing how sinful he is and that God chose Him by sheer sovereign grace and not for anything good in him. Christians should never lose the humble awe that God saved them by grace. Spurgeon: "I seem as if I can understand God's having chose you, but I shall never cease to wonder that he hath chosen me."[20]

Delving into what Scripture says about the depths of our depraved hearts also humbles us. God chose wicked sinners, not nice saints. This has special bearing on the debate over the order of the decrees — God chose from the mass of fallen humanity (infralapsarianism), not from a mass of pure unfallen humanity (supralapsarianism). Arminianism is tempted to pride because it says that God chose us based on our foreseen faith. But Calvinism produces humility because it asserts that God chose us by mere sovereign grace, and even our faith is a gift of God's grace.

Holiness

Ephesians 1:4 says that God chose us to be holy, and holy we shall be in Heaven. This has ethical implications for the present. Ephesians 2:10 says, "For we are His workmanship, created in Christ Jesus for good works, which God prepared beforehand that we should walk in them." This does not mean sinless perfection (1 John 1:8; Philippians 3:12), which Arminians such as John Wesley but no Calvinist has ever taught. Christ chose us and ordained that we bear spiritual fruit (John 15:16).

We discern our election in part from self-examination of a holy life and attitudes (2 Peter 1:5–10; see 2 Corinthians 13:5). In turn, this assurance leads to further holiness, which in turn produces more assurance of election and security of future perseverance. True assurance, we repeat, does not lead to licentious behavior, as we are often falsely accused of teaching or living. There is a kind of assurance-holiness dynamo. Christopher Love explained: "The assurance of your election should be a motive to you to add grace to grace and not sin to sin."[21] The Reformed Christian abominates the idea of sinning because of grace (Romans 6:15; Galatians 5:13; Jude 4). It is also no coincidence that the pernicious errors of easy-believism and carnal Christianity were devised by Arminians, not Calvinists. Ironically, Arminianism and not Calvinism tends to lead to unholiness. This applies especially to those who consider themselves Calvinists because they believe in the preservation of the saints but not the perseverance

---

20 Spurgeon, *Metropolitan Tabernacle Pulpit*, 14:350.
21 Christopher Love, *Preacher of God's Word* (Morgan, PA: Soli Deo Gloria, 2000), 149.

of the saints in holiness. They are half-point Calvinists and four-and-a-half-point Arminians. To give them their due, however, many evangelical Arminians such as Arminius, Wesley, and Tozer also abominate easy-believism and carnal Christianity. We link arms with them in the call for personal holiness.

A person who claims to be elect but lives a life of flagrant sin is lying and self-deceived, as much as the person who claims sinless perfection (1 John 1:8). He cannot prove his salvation and therefore not his election. Indeed, he nullifies his profession of faith and proves he is not saved at all. The Synod of Dort seriously warns us:

> The consideration of this doctrine of election is so far from encouraging remissness in the observance of the divine commands, or from sinking men in carnal security, that these, in the just judgment of God, are the usual effects of rash presumption, or of idle and wanton trifling with the grace of election, in those who refuse to walk in the ways of the elect (1:13).

Praise

God chose us "to the praise of the glory of His grace" (Ephesians 1:6; see vv. 12 and 14). Assurance of one's election moves him to worship God. "Gaze with delight upon the praise of mercy, that is, the grace of God," wrote Augustine.[22] Such a look moves the Christian to reverent wonder and awesome adoration. Jay Adams, Christian counselor, urges us: "That He has chosen to save you, Christian, should not merely please you; it should astonish you."[23] Edward Polhill, Puritan, waxed especially eloquent here: "This grand truth of election should justly astonish us into eternal admiration. Oh, the heights and depths of divine love! All the elect of God may lose themselves in holy mazes and trances. My God! My God! (may every one of them say) Why hast thou chosen me?"[24]

The great biblical doctrine of election opens a bejeweled door to new vistas of the glory of God, which is the final goal of election. When God displays His glory, His people respond with worship. We glorify Him because He first glorified Himself to us. Election reveals glory and incites the response of worship. Predestination produces praise.

---

22 Augustine, *The Works of Saint Augustine* (Hyde Park: New City, 1997), I/23:191.
23 Jay Adams, *The Grand Demonstration* (Santa Barbara: EastGate, 1991), 50.
24 Edward Polhill, *The Works of Edward Polhill* (Morgan, PA: Soli Deo Gloria, 1998), 126.

Love

God chose the elect out of love and predestined them to an eternal ocean of love (Ephesians 1:4–6; 2:7). Between our conversion and our glorification, we enjoy this love in our hearts and are moved to love God in return: "We love Him because He first loved us" (1 John 4:19). That love began in predestination. The Synod of Dort includes love in its list of the blessings of assurance of election: "Adoring the depth of His mercies [. . .] who first manifested so great love towards them [. . .] and rendering grateful returns of ardent love to Him" (1:13).

When the elect bride hears the assurance from her Beloved, "There were many others whom I could have chosen, but I chose to love you," then warm love wells up in her heart for Him as never before. Gratitude, humility, praise, and especially love characterize the heart of a Christian who is assured of his election. A Christian with little love for God has little assurance of election. After all, is not love to God the chief virtue in the Christian life?

Conclusion

Assurance of election causes great joy: "Rejoice that your names are written in heaven" (Luke 10:20). Christians should not only love the God who elected them but love the doctrine of election as well. Edwin Palmer asked, "Be very honest now. Do you like the teaching of election? Why?"[25] Non-Calvinists do not like it; some even hate it. That is sad. They do not know what blessings they are missing. Some Calvinists only grudgingly accept it. We should joyfully believe it and love God for electing us.

---

25 Edwin Palmer, *The Five Points of Calvinism*, Rev. ed. (Grand Rapids: Baker, 1980), 39.

Chapter 44
The Doctrine of Reprobation

In his book *Chosen by God*, R. C. Sproul has a chapter entitled "Double, Double, Toil and Trouble. Is Predestination Double?"[1] He states, "It is not enough to talk about Jacob; we must also consider Esau."[2] Romans 9:13 says, "Jacob I have loved, but Esau I have hated." Jacob was elect; Esau was not elect but was reprobate.

What Is Reprobation?

This is one of the hardest doctrines in the Bible to understand and accept. Perhaps it was in Peter's mind when he referred to hard teachings in Paul's letters (2 Peter 3:16). Relatively few Christians believe in it. Some vigorously oppose it.

Louis Berkhof offered a useful definition: "Reprobation may be defined as that eternal decree of God whereby He has determined to pass some men by with the operation of His special grace, and to punish them for their sins, to the manifestation of His justice."[3] The Westminster Confession gives us this definition which has been taught for hundreds of years by Calvinists:

> The rest of mankind God was pleased, according to the unsearchable counsel of His own will, whereby He extendeth or withholdeth mercy as he pleaseth, for the glory of His sovereign power over His creatures, to pass by, and to ordain them to dishonor and wrath for their sin, to the praise of His glorious justice (3:7).

Reprobation is not the same as total depravity. All men are totally depraved; only some are reprobate. It is not the same as the foreordination of sin. God foreordained to allow sin to exist; reprobation is the foreordination of the punishment of some sinners. Nor is reprobation the same as the unpardonable sin, supralapsarianism, or Hyper-Calvinism. Simply put, reprobation is non-election.

---

1 R. C. Sproul, *Chosen by God* (Wheaton: Tyndale, 1986), 139–60.
2 Sproul, *Chosen by God*, 141.
3 Louis Berkhof, *Systematic Theology* (Grand Rapids: Eerdmans, 1988), 116.

A High and Humbling Doctrine

I know of no post-biblical writer who held to this doctrine before Augustine. Some scholars deny that Augustine taught it, but that he did indeed hold to it is evident from the following quotation: "To those whom he predestined to eternal life, he most mercifully gives grace, and to those whom he predestined to eternal death, he most righteously assigns punishment, not only on account of sins which they willingly add, but also on account of original sin."[4]

Isidore of Seville (560–636) was probably the first to use the term *double predestination*. Gottschalk later explicitly and repeatedly taught it. Mainstream medieval theologians taught a somewhat modified version of it. Luther explicitly taught a strong doctrine of reprobation in *The Bondage of the Will*. John Calvin set the theological trajectory for later Reformed theology by repeatedly teaching it. He called it a *decretum horribile*[5]— not a horrible decree, but a horrifying or fearsome decree. The subject should humble us and cause us to examine ourselves to make sure we are saved and elect and not lost and reprobate (2 Corinthians 13:5). This doctrine found credal expression in the Canons of the Synod of Dort, the Westminster Confession, the Baptist Confession of 1689, and others. It is explained in most of the standard Reformed systematic theologies. However, we still await the definitive monograph on the subject. The main thing is that it is taught in the infallible Word of God.

Reprobation in Romans 9

Romans 9 is the clearest passage on reprobation in the Bible.[6] Paul had just discussed the Golden Chain in 8:29–30 where he mentioned *foreknowledge* (the forelove of election) and *predestination*. Now he continues the theme by contrasting election with non-election. He addresses the question why some Jews are not saved, and some Gentiles are. The answer: God chose some persons to be saved and not others, according to His eternal purpose (v. 11).

He puts forth Jacob and Esau as examples. One was chosen; the other was reprobated. This happened before they were born and therefore before they did

---

4 Augustine, *The Works of Saint Augustine* (Hyde Park: New City, 1997), I/23:544.
5 John Calvin, *Institutes of the Christian Religion* (Philadelphia: Westminster, 1960), 3:23:7 (p. 955). The McNeill-Battles translation renders it "the decree is dreadful."
6 See John Piper, *The Justification of God* (Grand Rapids: Baker, 1993). See also Reformed commentaries on Romans 9. Also D. Martyn Lloyd-Jones, *Romans: An Exposition of Chapter 9, God's Sovereign Purpose* (Edinburgh: Banner of Truth, 1991). William Twisse wrote a huge treatise entitled *The Riches of God's Love Unto Vessels of Mercy, Consistent with His Absolute Hatred or Reprobation of the Vessels of Wrath.*

either good or evil. He quotes Malachi 1:2–3 in verse 13, "Jacob I have loved, but Esau I have hated." He is not speaking of the nations of Israel and Edom, as Malachi did, but of specific historical individuals. He selected them as examples for another reason: They were twins.

In Scripture *hated* can mean either "loved less" (as in Luke 14:26) or "not loved at all." God loved Esau and all the non-elect by common grace. But He loved Jacob and the elect by special grace. God chose Jacob and the elect by special grace and withheld it from Esau and the others. Even if the word means "loved less" here, that still means God made a significant difference between them that determined their final destiny. But it could also mean actual hatred because it is tied in with the wrath of God in verse 22.

Why then did God love one in this way and not the other? It had nothing to do with their character, for this occurred before they were created, and they had no good to commend themselves to God at any time anyway. The answer is simply stated in verse 15: "I will have mercy on whomever I will have mercy, and I will have compassion on whomever I will have compassion." God freely and sovereignly chose to show this special mercy and compassion to Jacob and the elect and not to Esau and the non-elect.

This can be deduced in a parallel way. If God now gives saving grace to some sinners and not to others, then we can rightly infer that He foreordained in eternity to give saving grace to some and not to others. What God does in time is always according to His eternal purpose of predestination.

Paul then gives another example of reprobation: Pharaoh (v. 17). You could postulate that God said, "Moses I have loved, but Pharaoh I have hated." God reprobated Pharaoh in eternity and hardened his heart in time, as He does with all the non-elect.[7] Hardening is the evidence and outcome of reprobation. We could multiply other biblical examples. God chose Abel, not Cain; Isaac, not Ishmael; Solomon, not Absalom; and other sets of brothers. This teaches, among other things, that neither election nor reprobation run in the family blood. Just because one's parents are elect does not guarantee that one's own self is elect. The converse is true with reprobation.

The Potter and the Clay

Then Paul uses the illustration of the potter and the clay, which the Jews would recognize from Isaiah 29:16; 45:9; 64:8; Jeremiah 18:2–6; and Lamentations 4:2.

---

7 We will discuss *hardening* in the next chapter.

God is the potter; mankind is the clay. Remember that God formed Adam from the dirt of the ground (Genesis 2:7; 3:19). Peter Martyr Vermigli commented: "God is compared to a potter who surely before he begins to work determines in his mind what kind of vessel he will make."[8]

God the Potter divided the lump of clay into two parts. Note that it is the potter and not the clay that did the dividing. God was active; we were passive (obviously passive, since we did not even exist yet). He then made some of the clay into beautiful vessels such as vases or bottles for precious wine or perfume. These are the "vessels of mercy" (v. 23). This is election.

The Potter then uses the rest of the clay to mold "vessels of wrath" (v. 22). These are dishonorable containers such as garbage cans, chamber pots, or spittoons. This twofold division into pottery is mentioned in 2 Timothy 2:20: "But in a great house there are not only vessels of gold and silver, but also of wood and clay, some for honor and some for dishonor." That he there mentions different material does not alter his basic point.

Both vessels come from the exact same lump of clay. The elect and the non-elect are both born from the same mass of humanity — and a dirty one at that. This disproves the popular Arminian theory that "the same sun hardens clay but melts wax." No wax is in view here, only clay. God made the difference, not man. The Potter had the final say, not the clay.

And what was the final purpose of this division? It was to display His glory — the glory of mercy on some (v. 23) and the glory of power and wrath on others (v. 22). Paul uses this illustration to show that the elect are like Jacob in being vessels of mercy, while the reprobate are like Esau in being vessels of wrath. The elect are climbing Jacob's ladder to Heaven, while the non-elect are descending Esau's ladder to Hell.

Other Texts on Reprobation

First Thessalonians 5:9 says, "For God did not appoint us to wrath, but to obtain salvation through our Lord Jesus Christ." Some have misunderstood this as meaning that God has not appointed anyone at all to wrath, but they fail to correctly identify the "us." They are believers, who are elect (1:4). God appointed some sinners to eternal life (Acts 13:48) and the rest to eternal wrath.

We can deduce reprobation from other texts on election. Ephesians 1:4 says,

---

8 Peter Martyr Vermigli, *The Peter Martyr Library* (Kirksville, MO: Truman State University Press, 2003), 8:14.

"He chose us." That is not all humanity. That some were chosen means others were not chosen. The same can be applied to 2 Thessalonians 2:13 and other texts.

In John 13:18, Jesus said to the twelve apostles: "I do not speak concerning all of you. I know whom I have chosen." After Judas left, He said to the eleven: "You did not choose Me, but I chose you" (15:16). Jesus chose the eleven — not including Judas. Judas was never saved (John 6:70; 17:12). He was reprobate. Look also at John 15:19: "I chose you out of the world." He did not choose everyone in the world and therefore did not pray for the whole world in 17:9. Jesus could have said, "Peter I have loved, but Judas I have hated."

After mentioning the elect in 1 Peter 1:2, Peter speaks of the others in 2:8: "They stumble, being disobedient to the word, to which they also were appointed." Then he contrasts them with the "chosen" ones in verse 9 who obtained mercy in verse 10. Thus, some sinners were predestined to be disobedient to the Word and fall without salvation.

Simeon said of the baby Jesus, "Behold, this child is destined for the fall and rising of many in Israel" (Luke 2:34). Christ was predestined to be the Messiah. Some persons were predestined to rise in faith in Him, while others were predestined to fall in condemnation.

Second Peter 2:12 is sometimes cited as a text for reprobation: "But these, like natural brute beasts made to be caught and destroyed." By nature, we are all beastly sinners, but some are specifically made to be transformed into lambs, while others are destined to remain swine for the slaughter.

Jude 4 is also sometimes cited, but there is a translation problem. It could mean "certain men have crept in unnoticed, who long ago were marked out for this condemnation" (NKJV). That is, they were marked out in eternal reprobation. Other translations render it "written about" (NIV) or "written of beforehand" (ASV). Some use the word "designated" (ESV, RSV). This translation implies that the sinners in view were prophesied about in prophecy written in the Old Testament. In other words, they were spoken about in prophecy, not predestinated. If the first translation is used, it clearly means reprobation. But if the latter is true, reprobation is taught indirectly. Assuming it means prophecy, we see that the prophets predicted the doom of these sinners because God had told them of it. How did God know it? Because He foreordained and foreknew it. And that means reprobation. Just as Old Testament prophecies "had to be fulfilled" (Luke 24:44; see Acts 2:28), so the prophecies of doomed sinners had to be fulfilled because they were not only predicted but predestined.

Still More Texts

Matthew 11:25–26 refers to the temporal effects of election and reprobation: "You have hidden these things from the wise and prudent and have revealed them to babes. Even so, Father, for so it seemed good in Your sight." Christ revealed the Father to the elect, and it was His sovereign right to do so (v. 27). He did not do so with the rest.

Earlier in Matthew 7:23 Jesus fast-forwarded to Judgment Day, when He will condemn lost sinners with the words "I never knew you." Certainly He knew who they were and foresaw everything about them back in eternity. But as we saw in previous chapters on foreknowledge and election, Christ *foreknew* His people by way of forelove election. He did not forelove those He did not choose or save. He *forehated* them in reprobation.

One is tempted to cite Luke 17:34: "The one will be taken and the other will be left." Whether this refers to the rapture or the Judgment Day, we can detect election and reprobation behind it. Some sinners are taken to Heaven because they were chosen in election, while other sinners are left to go to Hell because they were left in their sins in non-election.

If Romans 8:29–30 is the Golden Chain of Salvation, then by good and necessary consequence we can deduce what I call the *Black Chain of Reprobation*.[9] The personal pronoun *whom* there means "all of whom," not "some of whom," otherwise Paul's whole argument crumbles. If, then, all who were predestined will be glorified, and not all humans will be glorified, it necessarily follows that some were not predestined to glorification. We could count backward: "Those who will not be glorified were not justified, were not called, were not predestined, were not foreknown."

Earlier we discussed how God chose some sinners to eternal life and wrote their names in the Book of Life. Revelation 13:8 explicitly speaks of the non-elect: "whose names have not been written in the Book of Life of the Lamb slain from the foundation of the world" (see also 17:8). Using theological poetical license, I say that they were written in the Book of Death, or what Thomas Watson called "the black book of reprobation."[10]

---

9 Thomas Watson: "God has [. . .] iron chains, which are partly His decree in ordaining men to destruction and partly His power in bridling and chaining them up under wrath." *The Mischief of Sin* (Morgan, PA: Soli Deo Gloria, 1994), 11.

10 Thomas Watson, *Discourses on Important and Interesting Subjects* (Ligonier, PA: Soli Deli Gloria, 1990), 1:122.

God foresaw everything that would come to pass because He foreordained all that would come to pass. He foreordained absolutely everything. That must include the final damnation of lost sinners. Proverbs 16:4: "The Lord has made all for Himself, yes, even the wicked for the day of doom." The reprobate were made for Doomsday.

Preterition and Pre-damnation

To be sure, Reformed theologians point out two stages in non-election. This parallels how God first chose the elect in forelove then set them on the road to Heaven (Romans 8:29). For the others, God first decreed to pass them by. This is usually called *preterition*, sometimes *rejection*. God declined to give those sinners saving grace but rather decreed to leave them in their sins.

The second stage is *pre-damnation*. It is vital to remember that this involved foreordained humans that would be created and allowed to fall into sin. God reprobated sinners, not sinless beings. Christopher Love put it thus: "The decree of non-election is to be distinguished from the decree of destination to punishment. [. . .] The first is an act of God's sovereignty, the latter an act of His justice."[11]

Note the divine justice in reprobation. God gave mercy to the elect, but He did not give injustice to the non-elect. He was just in both choices. This is fundamental to remember when answering the objection that reprobation is unfair. Augustine wrote long ago, "His generosity toward some did not, of course, mean that he was unjust toward the others. [. . .] By not giving it to everyone, he showed what all merited."[12] Nobody deserves election. Everyone deserves reprobation. Just as God does not send mere *people* to Hell but sends *sinners* there, so He reprobated *sinners* and not morally neutral or impersonal *people*. Once this is understood, all falls into place. If it will not be unjust of God to send unrepentant sinners to Hell at Judgment Day (Matthew 25:41; Romans 3:5–6), it was not unjust of God to foreordain to do so back in eternity (Romans 9:14). God was, is, and always will be absolutely just.

Edward Polhill calls our attention to a very fine point here regarding the foreordination of sin and reprobation:

> There is a great difference between reprobation of sin and the reprobation of sinners: the reprobation of sin issues from the sanctity and holiness

---

11 Christopher Love, *Preacher of God's Word* (Morgan, PA: Soli Deo Gloria, 2000), 132.
12 Augustine, *Works*, I/26:200, 208.

of God's will; but the reprobation of sinners issues from the sovereignty and justice thereof. The reprobation of sin is universal, and without any distinction of persons [. . .] but the reprobation of sinners is particular.[13]

Later he made another point: "Original sin makes all men reprobatable [. . .] but it makes no man a reprobate."[14]

I hasten to add that not every use of the word *reprobate* in Scripture refers to eternal non-election. Sometimes it refers to a temporal rejection and judgment. Likewise, when God is said to "give over" some sinners, this often means surrendering them to their own sins. Some of those sinners later repented and believed, thus verifying they were elect. Exegesis of places where such words are used is not based mainly on etymology so much as context, use, and theology.

Sin is not the cause but only the occasion of reprobation, as Vermigli explains: "If sin were the true cause of reprobation, then no one would be chosen, since God foreknows that all are defiled with it."[15] God chose some sinners to be saved and left others to be judged for their sins, but in neither case was sin the final deciding factor. The final factor was the sovereign will of God. This has bearing on the question of the order of the decrees, which I will discuss later.

Unconditional Reprobation

Reprobation is as unconditional as election in this specific sense: that God made the choice, not sinful man. This is one of the points Paul made in Romans 9. Just as eternal election is not finally based on foreseen faith in time, so eternal non-election is not based on foreseen unbelief or other sins. William Perkins explained, "If that faith foreseen be not the cause of the decree of election, it cannot be that the want of faith foreseen, should be the cause of the decree of reprobation; but rather as faith doth in order of causes follow after election, so must [unbelief] reprobation."[16] God was the First Cause of reprobation unto damnation even as He was the First Cause of election unto salvation and glorification. Unbelief is the instrumental cause of damnation even as faith is the instrumental cause of salvation. And the final cause of both is the glory of God.

In election, God sovereignly chose to give special love to some and not to all. Christopher Love again: "God's decrees, or appointing some men to be

---

13 Edward Polhill, *The Works of Edward Polhill* (Morgan, PA: Soli Deo Gloria, 1998), 132.
14 Polhill, 134.
15 Vermigli, *The Peter Martyr Library*, 8:51.
16 William Perkins, *A Golden Chaine* (n.p.: Puritan Reprints, 2010), 255.

objects of His wrath, do not infuse any sin or evil into such persons, but only withholds His grace from them."[17] This refers to special grace, not common grace. Arminians fail to distinguish those graces and therefore miss scriptural teaching on both election and reprobation.

Does not God have the right to choose to whom He will bestow His love? Or do only humans have that right? God does this in election and reprobation, as William Ames said, "Just as there is love which sets apart election, so there is a denial of love which sets apart or contrasts in reprobation."[18]

As we saw earlier, in the covenant of redemption God chose the elect. He did not choose the reprobate. Klaas Schilder somewhat boldly put it like this: "There is a *pactum salutis*, but also a *pactum damni*, a counsel of peace, but also a counsel of damnation."[19] Though it is not expressly stated in Scripture, we could say that since God always works in covenantal ways, it could be surmised that His promise to damn the reprobate entailed a covenant of reprobation.

If Christ was predestined to be the Head of the elect, the opposite is true for the non-elect. John Calvin: "Christ contrasts Himself with the devil, who is the head of the reprobate."[20] Gottschalk said that as the elect are the body of Christ, the reprobate are "members of the Devil and the body of Antichrist."[21] Election is in Christ; non-election is in Satan. Contrary to Karl Barth's error that Christ is the "Reprobate One" for all men, in truth Satan is the Reprobate One for all the non-elect.

We must be careful in differentiating election in Christ, "the Light of the world," (John 8:12) and reprobation in Satan, the Prince of Darkness (Cf. Ephesians 2:2; 6:12). Reprobation does not issue from any alleged dark side of God, for "God is light and in Him there is no darkness at all" (1 John 1:5). Rather, it is a matter of the relation of the holiness of God's love and of His wrath. He is holy and sovereign in both. Yet God's wrath is displayed in the outer darkness of Hell (Matthew 8:12), the destiny of reprobation. The darkness is in our sin, not in God's light.

John Lafayette Girardeau, the great nineteenth-century Southern

---

17 Love, *Preacher of God's Word*, 133.

18 William Ames, *The Marrow of Theology* (Boston: Pilgrim Press, 1968), 156.

19 Quoted in G. C. Berkouwer, *Divine Election* (Grand Rapids: Eerdmans, 1960), 169.

20 John Calvin, *Commentary on a Harmony of the Gospels: Matthew, Mark and Luke* (Grand Rapids: Eerdmans, 1980), 3:117.

21 *Gottschalk and a Medieval Predestinarian Controversy: Texts Translated from the Latin*, ed. by Victor Genke and Francis X. Gumerlock (Milwaukee: Marquette University Press, 2010), 113.

Presbyterian, perceptively drew this analogy. Election and reprobation are like "two hemispheres of the same globe, one bright side with the light of divine love and of the beauty of holiness, the other dark with the judicial frown of God and the dreadful deformity of sin."[22] This is why supralapsarianism borders on making God the author of sin, for it posits a reprobation of unfallen persons, which seem to point to some hidden and malevolent darkness in God rather than in man. Perish the very idea.

Both Election and Non-Election Are Biblical

Non-Calvinists, of course, have substantially different views of both election and reprobation than Calvinists teach. But some Calvinists balk at the idea of reprobation and hold to a supposed *single predestination*. For example, D. Martyn Lloyd-Jones preached: "I do not believe in 'double predestination.'"[23] My guess is that such Calvinists are rejecting the supralapsarianism scheme rather than the infralapsarianism view. Others, such as Arthur C. Custance, follow Heinrich Bullinger in saying that while election is not based on foreseen faith, reprobation is indeed based on foreseen unbelief.[24] Historic Lutheranism and some Amyraldians apparently held to something like this, though not Luther himself.

Calvin hit the nail on the head: "Election itself could not stand except as set over against reprobation."[25] George Whitefield agreed: "Without doubt, the doctrines of election and reprobation must stand or fall together."[26] More recently, Edwin Palmer: "Election without preterition is theological gobbledygook, a mythical inanity of an uncritical mind."[27] Single predestination is as absurd as a one-sided coin or the sound of one hand clapping. It is both theological nonsense as well as unbiblical error.

Romans 9 teaches both election and non-election. When it comes to predestination, one could say, "It is double or nothing." God could have elected

---

22 John Lafayette Girardeau, *Calvinism and Evangelical Arminianism* (Harrisonburg: Sprinkle, 1984), 174.

23 D. Martyn Lloyd-Jones, *The Final Perseverance of the Saints* (Edinburgh: Banner of Truth, 1975), 267. J. C. Ryle said, "I cannot find in Scripture any clear proof that there is any decreed reprobation. I hold that the destruction of those who are lost is the consequence of their own sins, and not of God's predestination." *Expository Thoughts on the Gospel: St. Luke—Volume II* (Cambridge: James Clarke, 1976), 172.

24 Arthur C. Custance, *The Sovereignty of Grace* (Phillipsburg, NJ: P&R, 1979), 143.

25 Calvin, *Institutes*, 3:23:1 (p. 947).

26 George Whitefield, *The Works of the Reverend George Whitefield, M.A.* (London: 1771), 4:58.

27 Edwin Palmer, *The Five Points of Calvinism*, Rev. ed. (Grand Rapids: Baker, 1984), 106.

all, some, or none. Obviously, He did not elect all, for some go to Hell. And equally obviously, He did not elect none, for some go to Heaven. If He elected only some, then He necessarily did not elect all — and that means double predestination. Single predestination could imply universalism. Some scholars retreat from the obvious, such as F. F. Bruce who wrote: "According to the general tenor of the Scriptures, the election of some does not necessarily involve the damnation of the rest."[28]

That option is not biblical. Election of only some necessarily means the non-election of the others. For example, God chose David to be the second king of Israel. When Samuel looked at each of David's brothers, he said, "Neither has the Lord chosen this one" (1 Samuel 16:8, 10). Choosing some means rejecting others. When a man chooses and marries a bride, he "forsakes all others," as stated in the traditional wedding vow. This is also seen in the election of Israel: "But you, Israel, are My servant, Jacob whom I have chosen. [. . .] I have chosen you and have not cast you away" (Isaiah 41:8–9). God cast other nations away; they were reprobate nations. In choosing Israel, God did not choose others (Acts 14:16). In choosing some sinners, He chose not to choose other sinners.

This dichotomy is blurred in Karl Barth's so-called Super-supralapsarianism. He taught the novel theory that all men are elect in Christ and non-elect in Christ. This is not the same as Arminianism. It is not a paradox either but a linguistic, logical, and unbiblical self-contradiction. It is nonsense. One is either elect or non-elect. He cannot be both or neither. It is the same as Heaven and Hell, the eternal destinies of the elect and reprobate. One ends up in either Heaven or Hell, not both or neither (Matthew 25:46). Barth elsewhere tips his hand in favor of universal salvation in the notion that Christ's grace triumphs over sin, and therefore universal election trumps universal reprobation. It boggles the mind to try to understand why some theologians think this is any kind of Reformed theology. It is not Calvinism nor even good Arminianism.

Objections

Objection 1: *"Reprobation is another term for the unforgivable blasphemy of the Holy Spirit."*

No, the two are separate things. All who commit that unpardonable sin are

---

28 F. F. Bruce, *Answers to Questions*, Rev. ed. (Grand Rapids: Zondervan, 1972), 114. He goes on to disagree with Calvin's interpretation of 1 Timothy 2:4.

obviously reprobate, but not all who are reprobate commit that sin. That sin includes the apostasy of Hebrews 6 and 10.

Objection 2: *"Reprobation makes God the author of sin."*

As said earlier, it is my opinion that supralapsarianism borders on this great error, but that is not the mainline Reformed position. The historic view was stated in the Canons of the Synod of Dort: "Reprobation [. . .] does not at all make God the author of sin (a blasphemous thought!) but rather its fearful, irreproachable, just judge and avenger" (1:15). The Synod censured Johannes Maccovius for his extreme supralapsarian and scholastic view that implied God was the author of sin.

Objection 3: *"The Reformed doctrine of reprobation presents God as capriciously and maliciously saying, 'Now whom am I going to damn today?'"*

This is as false as the previous objection. It forgets that we are all guilty and damnable sinners under the wrath of God until we are saved (Ephesians 2:3). God did not reject some sinners by flipping a coin any more than He did so in electing others. He did both by the wise and just counsel of His holy will. Even when God shows justice and wrath, He is not cruel or malevolent.

Objection 4: *"Election is eternal by God, but reprobation is temporal by man."*

No, both are eternal by God. See Ephesians 1:4; 2 Thessalonians 2:13; Revelation 13:8, 17:8.

Objection 5: *"Only Christ is reprobate."*

Christ is said to be the Elect One, but never the Reprobate One. Even when Christ was treated as the world's worst sinner on the cross because our sins were imputed to Him (2 Corinthians 5:21; Galatians 3:13), as Luther said, He was not actually made a sinner, nor was He reprobated. Satan, not Christ, is the Reprobate One. But he is not the only one reprobated.

Objection 6: *"The doctrine of reprobation gives lost sinners an excuse at Judgment Day: "You can't condemn me. I never had a chance. You did not elect me. You created me only to damn me."*

Yet God does not condemn a person only for being reprobate but for being an unrepentant sinner. Remember, nobody wants to be elected any more than he wants to be saved, until God changes his heart.

Objection 7: *"Doesn't God will everyone to be saved?"*

Yes, in the revealed will of the gospel but not in the secret will of predestination. It somewhat parallels sin. God strictly forbids it in the revealed will but foreordained its existence in the secret will. It is necessary to grasp the Reformed teaching of the twofold will of God to understand our answer.

Objection 8: *"Reprobation isn't fair!"*

This objection is used against many Reformed teachings, such as election and non-election. It was raised against Paul in Romans 9 in the very context of his teaching reprobation. The objection actually proves our point, for nobody would charge Arminianism with being unfair. The Reformed view of Romans 9 only appears unfair when one overlooks the universal guilt of man and the just and holy sovereignty of God. Notice Paul's answer to this objection: "But indeed, O man, who are you to reply against God?" (v. 20). The objection accuses God of injustice, which is blasphemy. Calvin noted this in his strong rebuke: "God is free to reprobate whom he pleases, the same way he also elects those he wishes, according to his counsel and his pure goodness. That teaching will be condemned by many lunatics whose venomous tongues are sharpened against God to spew their blasphemies."[29] The same attitude behind this objection lurks behind the objection to the scriptural doctrine of Hell as well.

Just as God owes grace to nobody, He owes election to nobody. He is just when He sovereignly withholds it from the reprobate. Peter Martyr Vermigli wrote: "God does no injury to anyone, although he does not bestow mercy on some, for he is not bound to any man by any law, nor is he compelled by duty to have mercy on anyone."[30] He has mercy on whomever He pleases to have mercy on.

Those who offer this objection are in no place to do so. We are guilty sinners. D. A. Carson succinctly said, "The horribleness of the so-called *decretum horribile* largely disappears if men remain responsible for their sin and choice."[31] God would have been absolutely just if He had reprobated everyone. The wonder is not that He reprobated some but that He elected any. In the famous words of C. H. Spurgeon: "I am not at all surprised that God hated Esau, but I am greatly amazed that God loved Jacob." Nobody deserves election; we all

---

29 John Calvin, *Sermons on Genesis, Chapters 1:1–11:4* (Edinburgh: Banner of Truth, 2009), 797–98.
30 Vermigli, *The Peter Martyr Library*, 8:24.
31 D. A. Carson, *Divine Sovereignty and Human Responsibility* (Atlanta: John Knox, 1981), 197. This is a virtual quotation from Joseph Bellamy, *The Works of the Rev. Joseph Bellamy, D.D.* (New York: 1811), 2:197.

deserve reprobation. The least of God's mercies are not deserved by the best of sinners, as Jacob learned (Genesis 32:10).[32]

I would ask the objector: Was it unfair of God not to elect Satan? Or the demons? Why not? They are greater sinners than humans only in quantity, not quality. And surely nobody but Origen and other heretics think that God actually elected the Devil.

John Wesley called reprobation a "cloven foot" of the Devil,[33] and other Arminians have considered it devilish and satanic. Actually, the objection itself is devilish, for the Devil hates reprobation because he knows he is reprobate (see Revelation 12:12 and chapter 49, "The Election of Angels"). Satan and unredeemed sinners despise God precisely for His sovereignty, and this is displayed in their antipathy to both election and reprobation. Those in Hell hate it even though they know they are reprobate. God could have said, "Michael I have loved, but Lucifer I have hated."

Homer Hoeksema was right: "God is *a priori* irreprehensible" in both election and reprobation.[34] He is beyond reproach.

Augustine echoed Paul in Romans 9 and presaged later believers in the doctrine of reprobation. Hear his wise words: "Nor was God unjust in not willing to save them, since they could have been saved had they wished."[35] Remember, the reprobate never wish to be saved. Their unwillingness renders them without excuse and without a foundation to blame God for their reprobation. God would indeed have been unjust to reprobate anyone who was willing to believe, but He was under no obligation to elect those who only theoretically might have believed (Matthew 11:21–24). Then Augustine added: "Who but a fool would think God is unfair whether he passes adverse judgment on one who deserves it or shows mercy to one who is unworthy?"[36] A few words later he commented on Romans 9:20 vis-à-vis reprobation: "God's judgment [. . .] is so just that, even if nobody were to be released from that condemnation, nobody would have any right to criticize God's justice."[37]

---

32 C. H. Spurgeon, *An All-Round Ministry* (London: Banner of Truth, 1960), 289.

33 Quoted by John Gill in his debate with Wesley, *Sermons and Tracts*, 2nd edition (Streamwood: Primitive Baptist Library, 1981), 3:119.

34 Homer Hoeksema, *The Voice of Our Fathers* (Grand Rapids: Reformed Free Publishing Association, 1980), 242.

35 Augustine, *Works*, I/8:327.

36 Augustine, *Works*, I/8:330.

37 Augustine, I/8:331.

Conclusion

We must not blame God but rather thank God if we know we are elect. We must examine ourselves to be sure (2 Corinthians 13:5). We can biblically discover if we are elect (2 Peter 1:10), but no man can know if he is reprobate, for he may be an elect who is not yet converted. The Bremen Consensus of 1595 gave us this wise caution:

> One also ought not to be precipitant in accounting someone to be among the reprobate, unless until the close of his life and till death he persists in obstinate wickedness and a stiff-necked spirit and finally shows himself to be a blasphemer, enemy, or scorner of God and of His Holy Word.[38]

There is something spiritually challenging, even disturbing, about this sobering doctrine. It challenges our flippancy and lethargy. "What if I am one of the reprobate?" This is why John Calvin called it a "dreadful decree." It can keep us awake at night. William Cowper often worried that he was one of the reprobate. It strikes a holy fear in our hearts. It disturbs our apathy.

Homer Hoeksema spoke soberly:

> One can surely never think or speak of reprobation, whether it be the reprobation of himself or of his fellow man, coldly. And the terror of reprobation is increased when we remember that according to the Reformed view, the view of Scripture, reprobation is sovereign, unchangeable, inflexible. [. . .] Reprobation is indeed terrible to contemplate. As terrible to contemplate it is, as the grace of election is wonderful.[39]

When we feel the power of this doctrine on our soul, we should flee to Christ for the comforting assurance of grace and election. None of the reprobate will ever believe. If we believe, that is proof we are not reprobate.

---

38 In James T. Dennison Jr., ed., *Reformed Confessions of the 16th and 17th Centuries in English Translation* (Grand Rapids: Reformation Heritage Books, 2012), 3:673.
39 Hoeksema, *The Voice of Our Fathers*, 254.

Chapter 45
The Hardening of the Reprobate

God elected some sinners in eternity and works in their hearts in time to regenerate them to prepare them for Heaven. But God also reprobated others in eternity and hardens their hearts in time to prepare them for Hell. In one sense, God merely leaves them with the hard, sinful hearts in which they were born. But there is a further hardening — a double hardening, as it were — that God does in the reprobate. The Westminster Confession sums it up:

> As for those wicked and ungodly men, whom God as a righteous judge, for former sins, doth blind and harden, from them he not only withholdeth his grace, whereby they might have been enlightened in their understandings, and wrought upon in their hearts; but sometimes also withdraweth the gifts which they had, and exposeth them to such objects as their corruption makes occasion of sin; and withal, gives them over to their own lusts, the temptations of the world, and the power of Satan: whereby it comes to pass, that they harden themselves, even under those means which God useth for the softening of others (5:6).

God Blinds Their Minds

We have seen that all sinners are born spiritually blind and need eyesight and not merely eyeglasses. The Bible says there is a further blindness that God imposes on the non-elect. Some call it *judicial blinding*. Isaiah 6:9–10 are the crucial verses. Isaiah saw God in Heaven, confessed his sin, and was cleansed. God commissioned him to go back and preach. But note the sobering words: "Keep on hearing, but do not understand; keep on seeing, but do not perceive. Make the heart of this people dull, and their ears heavy, and shut their eyes; lest they see with their eyes, and hear with their ears, and understand with their heart, and return and be healed."

Isaiah 44:18 records how this came to pass: "They do not know nor understand; for He has shut their eyes, so they cannot see, and their hearts, so they cannot understand." The people become like their dead idols, which have eyes and ears but cannot see or hear (Psalm 115:4–8). This is poetic justice and existential irony. God made man in His image (Genesis 1:26), but fallen man makes gods in his image, idols that can neither see nor hear. Fallen sinners are as spiritually lifeless as the stump of wood of their idols. They are as blind as a statue.

The prophecy of Isaiah 6:9–10 is quoted in John 12:39–40. First, John says in verses 37–38 that this is the fulfillment of Isaiah 53:1. The Jews remained spiritually blind and deaf even when their promised Messiah was right in front of them doing miracles. John explains why they did not believe: "They could not believe" because God blinded their eyes and hardened their hearts. Note the cause-and-effect order. The cause: God's blinding and hardening. The effect: They were blind, hardened, and unable to believe. The purpose: "Lest they should see with their eyes, lest they should understand with their hearts and turn, so that I should heal them."

It does not say that they themselves shut their eyes and hardened their hearts. The action was neither active nor reflexive (middle voice) on their part. Rather, God is the subject, and they are the object. God did this for a purpose, as Calvin explained:

> Observe that God directs his voice to them but in order that they may be even more deaf; he kindles a light but that they may be even more blind; he sets forth doctrine but that they may grow even more stupid; he employs a remedy but so that they may not be healed.[1]

In his commentary he applies this to others: "He will strike the ungodly with stupidity and dizziness that he may take vengeance on their malice. [. . .] He intends that his Word to be a punishment to the reprobate that it may make their blindness worse and plunge them in deeper darkness."[2] This explains the spiritual blindness of the Pharisees in John 9 as well as the judicial blindness on all other reprobates who reject Christ, the Light of the World.

Blinded Reprobates

God creates humans with good, poor, or no eyesight (Exodus 4:11). He does something similar in the spiritual realm as well. He actually does something to prevent the reprobate from spiritually seeing. He prevents them from believing and repenting. Of course, they are quite pleased to stay that way, for they love their sinful darkness (John 3:19). They call light darkness and darkness light

---

1 John Calvin, *Institutes of the Christian Religion* (Philadelphia: Westminster, 1960), 3:24:13 (p. 980).
2 John Calvin, *The Gospel According to St. John 11–21 and the First Epistle of John* (Grand Rapids: Eerdmans, 1979), 2:46–47.

(Isaiah 5:20). It is not that they yearn for spiritual light — indeed, they scorn and reject it.

The verses in Isaiah 6 are quoted by Christ in Matthew 13:14–15 (same as Mark 4:12 and Luke 8:10). Jesus says in verses 11 and 16 that it had been sovereignly given to the disciples to believe. This had not been given to others. This is why He spoke in parables (v. 13). Christ used parables to give sight to some and to blind others. The word of God in the gospel does that today. It enlightens and regenerates the elect, but it blinds and hardens the reprobate.

It is the same word that accomplishes both actions and purposes (Isaiah 55:11). It softens some, hardens others. Second Corinthians 2:15–16 says the gospel saves those who are being saved and condemns those who are being lost. It is a sweet aroma of life to the elect, but a foul odor of death to the reprobate. At first even the elect are repelled by it, for they are born in the same sinful state as the non-elect (Ephesians 2:3). God not only opens the eyes and ears of the heart of the elect but also opens their spiritual noses, as it were. They smell the sweet aroma of the beauty of Jesus Christ and are irresistibly drawn to Him. But the reprobate hate it more each time they hear it. This may be illustrated by the two thieves who were crucified next to Christ — they typify believers and unbelievers, the elect and the reprobate (Luke 23:39–43).

Paul quoted Isaiah 6:9–10 in Acts 28:26–27 to explain why some of his Jewish hearers believed and some did not (v. 24). Preachers today can take note of this as the same reason why some people in their church do not believe even after hearing hundreds of accurate Bible expositions. They are spiritually blind and deaf. If they are not elect, God has been using those messages to confirm their reprobation and harden their hearts.

Blinded Minds and Hearts

Romans 11:8–10 quotes Isaiah 29:10 to the same effect. Note the context of the quotation. Isaiah 49:9 says, "Pause and wonder! Blind yourselves and be blind!" Then verse 10: "For the Lord has poured out on you the spirit of deep sleep, and has closed your eyes, namely, the prophets; and He has covered your head, namely, the seers." God blinded their false prophets who preached lies that the people believed, resulting in their blindness. They blinded themselves as the result of God blinding them through the blind prophets. Romans 11:8 then applies it to Paul's day: "God has given them a spirit of stupor." Therefore, they are stupid. They are blind men leading other blind men into the ditch of Hell (Matthew 15:14).

Then Paul quotes Psalm 69:22–23. God sets a snare and a trap for certain sinners and lays a stumbling block before them. The New Testament often says that Christ is that stumbling block of offense (Romans 9:32–33; 1 Corinthians 1:23; 1 Peter 2:8). He is a stepping stone for the elect but a stumbling block to the non-elect. The elect are set free, but the non-elect are ensnared and entrapped.

Paul indirectly alludes to Deuteronomy 29:4, "The Lord has not given you a heart to perceive and eyes to see and ears to hear, to this very day." Paul, John, and Jesus applied the inspired words of Isaiah, David, and Moses to the unbelieving Jews in their day. We can apply the words of all these speakers to unbelievers in our own day. They apply to the reprobate of all ages.

God Hardens the Hearts of the Reprobate

God not only blinds their minds but hardens their hearts. Deuteronomy 2:30 says, "The Lord your God hardened [Sihon's] spirit and made his heart obstinate." Why? "That He might deliver him into your hand, as it is today." God hardened Sihon's heart to prepare him for judgment at the hands of the Israelites. Subject: God. Object: Sihon. Purpose: Punishment. This happens with all the reprobate.

Similar to this is Joshua 11:20. In previous verses we are told that Joshua was successful in his exploits. Why? Because God hardened the hearts of the Canaanites for two purposes: "that they might receive no mercy, but that He might destroy them." This is a type of God's hardening the hearts of the non-elect so that they do not receive mercy but are prepared for destruction (Romans 9:22).

The Case of Pharaoh

Romans 9 is the clearest chapter in the entire Bible on the doctrine of reprobation. It is also the clearest chapter on the hardening of the reprobate. Paul uses the case of Pharaoh to illustrate what God does to all the non-elect.

Let us first do a brief survey of what the Bible teaches about hard hearts in general. Sinners have a hard spirit (Deuteronomy 2:30); hard faces (Jeremiah 5:3); hardened or stiff necks (Exodus 32:9; 33:3, 5; 2 Kings 17:14; Nehemiah 9:16–17, 29; Jeremiah 7:26; 17:23; 19:15; Deuteronomy 10:16; Acts 7:51; Proverbs 29:1; 2 Chronicles 30:8; 36:13, etc.); and "hard hearts" (Matthew 19:8; Mark 3:5; 6:52; 10:5; 16:14; Romans 2:5, etc.). We have spiritual cardiac sclerosis — hardening of the heart. Sinners are "hardened through the deceitfulness of sin" (Hebrews

3:13). We are stubborn, impudent, and hard-hearted (Ezekiel 2:4; 3:7). We have both stiff necks and hard hearts, like Zedekiah in 2 Chronicles 36:13. God warns us: "Do not harden your hearts" (Psalm 95:8; Deuteronomy 15:7; Hebrews 3:8; 4:7).

This hardness of heart is what we Calvinists call *total depravity* and *spiritual inability*. Natural man can no more have a tender heart than a stone can feel compassion. Our hearts are as hard as granite toward God. God must replace our heart of stone with a heart of flesh in regeneration (Ezekiel 36:26).

Now let us examine Pharaoh. The Bible says that God hardened his heart and that Pharaoh hardened his own heart. This is more than the naturally hard heart that he was born with, but the result of hearing God's word through Moses. Which came first — God or Pharaoh hardening the heart?

One novel theory was put forth by Roger T. Forster and V. Paul Marston in their book *God's Strategy in Human History*.[3] They argue that the Hebrew word for *hardening* in Exodus could be translated "strengthened," as it is elsewhere. Joshua 11:20 would then mean "God gave the Canaanites courage to resist when all was lost." Thus, God emboldened and encouraged Pharaoh's heart so that he had courage to stand firm in the face of terrifying miracles. God actually helped Pharaoh in mercy, not judged him. But Pharaoh misused this assistance.

This strange theory is not difficult to refute. We grant that the word *chazaq* occasionally can mean *strengthen* in a good sense. But in many other places it clearly means *harden* in a bad sense. No major translation of those places renders it as "strengthen." Also, Pharaoh did this to himself. Are we to believe that he strengthened himself in a good sense while directly opposing God? Quite the contrary. It would be more appropriate to suggest that God strengthened Moses, not Pharaoh. Furthermore, Romans 9:18 uses a Greek word that is almost universally translated as *hardened* in a bad sense rather than *strengthened* in a good sense. The Calvinist is likely to echo the words of F. F. Bruce in his foreword to Forster and Marston's book. Confessing to be an "impenitent Augustinian," he writes: "This is not to say I am convinced by all their arguments; perhaps my heart, like Pharaoh's, has been 'strengthened.'"[4]

---

3 Roger T. Forster and V. Paul Marston , *God's Strategy in Human History* (Wheaton: Tyndale, 1973), 70–75, 155–75. Other Arminians have held to this theory: Jerry L. Walls and Joseph R. Dongell, *Why I Am Not a Calvinist* (Downers Grove, IL: InterVarsity, 2004), 89; Dave Hunt, *What Love Is This?* 3rd Edition (Bend, OR: The Berean Call, 2006), 334–35; Dave Hunt, in Dave Hunt and James White, *Debating Calvinism* (Sisters, OR: Multnomah, 2004), 105–06.
4 Forster and Marston, *God's Strategy in Human History*, vii–viii.

Arminians frequently argue that Pharaoh first hardened his own heart before God did so (Exodus 8:15, then 8:32; 9:34). They conclude that God hardened Pharaoh's heart as a response (Exodus 9:12; 10:20, 27; 11:10; 14:8). But we need to point out some places they fail to notice. For one, Exodus 7:13 and 7:22 say Pharaoh's heart "grew hard." This could be a passive effect caused by another, not a reflexive act done by oneself. And this preceded 8:15 where he hardened his own heart. See also 8:19, 9:7, and 9:35. More decisive is the Lord's word before Moses even confronted Pharaoh: "I will harden his heart" (7:3; see 14:4). In 14:17 God also promised to harden the hearts of the rest of the Egyptians, who responded by hardening their hearts.

The conclusion, then, is that God initiated the hardening, and Pharaoh responded with self-hardening, not vice versa as Arminians contend. This is a type of God's hardening all other reprobates. In 1 Samuel 6:6 God asked Israel: "Why then do you harden your hearts as the Egyptians and Pharaoh hardened their hearts?" The hardening of Romans 9 is parallel with the potter and clay model, in which the potter is active, and the clay is passive.

God Gives the Reprobate Over

God restrains some sin (Genesis 20:6; 1 Samuel 25:26, 34). He is under no compulsion to do so in every case. He also takes the restraints off, and we sin. In this God is just, and we are culpable.

Several places speak of God "giving over" men to sin (Psalm 81:11–12; Acts 7:42; Romans 1:24, 26, 28). He permits them to go their own way (Acts 14:16). He temporarily does this in the elect before their conversion but permanently does this in the non-elect. Calvin put it like this: "The others, whom he, in his righteous judgment, passes over, waste away in their own rottenness until they are consumed."[5]

God Withholds Grace from Them

Romans 11:8 quotes Deuteronomy 29:4 to prove the hardening of the reprobate: "Yet the Lord has not given you a heart to perceive and eyes to see and ears to hear, to this very day." He gives blindness by withholding sight. The reprobate do not deserve it, nor do they ask for sight. God therefore is not unjust to withhold it from them. Even the elect do not deserve it. God withholds the

---

5 Calvin, *Institutes*, 2:5:4 (p. 320).

effectual means of sight and salvation from the reprobate for the simple reason that He did not choose them for salvation.

Saving grace is irresistible. The withholding of grace produces a hardening that is also irresistible. The non-elect not only do not resist this hardening, they welcome it.

Joshua 11:20 states that God hardened certain people so that they would receive no mercy. God withheld softening saving grace from them. In Matthew 11:25, Jesus praised the Father for hiding spiritual illumination from some sinners (cf. Job 17:4). In fact, God even takes away what light and sight they had by nature (Matthew 13:12; 25:29). Special revelation enlightens the elect but further blinds the reprobate and removes some of the light of general revelation from them. They are thus doubly blind. The reprobate who rejects the gospel is worse than before he ever heard it — worse than those who never hear it. His sin is compounded, and his reprobation is confirmed in this life.

Augustine wrote: "Thus he imposes nothing whereby a person may become worse, but nothing is given to the person whereby he may become better."[6] Also, "He hardened certain sinners because he does not have mercy on them, not because he forces them to sin."[7] Divine hardening does not make God the author of sin. Jerome Zanchius said, "Now, if it was the will of God in time to refuse them this grace, it must have been His will from eternity, since His will is, as Himself, the same yesterday, today, and forever."[8] Hardening in time is the outcome of reprobation in eternity. Jonathan Edwards: "God makes wicked men in no other sense than he creates darkness, which is not by any positive effecting, but only ordering by withholding light, for darkness is only a negative."[9] Augustine's theory of the origin of sin is apparent here. William Lyford, Puritan, said that God hardens "by not showing mercy, as in the winter by the absence of the sun, the natural coldness of the air and earth causes frost and ice."[10]

God Turns Their Hearts

Proverbs 21:1 says, "The king's heart is in the hand of the Lord, like rivers of

---

6 Augustine, *The Works of Saint Augustine* (Hyde Park: New City, 2008), I/12:197.

7 Augustine, I/12:198.

8 Jerome Zanchius, *The Doctrine of Absolute Predestination* (Grand Rapids: Baker, 1977), 105.

9 Jonathan Edwards, *The Works of Jonathan Edwards* (New Haven: Yale University Press, 2006), 24:561.

10 William Lyford, *The Instructed Christian* (Morgan, PA: Soli Deo Gloria, n.d.), 106.

water; He turns it wherever He wishes." He did so in Egypt. He turned the heart of Prince Moses to serve God, but He also turned the heart of Pharaoh to disobey the Lord. Psalm 105:25 applied this to the earlier Egyptians: "He turned their heart to hate His people." The reprobate hate God's people because they hate God. This is because God sovereignly gave them over and turned their hearts in this direction. Yet in it all, God is sovereign, holy, and just, while they are responsible and guilty.

God not only withholds grace and mercy, He sovereignly permits the entrance of sin and unbelief into the hearts of the reprobate. We saw this regarding the origin of sin and the problem of evil. This is more than just "giving them over." Revelation 17:17 is sobering: "For God has put it into their hearts to fulfill His purpose, to be of one mind, and to give their kingdom to the beast, until the words of God are fulfilled." What is true eschatologically is also true experientially in all the reprobate. God puts it into their hearts to give the personal allegiance of their heart over to Satan to be their king and to be of one mind with him. This fulfills God's purpose of condemnation according to reprobation.

This is also seen in 2 Thessalonians 2:11–12, another prophecy of the Man of Sin who is usually identified with the Beast of Revelation 17. God sends some sinners "a strong delusion, that they should believe the lie, that they all may be condemned who did not believe the truth but had pleasure in unrighteousness." God gives the reprobate enough rope to hang themselves. And they do it willingly.

God Uses Satan and Demons

Satan is God's Devil. God righteously turns the reprobate over to Satan and allows the Devil and demons to have a damning influence in the hearts of the reprobate. Peter Martyr Vermigli said, "God often sends thoughts and offers occasions, by himself or by evil angels, which would be for the best if we were righteous, but since we are not renewed, they drive us to evil, and afterwards, damnation for sin follows, justly and righteously."[11] Calvin ties in the "giving over" principle to the reprobate and Satan: "So by His righteous judgment He gives up to a reprobate mind (Romans 1:28) those whom He has appointed to destruction, so that they may as though hypnotized hand themselves over to be

---

11 Peter Martyr Vermigli, *The Peter Martyr Library* (Kirksville, MO: Truman State University Press, 2003), 8:53.

deceived by Satan and his ministers with their eyes tight shut and their mind devoid of reason."[12]

This is seen, for instance, in Judges 9:23–24, 1 Samuel 16:14, 1 Kings 22:19–23, and 2 Chronicles 18:18–22. In each case God sent an evil spirit to deceive certain persons so their sin would increase and thereby hasten their judgment. Note 2 Chronicles 18:22 in particular: "The Lord has put a lying spirit in the mouth of those prophets of yours, and the Lord has declared disaster upon you." God still uses not only Satan and demons but also false teachers, preachers, and theologians to this effect today (2 Corinthians 11:14–15). All in all, God is First Cause using sinful second causes in such a way that He is not the author of sin.

This hardening is not always demon-possession. Sinners are already possessed by the Devil as slaves. God leaves the reprobate in that state and grants Satan greater power over them. The Devil exercises increasing evil dominion over the non-elect by taking away the seed of the gospel (Matthew 13:19), binding their minds further (2 Corinthians 4:4), and deceiving them with lies (John 8:44) and false prophets (1 John 4:1) as he leads them merrily to perdition. Jesus the Good Shepherd leads His sheep to Heaven. Satan is the Great Butcher who leads his flock of goats to Hell.

John Calvin observed: "God himself is said to harden and blind, when he gives men to be blinded by Satan, who is the minister and executioner of his wrath."[13] The Bohemian Confession (1575/1609) put it this way: "However, among all of God's punishments in this life, the greatest is when God punishes sin with sin."[14] Lest we be misunderstood, Calvinists categorically emphasize that God does no injustice to the reprobate nor approve of their sin. He remains absolutely just, and they remain responsible and guilty, as do Satan and the demons, who are also reprobate.

Conclusion

What is all this leading to? Twice in Joshua 11:20 we are told why God hardens hearts in this way: "that He might utterly destroy them." God does this in the non-elect "because the Lord desired to kill them" (1 Samuel 2:25). God is

---

12 John Calvin, *The Epistles of Paul the Apostle to the Romans and to the Thessalonians* (Grand Rapids: Eerdmans, 1980), 407.

13 John Calvin, *Commentary on the Book of the Prophet Isaiah* (Grand Rapids: Eerdmans, 1956), 4:356.

14 In James T. Dennison Jr., ed., *Reformed Confessions of the 16th and 17th Centuries in English Translation* (Grand Rapids: Reformation Heritage Books, 2012), 3:415.

fattening up the reprobate swine for the slaughter (see especially 2 Peter 2:12, 22). He is letting them have their fill of sin so that He will be glorified in punishing them in Hell one day. God is now allowing them to fill up their cup of sin (Genesis 15:16; Matthew 23:32; 1 Thessalonians 2:16). When they are full, judgment will come.

If God works all things for good to those who love Him and are called according to His purpose (Romans 8:28), then God also works all things for bad to those who hate Him and are not called according to His purpose. Even the good things that God gives the reprobate in this life by common grace redound to their future punishment in Hell (Luke 16:25). Good spiritual corn produces more fat for the slaughtered hogs.

It behooves all sinners to examine their heart to see if they be hardened in this way. Christ asks all of us, "Is your heart still hardened?" (Mark 8:17). Christ alone can unharden the heart of stone and give spiritual light and sight to the spiritually blind. To the one who willingly stays hardened, the Word of God gives this serious warning: "He who is often rebuked, and hardens his neck, will suddenly be destroyed, and that without remedy" (Proverbs 29:1; see 28:14).

Chapter 46
The Destiny of the Reprobate

Earlier we saw that the destination of the predestination of the elect is the glorification of God in the ocean of love in Heaven forever. That is their last link in the Golden Chain of Romans 8:29–30. But what about the Black Chain of Reprobation? Its first link was reprobation, its middle link is divine hardening, and the last link will be the glorification of God's wrath in their eternal conscious suffering in the Lake of Fire called Hell.

Hell Is Real

Hell is not a myth, for God Himself warns of myths (1 Timothy 1:4; Titus 1:14; 2 Peter 1:16). It is not a fable nor superstition nor a deceitful ruse to scare sinners into believing in Christ. It is the place of eternal torment for unrepentant demons and humans (Matthew 25:41). Only sinners go to Hell, and all who are in Hell are sinners. They receive the punishment we all deserve, the elect as well as the non-elect. Some persons sin more or in longer lives, so they will be punished more but not longer, for all suffer eternally (Luke 12:47–48). There are degrees of guilt and punishment but not of reprobation.

Souls of the lost are now suffering in Hades (Luke 16:23). After their resurrection in sin-infested bodies, they will be cast body and soul into eternal Gehenna (Matthew 10:28). It is perpetual and permanent. They are conscious and not asleep. There is no escape, mitigation of pain, Purgatory, reincarnation, or second chance. Hell's punishment is penal and punitive, not reformatory or medicinal. It is a "place of torment" (Luke 16:28), not a hospital or a school. There is no water there (Luke 16:24), only lava from the Lake of Fire. The tears of the damned cannot extinguish Hell's flames, for they are never quenched (Mark 9:43).

Christopher Love gave a good definition that represents historic Reformed theology:

> Hell is a place of torment ordained by God for devils and reprobate sinners wherein, by His justice, He confines them to everlasting

punishment, tormenting them both in body and soul, being deprived of God's favor, objects of His wrath under which they must lie to all eternity.[1]

Hell Is Eternal

The Bible clearly and repeatedly teaches that Hell is everlasting. Augustine taught it, and so have historic Catholicism, Lutheranism, and Arminianism. The Reformers, Puritans, Dutch Reformed, New England theologians, and Princetonians taught it. Jonathan Edwards taught it more clearly and in more penetrating depth than anyone before or since.[2] No orthodox Calvinist has taught universal salvation any more than universal election.

However, one or two otherwise orthodox Calvinists have toyed with the error of annihilationism. One was Arthur C. Custance in *The Sovereignty of Grace*, an exposition of the five points of Calvinism.[3] He questioned whether Hell is eternal. It does not appear that he committed himself to annihilationism, but he was tending in that direction. He argued that Christ suffered and appeased the infinite wrath of God in a finite period of time; therefore, it is possible for a sinner to suffer the wrath of God in a limited time and then be put into non-existence. Divine justice would be served, and there would then be only the elect in existence for eternity.

There are several serious flaws with this argument. It overlooks the vast difference between Christ and humans. Christ was sinless and divine; humans are neither. His suffering was propitiatory; those of the damned in Hell are not. Reprobates in Hell realize they are getting what they deserve, but Christ had no such realization for He was innocent (unless one holds to the heterodox error of John M'Leod Campbell and Thomas F. Torrance that Jesus somehow repented vicariously on the cross).[4] Christ suffered and died in His humanity, not His deity, for deity is both impassible and immortal. His pure deity gave infinite value to His suffering and death, thereby paying the infinite debt of

---

1 Christopher Love, *The Works of Christopher Love* (Morgan, PA: Soli Deo Gloria, 1995), 1:565.
2 See *The Torments of Hell: Jonathan Edwards on Eternal Damnation*, ed. by William Nichols. (Ames, IA: International Outreach, 2006). Also, Jonathan Edwards, *The Wrath of Almighty God* (Morgan, PA: Soli Deo Gloria, 2004).
3 Arthur C. Custance, *The Sovereignty of Grace* (Phillipsburg, NJ: P&R, 1979), 313–55. See also his *Journey Out of Time* (Brockville, Ontario: Doorway, 1987), 79–93; *The Seed of the Woman* (Brockville, Ontario: Doorway, 1980), 369–407; and *The Doorway Papers* (Grand Rapids: Zondervan, 1977), 6:45–49.
4 See Andrew Purves, *Exploring Christology and Atonement: Conversations with John McLeod Campbell, H. R. Mackintosh and T. F. Torrance* (Downers Grove, IL: InterVarsity, 2015).

the elect. Puritan Obadiah Grew pointed out that no mere human, even a sinless one, could pay such a debt, therefore they must suffer eternally in Hell.[5] Besides, they continue to sin and increase their debt and suffering. And if they actually could pay the debt, as Custance suggested, why are they annihilated? That would be like killing a prison inmate after he has served his sentence. Why would they not be released to Heaven? If so, then Hell becomes Purgatory. Rather, Hell is an eternal life sentence.

Hell Is Forever

There are many biblical proofs that Hell is both eternal and everlasting. First, the same Greek word *aionios* is used for both Heaven and Hell (Matthew 25:41, 46). Next, Revelation 14:10–11 uses the words "forever and ever" and "day and night." Thirdly, Luke 16 is clear that the rich man did not cease to exist in Hades. Revelation 19:20 says that the Beast and False Prophet will be sent to the Lake of Fire, and 20:10 says they are still there a thousand years later when the Devil and lost sinners join them there. The reprobate go to the same place as Satan and the demons (Matthew 25:41). They will share the same doom: "And they will be tormented day and night forever and ever" (Revelation 20:10). Nothing could be more explicit unless words lose their meaning.

Fifthly, *degrees of punishment* does not mean different lengths of time in Hell but rather degrees of intensity of pain. All suffer eternally, but some suffer more than others. The Bible nowhere suggests that some stay there shorter or longer than others. Next, annihilation would be a respite, not a punishment. It would be a mercy, but there is no mercy in Hell. God's wrath is poured out unmixed without any mercy whatsoever (Revelation 14:10; Luke 16:24). Remember, the reprobate were foreordained to receive wrath, not mercy (Romans 9:22). There is no love there either. Hell is an eternal echo of Hosea 9:15: "There I hated them. [. . .] I will love them no more."

Seventh, since the reprobate die in a state of unregenerate total depravity and spiritual inability, they will continue to sin forever. They will never repent or believe but will only continue in hatred of God and love of sin. Thomas Watson said, "As a sinner's heart will never be emptied of sin, so God's vial shall never be emptied of wrath."[6] Christopher Love: "If a wicked man could be fetched out of hell and brought back into a capacity of mercy, yet he would in a second

---

5 Obadiah Grew, *The Lord Our Righteousness* (Morgan, PA: Soli Deo Gloria, 2005), 8.
6 Thomas Watson, *Discourses on Important and Interesting Subjects* (Ligonier, PA: Soli Deo Gloria, 1990), 2:37. Also, *The Puritan Pulpit* (Morgan, PA: Soli Deo Gloria, 2004), 105.

life follow his lusts and sin himself into hell again."[7] Also, "Now, if there be continuous sinning in hell, you must continuously be punished in hell."[8] Hell never reforms anyone. It is not meant to. It does not do anyone good. It is only meant to do them pure justice.

Ninth, as Jonathan Edwards put it: "Now punishment can't be infinite in the degree of pain and misery, because a finite creature is not capable of it. Therefore "tis infinite in its continuance."[9] Infinite time is eternity. Edwards often used this biblical logic for a variety of purposes. Sin incurs infinite wrath, not because we are infinite or have an infinite number of sins but because sin is committed against an infinite and holy God. Since humans cannot suffer infinite pain, they must suffer pain in infinite duration.

The Bible frequently states that Hell is eternal. To apply Christ's words in John 14:2 to Hell, He could have said, "If it were not so, I would have told you." None spoke more boldly about eternal Hell than Jesus Christ.

The evangelical Arminian who believes in Hell sits on the horns of his own free will dilemma. If man always has libertarian free will and is able to repent, believe, and obey God when unconverted, then we ask if he would be able to use that free will in Hell and repent and believe? If he did, would not God be bound to release him? And if one sinner did that, why not all? Then Hell would be emptied. On that basis, Arminian Hell becomes Protestant Purgatory. Some ex-evangelical Arminians use this argument to teach universalism. Historic Calvinists deny it completely. This dilemma parallels the Arminian problem of those in Heaven conceivably using their free will to sin and be cast out of Heaven. Logically, such a view could have all in Heaven end up in Hell, and all in Hell end up in Heaven. But Luke 16:26 clearly says no one goes from either place to the other. Moreover, the Arminian dilemma only shows the fallacy of their error of conditional election and non-election. Reformed theology teaches unconditional election and reprobation and, therefore, permanent Heaven and Hell.

The Last Link in the Black Chain

The last link is not only damnation of the reprobate but the glory of God. It coincides with the last link in the Golden Chain. Both show the glory of God,

---

7 Christopher Love, *The Mischief of Sin* (Pittsburgh: Soli Deo Gloria, 1994), 57.
8 Christopher Love, *The Works of Christopher Love* (Morgan, PA: Soli Deo Gloria, 1995), 1:591.
9 Jonathan Edwards, *The Works of Jonathan Edwards* (New Haven: Yale University Press, 1997), 14:188.

for God foreordained everything for the display of His own glory (Romans 11:36).

God will be glorified in the revelation of His glorious grace in the elect (Ephesians 1:6). Conversely, He will be glorified in His wrath in the non-elect (Romans 9:22). If either elect or non-elect ceased to exist, God's plan of predestination would fail (perish the thought!), and God would be robbed of His glory. But just as God does not give His glory to idols (Isaiah 42:8; 48:11), He does not allow the reprobate to steal His glory in the end. The annihilationist heresy would do that by giving the damned one last hate-filled wish: "At least I will cheat God out of the glory of punishing me forever." But it will never be.

It is no coincidence that Arthur C. Custance also denied double predestination. He said that election is eternal and unconditional, but reprobation is conditioned by man in time.[10] Reprobation was based on foreseen unbelief. This is a quasi-Arminian theory that in some respects sounds Amyraldian. A weakened view of reprobation goes together with a weakened view of eternal Hell. For example, Arminians are far more likely to deny Hell than historic Calvinists are.

They fail to see that God is glorified in both election to Heaven and reprobation to Hell. If, for the sake of argument, we suppose that election and Heaven alone glorify God, then we are forced to blaspheme God's wisdom in choosing only some and not all men. It faults God with ordaining a system that does not produce maximum glory. But God displays His wisdom as well as His glory, grace, and wrath in the dual destinies of mankind.

If God elected all, where would be the glory of His wrath? If He reprobated all, where would be the revelation of His grace? The reprobate were foreordained to glorify divine power and wrath. As Edwards put it in soul-sobering words: "Wicked men answer the ends of their beings in no other way but in their suffering."[11] They are only valuable as fuel for the fires of Hell, whose light and heat eternally display the glorious wrath and power of God Almighty.

How the Reprobate Glorify God in Hell

God will love the elect forever and hate the reprobate forever. The elect will love God forever, and the reprobate will hate God forever. One will be confirmed in permanent holiness, the other in permanent unholiness (Revelation 22:11). How then do the reprobate glorify God in their sinful state?

---

10 Custance, *The Sovereignty of Grace*, 143.
11 In John Gerstner, *Unless You Repent* (Orlando: Soli Deo Gloria, 2005), 55.

Philippians 2:5–11 says that Christ will be rewarded for His Messianic obedience and atonement by having all men everywhere kneel and acknowledge that He is Lord. Every reprobate mouth will be shut so that no further excuses can be given (Matthew 7:22). Instead, the reprobate will use their tongues to confess that they are getting what they deserve (cf. Luke 23:41) and that Christ is Lord. Since they will know they have been reprobated justly, they will be forced to acknowledge that God was just not only to damn them but to reprobate them. The elect will have only God to thank for their election; the non-elect will have only themselves to blame for the reprobation. Justice will be served at last. This glorifies God.

Men glorify God in the manner appropriate to the revelation of divine glory. The elect, for example, glorify God in love as the reflection of divine love, including electing love. Likewise, the reprobate will reflect back to God "in kind" and appropriately to the revelation of His wrath and hatred their groans and self-cursing. That will glorify God's justice.

The elect will read their names in the Book of Life and rejoice (Luke 10:20). The reprobate will read their names in the Book of Death and shudder in anguish and agony. Then the Black Chain of Reprobation, as it were, will bind them hand and foot more tightly than the chains and fetters that enveloped Jacob Marley in Dickens's *A Christmas Carol*. Thus bound, they will be cast body and soul into the Lake of Fire to begin an eternal sentence of glorifying God in their punishment (Matthew 22:13).

It is vital to see that God is both glorified in Hell in wrath as He is in Heaven in grace. Calvin said, "The pious mind realizes that the punishment of the impious and wicked and the reward of life eternal for the righteous equally pertain to God's glory."[12] Will the reprobate realize this? Indeed they will, as Jonathan Edwards pointed out: "And as the damned have such manifestations of God's hatred, so they know that he never intends them any mercy; they know that he hates them with an eternal hatred. God's eternal decrees are now made known to them."[13]

But even that will not move them to repent. God gives no gift of repentance to anyone in Hell. The reprobate will not regret sinning, but they will regret the extra punishment that each sin brought to them. In the chilling words of Jonathan Edwards: "The damned in Hell would be ready to give worlds if they

---

12 John Calvin, *Institutes of the Christian Religion* (Philadelphia: Westminster, 1960), 1:2:2 (p. 43).

13 Edwards, *The Torments of Hell*, 212.

could to have the number of their sins to have been one less."[14] And since they die totally depraved in all parts of their being, every part of their being will be tormented with the fire of divine wrath forever. And thus, with poetic justice and theological irony, they glorify God in their whole being.

The Glory of God's Wrath

Romans 9:17 says that God will be glorified in the display of His power in the non-elect. God will, of course, be glorified in the irresistibility of His grace in the elect, and this will continue into eternity. The non-elect will be the recipients of divine power in another and converse way. First, they were irresistibly hardened by God in this life. Second, they will suffer irresistibly in Hell. They will be helpless to resist. Furthermore, they will be forced by divine power to kneel and confess that Jesus Christ is Lord.

Such glory also includes the glory of God's wrath on the predestined "vessels of wrath" (Romans 9:22). God did not foreordain the elect to wrath, but He most certainly did foreordain the non-elect to wrath (1 Thessalonians 5:9). They will actually, internally, existentially, and eternally receive the holy wrath of God into their very beings, like heat transferred into a red-hot poker. This is the "dishonorable use" for which they were predestined by the great Potter (Romans 9:21). Wrath is poured into the hearts of the non-elect in a converse manner as the love of God is poured into the hearts of the elect (Romans 5:5). They drink the cup of God's wrath in full strength, not diluted with even a single drop of common grace (Revelation 14:10; Psalm 75:8; Jeremiah 25:15).

This is according to Proverbs 16:4, "The Lord has made all for Himself, even the wicked for the day of doom." God foreordained the wicked reprobate for doomsday to glorify Himself by their receiving wrath for their sins.

An objection may be raised: Does not the Bible say that God has no pleasure in the death of a sinner? (Ezekiel 33:11). Yes, indeed. This has to do with the revealed will of God, not the secret will. Also, even in the secret will we say that God reveals glory and wrath but receives no positive pleasure in it. There is no joy in wrath. God is not a sadist. Satan is the celestial sadist, not God. God receives pleasure in the glorified elect and smiles on them forever. But He is glorified with an angry countenance toward the non-elect. The elect rejoice

---

14 Jonathan Edwards, *The Puritan Pulpit: Jonathan Edwards* (Morgan, PA: Soli Deo Gloria, 2004), 109. After millions of years in Hell, sinners will wish to be turned into nothing or even into toads and serpents rather than stay humans. "Ezekiel 8:8 (Sermon 477)," Jonathan Edwards Center at Yale University, accessed February 9, 2018, http://edwards.yale.edu/.

at God's smile, but the reprobate are terrified in tears as they forever behold the angry countenance of God's wrath (Revelation 6:16; 14:10). The elect enjoy the beatific vision — the vision of God that brings exquisite bliss — while the reprobate suffer the agonizing vision that brings torment.

The final links of the two chains of predestination, then, are not merely the happiness of the elect or the torment of the reprobate. The final goal is the glory of God revealed and reflected back. In this sense, Psalm 145:10 says, "All Your works shall praise You, O Lord."

The Echo of Glory

There is an eschatological *echo of glory* in eternity, as it were. The glory revealed to the elect and non-elect will complement each other. It has to do with how they see each other from Heaven and Hell to the glory of God.

It will surprise many Christians (and anger non-Christians) to read the several places in the Bible that tell us that both see each other in the next life and respond accordingly. The saints in Heaven will praise God as they view the damned in Hell. Revelation 15:3 says they will sing the Song of Moses, which the Israelites sang as they worshiped God for drowning Pharaoh and the Egyptians in the Red Sea (Exodus 15:1–21). They even danced with tambourines (v. 20). This is a type of the elect glorifying God as they see the reprobate who were typified by Pharaoh (Romans 9:17).

Isaiah 66:24 is quoted by Jesus in Mark 9:44 to refer to Hell. The first part of the verse says, "And they shall go forth and look upon the corpses of the men who have transgressed against Me." The elect will view the corpses of the reprobate at the Second Coming and later see their resurrected bodies at Judgment Day enter eternal fire. This will all cause the elect to glorify God. It may be compared with the Allies who celebrated the fall of the Axis powers at the end of World War II.

Revelation 19:1–7 records the heavenly scene in which both angels and saints witness the destruction of Mystery Babylon, Satan's evil empire. They shout and sing, "Amen! Hallelujah!" That kingdom consists of all reprobate humans and demons. This chorus will doubtlessly be repeated at Judgment Day. Psalm 52:6: "The righteous also shall see and fear; and shall laugh," just as God Himself will have the last laugh on unrepentant sinners who laugh at Him (Psalms 2:4; 37:13; 59:8; Proverbs 1:26). Proverbs 11:10: "When the wicked perish, there is jubilation." This will be the prophetic fulfillment of the imprecatory psalms.

Calvin cautioned us to wait until then, for we are still sinners though saints and would be tempted to gloat sinfully rather than glorify God righteously.[15] We should now grieve like Christ (Luke 19:41), not gloat. In Heaven, however, there will be no such sinful temptation. The elect will see the reprobate as God sees them: evil, totally degenerate, Hell-deserving sinners. We will share God's holy attitude of wrath.

This will have a humbling effect on the elect, as if they say, "There but for electing grace go I." The great Puritan Jeremiah Burroughs briefly explained that the elect in Heaven will have their hearts inflamed in love to God as they eternally behold the damned reprobate in Hell. This particularly displays "the top of His grace."[16] The reprobate will thus be an eternal reminder to the elect of what God saved them from.

The converse is true with the reprobate in Hell as they view the elect in Heaven. They will be moved to glorify God as they see the bride of Christ adorned with grace and holiness. This does not mean they will envy her or repent of their sins. Rather, they will hate her even as they hate God. The reprobate will acknowledge God's right to choose the elect. This will serve to vindicate the elect.

Conclusion

Our attitude toward these things should be God's attitude. We should not secretly wish it were not so, like the shallow statement, "I wish there was no such place as Hell." Are we wiser than God? Such an attitude implies, "I am holier than Thou, God." Christ glorified God for reprobating the non-elect and withholding grace from them (Matthew 11:25). We should humbly confess that God does all things well.

No man can know in this life that he is reprobate. But he can know that he is guilty and lost and deserves Hell. He will surely go there if he does not repent (Luke 13:3). Meditating on the destiny of the reprobate should cause each of us urgency to make our calling and election sure (2 Peter 1:10) by firmly believing in Jesus Christ.

Contemplating Hell warns the lost: "You may not glorify God now in faith, love, and obedience. But if you die lost, you will most assuredly glorify God in

---

15 John Calvin, *Sermons on the Book of Micah* (Phillipsburg, NJ: P&R, 2003), 411–13.

16 Jeremiah Burroughs, *Gospel Remission* (Morgan, PA: Soli Deo Gloria, 1995), 106.

your damnation." It is a fearful thing to fall into the hands of the living God (Hebrews 10:31).

Chapter 47
The Relation of Election and Reprobation

Having established the biblical teaching on election and reprobation, it remains for us to address a few less important questions.

Are the Elect and Reprobate in Any Way Related Now?

The elect are the family of God. The reprobate are the family of the Devil (John 8:44). But is there any overlap between spiritual and biological relationships? In brief, the Reformed position is that the elect and the reprobate are mixed together in the world, but it is not an even mixture. Jacob and Esau were twins; one was elect, and one was reprobate. The same was true with Abel and Cain, Isaac and Ishmael, Solomon and Absalom, and other brothers. God was not pleased to put the elect in separate biological families from the reprobate.

In fact, families are often divided like this (Matthew 10:35). It is rare to find a family in which all members are regenerate. Many whole families die lost, thereby confirming their reprobation. Yet even reprobate parents can have elect children, and elect parents can produce non-elect offspring. The Synod of Dort said that godly parents ought not to doubt the election of their children (1:17), at least their dying children. I respectfully disagree. That view could open the door to presumptive regeneration. Abraham Kuyper, for example, held that we ought to baptize our children on the assumption they are elect. To some Calvinists, that borders on baptismal regeneration. Instead, it would be wiser to assume our children are unregenerate and wait until they display marks of regeneration before baptizing them. The same applies to Communion. Some hyper-covenantalists practice paedo-Communion based on presuming that their children are regenerate and elect. But Scripture says that one must be able to examine himself (1 Corinthians 11:28), discern the Lord's body (1 Corinthians 11:29), and remember the Lord's death (1 Corinthians 11:24) to partake of Communion in a worthy way. Infants can do none of these.

Still, there is an interesting pattern to be noticed from a human perspective. Everything else being equal, children raised in a godly Christian family are more likely to become Christians than those raised in a non-Christian family. They are reared with Bible reading, prayer, and godly examples in their parents. When the elect meet in Heaven, there will be a large number of them who had been physically related on earth. I call these "clusters of the elect."

There is no "elect race" per se in which all or even most of its members are elect. Take Israel. God chose it as a special race (Deuteronomy 4:37), but that was no guarantee that all or even most Jews were elect. Indeed, most have not been elect down to the present day. True Jewish believers have always been a small remnant (Romans 11:5). They are an Israel within Israel (Romans 2:28–29; 9:6). This disproves the ultra-Pharisaic idea that all Jews were elect, and all Gentiles were non-elect.

There were elect persons, such as Enoch, prior to Abraham, the father of Israel. There were also some elect who were not physical Jews at the time of Abraham, such as Melchizedek and possibly Job. Other Gentile elect married into Israel, such as Ruth. Yet during the old covenant, far more of the elect were Israelites than Gentiles. But for the last two thousand years, very few physical Jews have been Christians and, therefore, elect. Romans 11 promises the day when God will move in a great way and a large number of Jews will become Christians.[1] "All Israel shall be saved" (v. 26). This does not mean every single Jew but probably a majority. We cannot say that this will tip the historical scales so that in the end converted Jews will have outnumbered unconverted Jews.

It has been a matter of debate whether Kuyper's views influenced certain persons in the South African Dutch Reformed Church to hold to a kind of "elect race" perspective underlying apartheid. Perhaps some Afrikaners once did, but that has been discredited and discarded. The same would go for any kind of white supremacy in America or Europe. Even the most ardent supporters of slavery in the Old South did not hold that most whites were elect.

Among Gentiles there has been a gradual development of Christianity as the gospel has gone worldwide. For most of the last twenty centuries, far more converted elect were to be found in Europe than the rest of the world combined. That has rapidly changed, first with America and then Africa, the Far East, and elsewhere. True Christianity is now a tiny minority in Europe. Perhaps there will one day be far more Christians in China or India than in Europe and America combined. Heaven will contain elect from every nationality and race (Revelation 5:9; 7:9).

---

1 See Iain H. Murray, *The Puritan Hope* (London: Banner of Truth, 1971).

If there has been no "elect race," there has also been no "reprobate race." The curse on Canaan (Genesis 9:25) was not placed on Africans but on Canaanites. But even so, there were some Canaanites such as Rahab and Uriah that proved their election by faith in the one true God. So, since God has mingled the elect in all races, we should preach the gospel to all people everywhere (Matthew 28:19–20; Mark 16:15; Luke 24:47; Acts 1:8).

Could They Have Been Reversed?

Could God have reversed the objects of election and reprobation? Could God have loved Esau and hated Jacob? Could God have chosen Judas and not Peter? In one sense, yes, for there was no higher law that dictated to God whom He must choose. Nor were there any qualifications or disqualifications in any member of the human race. Election was a free sovereign act of God.

God made the decision according to the wise counsel of His will (Ephesians 1:11). So, in this sense it could not have been otherwise, else the alternative would have been wiser than this one. This does not open the door to Middle Knowledge nor give credence to Gottfried Leibniz's idea that this is necessarily the best of all possible worlds.

This relates to the question: Could God have elected all and reprobated none or elected none and reprobated all? In one sense, yes, for He is sovereign and shows mercy on whom He will show mercy (Romans 9:15). After all, God chose none of the fallen angels. He could have elected all of them. He could have chosen Lucifer and not Michael. God could have chosen the entirety of humanity, but He did not. The Debrecen Synod of 1567 condemned *holopredestination* — that is, universal election. [2]

God chose some, not all. Why? It has to do with His ultimate purpose for which election and reprobation are proximate means. God foreordained everything to display His glory — the glory of grace to the elect and the glory of wrath to the non-elect. Hence, only some glory would have been revealed if He had chosen all or none. If all were elect, where would the glory of His wrath be? If all were reprobate, where would the glory of His grace be? [3] One must be careful not to insist that this necessitated that God had to elect and reprobate in this specific way. One wonders if He could wisely have done it in another unrevealed or unimagined way, but that would be the kind of futile

---

2 James T. Dennison Jr., ed., *Reformed Confessions of the 16th and 17th Centuries in English Translation* (Grand Rapids: Reformation Heritage Books, 2012), 3:41.
3 See Samuel Storms, *Chosen for Life*, 2nd ed. (Wheaton: Crossway, 2007), 184–97.

speculation that Calvin frequently warned against (see Deuteronomy 29:29). The truth seems to lie in the perfect harmony of the divine attributes within the divine Being. These attributes are revealed in foreordination, creation, salvation, and damnation. A different mixture of election and reprobation would indicate a different balance of divine attributes. This has obvious implications for the echo of glory mentioned in the previous chapter.

This takes us back to the unfathomable mystery of why God decreed and created anything at all. Philosophers like to ask the question, "Why is there something instead of nothing?" We ask, "Why did God foreordain this instead of nothing?" God was already perfectly happy and glorified in Himself in eternity. He beheld His glory and enjoyed perfect love within the Trinity. It has been theorized by Jonathan Edwards and others that there is something in the divine nature that necessitated the outflow of glory. Some say it is life; others, love. But we must be extra careful with this line of reasoning, for it could easily lead to a Reformed kind of *process theology*. Arminianism is frequently favorable to that heresy in the form of Open Theism. We need to keep the door shut. It would be safer and wiser to simply leave the matter to the unrevealed secrets of God. He will tell us the answer in Heaven.

Returning to the realm of revealed truth, we can affirm with certainty that God has not decreed any changeover from election to reprobation. There is, to be sure, a drastic changeover from being unregenerate to regenerate, from wrath to grace, among the elect. But that is not the same as a change from election to reprobation or vice versa. Here is where we see a dramatic difference between Calvinism and Barthianism and some forms of Arminianism. The latter suggests that one can be lost, found, and lost again, perhaps several more times after that. That might imply change from elect to non-elect or a move from Heaven to Hell or the opposite, contrary to Luke 16:26. The truth is that a person is either elect or non-elect, not both and not neither. One is permanently elect or reprobate, for both are unconditional on man. Once elect, always elect. One cannot change from the Golden Chain to the Black Chain or from the Book of Life to the Book of Death or vice versa. And it would be well to remember that the elect were chosen from the same lump of sinful humanity as the reprobate (Romans 9:20–21; see Ephesians 2:3). The elect were not any better or worse than the non-elect. In fact, many of the elect were worse sinners.

Are There More Elect or Reprobate?

Granted that God chose only some, the question arises whether He chose more or less than He did not choose. The divine Potter divided the lump of clay, but which part was larger? Will there be more saved or damned, more in Heaven or in Hell, more sheep or goats, more in the Book of Life or the Book of Death?

There is no unanimity among Calvinist leaders. On the one hand, Charles Hodge, William G. T. Shedd, Robert Lewis Dabney, J. C. Ryle, B. B. Warfield, and many others are of the mind that there are far more elect than reprobate, and therefore there will be far more in Heaven than in Hell. See Warfield's influential essay, "Are There Few that Be Saved?"[4] Some suggest that the final universe will resemble a city in which the general populace far outnumbers the criminals in the local prison.[5]

On the other hand, other leading Reformed theologians argue that there are far more reprobate sinners than elect believers. Calvin was one: "How is it that the greatest number go to destruction, and that there is but an handful of people which God reserveth to himself?"[6] He sometimes lamented that barely one in a hundred persons even in Geneva was a true believer. A century later another great Swiss Reformed divine, Johann Heinrich Heidegger, wrote: "Not only did God not elect all, but not even most, but a few. For, although the elect are, absolutely, sufficient many [. . .] yet, comparatively to those who are not elect, the elect are said to be few."[7] Abraham Kuyper was equally explicit: "Those who die saved in Jesus among the millions and millions who go down to the grave are by far the fewer in number!"[8] Samuel Rutherford was even more insistent: "Few are saved; men go to heaven in ones or twos, and the whole earth lieth in sin." The elect are but "a handful and remnant" compared with the reprobate who are "like the sand of the sea"; therefore, "Few, few, yea very few are saved."[9]

All sides agree that the number of the elect is in itself "a great multitude which no one could number" (Revelation 7:9). But that is not the state of the question. The point in debate is whether that number exceeds or is exceeded by the number of the reprobate. Interestingly, few Calvinists who address the subject say that the answer has not been revealed to us.

---

4 B. B. Warfield, *Biblical and Theological Studies* (Phillipsburg, NJ: P&R, 1968), 334–50.

5 Charles H. Spurgeon, *Metropolitan Tabernacle Pulpit* (Pasadena, TX: Pilgrim Publications, 1970), 43:436–37.

6 John Calvin, *Sermons on Election and Reprobation* (Audubon: Old Paths, 1996), 53.

7 Quoted in Warfield, *Biblical and Theological Studies*, 335.

8 Abraham Kuyper, *Particular Grace: A Defense of God's Sovereignty in Salvation* (Grandville: Reformed Free Publishing Association, 2001), 238.

9 Samuel Rutherford, *Letters of Samuel Rutherford* (Edinburgh: Banner of Truth, 1984), 407, 428, 548.

One factor affecting the debate is one's millennial position. Postmillennialists such as Hodge, Shedd, Dabney, and especially Warfield usually posit that believers will one day greatly outnumber unbelievers on earth. This will tip the scales of the historical census on the matter. Premillennialists, by contrast, usually argue the opposite, though a few like John Gill were optimistic premillennialists who expect a golden age of revival before the Second Coming.[10] Amillennialists tend to say that the overall proportion will stay the same to the end. A few writers have appealed to the parable of the ten virgins in Matthew 25. Five were elect, five were not elect. But almost everyone agrees that non-Christians have hitherto far outnumbered Christians through history so far.

What saith the Scriptures? In Matthew 7:13–14 our Lord contrasts the many on the road to destruction with the few on the road to eternal life. The elect were once on the road to perdition, but God moved them to the right road. Christ obviously taught that there will be more in Hell than in Heaven. Some such as Warfield and the Second Helvetic Confession (chap. 10) reply that Christ really did not answer the question here. Instead, He directed His hearers to make sure they were on the road to life. That is weak exegesis. Jesus said "many" and "few," not merely "some."

Matthew 22:14 is also explicit: "Many are called, but few are chosen." This is the general call of the gospel, not the specific call of saving grace. All who are effectually called will be justified (Romans 8:30). Matthew 22:14 clearly teaches that the elect are fewer in actual number than the called. And remember, not everyone hears the call. Few hear it, and fewer believe it. In this sense, "Many are reprobate, but few are elect."

This is also seen in the general pattern of biblical history. Only a "few" were saved in Noah's day (1 Peter 3:20). Only a few were saved between Adam and Noah, between Noah and Abraham, and between Abraham and Christ. There were very few elect even among the elect nation Israel. Even if we allow a future revival in Israel that will overflow to Gentiles, the last generation will revert to being like that of Noah's day (Matthew 24:37–39; see 1 Peter 3:20; 2 Peter 3:1–7). Christ asked the rhetorical question, "When the Son of Man comes, will He really find faith on the earth?" (Luke 18:8). The church is and always will be "a little flock" (Luke 12:32), fewer than the goats even though more sheep would be called into the flock after the Good Shepherd returned to Heaven (John 10:16).

Some appeal to the parable of leaven in Matthew 13:33 to argue that the

---

10 John Gill, *A Complete Body of Doctrinal and Practical Divinity* (Paris, AR: Baptist Standard Bearer, 1984), 448–53, 643–67.

whole lump of humanity will become Christians one day. I prefer to interpret it to mean that Christians will gradually permeate the world but not necessarily outnumber non-Christians.

The question of the destiny of dying infants also has some bearing on the question. Warfield and Hodge contend that since all dying infants are elect, and at least half of all infants in history have died in infancy, there will ultimately be more elect in Heaven then reprobate in Hell. We reply that granting the salvation of dying infants does not necessarily alter the balance. History may well continue for hundreds of centuries and overcome most infant mortality. In any case, this argument cannot outpace the clear teaching of Matthew 7 and 22.

If there are more elect than non-elect, then we must ask: What bearing does this have on the nature and purpose of election and reprobation? Several interesting insights have been offered. John Calvin said, "His kindness is all the more precious considering that many are allowed to be lost, and that he nevertheless preserves a seed, so as to show that he is the author of salvation."[11] Christopher Love points out that this proves the excellency of electing grace: "Ordaining most men unto wrath in no way impeaches the mercy of God, because God would show more mercy should He save one man in the world than He would show severity of justice should He condemn all the rest."[12] And elsewhere: "Every man upon the earth deserves death and damnation, and if God calls out any of the mass of mankind to save them, He shows more mercy than he would have done rigorous justice should He have destroyed all, because He is bound to save none at all."[13]

Thomas Doolittle, another Puritan, had this observation:

> The infiniteness of God's mercy is not to be judged by the number of the saved; but by the way and manner whereby freeth any from these tormenting flames. More shall be damned, than shall be saved, and yet God's mercy is infinite in saving a few, as well as his justice, in condemning the most. If God had saved but one of all lost mankind, it would have been

---

11 John Calvin, *Songs on the Nativity* (Edinburgh: Banner of Truth, 2008), 191.

12 Christopher Love, *Preacher of God's Word* (Morgan, PA: Soli Deo Gloria, 2000), 133; see also 134, 164.

13 Christopher Love, *A Treatise of Effectual Calling and Election* (Morgan, PA: Soli Deo Gloria, 1998), 293. So also *The Works of Christopher Love* (Morgan, PA: Soli Deo Gloria, 1995), 1:630–31.

a demonstration of his infinite mercy and goodness. The infiniteness of God's attributes is not to be judged by the plurality of objects.[14]

Another great Puritan, Jeremiah Burroughs, said that election shows the glory of God's grace, and reprobation shows the glory of His justice in due proportion to His holy nature:

> If God will observe a proportion between His mercy and justice so that He will have His justice appear as well as His mercy, then more must be damned than saved. [. . .] Because the glory of God's justice in damning two thousand is not so much as the glory of His mercy in saving two. [. . .] The reason is that there is something in the creature that calls for God's justice. [. . .] But there is nothing in the creature that requires His mercy. [. . .] But if He should save as many as He condemns, the mercy of God would be beyond all proportion to His justice. But that cannot be, hence it is that few are saved and many damned.[15]

Equal Ultimacy

Are the doctrines of election and reprobation equally ultimate? This refers to what is known in Reformed theology, especially in twentieth-century Dutch Calvinism, as *equal ultimacy*.[16] Briefly stated, it is this: In the mind and purpose of God, which is more important to the manifestation of His glory — election or reprobation? Is either one primary, or are they equal? It is not a matter of whether both are true, but whether either one had logical priority in foreordination. I know of nobody who suggests that reprobation is primary. Most say election is primary. But some, usually supralapsarians, say they are ultimately equal. Gordon Clark said, "Election and reprobation are equally ultimate."[17] Cornelius Van Til, another supralapsarian, said, "Reprobation is surely equal with election; it is the negative aspect of election. If reprobation is not equal with election, then election itself depends upon a prior deed on the part of man."[18] Alvin Baker criticized G. C. Berkouwer and argued, "In the sense of God's sovereignty, there is an 'equal ultimacy.' Reprobation is just

---

14 Thomas Doolittle, *Rebukes for the Burning of the Wicked in Hell* (Ames, IA: International Outreach, 2011), 36–37.

15 Jeremiah Burroughs, *Gospel Remission* (Morgan, PA: Soli Deo Gloria, 1995), 104–05.

16 For a cursory introduction, see R. C. Sproul, *Chosen by God* (Wheaton: Tyndale House, 1986), 142–48.

17 Gordon Clark, *Religion, Reason and Revelation* (Jefferson: The Trinity Foundation, 1986), 238.

18 Cornelius Van Til, *The Defense of the Faith*, 1st ed. (Phillipsburg, NJ: P&R, 1981), 416.

as ultimate and real as election."[19] Most Calvinists who discuss election do not even address the matter.

It may all be just a matter of slight semantic differences of emphasis. Both sides agree that God elected some and not others, irrespective of which are more. Both see election and reprobation as eternal decrees resulting in two eternal destinies. Both decrees are irreversible. As for myself and most other infralapsarians, I see more scriptural weight on the side of the supremacy of election over reprobation. They are not equally ultimate, though both are true.

Look at the lump of clay in Romans 9. Election logically preceded reprobation. God chose some sinners out of the fallen mass of humanity and left the rest to be damned. Compare Romans 11:7, "The rest were blinded." As D. A. Carson put it in another context, "John nowhere states that Jesus chose men to be condemned; rather, he chose some 'out of the world.'"[20] God obviously did not first select which would be damned and then left the others to be saved. Election and non-election are necessarily related, but election has the priority. Berkouwer quotes Klaas Dijk's important (and unfortunately untranslated) study of the supralapsarian/infralapsarian debate in this context: "These two parts of God's predestination may not be placed beside each other as coordinate, for rejection is subordinated to election but, at the same time, rejection is the necessary result of election."[21]

This is related to the Reformed understanding that there is a sense in which the reprobate serve the elect. Pointing to Esau as representative of the reprobate and Jacob as representative of the elect, Romans 9:12 says, "The older shall serve the younger." John Gill applied this to our question: "Esau was serviceable to Jacob, even in spiritual things, as reprobates are to the elect; for all things are for their sake, and all things work together for their good."[22] Herman Hoeksema, like Gill a supralapsarian, agreed: "For even as the chaff must serve the wheat, so the reprobate must be subservient to the realization of the glorification of the elect Church of Christ."[23] The infralapsarian Steve Lawson said, "To be sure, reprobation serves as the black velvet backdrop upon which the diamond of

19 Alvin Baker, *Berkouwer's Doctrine of Election* (Phillipsburg, NJ: P&R, 1981), 161.
20 D. A. Carson, *Divine Sovereignty and Human Responsibility* (Atlanta: John Knox, 1981), 196.
21 G. C. Berkouwer, *Divine Election* (Grand Rapids: Eerdmans, 1960), 178.
22 John Gill, *The Cause of God and Truth* (Grand Rapids: Baker Book House, 1980), 83.
23 Herman Hoeksema, *God's Eternal Good Pleasure* (Grand Rapids: Reformed Free Publishing Association, 1979), 21, see also 85.

God's election shines forth most brilliantly."[24] God is glorified in both Heaven and Hell, in grace and in wrath, but there remains a priority of the former over the latter.

This is not at all the Christian equivalent of the Talmud's idea that all Jews are elect, all Gentiles are reprobate, and therefore all Gentile dogs must one day serve the Jews and have no rights or should be shown no mercy. Rather, Christians are to love their enemies. Yet, as Gill said, God uses reprobation as one of the "things" of Romans 8:28 to bless the elect for good, as we saw in the echo of glory earlier. The reprobate are tending our garden until we inherit it (Matthew 5:5). We will receive by grace what they forfeited by sin. Whatever God has done for the reprobate by way of common grace will redound to their condemnation but go to the glorification of the elect. A few appeal to Isaiah 43:3–4: "I gave Egypt for your ransom, Ethiopia and Seba in your place. [. . .] Since you were precious in My sight, you have been honored, and I have loved you; therefore I will give men for you and people for your life." Even the damnation of the reprobate will serve the elect by increasing their humble love and gratitude to God for graciously choosing them despite their sin which they shared with the reprobate.

It appears that much of the debate revolves around the order of the decrees. Those who hold to equal ultimacy tend to be supralapsarian, while those who do not are usually infralapsarian. Before we discuss that in the next chapter, let D. A. Carson give us a good summary of the best solution: "The mode of divine 'ultimacy' has a built in asymmetry to it. The manner in which God stands behind evil and the manner in which he stands behind good are not precisely identical; for he is to be praised for the good, but not blamed for the evil."[25] He correctly ties the whole matter in with divine foreordination of good and evil.

Conclusion

Jacob and Esau were types of the elect and the non-elect. They were eventually reconciled (Genesis 33:1–16). But the elect and reprobate will never be reconciled in eternity, any more than Heaven and Hell will be one. But they will both continue forever to display the one ultimate glory of God.

---

24 Steven J. Lawson, *Foundations of Grace* (Orlando: Reformation Trust, 2006), 356.
25 Carson, *Divine Sovereignty and Human Responsibility*, 212.

Chapter 48
The Order of the Decrees

We now come to one of the deeper areas of the Reformed doctrine of predestination. It was debated more in the past than today, and many now just ignore it completely. The Bible does not explicitly address it, but its view can be legitimately deduced just as we can formulate the doctrine of the Trinity from various biblical passages.

The State of the Question

The state of the question is *not* whether God foreordained the Fall, whether predestination was single or double, whether the glory of God is the goal of all decrees, nor when the decrees occurred.

The state of the question revolves around three points: (1) whether the decree of election was logically before or after the decree of the Fall, (2) whether the decree of election was logically before or after the decree of the atonement, and (3) whether the decree of creation was logically first or last in the order of the decrees.

Note that we are talking about a logical and not a chronological order. The decrees all took place in eternity, not history. Though there is something "before" about what may be termed "eternity past" (Ephesians 1:4; John 17:5; Matthew 25:34; 2 Timothy 1:9), eternity is not merely prehistorical time. While we realize the limitations of expression on the subject, Scripture itself speaks about some kind of order in God's foreordination. For example, the first two links of the Golden Chain of Romans 8:29–30 are in eternity past, and the last link is in eternity future. So, the order is mainly logical, not chronological. This must be understood at the start. Some novices think, "Well, I must be supralapsarian because I believe that election took place before time began, and infralapsarianism says it happened in history after the Fall." All Calvinists agree that all the decrees happened in eternity past; none say they happened in time.

As we showed in the previous chapter, the decree of election logically preceded the decree of reprobation. We will not extend that discussion here, except to note that supralapsarianism tends toward equal ultimacy regarding the decrees of election and reprobation, producing several problems. As far as I can discern, most if not all infralapsarians deny equal ultimacy and thus avoid these problems. Amyraldism also rejects it but creates problems of its own. The debate also concerns the nature of decrees, not just their logical order.

The debate is over the order of the decrees (Latin, *ordo decretorum Dei*) and not the order of salvation (*ordo salutis*). The first was in eternity; the second, in time. They overlap in the Golden Chain, as it were. Infralapsarians say that they follow a similar order, while supralapsarians say they follow an opposite order.

The Three Main Reformed Positions

The three main Reformed positions have been the Amyraldian, the infralapsarian, and the supralapsarian positions. I call the first *Low Calvinism*, the second *mainstream Calvinism*, the third *High Calvinism*.[1] The first may also generally be called *hypothetical universalism*. All the great Reformed confessions of faith are infralapsarian; none are supralapsarian or Amyraldian. Yet it has often been suggested that they were worded in such a way that both supralapsarians and Amyraldians could sign them in good conscience. For instance, Gomarus, Voetius, and Maccovius were leading participants and signers of the Canons of the Synod of Dort yet were supralapsarians. Davenant and Martinus were more akin to Amyraldism and also signed them. Curiously, some supralapsarians such as Herman and Homer Hoeksema admit the canons were infralapsarian.[2] One wonders how they can subscribe to them. The Westminster Confession also sounds infralapsarian, but there were supralapsarians (such as Rutherford and Goodwin) and Amyraldians (such as Vines and Calamy) who produced and signed it.

It is not always easy to discern a theologian's position if he does not state it. Some also seem to misunderstand the question. Some argue that Augustine, Calvin, and Edwards were supralapsarian, but in my opinion they definitely were not. Calvin taught, "God chose whom He would out of the lost mass of mankind, and had reprobated whom He would."[3] Edwards: "The decrees of God must be conceived of in the same order, and as antecedent to and

---

1 As Peter Toon, *The Emergence of Hyper-Calvinism in English Nonconformity, 1689–1765* (London: The Olive Tree, 1967).

2 Herman Hoeksema, *Reformed Dogmatics*, 2nd ed. (Grandville: Reformed Free Publishing Association, 2004), 1:234–35; Homer Hoeksema, *The Voice of Our Fathers* (Grand Rapids: Reformed Free Publishing Association, 1980), 23, 121–22, 136, 143, 151–53, 163–67, 190, 235, 239, 249. Dort's clear infralapsarianism is seen in 1:10 and 14.

3 John Calvin, *Calvin's Calvinism* (Grand Rapids: Reformed Free Publishing Association, 1991), 116–17.

consequent on one another, in the same manner as God's acts in execution of those decrees."[4]

As far as I can tell, all Hyper-Calvinists (such as John Gill and Herman Hoeksema) have held to supralapsarianism. But not all supralapsarians have held to Hyper-Calvinism (such as Kuyper). Theonomists evidently are usually supralapsarian,[5] as were the so-called Antinomians. I would estimate that approximately 80 percent of Calvinists have been infralapsarian, 5 percent supralapsarian, and 15 percent Amyraldian. Unfortunately, some writers such as John Gill used the outdated term *sublapsarian* for what others called infralapsarian, while several have followed Augustus Hopkins Strong's error in differentiating sublapsarianism and infralapsarianism.[6] The term *sublapsarianism* should be retired once and for all. There is enough confusion surrounding the debate as it is.

Amyraldism

The first position we will discuss is the general view variously known as hypothetical universalism, Low Calvinism, or most popularly, Amyraldism. While admitting that there are definite differences among these often categorized as such, and not all of them addressed the order of the decrees, I will use the term *Amyraldism* as a moniker for four-point Calvinism.

Basically this position puts forward the following order: creation, Fall, universal atonement, election and reprobation, application of redemption. It agrees with infralapsarianism in putting creation first — otherwise, how could God logically decree anything on the basis of things not yet conceived as existing?

The key point with this position is that the decree of election follows the decree of atonement, not vice versa as the other two posit. It says that God foreordained the Fall and then Christ to die for all sinners equally. Then God chose the elect not only from a fallen mass but from a mass of humanity for whom Christ died equally. Christ died for sinners as sinners, not as elect

---

4 Jonathan Edwards, *The Works of Jonathan Edwards* (New Haven: Yale University Press, 2000), 18:318.

5 Greg Bahnsen confirmed this to me in a letter before he died, but elsewhere he seemed to prefer Bavinck and Berkhof's both/and position.

6 John Gill, *A Complete Body of Doctrinal and Practical Divinity* (Paris, AR: Baptist Standard Bearer, 1984), 184; Augustus Hopkins Strong, *Systematic Theology* (1907; repr., Old Tappen: Fleming H. Revell, 1979), 777.

sinners. Then God chose some and rejected others. He then decreed to apply redemption in salvation to the elect alone and withhold it from the non-elect. The limitation, then, was in the application and not in the intent or execution of the atonement. This also means that Christ died for the reprobate, who are damned for lack of faith and not lack of atonement. With some variations, this may be termed the general Amyraldian position.

This presents several problems. One is its straightforward doctrine of universal atonement as well as the nature of the atonement. It suggests that Christ merely provided atonement, not guaranteed redemption for those for whom He died.

Charles Hodge challenged this order of the decrees:

> At first it might seem a small matter whether we say that election precedes redemption or that redemption precedes election. In fact, however, it is a question of great importance. The relation of the truths of the Bible is determined by their nature. If you change the relation you must change their nature. If you regard the sun as a planet instead of the center of our system, you must believe it to be something very different in its constitution from what it actually is. So in a scheme of thought, if you make the final cause a means, or a means the final cause, nothing but confusion can be the result.[7]

The main problem with this order is that it seems to make some of the decrees hypothetical, conditional, and virtual rather than definite, unconditional, and actual. Thus it is often called *hypothetical universalism*, mainly in reference to the universality of the atonement. Mainstream Calvinism, however, denies that any of the decrees are hypothetical. They are unconditional because God fulfilled all conditions. A hypothetical decree resembles the Arminian idea of basing election on foreseen faith. Critics of this system sometimes charge it with having God change from Plan *A* to Plan *B*.

The Amyraldian theory tends to overreact to supralapsarian errors and is somewhere between mainstream Calvinism and Arminianism. But it most definitely is not Arminian, for it still upholds unconditional election and denies that election is based on foreseen faith.

---

7 Charles Hodge, *Systematic Theology* (Grand Rapids: Eerdmans, 1979), 2:322.

Supralapsarianism

On the other side of the mainstream is supralapsarianism. Theodore Beza is often considered the first to develop it, though ironically Duns Scotus taught certain features of it in the thirteenth century. Later it would be taught by Amandus Polanus, Johannes Maccovius, Franciscus Gomarus, Gisbertus Voetius, and other continental Calvinists. It was taught in Scotland by Samuel Rutherford; in England by William Perkins, William Whitaker, William Ames, William Twisse, Thomas Goodwin, Isaac Chauncey, and others; and by Samuel Willard in America. In the eighteenth century it was advocated by Alexander Comrie, Augustus Toplady, John Gill, and others. In the next century it was in decline but was still maintained by Abraham Kuyper, the Hyper-Calvinists, and others. In the twentieth century it was the view of Gordon H. Clark, Arthur W. Pink, Herman and Homer Hoeksema, David Engelsma, Klaas Schilder, Robert Reymond (surprisingly), the Hyper-Calvinists, and others.

The name comes from the Latin words *supra* (above) and *lapsus* (fall). Thus, it is said that the decree of election was logically before the decree of the Fall, and both were prior to the decree of creation. It has a certain kind of logic all its own and appeals to some Calvinists because it appears to give more emphasis to divine sovereignty and glory than the other theories.

It has several arguments. One is that what is first in intention is last in execution. The end is first decided, and then, the means (the end justifies the means). By analogy, a man draws up a blueprint before he builds a house (see Luke 14:28–30). He does not make it up as he goes along. If the house is to be made of wood, it will need nails to hold the boards together and then hammers to drive the nails in, and hammers must be bought, and there must be carpenters to use them, and so on. The bottom line is first drawn, then the details are added backward, as it were.

Similarly it says, "The order of history is, so to speak, infralapsarian; but the order of decrees is supralapsarian, so that history unfolds in exactly the opposite order of the decrees" (Homer Hoeksema).[8] We can look at the order of history and deduce backward what the logical order of the decrees was. Therefore the creation decree was last in order, for creation was first in history.

Next, it agrees that the Fall preceded salvation in time, therefore election to salvation preceded the decree of the Fall in the eternal order of the decrees. When God chose who would be saved, He made the choice from an unfallen

---

8 Hoeksema, *The Voice of Our Fathers*, 151–52.

pure mass of humanity. This is a critical point in the theory. The lump of clay in Romans 9:20–23 is formless stuff and unfallen bare humanity, somewhat like the amorphous original creation of Genesis 1:2 which was without form and void. Some contend that it was holy and innocent, like Adam before the Fall, while others appeal to Romans 9:11 and say it was neither bad nor good but just bare humanity, whatever that means. From this mass God chose some and reprobated others. To be sure, God did not choose some sinners and reprobate other sinners, but rather chose and reprobated innocent persons, for He had not yet foreordained the Fall. Then God predestined the Fall as a means to provide the occasion for the elect to be saved from sin and the non-elect to be punished for sin.

Thus, both election and reprobation are by bare sovereignty, not out of grace for the elect or justice for the non-elect. Proponents say this acknowledges more sovereignty than the other systems and gives God greater glory. Some suggest the other systems give too much responsibility to man and border on Arminianism.

Advocates of infralapsarianism respond as follows. First, if the creation decree was last, then the previous decrees of election and reprobation only dealt with men as merely potential and not as actual persons. Nothing can be predicated or predestined concerning a non-being. A potential person can be neither elected nor reprobated. In fact, this rather resembles the Amyraldian idea of hypothetical decrees. James Henley Thornwell was right: "The decree of creation must be first in order of nature, or election and reprobation will be concerned not about men but nonentities."[9] One supralapsarian reply is that men were viewed as "creatable" but not created, a concept without parallel anywhere in biblical theology.

Next, the supralapsarian view of unfallen man as neither good nor bad sounds dangerously like Pelagius' idea that Adam was created morally neutral and not righteous or holy. Such a view is anathema to historic Calvinists.

Then infralapsarians argue that chronological history follows the logical order of the decrees and is not in the opposite order. The first two links of the Golden Chain of Romans 8:29–30 follow a logical order, and the next links follow a chronological order. If the supralapsarian principle was true, then history would have Christ dying before the Fall, for the atonement decree followed the Fall decree. Infralapsarians sometimes say that supralapsarians have everything

---

9 James Henley Thornwell, *The Collected Writings of James Henley Thornwell* (Edinburgh: Banner of Truth, 1974), 2:116.

backward. Roger Nicole commented: "If the supralapsarians are correct in ordering the decrees by a backward unrolling of history, then everybody who is saved should be on the same side of the cross — but this is not the case."[10] As Edwards said above, the order of execution follows the order of the decrees.

The real problem with the theory is its view of the nature of election and reprobation from a mass of unfallen humanity. Thornwell again put his finger on the fatal flaw: "An election to salvation or to deliverance from guilt and misery necessarily presupposes guilt and misery in its objects as healing implies a disease or cooling implies heat."[11] Edward Polhill the Puritan wondered why there was a need for mercy where there was no misery.[12] Scripture repeatedly says that election was by grace and mercy (Ephesians 1:4–6; Romans 9:13, 15, 16, 18, 23; 2 Timothy 1:9). Romans 11:5 is especially explicit in calling it "the election of grace." Grace and mercy have to do with God's love for guilty and miserable sinners, not innocent and happy saints. At best, supralapsarianism has an election of love but not of grace or mercy. It resembles the election of angels, as we shall see in the next chapter.

The implications of this system for its view of salvation are somewhat troubling. Berkouwer chided Hoeksema because his supralapsarianism did not allow a transition from wrath to grace.[13] To the supralapsarian, the elect were always under love and never under wrath, which is directly contrary to Ephesians 2:3. To be consistent, the scheme must also posit that the non-elect have never been under any kind of love, favor, or grace, which is exactly why Hoeksema denied all forms of common grace. But if there is a common grace, supralapsarianism fails.

It is even worse when it comes to reprobation. Thornwell again: "The Supralapsarians, by their arbitrary reduction of creation and the fall to the category of means, really makes sin the consequence of damnation and not its ground. Man is not condemned because he sins, but sins that he may be condemned."[14] Christopher Ness, Puritan, likewise said, "'Tis a mere fallacy: as if the decree of non-election was the procuring cause of man's damnation. Sin is the cause of damnation, but reprobation is not the cause of sin."[15]

10 Roger Nicole, *Our Sovereign Saviour* (Fearn: Christian Focus, 2002), 44.
11 Thornwell, *The Collected Writings of James Henley Thornwell*, 2:23–24.
12 Edward Polhill, *The Works of Edward Polhill* (Morgan, PA: Soli Deo Gloria, 1998), 121.
13 G. C. Berkouwer, *Divine Election* (Grand Rapids: Eerdmans, 1960), 254–77.
14 Thornwell, *The Collected Writings of James Henley Thornwell*, 2:24.
15 Christopher Ness, *An Antidote to Arminianism* (Choteau, MT: Old Paths Gospel, n.d.), 51.

Augustine saw the problem over a thousand years before later Reformers developed supralapsarianism. He wrote: "But it is unjust that he would have hated Esau when there was no unrighteousness to merit it. [...] God, therefore, does not hate Esau the human being, but God does hate Esau the sinner."[16] The supralapsarian theory would have God first hate innocent Esau and then predestine a reason to hate him. This sounds dangerously like John 15:25: "They hated Me without a cause." But does God hate a sinless person? Does a just God have wrath on an innocent man? That would resemble an angry father taking out his anger by beating his innocent child. To use another picture, it would be like a crooked policeman who plants evidence on an innocent person to frame him then forces the man to commit the crime. Or it is like a lynch mob that punishes a man without a trial. It is like the Red Queen in *Alice in Wonderland* when she cried, "Verdict first, trial afterward!" See John 7:51. That is not the God of the Bible.

Some supralapsarians sound as if sin was only an arranged means to a previously predestined end to condemn the reprobate, as if sin was not even necessary for reprobation in the first place. It thus says that a good end justifies a bad means, contrary to Romans 3:8. Herman Bavinck refers to an intemperate remark by Augustine that God could have justly damned the innocent human race.[17] This harks back to the medieval debates regarding absolute power versus ordained power.[18] Certain scholastics argued that God has the former and can do anything at all, including punishing an innocent man, forgiving an unrepentant sinner, granting salvation without an atonement, accepting something other than the death of Christ for redemption (even the death of a pig), and so on. The Dominicans and most Augustinians and Reformers totally rejected this Semi-Pelagianism as blasphemy. But some supralapsarians — such as Rutherford and Twisse — employed the error of absolute power in their system, for which they were rebuked by infralapsarian John Owen. Duns Scotus proposed a form of proto-supralapsarianism. As the old proverb says, "Consider the source."

This is why supralapsarianism has often been charged with making God the author of sin. Even moderate supralapsarians at Dort felt the need to censure Maccovius for his unguarded scholastic extremes in this area. Later the Hyper-Calvinists followed supralapsarianism with non-Reformed results, such as the

---

16 Augustine, *The Works of Saint Augustine* (Hyde Park: New City, 2008), I/12:192, 200. This shows that Augustine was infralapsarian, not supralapsarian.

17 Herman Bavinck, *Reformed Dogmatics* (Grand Rapids: Baker, 2004), 2:395.

18 See my discussion above in chapter 20, "The Sovereignty of God."

denial of the free offer. Here is where we see a difference between the supra and infra schools regarding the foreordination of sin. Infralapsarians such as William G. T. Shedd and Robert Alexander Webb accuse the supralapsarians of saying that God positively foreordained sin and actively brought it about in the Fall — the very essence of being the author of sin.[19] In the infralapsarian system, God foreordained sin by permission to allow it to exist and negatively removed the restraint in Eden. It would be the difference between throwing a stone down and dropping a stone and letting it fall under its own weight.

When supralapsarians argue that their view exalts divine sovereignty more, they overlook the fact that all divine attributes are equal and work together. Sovereignty works with grace and justice. God elected out of sovereign grace, not naked sovereignty. He reprobated out of sovereign justice, not raw sovereignty. Sovereignty without justice is sovereign injustice. It could be said that the supralapsarian theory makes God a tyrant with neither justice nor mercy, for there was no mercy in election nor justice in reprobation. Thus, the question of the order of the decrees is not an irrelevant discussion but has serious implications for our doctrine of God. Furthermore, we tend to imitate our conception of God. Supralapsarianism can lead to the cold denial of common grace and the free offer, producing an unloving and unjust attitude to lost sinners.

Infralapsarianism

Infralapsarianism is in the middle between the other two theories and is by far the mainstream report among Reformed theologians. Warfield noted: "Supralapsarianism errs therefore as seriously on one side as universalism does on the other. Infralapsarianism offers the only scheme which is either self-consistent or consistent with the facts."[20] Logically one can prove it by process of elimination of the other two, but let us go further.

In John 15:19, Christ said, "I chose you out of the world." In John's Gospel, the world is a sinful state of being. Christ saved sinners out of it according to the decree to elect sinners out of the sinful mass of God-hating mankind (v. 18). The lump of clay in Romans 9:21 is a sinful lump — after all, it is dirt and not gold. Election is to salvation (2 Thessalonians 2:13), not preservation from sinning as

---

19 William G. T. Shedd, *Dogmatic Theology*, 3rd ed. (Phillipsburg, NJ: P&R, 2003), 342; Robert Alexander Webb, *Christian Salvation* (Harrisonburg: Sprinkle, 1985), 39.

20 B. B. Warfield, *The Plan of Salvation* (Grand Rapids: Eerdmans, 1970), 28.

in the election of unfallen angels. Salvation presupposes sin to be saved from, therefore the decree to save followed the decree to allow the Fall.

This bears on the atonement. Infralapsarianism holds to particular redemption. If the Bible teaches it, then the Amyraldian theory cannot stand. Even allowing for universal benefits in the atonement better fits into the infralapsarian system than the supralapsarian system, which generally holds to a strictly limited atonement without any universality.

The infralapsarian order of decrees follows the historical order of events. God foreordained everything that will come to pass. He predestined creation. He predestined to permit the Fall. He chose some sinners to be saved and left the rest to be punished for their sin. God then provided redemption for the elect and not the non-elect, though with universal benefits for all. He then predestined to send the Holy Spirit to apply Christ's atonement to the elect and efficaciously produce regeneration, faith, and repentance. Then He foreordained that the elect would persevere and be glorified in Heaven, to the glory of God's grace. It fits.

Alternative Theories

Herman Bavinck and Louis Berkhof saw good features in both the supra and infra positions and put forth a theory that was in some respects both and neither.[21] Upon close examination, their view still leaned more toward infralapsarianism. Earlier John Gill also put forth a kind of supra-infra system but basically came down on the supralapsarian side.[22] Both of these approaches have had only limited appeal in the Reformed community.

Some argue that the decrees are not to be seen in a logical order as such, for that implies chronology which does not exist in eternity. A logical order also implies that God learns rather than knows all things at once. So some put forth a coordinate relationship of the decrees rather than a subordinate order. Sometimes it is compared with a wheel in which all the spokes move at the same time. But the other proponents argue that the spokes are in a certain order, are they not? Does not the Golden Chain of Romans 8:29–30 teach a subordinate rather than coordinate order of the links? God could not have justified someone unless He had first called him and before that had

---

21 Bavinck, *Reformed Dogmatics*, 2:383–93; Louis Berkhof, *Systematic Theology* (Grand Rapids: Eerdmans, 1988), 118–25. Cornelius Van Til seemed to hold a similar view in *Common Grace and the Gospel*. (Phillipsburg: Presbyterian and Reformed, 1974).

22 Gill, *Body*, 185.

predestined and foreknown him. Compare Paul's logical order in Romans 10:14. Further, the decree of Christ's work on the cross presupposes a prior decree to allow sin and choose those for whom Christ died. Surely Christ had someone in mind in His substitutionary death, not "To whom it may concern."

G. C. Berkouwer was not impressed with the lapsarian debates.[23] He reinterpreted the relationship of the decrees to one another and then their nature and thus opened the door to a non-Reformed view of election and the other decrees. He rejected the idea of an overarching decree, then he modified the "before" of predestination and the decrees in light of a different view of eternity. He concluded that the traditional Reformed view renders history meaningless. Alvin Baker took him to task and argued that Scripture itself speaks of election "before the foundation of the world" (Ephesians 1:4).[24] Grace was given to the elect in Christ "before time began" (2 Timothy 1:9). Even if this is God speaking after the manner of man, it still indicates a logical order and a cause-and-effect relationship between ideas and decrees and their fulfillment in time. As Thornwell put it:

> But while, owing to the simplicity and eternity of the Divine nature, there cannot be conceived in God a succession of time, nor consequently various and successive decrees, yet we may justly speak of His decrees as prior or posterior in point of nature. Though they all constitute but one eternal act of Divine will, the objects about which they are concerned are connected with each other by various relations, and the decrees themselves may be spoken of in a language accommodated to these diversified relations.[25]

Berkouwer confessed to being influenced by Barth, whose "Super-supralapsarianism"[26] includes non-Reformed views of election and reprobation of all men, the election and reprobation of Christ, and other errors. Berkouwer's *Divine Election* and Barth's *Church Dogmatics* include helpful discussions of the history of the supralapsarian/infralapsarian debate but must be used with caution.[27]

---

23 Berkouwer, *Divine Election*, 254–77.
24 Alvin Baker, *Berkouwer's Doctrine of Election* (Phillipsburg, NJ: P&R, 1981).
25 Thornwell, *The Collected Writings of James Henley Thornwell*, 2:124.
26 Homer Hoeksema uses the term "supersupralapsarianism" in the sense of a subordinate order of the decrees of election and reprobation, but not in a Barthian sense. *The Voice of Our Fathers*, 238, 249.
27 Karl Barth, *Church Dogmatics* (Edinburgh: T. and T. Clark, 1957), II, Part 2, 127–45.

The roots of supralapsarianism go back to Duns Scotus' view regarding the predestination of Christ's Incarnation. This was later picked up by nineteenth-century German Reformed theologians such as Friedrich Schleiermacher and Isaak Dorner, then later by Karl Barth.[28] In sum, they proposed that Christ would have become a man even if Adam had never fallen. The Incarnation was not exclusively for redemption. In Reformed terms, this meant the decree of the Incarnation preceded the decrees of election and the Fall. This strange doctrine reflects its proponents' very non-Reformed errors in several other areas as well. For example, Schleiermacher renounced the German Reformed theology of his upbringing and denied the orthodox doctrines of particular election, substitutionary atonement, and everlasting Hell. He said that God elected everyone and that everyone would be saved, so the death of Christ was not propitiatory after all.[29] While Barth opposed him on various issues, they were more alike than he wanted to admit.

It is easy to debunk this theory. "Christ came into the world to save sinners" (1 Timothy 1:15). He did that by dying a substitutionary penal death on the cross for those whom God had chosen for salvation. He was born to die. If nobody had sinned, Christ would not have had to die and thus would not have become a man. Other purposes of the Incarnation are subsidiary to this one. A point to ponder: Christ did not become an angel, for the good angels needed no salvation, and there was no salvation decreed for the fallen angels. Would Schleiermacher suggest that Christ would have become an angel anyway? This contradicts Hebrews 2:14–17.

Even the supralapsarian Abraham Kuyper rejected the theory.[30] In one place Calvin denounced it as sacrilege and abomination, though the editor thinks he is referring to the error of the Lutheran Andreas Osiander.[31] Others have toyed with the idea of an incarnation without a Fall or redemption without Christ's death. Bradwardine and Rutherford held to a form of absolute power and said that God could have foreordained to be appeased in a way other than the death of Christ. On at least one occasion Calvin himself seemed to hold to the idea of incarnation without a Fall: "For supposing Adam had not fallen

---

28 See Edwin Chr. Van Driel, *Incarnation Anyway: Arguments for Supralapsarian Christology* (Oxford: Oxford University Press, 2008).

29 Friedrich Schleiermacher, *On the Doctrine of Election* (Louisville: Westminster John Knox Press, 2012).

30 Abraham Kuyper, *The Work of the Holy Spirit* (Grand Rapids: Eerdmans, 1969), 11–12, 274, 330.

31 John Calvin, *Sermons on Genesis 1:1–11:4* (Edinburgh: Banner of Truth, 2009), 100–101. He clearly rejected the idea in *Institutes*, 2:12:4 (p. 467).

into the ruin into which he has drawn us with him, yet God's Son would have been always as the first-born of creatures. [. . .] Even if we had no need of a redeemer, yet our Lord Jesus Christ would have been established as our head."[32] Statements such as these led J. V. Fesko and others to suggest that Calvin was supralapsarian.[33] My opinion is that these unguarded pronouncements are outweighed by many more in which he spoke of election from a fallen mass of humanity and the necessity of the Incarnation for the atoning death of Christ to achieve redemption.

Another bizarre theory with a strange Christology was the rare theory known as *Pre-Existerianism*,[34] which Peter Toon called "Supralapsarian Christology."[35] Thomas Goodwin and Arthur Pink held to a mild form of it. The main proponent was Joseph Hussey in *The Glory of Christ Unveiled or The Excellency of Christ Vindicated* (1706), which by no coincidence was the first Hyper-Calvinist book in that it was the first to deny the free offer of the gospel. The theory was later promoted by Hyper-Calvinists such as Samuel Eyles Pierce and John Stevens. But not all who held to it were supralapsarians. Isaac Watts and to a lesser extent Philip Doddridge accepted it, and their theology was somewhat Amyraldian.

Pre-Existerianism relates the order of the decrees to the covenant of redemption. In that eternal covenant, the Son pledged to become a man to die for the elect. Goodwin said that further stipulations were based on this promise, and Christ was treated as if He were the God-man, though He was only virtually and not actually a man yet. This was Pink's idea as well. Hussey and Watts, however, claimed that the second person of the Trinity actually took on a human soul in the eternal covenant of redemption. In the Incarnation, He only took on a human body. This has some similarity to the "Incarnation without a Fall" idea. Hussey tied it in with the election of Christ prior to the decrees of election and the Fall. Fortunately, this strange theory died out long ago.

Luther did not engage in discussion over the order of the decrees, but later

---

32 John Calvin, *Sermons on the Epistle to the Ephesians* (London: Banner of Truth, 1973), 120, 262.

33 J. V. Fesko, *Diversity Within the Reformed Tradition: Supra- and Infralapsarianism in Calvin, Dort, and Westminster* (Greenville, SC: Reformed Academic, 2001).

34 See my "Hyper-Calvinism and John Gill," PhD diss., University of Edinburgh, 1983, 246–60.

35 Peter Toon, "The Growth of a Supralapsarian Christology," *Evangelical Quarterly*, 39 (1967), 23–29.

Lutherans did. Their order rather resembled that of the Arminians. The main Arminian one was this: (1) creation, (2) permission of the Fall, (3) universal atonement, (4) sufficient grace to all, and (5) election by foreseen faith of those who persevere to the end.[36] Christopher Ness commented on the Arminian view:

> The Arminians, by the law of retaliation, may be called sub-mortuarians, for their holding no election till men die; and post-destinarians, for placing the eternal decree behind the race of man's life. Surely when believers die they are subjects of glorification, not of election. [. . .] And may they not also be styled re-lapsarians, for saying that the elect may totally and finally fall away.[37]

Conclusion

The correct order of the decrees is this:

1. Decree to create mankind

2. Decree to permit the Fall

3. Decree to choose some sinners to salvation

4. Decree to pass by other sinners in reprobation

5. Decree to send Christ to die for the elect

6. Decree to send the Holy Spirit to efficaciously apply redemption to the elect

7. Decree to harden the reprobate

8. Decree to glorify God through the glorification of the elect and the damnation of the reprobate

Some Reformed theologians, such as John Frame,[38] accept no order of the decrees because they feel the whole subject is too speculative and pries into unrevealed secrets. We await the standard treatment of the subject, but it is hoped that this chapter may help answer some questions within the bounds of orthodox biblical and Reformed theology.

---

36 See the chart in Warfield, *The Plan of Salvation*, 31.
37 Ness, *An Antidote to Arminianism*, 56.
38 John Frame, *Systematic Theology* (Phillipsburg, NJ: P&R, 2013), 224–28.

Chapter 49
The Election of Angels

Three hard cases arise regarding election and reprobation. The first is angels. The Westminster Confession says:

> By the decree of God, for the manifestation of His glory, some men and angels are predestined unto everlasting life, and others foreordained to everlasting death. These angels and men, thus predestined and foreordained, are particularly and unchangeably designed; and their number is so certain and definite, that it cannot be either increased or diminished (3:3–4).

The Westminster Larger Catechism adds more details:

> God by His providence permitted some of the angels, willfully and irrevocably, to fall into sin and damnation, limiting and ordering that, and all their sins, to His own glory; and established the rest in holiness and happiness; employing them all, at His pleasure, in the administrations of His power, mercy and justice (Answer 19).

Johannes Wollebius offered another summary: "The predestination of angels means that God has determined to preserve some of them in original happiness, in Christ the head, forever, and to punish others eternally for abandoning their station of their own accord, in order to reveal the glory of his grace and justice."[1] One could say it was, "Michael I have loved, but Lucifer I have hated."

The Elect Angels

The only explicit biblical reference to "elect angels" is 1 Timothy 5:21, but we can deduce more by good and necessary inference from what is said about angels and demons and the election and reprobation of humans. The term *elect angels* does not refer to ranks of angels (Romans 8:38; Ephesians 1:21; Colossians 1:16) nor to a group within the unfallen angels. All the holy angels are elect. Just as elect humans are chosen to be holy (Ephesians 1:4), so the elect angels are called "holy angels" (Mark 8:38; Luke 9:26) because they are already holy. John Gill

---

1 In John W. Beardslee III, ed., *Reformed Dogmatics* (New York: Oxford University Press, 1965), 50.

thought that the phrase "angels of God" in Luke 12:8–9 implied their election "not merely because they are His creatures, so are the evil angels; but because they are His chosen, His favourites, and appointed to be happy with Him to all eternity."[2]

We immediately see a difference between elect men and angels. All men are sinners, including the elect; none of the elect angels have ever sinned or ever will sin. There is not the slightest indication that God chose any of the sinful angels. Salvation is the product of election (2 Thessalonians 2:13), and none of the fallen angels will ever be saved (Matthew 25:41). Therefore it follows that none of the fallen angels were elected. Elect angels never sinned but rather "always see the face of My Father who is in heaven" (Matthew 18:10; see Luke 1:19; Isaiah 6:2–3; Daniel 7:10; Revelation 4:6–9, 5:11–12).

Their election is linked to the decree to keep them from falling. William G. T. Shedd explained, "It is not, in this case, a decree to deliver from sin, but to preserve from sinning."[3] This decree had two stages: preservation from falling, thus guaranteeing impeccability, and predestination to happiness and glory. Calvin said that the elect angels "have persevered, I acknowledge, to be due to the election of God, who hastened to love them, and embrace them with his goodness, by bestowing upon them the power of remaining firm and steadfast."[4]

A number of Reformed theologians suggest that all the angels were placed on a kind of probation in their sinless state, similar to Adam and Eve in the garden of Eden. Robert Lewis Dabney and Jonathan Edwards even say this involved a covenant. The stipulation was that if they obeyed, they would pass the test and be made impeccable and confirmed in holiness, with the guarantee they would never fall or even be subject to temptation. Some passed, and some failed.

Others favor another theory. They suggest that the elect angels were created impeccable, and the non-elect angels, like Adam and Eve, were not. Hence, the two were created differently. God did not create the non-elect angels as sinful, any more than Adam and Eve. But being peccable, they eventually all fell.

All Calvinists who address the subject agree that this election took place in eternity, their number is definite and fixed, no more are being elected, and so

---

2 John Gill, *A Complete Body of Doctrinal and Practical Divinity* (Paris, AR: Baptist Standard Bearer, 1984), 176.
3 William G. T. Shedd, *Dogmatic Theology*, 3rd ed. (Phillipsburg, NJ: P&R, 2003), 326. Roman Catholicism erroneously says the same about Mary.
4 John Calvin, *Selected Works of John Calvin* (Grand Rapids: Baker, 1983), 1:130.

on. Just as converted men may know that they are elected (2 Peter 1:10), so the elect angels already know they are elect, impeccable, and predestined to glory. This is their true happiness, as Augustine remarked: "If we could know from the holy Scriptures that no holy angel will fall anymore, how much more do they themselves know this, since the truth is revealed to them in a more lofty manner! We, of course, are promised happy life without end and equality with the angels."[5]

The Reprobate Angels

As with humans, the election of some logically means the non-election of others. God could have chosen all, some, or none of the angels. He chose only some. So said Calvin:

> Paul calls the elect angels who stood in this uprightness 'elect' (1 Timothy 5:21); if their steadfastness was grounded in God's good pleasure, the rebellion of the others proves the latter were forsaken. No other cause of this fact can be adduced but reprobation, which is hidden in God's secret plan.[6]

The reprobation of fallen angels was in three stages: (1) They were foreordained to fall into sin, (2) they were passed over by God in preterition, and (3) they were predestined to suffer punishment for their sin. The consequences happened in history in a like order: (1) They sinned and were cast out of Heaven, some were cast onto the earth, and others reserved in chains in Hades, (2) God provided no atonement or salvation for them, and (3) they will all eventually be cast into the Lake of Fire.

There are various opinions as to when the angels were created. Was it before or during the first week of Genesis 1? It appears that Lucifer was equal to Michael, since they are the highest of the good and bad angels (Jude 9; Revelation 12:7). Michael, not Jesus, is the equal opposite of Lucifer. Lucifer was puffed up in pride and aspired to become God. He thus sinned and became Satan (John 8:44; 1 Timothy 3:6).[7] A third of the angels followed him and also fell (2 Peter 2:4; Jude 6).[8] Job 4:18 says, "He charges His angels with error." Augustine had a curious theory:

---

5 Augustine, *The Works of Saint Augustine* (Hyde Park: New City, 1999), I/26:127.
6 John Calvin, *Institutes of the Christian Religion* (Philadelphia: Westminster, 1960), 3:23:4 (p. 952).
7 Some take Luke 10:18; Isaiah 14:12–17; and Ezekiel 28:11–19 to refer to this fall also.
8 Some add Genesis 6:1–4 and Revelation 12:4–12.

The angels were created when that first light was made, and that a separation was made between the holy and the unclean angels, as is said, "God divided the light from the darkness; and God called the light Day, and the darkness He called Night." For He alone could make this discrimination, who was able also before they fell, to foreknow that they would fall, and that being deprived of the light, which is the holy company of the angels spiritually radiant with the illumination of the truth, and that opposing darkness, which is the noisome foulness or the spiritual condition of those angels who are turned away from the light of righteousness, only He Himself could divide, from Whom their wickedness (not of nature, but of will), while yet it was future, could not be hidden or uncertain. [. . .] The light alone received the approbation of the Creator, while the angelic darkness, though it had been ordained, was not yet approved.[9]

All these demons are doomed. All are reprobate; none will ever be saved. God did not have to preserve them from falling, and He did not have to elect or save any. He chose to leave them as a class in their sin, even as He chose to preserve all the others as a class. Here they differ from humans. All elect humans are sinners; none of the elect angels are sinners. Reprobate men are like the reprobate angels — sinful. Samuel Rutherford argued that it was not because of a deficiency in divine mercy that rendered God incapable of choosing them but because of His sovereign prerogative: "He can, if He would, forgive all the devils and damned reprobates, in respect of the wideness of His mercy."[10] Edward Polhill was in awe and wondered, "Why a philanthropy rather than a philangely?"[11] Jonathan Edwards posited that the fall of the angels from such a lofty position was such a deliberate and conscious evil that it was as unforgivable as the unpardonable blasphemy of the Holy Spirit that some humans commit. This explains why all fallen angels are rejected as a class, but not all humans are rejected as a class. Hence, there is an offer of salvation to humans but not to reprobate angels.[12] I add that this is also why we are not to love them or pray for their salvation. That would be like praying for someone already in Hell, which is contrary to the revelation in Scripture. The revealed will of God for salvation includes all humans but no demons.

---

9 Saint Augustine, *The City of God*, 11:19, in Philip Schaff, ed. *A Select Library of Nicene and Post-Nicene Fathers of the Christian Church*, First Series (Grand Rapids: Eerdmans, 1979), 2:215.

10 Samuel Rutherford, *The Letters of Samuel Rutherford* (Edinburgh: Banner of Truth, 1984), 314.

11 Edward Polhill, *The Works of Edward Polhill* (Morgan, PA: Soli Deo Gloria, 1998), 144.

12 Jonathan Edwards, *The Works of Jonathan Edwards* (New Haven: Yale University Press, 1994), 13:385.

No man in this life may know he is reprobate, for he may yet believe in Christ and thereby show his election. But all the reprobate angels know they are reprobate and that they will never repent or believe. In this sense they are like reprobate men already in Hell, knowing their eternal destiny is hopeless torment. Revelation 12:12 indicates that Satan knows his time is short. He does not know how short, for it happens after the Second Coming, of which date only the Father knows (even the good angels do not know, Matthew 24:36). The demons also know they are doomed (Matthew 8:29). This only increases their present anguish and hatred for God and man. They want to take as many humans to Hell with them as possible. Reprobation loves company. Francis Turretin explained:

> The fallen angels are now so constituted in the penal state, that their reprobation is known by them, and they know (to increase their desperation) that no spark of hope is left for them. Here also they differ from reprobate men whose reprobation (although sure from eternity and immutable) is however infallibly known by no one while on earth. Yet the devils so bear the punishment of damnation as to know that they have no hope of pardon. Thus to wish to condole with their misery (as preposterously as to hope with Origen for their restitution after many revolutions of ages) is a ridiculous hope.[13]

All the elect angels know they are elect. All the reprobate angels know they are reprobate. And they know the state of each other.

Loraine Boettner applied the reprobation of angels to the defense of the reprobation of humans: "If it was consistent with God's infinite goodness and justice to pass by the whole body of fallen angels and to leave them to suffer the consequences of their sin, then certainly it was consistent with His goodness and justice to pass by some of the fallen race of men and to leave them in their sin."[14] Arminians often say Calvinism's doctrine of reprobation is unfair. Do they also complain that the reprobation of Satan and demons was unfair? In siding with reprobate humans, they are in danger of siding with reprobate demons.

As Satan is the leader of the reprobate demons (Matthew 25:41; Revelation 12:7–9), so he is the Reprobate Angel. One could theoretically surmise that the other demons were reprobated in him, as elect humans were elected in Christ.

---

13 Francis Turretin, *The Institutes of Elenctic Theology* (Phillipsburg, NJ: P&R, 1992), 1:341.
14 Loraine Boettner, *The Reformed Doctrine of Predestination* (Philadelphia: Presbyterian & Reformed, 1932), 268.

Contrary to Karl Barth's serious error, it is Satan and not Jesus Christ who is the Reprobate One. Christ was not reprobate for all humans, for some are elect. Propitiation is not reprobation. Gottschalk spoke to the question twelve hundred years ago:

> God, omnipotently and unchangeably [. . .] has, by His most just judgment, predestined the devil, who is the head of all the demons, with all his apostate angels and also with reprobate men, who are his members, on account of their foreknown particular future evil deeds, to merited eternal death.[15]

Just as Satan is the father of fallen sinners, he is the head of reprobate humans (John 8:44). A more horrible condition could hardly be imagined.

Angelic Supralapsarianism

Since the elect angels never sinned, some supralapsarian Calvinists buttress their case by saying that the election of humans was from an unfallen mass. If the supralapsarian election of angels was not unfair, why is the supralapsarian election of humans considered unfair? But there are several important differences. First, only some of the angels fell, but all humans fell in Adam. No elect angel fell, and no fallen angel was elect, while all elect humans have fallen. The election of angels was of love, not grace, but the election of humans was "the election of grace" (Romans 11:5), which presupposes sin. True, the elect angels did not merit their election, even if one supposes they passed a probationary test. But neither did they demerit election, as reprobate men and angels did. In a sense, the election of good angels was somewhat like the election of the sinless humanity of Christ. The members of the Trinity show love but not grace to each other ontologically or in the covenant of redemption.

God did no injustice in allowing the non-elect angels to fall and in passing them by. He gave them no restraining grace or electing grace. So, in one sense the election of good angels was supralapsarian, but we cannot argue the same for humans. Perhaps it would be more appropriate to say that angelic election was "nonlapsarian." It obviously was not infralapsarian.

As for the reprobation of the other angels, they are different from the elect angels. The reprobate angels sinned; the elect angels did not. But all humans

---

15 Gottschalk, *Gottschalk and a Medieval Predestination Controversy: Texts Translated from the Latin* (Milwaukee: Marquette University Press, 2010), 71. So too Calvin, *A Harmony of the Gospels: Matthew, Mark and Luke* (Grand Rapids: Eerdmans, 1980), 3:117.

have sinned. Turretin said, "The predestination of men supposes sin. [. . .] Therefore the angelic reprobation also presupposes sin." He refers to 2 Peter 2:4 and Jude 6 and adds,

> Therefore, they are conceived to have sinned and left their first estate before they could be conceived as reprobated. [. . .] He did not reprobate and devote to eternal punishment those whom he would permit to fall; but those whom he had permitted to fall by their own fault, he reprobated and relinquished forever.[16]

I would add that the same theodicy in defending God's foreordination of sin in humans would apply to His foreordination to the fall of Satan and the demons as well as their reprobation.

In the logical order of the decrees for the reprobate angels, God could theoretically have elected all, none, or some of the fallen angels. He sovereignly elected none. Supralapsarians would do well to note that this was an infralapsarian reprobation of angels. We could chart the decrees as follows:

1. Decree to create all the angels

2. Decree to preserve some angels in holiness

3. Decree to permit the others to fall

4. Decree not to elect any of the fallen angels

5. Decree to predestine the fallen reprobate angels to eternal punishment

The Elect Angels and Christ

Since the elect angels never sinned, they did not need election to salvation nor a Savior. They were therefore not elected "in Christ" to salvation (Ephesians 1:4). Louis Berkhof said, "The angels were not elected or predestined in Christ as Mediator, but in Him as Head, that is, to stand in a ministerial relation to Him."[17] So also said Calvin.[18] See Ephesians 1:21–23; Colossians 1:16; 2:10; Hebrews 2:14–16; and 1 Peter 3:22.

This has bearing on the Incarnation and the atonement. Hebrews 2:14–16 says Christ became a man to save men (i.e., the elect). If no humans were elect, He would not have become a man, nor would He have become a man if

---

16 Turretin, *Institutes of Elenctic Theology*, 1:336.
17 Louis Berkhof, *Systematic Theology* (Grand Rapids: Eerdmans, 1988), 113.
18 John Calvin, *Sermons on the Epistle to the Ephesians* (London: Banner of Truth, 1973), 45, 63.

nobody sinned. He did not become an angel, for elect angels are unfallen and do not need salvation, and no fallen angel was elected to salvation. This is a good argument in favor of limited atonement. Would an Arminian complain that Christ did not die for Satan nor the demons?

Arthur Custance offered another opinion. Unlike humans, who have organic unity in Adam, all angels (elect as well as non-elect) were created separately without organic unity to each other. There are no angelic fathers, sons, or brothers. They are not married to each other (Matthew 22:30). If Christ were to elect any fallen angels to salvation, He would have to become many angels — one for each angel elected from a fallen state.[19] That may be undue speculation. But a sounder observation could be made here. If all indications are that angels are male (male names and pronouns are used) and none marry, then neither may male humans marry each other. Indeed, same-sex marriage would be demonic, not angelic, as Genesis 6:1–6 and Jude 6–7 associate demons with sexual licentiousness, including homosexuality.

The Relation Between Elect and Reprobate Angels and Humans

How many angels are there? It is a definite and large number, not increasing through procreation nor decreasing through death (Matthew 22:30). God ceased all creation at the end of Genesis 1. They are described as a "multitude" (Luke 2:13); "more than twelve legions" (Matthew 26:53); and "an innumerable company of angels" (Hebrews 12:22). Revelation 5:11 speaks of "the number of them was ten thousand times ten thousand, and thousands of thousands." Revelation 9:16 may refer to two hundred million angels as apocalyptic horsemen. Deuteronomy 33:2 probably refers to angels rather than humans: "ten thousands of saints," or holy ones. Daniel 7:10 says, "A thousand thousands ministered to Him; ten thousand times ten thousand stood before Him."

We showed earlier that there are more non-elect than elect humans — but are there more elect or non-elect angels? In 2 Kings 6:16, Elisha said to his assistant, "Do not fear, for those who are for us are more than those who are with them." That may only refer to the angels and demons that were present. Elect and reprobate angels are involved in spiritual battle (Ephesians 6:10–17). Revelation 12:4 tells us that the elect angels outnumber reprobate angels by a proportion of two to one. If so, then there is a difference between elect and

---

19 Arthur C. Custance, *Two Men Called Adam* (Brockville, Ontario: Doorway Publications, 1983), 23.

non-elect humans regarding their proportion. We probably cannot determine whether there are more angels or humans, either throughout history or at any given moment. The number of humans is growing but not that of angels.

Augustine taught that God chose the elect angels to replace the ranks of the fallen angels.[20] Anselm later taught it. Spurgeon held to it in one place[21] but elsewhere did not. This is not to say they believed that elect humans become angels. That unusual view has been held by some heterodox Greek Orthodox priests and the Romanian Lutheran Richard Wurmbrand[22] based on a misunderstanding of Matthew 22:30. Christ said we become "like the angels," not "become angels." We are created lower than angels (Psalm 8:5) but will be exalted higher than them. They are servants of Christ; the elect are the bride of Christ. Men do not become angels any more than animals become men or angels become God.

Jonathan Edwards thought that one reason why God chose fallen humans rather than fallen angels was "that his grace might be the more conspicuous in being exercised toward a nature so inferior."[23] He also said that the election of sinful men was the occasion for Lucifer and other angels to be jealously offended and thus fall into sin. Election, of course, had already happened, so this could only be true if it referred to their first hearing of it.

Without speculating too far, it seems that the election and reprobation of angels logically preceded the election and reprobation of men, for the logical order of the decrees matches the historical enactment, and angels sinned before Adam and Eve sinned. Lastly, while elect and non-elect angels know which angels are elect or reprobate, it is unlikely that either of them know which humans, until they believe, are elect, and which humans, until they die, are reprobate, unless angels can discern who commits the unpardonable sin. So said Thomas Watson.[24]

---

20 Augustine, *Works*, I/8:291–92.

21 Charles H. Spurgeon, *Metropolitan Tabernacle Pulpit* (Pasadena, TX: Pilgrim Publications, 1974), 34:140

22 Wurmbrand expressed this opinion in an entire sermon which was available on tape but not in print.

23 "The Terms of Prayer (Sermon 473)," Jonathan Edwards Center at Yale University, accessed February 9, 2018, http://edwards.yale.edu/. Also, God has a greater love for elect saints than for angels, for Christ died for them but not for angels. Ibid., "Hebrews 12:22–24c (Sermon 546)."

24 Thomas Watson, *Discourses on Important and Interesting Subjects* (Ligonier, PA: Soli Deo Gloria, 1990), 2:71.

Their Predestined Destinies

Elect angels are predestined to happiness and glory, but all reprobate angels will be sent to eternal Hell with reprobate men (Matthew 25:41; Revelation 20:10). Like reprobate men, they will glorify God in being justly tormented forever for their sins. Since they are older, never sleep, and have sinned far more than any human, they will be tormented far more. Like reprobate men, they will be forced to bow the knee and confess that Jesus Christ is Lord, to the glory of God the Father (Philippians 2:10–11). Some apply Hebrews 1:6 to them: "Let all the angels of God worship Him." They will offer forced and grudging worship to Christ, even as they were forced to submit to Him when He cast demons out and overthrew Satan on earth. The elect angels, by contrast, willingly worshiped Christ at His birth (Luke 2:13–14) and continue to do so in Heaven (Revelation 5:11–12; and Isaiah 6:1–3 with John 12:41).

Both kinds of angels reside in God's universal theater of glory, only the elect sit in different sections than the reprobate. Both witnessed the death of Christ and see the conversion of the elect. Elect angels rejoice (Luke 15:10); reprobate angels curse.[25] They also all witness the death and damnation of reprobate humans. This coincides with the echo of glory among elect and reprobate humans in the afterlife. The elect angels not only praise God for punishing reprobate men (Revelation 19:1–3) but also for punishing reprobate angels. Conversely, reprobate angels give glory to God grudgingly for His electing angels and men. Jonathan Edwards put it like this in his own inimical way:

> The elect angels are greatly increased, both in holiness and happiness, since the fall of those angels that fell, and are immensely more holy than Lucifer and his angels were. For perfection in holiness, i.e. a sinless perfection, is not such in those that are finite, but it admits of finite decrees. The fall of the angels, as it increased their knowledge of God and themselves, gave 'em the knowledge of good and evil, and was a means of their being emptied of themselves and brought low in humility. And they increased in holiness by persevering in obedience.[26]

Moreover, we can surmise that elect men will glorify God for choosing and using the elect angels, such as their ministry to them (Hebrews 1:14). Elect angels will be amazed at the glorification of such unworthy human sinners. Now they are curious (1 Peter 1:12) and rejoice when each elect human is saved

25 See Jonathan Edwards' comments on Ephesians 3:10 in *Our Great and Glorious God* (Morgan, PA: Soli Deo Gloria, 2004), 121–49.
26 Edwards, *Works*, 20:199.

(Luke 15:10). How much more will they rejoice and worship when elect humans reach their eschatological glorification. Ephesians 3:10 indicates that they will glorify God as they are shown the details of how He worked out His eternal purpose in them.

Elect angels and men will not only glorify God as they view the final damnation of reprobate men and angels (Revelation 19:1–3), but elect men will participate in their condemnation at Judgment Day (1 Corinthians 6:2–3). Reprobate men and angels will be forced to render glory to God as they view elect men and angels in Heaven.

Conclusion

Consider the observations of Charles Haddon Spurgeon from his insightful sermon "Men Chosen — Fallen Angels Rejected":

> Men and devils have both sinned and have both deserved to be damned for their sins; God, if he shall so resolve, can justly destroy them all, or he may save them all, if he can do it with justice; or, he may save one of them if he pleases, and let the others perish; and if as he has done, he chooses to save a remnant, and that remnant shall be men, and if he allows all the fallen angels to sink to hell, all that we can answer is, that God is just, and he has a right to do as he pleases with his creatures. [. . .] We must fall down, and breathlessly admire the infinite sovereignty that passed by angels, and saved men.[27]

---

27 Charles H. Spurgeon, *New Park Street Pulpit* (Pasadena, TX: Pilgrim Publications, 1981), 2:293–94.

Chapter 50
The Election of Dying Infants

Lewis Sperry Chafer once wrote, "No theology is established or complete which does not account for the salvation of those who die in infancy."[1] Reformed theology addresses the issue, but there is not a unanimous consensus, only a general tendency and majority report. This is the second of three hard cases relating to election. If all dying infants are saved, they are all elect. If none are saved, they are all reprobate. If some are saved and not others, some are elect, and others are not. I hasten to add at the outset that the discussion is over infants who die in infancy, not those who reach childhood or adolescence.

The Options

There are several possible options to the question, "Are dying infants saved?"

1. We do not know. The Bible does not explicitly tell us or give us sufficient information from which we can deduce the answer. It is an unrevealed secret (Deuteronomy 29:29).[2]

2. All dying infants are lost. I know of no theologian, Reformed or otherwise, who holds this position.

3. Some dying infants are saved, and some are not. William Perkins spoke of "reprobate infants,"[3] but this does not necessarily refer to those who die in infancy. The reprobate all started out as reprobate infants. A very small number of Calvinists have held this position.

4. All baptized infants are saved, and all unbaptized infants are lost.

---

1 Lewis Sperry Chafer, *Systematic Theology* (Dallas: Dallas Seminary Press, 1975), 7:196.
2 For example, John Gill, *The Cause of God and Truth* (Grand Rapids: Baker Book House, 1980), 152, 158.
3 William Perkins, *The Work of William Perkins*, ed. by Ian Breward (Appleford: Sutton Courtenay, 1970), 251; cf. *A Golden Chaine* (n.p.: Puritan Reprints, 2010), 241–42. The Hungarian Confessio Catholica (1562) said: "Those born prematurely and infants of the vessels of wrath not elect will perish," citing Augustine. In James T. Dennison Jr., ed., *Reformed Confessions of the 16th and 17th Centuries in English Translation* (Grand Rapids: Reformation Heritage Books, 2010), 2:647.

A few Calvinists have held this view, though it borders on baptismal regeneration.

5. All dying infants of believing parents are saved, while all dying infants of unbelieving parents are lost. Baptism is irrelevant here. One wonders what proponents of this view say about infants with one believing parent and one unbelieving parent, illegitimate or adopted infants, those born from artificial insemination or surrogate motherhood, and other cases.

6. Some dying infants are saved, but we cannot say all are saved. A good number of Reformed theologians take this view, such as Francis Turretin and Herman Hoeksema.

7. All dying infants are saved. This is by far the view of most Calvinists, such as Charles Hodge, Benjamin B. Warfield, Charles Haddon Spurgeon, Augustus Toplady, Huldrych Zwingli, William G. T. Shedd, Loraine Boettner, and many more.

The classic confessional statement on the matter is from the Westminster Confession: "Elect infants, dying in infancy, are regenerated and saved by Christ through the Spirit, who worketh when, and where, and how He pleaseth. So also other elect persons, who are incapable of being outwardly called by the ministry of the Word" (12:3). Some interpret this to mean option 6 above, but in my view far more take it to mean option 7. In 1903, the Presbyterian Church in the United States of America gave this Declaratory Statement stating their official interpretation: "It is not to be regarded as teaching that any who die in infancy are lost. We believe that all dying in infancy are included in the election of grace, and are regenerated and saved by Christ through the Spirit, who works when and where and how he pleases."[4]

The Canons of the Synod of Dort only address dying infants of Christian parents: "Godly parents ought not to doubt the election and salvation of their children whom God calls out of this life in infancy" (1:17).

It is not enough to appeal to such confessions alone, nor the majority of theologians, public opinion, or one's feelings. Nor do we dare hold to a hope of a second chance after death, universal salvation, or reincarnation. The big question is: "What saith the Scriptures?"

---

4 Presbyterian Church of the United States of America, *Book of Confessions: Study Edition* (Louisville: Geneva Press, 1996), 216.

Original Sin

The first problem that arises is: "If all infants are born with original sin, then how can dying infants be saved?" Inborn sin and not just acts of conscious sin make us culpable and liable to Hell. God would be absolutely just to punish any or all dying infants if He chose to. But did He?

Jonathan Edwards discussed this in his masterful *Original Sin*.[5] He argued that the fact that some infants die in infancy is due to original sin. It proves they are guilty and deserve death, otherwise God would be unjust to allow innocent persons to die. So, if any are saved, it is not because of any supposed innocence, but the grace of God. William G. T. Shedd observed: "The 'salvation' of infants supposes their prior damnation."[6]

The Question of Baptism

Some link infant salvation with baptism. Charles Hodge once linked baptism with putting the infant's name in the Book of Life.[7] Many early Calvinists held to a moderate form of baptismal regeneration. For example, some said all baptized infants are regenerated; others said only some are regenerated, for the efficacy of regeneration is in the Spirit and not the water. This differed from the Lutheran and Catholic views. Gradually most Reformed theologians rejected anything hinting at baptismal regeneration. Others, such as Abraham Kuyper, interpreted Scripture and the Canons of Dort to teach *presumptive regeneration* — that is, Christian parents should presume their infants are regenerate until they grow up and give evidence to the contrary. In my view this goes too far. It would be safer to assume they are unregenerate until they give evidence they are regenerate, at which time the covenantal sign should be given. But even the presumptive regeneration theory allows that some baptized infants of Christian parents are not regenerate; some grow up and prove to be unregenerate and even reprobate. If all infants of believers are automatically born regenerate, then procreation becomes a form of evangelism that guarantees conversion.

Reformed Baptists, of course, deny infant baptism and thus separate it from the question of infant salvation. And generally speaking, the majority of Reformed theologians agree with the wise statement of Charles Hodge where he elsewhere said, "All who die in infancy are saved. [. . .] The Scriptures

---

5 Jonathan Edwards, *The Works of Jonathan Edwards*, Vol. 3 (New Haven: Yale University Press, 1970).

6 William G. T. Shedd, *Dogmatic Theology*, 3rd ed. (Phillipsburg, NJ: P&R, 2003), 910.

7 Charles Hodge, *Systematic Theology* (Grand Rapids: Eerdmans, 1979), 3:588.

nowhere exclude any class of infants, baptized or unbaptized, born in Christian or heathen lands, of believing or unbelieving parents, from the benefits of the redemption of Christ."[8] All dying infants are saved, period.

The Roman Catholic View

The official Roman Catholic view goes back to Augustine's strong view of both original sin and baptismal regeneration. He taught that all dying infants who have been baptized are saved, but all the rest are not. "Little ones who leave the body without baptism will be under the mildest condemnation of all."[9] This was taught by Aquinas, Lombard, and even the Jansenists. Gregory of Rimini was given the epithet *tortor infantium*, or infant torturer.

Other Catholic theologians modified it. This coincided with the development of the theory of Limbo (*limbus infantium*). This is not Hell per se nor Heaven in its fullness nor Purgatory. The Council of Trent approved the idea of Limbo, but the Catholic Church has never officially defined it. Some say that infants in Limbo are not in pain but do not get to see God in the beatific vision. Others say that infants only suffer deprivation of Heaven's blessings but not any positive punishment. Some say it is more like Heaven than Hell; some say it is like the garden of Eden before Adam fell. Others, such as Augustine, say Limbo is the mildest part of Hell. Still others say it is neither Heaven nor Hell but a third place. More and more Catholic theologians suggest that there might be a mysterious way in which God could save all dying infants, but He has not told us what it is.

Calvinists reject almost all the Catholic explanations as unbiblical. There is only Heaven and Hell (Matthew 25:46). All in Heaven see God (Revelation 22:4). All in Heaven are blessed, and all in Hell are cursed. There are degrees of blessing and cursing, but that does not allow for Limbo.

Non-Reformed Views

The Greek Orthodox Church and other Eastern Orthodox churches basically teach the Roman view, though they trace it to Gregory of Nazianzen and other Eastern divines rather than Augustine. High Church Anglicans and Episcopalians sometimes take the Catholic view.

Martin Luther and historic Lutherans have held to the basic position of

---

8 Hodge, *Systematic Theology*, 1:26.
9 Augustine, *The Works of Saint Augustine* (Hyde Park: New City, 1997), I/23:45.

Augustine but with a few modifications. Like Augustine and the Catholics, they hold to baptismal regeneration as the means of cleansing original sin, but they generally add that baptism also implants the seed of faith in the infant. A few, such as Luther, cherished the hope that God might save unbaptized children in a way God has not revealed, but the more conservative Lutherans are wary of such speculations.

Anabaptists naturally rejected both the Catholic and Lutheran theories. And even some sixteenth-century Reformed churches began the move away from the Catholic view, such as the Scottish King's Confession of 1581, which said: "We detest [. . .] [the pope's] cruel judgments against infants departing without the sacrament."[10]

The Question of Infant Faith

Can infants believe? Historic Lutherans and some Calvinists believe that God gives *seminal faith*, or the seed of faith, to some infants. Shedd defended it:

> The regenerate child, youth, and man believes and repents immediately. The regenerate infant believes and repents when his faculties will admit of the exercise and manifestation of faith and repentance. In the latter instance regeneration is potential or latent faith and repentance.[11]

Reformed Baptists and some paedobaptists disagree. They contend that infants are constitutionally and mentally incapable of faith, even as they are physically incapable of procreation. Faith comes by hearing of the word (Romans 10:17), not by baptism, and this requires some minimum of understanding that infants cannot have. Faith is not given in a mystical or magical way that bypasses either Scripture or the mind, otherwise why not read a Chinese Bible to a German baby? 1 Corinthians 14:9 and 16 say we must understand words before we can say the *amen* of faith. To say that Scripture gives regeneration without our understanding would be like agreeing with something that someone said while speaking in tongues. It profits nothing. Scripture says nothing about seminal faith, only the faith that agrees and trusts.

What about John the Baptist, who was filled with the Holy Spirit from when he was in his mother's womb (Luke 1:15, 41, 44)? Explanations vary. Some say he was filled but not regenerate, akin to Balaam or Saul when they prophesied in the power of the Spirit. That is unlikely. Many say John was an example

---

10 In Dennison Jr., ed., *Reformed Confessions*, 3:609.
11 Shedd, *Dogmatic Theology*, 782.

of infant regeneration and seminal faith. Others say John was an exception, not an example.[12] Then there are the cases of Jeremiah (Jeremiah 1:5) and Paul (Galatians 1:15–16). But the first refers to eternal calling even before conception, and the second does not say Paul was regenerated in the womb. Paul was not converted until he was an adult (Acts 9).

William Hendriksen urges caution in attributing "the possibility of propositional religious knowledge" to any infant, including unborn infants in the womb. Yet he grants that the Holy Spirit can be actively present in some way in an infant.[13] Another point bears mention. As we shall see later, regeneration precedes faith in the order of salvation. To some, this implies there may be a time lag between them; infants may be regenerate but not yet believe. This looks like special pleading without biblical foundation. It would be safer to say that regeneration and faith are inseparable, and therefore neither happens in infants. Christopher Love made yet another observation that confronts Arminianism: "If election depends upon foreseen faith or works, then infants so dying cannot be elect because they never have faith nor good works; but many infants are elect."[14]

The Age of Reason

Many Christians speak of the *age of accountability*, but that might imply that infants before that age are innocent. I prefer the term *age of reason*. Some use the phrase *age of consciousness*. Whichever term is used, Scripture does speak of a transition from unconscious infancy to conscious childhood. Deuteronomy 1:39 says, "Moreover your little ones and your children, who you say will be victims, who today have no knowledge of good and evil, they shall go in there." These infants were allowed into the Promised Land because they did not disbelieve the word of the Lord as their parents did. Some see a parallel with dying infants entering the heavenly Promised Land.

Jonah 4:11 speaks of more than 120,000 persons "who cannot discern between their right hand and their left." Since there were far more than that number of adults in Nineveh at that time, this refers to infants. Adults certainly can tell their right hand from their left. But something more is in view. Carl F. Keil, the

---

12　E.g., John Trapp's commentary on Luke 1:44. *A Commentary on the Old and New Testaments* (Eureka, CA.: Tanski, 1997), 5:306.

13　William Hendriksen, *New Testament Commentary: The Gospel of Luke* (Edinburgh: Banner of Truth, 1978), 97, 99 (on Luke 1:44).

14　Christopher Love, *Preacher of God's Word* (Morgan, PA: Soli Deo Gloria, 2000), 154. Also, *A Treatise of Effectual Calling and Election* (Morgan, PA: Soli Deo Gloria, 1998), 263, 293–94.

renowned commentator explains: "Not to be able to distinguish between the right hand and the left hand is a sign of mental infancy."[15] Their mental infancy parallels their inability to differentiate good and evil (cf. Adam and Eve in the garden of Eden). In Scripture, the right hand stands for good and the left, for evil (Matthew 25:33–34, 41).

Isaiah 7:15–16 prophesied Christ's birth, and it is even more explicit. "Curds and honey shall He eat, [until] He may know to refuse the evil and choose the good. For before the child shall know to refuse the evil and choose the good," and so on. Note the element of conscious knowledge in choosing good.

Some think that Romans 7:9 refers to this differentiation and transition: "I was alive once without the Law, but when the commandment came, sin revived and I died." This view says that original sin is inherent but latent in a person, then revives at a certain age and produces actual sin. Some link it with the Jewish *bar mitzvah* at age thirteen or perhaps puberty at about that age. The Mishnah said, "At five years old, one is fit for the Scripture, at ten for the Mishnah, at thirteen for the fulfilling of the commandments" (Avot 5:21).

The element of conscious knowledge is the key in these verses and the state of the question. James 4:17 says, "Therefore, to him who knows to do good and does not do it, to him it is sin." Numbers 15:22–31 speaks of sins of ignorance and sins of deliberation. It would seem that infants may be capable of the former but not the latter. Arthur Custance offers an explanation:

> There is a transitional period in here, and about all we can say on the basis of what is written in Scripture is that the time at which a child first discovers there is a difference between right and wrong seems to mark the age of accountability. When the time comes to make an actual choice between the two, a previous age of innocence becomes an age of virtue if the choice is made correctly, but an age of culpability if the choice is wrongly made. This may not, of course, actually occur at the same time of life for each individual.[16]

That sounds fine, except that Custance says that infants are innocent.

We go through various stages from conception in the womb to death in the tomb: prenatal, infancy, childhood, adolescence, teenagehood, young adulthood,

---

15 Carl F. Keil, *Biblical Commentary on the Old Testament: The Twelve Minor Prophets* (Grand Rapids: Eerdmans, 1967), 1:416.
16 Arthur C. Custance, *The Sovereignty of Grace* (Phillipsburg, NJ: Presbyterian and Reformed, 1979), 106.

middle age, and old age. The age in question has to do with the first two, especially the second. When does it change? Some say puberty; others, eighteen. Almost everyone says it varies. I put it much before adolescence and do not tie it in with puberty. Perhaps it is associated with a youngster's understanding of what he is saying as opposed to merely repeating words like a parrot.

Some persons never reach that transition point. Some infants have severely underdeveloped brains that keep them as permanent infants. They never mentally become even preadolescent children but remain babies in mind while their body grows up. If dying infants are saved, then certainly these are as well. This is what the Westminster Confession had in mind by referring to persons who are incapable of understanding the gospel call (12:3).

This transition would also be the age at which faith is possible. The child that is old enough to consciously sin is old enough to consciously believe in the Savior of sinners. Thus, childhood but not infant conversions are possible. Many Christians can testify of it in their own lives and in the lives of some of their children.

Are Dying Infants Saved?

The preponderance of Scripture strongly implies, if not makes certain, that all dying infants are saved. Several verses speak to the issue. Second Samuel 12:23 describes the death of David's son at the age of only seven days. David stopped mourning and was comforted by knowing he would one day see his son again. Contrast this with David's anguish over the death of wicked Absalom (2 Samuel 18:33). The infant had not been circumcised, for that was done on the eighth day by the Jews (Philippians 3:5), so the covenantal sign had no bearing on the matter. It is usually concluded that David knew the boy was in Heaven because all dying infants go to Heaven.

Matthew 18:1–14 (same as Mark 9:36–37, 42 and Luke 9:46–48) relates Jesus taking children His arms. It does not say their age, except that His calling them to Himself (Matthew 18:2) might imply they were old enough to recognize their names and come to Him by themselves. The text also says they believed in Him (Matthew 18:6; Mark 9:42). Some take this to refer to "baby Christians," that is, newly converted believers instead of infants. Verse 14 says, "It is not the will of your Father who is in heaven that one of these little ones should perish."

More to the point is Matthew 19:13–15 (same as Mark 10:13–16 and Luke 18:15–17). Verse 13 says the children were brought to Jesus, perhaps implying they were carried as infants. Then Jesus blessed them but did not baptize them. Matthew and Mark both used the Greek word *paideia* as in the earlier story. It is a general word like the English word *child*. It can include infants to teenagers. However, Doctor Luke uses the more precise word *brephos* (Luke 18:15). Most uses of this word are in Luke's account of the births of John the Baptist and Jesus. The word usually refers to infants still suckling at their mother's breast. It is used of Jesus both before and after birth. These are infants, not adolescents.

The crux is in Matthew 19:14 when Jesus said, "Let the little children come to Me and do not forbid them; for of such is the kingdom of heaven." This is more than saying that adults must become like little children (18:3). Here Jesus seems to be saying that infants are in a state compatible with heavenly citizenship. If they die in that state, they go to Heaven.

Matthew 21:16 says, "Out of the mouth of babes and nursing infants You have perfected praise." This may include children old enough to sing and shout (v. 15) but also nursing infants. *Theelazo* means a nursing baby at the breast. Spurgeon commented on this verse: "Does not that text seem to say that in heaven there shall be 'perfect praise' rendered to God by multitudes of cherubs who were here on earth — your little ones fondled in your bosom — and then snatched away to Heaven."[17]

Other Texts and Arguments

Spurgeon and others pointed to Ezekiel 16:21 where God rebuked the Israelites for sacrificing children to Moloch: "You have slain My children." This is not conclusive, for it could just refer to children as members of the community of Israel. Similarly, Jeremiah 19:4 condemns the taking of "the blood of the innocents." Infants are innocent of actual sin but not of original sin.

Job wished he had died as an infant or stillborn baby, for then he would be at rest (Job 3:11–16). This could conceivably imply that all dying infants are at rest with God. Ecclesiastes 6:3 says a stillborn child is better than hopeless old people, implying that they have life after death with God.[18] Some might appeal to Matthew 26:24: "It would have been good for [Judas] if he had not been born." Thus, a dying preborn infant goes to Heaven, and Judas went to Hell. That is not a necessary interpretation. It more likely seems that it would have

---

17 Charles H. Spurgeon, *New Park Street Pulpit* (Pasadena, TX: Pilgrim Publications, 1969), 6:508.

18 Cf. Craig Brown, *The Five Dilemmas of Calvinism* (Orlando: Ligonier Ministries, 2007), 115–16.

been better for Judas never to have existed at all than to have existed and gone to Hell.

In his useful book *The Theology of Infant Salvation*, Robert Alexander Webb appeals to such verses, but he often simply compiles possible interpretations to infer probabilities. For example, Isaiah 11:6–9 speaks of infants, but this refers to either the millennium or the eternal state. Acts 2:39 mentions children but has no reference to their death as such and in light of 16:31 probably refers to the promise of salvation received by faith. Spurgeon mentions 2 Kings 4:26–37, but the child there was no infant.

Romans 9:11 speaks of Jacob and Esau, but this refers to God electing them in eternity, not saving them as dying infants in time. Proverbs 22:6 speaks of raising children but does not say anything about their destiny if they died in infancy. Some appeal to 2 Timothy 3:15, but it only says that Timothy was taught the Scriptures from early youth, not that he was saved as an infant (and besides, he obviously did not die as an infant). Chafer points to the large multitudes in Heaven in Revelation 5:9 and concluded, "It is probable that the elect company, in order for it to be from every kindred, tribe and people, will be built up in part of those who die in infancy."[19] That might be true, but it more likely means people who would be saved as the church preaches the gospel to every nation (Matthew 24:14; 28:19).

Webb posits that if a supposed non-elect infant died and went to Hell, it would not understand why it was there. To turn this argument on its head, would an elect infant understand why it was in Heaven? God can educate both, so the argument is a *non sequitur*. All these texts are interesting but inconclusive to the state of the question. The cumulative weight of mere possibilities does not amount to a probable conclusion.

Problems

Some ask, "If all dying infants are saved, why are abortion and infanticide wrong? After all, wouldn't that simply send them to Heaven? They might otherwise grow up and end up in Hell." This is bad logic. It overlooks one big fact: God condemns murder (Exodus 20:13). If this argument were valid, it would also justify killing adult Christians to send them to Heaven.

Someone else might ask: "If they die as infants, what age will they be in Heaven?" This is difficult to answer. We can only speculate that they might be

---

19 Chafer, *Systematic Theology*, 7:199. So too Spurgeon, *New Park Street Pulpit*, 6:508.

granted immediate consciousness and later be resurrected in adult bodies. But the question does not address the specific issue.

In his often-helpful book *Heaven for Those Who Can't Believe*, Robert Lightner raises the unusual problem of what happens to unborn babies and their unsaved mothers at the time of the rapture. One can only speculate, if he cares to.

Calvin briefly addressed the question why all the elect are not saved in infancy. He answered that if all the elect were saved in infancy, it would not be obvious that salvation was completely by the Holy Spirit. God allows some of the elect to be saved in infancy but wisely waits until most reach maturity before saving them.[20] His discussion has more relevance for the question of infant regeneration than that of dying infants.

How Are Dying Infants Saved?

If all dying infants are saved, the question arises as to how this happens. The answer is that they are part of the Golden Chain together with non-infants. If saved, they were predestined. Peter Martyr Vermigli noted that the salvation of dying infants is proof that election is not based on foreseen works, for they have none.[21] I would add that it is not by foreseen faith either.

The key to the whole discussion is that dying infants were elected as a class. God could have elected all, none, or some. It appears He elected all, just as He elected all unfallen angels as a class and reprobated all fallen angels as a class. There are no exceptions in these cases, unlike humans who survive infancy, since most of them are reprobate and few are elect.

One thought is worth pondering. There may be something in the pattern that God elected none of the fallen angels, only a few fallen humans, and all dying infants. This could be seen in a pyramid diagram that displays God's electing grace in choosing the most helpless humans as a class.

If all dying infants are saved, then other inferences can be made. For reasons not entirely revealed to us and for His own glory, God decreed to place a large number of the elect in human bodies that would die in infancy. This is admitted even by those who say that only some dying infants are saved. God could have guaranteed that none of the elect would die in infancy, but He did not so decree. Spurgeon noted: "It is saved because it is elect. In the compass of election, and

---

20 John Calvin, *Sermons on the Epistle to the Ephesians* (London: Banner of Truth, 1973), 35–36.
21 Peter Martyr Vermigli, *The Peter Martyr Library* (Kirksville, MO: Truman State University Press, 2003), 8:32.

the Lamb's Book of Life, we believe there shall be found written millions of souls who are only shown on earth, then stretch their wings for heaven."[22] The Reformed view of unconditional election, then, is the key that opens the lock of the problem to the destiny of dying infants. The hard case actually sheds light on election.

Arminians who believe in the universal salvation of dying infants cannot base their theory on foreseen faith or good works. They usually base it on their weak view of original sin. Some deny original sin entirely, in which case they are Pelagians and not Arminians. Others suggest that dying infants have original sin but not guilt, which to the Reformed is as impossible as water without hydrogen and oxygen or fire without heat and light. How can there be sin without guilt? The Arminian theory puts all the emphasis on actual sins and fails to see the desperate sinfulness of infants with original sin. Even some Calvinists verge on this error when they suggest that unconscious original sin is not damnable. They forget that Numbers 15:27–31 says that sins of ignorance are still culpable and require atonement for forgiveness. So, the question of the destiny of dying infants touches on the first two points of Calvinism. It also touches on the fourth point, since it should be conceded that God irresistibly saves dying infants by efficacious grace. This was discussed by Augustine and the medieval Augustinians and Dominicans in the context of defending operative grace irresistibly regenerating infants through baptism.

Strong and Lightner argue for universal salvation for dying infants and say this necessitates a universal atonement. Not so, say mainstream Calvinists. It could only mean that Christ died for all the elect, including elect dying infants. Strong and Lightner were more or less Amyraldian, and often Amyraldians have a weakened view of original sin. Lightner, however, did make a good point: "Since Christ died in the place of those who can't believe, they will certainly receive salvation in Christ, the last Adam, as they received sin and condemnation in the first Adam."[23] Christ atoned for the original sin of the elect and not merely their actual sins.

If all dying infants are saved, it is because of Jesus Christ, for there is salvation in no one else (Acts 4:12). But what about the necessity of saving faith? Unbelievers are damned (Mark 16:16). Several answers have been put forth.

---

22 Charles H. Spurgeon, *Metropolitan Tabernacle Pulpit* (Pasadena, TX: Pilgrim Publications, 1969), 7:507.

23 Robert Lightner, *Heaven for Those Who Can't Believe* (Schaumburg, IL: Regular Baptist Press, 1987), 15. So also Augustus Hopkins Strong, *Systematic Theology* (Old Tappan: Fleming H. Revell, 1979), 662.

J. Oliver Buswell suggested that dying infants are given sufficient consciousness shortly before death to enable them to receive the gift of faith.[24] A. H. Strong said they are given faith immediately after death, and this is concurrent with their first sight of Christ.[25] Others are content to leave the matter unresolved in the secrets of God.[26]

Scripture says that faith is necessary to be justified and enter Heaven. Some say this only applies to persons capable of faith, not infants, while others say this proves the necessary existence of seminal faith. Others posit that since regeneration precedes faith, God might theoretically regenerate an infant at the moment of death and give him faith as he enters glory. Seen this way, infants are justified by faith consciously but not while on earth. In any case, the death of an infant confirms its election, for none of the reprobate die in infancy.

Conclusion

Grieving parents may take comfort that their beloved baby is safe in the arms of Jesus. But even those who are not convinced that all dying infants are saved may receive heavenly comfort. True comfort is not ultimately dependent on knowing if a loved one of any age is in Heaven. True, it is comforting to know that a Christian is now in Heaven (1 Thessalonians 4:18), but in many cases we just do not know if the loved one had been saved long before or even at the last moment. In some cases, like David with Absalom, we know they died lost.

But we do know that God is a good God who offers His very own peace to all who mourn. Jesus wept for His friend Lazarus (John 11:35) and doubtlessly wept when His stepfather, Joseph, died. He knows what it is to weep. He sympathizes. He cares.

---

24 J. Oliver Buswell, *A Systematic Theology of the Christian Faith* (Grand Rapids: Zondervan, 1962), 2:161–62.
25 Strong, *Systematic Theology*, 663.
26 So Isaac Ambrose, *The Christian Warrior* (Morgan, PA: Soli Deo Gloria, 1997), 20; Christopher Love, *A Treatise on Hell's Terrors* (Coconut Creek: Puritan Publications, 2012), 92; Spurgeon, *New Park Street Pulpit*, 6:507.

Chapter 51
The Destiny of the Unevangelized

We come now to the third hard case concerning election and reprobation. What is the eternal destination of those who never hear the gospel? Are they in the same situation as dying infants? If some are saved, they are elect; if not, non-elect. The issue touches on other issues relevant to the debate on the distinctive doctrines of Calvinism.

The Reformed Position

The question is not at all the same as for dying infants. Infants have original sin but no actual sins. The unevangelized have both (we are discussing the unevangelized past the age of reason in this chapter). Dying infants are saved, but that does not mean that the unevangelized are necessarily saved as well. If, as we argued in the previous chapter, infants are incapable of faith, this is a major difference with the unevangelized. The unevangelized are presently in a state of unbelief as well as sin. Unless a sinner repents and believes in Jesus Christ, he will perish (Luke 13:3).

One popular but erroneous way of addressing the question asks, "What happens to the innocent person who never hears the gospel?" But there are no innocent persons. The unevangelized are not like Adam before the Fall. There is no sinless "noble savage," no godly heathen. The unevangelized die lost.

Calvinists and other evangelicals outright deny universal salvation. Scripture clearly teaches that many sinners die lost and go to Hell. We also deny that there is any kind of second chance after death.

The Roman Catholic position has been changing. At one time, Rome officially taught that there is no salvation outside the Catholic Church. One must submit to the pope to be saved. The sacraments were necessary means of salvation. Some older Catholic theologians cherished the hope that the non-Catholic could somehow be saved, but this was a minority position. The big change happened at the Vatican II Council in the 1960s. That council officially proclaimed: "Those also can attain to everlasting salvation who through no fault of their own do not know the gospel of Christ or His Church, yet sincerely seek God and, moved by grace, strive by their deeds to do His will as it is known to them through the dictates of conscience."[1] It added that there is no salvation for anyone who knowingly and willfully rejects the gospel of Catholicism.

This acknowledged that some Protestants are "separated brethren." The perspective then broadened into a trans-religious ecumenism that recognizes all religions as valid, though Catholicism is still the best. Hans Kung was the foremost advocate of this position, which would have been unheard of a century ago. There is now open acknowledgment of "godly Hindus" as Catholic missionaries teach Zen Catholicism and other theologies. Karl Rahner and Don Cupitt popularized the idea of "anonymous Christians" — members of other religions who are somehow true Christians without knowing it. The observant Jew can be saved without the Church, the sacraments, or Christ. It is now religiously impolite to speak of the lost heathen. Diehard traditionalists, however, still adhere to the old approach and deny that Protestants and non-Christians are Christians.

A parallel perspective has been growing in Protestantism. Liberalism, of course, has for years denied that the unevangelized are lost. For example, this was at issue in the case of Pearl Buck and the Presbyterian church in the 1930s that led to the expulsion of J. Gresham Machen over missions. Gradually numerous erstwhile evangelicals took the liberal position. Previously they would disavow being evangelical or fundamentalist, but now they claim to still adhere to evangelical theology.

This movement has even affected Reformed circles. Some have tried to claim Huldrych Zwingli for their cause that there can be salvation for the unevangelized. Perhaps Zwingli made some remarks that could be taken in this direction, but his most explicit statement on the matter is expressly stated in his Seventy-Seven Articles of 1523: "Christ is the only way of salvation for all who have ever lived, do live or ever will live. He who seeks or points to another door does err — yea, is a murderer of souls and a robber."[2] Moyse Amyraut pondered whether God could save an unevangelized person by Christ without the gospel. He was refuted by the Formula Consensus Helvetica, which said that there are "innumerable myriads of men to whom Christ is not made known even by rumor" (Article 17). The gospel is the only means by which God calls sinners (Article 19), not the works of nature and providence (Article 20).

The Second Helvetic Confession opened the door a little: "At the same

---

1 Walter M. Abbott, ed., *The Documents of Vatican II* (New York: Herder and Herder, 1966), 35.

2 Arthur C. Cochrane, ed., *Reformed Confessions of the 16th Century* (Philadelphia: Westminster, 1966), 36.

time we recognize that God can illuminate whom and when He will, even without the external ministry, for that is His power; but we speak of the unusual way of instructing men, delivered unto us from God, both by commandment and example" (1:7). William G. T. Shedd also acknowledged the possibility of salvation for the unevangelized, though that number is small.[3] Elsewhere he clearly taught there was no salvation for those who never hear the gospel, therefore we must send them the gospel.

The loosely-aligned American movement known as the Primitive Baptists has always been emphatically Calvinist and often even Hyper-Calvinist. But one of its distinctive views is that there are many elect who are saved without ever hearing the gospel. They appeal to the absolute sovereignty of God and their idea of immediate regeneration. They oppose *mediate regeneration* as *gospel regeneration*. One does not need to hear the gospel to be regenerated, they argue. Thus, they do not send missionaries or evangelists nor support Bible societies or even Sunday schools. A few in the movement, however, take the more exclusive missionary view.

Some Calvinists interpret the Westminster Confession to teach that there may be a way for the unevangelized to be saved. They appeal to the following: "Elect infants, dying in infancy, are regenerated and saved by Christ through the Spirit, who worketh when, and where, and how He pleaseth. So also are all other elect persons, who are incapable of being outwardly called by the ministry of the Word" (10:3). Earlier we saw that the second sentence refers to mentally underdeveloped persons, not the unevangelized. The Confession goes on:

> Others, not elected, although they may be called by the ministry of the Word, and may have some common operations of the Spirit, yet they never truly come unto Christ, and therefore can not be saved: much less can men, not professing the Christian religion, be saved in any other way whatsoever, be they never so diligent to frame their lives according to the light of nature and the law of that religion they do profess. And to assert and maintain that they may, is very pernicious, and to be detested. (10:4)

By far the mainline Reformed view is that there is no salvation for those who never hear the gospel. John Calvin was most explicit and emphatic: "Those who have not heard about the Lord Jesus Christ will still perish without

---

3 William G. T. Shedd, *Calvinism: Pure and Mixed* (Edinburgh: Banner of Truth, 1986), 116–31; Augustus Hopkins Strong, *Systematic Theology* (Old Tappan: Fleming H. Revell, 1979), 564, 843.

mercy — they cannot hide behind their ignorance."[4] Such statements abound in the writings of Charles Hodge, Jonathan Edwards,[5] and many others. The Bohemian Confession of 1575/1609 stated: "We absolutely believe and profess from the bottom of our hearts that one can enter into this eternal life through no other means, nor attain it by any other path, than through Jesus Christ."[6]

I for one agree with the mainline view. The question is, "What saith the Scriptures?"

All Men Are Already Under God's Wrath

The theme of Romans is justification by faith. Paul lays the backdrop in chapters 1 through 3. In Romans 1:14–17 he says he is ready to preach the gospel, for it is the power of God unto salvation and through it is revealed the righteousness of God. Then in verses 18–32 he describes the hopelessness of sinful mankind. God has revealed His existence and some of His attributes to all men everywhere. They are guilty and without excuse. They are under a sentence of divine wrath. Creation reveals the problem but not the answer. The answer is in the gospel. The righteousness of God is revealed in the gospel, not in nature.

Paul continues in 2:1–11 to show that all men, both Jew and Gentile, are without excuse. The Jews have the written law and are guilty. The Gentiles have the law on their consciences and are guilty. In Ephesians 2:11–12 Paul says they are "without hope" and "without God." In Ephesians 4:17 he says they are spiritually blind. In 1 Corinthians 10:20 he says that non-Christian religions are demonic. This is the problem of universal sinfulness.

Then in Romans 2:12–16 Paul explains that the Gentiles have two condemning witnesses: external nature and internal conscience. They will not be judged by the written law they do not have but by the unwritten law they do have. Verse 12 is conclusive: They will perish without the written law. They do not need it to be

---

4 John Calvin, *Sermons on Galatians* (Edinburgh: Banner of Truth, 1997), 214.
5 Michael McClymond and Gerald McDermott wrongly claim that Edwards possibly allowed the salvation of some who never hear the gospel. *The Theology of Jonathan Edwards* (Oxford: Oxford University Press, 2012), 580–98. Edwards' unpublished sermon #235 on Matthew 22:14 explicitly argues that few who hear the gospel are saved, and there is no salvation for those who never hear the gospel; therefore, the dying unevangelized are all excluded and show they were not chosen to salvation. "Matthew 2:14 (Sermon 235)," Jonathan Edwards Center at Yale University, accessed February 9, 2018, http://edwards.yale.edu/.
6 In James T. Dennison Jr., ed., *Reformed Confessions of the 16th and 17th Centuries in English Translation* (Grand Rapids: Reformation Heritage Books, 2012), 3:428.

condemned; they are condemned already. Therefore, they are guilty and under condemnation even before they hear the gospel. They are lost.

Then in chapter 3 he quotes several Old Testament verses to show that all men everywhere, Jew and Gentile, are guilty of sin. In chapter 5 he explains that they are also guilty because of original sin inherited from Adam.

The Only Answer

Starting in 3:21, Paul begins to show the answer — justification by faith in Jesus Christ. We are justified by faith alone, not by good works (3:20, 28). That includes not only works of the law of Moses but works of the law of nature and conscience. It would be very odd if Paul said a person could be saved by obeying the law of nature but not the law of Moses.

We are saved by Christ's death (3:24–26; 5:8). His atonement is applied to us by the gift of faith. Faith is given to us through the gospel, not through nature or conscience, let alone non-Christian religions. Romans 10:14–15 presents a chain like 8:29–30. It could be called the *Silver Chain of Evangelism*. In the Golden Chain of 8:30 he mentioned "calling," which he mentions again in 10:13–14. All who call on the name of the Lord will be saved. As with 8:29–30, this means "all and only" without exception. But to call upon requires faith, and to have faith one must have hearing. And to hear one must have something to hear and someone to tell them the message. And those messengers must be sent. It is an airtight logic. No gospel, no faith; no faith, no salvation.

Then in verses 16–17 he states that not all who hear the gospel believe it. He quotes Psalm 19:4, which refers to natural revelation as in Romans 1. All people hear the inaudible truth that God exists, and therefore, they are accountable to Him. Note that verse 17 is explicit: Saving faith is a gift given only through the Word of God (some manuscripts and translations have "a word" or "preaching" about Christ). Without the gospel, they not only lack a Christ to believe in but also faith itself.

Robert Haldane spoke for the Reformed position here: "Men are not only saved through Christ, but they are saved through the knowledge of Christ."[7] Donald Grey Barnhouse said, "There is no hope for any man outside of Christ, whether that man has lived beyond the bounds of the gospel call or within its bounds."[8]

---

7 Robert Haldane, *The Epistle to the Romans* (London: Banner of Truth, 1966), 513.
8 Donald Grey Barnhouse, *Exposition of Bible Doctrine, Volume 2: God's Wrath* (Grand Rapids:

Christ Alone

One of the five great *sola* doctrines of Scripture that was rediscovered by the Protestant Reformers is "Christ alone" (*solus Christus*). We are saved by Jesus Christ alone, not by priests, popes, preachers, philosophers, parents, or ourselves. This is repeatedly and explicitly taught in the Bible. Jesus said, "I am the way, the truth and the life. No one comes to the Father except through Me" (John 14:6). He said that He is the only door (John 10:7, 9). Acts 4:12 says, "Nor is there salvation in any other, there is no other name under heaven given among men by which we must be saved." Christ is the only mediator between God and mankind (1 Timothy 2:5). There is no salvation for unbelievers who reject the gospel nor for nonbelievers who never hear the gospel (Mark 16:16; John 3:18, 36; 1 John 5:12). Abraham Kuyper was right: "Whom Jesus does not save can not be saved."[9]

We believe in Jesus by believing the gospel, for the gospel alone tells us about the person and work of Christ (1 Corinthians 15:1–4). God has been pleased to inseparably link the gift of saving faith with the content of the gospel. One simply cannot believe in Jesus Christ without believing the gospel. Charles Hodge put it well:

> The call in question is made only through the Word of God, as heard or read. That is, the revelation of the plan of salvation is not made by the works or by the providence of God; nor by the moral constitution of our nature, nor by the intuitions or deductions of reason; nor by direct revelation to all men everywhere and at all times; but only in the written Word of God. . . . The Scriptures do teach that saving knowledge is contained only in the Bible, and consequently that those ignorant of its contents are ignorant of the way of salvation.[10]

Objections

Objection 1: *"God is sovereign and is not limited to the gospel."*

This is position of the Primitive Baptists and a few others. The answer is in 1 Peter 1:23 and James 1:18. The gospel is God's appointed means of regenerating His elect. He could have theoretically chosen other means, but He has not so decreed.

Eerdmans, 1973), 69.

9 Abraham Kuyper, *The Work of the Holy Spirit* (Grand Rapids: Eerdmans, 1969), 605.

10 Charles Hodge, *Systematic Theology* (Grand Rapids: Eerdmans, 1979), 2:646.

Objection 2: *"The heathen who never hear the gospel are like Old Testament saints who never heard but were still saved."*

But the Bible says there has always been only one way of salvation and one gospel. Old Testament saints believed the same basic gospel (Galatians 3:8). Hebrews 4:2: "For indeed the gospel was preached to us as well as to them." Genesis 3:15 was the so-called *Proto-Evangelium*, and God progressively revealed more details through other prophecies such as Isaiah 53 (see Luke 24:44; Acts 10:43). Those that do not hear the gospel today are in an entirely different situation.

Objection 3: *"Did not Christ say that many will come from the east and west (Matthew 8:11) and that He had 'other sheep' (John 10:16)?"*

Those verses refer to Gentiles who had not yet been called but would believe when they heard. The book of Acts mentions many of them. Christ has only one flock — His believers.

Objection 4: *"What about Cornelius the Gentile who is called a God-fearer in Acts 10:2?"*

He was a Gentile who attended the synagogue, for Jews in that day called such Gentiles "God-fearers" because they believed in the one true God but had not yet become proselytes into Israel. Cornelius was not converted until Peter came and preached the gospel to him later in the chapter.

Objection 5: *"What about the good Muslim or the good Hindu?"*

Jesus said, "No one is good but One, that is, God" (Mark 10:18). God condemns all non-Christian religions as false religions. Just read the Old Testament. Muslims and Hindus worship demons, not the one true God (1 Corinthians 10:20). Those religions lead to Hell, not to Heaven (Matthew 7:13–14). Christ, not Muhammad, is the only way to God (John 14:6). Therefore, we must tell them the gospel.

Objection 6: *"What about non-Christian Jews?"*

The Jews acknowledge the one true God of Abraham, Isaac, and Jacob. But in denying the Trinity they show they do not have true faith in God. Paul said the gospel is for both Jew and Gentile (Romans 1:16). The unbelieving Jew needs Christ as much as the unbelieving Gentile. All are lost sinners (Romans 3:23). The modern "two covenants" error says that observant Jews who obey the law of Moses can be saved without faith in Christ because they are under a different covenant from the Gentiles. This is very wrong. The old covenant demanded faith in the coming Messiah. It has been abolished, but the gospel continues. As Romans, Galatians, and Ephesians say, nobody has ever been saved by obeying the law nor ever will be. This extreme dispensational error contradicts the Word of God and denies Christ is the only way.

Objection 7: *"What about the Greek philosophers?"*

Justin Martyr in the second century and, to some extent, Thomas Aquinas in the thirteenth century held that some Greek philosophers were unconscious "pre-Christians," as it were. Some may have had access to the Old Testament. But the Bible says that philosophy is vain deceit and does not hold to Christ (Colossians 2:8). Acts 17, 1 Corinthians 1, and Romans 1 describe the futility of philosophy. The philosophers died lost.

Objection 8: *"Middle Knowledge gives the answer how the unevangelized might be saved."*

This theory takes two forms. Some say that at least some of those who never hear the gospel will be saved because God knows that they would have believed had they heard. This is unbiblical. They still did not believe. God justifies believers, not those who hypothetically would have believed. Olympic gold medals are not awarded to athletes who would have won their races had they competed but to those runners who ran and won (see 1 Corinthians 9:24).

Another form of this objection says that God knew by Middle Knowledge that those who never hear the gospel would not have believed had they heard, so God is righteous in punishing them.[11] But does God punish unbelievers for unbelief in the gospel who never hear the gospel? No. The theory directly contradicts Matthew 11:21–24, where Christ says that the Sodomites would have believed and repented had they seen miracles. But God did not send them miracles because He did not elect them to salvation. Likewise, God can justly judge someone who does not repent or believe today, even if that person theoretically might have done so had he heard. God does not work by theoretical knowledge. Those who never hear the gospel are condemned for their original sin and actual sins against the law of nature. God does not condemn them for what they did not do. Peter Martyr Vermigli said, "Civil

---

11 E.g., Donald M. Lake, "He Died for All: The Universal Dimension of the Atonement." In Clark H. Pinnock, ed., *Grace Unlimited* (Minneapolis: Bethany House, 1975), 43; William Lane Craig, *The Only Wise God* (Grand Rapids: Baker, 1987), 150–51; "'No Other Name': A Middle Knowledge Perspective on the Exclusivity of Salvation through Christ," *Faith and Philosophy*, 6 (1989), 184–89.

judges will not punish people for those faults they might have committed if they had not been prevented."[12]

Objection 9: *"Since Christ died for everyone, nobody is condemned except for rejecting the gospel."*[13]

First, Christ did not die equally for all men. Next, they are condemned for sin, not just unbelief. Third, if this theory were true, then we should not preach the gospel to anyone, for then they might disbelieve and be damned. Next, the theory is incipient universalism for all who never hear.

Objection 10: *"There is a second chance after death (1 Peter 3:19) or reincarnation. Eventually everyone hears. God owes everyone the right to hear the gospel."*

Some proponents say that everyone will eventually believe and be saved, while others say that some still will never believe. Both are wholly unbiblical. First Peter 3:19 only speaks of Christ making a victorious proclamation to doomed demons and sinners in Hades on Holy Saturday, not preaching the gospel to them. Nobody goes from Hell to Heaven (Luke 16:26). There is no reincarnation (Hebrews 9:27), only resurrection to damnation (Daniel 12:2; Revelation 20:5). God does not owe anyone the gospel. It is a privilege, not a right. The time to believe is before death, not after (see 2 Corinthians 6:2 and Hebrews 9:27).

Objection 11: *"Does God not bring the gospel to people in ways other than the Bible?"*

No, He does not. The gospel is not revealed in the stars but in Scripture — "Christian astrology" is as ungodly as "Christian adultery." Nor is the gospel revealed through the pyramids, as some cults believe, for the pyramids were built by demon-worshiping Egyptians. The gospel is not in tree rings, the Chinese alphabet, frog DNA, or other such things. Nature testifies to the Creator's existence (Acts 14:17; Romans 1:19–21; Psalm 19:1) but does not reveal the way of salvation. The way is revealed only through the gospel in Scripture (1 Peter 1:25; Romans 1:16).

---

12 Peter Martyr Vermigli, *The Peter Martyr Library* (Kirksville, MO: Truman State University Press, 2003), 8:32.

13 Lake, "He Died for All," 47; Dave Hunt, *What Love Is This?*, 3rd ed., (Bend, OR: The Berean Call, 2006), 311.

Objection 12: "*Could God not bring them the gospel by dreams, visions, and angels as He did in the Old Testament?*"

He could, but He does not. He used those means to give special revelation, which has ceased with the closing of the biblical canon (see Hebrews 1:1–2). Angels do not bring the gospel. Note that even the angel in Acts 10 appeared to Cornelius but did not bring the gospel. Peter told him the gospel. Nor can we say that angels will preach the gospel everywhere according to Revelation 14:6. God commissions Christians, not angels, to tell people the good news.

Objection 13: "*What about the many stories of non-Christians who were saved by faith before they heard the missionaries?*"

Such stories and rumors abound, such as in Don Richardson's book *Eternity in Their Hearts*.[14] Some preachers believe the rumors and think that they help missions, but in reality if they were true there would be no need for missions.

Objection 14: "*If a person who never hears the gospel lives up to the light that he has, God will get the gospel to him so that he can believe and be saved.*"

John MacArthur[15] and others teach this theory. It does not say that the unevangelized are saved without the gospel, for proponents agree that there is no salvation without faith in Christ and the gospel. But the theory is based on a faulty interpretation of Acts 10. It overlooks one inescapable fact: Nobody lives up to the light he already has. They all hate and reject the light (John 3:19).

Objection 15: "*It would not be fair of God to condemn those who never hear of Christ.*"

This is related to the basic Arminian objection to all five points of Calvinism. We respond that God is always just. He is also sovereign. He chose whom to save and decided what is the means of saving them. He did not choose everyone, nor did He choose another means of salvation other than faith in Jesus Christ according to the gospel.

The gospel comes as good news to lost sinners who are already condemned, not to make them accountable and condemnable. They are "condemned already" (John 3:18). Rejecting Christ compounds their guilt, not makes them guilty for the first time. Arthur Pink said, "The heathen will not perish because they have

---

14 Ventura, CA: Regal Books, 1981.
15 For example, *The MacArthur New Testament Commentary, Acts 1–12* (Chicago: Moody, 1994), 293–94.

not believed in Christ, but because they failed to live up to the light which they did have — the testimony of God in nature and conscience."[16]

In his own straightforward way, John Gerstner struck at the root of this objection:

> Assuming that God does damn such persons, why is it unjust of Him to do so simply because they have no opportunity to be saved? If these persons are damned, they are damned because they are sinners; they are not damned because they have had an opportunity to be saved and have not utilized it. Their opportunity, or the lack of it, has nothing to do with their being damned; they are damned because they are sinners. What is unfair in God's damning sinners? [. . .] Some will say: Granted that God could damn men for their sins they have committed even though they did not hear the gospel and there would be no injustice in that as such. But, does not God have an obligation to offer salvation to everyone? But, we ask, why? Why does God have any obligation to offer salvation to any sinner? Grace, by definition, is undeserved. If it were deserved, it would not be a gospel; it would not be grace.[17]

This applies to the strange view that says, "God owes everyone the gospel. If they do not hear it in this life, God owes it to them in the next life." God owes sinners nothing but wrath. Grace is a free sovereign gift. So is the gospel.

All these objections seek to avoid the plain biblical teaching accepted by the vast majority of Calvinists as well as evangelical Arminians and Lutherans. The plain fact is that there is no salvation outside of Christ and no way to have faith in Christ except through the gospel. Those who never hear are lost. If they die lost, they go to eternal Hell.

Election and the Problem

If all who never hear die lost, then it follows that they were reprobated and not foreordained to hear and believe. None are elect. They go to Hell because of their sins. God predestined to pass them by in the decree of reprobation.

Therefore, we see there are two kinds of reprobate: those who never hear the gospel and those who hear but do not believe. Condemnation will be greater for the latter than for the former (Luke 12:48; Matthew 10:15; 11:22). The reprobate, child-sacrificing, homosexual rapists of Sodom and Gomorrah will be punished

---

16 Arthur W. Pink, *The Sovereignty of God* (Grand Rapids: Baker, 1973), 200.
17 John Gerstner, *Reasons for Faith* (New York: Harper and Row, n.d.), 151–52.

less than religiously hypocritical Jews in Christ's day or unbelieving churchgoers today (Matthew 11:20–24). There are not degrees of reprobation, but there are indeed degrees of punishment.

Conversely, if a person must hear and believe the gospel to be saved, it follows that all the elect will hear and believe the gospel sooner or later. As we shall see later, the Reformed doctrine of election is an incentive, not a hindrance, to the spread of the gospel. We know that someone out there will believe it, because God has foreordained that the elect will believe it.

Conclusion

If the unevangelized have any other way of salvation, then the need for evangelism and missions would be killed at once. A true view of the lost state of the unevangelized and the good news of the gospel gives us a greater encouragement and urgency to bring the gospel to everyone. Charles Hodge observed: "The proper effect of the doctrine that the knowledge of the gospel is essential to the salvation of adults, instead of exciting opposition to God's Word or providence, is to prompt us to greatly increased exertion to send the gospel to those who are perishing for lack of knowledge."[18]

We should also beware the words supposedly spoken by the Hyper-Calvinist John Collett Ryland to a young William Carey when Carey proposed to send out missionaries: "Sit down, young man. When God wants to save the elect, He'll do so in His own good time without you or me."[19] Fortunately, most Hyper-Calvinists do not believe that, but few of them send missionaries out, support evangelism, or tell the gospel far and wide.

The unevangelized are not just in so-called deep, dark Africa, for there are millions of Christians there. There are millions of unevangelized non-Christians in "Christian Europe" and "Christian America." Let us bring the gospel to all of them.

---

18 Hodge, *Systematic Theology*, 2: 648–49.
19 That he said this was denied by his son John Ryland Jr. and more recently was challenged by Iain H. Murray. But similar sentiments have been expressed by others.

Chapter 52
The Extent of the Atonement

The third point of Calvinism has been the most misunderstood and opposed of all the five points. This is unfortunate, for such misunderstanding misses the glorious truth contained in it. Most but not all Calvinists have believed in it, but no non-Calvinist does. It is usually the last of the five points that a new Calvinist accepts. When someone says, "I am a four-point Calvinist," we know automatically which point he does not accept.

It is sad that the debate has sometimes been rancorous. Participants on all sides sometimes resemble the soldiers who argued over Christ's robe while ignoring the sacred significance of the suffering Savior.

History of the Debate

There are basically three positions among Reformed theologians:

1. Christ died only for the elect and in no way whatsoever for the non-elect.

2. Christ died especially for the elect, and there is a general aspect for all men.

3. Christ died equally for all men.

It is difficult to ascertain the views of Augustine. Sometimes he seems to teach limited atonement; other times, universal atonement. Gottschalk seems to have been the first to explicitly teach the first view above in no uncertain terms. This view was also expressed in the Reformation by Theodore Beza and then by many subsequent Calvinists. John Owen wrote the classic *The Death of Death in the Death of Christ* upholding the strictly limited position with virtually no universal aspects. This became the view of most supralapsarians and all Hyper-Calvinists. Homer Hoeksema wrote, "If Christ died for the elect only, then there are no possible benefits in that death of Christ for anyone else but for those for whom He died."[1]

The Canons of the Synod of Dort tend to take a rather strictly limited view,

---

1 In Herman Hanko, Homer C. Hoeksema, and Gise Van Baren, *The Five Points of Calvinism* (Grand Rapids: Reformed Free Publishing Association, 1976), 61.

but they do allow for infinite value and universal sufficiency in the atonement (3:3–4). The Westminster Confession does not directly address the issue but could imply the more limited view (8:5, 8), as does the Larger Catechism (Q. 59). Yet there were divines at both assemblies who signed the standards while not holding to the strictly limited theory (such as the delegates from Britain and Germany at Dort and Vines, Arrowsmith, and Calamy at Westminster).

Theologians and historians have debated for centuries what the view of John Calvin was. I am inclined to believe he taught universal atonement, though he accepted the Lombardian formula in several places.[2] Moyse Amyraut and others of his school taught that Christ died *equally* for all. This seems to have been the position of the Thirty-Nine Articles of the Church of England (articles 2, 15, and 31) and possibly also the Heidelberg Catechism (Q. 37). Later the strictly universal position was advocated by post-Edwardsean New England theologians. It was taught by the so-called Low Calvinists in nineteenth-century Scotland, such as John M'Leod Campbell, James Morison, and Ralph Wardlaw. This general approach has been called Amyraldism, hypothetical universalism, or four-point Calvinism. It is popular with many dispensationalists. Augustus Hopkins Strong and Robert Lightner would be of this persuasion.[3]

It is not always easy to ascertain the views of some Reformed writers. Many do not address the issue. Some may have changed their views over time. Some stated their opinions in ways subject to misunderstanding. Caution must be exercised in studying both historical Reformed theology and true biblical theology on the matter.

The Mainstream Position

There have been a large number of leading Calvinists who hold what I consider to be the true biblical position. This may be called *moderate limited atonement* as opposed to the strictly limited view on the one hand or the strictly universal view on the other. Below is a catalog of just a few quotations that could be culled from leading Reformed theologians who by no means could be categorized as strictly limited or universal redemptionists. They taught that Christ died primarily for the elect, but there is a universal aspect for all men as well.

---

2 Curt Daniel, "Hyper-Calvinism and John Gill," PhD diss., The University of Edinburgh, 1983, 777–828.

3 Augustus Hopkins Strong, *Systematic Theology* (Old Tappan: Fleming H. Revell, 1979), 771–73; Robert Lightner, *The Death Christ Died: A Case of Unlimited Atonement* (Schaumburg, IL: Regular Baptist Press, 1967).

The earliest reference to limitation in the atonement was stated by Augustine's mentor, Ambrose: "Although Christ suffered for all, yet He suffered for us particularly, because He suffered for the church."[4] Peter Lombard put forth the formula that became a standard for much of medieval theology: "He offered himself on the altar of the cross not to the devil, but to the triune God, and he did so for all with regard to the sufficiency of the price, but only for the elect with regard to its efficacy, because he brought about salvation only for the predestined."[5]

Luther frequently asserted the universality of the atonement. For example: "He bore the sins of the entire world. [. . .] He has and bears all the sins of all men in his body. [. . .] He bears all the sins of the world from its inception. [. . .] Christ has taken away not only the sins of some men but your sins and those of the whole world."[6] Yet in at least one place he placed limitation in the work of Christ: "For in an absolute sense Christ did not die for all."[7] Subsequent Lutherans all taught a strictly universal atonement.

Zacharias Ursinus exemplified how many Reformed theologians used the Lombardian formula: "He died for all, as touching the sufficiency of the ransom which he paid; and not for all; but only for the elect, or those that believe, as touching the application and efficacy thereof. [. . .] Christ died in a different manner for believers and unbelievers."[8] Jerome Zanchius taught: "It is not false that Christ died for all men: for the passion of Christ is offered to all in the Gospel. But he died effectually for the elect alone, because indeed they only are made partakers of the efficacy of the passion of Christ."[9] The German Reformed perspective was also seen in the Bremen Consensus of 1595: "Indeed, that Christ has died for all and not for all are both true and both are found in Scripture and each must be taken in its proper sense."[10]

---

4 St. Ambrose, *Exposition of the Holy Gospel According to Saint Luke* (Etna, CA: Center for Traditionalist Orthodox Studies, 1998), 201.

5 Peter Lombard, *The Sentences, Book 3: On the Incarnation of the Word* (Toronto: Pontifical Institute of Medieval Studies, 2008), 86.

6 Martin Luther, *Luther's Works* (St. Louis: Concordia, 1955–), 26:285, 277; 22:169; 26:35, 38.

7 Luther, 25:376.

8 Zacharias Ursinus, *The Commentary of Dr. Zacharias Ursinus on the Heidelberg Catechism* (Phillipsburg, NJ: Presbyterian and Reformed, n.d.), 223. This sheds light on what the catechism meant in question 37's apparently universal redemption.

9 In John Davenant, *A Dissertation on the Death of Christ* (Weston Rhyn: Quinta Press, 2006), 191.

10 In James T. Dennison Jr., ed., *Reformed Confessions of the 16th and 17th Centuries in English Translation* (Grand Rapids: Reformation Heritage Books, 2012), 3:663.

In Great Britain, the "both/and" duality was expressed by George Abbot, the Puritan Archbishop of Canterbury who sent delegates to Dort: "Although we do not deny that Christ died for all men, yet we believe that he died specially and peculiarly for the Church, nor does the benefit of redemption pertain in an equal decree to all."[11] James Ussher: "So, in one respect he may be said to have died for all, and in another respect not to have died for all."[12] John Davenant, delegate to Dort, wrote the influential book *A Dissertation on the Death of Christ* to defend particular redemption with universal benefits. It was his opinion that this was in keeping with the Canons of Dort. Here is a summary:

> Christ suffered on the cross and died for all men or for the whole human race. We add, moreover, that this mediator, when he had determined to lay down his life for sin, had also this special intention, that, by virtue of his merits, he would effectually and infallibly quicken and bring to eternal life, some persons who were specially given to him by the Father. And in this sense we contend that Christ laid down his life for the elect alone, or in order to purchase his Church; that is, that he died for them alone, with the special and certain purpose of effectually regenerating and saving them by the merit of his death. Therefore, although the merit of Christ equally regards all men as to its sufficiency, yet it does not as to its efficacy.[13]

Controversial Richard Baxter's views are sometimes convoluted, but he wrote the large *Universal Redemption of Mankind* and others to share this view, such as: "Christ therefore died for all, but not equally for all, or with the same intent, design or purpose."[14] Edward Polhill, another Puritan, wrote:

> Now Christ's death was paid down by him and accepted by God as a price with a double respect. As for all men it was paid and accepted as a price, so far forth, as to procure for them a ground for their faith, viz., that they might be saved on gospel terms. And as for the elect it was further paid and accepted as a price, so far as to procure the very grace of faith for them. [. . .] Christ suffered between two thieves, a type of the elect and

---

11 In Davenant, *A Dissertation*, 198.

12 James Ussher, *The Whole Works of the Most Rev. James Ussher, D.D.* (Dublin, 1847), 12:559.

13 Davenant, *A Dissertation on the Death of Christ*, 198. Davenant's views were popularized in the twentieth century by Norman Douty, *The Death of Christ*, 1st ed. (Swengal, PA: Reiner, 1972), reprinted as *Did Christ Die Only for the Elect?* (Eugene, OR: Wipf and Stock, 1998); 2nd ed. (Irving, TX: Williams & Watrous, 1978) different pagination.

14 Richard Baxter, *Catholick Theologie*, Part II (London, 1675), 53. See *Universal Redemption of Mankind* (London, 1694).

reprobate world; but who dare say that he had as much respect to the one as to the other?[15]

The great William Ames also used the Lombardian formula: "As for the intention of application, it is rightly said that Christ made satisfaction only for those whom he saved, though in regard to the sufficiency in the mediation of Christ it may also rightly be said that Christ made satisfaction for each and all."[16]

Jonathan Edwards:

> From these things it will inevitably follow, that however Christ in some sense may be said to die for all, to redeem all visible Christians, yea, the whole world by His death; yet there must be something particular in the design of his death, with respect to such as he intended should actually be saved thereby. [. . .] Christ did die for all in this sense, that all by his death have an opportunity of being [saved].[17]

Charles Haddon Spurgeon often affirmed limited atonement, but he also believed in a universal side:

> The Saviour did, indeed, in a certain sense, die for all; all men receive many a mercy through his blood, but that he was the Substitute and Surety for all men, is so inconsistent, both with reason and Scripture, that we are obliged to reject the doctrine with abhorrence.[18]

> There is a wide, far-reaching sacrificial atonement which brings untold blessings to all mankind, but by that atonement a special divine object was aimed at, which will be carried out, and that object is the actual redemption of his own elect from the bondage of their sins, the price being the blood of Jesus Christ.[19]

> Then Christ died for them, and for them only. But in a certain sense he died for all, that all might be his property; and they are all his property.[20]

---

15 Edward Polhill, *The Works of Edward Polhill* (Morgan, PA: Soli Deo Gloria, 1998), 166, 171; cf. 172.

16 William Ames, *The Marrow of Theology* (Boston: Pilgrim Press, 1968), 150.

17 Jonathan Edwards, *The Works of Jonathan Edwards* (1957; repr., New Haven: Yale University Press, 1994), 1:435; 13:478.

18 Charles H. Spurgeon, *Metropolitan Tabernacle Pulpit* (Pasadena, TX: Pilgrim Publications, 1977), 46:7. See also 49:110.

19 Spurgeon, *Metropolitan Tabernacle Pulpit*, 21:176.

20 Terence Peter Crosby, ed., *C. H. Spurgeon's Sermons Beyond Volume 63* (Leominster: Day One, 2009), 615.

Spurgeon's views are summed up in his sermon "General and Yet Particular."[21]

Robert Lewis Dabney writes:

> There is no passage in the Bible which asserts an intention to apply redemption to any other than the elect, on the part of God and Christ; but there are passages which imply that Christ died for all sinners in some sense, as Dr. Ch. Hodge has so expressly admitted. [. . .] Redemption is limited, i.e., to true believers, and is particular. Expiation is not limited.[22]

He refers to the words of Charles Hodge: "There is a sense, therefore, in which He died for all, and there is a sense in which He died for the elect alone."[23] His son A. A. Hodge said:

> Nor is there any debate as to the universal reference of some of the benefits purchased by Christ. Calvinists believe that the entire dispensation of forbearance under which the human family rest since the fall, including the unjust as well as the just temporal mercies and means of grace, is part of the purchase of Christ's blood. They admit also that Christ did in some sense die for all men, that he thereby removed all legal obstacles from the salvation of any and every man, and that his satisfaction may be applied to one man as well as to another if God so wills it.[24]

William G. T. Shedd summed up his position: "Atonement is unlimited, and redemption is limited. This statement includes all the Scripture texts: those which assert that Christ died for all men, and those which assert that he died for his people."[25]

William Cunningham has a lengthy and useful discussion on the history of the debate and argues for particular redemption. But he also allows the following: "It is not denied by the advocates of particular redemption, or of a limited atonement, that mankind in general, even those who ultimately perish, do derive some advantage or benefits from Christ's death."[26] His friend and predecessor Thomas Chalmers expressed this position in *The Institutes of Theology*.

---

21 Spurgeon, *Metropolitan Tabernacle Pulpit*, 10:229–40.

22 Robert Lewis Dabney, *Systematic Theology* (Edinburgh: Banner of Truth, 1985), 527, 529.

23 Charles Hodge, *Systematic Theology* (Grand Rapids: Eerdmans, 1979), 2:546.

24 A. A. Hodge, *Outlines of Theology* (Edinburgh: Banner of Truth, 1973), 416. His fuller views are expressed in his large book, *The Atonement*.

25 William G. T. Shedd, *Dogmatic Theology*, 3rd ed. (Phillipsburg, NJ: P&R, 2003), 743.

26 William Cunningham, *Historical Theology* (London: Banner of Truth, 1969), 2:332.

J. C. Ryle is often cited as believing in universal atonement, but he actually took the mainstream line regarding limitation and universality. For example:

> To say, on the one hand, that Christ's death is efficacious to none but the elect and believers, is strictly true. [. . .] But to say, on the other hand, that in no sense did Christ do anything at all for the whole world, but that he did everything for the elect alone, seems to me utterly irreconcilable with this text (John 12:4). Surely Christ came to provide a salvation sufficient for the whole 'world.'"[27]

Later Anglican Calvinists such as W. H. Griffith Thomas expressed similar views.

Most supralapsarians hold to the stricter view of limited atonement with no universal aspects, but even the staunch Abraham Kuyper could write: "It is stated in Scripture, in words that are certainly not subject to two different interpretations, both that Christ died for all, and that he did not die for all."[28] His friend and successor Herman Bavinck said, "Although vicarious atonement as the acquisition of salvation in its totality cannot therefore be explained to include all persons individually, this is not to say that it has no significance for those who are lost."[29]

James Petigru Boyce:

> Christ did actually die for the salvation of all, as that he might be called the Savior of all; because his work is abundantly sufficient to secure the salvation of all who will put their faith in him. Christ died, however, in an especial sense for the Elect; because He procured for them not a possible, but an actual salvation.[30]

John Broadus, another important early Southern Baptist theologian, said:

> In one sense, Jesus 'gave himself a ransom for all' (1 Timothy 2:6), and to 'taste death for every man' (Hebrews 2:9; comp. 1 John 2:2), making salvation objectively possible for all; in another sense, his atoning death definitely contemplated the salvation of the elect.[31]

---

27 J. C. Ryle, *Expository Thoughts on the Gospels: St. John* (Cambridge: James Clarke, 1976), 2:429.
28 Abraham Kuyper, *Particular Grace: A Defense of God's Sovereignty in Salvation* (Grandville: Reformed Free Publishing Association, 2001), 272.
29 Herman Bavinck, *Reformed Dogmatics* (Grand Rapids: Baker, 2006), 3:470.
30 James Petigru Boyce, *Abstract of Systematic Theology* (Cape Coral, FL: Founders, 2007), 340.
31 John Broadus, *Commentary on the Gospel of Matthew* (Philadelphia: American Baptist

In what was perhaps the most influential Reformed systematic theology of the twentieth century, Louis Berkhof wrote: "All that natural man receives other than curse and death is an indirect result of the redemptive work of Christ."[32] Berkhof there and in *Vicarious Atonement Through Christ* defended the limited side of the atonement.

Loraine Boettner wrote what may have been the most influential work on the five points during the last century, *The Reformed Doctrine of Predestination*, and defended the limited aspect as well as the general aspect: "There is, then, a sense in which Christ died for all men."[33] Iain Murray, founder of the Banner of Truth, said: "But if the Gospel texts speak of the death of Christ in terms of the particular, there are others which direct us to the universal."[34]

The renown New Testament scholar D. A. Carson agreed with the basics of Reformed theology in numerous books, and gave a useful explanation of the duality of the atonement:

> I argue, then, that both Arminians and Calvinists should rightly affirm that Christ died for all, in the sense that Christ's death was sufficient for all and that Scripture portrays God as inviting, commanding, and desiring the salvation of all, out of love. [. . .] Further, all Christians ought also to confess that, in a slightly different sense, Christ Jesus, in the intent of God, died effectively for the elect alone, in line with the way the Bible speaks of God's special selecting love for the elect.[35]

John Murray defended the historic doctrine in *Redemption Accomplished and Applied*, and added these comments elsewhere: "In this sense, therefore, we may say that Christ died for non-elect persons. [. . .] The atonement was designed for those, and for those only, who are ultimately the beneficiaries of what it is in its proper connotation."[36] One of his successors at Westminster Theological

---

Publication Society, 1886), 531.

32 Louis Berkhof, *Systematic Theology* (Grand Rapids: Eerdmans, 1988), 393–94, 439.

33 Loraine Boettner, *Studies in Theology* (Philadelphia: Presbyterian and Reformed, 1973), 325. So also *The Reformed Doctrine of Predestination* (Philadelphia: Presbyterian and Reformed, 1932), 295.

34 Iain Murray, *The Cross: The Pulpit of God's Love* (Edinburgh: Banner of Truth, 2008), 10; cf. 16.

35 D. A. Carson, *The Difficult Doctrine of the Love of God* (Wheaton: Crossway, 2000), 77.

36 John Murray, *The Collected Writings of John Murray* (Edinburgh: Banner of Truth, 1976), 1:68–69.

Seminary, John Frame, said: "Christ died to guarantee salvation to the elect and to provide the opportunity of salvation for all."[37]

One of the most well-known and influential Calvinist preachers and writers has been John Piper. He made these observations: "We do not deny that Christ died to save all in some sense. [. . .] What we deny is that the death of Christ is for all men in the same sense. And he sent Christ to save those who believe in a more particular sense. God's intention is different for both."[38] And again: "Christ died for all, but especially for His bride."[39] Wayne Grudem wrote the best-selling Calvinist *Systematic Theology* and said this on the subject: "The statements 'Christ died for his people only' and 'Christ died for all people' are both true in some senses."[40]

R. C. Sproul has undoubtedly been the most influential popularizer of Reformed theology since the mid-1970s. He often defended limited atonement, but in at least one place admitted the universal aspect: "There is a universal effect of the cross, in the sense that everybody benefits from the death of Christ, although not in the full sense of being saved by it."[41] D. Martyn Lloyd-Jones is almost universally admitted to have been the greatest Calvinist preacher of the last hundred years. In some writings he speaks to the universal aspect, and in others, the limited aspect. He summed up his view in these words: "His death, as Calvin and other expositors remind us, because it was eternal and because He is the Son of God, is sufficient for the whole world; but it is efficient only for the church."[42]

R. B. Kuiper taught at both Westminster Theological Seminary and Calvin Theological Seminary in their golden days. He wrote what was perhaps the best short defense of limited atonement, *For Whom Did Christ Die?* He presented a fair and balanced treatment of the subject biblically and theologically. Here are a few representative statements on the matter:

> According to the Reformed faith the divine design of the atonement
> is in an important respect limited. But the Reformed faith also insists

---

37 John Frame, *The Doctrine of God* (Phillipsburg, NJ: P&R, 2002), 420.

38 John Piper, *Five Points* (Fearn: Christian Focus, 1995), 40.

39 John Piper, *A Godward Life: Book Two* (Sisters, OR: Multnomah, 1999), 352.

40 Wayne Grudem, *Systematic Theology* (Grand Rapids: Zondervan, 1994), 601.

41 R. C. Sproul, *Mighty Christ* (Fearn: Christian Focus, 1995), 132.

42 D. Martyn Lloyd-Jones, *Life in the Spirit* (London: Banner of Truth, 1973), 145–46. J. E. Hazlett Lynch argues in a whole book that Lloyd-Jones believed in universal atonement: *Lamb of God, Saviour of the World: The Soteriology of Rev. Dr. Martyn Lloyd-Jones* (Bloomington, IN: WestBow, 2015). R. T. Kendall has asserted this for years, while Iain Murray denies it.

that in other respects it is universal. It can be shown without the slightest difficulty that certain benefits of the atonement, other than the salvation of individuals, are universal. [. . .] Therefore the statement, so often heard from Reformed pulpits, that Christ died only for the elect must be rated a careless one. [. . .] The particular design of the atonement and its universal design in no way contradict each other. Nor do they merely complement each other. They support and strengthen each other. In the final analysis they stand and fall together.[43]

Similar quotations could be given from these and many other leading Reformed theologians. Many "new Calvinists" are not aware of them because they have only read a few short introductions to the five points. Some advocates of the strictly limited view casually dismiss these kinds of statements as either Amyraldian or Arminian. But if the above are not fully fledged Reformed theologians, then nobody is. They represent the cream of the leading Calvinists across the centuries and from different traditions (Puritan, Dutch, Presbyterian, Baptist, Anglican, etc.).

This is not to say that all of these agreed on what are the specific limited and universal aspects. The universal aspects will be discussed below and the limited side in the next chapter.

The Biblical Balance

There are number of important biblical teachings that have a dichotomy of truths that must be kept in balance: the oneness and threeness of the Trinity, the two natures of Christ, divine sovereignty and human responsibility, and the twofold will of God, to name a few. The same is true with the multifaceted work of Christ. In that one death He showed the love of God, defeated Satan, propitiated the Father, and more.

The atonement flows from the love of God (John 3:16; Romans 5:8; Galatians 2:20; 1 John 3:16, 4:9–10). Reformed theology teaches that Scripture presents a twofold love of God. He has a general love for all men as His creatures. It would not be inconsistent, then, for there to be a general aspect of the atonement for all men. But God also has a special love for the elect only, and this is shown in the limited side of the atonement. It is sometimes said that out of these two loves, the death of Christ provides salvation for all but guarantees it for the elect alone.

---

43 R. B. Kuiper, *For Whom Did Christ Die?* (Grand Rapids: Baker, 1982), 78–79.

This duality is reflected in 1 Timothy 4:10: "The living God, who is the Savior of all men, especially of those who believe." Christians are to reflect the love of God to all men (Matthew 5:44) and especially the brethren (John 13:34). Galatians 6:10 says, "Therefore, as we have opportunity, let us do good to all, especially to those who are of the household of faith." R. B. Kuiper wisely encouraged us to speak of Christ's death as being "especially" rather than "only" for the elect. That is also preferable to saying it was "equally" for all.

Matthew 13:44 might provide an illustration of this. In the parable, a man buys a field with the main purpose of obtaining the hidden treasure. In a like manner, Christ purchased the whole world with the main intent of attaining the elect and their salvation.

Substitutionary Atonement

Of course, this presupposes several other precious Bible truths. For one, God is justly angry with sinners and will not forgive anyone without atoning satisfaction. Anselm taught that God became a man to satisfy the infinite honor of God, which no mere man could accomplish, nor could God as God. Calvinists have more or less accepted this approach and added the dimension of penal substitution. Christ died as our legal substitute. He also paid our debt. Those who deny either divine wrath or penal substitution not only reject historic Calvinism but doctrines that are essential to biblical Christianity. Substitutionary atonement is a fundamental tenet of the gospel (1 Corinthians 15:1–4). Those who deny it deny the faith and prove to be unbelievers and heretics. It is that important.

Some Calvinists, such as Samuel Rutherford, toyed with the medieval theory of absolute power to say that God could forgive the elect without an atonement or with another person (a sinless man, an angel) or even with an animal (as in the Old Testament, even a pig). John Owen apparently once considered holding this theory but then rejected it and successfully refuted it.[44] There was no other way for God to be satisfied, as Christ prayed in Gethsemane (Matthew 26:39; Mark 14:36; Luke 22:42). Hebrews 9:22 teaches that without the shedding of blood, there can never be forgiveness. Election was a free act of God, but for salvation to be effected in the elect, an atoning sacrifice of the God-man was necessary.

Christ died *for* sinners as a substitute, not merely as an example of divine

---

44 John Owen, *The Works of John Owen* (London: Banner of Truth, 1967), 10:482–624, especially 574–607.

love to move them to repentance (as Abelard taught) nor as a martyr to a good cause (as many liberals have taught) nor merely as a goal. He suffered and died *for* them as their substitute and in their place (see Isaiah 53:4–12; Galatians 2:20; Romans 5:6, 8; and especially 1 Peter 3:18). It would be futile to debate "For whom did Christ die?" if He did not die for anyone. Historic Calvinists and Arminians agree here, though they disagree as to whether the atonement guaranteed salvation or merely provided for it. Tragically, in recent years many Arminians and ex-Calvinists have rejected the precious doctrine of penal substitutionary atonement. Many erroneously still claim to be evangelical while denying an essential of the evangel. No substitution, no salvation! We do not deny other aspects of the salvific work of Christ, such as *Christus Victor*. But neither should they deny this aspect. To deny one at the expense of the other would be as fatal as denying either the oneness or threeness of the Trinity or either of the two natures of Christ. What God has joined together, we dare not put asunder. However they identify those for whom the Savior died, historic Calvinists have firmly believed in substitutionary atonement. He died for us. We would die for this great truth.

Infinite Value and Universal Sufficiency

Most Calvinists have accepted Peter Lombard's formula: "Christ died sufficiently for all, but efficaciously only for the elect." Theodore Beza and Johannes Piscator rejected it because they thought it taught universal atonement.[45] Others who hold to the strictly limited view also sometimes reject it. Lombard built upon Anselm's theory that only an infinite being could satisfy God. God alone is infinite, so God became a man. In sum, the formula says that Christ's work was sufficient for all because it had infinite value. This is the main ingredient of the universal aspect of the atonement.

Martin Luther commented, "Just one drop of this innocent blood would have been more than enough for the sins of the whole world."[46] Edwards taught that we owe an infinite debt, not because we are infinite or have an infinite number of sins, nor are there infinite number of sinners, but because each sin is committed against God who is infinite in His being and holiness. Christ gave His life, blood, and death as an infinite payment: "All created beings are

---

45 Calvin accepted it in his commentary on 1 John 2:2 but said it was not applicable to that text. He employed it in other places and hinted at it in even more. John Gill rejected the formula: *The Cause of God and Truth* (Grand Rapids: Baker Book House, 1980), 98.
46 Luther, *Luther's Works*, 30:36.

nothing worth to God in comparison to the least drop of Christ's blood."[47] He did not suffer an infinite amount, for He suffered in His finite humanity and not in His impassible deity. Nor did He suffer an eternal duration. His infinite deity gave infinite value to His blood, suffering, and death.

The Scots Confession put it thus:

> Because the Godhead alone could not suffer death and neither could manhood overcome death, he joined both together in one person, that the weakness of one should suffer and be subject to death — which we had deserved — and the infinite and invisible power of the other, that is, of the Godhead, should triumph, and purchase for us life, liberty, and perpetual victory (Article 8).

Finite angels could not provide an infinite atonement sufficient for anyone, not even another angel. Calvin remarked: "For even if all the angels of heaven were made answerable for us, the price they would pay would be insufficient," and later added, "a hundred worlds [...] would not be sufficient to erase one offense that we have committed against God."[48] Matthew Henry said Christ "paid a price sufficient to redeem as many world of sinners as there are sinners in the world."[49] The saintly Robert Murray M'Cheyne said, "I ought to see that in Christ's blood shedding there is an infinite over-payment for all my sins. Although Christ did not suffer more than infinite justice demanded, yet He could not suffer at all without laying down an infinite ransom."[50]

Another great Scotsman, Samuel Rutherford, wrote: "There is as much merit in Christ as will buy a thousand heavens."[51] Elsewhere he noted that though the price was infinite and the suffering great, even now Christ has no regrets for what He paid or paid for: "Though ye give no hire for Him, yet hath He given a great price and ransom for you; and if the bargain were to make again, Christ would give no less for you than what He hath already given."[52]

---

47 Edwards, *Works*, 10:599. That the atonement required an infinite payment that only the God-man could make was taught in Reformed theology at least as early as Theodore Beza. Dennison Jr., ed., *Reformed Confessions of the 16th and 17th Centuries*, 2:248.

48 John Calvin, *Sermons on Galatians* (Edinburgh: Banner of Truth, 1997), 286, 395.

49 Matthew Henry, *Commentary on the Whole Bible* (Old Tappan: Fleming H. Revell, n.d.), 6:1045 (on 2 Peter 2:1).

50 Andrew Bonar, *Memoir and Remains of Robert Murray M'Cheyne* (Edinburgh: Banner of Truth, 1978), 151.

51 Samuel Rutherford, *Fourteen Communion Sermons* (Edinburgh: James Dickson, 1986), 256.

52 Samuel Rutherford, *Letters of Samuel Rutherford* (Edinburgh: Banner of Truth, 1984), 610.

Charles Hodge summed up an important principle at this juncture: "All that Christ did and suffered would have been necessary had only one human soul been the object of redemption; and nothing different and nothing more would have been required had every child of Adam been saved through His blood."[53] Perhaps he was rebuking the tiny group of strict limitarian Calvinists who taught the minority theory called *equivalentism*. That position says that Christ suffered a specific finite amount and would have had to suffer more or less pain if more or less sinners had been elected.[54]

The Canons of the Synod of Dort sum up the Reformed doctrine on the infinite value and universal sufficiency of the work of Christ:

> The death of the Son of God is the only and most perfect sacrifice and satisfaction for sin; and is of infinite worth and value; abundantly sufficient to expiate the sins of the whole world. This death derives its infinite value and dignity from these considerations, because the person who submitted to it was not only really man, and perfectly holy, but also the only begotten Son of God, of the same eternal and infinite essence with the Father and the Holy Spirit, which qualifications were necessary to constitute him a Savior for us; and because it was attended with a sense of the wrath and the curse of God due to us for sin. (2:2–3)

The delegates to Dort from Britain (especially Davenant) and Germany (such as Martinus) appealed to these words in arguing for a universal dimension of the atonement as well as a particular aspect. The historic Reformed view teaches the infinite value and universal sufficiency of the one glorious atoning work of Christ.

Universal Benefits

There are various universal benefits beyond the guaranteed salvation of the elect. One is common grace. In one sense it flows freely from the divine nature, for "God is love." But since mankind is fallen and deserves eternal wrath, there must have been something in the cross whereby God's general love for all must be met with satisfaction. If there is no universal aspect, there could be no common grace to us. Of course, Hyper-Calvinists such as Herman Hoeksema turn this around and argue there is no universal aspect or common grace, but that is a minority opinion in the Reformed community.

---

53 Hodge, *Systematic Theology*, 2:545.
54 See my "Hyper-Calvinism and John Gill," 551.

As Spurgeon once put it: "Christ hath bought some good things for all men — the common mercies of life."[55] Edward Polhill expressed it with typical Puritan eloquence: "Every bough of nature hangs upon the cross, every crumb of bread swims in his blood, every grape of blessing grows on his crown of thorns, and all the sweetness in nature streams out of his vinegar and gall."[56] He went on to say that Christ took the curse of creation and will renovate creation based on His atonement. Some see typological significance in Christ's wearing the crown of thorns (Matthew 27:29), for thorns represent the curse on creation (Genesis 3:18). Thus, His sacrifice had cosmic significance beyond humanity.

Next, all sinners deserve immediate judgment and instant wrath. Not only do all men receive many good things that they do not deserve (Luke 16:25; Acts 14:17), but they are not now receiving the wrath they do deserve. The very fact that they are not already in Hell is due in part to the death of Christ. Christ purchased a stay of execution for all men, as it were, but bought a guaranteed pardon for the elect alone. Lost sinners should thank God for every moment they are not in Hell, for anything short of Hell is a mercy bought by the blood of Christ. It had to be paid for, and Christ did just that.

This is related to another universal non-saving benefit. Romans 14:9 says, "For to this end Christ died and rose and lived again, that He might be Lord both of the dead and of the living." Christ was rewarded for His humiliating death by the Father with the honor of being Lord of all men, saved and lost, elect and non-elect (Philippians 2:5–11). He is the "heir of all things" (Hebrews 1:2).

Calvinists generally ground the universal free offer of the gospel in the infinite value and universal sufficiency of the atonement. Others who hold to the stricter limitation tended to deny this foundation or even reject the free offer altogether. But historic Calvinists contend that since a proclamation of the gospel is an invitation to a feast, there must be something on the banquet table that is infinitely sufficient for all to whom the invitation is extended (Matthew 22:2–14; Luke 14:16–24) — "Come, for all things are now ready."

The State of the Debate

To recount, there are basically three Reformed positions. Christ died (1) only for the elect, (2) for all men but especially the elect, and (3) equally for all men. They all deny that all men will be saved in the end, for they all believe

---

55 Charles H. Spurgeon, *Anecdotes and Stories* (London: Houlston and Wright, 1866), 140.
56 Polhill, *The Works of Edward Polhill*, 158.

in the Reformed doctrines of election and reprobation. A few New England ex-Calvinists such as Joseph Huntington[57] argued that all men will be saved because Christ died efficaciously for all. But that is universal salvation, not merely universal redemption or unlimited atonement. It is not even evangelical Arminianism, for Arminius and Wesley firmly believed in Hell. Moreover, we believe that God has not elected all.

David Allen misses the point on the very first page of *The Extent of the Atonement: A Historical and Critical Review*: "There are only two options: either Jesus substituted for the sins of all people, or he substituted for the sins of only some people."[58] In what is certainly the largest defense of Arminian universal atonement and attack on the Reformed doctrine of particular redemption, he fails to see the variations among Calvinists who hold to particularity according to positions 1 or 2. Consequently, he errs in classifying Jonathan Edwards, Charles Hodge, Robert Lewis Dabney, J. C. Ryle, and many others quoted above — including myself — as advocating universal atonement. Other writers, especially of the strictly limited position (1), make the same mistake by classifying the advocates of position 2 as promoting universal atonement (3). Still others class these theologians as belonging to group 1, overlooking their repeated and clear affirmations of universal aspects in the atonement. Though Allen and these writers offer many useful observations and documentations, they muddy the waters of discussion by failing to appreciate category 2.

The debate is not merely about the atonement's universal aspects, infinite value, or universal sufficiency nor even primarily about the identity of those for whom Christ died. The real question is over the nature of the atonement as to the efficacy at the point at which it was made at Calvary. Did Christ merely provide for redemption, or did He guarantee it for the elect? Did He actually propitiate the Father, or did He merely provide a sacrifice that would allow the Father to grant salvation to whom He chooses? Those who believe in the strictly limited view and those who teach the both/and view differ with the "equally for all" view on this critical point. We hold that Christ did actually satisfy the Father's wrath for the elect alone in such a way that guaranteed their salvation.

---

57 Joseph Huntington, *Thoughts on the Atonement of Christ* (Newburyport: John Mycall, 1976); *Calvinism Improved; or, The Gospel Illustrated as a System of Real Grace, Issuing in the Salvation of All Men* (New London: Samuel Green, 1976).
58 David L. Allen, *The Extent of the Atonement: A Historical and Critical Review* (Nashville: B&H Academic, 2016), ix.

Conclusion

In the next chapter we will discuss the biblical teaching on the particular aspect of the atonement for the elect alone. This is a distinctive element of mainstream Calvinism that is not shared with any other variety of evangelical theology.

Chapter 53
Limited Atonement

All true evangelical Christians believe "Christ died for us" (Romans 5:8). While there are many beautiful aspects of the atonement that shine like facets on a diamond, the aspect of substitution is especially prominent. Christ died as a substitute for others, not merely as an example of God's love, as a martyr to a good cause, or as victor over the Devil. There have been various theories regarding substitution, such as the satisfaction theory of Anselm, the governmental theology of Grotius, or the penal satisfaction theory. But there can be no doubt that substitution is essential to the scriptural teaching of the atonement (Isaiah 53:4–12; Matthew 20:28; 26:28; Mark 10:45; 14:24; Luke 22:19–20; Romans 5:6, 8; 1 Corinthians 15:3; 2 Corinthians 5:21; Galatians 3:13; Ephesians 5:2, 25; 1 Timothy 2:6; Hebrews 2:9; 9:28; 1 Peter 2:21, 24; 3:18).

The question then is, "For whom did Christ die?" But it is more than that. Earlier we saw that there are universal aspects involved. It is not just a question of extent but intent. More importantly, it has to do with the nature of the atonement. It is widely agreed that the term *limited atonement* is unfortunate. We use it because of the popular TULIP acrostic. To some persons the phrase seems to imply a deficiency in the work of Christ. As we shall see, the deficiency is in the non-Reformed theory. Many Calvinists prefer the terms *definite atonement* or *particular redemption* in order to bring out the perfection and particularity of redemption. This chapter will concisely present the main biblical and theological proofs for this precious truth.

Election and the Atonement

There is a close relation between unconditional election (the second point of Calvinism) and particular atonement (the third point). Both have to do with salvation. God chose the elect to be saved (2 Thessalonians 2:13). Christ died so that sinners could be saved. God did not foreordain to save the elect without an atonement. William Twisse, Samuel Rutherford, and a few other supralapsarians suggested that God could have saved the elect by sheer sovereignty without an atonement. Even Calvin toyed with this theory in at least one place.[1] But

---

1 John Calvin, *Sermons on Isaiah's Prophecy of the Death and Passion of Christ* (London: James Clarke, 1956), 125.

mainstream Reformed theology has said otherwise. Election was a free act of God — God did not have to elect anyone. But having elected them, His holy nature required satisfaction by atonement as necessary for the salvation of the elect. Thomas Watson said, "It was a far greater expression of love in God to give His Son to die for us than if He had voluntarily acquitted us of the debt without any satisfaction at all."[2]

In the covenant of redemption, the Father gave a select group of people to Christ and ordained that Christ would die to purchase their redemption. In the First London Baptist Confession of 1644 we read: "Christ Jesus by his death did bring forth salvation and reconciliation only for the elect, which were those which God the Father gave him" (Article 21; cf. Article 17). Christ agreed to this stipulation and in time died for them.

This means that the decree to elect logically preceded the decree of atonement. Christ did not come to die for a hypothetical group of people — to whom it may concern — but a specific group in particular. We could insert the atonement in the Golden Chain of Romans 8:29–30 between predestination and calling, thus: "Whom He predestined, He sent Christ to die for; and Christ died for those He also called and justified." At the least, Christ did not die for those whom He foreknew would not believe, so Jonathan Edwards argued.[3]

Atonement for the Elect Bride

The relationship between election, atonement, and salvation is especially seen in Ephesians 1 and 5. Ephesians 1:4 says that God chose the elect for the purpose of making them holy and without blemish. This is echoed in 5:25–27 where Paul says that Christ died to make His bride holy and without blemish. The two are inseparable. The atonement is the means by which God brings the elect to the predestined end. Ephesians 5:25–27 is, in my opinion, probably the most explicit and convincing presentation of particular and definite atonement in the Bible.

Though Christ has a general love for all men as His creatures, He has a special and particular love for the elect, His bride. He died for her in a way that He did not die for the non-elect, which are not His bride. We see this even in human relations. A man will do some things out of love for his wife that he will not do for other women. He is called to die for her but not for others.

---

2 Thomas Watson, *The Mischief of Sin* (Pittsburgh: Soli Deo Gloria, 1994), 118.
3 Jonathan Edwards, *The Works of Jonathan Edwards* (New Haven: Yale University Press, 1994), 13:211.

This also follows the Hebrew marriage custom. Two fathers make a covenant that their son and daughter will be married one day. Later, the young man proves himself worthy and pays a bride price to the father of the young woman (Genesis 29:15–21, 30; Exodus 22:16; Deuteronomy 22:28–29). He does not pay it for other women, only for the chosen one. When the price is paid, the betrothal is sealed. This illustrates how Christ paid the bride price for the elect to guarantee her salvation and union with Him. But not every sinner is part of this bride. Therefore, Christ did not die for them. If He did, their salvation would be guaranteed.

This is the full display of Christ's love, which husbands must imitate (Ephesians 5:25). Christ showed ultimate love for the bride in a way He did not for the non-bride (Romans 5:8; Galatians 2:20; 1 John 3:16; 4:9–10). This is special grace, not common grace. John Gill commented: "Those for whom Christ died, he loves with the greatest love; but he does not love every individual man with the greatest love; therefore he died not for every individual man."[4] In his typically eloquent way, John Piper put it like this:

> Christians are able to cherish the death of Christ as an act of omnipotent love by which Christ, our husband, pays for us, pursues us, overpowers us with love, and preserves us as his uniquely loved bride forever. The Lover of our souls paid his own blood, not just to make his marriage possible, but to break down doors of the prison and take his beloved to himself. Strength and stability and joy and courage flow from knowing ourselves loved like this.[5]

John 11:52 uses another metaphor and a similar argument. Christ died to gather the children of God. A father will do some things for his children that he will not do for other children, such as chasten them (Hebrews 12:5–11). Christ died in such a way as to guarantee the gathering (salvation) of His children. But not all people are His children; only the elect are. The non-elect remain lost sinners (Hebrews 2:13–17).

The Shepherd and the Sheep

There are several verses that speak of a particular group that Christ died for that explicitly excludes the rest. This is seen in John 10:11: "I am the good shepherd. The good shepherd gives His life for the sheep" (see also v. 15). Later He said to the unbelieving Jews present, "You are not of My sheep" (v. 26). The Good

---

4 John Gill, *The Cause of God and Truth* (Grand Rapids: Baker, 1980), 104.
5 John Piper, *A Godward Life: Book Two* (Sisters, OR: Multnomah, 1999), 354.

Shepherd died for His sheep, not for the wolves and goats (v. 12). Indeed, He died to save the sheep *from* the wolves and thieves. Perhaps He was thinking of the wolves in sheep's clothing of Matthew 7:15. The thieves would be those who live and die as children of the Devil (John 8:44). Gottschalk said that Christ died for His sheep, not for the Antichrist's goats.[6] Matthew 25:32–33 records how Christ will separate His sheep from the Devil's goats at Judgment Day.

Christ Died for His People

Several verses speak of Christ dying for His "people," such as Titus 2:14: "who gave Himself for us, that He might redeem us from every lawless deed and purify for Himself His own special people, zealous for good works." This directly parallels the wording of Ephesians 5:25–27. Not all sinners are His "people." Only the elect are. It follows that He died for His people in this special way that He did not for those who are not His people.

This is the *people of God* motif in Scripture. Israel was chosen to be the people of God but failed. In the fullness of the new covenant, the people of God consist of believers, the elect, the church. It does not include everyone. For example, 1 Peter 2:9: "You are a chosen generation. [. . .] His own special people" (see v. 10). Isaiah 53:8 says the atonement was for them: "For the transgressions of My people He was stricken," which clarifies the identity of those for whom Messiah died in verses 4–6 and 11–12. Hebrews 2:17 says this also: "to make propitiation for the sins of the people."

The phrase *My people* in the Old Testament sometimes refers to physical Israel, or "Israel after the flesh" (1 Corinthians 10:18). In other places it refers to the true spiritual Israelites, an Israel within Israel (Romans 9:6). This is crucial to understanding Hebrews 2:17. Hebrews explains how the Old Testament sacrifices were types of the one great sacrifice of Christ on the cross for His "people."

In surveying the Old Testament, we see that God provided atoning sacrifices for the people of Israel and not for the Gentiles (Deuteronomy 21:8). This is a type of Christ atoning for His elect people and not for the non-elect. He died for spiritual Israel, not for non-elect spiritual Gentiles. We see other limitations in the Old Testament. God provided atonement for some transgressors but not all. There is no atonement for those who were guilty of extreme and deliberate sins (Leviticus 27:29; Numbers 15:22–31).

---

6 Gottschalk, *Gottschalk and a Medieval Predestination Controversy*, ed. by Victor Genke and Francis X. Gumerlock (Milwaukee: Marquette University Press, 2010), 165.

Psalm 65:3 says, "As for our transgressions, You will provide atonement for them." Yet 1 Samuel 3:14 says, "The iniquity of Eli's house shall not be atoned for by sacrifice or offering forever." This is clearly a limitation of atonement, as is Jeremiah 18:23: "Provide no atonement for their iniquity." This is what Hebrews 10:26 refers to: "If we sin willfully after we have received the knowledge of the truth, there no longer remains a sacrifice for sins."

God provided the sacrificial Passover lamb for the Israelites, not the Egyptians (Exodus 12:13). Christ is our Passover Lamb (1 Corinthians 5:7; John 1:29). He is the Passover Lamb for spiritual Israel (Galatians 6:16), not for spiritual Egypt (Revelation 11:8). Furthermore, the Jewish high priest bore the names of the twelve tribes of Israel on his breastplate over his heart (Exodus 28:21). That did not include the Babylonians, Assyrians, or Canaanites. This was a type of Christ the Great High Priest who bore on His heart the names of His people, the true twelve tribes of spiritual Israel (James 1:1; 1 Peter 1:1). He did not include the names of the non-elect on His heart when He went to the cross. All the Old Testament sacrifices typified Christ's atoning sacrifice (Colossians 2:17 and much of Hebrews). Ephesians 5:2 says, "Christ has loved us and given Himself for us, an offering and a sacrifice to God for a sweet-smelling aroma." The "us" in Ephesians refers to the elect (1:4) — believers, the bride, His body — not all men. The great sacrifice is limited to His people.

Other verses indicate limitation by specifying those for whom Christ died. In John 15:13–14, Christ said He would die for His "friends." This means He did not die for those who are finally His enemies and not His friends. The elect were born enemies but are transformed into friends and reconciled by virtue of His death (Romans 5:10). The reprobate are never His friends; therefore, Christ did not die to reconcile them to Himself.

Acts 20:28 is an echo of Ephesians 5:25, in which elders are told to "shepherd the church of God which He purchased with His own blood." Christ purchased the flock, His church. Elders are to shepherd the sheep, not the goats or wolves. This alludes back to John 10. All these and others point to a limited group for whom Christ died in a special sacrificial way.

Deliverance from Evil and the Evil One

Galatians 1:4 says, "Who gave Himself for our sins, that he might deliver us from this present evil age, according to the will of God." The *our* and *us* refer to believers, not unbelievers. Note the goal of Christ's death. It is parallel to Ephesians 5:25–27 and Titus 2:14.

Christ died to defeat Satan and free His people (Genesis 3:15; Hebrews 2:14–16; 1 John 3:8; Colossians 2:15). He was successful. He guaranteed the fall of the Devil and the deliverance of His people from him. If His death did not accomplish one, it did not accomplish the other. If even one of those for whom Christ died in this way remains in Satan's grasp, then Christ failed, and Satan won. Perish the thought! Indeed, the *Christus Victor* motif alludes to Goliath's challenge (1 Samuel 17:8–9). If Christ failed, then the elect must serve Satan. But Christ won and so guaranteed that His people would be delivered to serve Him.

This reminds us of what we discussed earlier in the chapter on the election of angels. Christ did not die for Satan or the demons (Hebrews 2:14–16). The non-Calvinist has to admit that there is a limitation in that area, at the very least. But non-elect humans are in the same ultimate situation. They go to the same final destiny as "the Devil and his angels" (Matthew 25:41). Mainstream Calvinists reject Gary North's strange theory that Christ died to secure common grace for both reprobate humans and Satan, while not purchasing special grace for either.[7] We believe that Christ's atonement did indeed bring common grace to all humans, but this does not include the demons and their evil leader. There is no hint that there is any kind of grace for Satan and his angels.

Effectual Atonement

What God does, He always does as a Trinity. The Father effectually elected a definite and limited number of sinners, not all. The Holy Spirit effectually draws this same limited number to Christ. It follows that the second person of the blessed Trinity effectually redeemed those same elect and them alone. The Father has a general love for all and a special electing love only for the elect. The Spirit gives a general call to all and a special call only to the elect. Christ died in a general way for all men but in a special way for the elect alone.

This is what the formula of Peter Lombard refers to when it says, "Christ died sufficiently for all but efficiently only for the elect." Arminians do not seem to be able to grasp just what this efficiency and effectuality means. They do not believe in the definite and sovereign election by God alone nor the effectual and irresistible calling of the Holy Spirit. Therefore, they cannot comprehend the effectual definiteness of the atonement for Christ's people.

This is the real heart of the question. Mainstream Reformed theology teaches

---

7 Gary North, *Dominion and Common Grace* (Tyler, TX: Institute for Christian Economics, 1987), 43–44.

that Christ actually and effectually secured the redemption of His people. He died to guarantee their salvation, not merely make it possible, as Arminians teach. He "obtained" redemption absolutely, not tentatively (Hebrews 9:12). This is the thesis of John Murray's classic work *Redemption Accomplished and Applied*.[8] The accomplishment of propitiation and satisfaction is past and only awaits the application by the Spirit to effect regeneration and justification in the elect.

By contrast, the Arminian and Amyraldian theories only posit a tentative atonement. Lewis Sperry Chafer, a self-confessed Amyraldian, said: "Christ's death does not save either actually or potentially; rather it makes all men savable."[9] We grant that no one is personally justified before the atonement is applied by the Spirit effectually, but that is not the point. The state of the question is: Did Christ actually accomplish redemption when He cried, "It is finished" (John 19:30), or is there something else that must be done to accomplish redemption? Roman Catholicism contends, based on a faulty exegesis of Colossians 1:24, that the atonement was not enough; it needs to be finished through the Mass and our own redemptive suffering. This is a deficient view of Christ's perfect atonement. Historic Calvinists suggest that Arminianism offers a similar defective view, though much better than the Roman error.

Wayne Grudem argues that the real question is not the intent of the atonement based in election but its actual accomplishment in time. He argues that Christ fully and completely paid for the sins of the elect and not of the non-elect.[10] His point is well taken and has much merit in it as far as it goes. But it does not go far enough. It overlooks the fact that Christ's atonement in history was precisely according to eternal foreordination (Acts 2:23; 4:28). Christ did not accomplish redemption for any but the elect, for they alone were predestined to salvation. The main purpose of the atonement was to accomplish that atonement — and He most certainly did accomplish it.

William Cunningham perceptively observed, "The nature of the atonement settles or determines its extent."[11] I would add that the special intent of the atonement is the basis for its limited extent.

---

8 There are two editions with different paginations: 1955 and 1961, both by Eerdmans of Grand Rapids. The latter has been reprinted by Banner of Truth.
9 Quoted in Michael Horton, *Putting Amazing Back into Grace* (Grand Rapids: Baker, 1994), 128. See Lewis Sperry Chafer, *Systematic Theology* (Dallas: Dallas Seminary Press, 1975), 3:183–205.
10 Wayne Grudem, *Systematic Theology* (Grand Rapids: Zondervan, 1994), 601.
11 William Cunningham, *Historical Theology* (London: Banner of Truth, 1969), 2:325.

We are not merely saying, as evangelical Arminians say, that nobody could be saved without the death of Christ on the cross. Those who say otherwise are denying the very essence of the gospel, "Christ died for our sins" (1 Corinthians 15:3). Christ died to definitely secure the salvation of those for whom He died in this special way. The alternative is to put forth an indefinite atonement for nobody in particular or a universal atonement for all which guarantees salvation for nobody.

This is what we mean when we say that everyone except strict universalists believes in some limitation. It is a matter of where they place the limitation. Spurgeon summed it up: "I would rather believe in a limited atonement that is efficacious for all men for whom it is intended, than a universal atonement that is not efficacious for anybody, except the will of man be joined with it."[12] Elsewhere he showed that it is the indefinite Arminian universal theory that limits the efficacy of the atonement, while the Calvinist view has a perfect definiteness and efficacy. Who then teaches a limited "deficient" view of the atonement? The Arminian, not the Calvinist.[13] Loraine Boettner: "The Calvinist limits it quantitatively, but not qualitatively; the Arminian limits it qualitatively, but not quantitatively."[14] It is like the difference between two bridges. The Arminian bridge is very wide but only goes halfway across the river, while the Calvinist bridge is narrow but goes all the way across.

The Special Intent

Scripture repeatedly speaks of the special intent of the atonement that is limited to believers. First Peter 2:24: "Who Himself bore our sins in His own body on the tree, that we, having died to sins, might live for righteousness." We live because He died. First Peter 3:18: "Christ also suffered once for sins, the just for the unjust, that He might bring us to God." He came to save sinners (Matthew 1:21; 1 Timothy 1:15), not merely make them savable, as Chafer said. He died to deliver us (Hebrews 2:15), not merely make us deliverable. He died to redeem and adopt us, and so He did (Galatians 4:4–6). He died to reconcile us to God, and so He did (2 Corinthians 5:19; Romans 5:10).

Another way of putting it is this: The work of Christ on the cross guaranteed its own application. It was efficacious with the Father by means of the Holy

---

12 Charles H. Spurgeon, *New Park Street Pulpit* (Pasadena: Pilgrim Publications, 1981), 4:70.
13 Spurgeon, *New Park Street Pulpit*, 4:135. This is from his helpful sermon "Particular Redemption."
14 Loraine Boettner, *The Reformed Doctrine of Predestination* (Philadelphia: Presbyterian & Reformed, 1932), 153.

Spirit (Hebrews 9:14). This guaranteed that it would be efficacious in His people when the Spirit applies it to them. The number of those for whom He was substitute is the same — no more and no less — as those who actually benefit from it. As Herman Bavinck put it: "The application of salvation must therefore extend just as far as its acquisition. The application is comprehended in it and is its necessary development."[15]

Related to this principle is Romans 8:32: "He who did not spare His own Son, but delivered Him up for us all, how shall He not with Him also freely give us all things?" Earlier Paul described the Golden Chain (vv. 29–30) and would later show that nothing can separate us from the love of God (vv. 35–39). In verse 32 we see the necessary cause-and-effect relation between the cross and these other great spiritual benefits. He uses the argument from the greater to the lesser. If God gave us the greater gift (Christ), it necessarily follows that He will give all lesser gifts as well. But if Christ died equally for all men and with the same intent, it would follow that God gives all spiritual benefits to all men. But He does not do so. Therefore, He did not give Christ for all men. The "us all" must refer to the subjects of the rest of the chapter and the whole book: Christians. If the "us" in verse 32 means all men everywhere, then it must mean that in verse 35. If so, then all men would be saved. But not all men will be saved. Therefore, Christ was not delivered up for all men, but only for the "elect" (see v. 33).

The outcome of the atonement will be the same as its intention. All men will not be saved by the death of Christ; therefore, God did not intend all men to be saved in His decrees and intent of atonement. So argued Abraham Kuyper.[16]

The atonement was full payment, not a refundable down payment in part. "It is finished" (*Tetelestai*, John 19:30) means "Done. Completed. Paid in full." Christ will own exactly what He paid for (Isaiah 53:11). Otherwise He died in vain. He bought Christians out of slavery, and they therefore belong to Him (1 Corinthians 6:20). He won. He did not fail. The title of Michael Horton's book on the atonement is appropriate: *Mission Accomplished.*[17]

The Double Payment and Triple Option

Two further arguments in favor of particular redemption are related. The first is

15 Herman Bavinck, *Reformed Dogmatics* (Grand Rapids: Baker, 2016), 3:467.
16 Abraham Kuyper, *Particular Grace: A Defense of God's Sovereignty in Salvation* (Grandville: Reformed Free Publishing Association, 2001), 238.
17 Darlington, England: Evangelical Press, 1990.

the "no double payment" argument, summed up by Thomas Watson: "The blood of Christ is a price paid not only meritoriously, but efficaciously for all that believe. [. . .] God will not require the debt twice, both of the surety and the debtor."[18] Augustus Toplady's famous hymn "Rock of Ages" has these words: "Payment cannot God twice demand, first at my bleeding surety's hand, and then again at mine."

Christ was the surety for His people (Hebrews 7:22). A surety is a person who cosigns a loan and guarantees that he will pay if the other person is not able to pay. We are not able to pay our debt to God. Christ paid for us. That released us from the obligation and penalty. We are released. But not every person is released, for Christ was not everyone's surety. This suretyship is parallel to the Holy Spirit being the *arabon*, "the guarantee of our inheritance until the redemption of the purchased possession, to the praise of His glory" (Ephesians 1:14). The Son guaranteed payment, and the Spirit guarantees its application and completion. Arminians make both a tentative wish; we make them a definite certainty.

It was the Puritan John Owen who popularized the triple option argument:

> Christ imposed his wrath due unto, and Christ underwent the pains of hell for, either all the sins of all men, or all the sins of some men, or some sins of all men. If the last, some sins of all men, then have all men some sins to answer for, and so shall no man be saved. [. . .] If the second, that is it which we affirm, that Christ in their stead and room suffered for all the sins of all the elect of the world. If the first, why, then are not all freed from the punishment of all their sins? You will say, "Because of their unbelief; they will not believe." But this unbelief, is it a sin or not? If not, why should they be punished for it? If it be, then Christ underwent the punishment due to it, or not. If so, then why must that hinder them more than their other sins for which he died from partaking of the fruit of his death? If he did not, then he did not die for all their sins.[19]

Both arguments are based on the justice of God. It would be unjust of God to punish a person for whom Christ died. This relates to the ransom argument.

---

18 Thomas Watson, *The Beatitudes* (London: Banner of Truth, 1971), 253. The argument was used at least as early as the Confession of Tarcal and Torda (1562–63), in James T. Dennison Jr., ed., *Reformed Confessions of the 16th and 17th Centuries in English Translation* (Grand Rapids: Reformation Heritage Books, 2010), 2:672.

19 John Owen, *The Works of John Owen* (London: Banner of Truth, 1967), 10:173–74; repeated on p. 249.

Christ died to pay the ransom for us (Matthew 20:28; Mark 10:45; 1 Timothy 2:6). He paid the ransom to the Father, not to the Devil, as some early church fathers thought. The Father accepted the ransom price and released the elect from wrath. Job 33:24 gives us the critical principle: "Deliver him from going down to the Pit; I have found a ransom." It would be unjust of God not to release a prisoner for whom the ransom (Hebrew: *kophar*, "covering, atonement") was paid. God is not like evil kidnappers who murder the kidnapped child once the ransom has been paid so that he cannot identify them.

Miscellaneous Proofs

There is a necessary relationship between atonement and justification. We are justified based on Christ's atoning death on our behalf (Isaiah 53:11; Romans 3:24–25; 5:9; 8:32–34). Not all men are justified. Therefore, Christ did not atone for them. If He atoned for them, they would necessarily be justified. The sins of the elect alone were imputed to Christ, and His righteousness is imputed to them. The two imputations match. Gottschalk was perhaps the first to use this argument.[20] He also argued that Christ bore the curse of the law for the elect alone (Galatians 3:13), for if He bore the curse of the reprobate, then they will surely be freed from the curse. But that the reprobate will finally be cursed is clear from Matthew 25:41. Therefore He bore the curse only of those who will not finally be cursed — that is, the elect.[21]

In John 17:9, Christ said to the Father, "I do not pray for the world, but for those whom You have given Me." His special High Priestly Prayer matches His sacrifice — He died for all His people and only His people. See Romans 8:34 and 1 John 2:1–2. As Christopher Love explained: "If Jesus Christ would not spend His breath to pray for them, then surely He would not spend His precious blood to purchase heaven for them!"[22] It is true that Christ prayed in a general way for those who crucified Him (Luke 23:34), and by extension for all men in the general sense. Some Calvinists argue that all those who actually crucified Christ were later saved. But this is unlikely in light of Acts 3:14–15; 4:10; 7:52; and 1 Thessalonians 2:15.

One popular argument put forth by some Calvinists lacks merit. It says that Christ died for "many" (Isaiah 53:12; Matthew 20:28; 26:28; Mark 10:45, 14:24; Hebrews 9:28) and not for all. However, the New Testament generally contrasts

---

20 Gottschalk, *Gottschalk and a Medieval Predestination Controversy*, 106.

21 Gottschalk, 105.

22 Christopher Love, *Preacher of God's Word* (Morgan, PA: Soli Deo Gloria, 2000), 5.

"many" with "few" (Matthew 7:13–14; 22:14), not with "all." These verses, then, do not mean "He died for many and therefore not all" but rather "He died for a large number as opposed to a small number." Nor can they mean "He died for all instead of only a few." They simply refer only to a large number of persons. This parallels our previous discussion on the ratio of elect to non-elect. The elect are outnumbered by the non-elect, but their number is still very large (Revelation 7:9). In any case, these verses do not address the question of the extent of the atonement.

Revelation 5:9 also parallels 7:9: "You were slain, and have redeemed us to God by your blood out of every tribe and tongue and people and nation." He purchased us "out of" a larger group; He did not purchase everyone in that group.

Hebrews 10:14 is another good text: "For by an offering He has perfected forever those who are being sanctified." Not all men are perfected or sanctified; therefore, Christ did not present a perfect sacrificial offering for them.

A less obvious argument could be adduced from Isaiah 49:16: "See, I have inscribed you on the palm of My hands." This is shortly before the great prophecy of chapter 53. It could be argued that it is fulfilled in the crucifixion wounds in Christ's hands (Luke 24:39; John 20:27; Psalm 22:16). As with the high priest's breastplate, Christ bore the names of only His people when He made the great sacrifice in His body and blood.

Some Calvinists use this argument: "Christ did not die for those already in Hell; therefore, He did not die for all men." One could turn it around thus: "Did Christ die for those already in Heaven?" The argument is not watertight, but it does point to something important. Christ's work was retroactively applied to those already in Heaven but was not nor ever will be applied to those in Hell. Those in Heaven are elect; those in Hell are not.

Christ did not die for Judas, who hanged himself and went to Hell before Jesus died (Matthew 27:5; John 17:12; Acts 1:18–19). Spurgeon said:

> I thank God I do not believe that I was redeemed in the same way that Judas was, and no more. If so, I shall go to hell as Judas did. General redemption is not worth anything to anybody, for of itself it secures to no one a place in heaven; but the special redemption which does redeem, and

redeems men out of the rest of mankind, is the redemption to be prayed for, and for which we shall praise God forever and ever.[23]

Luther had a high view of the infinite value of Christ's death. If Christ paid such a high price, He will surely get what He paid for. Luther accused Erasmus and the Pelagians of "cheapening and debasing their own Pelagianism, by reducing the price of salvation."[24] One wonders if he would have leveled this charge against his associate Philip Melanchthon's synergism which somewhat resembled later Arminianism.

Calvinists have a higher vista on the infinite worth of Christ's atonement than others. Who but Jonathan Edwards would have said, "God's justice is more gloriously manifested in the sufferings of Christ for the elect than in the damnation of the world"?[25] And again:

> The wonderful things designed and virtually accomplished in what Christ did when on the earth are so manifold as to be sufficient to employ the contemplation of saints and angels to all eternity, who will discover more and more of the manifold wisdom of God therein, and yet never discover all.[26]

Conclusion

Not all Calvinists who believe in particular redemption accept all the preceding arguments. There are still other arguments, some strong and some weak. Spurgeon argued that the whole question gets back to the nature of God Himself: "Unless God can undeify himself, every soul that Christ died for he will have."[27]

---

23 Charles H. Spurgeon, *Metropolitan Tabernacle Pulpit* (Pasadena, TX: Pilgrim Publications, 1980), 21:175–76.
24 Martin Luther, introduction to *The Bondage of the Will* (Grand Rapids: Fleming H. Revell, 2005), 49–50.
25 Edwards, *Works*, 24:1024.
26 Edwards, 15:287.
27 Spurgeon, *Metropolitan Tabernacle Pulpit*, 58:124.

Chapter 54
Objections to Limited Atonement

There have been many objections to the doctrine of particular redemption from several quarters: Arminians, Amyraldians, Lutherans, even Roman Catholics. Defenders offer a variety of answers.

Objection 1: *What about the "perishing" passages?*

Romans 14:15 and 1 Corinthians 8:11 speak of certain persons perishing for whom Christ died. If the atonement guarantees the salvation of all for whom Christ died, how can we speak of some of them perishing?

The answer is quite simple. Both verses specifically say that the person in question is a "brother" — that is, a Christian. Unbelievers who never repent and believe will most certainly perish in Hell (Luke 13:3). A true believer never perishes like that (John 3:16; 10:28). These verses, then, cannot be speaking about one's dying lost and going to Hell. They warn Christians not to offend another Christian's conscience. If we do, the brother is said to perish. The damage is a wounded conscience, not a lost soul. It would be difficult to see how offending someone's conscience causes him to either die or go to Hell.

These verses might even be taken to support particular redemption, for they speak of *brothers* as those for whom Christ died. They say nothing about Christ dying for *non-brothers*.

Objection 2: *2 Peter 2:1 says Christ bought false teachers who are unbelievers.*

The chapter warns against false teachers who are on their way to Hell. They are reprobate, not elect. Does verse 1 mean that Christ bought them and therefore did not die only for the elect? Several answers have been offered. Some mistranslate the phrase as "even denying that the Lord bought them." That is forced eisegesis. The text says the heretics denied "the Lord," not "that the Lord." They denied the Lord Himself with their wicked lives, though not with their words (see Titus 1:16).

Another answer says that "bought" here refers to God's purchasing Israel out of Egypt (Deuteronomy 32:6) and not Christ buying people at the cross. That too is eisegesis. *Lord* in the New Testament generally refers to the Lord Jesus Christ, and He is often said to buy people (such as Acts 20:28 and 1 Corinthians 6:20). Another weak view says that the heretics only *thought* that the Lord bought them. But the text clearly says, "the Lord who bought them," not "the Lord whom they mistakenly thought bought them."

The best solution refers this verse to the general aspect of the atonement respecting all men everywhere, including heretical false teachers. Christ purchased all men and is their owner and master. Peter uses the Greek word *despotes*. Christ owns everyone, not just the elect. This verse does not refer to propitiation and salvation but to possession of men who are sinners.

Objection 3: *What about the verses that say Christ died for "all"?*

Several verses say Christ died for all (2 Corinthians 5:14–15; 1 Timothy 2:6; Hebrews 2:9). Some Calvinists refer these verses to the general aspect of the atonement for all men. Others give other answers. A popular answer is that the words translated *all* (*pas, pasan, pasa, pan, panta*) do not necessarily mean "each and every one" or "all without exception." They can sometimes mean "all without distinction" or "all kinds." For example, Acts 2:17 says that God will pour out His Spirit on "all (*pasan*) flesh." We know that not every person will receive the Spirit. "All" there must mean "all kinds," which is what Peter means in quoting Joel 2:28–32. God will pour out His Spirit on sons and daughters, young and old men, male and female servants, and people from various lands outside of Israel (vv. 9–11, 17–18). Christ redeems people from all kinds of nations, tribes, tongues, and peoples (Revelation 5:9; 7:9). "All" clearly means "all kinds" in 1 Timothy 6:10, usually translated as "the love of money is a root of all kinds of evil." Surely the love of money was not the root of Adam and Eve's first sin, for money did not exist yet. So, it is at least exegetically possible that the above verses could mean Christ died for all kinds of people.

In other places, *all* is a legitimate hyperbole in both Greek and English. For example, Mark 1:5 says "all" (*pasa*) the land of Judea and Jerusalem went out to hear John the Baptist and were baptized by him. But Luke 7:30 says that some of the Pharisees were not baptized. Are we to think that each and every person, including the elderly, infirm, and infants, went out there? This is obviously a hyperbole for "a large number," as in Matthew 10:22; John 8:2; Acts 22:15, 26:4, and elsewhere. Thus, the *all* passages above could simply mean Christ died for very large number of people.

We can dismiss any appeal to the verses which say Christ died "once and for all" (Hebrews 7:27; 9:12; 10:10). They do not specifically speak of substitution but finality. Christ died once and does not need to die again. The word *once* (*hapax* and derivatives) is so used in 9:7, 26, 27, 28, 10:2, 12:26 and 27. In fact, the Greek of 7:27, 9:12, and 10:10 does not even have any words for *all*.

Sometimes *all* refers to "all the persons in view in this context" — that is, all those the writer is referring to and not "all men everywhere." This is how some Reformed interpreters view 2 Corinthians 5:14–15. They would paraphrase it as follows: "Christ died for all believers. They died in His death. They should therefore live for Him." Others take these verses to refer to the universal aspect of the atonement. The limitation is in the second clause of verse 15, in which case the passage means "One died for everyone, for everyone was spiritually dead. But He died for everyone so that those who are spiritually alive should live for Christ."

Hebrews 2:9 uses *panta* which is translated as either "every" or "all." Interpretations vary. To some, it means "Christ tasted but did not experience death for everyone," which is a strange opinion. Others take it to refer to the universal aspect of the atonement. Still others take it to refer to all those in context: believers, the children of God, brethren, those being sanctified, the seed of Abraham, the people of God (vv. 10–17). A somewhat rare view has *all* meaning the "all" of verses 8 (three times) and 10 (twice). The "all things" include everything in the universe and not just people. Granted that there are cosmic implications of Christ's death, but I find this view to be inadequate.

Likewise, 1 Timothy 2:6 has several interpretations from Reformed scholars. There are two main ones. First, Paul tells us to pray for all kinds of people, including kings and others in authority (vv. 1–2). God desires all kinds of people to be saved (v. 4). This refers to predestination of the elect alone, not all men everywhere. Thus, Christ gave Himself for all the elect. Just as Christ did not pray for all men (John 17:9), we need not pray for all men (1 John 5:16). God chose the elect from all kinds of people, and Christ died for them alone.

Another interpretation of 1 Timothy 2:1–6 takes *all* to mean "each and every human." We are to pray for everyone in authority, not just some of them. The second "all" of verse 2 does not mean "all kinds" when it says, "all godliness and reverence." We can pray for everyone in the sense that Christ prayed even for those who crucified Him (Luke 23:34). God desires literally all sinners to be saved, not just some from all kinds. This is the revealed will of the gospel, not the secret will of predestination. In this sense Christ paid a ransom for all men everywhere. Paul's use of *all* in the Pastoral Epistles verifies that he means literally "all" and not "some from all kinds." This is the interpretation favored by John Piper[1] and others.

Objection 4: *What about the places where it says Christ died for "many"?*

The objection says that *many* means "all" as opposed to only a few. In Romans 5:12–21 Paul uses both "all" (vv. 12 twice, 18) and "many" (vv. 15 and 19 twice) synonymously. However, the section does not directly address the extent of the atonement, nor does the parallel in 1 Corinthians 15:22. But it does bear on the general subject. Some take Calvin's view: "Paul makes grace common to all men, not because it in fact extends to all, but because it is offered to all. Although Christ suffered for the sins of the world, and is offered by the goodness of God without distinction to all men, yet not all receive him."[2] The passage cannot teach universal justification. Paul is simply saying that all men were in Adam when he sinned and died (v. 12), whereas all who are in Christ will be justified. The two are not coextensive. Adam's sin brought death to a large number ("many"), and Christ's death also brought life to a large number. If these verses teach universal atonement, they would also teach universal justification. The main point is the relationship between Christ's death and the justification of His people.

Romans 5 may be an echo of Isaiah 53 verses 6 and 11–12. The death of the Messiah brings justification (v. 11). The Arminian usually takes the "all" of verse 6 to mean all men everywhere, for Scripture often says all men have sinned. Therefore, it is argued, Christ also died for all men. But they fail to see that Isaiah is not speaking of all men everywhere when he says "our." He is speaking of God's people. Some Reformed interpreters such as Calvin and Matthew Henry take this in a universal sense. The problem is that the *all* seems to be equated with the "many" who are justified by Messiah's death. But that surely does not include all men everywhere. Perhaps it would be more accurate to say that *all* means "all God's people" or a large number, that is, "many."

I have already referred to other places in which Christ is said to have died for "many" (Matthew 20:28; 26:28; Mark 10:45; 14:24; Hebrews 9:28). The many are contrasted with the few (Matthew 7:13–14; 22:14), not the all. They only say that Christ died for a large number of people. They do not teach that Christ died for a few or for all. The question of extent is not in view.

---

1 John Piper, *Does God Desire All to Be Saved?* (Wheaton: Crossway, 2013).
2 John Calvin, *The Epistles of Paul the Apostle to the Romans and to the Thessalonians* (Grand Rapids: Eerdmans, 1973), 117–18.

Objection 5: *What about the verses that say Christ died for "the world"?*

There are several verses that associate Christ's death with "the world": John 1:29; 3:16; 4:42; 6:51; 2 Corinthians 5:19; and 1 John 2:2. The question hinges on the meaning of the Greek word *kosmos*. Five of the six occurrences in question are in John's Gospel and first epistle. John frequently uses *kosmos* in a very general way for the entire universe (John 1:9–10; 8:23; 9:32; 13:1; 17:5, 11–13, 15, 18, 24, 18:36–37; 21:25; cf. Ephesians 1:4). Other places use it to refer to mankind at large, often with the nuance that it is a sinful world (John 1:10; 7:4, 7; 8:12; 12:19, etc.). It is the world out of which Christians have been chosen (John 15:18). In John 4:42, it could mean Gentiles as opposed to Jews, which is how Paul sometimes uses it. But it never means Christians as opposed to non-Christians. Indeed, sometimes it means the very opposite — the world of unbelievers (1 John 5:19).

Reformed interpretations vary. Some take the six verses to refer to "the world at large, but not everyone in the world." This was popularized by B. B. Warfield. Another view says it means the world of the elect. But the problem with that view is that *kosmos* is never used in that sense at all.[3] Such interpretations are special pleading and indicate a forced exegesis.

Most of the debate revolves around John 3:16, for many the most beloved verse in the Bible. It will not do to say, as some have, "Atonement isn't in view in that verse," for the death of Christ has been mentioned in verse 14. God the Father gave the Son at the cross. First John 4:9–10 is a close parallel to John 3:16 and certainly mentions propitiation.

I would follow the view of John Calvin, D. A. Carson, Iain Murray, John MacArthur, J. C. Ryle, C. H. Spurgeon, R. L. Dabney, and many other Reformed interpreters. John 3:16 is indeed universal in scope and does not limit all the atonement to the elect. It is speaking of the universal dimension of the atonement. This does not mean a strictly universal atonement, however, for other verses speak to the limited intent and extent. Iain Murray commented: "For if the elect are 'the world' that God loves, why is it that only some of that world ('whosoever believes in him') come to salvation? There is surely a distinction in the text between the larger number who are the objects of love and the smaller number who believe."[4] Robert Lewis Dabney explained:

The solution, then, must be in this direction, that the words, 'so loved the

---

3 See D. A. Carson, *The Difficult Doctrine of the Love of God* (Wheaton: Crossway, 2000), 17.
4 Iain Murray, *The Cross: Pulpit of God's Love* (Edinburgh: Banner of Truth, 2008), 16.

world,' were not designed to mean the gracious decree of election, though other scriptures abundantly teach there is such a decree, but a propension of benevolence not matured into the volition to redeem, of which Christ's mission is a sincere manifestation to all sinners.[5]

The eminent J. C. Ryle also took this approach:

> The 'world' means the whole race of mankind, both saints and sinners, without any exception. The word, in my opinion, is so used in John i.10, 29; vi.33, 51; viii.12; Rom. iii.19; 2 Cor. v.19; 1 John ii.2; iv.14. The 'love' spoken of is that love of pity and compassion with which God regards all His creatures, and especially regards mankind. It is the same feeling of 'love' which appears in Psalm cxlv.19, Ezek. xxxiii.11, John vi.32, Titus iii.4, 1 John iv.10, 2 Pet. ii.9, 1 Tim. ii.4. It is a love unquestionably distinct and separate from the special love with which God regards His saints. It is a love of pity and not of approbation or complaisance. But it is not the less a real love.[6]

John Calvin regularly interprets John 3:16 in this matter, as did the great Matthew Henry: "Though many of the world of mankind perish, yet God's giving his only-begotten Son was an instance of his love to the whole world, because through him there is a general offer of life and salvation made to all."[7] Such quotations could be made from other major Reformed theologians on John 3:16 and the other passages.

Also very relevant is 1 John 2:2. The same author of John 3:16 also wrote this verse, and his first epistle echoes some of the same words and themes as his Gospel. Some of the stricter limitarians who see little or no benefits in the atonement for the non-elect sometimes interpret it along the lines of Warfield's "the world but not everyone in the world" view. Others take it to mean "the world of Gentile believers and not just Jewish Christians." They appeal to Galatians 2:7–9 where John is said to be an apostle to the Jews.

Three linguistic points militate against those interpretations. First, *world* in John's writings never means Gentiles as opposed to Jews, except possibly John

---

5 Robert Lewis Dabney, *Discussions* (Harrisonburg: Sprinkle, 1982), 1:313. Elsewhere he wrote: "Christ's mission to make expiation for sin is a manifestation of unspeakable benevolence to the whole world, to man as man and a sinner, yet designed specifically to result in the actual salvation of believers." *Systematic Theology* (Edinburgh: Banner of Truth, 1985), 535.
6 J. C. Ryle, *Expository Thoughts on the Gospels, St. John* (Cambridge: James Clarke, 1975), 1:158–59.
7 Matthew Henry, *Commentary on the Whole Bible* (Old Tappan, Fleming H. Revell, n.d.), 5:888.

4:42. There is no indication in 1 John that he has in mind the Jew/Gentile difference, which is a major theme rather in Paul. Note that he specifically says, "*whole* world" (*holou kosmou*), which is also used in 5:19: "We know that we are of God, and the whole world lies under the sway of the wicked one." That is the world out of which believers have been saved and should put behind them (2:15–17).

Second, the "our" and "ours only" of 2:2 are basically the same as "we" and "our" of the rest of the epistle. He regularly contrasts *we/us/our* with *they/them/their*. It is never Jewish Christians versus Gentile Christians but rather Christians versus non-Christians. Thus, 2:2 would mean "He Himself is the propitiation for the sins of believers, but not believers only, but for the whole world of unbelievers."

Third, another keyword is often overlooked: *for*. It is the Greek word *peri*, meaning "respecting, regarding, concerning, with reference to." It does not specifically refer to substitution, as the other words usually used in the New Testament (*huper* and *anti*). The verse, then, is not directly addressing the identity of those for whom Christ was a substitute so much as Christ being the only propitiation available for anyone in the world, unbelievers as well as believers.[8] Galatians 1:4 also uses *peri*: "He gave Himself for our sins." First John 3:16 uses *huper*, then 4:10 reverts to *peri*. Christ is the only propitiation there is for anyone. This fits in with John's universal dimension of Christ's mission and does not of itself negate the more particular aim of Christ's work, as in John 17.

Lastly, there is 2 Corinthians 5:19. This would parallel the three uses of *all* in verses 14–15. Outright advocates of universal redemption say it obviously means "all men everywhere." But that presents the problem of the context. That view could lead to a universal reconciliation of all the world, which Scripture does not teach. Others take it to mean a kind of hypothetical reconciliation of all men. Still others use the "the world but not all in the world" argument. Perhaps the best would be parallel to John 3:16.

Objection 6: *The free offer of the gospel is universal, so the atonement must also be universal.*

Ironically, Hyper-Calvinists turn this around: Since the atonement is strictly

---

8 Compare Wayne Grudem's comment that in 1 John 2:2, "Christ is the atoning sacrifice that the gospel now makes available for the sins of everyone in the world." *Systematic Theology* (Grand Rapids: Zondervan, 1994), 598–99.

limited to the elect, there is no free offer to non-Christians. But mainstream Calvinists agree that the Bible does indeed teach a universal free offer of the gospel.

Again, Reformed answers vary. Some argue that there is no relation between the extent of the atonement and the free offer. Others say it is a mystery and a paradox how we can offer it to all, though Christ died only for some. Roger Nicole had a novel answer. He said the free offer is like a newspaper advertisement for a sale on sofas. Tens of thousands of people will read the ad, but the furniture store does not need to have tens of thousands of sofas in stock. The owner does good market research and stocks up what he thinks he can sell. The offer is in good faith and will be honored. Thus, the free offer of the gospel is of larger extent than the atonement.[9] But there are several problems with this theory. For one, God does not do market research. Furthermore, what would the store owner do if more buyers came in than he had available sofas for? Would he turn them away? Order more sofas from the factory?

The best answer has to do with the universal dimension of the atonement. It has infinite value and universal sufficiency; therefore, there is more than enough to cover the free offer to all, even a billion times the world's population. To rephrase Nicole's illustration, it would be like a store which had a million sofas, and the ad would be read by only a hundred people.

The objection does bring up a valid point. Christ often spoke of the invitation to a great banquet feast. "Come, for all things are ready" (Luke 14:17). In offering the gospel to all, we know there is indeed more than enough on the banquet table to provide for all comers. There is enough if everyone everywhere came, though of course that will not happen. This indicates that the atonement is not strictly limited, such as in the Equivalentist theory that Christ suffered only a small amount and shed only so much blood but would have had to do more had more sinners been elect. Would He also have had to die twice if twice as many were elected?

This answer fits in well with other replies to some of these objections. When one denies a universal aspect of the atonement, he is on the horns of a dilemma. He can easily back into Hyper-Calvinism without realizing it. On the other hand, others admit the universal dimension but fail to remember the restricted aspect for the elect alone. They face the danger of backing into Amyraldism or Arminianism. It is best to keep the balance of both aspects.

---

9 Roger Nicole, *Standing Forth: Collected Writings of Roger Nicole* (Fearn: Mentor, 2002), 337–38.

Objection 7: *If Christ died only for the elect, then nobody can believe Christ died for him until he first knows he is one of the elect. But nobody can know he is elect until he first believes in Christ. One must believe Christ died for him to be saved.*

This objection touches not only on the free offer but also the matter of personal assurance of election. One theory says that a lost sinner does not have to believe Christ died for him. He is called on to believe in Christ — that is all. This view says that we do not preach "Christ died for you," a phrase not found in the New Testament. The persuasion "Christ died for me" belongs to later assurance, not the essence of saving faith. Faith simply trusts in Christ, not that Christ died for him in particular.

A better approach is as follows. First Corinthians 15:1–4 recounts the gospel that Paul preached to the Corinthians before they believed (2:1–2). He preached that faith in this gospel was necessary to be saved. Note the words he used when presenting the gospel: "Christ died for our sins" (v. 3). The word *our* means "yours and mine." He is not saying "the sins of you and me as believers," for they had not been believers when they heard the gospel. The proclamation is tantamount to saying, "Christ died for us, that is, you and me." So, the Christian can and must be able to say, "Christ died for you." The persuasion "Christ died for me" is therefore at least implicit in saving faith, not a secondary persuasion which may or may not be arrived at later. When a sinner believes, he says, "The Son of God loved me and gave Himself for me" (Galatians 2:20). Both Calvin and Luther taught that a sinner must believe "Christ died for me" to be saved, and this is based on the universal aspect of the atonement in the proclamation "Christ died for us."[10]

This relates to the question of the extent of the atonement. There must be a universal dimension of the atonement upon which we may preach this personal proclamation. If there is not, one must resort to vague statements like "Christ died for sinners," which the unsaved listener will probably take to mean "all sinners, including you." Some will say, "But the book of Acts does not record statements such as 'Christ died for our sins.'" But a basic rule of hermeneutics is that the didactic portions of Scripture take precedence over narrative portions

---

10 E.g., Luther, *Luther's Works* (St. Louis: Concordia, 1972), 17:221–25, 229; Calvin, *Sermons on Galatians* (Edinburgh: Banner of Truth, 1997), 212–13; *The Epistles of Paul the Apostle to the Galatians, Ephesians, Philippians, and Colossians* (Grand Rapids: Eerdmans, 1980), 44. See the moving story of Luther in A. H. Strong, *Systematic Theology* (Old Tappan: Fleming H. Revell, 1979), 765.

in formulating theology. First Corinthians 15:1–4 is such a didactic portion that directly addresses the subject.

Objection 8: *But there is no verse anywhere in the Bible that says, "Christ died only for the elect."*

A quick reply would be: There is also no verse that says, "Christ died equally for all men." Neither adverb (*only* or *equally*) is used. Instead, 1 Timothy 4:10 uses the adverb "especially," which would include a universal dimension as well as a particular aspect. This would be the preferable word for the discussion.

The objection is sophomoric. It is akin to the Jehovah's Witness objection: "There is no verse that says, 'Jesus is God,' or 'God is a Trinity.'" This pedestrian method fails to see how we formulate theology based on correctly exegeting several verses and then comparing them with each other. Calvinists acknowledge that we can legitimately formulate doctrine by "good and necessary consequence" (Westminster Confession 1:6). In the previous two chapters, I exegeted several passages and showed how the particular and universal aspects of the atonement are legitimately deduced from the Bible. The objection is without foundation.

Conclusion

Not all Calvinists use all the above replies to objections. But many do. However we reply, let us have the same attitude of Robert Murray M'Cheyne: "Adore Jesus, that He passed by millions, and died for you."[11]

---

11 Andrew Bonar, *Memoir and Remains of Robert Murray M'Cheyne* (Edinburgh: Banner of Truth, 1978), 392.

Chapter 55
Irresistible Grace

Whatever God does, He does as a Trinity. The Father has a general love for all mankind but has a special love with which He elected some to be saved. The Son provided an infinitely valuable atonement sufficient for all mankind but died primarily to guarantee the salvation of the elect. Likewise, the Holy Spirit gives a general call to all who hear the gospel but gives a special call only to the elect whereby they are irresistibly drawn to Christ and are saved. This salvation by grace is thus both trinitarian and effectual.

What Is Irresistible Grace?

There seems to be a dilemma between the first and second points of Calvinism. If God has chosen the elect to salvation, and the elect are unable to believe and be saved, then how can they be saved? The answer is in the fourth point — the special grace of the Holy Spirit. This is called *irresistible grace* by some, *efficacious* or *effectual grace* by others, or even *invincible grace* by still others. Matthew Henry preferred the term "victorious grace."[1] The Westminster Confession gives a good summary of it:

> All those whom God hath predestined unto life, and those only, He is pleased in His appointed and accepted time, effectually to call, by His Word and Spirit, out of that state of sin and death, in which they are by nature, to grace and salvation by Jesus Christ; enlightening their minds, spiritually and savingly, to understand the things of God; taking away their heart of stone, and giving unto them an heart of flesh; renewing their wills, and by His almighty power determining them to that which is good, and effectually drawing them to Jesus Christ; yet so as they come most freely, being made willing by His grace (10:1).

The Synod of Dort called it "a most powerful and most pleasing, a marvelous, hidden, and inexpressible work, which is not lesser than or inferior in power to that of creation or raising the dead" (3/4:12). John Owen noted that it is "such an unconquerable efficacy of grace as always and infallibly produceth

---

1 Matthew Henry, *Commentary on the Whole Bible* (Old Tappan: Fleming H. Revell, n.d.), 6:89, commenting on Acts 7:51.

its effect."[2] Catholic Augustinians call it *operative grace* as opposed to the *cooperative grace* of Semi-Pelagianism. Medieval theologians such as Thomas Aquinas often described it in terms of Aristotle's categories of causation. But we do not need to appeal to pagan philosophers to explain and defend what the Bible repeatedly and explicitly teaches.

Special Calling

The Bible speaks of two kinds of calls.[3] The first is the universal call of the gospel as part of the Great Commission to all people and nations (Matthew 28:19–20; Mark 16:15–16; Luke 24:47; Acts 1:8). God calls all who hear the gospel to repent and believe in Christ and be saved (Mark 1:15; 16:16). This is the free offer of the gospel, the *general call*.

But there is another call that is given only to the elect. The general call is external; the *special call* is internal. Men give the general call; the Spirit gives the special call. This calling is the middle link of the Golden Chain of Romans 8:29–30. Paul said that he was "called through His grace" (Galatians 1:15). Irresistible grace is given through this special call, in which lost sinners are called out of darkness into salvation (1 Peter 2:9). God "saved us and called us with a holy calling" (2 Timothy 1:9). Thus, eternal election finds its effect in the elect through this special call. Calvin observed: "For what else is effectual calling but the fulfillment of the election that was previously hidden?"[4] As the elect were chosen from the fallen mass of humanity in eternity, so they are called out of it in time by the Spirit.

Generally speaking, the Gospels refer to the general call, not the special call. For example: "Many are called, but few are chosen" (Matthew 22:14). On the other hand, the Epistles generally speak of the special call rather than the general call (Romans 1:7; 8:30; 9:24; 1 Corinthians 1:9, 26, Galatians 1:15; 5:13; Ephesians 4:1, 4; Colossians 3:15; 1 Thessalonians 2:12; 4:7; 1 Timothy 6:12; 2 Timothy 1:9; 1 Peter 2:21; 2 Peter 1:10, etc.).

There are three passages that illustrate the relationship between the two calls. First, Acts 16:14: "The Lord opened her heart to heed the things spoken by Paul." Others heard Paul's words with their ears, but only Lydia heard them with her heart. The Spirit opens hard hearts by special calling and efficacious

---

2 John Owen, *The Works of John Owen* (London: Banner of Truth, 1967), 10:134.
3 The distinction goes back at least as far as John Calvin. See *Institutes of the Christian Religion* (Philadelphia: Westminster Press, 1960), 3:24:8, p. 974.
4 John Calvin, *Concerning Scandals* (Grand Rapids: Eerdmans, 1978), 54.

grace. Second, in John 10:27, Jesus said, "My sheep hear My voice" (cf. v. 16). The wolves and goats heard Him externally and disbelieved, while the sheep heard Christ internally and followed Him. Third, in the parable of Luke 14:16–24, messengers give two calls. The first is rejected; the second is accepted because the master tells the messengers to "compel them to come in" (v. 23). Men give the first invitation; the Spirit alone gives the second. Medieval Catholicism erred by appealing to this parable to defend the torture of the Inquisition to compel lapsed Catholics to return. But in truth, Christians can persuade (2 Corinthians 5:11) but not torture. Unlike Muslim fanatics, we use the Word and not the sword. The parable illustrates how the Spirit effectually brings the elect in to the banquet of salvation. None of the elect are left out, and none of the non-elect are brought in.

The Spirit's chosen means is the Bible, especially the gospel (the general call). In his own eloquent way, Samuel Rutherford put it like this: "He rides upon the white horse of the gospel, and shoots the arrow of the irresistible word of God into the hearts of God's elect, so that they must obey and become the Lord's prisoners, His conquered, ransomed and bought ones by virtue of the Father's decreet."[5] Calvin sometimes spoke of this as "double grace," that is, the grace of the preached word must be completed by the irresistible grace of the Holy Spirit, thus effecting salvation in the elect.[6]

The Drawing of the Spirit

John 6:44 is the key verse: "No one can come to Me unless the Father who sent Me draws him." The Father draws men to Christ by the Holy Spirit. In a previous chapter I showed how this verse teaches total inability of the human will. Fallen man is unable and unwilling to come to Christ for salvation (John 5:40). God does for the sinner what he is not able to do by himself. He "draws" the sinner to Christ. The Greek word is *helko*, to drag. It does not mean simply to entice or assist, as Arminians say. It is used in John 21:6 and 11 of fishermen dragging a net, hence, a *dragnet* (the same idea but a different word is used in Matthew 13:47–48). In John 18:10, Peter "drew out" his sword, not merely asked it to get out of the scabbard. In Acts 16:19 and 21:30 it is used of Paul and Silas being "dragged" by a mob. James 2:6 employs it of rich men "dragging" the poor into court.

---

5 Samuel Rutherford, *Fourteen Communion Sermons* (Edinburgh: James Dickson, 1986), 72; cf 130, 304–05. A footnote in the text explains a *decreet* as "a writ ordering the arrest of a person."
6 John Calvin, *Sermons on the Epistle to the Ephesians* (London: Banner of Truth, 1973), 27.

The word means to drag, pull, compel, force, and overwhelm with superior force. Note the following examples from ancient extra-biblical Greek: to drag a dead body by the foot, to drag away a prisoner, to drag a felled tree, to draw ships down to the sea, to pull a chariot, to pull a plow, to drag chains, to pull a cloak behind oneself, to draw a bow string, to hoist sails, to lift up scales, to pull a barge pole, to tow a ship, and to compel a person to work for you. In every case, a superior force is exerted effectually and successfully.

So, John 6:44 teaches that the Father efficaciously drags the elect to Christ. Sam Storms poignantly notes, "Jesus also says that it is impossible for someone whom the Father 'draws' not to come to him."[7] Someone might object: "You can lead a horse to water, but you can't make him drink." We reply that the Good Shepherd does indeed make the sheep drink (Psalm 23:2). The Good Shepherd also goes out, picks up, and carries the lost sheep, not just calls out to them (Luke 15:5; Isaiah 40:11).

Power Grace

The reason that this grace is always successful is that it is backed up with divine omnipotence. Jeremiah 20:7: "O Lord, You induced me, and I was persuaded; You are stronger than I, and have prevailed." Thomas Watson said the Spirit has a "magnetic virtue" whereby He draws us.[8] Some time ago, John Wimber wrote about "Power Evangelism" but did not believe in what I call "power grace." This is the true power in evangelism. Note 1 Thessalonians 1:5: "Our gospel did not come to you in word only, but also in power, and in the Holy Spirit." It is the same power that raised Christ from the dead that effectually raises dead sinners from spiritual death (Ephesians 1:19). Ephesians 3:7 calls it "the effective working of His power." It is always effectual and successful.

Philosophers debate what would happen if an unstoppable force met an immovable object. Theologically, the dead sinner appears immovable, but the Spirit is stronger and therefore unstoppable. Scripture sometimes speaks of God dealing with men in a give-and-take manner but also in an overwhelming way that overcomes all human obstacles. Second Chronicles 20:6: "In Your hand is there not power and might, so that no one is able to withstand You?" That is precisely what is involved in special grace.

Psalm 110:3 says, "Your people shall be volunteers in the day of Your power." The KJV renders it "shall be willing." When God exerts power grace, sinners

---

7 Sam Storms, *Chosen for Life*, Rev. ed. (Wheaton: Crossway, 2007), 92.
8 Thomas Watson, *Heaven Taken by Storm* (Orlando: The Northampton Pulpit, 2007), 143.

respond willingly and volunteer to believe. God makes us willing, as in Philippians 2:13: "It is God who works in you both to will and to do for His good pleasure." As we saw in an earlier chapter, the human will is not off-limits to God. God has the right to intervene and turn it around if He chooses. As Spurgeon put it, "A man is not saved against his will, but he is made willing by the operation of the Holy Ghost."[9] Just as the Holy Spirit irresistibly "carried along" the writers of Scripture to infallibly write down God's words (2 Peter 1:21), so the Spirit irresistibly carries humans along so that they believe those words and are saved.

A Holy and Loving Violence

This raises the question of whether this power is violent or not. On the one hand, it is not violent in the sense of being malignant or malicious. Heinrich Bullinger commented that Christ does not drag men "by the hair" to Himself, though He did so with Saul on the Damascus road.[10] Curiously, even the very non-Calvinist C. S. Lewis said that God brought him "kicking, struggling, and resentful,"[11] like Saul of Tarsus who "kicked against the pricks" in Acts 9:5. Maurice Roberts: "It is a secret exercise of omnipotence on the hidden man of the heart coaxing and alluring him to salvation and glory by Christ. It is always effectual but it is never brute strength."[12] Calvin remarked, "God seeks to draw us to himself gently and lovingly," but because "we, like savage beasts, refuse to be led [. . .] it is often necessary for him to use force,"[13] and "so far as the manner of drawing goes, it is not violent so as to compel men by an external force; but yet it is an effectual movement of the Holy Spirit, turning men from being unwilling and reluctant into willing."[14] Wrong violence is external, but gracious force is internal. Calvin referred to it as "a secret impulse."[15]

In another sense, there is a "holy violence" involved. A mother will lovingly but violently grab her baby who has crawled out into the street. Does not a

9 Charles H. Spurgeon, *Metropolitan Tabernacle Pulpit* (Pasadena, TX: Pilgrim Publications, 1981), 10:307.

10 Heinrich Bullinger, *The Decades of Henry Bullinger* (Grand Rapids: Reformation Heritage Books, 2004), 3:190. Calvin said that in some cases God has to pull us by the hair. *Sermons on Genesis, Chapters 11:5–20:7* (Edinburgh: Banner of Truth, 2012), 516.

11 C. S. Lewis, *Surprised by Joy* (New York: Harcourt Brace Jovanovich, 1955), 228–29. Quoted in Janine Goffar, ed., *C. S. Lewis Index* (Carlisle: Solway/Paternoster Publishing, 1995), 114.

12 Maurice Roberts, *The Thought of God* (Edinburgh: Banner of Truth, 1993), 21.

13 John Calvin, *Sermons on Galatians* (Edinburgh: Banner of Truth, 1997), 219.

14 John Calvin, *The Gospel According to St. John 1–10* (Grand Rapids: Eerdmans, 1979), 164.

15 Calvin, *Sermons on the Epistle to the Ephesians*, 102.

loving Father God rescue His children with loving violence? John Trapp called it "a merciful violence."[16] When a lost sinner sees he is going to Hell, he gets desperate and violently seeks salvation. Matthew 11:12: "The kingdom of heaven suffers violence, and the violent take it by force." This is the result of the Spirit working powerfully in his heart. Conviction of sin and the new birth certainly involve gracious violence, for they are spiritually dramatic and life-changing. The angels used a holy violence when they pulled Lot and his family by the hand out of Sodom to save them from fire and brimstone. Genesis 19:16 explains why: "the Lord being merciful to them." 2 Peter 2:6–9 says this was a type of God delivering others.

This is similar to how the Spirit "came upon" prophets and judges in the Old Testament (Numbers 11:25–29; 1 Samuel 10:6, 10; 11:6; 16:13; 19:20, 23; Judges 3:10; 6:34; 11:29; 13:25; 14:6, 19; 15:14; 1 Chronicles 12:18; 2 Chronicles 15:1; 20:14; 24:20; Isaiah 61:1; Ezekiel 3:24; 11:5). The Spirit enabled them to work miracles they could not otherwise be able to do. He overcame their reluctance to prophesy. Likewise, the Spirit "comes upon" an elect sinner and enables him — yes, even compels him — to believe and be saved.

God Overcomes Our Resistance

Fallen man always resists the Holy Spirit (Acts 7:51). This illustrates the first point of Calvinism, not disproves the fourth. In effectual calling, the Spirit overcomes this resistance with special grace. Police are trained to meet resistance with superior force, such as in the "swarm" tactic. John Owen wrote, "It doth not so much take away a power of resisting as give a will of obeying, whereby the powerful impotency of resisting is removed."[17]

A popular notion is that Christ is a gentleman and does not use force. He knocks on the door of our hearts; He does not bash the door down. Usually reference is made to Revelation 3:20, forgetting that this verse is referring to Christians, not non-Christians (cf. Song of Solomon 5:2–4). Calvinists point out that it was the Spirit that opened the door to Lydia's heart in Acts 16:14. Just as Christ miraculously entered the room where the apostles were hiding behind locked doors (John 20:26), so He miraculously enters the sinner's heart and opens it from the inside. You could say that Christ knocks on the door with one hand and opens it from the inside with the other. He causes the door to open;

---

16 John Trapp, *A Commentary on the Old and New Testaments* (Eureka: Tanski, 1997), 5:363, commenting on John 6:44.

17 Owen, *The Works of John Owen*, 10:134, 380.

we do not (cf. Acts 12:10). He opens, and no man can close (Revelation 3:7). He has all the keys (Revelation 1:18). We open in response to Christ opening our hearts.

The historic Lutheran position — though perhaps not the position of Luther himself — is that a person is not able to actively come to Christ, but he is able to cease resisting the Holy Spirit's overtures by his free will, thereby allowing the Spirit to draw him. Some Arminians suggest a similar idea. But that is not so. As we saw in discussing total depravity and inability, fallen man is not able to *not* resist. He always resists until met with a superior power — namely, that of the Holy Spirit. God melts our resistance and transforms us from resisting enemies into willing friends. He sovereignly removes the hard heart of resistance and replaces it with a loving and submissive heart of flesh (Ezekiel 36:26).

Irresistible Love

We need to remember that it is irresistible grace, not mere power. It was out of love that the Father chose the elect (Ephesians 1:4–5) and out of love that the Son died for them (1 John 3:16). Even so, it is the love of the Spirit poured into the elect's hearts that brings them to salvation (Romans 5:5). Jonathan Edwards often pointed out that a sinner comes to Christ not just out of a fear of Hell but out of a sight of the love and loveliness of Jesus Christ.[18] Irresistible grace is power love and powerful love.

In his lovely book, *The Best Match*, Puritan Edward Pearse describes how Christ the Lover "woos" His elect bride effectually with overtures of love, with "a secret touch" and "admirable sweetness."[19] This is well shown in the Song of Solomon and verses such as Jeremiah 31:3: "I have loved you with an everlasting love. Therefore with lovingkindness have I drawn you." The Greek Septuagint used the word *helko* there. Then there is Hosea 11:4: "I drew them with gentle cords, with bands of love." Samuel Rutherford, whom someone said had "an almost womanly love for Christ," often waxed eloquent along these lines. He once wrote that just as faith works by love (Galatians 5:6), so God's irresistible grace works by love in wooing His elect bride by awakening her so that she comes most freely to her beloved.[20] An old hymn had the words, "Twas the

---

18 Jonathan Edwards, *The Works of Jonathan Edwards* (New Haven: Yale University Press, 2006), 25:635; also, "Matthew 25:1 (Sermon 448)," Jonathan Edwards Center at Yale University, accessed February 9, 2018, http://edwards.yale.edu/.

19 Edward Pearse, *The Best Match* (Morgan, PA: Soli Deo Gloria, 1994), 38, 101, 381.

20 Rutherford, *Fourteen Communion Sermons*, 214, 254–56.

same love that spread the feast that sweetly forced me in." It is the magnet of love.

Spurgeon commented, "We yield to the drawings because they come from the Lord's own hand, and their power lies in his love."[21] An old love song had the words: "You made me love you. I didn't want to do it, but you made me love you." 1 John 4:19 puts it better: "We love Him because He first loved us." It is this work of love in special grace that gives us life, faith, and love for Christ. The eighteenth-century Calvinist hymn writer Anne Steele was right to call it the "resistless power of love divine."[22] William Greenhill the Puritan put it like this: "He sweetens their wills, and overcomes them with kindness and Truth. God does not force a man's will, but He sweetly and lovingly takes away the unwilling part of his will, the corruption of his will."[23] John Gill compared it with three things: "Music draws the ear, love the heart, and pleasure the mind."[24] Jonathan Edwards: "Christ don't drive, he draws the heart; he draws by light and love."[25]

Objections Answered

In light of such a wonderful doctrine of loving grace, Calvinists are offended by the accusation of Norman Geisler that the Reformed view of irresistible grace makes God a divine rapist.[26] Nothing could be further from the truth. In forcible rape, the rapist acts illegally, out of selfish lust, often with anger or hatred, sometimes with deception or threats, and not out of love or concern for the well-being of the victim. The victim is harmed, shamed, reacts with fear and anything but love for her attacker. By contrast, in irresistible grace God works legally, lovingly, honestly, and generously, with everlasting concern for the well-being of the elect sinner, who responds gratefully, submissively, lovingly, and joyfully. Effectual grace is not a shameful disgrace but true spiritual romance.

There are other objections such as: "God gives sufficient grace to all men, or at least all who hear the gospel, whereby they are enabled to believe freely

---

21 Spurgeon, *Metropolitan Tabernacle Pulpit*, 36:334.

22 Anne Steele, *Hymns* (Palmers Green: Gospel Standard Baptist Trust, 1967), 73.

23 William Greenhill, *Sermons on Christ's Last Discourse of Himself* (Morgan, PA: Soli Deo Gloria, 1999), 150.

24 John Gill, *The Cause of God and Truth* (Grand Rapids: Baker Book House, 1980), 111.

25 Jonathan Edwards, *The Works of Jonathan Edwards* (New Haven: Yale University Press, 1997), 14:432.

26 Norman Geisler, "God Knows All Things." In David and Randall Basinger, eds., *Predestination and Free Will* (Downers Grove, IL: Intervarsity, 1986), 69.

without so-called effectual grace." This is the historic Arminian position. It takes completely out of context the phrase, "My grace is sufficient for you" (2 Corinthians 12:9), which applies to those who are already saved, not lost sinners. There is not a shred of biblical evidence anywhere that God gives this so-called sufficient grace. Blaise Pascal, the French Jansenist who came as close to being a Calvinist as a Roman Catholic could, mocked this as "sufficient grace that is not sufficient."[27] We need efficient grace that always succeeds, not sufficient grace that only tries and fails. Scripture teaches general grace and special grace but not something in between.

Perhaps the most common objection is that it violates man's free will. But we have already proved from the Bible that fallen man does not have free will. He is a slave to sin. Efficacious grace frees him from that slavery. Moreover, Scripture also repeatedly teaches that God does indeed interfere with man's will, both before and after conversion.

Another objection argues that God patiently waits for the lost sinner to believe, sometimes referring to Isaiah 30:18. We respond that this is true with the free offer of the gospel, but not the special call of irresistible grace. God waits all day for lost sinners (Romans 10:21). They stubbornly refuse to come to Him. At the end of the day, God either calls them efficaciously or judges them in wrath.

Norman Geisler represents classic Arminianism when he offers this objection: "God's grace works synergistically on free will. That is, it must be received to be effective. [. . .] God's justifying grace works cooperatively, not operatively."[28] This was also basically the view of Philip Melanchthon, who differed with Luther. The debate goes all the way back to Augustine (operative grace) as opposed to the Semi-Pelagians (cooperative grace). It is strange that Geisler, a student of Augustine's theology, claims to be a moderate Calvinist and charges that those who believe in efficacious grace are Hyper-Calvinist. The truth of the matter is that synergism comes dangerously close to making man a co-savior with God, almost like the Roman Catholic idea that Mary is co-redemptrix with Christ. Calvinism teaches that the effectiveness of grace is dependent on God, not fallen man. Scripture teaches *monergism* (God works alone) rather than *synergism* (God and man accomplish salvation).[29] The Puritan Christopher

---

27 Blaise Pascal, *Pensees, The Provincial Letters* (New York: Random House, 1941), 337.
28 Norman Geisler, *Chosen but Free*, 3rd ed. (Minneapolis: Bethany House, 2010), 284.
29 A good book on monergism is Matthew Barrett, *Salvation by Grace: The Case for Effectual Calling and Regeneration* (Phillipsburg, NJ: P&R, 2013).

Love said, "You have not been your own converters."[30] Conversion is produced by the effectual grace of the Spirit, not human free will.

Another objection says, "Doesn't John 12:32 say that Christ will draw all men to Himself?" Some Calvinists suggest that this refers to the general call of the gospel, but since the verse uses the word *helko*, it is safer to say it refers to efficacious drawing of "all kinds" of people (cf. Acts 2:17). Note the context. In verses 20 and 21, some Greeks came to meet Jesus. They were being irresistibly drawn to Christ. Jesus was drawing Greeks as well as Jews to Himself. If He irresistibly did this to literally every human being, then every human being would be saved. But we know that is not the case. He efficaciously draws some individuals of all groups of men, not all individuals of all groups.

The foundation for most objections is this: "It is not fair for God to efficaciously draw some and not others." We have seen this objection time and time again in this volume and have answered it the same each time. Does God not have the right to efficaciously draw whomever He wishes? Has He relinquished that right to sinful man? Or has it always been in the hand of sinners and not in the hands of Almighty God? The Canons of the Synod of Dort tersely replied with these words: "God is under no obligation to confer this grace upon any" (3/4:15). No man deserves irresistible grace, and God is not unfair to withhold it from some and give it to others. Rather than object, we should fall on our knees and thank God for it.

Conclusion

Effectual calling and irresistible grace is a wonderful blessing. Consider Psalm 65:4: "Blessed is the man You choose, and cause to approach You" (cf. Numbers 16:5). That is both unconditional election and irresistible grace. When all is said and done, there is still much mystery in all this. As a popular old hymn put it, "I know not how the Spirit moves, convincing men of sin; revealing Jesus through the Word, creating faith in Him." The words of the Synod of Dort are again applicable: "The manner of this operation cannot be fully comprehended by believers in this life. Notwithstanding which, they rest satisfied with knowing and experiencing, that by this grace of God they are enabled to believe with the heart and love their Savior" (3/4:13).

Praise God for irresistible grace.

---

30 Christopher Love, *The Works of Christopher Love* (Morgan, PA: Soli Deo Gloria, 1995), 1:17.

Chapter 56
The New Birth

In this chapter, I will concentrate on certain aspects of the doctrine of regeneration that bring out Calvinism's distinctive view of irresistible grace and other teachings.

What It Is and Is Not

The Bible says that there is an experience known as being *born again* or *born of the Spirit*. It is popularly called the *new birth* and theologically called *regeneration*. It is not reincarnation. Some who believe in reincarnation mistakenly think they have been born again. Regeneration is biblical; reincarnation is not.

Regeneration is also not moral reformation. It is divine innovation, not personal renovation. We are remade by God, not remodeled by ourselves. Nor is it self-reformation or making resolutions to be a better person. Neither is it brought about by obeying the Ten Commandments or the Golden Rule. Galatians 3:21 says, "For if there had been a law given which could have given life, truly righteousness would have been by the law."

Regeneration is also not deification or divinization. God does not make us little gods, contrary to Satan's lie in Genesis 3:5. Some extreme Pentecostals teach that "dogs beget puppies, cats beget kittens, and God begets little gods." Mormons also believe that Mormon men may become gods. All these grossly interpret John 10:34–35 and 2 Peter 1:4. We are God's — not gods.

Regeneration happens in this life, not at the point of death or after death by reincarnation. Some have the unbiblical notion expressed in the famous prayer of Francis of Assisi that we are born again as we leave the womb of this world and enter the next. But the Bible says that Christians have already been born again (1 Peter 1:23). It is past, not future.

Others mistakenly link it with Christ's personal experience. Some say that our regeneration is like His virgin conception and birth. But they fail to see that Christ was generated in His humanity but not regenerated in His spirit. Others think He was regenerated at His baptism or resurrection. But regeneration is spiritual and not physical resurrection.

The New Birth in John 3

John 3 is the classic passage on regeneration. Unfortunately, many readers are as baffled about it as was Nicodemus. But others truly understand it and experience it like Nicodemus did between John 3 and 19:39. In verses 3 and 5, Jesus said that regeneration is absolutely essential to enter or even see the kingdom of Heaven. To underscore this He added, "You must be born again" (v. 7). That was George Whitefield's favorite verse to preach on. When asked why he kept preaching, "You must be born again," he replied, "Because you *must* be born again."

The kingdom of Heaven, also called the kingdom of God, is not an earthly Jewish empire nor merely the future millennium after the Second Coming. It is the present realm of King Jesus in the hearts of His people. He delivers His saints from Satan's evil kingdom and transfers them to His own kingdom (Colossians 1:13). Those who are not born again and remain in the Devil's domain will end up in Hell with Satan and the demons (Matthew 25:41), which is the "second death" (Revelation 20:5–6). Regeneration brings a person into the kingdom of God now and into Heaven later. As the old saying goes, "He that has been born once dies twice, but he that has been born twice dies once" (see John 11:26).

The word *again* (*anothen*) in John 3:7 can mean either "again" or "from above." It may be a double entendre meaning "born again from above." James 1:17 uses it to mean "from above" — in that a good gift comes down from the Father. Then in verse 18, James mentions the new birth as such a gift.

Nicodemus mistakenly thought that Jesus was speaking of a second physical birth. But it is a spiritual experience, not a physical one. Christ then emphasized that it is produced by the Holy Spirit alone, not by one's own self or another person. The Spirit blows like the wind of Ezekiel 37 in giving life to the spiritually dead. Note that He does this by His own sovereign will (see 1 Corinthians 12:11). We cannot produce it or induce it or even predict it in ourselves or others. It is therefore by God's grace alone, not by our efforts or good works. The Son is also involved, for "the Son gives life to whom He will" (John 5:21; see Matthew 11:27). We must not think that regeneration merely implants an impersonal principle of life in us. Rather, regeneration is the implanting of a person — the Holy Spirit. And He produces the new birth when He comes into the heart of a dead sinner.

The New Birth in 1 John

There are six places in which 1 John mentions the new birth: 2:29; 3:9; 4:7; 5:1, 4, and 18. In them John makes two complementary points. The positive point is that the person who has been spiritually reborn practices righteousness as a way of life (2:29; 3:9), as evidenced by a life of love (4:7) and overcoming sin (5:4). The negative point is that regeneration prevents one from living in perpetual sin (3:9; 5:18). This has great implications for the Reformed doctrine of the perseverance of the saints. Those who deny the doctrine of perseverance necessarily have a defective view of regeneration, for regeneration guarantees perseverance.

Three Metaphors

The new birth is a spiritual resurrection. Sinners are spiritually dead. They need life, not medicine; they need resurrection, not resuscitation (see Ephesians 2:1, 5; Colossians 2:13). First John 3:14 describes it as passing from death to life. Christ first raises us spiritually in regeneration and then later physically in physical resurrection (John 5:24). This was typified in the wind blowing on the dry bones of Ezekiel 37. Note verse 14: "I will put my Spirit in you, and you shall live."

The second metaphor is that of a new creation (2 Corinthians 5:17; Galatians 6:15). It is as radical as the creation of Adam and the universe. God made Adam out of the dirt and breathed life into him (Genesis 2:7). God breathes the Holy Spirit into dead and dirty sinners and recreates them into saints. Petrus van Mastricht said it would have been better not to have been born at all than to not have been born again (see Matthew 26:24) and better not to have been created than not to have been recreated.[1]

The third metaphor is that of receiving a new heart (Ezekiel 11:19; 36:26). Our old hearts are rock-hard, hard as granite. In regeneration God gives us a tender heart of flesh in a divine heart transplant so that we will personally know Him. Jeremiah 24:7 promises, "I will give them a heart to know Me [. . .] for they shall return to Me with their whole heart." Deuteronomy 10:16, 30:6, and Jeremiah 4:4 use a slightly different metaphor — a spiritual circumcision of the heart (Cf. 32:39).

Qualities of the New Birth

The new birth is always preceded by increasing conviction of sin, like a woman

---

1 Petrus van Mastricht, *A Treatise on Regeneration* (Morgan, PA: Soli Deo Gloria, 2002), 64.

in labor. The gradual preparation culminates in an instantaneous experience. The preparation is progressive, but the birth itself happens in the twinkling of an eye. There are not degrees of regeneration. One is either regenerated, or he is not. He is either spiritually alive or dead. One cannot be both or neither. It is also unrepeatable. One may be born again but not born again and again and again, as Arminians think (I met one who claimed to have been born again five times). Also, regeneration is complete in itself, like a newly born baby in good health. It then expresses itself in the process of spiritual growth (1 Peter 2:2). Note that the passages in 1 John are all in the perfect tense — something happened in the past with continuing results into the present.

There is no "dormant regeneration" in which a person can be regenerated but not have any signs of life yet, such as faith or repentance or spiritual fruit. Abraham Kuyper taught something like that in his theory of presumptive regeneration. Some extreme Primitive Baptists also teach something similar regarding their view of the immediate regeneration of the elect long before they hear the gospel. One explanation they offer is that the new birth takes two stages like physical birth — one may have spiritual life, followed later by spiritual birth when those qualities are manifested. And some Calvinists hold to a view similar to Lutheranism in holding that some infants are regenerate but do not have conscious faith, only the principle of faith in them. Others even say such a baby is regenerate and may not have any faith at all for years to come. The proper view says that regeneration precedes faith but is never separate from faith.

The new birth itself is the same in all who experience it. Nobody is more born again than anyone else or has a different regeneration. The outward circumstances may differ, and some may go through much longer or deeper conviction of sin than others. But the internal experience is always the same. Further, only Christians have been born again, for this is what makes a person a Christian in the first place. By definition, a non-Christian has not been born again. The phrase *born-again Christian* is redundant and should not be taken to mean that only some Christians are born again any more than some born-again people are not Christians.

Regeneration happens simultaneously with the baptism of the Holy Spirit. When the Spirit baptizes us into Christ, Christ baptizes us into the Spirit. The result is that we are in Christ, and Christ is in us, and we are in the Spirit, and the Spirit is in us. See 1 Corinthians 12:13. Spirit-baptism, therefore, is not a second blessing that only some Christians have experienced, be it a supposed

Pentecostal/charismatic speaking in tongues, a post-conversional sealing that produces assurance (as taught by Martyn Lloyd-Jones), or being made a spiritual Christian instead of a carnal Christian.

The new birth does not remove original sin or indwelling sin, so regeneration is not the error of sinless perfection (Philippians 3:12; Hebrews 12:23; 1 John 1:8). But regeneration does begin to reverse the effects of sin in us. As original sin and total depravity affect all aspects of our being, so regeneration affects all aspects as well and keeps growing. Sinful leaven leavens the whole lump, but the growth of the spiritual leaven of regeneration is never complete in this life.

Regeneration is not the same as justification or adoption. Regeneration affects our nature. Justification changes our legal standing with God, and adoption changes our relationship with God. But the three are inseparable. One cannot have one without the other two. All Christians have all three.

The new birth does more than restore us to a kind of life that Adam had before the Fall. He was sinless then, but we do not become sinless until we die or experience physical resurrection at the Second Coming. But as we saw in the discussion on the *Felix Culpa*, a regenerate Christian has something greater than unfallen Adam had. A Christian has Christ and the Spirit indwelling him.

Lastly, while we are conscious of the effects of regeneration, we are not conscious of the act of regeneration itself. It happens beneath the radar of our consciousness, as it were. Yet we quickly begin to realize we are new creatures in Christ. It remains a deep, deep mystery to us. Calvin said, "When the Lord breathes faith into us He regenerates us in a hidden and secret way that is unknown to us."[2]

The Means of Regeneration

The entire Trinity is involved in this blessed experience, but especially the Holy Spirit. Just as the Father is primarily the one who elects who will be saved (Ephesians 1:4), and the Son dies especially for them (Ephesians 5:25), so it is mainly the work of the Holy Spirit to apply redemption to the elect through regeneration. Jesus specifically referred to it as being "born of the Spirit" (John 3:5–6). John 6:63: "It is the Spirit who gives life." See 2 Corinthians 3:6. The Spirit produces the new birth through irresistible grace. And 1 Samuel 10:6: "Then the Spirit of the Lord will come upon you and you will [. . .] be turned into another man."

---

2 John Calvin, *The Gospel According to St. John 1–10* (Grand Rapids: Eerdmans, 1979), 19.

This does *not* at all mean that the Holy Spirit is a mother in the new birth. All members of the Trinity are masculine: *He*, not *she*. Even in the virgin birth of our Lord, it was Mary and not the Spirit that was the mother (see Luke 1:35). Ultra-feminist "theologians" and even some gullible evangelicals like to say that the Spirit is the mother in the Father-Mother-Son Trinity. But that resembles the pagan triads such as the Egyptian Osiris-Isis-Horus false deities rather than the one true God. This heresy would make God a hermaphrodite bisexual male-female and thereby legitimatize homosexuality and lesbianism. This is blasphemy. The Spirit produces the new birth but not as a mother. A human mother is passive in conception; the father is active. A father does the begetting (Matthew 1). The Spirit is the means by which the Father produces new life in the womb of our heart.

The means the Spirit uses is not water baptism, as many think. Baptismal regeneration has been taught by Catholicism for centuries. Lutheranism holds to it, and some of the early Calvinists did as well. The error is based on a misunderstanding of John 3:5 and Titus 3:5. It is actually an occult and magical idea, in which the Spirit uses "holy water" to produce a miracle. A better exegesis of John 3:5 takes the water to mean the word of God (as Ephesians 5:26), the Holy Spirit (*and* can mean "even"), or natural birth (we must be born spiritually by the Spirit and not just physically in the water of a mother's womb).

The true means is the Word of God. The Spirit inspired it and uses it to produce the new birth in the elect. First Peter 1:23 and James 1:18 explicitly teach this. Luke 8:11 says, "The seed is the word of God." Faith is given in regeneration by means of the word, not the water (Romans 10:17). Not all who hear or read the Bible become regenerate, of course, but nobody is regenerated without it. First Thessalonians 1:5 and 2:13 describe the relation of the two: "Our gospel did not come to you in word only, but also in power and in the Holy Spirit and in much assurance [. . .] the word of God effectively works in you who believe." The Spirit irresistibly works regeneration in the elect through the gospel contained in the Bible.

Primitive Baptists are strongly Calvinistic (some even Hyper-Calvinistic) and teach *immediate regeneration*. This theory says that God regenerates the elect directly without any means at all. Consequently, they say, God regenerates many people who never hear the gospel; there is no need to send missionaries or evangelists or support Bible societies. They deride the orthodox Reformed doctrine as *gospel regeneration*. But this is an unbiblical theory. God's ordained means is the Bible. Just as God created the universe by speaking the word of power (Genesis 1), so He produces the new creation of regeneration by His inspired Word. The Holy Spirit uses Holy Scripture to effect holy regeneration.

God Is Active; Man Is Passive

"In regeneration man is 100% passive, and the Holy Spirit is 100% active," wrote Edwin Palmer.[3] Regeneration is *monergistic*, not *synergistic*. It is produced by God alone, not in a cooperative manner by God and us. And it certainly is not a monergism of self. Calvinists have always firmly believed in monergism — God alone works. Semi-Pelagianism, Melanchthonian Lutherianism (but not Luther), and Arminianism believe in synergism — the work of God and man. Abraham Kuyper put it well: "Hence, in regeneration, man is neither worker nor co-worker; he is merely wrought upon; and the only Worker in this matter is God."[4]

John 1:12–13 emphasizes this point. Some zealous but naïve evangelists think verse 12 implies that the lost sinner does something to bring about the new birth. He believes in order to be born again. But that is exactly what John is *not* saying but rather denying. That is why he added verse 13. One is not born again by anything human, be it natural birth, his parents' will, or his own will. It is done solely by the will of God. Romans 9:16 says, "So it is not of him who wills, nor of him who runs, but of God who shows mercy." It is a divine miracle, not a human achievement, nor even a divine-human synergism. A person can no more cooperate in producing spiritual birth than he can help in producing his natural birth. His parents did the work. He is the effect, not the cause.

The new birth is something done to us, not by us. God alone is active; we are passive. God is the subject; we are the object. The Westminster Confession says we are "altogether passive" (10:2). The resulting effect is that we actively repent and believe. Petrus van Mastricht put his finger on the crux of the matter: "For if he did anything toward begetting life in himself, he must be already alive, since a dead person cannot act; and if he is already alive, then surely life is not begotten in him."[5] This disproves the Arminian error that a lost sinner can help bring about his own regeneration.

This is illustrated in the resurrection of Lazarus in John 11. Christ alone was active; Lazarus was utterly passive. Contrary to a widespread misunderstanding, God does not command lost sinners to be born again. John 3:7 is a statement

---

3 Edwin Palmer, *The Holy Spirit* (Philadelphia: Presbyterian and Reformed, 1964), 84.
4 Abraham Kuyper, *The Work of the Holy Spirit* (Grand Rapids: Eerdmans, 1969), 306.
5 van Mastricht, *A Treatise on Regeneration*, 27.

of fact, not a command. It is an indicative sentence, not an imperative. A dead sinner can no more give himself life than the Ethiopian (or anyone else) can change the color of his skin or a leopard change his spots, says Jeremiah 13:23. John Piper explains that the gospel command to live is what creates life in a dead soul, just as a loud voice shouting, "Wake up!" is what wakes a sleeping person from his slumber[6] (see Ephesians 5:14). Christ "shouted with a loud voice, 'Lazarus, come forth!'" (John 11:43).

Regeneration Precedes Faith

Here is where we come to one of the most controversial and distinctive tenets of Reformed theology. We believe that Scripture teaches that regeneration logically precedes and produces faith, not vice versa. The popular Arminian theory is "Faith is logically prior to regeneration" (Norman Geisler).[7] The Statement of Faith of Dallas Theological Seminary says, "We believe that when an unregenerate person exercises that faith in Christ which is illustrated and described as such in the New Testament, he passes immediately out of spiritual death into spiritual life, and from the old creation into the new."[8] This was popularized in the book *How to Be Born Again* by Billy Graham. How? Believe. A Calvinist would say, "How to believe? Be born again."

The problem with the Arminian theory is that it fails to see that a fallen sinner is spiritually dead and morally incapable of exercising saving faith, indeed, of doing anything spiritually good at all. Rejection of the fourth point of Calvinism goes together with rejection of the first point. Semi-Pelagianism says man takes the first step; Arminianism says he takes the second step. Calvinism says God takes all the steps and carries the sinner. Theodore Beza wrote, "It has been as impossible for us to believe of ourselves (John 12:38–39) as it is impossible for a man that is dead to fly."[9]

First John 5:1 is the key verse: "Whoever believes that Jesus is the Christ is born of God." The grammar is crucial. The Greek verb *believes* (*pisteuon*) is in the present tense: is believing. The verb is *born* (*gegennetai*) is in the perfect tense: has been born and still is. We could paraphrase it as follows: "Whoever now is believing that Jesus is the Christ was born by God in the past with

---

6 John Piper, *The Godward Life* (Sisters, OR: Multnomah, 1997), 249.

7 Norman Geisler, *Chosen But Free*, 3rd ed. (Minneapolis: Bethany House, 2010), 284.

8 "DTS Doctrinal Statement," Article VIII, Dallas Theological Seminary website, accessed February 23, 2018, https://www.dts.edu/about/doctrinalstatement.

9 In James T. Dennison Jr., ed., *Reformed Confessions of the 16th and 17th Centuries in English Translation* (Grand Rapids: Reformation Heritage Books, 2010), 2:253.

the result that he is now in a state of spiritual life." And 1 John 2:29 has the same grammatical structure: "Everyone who practices righteousnesses is born of Him." Clearly the practice of righteousness follows and not precedes being born of God, does it not? Otherwise good works produce regeneration, which is clearly false. First John 5:1 does not say, "Whoever believes will be born of God," but "has been." This significant point is missed by several popular translations. In light of 1 John 5:1, Dave Hunt is clearly wrong to claim, "There is not one scripture that states clearly the doctrine that regeneration comes first and then faith follows — not one."[10]

This is according to the order of Psalm 80:18: "Revive us and we will call upon Your name." In context this refers to the restoration of backsliders, but the same principle applies to regeneration. We could apply it like this: "Regenerate us, and we will call upon you in faith to be saved" (see Romans 10:13).

At this point opponents sometimes resort to their misunderstanding of John 1:12–13. They mistakenly see regeneration in both verses. In truth, verse 12 speaks of adoption and verse 13 speaks of regeneration. Again, the tenses bring this out: "To those who receive Christ by faith, He gave the right to be adopted as children of God, and they had already been born by the will of God and not by themselves." Calvin put it well: "God, therefore, deems those worthy of the honour of adoption who believe in His Son, but whom He had formed for Himself to be His sons, those He at length declares to be such."[11] The Greek word is *exousian* (authority), not *dunamis* (power). The former is a legal term pertaining to adoption, whereas the latter is an existential term more suited to regeneration (as Romans 1:16).

Thomas Bradwardine said this more than a hundred years before the Reformation: "He did not say, 'He gave them power to make themselves sons of God,' but 'to be made sons of God.'"[12] The cause and effect are vital. As we shall shortly see in the chapter on the order of salvation, the logical order is: regeneration→ faith→ adoption.

Conclusion

This brings us to the subject of faith. If regeneration is a sovereign and

---

10 Dave Hunt, *What Love is This?*, 3rd ed. (Bend, OR: The Berean Call, 2006), 116.

11 John Calvin, *Calvin's Calvinism* (Grand Rapids: Reformed Free Publishing Association, 1991), 51.

12 Quoted in J. V. Fesko, *Diversity Within the Reformed Tradition* (Jackson, Miss.: Reformed Academic, 2001), 43.

monergistic act of God, then it follows that saving faith is a sovereign gift of God as well.

Chapter 57
The Gift of Faith

Calvinists have always believed that saving faith is a sovereign gift of God that is freely bestowed on the elect and them alone. It is "the faith of God's elect" (Titus 1:2). Saving faith is the condition of salvation: "Believe on the Lord Jesus Christ and you shall be saved" (Acts 16:31). It does not mean that we are saved because there is any merit in faith or that faith is a kind of righteous substitute for obedience to the law. All the merit is in Christ.

Faith Alone

One of the key issues of the Reformation was whether we are saved by faith alone or faith plus something else. The Reformers insisted that we are saved by "faith alone" (*sola fide*), according to Romans 3:20 and 28; Galatians 2:16; Ephesians 2:8–9; 2 Timothy 1:9; and Titus 3:5. Roman Catholicism taught — and still teaches — that faith is needed but it is not enough. We must also do the sacraments, do good works, suffer to prove ourselves worthy, and so forth. Sadly, even some Protestants add conditions. The three so-called Restorationist church groups (Church of Christ, Christian Church, and Disciples of Christ) say that one must repent and believe, but he is not saved until he is baptized. That adds a work to the condition and is condemned by Galatians 1:9. The so-called New Perspective on Paul also denies faith alone in the Reformation sense. It says that faith is really faithful obedience to covenantal requirements of the law. They reject the "old perspective" of the Reformation and present a position very close to that of the Pharisees — faith plus works. The true Pauline order is faith-justification-works, not faith-works-justification.

In the previous chapter we saw that the Bible teaches that regeneration is the monergistic sovereign work of God and logically precedes and produces faith. Regeneration and faith are inseparable. One cannot be regenerate without faith any more than one can have faith and be unregenerate. Both are the free gift of God given to all Christians. This is essential to the fourth point of Calvinism. The Canons of the Synod of Dort sum up our position:

> Faith is therefore to be considered the gift of God, not on account of its being offered by God to man, to be accepted or rejected at his pleasure; but

because it is in reality conferred, breathed, and infused into him; or even because God bestows the power or ability to believe, and then expects that man should by the exercise of his own free will, consent to the terms of salvation, and actually believe in Christ; but because he who works in man both to will and to do, and indeed all things in all, produces both the will to believe, and the act of believing also (3/4:14).

Ephesians 2:8–9

This is usually the first passage appealed to in the debate: "For by grace you have been saved through faith, and that not of yourselves; it is the gift of God, not of works, lest anyone should boast." There are several interpretations as to the meaning of "that." The first says it refers to *faith*, which is the immediate antecedent. This was the position of Augustine, Theodore Beza, Johannes Cocceius, Abraham Kuyper, and others. The difficulty with this view is that the Greek word for *that* is a neuter demonstrative pronoun and *faith* is a feminine noun. In Greek, a pronoun must agree in gender with the antecedent noun it modifies. Gordon Clark, who says faith is the gift, argues that there are exceptions to this rule.[1] He points to Acts 8:10; 1 Corinthians 6:11; 10:6, 1 Peter 2:19; 2 Peter 2:17; and Jude 12. Opponents says that these references are not exact parallels, and even if they were they would be rare exceptions to the rule. Moreover, this interpretation would render the ensuing clause in an awkward manner: "and faith is not of works, lest anyone should boast." The Scottish Calvinist John Eadie remarked, "You may declare that salvation is not of works, but you cannot with propriety say that faith is not of works."[2] The interpretation is very unlikely.

Another unlikely view argues that the faith in question is not ours but God's faith or faithfulness. Exponents allude to verses that speak of the faith of God or of Christ (Mark 11:22; Galatians 2:16). Some think this is what Romans 1:17 means: "from God's faith to our faith." Those of the school of Thomas F. Torrance and others who hold to the vicarious faith and repentance of Christ promote this opinion. Whether that may or may not be true, it is extremely unlikely that this is what Paul had in mind in Ephesians 2:8–9.

Still another suggestion is that "that" refers to *grace*. But that would be redundant, for grace is by definition a free gift from God to us. Also, like the

---

1 Gordon Clark, *Predestination* (Phillipsburg, NJ: Presbyterian & Reformed, 1987), 103. See also his *Ephesians* (Jefferson: Trinity Foundation, 1985), 72–74.
2 John Eadie, *Commentary on the Epistle to the Ephesians* (Grand Rapids: Zondervan, 1977), 152.

Greek word for *faith*, the word for *grace* is also feminine and does not match the neuter word *that*.

The best interpretation is that the word "that" there refers to the whole preceding sentence. This was the position of Calvin, Matthew Henry, John Gill, John Eadie, and many others. This has the fewest difficulties and the best grammatical parallels. First Corinthians 6:6 and 8 and Philippians 1:28 use a very similar grammatical construction with the word *that* and refer to the whole preceding clause and not just a single word, let alone one with a different gender. Thus it takes Ephesians 2:8–9 to mean: "By grace you have been saved through faith, and this salvation-by-grace-through-faith is not of yourselves, but is the free gift of God and not by works lest anyone should boast." Strangely, some Arminians take this line but contend that it denies that faith is a gift. They fail to see that the gift is the entire salvation process from grace through faith. Therefore, the verses do indeed teach that faith is a gift but not in the way that some think.

Other Verses

I am not aware of any verses in the Old Testament that speak of faith as a gift. There are, however, several in the New Testament that directly or indirectly teach that faith is a gift from God. Second Peter 1:1 is perhaps the most explicit: "To those who have obtained like precious faith with us." If obtained, it was given. Note that Peter says it is given to all Christians.

Philippians 1:29 is also explicit: "For to you it has been granted on behalf of Christ, not only to believe in Him, but also to suffer for His sake." This does not mean: "The gospel commands you to believe, and if you do, you will suffer." That is true, of course, but Paul means more. "Granted" refers to a gift, not a demand. God gives faith in Christ and suffering for Christ to the elect. Faith as a grant-gift is also taught in John 6:65: "No one can come to Me unless it has been granted to him by My Father." Coming to Christ is faith (vv. 37 and 45; see Matthew 11:28).

John 3:27 says, "A man can receive nothing unless it has been given to him from heaven." This is an axiom applicable to all God's gifts. All good things come down from the Father (James 1:17), and faith is such a good gift. God gives, we receive. That we receive means it is a gift. You cannot receive what is not given. On *receive*, see 2 Peter 1:1 again.

First Corinthians 4:7 was a favorite verse of Augustine:[3] "For who makes you differ from another? And what do you have that you did not receive? Now if you did indeed receive it, why do you boast as if you had not received it?" The forbidden boasting is parallel to Ephesians 2:8–9. No one can boast of a free gift; boasting assumes earning it. Those who deny that faith is a gift are in effect boasting, "Well, at least I contributed my part to my salvation." Never! Whoever boasts should boast only in the Lord (1 Corinthians 1:31) and in His work on the cross (Galatians 6:14). We boast in Christ's works, not ours. To say that faith is not a gift implies that it is our own work, and that robs God's glory and takes it to oneself.

First Corinthians 12:3 says, "No one can say that Jesus is Lord except by the Holy Spirit." Obviously Paul means the confession made in faith, not merely speaking the words "Jesus is Lord" (see Romans 10:9–10). Paul then lists several spiritual gifts that are sovereignly and freely given by the Spirit, including faith (v. 9). This is not saving faith, for that is given to all Christians, and these spiritual gifts are not given to every Christian. It could refer to the faith to work miracles or the strong faith in intercessory prayer (George Mueller is often cited as the example). But the underlying principle is the same. The Spirit gives *all* His gifts sovereignly and freely (v. 11). None are earned or produced by ourselves.

Galatians 5:22 lists faith as one of the fruits of the Spirit, but it is probably referring to faithfulness in perseverance rather than saving faith. Still, like spiritual gifts, the fruits of the Spirit are produced by the Holy Spirit and not by ourselves.

Two verses speak of faith coming to a person. Romans 10:17: "Faith comes by hearing and hearing by the word of God." In context, this means saving faith. It is bestowed on us by the Word of God, which we previously saw is also the means of regeneration. Faith and the new birth are given simultaneously through the Spirit-inspired Holy Scriptures. The other verse is Galatians 3:23: "Before faith came, we were kept under the law." This is a difficult verse to interpret. In context Paul is speaking of freedom in the new covenant after the dispensation of the law. When Christ came, the old covenant passed away, including certain features of the law, such as the ceremonies. A similar thing happens in the life of an individual. The law convicts him; the Spirit converts him and frees him. When the Spirit does this, He gives faith. Perhaps this verse

---

3 Augustine, *The Works of Saint Augustine* (Hyde Park: New City, 1999), I/26:152–56.

should not be pressed too far to show that personal saving faith is a gift, but the underlying principle is implicit if not explicit.

Then Matthew 13:11 says, "It has been given to you to know the mysteries of the kingdom of heaven, but to them it has not been given." This refers to spiritual illumination, which is part of saving faith. It is sovereignly given to some people and not to others.

Acts 18:27 says, "He greatly helped those who had believed through grace." Why did they believe? It was because God graciously gave them faith. Earlier Luke recorded Peter's words in 3:16: "through faith in His name [. . .] the faith which comes through Him." We have faith in Christ because it has been given to us by Christ.

Romans 12:3 says, "God has dealt to each one a measure of faith." This probably refers to serving faith rather than saving faith, but again the principle is the same. All God's gifts are free gifts.

Hebrews 12:2 calls Jesus "the author and finisher of our faith." This does not refer to "the faith" as the content of saving faith, as in Jude 3. Rather, it means the act of faith. Faith believes and follows, as in chapter 11. Jesus is the author — He gave it. He is the finisher — He keeps giving it. He will complete it, as per Philippians 1:6.

Remember that fallen man is spiritually unable to believe. A dead man cannot do anything. A fallen sinner cannot believe. He is not able to "work up" faith. As Calvin noted, "Faith has been granted to us because we could not have manufactured it within ourselves."[4]

How Faith Is Given

We are blind and "could not believe" (John 12:39–40). How is it then that some people believe, and others do not? It is not a matter of intelligence, willpower, upbringing, or anything else that is human. It is only because God chose to give a person the gift of faith.

Faith is given in the same way that regeneration is given — by the Holy Spirit through Holy Scripture.[5] God sovereignly bestows the three elements of saving faith: knowledge, assent, and trust. God commands us to believe,

---

4 John Calvin, *Sermons on Galatians* (Edinburgh: Banner of Truth, 1997), 392.
5 Calvin agreed with Augustine: "Faith is conceived from the Scriptures." *Selected Works of John Calvin* (Grand Rapids: Baker, 1983), 3:70.

and He gives what He commands, as Augustine said in his famous prayer. The Confession of Tarcal and Torda said, "He creates that faith in us which He earnestly demands from us."[6]

The Gift of Repentance

Sometimes we are told to repent to be saved (Acts 3:19), other times to believe to be saved (Acts 16:31), and sometimes both (Mark 1:15; Acts 20:21). We are not saved by faith without repentance any more than repentance without faith. It is a repentant faith and a believing repentance. They are two sides of the same coin, and the coin is a gift from God. They are given together. Calvin said that faith and repentance can be differentiated but never separated.[7]

Repentance is a gift sovereignly bestowed by God. Acts 5:31: "Him God has exalted to His right hand to be Prince and Savior, to give repentance to Israel and forgiveness of sins." Acts 11:18: "Then God has also granted to the Gentiles repentance to life." God commands all men everywhere to repent (Acts 17:30) and gives the gift of repentance to the elect.

Second Timothy 2:25: "In humility correcting those who are in opposition, if God perhaps will grant them repentance, so they may know the truth." It is God's sovereign prerogative to give or withhold the gift of repentance, even as He gives or withholds faith, mercy, and salvation (Romans 9:15). Calvin noted, "God is not called the helper in repentance, but the author of it."[8]

Saving repentance goes hand in hand with saving faith. First, it is a change of mind, then a mourning for sin, then a turning from sin. There is a non-saving repentance just as there is a non-saving faith, such as in the case of Judas (Matthew 27:3; 2 Corinthians 7:10). That can and does often happen in unregenerate sinners who mistakenly think they truly repented. But true repentance is the fruit of regeneration. Asahel Nettleton preached a powerful sermon entitled "Genuine Repentance Does Not Precede Regeneration."[9] God gives repentance in the gift of regeneration, and logically regeneration precedes repentance as it precedes faith.

---

6 In James T. Dennison Jr., ed., *Reformed Confessions of the 16th and 17th Centuries in English Translation* (Grand Rapids: Reformation Heritage Books, 2010), 2:667.

7 John Calvin, *Commentaries on the Book of the Prophet Jeremiah and Lamentations* (Grand Rapids: Eerdmans, 1950), 3:336.

8 Calvin, 3:229.

9 Asahel Nettleton, *Sermons from the Second Great Awakening* (Ames, IA: International Outreach, 1995), 60–73.

Objections

One objection runs: "God only *offers* the gift of faith and repentance. We must first ask for it. But we can also reject it." We reply that salvation is both offered and given, but faith and repentance are given and not offered. The Arminian says we must first ask for the gift. This overlooks the principle of James 1:6–7 where we are told that we must ask for something in faith, or we will not receive it. But the unbeliever by definition does not have any faith with which to ask God for the gift of faith. A Christian by definition is a believer and can use his faith to ask for more faith (Luke 17:5). But the unbeliever must first be given faith before he can ask for anything. Without faith, all he does or asks is sin (Romans 14:23).

Another objection contends, "All men already have faith, but only some put that faith in Christ." Sometimes they quote Romans 12:3: "God has dealt to each one a measure of faith." That is faulty exegesis, for Paul is speaking of believers and not unbelievers. An unbeliever has no faith, and without faith it is impossible to please God (Hebrews 11:6). Believing in God is the first step he must take, but he cannot make that step until it has been given to him. Second Thessalonians 3:2 also answers this objection thus: "Not all have faith." Many have false faith. Luke 18:9 speaks of those who "trust in themselves" and not in God, but that clearly is not a misplaced saving faith but proud self-confidence.

Still another objection says, "We are commanded to believe. It cannot be both a duty and a gift." This was Pelagius' position. If God commands something, we are able to do it. He violently rejected Augustine's view that God gives what He commands. Oddly, many Hyper-Calvinists use a similar wrong logic in reverse. They say that something cannot be both a gift and a duty. Since faith is a gift, it is therefore not a duty. But the Bible says that faith is both. Augustine was right after all.

One last objection should not surprise us, for it is offered time and time again to the teachings of Calvinism: "It is not fair to give faith to some and not to others!" But who says so? Can God not give faith to whomever He pleases? As the Synod of Dort pointed out, "God is under no obligation to confer this grace upon any" (3/4:15). No man deserves the gift of faith and repentance. Therefore, nobody can charge God with unfairness in withholding it from them. The objection springs from the same proud heart that boasts of its freedom to believe anything he wants to. But those who truly believe are humbly grateful to God for giving them the faith to be saved and which they did not deserve. They boast in God, not in themselves.

Conclusion

Curiously, the Arminians Jerry Walls and Joseph Dongell are right when they admit, "If faith is not our doing but God's gift, then the well-known features of Calvinism fall into place."[10] Unfortunately, they deny that faith is a gift, and so they reject the wonderful doctrines of grace. If faith is not a gift of grace, then what is it but a work of man? If so, we are saved by works, not by grace, contrary to Ephesians 2:8–9.

God gives the dual gift of faith and repentance irresistibly to all the elect and only to the elect. It is as effectual as regeneration. Faith is the hand that receives Christ, and even that hand is the gift of God. God alone gives this gift. We cannot give it to another person any more than we can give it to ourselves. The Bible knows nothing of proxy faith or claiming someone for Christ.

If we have faith, let us thank God for giving it to us.

---

10 Jerry Walls and Joseph Dongell, *Why I Am Not a Calvinist* (Downers Grove, IL: InterVarsity, 2004), 77.

Chapter 58
The Order of Salvation

Earlier we discussed the order of the decrees; now we look at the order of salvation. The two are related but should not be confused. The first is the eternal plan of salvation; the second is the historical enactment of salvation. They are both part of the Golden Chain of Romans 8:29–30. There are other links as well.

Jacob Karpov, an eighteenth-century Lutheran, is generally credited with coining the term *ordo salutis*, but the question was debated long before him. Theodore Beza, William Perkins, and John Bunyan produced detailed charts on the order of salvation as they saw it. Karl Barth dismissed the whole idea as crass scholasticism, and G. C. Berkouwer was not far behind in his opinion. Non-Reformed theologians often dismiss or ignore it. While there are different opinions among the Reformed on some points, a consensus exists.

Is There a Biblical Order?

Scripture speaks of salvation in a general way and uses various words for its constituent elements. Paul tended to speak in terms of justification; John, in terms of regeneration. All the elements are necessary and inseparable but must be differentiated and not confused with each other. Justification has to do with our legal standing before God; regeneration, our experiential state — and both are necessary for salvation.

Reformed writers sometimes say that the historical links, like those in eternity, are united in a logical but not chronological order. While there is much truth in this, there is still something chronological in the order because we live in chronological time and not infinite eternity. This does not mean there is any time lag between the links. Salvation happens in an instant, though there are varying degrees of preparation and follow-through in sanctification along the way to glorification.

One cannot be justified without being regenerated, any more than one can have faith and not repentance or faith and not justification. The links are divinely and permanently welded together. If there was an interval, what would happen if a person died in that interval? What if he was regenerate but did not yet believe and been justified? He could not go to Hell, for he had been regenerated, but he could not enter Heaven, for he had not been justified. Lutherans tend to say it is a mystery best left to God, but Calvinists go deeper. At any given moment a person is either a Christian, or he is not. He cannot be both or neither. There is no such thing as a half-Christian. Even pseudo-Christians are non-Christians.

Anthony Hoekema[1] and others propose a coordinate rather than subordinate order, similar to their theory of a coordinate order of decrees. All the spokes on a wheel turn at the same time, they say. We reply that it matters in what order the spokes are placed and in what direction the wheel turns. In some cases, reversing the order produces a false gospel and non-salvation, as in putting works before justification.

Sinclair Ferguson rightly comments: "The 'ordo salutis' seeks to establish, on the basis of Scripture, a pattern common to all believers, although experienced with different degrees of consciousness by each individual."[2] The same elements happen in every Christian, for there is only one salvation. There are not degrees of salvation — nobody is more saved than anyone else.

It sometimes happens that the differences of opinions on the order of the decrees are reflected in one's view of the order of salvation. For instance, some supralapsarians argue for justification before faith, which no infralapsarian would dare suggest. The supralapsarian scheme presents other problems it does not resolve.

The Roman Catholic Order

The Protestant Reformers rejected the Roman Catholic order as unbiblical and heretical. In general, Catholic dogma puts forth the following order according to their sacramental system:

1. *Baptism.* One is regenerated in baptism, usually as an infant. Grace is sacramentally infused, and original sin is forgiven.

2. *Confirmation.* As the baptized child grows, he develops infused grace by learning his catechism, doing good works, and believing whatever the Catholic Church teaches. This is verified by a priest around the time of puberty, and the priest or bishop breathes the Holy Spirit into him. He is now eligible for the Eucharist.

---

1 Anthony Hoekema, *Saved by Grace* (Grand Rapids: Eerdmans, 1989), 11–27.
2 Sinclair Ferguson, "Ordo Salutis." In Martin Davie, et al, eds., *New Dictionary of Theology*, 2nd ed. (Downers Grove, IL: InterVarsity, 2016), 633.

3. *The Eucharist*. When a Catholic partakes of the transubstantiated bread and wine that is the literal and physical body and blood of Jesus, he receives still more grace. This is the most important sacrament of all, and the primary means of saving grace.

4. *Penance*. When a Catholic sins, especially mortal sin, he must do penance prescribed for him by a priest following confession before he partakes of the Eucharist again. Penance is a good work, such as giving money to the church, visiting the sick, or just saying so many "Hail Mary" prayers. The Catholic repeats this over and over throughout his lifetime. He must have faith and works. Suffering can also be useful as self-atonement. One is gradually made righteous in this process, which Catholicism considers justification. One is not finally pronounced righteous until Judgment Day.

5. *Extreme Unction*. When a Catholic nears death, he must confess his sins to a priest and receive Last Rites for forgiveness. There is no ratchet effect on any of this, for a Catholic may commit a mortal sin at any stage and die lost.

6. *Purgatory*. If a Catholic dies in a state of grace, he goes to Purgatory to suffer for his sins and have original sin burned out of him. But he will eventually make it to Heaven, even if he must spend thousands of years in Purgatory.

More liberal Catholic theologians dilute the above, especially as they acknowledge salvation in Protestant and even non-Christian religions. Traditional Catholics have official dogma on their side in accepting the above. For them, there is no salvation outside the Catholic Church and its method of salvation.

The Arminian Order of Salvation

There are variations within Arminianism, but the mainline order is as follows:

1. God gives sufficient grace to all people (or at least all who hear the gospel), thus counter-balancing human depravity and enabling them to believe if they will.

2. Some people use sufficient grace by using free will, and so they believe and repent.

3. God gives regeneration on the basis of faith. He infuses righteousness, and believers are made partly righteous.

4. Some Arminians say God imputes the righteousness of Christ to believers.

5. God accepts this righteousness and pronounces the believer pardoned.

6. God then adopts the pardoned sinner.

7. But this must be maintained by free will perseverance, or all will be lost.

Preparatory Stages

The Reformed *ordo salutis* begins with what God does before saving a sinner. First there must be conviction of sin, sometimes called the needle that pulls the thread of salvation. God gradually shows a sinner that he is lost, deserves Hell, and cannot save himself. This is produced by the Holy Spirit through the law (Galatians 3:24). The Puritans called this a *law work*, not to be confused with a work of the law. This process culminates in conversion in the elect. But even a non-elect person can experience conviction. There is no conversion without conviction, but there can be conviction without conversion.

Unlike Pelagianism and other errors, Calvinism has always taught that God requires no good works whatsoever to contribute to the sinner's salvation. Salvation is entirely of grace — *sola gratia* (Ephesians 2:8–9). It would be incorrect to suppose that a person with many good works is more likely to become saved than another sinner with only a few good works, for the simple reason that no unregenerate sinner has any good works at all. Good works follow salvation, not precede it or produce it.

The American Puritans in particular taught what is called *preparationism*. They did not call on lost sinners to do good works to prepare themselves for salvation. Rather, they preached the gospel to them and urged them to read the Bible, listen to good sermons, attend church, and examine their hearts to see what sins were keeping them from repenting and believing in Christ. Some advocates of this approach went too far and bordered on legalism. Sometimes sinners presumed they had been converted because they had gone through certain preparatory stages of conviction and had outward morality. Jonathan Edwards clarified biblical preparationism while not dismissing it as some Arminians have done.

Some Hyper-Calvinists also err in a kind of preparationism. They say that we cannot invite all sinners to Christ; we can invite only "sensible sinners," or those who have been deeply convicted of their sins. Some Hyper-Calvinists say that this is evidence that they have already been regenerated without knowing it. For them, faith is simply the realization that one has already been saved. This fits in with their view that justification precedes faith.

Also preparatory is the understanding of the gospel. Faith is given through the Word, but not all who hear or read the gospel are given faith. The key is enlightenment. The Spirit supernaturally enlightens a lost and convicted sinner of his doom and thus enables him to see his need for a Savior. Then the Spirit enlightens his mind to see the truth of the gospel. He then knows the gospel is true but has not yet been saved. Many Reformed men, such as Edwards, say that if a sinner violently resists and blasphemes the Spirit at this stage, he commits the unpardonable blasphemy of the Spirit according to Hebrews 6 and 10. Such a person is branded a reprobate by the Spirit and will never become converted. He proves that he was never regenerate, as opposed to Arminian theories to the contrary. Though this experience is extreme, fortunately it is rare.

Regeneration and Adoption

Scripture teaches that both regeneration and adoption are essential parts of salvation. Both are metaphors for being children of God, but they are not identical. Regeneration is an experiential work of God *in* us, while adoption is a legal act of God *for* us. Which logically comes first?

Some Hyper-Calvinists taught eternal adoption, such as James Wells, John Brine, and especially John Gill, who wrote: "As the will of God to elect is his election of them, so his will to adopt the same is his adoption of them. Adoption is before regeneration; the one is an act of God in eternity, the other is an act and work of his grace in time; the one is the cause, the other the effect."[3] But he overlooks Galatians 3:26: "You are all sons of God through faith in Jesus Christ." That is adoption, not regeneration. Faith must logically precede adoption. We are adopted by faith just as we are justified by faith. And since regeneration precedes faith, the order is regeneration-faith-adoption. Regeneration precedes adoption in the *ordo salutis*.

Related to the theory of eternal adoption is the theory of *eternal union*. It was taught by John Gill, William Huntington, J. C. Philpot, A. W. Pink, and others, who are usually Hyper-Calvinists. It says that God united the elect with Christ in the eternal covenant of redemption. Mainstream Calvinists agree that the elect were federally united with Christ then but deny that we were personally or experientially united with Him until regeneration. In Romans 16:7, Paul said that Andronicus and Junias were "in Christ before me." That could not be true if all the elect were actually in Christ from eternity. Actual union does not occur

---

3 John Gill, *A Complete Body of Doctrinal and Practical Divinity* (Paris, AR: Baptist Standard Bearer, 1984), 201–02.

until regeneration. God unites the elect to Christ by the Spirit at the point of regeneration. Reformed theologians differ whether union or regeneration logically comes first.

This is just one of several areas in which Hyper-Calvinists tend to push things out of time back into eternity in the name of sovereign grace. G. C. Berkouwer accused them of making salvation history meaningless.[4] In the name of denying human credit for salvation, they not only make us completely passive but put several elements of our salvation completely outside of our experience in time. This reflects their imbalanced view of divine sovereignty and human responsibility.

It is true that the decision to elect is election, but the decision to adopt is not adoption any more than the decree to create is the same as the act of creation in time. Otherwise, one has creation before creation. The Hyper-Calvinist follows the inconsistencies of his supralapsarianism and claims that certain parts of salvation are divine works within God in eternity rather than works from God in time.

Calling and Justification

The Golden Chain of Romans 8:29–30 clearly puts effectual calling before justification. The Silver Chain puts calling before faith in Romans 10:14–17. We call on God because He first called us. There is a slight difference of opinion among some Reformed theologians regarding the logical order of calling and regeneration. Does calling precede and produce regeneration (as typified in Lazarus in John 11)? Or are we regenerated in order to hear the call? Likewise, where does vital union with Christ come in with these two?

Justification and Faith

All the Protestant Reformers and later Calvinists have taught justification by faith alone without works of the law. This was a major difference between Protestant evangelicalism and Roman Catholicism — and still is. We hold that justification includes the pardon of sin and the imputation of the twofold righteousness of Christ. On this fine point it is debated whether the logical order is pardon (legal removal of guilt) and then imputation (putting Christ's righteousness in the place of the removed guilt) or vice versa. Even more specifically, it would appear that the passive obedience of Christ (His death)

---

4 G. C. Berkouwer, *Faith and Justification* (Grand Rapids: Eerdmans, 1979), 25–36, 143–68; and *Divine Election* (Grand Rapids: Eerdmans, 1960).

is logically imputed first before His active obedience (His holy life), assuming there is such an order.[5]

All historical Calvinists believe that justification is by imputation, not infusion, as taught by Romanism. God does indeed infuse righteousness into the sinner when He regenerates him, for the Spirit enters his heart and transforms it to begin the process of sanctification. But — and this is vital — God justifies the sinner on the basis of what Christ did *for* him rather than what He does *in* him. Rome confuses justification with sanctification by making it a process whereby God makes us holy. In Reformed terms, this puts sanctification before justification, which is a deadly error. The Neonomianism of Richard Baxter and Daniel Williams bordered on this heresy by apparently combining imputed righteousness with infused righteousness as the twin ground of justification. They attempted a reunion not only of Calvinism, Arminianism, and Lutheranism but a reunion of all three with Roman Catholicism.

Though there are variations among Arminians, and some believe in imputation, their mainline position of infusion is closer to Rome than they realize. Rome teaches that *to justify* means "to make righteous." Historic Lutheranism and Calvinism have always taught that it means "to legally declare righteous." It is a legal and not an experimental word. This is borne out by Exodus 23:7; Deuteronomy 25:1; 1 Kings 8:32; Proverbs 17:15; and Isaiah 5:23. The opposite of justification is condemnation, which is not making a person unrighteous but declaring that he is unrighteous.

Moreover, neither Rome nor Arminianism say that the infusion of grace and righteousness makes a person sinless, though both sometimes admit that there may be a later second blessing in which a person is made sinlessly perfect. They say that regeneration forgives but does not eradicate original sin and indwelling sin. The result — which they generally do not admit — is a system of salvation in which God forgives and saves sinners based on an incomplete righteousness. The Neonomians seemed to say that God lowers His standard from the old law to the new law. But historic Calvinists are horrified at the implications of these errors. God most certainly does not compromise His absolute holiness. He demands a perfect righteousness. To their credit, evangelical Arminians deny that there is sacramentally infused grace as taught by Rome, though some Anglican and Episcopalian Arminians teach just that. Lutheranism, on the other hand, teaches baptismal regeneration but counterbalances this with justification by imputed and not infused righteousness. Fortunately, evangelical Arminians also deny

---

5 I will discuss the twofold obedience of Christ in a later chapter.

that there is any personal salvific merit in infused righteousness. John Wesley disagreed with Baxter on this, to his credit. All the merit must be in Christ, or we are back in the morass of Pharisaism, Pelagianism, and Roman Catholicism.

All of this has been challenged in recent decades by the so-called New Perspective on Paul. This serious error arose from non-evangelicalism and non-Reformed sources such as E. P. Sanders and James D. G. Dunn. It made inroads into erstwhile evangelical and Reformed circles mainly through the ex-Calvinist N. T. Wright. Curiously, Wright was one of the "Four Oxford Students" who authored the fine little book *The Grace of God in the Gospel* published by Banner of Truth in 1972. This system fundamentally disagrees with the "old perspective" of the Reformers and historic Calvinists on several points. It downplays or denies divine wrath, outright denies the imputation of Christ's righteousness, redefines faith as *covenantal faithfulness* (that is, obedience to God's laws), and defends the Pharisees and thereby medieval Catholicism from the charge of legalism. The old perspective, it is argued, was anti-Semitic and fundamentally misunderstood Judaism at the time of the New Testament as well as totally misunderstood Paul on his major contribution to theology. In effect, the New Perspective ends up teaching the very heresy that Calvinists argue that Paul opposed: justification by works. It is a repudiation of the Reformation as well as the gospel. It is the road back to Pharisaism and Catholicism. Fortunately, stalwart Calvinists have seen this error for what it is and reject it in no uncertain terms. The old and true gospel of justification by faith alone is preferable to the new and false gospel of justification by faithful works. See Galatians 1:8–9.

Another question has been discussed in Reformed circles regarding the *ordo salutis* and justification by faith: Does faith precede or follow justification?[6] By far most historic Calvinists agree with historic Lutherans and even evangelical Arminians in teaching that faith logically precedes justification. We are justified by faith (Romans 3:20, 28; 5:1; Galatians 2:16). However, a few Hyper-Calvinists such as John Gill, the so-called Calvinistic Antinomians such as Tobias Crisp and John Eaton, and some other supralapsarians have taught that justification precedes faith. Alexander Comrie and Abraham Kuyper taught it within Dutch Reformed theology with a few twists. The theory seems to lurk around the fringes of supralapsarianism. I do not know of any infralapsarians who hold to it, nor have all supralapsarians accepted it.

The theory has two aspects, one affecting their view of the order of the decrees

---

6 See Curt Daniel, "Hyper-Calvinism and John Gill," PhD diss., The University of Edinburgh, 1983, 305–30.

and the other the order of salvation. In the first, they teach that justification is an eternal and internal work of God, like eternal adoption and eternal union. It is part of the covenant of redemption. Justification is in God and is not an experience within us; therefore, it was not necessary that we exist yet. It is as eternal as predestination. Gill said that as the decree to elect is election, so the decree to justify is justification. The elect are first justified in the "court of Heaven" in eternity, and then later justified in "the court of conscience" in time.[7] Francis Turretin represented historic Calvinism in rebutting this view. He showed that the decree to justify is no more the legal act of justification than the decree to create is the act of creation.[8] If justification is eternal, then the sinner is justified before he has sinned, yea, even before he exists. This is but one example of how the supralapsarian theory leads to confusion in various areas. To their credit, however, some advocates of eternal justification explain that the elect are decretively justified in eternity, virtually justified in the resurrection of Christ, and actually justified at the point of faith in the elect.

But this leads to another fog of confusion. Advocates of eternal justification often argue that justification logically precedes faith in the *ordo salutis*. As Kuyper put it, "Wherefore God does indeed declare the ungodly just before he believes, that he may believe, and not after he believes."[9] Gill and the Antinomians insisted that faith is a blessing, not a condition per se, of justification. We believe that we have already been justified; we do not believe to become justified.

This can be refuted in several ways. First, the Bible clearly teaches that we are justified "by" faith (Romans 5:1). We believe "through grace" (Acts 18:27), but it would not be scripturally correct to say that we believe through justification. Faith logically precedes justification in a legal cause-and-effect manner. To say the opposite is to get the cart before the horse. Also, it appears that the "justification before faith" theory is always promoted by supralapsarians. But they thereby show their own inconsistency with the supralapsarian dictum that "What is first in intention is last in execution." If justification precedes faith in the order of the decrees, it would have to follow it in the historical order of salvation — the very thing they deny. Their whole approach reveals an imbalanced view of divine sovereignty and human responsibility, an overemphasis on God's internal and eternal acts, and a muddled and inconsistent logic.

---

7 Gill, *Body*, 203–09.

8 Francis Turretin, *The Institutes of Elenctic Theology* (Phillipsburg, NJ: P&R, 1992), 2:682–85.

9 Abraham Kuyper, *The Work of the Holy Spirit* (Grand Rapids: Eerdmans, 1969), 376; cf. 367–71.

The question parallels the practical matter of forgiving someone who sins against us (e.g., Matthew 6:12–15). One often hears words like, "Forgive him, even if he does not repent and apologize." That sounds very spiritual, but it is not biblical. Ephesians 4:32 says, "Forgiving one another, even as God in Christ forgave you." Our forgiving others should imitate God forgiving us (5:1). But God does not forgive and justify us before we repent and believe but rather after (Acts 3:19). God does not forgive without repentance any more than He justifies without faith. Jesus said, "If your brother sins against you, rebuke him; and if he repents, forgive him" (Luke 17:3). The "if" is the crucial condition in both God forgiving us and our forgiving others. To say that we should forgive others even when they do not repent implies that God forgives us without repentance. James B. Torrance used to say that in preaching the gospel, we are not to say, "If you repent, God will forgive you," but rather "Repent because God has already forgiven you." This Neo-Orthodox approach says God has already forgiven the human race, whether they know it or not and whether they repent or not. Still, Christians should imitate God by sincerely desiring that others repent of their sins against us (cf. 2 Peter 3:9). We should lovingly rebuke them and offer forgiveness. Of course, only God can give repentance. We can only plead, pray, and wait. And we should.

Faith and Repentance

We have already shown that Scripture teaches that both faith and repentance are sovereign gifts of God and are the twofold condition of justification. Non-Calvinists sometimes deny that repentance is part of faith and that it is a necessary condition of salvation. To them, our position is at odds with *sola fide* by making repentance a second condition. Some even say that repentance is a work, and to make it a condition of salvation is to add works to faith as a condition, which is clearly unbiblical. Therefore, it is argued, repentance must always follow justification. Indeed, extreme advocates of this error sometimes go so far as to say that it is an optional extra. Some believers never repent, they say. Historic Calvinists could not disagree more strongly. Just as a sinner will perish if he does not believe (John 3:16), he will perish if he does not repent (Luke 13:3).

Repentance is part of conversion (Acts 3:19). Repentance is a change of mind, a change of heart, and a change of direction. It is a turning from sin to God (1 Thessalonians 1:9; Acts 14:15; 20:21; 26:20). One must forsake sin to receive saving mercy and salvation (Proverbs 28:13). There is no salvation without conversion (Matthew 18:3) or repentance (Luke 13:3).

But which logically comes first: faith or repentance? Great Reformed divines have differed. Some, such as Robert Lewis Dabney, Arthur W. Pink, Geerhardus Vos, Abraham Kuyper, and James Petigru Boyce have taught that repentance logically goes before faith. They appeal to Mark 1:15; Acts 20:21; and 2 Timothy 2:25–26. Turning from sin logically and directionally precedes turning to God.

Others, such as Calvin, William G. T. Shedd, Herman Hoeksema, John Gill, R. A. Webb, and A. A. Hodge have taught that faith logically precedes repentance. They point to Acts 11:21: "A great number believed and turned to the Lord." Romans 14:23 says, "Whatever is not of faith is sin," so repentance must follow faith, or it is sin. Hebrews 11:6 says the first step is belief in God. Some say that repentance is the effect of faith, not its cause.[10] Calvin said, "Repentance not only constantly follows faith, but is also born of it."[11] Repentance is the tear that falls from the eye of faith, as per Zechariah 12:10.[12]

A third position parallels the theory of a coordinate rather than subordinate order of decrees and salvation. In other words, faith and repentance are not only simultaneous (which all parties accept), but neither of them logically precedes the other because they are part and parcel of each other. Rather than one being the first step followed by the other, it is a two-footed jump, as it were. John Murray said, "The faith that is unto salvation is a penitent faith and the repentance that is unto life is a believing repentance."[13] Spurgeon: "No man can repent of sin without believing in Jesus, nor believe in Jesus without repenting of sin."[14] Jonathan Edwards: "Faith and repentance are implied in the nature, the one of the other. The soul, in repenting, believes, and in believing, repents. Faith is necessary in order to repentance, and repentance is necessary in order to faith."[15] Calvin again: "We cannot have faith without repentance, and we cannot have repentance without faith."[16]

---

10 See James T. Dennison Jr., ed., *Reformed Confessions of the 16th and 17th Centuries in English Translation* (Grand Rapids: Reformation Heritage Books, 2010), 2:500.

11 John Calvin, *Institutes of the Christian Religion* (Philadelphia: Westminster, 1960), 3:3:1 (p. 593).

12 Charles H. Spurgeon, *Metropolitan Tabernacle Pulpit* (Pasadena, TX: Pilgrim Publications, 1981), 10:341–52; 50:445–54.

13 John Murray, *Redemption Accomplished and Applied* (Grand Rapids: Eerdmans, 1955), 140.

14 Spurgeon, *Metropolitan Tabernacle Pulpit*, 35:522.

15 Jonathan Edwards, *The Works of Jonathan Edwards* (New Haven: Yale University Press, 2006), 24:862.

16 John Calvin, *Sermons on Genesis 1:1–11:4* (Edinburgh: Banner of Truth, 2009), 439.

Conclusion

There are other elements in salvation not included here, such as reconciliation. The mainstream Reformed order would be this: calling → union with Christ → regeneration → faith/repentance → justification → adoption. All these are preceded by the process of conviction of sin and enlightenment of the gospel and then followed by the process of sanctification. It all leads inevitably to glorification as the final link in the Golden Chain of Romans 8:29–30.

Chapter 59
Common Grace

First Peter 4:10 describes the grace of God as "manifold," or literally "multi-colored." God's favorable attitude toward mankind consists of grace, mercy, love, kindness, and other wonderful aspects. Reformed theologians differentiate two main kinds of grace: special saving grace for the elect and common grace for all mankind, including the non-elect. God loves all men with some love but loves the elect with all love.

One of the key points of the Reformation was *sola gratia* — grace alone. We are saved by God's grace alone, not by our good works (Ephesians 2:8–9). Evangelical Arminians agree but generally believe only in common grace and make it saving but resistible. This can be seen, for instance, in two books edited by Clark Pinnock: *Grace Unlimited* and *The Grace of God, The Will of Man*.[1] We have already discussed special grace; now we will look at common grace.

Common Grace for All Mankind

The basic element in common grace was noted by Iain Murray: "True Calvinism teaches that God has a general love for all and a special love for his elect."[2] The great J. C. Ryle repeated this over and over, as when he said:

> He has compassion even on those who are not His people — the faithless, the graceless, the followers of this world. He feels tenderly for them, though they know it not. He died for them, though they care little for what He did on the cross. He would receive them graciously, and pardon them freely, if they would only repent and believe on Him. Let us ever be aware of measuring the love of Christ by any human measure. He has a special love, beyond doubt, for His own believing people. But He also has a general love of compassion, even for the unthankful and evil.[3]

God loves even the reprobate in this sense. He loved the nation of Israel

---

1 Clark Pinnock, *Grace Unlimited* (Minneapolis: Bethany House, 1975); *The Grace of God, The Will of Man* (Grand Rapids: Zondervan, 1989).

2 Iain Murray, *Heroes* (Edinburgh: Banner of Truth, 2009), 274.

3 J. C. Ryle, *Expository Thoughts on the Gospels: St. Mark* (Cambridge: James Clarke, 1973), 154.

(Deuteronomy 7:8), but not all the Israelites were elect. As Ryle observed above, this general love is reflected in the general aspect of the atonement.

Scripture teaches that God displays this common grace through creation and providence. In Matthew 5:44–45, Christ tells us to love our enemies and do good to them, for in so doing we imitate God who sends sunshine and rain on all men. Would God command us to love all men if He Himself did not love all men? The second greatest of God's commandments is to love our neighbor (Matthew 22:39), and that includes non-Christians and non-elect. The parallel in Luke 6:35–36 adds that God is kind and merciful to all men, even those who never thank Him. God loves even the reprobate as His creatures. And since this is a love for sinners, it is undeserved and therefore a kind of grace.

This general love is seen in the bounties of providence that God bestows on all mankind. Acts 14:17: "He did good, gave us rain from heaven and fruitful seasons, filling our hearts with food and gladness." This is described in Job 37–39 and often in the Psalms (33:5, 65:5–13, 104:1–30, 136:25, 145:14–16). Psalm 145:9: "The Lord is good to all, and His tender mercies are over all His works." David exclaimed, "The earth is full of the goodness of the Lord" (Psalm 33:5). God does good to all mankind, especially the household of faith, and so should we (Galatians 6:10).

Creation tells us something about the Creator, including His goodness to mankind (Psalm 19:1–3; Romans 1:18–21; 2:4). And 1 Timothy 4:4: "Every creature of God is good" (echoing Genesis 1:31). James 1:17: "Every good gift and every perfect gift is from above, and comes down from the Father of lights." Abraham told the reprobate rich man in Hades, "Son, remember that in your lifetime you received your good things" (Luke 16:25).

There are four reasons for this benevolent and universal love. First, all mankind bears the image of God, though marred by sin. God loves His own image and those who bear it. Second, the elect and reprobate are mingled together in the world. He sends rain over an entire area, not just on the elect. The elect are no different before their conversion than the non-elect — they are all "children of wrath" (Ephesians 2:3). Third, God blesses the reprobate because of the elect, as in Genesis 39:5: "The Lord blessed the Egyptian's house for Joseph's sake, and the blessing of the Lord was on all that he had in the house and in the field." Fourth, and most importantly, as Calvin said, "His nature is to love men."[4] God

---

4 John Calvin, *The Gospel According to St. John 11–21 and the First Epistle of John* (Grand Rapids: Eerdmans, 1979), 290.

gives good to all because He is good in Himself. Psalm 119:68: "You are good and do good." Truly God is good.

Christ is the perfect revelation of God. He regularly showed mercy and compassion on the multitudes at large (Matthew 9:36; 14:14; Mark 6:34, etc.). It will not do to say this was only in His humanity, for His holy humanity was in perfect accord with His deity. God has a general love of compassion and pity on all who suffer and are lost (Jonah 4:2, 11).

After citing these and other verses, Louis Berkhof answered the Hyper-Calvinists who deny common grace with this statement: "If such passages do not testify to a favorable disposition in God, it would seem that language has lost its meaning, and that God's revelation is not dependable on this subject."[5]

Restraining Grace

If all mankind is totally depraved and wicked, why are we not as sinful as we would like to be? Why do we not murder each other? If Calvinism is true, the world goes better than we would expect. This is not due to any supposed good in us, for there is none (Romans 8:7; Mark 10:18). Rather, it is because God is good and restrains evil in the world. This is an important element of common grace.

Genesis 20:6: "I withheld you from sinning against me." God can and does intervene in the human will and external circumstances to restrain sin and sinners. He restrained Sennacherib in 2 Kings 19:27–28 and restrained David in 1 Samuel 25:26, 33–34. God restrains sin in both the elect and the non-elect. He uses restraining grace to protect people (Genesis 31:7). He draws the line on how far He will allow men to fall into sin by sovereignly saying, "This far you may come, but no farther" (Job 38:11). Second Thessalonians 2:6–7 mentions "what is restraining" the Man of Sin from appearing. He also restrains men of sin everywhere.

Fallen man is led by his evil nature (James 1:14–15), which in turn is led captive by Satan (2 Timothy 2:26; Ephesians 2:1–3; John 8:44). Job 1:12 and 2:6 tell us that God sovereignly controls and restrains even the Devil. God's restraints are like a leash on a dog or bridle on a horse, as Calvin said: "God restrains them by hidden bridle and rules their hands and their hearts."[6]

---

5 Louis Berkhof, *Systematic Theology* (Grand Rapids: Eerdmans, 1988), 446.
6 John Calvin, *Commentaries on the Book of the Prophet Jeremiah and the Lamentations* (Grand Rapids: Eerdmans, 1950), 3:328.

God can pull in the reins on Satan and sinners or give them slack and allow them to sin. We discussed this in chapter 30 on the problem of evil. When God removes the restraints, men necessarily fall into sin. This even includes Christians. If God took all the restraints off, even the best of saints would tumble into horrendous evil. Remember David. Jonathan Edwards observed:

> There are in the souls of wicked men those hellish principles reigning, that would presently kindle and flame out into hell-fire, if it were not for God's restraints. There is laid in the very nature of carnal men, a foundation for the torments of hell; there are those corrupt principles, in reigning power in them, and in full possession of them, that are the beginnings of hell-fire. These principles are active and powerful, exceeding violent in their nature, and if it were not for the restraining hand of God upon them, they would soon break out, they would flame out after the same manner as the same corruptions, the same enmity does in the hearts of damned souls, and would beget the same torments in them as they do in them.[7]

Though this restraining grace is generally irresistible, it is not saving. Saints receive it and are already saved; the lost experience it and remain unconverted. Christopher Love: "Restraining grace to a wicked man is just as a chain to a lion or a prison to a thief. It restrains the rage of one and the theft of the other, but does not at all change the nature of either."[8] He added: "Though they shall go to hell, yet they have cause to bless God for restraining grace on earth. For though it will not make you good, yet it will and does make you less evil."[9] It thereby results in less punishment. But lost sinners never thank God for it. Christians ought to thank God more than they do.

Some admit that God restrains sin in the reprobate but deny that this is any kind of grace. Others deny restraining grace but thereby are forced to redefine or even deny total depravity. After all, if God is not restraining sinners, then they are capable of restraining themselves and are not therefore bound by sin. They are not "that bad." Neither view is historically Reformed.

Enabling Grace to Do Outward Good

By common grace God enables the unregenerate to do outward good, even though their inner hearts remain wicked. Matthew 7:11: "If you, being evil,

---

7 Jonathan Edwards, *The Works of Jonathan Edwards* (New Haven: Yale University Press, 2003), 22:407.
8 Christopher Love, *The Works of Christopher Love* (Morgan, PA: Soli Deo Gloria, 1995), 1:312.
9 Love, 1:323.

know how to give good gifts to your children." See Luke 6:33 and Romans 2:14–15. Unbelievers do outward good with the wrong motives, for whatever is not done in faith (Romans 14:23) or to the glory of God (1 Corinthians 10:31) is sin. By definition, an unbeliever does not have faith.

In this way God provides for the ongoing progress of the world. Robert Murray M'Cheyne said, "All the decency and morality of unconverted men is to be attributed to the restraining grace of the Holy Spirit."[10] These are what Calvinists sometimes call "bad good works." They are outwardly good but done with inwardly bad motives, such as pride. But God overrules the inwardly bad to use the outwardly good to do good for bad people in the world.

God sometimes gives extra common grace to a locality where Christians are in abundance. Americans sing, "America, America, God shed His grace on thee." This works together with their being salt and light in the world (Matthew 5:13–16). But if they lose their saltiness and dim their light, they may forfeit the benefits of God's common grace.

Common Grace and Culture

Abraham Kuyper developed another aspect of common grace in a controversial way. He discussed it at length in his *Common Grace*[11] and summed it up in his Stone Lectures at Princeton Theological Seminary, published as *Lectures on Calvinism*. He defined common grace as "that act of God by which negatively He curbs the operations of Satan, death, and sin, and by which positively He creates an intermediate state for this cosmos, as well as for our human race, which is and continues to be deeply and radically sinful, but in which sin cannot work out its end."[12] The nature of this "intermediate state" has aroused much controversy.

God keeps order in the world by various means, such as civil rulers. They are ordained by God to establish a certain measure of civil righteousness by rewarding good and punishing evil (Romans 13:1–6; 1 Peter 2:13–14; 1 Timothy 2:1–2). This does not necessitate a theocracy nor require that every civil ruler be a Christian. Scripture gives several examples of civil rulers who ruled well but with unregenerate hearts (2 Kings 10:29–30; 12:2–3; 14:3–4).

---

10 Andrew Bonar, *Memoir and Remains of Robert Murray M'Cheyne* (Edinburgh: Banner of Truth, 1978), 463.

11 Abraham Kuyper, *Common Grace* (Bellingham: Lexham Press, 2016).

12 Abraham Kuyper, *Principles of Sacred Theology* (Grand Rapids: Eerdmans, 1969), 279.

By common grace God enables sinners to do outward good that contributes to culture above what they are naturally able to do. This is why an unregenerate artist can paint a beautiful portrait, or an atheist scientist can discover a great wonder medicine. Not all builders of the Old Testament temple were Israelites, nor were all Israelites regenerate. But God enabled both to do the job. God gives good talents to bad sinners.

Kuyper applied this to the various "spheres" of society, such as education, government, the arts, the family, science, and others. Unfortunately, some later Kuyperians took his theory far beyond what he would have approved. For example, some misuse it to approve what Scripture forbids, such as homosexuality. Others so emphasize common grace without evangelism that they end up with a distorted Calvinistic version of the liberal "social gospel." Many Kuyperians are quite liberal in their ethics and politics. Though Kuyper became prime minister of the Netherlands, his common grace experiment failed, and the Netherlands today is extremely non-Christian in almost all its "spheres." But then, one could say the same for the failures of the Genevan theocracy, the Puritan semi-theocracies in both England and New England, South Afrikaner Kuyper-Calvinism, and others. One reason may be that Kuyperians tend to try to make godly bricks without Christian straw. Without a corresponding biblical evangelism and Reformed experimental spirituality, Kuyperianism pulls up its anchor and drifts into a compromised system. It loses its saltiness.

The Rejection of Common Grace

Kuyper's Neo-Calvinism, as it has been called, became very popular in Dutch-American Calvinist circles early in the twentieth century. After much discussion and debate, the Christian Reformed Church officially approved the "Three Points of Common Grace" in 1924. Because of their importance and ongoing controversial nature, they deserve to be quoted:

> Concerning the first point, touching the favorable attitude of God toward mankind in general, and not alone toward the elect, Synod declares that it is certain, according to Scripture and the [Belgic] Confession, that there is, besides the saving grace of God, shown only to those chosen to eternal life, also a certain favor or grace of God which He shows to his creatures in general. This is evident from the quoted Scripture passages and from the Canons of Dort, II, 5, and III and IV, 8 and 9, where the general offer of the Gospel is discussed; while it is evident from the declarations

of Reformed writers of the period of florescence of Reformed theology that our Reformed fathers from of old have championed this view. (Psalm 145:9; Matthew 5:44, 45; Luke 6:35, 36; Acts 14:16, 17; 1 Timothy 4:10; Romans 2:4; Ezekiel 33:11; Ezekiel 18:23)

Concerning the second point, touching the restraint of sin in the life of the individual and in society, the Synod declares that according to Scripture and the Confession, there is such a restraint of sin. This is evident from the quoted Scripture passages and from the Belgic Confession, articles 13 and 36, where it is taught that God through the general operations of His Spirit, without renewing the heart, restrains sin in its unhindered breaking forth, as a result of which human society has remained possible; while it is evident from the quoted declarations of Reformed writers of the period of florescence of Reformed theology that our Reformed fathers of old have championed this view (Genesis 6:3; Psalm 81:11, 12; Acts 7:42; Romans 1:24, 26, 28; 2 Thessalonians 2:6, 7).

Concerning the third point, touching the performance of so-called civic righteousness by the unregenerate, the Synod declares that according to Scripture and the Confession the unregenerate, though incapable of any saving good (Canons of Dort, III, IV, 3), can perform such civic good. Thus it is evident from the quoted Scripture passages and from the Canons of Dort, III, IV, 4, and the Belgic Confession, where it is taught that God, without renewing the heart, exercises such influence upon man that he is enabled to perform civic good; while it is evident from the quoted declarations of Reformed writers of the period of florescence of Reformed theology, that our Reformed fathers from of old have championed this view. 2 Kings 10:29, 30; 2 Kings 12:2 (compare 2 Chronicles 24:17–25); 2 Kings 14:3 (compare 2 Chronicles 25:2 and vss. 14–16, 20, 27); Luke 6:33; Romans 2:14 (compare vs. 13. Also Romans 10:5 and Galatians 3:12).[13]

Herman Hoeksema and others vehemently rejected these three points. Their opposition became so heated that they were expelled from the Christian Reformed Church. They then founded the Protestant Reformed Church which continues to this day to reject the three points and all notions of common grace — period. They strongly deny that there are favorable bounties of providence as evidence of a general favor of God for all men. They also reject the free offer of the gospel, a universal saving desire of God for all men, restraining

---

13 Quoted from Cornelius Van Til, *Common Grace and the Gospel* (Philadelphia: Presbyterian and Reformed, 1974), 19–21.

grace, and sphere-sovereignty common grace. They deny the very essence of common grace — namely, that God has a general love for all men, including the reprobate. Hoeksema and his followers have denounced the whole idea of common grace as Arminianism and a false gospel.

But Hoeksema was historically, confessionally, and biblically wrong. Kuyper and the Kuyperians may have embellished the idea of common grace in certain questionable ways, but the basic doctrine is sound. Hoeksema and the Protestant Reformed Church have insisted that God has no love or grace whatsoever on the reprobate. This was certainly not Calvin's view. Calvin regularly and explicitly taught that God has a general love for all men as His creatures. For example:

> Thus, although the love of God is shown to all men by virtue of the fact that we were created in his own image, and although he causes the sun to rise upon all, provides food for all, and watches over all, yet this is nothing compared to that special love which he reserves for his elect, his flock.[14]

James William Anderson[15] and Herman Kuiper[16] have collected hundreds of such quotations from Calvin. I have found still more.

It is neither Arminianism nor Amyraldism to hold to common grace, as the Hoeksemites contend. This is mainstream Reformed theology. The Christian Reformed Church knew its history when it said that great Reformed theologians of the golden age past (the sixteenth and seventeenth centuries) held to this theology. It is the deniers of common grace, not the upholders of it, that are out of the historic mainstream.

Hoeksema and his followers linked the rejection of common grace with their denial of the free offer of the gospel, resulting in a distinct Dutch Reformed version of Hyper-Calvinism that went beyond the Hyper-Calvinism of John Gill and other English Hyper-Calvinists. Gill and others at least held to a modified form of common grace. Curiously, Hoeksema's successor David Engelsma claims that the Protestant Reformed Church is true Calvinism and is not Hyper-Calvinism, when in fact they are more Hyper than their English compatriots.

Theonomists have had yea/nay opinions on common grace but do not usually deny the free offer. Gary North rejected the first of the Three Points of 1924 by

---

14 John Calvin, *Sermons on Galatians* (Edinburgh: Banner of Truth, 1997), 18.
15 James William Anderson, "The Grace of God and the Non-Elect in Calvin's Commentaries and Sermons," Ph.D. diss., New Orleans Baptist Theological Seminary, 1976.
16 Herman Kuiper, *Calvin on Common Grace* (Goes: Oosterbaan and Le Cointre, 1928).

arguing that God gives "favors" but not "favor" to the unregenerate reprobate, and he admits a sympathy for the Protestant Reformed Church.[17] Theonomist literature says far more about law than grace, but few if any of them would correctly be classified as Hyper-Calvinists.

Common Grace and Salvation

We now come to the question of how common grace bears on salvation. Earlier we saw how historic Calvinism teaches that God sincerely desires the salvation of all men according to His revealed will. We also explained how this bears on the universal aspect of the atonement. Common grace is not irresistibly salvific, but it does have implications for salvation.

Romans 2:4 says to all men: "Or do you despise the riches of His goodness, forbearance, and longsuffering, not knowing that the goodness of God leads you to repentance?" The gifts of common grace are incentives for lost sinners to turn from sin and toward God for salvation. In Acts 14:15–17, Paul pointed to the good gifts of providence in the very context of preaching the gospel (v. 7). So should we.

God does indeed have a general love for all men as His creatures and earnestly desires their salvation. Jesus "loved" the rich young ruler (Mark 10:21) and wept over lost Jerusalem (Luke 13:34; 19:41; Matthew 23:37). God takes no pleasure in the death of lost sinners but rather desires that they repent and be saved (Ezekiel 18:23, 32; 33:11; Jonah 4:2, 11). This is the general call and free offer but not the special call of effectual grace. On the one hand, Arminianism errs by denying special and irresistible grace. On the other, Hyper-Calvinism errs by denying the free offer. The truth is between these two opposite errors.

Prevenient Grace

Because He desires the salvation of all men, God strives with them graciously but not always efficaciously. This precedes efficacious saving grace, as William G. T. Shedd explained: "There is a grace of God that goes before regenerating grace and makes the soul ready for it. It is common or prevenient grace."[18]

The Reformed view is substantially different than the Arminian and Lutheran views. Those theories argue that prevenient grace is universal and saving but is

17 Gary North, *Dominion and Common Grace* (Tyler, TX: Institute for Christian Economics, 1987), 21–22.

18 William G. T. Shedd, *Dogmatic Theology*, 3rd ed. (Phillipsburg, NJ: P&R, 2003), 773.

resistible because the final say depends on the lost sinner's free will. Arminians tend to prefer the term *sufficient grace*. Some say they agree with Calvinism on total depravity and inability (which is open to debate) but add that God gives a sufficient grace to all (or at least all who hear the gospel). This enables them to repent and believe. The term has the appearance of being based on 2 Corinthians 12:9, "My grace is sufficient for you." But that verse is speaking of a saved believer and has nothing to do with salvation or depravity. Others say their theory is bolstered by John 1:9, but that too is special pleading and poor exegesis.

In a very real sense this is the key difference between Calvinism and Arminianism, as it was between Augustinianism and Semi-Pelagianism and later Jansenism and the Jesuits. In his famous second *Provincial Letter*, the Jansenist Blaise Pascal put his finger on the state of the question:

> The Jesuits maintain there is a grace given generally to all men subject in such a way to free-will that the will renders it efficacious or inefficacious at its pleasure, without any additional aid from God, and without wanting anything on his part in order to act effectively; and hence they term this grace sufficient, because it suffices of itself for action. The Jansenists, on the other hand, will not allow that any grace is actually sufficient which is not also efficacious; that is, that all those kinds of grace which do not determine the will to act effectively are insufficient for action; for they hold that a man can never act without efficacious grace.[19]

It may be debated whether Arminius borrowed from Luis de Molina or other Jesuit Semi-Pelagians, but the Arminian idea is much the same as theirs. As for Lutheranism, it veered away from Luther's robust Augustinianism on efficacious grace and developed its own version of sufficient grace, mainly due to the influence of Philip Melanchthon's synergistic approach to grace. The Lutheran scholastics did not argue that sufficient grace enabled a lost sinner to actively believe. Rather, they contended that lost sinners are able to cease resisting God's overtures of grace by passive surrender, which in turn removes the hindrance to the gift of faith. When they do this, special grace becomes effectual, and salvation results. Arminianism and Lutheranism have more similarities on this point than they generally realize — and share a dangerously similar view with the Semi-Pelagian Jesuits and their theological ancestors.

Calvinism and Augustinianism, by contrast, hold that fallen man, because

---

19 Blaise Pascal, *Pensees/The Provincial Letters* (New York: Random House, 1941), 336–37.

of his depravity and inability, always resists the Holy Spirit (Acts 7:51). He is not able to not resist until special efficacious grace is given to overcome his resistance and guarantee regeneration. This key point must be understood to grasp what the whole debate is all about.

Is there then no prevenient grace that prepares for special grace? Listen to Shedd again explain:

> The reprobate resist and nullify common grace: and so do the elect. The obstinate selfishness and enmity of the human heart defeats the Divine mercy as shown in the ordinary influence of the Holy Spirit, in both the elect and the non-elect. [. . .] The difference between the two cases is, that in the instance of the elect, God follows up the common grace which has been resisted, with the regenerating grace which overcomes resistance; which in the instance of the reprobate, he does not.[20]

Common grace, then, is good but not good enough. Fallen man needs more, and God gives that more to the elect. Common grace prepares the way for special grace in the elect. But the common grace that the reprobate resist will one day redound to their damnation. There can be prevenient grace without special grace, but there is no special grace without prevenient grace.

Conclusion

Unregenerate sinners should thank God for all forms of common grace and use them properly. Regenerate sinners should also thank God for common grace that was given to them both before and after their conversion. We can also thank God especially for special grace that efficaciously brought us to Jesus Christ, who is God's greatest gift of grace.

---

20 Shedd, *Dogmatic Theology*, 35.

Chapter 60
Preservation of the Saints

At one time or another, every Christian has asked the question: "Can I lose my salvation?" There are three possible answers: yes, no, or we cannot know. Many churches give the affirmative answer, including Methodists, Nazarenes, the Church of Christ, most Pentecostals and charismatics, most Lutherans, Roman Catholics, and others. Historic Calvinists have always answered no, but so have some inconsistent Arminians, as we shall see.

The fifth point of Calvinism is well summarized by the Westminster Confession: "They whom God hath accepted in His Beloved, effectually called and sanctified by His Spirit, can neither totally nor finally fall away from the state of grace; but shall certainly persevere therein to the end and be eternally saved" (17:1; see the Larger Catechism, question 79). As seen in this statement, the fifth point includes both the preservation and perseverance of the saints. Many Arminians hold to the first but not the second, but true Calvinists hold to both.

This doctrine is sometimes called *eternal security*, in contrast with temporary security or eternal insecurity. Some employ the oft-misused phrase, "Once saved, always saved," which is generally used by those who accept preservation without perseverance. Both truths are inseparable and promised by God in Jeremiah 32:40: "And I will make an everlasting covenant with them, that I will not turn away from doing them good; but I will put My fear in their hearts so they will not depart from Me."

God Preserves His People

Scriptures frequently states that God preserves, keeps, sustains, protects, and guards His people. He does not abandon, forsake, or discard them. Consider the following:

- "The Lord loves justice, and does not forsake His saints" (Psalm 37:28).

- "Who keeps our soul among the living, and does not allow our feet to be moved" (Psalm 66:9).

- "For the Lord will not cast off His people, nor will He forsake His inheritance" (Psalm 94:14).

- "He preserves the souls of His saints; He delivers them out of the hand of the wicked" (Psalm 97:10).

- "He who keeps you will not slumber. [. . .] The Lord shall preserve you from all evil; He shall preserve your soul. The Lord shall preserve your going out and your coming in from this time forth, and even forevermore" (Psalm 121:3, 7–8).

- "The Lord upholds all who fall, and raises up all who are bowed down" (Psalm 145:14).

- "The Lord preserves all who love Him" (Psalm 145:20).

- "He guards the paths of justice, and preserves the way of His saints" (Proverbs 2:8).

The New Testament has two verses on this subject in which the Greek text has multiple negatives for emphasis, as if the promise is written in capital letters, bold print, and underlined. John 6:37: "All that the Father gives Me will come to Me, and the one who comes to Me I will by no means cast out" (two negatives). Hebrews 13:5: "I will never leave you nor forsake you" (three negatives).

First Peter 1:5 is explicit: "who are kept by the power of God, through faith for salvation ready to be revealed in the last time." Our eternal inheritance is "reserved in heaven" (v. 4), and we are reserved for Heaven. We are both reserved and preserved. Ultimately our preservation depends on God's power to hold us, not our power to hold God, otherwise we would surely lose it. John Calvin said, "The salvation of all the elect is as certain as God's power is invincible."[1] We are safe because God is strong.

Christians can not only know they were elected (2 Peter 1:10) and that they are presently saved, but they can also know that they will always be saved. If saved, then safe. Second Timothy 1:12: "I know whom I have believed and am persuaded that He is able to keep what I have committed to Him until that Day." We know because God is faithful to keep His promise to keep us (1 Thessalonians 5:23–24). He keeps us in a safe place, yea, the safest place of all: God. Colossians 3:3: "Your life is hidden with Christ in God."

There is a sense in which we keep ourselves (human responsibility). There is

---

1 John Calvin, *The Gospel According to St. John 1–10* (Grand Rapids: Eerdmans, 1979), 273.

also a sense in which we are being kept (divine sovereignty). We keep because we are being kept, not vice versa as Arminianism would have it. Both senses are in the Letter of Jude: "Keep yourselves in the love of God. [. . .] Now to Him who is able to keep you from stumbling, and to present you faultless before the presence of His glory with exceeding joy" (vv. 21, 24).

First John 5:18 is rendered "he who has been born of God keeps himself" in the New King James Version and others. Some translations and commentators take the subject to be *Christ*, the only begotten Son of God (1 John 4:9), and the object to be *believers*. That is a truth, but another interpretation says the subject and the object are the same — *believers*, as in the preceding clause. Either way, Christ the only begotten Son keeps the sons and daughters who have been begotten by God in regeneration, who then also keep themselves.

This preservation is in accord with Christ's prayer in John 17. Twice He prayed that the Father would "keep" His people (vv. 11, 15). While He was on earth, Jesus "kept" those whom the Father had given to Him (v. 12). The only exception was Judas, who was an imposter and never truly believed in Christ (v. 12). This prayer/promise applies to all future believers, not just the early disciples (v. 20), but it excludes unbelievers in the world at large (v. 9).

Preserved from Satan

John 17 also records Christ's prayer that the Father keep disciples from Satan (v. 15). If even one were to be lost, then the Father did not answer Christ's prayer, and Satan won. May it never be! The Father always answered the Son's prayers (John 11:42). God preserves and keeps believers from the Devil, not just from Hell and eternal damnation. We are permanently in Christ's kingdom, never to return to Satan's kingdom of darkness (Colossians 1:13).

Satan tries to hold on to sinners and keep them in his evil control. He is going to Hell and wants to take as many people with him as possible. He never surrenders even one without a fight. They are in his evil grip because of their sinful nature (Ephesians 2:1–3; 1 John 5:19). Christ rescues the elect from Satan. The Devil seeks to get them back, but Christ is stronger and never releases even one. The Evil One wanted Peter back, but he failed because Jesus prayed for Peter (Luke 22:31–32). He does the same for all His saints.

Spurgeon said, "If God lights the candle, none can blow it out."[2] Satan seeks to do just that but fails. He has never reclaimed even one saved sinner.

---

2 Quoted in John Blanchard, *More Gathered Gold* (Welwyn: Evangelical Press, 1986), 85.

Remember the picture in John Bunyan's *The Pilgrim's Progress* in which Satan tried to blow out a fire, but God kept pouring oil on it to keep it going. God supplies us with the Holy Spirit to keep us from the Evil Spirit. Ironically, God even uses Satan to keep Christians. George Whitefield commented that as a shepherd uses a sheepdog to fetch straying sheep, so the Good Shepherd uses the Devil to "bark" at straying Christians and thus, instead of driving them away, brings them back to Christ.[3] Samuel Rutherford: "I am sure that Christ hath by His death and blood casten the knot so fast, that the fingers of the devils and hell-fulls of sins cannot loose it."[4]

If any of the elect were to be finally lost, we could rightly conclude that Satan won the tug-of-war with God. Those who say that God and Satan are engaged in "cosmic chess" with human pawns must logically conclude that Satan wins some pieces and could theoretically win the game. That is bad Arminianism. If Satan could win anything from God, he would be stronger and smarter than God, and we should follow him rather than the Lord (1 Kings 18:21). Remember Goliath's challenge. But God is infinitely stronger than Satan (1 John 4:4). Satan is stronger and cleverer than we saints are, but God is vastly stronger and wiser than Satan. God will not relinquish even one believer.

A true disciple can never become demon-possessed or possessed by the Devil again. Some Arminians appeal to Luke 11:24–26, but Calvinists point out that this case describes someone who was never saved to begin with. His house was still empty, not inhabited by Christ. Then there is the case of Job, a type of Christians in general. God tested him by allowing Satan to tempt and assault him, but God preserved him to the glorious end.

Preservation and Eternal Life

The Gospel and epistles of John promise preservation because God gives eternal life to His people. A believer already has it as a present possession (John 6:47). This ensures security from condemnation (John 5:24). This life is given in regeneration and will never be forfeited by the believer or taken back by God who gave it. Otherwise, it would be *temporary* life and not *eternal* life. It would end in death, not life. But a Christian will never die spiritually, even though he will die physically (John 11:25–26).

---

3 George Whitefield, *Sermons of George Whitefield*, ed. by Lee Gatiss (Wheaton: Crossway, 2012), 2:450.
4 Samuel Rutherford, *The Letters of Samuel Rutherford* (Edinburgh: Banner of Truth, 1984), 180.

John 10:28–29 is perhaps the most explicit place in the entire Bible to teach eternal security: "And I give them eternal life, and they shall never perish; neither shall anyone snatch them out of My hand. My Father, who has given them to Me, is greater than all; and no one is able to snatch them out of My Father's hand." First, Christ uses a double negative in Greek for emphasis: "They shall never ever perish." Millard Erickson offers this translation: "They shall not, repeat, shall not ever perish in the slightest."[5] Divine preservation prevents perishing. See John 3:16: "shall not perish." If even one perishes, then they were not preserved. Once a sheep, always a sheep. A sheep never becomes a goat.

Then Christ promised that no one can take His sheep from either His or His Father's hand. In context, this refers to the Pharisees' attempt to turn Christ's disciples away from Him like a wolf snatching sheep from a shepherd. It also applies to Satan and the demons. But no one "shall" (v. 28) because no one is "able" (v. 29). Samuel Rutherford said, "Hell, devils, the wrath of God, the curse of the law, could not loose His grips of you. [. . .] Christ took a hearty grip of you upon the cross; He let you not slip out of His fingers again."[6] Adam fell in Eden, but nobody can fall from Christ's hand.

Arminians suggest several misinterpretations of John 10:28. First, some say that nobody can take us, but we can take ourselves out of Christ's hand by free will. We disagree. If one could, why not all? If all, Christ has none left, and Satan takes everyone to Hell. Second, some Arminians say that nobody can take us, but we can slip, be dropped, or jump out of Christ's hand. This is a foolish and desperate attempt to twist the obvious meaning.

Christians fall into sin, but we never fall from Christ's hands. It is like a father holding his little boy's hand as they take a walk. The boy stumbles and lets go, but the father still holds him tightly and keeps him from falling to the ground. This is precisely what is promised in Psalm 37:24: "Though he fall, he shall not be utterly cast down; for the Lord upholds him with His hand." Proverbs 24:16 adds that if a believer falls, he will arise. In the Christian life, what goes down must come up again.

Then John 10:29 adds that we are held by both Christ and the Father. Two divine hands hold us. Even if one of them theoretically let loose, the other has

---

5 Millard Erickson, *Christian Theology* (Grand Rapids: Baker, 1985), 992.
6 Samuel Rutherford, *Fourteen Communion Sermons* (Edinburgh: James Dickson, 1986), 280, 284.

a firm grip. We could add that the Spirit also holds us. Would anyone ever presume to think anything could take us from such a strong grip of love?

It is as if God says to each of His children, "I love you too much to let you go." It was the blind Scottish preacher George Matheson who wrote the great hymn, "O Love That Will Not Let Me Go." Edwin Palmer put it like this: "It is because God perseveres in His love toward His Church that the Church perseveres in its love toward Him."[7] See 1 John 4:19.

Preservation and Predestination

Predestination promises preservation. Election guarantees eternal security. Louis Berkhof sums up our position: "Election does not merely mean that some will be favoured with certain external privileges and may be saved, if they do their duty; but that they who belong to the number of the elect shall finally be saved and can never fall short of perfect salvation."[8]

Romans 8:28–30 is conclusive here. First, verse 28 tells us that absolutely all things work together for the good of God's people. This is God's "purpose" that never fails to come to pass. If someone objects, "It is conditional on our loving God," we reply that God Himself guarantees that we will meet that condition. He continues to supply us with all necessary love. He never stops loving us. We love because He first loved us (1 John 4:19); therefore, He keeps us loving Him. Besides, if a believer stops loving God, how does that work together for his good?

Then verses 29–30 contain the unbreakable Golden Chain. God foreordained all the links. If one could be broken, all could be broken (compare James 2:10; Galatians 3:10). A chain is only as strong as its weakest link. But it is an unbreakable whole, as James Henley Thornwell explained: "Salvation is one great whole, and wherever it begins to exist it takes hold upon eternity."[9] All, not some, who have been predestined will be justified and glorified.

A similar chain is in Romans 8:35–39. Nothing can separate the elect from the love of God or the God of love. Note that Paul includes "any other created thing" (v. 39), which includes even the believer himself. To deny the unfailing

---

7 Edwin Palmer, *The Five Points of Calvinism*, 2nd ed. (Grand Rapids: Baker, 1980), 68.

8 Louis Berkhof, *Systematic Theology* (Grand Rapids: Eerdmans, 1988), 547.

9 James Henley Thornwell, *The Collected Writings of James Henley Thornwell* (Edinburgh: Banner of Truth, 1974), 2:122.

preservation of the believer is to grossly underestimate the love of God for His people.

Augustine taught an unusual variation of this doctrine. He posited that one of the non-elect might believe and be justified but would fall away and not be preserved because he was not elected. But all the elect will persevere: "As God can never make a mistake, so none of the predestined can fail to be saved."[10] Reformed theology improves this and proves that none of the non-elect will ever believe or be justified. All who believe were predestined, and they shall all persevere and be preserved unto glorification.

Preservation is also guaranteed in the eternal covenant of redemption. Jesus stated in John 6:39, "This is the will of the Father who sent Me, that of all He has given Me I should lose nothing, but should raise it up at the last day." The Father gave them to the Son in eternity past and presents them personally to Christ in time through the Spirit (see John 17:2, 6, 11, 12, 24).

There will be no empty seats in Heaven, for all who are effectually called will most certainly come to the great banquet. Calvin said, "Where God's calling is effectual, perseverance will be certain."[11] Effectual calling is also an unbreakable link in the Golden Chain (Romans 8:30).

Miscellaneous Proofs

Salvation has an irreversible ratchet effect. Once a person is saved, he can never be unsaved. "The gifts and the calling of God are irrevocable" (Romans 11:29; see Numbers 23:19 and Ecclesiastes 3:14). This is especially the case with justification. "There is therefore now no condemnation to those who are in Christ Jesus" (Romans 8:1). "Much more then, having now been justified by His blood, we shall be saved from wrath through Him" (Romans 5:9; see v. 10). If Jesus did so much to save us, will He not do as much to keep us saved? See Romans 8:32. Nobody can condemn those whom God has justified (Romans 8:33). Those who have eternal life can never again be under condemnation (John 5:24).

There is no double jeopardy for the elect. We have been completely and finally pardoned, not paroled on condition of good behavior. We cannot be

---

10 Quoted in Martin Bucer, *Common Places of Martin Bucer*, ed. by D. F. Wright (Appleford: Sutton Courtenay, 1972), 103.

11 Calvin, *The Gospel According to St. John 11–21 and The First Epistle of John* (Grand Rapids: Eerdmans, 1979), 258.

tried twice. All, not some, of our sins have been forever forgiven (Isaiah 1:18; Micah 7:19; Psalm 103:3; 1 John 1:7). We will never commit the unforgivable sin of Matthew 12:32, for *all* our sins have been forgiven. God will never revoke His decision to justify us, nor will He tear up our new birth certificate, annul our adoption, or divorce us. Thomas Watson asked, "What were a man the better for the king's pardon if he were condemned after he were pardoned?"[12] Only Christ could legally condemn us, but He died to justify us and not to condemn us (Romans 8:34).

God puts His personal seal on Christians when He saves them (Ephesians 1:13; 4:30; 2 Corinthians 1:22). This is the Holy Spirit. Caspar Olevianus said that Christ has "branded" His lambs with the mark of the Spirit.[13] In ancient days, a royal seal was meant to keep intruders out at the peril of their life (Daniel 6:17; Matthew 27:65–66). The seal of the Spirit keeps Satan from plundering our souls from God. The seal proves that we belong to God (Romans 4:11; Revelation 7:3). To be sure, the Spirit is the *arabon*, the down payment that God gives to guarantee that He will complete the transaction (Ephesians 1:14). God pledges that all conditions will be met, and He never breaks a promise.

The Bible knows only two categories of men: those who are lost and those who are saved. There are elect who are not yet saved, but there are no "ex-saved" persons or "ex-Christians" (see 1 John 2:19). Otherwise there could be an Arminian version of the Calvinist hymn, "I once was saved but now am lost, once could see but now am blind." Some Arminians mistakenly think they have been saved and lost several times. Such a view cannot bring any personal assurance or security, but only constant fear that one may have lost his salvation without knowing it or may yet lose it and end up in Hell. Is such a dreadful life really what Christ promised His beloved children? The idea of repeated salvations and apostasies almost resembles repeated reincarnations.

Reformed theology teaches that the new birth is unrepeatable. It is like the atonement "once for all" (Hebrews 9:12). Sadly, many people think they lost their salvation, when they were never saved to begin with. Once saved, always saved — better yet, *if* saved, always saved.

Our vital union with Christ is also unbreakable. We are members of His body — will Christ amputate His own limbs? Thomas Watson asked, "If one believer may be broken off from Christ, then, by the same rule, who not another? Why

---

12 Thomas Watson, *The Beatitudes* (London: Banner of Truth, 1971), 254.
13 Caspar Olevianus, *A Firm Foundation* (Grand Rapids: Baker, 1995), 85–86.

not all? And so Christ would be a head without a body."[14] Also, "Every child of God is a part of Christ. He is 'Christ mystical.' Now, shall a member of Christ perish? A child of God cannot perish but Christ must perish. Jesus Christ who is the Husband, is the Judge, and will he condemn his own spouse?"[15] Nor will Christ divorce His wife (Hosea 2:19). The phony "conversions" of the non-elect, however, will all be annulled one day.

If we could lose our salvation on earth by free will, why not also in Heaven? Or will God take away free will up there? If one could lose salvation in Heaven, why not everyone? The result would be an empty Heaven and a full Hell. Furthermore, it would mean a defeated God and a victorious Devil. Does any Christian take such a possibility seriously?

Saints on earth are as secure, though not as happy, as saints in Heaven. Indeed, we are as secure as the elect and unfallen angels. Again, hear Thomas Watson: "He who hath true grace, can no more fall away than the angels, which are fixed stars in their heavenly orbs."[16] Samuel Rutherford: "Were I in heaven, and had the crown on my head, if free-will were my tutor, I should lose heaven."[17] But as we saw earlier, the elect will be made impeccable. Arminian theology always insists on free will and cannot consistently hold to impeccability in Heaven, though some of them put forth the erroneous idea of sinless perfection on earth.

It is true that saints fall into sin on their way to Heaven, but that does not cancel their salvation. Otherwise, they would lose their salvation every time they sin, and we all sin many times a day (James 3:2). Does such a person have to be born again every time he sins? Spurgeon was reputed to have said, "The believer, like a man on shipboard, may fall again and again on the deck, but he will never fall overboard."[18] Christ always catches us in His "everlasting arms" (Deuteronomy 33:27) and makes us stand again (Romans 14:4). Rutherford again: "We are aye falling, and Christ is aye setting us to our feet again."[19] See

---

14 Thomas Watson, *A Body of Divinity* (Edinburgh: Banner of Truth, 1974), 282.

15 Watson, *The Beatitudes*, 253.

16 Thomas Watson, *Discourses on Important and Interesting Subjects* (Ligonier: Soli Deo Gloria, 1990), 2:92.

17 Rutherford, *Letters*, 498.

18 Quoted in Loraine Boettner, *The Reformed Doctrine of Predestination* (Philadelphia: Presbyterian & Reformed, 1932), 188–89.

19 Rutherford, *Fourteen Communion Sermons*, 183.

Proverbs 24:16. Calvin said, "God keeps His elect by a secret bridle, that they may not fall to their destruction."[20]

Like Mary of Bethany, the Christian has chosen Christ because Christ has first chosen them. Luke 10:42: "Mary has chosen that good part, which will not be taken away from her." Satan's crows may steal the seed of the gospel from the non-elect (Matthew 13:19), but they can never steal those seeds from the hearts of the elect once they have germinated and begun to grow.

God finishes what He starts in salvation (Philippians 1:6). Augustine asked, "But, if God produces our faith, working in a marvelous manner in our hearts in order that we believe, need we fear that he cannot do the entire work?"[21] Jesus is both "the author and finisher of our faith" (Hebrews 12:2). Unlike the man in Christ's parable, Christ will not fail to complete the building of salvation in us (Luke 14:28–29), otherwise He would be the laughingstock of Hell's foes. Christ also continues to supply daily repentance which is essential for both justification and a life of sanctification. Calvin said, "For as he begins repentance in us, so he also gives us perseverance."[22] Luther said in the first of his Ninety-five Theses that the whole life of a Christian is one of repentance.

Then there is the ironclad promise of the new covenant (Jeremiah 32:40; Hebrews 8:9–10). Part of the weakness of the old covenant was that it could be broken. But as John Piper points out, "The new covenant is radically different in that it is not vulnerable to our weakness. Rather, it assures us that God's sovereignty will overcome our weakness and prevent us from breaking the covenant."[23] God backs up the promise of perseverance in the new covenant with His invincible omnipotence. Augustine said that "If any of these perishes, God is defeated by human sinfulness, but none of them perishes because God is not defeated by anything."[24]

God always retrieves straying Christians, both to prevent extended backsliding (Hosea 14:4) and to preserve them for Heaven. There is truth in the popular adage: "God will either bring the backslider back or bring him home." See 1 Corinthians 11:30 and 1 John 5:16.

Salvation is like a race (Hebrews 12:1). We began running, we are running, and we will complete the race. All the elect will be able to say with Paul, "I have

---

20 Calvin, *The Gospel According to St. John 11–21 and The First Epistle of John*, 210.

21 Augustine, *The Works of Saint Augustine* (Hyde Park: New City, 1999), I/26:152.

22 Calvin, *The Acts of the Apostles 1–13* (Grand Rapids: Eerdmans, 1982), 149.

23 John Piper, *A Godward Life: Book Two* (Sisters, OR: Multnomah, 1999), 248.

24 Augustine, *Works*, I/26:118.

finished the race" (2 Timothy 4:7). Paul knew the inside secret: "It is not of him who wills, nor of him who runs, but of God who shows mercy" (Romans 9:16). God has guaranteed that we will win the race. The glory of God is at stake, said Calvin: "He has permanently attached His glory to our salvation and therefore God says, 'You cannot perish, unless my glory would likewise perish.'"[25]

Jonathan Edwards had a moving observation:

> God will sooner at one blow destroy all the wicked of the world than that one of his saints should be lost. [. . .] If you are assured of your conversion, you may withal be assured that God, the supreme Lord of heaven and earth, sets a higher value upon you than upon all the reprobates of the world, that God has set so high a value upon you that the has given the blood of his own Son for your ransom.[26]

As many a godly pastor can testify in his ministry, God keeps the precious souls of His elderly children even through dementia and Alzheimer's disease. No physical or mental affliction can ever separate the elect from Him who chose them (Romans 8:35–39).

Angels rejoice over a sinner who repents (Luke 15:10). This proves they believe in the preservation of the saints, as Spurgeon observes: "And if I were an Arminian, I should recommend the angels not rejoice over a sinner that repenteth, for he might fall from grace, and perish, and then they would have to ring the bells of heaven backward, or to toll them, and to recall their songs, and say, 'We rejoiced too soon.'"[27]

Conclusion

The promise of permanent preservation gives great personal assurance to the believer amid trials and doubts. There is no greater feeling than knowing God loves you and will never let you go. Let Spurgeon have the last word:

> Our Arminian friends say that you may be a child of God to-day and a child of the devil to-morrow. Write out that statement, and place at the bottom of it the name 'Arminian,' and then put the scrap of paper in the

---

25 John Calvin, *Commentary on the Book of the Prophet Isaiah* (Grand Rapids: Eerdmans, 1948), 3:344.

26 Jonathan Edwards, *The Works of Jonathan Edwards* (New Haven: Yale University Press, 1999), 17:311–12.

27 Charles H. Spurgeon, *Metropolitan Tabernacle Pulpit* (Pasadena, TX: Pilgrim Publications, 1977), 48:379.

fire: it is the best thing you can do with it, for there is no truth in it. Jesus says, 'whosoever liveth and believeth in me shall never die.'"[28]

28 Spurgeon, *Metropolitan Tabernacle Pulpit*, 30:503.

Chapter 61
Perseverance of the Saints

Occasionally we hear the question, "Just where is this supposed 'perseverance of the saints' in the Bible anyway?"[1] The ready answer is in Revelation 14:12: "Here is the perseverance of the saints who keep the commandments of God and their faith in Jesus" (NASB; see 13:10). The phrase is found in the Bible, and so is the doctrine it represents.

Old Paul told young Timothy to "continue" (1 Timothy 4:16). Scripture is replete with exhortations to continue, keep on keeping on, not to grow weary in well-doing, not to give up, to run the race — in a word, to *persevere*. The fifth point of Calvinism is not merely that God preserves His people but that He guarantees that they will persevere in faith and obedience to the end. Perseverance is evidence not only of regeneration and justification but of preservation. Preservation and perseverance are two sides of the same coin. They require, imply, and complement each other. It would be unbiblical and reckless to deny either truth, for both have important theological and practical implications.

Perseverance in Faith and Repentance

The truly regenerate soul will persevere through the trials of life and continue to believe and repent. He may slip and fall, develop bad habits, struggle with besetting sins, and wrestle with doubts. But he will continue in faith and repentance to the end of his life on earth.

The gospel commands us to "Repent, and believe the gospel" (Mark 1:15). It never says, "Believe only once," but rather, "Start believing and continue believing." Of course, as we showed earlier, God gives us the gift of faith. Once it is received, the sinner is justified in an instant and forevermore. But a true believer always continues to believe, otherwise he is not a true believer. The Greek word for *believes* in John 3:16 and elsewhere is in the present continuous tense. The French Confession of 1559 said, "He never gave faith unto the elect only once to bring them to the good way; but also to cause them to continue

---

1 For example, Dave Hunt denies that this phrase is in the Bible. *What Love is This?* 3rd ed. (Bend, OR: The Berean Call, 2006), 113.

in it unto the end."[2] As Spurgeon put it: "This proves the final perseverance of the saints; for if the believer ceased to be a believer he would perish; and as he cannot perish, it is clear that he will continue a believer."[3] John 3:16 and 10:28 are of one cloth.

For this reason, Calvinists have always strongly rejected "easy-believism," the heresy that says a sinner needs to believe only once and can remain a Christian without ever believing again, let alone obeying God. But Christ calls a sinner to a life of faith, not just an act of faith.

The same is true with repentance. Repentance is as essential to salvation as faith. Compare Luke 13:3 with John 3:16. Both require the condition to be fulfilled lest we "perish." Some who claim to be evangelical and even Reformed teach that repentance is not even required once! Others say once is enough. True evangelicals — Calvinist as well as Arminian — heartily agreed with the first of Martin Luther's Ninety-five Theses: "Our Lord and Master Jesus Christ in saying 'Repent ye,' intended that the whole life of believers should be repentance." Christ commanded both faith and repentance. He gives both to the elect. He continues to give them. And the converted continue in both.

God picks the fallen Christian up and works faith and repentance in him so that he repents and gets back to living the life of faith. The Canons of Dort summarize our position:

> For in the first place, in these falls He preserves in them the incorruptible seed of regeneration from perishing, or being totally lost; and again, by His Word and Spirit, certainly and effectually renews them again to repentance, to a sincere and godly sorrow for their sins, that they may seek and obtain remission in the blood of the Mediator, may again experience the favor of a reconciled God, through faith adore His mercies, and henceforward more diligently work out their own salvation with fear and trembling (5:7).

Perseverance and Obedience

Scripture repeatedly teaches that the regenerate saint will also persevere in the fruit that faith produces — that is, a godly life of obedience to our heavenly Father. In this sense sanctification is a necessary corollary and not an optional

---

2 In James T. Dennison Jr., ed., *Reformed Confessions of the 16th and 17th Centuries in English Translation* (Grand Rapids: Reformation Heritage Books, 2010), 2:147–48.
3 Charles H. Spurgeon, *Metropolitan Tabernacle Pulpit* (Pasadena, TX: Pilgrim Publications, 1973), 31:394.

extra that only some Christians have. It is not a meritorious condition but a necessary evidence. Salvation without sanctification following is no salvation. Justification without sanctification is phony justification that leads to damnation. Or to be plain about it, anyone who thinks he can believe and then live in sin as he pleases is damnably deceived. He is still lost.

The life of obedience is characterized by an internal experiential holiness as well as an external godly lifestyle. Hebrews 12:14 says, "Pursue peace with all people, and holiness, without which no one will see the Lord."[4] This refers to the practical holiness of sanctification, not the imputed righteousness of Christ given in justification. One does not have to pursue the latter once he already has it. The verse also does not mean, "Without holiness the non-Christian will not see the Lord in us" — a strange and novel misinterpretation if there ever was one. And it certainly does not mean that without holiness a Christian is saved but does not get to see God when he gets to Heaven. All Christians see God there (Revelation 22:4; Matthew 5:8; Psalm 17:15; 1 John 3:2). Note the verb of Hebrews 12:14, "pursue." That means to run after, continue in, persevere in.

The great nineteenth-century Scottish theologian William Cunningham offered the following incisive observation that explains that the Reformed doctrine of perseverance includes obedience and not just faith and repentance:

> The perseverance which we contend for [. . .] is just a perseverance in faith and holiness — a continuing steadfast in believing, and in bringing forth all the fruits of righteousness. Perseverance is not merely a continuing for some time upon earth after faith and regeneration have been produced, and then being admitted, as a matter of course, to heaven, without any regard to the moral experience of faith and in the practice of holiness. This, we say, has been provided for, and will be certainly effected.[5]

One could express it in a trinitarian way. The Father demands holiness and predestines it in the elect. The Son purchased it at the cross. The Holy Spirit produces it in the elect. After all, are not Christians often called "saints" in the Bible? Scripture knows nothing of unsanctified saints, unbelieving believers, or unrepentant penitents.

---

4 I heartily recommend that all readers read the classic book *Holiness* by J. C. Ryle, frequently reprinted by various publishers.
5 William Cunningham, *Historical Theology* (London: Banner of Truth, 1969), 2:495.

The Inevitability of Perseverance

Job 17:9 says, "Yet the righteous will hold to his way, and he who has clean hands will be stronger and stronger." Note "will" (twice), not "might" or "should."

We continue to hold on to Christ, and He continues to hold on to us. True disciples will hold on to the way of righteousness. If he falls, he will bounce back up, as Proverbs 24:16 says, "For a righteous man may fall seven times and rise again." Micah 7:8: "When I fall, I will rise." It is as inevitable as the law of gravity in reverse: What goes down must come up.

Our opponents often cite Matthew 10:22 and 24:13: "He who endures to the end will be saved." One could debate how this applies to saints in the siege of Jerusalem as well as to all saints thereafter, but the experimental principle applies to both. Actually, we basically agree with evangelical Arminians on this point. Only those who endure in faith, repentance, and holiness to the end will be saved when they die. Then we disagree — Arminians say that not all who initially believe and repent will endure, while we argue that they all *do* endure. All who start will certainly finish. One could turn the verse around: "He who is saved will endure to the end."

Likewise, we agree with them on John 8:31: "If you abide in My word, you are My disciples indeed." Christ here differentiated true and false disciples, not spiritual versus carnal Christians. A true disciple always abides in Christ's words by perseverance. He who does not do so was never a true disciple to begin with.

When God regenerates a person, He gives him a new principle of life that necessarily results in a radical change of internal attitudes and external lifestyle. Once he loved sin and hated God; now he hates sin and loves God. First Corinthians 6:9–11 contrasts the radical difference between the old and the new life. Note the words "such *were* some of you," not "are." Paul insists that those who have no such radical change will not inherit Heaven, as he repeats in Ephesians 5:5.

Romans 8 contrasts the one who regularly walks according to the sins of the flesh with the one who regularly walks in the Spirit (vv. 5–10). The former will die and go to Hell (v. 13). But since the elect will never go to Hell, we must conclude that a regenerate person will never live a life of perpetual sin in the flesh.

In Matthew 7:17–18, our Lord contrasts two kinds of trees, representing the saved and the lost. The good tree bears good fruit, for that is its nature. The bad tree bears bad fruit, for that is its nature as well. Christ's point is that God changes our nature when He saves us, and this always results in a change of fruit. Receiving eternal life means receiving a new lifestyle. It would be directly contrary to Christ's words to suggest that a Christian can never have good fruit and always have bad fruit. Such is existentially impossible. It is as impossible as for a totally depraved and morally unable sinner to bear good fruit.

In this sense, we argue, sanctification is the necessary evidence and corollary of justification. We are not justified because we have been sanctified, as Roman Catholicism teaches. But neither are we justified without sanctification following. No sanctification following means no justification preceding. The Scots Confession states: "For we must boldly affirm that it is blasphemy to say that Christ abides in the hearts of those in whom is no spirit of sanctification" (Article 13). Sanctification means perseverance in holiness. John Murray wrote, "The perseverance of the saints reminds us very forcefully that only those who persevere to the end are saints."[6]

There is more at stake in this than many realize. To assert that a Christian is able to live a continuous life of sin minimizes or denies the drastic change that God produces in him through regeneration. More significantly, it grossly underestimates or eliminates the work of the Holy Spirit. The same Spirit that gives regeneration produces sanctification. One always follows the other as night follows day. To say that a believer is able to live a nonstop life of unholiness is to insult the Spirit of holiness Himself.

Perseverance in 1 John

Nowhere is Holy Writ more explicit on this than in 1 John 3:4–12. First, John defines sin as lawlessness — the breaking of God's law (v. 4). Christ appeared to take away sin (v. 5). Therefore, those who are in Christ *cannot* (not merely *may not*) stay in constant sin. This is the crucial point in his whole argument against the Gnostics who claimed that their revelations freed them from ethical implications. Note the following strong words: "Whoever abides in Him does not sin. Whoever sins has neither seen Him nor known Him. [. . .] He who sins is of the devil. [. . .] Whoever has been born of God does not sin, for His seed remains in him; and he cannot sin, because he has been born of God" (vv. 6, 8, 9). Verse 10 is the clincher: "In this the children of God and the children of the

---

6 John Murray, *Redemption Accomplished and Applied* (Grand Rapids: Eerdmans, 1955), 155.

devil are manifest: Whoever does not practice righteousness is not of God, nor is he who does not love his brother."

A true Christian has been born of God and cannot remain in perpetual sin. Whoever stays in perpetual sin thereby proves that he is still in the grip of a sinful nature and in the hands of Satan (see 5:19). Homer Hoeksema observed: "Regeneration, rightly understood, is the essence of perseverance; and perseverance is but the extension of the wonder of regeneration."[7] What many readers miss is the tense of the verbs *sins* and *practices* in this section. They are present continuous verbs, indicating an ongoing pattern. By contrast, the person who has the opposite pattern proves that he is not righteous, regenerate, or a true believer. A true Christian always practices righteousness as a general way of life.

Earlier John applied this to the Gnostic heretics: "They went out from us, but they were not of us; for if they had been of us, they would have continued with us; but they went out that they might be made manifest, that none of them were of us" (2:19). This parallels the "manifest" of 3:10. The heretics claimed to be true believers, but their lifestyles gave the lie to their profession (compare Titus 1:16). They eventually left the fold of true Christians. They did not lose their salvation — they never had it to start with. If they had it, they would have persevered in righteousness and continued with other Christians. But they did not. They committed apostasy.

John himself witnessed the same thing when he followed Jesus Christ. In John 6:66, he recorded, "From that time many of His disciples went back and walked with Him no more." They were never true disciples, for true disciples continue to follow Christ (John 8:31).

Perseverance in James 2

James 2 discusses the relation of faith and works, which is much the same as the relation of justification and sanctification. We know that we are justified by faith without works (Romans 3:28; Galatians 2:16; Ephesians 2:8–9). Paul and James were both infallibly inspired by God, so they complement and not contradict each other. Paul discussed what precedes justification; James, what follows. Paul taught that we do not need works before justification as a meritorious ground; James says we need works after justification as evidence. They do not oppose

---

7 Homer Hoeksema, *The Voice of Our Fathers* (Grand Rapids: Reformed Free Publishing Association, 1980), 826.

each other face to face but stand back to back against opposite errors of legalism and license.

Faith without works is dead (2:17, 20, 26). A dead faith cannot save (v. 14). Unfortunately, many translations leave out the definite article *the* or *that* in verse 14, which should read, "Can *that* faith save him?" Can the faith without works save anyone? The obvious answer is no. Saving faith always produces works. Lack of works proves lack of faith. He who has been justified by faith will then persevere in works of obedience. He who does not do so thereby proves that he was never justified by faith. The old Reformation formula was: "We are justified by faith alone, but the faith that justifies is never alone." The Anglican Catechism of 1553 says, "And although good works cannot deserve to make us righteous before God, yet do they so cleave unto faith that neither can faith be found without them, nor good works be anywhere without faith."[8]

In sum, the Reformed view is this: Justification precedes sanctification, and justification always produces sanctification. No sanctification, no justification. Or as the title of one book has it: *No Holiness, No Heaven!*[9]

Mistaken Notions about Perseverance

Any Bible truth is subject to misunderstanding, and many anti-Calvinists greatly misunderstand what we and the Bible teach on this subject. One is this: "Calvinists demand sinless perfection for justification." No historic Calvinist has ever taught the serious error of sinless perfectionism. But many Arminians, such as John Wesley, have taught it. Fortunately, evangelical Arminianism does not lay down sinless perfection as a condition of salvation. Calvinists do not demand a sinless life as evidence of conversion. We speak only of a general consistency of faith, repentance, and obedience. Christians are not sinless, but they do sin less. Sinless perfectionism is disproved by Philippians 3:12, James 3:2, and 1 John 1:8. The only "Second Blessing" that brings sinless perfection is death (Hebrews 12:23).

Nor do we teach that perseverance is by one's own self-effort. Left to ourselves, even Christians would only sin. We persevere in holiness only because God perseveres in supplying us with holiness by the Holy Spirit through Holy Scripture. If God let us do it ourselves, we would sin our way to perdition. The Synod of Dort wisely pronounced, "With respect to themselves this not only

---

8 In Dennison, *Reformed Confessions*, 2:31.
9 Richard Aldersen, *No Holiness, No Heaven! Antinomianism Today* (Edinburgh: Banner of Truth, 1986).

could happen, but also undoubtedly would happen; but with respect to God cannot possibly happen" (5:8). Here we see how preservation and perseverance work together.

Another false notion is: "Perseverance is the ideal but not the norm. Some Christians just do not meet that ideal." We reply: Sinlessness is the ideal; perseverance is the norm. Some Christians grow in holiness more than others, but all grow some, or they are dead. Even the youngest or weakest Christian perseveres.

Nor do we teach that Christians never backslide, fall into heinous sins, or grow spiritually cold. This should be obvious from experience as well as Scripture. The Bible records sad examples of the sins of great saints (Noah, Moses, Samson, David, Solomon, Peter, and others). A Christian might even commit worse sins after his conversion than before. This is particularly true with those who were converted as children. All Christians still have indwelling sin, but as Thomas Watson said, "Though sin lives in him, yet he doth not live in sin."[10]

No Perpetual Backsliding

A widespread error held by many is the idea that a Christian can backslide long and hard his whole life, but God will bring him back shortly before he dies. This is incorrect. It is true that God restores backsliders (Hosea 14:4), but He does so within a reasonable period of time and not after decades of flagrant sin. Backsliding can be compared to holding one's breath — you can do it for a short while but not for years. God uses chastening, providential hindrances, and the Holy Spirit working on our consciences to bring the backslider back.

It is sheer presumption to suggest that a perpetually sinning person is only backslidden. Orthodox Calvinists utterly oppose the error of the "carnal Christian." That error takes various forms: asserting faith without repentance, repeating the Sinner's Prayer or "going forward" at an altar call without true conversion, supposing one can be justified without sanctification following, not having any fruit of the Spirit but only increased evil fruit, and the like. This notion is widespread in evangelical, fundamentalist, and charismatic churches. Sadly, it even has crept into a few Reformed churches and in even more pseudo-Reformed churches. The blame for this error is to be laid squarely at the door of an antinomian mindset. It is not even good Arminianism, for it

---

10 Thomas Watson, *Discourses on Important and Interesting Subjects* (Ligonier: Soli Deo Gloria, 1990), 1:518.

would have been utterly abominated by Arminius and Wesley. A. W. Tozer, a godly Arminian, addressed it and cried, "I call it heresy!"[11]

Unfortunately, there are some who claim to be Calvinist while holding to this dangerous error. They generally profess to be four-point Calvinists, but upon further investigation they usually believe in free will, election without reprobation, no limited atonement, and preservation without perseverance. That is far more Arminian than Reformed. And it is not even good Arminianism. They assert what James 2 explicitly condemns — faith without works.

It often goes by the innocuous title "Once saved, always saved." In the correct sense that term is acceptable but not in the popular usage. It is often associated with a kind of shallow evangelism by overzealous and unwise pastors, evangelists (especially on television), and youth workers. They often boast of the large numbers of their "converts." When those converts fail to show any change in their lives, they are pronounced so-called carnal Christians who are still saved. But according to the Word of God, they are carnal non-Christians. It is sheer licentiousness and antinomianism, fundamentally no different from the ancient Gnostics opposed by John or the Antinomians who say God's law has been totally abolished. Practitioners of this method urge their converts never to doubt their salvation, even after years of sinful behavior. But Scripture urges us, "Examine yourselves as to whether you are in the faith" (2 Corinthians 13:5). Promoters of this error sometimes use it as a reason to reject orthodox Calvinism. The feeling is mutual.

Jesus warned about this kind of danger in the very context of warning of false prophets (Matthew 7:15–23). "You will know them by their fruits" (v. 16). Peter did the same in 2 Peter 2. Christ clearly stated that a good tree cannot bear bad fruit — the very thing that the carnal Christian error asserts. A bad tree will end up in the fire of Hell (v. 19), not the glory of Heaven. Then Christ went on to forewarn "you who practice lawlessness" — they too will be consigned to Hell (v. 23). Note that those souls claimed to be Christians. Doubtlessly there will be many who will claim to be carnal Christians at Judgment Day. Imagine their terror when they discover they believed a false gospel and were never truly converted.

The Protestant Reformation was ignited by a godly revulsion against the licentiousness of the Roman Catholic heresy of peddling indulgences, which sold licenses to sin. In my opinion, the modern purveyors of antinomianism,

---

11 A. W. Tozer, *I Call It Heresy!* (Camp Hill, PA: Christian Publications, 1991).

easy-believism, and carnal Christianity are no better. We need a new Reformation to expose and excise it.

Moreover, this gross error is just what Jude warned about. False prophets proclaim, "Free grace!" but actually turn the grace of God into licentiousness (v. 4). They promote cheap grace, which is no grace. Cheap grace is disgrace. True grace leads to holiness (Titus 2:11–12). The root of the error is a rejection of the biblical doctrine of the perseverance of the saints.

The Reformed doctrines of preservation and perseverance solve a common problem faced by Christian parents. Too often they raise a child by the Bible, and it looks like he is a Christian. He may have repeated "the sinner's prayer" at a young age, been baptized, and was even active in church, prayer, Bible study, and evangelism. But then he radically changes when he leaves home at eighteen to go to college, join the military, or get married. He soon leads a flagrantly non-Christian lifestyle and may even become a homosexual, criminal, or atheist. The parents naively but with good motives say he is a backslidden "carnal Christian" who is still saved. They may say, "He is still a child of the covenant." Or they may say he lost his salvation. They should realize that the son was never truly converted to begin with. He only looked like it. The Reformed doctrines of preservation and perseverance give the correct diagnosis. The parents are urged to earnestly speak with their son about the gospel and sincerely pray for his salvation.

Evangelical Arminians say, "You must persevere to be preserved." The Antinomian says, "You need not persevere to be preserved." Calvinism teaches, "The true Christian will be preserved by God and will persevere to the end."

Conclusion

The fifth point of Calvinism could be retitled "The Perseverance of the Savior." We keep on because we are kept by the Savior. It is His promise that keeps the saints persevering, not their own efforts. This is the meaning of Philippians 1:6: "Being confident of this very thing, that He who has begun a good work in you will complete it until the day of Jesus Christ." See also Jude 24.

The great Calvinist hymn writer Augustus Toplady united perseverance and preservation in the lines of one of his hymns:

> My name from the palms of his hands eternity will not erase,
> Impressed on his heart it remains, in marks of indelible grace.

Yes, I to the end shall endure, as sure as the earnest is giv'n,
More happy, but not more secure, the glorified spirits in heav'n.[12]

---

[12] Augustus Toplady, *A Debtor to Mercy Alone*, 1771.

Chapter 62
Objections to Eternal Security

There are a number of objections to the fifth point of Calvinism, especially preservation. It is fitting that we answer them for the benefit of non-Calvinists, semi-Calvinists, and wavering Calvinists.

Objections from the Old Testament

The first concerns Psalm 51:11: "Do not cast me away from Your presence, and do not take Your Holy Spirit from me." It is argued that David was in danger of losing the Spirit and salvation and being cast away. We reply that David repented and was not cast away. The same is true for every sinning Christian. Some suggest that the Spirit was not given permanently to Old Testament believers, but David certainly had the Spirit, as do all true believers (Romans 8:9). Psalm 51 records David's agonizing repentance after his sin with Bathsheba. Repentant Christians mourn like this as well.

The main Old Testament passage used as an objection is Ezekiel 18:24. The argument is that a righteous person can turn away from righteousness and be lost. Calvinists offer several replies. Some put forth the unlikely view that Ezekiel is speaking only of external righteousness, like that of the Pharisees. Another says the case is only a hypothetical case because no one is righteous of himself (Romans 3:10). A better answer is that the case is hypothetical but impossible. If a Christian truly forsook Christ, then he would certainly forfeit salvation. But that will never happen because Christ guarantees that the elect will never apostatize.

Objections from the Gospels

Matthew 5:13 says Christians are the salt of the earth but will be thrown away if they lose their saltiness. Arminians sometimes say this means loss of salvation. But salvation is not in view here. A Christian can lose his salty impact on the world by imitating the world, avoiding all contact or confrontation, or just staying in the salt shaker.

Then there is Matthew 10:33: "Whoever denies Me before men, him I will deny before My Father who is in heaven" (see 2 Timothy 2:12). It is argued that this means that a Christian can deny Christ and be denied before the Father. But this is not what Christ meant. He is not speaking of believers. Peter denied Christ three times but was restored. He did not forfeit salvation nor need to be saved three more times. All Christians falter like that at times. Jesus is speaking to unbelievers who consistently deny Christ by word or life (see Titus 1:16).

This raises the question of those who once claimed to be Christians but now deny they are Christians. Arminians are quick to assume that they were truly saved. By contrast, Antinomians will say that these deniers may still be Christians even when they deny the faith. One has been reported as teaching, "You can even become an atheist, but if you once accepted Christ as Savior, you cannot lose your salvation, even though you deny God."[1] That is the logical conclusion of the carnal Christian error, but it flatly contradicts Matthew 10:33.

Some interpret Matthew 13:3–23 to teach that some accept the seed of the gospel and are saved, then later fall away and become lost. In his excellent book *The Gospel According to Jesus*,[2] John MacArthur gives the best answer. The first three soils in the parable represent three kinds of unbelievers. Two of them pretended to be Christians but then fell away from their false profession of faith. The latter three soils represent three kinds of Christians as to their degree of service. Note that all three did truly bear good fruit, which disproves the notion that a Christian can bear all bad fruit and no good fruit.

Then there is the parable of the ten virgins in Matthew 25:1–13. Some Arminians say that all ten were believers, for they all had the oil of the Holy Spirit. But half of them lost the Spirit and forfeited salvation. The better interpretation is that five were saved, but the other five only pretended to be saved. The great American Puritan Thomas Shepard published a remarkable series of sermons on this parable that has challenged false believers for centuries.[3]

What we see again and again is the Arminian proclivity to pronounce a person a Christian based on a quick and shallow profession of faith. When he "falls away," that is taken as proof the Christian can become a non-Christian. The Antinomian promoter of easy-believism and the carnal Christian theory takes the opposite error and contends that this person is still saved. The Calvinist avoids ditches on both sides of the road. The person in question proves he

---

1 Richard Aldersen quotes these words from Bob Thieme in *No Holiness, No Heaven! Antinomianism Today* (Edinburgh: Banner of Truth, 1986), 58.

2 Grand Rapids: Zondervan, 1988. Revised edition, 2008.

3 Thomas Shepard, *The Parable of the Ten Virgins* (Ligonier, PA: Soli Deo Gloria, 1990). Jonathan Edwards preached a similar series, but as yet the sermons remain unpublished.

was never saved to begin with. We should be far more careful in pronouncing someone saved.

This is seen in John 6:66: "From that time many of His disciples went back and walked with Him no more." These were not true believers before or after this departure. Jesus went on to state categorically that true disciples continue to abide in His word (John 8:31). Perseverance is a necessary evidence of preservation and true conversion. The false disciples of chapter 6 only wanted free food, miracles, and a worldly king. They resemble the multitudes of pseudo-converts today who only want material blessings, not salvation. They believe the false "prosperity gospel" rather than the true gospel. They are like the "rice Christians" on the mission field who claim to be Christians only for the free rice but forsake that profession of faith when the rice runs out or the missionaries move on.

This brings us to John 15:1–8. Arminians often say that verses 2 and 6 prove that a person who was once spiritually united with Christ can be cut off and thrown into Hell. Some Calvinists reply that this refers rather to God's pruning of believers to make them more fruitful. Actually, that truth is taught in the second half of verse 2, not the first. The dead branches that are cut off and destroyed are again false believers. They were "hangers on" like in chapter 6. Note that they had no spiritual fruit, and the true branches did (v. 8).

Objections from Paul's Epistles

Romans 11:17–24 is somewhat like John 15:1–8 in that it too speaks of branches being removed from a tree. But the contexts are different. Here Paul is not speaking of individuals, but groups — Jews and Gentiles. There is one people of God, not two as dispensationalists say. In the old covenant, almost all true believers were Jews. Only a few Gentiles were saved, such as Melchizedek, Job, Ruth, and Jethro. When Christ came, Israel at large rejected Him (John 1:11), though a few did accept Him. Consequently, Israel lost its favored status and was replaced by the church which is predominantly Gentile. Over the centuries there have always been a few Jewish Christians, and Romans 11 promises the day when Israel at large will believe in Jesus as Messiah. The Jewish branch will be grafted back in. This has nothing to do with individual Jews or Gentiles losing salvation.

A somewhat rare opinion of 1 Corinthians 6:9–10 and Ephesians 5:3–5 holds that a Christian can lose his salvation if he commits even one of the sins listed there. But if this proves anything, it proves too much. If true, it would mean that we can forfeit salvation for coveting, lying, lusting, stealing, or getting drunk even once. One Arminian who holds to this opinion said he has lost and regained his salvation many times. One wonders how he or other Arminians can sleep at night. Some fear they may have lost their salvation without knowing it. This resembles the Roman Catholic who is afraid that he may die in mortal sin and go to Hell. Reformed theology offers solid assurance of preservation, perseverance, and a good night's sleep.

But did not Paul himself worry that he might become an apostate "castaway" in 1 Corinthians 9:27? No, he only was concerned that he might seriously harm his ministry. He had great assurance that Christ would keep him to the end (Philippians 1:6; 2 Timothy 1:12). This raises the related issue of disqualified preachers. Generally speaking, Arminians tend to be quicker to restore fallen preachers to office than Calvinists, for we generally hold to a higher and more biblical standard of ministerial qualifications.

Next, 1 Corinthians 10:12 warns, "Therefore let him who thinks he stands take heed lest he fall." This is a warning of falling into sin because of pride, not falling from salvation. Verse 13 contextually mentions sin, not apostasy.

Does 1 Corinthians 11:29 mean that a Christian who commits sacrilege (such as drunkenness) at the Lord's Supper brings ultimate damnation upon himself? No, Paul speaks of "judgment" (v. 30) as part of divine chastening even unto death. As we shall see later, Calvinists generally "fence" the Lord's Table far more cautiously than Arminians by restricting it from believers who are being disciplined by their local church. We often urge unbelievers not to partake, for it would add to their condemnation. One does not often hear such cautions at non-Reformed Communion services.

Arminians frequently cite Galatians 5:4: "You have become estranged from Christ, you who attempt to be justified by law; you have fallen from grace." Paul here addresses the same legalists in previous chapters who preached the false gospel of faith and works. He did not at all consider them to be true believers. Whoever thinks he is justified by works of the law will be condemned by the law. The true Christian is justified by grace alone and faith alone (Ephesians 2:8–9). Paul warns the true believers to avoid the error of the false gospel of the Galatian Judaizers. A true Christian may fall *in* grace but never fall *from* grace. He may be chastened *by* Christ, but never severed *from* Christ.

Colossians 1:23 and 1 Corinthians 15:1–2 emphasize the "if" condition of faith. On this we agree with evangelical Arminians against pseudo-Calvinist

Antinomians. One will not die saved if he has not truly believed and continued in faith. These verses do not assert or imply that a true believer can stop believing.

Second Thessalonians 2:3 predicts the future "falling away" which Arminians sometimes think refers to Christians losing their salvation. They have a different understanding of apostasy than Calvinists have. They speak of losing salvation. We speak of false believers turning away from their profession or from the true gospel. This verse, like 1 Timothy 4:1, warns of a then-future growth of heresy and false gospels. This does not predict true Christians falling away but rather many false believers accepting false gospels. Jude 3 also warned of those who fall away from "the faith" — the gospel.

I mention in passing a very rare interpretation of "the lie" in 2 Thessalonians 2:11. It has been suggested that this refers to Satan's lie to Eve, "You shall not die" (Genesis 3:4). It suggests that Calvinists believe "the lie" that they can sin with immunity and not lose their salvation. But 2 Thessalonians 2:11 is speaking of the lie that the Man of Sin is a great hero. It says nothing of losing salvation.

Objections from the Book of Hebrews

Hebrews contains several severe warning passages (2:1–3; 3:6, 14; 4:14; 6:4–12; 10:26–31, 38). They must be interpreted in context. The writer is addressing a congregation of Jews who professed to follow Christ. Some were having second thoughts and were about to reject Him and return to the old covenant sacrifices and law. The writer warns that they would die in the wilderness like their ancestors. Jesus is the promised Messiah, surpassing even Moses and Abraham. To reject Him brings worse condemnation than even rejecting Moses. Denying the gospel is worse than breaking the law. A true believer proves he is such by continuing in faith to the end, like the examples of chapter 11. Those who go back prove they were not true believers.

This sets the context for 6:4–12 and 10:26–31, texts frequently cited as proof that one can be saved and later damned. There are several Reformed answers. Some say the passages are only hypothetical — God would indeed take away salvation from someone who committed such an apostasy, but it will never happen. A better and more popular explanation argues that the writer is not speaking of true believers but false believers who experienced something of the Spirit just short of salvation. They then pulled away violently and opposed Christ and Christianity. This is a rare case of extreme apostasy, not like the more common rejection by false converts. These persons had what Calvin called a temporary faith,[4] not true faith that continues.

Note that 6:6 says that those who commit this apostasy cannot ever be renewed to repentance again. Very few Arminians say that a person who loses his salvation can never be saved again. Calvinists often say these verses teach a rare and extreme apostasy akin to the unforgivable blasphemy of the Holy Spirit (Matthew 12:32). Note that the person "insults" the Holy Spirit (10:29). This confirms his reprobation in this life. Nobody who has gone this far was ever saved or will ever be saved. Hebrews 6:9–12 clarifies that the writer is not speaking of true believers in those warnings. Apostates are in verses 4–8; true believers in 9–12. These passages, then, do not teach that a true believer can commit the unpardonable sin of extreme apostasy resulting in the loss of his soul.

Objections from the Catholic Epistles

Some think that 2 Peter 2:4 and Jude 6 teach that a Christian can lose his salvation like the angels who fell from Heaven. Not so. For one thing, as we saw earlier, all the angels who fell were non-elect; none will ever be saved. By contrast, all men are born sinful. Some are saved from it. None fall back into a lost state.

Peter continues his warning of false teachers and apostates who want to lure Christians away from the truth. Peter's whole point is that they were never true believers. They were hogs and dogs, not sheep. The false believers and teachers will eventually imitate the fallen angels by returning to a life of sin consistent with their true nature.

By common consent 1 John 5:16–17 is hard to interpret. Some Arminians take it to mean what Roman Catholicism takes it to mean — losing salvation by means of a mortal sin. Calvinists usually argue that it refers rather to a Christian who has not repented of a gross sin and faces chastening by death, as in 1 Corinthians 11:29–30. When it is obvious that a person is in that situation, prayer for him is ineffectual.

Objections from Revelation

The main objection from Revelation is based on Revelation 3:5 and 20:15. It is

---

4 E.g., *Calvin's Ecclesiastical Advice* (Louisville: Westminster John Knox Press, 1991), 29–31, and his comments in the pertinent commentaries and *Institutes*.

argued that God will remove names from the Book of Life when a Christian sins too far, stops believing, or otherwise forfeits salvation. We have already discussed the Book of Life in chapter 38, "The Election of Grace." God sovereignly wrote the names of the elect in the Book of Life back in eternity. He promises never to erase the names, nor can we. Revelation 3:5 describes Christians as overcomers. All Christians are overcomers, not just some who persevere. See Romans 8:37; 1 John 2:13; 4:4; and Revelation 21:7. Of such God gives this great promise: "I will not blot out his name from the Book of Life." That is a promise of preservation, not a warning of losing salvation.

Other passages that speak of being removed from the Book of Life could refer to the roll of the living. When God takes a person's life, He erases him from the list of the living. Some Old Testament references could refer to the census of Israel, from which a person could be removed by excommunication or death. They do not speak of a true believer committing apostasy and losing salvation.[5]

Objections from Personal Examples

Arminians frequently refer to two kinds of personal examples. The first are in Scripture: Saul; Demas (2 Timothy 4:10); Hymenaeus, Alexander, and Philetus (1 Timothy 1:19–20; 2 Timothy 2:17); Simon Magus (Acts 8); Esau (Hebrews 12:15–17); and others. It is held that these were all once true believers who later sinned away their salvation.

Calvinists and some Arminians take differing views on Saul. Some say he had been saved and died a failure. Others deny he was ever saved. A few suggest that Saul lived in the old covenant era when one could lose salvation, unlike those in the new covenant. The associates of Paul may have been backslidden or afraid to stand with Paul like Luke did (2 Timothy 4:11). They would resemble the apostles who fled when Christ was arrested. Others take them to be apostates who were never truly converted. But we deny that any of these were true believers who became unbelievers.

Simon Magus was obviously a false convert. He "believed" only externally and temporarily, for his heart was still bound in sin (Acts 8:21–23). Even demons believe like Simon (James 2:19). As for Esau, Hebrews 12:17 says he grieved and sought repentance in vain. Perhaps he was an example of the extreme apostasy

---

5 See John Piper, *A Godward Life: Book Two* (Sisters, OR: Multnomah, 1999), 203–06.

of chapters 6 and 10. Romans 9:13 says he was non-elect and therefore never saved.

Some, but not all Arminians, point to Judas as an example of an ex-Christian. It baffles Calvinists that anyone would seriously think he was ever truly saved. He is described as a "devil" (John 6:70), a thief who only followed Christ for money (John 12:6), and a traitor for money. He was a "son of perdition" (John 17:12) who died and went to Hell where he belonged. He fell from apostleship, not from salvation. He committed the extreme apostasy of the unpardonable sin. Adam Clarke, the popular Arminian Bible commentator, took the novel view that Judas actually repented and was again saved.[6] We disagree. Judas only "repented" in the sense of mourning by way of a guilty conscience, not out of godly sorrow (2 Corinthians 7:10). If he truly repented, why did he then commit suicide? He went to Hell (Acts 1:25).

Arminians buttress their case by appealing to another group of examples — namely, persons they knew personally. One often hears words like these: "I knew someone who was saved and then lost. You can't tell me he was never saved. I know better. He loved Jesus, went to church, even did some witnessing. And you can't tell me he is now saved, for he lives a life of flagrant sin, curses Christ, and denies being a Christian." First, we reply that we base our theology on Scripture alone, not personal experience or observation. We evaluate such cases in the light of Scripture. The conclusion in the vast majority of such cases is that the person in question was not a true Christian to begin with. He was only another false convert who turned his back on Christianity. He never lost what he never had.

This relates to another all-too-common case: encountering those persons themselves who think they were once Christians and now are not. They may say with bitter spite, "I tried it. I was 'saved' like you are. Then I woke up and stopped believing in Jesus like I stopped believing in Santa Claus. I'm not interested. Leave me alone!" The sad thing is that such a person is very hard to speak with; few ever become truly saved. The reason is they do not realize they were swindled with a cheap evangelistic method and phony profession of faith. Easy-believism multiplies such cases. They are like the persons in 2 Peter 2:20–21. It would be easier to direct them to Christ for salvation if they had never claimed to have been a Christian than to have made a false profession

---

6 Adam Clarke, *The New Testament of Our Lord and Saviour Jesus Christ* (Nashville: Abingdon, n.d.), 5:686–91.

and then gone back on it. The doctrines of grace and other biblical truths help prevent such tragedies from happening and assist those who fall into them.

Conclusion

Lastly, what about free will? This seems to be the recurring objection to most of the doctrines of grace. We have already refuted the error of free will. If left to free will, all Christians would indeed lose their salvation. But our wills have been freed from being sin-slaves and are now Christ-slaves of righteousness (Romans 6:16–22). Christ has us bound in chains of grace and loves us too much to let us go. His will is stronger than ours and guarantees that He will both preserve us and make us persevere to the end.

Chapter 63
Holy Scripture

For the remainder of this volume we will discuss certain aspects of Reformed distinctives on selected doctrines. We start with Scripture. Calvinists have always had a high view of Holy Scripture second to none. We believe in *sola Scriptura* — Scripture alone is our highest and final authority in all matters of faith and practice.

Biblical Infallibility

Historical Calvinism believes in the absolute trustworthiness of the Bible. Two of the best books ever written to defend biblical inerrancy were written by Calvinists: *The Inspiration and Authority of the Bible* by Benjamin Breckinridge Warfield and *Thy Word is Truth* by Edward John Young. Thomas Vincent the Puritan summed up our position: "That the Scriptures are true is evident, because they are the Word of God, who is a God of truth and cannot lie; who can as soon cease to be God as to be true."[1]

Some critics — even some who profess to be Reformed — have argued that John Calvin held to a fallible and errant Bible and that the idea of infallibility and inerrancy was invented by later scholastics such as Francis Turretin.[2] This flawed opinion appears to twist the great Reformer's clear doctrine to conform with that of the critics. The Reformers all held to full biblical inspiration, infallibility, inerrancy, and authority. They would have condemned anyone who denied it. Hear Calvin's own words: "There is such a perfection in the word of God, as that nothing can be found therein, but all purity and sincerity; and to be so infallible a truth [. . .] we say that it is infallible."[3] When he says that God "lisps" to us in the Bible, he did not mean that it has errors, as some suppose. Rather, he meant that this is how God condescends to tell us "his secrets after a

---

1 Thomas Vincent, *Christ's Sudden and Certain Appearance to Judgment* (Morgan, PA: Soli Deo Gloria, 1996), 182.
2 So Jack B. Rogers and Donald K. McKim, *The Authority and Inspiration of the Bible* (San Francisco: Harper & Row, 1979). They were refuted by John Woodbridge, *Biblical Authority: A Critique of the Rogers/McKim Proposal* (Grand Rapids: Zondervan, 1982).
3 John Calvin, *Sermons on Psalm 119* (Audubon: Old Paths Publications, 1996), 353, 239. See also pages 68, 124, 201.

sweet and living fashion, as if one wishing to feed a little babe should chew his meat for him, in order that he should have no more to do but swallow it down."[4] "Thy Word is truth!" (John 17:17)

The Internal Testimony of the Holy Spirit

More than other systems of theology, Calvinism has taught that the ultimate reason why we believe the Bible is the inspired word of God is because God Himself proves it through the internal testimony of the Holy Spirit (*testimonium internum Spiritus Sancti*). The Westminster Confession explains:

> We may be moved and induced by the testimony of the Church to a high and reverent esteem of the holy scripture, and the heavenliness of the matter, the efficacy of the doctrine, the majesty of the style, the consent of the parts, the scope of the whole, (which is to give all glory to God) the full discovery of it makes of the only way of man's salvation, the many other incomparable excellencies, and the entire perfection thereof, are arguments whereby it does abundantly evidence itself to be the word of God; yet, notwithstanding, our full persuasion and assurance of the infallible truth, and divine authority thereof, is from the inward work of the Holy Spirit, bearing witness by and with the word in our hearts. (1:5)

This is in opposition to the Roman Catholic position that we know the Bible is divinely inspired because the Catholic Church tells us it is. That would make the Catholic hierarchy the final authority. Nor do we believe it is inspired because of its fulfilled prophecies, for we would not know about those prophecies or fulfillments unless they were infallibly recorded in Scripture. Nor do miracles prove the Bible, for if scoffers do not believe the Bible, they will not believe in miracles (Luke 16:31). Scripture proves miracles, not vice versa.

This testimony is not an audible voice or mystical experience, let alone the Mormon "burning in the bosom" that allegedly proves the Book of Mormon. The testimony does not add any new information to the Bible, such as identifying the anonymous author of the book of Hebrews. The Spirit bears witness "by and with the scriptures in the heart of man" (Westminster Larger Catechism, Q. 4). It is closely related to the illumination of faith.

God does not give this testimony through the Qur'an, the Apocrypha, the Rig Veda, or even the Apostolic Fathers. He does it only through the inspired and canonical sixty-six books of the Bible. The French Confession of 1559

---

4 John Calvin, *Sermons on the Epistle to the Ephesians* (London: Banner of Truth, 1973), 423.

says, "We know these books to be canonical [. . .] by the testimony of inward illumination by the Holy Spirit, which enables us to distinguish them from other ecclesiastical books" (Article 4).

Calvin said that it is not right or necessary to subject the Bible to the proofs of man. The testimony excels all human reason. Just as God alone can prove His own existence, so only God can prove the inspiration of Scripture. The same Spirit who inspired the prophets to write it still speaks through it today to authenticate it. Every Christian senses this testimony.[5]

This has great implications for apologetics. Abraham Kuyper, the founder of presuppositional apologetics, said that the supernatural character of Scripture precludes it from natural proof: "Do not men see and understand, then, that the evidence of the divine authority of the Scripture must come to us in such a manner that the simplest old woman in the poorhouse can see it as well as I can?"[6] If all Christians perceive it, it is strange that so many resort to human proofs through evidences, logical arguments, opinion polls, and the like.

John Owen pointed out that one does not have to prove the sunlight by a candle.[7] Ephesians 5:13: "For whatever makes manifest is light." The Bible is spiritual light and proves itself by giving light (Psalm 119:105; Proverbs 6:23; 2 Peter 1:19). The best proof of the Bible is the Bible itself. The Spirit who inspired it continues to speak through it today (Hebrews 3:7; 10:15), just as He did through the preaching of the apostles (1 Thessalonians 1:5; 2:13). This is how the Good Shepherd calls His sheep (John 10:4, 16, 27).

As Owen said, "Being what they are, they declare whose they are."[8] The Bible bears the fingerprints of God. John Murray: "The Holy Spirit may be said to bear perpetual witness to the divine character of that which is his own handiwork,"[9] even as an artist signs his paintings. Thomas Manton said, "The same Holy Ghost which inspired the penman of the scriptures, inclines our hearts to believe them."[10] There is a sense in which unbelievers feel the force of the Spirit's testimony, as they did when the prophets spoke (Ezekiel 2:5; cf.

---

5 John Calvin, *Sermons on Galatians* (Edinburgh: Banner of Truth, 1997), 492; *Institutes of the Christian Religion* (Philadelphia: Westminster, 1960), 1:7:2 (pp. 76–81).

6 Abraham Kuyper, *The Work of the Holy Spirit* (Grand Rapids: Eerdmans, 1969), 176, 191.

7 John Owen, *The Works of John Owen* (London: Banner of Truth, 1976), 16:311.

8 Owen, *The Works of John Owen*, 16:311.

9 In Ned B. Stonehouse and Paul Woolley, eds., *The Infallible Word* (Phillipsburg, NJ: P&R, 2002), 49.

10 Thomas Manton, *The Works of Thomas Manton, D.D.* (Worthington: Maranatha Publications, n.d.), 10:448.

33:33). This parallels how all men everywhere perceive God's testimony of His existence and attributes through creation, though they suppress it (Romans 1:18–21). There is also another sense in which only God's people sense the testimony (John 10:26–27; 1 Corinthians 2:14).

This testimony is closely related to the testimony of the Spirit given to believers for assurance of salvation (Romans 8:16; Galatians 4:6; 1 John 3:20–21, 24; 4:13; 5:10). The Spirit speaks through Scripture and produces an echo of faith, as it were, in the hearts of the elect. First John 5:6 says, "It is the Spirit who bears witness, because the Spirit is the truth." This is greater than mere human testimony (v. 9). Therefore, to disbelieve God's Word is to call Him a liar (v. 10). To deny biblical inspiration and infallibility is to insult the Spirit's testimony and is therefore blasphemy.

The Perspicuity of Scripture

Another important aspect of the Reformed doctrine of the Bible is the *perspicuity* of Scripture. The Westminster Confession explains:

> All things in Scripture are not alike plain in themselves, nor alike clear unto all; yet those things which are necessary to be known, believed, and observed, for salvation, are so clearly propounded and opened in some place or Scripture or other, that not only the learned, but the unlearned in a due use of the ordinary means, may attain unto a sufficient understanding of them. (1:7)

Some parts of the Bible are harder to understand than others (2 Peter 3:16). But God has made the basic gospel understandable to all, even the illiterate. The Bible was not written to Greek philosophers but to the common man. We are commanded to read the Bible aloud in local churches, which by and large contain members who are not great intellectuals (Colossians 4:16; 1 Thessalonians 5:7; 1 Corinthians 1:26). Everyone is commanded to read the Bible for himself (John 5:39; Acts 17:11).

The Bible gives light to the simple and makes us wise to salvation (Psalms 19:7; 119:98–100, 130; 2 Timothy 3:15–17). William Tyndale, the early English Bible translator, once said to a Roman Catholic prelate, "If God spare my life, ere many years I will cause a boy that driveth a plow should know more of the Scriptures than thou dost." The basic gospel in Scripture is clear to all, for all are commanded to believe it and be saved (Mark 1:15; 16:15–16).

The Analogy of Faith

Related to the above is the doctrine known as the *analogy of faith*. This means the basic message of the Bible is to be used as a hermeneutical tool in interpreting the rest of the Bible. Early proponents pointed to Romans 12:6: "Let us prophesy in proportion to our faith." The Greek is literally "the analogy *(analogian)* of the faith." Calvin commented: "By the word *faith* he means the first principles of religion, and any doctrine that has been found not to correspond with these is condemned as false."[11]

The gospel is of first importance and must be believed for one to be saved (1 Corinthians 15:1–4). It is "the faith" — that is, the content and not the act of faith that is in view here (Acts 6:7; 1 Timothy 4:1; Jude 3). Any interpretation of any part of Scripture that contradicts the gospel is necessarily wrong. The same goes for any interpretation that assumes the text is in error. The implications for exegesis are obvious, enormous, and serious.

This relates to systematic theology, an area in which Calvinists have excelled for centuries. Paul speaks of revealed truth as sound doctrine (1 Timothy 1:10; Titus 2:1); the words of faith and of the good doctrine (1 Timothy 4:6); the pattern of sound words (2 Timothy 1:13); the doctrine which accords with godliness (1 Timothy 6:3); "the faithful word [. . .] sound doctrine" (Titus 1:9); and "that form of doctrine to which you were delivered" (Romans 6:17). Biblical exegesis produces biblical theology and, in turn, systematic theology. The various doctrines of the many books of the Bible can be related to each other to get the whole counsel of God.

The analogy of faith is related to the *analogy of Scripture*. Scripture is to be interpreted by Scripture. The Bible is its own best commentary. Again the Westminster Confession explains: "The infallible rule of interpretation of Scripture is Scripture itself; and therefore, when there is a question about the true and full sense of any Scripture, (which is not manifold, but one) it must be searched and known by other places that speak more clearly (1:9)".

The clear passages (such as didactic places) interpret the unclear (such as prophecy or parables), not vice versa. The New Testament is God's inspired and infallible commentary on the Old Testament. Some non-Calvinists reject this, arguing that the readers of the Old Testament did not have the New Testament in front of them. Some even insinuate that it is unnecessary to consult the New

---

11 John Calvin, *The Epistles of Paul the Apostle to the Romans and to the Thessalonians* (Grand Rapids: Eerdmans, 1980), 269.

when studying the Old, or even that the New misinterprets the Old. This is to ignore or deny biblical infallibility. Heinrich Heppe said, "The obscure passages are to be explained by the unambiguously clear ones or by the *analogia fide* [analogy of faith] based on them."[12]

One application of all of this is that Old Testament believers were saved by believing the same basic gospel that New Testament saints believed (Galatians 3:8; Luke 24:44–46; Acts 10:43; Hebrews 4:2). There is and always has been only one true gospel (Galatians 1:9). This contradicts a fundamental principle of dispensationalism — namely, that old covenant believers were not saved by faith in the person and work of Christ. Some say that message was not revealed until the new covenant era, while others admit it was revealed through types and prophecies, but nobody understood them (thereby misunderstanding 1 Peter 1:10–11). But Christ explicitly rebuked those who failed to believe the gospel of His person, death, and resurrection as repeatedly promised in the Old Testament (Luke 24:25–26, 44, 46).

Yet another related principle emphasized by Reformed theology is the use of deduction from exegesis to produce theology. The standard explanation is that of the Westminster Confession: "The whole counsel of God, concerning all things necessary for His own glory, man's salvation, faith and life, is either expressly set out in Scripture, or by good and necessary consequence may be deduced from Scripture (1:6)."

This principle can be traced back at least as far as Martin Bucer, who wrote: "Concerning the things of God, nothing is to be taught unless it is either expressly set out in the Scriptures, or may be truly and certainly proved from the same."[13] This is a contributing factor in systematic theology. Some early scholastics may have abused it by going too far, but it is valid nonetheless. It means that we can formulate doctrines by cross-referencing several verses together, where the formulated doctrine is not stated in just one place. For example, the Trinity is not taught in any one verse, but is seen by comparing several verses together. Some non-Reformed critics reject this principle, saying "We cannot say something is biblical unless it is explicitly said to be such." For example, some dispensationalists reject the idea of the covenant of works because the term is not found in Scripture, yet they themselves use the extra-

---

12 Heinrich Heppe, *Reformed Dogmatics* (Grand Rapids: Baker, 1978), 34.
13 Martin Bucer, *Common Places of Martin Bucer*, ed. by D. F. Wright (Appleford: Sutton Courtenay, 1977), 78.

biblical term *dispensation of innocence*. Theology would be greatly minimized if it were to be restricted to only the explicit statements in the Bible.

Providential Preservation

Historic Calvinists not only teach that God inspired His Word but that He has providentially preserved it over the centuries and will continue to do so until the Second Coming. The Westminster Confession states that the words of God have been "by His singular care and providence kept pure in all ages" (1:8). The Formula Consensus Helvetica explains it as follows: "God, the Supreme Judge, not only took care to have his word, which is the "power of God unto salvation to everyone that believes' (Romans 1:16), committed to writing by Moses, the Prophets and the Apostles, but has watched and cherished it with paternal care from the time it was written up to the present, so that it could not be corrupted by craft of Satan or fraud of man."[14]

Jesus said that His words will never pass away (Matthew 5:18; 24:35; Mark 13:31; Luke 16:17; 21:33). First Peter 1:25 quotes Isaiah 40:8: "But the word of the Lord endures forever" (see also v. 23). Romans 3:2 and 9:4 say that the Hebrew Scriptures were entrusted to the Jews. God preserved His Word through the Jews up to the time of Christ, and He has entrusted the New Testament to the church as well. But ultimately, God Himself guarantees their preservation.

This does not mean that every Hebrew or Greek manuscript is perfect, for there are scribal errors in all of them. But it does mean that God's inspired words have not been lost. God has preserved all canonical books and inspired verses, words, and even the letters. There are no "lost books of the Bible" or even lost letters. God did not grant providential preservation to non-inspired books of the prophets or apostles, such as Paul's other letters to the Corinthians (1 Corinthians 5:9) or the non-inspired books mentioned in the Old Testament such as the "Book of the Wars of the Lord" (Numbers 21:14).

Just as God preserves His saints and guarantees their perseverance, so He preserves His holy words, and they continue always. The Bible is God's means of salvation, sanctification, and guidance, among many other great blessings. Without them, none of the elect would be saved. Francis Turretin elaborated:

> But if not even one tittle (or the smallest letter) could fail, how could several canonical books perish? [. . .] From the providence of God

---

14 In James T. Dennison Jr., ed., *Reformed Confessions of the 16th and 17th Centuries in English Translation* (Grand Rapids: Reformation Heritage Books, 2014), 4:520.

perpetually keeping watch for the safety of the church (which cannot be conceived to have allowed her to suffer so great a loss). Otherwise what would become of the wisdom and goodness and power of God if he had willed that such a precious treasure should be shown to his church and then taken away; and that the body of Scripture should exist at this day mutilated and defective?[15]

Some Calvinists have applied this principle to textual criticism to defend the Masoretic Hebrew Old Testament and the Majority Greek New Testament or the *Textus Receptus*. This was the position of John Owen,[16] Robert Lewis Dabney,[17] Edward F. Hills,[18] Jakob Van Bruggen,[19] and others. On the other hand, B. B. Warfield accepted providential preservation but held to an eclectic critical text of the Greek New Testament.[20] Interest in the Majority Greek Text has been growing in Reformed circles in recent decades.

Conclusion

These are just a few areas in which Reformed theology has taken the lead among evangelicals. Some Calvinists are not aware of these areas, or they have offered alternative options. But we would do well to learn from our wise and godly theological forefathers who held to a high view of Holy Scripture.

---

15 Francis Turretin, *The Institutes of Elenctic Theology* (Phillipsburg, NJ: P&R, 1992), 1:96.

16 Owen, *The Works of John Owen*, 16:296–421.

17 Robert Lewis Dabney, *Discussions* (Harrisonburg: Sprinkle, 1982), 1:350–98.

18 Edward F. Hills, *The King James Version Defended* (Des Moines, IA: Christian Research Press, 1956).

19 Jakob Van Bruggen, *The Ancient Text of the New Testament* (Winnipeg: Premier Publishing, 1976).

20 B. B. Warfield, *An Introduction to the Textual Criticism of the New Testament* (London: Hodder & Stoughton, 1907).

Chapter 64
The Two Natures of Christ

All evangelicals have always held to the full deity and humanity of Christ — two natures in one person. Historic Calvinists and Lutherans have believed in both truths but have differed with each other on how they are related in the one person. In this chapter we will look at these and a few other related points.

Very God and Very Man

The Bible explicitly calls Jesus "God" (Isaiah 9:6; John 1:1; 20:28; Romans 9:5; 1 Timothy 3:16; Titus 2:13; Hebrews 1:8). He Himself claimed to be the great "I Am" (John 8:24, 58). There are many other proofs that Jesus Christ was and is fully God.[1]

The Bible also says that He is "Man" (Isaiah 53:3; John 8:40; 19:5; Acts 2:22; 17:31; Romans 5:15–19; 1 Timothy 2:5). He had a human body and a human soul. The only way in which His humanity was different from ours is that He had no sin. He was the only permanently sinless man who ever lived.

Some verses speak of both His deity and humanity (Romans 1:3–4; 9:5; 1 Timothy 3:16). He is the *theanthropos*, the God-man. He is not half God and half man but fully God and fully man. He was first God, to be sure, but took on a human nature in the Incarnation (John 1:1, 14). He did not cease to be God when He became a man, nor did He cease to be a man when He returned to Heaven. He received a human nature from his mother Mary but did not receive a divine nature from God the Father, for He had already been eternally God. He was born of a virgin (Matthew 1; Luke 1). He had a heavenly Father and an

---

1 In addition to the standard Reformed systematic theologies, good Reformed defenses of the deity of Christ include the following: Stephen Wellum, *God the Son Incarnate: The Doctrine of Christ* (Wheaton: Crossway, 2016); Robert Reymond, *Jesus, Divine Messiah* (Fearn: Mentor/Christian Focus, 2003); Benjamin Breckinridge Warfield, *The Lord of Glory* (New York: American Tract Society, 1907), often reprinted by various publishers; Christopher W. Morgan and Robert A. Peterson, eds., *The Deity of Christ* (Wheaton: Crossway, 2001); Daniel R. Hyde, *God with Us* (Grand Rapids: Reformation Heritage Books, 2007); Stuart Olyott, *Jesus is Both God and Man* (Darlington: Evangelical Press, 2000). I hope to publish a short book soon presenting one hundred biblical proofs of the deity of Christ.

earthly mother, not a heavenly mother or an earthly father. He was as old as His Father and older than His mother.

This union of the two natures in one person is called the *hypostatic union*. It is totally unique, for this was the only time God became a man, and the only man that was God. He was not a man who became a god, as Mormonism teaches, but He was God who became the God-man. He is unique. Contrary to some heretical notions, Christians do not become little gods when they are born again. Only Jesus Christ will ever be the God-man.

Reformed theology says that the hypostatic union is the second greatest of all theological mysteries. It is second only to the mystery of the Trinity. Note how they overlap. In the one, God has three persons in one divine nature, while in the other, Christ has two natures in one person. We cannot fully understand either mystery, but there are some things that the Bible says about them. The classic statement on the hypostatic union is the Chalcedonian Formula, also known as the Creed of Chalcedon. The heart of this great statement is as follows:

> Perfect in Deity and Perfect in Humanity, truly God and truly Man, of a rational soul and body, consubstantial with the Father according to His Deity, consubstantial with us according to His Humanity [. . .] to be acknowledged in two natures without confusion or change, without division or separation, the difference of the natures being by no means removed by the union, but rather the property of each nature being preserved and concurring in one Person and one subsistence not parted or divided into two persons.

Evangelical believers defended both the Trinity and hypostatic union in the great debates of the early church. Augustine wrote what has been the most influential book ever written on the Trinity but also offered profound insights on the hypostatic union that have affected both Catholic and Protestant churches ever since. For example, he made the following statements:

> "The Lord Jesus, who is the wisdom of God, was both in his mother's womb and in heaven."[2]

> "And thus by reason of the distance between the divinity and human weakness, the Son of God remained in heaven, and the Son of Man lived on earth."[3]

---

2 Augustine, *The Works of Saint Augustine* (Hyde Park: New City, 2008), I/12:56.
3 Augustine, I/12:69.

"Behold, He was here, and was also in heaven; was here in the flesh, in heaven by His divinity; yea, everywhere by His divinity."[4]

"When He chose to be in the form of a servant, and lower than the angels, that He might be our Mediator, He remained higher than the angels, in the form of God — Himself at once the way of life on Earth and life itself in Heaven."[5]

No Calvinist could have expressed it better.

The Historic Lutheran Position

The historic Lutheran doctrine was officially formulated in credal form in the Formula of Concord and was discussed most fully in Martin Chemnitz's massive volume *The Two Natures of Christ*. This position quickly became a point of difference not only with Rome but with the Swiss, French, and German Reformed churches and then with the Dutch, English, and Scottish Calvinists. When some moderate Lutherans expressed slight sympathy for the Reformed position — or were suspected to be sympathetic — they were branded as "Crypto-Calvinists." The Lutherans sometimes debated among themselves, but the majority opinion won out and is still the official position to this day in traditional Lutheran churches.

Basically, the position says that in the Incarnation, certain divine attributes were communicated or infused into the human nature of Christ. His humanity was deified or divinized to some extent. The Lutherans debated to what extent this communication of attributes was affected. Not all the divine attributes were communicated — for example, spirituality, for Christ's body remained physical — but omnipresence, omniscience, and omnipotence were transmuted in such a way that the human nature of Christ is everywhere, knows everything, and can do anything. Catholics and Calvinists accused them of contradicting Scripture and the Chalcedonian formula by advocating a kind of *Eutychianism*. That is, they seemed to teach a fusion of the two natures to produce third hybrid, something like how parents produce a baby through procreation.

The classic Lutheran illustration is of an iron rod placed in a fire. Heat is communicated to the iron, but the iron remains iron and the heat remains heat. This is alleged to reflect the inter-trinitarian relationships of the three divine

---

4 In Philip Schaff, ed., *A Select Library of the Nicene and Post-Nicene Fathers of the Christian Church*, First Series (Grand Rapids: Eerdmans, 1978), 7:84.
5 Schaff, 2:174.

persons known as *perichoresis* or *interpenetration*, in which each of the three is "in" the other two but keeps His own distinctive personality.

The communication is seen to be one way from the divine to the human. No Lutheran, to my knowledge, has suggested that any of Christ's human attributes were transfused into His divine nature. This does, however, have bearing on the question of divine simplicity and especially divine impassibility. Were they also communicated?

What is of special interest to the Lutherans is the communication of divine omnipresence, or what they generally call *ubiquity*. Thus, Christ is said to be everywhere in His humanity and not just in His deity, else the two natures are separated. There is no place in the universe where His deity is present that His humanity is not, they argue. Their formula is, "The Logos is not beyond the flesh" (*Logos non extra carnem*). The humanity of Christ was expanded to match His deity, not His deity shrunk to be compressed into a finite humanity. This includes His physical body as well as His soul. Stressing such verses as Colossians 2:9 and Ephesians 1:23 and 4:10, they teach that Christ's body is literally everywhere.

This communication of properties is said to have occurred instantaneously in the miracle of the Incarnation, though some seemed to have put it in the glorification of the resurrection or Ascension. Christ veiled His deity for thirty-three years and did not make full use of His deified humanity. Later extreme Lutherans developed the heterodox theory of the Kenosis of Christ, in which He did not make any use of His deity but left it in Heaven. But the mainstream view is that Christ never acted as just man or God but as both through the hypostatic union.

The main reason for this position is to validate their distinct view of the Lord's Supper. Lutheranism rejects the Catholic idea of transubstantiation — that is, the bread and wine literally become the physical body and blood of Christ. Instead, they teach *consubstantiation*. The elements do not change, but the Mystical Presence of Christ is in, with, and under the elements. This presence includes both natures. Consequently, Christ must have an omnipresent humanity to be present at Communions around the world at the same time. One could call this *consubstantial ubiquitarianism*.

The Reformed View

God became a man to save sinners (1 Timothy 1:15). The infinite God demanded satisfaction from man by suffering and death. God is impassible and immortal, so God became a man to suffer and die and provide satisfaction. The Confession of Faith used in the English Congregation at Geneva (1556) put it like this: "Inasmuch as He, being only God, could not feel death, neither being only man, could overcome death, He joined both together, and allowed His humanity to be punished with most cruel death."[6] This unites the Incarnation and the atonement. Calvinists say that Christ suffered and died in His humanity, not His deity, and that His one person was made a curse for His people (Galatians 3:13). Therefore Jesus Christ was fully God and fully man.

We hold that Christ took on a second nature without any co-mingling of deity and humanity. The Incarnation did not produce a hybrid or anything like a child conceived by two parents. The divine attributes were not communicated to Christ's humanity, but the attributes of His deity and humanity resided in His person. His humanity was no more deified than His deity was humanized. His humanity was glorified in the resurrection, to be sure. But that will happen in resurrected Christians as well (Philippians 3:21). We will not become divine. To say His humanity was deified implies that the humanity of Christians will also be deified.

Yet we confess that the *person* of Christ was omniscient, omnipotent, and omnipresent. The Westminster Confession summarizes our position well: "So that the two whole, perfect and distinct natures, the Godhead and the manhood, were inseparably joined together in one person, without conversion, composition or confusion" (8:2). The Second Helvetic Confession: "These are bound and united with one another in such a way that they are not absorbed, or confused, or mixed, but are united or joined together in one person — the properties of the natures being unimpaired and permanent" (Ch. 11). The French Confession of 1559 specifically counters Lutheranism: "The human nature remains finite, having its form, measure and property."[7]

Calvin was very young when Luther was old, and he often presented the Reformed view in his writings. For example: "We affirm his divinity so joined and united with his humanity that each retains its distinctive nature unimpaired, and yet these two natures constitute one Christ."[8] Answering Lutheran critics, he said,

---

6 In Arthur C. Cochrane, ed., *Reformed Confessions of the Sixteenth Century* (Philadelphia: Westminster, 1966), 132.

7 In James T. Dennison Jr., ed., *Reformed Confessions of the 16th and 17th Centuries in English Translation* (Grand Rapids: Reformation Heritage Books, 2010), 2:146.

8 John Calvin, *Institutes of the Christian Religion* (Philadelphia: Westminster, 1960), 2:14:1 (p. 482).

> Thus it does not follow that, if the divinity of Christ is infinite, hence his body must be also. In speaking thus, we do not divide Jesus Christ, but only distinguish the properties of his two natures which are entire in him, as without dividing a man one may point to the differences between soul and body.[9]

Calvin rightly contended that if the Incarnation necessitated that the divine qualities were infused into His humanity, then human qualities such as physicality and passibility could be transfused into His deity. But that could never be, for God would no longer be God.[10] The incommunicable attributes of God are not even communicated to the holy and sinless humanity of Christ.

There are no perfect parallels, but some have been suggested. One is Calvin's analogy referred to above: soul and body. But they are separated at death, while Christ's deity and humanity were never separated, even at the cross, as the Belgic Confession states (Article 19). Another weak analogy is the two natures in a Christian — sin and grace. But that too is inadequate. To be precise, those are properties, not natures. Once we were totally infected by sin, presently there is a combination of the two, and one day there will only be grace and holiness.

The perichoresis of the Trinity has bearing on the hypostatic union. There is only one divine nature, and the three persons are forever united but distinct. When it is said that they are each "in" the other, it cannot legitimately be said that the distinct qualities of each is transferred to the other. If the Lutheran idea were correct, one might logically suppose the first person's distinct Fatherhood is transferred into the Son, which if carried out throughout the Trinity would erase the distinctive qualities of each person, leaving a Modalist non-Trinity. The trinitarian perichoresis is a deep mystery but must not be misunderstood so as to minimize or eliminate the three distinctive personalities. Nor does the shared divine nature minimize the distinctiveness of the persons. Neo-Orthodox speculation in this area is sometimes too speculative and unhealthy.

The *Extra Calvinisticum*

The early Lutherans gave a name to the Reformed position: The *Extra Calvinisticum*, or "The Calvinistic Extra." Richard Muller explains: "The Reformed argued that the Word is fully united to but never contained within the human nature and therefore, even in incarnation, is to be conceived as being

---

9 John Calvin, *Calvin: Theological Treatises* (Philadelphia: Westminster, 1954), 43.

10 John Calvin, *Commentaries on the Book of the Prophet Jeremiah and Lamentations* (Grand Rapids: Eerdmans, 1950), 1:xviii–xx. On why God became a man, see *Institutes*, 1:2:12 (pp. 464–74).

beyond or outside of (*extra*) the human nature."[11] As the Heidelberg Catechism puts it: "Since divinity is incomprehensible and everywhere present, it must follow that the divinity is indeed beyond the bounds of the humanity which it has assumed, and is nonetheless even in that humanity as well, and remains personally united to it" (Q. 48).

In contrast to the Lutheran formula, the Reformed formula is: "The finite is incapable of the infinite" (*Finitum non capax infinitum*). Human nature — both soul and body — is by definition and nature finite and therefore not omnipresent, even in the hypostatic union of Christ. Hebrews 2:14 says He took on the same humanity as we have. Is our present or future humanity infinite? Likewise, it is not eternal or immutable or possessive of other incommunicable divine attributes. As Spurgeon said in another context, "You cannot put the ocean into a teacup."[12] The sea fills the cup, and the cup is in the sea, but far more is outside the cup than is in it. To use another analogy, a man's hand fills his glove, but there is far more of the man outside (*extra*) the glove. It is like God filling the whole universe, but also overflowing it (1 Kings 8:27). Calvin put it like this:

> For even if the Word in his immeasurable essence united with the nature of man into one person, we do not imagine that he was confined therein. Here is something marvelous: the Son of God descended from heaven in such a way that, without leaving heaven, he willed to be borne in the virgin's womb, to go about the earth, and to hang upon the cross; yet he continuously filled the world even as he had done from the beginning.[13]

Calvin was obviously strongly influenced by Augustine in these sentiments, as seen from the quotes by Augustine at the beginning of this chapter. It is curious that Martin Luther, a converted Augustinian monk, departed from the African Bishop on such a point. Zwingli said, "What is infinite is also eternal. Christ's humanity is not eternal; therefore it is not infinite."[14] God fills all time, but is not limited to or contained within chronological time (this provides the model for other Reformed perspectives on theological issues relating to eternity). The same could be said about the logical necessity of the other divine attributes. If Christ's humanity was made omnipresent, then it follows

---

11 Richard Muller, *Dictionary of Latin and Greek Theological Terms, Drawn Principally from Protestant Scholastic Theology,* 2nd ed. (Grand Rapids: Baker Academic, 2017), 116.

12 Charles H. Spurgeon, *Commenting and Commentaries* (London: Banner of Truth, 1969), 43.

13 Calvin, *Institutes,* 2:13:4 (p.481).

14 In Dennison Jr., ed., *Reformed Confessions of the 16th and 17th Centuries in English Translation,* 1:188. See also pages 126–28.

it must have also been made omniscient and omnipotent. But we read in the Gospels that Christ was not omniscient nor omnipotent in His humanity. If it is argued that He was given immortality, then the Lutheran trips over his own beard. If Christ was made immortal at the Incarnation, how could He die at Calvary? Also, Christians will also be granted immortality in the resurrection (1 Corinthians 15), which proves that immortality is a communicable attribute, not an incommunicable attribute like omnipresence. We will not be everywhere in our glorified body nor know everything nor be able to do everything.

While He was on earth in His humanity, Christ was still present in Heaven in His deity. Most Greek manuscripts and English translations read John 3:13 as follows: "No one has ascended to heaven but He who came down from heaven, that is, the Son of Man who is in heaven" (so the KJV, NKJV; cf. the ASV, NEB, and others). Some Calvinists also appeal to John 1:18: "The only begotten Son, who is in the bosom of the Father, He has declared Him." Others take both verses to refer to Christ's post-Ascension session in Heaven.

Christ is indeed omnipresent (Matthew 18:20; 28:20), but that is in His deity and not His humanity. That His humanity was not omnipresent before and after His resurrection can easily be proved. The angel said, "He is not here" (Matthew 28:6; Mark 16:6). He was not with Mary and Joseph but was in the temple (Luke 2:43, 46). He said, "The poor you have with you always, but you do not have Me always" (John 12:8; Matthew 26:11), and "I leave the world and go to the Father" (John 16:28; see 16:7 and 17:11). Jesus walked. He moved from one place to another. Therefore, He was not everywhere in His humanity.

What about Colossians 2:9 — "For in Him dwells all the fullness of the Godhead bodily" — a text often cited by our Lutheran brethren? In addition to teaching Christ's full deity, it tells us that His deity was united with His body and not just His soul. The word *fullness* should not be taken to mean all infinite deity, otherwise why not say that all the deity and personality of the Father and the Spirit were present in His body and soul? An extreme distortion of incarnational perichoresis could lead to the Barthian Christomonism or even Sabellianism. If taken to such extremes, one would have to say that the Father died on the cross (*patripassionism*) or even that the Spirit died there (*pneumatipassionism*). But it was Christ alone who was incarnated and died.

Lutherans also appeal to Ephesians 1:23: "the fullness of Him who fills all in all" and 4:10: "that He might fill all things." Calvinists say that these texts refer to filling all Christians or to His deity.

Christ was omniscient in His deity (John 21:17) but not in His humanity (Mark 13:32; Luke 2:40, 52). He is omnipotent in His deity (Matthew 28:18) but not in His humanity, for He became tired. We shall be like Him in glorified immortality and holiness (1 John 3:2) but will not be divine.

Perhaps another parallel could be seen in the paradox of divine sovereignty and human responsibility. Both are true, but divine sovereignty precedes and governs human responsibility, not vice versa. Christ's deity preceded and governed His humanity so as not to destroy or deny it. Hyper-Calvinism seriously weakens human responsibility by overemphasizing divine sovereignty, which could almost lead to a docetic view of Christ's humanity.

Caspar Olevianus argued that Satan always attacks both natures of Christ. In propounding the Lutheran view, the Devil diminishes Christ's true humanity and almost makes it a ghost, which undermines the physical resurrection. It also undermines the virgin birth (for He was in only one womb), the atonement (for He died in only one place), His burial (for He was buried only in Joseph's grave), and the Ascension (for He is up there and not down here in His humanity).[15]

Christ's two natures are distinguishable but not divisible. Calvin echoed Chalcedon: "It is no more permissible to co-mingle the two natures in Christ than to pull them apart."[16] Quite so. Lastly, one could speculate whether the Holy Spirit was the glue that united Christ's two natures via the virgin birth (Luke 1:35), even as He is the mutual binding love between the Father and the Son. Augustinian discussion on this point would prove fascinating.

The Ascension

The question has obvious bearing on Christ's Ascension. Forty days after He rose from the dead, He went back to Heaven to sit at the Father's right hand (Mark 16:19; Luke 24:51; Acts 1:9–11; Ephesians 4:8–9), just as He promised the apostles (John 16:28). He ascended in His human body and soul, not His deity which was already in Heaven and is still with us here on earth (Matthew 18:20; 28:20). Hebrews 8:4, which alone would refute Lutheran ubiquitarianism, says, "For if He were on earth, He would not be a priest." He ascended to Heaven to serve as our Great High Priest in His dual natures.

When He was on earth in His humanity, He was still in Heaven in His deity. Conversely, He is now in Heaven in His humanity but still on earth in

---

15 Caspar Olevianus, *A Firm Foundation* (Grand Rapids: Baker, 1995), 59–62.
16 Calvin, *Institutes*, 2:14:4 (p. 487).

His deity. He is not now here physically any more than He was in Heaven physically before the Ascension. Calvin appropriately quoted Augustine: "For one person is God and man, and both one Christ; everywhere, through the fact that he is God; in heaven, through the fact that he is man."[17] The Heidelberg Catechism: "As a man he is no longer on earth, but in his divinity, majesty, grace, and Spirit, he is never absent from us" (Q. 47).

This illustrates the *Extra Calvinisticum* in a fascinating way. After the Incarnation, there was something "extra" about Christ still in Heaven — His deity. After the Ascension, He is with us here in His deity, but there is something "extra" about Him that is not here — His humanity.

Calvinists have always given special attention to the heavenly "session" of Christ. He intercedes for us as the God-man (Hebrews 7:25). "But," a Lutheran may object, "does not Hebrews 4:16 say that we can draw near to Christ even now? That assumes He is near in both natures." We answer that we can touch the person of Christ, as it were, not His humanity that is in Heaven. Would the Lutherans say that we can touch His body, consubstantiation notwithstanding? Remember that Christ told Mary Magdalene to stop holding Him, for He had not yet ascended. This implies that after the Ascension we cannot hold His body. We touch His deity, for He is everywhere. Granted that there is still much mystery as to *where* Heaven is, but it certainly is not literally here on Earth.

Perhaps there may be another parallel. God is everywhere, but sinners are said to be separated from His gracious presence (Ephesians 2:12) and will continue so in eternal Hell (Matthew 7:23; 25:41). They will, however, suffer in the presence of the Lamb (Revelation 14:10–11). Scripture also speaks of the omnipresent God being in some places more than others, such as the Holy of Holies. Christ is everywhere in His deity but manifests Himself specially in His humanity that is localized in Heaven.

Where is Jesus? Christians reply, "In my heart," or "Among believers when they meet," or "Everywhere," or "In Heaven." These are all true in different respects. When Lutherans ask, "Where in the universe is Christ in His deity without His humanity?" the Calvinist replies, "He is everywhere in His deity without His humanity, except in that special place at the Father's right hand in Heaven."

Robert Murray M'Cheyne answered the popular Lutheran objection that

---

17 Calvin, *Institutes*, 4:17:28 (p. 1397).

we divide the two natures of Christ, thus leaving His humanity incapable of touching us now:

> His human nature is at the right hand of God upon the throne — a lamb as it had been slain. But His divine nature is unlimited, fills all worlds, and is present in every dwelling of every disciple in this world. His divine nature thus brings in continual information to His human heart of everything that is going on in the heart and history of His people; so that His human heart beats towards us just as if He were sitting by our side.[18]

Christ's heavenly session offers great comfort and encouragement to believers, as the Belgic Confession says, "For neither in heaven nor among the creatures on earth is there anyone who loves us more than Jesus Christ does" (Article 26).

Some Reformed Deviations

Before we conclude, it would be appropriate to mention a few minority opinions that deviate from the majority report. Early Arminians were often friendly toward Socinianism and its denial of Christ's full deity. This reflects their overemphasis on human responsibility and weakening of divine sovereignty. More than a few advocated the ancient error of subordinationism.

Over the centuries, when Calvinism began to wane in some places, forms of Socinianism came in usually after the ex-Calvinists became Arminian. Witness how so many post-Puritan English Presbyterians went Arian or post-Edwardsean New Englanders went Unitarian. Without painting with too broad a brush, we can point out that it would be possible to be Arminian on their five points and deny Christ's deity but impossible to deny Christ's full deity while holding to the five points of Calvinism. I am not familiar with any person, theologian, or church that holds to the doctrines of grace and rejects Christ's deity.

Joseph Hussey, the first Hyper-Calvinist, popularized an earlier error regarding the two natures of Christ called *Pre-Existerianism*. Isaac Watts and John Stevens also advocated it, and Thomas Goodwin and Arthur W. Pink taught a modified form of it. This unusual error contended that Christ was both God and man in eternity. Christ took on a human soul in the eternal covenant of redemption and later assumed a human body in the Incarnation. This novel theory obviously had implications for the Reformed view of the hypostatic

---

18 Andrew Bonar, *Memoir and Remains of Robert Murray M'Cheyne* (Edinburgh: Banner of Truth, 1978), 286.

union and the *Extra Calvinisticum*. I know of no one who holds this theory today. It would result in a two-stage hypostatic union.

In the eighteenth century, Thomas Ridgley of England taught the doctrines of grace, but advocated a theory of the divine Sonship of Christ which rejected the orthodox doctrine of eternal generation. He argued that Christ was eternally and fully God but was called "Son of God" only by virtue of the Incarnation. John MacArthur also once taught this but later retracted his opinion and came to hold the orthodox doctrine of eternal generation. J. Oliver Buswell also evidently held to Ridgley's opinion. It is a fine point, for none of these denied Christ's deity or humanity, but in rejecting eternal generation, they somewhat reworded the hypostatic union at some points.

Bruce Ware has proposed a new model of Christ's deity and relationship with the Father.[19] While professing to uphold the full deity of Christ, he has put forth what we might term *Reformed subordinationism*. He says this resolves the question of male-female roles within marriage. He proposes that Christ and the Father are equal in divine nature, but the person of Christ is subordinate to the person of the Father within the ontological and eternal Trinity. Thus, husbands and wives are equal in nature and value, but the wife is to be subordinate to the husband within marriage as Christ is to the Father within the Trinity. He specifically appeals to 1 Corinthians 11:3. The theory has not gained widespread acceptance in Reformed circles. For one thing, most Calvinists would be reluctant to accept any kind of subordination within the Trinity. All three persons are equal in person as well as in nature. Ware does not advocate full-blown subordinationism, which would posit that Jesus is somehow less divine than the Father by nature, but his theory could be construed as putting the key into the lock to open the door to subordinationism. His theory has something in common with his unusual theory of "Reformed Middle Knowledge," which also has not gained much acceptance in Calvinist circles.

We need not enter into debate with the various Neo-Orthodox post-Reformed theories. On the one hand, Karl Barth and others strongly defended the deity and humanity of Christ. Sometimes their discussions on the hypostatic union and trinitarian perichoresis are thought-provoking,[20] even if one does not accept all their speculations. But one can discern a tendency to novelty

---

19 Bruce A. Ware, *Father, Son, & Holy Spirit: Relationships, Roles, & Relevance* (Wheaton: Crossway, 2005).

20 E.g., Alan J. Torrance, *Persons in Communion: Trinitarian Description and Human Participation* (Edinburgh: T. and T. Clark, 1996).

in reacting against historical Reformed Christology, even while defending the full deity of Christ. One glaring example is the heretical theory of Edward Irving and Thomas F. Torrance. That error says that Christ assumed a fallen human nature but never actually sinned. Their attempts to say that this did not corrupt the hypostatic union are not convincing. How could anyone realistically suggest that Christ would dare unite His holy divine nature with an unholy human nature? It is one thing to say that Christ was metaphorically made sin (2 Corinthians 5:19) and a curse (Galatians 3:13) for us, but it is quite another thing to say that He possessed an ontological and personal union of deity and sin.

Conclusion

One day Christ will leave the Father's right hand and return to earth just as He had ascended so many centuries ago (Acts 1:11). This alone would disprove the Lutheran idea of ubiquity. If Christ is already everywhere in His humanity, what need is there for the Second Coming? The Lutheran idea of a secret and unmanifested ubiquitous humanity somewhat resembles the errors of extreme Preterism (that says Christ came literally in AD 70) and that of the Jehovah's Witnesses (who said He came literally in 1914 and is with us invisibly).

The Reformed view is that of the Apostles' Creed: "He ascended into heaven, and sitteth at the right hand of God the Father Almighty; from thence He shall come to judge the quick and the dead." Premillennial Calvinists say that His humanity will be limited to a specific place during the millennium on earth. In any case, the permanence of the hypostatic union means that Christ will remain the God-man forever and ever.

One last blessed thought is worth pondering. One wonderful part of the beatific vision will be that glorified saints will be able to see God through the God-man, including His human body and soul. He gave a foretaste of this on the Mount of Transfiguration. We will indeed see Him as He is (1 John 3:2), the glorious God-man. Calvinists and Lutherans will enjoy this glorious vision together.

Chapter 65
The Active and Passive Obedience of Christ

There is a fine point in theology regarding the link between atonement and justification. No evangelical believes we are justified by our own righteousness. Some who claim to be evangelical deny that we are justified by the imputed righteousness of Christ. Some evangelicals believe we are justified by only the imputed righteousness of the passive obedience of Christ. Most Calvinists have believed in justification by the double imputation of both the active and passive obedience of Christ, while most non-Calvinists do not. There are exceptions on both sides.

The *active obedience* of Christ refers to His entire life of holy obedience to the Father, while His *passive obedience* refers to His submission to die on the cross to make atonement. The terms are often misunderstood. Christ was *active* in all He did, and *passive* should not be taken to mean a nonchalant attitude. Some prefer the terms *preceptive* and *penal obedience*.

Survey of Reformed Views

Before the Reformation, almost all theologians taught that we are justified in the sense of being made righteous by the infusion of grace in infant baptism. The Christian must then develop this righteousness by the sacraments, good works, and suffering to make it to Heaven. This was especially taught in detail by medieval Catholic scholastics and their "merit theology" (condign merit, congruous merit, treasury of merits, etc.).

Martin Luther rejected this whole approach and rediscovered the true biblical doctrine. Though he still held to baptismal regeneration, he utterly denied that we have any merits or righteousness that put us right with God. All the merit is in Christ, not us. Moreover, Christ's righteousness is imputed to the believer legally and not infused into him for justification. He stressed that *to justify* means "to legally declare righteous" and not "to experientially make righteous." In this he disagreed with Augustine yet held to Augustine's controversial prayer that ignited the Pelagian controversy: "Give what you command and command what You will." God demands perfect righteousness to declare a sinner righteous, and He gives that righteousness to believers. The believer is simultaneously just and unjust — just in Christ and unjust in his own personal righteousness. Most Lutherans followed him in this position, though some such as Andreas Osiander believed in justification by both imputed and infused righteousness.

John Calvin basically accepted this view. Some recent critics have argued that Calvin did not accept the imputation of Christ's active obedience, when in fact he certainly did but did not elaborate it as much as later Reformed theologians. For example:

- "It behooved our Lord Jesus Christ to be subject to the law, to the intent that his obedience might now be imputed unto us, and God accept thereof as though we brought the like obedience of our own."[1]

- "He lived a life of perfect obedience on our behalf."[2]

- "Thus stripped of our own righteousness, we are clothed with Christ's righteousness."[3]

This became the majority Reformed position. The Belgic Confession said, "But Jesus Christ's imputing to us all His merits, and so many holy works which He has done for us and in our stead, is our righteousness" (Article 22). The Heidelberg Catechism: "What benefit do you receive from the holy conception and birth of Christ? That He is our Mediator, and that, in God's sight, He covers over with His innocence and perfect holiness the sinfulness in which I have been conceived" (Q. 36). The Westminster Confession says that God justifies us "by imputing the obedience and satisfaction of Christ unto them" (11:1). The Westminster Larger Catechism says we are justified "only for the perfect obedience and full satisfaction of Christ, by God imputed to them" (Q. 70). The Second London Baptist Confession of 1689 amplifies the Westminster Confession on this article: "Those whom God effectively calleth, he also freely justifieth, not by infusing righteousness into them [. . .] but by imputing Christ's active obedience unto the whole law, and passive obedience in his death for their whole and sole righteousness by faith" (11:1). Similar words are found in the Savoy Confession under the influence of John Owen. The Irish Articles,

---

1 John Calvin, *Sermons on Deuteronomy* (Edinburgh: Banner of Truth, 1987), 763.

2 John Calvin, *Sermons on Galatians* (Edinburgh: Banner of Truth, 1997), 144.

3 John Calvin, "Calvin's Catechism of 1538," chapter 16 in James T. Dennison Jr., ed., *Reformed Confessions of the 16th and 17th Centuries in English Translation* (Grand Rapids: Reformation Heritage Books, 2008), 1:422; see also p. 515.

mainly the work of James Ussher, states: "Christ is now the righteousness of all them that truly believe in him. He, for them, paid their ransom by his death. He, for them, fulfilled the law in his life."[4]

Some Calvinists such as Johannes Piscator accepted only the imputation of Christ's passive obedience — His death and not His life. He was followed by David Pareus the disciple of Zacharias Ursinus and later by Thomas Gataker and Richard Vines, two prominent members of the Westminster Assembly. Later Calvinists denied or dramatically reworded the covenant of works and tended to deny the imputation of Christ's active obedience. John Murray, on the other hand, greatly reworded the covenant of works with Adam but strongly defended double imputation.

The Socinians totally denied all imputed righteousness and proposed a radically different idea of justification. The Anabaptists showed some Socinian influence, as did some of the early Arminians. Some Arminians have believed in double imputation, but they are relatively few. Some accept single imputation, while others propose justification by infused righteousness or a combination of imputed and infused righteousness. This has been a frequent point of dispute between Arminianism and Calvinism, with historic Lutherans mostly in agreement with the latter. The so-called Antinomians of the seventeenth century strongly emphasized the imputation of Christ's active obedience, to a large extent under the influence of Luther. But they sometimes tended to weaken the infusion of righteousness, even when they denied it had any part in justification. Later the Neonomians such as Richard Baxter tried to unite Calvinism, Arminianism, Lutheranism, and even Catholicism in a heterodox theory. In the main they propounded a combination of imputed passive obedience together with infused righteousness and cooperative faith unto justification. This was vehemently denied by John Owen and others.

Later, most dispensationalists of a somewhat Amyraldian perspective have denied double imputation because they generally deny the existence of a covenant of works.[5] Late in the twentieth century the so-called New Perspective on Paul threw out the whole idea of imputation and radically redefined justification. Discarded was the old perspective of Luther and Calvin. Instead, there is no legally declarative justification by faith nor imputation of either Christ's active or passive obedience. Instead, we are made righteous by our "faithfulness" to

---

4 In Philip Schaff, ed., *The Creeds of Christendom* (Grand Rapids: Baker, 1966), 3:532.
5 Dispensationalists often reject the covenant of works because the term is not found in the Bible. Instead, they use the term *Dispensation of Innocence*, which is also not found in the Bible.

covenantal obligations. Traditional Calvinists have sometimes charged this error with Pharisaism, Pelagianism, and medieval merit theology.

To my knowledge, nobody has suggested that believers are justified by the imputation of Christ's active obedience without His passive obedience. The closest to this perhaps would be liberals who say that God accepts us for our godly life of imitating Christ. Even evangelical Arminians reject that. In the nineteenth century a tiny group of English Hyper-Calvinists taught *imputed sanctification*, which was evidently an echo of the old antinomian view of John Eaton and others. This error overreacted to the Arminian doctrine of justification by infused righteousness and came up with the novel notion of non-experiential sanctification. That is, we are sanctified only by the righteousness of Christ outside us, not inside us. Some in the more recent "free grace" movement popularized by Zane Hodges teach something akin to this. They deny that any perseverance in holiness is necessary as an evidence of justification. They seem to say that there are no necessary dramatic changes in regeneration. A believer has no infused righteousness in sanctification, only imputed righteousness in justification. Historic Calvinists have rejected all these options as dangerous if not heretical.

Romans 5:12–21

Paul draws a parallel between Adam and Christ in these verses. God put Adam under the covenant of works on behalf of all humanity. If he obeyed, he would be rewarded. If he failed, he would bring in sin and death for himself and all humanity. His sin is thus passed on to all men. We cannot get right with God by trying to keep the covenant of works (the law) in part or in whole.

Christ came to save us from that doom. He surpassed the first Adam, for He was the God-man. He fully obeyed the law and, in that sense, kept the covenant of works. He also took upon Himself the punishment for His people's breaking the law. His holy life and death provide the righteousness that God requires. God imputes both to believers and declares them righteous.

Note verse 19, "the obedience of one." Mainline Calvinists take this to include both His life of obedience to the law and of the specific obedience to the Father's command to die. In other words, it includes both His active and passive obedience, both of which are imputed to believers in justification. As Calvin put it: "It is true that the whole life of our Lord Jesus Christ has become our ransom, for the obedience which He yielded in this world to God his Father was to make amends for Adam's offence and for all the iniquities for which we are in debt."[6] He gave His whole life *for* us in redemption and gives it *to* us in justification.

Philippians 2 and 3

Philippians 2:6–8 says that the divine Christ became a man, humbled Himself, and was "obedient unto death." He obeyed the Father's command to come into the world and die as well as to live a holy life. The result is that He was raised and exalted as Lord (v. 11).

This has bearing on justification in a way often overlooked by commentators. Philippians 3:9 says, "Not having my own righteousness, which is from the law, but that which is through faith in Christ, the righteousness which is from God by faith." This is an allusion to Isaiah 53:11 in which our justification is based on Messiah's death. It is legitimate to link the obedient life and death of Christ in 2:6–8 with the imputed righteousness of 3:9. In other words, the righteousness that God bestows on believers includes Christ's whole obedient life unto death — or what we call His active and passive obedience.

The Covenant of Works and of the Law

God has always demanded perfect righteousness, for He is absolutely righteous and will not lower His standard for anyone. He required full obedience from Adam. Adam failed. The holiness of God then demanded his death. But God graciously forgave Adam by covering him with animal skins (Genesis 3:21). Those skins came from a sacrificial animal — probably a lamb. This typifies how the righteousness of Christ is imputed to believers to cover their sins in justification.

The *moral law* is the core of the covenant of works. Though it has been annulled as a means of salvation, it continues as a means of damnation. Without a life of perfect obedience to the law, we are doubly damned — damned in Adam (original sin) and in ourselves (actual sins). We owe God both our life and our death. This is one purpose of the law. If we could obey perfectly, we would live and be declared righteous. Leviticus 18:5: "You shall therefore keep My statutes and My judgments, which if a man does, he shall live by them." This is repeated in Nehemiah 9:29; Ezekiel 20:11, 13, and 21; and significantly in Romans 10:5. Jesus said in Matthew 19:17, "If you want to enter into life, keep the commandments." Also, "Do this and you will live" (Luke 10:28). Paul

---

6 John Calvin, *Sermons on the Epistle to the Ephesians* (London: Banner of Truth, 1973), 53.

repeated this principle in Romans 2:13: "For not the hearers of the law are just in the sight of God, but the doers of the law will be justified." But as he also said in Galatians 3:10–11, a person would have to obey every one of God's commandments for his entire life without exception (he quotes Deuteronomy 27:26 for proof; see also Deuteronomy 6:25). Romans 5 leaves us even worse off, for there Paul says that we inherit Adam's sin in our birth. We cannot even begin to live a life of obedience, for we are born sinful and damned. That is the utter plight of mankind.

No man except Jesus Christ has ever kept God's holy law perfectly. He is thereby a second or last Adam (Romans 5:14–19; 1 Corinthians 15:22, 45–49). Unlike the rest of us, He was born without original sin (Luke 1:35). He perfectly obeyed the entire law of God. As a Jew, He kept the ceremonial laws as well as the moral laws encapsulated in the Ten Commandments and the two love commandments. Here is where Reformed theology goes beyond most other theologies. We see that Christ not only obeyed the law for Himself but also for His people. Further, the glory of His grace is seen in His suffering the penalty for our sin as well. He had to both live and die for us to grant us justification. He had to fulfill both the demands and the penalties of the law for us — and He did. Thus, He grants both His holy life (active obedience) and death (passive obedience) to His people in justifying them. The covenant of works is fulfilled by Christ and thereby provides for the covenant of grace for believers.

Leviticus is that part of the law dealing with animal sacrifices. Those animals had to be without blemish. The book of Hebrews says that this typified the life and death of Christ. His perfect life was necessary for Him to die a perfect substitutionary death for us. His deity was also involved, not in dying (for deity is immortal) but in giving infinite value to His sacrifice. His holy deity also safeguarded His sinless humanity, otherwise He might have sinned. This is one reason why mainline Calvinists have believed in the impeccability of Christ and not merely His sinlessness. James Ussher pointed out that there are two aspects of Christ's active obedience. First, Christ had *original righteousness* rather than original sin. His very nature was impeccably pure, for He was God. Second, Christ had *actual righteousness* — a life of perfect obedience.[7]

Just as one cannot separate Christ's holy life from His holy death in atonement, so we cannot separate His life from His death in justification. What God has joined together, let us not put asunder. Just as we dare not separate His

---

7 James Ussher, *A Body of Divinity* (Birmingham: Solid Ground Christian Books, 2007), 155–56.

two natures in one person, we must not separate His imputed life and death in justification.

The Active Obedience of Christ

As a man, Christ obeyed the law and thereby merited what the law promised. But He did this for His people and not only for Himself, for He was a "public person." He was our legal covenantal representative, as Adam had been. Adam merited death for himself and his progeny; Christ merited life for Himself and His people. His holy life was therefore both vicarious and meritorious. William G. T. Shedd explained it:

> The chief function of Christ's obedience of the moral law is to earn a title for the believer to the rewards of heaven. This part of Christ's agency is necessary, because, merely to atone for past transgressions would not be a complete salvation. It would, indeed, save man from hell, but it would not introduce him into heaven. He would be delivered from the law's punishment, but would not be entitled to the law's reward.[8]

Theoretically Christ could have appeared on earth as a full-grown man like Adam and gone straight to the cross. But He did not. He humbled Himself to be incarnated as a tiny fertilized egg and fetus in Mary's womb and then go through all the stages of human development for thirty years (see Luke 2:40, 52). He obeyed the Father perfectly at every stage. If only His death was needed for atonement and justification, why was He not put to death in the womb?

Christ lived His whole life in "the shadow of the cross." Referring to Philippians 2:6–8, the Formula Consensus Helvetica said that "Christ's life was nothing but a continuous emptying of self, submission and humility. [. . .] Christ in our stead satisfied the law and justice by His most holy life" (Article 15). His whole life was one of self-denying atonement for us. Herman Bavinck: "The obedience of Christ accorded to the law, therefore, was totally voluntary. Not his death alone, as Anselm said, but his entire life was an act of self-denial, a self-offering presented by him as head in the place of his own."[9] His death was the culmination of His obedience, not the totality of it.

---

8 William G. T. Shedd, *Dogmatic Theology*, 3rd ed. (Phillipsburg, NJ: P&R, 2003), 721. Edwards said that it would be only a half redemption if Christ only bought deliverance from Hell. Full redemption means He purchased entrance to Heaven for us. "John 10:18 (Sermon 387)," Jonathan Edwards Center at Yale University, accessed February 9, 2018, http://edwards.yale.edu/.

9 Herman Bavinck, *Reformed Dogmatics* (Grand Rapids: Baker, 2006), 3:379.

In the eternal covenant of redemption, it was agreed that the Son would provide both a holy life and a holy death for the justification of God's elect. The law requires both our life and our death; Christ provided both. John Murray commented: "It is the active and passive obedience of Christ that is the price of their redemption, active and passive obedience because he was made under the law, fulfilling all the requirements of righteousness and met all the sanctions of justice."[10]

The Heidelberg Catechism indicates that Christ's whole life included suffering of a propitiatory nature: "That throughout his life on earth but especially at the end of it, he bore in body and soul the wrath of God against the sin of the whole human race" (Q. 37). His whole life was one of increasing suffering, from His birth, circumcision, and mockery of men to Gethsemane and Calvary.

Jonathan Edwards underscored this theme:

> All Christ's sufferings from his first incarnation were of a propitiatory nature, as every act of obedience from his first incarnation was meritorious. Indeed his last sufferings were his principal sufferings, and so 'tis by them principally that we have propitiation. So it was by his last act of obedience, viz., in yielding himself to death, that was as much his principal act of obedience, and so that which principally he merited heaven.[11]

Elsewhere he noted that Christ was active as priest and passive as sacrifice at the cross,[12] which is an amazing and profound observation.

Double Obedience and Justification

Christ both obeyed and died for us, and this dual obedience is imputed to us in justification. As there are two aspects of His obedience, there are two corresponding aspects of justification. First, Christ's death (passive obedience) provides for the forgiveness and removal of our sins. Second, His life (active obedience) provides a perfect righteousness in the place of our imperfect unrighteousness. All true evangelicals accept the first, but many overlook the second. To use a simple illustration, Christ's obedience is like a pencil. His

---

10 John Murray, *Redemption Accomplished and Applied* (Grand Rapids: Eerdmans, 1955), 51.
11 Jonathan Edwards, *The Works of Jonathan Edwards* (New Haven: Yale University Press, 2001), 19:514.
12 Jonathan Edwards, *Sermons on the Lord's Supper* (Orlando: The Northampton Press, 2007), 37.

passive obedience erases our sins, and His active obedience writes righteousness in the place of our sins.

This follows the "garment motif" in Scripture. God removed Adam's fig leaves and gave him animal skins (Genesis 3:21). Our sins are like filthy rags (Isaiah 64:6). God removes them and replaces them with the beautiful, seamless, holy robe of Christ's righteousness. Isaiah 61:10: "He has clothed me with the garments of salvation, He has covered me with the robe of righteousness." Zechariah 3:4–5 describes how God replaces filthy rags with a beautiful garment. Paul said in Galatians 3:27 that we "put on Christ." He uses a word that is often used of putting on clothing. We are to repent, that is, "put off" the filthy garments (Ephesians 4:22; Colossians 3:9). The KJV and NKJV of Romans 3:22 employees the Majority Text of Greek manuscripts in saying that the righteousness of God is given both "to" and "on" us. One could say that the dual obedience of Christ forms the warp and woof of the woven righteous robe. Thomas Watson: "This robe doth not only cover, but adorn: having on this robe we are reputed righteous, not only as angels, but as Christ, 2 Corinthians v. 21."[13] God forbade the Jews from wearing mixed-blended clothes (Deuteronomy 22:11). Likewise, God forbids us from attempting to be justified by a mixture of Christ's righteousness and our own. There is not a single thread in this exquisite garment that is our own. It is all Christ's.

Salvation is both positive and negative. God gives us what we do not deserve and withholds from us what we do deserve. Acts 26:18 says we receive both forgiveness (negative) and an inheritance (positive). Christ died to bring us both redemption and adoption (Galatians 4:4–5; see 3:13–14). His "reconciliation for iniquity" not only takes away our sin but brings in "everlasting righteousness" (Daniel 9:24). Romans 5:10 links Christ's life and death for our salvation: "For if when we were enemies we were reconciled to God through the death of His Son, much more, having been reconciled, we shall be saved by His life."

Reformed theology often argues that if only the passive obedience of Christ is imputed to us, then we would only be put back on the probationary status of Adam before the Fall. The Arminian rejection of the preservation of the saints resembles that weak promise. Louis Berkhof was right: "If Christ had suffered only the penalty imposed on man, those who shared in the fruits of His work would have been left exactly where Adam was before he fell. Christ merits more

---

13 Thomas Watson, *Discourses on Important and Interesting Subjects* (Ligonier, PA: Soli Deo Gloria, 1990), 1:613.

for sinners than the forgiveness of sins."[14] We are given more than what Adam lost: a perfect divine-human righteousness. Adam lost his own righteousness, but the elect will never lose the imputed righteousness of the Second Adam. In a debate at the Westminster Assembly in favor of the imputation of Christ's active obedience, Theodore Bathurst said, "Making righteousness is more than mere making innocent."[15] Justification is far more than being "just as if I had never sinned." It is "as if I had the very holiness of Jesus Christ."

The great nineteenth-century Scottish theologian James Buchanan rightly said that Piscator's view of single imputation "left a door open for the introduction of his own personal obedience, as the only ground of his future hope, after he had obtained the remission of his past sins."[16] The Neonomians were in danger of going through that door. It is insufficient that Christ's death only removed our sins, to be replaced with our own righteousness, even if it is by the infused righteousness of Christ. For one thing, infused righteousness is incomplete in this life. God will not accept an imperfect righteousness.

In his own eloquent way, Robert Murray M'Cheyne observed:

> I must not only wash in Christ's blood, but clothe me in Christ's obedience. For every sin of omission in self, I may find a divinely perfect obedience ready for me in Christ. For every sin of commission in self, I may find not only a stripe or a wound in Christ, but also a perfect rendering of the opposite obedience in my place, so that the law is magnified, its curse more than carried, its demand more than answered.[17]

M'Cheyne was one of the few to point out the relation between dual obedience of Christ and our dual sins of commission and omission.

To be sure, the order of salvation here is: regeneration → infused righteousness → gift of faith → justification. But this is crucial: the elect are not justified on the basis of what Christ does *in* us but rather *for* us. We are justified based on what Christ did for us two thousand years ago at Calvary, not based on what the Holy Spirit does in us today. Infused righteousness leads to gradual sanctification, not to instant justification. Failure to see this has tragic consequences.

---

14 Louis Berkhof, *Systematic Theology* (Grand Rapids: Eerdmans, 1988), 380.
15 Chad Van Dixhoorn, ed., *The Minutes and Papers of the Westminster Assembly, 1643–1652* (Oxford: Oxford University Press, 2012), 2:54.
16 James Buchanan, *The Doctrine of Justification* (Edinburgh: Banner of Truth, 1997), 175.
17 Andrew Bonar, *Memoir and Remains of Robert Murray M'Cheyne* (Edinburgh: Banner of Truth, 1978), 152.

There is another aspect of imputed righteousness that is rarely discussed. It has to do with the relationship between the two natures of Christ and justification — that is, between the hypostatic union and the dual obedience of Christ that is imputed to believers. Christ is both God and man. He died in His humanity, not His deity. Moreover, being man, He could be tempted, but being God, He could not sin. The two natures can be distinguished but never separated, not even in His atoning death. His life of obedience, then, was that of the divine-human who was impeccable and not merely sinless. He had positive holiness, not just negative sinlessness. And just as we cannot separate His active and passive obedience, neither can we separate His divine holiness from His sinless and impeccable humanity. This means that it is not just His sinless human obedience that is imputed to us but also His divine holiness. It was His divine holiness that guaranteed His virgin-born humanity would be impeccable and have infinite worth in the atonement. This adds a staggeringly glorious luster to His imputed righteousness. Has anyone ever plumbed the depths of how perfect this righteousness really is? It is not just that of a sinless life and substitutionary death of a mere man but that of the God-man. It is "the righteousness of God" (Romans 1:17).

Some Unusual Variations

There are three unusual variations that have been proposed from the periphery of the Reformed theological community, with varying degrees of error. The first has been popularized by Thomas F. Torrance and others. It is the *vicarious faith* theory. Alluding to Galatians 2:16 and 20, proponents argue that the Greek text reads "the faith of Jesus Christ" (*pisteos Iesou Christou*). Some refer to Mark 11:22 and render it "have the faith of God" (*echete pistin Theou*). They do not merely say that this means that faith is a gift from God. Rather, it is proposed that these texts mean that we are justified by Christ's faith, not ours. Some relate "the faith of God" to their understanding of Romans 1:17, "from God's faith (or faithfulness) to our faith." This sometimes leads to a universalism in which Christ believed for all men and not just the elect.

But most translations and commentators argue that the genitive should mean "in" referring to an object rather than "of" referring to the source. The context of these verses is not Christ or God believing for us but our believing in Christ and God (see 1 Peter 1:21; John 14:1). We are justified by believing *in* Christ, not by Christ believing *for* us.

The second unusual variation is *vicarious baptism*. Matthew 3:15 says that

Christ was baptized to "fulfill all righteousness." Verse 14 says Christ did not have to be baptized, for He had no sin from which to repent. He was, the theory says, baptized on our behalf. This almost resembles the Mormon heresy of vicarious baptism for the dead based on a wrong interpretation of 1 Corinthians 15:29. I once heard R. T. Kendall preach at Westminster Chapel that God requires us to be baptized, but Christ fulfilled that for us. Being a Baptist, Kendall was not denying the command to be baptized after conversion but seemed to imply that God requires baptism for salvation. Was Christ really baptized vicariously so we could be saved? Abraham Kuyper hinted at this in his curious statement, "That Christ's Baptism was not a mere form, but the fulfilling of all righteousness proves that he descended into the water burdened with our sins."[18] It would be better to say that Christ was baptized in the wrath of God for our sins at the cross than in the water of the River Jordan (Mark 10:38). The idea of vicarious baptism has not gained many adherents in the Reformed fold.

The third and most suspect error is *vicarious repentance*. A few of the so-called Calvinistic Antinomians of seventeenth-century England verged on this strange theory, but it was more explicitly taught by the controversial nineteenth-century Scot named John M'Leod Campbell. Thomas Torrance and others picked it up because they felt that Campbell was the most significant theologian between Calvin and Barth (!). Even the otherwise orthodox Arthur C. Custance held to a form of this view: "I think that when we are told that He bore our sins, we are to understand that He really in His own heart and mind became consciously guilty as though He had really committed those things."[19]

The theory turns on several points. First, Christ was baptized for us. Baptism requires repentance, therefore, Christ repented for us. Second, Christ was "made sin" (2 Corinthians 5:21) and "a curse" (Galatians 3:13) for us on the cross. Such suffering, it is alleged, somehow entailed the personal anguish of repentance. Perhaps the proponents of this view were thinking of how the high priest confessed the sins of the people onto the sacrificial lamb or how some of the prophets confessed in grief the sins of the people or even their ancestors. In the school of Torrance, the theory overlaps with the error taken from Edward Irving that Christ was born with a sinful nature, though He never committed actual sin. This vicarious repentance is supposed to be essential for His suffering and death to be acceptable to God for atonement.

---

18 Abraham Kuyper, *The Work of the Holy Spirit* (Grand Rapids: Eerdmans, 1969), 98.
19 Arthur C. Custance, *Two Men Called Adam* (Brockville, Ontario: Doorway Publications, 1983), 188. See also pp. 184–90.

Mainline Calvinists find this last theory to be unbiblical, repugnant, and perhaps even blasphemous. We agree that Christ lived and died for us and that His baptism was to fulfill all righteousness, even if it was not vicarious. But we then ask, "How in the world can a person repent in the place of another person if he did not personally participate in his sin?" Lutherans and others sometimes posit some kind of vicarious faith by a parent or godfather (which the Reformed rarely accept). And indeed, Christ did suffer enormous wrath from the Father. But did the dereliction of His anguish really mean that He repented of our sins? After all, our sins were legally imputed *onto* Him, not experimentally infused *into* Him. Such a misunderstanding led to various errors among the seventeenth-century Antinomians. Saving repentance includes a change of mind, contrite mourning for sin, and a resolute turning from sin. Christ experienced none of these, for His mind, heart, and direction were always toward God. Christ suffered for us (1 Peter 2:21) and prayed for us (1 John 2:2) as Mediator, but there is no hint that He repented for us. Rather, He died for us and calls on us to repent.

Conclusion

Several great hymns incorporate the wonderful truth of imputed righteousness:

> When He shall come with trumpet sound,
> O may I then in Him be found.
> Dressed in His righteousness alone,
> Faultless to stand before the throne.[20]

> Jesus thy blood and righteousness,
> My beauty are, my glorious dress.
> Mid flaming worlds, in these arrayed,
> With joy shall I lift up my head.[21]

> No condemnation now I dread.
> Jesus, and all in Him, is mine.
> Alive in Him, my living Head,
> And clothed in righteousness divine,
> Bold I approach the eternal throne
> And claim the crown, through Christ my own.[22]

---

20 Edward Mote, "The Solid Rock," ca. 1834.
21 Nicholas von Zinzendorf, "Jesus, Thy Blood and Righteousness," 1739.
22 Charles Wesley, "And Can It Be That I Should Gain?" *Psalms and Hymns*, 1738.

At the close of his life, J. Gresham Machen wrote these words to his friend John Murray: "Thank God for active obedience of Christ. No hope without it."[23] How true.

23 Ned. B. Stonehouse, *J. Gresham Machen: A Biographical Memoir* (Edinburgh: Banner of Truth, 1977), 508.

Chapter 66
The Law

When one reads the Bible through for the first or the hundredth time, he is made aware of the prominent place of the holy law of God. Reformed theology has always had a high view of God's law because of its high view of the holiness and sovereignty of God. A brief survey of the historical and theological landscape is in order, with special attention to certain salient points.

The Reformation Debate

All branches of the Protestant Reformation believed in the law of God, with varying emphases. Luther and the Lutherans emphasized the law as a means of conviction of sin and preparation for conversion. They accepted the law as useful for Christians — after all, Luther's catechisms discussed the Ten Commandments. But they feared that too much stress on the law could lead to works-righteousness that would threaten the doctrine of justification by faith alone. Yet the early Lutherans also opposed Johann Agricola's low view of the law. It is probable that Luther himself coined the word *antinomian* to oppose Agricola's views. Gradually historical Lutheranism tended to see law and gospel as contradictory, while the Reformed see them as complementary.[1]

There are indications that the Anabaptists — perhaps because of their "spiritualist" emphasis — tended to downplay the law in favor of a more mystical approach to ethics. This does not mean they approved of licentious living, for in some areas they were overly strict. The historical Roman Catholic view of the law was seen by the Protestants as being somewhat pharisaic — too legalistic, ethical loopholes allowed (especially among the Jesuits), works of the law being essential to be saved, and the like. The Reformed, then, saw themselves between the Scylla of a lesser view of the law and the Charybdis of Catholicism's legalistic view.

Theonomy

Though there were some precursors, the *theonomy* movement began in the 1960s

---

1 The best summary of the historic Lutheran doctrine is still *The Proper Distinction Between Law and Gospel* by C. F. W. Walther. (St. Louis: Concordia, often reprinted).

with Rousas John Rushdoony.[2] His large volume *The Institutes of Biblical Law*[3] is considered the primary handbook of the movement. His son-in-law Gary North was another controversial writer. The third member of the theonomic triumvirate was Greg Bahnsen. His book *Theonomy in Christian Ethics*[4] is the fullest defense of theonomy, "the Law of God." Lesser theonomists have included James Jordan, Ray Sutton, David Chilton, and Kenneth Gentry. The movement reached its high point around 1990 and has since diminished considerably. Gary DeMar, Joseph Morecraft, and Mark Rushdoony are the current leaders. It has never been a large movement and has thrived mainly on the outskirts of conservative American Presbyterianism.

The key doctrine of theonomy is that the law of God has never and can never change. It is still applicable in all areas of life and society. They appeal especially to Matthew 5:17–19. But they are on the horns of a dilemma. If the law has not changed *at all*, why do we not have animal sacrifices and other ceremonies that the New Testament says have passed away? More problematic and controversial is the theonomic argument that the Old Testament judicial laws are still valid today for Gentile nations. Some theonomists even say that the kosher food laws and the Jubilee year are valid for today. Some seem to call for a theonomic theocracy. Opponents sometimes have accused the movement of Pharisaism — legalism on some things, yet antinomian on others (such as defending lying, Jacob cheating Esau, loopholes for divorce, etc.). Some theonomists frequently scorn Pietism and devotional experimentalism as emotional sentimentalism. The doctrine of theonomy is one of the three pillars of Christian Reconstruction: theonomy, postmillennialism, and presuppositional apologetics. The leaders are usually supralapsarian and sometimes border on Hyper-Calvinism.[5]

Some in the movement, such as James Jordan, became increasingly sacramental and liturgical. Others developed the controversial *Federal Vision*

---

2 An informative critique by an outsider is *Christian Reconstruction: R. J. Rushdoony and American Religious Conservation* by Michael J. McVicar (Chapel Hill: University of North Carolina Press, 2015). The faculty of Westminster Theological Seminary gave a generally negative response to the movement in *Theonomy: A Reformed Critique*, ed. by William S. Barker and W. Robert Godfrey (Grand Rapids: Zondervan/Academic Books, 1990).

3 R. J. Rushdoony, *The Institutes of Biblical Law* (Philadelphia: Presbyterian and Reformed, 1973).

4 Greg Bahnsen, *Theonomy in Christian Ethics*, 2nd ed. (Phillipsburg, NJ: Presbyterian and Reformed, 1984).

5 For example, Rushdoony scorned the idea of a "well-meant offer of the Gospel," not so much because of predestination but because God only commands, not offers. *The Roots of Reconstruction* (Vallecito, CA: Rose House Books, 1991), 18–19.

(Steve Wilkins, Steve Schlissel, Peter Leithart, Douglas Wilson, Rich Lusk). Some have been influenced by Norman Shepherd, who was ousted from Westminster Theological Seminary because of his controversial views on the place of works in justification. To give the movement its due, the main writers have often offered profound insight on subjects nobody else would discuss. But in the end, the movement was considered too legalistic by most mainstream Calvinists.

The Opposite Tendency

The opposite tendency goes back to Agricola and the Anabaptists. The so-called Antinomians of the 1630s American colonies (especially Mrs. Anne Hutchinson) and 1640s England (John Eaton, Tobias Crisp, William Dell, John Saltmarsh) did not actually deny the law so much as minimize it. Later William Huntington and the Gospel Standard Baptists (William Gadsby, Joseph Charles Philpot) taught a Hyper-Calvinistic form of doctrinal antinomianism. To them, the gospel and not the law is the standard for Christians. But they have abhorred antinomianism in practice and generally live very godly lives.

Very few traditional Calvinists have accepted dispensationalism, and one reason is its low view of the law.[6] It tends to say that the law has been abolished, and only those laws that are repeated in the New Testament are still valid today. The general Reformed view is that Old Testament laws continue unless abolished in the New Testament. John Gerstner[7] and the theonomists charged dispensationalism with being inherently antinomian in theory and opening the door to practical antinomianism. For instance, it was dispensationalism and not Calvinism that gave rise to the "non-Lordship theology" of Charles C. Ryrie and Zane Hodges, also known as the "free grace movement." This viewpoint says that a sinner need not submit to Christ as Lord or repent of sin to become a Christian, for that would be to bring in works-righteousness. Sometimes dispensationalists seem to imply that the old covenant was all law and no grace, and the new covenant is all grace and no law. To bring the law in to the new would be the Galatian heresy of mingling law and grace. There are some notable exceptions, of course. John MacArthur, for one, is a traditional dispensationalist who strongly affirms Lordship salvation and holds to a generally Reformed view of the law.

---

6 A useful short summary of the dispensational view of the law is Alva J. McClain, *Law and Grace* (Chicago: Moody Press, 1967).

7 John Gerstner, *Wrongly Dividing the Word of Truth* (Morgan, PA: Soli Deo Gloria, 2000).

The New Covenant branch of Reformed Baptists holds to a view of the law similar to dispensationalism without its eschatology and non-Lordship views. Among its leaders are Jon Zens, John Reisinger, and Fred Zaspel. D. A. Carson has had much influence in this small movement as well.

Overall, the theonomists and others above are in general agreement on the basic distinctives of Reformed theology on most points. Mainstream Calvinists steer a center course between theonomists on the one hand and those who hold to a lesser view of the law on the other.

The Reformed View

The mainline Reformed position can be gleaned from the leading Calvinist confessions and theologians, many of which have detailed expositions of the Ten Commandments. Here are some of its main features.

First, the law has three divisions. The moral law is revealed in creation and conscience and is summed up in the Ten Commandments and the two love commands. It is binding on all people everywhere at all times. It is the essence of the covenant of works: "Do this and you will live" (Luke 10:28). It never changes because it is founded directly on the unchanging holy nature of God.

Second, the ceremonial law includes certain ceremonies which are primarily symbolic and typological in nature, such as animal sacrifices, food laws, certain holy days, and circumcision. They were never binding on Gentiles and were abolished when Christ came. They have been replaced by the two simple ordinances of baptism and the Lord's Supper.

The third division is the civil law, such as the case laws of Exodus 21–23. Most of these have been abolished because they primarily pertained to Israel as a unique and temporary theocracy. Some of the civil laws, such as capital punishment, continue because they are based directly on moral laws. The Westminster Confession says that the "general equity" of the civil law continues but not the entire body of it (19:4).

Next, mainline Calvinism says there are three main uses of the law, primarily the moral law. The first use is to restrain sin in society. This overlaps with the binding laws of the third division. Civil governments can and should enforce laws against theft, murder, vice, and other sins which are crimes. This works closely with common grace and should restrain sin and promote peace and righteousness in society.

The second use is that the law convicts of sin to lead a sinner to Christ by showing him his need of a Savior (Galatians 3:24). This use somewhat reflects the historical giving of the law at Sinai before the coming of Christ. It tells us what sin is (Romans 3:20; 1 John 3:4). Christ directed the rich young ruler to the law in this respect (Mark 10:19). The Holy Spirit uses the law to convict of sin (John 16:7–11; James 2:9) and shuts all mouths (Romans 3:19). The Puritans called this a *law work*, not to be confused with a work of the law. Once a sinner is converted, the main purpose of this use is fulfilled. Some say that a secondary application of this use is to touch the conscience of a sinning Christian to urge him to repent back to Christ.

The third use of the law is to instruct the Christian in how to obey his heavenly Father. It reveals the will of God for our sanctification (1 Thessalonians 4:3) and tells us how we may express our loving gratitude to God for saving us. This use has been minimized by Lutherans and the above-mentioned Calvinists.

Two Specific Laws

There are two laws in particular that historic Calvinists have given special attention to more than our non-Reformed brethren. The first is the Sabbath. It is included in the abiding moral law summed up in the Ten Commandments and is based on the creation ordinance of Genesis 2:3. Certain aspects were only for Israel, such as the feasts and Jubilee (Colossians 2:16–17), but the one-in-seven-day principle continues for Christian and non-Christian alike (Revelation 1:10; 1 Corinthians 16:2). Christ changed the day from the last to the first day of the week to commemorate His resurrection. The Old Testament emphasized "Do not work." The New Testament emphasizes "Do worship." These two are complementary, not contradictory.

Unfortunately, there are ditches on both sides of the road on God's law (Deuteronomy 5:32), including the Sabbath. On the one hand, some Calvinists have become legalistic regarding various activities on the Lord's Day. For example, some overly zealous believers will not take walks or eat cooked meals on Sunday. On the other hand, others have become far too loose, even denying the Sabbath altogether (such as the New Covenant Baptists and dispensationalists). But historically, mainstream Calvinists have observed the Lord's Day as a delight (Isaiah 58:13).

The other case has to do with the second of the Ten Commandments. Historical Calvinists have almost been alone in seeing that God forbids all pictures and statues of our Lord Jesus Christ.[8] This is explicitly taught in several Reformed standards. The Westminster Larger Catechism says the second commandment forbids "the making of any representation of God, or all or any of the three persons" (Q. 109). The Second Helvetic Confession said that "although Christ took upon Him man's nature, yet He did not, therefore, take it that He might set forth a pattern for carvers and painters" (Ch. 5). The Reformed Protestants disagreed with Lutherans, Catholics, and Greek Orthodox on this point. Today there are very few evangelicals except traditional Calvinists who reject the use of images of Jesus, and even some otherwise conservative Calvinists still use them. But traditional Calvinists reject as idolatry the use of pictures, movies, crucifixes, and other representations of our Lord Jesus Christ, even in art or education.

We have no true or accurate photographs or portraits of Christ, only pictures based on the fallen imagination of artists (Acts 17:29). Some are made from the likeness of unbelieving male models. In his classic book *Knowing God*, J. I. Packer put it well:

> This categorical statement rules out, not simply the use of pictures and statues which depict God as an animal, but also the use of pictures and statues which depict Him as the highest created thing we know — a man. It also rules out the use of pictures and statues of Jesus Christ as a man, although Jesus Himself was and remains Man; for all pictures and statues are necessarily made after "the likeness" of ideal manhood as we conceive it, and therefore come under the ban which the commandment imposes.[9]

The deity of Christ cannot be portrayed for it is invisible (Deuteronomy 4:15–16) until we behold the beatific vision in Heaven (Matthew 5:8). God is spirit and must be worshiped in spirit and truth, not in pictures and statues. The use of pictures wrongly assumes that faith is helped by sight, whereas the Bible says that faith is based on the Bible and not physical sight (John 20:29; 2 Corinthians 5:7). Paul "portrayed" Christ with words, not pictures (Galatians

---

8 See John Calvin, *Institutes of the Christian Religion* (Philadelphia: Westminster, 1960), 1:11–12:3 (pp. 99–120); Daniel R. Hyde, *In Living Color: Images of Christ and the Means of Grace* (Grandville: Reformed Fellowship, Inc., 2009); Peter Barnes, *Seeing Jesus: The Case Against Pictures of Our Lord Jesus Christ* (Edinburgh: Banner of Truth, 1990); Carlos M. N. Eire, *War Against the Idols* (Cambridge: Cambridge University Press, 1986); Giuseppe Scavizzi, *The Controversy on Images from Calvin to Baronius* (New York: Peter Lang, 1992); and William A. Dyrness, *Reformed Theology and Visual Culture: The Protestant Imagination from Calvin to Edwards* (Cambridge: Cambridge University Press, 2004).

9 J. I. Packer, *Knowing God* (Downers Grove, IL: InterVarsity, 1973), 39.

3:1). So should we. Catholicism defends pictures and statues as "aids for the illiterate and ignorant," but Calvinists point out that this is exactly the rationale of pagan idolaters. Did not God forbid idols to the Israelites, most of whom could not read or write? Pictures of Christ are superstitious idols and a kind of religious pornography — enticing but forbidden and always sinful.

The elements of Communion are "visible words of God," said Peter Martyr Vermigli and Martin Bucer, but they are symbols and not actual pictures. Christ is the perfect and personal image of God (Colossians 1:15), and Christians are refashioned into the image of Christ when they are saved (Romans 8:29; 2 Corinthians 3:18). Reformed worship services have generally been non-ornamental and simple so as to be spiritual and not carnal. The Word of God, not pictures or statues, is central. Pictures have a way of pushing the Word of God aside. Our high view of the exalted majesty of God explains our jealousy for the purity of worship and condemnation of all idolatry, including pictures and statues of Christ.

Conclusion

These are the main features of the mainstream Reformed view of the law. The wealth of Calvinist discussions of the law in Reformed confessions, systematic theologies, and expositions of the Decalogue testify to our high regard for the law of God. Like David we confess, "O how I love Your law!" (Psalm 119:97), and with Paul, "Therefore the law is holy, and the commandment holy and just and good" (Romans 7:12).

Chapter 67
Covenant Theology

No discussion of Calvinism is complete without some mention of *covenant theology*. The two are not exactly synonymous — some Calvinists prefer other options, and some who believe in covenant theology are non-Reformed. But there has been a close relationship between the two for centuries.

History of Covenant Theology

While Christians in all ages have believed something about the biblical covenants, it was not until the Reformation that theologians began to link them together in a unifying system that explains God's dealings with mankind over the span of history. The earliest roots go back to the German-speaking side of Reformed Protestantism. Huldrych Zwingli taught that God made a covenant with Adam and then later covenants with other persons. He used this preliminary covenant model mainly to reply to Anabaptists in Switzerland. But he did not elaborate much further.

Recent historians frequently consider Zwingli's successor Heinrich Bullinger to be the actual father of covenant theology.[1] In his important work *Of the Eternal Testament or Covenant of God* (1534) he taught that all the biblical covenants are related to each other and find their final fulfillment in Christ and the new covenant. John Calvin spoke of the covenants as having an organic unity and compared the progression of covenants in history to the rise of the sun reaching its zenith in Christ.[2] But he did not emphasize this approach as a unifying system as much as Bullinger did. There is disagreement in the "Calvin versus Calvinism" debate over the extent to which Calvin held to covenant theology.

Caspar Olevianus, coauthor of the Heidelberg Catechism and an important early German Reformed theologian, took the system a step further.[3] He said

---

[1] Charles S. McCoy and J. Wayne Baker, *Fountainhead of Federalism: Heinrich Bullinger and the Covenant Tradition* (Louisville: Westminster John Knox Press, 1991); J. Wayne Baker, *Bullinger and the Covenant* (Athens: Ohio University Press, 1980).

[2] Peter A. Lillback, *The Binding of God: Calvin's Role in the Development of Covenant Theology* (Grand Rapids: Baker Academic, 2001).

[3] R. Scott Clark, *Olevianus and the Substance of the Covenant* (Grand Rapids: Reformation

that there is one main covenant of grace that is gradually revealed from the eternal inter-trinitarian covenant with Christ as the Head and representative of the elect. It is a covenant of grace to us, for faith itself is a condition fulfilled by God as a gift to us. God made a covenant of works with Adam, which Adam broke. Salvation comes only through the covenant of grace through Christ in all ages, especially in the fullness of the new covenant. He explained his views in *Concerning the Nature of the Covenant of Grace Between God and the Elect* (1585).

In *Questions and Answers Respecting the Covenant of God* (1596), Robert Rollock of Scotland taught that all of God's dealings with man are through covenants. The covenant of works with Adam was summed up in the moral law written on his heart and later shown to mankind in their heart and in creation. This covenant was more explicitly revealed in the Ten Commandments and the covenant with Israel. Every covenant has a sacrament attached to it as a sign.

Johannes Cocceius was a German Reformed professor at the universities of Franeker and Leiden in the Netherlands.[4] He opposed the theological method of Reformed scholasticism and advocated a more exegetical-based theology. He is sometimes considered the father of what has come to be known as *biblical theology* as opposed to systematic theology. An extremely able scholar and prolific writer, he summed up his views in *The Doctrine of the Covenant and Testament of God* (1648).[5] Among his controversial views were that sins were only covered and not removed in the old covenant and that the Sabbath was a covenantal sign only for Israel and is not in effect in the new covenant. He was opposed particularly by Gisbertus Voetius, and the debate between the Cocceians and Voetians continued throughout the century in the Netherlands.

Herman Witsius merged covenant theology with the Dutch Puritanism known as the *Nadere Reformatie*. His *The Economy of the Covenants*[6] is often considered the high-water mark of covenant theology.

Covenant theology also grew in England through such writers as John Ball in *A Treatise on the Covenant of Grace* (1645) and John Preston in *The New*

Heritage Books, 2005); Lyle D. Bierma, *German Calvinism in the Confessional Age: The Covenant Theology of Caspar Olevianus* (Grand Rapids: Baker, 1996).

4 Willem J. van Asselt, *The Federal Theology of Johannes Cocceius (1603–1669)* (Leiden: Brill, 2001); Brian J. Lee, *Johannes Cocceius and the Exegetical Roots of Federal Theology* (Gottingen: Vandenhoeck & Ruprecht, 2009).

5 Johannes Cocceius, *The Doctrine of the Covenant and Testament of God* (Grand Rapids: Reformation Heritage Books, 2016).

6 Herman Witsius, *The Economy of the Covenants Between God and Man* (Escondido, CA: den Dulk Foundation, 1990).

Covenant, or The Saint's Portion (1629). It found explicit confessional status in the Westminster Confession (Ch. 7) and *The Sum of Saving Knowledge*. By the end of the seventeenth century, Reformed orthodoxy was in decline. The Leiden school took covenant theology into non-Reformed areas, which the Voetians had warned against. In some quarters this approach downplayed divine revelation and emphasized human and cultural development of religion in the Bible.

In the next century, John Gill taught a traditional covenant theology with a Baptist flavor.[7] His emphasis on identifying the eternal covenant of redemption with the historical covenant of grace featured in his Hyper-Calvinism. For example, he taught that faith is a blessing and not a condition of the covenant of grace, for that covenant is unconditional on us. This meant that saving faith is not a duty of all men, for if it is a duty then the covenant is based on works and not grace. Further, the covenant is made with Christ as Head of the elect and is not offered to sinners.

Traditional covenant theology was emphasized in the Princeton Theology, especially through Charles Hodge,[8] who merged covenant theology with the Reformed scholasticism of Francis Turretin. In the twentieth century Louis Berkhof[9] and others popularized a kind of Dutch-American form of covenant theology. Meredith G. Kline[10] wrote several significant works on the biblical covenants in light of ancient Near East customs. He taught that they follow the *suzerainty-vassal* pattern of ancient treaties and covenants. The suzerain (war-lord king) promised to protect and do good to the vassals (citizens) if they promised to serve him alone. The essence of such treaties was: "I will be your protective lord, and you will be my submissive people." John Murray[11] and Herman Hoeksema made modifications to traditional covenant theology by speaking of the covenant with Adam as more of a promissory personal relationship than a contractual covenant. O. Palmer Robertson also made significant modifications to covenant theology.

---

7 John Gill, *A Complete Body of Doctrinal and Practical Divinity* (Paris, AR: Baptist Standard Bearer, 1984), 209–50, 345–60; Curt Daniel, "Hyper-Calvinism and John Gill," PhD Diss., University of Edinburgh, 1983, 218–94.

8 Charles Hodge, *Systematic Theology* (Grand Rapids: Eerdmans, 1979), 2:117–22, 354–77.

9 Louis Berkhof, *Systematic Theology* (Grand Rapids: Eerdmans, 1988), 262–301.

10 See especially Meredith G. Kline, *Kingdom Prologue* (Overland Park: Two Age Press, 2006); Howard Griffith and John R. Muether, eds., *Creator, Redeemer, Consummator: A Festschrift for Meredith G. Kline* (Jackson, Miss.: Reformed Theological Seminary, 2000).

11 John Murray, *The Covenant of Grace* (Phillipsburg, NJ: Presbyterian & Reformed, 1988).

Arthur W. Pink taught a traditional Baptist form of covenant theology.[12] Most contemporary Reformed Baptists follow this model, but the so-called New Covenant Baptists prefer an approach more like dispensationalism. To them, the law was integral to the old covenant and therefore has been superseded by the laws of Christ in the new covenant.

Michael Horton[13] has written a number of books on covenant theology under the influence of Meredith G. Kline and Geerhardus Vos. He seems to see covenants everywhere and in every subject, perhaps the counterpart to the dispensational overemphasis on pigeon-holing every biblical topic by the various dispensations. Horton has been criticized for bringing in some non-Reformed elements, but he does offer many useful contributions to the discussion.

The Biblical Covenants

While there are variations within traditional covenant theology, the following is a general summary of the mainstream view. First, the word *covenant* means agreement, contract, treaty, testament. The Hebrew word is *berith*; the Greek word is *diatheke* (rarely, *suntheke*). The Latin words *testamentum* and *foedus* are also employed; hence, covenant theology is sometimes called *Federalism*. In a covenant, two parties agree to certain stipulations with conditions and promises. When it is a testament, like a human will, it is more unconditional (though the book of Hebrews speaks of it as a testament and emphasizes faith).

The first covenant was the covenant of redemption between the Father and the Son before time began.[14] The Father chose the elect and gave them to the Son, who agreed to become a man and die an atoning death to save them. He was their surety in the covenant (Hebrews 7:22). For Christ, this work was a covenant of works. He fulfilled the task and was rewarded with being exalted as Lord (Philippians 2:9–11). The Holy Spirit was the official witness of the covenant of redemption and promised to apply the work of Christ to the elect.

The first covenant in time was the covenant of works made with Adam as a representative for all mankind. Scripture does not explicitly call it a covenant (though some appeal to Hosea 6:7 where the Hebrew word is *adam*), but it has all the features of a covenant: promise, conditions, sacramental sign, and so forth. It is implied in Romans 5 and 1 Corinthians 15. Just as Christ was the

---

12 Arthur W. Pink, *The Divine Covenants* (Grand Rapids: Baker Book House, 1973).
13 See especially Michael Horton, *God of Promise: Introducing Covenant Theology* (Grand Rapids: Baker Books, 2006).
14 I discuss the covenant of redemption in chapter 40.

covenantal Head for His people, so Adam was for mankind. The Westminster Confession summarizes it: "The first covenant made with man was a covenant of works, wherein life was promised to Adam, and in him to his posterity, upon condition of perfect and personal obedience" (7:2). There is debate as to whether Adam was under the covenant for a temporary or perpetual period. The sacramental seal was the Tree of Life, which Adam forfeited when he broke the covenant.

If Adam obeyed, he would live. But he disobeyed and later died and brought sin and death to his posterity (Genesis 2:16–17; Romans 5:12). This covenant has been annulled so far as any possibility of salvation, but the effects of it continue in damnation. The law was the basic condition of this covenant, and the moral law continues as well.

Covenant theologians differ as to whether the covenant made at Mount Sinai was a repetition of the covenant of works or a mixture with the covenant of grace which began to be revealed after Adam fell. The promise of salvation continued through various covenants, as explained by the Westminster Confession:

> Man by his fall having made himself incapable of life by that covenant, the Lord was pleased to make a second, commonly called the Covenant of Grace: whereby he freely offereth unto sinners life and salvation by Jesus Christ, requiring of them faith in him, that they may be saved; and promising to give unto all those that are ordained unto life his Holy Spirit, to make them willing and able to believe (7:3).

Later covenants were a mixture of these two covenants. The basic promise of the covenants is the same: "I will be your God, and you will be My people." Faith is the condition, but it is also a gift. In this sense, God fulfills all the conditions by grace. Old Testament believers were saved by faith in the coming Messiah who would atone for their sins. Nobody was ever saved by keeping the law or the covenant of works. All the covenants find their fulfillment in Christ. The new covenant is the purest form of the covenant of grace and does away with certain temporary and typical features of previous covenants, such as the land promised to Israel.

All covenants have sacraments and ceremonies. Zwingli taught that children of believers are "in the covenant" in all ages, and therefore baptism should be given to covenantal children as circumcision was under the old covenant. Baptist covenantalists, however, argue that the fullness of the new covenant meant a change regarding children.[15] Physical children under the old covenant were entitled to the sign, but in the new covenant the sign is given only to spiritual children — that is, sinners who have been born again. All examples and commands for baptism in the new covenant require faith and repentance and exclude infants.

Covenant Theology and Dispensationalism

The main rival to covenant theology within evangelicalism has been the system known as dispensationalism. The former can be traced back to the sixteenth-century Reformation, while the latter is usually traced back to John Nelson Darby and the Plymouth Brethren in early nineteenth-century England. Both present theologies dealing with God's progressive plan of redemption in history. Both are based on a high view of biblical infallibility, and neither of them has found favor with liberal theologians or Roman Catholics. Though they disagree on certain key points, they actually have more in common than many people think.

The differences are not mainly in eschatology. While all dispensationalists are premillennial and believe in the pretribulation rapture, covenantalists may be amillennial, postmillennial, or premillennial, though they rarely accept the pretribulation rapture theory. The main issue is the relation of Israel and the church. The *sine qua non* of dispensationalism is that God has two separate and distinct peoples with different covenants and destinies. To confuse Israel and the church is akin to mingling grace and works or law and gospel. Covenant theology, on the other hand, holds that God has one people, not two. Romans 11:16–21 speaks of one tree, not two. That tree has Jewish and Gentile branches, and there will be a revival of Jews coming to Christ one day. Believers under the old covenant were part of the church in embryo (Acts 7:38), and the new covenant church is the true spiritual Israel (Galatians 3:29; 6:16; Romans 2:28–29; 9:6; Philippians 3:3). There is an organic spiritual relationship between believers in all time periods, for they are all elect and members of the body of Christ. Many dispensationalists, by contrast, argue that old covenant believers were not "in Christ," for that is a new covenant distinctive. Federalists reply that all believers are elect "in Christ" according to Ephesians 1:4.

Covenant theology emphasizes the progression of the related covenants,

---

15 See Paul K. Jewett, *Infant Baptism and the Covenant of Grace* (Grand Rapids: Eerdmans, 1978); Fred Malone, *The Baptism of Disciples Alone* (Cape Coral, FL: Founders, 2003); David Kingdom, *Children of Abraham* (Haywards Heath: Henry E. Walter and Carey, 1973).

while dispensationalists emphasize the differences and the time periods between the covenants. This leads to another significant difference. As we have seen, covenantalists teach that believers in the periods before Christ were saved by faith in the promised sin-bearing Messiah, for that is the essence of the one true gospel preached and believed in all eras (Galatians 3:8; Hebrews 4:2). By contrast, dispensationalists insist that pre-Christian believers were saved by faith in other promises, such as having a son, the Promised Land, and protection from enemies. It is generally taught that Old Testament saints did not understand the Messianic prophecies or types sufficiently to enable them to believe in Messiah as the atoning sacrifice. Some extreme dispensationalists have even taught that some were saved by works or that Jews today can be saved by keeping the old covenant. Covenantalists strongly disagree.

Dispensationalists say that the church is a New Testament institution completely separate from Old Testament Israel. Moreover, it is a parenthesis in God's history of redemption, a kind of temporary afterthought. Covenant theology, by strong contrast, says the church is the culmination of the previous covenants and periods. Dispensationalism seems to be saying that God will go back to the old covenant when the church is removed at the rapture. Covenant theology, however, says the old covenant has been forever abolished. Some dispensationalists say that the new covenant is not even in force yet, for it was promised to be made with Israel and not with the Gentile church (Jeremiah 31:31).

Dispensationalists also disagree on the continuation of the law. They generally say that it has been abolished (at least until after the rapture), while covenant theology argues that the moral law continues, while the ceremonial laws have been abolished and replaced by new covenant ordinances. One says the laws are abolished unless repeated in the new, while the other says they continue unless abolished in the new. It is a fine, but significant, point. To the one, dispensationalism appears to be antinomian, while to the other, covenant theology appears legalistic.

Dispensationalists usually teach that God will reinstitute animal sacrifices in the Jewish millennium after Christ's return (the church will be in Heaven, not on earth at that time). There is no feature of dispensationalism that is more offensive and repugnant to covenantalists than this. In light of the book of Hebrews presenting the perfect work of Christ's atoning death, to go back to the animal sacrifices would be tantamount to re-crucifying Christ (6:6), trampling underfoot the holy blood of Jesus Christ (10:29), and committing ultimate sacrilege and possibly unforgivable blasphemy. Christ offered the perfect sacrifice once and for all. It will not do to say, as some do, that the future animal sacrifices will only be "memorials." The Lord's Supper is the new covenant memorial ordinance. Sacrifices in the old covenant were typical memorials, but they have been abolished forever.

There are variations within both systems. Some Calvinists suggest a middle way that combines the best of both while excluding the weaknesses of both. This is often called *historical premillennialism* and was taught by numerous Puritans and other Calvinists, such as Horatius Bonar, James Montgomery Boice, and the present writer. They say the rapture happens at the time of the Second Coming, not seven years previously. God will send a revival to the Jews one day to be regrafted into the one covenantal tree of Romans 11. Animal sacrifices will not be brought back. There is an organic and spiritual relation between believers in all ages, and they have all been saved by faith in Jesus Christ as sin-bearing atonement.

It is a fact of history that very few five-point Calvinists have accepted dispensationalism. Most have believed in covenant theology. Dispensationalism can be held by Arminians. Some dispensationalists are Amyraldian, even though Moyse Amyraut himself believed in covenant theology. The debate continues.

Conclusion

Salvation has always been by grace and has been granted by the covenant-keeping God. Christ is the only covenantal Mediator, and through Him we receive all God's promised gifts.

Chapter 68
The Church

The Protestant Reformers rejected most of Roman Catholic ecclesiology, but each of the three branches of Protestantism developed its own view of the church. The Lutherans have frequently accepted bishops, while Anabaptists have always taught congregational government and believers-only membership. There is a general Reformed ecclesiology but with variations.

What Is the Church?

The Greek word for *church* is *ekklesia*, "called out ones." Calvinists tie this in with the second and fourth points of Calvinism. We are called out in election in eternity and then efficaciously called to Christ in time. The Westminster Confession states: "The catholick or universal church, which is invisible, consists of the whole number of the elect that have been, are, or shall be gathered into one, under Christ the head thereof" (25:1).

Unlike dispensationalism, mainstream Reformed theology teaches that there is an organic and spiritual relation between Old Testament Israel and the New Testament church. God has one united people, not two distinct peoples. Romans 11:16–24 speaks of the one tree with Jewish and Gentile branches. Ephesians 2:11–22 describes this one people as a commonwealth, a new man, and a temple. Gentile Christians will sit at the same table as Abraham, Isaac, and Jacob and other Hebrew believers from the old covenant (Matthew 8:11). In one sense, the church is the new Israel (Galatians 6:16). The kingdom of God was taken away from Israel and given to the church (Matthew 21:43). The church existed in embryonic form in the Old Testament but was properly born on the day of Pentecost (Matthew 16:18; Acts 2).

Ekklesia is used about seventy-five times in the Greek Septuagint and usually corresponds to the Hebrew word *qahal*, "congregation." Acts 7:38 speaks of the "congregation" in the wilderness, or as the KJV has it, "the church in the wilderness." *Sunagoge* is also used to translate *qahal*. Local synagogues were formed during the Exile in Babylon and continued when the people returned to the land. James 2:2 and Hebrews 10:25 use *sunagoge* as a term for the church.

Thus, the people of God in both testaments are part of the one family of God.

New Testament believers are the true children of Abraham, not unbelieving Jews (Galatians 3:29). They are the true *dispersion* (James 1:1; 1 Peter 1:1), the true circumcision (Philippians 3:3; Romans 2:28–29, 9:6), the true Jerusalem (Galatians 4:26; Hebrews 12:22). The church is basically the same as the kingdom of God (Matthew 16:18–19), from Adam onwards. There is no doubt that Christians are now in the kingdom (Colossians 1:13; Matthew 3:2; 4:17; 11:11–12, 12:28, 23:13; Luke 17:21; Romans 14:17), but the consummation of the kingdom is still future (Matthew 26:29).

The Visible and Invisible Church

While a few early fathers and medieval theologians spoke of the bifurcation of the *visible* and *invisible church*, the overwhelming majority identified both with the Roman Catholic Church. Most of the Reformers challenged this, especially the Calvinists. Just as not all who are of Israel are true Israel (Romans 9:6), so not all who are of the church are the true church.

More than the other branches of the Reformation, the Reformed branch has always taught the invisible church is the true church, the body of Christ. On the other hand, the visible local church is not yet pure — it may contain non-elect members and false brethren. It needs to be reformed and purified — hence the Reformation, Puritanism, and revivals. One may belong to the visible and not the invisible church, and conversely, one may be in the invisible church but not in a local visible church. Ideally the two should match, as they will in Heaven.

Contrary to official Catholicism, we teach that membership in a visible local church is not necessary for salvation, nor do we guarantee that all our members are saved. Calvinism is neither Catholic nor a cult. But since the invisible church consists of all and only true believers, membership in it is an essential part of salvation. There is no salvation outside of Christ (Acts 4:12), and salvation puts us into His body, the invisible church (1 Corinthians 12:13). Hence, there is a Reformed view that is different than the Catholic dictum, "There is no salvation outside the Church." Rome officially teaches that it is the only true church, and outside of it there is no salvation. However, this old dogma has been considerably weakened since the Vatican II Council and the ecumenical movement.

The Marks of the Church

Rome says that it alone has the four essential marks of the church: "The Church is one, holy, catholic and apostolic." Further, a person must be ecclesiastically related to the pope to be a true Christian. All the Reformers vehemently disagreed and cried, "*Solus Christus*! Salvation by Christ alone!" All the Reformers and most of the Puritans and later Calvinists considered the papacy to be the Antichrist and Roman Catholicism to be Mystery Babylon. It has been wryly said that the papacy is in the temple of 2 Thessalonians 2:4 but not in the church of Matthew 16:18. Rome has downplayed their historical dogma in recent decades but has never officially repudiated their centuries-old official pronouncements. Thousands of our Protestant ancestors were tortured and burned at the stake for denying Rome's claims. Rome has never repented nor apologized. Traditional Calvinists have never forgotten.

The Reformed generally agree that there are three definitive "marks" of the true church: "The true church can be recognized if it has the following marks: The church engages in pure preaching of the gospel; it makes use of the pure administration of the sacraments as Christ instituted them; it practices church discipline for correcting faults" (Belgic Confession, Article 29). Rome has none of these. Historic Lutherans have them to some degree. Some ultra-conservative Presbyterians and Dutch Reformed do not recognize Baptist churches — even Reformed Baptist churches — because of the difference on baptism.

The first mark concentrates on the gospel of salvation. A church need not be Calvinist in all its doctrines to be Christian, but it is no church if it preaches a false gospel (Galatians 1:9). As we shall see in the next chapter, there is variety among the Reformed regarding the second mark. The third mark is based on Matthew 18:15-20. Without discipline a church loses its identity — all that goes in the top of the barrel flows out the bottom unless it is guarded. This has bearing on church membership. All historic Reformed churches have taught the importance of church membership. Reformed Baptists, however, emphasize "believers-only membership" and do not consider infants of believers to be members in any sense.

The Regulative Principle

There is another matter over which historic Calvinists disagree with Catholics and Lutherans, indeed, with most non-Reformed Christians. The question is: "How should we worship together?" Rome emphasizes the sacraments and appeals to official tradition and canon law to tell us how to worship. Lutheran worship is less sacramental but more so than the Reformed. Its basic principle is: "Whatever is not explicitly forbidden in Scripture is allowed." The Anglican/ Episcopalian model is somewhere between the Catholic and Lutheran models:

"The church has the authority to institute new forms of worship as long as they do not contradict Scripture."

The Reformed position is notably different and far more biblical. It is "worship *sola Scriptura*" — worship as taught by Scripture alone. The Westminster Confession gives the classic definition of what has been called the *Regulative Principle of Worship*:

> The acceptable way of worshiping the true God is instituted by Himself, and so limited by His own revealed will, that He may not be worshiped according to the imaginations and devices of men, or the suggestions of Satan, under any visible representations, or any other way not prescribed in the holy Scripture (21:1).

God Himself regulates how He is to be worshiped. He does not leave it to man, a church, or the latest fad. The Regulative Principle has always been at the core of Reformed ecclesiology. The Reformers did not just reform doctrine, but they reformed worship as well, for worship is the highest duty and privilege of Christians and the main purpose of the church.

John Calvin laid the foundation for the Regulative Principle:

- "If all voluntary worship which we ourselves devise apart from God's commandment is hateful to him, it follows that no worship is acceptable to him except that which is approved by His Word."[1]

- "God hates nothing more than counterfeit worship."[2]

- "God disapproves of all modes of worship not expressly sanctioned by His Word."[3]

- "For anything that God has not commanded us to do, or put his stamp of approval upon, results in wages that can be collected only in hell [. . .] for we cannot invent forms of worship, based upon our fantasies, without at the same time inventing a new god [. . .] for we all possess the seed of idolatry in our nature."[4]

All unbiblical worship is idolatry. Our hearts are idol factories. God strictly

---

1 John Calvin, *Institutes of the Christian Religion* (Philadelphia: Westminster, 1960), 4:13:2 (pp. 1255–56).

2 Calvin, 4:13:7 (p. 1260).

3 John Calvin, *Selected Works of John Calvin* (Grand Rapids: Baker Book House, 1983), 1:128. See also Sermons on *Genesis 1:1–11:4* (Edinburgh: Banner of Truth, 2009), 478–79, 700.

4 John Calvin, *Sermons on the Book of Micah* (Phillipsburg, NJ: P&R, 2003), 36–37.

forbids idolatry in all forms and does not leave the form of worship up to us, otherwise worship quickly becomes idolatrous, as seen in the Old Testament. What we do in corporate worship must be taught in Scripture — no more, no less, none else. God forbids us to add to, subtract from, or substitute for what is in His Word (Deuteronomy 4:2; 12:32). The Old Testament gave specific and detailed requirements. Some of them carry over into the New Testament. Though New Testament worship is far less detailed, liturgical, or ritualistic than the Old, it is more spiritual. The Regulative Principle applies to both covenants. We must worship only as God has commanded us to worship. Unbiblical worship is not acceptable to God.

Self-invented worship is expressly forbidden in Colossians 2:23. Christ condemned the Pharisees for distorting the true worship of God by their tradition (Matthew 15:1–9). God slew Nadab and Abihu for offering "strange fire" that He had not commanded (Leviticus 10:1–3). God punished Uzziah for offering incense, which was commanded only of the priests (2 Chronicles 26:18–21). Uzzah was slain by God for touching the holy Ark of the Covenant, and David erred in transporting the Ark on an oxcart (2 Samuel 6:6–7). Unbiblical worship is potentially lethal. The Irish Articles (1615) said, "All worship devised by man's fantasy, besides or contrary to the Scriptures [. . .] has not only no promise of reward in Scripture, but contrariwise, threatenings and maledictions."[5] It is just that serious.

The same applies to the internal attitudes of the heart and mind. It is possible but impermissible to worship with correct outward form without the appropriate internal motives. True worship must be reverent both internally and externally. Reformed worship generally stands in stark contrast with cold liturgicalism on the one hand and silly emotionalism on the other. Acceptable worship must be in spirit and in truth (John 4:24), and the Regulative Principle zealously strives to be both.

This important principle is based on the second of the Ten Commandments. The Westminster Larger Catechism gives a good summary:

> The duties required in the second commandment are, the receiving, observing, and keeping pure and entire, all such religious worship and ordinances as God hath instituted in his word; particularly prayer and thanksgiving in the name of Christ; the reading, preaching, and hearing of the word; the administration and receiving of the sacraments; church

---

5 In James T. Dennison Jr., ed., *Reformed Confessions of the 16th and 17th Centuries in English Translation* (Grand Rapids: Reformation Heritage Books, 2014), 4:99.

government and discipline; the ministry and maintenance thereof; religious fasting; swearing by the name of God, and vowing unto him: as also the disapproving, detesting, opposing, all false worship; and, according to each one's place and calling, removing it, and all monuments of idolatry. (Q. 108)

The sins forbidden in the second commandment are, all devising, counseling, commanding, using, and any wise approving, any religious worship not instituted by God himself; tolerating a false religion; the making any representation of God, of all or any of the three persons, either inwardly in our mind, or outwardly in any kind of image or likeness of any creature whatsoever; all worshiping of it, or God in it or by it; the making of any representation of feigned deities, and all worship of them, or service belonging to them; all superstitious devices, corrupting the worship of God, adding to it, or taking from it, whether invented and taken of ourselves, or received by tradition from others, though under the title of antiquity, custom, devotion, good intent, or any other pretense whatsoever; simony; sacrilege; all neglect, contempt, hindering, and opposing the worship and ordinances which God hath appointed. (Q. 109)

Calvinists versed in Reformed history greatly appreciate the value of the Regulative Principle. Unfortunately, many new Calvinists have never heard of it and sometimes are slow to accept it because they are accustomed to man-made worship. Those who want to please God will search the Scriptures and obey God's way of worship.

False worship includes the superstitious sacramentalism of Roman Catholicism but also man-centered entertainment that masquerades as worship, such as what is widespread in modern evangelicalism. Just as we reject Rome's idolatry, we reject evangelical fads (puppet shows in the pulpit, silly drama, sensuous dancing, flashing lights, and smoke). The list seems endless and gets worse every year. Such pseudo-worship is not only unbiblical but is as repugnant to God as worshiping a stump of wood. Just as idolaters first invent idols in their hearts and fashion their idol-gods in their own image and to their own liking, so how we worship tells us much about the state of our own hearts and our attitude toward God who is holy. Too, how a church worships on the Lord's Day is a gauge as to not only its doctrinal orthodoxy but the state of its spirituality. Calvin said, "All who set up their own false rites to God worship and adore their own ravings."[6] John Owen thundered:

---

6 Calvin, *Institutes*, 1:4:3 (p. 49).

> Arrogant little humans are very prone to introduce into religious worship figments drawn from their own emotions, and to defend them by specious pretexts (particularly the use of philosophy and superstition — a fact to which all human experience will testify), and so it pleased God to render this theology absolutely inviolable and sacred for the future by confirming it by the terrible punishment of the first apostates from this command.[7]

There have been debates over certain specifics of worship within the parameters of the Regulative Principle. During the Vestments Controversy in the post-Reformation Church of England, most Puritans opposed the use of clerical garments. But others, such as Martyn Lloyd-Jones, have worn a Geneva gown while preaching. Most early Calvinists sang only psalms, but most today sing psalms, hymns, and spiritual songs according to Ephesians 5:19. Many great hymns were written by Calvinists such as John Newton, Isaac Watts, William Cowper, and Horatius Bonar. Some psalms-only churches insist on non-instrumental singing. Most paedobaptists reject paedocommunion, and Reformed Baptists reject paedobaptism because of their understanding of the Regulative Principle. A few churches allow the repeating of the Apostles' Creed or the Lord's Prayer; most do not. By far most do not allow speaking in tongues or "prophesying" because they believe those were temporary spiritual gifts only for the early church. Some allow choirs and solos; some do not. By far most end their worship services with a pastoral benediction, and almost no Reformed services include an altar call.

Church Government

It is in this area that we find the most variety in the Reformed family. The mainstream view follows a *presbyterial* system as taught by Calvin and other early Reformed writers. This is practiced by Presbyterians of Scottish heritage and those of a Dutch Reformed tradition. About half of the Puritans were Presbyterian. In this ecclesiology, every local church is led by elders, who together form a session or consistory, and are further united in a presbytery within a broad region. In turn, they are members of a national general assembly or synod. Charles Hodge taught that only teaching elders are part of the presbytery. Southern Presbyterians tend to follow James Henley Thornwell's view that all elders are part of the presbytery. It is sometimes said that the

---

7 John Owen, *Biblical Theology* (Pittsburgh: Soli Deo Gloria, 1994), 435.

Dutch Reformed tend to place more authority within the local congregation than the Presbyterians do.

Others have taught a more hierarchical government known as *Episcopalianism*, or rule by bishops over several churches. Many of the Puritans followed this model, such as William Perkins, Richard Sibbes, James Ussher, John Davenant, Joseph Hall, and others. Later Anglicans include George Whitefield, John Newton, and J. C. Ryle, and more recently W. H. Griffith Thomas and James I. Packer.

Others deny any church government outside the local church. Many of the Puritans were Independents, such as John Owen, Thomas Goodwin, Jeremiah Burroughs, and Joseph Caryl. In America they were called *Congregationalists* and included Thomas Shepard, John Cotton, Thomas Hooker, Solomon Stoddard, and Jonathan Edwards. A similar polity has been advocated by Calvinistic Baptists, such as John Bunyan, John Gill, and Charles Haddon Spurgeon.

Most Calvinists advocate multiple and equal elders within the congregation, as taught in Philippians 1:1; 1 Peter 5:1; James 5:14; 1 Timothy 5:17; Titus 1:5; Acts 11:30; 14:23; 15:2–6, 22–23; 16:4; 20:17, 28; and 21:18. This is a safeguard against a one-man rule on the one hand and unchecked democracy on the other. In the rediscovery of Reformed theology among Baptists in recent decades, most have come to accept multiple eldership rather than the more traditional model of the pastor and deacons among American Baptist churches. And by far most historic Calvinists have believed that only men are eligible to serve as elders.

Church-State Relations

At the time of the Reformation, there were several competing theories of church-state relations. Roman Catholicism basically taught that the church has authority over the state. Anabaptists taught complete separation of church and state and generally withdrew from civil government and advocated that government does not have authority over the church. They usually have refrained from voting, serving on juries, serving in the military, and the like. Lutheranism and Episcopalianism basically teach that the state has authority over the church. A few early Reformed theologians held this position, such as Heinrich Bullinger and Thomas Erastus (from whom the term *Erastianism* emerged).

Calvin and most Reformed have taught the "Two Kingdoms" position. Church and state are separate but equal realms. They overlap; Christians are citizens of both. Neither may encroach upon the other. The state has the power of the sword; the church has the power of the Word — and neither has both. The state receives taxes; the church receives tithes. The state's purpose is to punish crime and reward righteousness. The church's purpose is to worship God and preach God's Word. Some godly Calvinists supported a monarchy, while others taught a republic or democracy in society.

There have been some experiments in theocracy, such as in sixteenth-century Geneva and Scotland, the Puritan Commonwealth, and some of the pre-Revolutionary American colonies. The Dutch Reformed sometimes verged on theocracy, such as when the state ousted Arminian clergy after the Synod of Dort. Abraham Kuyper's idea of common grace and sphere sovereignty led to a semi-theocracy with him as prime minister. But all these experiments eventually failed. Switzerland, Scotland, the Netherlands, and America are examples of post-Christian degenerate society today. One analysis suggests that such efforts are always doomed to failure in the next generation. Too often Christians "engage" society in a way that leads to compromise. Instead of an engagement that results in marriage, there should be a prophetic engagement that leads to divorce — or at least involvement without contamination. Godly Christians should act as loving and righteous salt and light in their society.

Conclusion

In addition to the five *sola* doctrines, Calvinists have rallied around the banner "Reformed and always reforming." This means basing one's ecclesiology on Scripture alone and not departing from a solid biblical foundation. There's always room for improvement and vigilance against encroaching compromise.

Chapter 69
The Sacraments

The Protestant Reformers disagreed with Roman Catholicism on many things. One was the idea of priesthood. The Reformers taught the priesthood of all believers (Isaiah 61:6; 1 Peter 2:5, 9; Hebrews 13:15–16; Revelation 1:6; 5:10). Christ alone is the High Priest, not the pope. Elders are not a special class of priests. The Reformers also disagreed with Rome's teaching on sacraments, but they also disagreed with each other. And there has been variation even among the Reformed family on some points regarding the sacraments, though there is a mainline view.

The Sacraments

We believe Christ ordained only two sacraments, and so we reject five of the seven Roman Catholic sacraments. We believe in baptism and the Lord's Supper, but reject confirmation, penance, holy orders, marriage, and last rites as sacraments. We should interview candidates for baptism and church membership to discern their spiritual state, but that is not a rite of confirmation. Christians should confess their sins against another Christian and perhaps to a counselor or elder should church discipline be in view, but that is not confession and penance. Marriage and ordination to the eldership are biblical, but they are not sacraments. We should pray for dying Christians, but that is not last rites.

A tiny group of Christians have rejected all sacraments, such as the Quakers, the Salvation Army, some ultra-dispensationalists, a few of the seventeenth-century Antinomians (such as William Dell), and a few nineteenth-century Hyper-Calvinists. On the other hand, most Primitive Baptists have practiced foot-washing as a third ordinance.

Baptism

The earliest Reformed theologians accepted a modified form of baptismal regeneration. They disagreed with Catholicism and Lutheranism on a fine point. The Reformed taught that God *might* regenerate an infant during baptism but does not *always* do so. The efficacy is not dependent on the water but rather the Spirit and the Word. By the end of the seventeenth century, most

Reformed churches modified the earlier position. Since then, the vast majority of Calvinists have rejected baptismal regeneration.

A few have taught what has been called *presumptive regeneration*. Abraham Kuyper was the most prominent advocate and summed it up: "As a rule, every baptized person should be reckoned as belonging to the regenerated (but not always converted)."[1] Parents should presume that their baptized babies are elect and regenerate until they later give evidence to the contrary. The child may be regenerate but not have conscious faith, which grows gradually over the years. Some churches reject this approach in theory but imply it in practice. But most Reformed churches do not accept it in theory or practice.

Infant baptism has been the majority report in the Reformed family. It has been suggested that Huldrych Zwingli once considered whether *believer's baptism* might be biblical, but then strongly rejected it when the Anabaptists diverged from orthodox theology on several points. Unlike Rome and the Lutherans, he based infant baptism on the covenantal principle: Just as infants in the old covenant were given circumcision, so infants in the new covenant should be given baptism.

Baptism is the sign and seal of the covenant. Some have compared it with a wedding ring — a token of marriage, not the means of marriage. If baptism is done properly, it should not be repeated. Most paedobaptists have baptized by sprinkling, a few baptize by pouring, and a few will immerse adults on occasion. Curiously, John Calvin admitted that the Greek work *baptizo* means to immerse, and the early church practiced baptism by immersion.[2]

The Anabaptists poured or immersed, but their main argument was that baptism is reserved only for believers, not infants. Infants cannot believe; therefore, they may not be baptized. The early Anabaptists accepted the five *sola* doctrines but not the five points of Calvinism. They were a kind of pre-Arminian sort of evangelical Semi-Pelagians. Some were heretical. Michael Servetus and the Socinians rejected the Trinity and the deity of Christ. Consequently, both the Reformed and the Lutherans persecuted the Anabaptists. Many were even martyred by drowning (Switzerland) or burning at the stake (the Netherlands).[3] That was a sad and tragic chapter in Reformed history that has been regretted ever since.

---

1 Abraham Kuyper, *The Work of the Holy Spirit* (Grand Rapids: Eerdmans, 1969), 342; cf. 288.
2 John Calvin, *Institutes of the Christian Religion* (Philadelphia: Westminster, 1960), 4:15:19, (p. 1320).
3 Thieleman J. van Braght, *Martyrs Mirror* (Scottsdale, PA: Herald, 1950).

By the 1630s, English Baptists became primarily Calvinistic in soteriology. For example, the First and Second London Confession of Faith were strongly Calvinistic in almost everything but baptism. Over the centuries, Calvinistic Baptists have been a growing part of the Reformed community. The best-selling of all Puritan books was written by a Baptist — *The Pilgrim's Progress* by John Bunyan. John Gill was probably the most prominent English Reformed theologian in the eighteenth century. By common consent, Charles Haddon Spurgeon has been considered the "Prince of Preachers." More recently Martyn Lloyd-Jones has been accorded that honor. Many do not know that he began as a Welsh Calvinistic Methodist but changed to believer's baptism.[4] There are currently several varieties of Calvinistic Baptists: Reformed Baptist, Strict Baptists, Sovereign Grace Baptists, Primitive Baptists, and others. They would account for about a third of the worldwide Reformed community.

Much of the debate revolves around the nature of the biblical covenants. Most Calvinists have believed in covenant theology and say that the covenant of grace is the same in all periods. The family principle is the same for both the old and the new covenants, therefore infants of believers are entitled to the covenantal seal. Calvinistic Baptists, most of whom accept a slightly modified covenant theology, argue that there is a change in the family principle from the old to the new. All commands and examples in the New Testament are for believers. In other words, the covenantal sign is only for those who have been born again spiritually, not for those merely born physically of believing parents. Curiously, some dispensationalists have been paedobaptist, such as Donald Grey Barnhouse and Lewis Sperry Chafer, though more have been Amyraldian and have taught believer's baptism. The debate continues.[5]

The Lord's Supper

The second sacrament is variously called "the Lord's Supper" (1 Corinthians 11:20); "the table of the Lord" (1 Corinthians 10:21); "Communion" (1 Corinthians 10:16); and "the breaking of the bread" (1 Corinthians 10:16; Acts 2:42, 46, 20:7). Calvinists rarely call it the *Eucharist* (from the Greek word *eucharisteo*, to thank). We never call it the Mass. Rome teaches the heresy of *transubstantiation* — the bread and wine literally change into the physical body and blood of Christ. The elements are considered divine and, therefore, are elevated to be worshiped. The Mass is officially said to be a propitiatory sacrifice for sins. Grace is

---

4 Martyn Lloyd-Jones, *Great Doctrines of the Bible: The Church and the Last Things* (Wheaton: Crossway, 1998), 25–46.
5 See chapter 67 on covenant theology.

automatically and physically given through the Mass. Like historic Lutherans and Anabaptists, orthodox Calvinists have always considered the Catholic Mass to be superstition, blasphemy, and idolatry. Thousands of brave Protestants were tortured and burned at the stake by Roman Catholics for rejecting the Romish Mass. Our position was stated by Charles Hodge: "No doctrine of the Church of Rome is more portentous or more fruitful of evil consequences than this doctrine of the mass; and no doctrine of that Church is more entirely destitute of even a semblance of Scriptural support."[6] Similar strong statements abound among the Reformers and Puritans, but sadly are lacking in most contemporary evangelical and Reformed preaching and theology. We need to return to our biblical and historical roots.

Luther and his followers modified the Roman doctrine and proposed *consubstantiation*. That is, Christ is present (the *real presence*) at Communion "in, with and under" the bread and wine. The elements do not change. Whoever eats and drinks partakes of Christ in some way, even without faith. As we saw earlier, this view is linked with the Lutheran idea of the ubiquity of the humanity of Christ. Calvinists see the Lutheran theory as an improvement on Rome's heresy but say it does not go far enough from Rome and back to Scripture.

A third theory is associated with the father of Reformed theology, Huldrych Zwingli. It teaches that there is no real presence at Communion. The Lord's Table is only a meal of remembrance (Luke 22:19; 1 Corinthians 11:24–25). Though some scholars suggest that Zwingli also allowed a degree of spiritual presence and communion, most historians agree that he taught the memorial view alone. This position is the majority view among most evangelicals and fundamentalists today, especially among Baptists and charismatics. It would appear that the Anabaptists taught it also.

Spiritual Communion

The mainstream Reformed position goes back to Martin Bucer, John Calvin, and Peter Martyr Vermigli. They felt that Zwingli and the Anabaptists went too far and left out an important part of the Supper — namely, spiritual communion at Communion. We remember Christ in our minds and commune with Him in our hearts when we eat and drink in faith. The key verses are 1 Corinthians 10:16–21, especially verse 16: "The cup of blessing which we bless, is it not the communion of the blood of Christ? The bread which we break, is it

---

6 Charles Hodge, *Systematic Theology* (Grand Rapids: Eerdmans, 1979), 3:688.

not the communion of the body of Christ?" Paul says we have *koinonia* with the Lord — fellowship, spiritual communion, a heart-to-heart relationship. We do more than remember Him in the past; we commune with Him in the present. Paul contrasts it with the sacrificial meal of pagans, in which they consorted with demons (1 Corinthians 10:20).

Some but not all Reformed theologians see this in John 6:48–58. Christ is the Bread of Life (v. 35). True spiritual life comes from eating His flesh and drinking His blood. Contra Catholicism, this is not literal, or else it would be cannibalism, which is forbidden in Leviticus 17:11–16. Christ Himself corrected this misunderstanding in verse 63. When we truly receive Christ by faith, we metaphorically eat and drink the Bread of Life. We are not regenerated by the sacrament, but we are fed further spiritual life. It is one of several *means of grace*, like prayer, Bible reading, and worship. It cultivates and increases spiritual life. It is not automatic or magical, as Rome teaches. It is not salvific either. Calvinists sometimes say, "Communion is a special means of grace, but it is not a means of special grace." Calvin said, "Just as bread and wine sustain physical life, so are souls fed by Christ,"[7] and, "These benefits are to nourish, refresh, strengthen and gladden."[8]

In contrast with the Lutheran idea of the ubiquity of Christ's human body, the Reformed teach that Christ is present spiritually in His deity. The Second Helvetic Confession expressed it thusly:

> Yet the Lord is not absent from His Church when she celebrates the Supper. The sun, which is absent from us in the heavens, is notwithstanding effectually present among us. How much more is the Sun of Righteousness, Christ, although in His body He is absent from us in heaven, present with us, not corporally, but spiritually, by His vivifying operation, and as He Himself explained at His Last Supper that He would be present with us (Ch. 21).

Word and Spirit

Calvinism teaches the *spiritual presence* of Christ at Communion, not the real presence. It is real, of course, but not in a physical sense. Christ is present by the Spirit and the Word. This great biblical teaching was rediscovered and expounded in the Reformation primarily by Bucer and Vermigli. It has become a leading and distinctive feature of the Reformed doctrine of Communion.

---

7 Calvin, *Institutes*, 4:17:1 (p. 1361).
8 Calvin, 4:17:3 (p. 1363).

The Lord's Supper requires both the physical elements and the Word of God. It cannot be truly celebrated without either of them. Without the Word, the Table slides back into Romanism. Without the elements, Communion is in danger of being ignored or abolished. Appropriate Bible verses must be read and expounded, and those verses must say something about the person and/or work of Christ. Vermigli said that the elements are "visible words of God," but they are useless without the inspired Word. They would only be an uninterpreted parable. They are the only pictures of Christ that are allowed, as it were, but even then, they are only symbolic and not actual portraits.

Even the elements and the Word are futile unless they are blessed by the Holy Spirit. John 6:63: "It is the Spirit who gives life; the flesh profits nothing. The words that I speak to you are spirit, and they are life." The Spirit operates through the Spirit-inspired Scripture at the Lord's Table to bless believers and feed them with the ongoing life of Christ.

Faith is necessary to partake. We eat with the heart, not just the mouth. He who does not believe does not partake spiritually, contrary to both Rome and Lutheranism. The early Reformers — especially Calvin and Luther — insisted that the faith that feeds upon Christ at the Table must heartily believe "Christ died for me" (see Luke 22:19–20; Galatians 2:20). Later Calvinists downplayed this assurance at Communion, but urged that faith is strengthened at Communion nonetheless. The Belgic Confession said that faith is "the hand and mouth of the soul" (Article 35). The Westminster Larger Catechism explained the godly attitude involved in rightful partaking:

> It is required of them that receive the sacrament of the Lord's Supper, that, during the time of the administration of it, with all holy reverence and attention they wait upon God in that ordinance, diligently observe the sacramental elements and actions, heedfully discern the Lord's body, and affectionately mediate on His death and sufferings, and thereby stir up themselves to a vigorous exercise of their graces; in judging themselves, and sorrowing for sin; in earnest hungering and thirsting after Christ, feeding on Him by faith, receiving of His fullness, trusting in His merits, rejoicing in His love, giving thanks for His grace; in renewing of their covenant with God, and love to all the saints. (Q. 174)

Rightful Participants

The Table of the Lord is for the Lord's people — all Christians but only Christians, excepting those under church discipline. They must be able to remember Christ in faith, discern His body, and examine themselves. The unregenerate as well as believers with unrepented sin (1 Corinthians 11:27–32) are urged not to partake. A Christian with weak faith should still partake, for the Word strengthens faith.

How this is to be implemented has caused various controversies. The early New England idea was shown in the Halfway Covenant. Persons were to be admitted to the Table if they made a valid profession of faith and had no gross sin and had been baptized, even if they could not testify to a saving relation with Christ or give experimental and affectionate evidence. Jonathan Edwards came to reject and oppose this, but it continued in less orthodox forms of New England Theology. Other Calvinists, such as some Scottish Presbyterians, interviewed parishioners and issued "communion tokens" in the form of coins or cards as a kind of ticket to the Table. While one commends their zeal, one also wonders if this is what Christ and the apostles had in mind. The practice of tokens faded away, but some still use the interview process. Many Reformed churches practice closed Communion — only members may partake. Strict Baptists restrict Communion to those who have been baptized as believers. Many if not most Reformed Baptists and paedobaptists practice believers-only Communion, open to non-member believers.

It is the general practice to "fence the Table." Believers are invited, but unbelievers and unrepentant backsliders are urged to refrain from partaking. Historic Calvinists take a very serious attitude of reverence at Communion, in stark contrast with the flippant attitude common in many non-Reformed churches. It is serious because it is spiritual. A holy attitude must prevail, or sacrilege is committed.

Some extreme Calvinists, usually Presbyterian and never Baptist, have taught paedo-Communion. They reason that since we give the first sacrament to infants of believers, why not give the second sacrament? By far most Calvinists reject this somewhat bizarre practice. It is pointed out that infants cannot believe, remember Christ, discern the Lord's body, or examine themselves. Calvin noted: "A self-examination ought, therefore, to come first, and it is vain to expect this of infants."[9] There is neither command nor example of infant Communion in Scripture. Even Rome does not practice it, though some Eastern Orthodox churches do.

As to frequency, most Reformed churches celebrate Communion once a

---

9 Calvin, 4:16:3 (p. 1353).

month or once a quarter. A few do it only once or twice a year. A few, such as some Reformed Baptists (including the author's church), practice weekly Communion, which Calvin favored.[10]

Conclusion

The Reformed view of the sacraments was summed up by William Perkins the Puritan: "Sacraments do not confer grace, but rather confirm grace."[11] They are holy ordinances that God has instituted for His people to testify to His wondrous grace.

10 John Calvin, *Calvin: Theological Treatises* (Philadelphia: Westminster, 1954), 49.
11 William Perkins, *A Golden Chaine* (n.p.: Puritan Reprints, 2010), 224.

Chapter 70
Calvinistic Apologetics

Christians in every era have attempted to defend the faith against the assaults and objections of non-Christians.[1] The Reformers and Puritans did not encounter as many outright non-Christians, so their efforts were more in the area of polemics against Roman Catholicism, Socinianism, and other pseudo-Christian errors. Peter Ramus greatly simplified the Aristolelianism of Catholic scholasticism. But as non-Christian philosophy began to grow in the seventeenth century, Reformed theologians rose to the challenge. Over the subsequent centuries Calvinist writers have been involved in apologetics.

Calvinistic Rationalism

The first major challenge to Christianity after the Reformation came from the philosophy of Rationalism as taught by René Descartes (1596–1650). Nominally a Catholic, he tried to harmonize Christianity with philosophy far more than Thomas Aquinas had in the thirteenth century. His approach opened the door to Deism and the Enlightenment, which have only a vague resemblance to Christianity.

Two responses bear mentioning. Jonathan Edwards wrote against Deism in several works. His approach might be termed *Reformed Rationalism*. Among his arguments was the contention that Deism does not adequately answer the questions raised by modern thinkers. Christianity does. Christianity alone is logically consistent. He used some of Rationalism's very methods to refute Rationalism. Sometimes he did this by showing the absurdity of its conclusions.

Later in the eighteenth century, Thomas Reid (1710–96) of Scotland offered another variation in opposing his fellow Scotsman David Hume (1711–76). Hume proposed a philosophy more of empiricism than the older Rationalism, and so Reid's apologetic might be termed *Reformed Empiricism*. As with so many previous and subsequent apologists, Reid attempted to defend Christianity by employing what he thought was a Christian form of what he opposed. His system has been called *Scottish Realism* or *Common Sense Philosophy*. This

---

1 For a useful survey of the history of apologetics from a Reformed perspective, see William Edgar and K. Scott Oliphint, eds., *Christian Apologetics*, 2 vols. (Wheaton: Crossway, 2009).

became very popular among Calvinists such as the Princeton schools, including James McCosh and Charles Hodge. In Europe it was continued and made less Calvinistic by Sir William Hamilton (1788–1856) and Dugald Stewart (1753–1828).

In the twentieth century, this general approach was popular with evangelicals, including Calvinists such as J. Oliver Buswell Jr. (1895–1977). Buswell taught at Wheaton College and Covenant Theological Seminary and wrote *A Systematic Theology of the Christian Religion* and *A Christian View of Being and Knowing*. He leaned toward Christian empiricism in denying that man is born with innate ideas. The mind is blank until it receives data through experience, which is then processed by inference. He taught the usefulness of the *law of noncontradiction* (*A* cannot equal non-*A*), a basic theorem of Rationalism and logic. Through this approach one can conclude there probably is a Supreme Being who is the source of rational meaning and existence.

This use of evidences became very popular among evangelicals, such as Josh McDowell in his hugely popular *Evidence that Demands a Verdict*. But there is nothing distinctly Reformed about it; many Arminians have used it.

John Gerstner (1914–96) proposed a more Reformed view of Christian Rationalism. He took his cue from Edwards, not the Princetonians or Reid. Note the title of his three-volume magnum opus: *The Rational Biblical Theology of Jonathan Edwards*. In 1960 he wrote the short *Reasons for Faith*. Gerstner's main disciple was R. C. Sproul (1939–2017), who with Gerstner and Arthur Lindsley co-wrote *Classical Apologetics: A Rational Defense of the Christian Faith and a Critique of Presuppositional Apologetics*. Sproul had been perhaps the most well-known popular Calvinist writer since 1980 to the present. His book *Reason to Believe* resembles Gerstner's in both title and method.

This approach does not employ many empirical evidences but rather rational arguments. One is as follows: The Bible is a good history book, as verified by secular historians and archaeologists. At the least, it teaches that Jesus of Nazareth was a good man, as almost all readers of the Bible admit. But Jesus claimed to be God and asserted that the Bible is the word of God. Good men do not make such claims unless they are right. Therefore, Christ is (or probably is) who He claimed to be, and the Bible is (or probably is) the word of God. From there we go on to substantiate the truth claims of the gospel. Edwards, Gerstner, and Sproul argue that Christianity alone is rational and consistent with itself and the facts of history and observation. This approach could be considered Reformed Aristotelianism or Calvinistic Thomism. Gerstner used to ask, "Should old Aquinas be forgot?" and made the astounding assertion that Aquinas was a Protestant before the Reformation. But like other Christian Rationalists, this method can be adapted by Arminians, as has been done by Norman Geisler, J. P. Moreland, and William Lane Craig, all three of whom oppose historic Calvinism.

Presuppositionalism

In the late nineteenth century, a much more distinctly Reformed apologetic was developed by Abraham Kuyper (1837–1920). It has been called the Amsterdam Philosophy (Kuyper founded the Free University of Amsterdam), Neo-Calvinism, Kuyper-Calvinism, Calvinistic Philosophy, or *presuppositionalism*. Rather than employ the enemy's tools against him, Kuyper insisted that Christianity and non-Christianity are irreconcilable, and so we must recognize "The Antithesis." Apologetics should be antithetical, not synthetical, in method. God's ways and thoughts are not our ways and thoughts (Isaiah 55:8). This more resembles Tertullian's method than Justin Martyr's.

In the twentieth century, this apologetic school began to divide. The more liberal approach was spearheaded by Herman Dooyeweerd (1894–1977), director of the Abraham Kuyper Foundation and professor of law at the Free University of Amsterdam. He founded the Association for Calvinistic Philosophy and was editor of the *Philosophia Reformata* journal. His major work was the enormous *A New Critique of Theoretical Thought* (4 volumes). He aimed his guns more at Immanuel Kant than at René Descartes. Human thought is not neutral or uncritically theoretical, argued Dooyeweerd. Everyone has presuppositions, often without knowing what they are. Nobody is neutral, nor is our mind free from the noetic effects of sin. Man only pretends to be autonomous, when in fact he is biased against God and does not think straight.

The first wave of this branch was led by Dooyeweerd, Dirk Hendrik Th. Vollenhoven (1892–1978), professor of philosophy at the Free University of Amsterdam, and Hendrik G. Stoker (1899–1993) of South Africa. Others included H. van Riessen, J. P. A. Mekkes, and J. M. Spier. Stoker's influence was felt at Potchefstroom University for Christian Higher Education, especially through B. J. Van der Walt. In Canada, Dooyeweerdianism was continued leftward by the Institute for Christian Studies (Toronto) and through Hendrik Hart and C. T. McIntire, son of the controversial Presbyterian fundamentalist Carl McIntire. In the United States, it was continued at Dordt College and elsewhere, mostly among Dutch-Americans through the teaching of H. Evan

Runner, H. L. Hebden Taylor, and Robert Knudsen. William Young and David Hugh Freeman, the translators of Dooyeweerd's *New Critique*, later retreated from the direction of the more extreme exponents. The movement became increasingly speculative and obtuse. It resembled a liberal Calvinism mingled with secular humanism on philosophical and ethical issues and was sometimes accused of antinomianism and anti-experimental spirituality. Dooyeweerdianism still continues, but it is past its high point.

Cornelius Van Til

Van Til (1895–1987) was originally a member of Dooyeweerd's school of the so-called *Philosophy of the Cosmonomic Idea*, but he increasingly became disaffected with its leftward direction. His approach was notably more confessionally and traditionally Reformed. He first taught at Princeton Theological Seminary and helped found Westminster Theological Seminary. He wrote dozens of books, pamphlets, and unpublished syllabi, of which *The Defense of the Faith* was his most important. He was a vehement opponent of Karl Barth and Neo-Orthodoxy, which is curious because both Barth and Van Til have been charged with Fideism.

Van Til emphasized the Antithesis, *sola Scriptura*, "the self-attesting Christ of Scripture," the internal testimony of the Holy Spirit, the *sensus divinitatis*, and other Reformed tenets. He relegated proofs and evidences to a much lower place but did not entirely rule them out. He taught that we defend Christianity by exposing the absurdity of non-Christian presuppositions. We do not need to prove the existence of God or the Word of God, for they are self-attesting. There are no "brute facts" to which we appeal, but rather, we touch common ground in the image of God in all men. Sin has defaced that image and controls man's thoughts, but Scripture speaks to him and transforms him when used by the Holy Spirit.

Gerstner, Sproul, and others opposed this as Fideism — a non-rational leap of faith not based on verifiable facts. Unlike Dooyeweerdianism, Van Til's approach has continued and flourished in historic Reformed circles. Among its proponents are John Frame, K. Scott Oliphint, William White, Thom Notaro, Richard Platt, J. S. Halsey, William Edgar, and the theonomists, especially R. J. Rushdoony, Greg Bahnsen, and Gary North. It should be pointed out that presuppositionalism is held almost exclusively by evangelical Calvinists, rarely by non-Calvinists.

Variations of Presuppositionalism

Francis Schaeffer (1912–84) studied briefly under Van Til at Westminster Theological Seminary. He ministered in the Bible Presbyterian Church led by Carl McIntire until it split, and he linked up with the Reformed Presbyterian Evangelical Synod associated with Buswell. He then served as missionary evangelist to Switzerland in the L'Abri community he founded with his wife, Edith, in 1947. By the late 1970s he was extremely popular with young American evangelicals through his books, such as *The God Who Is There*, *Escape from Reason*, and *How Should We Then Live?* Later in his ministry he turned to addressing the ethical and philosophical implications of increasingly post-Christian society. He co-wrote the strongly pro-life *Whatever Happened to the Human Race?* with C. Everett Koop, who would later serve as Surgeon General in the Reagan administration. Schaeffer was also a leading defender of full biblical inerrancy in the "Battle for the Bible" during the 1970s and 1980s. His son Franky (later Frank) continued his legacy for a short time before becoming radically non-evangelical.[2] Others of the "Schaeffer School" were Os Guinness, Hans Rookmaker, Udo Middleman, and Dick Keyes. Unlike Van Til's following, Schaeffer's has waned considerably and bears only a little resemblance to the original vision, though the small Francis Schaeffer Institute located at Covenant Theological Seminary keeps the flame alive.

Less explicitly Reformed than Van Til, Schaeffer taught a modified presuppositionalism that was popular with Christian "baby boomers" who were confronted with the philosophy of existentialism. One feature of his approach was to push one's opponents to the brink of despair and even suicide by showing that their views led only to absurdity and hopelessness. Christianity alone offers true hope and meaning. But as existentialism was replaced by postmodernism as the philosophy *de jour*, Schaefferianism became outdated. Many later evangelical leaders, however, were greatly influenced by Schaeffer, such as Albert Mohler.

Gordon H. Clark (1902–85) presented another form of presuppositionalism, one that was more explicitly Reformed than that of Schaeffer but with certain notable differences with Van Til. Clark was a conservative Presbyterian who taught at Wheaton College and Butler University. A prolific author, perhaps the best summary of his apologetic was *A Christian View of Men and Things*. He strongly opposed empiricism, even in a Christian dress, and rejected evidentialist apologetics. He proposed what might be termed *rational presuppositionalism*.

---

2 Frank Schaeffer, *Dancing Alone* (Brookline, MA: Holy Cross Orthodox, 1994).

He accepted the Reformed theology of the *sensus divinitatis*, the internal testimony of the Holy Spirit, the noetic effects of sin, *sola Scriptura*, and others. He accepted far more logic than Van Til did — perhaps too much, as when he translated the *logos* of John 1:1 as "The logic was God."[3] Unlike Van Til, he deemphasized paradox and stressed the law of noncontradiction. Christianity alone is logical and self-consistent. Most of all, it is based on the inspired and self-authenticating Word of God. The Bible is the Christian's apologetic presupposition, argued Clark.

Van Til opposed Clark's ordination in the Orthodox Presbyterian Church over the issue of the incomprehensibility of God.[4] At Wheaton he exercised much influence over several young students who would later be major evangelical leaders, such as Carl F. H. Henry, Edward John Carnell, Ronald Nash, and Gordon Lewis, who were all only moderately Reformed. Clark's closest disciples have been John Robbins and Gary Crampton. His school has always been overshadowed by Van Til's, and while their rivalry has not always been friendly, they are both more explicitly Reformed in theology than most other kinds of evangelical apologetics.

Reformed Epistemology

Yet another school of Calvinistic apologetics appeared in post-war American evangelicalism. It developed in the more liberal wing of the Dutch-American Christian Reformed Church, mainly at Calvin College under the influence from G. C. Berkouwer of Holland and, initially at least, Herman Dooyeweerd. It might better be considered a cousin of presuppositionalism than a brother. Its leading proponents have been Alvin Plantinga (1932–), Nicholas Wolterstorff (1932–), William Alston, George Mavrodes, and Kelly James Clark. Much of the discussion revolves around epistemology — "How can we know what is true and right?"

Plantinga's main contribution has been in the area of "warrants," which is somewhere between conclusive proof and probable reasons. The system could be charted between presuppositionalism on the one hand and Scottish Common Sense Realism and Christian Rationalism on the other. It is far more philosophical than Van Tilian presuppositionalism. It has gained popularity in

---

3 Gordon H. Clark, *The Johannine Logos*, 2nd ed. (Jefferson, MD: The Trinity Foundation, 1989) and *Logic*, 2nd ed. (Jefferson, MD: The Trinity Foundation, 1988), 120–21.

4 See Fred H. Klooster, *The Incomprehensibility of God in the Orthodox Presbyterian Church Conflict* (Franeker: T. Wever, 1951).

the era of postmodernism and is one of the few modern Christian apologetics that has gained the attention of non-Christian philosophers.

It often discusses the problem of evil and employs the "Free Will Defense," which is certainly more Arminian than Reformed, even though Plantinga and the others still profess the Three Forms of Unity held by Dutch Calvinism. In this principle, love must be unforced to be true. God risked that man would fall in creating him with free will. Ultimately God uses sin for good (Plantinga accepted a form of the *Felix Culpa*). Natural philosophy has no answer to the problem of evil, but Christianity does, argued Plantinga.

We all believe certain things without convincing evidence. This is akin to presuppositions, but Plantinga prefers to address warrants than unconscious presuppositions. We regularly accept some things to be true without going through the scientific method of observation, theorizing, and validating or by logical deductions by syllogizing again and again. Also, we all have a common-sense perception of things and a sense of the divine. We do not have to prove that Christianity is true, for the *sensus divinitatis* and internal testimony of the Spirit provide sufficient warrant to believe. *Foundationalism* is inadequate to the task — that is, we can only believe something if it is self-evident or provable to the senses. Belief in God is "proper and basic" and does not require demonstrable evidence.

In the end, Reformed Epistemology has some strengths over Christian Rationalism but shares some of the weaknesses of presuppositionalism. Perhaps its greatest weakness is its obvious philosophical methodology rather than theological dogmatism. Like the others, it just is not biblical enough.

Miscellaneous Reformed Apologists

There have been other attempts at apologetics by Reformed theologians, but they are hard to classify into the above groups. David Wells, both Reformed and Episcopalian, wrote an incisive trilogy: *No Place for Truth, God in the Wasteland,* and *Losing Our Virtue.* His approach is somewhat similar to the latter Francis Schaeffer as well as Albert Mohler and James Montgomery Boice. He does not so much answer philosophical objections as address cultural dilemmas that have arisen from post-Christian and postmodern society that has lost its moral compass and truth map. Not presuppositionalist *per se*, he does address underlying assumptions and shows that Christianity alone solves the basic needs and problems of the world.

John Blanchard, the leading British evangelist for the last generation and a Reformed Baptist by conviction, wrote his masterpiece *Does God Believe in Atheists?* At times he sounds rationalist or evidentialist, occasionally presuppositional, somewhat Schaefferian, never boring. His strength is that he is far more evangelistic in his apologetics than the others — which must never be forgotten in the truth wars. We are not just out to win arguments but to win souls for Christ. On the other hand, one of his weaknesses is shared with Josh McDowell: He tends to buttress his arguments with quotations from "experts" and "authorities" as if to argue that Christians also have heavyweight intellectuals on their side. He mainly responds to the "New Atheism" of Richard Dawkins and Christopher Hitchens as well as scientists such as Stephen Hawking.

John Feinberg employed what is sometimes called the "Cumulative Position" of apologetics. Like Blanchard, he uses a variety of approaches, like a carpenter who selects just the right tool for the specific job at hand. His large volume *No One Like Him* is a traditional Calvinistic theology of God, and his approach can be seen in books like *Can You Believe It's True?*

Paul Helm is also hard to categorize. Like Plantinga he is primarily a philosophy professor and does not often quote or exegete Scripture. But this is balanced by his outspoken Reformed theology, such as his defense of historically orthodox views of eternity, the compatibility of divine sovereignty and human responsibility, and limited atonement. He has written a number of excellent studies of John Calvin.

Biblical Apologetics

All the above writers and systems have useful points and are within the broad circle of Calvinist doctrine. But, in my opinion, all tend to be overly philosophical and insufficiently biblical. They tend to be too timely and not timeless. They sometimes oppose objections that are already out of style, fighting battles that nobody is interested in anymore. Thus, they become dated and ignored by the very opponents they seek to answer. Further, they have a distinct tendency to imitate those they oppose by employing their opponents' methods. Hence, Christian Rationalism, Christian Empiricism, Christian Fideism, etc.

A small but growing number of historic Calvinists are dissatisfied with these attempts at Reformed apologetics. We prefer what I have coined as *Biblical*

Apologetics.[5] I plan to write at length on the subject. Back in the 1960s, Jay Adams began a revolution in Christian counseling by arguing that Christians should counsel from the Bible and do not need the methods of secular psychology. He did this by appealing to the infallible and sufficient Word of God. I say that we need a similar revolution in apologetics. We need to apply *sola Scriptura* to answering the objections of non-Christians. Scripture is sufficient of itself to answer the big questions. Evidences, arguments, logical syllogisms, and presuppositions are not enough. Using them instead of Scripture implies that Scripture is not sufficient — indeed, that it is not what it claims to be. At best, such methods and proofs can only win a stalemate (and often not even that), while a Bible-based apologetic alone can win the game.

Presuppositionalism, especially Clark's version, advocates Scripture over proofs, but fails at several points. It does not appeal to Scripture soon enough. True biblical apologetics is somewhat prophetic. We can quote Scripture and say, "Thus saith the Lord," and "It is written." "The Bible says" is better than "Logic proves that" or "The evidence demands it." Billy Graham popularized the phrase "The Bible says" in the context of evangelism, and the same method must be used in evangelistic apologetics. Without the evangelism note, apologetics quickly becomes a futile exercise in trying to score philosophical points.

Saving faith is given by means of the Bible (Romans 10:17). Christians need to give non-Christians the Bible, not arguments. Using "proofs" implies that the Bible is not good enough. Indeed, it logically implies that those proofs are the basis for our faith, not the Bible. But Scripture is our highest authority, not human wisdom. Reformed apologists believe in the infallibility and self-attestation of Scripture, but they rarely use it in debates. They try to prove the sword rather than using it. In effect they *yield* the sword rather than *wield* it. It is ironic that so many advocate the internal testimony of the Spirit in Scripture but do not rely on it. As Spurgeon is reported to have said, we do not have to defend a lion — just let it out of its cage, and it will defend itself. So with Scripture. Unbelievers may not agree with the Word, but they will feel the force of it (see Ezekiel 2:5; 33:3).

Biblical apologetics is basically very simple. Unlike other apologetic systems, it does not require extensive knowledge of philosophy. It can be used by any

---

5 The closest to my approach would be Clifford B. McManis, *Biblical Apologetics* (n.p.: XLibris Corp., 2012), revised as *Apologetics by the Book* (Sunnyvale, CA: GBF, 2017). A similar approach is in Voddie Baucham Jr., *Expository Apologetics* (Wheaton: Crossway, 2015).

Christian who believes the Bible is the inspired word of God. It works like this: We listen to the objection, boil it down to a basic point, search for the Scripture that most directly answers the objection, and then we quote and explain what God says in the Bible. We thus appeal to God alone as authority. To all objections we can say, "That is not what God says in the Bible. This is what God says."

Perhaps the basic question of all philosophy is "Why?" The Bible's answer is: "God." Why do we believe the Bible? Because God says it is His word. Why do we believe in God? Because God says He exists. Why do we exist? Because God created us for His own glory. Why do we believe Christ is the only way to God? Because God says so.

Other methods fight fire with fire. This method fights fire with water. When they pull a knife, we pull a gun. Using philosophy (even the "Christian Philosophy" of presuppositionalism) opens the door to liberalism, for liberalism is the mingling of Christianity with whatever philosophy is currently in vogue. The Bible uses the word *philosophy* only once (Colossians 2:8) — and then to warn against it. See Paul's estimation of human wisdom in 1 Corinthians 1. "Christian philosophy" is like "Christian adultery." One is reminded of Luther's opinion that philosophy is "the Devil's whore." Philosophy originates in the fallen mind of God-hating humanity and cannot be baptized into Christian service. Like adultery, it produces an illegitimate child.

Presuppositionalism is a great advance on the other Reformed apologetics but does not go far enough. Though its exponents are loath to admit it, they employ more philosophy than they realize. Their strength is in seeing "The Antithesis," the noetic effects of sin, and the failure of philosophy. But even Van Til admitted that he did not have enough biblical exegesis in his books.[6] To use non-Christian tools is to employ carnal weapons instead of spiritual (2 Corinthians 10:4).

Conclusion

We need to apply Bible doctrine to biblical apologetics. Calvinists need to take the lead in a "Back to the Bible" biblical apologetic.

---

6 Cf. Van Til's admission in *Jerusalem and Athens: Critical Discussions on the Theology and Apologetics of Cornelius Van Til*, ed. by E. R. Geehan (n.p.: Presbyterian and Reformed, 1971), 203.

Chapter 71
Reformed Evangelism

Like all Christians, Calvinists believe in evangelism. But it must be biblical in content and method. Our forefathers reformed the church in doctrine and practice in the Reformation, and we need another Reformation today in the realm of evangelism. The true gospel needs to be rediscovered. One could apply the Regulative Principle to evangelism as well as worship: We must evangelize only in the way that God has told us in the Bible. His way is best.

Calvinistic Evangelism

It is sometimes said that Arminians evangelize more, and Calvinists evangelize better. There is some truth in this, for there are far more Arminians than Calvinists in the churches today. Most popular evangelism is clearly Arminian in content and method. It is no surprise that many if not most Calvinists were converted under Arminian evangelism. Eventually, many rethink the subject in light of the Bible.

Arminians frequently charge us with being non-evangelistic with statements like "If I believed like you, I would never share the gospel with anyone." That is a gross misunderstanding if not deliberate misrepresentation. For instance, the Protestant Reformation was very evangelistic. Hundreds of thousands of sinners were saved. The Geneva church sent hundreds of preachers into France with the gospel and even sent missionaries to Brazil.

The Puritans were also evangelistic. Two best-selling evangelistic books were penned by leading Puritans: *An Alarm to the Unconverted* by Joseph Alleine and *A Call to the Unconverted* by Richard Baxter. John Eliot and David Brainerd were Calvinist missionaries to the American Indians. Most of the preachers of the Evangelical Awakening in Britain were Calvinists: George Whitefield, Howell Harris, Daniel Rowland, to name a few. Almost all the preachers in the Great Awakening in America were strongly Calvinistic: Jonathan Edwards, the Tennents, Theodorus Frelinghuysen, and others. Many preachers in the Second Great Awakening were Calvinists: Asahel Nettleton, Timothy Dwight, and more. The Great Missionary Movement was begun by five-point Calvinists: Andrew Fuller, William Carey, John Rippon, John Ryland Jr., and Samuel

Pearce. Charles Haddon Spurgeon was greatly used by God to the conversion of thousands. Alexander Duff, Adoniram Judson, and David Livingstone were famous nineteenth-century Calvinist missionaries. John Blanchard has been a world-renown Calvinist evangelist for over half a century. D. James Kennedy's *Evangelism Explosion* has impacted thousands of evangelistic Christians and helped convert many lost souls. A catalog of Reformed evangelists, preachers, and missionaries could go on and on.

It is simply not true that "Calvinism kills evangelism and missions." That accusation is only true of the approximately 1 percent of Calvinists who are Hyper-Calvinists. My belief in the doctrines of grace has by no means impeded my evangelism. I have preached well over a thousand evangelistic messages in churches, nursing homes, skid-row missions, and open-air street meetings for over forty years. Hundreds of Reformed pastors can also so testify.

Evangelism and the Sovereignty of God

In his excellent book *Evangelism and the Sovereignty of God*, J. I. Packer relates divine sovereignty and human responsibility to evangelism. God is absolutely sovereign and has foreordained all that comes to pass. But we are also responsible to believe and, when converted, to tell people the gospel. Those truths are complementary, not contradictory.

God chose only some sinners to be saved. That is the secret will of God in predestination. But in the revealed will, God sincerely desires all sinners to be saved and commands them to believe in Christ. It is a paradox — or as Packer calls it, an *antinomy* — but we dare not deny either truth, for they are both taught in Scripture. The revealed will includes both law and gospel. One tells us the problem; the other tells us the answer. We need to tell all people both of them.

Prayer should accompany evangelism. In evangelism we speak to men for God, and in prayer, we speak to God for men. We plant the seeds of the gospel, then water them by prayer. We pray for God to call in His elect through the gospel, and like Paul, we earnestly pray that God will save those who are lost (Romans 10:1).

We showed earlier that the Bible says there is no salvation for those who never hear the gospel nor for those who hear but do not repent and believe. Therefore it is imperative that all Christians obey the Great Commission far and wide. It is not just the job of the pastor, missionary, and evangelist but all

Christians (see Acts 8:4). All sinners need to hear; all Christians need to tell them.

Evangelism and the Five Points

Fallen man is guilty, deserves Hell, and is unable to save himself. He is not even able to repent and believe. But he is accountable to God to repent and believe. Repentance and faith are both gifts and duties. God gives them to the elect through the Word that is preached and thereby draws them to Christ for salvation. If the sinner was not totally depraved and morally unable, his situation would not be hopeless. The gospel would not be necessary. But he is, and it is. The first point of Calvinism, then, does not negate evangelism but makes it all the more important. Weakening this doctrine leads to weakening the need.

God has not told us who the elect are, only that all men everywhere are lost. The elect are mingled secretly among the reprobate. Our job is not to find out who the elect are and share the gospel with them only but to tell everyone. Peter Martyr Vermigli had a good insight here:

> Nor is it any obstacle to preaching that the number of the elect is certain and fixed, as it really is, for by preaching we do not go about trying to transfer men from the number of the reprobate into the number of the elect, but rather affirm that the elect, by the ministry of the Word, might be brought to their appointed end.[1]

As John Blanchard says, "Election is a doctrine I am called upon to believe; evangelism is a command I am called upon to obey."[2] Evangelism and election are both in Matthew 22:14: "Many are called, but few are chosen." Further, we do not need to tell the lost about election, but we do need to tell them about the gospel.[3] We must preach the revealed will first, then the secret will after they are saved. Election is an incentive, not a hindrance, to true evangelism. God has guaranteed that someone out there will believe the gospel. Paul said in 2 Timothy 2:10, "Therefore I endure all things for the sake of the elect, that they also may obtain the salvation which is in Christ Jesus, with eternal glory."

1 Peter Martyr Vermigli, *The Peter Martyr Library* (Kirksville, MO: Truman State University Press, 2003), 8:8.

2 John Blanchard, *More Gathered Gold* (Welwyn: Evangelical Press, 1986), 87.

3 D. Martyn Lloyd-Jones, *Romans: The Final Perseverance of the Saints* (Edinburgh: Banner of Truth, 1975), 195.

See Acts 18:10. Nobody believed in election more than Paul, and nobody was as zealous for evangelism as Paul. We must imitate him in both.

What about the third point? Many Calvinists base the free offer of the gospel on the infinite value and universal sufficiency of the atonement. In Christ's parable of the feast, there was more than enough on the banquet table to which people were invited (Luke 14:16–24). In preaching the gospel we say both, "Come, for all things are now ready" (Luke 14:17), and "Christ died for our sins" (1 Corinthians 15:3).[4]

Some apply the same parable to the fourth point. We invite lost sinners, but it is the Holy Spirit who effectually "compels them to come in" (Luke 14:23). They resist the general call, but the Spirit efficaciously melts and overcomes their resistance and makes them willing to come to Christ. The special irresistible call is a great incentive for Christians to share the gospel. There is more power in the gospel than we realize (Romans 1:16).

The Reformed doctrine of the perseverance and preservation of the saints is an encouragement to lost sinners who worry that they would not be able to hold on if they become a Christian. The gospel tells them that God has promised to hold them and guarantees that He will never let them go (John 10:28). The doctrine of perseverance also demands that we tell sinners that God does not command only a one-time decision but a lifetime commitment to Christ.

Arminian Abuses

There are several evangelistic errors that are promoted by well-meaning Arminians. Many are based on the unbiblical idea of free will. Some are misleading, manipulative, or even deceptive. Perhaps the most common abuse is what is sometimes called "decisional evangelism." It concerns the desired response of the lost sinner who hears the gospel. He is urged to repeat a prayer (sometimes called the "Sinner's Prayer" based on a misinterpretation of Luke 18:13). He may be told, "Open the door of your heart, and invite Jesus in." This is extremely widespread in popular evangelism. Sometimes those who do not employ this method are severely castigated as unloving or uninterested in winning souls for Christ. The problem is that there is absolutely no biblical support whatsoever for decisional evangelism. There are no commands or

---

4 The reader is advised to read Charles H. Spurgeon's sermon "Compel Them to Come In," *New Park Street Pulpit* (Pasadena, TX: Pilgrim Publications, 1981), 5:17–24. It was remarkably blessed by God in the conversion of many sinners, both when preached and later published.

examples in the Bible. We never find Christ, the apostles, the prophets, or even the average Christian in the Bible using anything resembling this practice.

Nobody led the tax collector of Luke 18:13 in the Sinner's Prayer nor the thief on the cross, the woman at the well, the Philippian jailer, or those who heard Peter preach on the day of Pentecost. It is curious that Robert Coleman wrote the generally useful book *The Master Plan of Evangelism* from an Arminian perspective and called on us to evangelize like the Master did, yet Coleman failed to note that the Master never used the method promoted by Arminians today. The gospel calls on sinners to repent and believe, not ask Jesus into their heart. It is Christ, not the sinner, who opens the heart (Acts 16:14). Revelation 3:20 is addressed to professing Christians, not non-Christians, and is an allusion to Song of Solomon 5:2 in which the husband desires deeper intimacy with his bride. When we substitute anything for faith and repentance, there can be no true salvation — only false conversions.

The same is true with the "altar call," also called "going forward," "hitting the sawdust trail," and other such terms. Not only are there no examples or commands for this widespread practice in Scripture, but nobody did it until the early nineteenth century. It appears that Charles Finney and other Arminians invented it to multiply the number of their converts in the Second Great Awakening, many if not most of whom later vanished like fog in the "burned-over district" of New York and elsewhere. The same pattern occurs today in mass evangelism. One never finds anything like Finney's "anxious bench" in the evangelism of Jonathan Edwards, George Whitefield, or even John Wesley. Asahel Nettleton practiced a far more biblical evangelism at the same time as Finney, and most of his converts proved to be true converts, not flash-in-the-pan, temporary converts like we find in Matthew 13:20–21 and John 6:66. The altar call is so uncritically accepted today that it has become almost a third sacrament, especially in Baptist churches. To stop it or even question it usually invites immediate wrath. The closest example in Scripture would be Moses calling on Jews to step out and join him in Exodus 32:26, but Moses then commanded them to slay others with a sword. Would anyone today issue such an altar call?

Arminianism frequently, though not always, practices "easy-believism." It lowers the cost of discipleship in several ways. One is by denying the absolute necessity for repentance, contrary to Christ's words in Luke 13:3 (see Luke 24:47). Others make repentance only a change of mind or a temporary requirement during the so-called dispensational "Kingdom offer" period of Christ's ministry. It may make faith only mental assent rather than personal trust in Christ. It frequently states that a sinner only has to believe in Jesus as Savior rather than submit to Him as Lord. It will say, "Give your heart to Jesus," rather than "Repent and believe" (Mark 1:15). This unbiblical and dangerous approach has been effectively disproved by John MacArthur in *The Gospel According to Jesus*; Walter Chantry in *Today's Gospel: Authentic or Synthetic?*; and Paul Washer in his trilogy, *The Gospel's Power and Message*, *The Gospel Call and True Conversion*, and *Gospel Assurance and Warnings*. Easy-believism does not urge the sinner to count the cost (Luke 14:28) or expect persecution (Matthew 24:9). It only occasionally talks about sin as breaking the law of God and deserving eternal Hell. It does not emphasize conviction of sin. Rather, it concentrates on "felt needs" such as loneliness. It certainly does not demand an absolute lifetime commitment but calls for a quick decision. It does not call on the sinner to deny himself, take up his cross, and follow Christ (Mark 8:34). Historic Calvinism has never advocated easy-believism but has been its severest critic. Fortunately, some Arminians like John Wesley and A. W. Tozer have not endorsed this deficient gospel.

Such Arminian abuses multiply false converts. When they do not "go on" or show lasting spiritual fruit, they are judged to be "carnal Christians." Calvinists consider them carnal non-Christians, for true Christians persevere to the end in faith, repentance, and obedience. A rediscovery of orthodox Calvinism usually leads to a reevaluation of Arminian evangelistic abuses. New Calvinists often reject them very quickly and practice more biblical evangelism.

Weaknesses Calvinists Face

Calvinists face certain weaknesses that non-Calvinists do not. One is Hyper-Calvinism, which we examined earlier in this volume. The definitive feature of this system is the denial of the free offer of the gospel. Related to that is the rejection of any desire of God for the salvation of all men. Many Hyper-Calvinists also reject common grace and the duty of all who hear the gospel to savingly believe in Christ. Many do not invite all sinners, only so-called "sensible sinners" who have already been convicted of sin and may already be unconsciously regenerate. The implications of this error for evangelism are obvious. Curiously, Jonathan Edwards said that Jesus Christ Himself invited those whom He knew were reprobate — and so we too can invite all sinners, even though we do not know who are elect or reprobate.[5]

---

5 Jonathan Edwards, *The Works of Jonathan Edwards* (New Haven: Yale University Press, 2004), 20:108.

It was Andrew Fuller's *The Gospel Worthy of All Acceptation* that not only checked the stultifying effects of English Hyper-Calvinism in the eighteenth century but opened the door to the Great Missionary Movement in 1792. When we minimize or deny God's universal will that all be saved, we too lose that will. We should heed Augustine's counsel: "For, not knowing who pertains to and who does not pertain to the number of the predestined, we ought to have such a spirit of love that we want all to be saved."[6] We should be like Paul (Romans 10:1). Some Calvinists seem to be hindered in their evangelism because they do not know who the elect are, wrongly presuming that they need to know such information. Sometimes that is only an excuse for laziness or lack of love, let alone obedience to the Great Commission. Their witnessing almost encourages unbelievers to delay believing in Christ until they know they are elect. Spurgeon offered good advice:

> I hear one say, 'Suppose I am not one of God's elect.' To him I say, 'Suppose you are.' Better still, suppose you leave off supposing altogether, and just go to Jesus Christ and see. [. . .] You come to Christ, and you shall know that you were given to Christ; for none come to Him but those who are His, and by this coming to Him they give the best evidence of their election.[7]

New Calvinists sometimes lose their former evangelistic zeal and prefer to just argue about theology, especially Calvinism. They prefer counting the petals on the TULIP to preaching the gospel. There is no excuse for such imbalanced zeal and laziness. Nobody believed the doctrines of grace more than the apostle Paul, and we would all do well to imitate his zeal for preaching the gospel (Romans 1:15). "Woe is me if I do not preach the gospel!" (1 Corinthians 9:16).

Unlike the Arminian, the Calvinist may struggle with the question: "If God has already predestined who will be saved, why evangelize?" The answer is simple: We evangelize because God commands us to and uses it to call His elect. It parallels why we should pray in light of the sovereignty of God.

Calvinists and Arminians alike need to be reminded of the sober warnings of Ezekiel 3 and 33. God has made us watchmen on the wall. We must blow the gospel trumpet and warn lost sinners of Hell. If they hear and do not believe, their blood is on their own head. If they hear and heed, they are safe. But God holds their blood on *our* head if we see the danger and do not warn them. Can

---

6 Augustine, *The Works of Saint Augustine* (Hyde Park: New City, 1999), I/26:141.
7 Charles H. Spurgeon, *Metropolitan Tabernacle Pulpit* (Pasadena, TX: Pilgrim Publications, 1985), 30:52–53.

any of us say with Paul that we are free of the blood of all men (Acts 20:26)? Knowing the fear of the Lord and the terrors of Hell should drive us to warn sinners, plead with them to repent, and tell them the gospel while there is still time (2 Corinthians 5:11). The love of Christ constrained Paul to preach the gospel (2 Corinthians 5:14). It should move us as well. Calvinists have a higher view of grace than non-Calvinists; therefore, we should have more reason to tell the gospel.

And the ultimate goal of evangelism? The glory of God.

Conclusion

Let us imitate Spurgeon who preached: "Oh, my brothers and sisters in Christ, if sinners will be damned, at least let them leap to hell over our bodies; and if they will perish, let them perish with our arms about their knees, imploring them to stay, and not madly destroy themselves."[8]

---

8 Spurgeon, *Metropolitan Tabernacle Pulpit*, 7:11.

Chapter 72
Arminianism

Throughout this volume we have interacted with Arminianism as well as Lutheranism, Catholicism, and a few others. Arminianism is the main rival to Calvinism within evangelical Protestantism. A few further comments remain to be made.

History

Just as Calvinism is named for John Calvin but existed as pre-Calvinism before him and is subsumed under Reformed theology in general, so there was a kind of pre-Arminianism before Jacob Arminius, and there were later variations of this general system.

Few writers in the first three centuries after the New Testament commented at any length on the issues where Calvinists and Arminians disagree. My opinion is that those who did tended to favor the doctrines of free will, predestination by foresight, universal atonement, resistible grace, and the possibility of final apostasy and loss of salvation. This was particularly the case in the east, mainly due to the influence of Origen.[1] There would not be anything resembling Reformed theology in the Eastern churches until Cyril Lucaris in the seventeenth century, and he was severely condemned and left no defenders or successors.

In the west there were a few who advocated a mild pre-Augustinianism, such as Cyprian and Ambrose. Pelagius went further than anyone before him in advocating free will and denying original sin, even more than Origen. Some Calvinists mistakenly have charged Arminianism with being Pelagianism revisited, when in fact some of Pelagius' strongest opponents were Semi-Pelagians, such as Jerome.[2] Augustine and his followers — both Augustinians like Prosper and semi-Augustinians like Gregory the Great — effectively refuted both Pelagianism and Semi-Pelagianism. The term *Semi-Pelagianism* was not actually coined until the late sixteenth century but has become the

---

1 See Benjamin Drewery, *Origen and the Doctrine of Grace* (London: Epworth, 1960).
2 It would be more precise to describe Jerome as anti-Pelagian than as Augustinian; he seemed to waver between Semi-Pelagianism and semi-Augustinianism.

accepted term to describe the theology of certain fourth-century Christians in Gaul who rejected both Augustinianism and Pelagianism. They were, in my view, closer to Pelagianism than they, or later critics, have acknowledged. For example, on the crucial issue of depravity, the Pelagians said man is well, the Semi-Pelagians said man is sick, and the Augustinians said man is dead. A well man and a sick man have more in common with each other than with a dead man, for they are both still alive.

I for one see close similarities between Arminianism and Semi-Pelagianism. Both teach cooperative grace that is resistible rather than operative grace that is irresistible. Both teach free will, election by foresight, the possibility of loss of salvation, universal atonement, and so on. To use what may be a hyperbolic analogy, Semi-Pelagianism taught that man must take the first step toward God, then God responds. Arminianism usually says God first enables man to take the next step. But both Augustinianism and Calvinism teach that God takes the first and second steps to carry man to Himself.

Both Semi-Pelagianism and Augustinianism were entrenched in Roman Catholic sacramentalism for the next millennium. Throughout the Middle Ages theologians wavered between these two poles (there were no Pelagians during that time). Gottschalk was the leading Augustinian until Thomas Bradwardine, John Wycliffe, and Jan Hus, and then Martin Luther.[3] Their opponents could be characterized as various forms of Semi-Pelagians, especially the Franciscans such as Duns Scotus and William of Ockham. Bradwardine opposed them in his large tome *De Causa Dei Contra Pelagium*, that is, *The Cause of God Against the Pelagians*. He showed their close affinity with both Pelagianism (which Rome condemned) and Semi-Pelagianism (which Rome allowed).

In the sixteenth century, the leading Catholic anti-Protestants were generally in the line of the previous Semi-Pelagians. They would include Desiderius Erasmus, Johann Eck, and Robert Bellarmine. Most of the Anabaptists were Semi-Pelagians without the sacramentalism. This, then, was the milieu from which there arose a Dutch reaction to the Reformed branch of the Reformation. Arminius was influenced by Dirck Coornhert, and many early Arminians were influenced by the Socinians.[4] For example, some Arminians taught subordinationism rather than the full and equal trinitarianism, echoing Origen's error that opened the door to Arianism. Other early Arminians were

---

3 See Guido Stucco, *God's Eternal Gift* (Bloomington: XLibris, 2009).
4 Martin Mulsow and Jan Rohls, eds., *Socinianism and Arminianism: Antitrinitarians, Calvinists, and Cultural Exchange in Seventeenth-Century Europe* (Leiden: Brill, 2005).

full Trinitarians, but it is significant that almost no Calvinist of any era has advocated subordinationism. One reason is that Reformed theology holds to a higher view of God than Arminianism ever has.

It was the more extreme Arminians that John Owen and Pierre du Moulin charged with outright heresy.[5] Jacob Arminius himself was more evangelical than Simon Episcopius and certainly more so than Philip Limborch. In England, the Arminians William Laud, John Goodwin, Edward Stillingfleet, Jeremy Taylor, John Tillotson, the Cambridge Platonists, and the Latitudinarians vigorously opposed Puritan Calvinism. By the end of the seventeenth century, English Calvinism was in retreat, and Arminianism became a dry moralism which opened the door to Deism. William Whiston and Daniel Whitby were leading Arminians that drifted into Arianism and Socinianism. Whitby in particular was a popular anti-Calvinist who defended the five points of the Remonstrants but was refuted by John Gill and Jonathan Edwards.[6] Extreme Arminianism took over the Reformed church in Switzerland at that time and spread throughout Europe.

In the next century, John and Charles Wesley produced a considerably more evangelical brand of Arminianism than even Jacob Arminius envisioned.[7] Perhaps it was due to their Puritan ancestors and strong revulsion to any kind of liberalism. But they and their followers, such as John Fletcher, bitterly opposed Calvinism. In the next generation moderate Arminians such as Richard Watson were leery of more radical Arminians like Adam Clarke. Later William Burt Pope and John Miley guided mainstream British Arminianism through a moderate course as the evangelistic fires died down. As in so many places, it became dry, moralistic, and tending toward whatever liberalism was then in vogue (Deism, the Enlightenment, Romanticism, German liberalism).

Arminianism did not take root in America to any noticeable degree until after the strongly Calvinistic Great Awakening in the mid-eighteenth century. By the turn of the century, Methodist circuit riders preached the gospel and taught Arminianism throughout the new nation. The Second Great Awakening

---

5 John Owen, *A Display of Arminianism* in *The Works of John Owen* (London: Banner of Truth, 1967), 10:1–137; Pierre Du Moulin, *The Anatomy of Arminianisme* (Norwood, NJ: Walter J. Johnson, 1976).

6 John Gill, *The Cause of God and Truth* (Grand Rapids: Baker Book House, 1980); Jonathan Edwards, *The Freedom of the Will* in *The Works of Jonathan Edwards, Volume 1* (New Haven: Yale University Press, 1957).

7 See Herbert Boyd McGonigle, *Sufficient Saving Grace: John Wesley's Evangelical Arminianism* (Carlisle: Paternoster, 2001).

was led in part by Arminians such as Barton Stone, Peter Cartwright, Alexander Campbell, and Charles Finney, who in some areas was more Pelagian than Semi-Pelagian. It was from this soil that much of modern fundamentalism and evangelicalism in America grew later in the century and up to today. Calvinism was initially much involved in the leadership of both movements but gradually declined.

When Calvinist orthodoxy recedes, Arminianism spreads. And when evangelical Arminianism cools off, it usually goes liberal or Pelagian or both. A similar pattern can be seen in the history of Lutheranism, Calvinism's closest cousin in the Reformation. Luther was closer to Calvin on the doctrines of grace than many historians realize. As Calvin had his Arminius, Luther had his Melanchthon. Arminianism and Melanchthonianism substituted semi-Pelagian synergism for Augustinian and Reformed monergism. Hyper-Calvinism went "higher" than Calvin, but no later Lutheran went "higher" than Luther. Melanchthonian synergism bore a remarkable resemblance to both Semi-Pelagianism and Arminianism. Later this unchecked trajectory led to the rise of German liberalism.[8] For centuries conservative Lutherans have been suspicious of both Calvinism and Arminianism. For instance, R. C. H. Lenski, the conservative Lutheran Bible commentator, took regular swipes at Calvinism in his commentaries, such as: "Thank God, Paul is neither an Arminian Calvinist nor Calvinist Arminian. The Arminians and Calvinists do better than that; each holds to only one error instead of combining the two. Paul held to neither error."[9] Earlier Lutheran dogmaticians from the Silver Age of Lutheran Orthodoxy such as Johann Gerhard and Johann Andreas Quenstedt regularly castigated Calvinism in virtually every chapter. Later in the nineteenth century, August Pfeiffer produced a virulent work entitled *Anti-Calvinism*. But for all their denials, historic post-Luther Lutheranism seems closer to Semi-Pelagianism and Arminianism than to Augustinianism and Calvinism.[10]

---

8 There is a need for a detailed comparison of the synergism of Melanchthonian Lutheranism, Arminianism, and Semi-Pelagianism. It has been suggested that the term *Semi-Pelagianism* was coined by the authors of the Lutheran *Book of Concord* in the sixteenth century.

9 R. C. H. Lenski, *The Interpretation of St. Paul's Epistles to Galatians, Ephesians and Philippians* (Minneapolis: Augusburg, 1961), 799. Lenski frequently disagreed with Calvinists but rarely with Arminians. A good comparison is Robert Kolb and Carl R. Trueman, *Between Wittenberg and Geneva: Lutheran and Reformed Theology in Conversation* (Grand Rapids: Baker Academic, 2017). A concise presentation of the Lutheran view of election may be found in Thomas Frizelle, *Chosen by God: Why Did God Choose Me?* (St. Louis: Concordia, 1991).

10 In several respects, such as baptismal regeneration, Luther was closer to Augustine than Calvin was.

Today, most Lutherans are liberal. Fortunately, the more evangelical Lutherans oppose this disastrous trend. Other liberals were once evangelical Arminians and espouse a liberal Arminianism in theory. A much smaller contingent came from orthodox Calvinism, which we will discuss later. My contention is that just as water runs downhill, unchecked Arminianism tends to lead to theological liberalism. And this is just what orthodox Calvinists have warned about for centuries. We applaud the noble evangelical Arminians who swim against the tide and oppose liberal apostasy, but they need to see that their very theology encourages this tendency.

Arminian Weaknesses

Just as Socinians and Arians cannot grasp how Christ can be both God and man and therefore must be only man, so Arminians cannot grasp how God can be absolutely sovereign and man be morally responsible, so they tilt the balance toward free will and weaken divine sovereignty. To the degree to which one overemphasizes one, he deemphasizes the other (witness how Hyper-Calvinism does this in reverse). Their protestations to the contrary, Arminianism has at least the appearance of being man-centered rather than God-centered. Has anyone ever made that accusation against any Calvinist?

This relates to the difference in our view of certain attributes of God. Erroll Hulse, the influential English Reformed Baptist, taught me many decades ago that all errors in doctrine and practice can be traced back to an imbalanced view of the attributes of God. Arminianism gives lip service to divine sovereignty, but certainly theirs is a limited and not an absolute sovereignty. For example, they recoil at the idea of an overarching, all-inclusive predestination of all things. They frequently assert that love is the primary attribute of God, though some of a more Wesleyan variety favor holiness. This explains their differences with Calvinism on several issues. They say love is always voluntary, never forced. It is not only undeserved but unconditional. God must love everyone equally, or He does not love anyone at all, argued Dave Hunt in *What Love Is This?* Man is therefore free to choose, and God never interferes. This imbalanced view tends to downplay divine wrath in the more popular and liberal Arminianisms. That results first in eschatological annihilationism and then universalism. History bears this out. Just as many of the early Arminians were friends of the Socinians, so many early American Arminians were friendly to Unitarianism and universalism.

As we have asserted repeatedly, Arminianism lowers God and raises man.

God has limited sovereignty, and man has free will. Calvinism, by contrast, has a robust view of the high majesty of divine sovereignty and a far lower view of sinful man, both more so than any other form of theology. By contrast, Arminianism posits a "big man" idea of God and a godlike view of man. This means a finite distance between God and man as well as a qualitative similarity. Calvinism by stark contrast teaches an infinite distance and an utter qualitative difference between Creator and creature.

The seventeenth-century Remonstrants put forth their five points before the anti-Remonstrants responded at Dort with the so-called five points of Calvinism. Semi-Pelagians such as John Cassian and Duns Scotus would probably have been able to sign the Remonstrance, while Augustine, Gottschalk, Bradwardine, and possibly even Luther might have affirmed the Dortian canons.

Arminianism dominates most of popular evangelicalism in the twenty-first century. Its good points have contributed much good in many areas. But it has also introduced many weaknesses that we have discussed in this volume. Its rejection of the Regulative Principle brought in the widespread acceptance of man-centered entertainment in the place of God-centered, reverent worship. Arminianism is certainly dominant in pop evangelism with its shallow gospel, easy-believism, altar calls, and multiplied false converts. It often promotes different approaches to sanctification, such as perfectionism, the "Higher Life" Keswick model, or the carnal Christian error. Fortunately, many evangelicals are waking up to these dubious trends and want something more biblical. They find it in historic Calvinism.

"Yes, But"

Arminianism has what I call the "Yes, but" tendency when it comes to answering Reformed theology. Take the five points. "Is man depraved? Yes, but he still has free will. Election? Yes, but it is based on God's foresight of man's free will. Atonement? Yes, but it must be equally for all, or God is not loving to anyone. Grace? Yes, but man's free will can stalemate it. Perseverance and preservation? A good ideal, yes, but man's free will can veto it." Free will is repeatedly used as the trump card to counter Calvinism, but Arminianism never investigates whether free will is actually taught in the Bible. It just cannot grasp how evil and horrible mankind really is.

Arminianism is inherently synergistic: God does His part, man does his part, and together they get the job done. Evangelical Arminianism stops short of the implications of synergism — namely, that man is his own co-savior. Evangelical Arminians also detest any suggestion that man's cooperating free will has any merit in justification, even while asserting that justification is through infused rather than imputed righteousness. But others cross that line into moralism and accept human merit as part of salvation — the very thing condemned by Paul, Augustine, Luther, Calvin, and all Calvinists in every era. Calvinistic monergism alone explains *sola gratia*. Again, we detect the Arminian "Yes, but" objection: "Salvation is completely by grace, yes, but man must do his part." We reply that if it is not all by God's grace, it is not by grace at all (see Romans 11:6). The Arminian insistence on free will comes precariously close to merit theology and salvation by works. It was Semi-Pelagianism that gave us merit theology. Dave Hunt's protests notwithstanding, Arminianism is closer to Catholicism than he realizes.[11]

The Arminian Pandora's Box

All sorts of theological errors have sprung from Arminianism, such as Pentecostalism. One case in point is Open Theism. This dangerous heresy became popular in the 1980s but is actually a reincarnation of sixteenth-century Socinianism. It came back when certain extreme Arminians such as Clark Pinnock violently reacted to the resurgence of Calvinism. Not satisfied with weakening divine sovereignty, they proceeded to deny divine omniscience — God does not know the future because the future is "open." This obviously goes beyond the rejection of the all-encompassing decree in which God unchangeably foreordained all that comes to pass. To their credit, some evangelical Arminians such as Norman Geisler have opposed Open Theism. But the major opponents have been Reformed, such as Bruce Ware, John Frame, and Robert Morey. One cannot cross from Calvinism to Open Theism without first becoming Arminian.

A more serious error incipient in Arminianism is its basic objection to point after point of Calvinism — namely, "That's not fair!" This is not a mere academic objection against absolute divine sovereignty but an immoral rebellion against God who is absolutely sovereign. Job learned the lesson and submitted (Job 42:2, 6). Oh, that our Arminian friends would do the same. We puny and depraved humans are in no place to question the ways of God. Such rebellion proves the Reformed doctrine of depravity and is the very essence of sin.

---

11 Hunt wrote against both Roman Catholicism and Calvinism but did not admit Arminianism is similar to Catholic Semi-Pelagianism.

Anti-Calvinist Arminianism

With the resurgence of Reformed theology in recent decades has come a backlash from other quarters, including Arminianism. Curiously, Lutherans and Catholics have not responded much to resurgent Calvinism.[12] The strongest attacks have come from fundamentalist Arminians (see our bibliography). The more serious attempts at refuting Calvinism have come from Norman Geisler, I. Howard Marshall, Dave Hunt, Jack Cottrell, Lawrence Vance, Robert Shank, Robert Picirilli, F. Leroy Forlines, and especially Roger Olson. Jerry Walls and Joseph Dongell's *Why I Am Not a Calvinist* is friendlier than many others, as is *Whosoever Will*, edited by David Allen and Steve Lemke. Others are extreme, misinformed, and rude and should be distasteful even to other Arminians. Some rebuttals might be classified as Hyper-Arminian, the overreactive counterpart of Hyper-Calvinism.

Some anti-Calvinists like Clark Pinnock have drifted into Open Theism. Roger Olson has written extensively against Calvinism and admits to holding to "evangelical synergism."[13] He rightly points out the differences between the evangelical Arminianism of Arminius and Wesley as opposed to the more extreme Arminianism of Limborch and others. He claims to respect Calvin and Calvinism but pulls no punches in his severest criticism: "What I mean is that if I were a Calvinist and believed what these people teach, I would have difficulty telling the difference between God and Satan."[14] He admits leaning toward Open Theism and may one day fully embrace it.[15] This proves our point.

C. Gordon Olson, not to be confused with Roger Olson, is typical of another kind of anti-Calvinist Arminianism. In *Beyond Calvinism and Arminianism: An Inductive Mediate Theology of Salvation*, he proposes a truce and a middle way that is neither Reformed nor Arminian. His "inductive exegetical" approach appears to be critical and fair but usually results in the same conclusions as historic Arminianism. This is typical of other writers such as Samuel Fisk. Some

---

12 Catholic works on predestination and grace sometimes disagree with Calvinism, such as John Cowburn, *Free Will: Predestination and Determinism* (Milwaukee: Marquette University Press, 2008); John Salga, *The Mystery of Predestination* (Charlotte: TAN Books, 2010); William G. Most, *Grace, Predestination, and the Salvific Will of God* (Front Royal, VA: Christendom, 1997); and especially Eduardo J. Echeverria, *Divine Election: A Catholic Orientation in Dogmatic and Ecumenical Perspective* (Eugene, OR: Pickwick Publications, 2016).

13 Roger Olson, *Arminian Theology* (Downers Grove, IL: InterVarsity, 2006), 18.

14 Roger Olson, *Against Calvinism* (Grand Rapids: Zondervan, 2001), 23. John Wesley is reputed to have said to Augustus Toplady, "Your God is my Devil."

15 "I consider Open Theism a legitimate and Arminian option even though I have not yet adopted it as my own perspective." Olson, *Arminian Theology*, 198.

claim to be neither, while others claim to be both: thus, "Calminianism."[16] That is not Amyraldism or even Baxterianism but yet another form of Arminianism.

Pseudo-Calvinist Arminianism

There is a strange theological anomaly that perhaps can be best described as "pseudo-Calvinist Arminianism." It does not openly attack Calvinism so much as pretends to be Reformed when it is not and thereby breeds confusion. There are many modern evangelicals that profess to be Calvinist when they are in fact quite Arminian without knowing it. I do not charge them with deceit — just ignorance. This phenomenon can be seen, for example, in their profession of eternal security, especially in the form of "once saved, always saved." One hears explanations such as, "Calvinists believe you can't lose your salvation, and Arminians say you can, so I guess I'm a Calvinist." They generally do not know that Arminius and many of his early followers left the question open. Too, many hold to "once saved, always saved" in preservation but deny the Reformed doctrine of perseverance and go on to deny the other four points. The result is four-and-a-half-point Arminianism that claims to be Calvinism!

Others tip their hand on the five points one by one. They profess to believe in total depravity but not moral inability; unconditional election but not reprobation; substitutionary penal atonement, but it is equally for all and guarantees salvation for none; salvation by grace alone, but it is resistible by free will; and of course preservation without perseverance. This is not even Amyraldism but Arminianism.

Curiously, there are large numbers of Christians who claim to be Calvinist yet are in fact Arminian, but the reverse is not true. There are no Calvinists who claim to be Arminian but are really Calvinists. It is like another pattern: Many liberals claim to be evangelical when they are not, but true evangelicals do not go around claiming to be liberal. More importantly, there are millions of pseudo-Christians who profess to be born-again Christians when they are not, but one does not encounter true Christians claiming to be non-Christians except when tortured or backslidden.

This general pattern is seen in Norman Geisler.[17] He insists he is a moderate

---

16 Some consider Richard Baxter's blend of Calvinism, Arminianism, and Lutheranism to be a kind of "Calminianism." But he denies being Arminian and is closer to Reformed theology than to Arminianism. Amyraldism is also not, as some think, simply "Arminianism in disguise." Amyraut stringently denied being Arminian.

17 See especially *Chosen But Free*, 3rd ed. (Minneapolis: Bethany House, 2010).

Calvinist and attacks as "ultra-Calvinist" anyone who holds to any or all of the five points. He displays a serious ignorance of true Hyper-Calvinism as well as mainline Calvinism. In reality, Geisler is not a moderate Calvinist at all but basically a Semi-Pelagian synergist and Arminian, except for preservation. Mainline Calvinists are not Hyper-Calvinists, as he charges, but the real thing. Sadly, Geisler's approach has spread confusion and ignorance to the debate. Outright Arminians like Roger Olson at least do not claim to be what they are not.

The Rediscovery of Jacob Arminius

Concurrent with the revival of anti-Calvinist Arminianism is a more respectable appreciation of Jacob Arminius in certain quarters. Keith Stanglin, Carl Bangs, and others have made worthwhile contributions to the study of the life and theology of Arminius. Such writers are favorable to his theology and are not outright hostile to Reformed theology.

Some have suggested that Arminianism should be accepted in the Reformed camp as another variety of Calvinism, even as Hyper-Calvinism is still within the fold. Some consider it to be "liberal Calvinism." After all, did not Arminius himself study in Geneva under Theodore Beza? Richard Muller and others have refuted this assertion by showing that the differences are not only on the five points as debated at the Synod of Dort but reveal fundamental differences going back to the Reformation itself.

Is Arminianism Evangelical or an Enemy?

The question that orthodox Calvinists must answer is: Are Arminians true Christians or heretics? Is Arminianism *ipso facto* damnable heresy regardless of whether it is moderate or extreme, or is it a tolerable error that still holds to the true gospel? Most Hyper-Calvinists insist that all Arminians are heretics and in the same damnable class as the cults, Roman Catholics, and Protestant liberals. Mainline Calvinists, however, are not so critical in their estimation.

Iain Murray speaks for many: "[A] person does not have to be a Calvinist to be a Christian. An evangelist of Arminian persuasion preaches the same Saviour as the Calvinist."[18] He thus agrees with John Newton and Charles Spurgeon.[19] George Whitefield the Calvinist strongly disagreed with John Wesley the Arminian and ceased working with him but still considered him

---

18 Iain Murray, *Heroes* (Edinburgh: Banner of Truth, 2009), 277.
19 Murray, 102–04.

a revered brother in Christ and effective preacher of the gospel. Spurgeon admired D. L. Moody. Many Calvinists such as Martyn Lloyd-Jones respected Billy Graham, his altar calls and ecumenism notwithstanding.

By contrast, some extreme Arminians deny that Calvinists are Christians. Lawrence Vance appears to hold this opinion when he wrote "Calvinism is the greatest 'Christian' heresy that has ever plagued the church."[20] Greater than Arianism? Or Pelagianism? Or Catholicism or Mormonism? Perhaps he exaggerates. But many if not most Hyper-Calvinists reply in kind by claiming that anyone who denies any of the five points is not a true Christian. Mainstream Calvinists would calmly remind them that however important the five points are, they are not of the essence of the gospel as recorded in 1 Corinthians 15:1–4 and elsewhere. Evangelical Arminians preach the same basic gospel as historic Calvinists. That does not, of course, apply to the more extreme Arminians who advocate liberalism, Socinianism, Open Theism, or other poisonous heresies and false gospels.

William Ames — Puritan, supralapsarian, and advisor at the Synod of Dort — perceptively observed:

> The view of the Remonstrants (Arminians) as it is taken by the mass of their supporters, is not strictly a heresy, but a dangerous error tending toward heresy. As maintained by some of them, however, it is the Pelagian heresy: because they deny that the effective operation of inward grace is necessary for conversion.[21]

Extreme Arminianism is not evangelical. It goes beyond Semi-Pelagianism, adds merit to free will, and goes beyond mere synergism into a co-saviorhood with God or even a monergism of man. That clearly is a false gospel deserving damnation (Galatians 1:9). But evangelical Arminians usually condemn it as strongly as we do.

R. C. Sproul put it like this: "People often ask me if I believe Arminians are Christians. I usually answer, 'Yes, barely.' They are Christians by what we call a felicitous inconsistency."[22] Many Reformed leaders have respected Arminian leaders such as A. W. Tozer as spiritual giants. Iain Murray, cofounder of The Banner of Truth, wrote a sympathetic biography of John Wesley, which pointed out his numerous errors but also his godliness and orthodoxy on the gospel.

---

20 Lawrence Vance, *The Other Side of Calvinism*, Rev. ed. (Pensacola: Vance, 1999), X.

21 Quoted in Alan P. F. Sell, *The Great Debate* (Grand Rapids: Baker Book House, 1983), 23.

22 R. C. Sproul, *Willing to Believe* (Grand Rapids: Baker Book House, 1997), 25.

Mainstream Calvinists accept evangelical Arminians as brothers. We hope they repay the compliment. Most do.

Conclusion

Mainline Calvinists may inadvertently claim, "I am of Calvin," and evangelical Arminians may seem to cry, "I am of Arminius." But deep down, both believe "We are both of Christ." Their differences are real and cannot be ignored, but neither should they be exaggerated beyond measure, or they are in danger of bearing false witness against brothers in Christ.

Chapter 73
The Practical Application of Calvinism

We have occasionally made practical applications of Reformed history and theology throughout this volume. It is fitting to give a few last lessons for those who believe in the distinctive teachings of Calvinism. All theology must not only be doxological (worshipful) but practical and experiential.

A Reformed Worldview

We need a distinctive biblical and Reformed *weltanschauung*, or world-and-life-view. Augustine, Calvin, Kuyper, and others addressed how Christians can live in society as salt and light so as to influence the world for good. They attempted to bring about a godly society.

Abraham Kuyper has had a major influence through his view of common grace and sphere sovereignty. His plan is summed up in his *Lectures on Calvinism.*[1] Note the chapter titles: "Calvinism as a Life-system," "Calvinism in Religion," "Calvinism and Politics," "Calvinism and Science," "Calvinism and Art," and "Calvinism and the Future." He edited a Christian weekly newspaper, founded a Christian university, wrote dozens of books and hundreds of articles, and even became prime minister of the Netherlands. But as the twentieth century progressed, Christian influence in Holland waned to the point where the Netherlands is now one of the most decadent nations on earth. Kuyper had a good *weltanschauung*, but the weakness of his system led to the crumbling of Dutch Reformed society. One thing he did not fully appreciate was the inherently hostile resistance by non-Christians to Christianity. You cannot make a Christian society out of non-Christians any more than you can make bricks without straw.

The same happened in Geneva a century after Calvin, the Puritan Commonwealth after Cromwell, Knox's Edinburgh, the Puritan experiment in the American colonies, South Africa, and elsewhere. A Calvinist worldview, then, must take the doctrine of total depravity more seriously. Common grace will restrain the sinner outwardly but cannot convert him. When common

---

1 See Peter S. Heslam, *Creating a Christian Worldview: Abraham Kuyper's Lectures on Calvinism* (Grand Rapids: Eerdmans, 1998).

grace withdraws, a post-Christian society often becomes worse than ever. We should pray for common grace for our society ("God shed His grace on thee") but pray even more for special grace. Pray for revival; work for reformation.

A Reformed worldview remembers that God is sovereign over all aspects of society. "This Is My Father's World." It does not belong to man or chance. We are only the caretakers. Someone has said, "Creation belongs to God, and He wants it back." Prayer should work together with providence in using the world properly to the glory of God.

The center of gravity in Reformed theology is *soli Deo gloria*. A biblical worldview emphasizes that everything must be done to the glory of God (1 Corinthians 10:31). That includes art, science, industry, family, and government. Take economics. Max Weber put forth the thesis in *The Protestant Ethic and the Spirit of Capitalism* that Calvinism laid the foundation for modern democracy and free enterprise.[2] In spite of some of his erroneous observations, he had a point. Nations where Calvinism has had its greatest influence also have enjoyed great prosperity and freedom, such as Switzerland, the Netherlands, England, Scotland, and America.

The movement known as Christian Reconstruction (theonomy) has numerous flaws, but it is correct in reminding us of the *creation mandate* of Genesis 1:28. Even if we cannot bring about a theonomic theocracy, the theonomists address some issues that many others ignored. On the other hand, they often fail to put the creation mandate alongside the Great Commission. The latter is more important than the former. What good is a godly society if there are very few Christians in it? We dare not minimize or omit evangelism from our worldview and mission in the world.

Pitfalls Peculiar to Calvinists

Every Christian tradition has its pitfalls, and that includes the Reformed community. One is pride. All Christians must resist this evil poison. It takes on a particularly foul odor when a person becomes proud of holding to the doctrines of grace. Some seem to take pride in being one of the elect, forgetting that election is by grace, and we are the *elect* and not the *elite*. Others seem to confine the elect to Calvinists. If Ephesians 2:8–9 leaves no room for boasting of

---

2 Max Weber, *The Protestant Ethic and the Spirit of Capitalism* (New York: Scribner, 1930). More recently and from a Reformed perspective, see Douglas F. Kelly, *The Emergence of Liberty in the Modern World: The Influence of Calvin on Five Governments from the 16th through the 18th Centuries* (Phillipsburg, NJ: P&R, 1992).

salvation by grace, then Ephesians 1:4–6 leaves no room for boasting of election by grace. We must remember one of Augustine's favorite verses: "For who made you to differ from another? And what do you have that you did not receive? Now if you did indeed receive it, why do you boast as if you had not received it?" (1 Corinthians 4:7). "He who glories, let him glory in the Lord" (1 Corinthians 1:31). "Therefore, as the elect of God, put on humility" (Colossians 3:12).

The Calvinist must not look down on non-Calvinists. Some take a special glee in attacking Arminians. One such overzealous brother was heard to say, "The only good Arminian is a dead Arminian." Sad to say, there was a fistfight between a Calvinist student and an Arminian student at a leading evangelical seminary some years ago. Worse, one of the Calvinist delegates to the Synod of Dort challenged another Calvinist delegate to a duel over a disagreement on a relatively small point of theology. May it never be! We Calvinists need the humility to not only recognize our Arminian brothers but to acknowledge and applaud numerous Arminian spiritual giants such as A. W. Tozer, as Martyn Lloyd-Jones did.

There seems to be a kind of Calvinist gnosticism in some quarters. Such persons seem to think they have undergone a special initiation into the deeper mysteries to which ignorant non-Reformed brothers have not been enlightened. Some speak of it as almost a second conversion. Some have used the quip: "I asked John Calvin into my heart." Sometimes this is evidenced by a proud air of intellectualism that disdains experimental heart religion. It may overindulge in heady scholasticism, as if discerning the order of the decrees is more important than godly living. It may be guilty of prying into unrevealed secrets (Deuteronomy 29:29). That resembles the obsession over eschatology that other Christians have, leading to a lack of interest in evangelism (Acts 1:6–8).

And then there is hero worship. While we should honor and learn from Reformed writers of the past, we must not idolize them, or we end up canonizing them as Calvinist saints. They are not infallible semi-divine angels but men with like passions as ourselves. Take John Calvin. Lloyd-Jones was wise to caution us: "It would be a pathetic condition if we found ourselves saying that Calvin could not be wrong."[3] And again, "We must not turn him into a pope! He was as liable to error as anybody else."[4] The same goes for Jonathan Edwards, John

---

3 D. Martyn Lloyd-Jones, *Knowing the Times* (Edinburgh: Banner of Truth, 1989), 194.
4 D. Martyn Lloyd-Jones, *Romans: An Exposition of Chapter 5, Assurance* (Edinburgh: Banner of Truth, 1971), 205.

Owen, John Gill, Cornelius Van Til, Herman Hoeksema, R. C. Sproul, and Lloyd-Jones himself. This tendency resembles 1 Corinthians 1:12. Even the use of the term *Calvinism* can be misused: "I belong to Calvin." As stated in the quote from Spurgeon early in this volume, we use these terms only for a kind of shorthand, not to lionize Calvin as our great guru.

Spurgeon lampooned a certain kind of Calvinist who was obsessed with the five points to the detriment of other doctrines and practices: "They have a kind of barrel-organ that only plays five tunes, and they are always repeating them."[5] Others are more zealous to make Calvinists out of Arminians than to make Christians out of non-Christians. John Wesley lamented, "Oh that our brethren were as zealous to make Christians as they are to make Calvinists!"[6] Iain Murray: "The preacher ought to have a higher aim than to make people Calvinists; and if people are only made Calvinists in their heads they invariably become a blot on the unity and catholicity that ought to mark every true Christian."[7]

Then there is what may be termed the "New Calvinist Syndrome." Some believers were converted under Arminian auspices and came to see its weaknesses, then glow with delight when they discover the doctrines of grace. Fair enough. But they often — too often — offend their non-Calvinist and even non-Christian friends in their zeal that lacks Christian courtesy. Some are just plain rude. They owe a lot of apologies to a lot of people, including the Lord. This is not limited to the "Young, Restless, and Reformed" crowd either nor to those who wander into Hyper-Calvinism. It can infect anyone.

For some, Calvinism is just another religious fad. (I knew one young man who went from Greek Orthodoxy to Pentecostalism to Calvinism to Neo-Orthodoxy within the space of five years, and who knows where he went after that.) They are immature butterflies that flit and fly from one flower to the next. They often lack discernment, "tossed to and fro by every wind of doctrine" (Ephesians 4:14), having itching ears for something new (Acts 17:21; 2 Timothy 4:3). Often, they never commit to a local church, preferring to stay home and read books or listen to messages by great preachers rather than by a dedicated but unfamous, hardworking, and often underappreciated pastor. They need to grow up.

---

5 Charles H. Spurgeon, *C. H. Spurgeon's Forgotten Prayer Meeting Addresses* (Leominster: Day One, 2011), 173.
6 Quoted in T. Ferrier Hulme, *John Wesley and His Horse* (London: Epworth, 1933), 69.
7 Iain Murray, *Heroes* (Edinburgh: Banner of Truth, 2009), 103.

Others get locked into a staid and stale Reformed traditionalism. They dare not disagree with the Reformed confessions on anything or even to study to see if those confessions are biblical (1 Thessalonians 5:21; Acts 17:11). As great as the confessions are, they are neither inspired nor infallible.

Then others live in the past, wishing they could live in Calvin's Geneva or the Puritan Commonwealth. They forget that God has placed them when and where they are today for a reason. The good old days when Calvinism was more widespread were not always so good (Ecclesiastes 7:10). Sometimes you can tell, by their stilted English, when a young Calvinist has been reading old Puritan books or old *Nadere Reformatie* writers. One almost expects them to break out with a "Forsooth!" Sermons sometimes become dry lectures, and prayers become flowery theological expatiations. God is not impressed. When they speak in old-fashioned King James English, they may as well be speaking in tongues.

Some Calvinists are given to over-introspection, carrying self-examination too far without developing spiritual fruit. Many are obsessed with worrying whether they are elect. Some are like poor old William Cowper, dreading that they are reprobate or have committed the unpardonable sin.

Others overemphasize divine sovereignty and weaken human responsibility and become lethargic (read: lazy). This becomes a kind of Calvinist "Let go and let God" passivity that is unbiblical and unhealthy. More than a few get discouraged when they do not measure up to a David Brainerd or Robert Murray M'Cheyne, both of whom died before they turned thirty. Those examples should encourage us, not discourage us.

Some become emotionally and spiritually cold. There is some truth in the criticism that Calvinists are the "frozen chosen." Well, many are cold, but few are frozen. Calvinists should not be stoics but the warmest of Christians. James Montgomery Boice was one of the friendliest persons I ever met. Christians should be friendly and imitate the One who was called "the friend of sinners" (Matthew 11:19). Would our non-Calvinist friends say we are friendly or standoffish, sweet or sour, warm or cold?

We have already warned against Hyper-Calvinism. There is also a practical Hyper-Calvinism. Many Calvinists believe in the free offer. The trouble is, they never give it to anyone. Others back into Hyper-Calvinism in theory or practice by overreacting to Arminianism, easy-believism, or shallow evangelism. Even when they do tell the gospel, it is ice-cold: "Take it or leave it." One of George

Whitefield's assistants said that he never heard him preach but that Whitefield wept for sinners. Jesus wept for the lost (Luke 19:41). Do we?

God warns His children of dangers on both sides of the road (Joshua 1:7). Reformed Christians need to beware of a kind of Calvinistic legalism on the one side and Calvinistic antinomianism on the other. Let us never turn the holy law of God into self-righteousness or a club to hit people over the head with nor misuse grace as an excuse for sin. Nor should we swing from one extreme to the other. Let us avoid both Hyper-Calvinism and Amyraldism and stick with mainstream Calvinism.

Appropriate Attitudes

Realizing that God is truly sovereign, we should joyfully submit to both the secret and revealed wills. This should be a grateful trust in our loving heavenly Father, not a grudging acquiescence to an impersonal or cruel dictator. In his book *The Sovereignty of God*, Arthur Pink wrote: "True recognition of God's sovereignty humbles us as nothing does or can humble, and brings the heart into lowly submission before God, causing us to relinquish our own self-will and make us delight in the perception and performance of the divine will."[8]

The doctrines of grace are comforting doctrines. Romans 8:28 bears new luster when we realize that God does indeed control everything for our good. Arthur Custance rightly said,

> Now surely, one of the most comforting things about any faith in the absolute sovereignty of the grace of God ought to be the assurance we derive from that faith that God is still on the throne even in our most dismal defeats and that the clouds we so much dread are waiting to pour only showers of blessing on our head.[9]

When we are assured of our election, we will also be assured of our preservation, perseverance, and glorification. Nothing can hinder the invincible love of God for His elect. We can lay our heads on the soft pillow of Romans 8:28–30 when our time comes to die.

Seeing that the doctrines of grace are indeed biblical brings great encouragement along the road to glory. It sheds light in the dark valleys and hope amid adverse circumstances. As one put it, "Theology is strong or weak, virile

8 A. W. Pink, *The Sovereignty of God* (Grand Rapids: Baker Book House, 1973), 221.
9 Arthur C. Custance, *The Sovereignty of Grace* (Phillipsburg, NJ: Presbyterian and Reformed, 1979), 231.

or feeble, deep or shallow in proportion to its Calvinistic spirit. Calvinism [. . .] puts iron in the blood, and gives muscle and fibre to conviction and Christian experience."[10] Spurgeon once said, "When my spirit gets depressed, nothing will sustain it but the good old-fashioned Calvinistic doctrine."[11]

These truths are for the heart and not just the head and hands. William Masselink wisely commented: "Calvinism in the head is good, but true Calvinism in the heart is far better."[12] Seventeenth-century Reformed scholasticism needed the heart religion of the Puritans and the *Nadere Reformatie* to balance its deep theology. Too much doctrine in the head without humble heart religion can lead to pride and a fall (Proverbs 16:18; 1 Corinthians 8:1). Fortunately, the revival of Calvinism in the second half of the twentieth century brought with it the rediscovery of Reformed experimental spirituality, as witnessed by new publishers such as The Banner of Truth, Soli Deo Gloria, Reformation Heritage Books, and EP Books (Evangelical Press). Likewise, true Calvinistic preaching will feed the heart, not just educate the head.

John Piper emphasizes that the doctrines of divine sovereignty and grace rightly understood will lead us to "glorify God and enjoy him forever" (Westminster Shorter Catechism, Q. 1). He advocates what he calls "Christian Hedonism"— taking joy in God Himself. In a delightful expression of such joy, he put it like this in relation to the five points:

> We need to make plain that total depravity is not just badness, but blindness to beauty and deadness to joy; and unconditional election means that the completeness of our joy in Jesus was planned for us before we ever existed; and that limited atonement is the assurance that indestructible joy in God is infallibly secured for us by the blood of the covenant; and irresistible grace is the commitment and power of God's love to make sure we don't hold on to suicidal pleasures, and to set us free by the sovereign power of superior delights; and that the perseverance of the saints is the almighty work of God to keep us, through all affliction and suffering, for an inheritance of pleasures at God's right hand forever.[13]

---

10 H. Tydeman Chilvers, *Is There a Future for Calvinism?* (London: Arthur H. Stockwell, 1929), 7. Valentine Hepp remarked, "Calvinism is characterized by virility, but also by sensitivity and tenderness." In Valentine Hepp, et al, *Tweede International Congres van Gereformeerden (Calvinisten)* ("s-Gravenhage: Martinus Nijhoff, 1935), 21.

11 Charles H. Spurgeon, *Metropolitan Tabernacle Pulpit* (Pasadena, TX: Pilgrim Publications, 1979), 58:380.

12 William Masselink, *Sermons on the Commandments* (Grand Rapids: Zondervan, 1934), 34.

13 John Piper, *A Godward Life: Book Two* (Sisters, OR: Multnomah, 1999), 81–82.

Sam Storms[14] and others emphasize holy joy as the fruit of beholding the awesome sovereignty of God. Augustine taught it more than fifteen hundred years earlier. He said we should enjoy God for His own sake, not as a means to an end. God Himself is the greatest end.[15]

This leads to worship. When we are awed by God's sovereign majesty, how can we not praise Him for His magnificence and glory? Reformed worship should be deeper and higher than others, for we have a deeper and higher vista of the sovereign glory of God. We study theology to make fuel for doxology. Our mind is the mouth of the soul to the heart, and good Bible doctrine should produce greater worship. But sooner or later we reach the limit of what God has revealed and what our little mind can comprehend. At that point, said Theodore Beza, "Adore what you cannot grasp."[16]

Calvin often warned against prying into unrevealed divine secrets as per Deuteronomy 29:29. Do not judge God by human standards, said he.[17] Do not resist God.[18] Let God be God, as Luther said. Bow in awe before the infinite beauty and majesty of God.[19] Any theology that does not produce such worship is not biblical. Reformed theology is not only God-exalting but should produce God-intoxicated Christians who love to worship.

If humility is sometimes said to be the queen of virtues, then love is the king of virtues. This is the greatest commandment of all (Matthew 22:37–38). It is our highest privilege as well as our greatest duty. God loves us in election by the Father, redemption by the Son, and efficacious grace by the Spirit. We should respond with love for Him who first loved us (1 John 4:19). Calvinists have all the more reason to excel as God-lovers. Witness Samuel Rutherford in his classic letters, which should be required reading for all Christians, especially Calvinists. A theological giant with the boldness of a lion, he was once described as being "almost womanly" in his sweet spiritually-romantic interludes with Jesus Christ

---

14 Sam Storms, *One Thing: Developing a Passion for the Beauty of God* (Fearn: Christian Focus, 2004).

15 Augustine, *The Works of Saint Augustine* (Hyde Park: New City, 2005), I/11:107–09, 114–15.

16 Theodore Beza, *A Little Book of Christian Questions and Responses* (Allison Park, PA: Pickwick, 1986), 9.

17 John Calvin, *Calvin's Calvinism* (Grand Rapids: Reformed Free Publishing Association, 1991), 21–22, 274.

18 John Calvin, *The Institutes of Christian Religion* (Philadelphia: Westminster, 1960), 1:17:2 (pp. 212–14).

19 Calvin, *Calvin's Calvinism*, 214.

as our heavenly husband. Is this not a foretaste of Heaven, in which the elected bride will be united in heavenly eternal love with the Beloved?

Jonathan Edwards often waxed eloquent on love for God, both theologically and personally. In one of the most profound statements in all Reformed theology, he offered this observation: "A being that loves himself, necessarily loves Love to himself. If holiness in God consist chiefly in love to himself, holiness in the creature must chiefly consist in love to him. And if God loves holiness in himself, he must love it in the creature."[20]

Conclusion

Edwards was perhaps the greatest Reformed theologian who ever lived. He wrote his masterpiece *A Treatise on Religious Affections*[21] to examine false evidences of conversion and describe true evidences. The real proof of being saved is not just emotions, actions, or even right doctrine. The ultimate testimony is a godly heart that has been gloriously saved by grace. And the chief virtue of that heart is love for God.

---

20 Jonathan Edwards, *The Works of Jonathan Edwards* (New Haven: Yale University Press, 1989), 8:456.
21 Jonathan Edwards, *A Treatise on Religious Affections* in *The Works of Jonathan Edwards*, Volume 2.

Chapter 74
Calvinism Today and Tomorrow

As we bring our study of Calvinism to a close, it is time to make a few final comments regarding the identity and future of Calvinism.

What Is Calvinism?

At its most basic level, Calvinism is simply the theology of John Calvin, just as pure Augustinianism is the theology of Augustine, and Lutheranism is the theology of Luther. While some try to posit a radical change in Calvin's early to later theology,[1] the consensus of most scholars is that he did not materially change in any major area. Some exaggerate the significance of his moving his discussion on predestination in various editions of the *Institutes*. Calvin was remarkably consistent throughout his life and career as pastor and theologian (a good example for us to follow). Augustine, on the other hand, gradually moved from a somewhat Semi-Pelagian position to a Pauline position on the issues of grace. If one wants to ascertain "Calvin's Calvinism,"[2] he need look no further than his catechism,[3] confession of faith,[4] or the *Institutes*, including its several abridgments.[5]

In another sense, *Calvinism* has been taken to refer more broadly to Reformed theology, that is, the theology of the Swiss Reformation as opposed to German Lutheranism or Anabaptism. There were slight variations among pre-Calvin Reformed theologians such as Zwingli and Bucer (e.g., on the Lord's Supper), and there would be yet more variations later. The Reformed tree has many branches; the Calvinist family has many children.

---

1 So Augustus Hopkins Strong, *Systematic Theology* (Old Tappan, NJ: Fleming H. Revell, 1979), 977.

2 This is the catchy title of the translation of two of Calvin's theological treatises edited by Henry Cole. Calvin obviously did not give his name to them or anything else.

3 See I. John Hesselink, *Calvin's First Catechism* (Louisville: Westminster John Knox Press, 1997); John Calvin, *Selected Works of John Calvin* (Grand Rapids: Baker Book House, 1983), 2:33–94.

4 See "Brief Form of a Confession of Faith," in *Selected Works of John Calvin*, 2:129–35; cf. 2:137–62.

5 E.g., John Calvin, *Truth for All Time: A Brief Outline of the Christian Faith* (Edinburgh: Banner of Truth, 1998).

One way of defining true Calvinism is by comparing the major Reformed confessions, catechisms, and creeds of the first two centuries. James T. Dennison's massive *The Reformed Confessions of the 16th and 17th Centuries* is an extremely useful resource and essential for all serious studies in Calvinist history and theology. The indexes help to trace the progression, debates, and variety of Reformed theology in its formative years. Special attention should be given to the Heidelberg Catechism, the Belgic Confession, the Canons of the Synod of Dort, and the Westminster Confession as the primary standards. Secondarily one should study the Thirty-Nine Articles, the Second Helvetic Confession, the Westminster Shorter Catechism, the French Confession of Faith, and the Second London Baptist Confession of Faith. The basic consensus of the Calvinist confessions expresses the essence of confessional, historic Reformed orthodoxy.

Calvinism shares some beliefs with traditional Roman Catholicism: the Trinity, miracles, the dual natures of Christ, the virgin birth, the resurrection, Heaven and Hell, and more. But it denies certain Roman errors, such as its view of papal supremacy, the sacraments, Marian sinlessness, and other errors. The main differences debated in the Reformation revolved around the five so-called *sola* doctrines.[6] The Reformers believed in *sola Scriptura* — Scripture alone is our final authority, not the papacy, fathers, councils, and bulls of Rome nor personal feelings, opinions, philosophy, or human traditions. Salvation is *sola gratia* and *sola fide* — by grace and faith alone (Ephesians 2:8–9), not by works, sacraments, or anything else. It comes by Christ alone — *solus Christus*[7]— not by priests, Mary, saints, parents, or even self. All the glory goes to God alone — *soli Deo gloria* — not to self, the Catholic Church, the pope, Mary, or anyone else. On these five points the three branches of the Reformation were in basic agreement. Anyone who later claimed to be a Calvinist but denied any of them cannot be considered a true Calvinist or even a true Christian.

The same is true with another set of five truths, sometimes called the *five fundamentals*: verbal inspiration of Scripture, the virgin birth of Christ, vicarious atonement, the victorious resurrection, and the visible return of Christ.[8] Fundamentals they are, and anyone who denies them is neither Calvinist

---

6 Kenneth J. Stewart, *Ten Myths about Calvinism* (Downers Grove, IL: IVP Academic, 2011) has traced the TULIP mnemonic to the early 1900s, but has anyone traced the origin of the five *solas* as such?

7 *Solus Christus* (nominative) means "Christ alone" saves, while *solo Christo* (ablative) means salvation is "by Christ alone." Thanks to Francis X. Gumerlock — Latin teacher, church historian, translator, and friend — for this helpful explanation.

8 The term is usually traced to the set of small books published under the title *The Fundamentals* during the Fundamentalist-Modernist controversy in early twentieth-century America.

nor Christian. These two sets of truths are of first importance to Christianity (1 Corinthians 15:1–4), without which one is left with a false and accursed gospel (Galatians 1:9). Evangelical Arminians, historic Lutherans, and Anabaptists accept the five fundamentals, as do some traditional Catholics but not most liberal Protestants.

There is a third group of five doctrines: the *five points of Calvinism*. While one does not have to believe any or all of them to be a Christian, it is my opinion that they form the heart of the *distinctive* doctrines of Reformed theology. No non-Calvinist accepts them, though Luther and Augustine came close. One slight modification would be with the third point, for Amyraldians reject it but accept the other four. There are slight variations on election regarding the order of decrees, but mainline Calvinism is remarkably consistent in the essence of these points.

There is a sixth point of Calvinism, as it were, that is basic to the other five and is also a distinctive tenet of Calvinism. I refer, of course, to our view of absolute divine sovereignty.[9] We teach that God is absolutely sovereign and has unchangeably foreordained whatsoever comes to pass solely on the basis of His sovereign will. If there is a "central dogma" of Reformed theology, this would have to be it. I do not say that all other Reformed doctrines are logically deduced from it, but rather that it has a singular place in our theology and a distinct flavor that differentiates ours from other theologies.

Varieties of Calvinism

There has always been a mainstream or mainline Reformed theology that closely resembles "Calvin's Calvinism." But the Reformed river has various cross-currents, eddies, and tributaries. One only has to see the variety of views on ecclesiology and eschatology.

Historians have sometimes charted "High" and "Low" Calvinism, or to be horizontal, right-wing and left-wing Calvinism (see Joshua 1:7). *High Calvinism* is usually traced to Theodore Beza, the supralapsarians, and Reformed Scholastics. They generally hold to a strictly limited atonement without any universal aspects and tend to deny that assurance is of the essence of faith. This is not necessarily to accept the "Calvin versus Calvinism" thesis of R. T. Kendall and others.[10] High Calvinism was obviously higher than Calvin and most early

---

9 As we showed earlier, *absolute sovereignty* is not to be equated with the theory of *absolute power* advocated by Duns Scotus.

10 R. T. Kendall, *Calvin and English Calvinism to 1649* (Oxford: Oxford University Press,

Reformed theologians on many issues, but it was not mainstream Calvinism. This High tendency later produced Hyper-Calvinism. Another debate would be "Calvin versus Hyper-Calvinism," where there are several obvious and significant differences.

By contrast, *Low Calvinism* would be a useful term for what is sometimes called Amyraldism or hypothetical universalism. It has a place at the table in the Reformed family, but it is "lower" than the mainstream on various issues. Overall, then, there is unity and diversity in the orthodox Reformed tradition.

The Great Calvinists

God used many great and godly men and women in the history of redemption in Bible days. The same is true in church history, including Reformed history. I use the analogy of David, his three closest associates, and the thirty mighty men of 2 Samuel 23:8–39. One could consider Augustine like David, then Calvin, Edwards, and Kuyper as the three most influential Reformed thinkers of all. Included in the thirty would be Zwingli, Bucer, Vermigli, Bullinger, Beza, Knox, and Cranmer in the sixteenth century. In the seventeenth century, Perkins, Owen, Bunyan, Voetius, Turretin, and van Mastricht stand out. In the next century were Whitefield, Gill, Boston, and Brakel. In the nineteenth century we find Spurgeon, Hodge, Dabney, Chalmers, Cunningham, Shedd, and Ryle. Since 1900, the giants include Warfield, Bavinck, Lloyd-Jones, Berkhof, Sproul, and MacArthur.

Of the great thinkers, Calvin, Edwards, and Kuyper excelled as creative geniuses, while others such as Beza, Owen, Turretin, Hodge, and Bavinck were best suited as organizers. Warfield and Bavinck were probably the most learned in many fields, but let us not ignore Beza, Ussher, and Owen. Others were leaders in realms beyond theology, such as Cromwell, Chalmers, and Kuyper. Of the great evangelists, Whitefield and Edwards stand highest. Of preachers, Spurgeon and Lloyd-Jones are the princes, followed by the Puritans Manton, Watson, and Sibbes. Calvinists may offer their own candidates for the three and the thirty, but these are my nominations.

Reformed theologians seem to swim in an ocean of ink. They have produced an enormous number of books that are still being read today. Augustine was the most prolific writer among the church fathers. Calvin produced a huge number of treatises, commentaries, sermons, letters, and others. Bullinger's thousands of

---

1979); Holmes Rolston III, *John Calvin Versus the Westminster Confession* (Richmond: John Knox, 1972).

letters are still being edited. Spurgeon published more sermons than anyone else, Reformed or otherwise, not to mention his dozens of books. Calvin, Spurgeon, and Kuyper were the most prolific Reformed writers of all. Baxter was the most published of the Puritans, even more than Owen or Manton. Bucer's output was huge, but unfortunately very little has been translated into English. The Yale edition of Edwards' published works is less than half of the manuscripts contained on the Jonathan Edwards Center at Yale University website.[11] More recently, Pink, Lloyd-Jones, Sproul, and MacArthur have authored dozens of books.

A directory of notable Reformed women must include Sarah Edwards, Susannah Spurgeon, and the "three Annes" — Anne Bradstreet, Anne Steele, and Anne Dutton (but *not* Mrs. Anne Hutchinson). Others were not as outspoken in their Reformed convictions, and still others served our Lord in the shadow of their more well-known husbands. Elisabeth Elliott and Edith Schaeffer were godly Calvinist giantesses in recent decades. Someone should compile a book on the great Reformed women over the centuries.

It is an interesting and significant fact that no notable Calvinist to my knowledge has ever apostatized. Yet they were not perfect. The best of men are but men at best. Witness Calvin's approval of the execution of Servetus, Augustine's approval of torture, and Cotton Mather's involvement in the Salem Witch Trials. These faults do not disqualify them as unreliable theologians, nor do they discredit Calvinism, for all religious traditions have their flaws (such as Wesley's less than ideal marriage or Luther's anti-Semitism).

The Two-Way Street

Using the road analogy again, we can see travel in both directions to and from Calvinism. Negatively, there are what may be considered "post-Calvinists" or even "ex-Calvinists." These are individuals who once claimed to be Reformed but changed their beliefs. Some who are raised in a Reformed church later become Arminian, Pentecostal, or even Lutheran. Some flit from church to church. One Austin Fischer wrote a small item entitled *Young, Restless, No Longer Reformed.*[12] Scott Hahn and Jerry Matatics claim to have once been confessional Presbyterians before joining the Catholic Church. Even the ultra-Arminian Open Theist Clark Pinnock said he was once a Calvinist. N. L. Rice made a poignant observation: "If any man or class of men professing to be

---

11 http://www.edwards.yale.edu
12 Eugene, OR: Cascade, 2014.

Calvinists, have abandoned the fundamental doctrines of Christianity, they have commenced their downward course by renouncing the doctrines peculiar to Calvinism."[13] As we said in the previous chapter, one might go from Calvinism to Arminianism to liberalism, but one almost never goes from Arminianism to Calvinism to liberalism.

A similar pattern can be detected in churches, denominations, and seminaries that are Reformed in name only. They may still be Presbyterian, for example, but deny the five points or, worse, the five *solas* or the five fundamentals. Surely, they are no longer Calvinist or even Christian.

Calvinism has had two errant children, as it were, that came out of the Reformed family and produced heterodox families of their own. The first *enfant terrible* was Arminianism. Some recent writers have suggested that Arminianism is still in the Reformed family; older writers called it "Liberal Calvinism." Richard Muller has disproved this theory. However one delineates Calvinist doctrinal parameters, Arminianism is as much outside the Calvinist circle as Lutheranism.

The same and more can be said about Neo-Orthodoxy. While Barth and Brunner came from a liberal German Swiss Reformed background and often quoted the older Calvinists (usually drawing from Heppe), I remain unconvinced that their system is true Calvinism. They denied so much that we hold dear and essential. They diluted the five points beyond recognition and held to grossly distorted views of the five *solas* and the five fundamentals. It would be more appropriate to consider Neo-Orthodoxy "bastardized Calvinism." I for one agree with Cornelius Van Til's assessment. As Machen considered liberalism to be a separate religion from true Christianity, hence his book *Christianity and Liberalism*, so Van Til wrote *Christianity and Barthianism*. The movement is past its heyday but still lingers on the fringes of the Reformed community. It is not a "new Orthodoxy" but, as Van Til entitled another exposé, *The New Modernism*. The same charge can be made against Scottish Neo-Orthodoxy (the Torrances), Dutch Neo-Orthodoxy (Kuitert, et al), and a host of American Neo-Orthodoxies in Presbyterian, Dutch Reformed, and even Baptist circles. These are not Reformed and moreover are not even evangelical. In this respect, they are further from the truth than is evangelical Arminianism, which at least still subscribes to the five *solas* and the five fundamentals.

But if some are departing, others are arriving. It is a two-way street. There

---

13 N. L. Rice, *God Sovereign and Man Free* (Harrisonburg: Sprinkle, 1985), 21–22.

have always been those coming into Calvinism from non-Christian and non-Reformed backgrounds. We thank God for the Reformed resurgence since the mid-twentieth century,[14] which has been growing more and more in the twenty-first century. It has widely spread in Baptist circles and even among charismatics, a tradition that has been overwhelmingly Arminian. More significantly, it has grown in non-European and non-American countries, especially South Korea. The massive growth of underground Christianity in China will probably lead to a widespread discovery of Reformed Christianity hitherto unmatched elsewhere.

The Future of Calvinism

Reports of the death of Calvinism are greatly exaggerated and perhaps betray the secret wishes of our critics more than the facts allow. Calvinism is alive and growing. It has not reached its zenith yet. The Golden Age of the Reformation and Puritan era may well be surpassed in the future. Who can tell if there might be further giants equal to the previously named three and thirty greatest Calvinists? There might arise a greater evangelist than Whitefield or a preacher beyond even Spurgeon. God is not finished.

Often a Christian discovers the beauties of Reformed teaching by being dissatisfied and even disgusted by shallow versions of evangelicalism, including Arminianism but also others. Some get tired of the emotionalism of Pentecostalism. They are fed up with cotton candy; they want meat. Others see through easy-believism. As many Christians mature, they discover the biblically sound foundation in Calvinism that they have been dreaming of and praying for. As those other sorry trends get worse, we can expect further departures from them and immigrants into the Reformed fold.

There may even be a radical revival of true Augustinianism within Catholicism, which gave birth to the Reformation. Perhaps some Catholics will not only rediscover Augustine but reevaluate Gottschalk and Cornelius Jansen and find out they were right after all. Guido Stucco is a case in point in his excellent *God's Eternal Gift*.[15] This could lead them to reevaluate Luther and then Calvin. One can dream — and pray.

In his *Lectures on Calvinism*, Father Abraham Kuyper[16] gave us these telling words:

---

14 See John J. Murray, *Catch the Vision* (Darlington: Evangelical Press, 2007).
15 Bloomington, Ind.: XLibris, 2009.
16 One well-known Dutch American theologian, David Engelsma, once smiled and said to

> Calvinism is not dead — that it still carries in its germ the vital energy
> of the days of its former glory. Yea, even as a grain of wheat from the
> sarcophagi of the pharaohs, when again committed to the soil, bears a fruit
> a hundredfold, so Calvinism still carries in itself a wondrous power for the
> future of the nations.[17]

As Calvinism was declining in England early in the twentieth century,
H. Tydeman Chilvers — pastor of Spurgeon's Metropolitan Tabernacle —
wrote these opening words in his small book *Is There a Future for Calvinism?*:

> If there is no future for Calvinism then there is no future for anything
> that is of any value or worth. Every system of religious thought based upon
> the Scriptures, and all theology that is worthy of the Christian Church,
> are marked by that which is derived directly or indirectly from Calvinistic
> doctrine. Theology is strong or weak, virile or feeble, deep or shallow, in
> proportion to its Calvinistic spirit. Calvinism, in the truest interpretation of
> that word, puts iron in the blood, and gives muscle and fibre to conviction
> and Christian experience; and the people who receive it because they
> believe it, and then prove it in heart and life, are such as possess gumptious
> inflexibility with grace, in what they conceive to be the truth of God. I
> honestly believe that the Church's great need at the present hour is a strong
> grip of what this particular theology stands for. (Emphasis his)[18]

Conclusion

If Reformed theology is the purest form of biblical Christianity, then we can
confidently expect our sovereign Lord to bless it in the future as He continues
to call in the elect, build His church, and spread His glory around the world
until the Second Coming. Until then, the cry and prayer of every Reformed
Christian will be:

Soli Deo Gloria!

---

me, "After all, we are all 'sons of Abraham.'"
17 Abraham Kuyper, *Lectures on Calvinism* (Grand Rapids: Eerdmans, 1931), 40.
18 H. Tydeman Chilvers, *Is There a Future for Calvinism?* (London: Arthur H. Stockwell,
1929), 1.

Calvinism vs. Arminianism Chart

The 5 Points of Calvinism	The 5 Points of Arminianism
TOTAL DEPRAVITY Sin controls every part of man. He is spiritually dead and blind and unable to obey, believe, or repent. He continually sins, for his nature is completely evil.	**FREE WILL** Sin does not control man's will. He is sick and near-sighted, but still able to obey, believe, and repent. He does not continually sin, for his nature is not completely evil.
UNCONDITIONAL ELECTION God chose the elect solely on the basis of His free grace, not anything in them. He has a special love for the elect. God left the rest to be damned for their sins.	**CONDITIONAL ELECTION** God chose the elect on the basis of their foreseen faith. He loves all men equally. God passed over no one but gives everyone an equal chance to be saved.
LIMITED ATONEMENT Christ died especially for the elect and paid a definite price for them that guaranteed their salvation.	**UNIVERSAL ATONEMENT** Christ died equally for all men and paid a provisional price that made salvation possible for all but guaranteed it for none.
IRRESISTIBLE GRACE Saving grace is irresistible, for the Holy Spirit is invincible and intervenes in man's heart. He sovereignly gives the new birth, faith, and repentance to the elect.	**RESISTIBLE GRACE** Saving grace is resistible, for God cannot interfere with man's free will. Man is born again after he believes, for faith and repentance are not gifts of God.
PERSEVERANCE OF THE SAINTS God preserves all the elect and causes them to persevere in faith and obedience to the end. None are continually backslidden or finally lost.	**FALLING FROM GRACE** Only a few Christians continue in faith and obedience to the end (Arminians are divided over whether one can actually lose his salvation).

Bibliography

The following bibliography is provided for those who wish to study the history and theology of Calvinism further. Many items listed have further bibliographies. Of special interest are the following:

Beeke, Joel R. *A Reader's Guide to Reformed Literature*. Grand Rapids: Reformation Heritage Books, 1999.

Martin, Robert P. *A Guide to the Puritans*. Edinburgh: Banner of Truth, 1997. (not limited to the Puritans)

I have generally limited this listing to books published after 1950, though some are reprints from before then. Most are still in print. I have not included journal articles, websites, or doctoral dissertations except my own. The more advanced works will direct more serious students to studies in German, French, Dutch, and Latin.

I have not included websites for several reasons. First, they are readily accessible by online search engines. Second, though many are valuable, too many others are simply personal blogs or shallow screeds. The same applies to many anti-Calvinist websites. Third, websites come and go too rapidly to list here, while books remain available in libraries even when they go out of print. Interested readers may easily borrow them from their local library by means of interlibrary loan.

Calvinists have written far too many Bible commentaries to list here. Readers may want to consult the main ones for the Scripture texts cited in this volume. John Calvin's commentary heads the list. He did not live to complete it, but his several series of expository sermons almost completed the project. Among Calvinists who commented on the whole Bible are Matthew Henry, Matthew Poole, John Gill, John Trapp, and Thomas Scott. Several Reformed commentary series include many authors, such as the Geneva series (Banner of Truth), the Reformed Expository Commentary (P&R), The Reformation Commentary on Scripture (IVP), Let's Study (Banner of Truth), and The Evangelical Press Study Commentary (Evangelical Press). Both the Synod of Dort and the Westminster Assembly produced large commentaries on the whole Bible, but only the former is still in print. The best Reformed commentary on the entire New Testament is *New Testament Commentary* by William Hendriksen and Simon Kistemaker. *The MacArthur New Testament Commentary* is also excellent. Of course, most commentaries are not a part of a series, such as John Owen on Hebrews or J. C. Ryle on the four gospels. For concise comments, see the various "study Bibles": *The Reformation Heritage KJV Study Bible*, *The Reformation Study Bible* (formerly *The New Geneva Study Bible*), *The Spirit of the Reformation Study Bible*, *The MacArthur Study Bible*, and the various reprints of the original *Geneva Bible*.

I have not included journal articles. For one thing, that would have greatly expanded the bibliography to include even a small sampling. Also, though they may be consulted at most good seminaries, they are not usually available for interlibrary loan. Most are still not available online. Most journals have book reviews of new books and keep the serious student informed of current discussions. Among the more important Reformed journals are the following: *Westminster Theological Journal*, *Calvin Theological Journal*, *Puritan Reformed Journal*, *Mid-America Journal of Theology*, *The Journal of Reformed Theology*, and *Banner of Truth*. The *Calvin Theological Journal* publishes an extensive annual listing of new books, articles, and dissertations relating to Calvin and Calvinism in many languages.

It is my hope that this bibliography will be of use to the Reformed community and others in their study of the history and theology of Calvinism.

General Studies

à Brakel, Wilhelmus. *The Christian's Reasonable Service*. 4 vols. Translated by Bartel Elshout. Ligonier: Soli Deo Gloria, 1992.

Alcorn, Randy. *Hand in Hand: The Beauty of God's Sovereignty and Meaningful Human Choice*. Colorado Springs: Multnomah Books, 2014.

Balserak, Jon. *Calvinism: A Very Short Introduction*. Oxford: Oxford University Press, 2016.

Barrett, Matthew. *Salvation by Grace*. Phillipsburg, NJ: P&R, 2013.

Barrett, Matthew, and Thomas J. Nettles, eds. *Whomever He Wills: A Surprising Display of Sovereign Mercy*. Cape Coral, FL: Founders Press, 2012.

Bavinck, Herman. *Reformed Dogmatics*. 4 vols. Grand Rapids: Baker Academic, 2003.

Beardslee, John W. III, ed. *Reformed Dogmatics*. New York: Oxford University Press, 1965.

Beeke, Joel R. *Puritan Reformed Spirituality*. Grand Rapids: Reformation Heritage Books, 2004.

Beeke, Joel R. and Paul M. Smalley. *Reformed Systematic Theology*. 4 vols. Wheaton: Crossway, 2019.

Belcher, Richard. *A Journey in Grace*. Colombia: Richbarry Press, 1990.

Belcher, Richard. *A Journey in Predestination*. Fort Mill, SC: Richbarry Press, 2013.

Benedetto, Robert, and Donald K. McKim. *Historical Dictionary of Reformed Churches*. 2nd ed. Lanham: Scarecrow Press, 2010.

Benedict, Philip. *Christ's Churches Purely Reformed: A Social History of Calvinism*. New Haven: Yale University Press, 2002.

Benton, John, and John Peet. *God's Riches:*

A Work-Book on the Doctrines of Grace. Edinburgh: Banner of Truth, 1991.

Berkhof, Louis. *Systematic Theology.* Grand Rapids: Eerdmans, 1988.

Boettner, Loraine. *The Reformed Doctrine of Predestination.* Phillipsburg, NJ: P&R, 1932.

Boettner, Loraine. *The Reformed Faith.* Phillipsburg, NJ: Presbyterian and Reformed, 1983.

Boice, James Montgomery. *Foundations of the Christian Faith.* Downers Grove, IL: IVP, 1986.

Boice, James Montgomery, and Philip Graham Ryken. *The Doctrines of Grace.* Wheaton: Crossway, 2002.

Boyce, James Petigru. *Abstract of Systematic Theology.* Cape Coral, FL: Founders Press, 2007.

Brown, Craig R. *The Five Dilemmas of Calvinism.* Orlando: Ligonier Ministries, 2007.

Bullinger, Henry (Heinrich). *The Decades of Henry Bullinger.* 4 vols. in 2. Grand Rapids: Reformation Heritage Books, 2011.

Buice, Josh, ed. *The New Calvinism.* Fearn: Christian Focus, 2017.

Cairns, Alan. *Dictionary of Theological Terms.* Greenville, SC: Ambassador Emerald International, 2002.

Calvin, John. *Institutes of the Christian Religion.* 2 vols. Edited by John T. McNeill. Translated by Ford Lewis Battles. Philadelphia: Westminster Press, 1960.

Cameron, Nigel M. de S., ed. *Dictionary of Scottish Church History & Theology.* Downers Grove, IL: IVP, 1993.

Clark, Gordon H. *Predestination.* Phillipsburg, NJ: Presbyterian and Reformed, 1987.

Clendenen, E. Ray, and Brad J. Waggoner, eds. *Calvinism: A Southern Baptist Dialogue.* Nashville: B&H Academic, 2008.

Coles, Elisha. *God's Sovereignty.* Grand Rapids: Baker Book House, 1979.

Cosby, Brian. *Rebels Rescued.* Fearn: Christian Focus, 2012.

Culver, Robert. *Systematic Theology.* Fearn: Mentor: 2005.

Cunningham, William. *Historical Theology.* 2 vols. London: Banner of Truth, 1969.

Dabney, Robert Lewis. *Systematic Theology.* Edinburgh: Banner of Truth, 1985.

Dabney, Robert Lewis, and Jonathan Dickinson. *The Five Points of Calvinism.* Harrisonburg, VA: Sprinkle Publications, 1992.

Dagg, J. L. *A Manual of Theology.* Harrisonburg, VA: Gano Books, 1990.

Dennison, James T., Jr., ed. *Reformed Confessions of the 16th and 17th Centuries in English Translation.* 4 vols. Grand Rapids: Reformation Heritage Books, 2008.

Edwards, Jonathan. *The Works of Jonathan Edwards.* 2 vols. Edinburgh: Banner of Truth, 1974.

Edwards, Jonathan. *The Works of Jonathan Edwards.* 26 vols. New Haven: Yale University Press, 1957.

Ella, George M. *More Mountain Movers.* Eggleston: Go Publications, 1999.

Ella, George M. *Mountain Movers.* Eggleston: Go Publications, 1999.

Foster, Greg. *The Joy of Calvinism.* Wheaton: Crossway, 2012.

Frame, John M. "Introduction to the Reformed Faith." In *John Frame's Selected Shorter Writings,* 1:77–99. Phillipsburg, NJ: P&R, 2014.

Frame, John M. *Systematic Theology.* Phillipsburg, NJ: P&R, 2013.

Gamble, Richard. C. *The Whole Counsel of God.* Phillipsburg, NJ: P&R, 2009.

Gamble, Richard. C., ed. *Articles on Calvin and Calvinism.* 14 vols. New York: Garland, 1992.

George, Timothy. *Amazing Grace: God's Pursuit, Our Response.* 2nd ed. Wheaton: Crossway, 2001.

Gerstner, John. *A Predestination Primer.* Grand Rapids: Baker Book House, 1960.

Gill, John. *The Cause of God and Truth*. Grand Rapids: Baker Book House, 1980.

Gill, John. *A Complete Body of Doctrinal and Practical Divinity*. Paris, AR: Baptist Standard Bearer, 1984.

Girardeau, John Lafeyette. *Calvinism and Evangelical Arminianism*. Harrisonburg, VA: Sprinkle Publications, 1984.

Girod, Gordon. *The Deeper Faith: An Exposition of the Canons of Dort*. Grand Rapids: Baker, 1949.

Good, Kenneth H. *God's Gracious Purpose as Seen in the Gospel of John*. Grand Rapids: Baker Book House, 1979.

Grudem, Wayne. *Systematic Theology*. Grand Rapids: Zondervan, 1994.

Hagopian, David G., ed. *Back to Basics: Rediscovering the Richness of the Reformed Faith*. Phillipsburg, NJ: P&R, 1996.

Hanko, Herman, Homer Hoeksema, and Gise Van Baren. *The Five Points of Calvinism*. Grand Rapids: Reformed Free Publishing Association, 1976.

Hansen, Collin. *Young, Restless, Reformed*. Wheaton: Crossway, 2008.

Hart, D. G. *Calvinism: A History*. New Haven: Yale University Press, 2013.

Hart, D. G., and Mark A. Noll, eds. *Dictionary of the Presbyterian & Reformed Tradition in America*. Phillipsburg, NJ: P&R, 2005.

Heppe, Heinrich. *Reformed Dogmatics*. Grand Rapids: Baker Book House, 1978.

Hodge, Charles. *Systematic Theology*. 3 vols. Grand Rapids: Eerdmans, 1979.

Hodges, Louis Igou. *Reformed Theology Today*. Columbia: Brentwood Christian Press, 1995.

Hoeksema, Herman. *Reformed Dogmatics*. 2 vols. 2nd ed. Grandville: Reformed Free Publishing Association, 2004.

Holder, R. Ward, ed. *The Westminster Handbook to Theologies of the Reformation*. Louisville: Westminster John Knox Press, 2010.

Horton, Michael. *The Christian Faith*. Grand Rapids: Zondervan, 2011.

Horton, Michael. *For Calvinism*. Grand Rapids: Zondervan, 2011.

Horton, Michael. *Putting Amazing Back into Grace*. Grand Rapids: Baker Books, 1994.

Hunt, Dave, and James White. *Debating Calvinism*. Sisters, OR: Multnomah, 2004.

Hyde, Daniel R. *Welcome to a Reformed Church*. Orlando: Reformation Trust, 2010.

Johnson, William Stacy, John H. Leith, and George W. Stroup, eds. *Reformed Reader: A Sourcebook in Christian Theology*. 2 vols. Louisville: Westminster John Knox Press, 1993.

Kapic, Kelly M., and Wesley Vander Lugt. *Pocket Dictionary of the Reformed Tradition*. Downers Grove, IL: IVP Academic, 2013.

Kuyper, Abraham. *Particular Grace: A Defense of God's Sovereignty in Salvation*. Grandville: Reformed Free Publishing Association, 2001.

Lawson, Steven J. *A Long Line of Godly Men*. 2 vols. Orlando: Reformation Trust, 2006.

Lems, Shane. *The Doctrines of Grace*. Phillipsburg, NJ: P&R, 2013.

Lloyd-Jones, D. Martyn. *Great Doctrines of the Bible*. 3 vols. Wheaton: Crossway, 2003.

MacArthur, John, and Richard Mayhue, eds. *Biblical Doctrine*. Wheaton: Crossway, 2017.

Machen, J. Gresham. *The Christian View of Man*. London: Banner of Truth, 1965.

Martin, Albert. *The Practical Implications of Calvinism*. Edinburgh: Banner of Truth, 1979.

Martin, Robert. *A Guide to the Puritans*. Edinburgh: Banner of Truth, 1997.

Matthews, John. *The Divine Purpose*. Vestavia Hills, AL: Solid Ground Christian Books, 2009.

McClarty, Jim. *By Grace Alone*. Smyrna, GA: GCA Publishing, 2007.

McKim, Donald K., ed. *Encyclopedia of the Reformed Faith*. Louisville: Westminster John Knox Press, 2001.

McKim, Donald K., ed. *The Westminster Handbook of Reformed Theology*. Louisville: Westminster John Knox Press, 2001.

McNeill, John T. *The History and Character of Calvinism.* New York: Oxford University Press, 1954.

Meeter, H. Henry. *The Basic Ideas of Calvinism.* 6th ed. Grand Rapids: Baker Book House, 1990.

Montgomery, Daniel, and Timothy Paul Jones. *PROOF: Finding Freedom Through the Intoxicating Joy of Irresistible Grace.* Grand Rapids: Zondervan, 2015.

Morecraft, Joseph, III. *Authentic Christianity.* 5 vols. Powder Springs, GA: Minkoff Family Publishing and American Vision Press, 2009.

Moulin, Peter (Pierre Du). *The Anatomy of Arminianisme.* Norwood: Walter J. Johnson, 1976.

Muller, Richard A. *Dictionary of Latin and Greek Theological Terms, Drawn Principally from Protestant Scholastic Theology.* 2nd ed. Grand Rapids: Baker Academic, 2017.

Muller, Richard A. *Post-Reformation Reformed Dogmatics.* 2nd ed. 4 vols. Grand Rapids: Baker Academic, 2003.

Murray, John. *The Collected Writings of John Murray.* 4 vols. Edinburgh: Banner of Truth, 1976.

Murrell, Adam. *Predestined to Believe.* Eugene: Resource Publications, 2008.

Ness, Christopher. *An Antidote to Arminianism.* Choteau, MT: Old Paths Gospel Press, n.d.

Nettles, Thomas J. *By His Grace and For His Glory.* Rev. ed. Cape Coral, FL: Founders Press, 2006.

Orrick, Jim Scott. *Mere Calvinism.* Phillipsburg: P&R, 2019.

Owen, John. *The Works of John Owen.* 24 vols. London: Banner of Truth, 1967.

Packer, J. I. *Evangelism and the Sovereignty of God.* Downers Grove, IL: InterVarsity Press, 1961.

Palmer, Edwin. *The Five Points of Calvinism.* Rev. ed. Grand Rapids: Baker Book House, 1984.

Parks, William. *Sermons on the Five Points of Calvinism.* Choteau, MT: Old Paths Gospel Press, n.d.

Payne, William E. *Life Transforming Truth: An Introduction to the Doctrines of Grace.* Dundas, Ontario: Joshua Press, 2001.

Perkins, William. *A Golden Chaine, or the Description of Theologie, Containing the Order of the Causes of Salvation and Damnation, According to God's Word.* N.p.: Puritan Reprints, 2010.

Peterson, Robert A., and Michael D. Williams. *Why I Am Not an Arminian.* Downers Grove, IL: IVP, 2004.

Phillips, Richard D. *What's So Great about the Doctrines of Grace?* Orlando: Reformation Trust, 2008.

Picken, Stuart D. B. *Historical Dictionary of Calvinism.* Lanham: Scarecrow Press, 2012.

Pink, Arthur W. *The Sovereignty of God.* Grand Rapids: Baker Book House, 1973.

Piper, John. *Five Points.* Fearn: Christian Focus, 2013.

Piper, John. *TULIP: The Pursuit of God's Glory in Salvation.* Wheaton: Crossway, 2009.

Polhill, Edward. *The Works of Edward Polhill.* Morgan: Soli Deo Gloria, 1998.

Reed, R. C. *The Gospel as Taught by Calvin.* Edinburgh: Banner of Truth, 2009.

Reisinger, Ernest C., and D. Matthew Allen. *Beyond Five Points.* Cape Coral, FL: Founders Press, 2002.

Reymond, Robert L. *A New Systematic Theology of the Christian Faith.* Nashville: Thomas Nelson, 1998.

Ryken, Philip G. *The Message of Salvation.* Downers Grove, IL: IVP, 2001.

Samson, John. *Twelve What Abouts: Answering Common Objections Concerning God's Sovereignty in Election.* Birmingham: Solid Ground Christian Books, 2012.

Schreiner, Thomas R., and Bruce A. Ware, eds. *The Grace of God, The Bondage of the Will.* 2 vols. Grand Rapids: Baker Books, 1995.

Schreiner, Thomas R. and Bruce A. Ware,

eds. *Still Sovereign*. Grand Rapids: Baker Books, 2000.

Seaton, Jack. *The Five Points of Calvinism*. London: Banner of Truth, 1970.

Selderhuis, Herman J., ed. *The Calvin Handbook*. Grand Rapids: Eerdmans, 2009.

Shaw, Robert. *The Reformed Faith*. Fearn: Christian Heritage/Christian Focus, 2008.

Shedd, William G. T. *Calvinism: Pure and Mixed*. Edinburgh: Banner of Truth, 1986.

Shedd, William G. T. *Dogmatic Theology*. 3rd ed. Phillipsburg, NJ: P&R, 2003.

Smith, Morton H. *Systematic Theology*. 2 vols. Greenville, SC: Greenville Seminary Press, 1994.

Sproul, R. C. *Chosen by God*. Wheaton: Tyndale House, 1986.

Sproul, R. C. *Grace Unknown*. Grand Rapids: Baker Books, 1997. (Reprinted 2005 as *What is Reformed Theology?*)

Sproul, R. C., Jr., ed. *After Darkness, Light*. Phillipsburg, NJ: P&R, 2003.

Spurgeon, Charles Haddon. *A Defence of Calvinism*. Edinburgh: Banner of Truth, 2008.

Spurgeon, Charles Haddon. "A Defence of Calvinism." In *C. H. Spurgeon Autobiography, Volume I: The Early Years 1834–1859*, 163–77. Edinburgh: Banner of Truth, 1976.

Spurgeon, Charles Haddon. *Exposition of the Doctrines of Grace*. Pasadena, TX: Pilgrim Publications, 1971.

Spurgeon, Charles Haddon. "Exposition of the Doctrines of Grace." In *Metropolitan Tabernacle Pulpit*, 7:297–304. Pasadena, TX: Pilgrim Publications, 1986.

Spurgeon, Charles Haddon. *Sermons on Sovereignty*. Pasadena, TX: Pilgrim Publications, 1990.

Steele, David, Curtis Thomas, and S. Lance Quinn. *The Five Points of Calvinism*. 2nd ed. Phillipsburg, NJ: P&R, 2004.

Stewart, Kenneth J. *Ten Myths About Calvinism: Recovering the Breadth of the Reformed Tradition*. Downers Grove, IL: IVP, 2011.

Storms, Sam. *Chosen for Life*. Rev. ed. Wheaton: Crossway, 2007.

Talbot, Kenneth G., and Gary Crampton. *Calvinism, Hyper-Calvinism and Arminianism*. Battle Ground, Wash.: Christian Resources, 1990.

te Velde, Dolf, ed. *Synopsis Purioris Theologiae: Synopsis of a Purer Theology*. 3 vols. Leiden: Brill, 2015.

Turretin, Francis. *Institutes of Elenctic Theology*. Edited by James T. Dennison Jr. 3 vols. Phillipsburg, NJ: P&R, 1992.

Tyson, Thomas E., and G. I. Williamson. *What is the Reformed Faith?* Willow Grove: The Committee on Christian Education of the Orthodox Presbyterian Church, 2007.

Ursinus, Zacharias. *The Commentary of Dr. Zacharias Ursinus on the Heidelberg Catechism*. Phillipsburg, NJ: Presbyterian and Reformed, n.d.

van Mastricht, Petrus. *Theological and Practical Theology*. Edited by Joel R. Beeke. Translated by Todd Rester. Grand Rapids: Reformation Heritage Books, 2018.

Venema, Cornelis P. *But for the Grace of God: An Exposition of the Canons of Dort*. Grandville: Reformed Fellowship, 2011.

Vos, Geerhardus. *Reformed Dogmatics*. 5 vols. Bellingham: Lexham Press, 2012.

Warburton, Ben A. *Calvinism*. Grand Rapids: Eerdmans, 1955.

Watson, Thomas. *A Body of Divinity*. Edinburgh: Banner of Truth, 1974.

Watts, Malcolm. *What is a Reformed Church?* Grand Rapids: Reformation Heritage Books, 2011.

Westminster Confession of Faith. Glasgow: Free Presbyterian Publications, 2003.

White, James R. *God's Sovereign Grace*. Southbridge, MA: Crowne Publications, 1991.

White, James R. *The Potter's Freedom*. Amityville, NY: Calvary Press Publishing, 2000.

White, James R. *The Sovereign Grace of God.* Lindenhurst: Great Christian Books, 2003.

Wright, R. K. McGregor. *No Place for Sovereignty.* Downers Grove, IL: IVP, 1996.

Wright, Shawn D. *40 Questions About Calvinism.* Grand Rapids: Kregel, 2019.

Zemek, George. *A Biblical Theology of the Doctrines of Sovereign Grace.* Little Rock: BTDSG, 2002.

Pre-Calvinism

Alexander, Archibald. "The Early History of Pelagianism." In Charles Hodge, et al. *Princeton versus the New Divinity*, 52–89. Edinburgh: Banner of Truth, 2001.

Augustine. *The Works of Saint Augustine.* 48 vols. Hyde Park: New City Press, 1997.

Boettner, Loraine. *The Reformed Doctrine of Predestination*, 318–323. Philadelphia: Presbyterian and Reformed, 1932.

Bonner, Gerald. *St. Augustine of Hippo: Life and Controversies.* Rev. ed. Norwich: Canterbury Press, 1986.

Bromiley, Geoffrey W. *Historical Theology*, 109–23, 159–70. Grand Rapids: Eerdmans, 1978.

Brown, Peter. *Augustine of Hippo: A Biography.* 2nd ed. Berkeley: University of California Press, 2000.

Busenitz, Nathan. *Long Before Luther: Tracing the Heart of the Gospel from Christ to the Reformation.* Chicago: Moody Publishers; and Los Angeles: The Master's Seminary Press, 2017.

Chadwick, Henry. *Augustine: A Very Short Introduction.* Oxford: Oxford University Press, 2001.

Chadwick, Henry. *Augustine of Hippo: A Life.* Oxford: Oxford University Press, 2009.

Cunningham, William. *Historical Theology*, 1:179–84, 321–58. London: Banner of Truth, 1969.

Custance, Arthur C. *The Sovereignty of Grace*, 13–50. Phillipsburg, NJ: Presbyterian and Reformed, 1979.

De Bruyn, Theodore. *Pelagius' Commentary on St. Paul's Epistle to the Romans.* Oxford: Clarendon Press, 1993.

Di Berardino, Angelo, ed. *Patrology*, 4:342–563. Westminster: Christian Classics, 1986.

Evan, Robert F. *Four Letters of Pelagius.* New York: Seabury Press, 1968.

Evan, Robert F. *Pelagius: Inquiries and Reappraisals.* New York: Seabury Press, 1968.

Ferguson, John. *Pelagius: A Historical and Theological Study.* Cambridge: W. Heffer and Sons, 1956.

Fitzgerald, Allan D., ed. *Augustine Through the Ages: An Encyclopedia.* Grand Rapids: Eerdmans, 1999.

Geisler, Norman, ed. *What Augustine Says.* Grand Rapids: Baker Book House, 1982.

Genke, Victor, and Francis X. Gumerlock, eds. *Gottschalk and a Medieval Predestinarian Controversy: Texts Translated from the Latin.* Milwaukee: Marquette University Press, 2010.

Gill, John. *The Cause of God and Truth*, 220–328. Grand Rapids: Baker Book House, 1980.

Harnack, Adolph. *History of Dogma*, 5:61–261, 292–302. Gloucester: Peter Smith, 1976.

Kelly, J. N. D. *Early Christian Doctrines*, 344–74. 2nd ed. New York: Harper & Row, 1960.

Krabbendam, Henry. *Sovereignty and Responsibility: The Pelagian-Augustinian Controversy in Philosophical and Global Perspective.* Bonn: Culture and Science Publishers, 2002.

Lawson, Steven. *A Long Line of Godly Men, Volume 2.* Orlando: Reformation Trust, 2011.

Leff, Gordon. *Bradwardine and the Pelagians.*

Cambridge: Cambridge University Press, 1957.

Levering, Matthew. *Predestination*, 36–97. Oxford: Oxford University Press, 2011.

Levering, Matthew. *The Theology of Augustine*. Grand Rapids: Baker Academic, 2013.

McCracken, George E., ed. *Early Medieval Theology*, 148–75. Library of Christian Classics, Volume IX. Philadelphia: Westminster Press, 1957.

McKitterick, Rosamond, ed. *The New Cambridge Medieval History*, 2:767–73. Cambridge: Cambridge University Press, 1995.

Needham, N. P. *The Triumph of Grace: Augustine's Writings on Salvation*. London: Grace Publications Trust, 2000.

O'Donnell, James J. *Augustine: A New Biography*. New York: HarperCollins, 2005.

Oberman, Heiko A. *The Harvest of Medieval Theology*. Grand Rapids: Baker Academic, 2000.

Ogliari, Donato. *Gratia et Certamen: The Relationship Between Grace and Free Will in the Discussion of Augustine with the So-Called Semipelagians*. Leuven: Leuven University Press, 2003.

Pelikan, Jaroslav. *The Christian Tradition*, 3:80–98. Chicago: University of Chicago Press, 1978.

Peterson, Robert A., and Michael D. Williams. *Why I Am Not an Arminian*, 20–41. Downers Grove, IL: IVP, 2004.

Pollmann, Karla, ed. *The Oxford Guide to the Historical Reception of Augustine*. 3 vols. Oxford: Oxford University Press, 2013.

Portalie, Eugene. *A Guide to the Thought of St. Augustine*. Chicago: Henry Regnery, 1960.

Rees, B. R. *Pelagius: The Letters of Pelagius and His Followers*. Woodbridge: Boydell Press, 1991.

Rees, B. R. *Pelagius: A Reluctant Heretic*. Woodbridge: Boydell Press, 1988.

Robson, J. A. *Wyclif and the Oxford Schools*. Cambridge: Cambridge University Press, 1961.

Schaff, Philip. *History of the Christian Church*, *Volume 3*. Grand Rapids: Eerdmans, 1984.

Schaff, Philip, ed. *A Select Library of the Nicene and Post-Nicene Fathers of the Christian Church*. First Series. 8 vols. Grand Rapids: Eerdmans, 1978.

Seeberg, Reinhold. *The History of Doctrine*, 1:328–82, 2:30–33. Grand Rapids: Baker Book House, 1978.

Shedd, William G. T. *A History of Christian Doctrine*, 2:92–110. Eugene: Wipf and Stock, 1998.

Sproul, R. C. *Willing to Believe: The Controversy Over Free Will*, 33–84. Grand Rapids: Baker Books, 1997.

Stucco, Guido. *God's Eternal Gift: A History of the Catholic Doctrine of Predestination from Augustine to the Renaissance*. N.p.: XLibris Corp., 2009.

Stucco, Guido. *Not Without Us: A Brief History of the Forgotten Catholic Doctrine of Predestination During the Semipelagian Controversy*. Tucson: Fenestra Books, 2006.

Stump, Eleonore, and Norman Kretzmann, eds. *The Cambridge Companion to Augustine*. Cambridge: Cambridge University Press, 2001.

Teske, Roland J. *Augustine of Hippo: Philosopher, Exegete, and Theologian*. Milwaukee: Marquette University Press, 2009.

Warfield, Benjamin B. *Calvin and Augustine*. Philadelphia: Presbyterian and Reformed, 1971.

Warfield, Benjamin B. *The Works of Benjamin B. Warfield*, 4:113–412. Grand Rapids: Baker Book House, 1981.

Weaver, Rebecca Hardin. *Divine Grace and Human Agency: A Study of the Semi-Pelagian Controversy*. Macon, GA: Mercer University Press, 1996.

The Reformation

Bagchi, David, and David C. Steinmetz, eds. *The Cambridge Companion to Reformation Theology*. Cambridge: Cambridge University Press, 2004.

Bainton, Roland. *Here I Stand: A Life of Martin Luther*. Nashville: Abingdon Press, 1950.

Balke, Willem. *Calvin and the Anabaptist Radicals*. Grand Rapids: Eerdmans, 1981.

Barrett, Matthew, ed. *Reformation Theology: A Systematic Summary*. Wheaton: Crossway Books, 2017.

Barth, Hans-Martin. *The Theology of Martin Luther*. Minneapolis: Fortress Press, 2013.

Benedict, Philip. *Christ's Churches Purely Reformed: A Social History of Calvinism*. New Haven: Yale University Press, 2002.

Boice, James Montgomery, and Benjamin E. Sasse, eds. *Here We Stand*. Grand Rapids: Baker Books, 1996.

Bromiley, G. W., ed. *Zwingli and Bullinger*. Library of Christian Classics, Volume XXIV. Philadelphia: Westminster Press, 1953.

Bucer, Martin. *The Common Places of Martin Bucer*. Edited by D. F. Wright. Appleford: Sutton Courtenay Press, 1972.

Bullinger, Henry (Heinrich). *The Decades of Henry Bullinger*. 4 vols. in 2. Grand Rapids: Reformation Heritage Books, 2004.

Burnett, Amy Nelson, and Emidio Campi, eds. *A Companion to the Swiss Reformation*. Leiden: Brill, 2016.

Cunningham, William. *The Reformers and the Theology of the Reformation*. Edinburgh: Banner of Truth, 1979.

D'Aubigne, J. H. Merle. *History of the Reformation in Europe in the Time of Calvin*. 8 vols. in 4. Harrisonburg, VA: Sprinkle Publications, 2000.

D'Aubigne, J. H. Merle. *History of the Reformation in the Sixteenth Century*. Grand Rapids: Baker Book House, 1976.

Dennison, James T., Jr., ed. *Reformed Confessions of the 16th and 17th Centuries in English Translation, Volume 1*. Grand Rapids: Reformation Heritage Books, 2010.

Donnelly, John Patrick. *Calvinism and Scholasticism in Vermigli's Doctrine of Man and Grace*. Leiden: Brill, 1976.

Eire, Carlos M. N. *Reformations: The Early Modern World, 1450–1650*. New Haven: Yale University Press, 2016.

Elton, G. R., ed. *The New Cambridge Modern History, Volume 2: The Reformation, 1520–1559*. Cambridge: Cambridge University Press, 1958.

Engelsma, David J., ed. *The Sixteenth-Century Reformation of the Church*. Jenison: Reformed Free Publishing Association, 2007.

Evans, G. R. *The Roots of the Reformation*. 2nd ed. Downers Grove, IL: IVP, 2012.

Gabler, Ulrich. *Huldrych Zwingli*. Philadelphia: Fortress Press, 1986.

Ganzer, Klaus, and Bruno Steiner, eds. *Dictionary of the Reformation*. New York: Crossroad, 2004.

George, Timothy. *Theology of the Reformers*. Nashville: Broadman Press, 1988.

Godfrey, W. Robert. *Reformation Sketches*. Phillipsburg, NJ: P&R, 2003.

Gordon, Bruce. *The Swiss Reformation*. Manchester: Manchester University Press, 2002.

Gordon, Bruce, and Emidio Campi, eds. *Architects of Reformation: An Introduction to Heinrich Bullinger, 1504–1575*. Grand Rapids: Baker Academic, 2004.

Greschat, Martin. *Martin Bucer: A Reformer and His Times*. Louisville: Westminster John Knox Press, 2004.

Hart, D. G. *Calvinism: A History*, 1–46. New Haven: Yale University Press, 2013.

Heinze, Rudolph W. *Reform and Conflict: From the Medieval World to the Wars of Religion, A.D. 1350–1648*. The Baker History of the Church, Volume 4. Grand Rapids: Baker Books, 2005.

Hillerbrand, Hans J., ed. *The Oxford Encyclopedia of the Reformation.* 4 vols. New York: Oxford University Press, 1996.

Hillerbrand, Hans J., ed. *The Reformation.* New York: Harper and Row, 1964.

Holder R. Ward, ed. *The Westminster Handbook to Theologians of the Reformation.* Louisville: Westminster John Knox Press, 2010.

James, Frank, III. *Peter Martyr Vermigli and Predestination.* Oxford: Clarendon Press, 1998.

Janz, Denis R., ed. *A Reformation Reader: Primary Texts with Introductions.* Minneapolis: Fortress Press, 2008.

Johnson, Gary L. W., and R. Fowler White, eds. *Whatever Happened to the Reformation?* Phillipsburg, NJ: P&R, 2001.

King, John B., Jr. *Predestination in Light of the Cross: A Critical Exposition of Luther's Theology.* Vallecito: Chalcedon Foundation, 2003.

Landry, Eric, and Michael S. Horton, eds. *The Reformation Then and Now.* Peabody: Hendrickson, 2017.

Lawson, Steven J. *The Heroic Boldness of Martin Luther.* Orlando: Reformation Trust, 2013.

Lawson, Steven J. *A Long Line of Godly Men, Volume 2.* Orlando: Reformation Trust, 2011.

Lindberg, Carter, ed. *The European Reformations Sourcebook.* Oxford: Blackwell, 2000.

Lindberg, Carter, ed. *The Reformation Theologians: An Introduction to Theology in the Early Modern Period.* Oxford: Basil Blackwell, 2002.

Lindsay, Thomas M. *The Reformation.* Edinburgh: Banner of Truth, 2006.

Luther, Martin. *The Bondage of the Will.* Translated by J. I. Packer and O. R. Johnston. Grand Rapids: Fleming H. Revell, 2005.

Luther, Martin. *Luther's Works.* 55+ vols. St. Louis: Concordia Publishing House, 1958.

MacCulloch, Diarmaid. *The Reformation.* New York: Viking, 2003.

McLelland, Joseph C. *The Visible Words of God: An Exposition of the Sacramental Theology of Peter Martyr Vermigli, A.D. 1500–1562.* Edinburgh: Oliver and Boyd, 1957.

Melanchthon, Phillip. *Melanchthon on Christian Doctrine.* New York: Oxford University Press, 1965.

Needham, N. R. *2000 Years of Christ's Power, Volume 3.* Rev. ed. Fearn: Christian Focus, 2016.

Nelson, Derek R., and Paul R. Hinlicky, eds. *The Oxford Encyclopedia of Martin Luther.* 3 vols. Oxford: Oxford University Press, 2017.

Nichols, Stephen. *The Reformation.* Wheaton: Crossway, 2007.

Pauck, Wilhelm, ed. *Melanchthon and Bucer.* Library of Christian Classics, Volume XIX. Philadelphia: Westminster Press, 1969.

Pelikan, Jaroslav. *The Christian Tradition, Volume 4.* Chicago: University of Chicago Press, 1984.

Potter, G. R. *Zwingli.* Cambridge: Cambridge University Press, 1976.

Preus, Robert D. *The Theology of Post-Reformation Lutheranism.* 2 vols. St. Louis: Concordia Publishing House, 1970.

Reeves, Michael. *The Unquenchable Flame.* Nashville: B&H Academic, 2009.

Reeves, Michael, and Tim Chester. *Why the Reformation Still Matters.* Wheaton: Crossway, 2016.

Robinson, William Childs. *The Reformation: A Rediscovery of Grace.* Grand Rapids: Eerdmans, 1962.

Roth, John D., and James M. Stayer, eds. *A Companion to Anabaptism and Spiritualism, 1521–1700.* Leiden: Brill, 2007.

Rupp, E. Gordon, and Philip S. Watson, eds. *Luther and Erasmus: Free Will and Salvation.* Philadelphia: Westminster Press, 1969.

Schaff, Philip. *History of the Christian Church,*

Volumes 7 and 8. Grand Rapids: Eerdmans, 1980.

Schiebert, Ernest G. *The Reformation.* Minneapolis: Fortress Press, 1996.

Selvaggio, Anthony T. *Meet Martin Luther.* Grand Rapids: Reformation Heritage Books, 2017.

Sproul, R. C. *Willing to Believe,* 87–102. Grand Rapids: Baker Books, 1992.

Steinmetz, David C. *Reformers in the Wings.* Philadelphia: Fortress Press, 1986.

Stephens, W. P. *The Theology of Huldrych Zwingli.* Oxford: Clarendon Press, 1986.

Sunshine, Glenn S. *The Reformation for Armchair Theologians.* Louisville: Westminster John Knox Press, 2005.

van den Berg, Machiel A. *Friends of Calvin.* Grand Rapids: Eerdmans, 2009.

Vermigli, Peter Martyr. *The Peter Martyr Library.* 10 volumes. Kirksville, MO: Truman State University Press, 1994.

Wengert, Timothy, ed. *Dictionary of Luther and the Lutheran Traditions.* Grand Rapids: Baker Academic, 2017.

Whitford, David M., ed. *Reformation and Early Modern Europe: A Guide to Research.* Kirksville, MO: Truman State University Press, 2008.

Williams, George Hunston. *The Radical Reformation.* 3rd ed. Kirksville, MO: Sixteenth Century Journal, 1992.

John Calvin

Battles, Ford Lewis. *Analysis of the Institutes of the Christian Religion of John Calvin.* Phillipsburg, NJ: P&R, 2001.

Battles, Ford Lewis. *Interpreting John Calvin.* Grand Rapids: Baker Books, 1996.

Beach, J. Mark. *Piety's Wisdom: A Summary of Calvin's Institutes with Study Questions.* Grand Rapids: Reformation Heritage Books, 2010.

Beeke, Joel R., David W. Hall, and Michael A. G. Haykin, eds. *Theology Made Practical: New Studies on John Calvin and His Legacy.* Grand Rapids: Reformation Heritage Books, 2017.

Beeke, Joel R., and Garry J. Williams, eds. *Calvin: Theologian and Reformer.* Grand Rapids: Reformation Heritage Books, 2010.

Beeke, Joel R., ed. *Calvin for Today.* Grand Rapids: Reformation Heritage Books, 2009.

Bouwsma, William J. *John Calvin: A Sixteenth-Century Portrait.* New York: Oxford University Press, 1989.

Calvin, John. *The Bondage and Liberation of the Will.* Edited by Anthony N. S. Lane. Grand Rapids: Baker Book House, 1996.

Calvin, John. *Calvin: Theological Treatises.*

Edited by J. K. S. Reid. Philadelphia: Westminster Press, 1954.

Calvin, John. *Calvin's Calvinism.* 2nd ed. Edited by Henry Cole and Russell Dykstra. Jenison: Reformed Free Publishing Association, 2009.

Calvin, John. *Calvin's Commentaries.* 45 vols. in 22. Grand Rapids: Baker Book House, 1978.

Calvin, John. *Calvin's New Testament Commentaries.* 12 vols. Edited by Thomas F. Torrance. Grand Rapids: Eerdmans, 1972.

Calvin, John. *The Deity of Christ and Other Sermons.* Grand Rapids: Eerdmans, 1950.

Calvin, John. *Institutes of the Christian Religion.* Edited by John T. McNeill. Translated by Ford Lewis Battles. 2 vols. Philadelphia: Westminster Press, 1960.

Calvin, John. *Selected Works of John Calvin.* 7 vols. Grand Rapids: Baker Book House, 1983. Also reprinted as *Tracts and Letters,* Edinburgh: Banner of Truth, 2009.

Calvin, John. *The Secret Providence of God.* Edited by Paul Helm. Wheaton: Crossway, 2010.

Calvin, John. *Sermons on Deuteronomy.* Edinburgh: Banner of Truth, 1987.

Calvin, John. *Sermons on Election and Reprobation*. Audubon: Old Paths Publications, 1996.

Calvin, John. *Sermons on First Timothy*. Edinburgh: Banner of Truth, 2018.

Calvin, John. *Sermons on Second Timothy*. Translated by Robert White. Edinburgh: Banner of Truth, 2018.

Calvin, John. *Sermons on Galatians*. Edinburgh: Banner of Truth, 1997.

Calvin, John. *Sermons on Job*. Edinburgh: Banner of Truth, 1993.

Calvin, John. *Sermons on the Epistle to the Ephesians*. London: Banner of Truth, 1973.

Calvin, John. *Sermons on the Epistles to Timothy and Titus*. Edinburgh: Banner of Truth, 1983.

Calvin, John. *Sermons on Titus*. Edinburgh: Banner of Truth, 2015.

Calvin, John. *Treatises Against the Anabaptists and Against the Libertines*. Grand Rapids: Baker Book House, 1982.

Chung, Sung Wook, ed. *John Calvin and Evangelical Theology*. Louisville: Westminster John Knox Press, 2009.

Cottret, Bernard. *Calvin: A Biography*. Grand Rapids: Eerdmans, 2000.

D'Aubigne, J. H. Merle. *History of the Reformation in Europe in the Time of Calvin*. 8 vols. in 4. Harrisonburg, VA: Sprinkle Publications, 2000.

Davis, Thomas, ed. *John Calvin's American Legacy*. Oxford: Oxford University Press, 2010.

De Greef, Wulfert. *The Writings of John Calvin: An Introductory Guide*. Rev. ed. Louisville: Westminster John Knox Press, 2008.

Dowey, Edward A., Jr. *The Knowledge of God in Calvin's Theology*. Grand Rapids: Eerdmans, 1994.

Engelsma, David J. *The Reformed Faith and John Calvin: The Institutes in Summary Form*. Jenison: Reformed Free Publishing Association, 2009.

Gamble, Richard C., ed. *Articles on Calvin*

and Calvinism. 14 volumes. New York: Garland, 1992.

Ganoczy, Alexandre. *The Young Calvin*. Philadelphia: Westminster Press, 1982.

George, Timothy, ed. *John Calvin and the Church*. Louisville: Westminster John Knox Press, 1990.

Godfrey, W. Robert. *John Calvin: Pilgrim and Pastor*. Wheaton: Crossway, 2009.

Gordon, Bruce. *Calvin*. New Haven: Yale University Press, 2009.

Hall, David W. *The Legacy of John Calvin*. Phillipsburg, NJ: P&R, 2008.

Hall, David, ed. *Tributes to John Calvin*. Phillipsburg, NJ: P&R, 2010.

Hall, David W., and Marvin Padgett, eds. *Calvin and Culture: Exploring a Worldview*. Phillipsburg, NJ: P&R, 2010.

Hall, David W., and Peter A. Lillback, eds. *A Theological Guide to Calvin's Institutes*. Phillipsburg, NJ: P&R, 2008.

Helm, Paul. *Calvin: A Guide for the Perplexed*. London: T. and T. Clark, 2008.

Helm, Paul. *Calvin at the Centre*. Oxford: Oxford University Press, 2010.

Helm, Paul. *John Calvin's Ideas*. Oxford: Oxford University Press, 2004.

Hirzel, Martin Ernst, and Martin Sallmann, eds. *John Calvin's Impact on Church and Society, 1509–2009*. Grand Rapids: Eerdmans, 2009.

Hunter, A. Mitchell. *The Teaching of Calvin*. London: James Clarke, 1950.

Johnson, William Stacy. *Calvin: Reformer for the 21st Century*. Louisville: Westminster John Knox Press, 2009.

Lane, Anthony N. S. *A Reader's Guide to Calvin's Institutes*. Grand Rapids: Baker Academic, 2009.

Lawson, Steven J. *The Expository Genius of John Calvin*. Orlando: Reformation Trust, 2007.

McGrath, Alister E. *A Life of John Calvin*. Oxford: Basil Blackwell, 1990.

McKim, Donald K., ed. *The Cambridge Companion to John Calvin*. Cambridge: Cambridge University Press, 2004.

McKim, Donald K., ed. *Readings in Calvin's Theology*. Grand Rapids: Baker Book House, 1984.

McNeill, John T. *The History and Character of Calvinism*. Philadelphia: Westminster Press, 1954.

Methuen, Charlotte. *What Luther and Calvin Really Said*. Grand Rapids: Kregel, 2010.

Muller, Richard A. *The Unaccommodated Calvin*. New York: Oxford University Press, 2000.

Murray, John. *Calvin on Scripture and Divine Sovereignty*. Grand Rapids: Baker Book House, 1960.

Niesel, Wilhelm. *The Theology of John Calvin*. Philadelphia: Westminster Press, 1956.

Parker, T. H. L. *Calvin: An Introduction to His Thought*. Louisville: Westminster John Knox Press, 1995.

Parker, T. H. L. *John Calvin: A Biography*. Philadelphia: Westminster Press, 1975.

Partee, Charles. *The Theology of John Calvin*. Louisville: Westminster John Knox Press, 2008.

Piper, John. *John Calvin and His Passion for the Majesty of God*. Wheaton: Crossway, 2009.

Piper, John, and David Matthis, eds. *With Calvin in the Theater of God*. Wheaton: Crossway, 2010.

Reymond, Robert. *John Calvin: His Life and Influence*. Fearn: Christian Focus, 2004.

Schaff, Philip. *History of the Christian Church*, 8:223–844. Grand Rapids: Eerdmans, 1984.

Selderhuis, Herman J., ed. *The Calvin Handbook*. Grand Rapids: Eerdmans, 2009.

Selderhuis, Herman J. *John Calvin: A Pilgrim's Life*. Downers Grove, IL: IVP, 2009.

Stroup, George W. *Calvin*. Nashville: Abingdon Press, 2009.

van't Spijker, Willem. *Calvin: A Brief Guide to His Life and Thought*. Louisville: Westminster John Knox Press, 2009.

Vollmer, Philip. *John Calvin, Man of the Millennium*. San Antonio: Vision Forum, 2008.

Walker, Williston. *John Calvin*. New York: Schocken Books, 1969.

Wallace, Ronald S. *Calvin, Geneva and the Reformation*. Grand Rapids: Baker Book House, 1988.

Warfield, Benjamin B. *Calvin and Augustine*. Philadelphia: Presbyterian and Reformed, 1956.

Warfield, Benjamin B. *The Works of Benjamin B. Warfield, Volume 5*. Grand Rapids: Baker Book House, 1981.

Wendel, Francois. *Calvin: The Origin and Development of His Religious Thought*. London: Collins, 1963.

The Spread of Calvinism

Andreas, Jakob, and Theodore Beza. *Lutheranism and Calvinism: The Classic Debate at the Colloquy of Montebeliard (1586)*. Translated by Clinton J. Armstrong. St. Louis: Concordia Publishing House, 2017.

Benedict, Philip. *Christ's Churches Purely Reformed*, 121–291. New Haven: Yale University Press, 2002.

Beza, Theodore. *The Christian Faith*. Lewes: Christian Focus Ministries Trust, 1992.

Beza, Theodore. *A Little Book of Christian Questions and Responses*. Allison Park: Pickwick Publications, 1986.

Bierma, Lyle D. *German Calvinism in the Confessional Age: The Covenant Theology of Caspar Olevianus*. Grand Rapids: Baker Books, 1996.

Clark, R. Scott. *Caspar Olevianus and the Substance of the Covenant*. Edinburgh: Rutherford House, 2005.

D'Aubigne, J. H. Merle. *History of the Reformation in the Time of Calvin*. 8 vols. in 4. Harrisonburg, VA: Sprinkle Publications, 2000.

D'Aubigne, J. H. Merle. *The Reformation in England*. 2 vols. London: Banner of Truth, 1963.

Duke, Alastair. *Reformation and Revolt in the Low Countries*. London: Hambledon Press, 1990.

Gamble, Richard C., ed. *Articles on Calvin and Calvinism*, Volumes 13 and 14. New York: Garland, 1992.

Greaves, Richard L. *Theology and Revolution in the Scottish Reformation*. Grand Rapids: Christian University Press, 1980.

Hart, D. G. *Calvinism: A History*, 47–71. New Haven: Yale University Press, 2013.

Heppe, Heinrich. *Reformed Dogmatics*. Grand Rapids: Baker Book House, 1978.

Hillerbrand, Hans, ed. *The Oxford Encyclopedia of the Reformation*. 4 volumes. New York: Oxford University Press, 1996.

Hirzel, Martin Ernest, and Martin Sallmann, eds. *John Calvin's Impact on Church and Society, 1509–2009*. Grand Rapids: Eerdmans, 2009.

Kendall, R. T. *Calvin and English Calvinism to 1649*. New York: Oxford University Press, 1979.

Knox, John. *The Reformation in Scotland*. Edinburgh: Banner of Truth, 1982.

Lindberg, Carter, ed. *The Reformation Theologians*. Oxford: Basil Blackwell, 2002.

Loane, Marcus. *Masters of the English Reformation*. Edinburgh: Banner of Truth, 2005.

M'Crie, Thomas. *The Story of the Scottish Church from the Reformation to the Disruption*. Glasgow: Free Church Publications, n.d.

MacLeod, John. *Scottish Theology*. Edinburgh: Banner of Truth, 1994.

Marshall, Peter. *Heretics and Believers: A History of the English Reformation*. New Haven: Yale University Press, 2017.

McNeill, John T. *The History and Character of Calvinism*, 237–330. New York: Oxford University Press, 1954.

Miller, Charles. "The Spread of Calvinism in Switzerland, Germany, and France."

In John H. Bratt, ed. *The Rise and Development of Calvinism*, 27–62. Grand Rapids: Eerdmans, 1968.

Muller, Richard A. *After Calvin: Studies in the Development of a Theological Tradition*. New York: Oxford University Press, 2003.

Muller, Richard A. *Post-Reformation Reformed Dogmatics*. 2nd ed. 4 vols. Grand Rapids: Baker Academic, 2003.

Olevianus, Caspar. *A Firm Foundation*. Grand Rapids: Baker Books, 1995.

Pettegree, Andrew, Alastair Duke, and Gillian Lewis, eds. *Calvinism in Europe, 1540–1620*. Cambridge: Cambridge University Press, 1994.

Prestwich, Menna, ed. *International Calvinism, 1541–1715*. Oxford: Clarendon Press, 2013.

Raitt, Jill, ed. *Shapers of Religious Traditions in Germany, Switzerland, and Poland, 1560–1600*. New Haven: Yale University Press, 1981.

Reid, W. Stanford, ed. *John Calvin: His Influence in the Western World*. Grand Rapids: Zondervan, 1982.

Ryle, J. C. *Light from Old Times*. Moscow, Idaho: Charles Nolan, 2000.

Schaff, Philip. *History of the Christian Church*, Volume 8. Grand Rapids: Eerdmans, 1984.

Selderhuis, Herman J., ed. *The Calvin Handbook*, 63–125, 472–76. Grand Rapids: Eerdmans, 2009.

Sunshine, Glenn S. *Reforming French Protestantism*. Kirksville, MO: Truman State University Press, 2003.

Ursinus, Zacharias. *The Commentary of Dr. Zacharias Ursinus on the Heidelberg Catechism*. Phillipsburg, NJ: Presbyterian and Reformed, n.d.

Visser, Derk. *Zacharias Ursinus*. New York: United Church Press, 1983.

Wright, Shawn D. *Our Sovereign Refuge: The Pastoral Theology of Theodore Beza*. Carlisle: Paternoster Press, 2004.

Wright, Shawn D. *Theodore Beza: The Man and the Myth*. Fearn: Christian Focus, 2015.

The Synod of Dort

Arminius, James. *The Writings of James Arminius.* 3 vol. Grand Rapids: Baker Book House, 1996.

Bangs, Carl. *Arminius: A Study in the Dutch Reformation.* Nashville: Abingdon Press, 1971.

Barrett, Matthew. *The Grace of Godliness: An Introduction to Doctrine and Piety in the Canons of Dort.* Dundas, Ontario: Joshua Press, 2013.

Bird, Benedict. "The Synod of Dort (1618–1619)." In *God With Us and For Us: Papers read at the 2017 Westminster Conference,* 87–110. Dewskbury: John Harris, 2017.

Boekestein, William. *The Glory of Grace: The Story of the Canons of Dort.* Grand Rapids: Reformed Fellowship, 2012.

Brian, Rustin E. *Jacob Arminus: The Man from Oudewater.* Eugene, OR: Cascade Books, 2015.

Clarke, F. Stuart. *The Ground of Election: Jacobus Arminius' Doctrine of the Work and Person of Christ.* Milton Keynes: Paternoster, 2006.

Cunningham, William. *Historical Theology,* 2:371–513. London: Banner of Truth, 1969.

De Jong, Peter Y., ed. *Crisis in the Reformed Churches.* Grand Rapids: Reformed Fellowship, 1968.

de Witt, John R. "The Arminian Conflict and the Synod of Dort." In J. I. Packer, ed., *Puritan Papers,* 5:3–23. Phillipsburg, NJ: P&R, 2005.

den Boer, William. *God's Twofold Love: The Theology of Jacob Arminius (1559–1609).* Göttingen: Vandenhoek & Ruprecht, 2010.

Dennison, James T., Jr., ed. *Reformed Confessions of the 16th and 17th Centuries in English Translation,* 4:41–48, 120–53. Grand Rapids: Reformation Heritage Books, 2014.

Ellis, Mark A., ed. *The Arminian Confession of 1621.* Eugene: Pickwick Publications, 2005.

Feenstra, Peter G. *Unspeakable Comfort: A Commentary on the Canons of Dort.* Winnipeg: Premier Publishing, 1997.

Gatiss, Lee. "The Synod of Dort and Definite Atonement." In David Gibson and Jonathan Gibson, eds. *From Heaven He Came and Sought Her,* 143–63. Wheaton: Crossway, 2013.

Godfrey, W. Robert. *Saving the Reformation: The Pastoral Theology of the Synod of Dort.* Orlando, FL: Reformation Trust, 2019.

Goudriaan, Aza, and Fred van Lieberg, eds. *Revisiting the Synod of Dort (1618–1619).* Leiden: Brill, 2011.

Gunter, W. Stephen. *Arminius and His Declaration of Sentiments.* Waco: Baylor University Press, 2012.

Haak, Theodore, trans. *The Dutch Annotations Upon the Whole Bible.* Leerdam: Gereformeerde Bijbelstichting, 2000.

Hoeksema, Homer. *The Voice of Our Fathers.* Grand Rapids: Reformed Free Publishing Association, 1980.

Hsia, R. Po-Chia, and Henk van Nierop, eds. *Calvinism and Religious Toleration in the Dutch Golden Age.* Cambridge: Cambridge University Press, 2002.

McComish, William A. *The Epigones: A Study of the Theology of the Geneva Academy at the Time of the Synod of Dort, with Special Reference to Giovanni Diodati,* 46–126. Allison Park, PA: Pickwick Publications, 1989.

Milton, Anthony, ed. *The British Delegation and the Synod of Dort (1618–1619).* Woodbridge: Boydell Press, 2005.

Moulin, Peter (Pierre Du). *The Anatomy of Arminianisme.* Norwood: Walter J. Johnson, 1976.

Muller, Richard A. *God, Creation, and Providence in the Thought of Jacob Arminius.* Grand Rapids: Baker Book House, 1991.

Mulsow, Martin, and Jan Roehls, eds. *Socinianism and Arminianism: Antitrinitarians, Calvinists, and Cultural*

Exchange in Seventeenth-Century Europe. Leiden: Brill, 2005.

Needham, N. R. *2000 Years of Christ's Power*, 4:127–42. Rev. ed. Fearn: Christian Focus, 2016.

Owen, John. "A Display of Arminianism." In *The Works of John Owen*, 10:1–137. London: Banner of Truth, 1967.

Packer, J. I. "Arminianisms." In *Honouring the People of God: The Collected Shorter Writings of J. I. Packer*, 279–308. Carlisle: Paternoster, 1999.

Peterson, Robert A., and Michael D. Williams. *Why I Am Not an Arminian*, 92–135. Downers Grove, IL: IVP, 2004.

Pinson, J. Matthew. *Arminian and Baptist.* Nashville: Randall House, 2015.

Platt, Eric. *Britain and the Bestandstwisten: The Causes, Course and Consequences of British Involvement in the Dutch Religious and Political Disputes of the Early Seventeenth Century.* Göttingen: Vandenhoeck & Ruprecht, 2015.

Pronk, Cornelis. *Expository Sermons on the Canons of Dort.* St. Thomas: Free Reformed Publications, 1999.

Robinson, John. "A Defence of the Doctrine Propounded at the Synod of Dort." In *The Works of John Robinson*, 1:261–471. Harrisonburg, VA: Sprinkle Publications, 2009.

Schaff, Philip, ed. *Creeds of Christendom*, 3:545–97. Grand Rapids: Baker Book House, 1966.

Schreiner, Thomas R. and Bruce A. Ware, eds. *The Grace of God, The Bondage of the Will*, 2:51–278. Grand Rapids: Baker, 1995.

Scott, Thomas. *The Articles of the Synod of Dort.* Harrisonburg, VA: Sprinkle Publications, 1993.

Sell, Alan P. F. *The Great Debate.* Grand Rapids: Baker Book House, 1983.

Sierhuis, Freya. *The Literature of the Arminian Controversy.* Oxford: Oxford University Press, 2015.

Stanglin, Keith D. "Arminian, Remonstrant, and Early Methodist Theologies." In Ulrich L. Lehner, Richard A. Muller, and A. G. Roeber, eds. *The Oxford Handbook of Early Modern Theology, 1600–1800.* Oxford: Oxford University Press, 2016.

Stanglin, Keith D. *Arminius and the Assurance of Salvation.* Leiden: Brill, 2007.

Stanglin, Keith D., Mark G. Bilby, and Mark H. Mann. *Reconsidering Arminius.* Nashville: Abingdon Press, 2014.

Stanglin, Keith D., and Thomas H. McCall. *Jacob Arminius: Theologian of Grace.* Oxford: Oxford University Press, 2012.

Treier, Daniel J. and Walter A. Elwell, eds. *Evangelical Dictionary of Theology*, 3rd ed., 212, 255–256, 739. Grand Rapids: Baker Academic, 2017.

van Leeuwen, Th. Marius, Keith D. Stanglin, and Marijke Tolsma, eds. *Arminius, Arminianism, and Europe.* Leiden: Brill, 2009.

Venema, Cornelis P. *But for the Grace of God: An Exposition of the Canons of Dort.* Grandville: Reformed Fellowship, 1994.

Wagner, John D., ed. *Arminius Speaks: Essential Writings on Predestination, Free Will and the Nature of God.* Eugene: Wipf and Stock, 2011.

Warburton, Ben A. *Calvinism*, 47–62. Grand Rapids: Eerdmans, 1955.

Seventeenth-Century Calvinism

à Brakel, Wilhelmus. *The Christian's Reasonable Service.* 4 vols. Translated by Bartel Elshout. Ligonier, PA: Soli Deo Gloria, 1992.

Abercrombie, Nigel. *The Origins of Jansenism.* Oxford: Clarendon Press, 1984.

Beardslee, John W. III, ed. *Reformed Dogmatics.* New York: Oxford University Press, 1965.

Beeke, Joel R. "Calvin as a Calvinist." In Joel R. Beeke, David W. Hall, and Michael A. G. Haykin, eds. *Theology Made Practical:*

New Studies on John Calvin and His Legacy. Grand Rapids: Reformation Heritage Books, 2017.

Beeke, Joel R. "The Dutch Second Reformation ("Nadere Reformatie")." In Wilhelmus à Brakel, *The Christian's Reasonable Service*, 1:lxxxv–cxl. Ligonier, PA: Soli Deo Gloria, 1992.

Beeke, Joel R. *Experiential Grace in Dutch Biography.* Sioux Center: Netherlands Reformed Book and Publishing Committee, 1984.

Beeke, Joel R. *The Quest for Full Assurance.* Edinburgh: Banner of Truth, 1999.

Beeke, Joel R., ed. *Sovereign Grace in Life and Ministry.* Sioux Center: Netherlands Reformed Book and Publishing Committee, 1984.

de Molina, Luis. *On Divine Foreknowledge.* Ithaca: Cornell University Press, 1988.

de Reuver, Arie. *Sweet Communion: Trajectories of Spirituality from the Middle Ages through the Further Reformation.* Grand Rapids: Reformation Heritage Books, 2017.

Escholier, Marc. *Port-Royal: The Drama of the Jansenists.* New York: Hawthorn Books, 1968.

Fesko, J. V. *Diversity Within the Reformed Tradition: Supra- and Infralapsarianism in Calvin, Dort, and Westminster.* Greenville: Reformed Academic Press, 2001.

Goudriaan, Aza. *Reformed Orthodoxy and Philosophy, 1625–1750: Gisbertus Voetius, Petrus van Mastricht, and Athonius Driessen.* Leiden: Brill, 2006.

Hadjiantoniou, G. A. *Protestant Patriarch: The Life of Cyril Lucaris (1572–1638), Patriarch of Constantinople.* Richmond: John Knox Press, 1961.

Hart, D. G. *Calvinism: A History*, 47–71. New Haven: Yale University Press, 2013.

Heppe, Heinrich. *Reformed Dogmatics.* Grand Rapids: Baker Book House, 1978.

Hsia, R. Po-Chia, and Henk van Nierop, eds. *Calvinism and Religious Toleration in the Dutch Golden Age.* Cambridge: Cambridge University Press, 2002.

Klauber, Martin I. *Between Reformed Scholasticism and Pan-Protestantism: Jean-Alphonse Turretin (1671–1737) and Enlightenment Orthodoxy at the Academy of Geneva.* Selinsgrove, PA: Susquehanna University Press, 1994.

Kolakowski, Leszek. *God Owes Us Nothing: A Brief Remark on Pascal's Religion and on the Spirit of Jansenism.* Chicago: University of Chicago Press, 1995.

Lehner, Ulrich L., Richard A. Muller, and A. G. Roeber, eds. *The Oxford Handbook of Early Modern Theology, 1600–1800.* Oxford: Oxford University Press, 2016.

Muller, Richard A. *After Calvin: Studies in the Development of a Tradition.* Oxford: Oxford University Press, 2003.

Muller, Richard A. *Christ and the Decree: Christology and Predestination in Reformed Theology from Calvin to Perkins.* Durham: Labyrinth Press, 1986.

Muller, Richard A. *Dictionary of Latin and Greek Theological Terms, Drawn Principally from Protestant Scholastic Theology.* 2nd ed. Grand Rapids: Baker Academic, 2017.

Muller, Richard A. *Post-Reformation Reformed Dogmatics.* 2nd ed. 4 vols. Grand Rapids: Baker Academic, 2003.

Muller, Richard A. "Reception and Response: Referencing and Understanding Calvin in Seventeenth-Century Calvinism." In Irena Backus and Philip Benedict, eds. *Calvin and His Influence*, 182–201. Oxford: Oxford University Press, 2011.

Neale, J. M. *A History of the So-Called Jansenist Church of Holland.* New York: AMS, 1970.

Needham, N. R. *2000 Years of Christ's Power*, 4:101–26, 475–520, 579–99. Rev. ed. Fearn: Christian Focus, 2016.

Pelikan, Jaroslav. *The Christian Tradition*, 4:374–85. Chicago: University of Chicago Press, 1984.

Platt, John. *Reformed Thought and Scholasticism: The Arguments for the*

Existence of God in Dutch Theology, 1575–1650. Leiden: Brill, 1982.

Schroeder, Carl J. *In Quest of Pentecost: Jodocus van Lodenstein and the Dutch Second Reformation.* Lanham, MD: University Press of America, 2001.

Sedgwick, Alexander. *Jansenism in Seventeenth-Century France.* Charlottesville: University Press of Virginia, 1977.

Selderhuis, Herman J., ed. *Handbook of Dutch Church History,* 259–360. Göttingen: Vandenhoeck & Ruprecht, 2015.

Sprunger, Keith. *Dutch Puritanism: A History of English and Scottish Churches of the Netherlands in the Sixteenth and Seventeenth Centuries.* Leiden: Brill, 1987.

Stoeffler, F. Ernest. *The Rise of Evangelical Pietism.* Leiden: Brill, 1971.

Strehle, Stephen. *Calvinism, Federalism, and Scholasticism: A Study of the Reformed Doctrine of Covenant.* Bern and New York: Peter Lang, 1988.

Taffin, Jean. *The Mark of God's Children.* Grand Rapids: Baker Academic, 2003.

te Velde, Dolf. *The Doctrine of God in Reformed Orthodoxy, Karl Barth, and the Utrecht School.* Leiden: Brill, 2013.

te Velde, Dolf, ed. *Synopsis Purioris Theologiae: Synopsis of a Purer Theology.* 3 vols. Leiden: Brill, 2015.

Teelinck, Willem. *The Path of True Godliness.* Grand Rapids: Baker Academic, 2003.

Trueman, Carl R., and R. S. Clarke, eds. *Protestant Scholasticism.* Carlisle: Paternoster, 1999.

Turretin, Francis. *Institutes of Elenctic Theology.* Edited by James T. Dennison Jr. 3 vols. Phillipsburg, NJ: P&R, 1992.

van Asselt, Willem J., ed. *Introduction to Reformed Scholasticism.* Grand Rapids: Reformation Heritage Books, 2011.

van Asselt, Willem J., and Eef Dekker, eds. *Reformation and Scholasticism.* Grand Rapids: Baker Academic, 2001.

Voetius, Gisbertus, and Johannes Hoornbeeck. *Spiritual Desertion.* Grand Rapids: Baker Academic, 2003.

Wisse, Maarten, Marcel Sarot, and Willemien Otten, eds. *Scholasticism Reformed.* Leiden: Brill, 2010.

Witsius, Herman. *The Economy of the Covenants between God and Man.* 2 vols. Escondido, CA: Den Dulk Foundation; and Phillipsburg, NJ: P&R, 1990.

Puritanism

Adair, John. *Founding Fathers: The Puritans in England and America.* Grand Rapids: Baker Book House, 1986.

Allen, Lewis and Tim Chester. *The Glory of Grace: An Introduction to the Puritans in Their Own Words.* Edinburgh: Banner of Truth, 2018.

Barker, William. *Puritan Profiles.* Fearn: Mentor, 1996.

Baxter, Richard. *The Practical Works of Richard Baxter.* 4 vols. Ligonier: Soli Deo Gloria, 1990.

Beeke, Joel R., and Mark Jones. *A Puritan Theology.* Grand Rapids: Reformation Heritage Books, 2012.

Beeke, Joel R., and Randall J. Pederson. *Meet the Puritans.* Grand Rapids: Reformation Heritage Books, 2006.

Bennett, Arthur, ed. *The Valley of Vision: A Collection of Puritan Prayers and Devotions.* Edinburgh: Banner of Truth, 2005.

Bremer, Francis J. *Puritanism: A Very Short Introduction.* Oxford: Oxford University Press, 2009.

Bremer, Francis J., and Tom Webster, eds. *Puritans and Puritanism in Europe and America: A Comprehensive Encyclopedia.* 2 vols. Santa Barbara: ABC-CLIO, 2007.

Brook, Benjamin. *The Lives of the Puritans.* 3 vols. Pittsburgh: Soli Deo Gloria, 1994.

Brooks, Thomas. *The Works of Thomas Brooks.* 6 vols. Edinburgh: Banner of Truth, 1980.

Brown, John. *The English Puritans*. Fearn: Christian Heritage, 1998.

Bunyan, John. *The Pilgrim's Progress*. Edinburgh: Banner of Truth, 1991.

Bunyan, John. *The Works of John Bunyan*. 3 vols. Edinburgh: Banner of Truth, 1991.

Carr, J. A. *The Life and Times of Archbishop James Ussher*. Green Forest: Master Books, 2006.

Dever, Mark E. *Richard Sibbes: Puritanism and Calvinism in Late Elizabethan and Early Stuart England*. Macon, GA: Mercer University Press, 2000.

Di Gangi, Mariano, ed. *A Golden Treasury of Puritan Devotions*. Phillipsburg, NJ: P&R, 1999.

Ferguson, Sinclair B. *John Owen and the Christian Life*. Edinburgh: Banner of Truth, 1987.

Flavel, John. *The Works of John Flavel*. 6 vols. Edinburgh: Banner of Truth, 1982.

Fraser, Antonia. *Cromwell the Lord Protector*. New York: Alfred A. Knopf, 1973.

Goodwin, Thomas. *The Works of Thomas Goodwin*. 12 vols. Eureka, CA: Tanski, 1996.

Gurnall, William. *The Christian in Complete Armour*. London: Banner of Truth, 1964.

Hall, David D., ed. *Puritans in the New World*. Princeton: Princeton University Press, 2004.

Harman, Allan. *Matthew Henry: His Life and Influence*. Fearn: Christian Focus, 2012.

Haykin, Michael A. G. *Kiffin, Knollys and Keach*. Leeds: Reformation Today, 1996.

Hindson, Edward, ed. *Introduction to Puritan Theology*. Grand Rapids: Baker Book House, 1976.

Hulse, Erroll. *Who Are the Puritans? And What Do They Teach?* Darlington: Evangelical Press, 2000.

Kapic, Kelly M., and Randall C. Gleason, eds. *The Devoted Life: An Invitation to the Puritan Classics*. Downers Grove, IL: IVP, 2004.

Kendall, R. T. *Calvin and English Calvinism to 1649*. New York: Oxford University Press, 1979.

Kevan, Ernest. *The Grace of Law*. Ligonier, PA: Soli Deo Gloria, 1993.

Lewis, Peter. *The Genius of Puritanism*. Haywards Heath: Carey Publications, 1979.

Lloyd-Jones, D. Martyn. *The Puritans: Their Origins and Successors*. Edinburgh: Banner of Truth, 1987.

Loane, Marcus. *Makers of Puritan History*. Grand Rapids: Baker Book House, 1980.

M'Crie, Thomas. *The Story of the Scottish Church from the Reformation to the Disruption*. Glasgow: Free Church Publications, n.d.

MacLeod, John. *Scottish Theology*. Edinburgh: Banner of Truth, 1974.

Martin, Robert P. *A Guide to the Puritans*. Edinburgh: Banner of Truth, 1997.

Mathes, Glenda Faye, and Joel R. Beeke. *Puritan Heroes*. Grand Rapids: Reformation Heritage Books, 2018.

Murray, Iain H., ed. *The Reformation of the Church: A Collection of Reformed and Puritan Documents on Church Issues*. Edinburgh: Banner of Truth, 1987.

Neal, Daniel. *The History of the Puritans*. 3 vols. Minneapolis: Klock and Klock, 1979.

Needham, N. R. *2000 Years of Christ's Power*, 4:175–444. Rev. ed. Fearn: Christian Focus, 2016.

Owen, John. *The Works of John Owen*. 16 vols. Edinburgh: Banner of Truth, 1976.

Packer, J. I. *Puritan Portraits*. Fearn: Christian Focus, 2012.

Packer, J. I. *A Quest for Godliness: The Puritan Vision of the Christian Life*. Wheaton: Crossway, 1990.

Packer, J. I. *The Redemption and Restoration of Mankind in the Thought of Richard Baxter*. Vancouver: Regent College Publishing, 2003.

Pastoor, Charles, and Galen K. Johnson, eds. *Historical Dictionary of the Puritans*. Lanham: Scarecrow Press, 2007.

Perkins, William. *The Works of William*

Perkins. 10 vols. Grand Rapids: Reformation Heritage Books, 2014.

Reid, James. *Memoirs of the Westminster Divines.* Edinburgh: Banner of Truth, 1982.

Rutherford, Samuel. *Letters of Samuel Rutherford.* Edinburgh: Banner of Truth, 1984.

Sibbes, Richard. *The Works of Richard Sibbes.* 7 vols. Edinburgh: Banner of Truth, 1979.

Thomas, I. D. E., ed. *A Treasury of Puritan Quotations.* Chicago: Moody Press, 1975.

Toon, Peter. *Puritans and Calvinism.* Swengel: Reiner Publications, 1973.

Tyacke, Nicholas. *Anti-Calvinism: The Rise of English Arminians c. 1590–1640.* Oxford: Clarendon Press, 1987.

Walker, James. *The Theology and Theologians of Scotland, 1560–1750.* Edinburgh: John Knox Press, 1982.

Wallace, Dewey. *Puritans and Predestination.* Chapel Hill: University of North Carolina Press, 1982.

Wallace, Dewey. *The Spirituality of the Later English Puritans: An Anthology.* Macon, GA: Mercer University Press, 1987.

The Westminster Assembly

Barker, William. *Puritan Profiles.* Fearn: Mentor, 1996.

Bower, John R. *The Larger Catechism: A Critical Text and Introduction.* Grand Rapids: Reformation Heritage Books, 2010.

Carson, John J., and David W. Hall, eds. *To Glorify and Enjoy God.* Edinburgh: Banner of Truth, 1994.

Clark, Gordon H. *What Presbyterians Believe.* Philadelphia: Presbyterian and Reformed, 1965.

Coldwell, Chris, ed. *The Grand Debate.* Dallas: Nephtali Press, 2014.

Dennison, James T., Jr., ed. *Reformed Confessions of the 16th and 17th Centuries in English Translation,* 4:231–72, 299–368. Grand Rapids: Reformation Heritage Books, 2014.

Dever, Mark, and Sinclair Ferguson. *The Westminster Directory for Public Worship.* Fearn: Christian Focus, 2009.

Dickson, David. *Truth's Victory over Error: A Commentary on the Westminster Confession of Faith.* Edinburgh: Banner of Truth, 2007.

Duncan, J. Ligon, ed. *The Westminster Confession into the 21st Century.* 3 vols. Fearn: Mentor, 2003.

Fesko, J. V. *The Spirit of the Age: The 19th Century Debate over the Holy Spirit and the Westminster Confession.* Grand Rapids: Reformation Heritage Books, 2018.

Fesko, J. V. *The Theology of the Westminster Standards.* Wheaton: Crossway, 2014.

Gerstner, John H., Douglas F. Kelly, and Philip Rollinson. *A Guide to the Westminster Confession of Faith: Commentary.* Signal Mountain: Summerton Texts, 1992.

Gillespie, George. *The Works of George Gillespie, Volume 2.* Edmonton: Still Waters Revival Books, 1991.

Hall, David W. *Windows on Westminster.* Norcross: Great Commission Publications, 1993.

Hendry, George S. *The Westminster Confession for Today.* London: SCM, 1960.

Heron, Alastair I. C., ed. *The Westminster Confession in the Church Today.* Edinburgh: St. Andrews Press, 1982.

Hetherington, William Maxwell. *History of the Westminster Assembly of Divines.* Edmonton: Still Waters Revival Books, 1993.

Hodge, A. A. *The Confession of Faith.* London: Banner of Truth, 1958.

Khoo, Jeffrey. *The Theology of the Westminster Standards: A Reformed-Premillennial Study of Christian Basics.* Singapore: Far Eastern Bible College Press, 1997.

Letham, Robert. *The Westminster Assembly*. Phillipsburg, NJ: P&R, 2009.

Morecraft, Joseph, C. III. *Authentic Christianity*, 1:1–112. Powder Springs, GA: Minkoff Family Publishing and American Vision Press, 2009.

Muller, Richard A., and Rowland S. Ward. *Scripture and Worship*. Phillipsburg, NJ: P&R, 2007.

Murray, John. "The Theology of the Westminster Confession." In John H. Skilton, ed., *Scripture and Confession*, 125–48. Phillipsburg, NJ: Presbyterian and Reformed, 1973.

Paul, Robert. *The Assembly of the Lord*. Edinburgh: T. and T. Clark, 1985.

Pipa, Joseph A., Jr. *The Westminster Confession of Faith Study Book*. Fearn: Christian Focus, 2005.

Powell, Hunter. *The Crisis of British Prostestantism*. Manchester: Manchester University Press, 2015.

Quigley, Lynn, ed. *Reformed Theology in Contemporary Perspective*. Edinburgh: Rutherford House, 2006.

Reid, James. *Memoirs of the Westminster Divines*. Edinburgh: Banner of Truth, 1982.

Schaff, Philip, ed. *Creeds of Christendom*, 1:727–816, 3:600–704. Grand Rapids: Baker Book House, 1966.

Shaw, Robert. *The Reformed Faith: Exposition of the Westminster Confession of Faith*. Fearn: Christian Heritage/Christian Focus, 2008.

Shedd, William G. T. *Calvinism: Pure and Mixed*. Edinburgh: Banner of Truth, 1986.

Smith, Morton H. *Harmony of the Westminster Confession and Catechisms*. Greenville, SC: Greenville Seminary Press, 1991.

Spear, Wayne R. *Faith of Our Fathers: A Commentary on the Westminster Confession of Faith*. Pittsburgh: Crown & Covenant Publications, 2006.

Sproul, R. C. *Truths We Confess: A Layman's Guide to the Westminster Confession of Faith*. 3 vols. Phillipsburg, NJ: P&R, 2006.

Suthers, Edwin B. *An Exhaustive Concordance to the Westminster Confession of Faith and Catechisms and Index to the Scripture Proofs*. Camp Hill: Presbyter Publications, 1994.

The Confession of Faith: The Larger and Shorter Catechism, with Scripture Proofs at Large. Glasgow: Free Presbyterian Publications, 1973.

Van Dixhoorn, Chad. *Confessing the Faith: A Reader's Guide to the Westminster Confession of Faith*. Edinburgh: Banner of Truth, 2014.

Van Dixhoorn, Chad. *God's Ambassadors: The Westminster Assembly and the Reformation of the English Pulpit, 1643–1653*. Grand Rapids: Reformation Heritage Books, 2017.

Van Dixhoorn, Chad, ed. *The Minutes and Papers of the Westminster Assembly, 1643–1653*. 5 vols. Oxford: Oxford University Press, 2012.

Vos, Johannes. *The Westminster Larger Catechism: A Commentary*. Phillipsburg, NJ: P&R, 2002.

Warfield, Benjamin B. *Selected Shorter Writings of Benjamin B. Warfield*, 2:370–410. Nutley: Presbyterian and Reformed, 1970.

Warfield, Benjamin B. *The Works of Benjamin B. Warfield, Volume 6*. Grand Rapids: Baker Book House, 1981.

Watson, Thomas. *A Body of Divinity*. Edinburgh: Banner of Truth, 1974.

Williamson, G. I. *The Shorter Catechism*. 2 vols. Philadelphia: Presbyterian and Reformed, 1970.

Williamson, G. I. *The Westminster Confession of Faith for Study Classes*. Philadelphia: Presbyterian and Reformed, 1964.

Amyraldism

Armstrong, Brian. *Calvinism and the Amyraut Heresy*. Madison: University of Wisconsin Press, 1969.

Boersma, Hans. *A Hot Pepper Corn*, 197–200. Zoetermeer: Uitgeverij Boekencentrum, 1993.

Bray, Gerald. *God Has Spoken*, 899–920. Wheaton: Crossway, 2014.

Cairns, Alan. *Dictionary of Theological Terms*, 3rd ed., 16, 218–20. Belfast: Ambassador Publications, 2002.

Clifford, Alan C. "Calvin and Calvinism: Amyraut et al." In Alan C. Clifford, ed. *John Calvin 500: A Reformation Affirmation*, 37–79. Attleborough: Charenton Reformed Publishing, 2011.

Clifford, Alan C. *Amyraut Affirmed*. Attleborough: Charenton Reformed Publishing, 2004.

Clifford, Alan C. *Calvinus: Authentic Calvinism. A Clarification*. Attleborough: Charendon Reformed Publishing, 1996.

Clifford, Alan C., ed. *Christ for the World: Affirming Amyraldism*. Attleborough: Charenton Reformed Publishing, 2007.

Crisp, Oliver D. *Deviant Calvinism*, 175–212. Minneapolis: Fortress Press, 2014.

Cunningham, William. *Historical Theology*, 2:323–70. London: Banner of Truth, 1969.

Davenant, John. *A Dissertation on the Death of Christ*. Weston Rhyn: Quinta Press, 2006.

Demarest, Bruce. "Amyraldianism." In Treier, Daniel J. and Walter A. Elwell, eds. *Evangelical Dictionary of Theology*, 3rd ed., 48. Grand Rapids: Baker Academic, 2017.

Dennison, James. T., Jr., ed. *Reformed Confessions of the 16th and 17th Centuries in English Translation*, 4:516–30. Grand Rapids: Reformation Heritage Books, 2014.

Djaballah, Amar. "Controversy on Universal Grace: A Historical Survey of Moise Amyraut's Brief Traitte de la Predestination." In David Gibson and Jonathan Gibson, eds. *From Heaven He Came and Sought Her*, 165–99. Wheaton: Crossway, 2013.

Frame, John. *The Doctrine of God*, 801–06. Phillipsburg, NJ: P&R, 2002.

Hamilton, Ian. "Amyraldism: Is it Modified Calvinism?" in Joseph A. Pipa Jr. and C. N. Willborn, eds. *Confessing our Hope*, 71–92. Greensville, SC: Southern Presbyterian Press, 2004.

Harding, Matthew. *Amyraut on Predestination*. Attleborough: Charenton Reformed Publishing, 2017.

Hodge, A. A. *Outlines of Theology*, 656–63. Grand Rapids: Zondervan, 1973.

Kendall, R. T. *Calvin and English Calvinism to 1649*. New York: Oxford University Press, 1979.

Klauber, Martin I., ed. *The Theology of the French Reformed Churches: From Henri IV to the Revocation of the Edict of Nantes*. Grand Rapids: Reformation Heritage Books, 2014.

Leith, John H., ed. *Creeds of the Churches*, 308–23. Chicago: Aldine, 1963.

Moore, Jonathan C. *English Hypothetical Universalism*. Grand Rapids: Eerdmans, 2007.

Moore, Jonathan D. "The Extent of the Atonement: English Hypothetical Universalism versus Particular Redemption." In Michael A. G. Haykin and Mark Jones, eds. *Drawn in Controversie: Reformed Diversity and Debates Within Seventeenth-Century British Puritanism*, 124–61. Göttingen: Vandenhoeck & Ruprecht, 2011.

Muller, Richard A. *Calvin and the Reformed Tradition*, 107–60. Grand Rapids: Baker, 2012.

Muller, Richard A. *Dictionary of Latin and Greek Theological Terms, Drawn Principally from Protestant Scholastic Theology*, 2nd ed., 381–83. Grand Rapids: Baker Academic, 2017.

Needham, N. R. 2000 Years of Christ's

Power, 4:143–55. Rev. ed. Fearn: Christian Focus, 2016.

Nicole, Roger. "Amyraldianism, Amyraldism, Amyraldus, Amyraut." In *The Encyclopedia of Christianity*, 1:184–93. Wilmington: National Foundation for Christian Education, 1964.

Nicole, Roger. "Amyraldism." In Martin Davie, et al, eds. *New Dictionary of Theology*, 21–22. 2nd ed. Downers Grove, IL: InterVarsity Press, 2016.

Nicole, Roger. "Brief Survey of the Controversy on Universal Grace." In *Standing Forth: Collected Writings of Roger Nicole*, 313–30. Fearn: Mentor, 2002.

Nicole, Roger. *Moyse Amyraut: A Bibliography*. New York: Garland, 1981.

Selderhuis, Herman J., ed. *A Companion to Reformed Orthodoxy*, 242–51, 579–85. Leiden: Brill, 2013.

Selderhuis, Herman J., ed. *The Calvin Handbook*, 477–79. Grand Rapids: Eerdmans, 2009.

Thomas, G. Michael. *The Extent of the Atonement: A Dilemma for Reformed Theology from Calvin to the Consensus*, 12–40, 162–247. Carlisle: Paternoster, 1997.

Turretin, Francis. *Institutes of Elenctic Theology*. 1:395–417. Phillipsburg, NJ: P&R, 1992.

Van Stam, F. P. *The Controversy over the Theology of Saumur, 1635–1650*. Amsterdam: APA-Holland University Press, 1988.

Warfield, Benjamin Breckinridge. *The Plan of Salvation*. Grand Rapids: Eerdmans, 1970.

Hyper-Calvinism

Brewster, Paul. *Andrew Fuller: Model Pastor-Theologian*. Nashville: B & H, 2010.

Brine, John. *A Treatise on Various Subjects*. Paris, AR: Baptist Standard Bearer, 1987.

Clark, R. Scott. "Janus, the Well-Meant Offer of the Gospel, and Westminster Theology." In David VanDrunnen, ed. *The Pattern of Sound Doctrine*, 149–80. Phillipsburg, NJ: P&R, 2004.

Dabney, Robert Lewis. *Discussions*, 1:282–313. Harrisonburg, VA: Sprinkle Publications, 1982.

Daniel, Curt D. "Hyper-Calvinism and John Gill," PhD Diss., University of Edinburgh, 1983.

Daniel, Curt D. "Hyper-Calvinism." In Martin Davie, et al, eds. *New Dictionary of Theology*, 432–33. 2nd ed. Downers Grove, IL: InterVarsity Press, 2016.

de Jong, A. C. *The Well-Meant Gospel Offer: The Views of H. Hoeksema and K. Schilder*. Franeker: T. Weaver, 1954.

Ella, George. *John Gill and the Cause of God and Truth*. Eggleston: Go Publications, 1995.

Ella, George. *William Huntington: Pastor of Providence*. Darlington: Evangelical Press, 1994.

Engelsma, David J. *Hyper-Calvinism and the Call of the Gospel*. 3rd ed. Jenison: Reformed Free Publishing Association, 2014.

Fuller, Andrew. *The Complete Works of the Rev. Andrew Fuller*. 3 vols. Harrisonburg, VA: Sprinkle Publications, 1988.

Fuller, Andrew. *The Works of the Rev. Andrew Fuller*, 1-vol. ed. Edinburgh: Banner of Truth, 2007.

Gamble, Whitney G. *Christ and the Law: Antinomianism and the Westminster Assembly*. Grand Rapids: Reformation Heritage Books, 2018.

Gay, David H. J. *Eternal Justification: Gospel Preaching to Sinners Marred by Hyper-Calvinism*. Bedford: Brachus, 2013.

Gay, David H. J. *The Gospel Offer is Free*. Biggleswade: Brachus, 2004.

Gay, David H. J. *Particular Redemption and the Free Offer*. Biggleswade: Brachus, 2008.

Gill, John. *The Cause of God and Truth*. Grand Rapids: Baker Book House, 1980.

Gill, John. *A Complete Body of Doctrinal*

and Practical Divinity. Paris, AR: Baptist Standard Bearer, 1984.

Gosden, J. H. *What Gospel Standard Baptists Believe*. Chippendam: Gospel Standard Societies, 1993.

Hassell, Cushing. *History of the Church of God*. Ellenwood: Old School Hymnal Co., 1983.

Haykin, Michael A. G. *'At the Pure Fountain of Thy Word': Andrew Fuller as an Apologist*. Carlisle: Paternoster, 2004.

Haykin, Michael A. G., ed. *The Life and Thought of John Gill (1697–1771): A Tercentennial Appreciation*. Leiden: Brill, 1997.

Hoeksema, Herman. *Reformed Dogmatics*. 2 vols. 2nd ed. Grandville: Reformed Free Publishing Association, 2004.

Hoeksema, Herman. *The Triple Knowledge*. 3 vols. Grand Rapids: Reformed Free Publishing Association, 1976.

Hulse, Erroll. *The Great Invitation*. Welwyn: Evangelical Press, 1986.

Hulse, Erroll. *Who Saves, God or Me?*, 91–115. Darlington: Evangelical Press, 2008.

Huntington, William. *The Select Works of the Late. Rev. William Huntington, S.S.* 6 vols. Harpenden: Gospel Standard Trust Publications, 1992.

Hussey, Joseph. *God's Operations of Grace But No Offers of Grace*. Abridged ed. Elon College: Primitive Publications, 1973.

MacLean, Donald John. *James Durham (1622–1658) and the Gospel Offer in its Seventeenth-Century Context*. Göttingen: Vandenhoeck & Ruprecht, 2015.

Mathis, James R. *The Making of the Primitive Baptists: A Cultural and Intellectual History of the Antimission Movement, 1800–1840*. New York: Routledge, 2004.

Morden, Peter J. *The Life and Thought of Andrew Fuller (1754–1815) and the Revival of Eighteenth-Century Particular Baptist Life*. Carlisle: Paternoster, 2003.

Murray, Iain H. *Spurgeon v. Hyper-Calvinism*. Edinburgh: Banner of Truth, 1995.

Murray, John. *The Collected Writings of John Murray*. 1:59–85, 4:113–32. Edinburgh: Banner of Truth, 1976.

Murray, John. *The Free Offer of the Gospel*. Edinburgh: Banner of Truth, 2001.

Naylor, Peter. *Picking Up a Pin for the Lord*. London: Grace Publications Trust, 1992.

Nettles, Thomas J. *By His Grace and For His Glory*. Rev. ed. Cape Coral, FL: Founders Press, 2006.

Oliver, Robert W. *History of the English Calvinistic Baptists, 1771–1892*. Edinburgh: Banner of Truth, 2006.

Philpot, J. C. *Letters and Memoir of Joseph Charles Philpot*. Grand Rapids: Baker Book House, 1981.

Philpot, J. C. *Sermons*. 10 vols. Harpenden: Gospel Standard Trust Publications, 1977.

Ramsbottom, B. A. *The History of the Gospel Standard Magazine, 1835–1985*. Carshalton: Gospel Standard Societies, 1985.

Ramsbottom, B. A. *William Gadsby*. Harpenden: Gospel Standard Trust Publications, 2003.

Rippon, John. *A Brief Memoir of the Life and Writings of the Late Rev. John Gill, D.D.* Harrisonburg, VA: Gano Books, 1992.

Ryle, J. C. *Old Paths*. Edinburgh: Banner of Truth, 2013.

Sarrells, R.V. *Systematic Theology*. Azle, Tex: Harmony Hill, 1975.

Sell, Alan P. F. *The Great Debate*. Grand Rapids: Baker Book House, 1983.

Shaw, Ian J. *High Calvinism in Action*. Oxford: Oxford University Press, 2002.

Silversides, David. *The Free Offer: Biblical and Reformed*. N.p.: Marpet Press, 2005.

Stebbins, Kenneth W. *Christ Freely Offered*. Glebe: Fast Books/Covenanter Press, 1978/96.

Toon, Peter. *The Emergence of Hyper-Calvinism in English Nonconformity 1689–1765*. London: The Olive Tree, 1967 (reprinted Eugene: Wipf and Stock, 2011).

Van Til, Cornelius. *Common Grace and the Gospel*. Phillipsburg, NJ: Presbyterian and Reformed, 1974.

Watson, T. E. "Andrew Fuller's Conflict

with Hypercalvinism." In David Martyn Lloyd-Jones, ed. *Puritan Papers, Volume*

1:1956–1959, 271–82. Phillipsburg, NJ: P&R, 2000.

Eighteenth-Century Calvinism

Bond, Douglas. *The Poetic Wonder of Isaac Watts*. Orlando: Reformation Trust, 2013.

Boston, Thomas. *The Complete Works of the Late Rev. Thomas Boston*. 12 vols. Wheaton: Richard Owen Roberts, 1980.

Boston, Thomas. *Memoirs of Thomas Boston*. Edinburgh: Banner of Truth, 1988.

Bull, Josiah. *"But Now I See': The Life of John Newton*. Edinburgh: Banner of Truth, 1998.

Clifford, Alan C. *The Good Doctor: Philip Doddridge of Northampton – A Tercentenary Tribute*. Attleborough: Charenton Reformed Publishing, 2002.

Comrie, Alexander. *The ABC of Faith*. Ossett: Zoar Publications, 1978.

Dallimore, Arnold. *George Whitefield*. 2 vols. Edinburgh: Banner of Truth, 1970.

Davidson, Noel. *How Sweet the Sound*. Belfast: Ambassador, 1997.

Deacon, Malcolm. *Philip Doddridge of Northampton 1702–51*. Northampton: Northamptonshire Libraries, 1980.

Doddridge, Philip. *The Rise and Progress of Religion in the Soul*. Orlando: Soli Deo Gloria, 2005.

Ella, George M. *Augustus Montague Toplady: A Debtor to Mercy Alone*. Eggleston: Go Publications, 2000.

Ella, George M. *William Cowper: Poet of Paradise*. Darlington: Evangelical Press, 1993.

Evans, Eifion. *Daniel Rowland and the Great Evangelical Awakening in Wales*. Edinburgh: Banner of Truth, 1985.

Ferguson, Sinclair B. *The Whole Christ: Legalism, Antinomianism, and Gospel Assurance – Why the Marrow Controversy Still Matters*. Wheaton: Crossway, 2016.

Fisher, Edward. *The Marrow of Modern Divinity*. Swengel: Reiner, 1978.

Fountain, David. *Issac Watts Remembered*.

Harpenden: Gospel Standard Baptist Trust, 1974.

Fuller, Andrew. *The Works of Andrew Fuller*. 3 vols. Harrisonburg, VA: Sprinkle Publications, 1988.

Gatiss, Lee, ed. *The Sermons of George Whitefield*. 2 vols. Wheaton: Crossway, 2012.

Gillies, John. *Historical Collections of Accounts of Revivals*. Edinburgh: Banner of Truth, 1981.

Johnston, E. A. *George Whitefield: A Definitive Biography*. 2 vols. Stoke-on-Trent: Tentmaker Publications, 2008.

Jones, David Ceri, Boyd Stanley Schlenther, and Eryn Mant White. *The Elect Methodists: Calvinistic Methodism in England and Wales 1735–1811*. Cardiff: University of Wales Press, 2012.

Jones, John Morgan and William Morgan. *The Calvinistic Methodist Fathers of Wales*. 2 vols. Edinburgh: Banner of Truth, 2008.

Kidd, Thomas S. *George Whitefield: America's Spiritual Founding Father*. New Haven: Yale University Press, 2014.

Lachman, David C. *The Marrow Controversy, 1718–1723*. Edinburgh: Rutherford House, 1988.

Lawson, Steven J. *The Evangelistic Zeal of George Whitefield*. Orlando: Reformation Trust, 2014.

Lawton, George. *Within the Rock of Ages: The Life and Work of Augustus Montague Toplady*. Cambridge: James Clarke, 1983.

M'Crie, Thomas. *The Story of the Scottish Church from the Reformation to the Disruption*. Glasgow: Free Church Publications, n.d.

MacGowan, A. T. B. *The Federal Theology of Thomas Boston*. Carlisle: Paternoster, 1997.

MacLeod, John. *Scottish Theology, 139–228*. Edinburgh: Banner of Truth, 1974.

Newton, John. *The Works of the Rev. John Newton.* 6 vols. Edinburgh: Banner of Truth, 1985.

Pollock, John. *George Whitefield and the Great Awakening.* London: Hodder and Stoughton, 1972.

Roberts, Richard Owen. *Whitefield in Print: A Bibliographic Record of Works By, For, and Against George Whitefield.* Wheaton: Richard Owen Roberts, Publishers, 1988.

Ryken, Philip Graham. *Thomas Boston as Preacher of the Fourfold State.* Carlisle: Paternoster, 1999.

Ryle, J. C. *Christian Leaders of the Eighteenth Century.* Edinburgh: Banner of Truth, 1978.

Selderhuis, Herman J., ed. *The Calvin Handbook,* 479–86. Grand Rapids: Eerdmans, 2009.

Selderhuis, Herman J., ed. *Handbook of Dutch Church History,* 361–434. Göttingen: Vandenhoeck & Ruprecht, 2015.

Tanis, James R. *Dutch Calvinistic Pietism in the Middle Colonies: A Study in the Life and Thought of Theodorus Jacobus Frelinghuysen.* "s-Gravenhage: Martinus Nijhoff, 1967.

Toplady, Augustus Montague. *The Complete Works of Augustus Toplady.* Harrisonburg, VA: Sprinkle Publications, 1987.

Tyerman, Luke. *The Life of the Reverend George Whitefield.* 2 vols. Azle, TX: Need of the Times Publishers, 1995.

Van Lieberg, Fred. *Living for God: Eighteenth-Century Dutch Pietist Autobiography.* Lanham: Scarecrow Press, 2006.

VanDoodewaard, William. *The Marrow Controversy and Seceder Tradition.* Grand Rapids: Reformation Heritage Books, 2011.

Walker, James. *The Theology and Theologians of Scotland, 1560–1750.* Edinburgh: John Knox Press, 1982.

Watts, Isaac. *The Works of the Reverend and Learned Isaac Watts, D.D.* 6 vols. New York: AMS Press, 1971.

Whitefield, George. *George Whitefield's Journals.* Edinburgh: Banner of Truth, 1978.

Wood, A. Skevington. *The Inextinguishable Blaze: Spiritual Renewal and Advance in the Eighteenth Century.* Grand Rapids: Eerdmans, 1960.

New England Theology

Bellamy, Joseph. *The Works of Joseph Bellamy.* 2 vols. New York: Garland, 1987.

Carden, Allen. *Puritan Christianity in America.* Grand Rapids: Baker Book House, 1990.

Cherry, Conrad. *The Theology of Jonathan Edwards.* Gloucester: Peter Smith, 1974.

Conforti, Joseph. *Samuel Hopkins and the New Divinity Movement.* Grand Rapids: Eerdmans, 1981.

Crisp, Oliver D. and Douglas Sweeney, eds. *After Jonathan Edwards: The Courses of the New England Theology.* Oxford: Oxford University Press, 2012.

Crisp, Oliver D. and Kyle C. Strobel. *Jonathan Edwards: An Introduction to His Thought.* Grand Rapids: Eerdmans, 2018.

Edwards, Jonathan. *The Works of Jonathan Edwards.* 2 vols. Edinburgh: Banner of Truth, 1974.

Edwards, Jonathan. *The Works of Jonathan Edwards.* 26 vols. New Haven: Yale University Press, 1957.

Emmons, Nathanael. *The Works of Nathanael Emmons.* 6 vols. New York: Garland, 1987.

Gerstner, John H. *Jonathan Edwards: A Mini-Theology.* Wheaton: Tyndale House, 1987.

Gerstner, John H. *The Rational Biblical Theology of Jonathan Edwards.* 3 vols. Orlando: Ligonier Ministries, 1991.

Guelzo, Allen C. *Edwards on the Will.* Middletown: Wesleyan University Press, 1989.

Hodge, Charles, et al. *Princeton versus the*

New Divinity. Edinburgh: Banner of Truth, 2001.

Holmes, Stephen R. *God of Grace and God of Glory: An Account of the Theology of Jonathan Edwards*. Edinburgh: T. and T. Clark, 2000.

Hooker, Thomas. *The Application of Redemption*. Ames, IA: International Outreach, 2008.

Hopkins, Samuel. *The Works of Samuel Hopkins*. 3 vols. New York: Garland, 1987.

Lawson, Steven J. *The Unwavering Resolve of Jonathan Edwards*. Orlando: Reformation Trust, 2008.

Lee, Sang Hyun, ed. *The Princeton Companion to Jonathan Edwards*. Princeton: Princeton University Press, 2005.

Lesser, M. X. *Reading Jonathan Edwards: An Annotated Bibliography in Three Parts, 1729–2005*. Grand Rapids: Eerdmans, 2008.

Lucas, Sean Michael. *God's Grand Design: The Theological Vision of Jonathan Edwards*. Wheaton: Crossway, 2011.

Marsden, George M. *Jonathan Edwards: A Life*. New Haven: Yale University Press, 2003.

McClymond, Michael J. and Gerald R. McDermott. *The Theology of Jonathan Edwards*. Oxford: Oxford University Press, 2011.

Murray, Iain H. *Jonathan Edwards: A New Biography*. Edinburgh: Banner of Truth, 1987.

Murray, Iain H. *Revival and Revivalism: The Making and Marring of American Evangelicalism 1750–1858*. Edinburgh: Banner of Truth, 1994.

Ryken, Leland. *Worldly Saints: The Puritans as They Really Were*. Grand Rapids: Academie Books/Zondervan, 1986.

Shepard, Thomas. *The Works of Thomas Shepard*. 3 vols. Ligonier, PA: Soli Deo Gloria, 1991.

Silverman, Kenneth. *The Life and Times of Cotton Mather*. New York: Harper and Row, 1984.

Stein, Stephen J., ed. *The Cambridge Companion to Jonathan Edwards*. Cambridge: Cambridge University Press, 2007.

Stoddard, Solomon. *A Guide to Christ*. Ligonier, PA: Soli Deo Gloria, 1993.

Stoddard, Solomon. *The Puritan Pulpit, The American Puritans: Solomon Stoddard*. Orlando: Soli Deo Gloria, 2005.

Storms, C. Samuel. *Tragedy in Eden: Original Sin in the Theology of Jonathan Edwards*. Lanham: University Press of America, 1985.

Stout, Harry S., ed. *The Jonathan Edwards Encyclopedia*. Grand Rapids: Eerdmans, 2017.

Sweeney, Douglas A. and Allen C. Guelzo, eds. *The New England Theology: From Jonathan Edwards to Edwards Amasa Park*. Grand Rapids: Baker Academic, 2006.

Sweeney, Douglas A. *Nathaniel Taylor, New Haven Theology, and the Legacy of Jonathan Edwards*. New York: Oxford University Press, 2003.

Tracy, Joseph. *The Great Awakening*. Edinburgh: Banner of Truth, 1976.

Tyler, Bennet and Andrew Bonar. *The Life and Labours of Asahel Nettleton*. Edinburgh: Banner of Truth, 1975.

Warfield, Benjamin Breckinridge. *Studies in Theology*, 515–38. Grand Rapids: Banner of Truth, 1988.

Warfield, Benjamin Breckinridge. *The Works of Benjamin B. Warfield*, 9:515–38. Grand Rapids: Baker Book House, 1981.

Ziff, Larzer. *Puritanism in America*. New York: Viking Press, 1973.

The Princeton Theology

Adams, Jay E. *The Christian Counselor's Manual*. Phillipsburg, NJ: Presbyterian and Reformed, 1973.

Adams, Jay E. *Competent to Counsel.* Phillipsburg, NJ: Presbyterian and Reformed, 1972.

Alexander, Archibald. *The Log College.* London: Banner of Truth, 1968.

Alexander, Archibald. *Thoughts on Religious Experience.* Edinburgh: Banner of Truth, 1978.

Alexander, James W. *The Life of Archibald Alexander, D.D.* Harrisonburg, VA: Sprinkle Publications, 1991.

Calhoun, David B. *Princeton Seminary.* 2 vols. Edinburgh: Banner of Truth, 1994.

Garrestson, James M., ed. *Pastor-Teachers of Old Princeton.* Edinburgh: Banner of Truth, 2012.

Gutjahr, Paul C. *Charles Hodge: Guardian of American Orthodoxy.* New York: Oxford University Press, 2011.

Hodge, A. A. *The Life of Charles Hodge.* Edinburgh: Banner of Truth, 2010.

Hodge, A. A. *Outlines of Theology.* Grand Rapids: Zondervan, 1973.

Hodge, Charles, et al. *Princeton versus the New Divinity.* Edinburgh: Banner of Truth, 2001.

Hodge, Charles. *Systematic Theology.* 3 vols. Grand Rapids: Eerdmans, 1979.

Hoffecker, W. Andrew. *Piety and the Princeton Theologians.* Phillipsburg, NJ: Presbyterian and Reformed, 1981.

Kerr, Hugh, ed. *Sons of the Prophets: Leaders in Protestantism from Princeton Seminary.* Princeton: Princeton University Press, 1963.

Loetscher, Lefferts A. *Facing the Enlightenment and Pietism: Archibald Alexander and the Founding of Princeton Theological Seminary.* Westport: Greenwood Press, 1983.

Machen, J. Gresham. *Christianity and Liberalism.* Grand Rapids: Eerdmans, 1946.

Machen, J. Gresham. *Selected Shorter Writings.* Edited by D. G. Hart. Phillipsburg, NJ: P&R, 2004.

Machen, J. Gresham. *The Virgin Birth of Christ.* Grand Rapids: Baker Book House, 1967.

Moorhead, James H. *Princeton Seminary in American Religion and Culture.* Grand Rapids: Eerdmans, 2012.

Murray, Iain H. *The Life of John Murray.* Edinburgh: Banner of Truth, 2007.

Murray, John. *The Collected Writings of John Murray.* 4 vols. Edinburgh: Banner of Truth, 1976.

Murray, John. *The Epistle to the Romans.* Grand Rapids: Eerdmans, 1983.

Noll, Mark. *The Princeton Theology, 1812–1921: An Anthology.* Phillipsburg, NJ: Presbyterian and Reformed, 1983.

Stewart, John W and James H. Moorhead, eds. *Charles Hodge Revisited.* Grand Rapids: Eerdmans, 2002.

Stonehouse, Ned. B. J. *Gresham Machen: A Biographical Memoir.* Grand Rapids: Eerdmans, 1954.

Van Til, Cornelius. *The Defense of the Faith.* Phillipsburg, NJ: Presbyterian and Reformed, 1955.

Vander Stelt, John C. *Philosophy and Scripture: A Study of Old Princeton and Westminster Theology.* Marlton: Mack Publishing Co., 1978.

Vos, Geerhardus. *Biblical Theology.* Edinburgh: Banner of Truth, 1975.

Vos, Geerhardus. *Redemptive History and Biblical Interpretation.* Phillipsburg, NJ: Presbyterian and Reformed, 1980.

Warfield, Benjamin Breckinridge. *The Works of Benjamin B. Warfield.* 10 vols. Grand Rapids: Baker Book House, 1981.

Wells, David F., ed. *The Princeton Theology.* Grand Rapids: Baker Book House, 1989.

Wells, David F., ed. *Reformed Theology in America, 15–132.* Grand Rapids: Eerdmans, 1985.

Woolley, Paul, ed. *The Infallible Word.* Phillipsburg, NJ: Presbyterian and Reformed, 1970.

Zaspel, Fred G. *The Theology of B. B. Warfield: A Systematic Summary.* Wheaton: Crossway, 2010.

Nineteenth-Century American Calvinism

Aubert, Annette G. *The German Roots of Nineteenth-Century American Theology.* Oxford: Oxford University Press, 2013.

Bouwer, Arie R. *Reformed Church Roots.* N.p.: Reformed Church Press, 1977.

Boyce, James Petigru. *Abstract of Systematic Theology.* Cape Coral, FL: Founders Press, 2007.

Bratt, James D. *Dutch Calvinism in Modern America.* Grand Rapids: Eerdmans, 1984.

Dabney, Robert Lewis. *Discussions.* 5 vols. Harrisonburg, VA: Sprinkle Publications, 1982.

Dabney, Robert Lewis. *Systematic Theology.* Edinburgh: Banner of Truth, 1985.

Farmer, James Oscar. *The Metaphysical Conspiracy: James Henley Thornwell and the Synthesis of Southern Values.* Macon: Mercer University Press, 1986.

Fortson, S. Donald, III. *The Presbyterian Creed: A Confessional Tradition in America, 1729–1870.* Milton Keynes: Paternoster, 2008.

Girardeau, John Lafeyette. *Calvinism and Evangelical Arminianism.* Harrisonburg, VA: Sprinkle Publications, 1984.

Girardeau, John Lafeyette. *Discussions of Theological Questions.* Harrisonburg, VA: Sprinkle Publications, 1986.

Hart, D. G. and John R. Muether. *Seeking a Better Country: 300 Years of American Presbyterianism,* 91–187. Phillipsburg, NJ: P&R, 2007.

Hart, D. G. *John Williamson Nevin: High-Church Calvinist.* Phillipsburg, NJ: P&R, 2005.

Hart, Darryl G. "Consistently Contested: Calvin Among Nineteenth-Century Reformed Protestants in the United States." In David W. Hall, ed. *Tributes to John Calvin,* 435–63. Phillipsburg, NJ: P&R, 2010.

Holifield, E. Brooks. *Gentlemen Theologians.* Durham: Duke University Press, 1978.

Johnson, Thomas Cary. *The Life and Letters of Benjamin Morgan Palmer.* Edinburgh: Banner of Truth, 1987.

Johnson, Thomas Cary. *The Life and Letters of Robert Lewis Dabney.* Edinburgh: Banner of Truth, 1977.

Kelly, Douglas. *Preachers with Power.* Edinburgh: Banner of Truth, 1992.

Lucas, Sean Michael. *Robert Lewis Dabney: A Southern Presbyterian Life.* Phillipsburg, NJ: P&R, 2005.

Marsden, George M. *The Evangelical Mind and the New School Presbyterian Experience.* New Haven: Yale University Press, 1970.

Nettles, Thomas J. *By His Grace and For His Glory.* Rev. ed. Cape Coral, FL: Founders Press, 2006.

Nettles, Thomas J. *James Petigru Boyce: A Southern Baptist Statesman.* Phillipsburg, NJ: P&R, 2009.

Nevin, John Williamson. *The Mystical Presence.* Eugene: Wipf and Stock, 2000.

Palmer, Benjamin Morgan. *The Life and Letters of James Henley Thornwell.* Edinburgh: Banner of Truth, 1974.

Schaff, Philip. *History of the Christian Church.* 8 vols. Grand Rapids: Eerdmans, 1985.

Shedd, William G. T. *Calvinism: Pure and Mixed.* Edinburgh: Banner of Truth, 1986.

Shedd, William G. T. *Dogmatic Theology.* 3rd ed. Phillipsburg, NJ: P&R, 2003.

Shriver, George. *Philip Schaff: Christian Scholar and Ecumenical Prophet.* Macon, GA: Mercer University Press, 1987.

Smith, Morton. *Studies in Southern Presbyterian Theology.* Phillipsburg, NJ: Presbyterian and Reformed, 1987.

Sweeney, Douglas A. "'Falling Away from the General Faith of the Reformation?' The Contest over Calvinism in Nineteenth-Century America." In Thomas J. Davis, ed. *John Calvin's American Legacy,* 111–46. Oxford: Oxford University Press, 2010.

Thompson, Ernest Trice. *Presbyterians in the South.* 3 vols. Richmond: John Knox Press, 1963.

Thornwell, James Henley. *The Collected Writings of James Henley Thornwell.* 4 vols. Edinburgh: Banner of Truth, 1974.

Van Oene, W. W. J. *Patrimony Profile: Our Reformed Heritage Retraced 1795–1946.* Winnipeg: Premier Publishing, 1999.

Wells, David F., ed. *Reformed Theology in America,* 133–243. Grand Rapids: Eerdmans, 1985.

Wells, David F., ed. *Southern Reformed Theology.* Grand Rapids: Baker Book House, 1989.

White, Henry Alexander. *Southern Presbyterian Leaders.* Edinburgh: Banner of Truth, 2000.

Nineteenth-Century European Calvinism

Atherstone, Andrew, ed. *Bishop J. C. Ryle's Autobiography: The Early Years.* Edinburgh: Banner of Truth, 2016.

Bebbington, David. "Calvin and British Evangelicalism in the Nineteenth and Twentieth Centuries." In Irena Backus and Philip Benedict, eds. *Calvin and His Influence,* 282–305. Oxford: Oxford University Press, 2011.

Bonar, Andrew. *Memoir and Remains of Robert Murray M'Cheyne.* Edinburgh: Banner of Truth, 1978.

Bouma, Henrik. *Secession, Doleantie, and Union: 1834–1892.* Neerlandia: Inheritance Publications, 1995.

Bratt, James D. *Abraham Kuyper: Modern Calvinist, Christian Democrat.* Grand Rapids: Eerdmans, 2013.

Campbell, John M'Leod. *The Nature of the Atonement.* Grand Rapids: Eerdmans, 1996.

Cunningham, William. *Historical Theology.* 2 vols. London: Banner of Truth, 1969.

Cunningham, William. *The Reformers and the Theology of the Reformation.* Edinburgh: Banner of Truth, 1979.

Dallimore, Arnold. *The Life of Edward Irving.* Edinburgh: Banner of Truth, 1983.

Haldane, Alexander. *The Lives of Robert and James Haldane.* Edinburgh: Banner of Truth, 1990.

Hamilton, Ian. *The Erosion of Calvinist Orthodoxy: Seceders and Subscription in Scottish Presbyterianism.* Edinburgh: Rutherford House, 1990.

Heppe, Heinrich. *Reformed Dogmatics.* Grand Rapids: Baker Book House, 1978.

Kamps, Marvin. *1834: Hendrik de Cock's Return to the True Church.* Jennison: Reformed Free Publishing Association, 2011.

Krummacher, Friedrich. *The Suffering Saviour.* Edinburgh: Banner of Truth, 2004.

Kuipers, Tjitze. *Abraham Kuyper: An Annotated Bibliography 1857–2010.* Leiden: Brill, 2011.

Kuyper, Abraham. *The Holy Spirit.* Grand Rapids: Eerdmans, 1969.

Kuyper, Abraham. *Lectures on Calvinism.* Grand Rapids: Eerdmans, 1931.

Kuyper, Abraham. *Principles of Sacred Theology.* Grand Rapids: Eerdmans, 1968.

Lawson, Steven J. *The Gospel Focus of Charles Spurgeon.* Orlando: Reformation Trust, 2012.

M'Crie, Thomas. *The Story of the Scottish Church from the Reformation to the Disruption.* Glasgow: Free Church Publications, n.d.

MacLeod, John. *Scottish Theology,* 229–332. Edinburgh: Banner of Truth, 1983.

McFarlane, Graham W. P. *Christ and the Spirit: The Doctrine of the Incarnation According to Edward Irving.* Carlisle: Paternoster, 1996.

McGoldrick, James E. *Abraham Kuyper: God's Renaissance Man.* Darlington: Evangelical Press, 2000.

Murray, Iain H. *J. C. Ryle: Prepared to Stand Alone.* Edinburgh: Banner of Truth, 2016.

Ryle, J. C. *Expository Thoughts on the Gospels.* 7 vols. London: James Clarke, 1975.

Ryle, J. C. *Holiness.* Cambridge: James Clarke, 1956.

Selderhuis, Herman J., ed. *Handbook of Dutch Church History*, 435–520. Göttingen: Vandenhoeck & Ruprecht, 2015.

Spurgeon, Charles Haddon. *Spurgeon's Autobiography.* 2 vols. Edinburgh: Banner of Truth, 1976.

Stevenson, Peter K. *God in Our Nature: The Incarnational Theology of John McLeod Campbell.* Carlisle: Paternoster, 2004.

Stewart, Kenneth J. *Restoring the Reformation: British Evangelicals and the Francophone 'Reveil' 1816–1849.* Milton Keynes: Paternoster, 2006.

Swieringa, Robert P. and Elton J. Bruins. *Family Quarrels in the Dutch Reformed Churches in the Nineteenth Century.* Grand Rapids: Eerdmans, 1999.

Wright, David F. and Gary D. Badcock, eds. *Disruption to Diversity: Edinburgh Divinity 1846–1996.* Edinburgh: T. and T. Clark, 1996.

Neo-Orthodoxy

Barnes, Peter. *A Handful of Pebbles.* Edinburgh: Banner of Truth, 2008.

Barth, Karl. *Church Dogmatics.* 14 vols. Edinburgh: T. and T. Clark, 1975.

Barth, Karl. *The Theology of John Calvin.* Grand Rapids: Eerdmans, 1995.

Barth, Karl. *The Theology of the Reformed Confessions.* Louisville: Westminster John Knox Press, 2002.

Berkouwer, G. C. *The Triumph of Grace in the Theology of Karl Barth.* Grand Rapids: Eerdmans, 1956.

Bloesch, Donald G. *Jesus is Victor.* Nashville: Abingdon, 1976.

Bolich, Gregory G. *Karl Barth & Evangelicalism.* Downers Grove, IL: IVP, 1980.

Brunner, Emil. *Dogmatics.* 3 vols. Philadelphia: Westminster Press, 1950.

Buis, Harry. *Historic Protestantism and Predestination*, 99–113. Philadelphia: Presbyterian and Reformed, 1958.

Cairns, Alan. *Dictionary of Theological Terms*, 134, 298–99, 483–85. 3rd ed. Belfast: Ambassador Publications, 2002.

Chung, Sung Wook. *Admiration and Challenge: Karl Barth's Theological Relationship with John Calvin.* New York: Peter Lang, 2002.

Clark, Gordon H. *In Defense of Theology*, 45–70. Milford: Mott Media, 1984.

Clark, Gordon H. *Karl Barth's Theological Method.* Philadelphia: Presbyterian and Reformed, 1963.

Colyer, Elmer M. *How to Read T. F. Torrance.* Downers Grove, IL: IVP, 2001.

Colyer, Elmer M. *The Nature of Doctrine in T. F. Torrance's Theology.* Eugene: Wipf and Stock, 2001.

Crampton, W. Gary. *A Concise Theology of Karl Barth.* Lakeland, FL: Whitefield Media Productions, 2012.

Gerstner, John H. *The Early Writings*, 2:77–80. Morgan, PA: Soli Deo Gloria, 1998.

Glomsrud, Ryan. "Karl Barth and Modern Protestantism: The Radical Impulse." In R. Scott Clark and Joel E. Kim, eds. *Always Reformed: Essays in Honor of W. Robert Godfrey*, 92–114. Escondido: Westminster Seminary California, 2010.

Hart, D. G. *Calvinism: A History*, 272–94. New Haven: Yale University Press, 2013.

Hausmann, William John. *Karl Barth's Doctrine of Election.* New York: Philosophical Library, 1969.

Henry, Carl F. H. *God, Revelation, and Authority*, 6:90–107. Wheaton: Crossway, 1999.

Hughes, Philip Edgcumbe, ed. *Creative Minds in Contemporary Theology*, 27–62, 99–130. Grand Rapids: Eerdmans, 1969.

Jewett, Paul K. "Neo-Orthodoxy." In Everett

F. Harrison, ed. *Baker's Dictionary of Theology*, 374–79. Grand Rapids: Baker Book House, 1960.

Jewett, Paul K. *Election and Predestination*, 48–54. Grand Rapids: Eerdmans, 1985.

Jewett, Paul K. *Emil Brunner: An Introduction to the Man and His Thought*. Chicago: InterVarsity Press, 1961.

Jewett, Paul K. *Emil Brunner's Concept of Revelation*. London: James Clarke, 1954.

Klooster, Fred H. *The Significance of Barth's Theology*. Grand Rapids: Baker Book House, 1961.

Kromminga, D. H. "The Sovereignty of God and the Barthians." In Jacob T. Hoogstra, ed. *The Sovereignty of God*, 65–92. Birmingham: Solid Ground Christian Books, n.d.

Machen, J. Gresham. *Selected Shorter Writings*, 533–43. Phillipsburg, NJ: P&R, 2004.

McDonald, Neil B. and Carl Trueman, eds. *Calvin, Barth, Reformed Theology*. Milton Keynes: Paternoster, 2008.

McGrath, Alister E. *T. F. Torrance: An Intellectual Biography*. Edinburgh: T. and T. Clark, 1999.

McKim, Donald K., ed. *How Karl Barth Changed My Mind*. Grand Rapids: Eerdmans, 1986.

Nicole, Roger. "The Neo-Orthodox Reductionism." In Gordon Lewis and Bruce Demarest, eds. *Challenges to Inerrancy*, 121–44. Chicago: Moody Press, 1984.

Polman, A. D. R. *Barth*. Philadelphia: Presbyterian and Reformed, 1960.

Ramm, Bernard. *A Handbook of Contemporary Theology*. Grand Rapids: Eerdmans, 1966.

Reymond, Robert L. *Barth's Soteriology*. Philadelphia: Presbyterian and Reformed, 1967.

Reymond, Robert L. *Brunner's Dialectical Encounter*. Philadelphia: Presbyterian and Reformed, 1967.

Reymond, Robert L. *Contending for the Faith*, 209–56. Fearn: Mentor/Christian Focus, 2005.

Runia, Klaas. *Karl Barth's Doctrine of Holy Scripture*. Grand Rapids: Eerdmans, 1962.

Ryrie, Charles C. *Neoorthodoxy*. Kansas City: Walterick Publishers, 1977.

Smith, David L. *A Handbook of Contemporary Theology*, 27–40. Wheaton: Bridgepoint, 1992.

te Velde, Dolf. *The Doctrine of God in Reformed Orthodoxy, Karl Barth, and the Utrecht School*. Leiden: Brill, 2013.

Torrance, Thomas F. *Karl Barth: Biblical and Evangelical Theologian*. Edinburgh: T. and T. Clark, 1990.

Torrance, Thomas F. *Space, Time and Incarnation*. London: Oxford University Press, 1969.

Torrance, Thomas F. *Space, Time and Resurrection*. Edinburgh: Handsel Press, 1976.

Torrance, Thomas F. *Theological Science*. New York: Oxford University Press, 1969.

Torrance, Thomas F. *The Trinitarian Faith*. Edinburgh: T. and T. Clark, 1988.

Traub, William C. "Karl Barth and the Westminster Confession of Faith." In J. Ligon Duncan, III, ed. *The Westminster Confession into the 21st Century*, 3:175–222. Fearn: Mentor/Christian Focus, 2009.

Treier, Daniel J. and Walter A. Elwell, eds. *Evangelical Dictionary of Theology*, 3rd ed., 581–83. Grand Rapids: Baker Academic, 2017.

Tseng, Shao Ki. *Karl Barth's Infralapsarian Theology*. Downers Grove, IL: IVP Academic, 2016.

Van Til, Cornelius. *Barth's Christology*. Philadelphia: Presbyterian and Reformed, 1962.

Van Til, Cornelius. *Christianity and Barthinianism*. Philadelphia: Presbyterian and Reformed, 1962.

Van Til, Cornelius. *Karl Barth and Chalcedon*. Philadelphia: Westminster Theological Seminary, 1960.

Van Til, Cornelius. *Karl Barth and Evangelicalism*. Nutley: Presbyterian and Reformed, 1964.

Van Til, Cornelius. *The New Modernism.* Philadelphia: Presbyterian and Reformed, 1947.

Webster, John, ed. *The Cambridge Companion to Karl Barth.* Cambridge: Cambridge University Press, 2000.

Wells, David F., ed. *Reformed Theology in America*, 245–98. Grand Rapids: Eerdmans, 1985.

Whitney, H. J. *The New Heresy.* Singapore: Yeat Sing Art Printing Co., n.d.

Twentieth-Century American Calvinism

Bahnsen, Greg. *Theonomy in Christian Ethics.* 2nd ed. Phillipsburg, NJ: Presbyterian and Reformed, 1984.

Barker, William S. and W. Robert Godfrey, eds. *Theonomy: A Reformed Critique.* Grand Rapids: Academie Books/Zondervan, 1990.

Beeke, Joel R. "Twelve Reasons Calvin is Important Today." In Joel R. Beeke, ed. *Calvin for Today*, 241–76. Grand Rapids: Reformation Heritage Books, 2009.

Berkhof, Louis. *Systematic Theology.* Grand Rapids: Eerdmans, 1988.

Boettner, Loraine. *The Reformed Doctrine of Predestination.* Philadelphia: Presbyterian and Reformed, 1932.

Borgman, Brian. *My Heart for Thy Cause: Albert M. Martin's Theology of Preaching.* Fearn: Mentor, 2002.

Carson, D. A. *The Difficult Doctrine of the Love of God.* Wheaton: Crossway, 2000.

Carter, Anthony J. *Being Black and Reformed.* Phillipsburg, NJ: P&R, 2003.

Carter, Anthony J., ed. *Glory Road: The Journeys of 10 African-Americans into Reformed Christianity.* Wheaton: Crossway, 2009.

Chantry, Tom and David D. Dykstra. *Holding Communion Together: The Reformed Baptists, The First Fifty Years - Divided and United.* Birmingham: Solid Ground Christian Books, 2014.

Chantry, Walter. *Today's Gospel: Authentic or Synthetic?* London: Banner of Truth, 1970.

Crocco, Stephen D. "Whose Calvin, Which Calvinism? John Calvin and the Development of Twentieth-Century American Theology." In Thomas J. Davis, ed. *John Calvin's American Legacy*, 165–88. Oxford: Oxford University Press, 2010.

DeKlerk, Peter and Richard De Ridder, eds. *Perspectives on the Christian Reformed Church.* Grand Rapids: Baker Book House, 1983.

DeKlerk, Peter, ed. *A Bibliography of the Professors of Calvin Theological Seminary.* Grand Rapids: Calvin Theological Seminary, 1980.

Dennison, Charles G. and Richard C. Gamble, eds. *Pressing Towards the Mark: Essays Commemorating Fifty Years of the Orthodox Presbyterian Church.* Philadelphia: The Committee for the Historian of the Orthodox Presbyterian Church, 1986.

Duncan, Ligon. "The Resurgence of Calvin in America." In Joel R. Beeke, ed. *Calvin for Today*, 227–40. Grand Rapids: Reformation Heritage Books, 2009.

Grudem, Wayne. *Systematic Theology.* Grand Rapids: Zondervan, 1994.

Hansen, Collin. *Young, Restless, Reformed.* Wheaton: Crossway, 2008.

Hart, D. G. *Calvinism: A History*, 248–94. New Haven: Yale University Press, 2013.

Hendriksen, William and Simon Kistemaker. *New Testament Commentary.* 14 vols. Grand Rapids: Baker Book House, 1996.

Hesselink, I. John. "The Charismatic Movement and the Reformed Tradition." In Donald K. McKim, ed. *Major Themes in the Reformed Tradition*, 386–99. Grand Rapids: Eerdmans, 1992.

Hodges, Louis Igou. *Reformed Theology Today.* Columbia: Brentwood Christian Press, 1995.

Hoogstra, Jacob T., ed. *American Calvinism: A Survey*. Grand Rapids: Baker Book House, 1957.

Jewett, Paul K. *Election and Predestination*. Grand Rapids: Eerdmans, 1985.

Johnson, E. A. *God's "Hitchhike" Evangelist: The Biography of Rolfe Barnard*. Asheville: Revival Literature, 2012.

MacArthur, John F. *The Gospel According to Jesus*. Rev. ed. Grand Rapids: Zondervan, 2008.

McGoldrick, James E. *Presbyterian and Reformed Churches: A Global History*. Grand Rapids: Reformation Heritage Books, 2012.

McVicar, Michael S. *Christian Reconstruction: R. J. Rushdoony and American Religious Conservatism*. Chapel Hill: University of North Carolina Press, 2015.

Muller, Richard A. *Post-Reformation Reformed Dogmatics*. 4 vols. 2nd ed. Grand Rapids: Baker Academic, 2003.

Murray, Iain H. *John MacArthur: Servant of the World and Flock*. Edinburgh: Banner of Truth, 2011.

Nettles, Thomas J. *By His Grace and For His Glory*. Rev. ed. Cape Coral, FL: Founders Press, 2006.

Nicole, Roger N. *Standing Forth: Collected Writing of Roger N. Nicole*. Fearn: Mentor, 2002.

North, Gary. *Crossed Fingers: How the Liberals Captured the Presbyterian Church*. Tyler: Institute for Christian Economics, 1996.

Palmer, Edwin H. *The Five Points of Calvinism*. Rev. ed. Grand Rapids: Baker Book House, 1984.

Piper, John. *Desiring God*. Portland: Multnomah Press, 1986.

Rushdoony, Rousas John. *The Institutes of Biblical Law*. Phillipsburg, NJ: Presbyterian and Reformed, 1973.

Schaeffer, Edith S. *The Tapestry*. Waco: Word, 1981.

Schaeffer, Francis A. *The Complete Works of Francis A. Schaeffer*. 5 vols. Wheaton: Crossway, 1982.

Schmidt, Corwin, Donald Luidens, James Penning, and Roger Nemeth. *Divided by a Common Heritage*. Grand Rapids: Eerdmans, 2006.

Smith, Frank J. *The History of the Presbyterian Church in America*. 2nd ed. Lawrenceville: Presbyterian Scholars Press, 1999.

Smylie, James H. *American Presbyterians: A Pictorial History*. Philadelphia: Prebyterian Historical Society, 1985.

Sproul, R. C. *The Holiness of God*. Wheaton: Tyndale House, 1986.

Sproul, R. C., Jr., ed. *After Darkness, Light*. Phillipsburg, NJ: P&R, 2003.

Thomas Geoffrey. *Ernest C. Reisinger*. Edinburgh: Banner of Truth, 2002.

Venema, Cornelis P. "Integration, Disintegration, and Reintegration: A Preliminary History of the United Reformed Churches in North America." In R. Scott Clark and Joel E. Kim, eds. *Always Reformed: Essays in Honor of W. Robert Godfrey*, 244–50. Escondido, CA: Westminster Seminary California, 2010.

Vincze, Charles. "The Future of Calvinism in America." In Jacob T. Hoogstra, ed. *The Sovereignty of God*, 208–13. Birmingham: Solid Ground Christian Books, n.d.

Walker, Jeremy. *The New Calvinism Considered*. Darlington: EP Books, 2013.

Williams, E. S. *The New Calvinists*. London: The Wakeman Trust, 2014.

Twentieth-Century British Calvinism

Bebbington, David. "Calvin and British Evangelicalism in the Nineteenth and Twentieth Centuries." In Irena Backus and Philip Benedict, eds. *Calvin and His Influence*, 282–305. Oxford: Oxford University Press, 2011.

Cameron, Nigel M. de S., David F. Wright, David C. Lachman, and Donald E. Meek, eds. *Dictionary of Scottish Church History & Theology*. Downers Grove, IL: IVP, 1993.

Helm, Paul. *Calvin and the Calvinists*. Edinburgh: Banner of Truth, 1982.

Lawson, Steven J. *The Passionate Preaching of Martyn Lloyd-Jones*. Orlando: Reformation Trust, 2016.

Lloyd-Jones, D. Martyn. *Romans*. 14 vols. Edinburgh: Banner of Truth, 1985.

MacLeod, John. *Scottish Theology*. Edinburgh: Banner of Truth, 1974.

Murray, Iain H. *D. Martyn Lloyd-Jones*. 2 vols. Edinburgh: Banner of Truth, 1982.

Murray, Iain H. *The Life of Arthur W. Pink*. Rev. ed. Edinburgh: Banner of Truth, 2004.

Murray, John J. *Catch the Vision: Roots of the Reformed Recovery*. Darlington: Evangelical Press, 2007.

Packer, J. I. *Collected Shorter Writings of J. I. Packer*. 4 vols. Carlisle: Paternoster, 1998.

Packer, J. I. *Evangelism and the Sovereignty of God*. Downers Grove, IL: InterVarsity Press, 1961.

Packer, J. I. *Knowing God*. Downers Grove, IL: InterVarsity Press, 1973.

Pink, Arthur W. *The Attributes of God*. Grand Rapids: Baker Books, 2006.

Pink, Arthur W. *The Sovereignty of God*. Grand Rapids: Baker Book House, 1973.

Ramsbottom, B. A., ed. *The History of the Gospel Standard Magazine 1835–1985*. Carshalton: Gospel Standard Societies, 1985.

Sell, Alan P. F. *The Great Debate*. Grand Rapids: Baker Book House, 1983.

Thomas, W. H. Griffith. *The Principles of Theology*. London: Church Book Room Press, 1956.

Twentieth-Century International Calvinism

Bale, Colin R. "Calvinism in Australia 1788–2009: a historical assessment." In Mark D. Thompson, ed. *Engaging with Calvin: Aspects of the Reformer's Legacy for Today*. Nottingham: Apollos, 2009.

Baugus, Bruce B., ed. *China's Reforming Churches*. Grand Rapids: Reformation Heritage Books, 2014.

Blair, William Newton and Bruce F. Hunt. *The Korean Pentecost and the Sufferings Which Followed*. Edinburgh: Banner of Truth, 1977.

Brown, G. Thompson. *Not By Might: A Century of Presbyterianism in Korea*. Atlanta: Presbyterian Church in the USA, 1984.

Chung, S. K. *A Study on Calvinism*. Seoul: Chongshin Publishing Co., 1995.

Chung, Sung-Kuh. *Korean Church and Reformed Faith*. Seattle: Time Printing, 1996.

Clark, Allen D. *A History of the Church in Korea*. Seoul: Christian Literature Society of Korea, 1971.

De Klerk, W. A. *The Puritans in Africa - A Story of Afrikanerdom*. London: R. Collings, 1975.

Deenick, J. W., ed. *A Church en Route: 40 Years Reformed Churches of Australia*. Geelong: Reformed Churches Publishing House, 1991.

Gill, Stewart D. "The Battle for the Westminster Confession in Australia." In J. Ligon Duncan, ed. *The Westminster Confession into the 21st Century*, 1:247–301. Fearn: Mentor, 2003.

Gombos, Gyula. *The Lean Years: A Study of Hungarian Calvinism in Crisis*. New York: The Kossuth Foundation, 1960.

Grayson, James Huntley. *Korea: A Religious History*. Rev. ed. Richmond: Routledge Curzon, 2002.

Kim, Jae Sung. "Calvinism in Asia." In David W. Hall, ed. *Tributes to John Calvin*, 487–503. Phillipsburg, NJ: P&R, 2010.

Kim, Young-Han, et al. *Reformed Theology Today*. N.p.: Poong-Man Publishing Co., 1989.

McGoldrick, James Edward. *Presbyterian and Reformed Churches: A Global History.* Grand Rapids: Reformation Heritage Books, 2012.

Murray, Iain H. *Australian Christian Life from 1788.* Edinburgh: Banner of Truth, 1988.

Selderhuis, Herman J., ed. *Handbook of Dutch Church History*, 521–644. Göttingen: Vandenhoeck & Ruprecht, 2015.

Shearer, R. E. *Wildfire: Church Growth in Korea.* Grand Rapids: Eerdmans, 1966.

Van der Walt, B. J. *Anatomy of Reformation.* Potschefstroom: Potschefstroom University for Christian Higher Education, 1991.

Van der Walt, B. J., ed. *Our Reformational Heritage.* Potschefstroom: Potschefstroom University for Christian Higher Education, 1984.

Van der Walt, B. J., et al. *Calvinus Reformator: His Contribution to Theology, Church and Soceity.* Potschefstroom: Potschefstroom University for Christian Higher Education, 1982.

Wang, Aiming. *Church in China: Faith, Ethics, Structure: The Heritage of the Reformation for the Future of the Church in China.* Bern: Peter Lang, 2009.

Ward, Rowland S. *The Bush Still Burns: The Presbyterian and Reformed Faith in Australia, 1788–1988.* Melbourne: Rowland S. Ward, 1989.

Ward, Rowland S. *Presbyterian Leaders in Nineteenth-Century Australia.* Melbourne: Rowland S. Ward, 1993.

Yim, Hee-Mo. *Unity Lost - Unity to Be Regained in Korean Presbyterianism: A History of Divisions in Korean Presbyterianism and the Role of the Means of Grace.* Frankfort-am-Main: Peter Lang, 1996.

The Sovereignty of God

Abendroth, Mike. *The Sovereignty and Supremacy of King Jesus.* Leominster: Day One, 2011.

Bavinck, Herman. *Reformed Dogmatics*, 2:228–49. Grand Rapids: Baker Academic, 2003.

Belcher, Richard P. *A Journey in God's Sovereignty.* Fort Mill: Richbarry Press, 2006.

Berkhof, Louis. *Systematic Theology*, 76–80. Grand Rapids: Eerdmans, 1988.

Boettner, Loraine. *The Reformed Doctrine of Predestination*, 30–34. Philadelphia: Presbyterian and Reformed, 1932.

Boice, James Montgomery. *Our Savior God.* Grand Rapids: Baker Book House, 1977.

Cairns, Alan. *Dictionary of Theological Terms*, 428–32. 3rd ed. Belfast: Ambassador Publications, 2002.

Carson, D. A. "How Can We Reconcile the Love and the Transcendent Sovereignty of God?" in Douglas S. Huffman and Eric L. Johnson, eds. *God Under Fire*, 279–312. Grand Rapids: Zondervan, 2002.

Charnock, Stephen. *The Existence and Attributes of God*, 2:356–471. Grand Rapids: Baker Book House, 1983.

Chase, Mitchell L. *Behold Our Sovereign God.* Brenham: Lucid Books, 2012.

Clarkson, David. *The Works of David Clarkson*, 2:454–516. Edinburgh: Banner of Truth, 1988.

Crisp, Oliver D. *Jonathan Edwards on God and Creation*, 57–76. Oxford: Oxford University Press, 2012.

Custance, Arthur C. *Time and Eternity and Other Biblical Studies*, The Doorway Papers, 6:121–74. Grand Rapids: Zondervan, 1977.

Drayson, F. K. "Divine Sovereignty in the Thought of Stephen Charnock." In D. Martyn Lloyd-Jones, ed. *Puritan Papers*, 1:213–24. Phillipsburg, NJ: P&R, 2000.

Edwards, Jonathan. "God Does What He

Pleases." In The Puritan Pulpit, 147–75. Morgan, PA: Soli Deo Gloria, 2004.

Edwards, Jonathan. Our Great and Glorious God, 39–53. Morgan, PA: Soli Deo Gloria, 2004.

Feinberg, John S. No One Like Him, 294–98, 625–734. Wheaton: Crossway, 2001.

Frame, John. The Doctrine of God, 21–115. Phillipsburg, NJ: P&R, 2002.

George, Timothy. Amazing Grace: God's Pursuit, Our Response, 15–33. Wheaton: Crossway, 2011.

Gill, John. A Complete Body of Doctrinal and Practical Divinity, 70–78. Paris, AR: Baptist Standard Bearer, 1984.

Grudem, Wayne. Systematic Theology, 216–18. Grand Rapids: Zondervan, 1994.

Helm, Paul. "Classical Calvinist Doctrine of God." In Bruce A. Ware, ed. Perspectives on the Doctrine of God, 5–52. Nashville: B&H Academic, 2008.

Hodge, Charles. Systematic Theology, 1:439–41. Grand Rapids: Eerdmans, 1979.

Hoogstra, Jacob T., ed. The Sovereignty of God. Vestavia Hills, AL: Solid Ground Christian Books, n.d.

Hughes, Philip Edgcumbe. "The Sovereignty of God — Has God Lost Control?" In R. C. Sproul, ed. Soli Deo Gloria: Essays in Reformed Theology, 26–35. Nutley: Presbyterian and Reformed, 1976.

Lawson, Steven J. "Our Sovereign Savior: Sermon on Revelation 5:1–14." In Matthew Barrett and Thomas J. Nettles, eds. Whomever He Wills, 3–15. Cape Coral, FL: Founders Press, 2012.

Lawson, Steven J. A Long Line of Godly Men, 1:27–35, 46–53, 74–78, 107–08, 115–19, 122–26, 135–39, 150–57, 167–170, 200–202, 209–11, 224–29, 244, 309–11, 542–44. Orlando: Reformation Trust, 2006.

Lawson, Steven J. Made in Our Image, 91–106. Sisters, OR: Multnomah, 2000.

Leahy, Frederick S. The Hand of God: The Comfort of Having a Sovereign God. Edinburgh: Banner of Truth, 2007.

MacArthur, John F. Our Awesome God, 111–20. Wheaton: Crossway, 1993.

MacLeod, Donald. "Sovereignty of God." In Sinclair B. Ferguson, David F. Wright, and J. I. Packer, eds. New Dictionary of Theology, 654–56. Downers Grove, IL: InterVarsity Press, 1988.

McDavid, Edmund R., III. God's Guarantee: Are You Saved by It? Birmingham: Hope Publishing Co., 2002.

McNeill, Robert E. God Indeed! Enumclaw: WinePress Publishing, 2002.

Muller, Richard A. Divine Will and Human Choice: Freedom, Contingency, and Necessity in Early Modern Reformed Thought. Grand Rapids: Baker Academic, 2017.

Muller, Richard A. Post-Reformation Reformed Dogmatics, Volume 3. 2nd ed. Grand Rapids: Baker Academic, 2003.

Murray, John. Calvin on Scripture and Divine Sovereignty. Grand Rapids: Baker Book House, 1960.

Murray, John. The Collected Writings of John Murray, 4:191–204. Edinburgh: Banner of Truth, 1982.

Oliphint, K. Scott. God with Us. Wheaton: Crossway, 2012.

Packer, J. I. Evangelism and the Sovereignty of God. Downers Grove, IL: InterVarsity Press, 1961.

Packer, J. I. Knowing God. Downers Grove, IL: InterVarsity Press, 1973.

Phillips, Richard D. What's So Great about the Doctrines of Grace?, 1–16. Orlando: Reformation Trust, 2008.

Pink, Arthur W. The Attributes of God. Grand Rapids: Baker Books, 2006.

Pink, Arthur W. The Sovereignty of God. Grand Rapids: Baker Book House, 1973.

Poythress, Vern S. Chance and the Sovereignty of God. Wheaton: Crossway, 2014.

Rice, N. L. God Sovereign and Man Free. Harrisonburg, VA: Sprinkle Publications, 1985.

Schreiner, Thomas R. and Bruce A. Ware,

eds. The Grace of God: The Bondage of the Will, 1:25–46, 203–48. Grand Rapids: Baker, 1995.

Scott, Thomas. The Rights of God. London: Forgotten Books, 2015.

Spiegel, James S. The Benefits of Providence. Wheaton: Crossway, 2005.

Sproul, R. C. Does God Control Everything? Orlando: Ligonier/Reformation Trust, 2012.

Sproul, R. C. Not a Chance. Grand Rapids: Baker Books, 1994.

Spurgeon, Charles Haddon. Metropolitan Tabernacle Pulpit, 10:301–12, 58:13–24. Pasadena, TX: Pilgrim Publications, 1981.

Spurgeon, Charles Haddon. New Park Street Pulpit, 2:185–92, 6:253–60. Pasadena, TX: Pilgrim Publications, 1981.

Spurgeon, Charles Haddon. Sermons on Sovereignty, 25–49. Pasadena, TX: Pilgrim Publications, 1990.

Storms, C. Samuel. The Grandeur of God. Grand Rapids: Baker Book House, 1984.

Thomas, D.W.H. "Sovereignty of God." In Martin Davie, et al, eds. New Dictionary of Theology, 858–60. 2nd ed. Downers Grove, IL: InterVarsity Press, 2016.

Treier, Daniel J. and Walter A. Elwell, eds. Evangelical Dictionary of Theology, 3rd ed., 829–31. Grand Rapids: Baker Academic, 2017.

Turretin, Francis. Institutes of Elenctic Theology, 1:250–253. Phillipsburg, NJ: P&R, 1992.

Vass, Larry Ivan. A Reformed View of the Sovereignty of God in a Postmodern World. Baltimore: Publish America, 2008.

Warburton, Ben A. Calvinism, 63–79. Grand Rapids: Eerdmans, 1955.

Ware, Bruce A. God's Greater Glory. Wheaton: Crossway, 2004.

Wells, Tom. God is King! Darlington: Evangelical Press, 1992.

Westblade, Donald J. "The Sovereignty of God in the Theology of Jonathan Edwards." In Sam Storms and Justin Taylor, eds. For the Fame of God's Name: Essays in Honor of John Piper, 105–25. Wheaton: Crossway, 2010.

White, James. The Sovereign Grace of God, 19–46. Lindenhurst: Great Christian Books, 2003.

Absolute Predestination

à Brakel, Wilhelmus. The Christian's Reasonable Service, 1:193–209. Ligonier, PA: Soli Deo Gloria, 1992.

Abendroth, Mike. The Sovereignty and Supremacy of King Jesus, 43–60. Leominster: Day One, 2011.

Ames, William. The Marrow of Theology, 94–100. Boston: Pilgrim Press, 1968.

Bac, J. Martin. Perfect Will Theology: Divine Agency in Reformed Scholasticism as Against Suarez, Episcopius, Descartes, and Spinoza. Leiden: Brill, 2010.

Basinger, David and Randall, eds. Predestination and Free Will. Downers Grove, IL: InterVarsity Press, 1986.

Bavinck, Herman. Reformed Dogmatics, 2:370–74. Grand Rapids: Baker Academic, 2003.

Beardslee, John W., III, ed. Reformed Dogmatics, 45–53, 335–459. New York: Oxford University Press, 1965.

Boettner, Loraine. The Reformed Doctrine of Predestination, 20–29. Philadelphia: Presbyterian and Reformed, 1932.

Boston, Thomas. The Complete Works of the Late Rev. Thomas Boston, 1:149–67. Wheaton: Richard Owen Roberts, 1980.

Boyce, James Petigru. Abstract of Systematic Theology, 115–24. Cape Coral, FL: Founders Press, 2007.

Calvin, John. Calvin's Calvinism. 2nd ed. Edited by Henry Cole and Russell

Dykstra. Jennison: Reformed Free Publishing Association, 2009.

Calvin, John. *Institutes of the Christian Religion*, 3:21–24 (pp. 920–87). Philadelphia: Westminster Press, 1960.

Calvin, John. *Sermons on the Epistle to the Ephesians*, 50–65. London: Banner of Truth, 1973.

Clark, Gordon H. *Predestination*. Phillipsburg, NJ: Presbyterian and Reformed, 1987.

Crabtree, J. A. *The Most Real Being: A Biblical and Philosophical Defense of Divine Determinism*. Eugene: Gutenberg College Press, 2004.

Culver, Robert. *Systematic Theology*, 122–40. Fearn: Mentor, 2005.

Cunningham, William. *The Reformers and the Theology of the Reformation*, 471–524. London: Banner of Truth, 1967.

Dabney, Robert Lewis. *Systematic Theology*, 211–46. Edinburgh: Banner of Truth, 1985.

Edwards, Jonathan. *Our Great and Glorious God*, 54–84. Morgan, PA: Soli Deo Gloria, 2004.

Edwards, Jonathan. *The Works of Jonathan Edwards*, 13:250; 18:392–98. New Haven: Yale University Press, 1994.

Feinberg, John S. "God Ordains All Things." In David Basinger and Randall Basinger, eds. Predestination & Free Will, 17–44. Downers Grove: InterVarsity Press, 1986.

Feinberg, John S. *No One Like Him*, 501–36, 625–76. Wheaton: Crossway, 2001.

Fesko, J. V. *The Theology of the Westminster Standards*, 95–124. Wheaton: Crossway, 2014.

Frame, John M. *The Doctrine of God*, 313–42. Phillipsburg, NJ: P&R, 2002.

Gerstner, John H. *Primitive Theology*, 161–220. Morgan, PA: Soli Deo Gloria, 1996.

Gill, John. *A Complete Body of Doctrinal and Practical Divinity*, 172–91. Paris, AR: Baptist Standard Bearer, 1984.

Grudem, Wayne. *Systematic Theology*, 315–51. Grand Rapids: Zondervan, 1994.

Helm, Paul. "Discrimination: Aspects of God's Causal Activity." In David E. Alexander and Daniel M. Johnson, eds. *Calvin and the Problem of Evil*, 145–67. Eugene: Pickwick, 2016.

Helm, Paul. "Of God's Eternal Decree." In Lynn Quigley, ed. *Reformed Theology in Contemporary Perspective*, 143–61. Edinburgh: Rutherford House, 2006.

Heppe, Heinrich. *Reformed Dogmatics*, 150–89. Grand Rapids: Baker, Book House, 1978.

Hodge, A. A. *Evangelical Theology*, 118–38. Edinburgh: Banner of Truth, 1990.

Hodge, A. A. *Outlines of Theology*, 200–13. Grand Rapids: Zondervan, 1973.

Hodge, Charles. *Systematic Theology*, 1:535–49. Grand Rapids: Eerdmans, 1979.

Hoeksema, Herman. *Reformed Dogmatics*, 1:219–28. 2nd ed. Grandville: Reformed Free Publishing Association, 2004.

Hunt, Dave and James White. *Debating Calvinism*, 35–62. Sisters, OR: Multnomah, 2004.

Kuyper, Abraham. *Common Grace*, 2:103–30. Bellingham, WA: Lexham, 2019.

Lloyd-Jones, D. Martyn. *Great Doctrines of the Bible*, 1:92–102. Wheaton: Crossway, 2003.

Machen, J. Gresham. *The Christian View of Man*, 24–113. London: Banner of Truth, 1965.

MacLeod, Donald. *Behold Your God*, 207–12. Fearn: Christian Focus, 1995.

Matthews, John. *The Divine Purpose*. Vestavia Hills, AL: Solid Ground Christian Books, 2009.

Morecraft, Joseph, III. *Authentic Christianity*, 1:395–420. Powder Springs, GA: Minkoff Family Publishing and American Vision Press, 2009.

Muller, Richard A. *Dictionary of Latin and Greek Theological Terms, Drawn Principally from Protestant Scholastic Theology*, 77, 87, 274–76. 2nd ed. Grand Rapids: Baker Academic, 2017.

Nettleton, Asahel. *Sermons from the Second*

Great Awakening, 180–89. Ames, IA: International Outreach, 1995.

Owen, John. *The Works of John Owen*, 10:14–22. Edinburgh: Banner of Truth, 1976.

Packer, J. I. "The Plan of God." In *Hot Tub Religion*, 19–45. Wheaton: Tyndale House, 1987.

Perkins, William. *A Golden Chaine*, 11–14. N.p.: Puritan Reprints, 2010.

Phillips, Richard D. *Chosen in Christ*, 127–40. Phillipsburg, NJ: P&R, 2004.

Pink, Arthur W. *The Sovereignty of God*. Grand Rapids: Baker Book House, 1973.

Polhill, Edward. *The Works of Edward Polhill*, 114–17. Morgan, PA: Soli Deo Gloria, 1998.

Rice, N. L. *God Sovereign and Man Free*. Harrisonburg, VA: Sprinkle Publications, 1985.

Rouwendal, Pieter. "The Doctrine of Predestination in Reformed Orthodoxy." In Herman J. Selderhuis, ed. *A Companion to Reformed Orthodoxy*, 552–89. Leiden: Brill, 2013.

Shaw, Robert. *The Reformed Faith*, 81–99. Fearn: Christian Heritage, 2008.

Shedd, William G. T. *Calvinism: Pure and Mixed*, 29–68. Edinburgh: Banner of Truth, 1986.

Shedd, William G. T. *Dogmatic Theology*, 311–26. 3rd ed. Phillipsburg, NJ: P&R, 2003.

Smith, Morton H. *Systematic Theology*, 1:155–62. Greenville: Greenville Seminary Press, 1994.

Sproul, R. C. *Chosen by God*, 7–76. Wheaton: Tyndale House, 1986.

Sproul, R. C. *Not a Chance*. Grand Rapids: Baker Books, 1994.

Spurgeon, Charles Haddon. *Metropolitan Tabernacle Pulpit*, 7:465–72. Pasadena, TX: Pilgrim Publications, 1981.

Turretin, Francis. *Institutes of Elenctic Theology*, 1:311–35. Phillipsburg, NJ: P&R, 1992.

Van Dixhoorn, Chad. *Confessing the Faith*, 43–58. Edinburgh: Banner of Truth, 2014.

van Genderen, J. and W. H. Velema. *Concise Reformed Dogmatics*, 193–96. Phillipsburg, NJ: P&R, 2008.

Vos, Geerhardus. *Reformed Dogmatics*, 1:77–96. Bellingham: Lexham Press, 2012.

Warfield, Benjamin Breckinridge. "Predestination." In *Biblical and Theological Studies*, 270–333. Phillipsburg, NJ: Presbyterian and Reformed, 1968.

Warfield, Benjamin Breckinridge. *Selected Shorter Writings of Benjamin B. Warfield*, 1:93–110. Philadelphia: Presbyterian and Reformed, 1970.

Warfield, Benjamin Breckinridge. *Studies in Theology*, 117–234. Edinburgh: Banner of Truth, 1988.

Wright, R. K. McGregor. *No Place for Sovereignty*. Downers Grove, IL: IVP, 1996.

Zanchius, Jerome. *The Doctrine of Absolute Predestination*. Grand Rapids: Baker Book House, 1977.

Foreknowledge

Basinger, David and Randall, eds. *Predestination & Free Will*. Downers Grove, IL: InterVarsity Press, 1986.

Berkhof, Louis. *Systematic Theology*, 66–68. Grand Rapids: Eerdmans, 1988.

Boettner, Loraine. *The Reformed Doctrine of Predestination*, 42–46. Philadelphia: Presbyterian and Reformed, 1932.

Boyce, James Petigru. *Abstract of Systematic Theology*, 86–92. Cape Coral, FL: Founders Press, 2007.

Charnock, Stephen. *The Existence and Attributes of God*, 1:406–97, especially 429–51. Grand Rapids: Baker Book House, 1983.

Clark, Gordon H. *Predestination*, 31–46. Phillipsburg, NJ: Presbyterian and Reformed, 1987.

Crabtree, J. A. "Does Middle Knowledge

Solve the Problem of Divine Sovereignty?" In Thomas R. Schreiner and Bruce A. Ware, eds. *The Grace of God, The Bondage of the Will*, 2:429–58. Grand Rapids: Baker Books, 1995.

R. Schreiner and Bruce A. Ware, eds. *The Most Real Being: A Biblical and Philosophical Defense of Divine Determinism*, 323–54. Eugene: Gutenberg College Press, 2004.

Edwards, Jonathan. *The Works of Jonathan Edwards*, 1:239–69. New Haven: Yale University Press, 1957.

Treier, Daniel J. and Walter A. Elwell, eds. *Evangelical Dictionary of Theology*, 3rd ed., 322–23. Grand Rapids: Baker Academic, 2017.

Erickson, Millard J. *What Does God Know and When Does He Know It?* Grand Rapids: Zondervan, 2003.

Feinberg, John S. *No One Like Him*, 149–83, 299–320, 735–75. Wheaton: Crossway, 2001.

Frame, John M. *The Doctrine of God*, 469–512. Phillipsburg, NJ: P&R, 2002.

Frame, John M. *No Other God*. Phillipsburg, NJ: P&R, 2001.

Frame, John M. *Systematic Theology*, 309–27. Phillipsburg, NJ: P&R, 2013.

Gill, John. *The Cause of God and Truth*, 202–220, 316–28. Grand Rapids: Baker Book House, 1980.

Grudem, Wayne. *Systematic Theology*, 190–93, 676–79. Grand Rapids: Zondervan, 1994.

Helm, Paul. "The Augustinian-Calvinist View." In James K. Beilby and Paul R. Eddy, eds. *Divine Foreknowledge: Four Views*, 161–89. Downers Grove, IL: InterVarsity Press, 2001.

Helm, Paul. "The Philosophical Issue of Divine Foreknowledge." In Thomas R. Schreiner and Bruce A. Ware, eds. *The Grace of God: The Bondage of the Will*, 2:485–97. Grand Rapids: Baker Books, 1995.

Helm, Paul. *Eternal God: A Study of God Without Time*, 73–143. Oxford: Clarendon Press, 1988.

Helm, Paul. *The Providence of God*, 55–60. Downers Grove, IL: IVP, 1994.

Heppe, Heinrich. *Reformed Dogmatics*, 69–81. Grand Rapids: Baker Book House, 1978.

Hodge, Charles. *Systematic Theology*, 1:393–401. Grand Rapids: Eerdmans, 1979.

Hoeksema, Herman. *Reformed Dogmatics*, 1:120–31. 2nd ed. Grandville: Reformed Free Publishing Association, 2004.

Howe, John. *The Works of the Rev. John Howe, M.A.*, 2:474–526. Ligonier, PA: Soli Deo Gloria, 1990.

Hughes, Philip Edgcumbe. *The True Image*, 152–58. Grand Rapids: Eerdmans, 1989.

James, Edgar C. "Is Foreknowledge Equivalent to Foreordination?" In Roy B. Zuck, ed., *Vital Theological Issues*, 21–25. Grand Rapids: Kregel, 1994.

Johnson Gary L. W. and R. Fowler White, eds. *Whatever Happened to the Reformation?*, 59–131. Phillipsburg, NJ: P&R, 2001.

MacArthur, John and Richard Mayhue, eds. *Biblical Doctrine*, 174–77. Wheaton: Crossway, 2017.

Morey, Robert. *Battle of the Gods*. Southbridge: Crown Publishing, 1989.

Muller, Richard A. *Dictionary of Latin and Greek Theological Terms, Drawn Principally from Protestant Scholastic Theology*, 243–44, 280–81, 324–26. 2nd ed. Grand Rapids: Baker Academic, 2017.

Muller, Richard A. *Post-Reformation Reformed Dogmatics*, 3:384–432. 2nd ed. Grand Rapids: Baker Academic, 2003.

Oliphint, K. Scott. *God with Us*, 93–109. Wheaton: Crossway, 2012.

Owen, John. *The Works of John Owen*, 10:22–40. Edinburgh: Banner of Truth, 1976.

Piper, John; Justin Taylor; and Paul Kjoss Helseth, eds. *Beyond the Bounds*. Wheaton: Crossway, 2003.

Sarot, Marcel. "Omniscient and Eternal God." In Maarten Wisse, Marcel Sarst, and Willemien Otten, eds. *Scholasticism Reformed*, 280–302. Leiden: Brill, 2010.

Schreiner, Thomas R. and Bruce A. Ware, eds. *The Grace of God, The Bondage of the*

Will, 1:183–200; 2:429–58, 485–97. Grand Rapids: Baker, 1995.

Storms, C. Samuel. "Open Theism in the Hands of an Angry Puritan: Jonathan Edwards on Divine Foreknowlege." In D. G. Hart, Sean Michael Lucas, and Stephen J. Nichols, eds. *The Legacy of Jonathan Edwards*, 114–30. Grand Rapids: Baker Academic, 2003.

Storms, C. Samuel. *The Grandeur of God*, 61–84, 173–80. Grand Rapids: Baker Book House, 1984.

Strimple, Robert B. "What Does God Know?" In John H. Armstrong, ed. *The Coming Evangelical Crisis*, 139–54. Chicago: Moody Press, 1996.

te Velde, Dolf. *The Doctrine of God in Reformed Orthodoxy, Karl Barth, and the Utrecht School*. Leiden: Brill, 2013.

Turretin, Francis. *Institutes of Elenctic Theology*, 1:206–18. Phillipsburg, NJ: P&R, 992.

Vos, Geerhardus. *Reformed Dogmatics*, 1:16–20. Bellingham: Lexham Press, 2012.

Ware, Bruce A. *God's Lesser Glory*. Wheaton: Crossway, 2000.

Ware, Bruce A., ed. *Perspectives on the Doctrine of God: 4 Views*. Nashville: B&H, 2008.

Warfield, Benjamin B. *The Works of Benjamin B. Warfield*, 2:71–100. Grand Rapids: Baker Book House, 1981.

White, James R. *The Potter's Freedom*, 53–74. Amityville: Calvary Press Publications, 2000.

White, James R. *The Sovereign Grace of God*, 149–83. Lindenhurst: Great Christian Books, 2003.

Wilson, Douglas. *Knowledge, Foreknowledge, & the Gospel*. Moscow, Ida.: Canon Press, n.d.

Wilson, Douglas, ed. *Bound Only Once*. Moscow, Ida.: Canon Press, 2001.

Wright, R. K. *No Place for Sovereignty*. Downers Grove, IL: IVP, 1996.

Providence

à Brakel, Wilhelmus. *The Christian's Reasonable Service*, 1:331–54. Ligonier, PA: Soli Deo Gloria, 1992.

Abendroth, Mike. *The Sovereignty and Supremacy of King Jesus*, 61–88. Leominster: Day One, 2011.

Ames, William. *The Marrow of Theology*, 107–13. Boston: Pilgrim Press, 1968.

Bavinck, Herman. *Reformed Dogmatics*, 2:374–80, 591–619. Grand Rapids: Baker Academic, 2003.

Beardslee, John, III, ed. *Reformed Dogmatics*, 58–61. New York: Oxford University Press, 1965.

Beeke, Joel R. and Mark Jones. *A Puritan Theology*, 161–77. Grand Rapids: Reformation Heritage Books, 2012.

Belcher, Richard. *A Journey in Providence*. Columbia: Richbarry Press, 1999.

Berkouwer, G. C. *The Providence of God*. Grand Rapids: Eerdmans, 1952.

Boettner, Loraine. *The Reformed Doctrine of Predestination*, 35–41. Philadelphia: Presbyterian and Reformed, 1932.

Boston, Thomas. *The Complete Works of the Rev. Thomas Boston*, 1:186–228. Wheaton: Richard Owen Roberts, 1980.

Boyce, James Petigru. *Abstract of Systematic Theology*, 217–29. Cape Coral, FL: Founders Press, 2007.

Brown, John. *The Systematic Theology of John Brown*, 177–91. Fearn: Christian Focus; Grand Rapids: Reformation Heritage Books, 2007.

Bullinger, Henry (Heinrich). *The Decades of Henry Bullinger*, 3:173–84. Grand Rapids: Reformation Heritage Books, 2004.

Calvin, John. *Calvin's Calvinism*. 2nd ed. Edited by Henry Cole and Russell Dykstra. Jennison: Reformed Free Publishing Association, 2009.

Calvin, John. *Institutes of the Christian*

Religion, 1:16–17 (pp.197–228). Philadelphia: Westminster Press, 1960.

Calvin, John. *The Secret Providence of God*. Edited by Paul Helm. Wheaton: Crossway, 2010.

Carson, Alexander. *History of Providence*. Grand Rapids: Baker Book House, 1977.

Charnock, Stephen. *Divine Providence*. Ames, IA: International Outreach, 2006.

Charnock, Stephen. *The Existence and Attributes of God*, 2:295–304. Grand Rapids: Baker Book House, 1979.

Charnock, Stephen. *The Works of Stephen Charnock*, 1:1–120. Edinburgh: Banner of Truth, 1985.

Custance, Arthur C. *Science and Faith, The Doorway Papers*, 8:48–98. Grand Rapids: Zondervan, 1978.

Dabney, Robert Lewis. *Systematic Theology*, 276–91. Edinburgh: Banner of Truth, 1985.

Erskine, Ralph. *The Works of Ralph Erskine*, 6:222–68. Glasgow: Free Presbyterian Publications, 1991.

Farley, Benjamin W. "The Providence of God in Reformed Perspective." In Donald K. McKim, ed. *Major Themes in the Reformed Tradition*, 386–99. Grand Rapids: Eerdmans,1992.

Farley, Benjamin W. *The Providence of God*. Grand Rapids: Baker Book House, 1988.

Feinberg, John S. *No One Like Him*, 625–76. Wheaton: Crossway, 2001.

Flavel, John. *The Mystery of Providence*. London: Banner of Truth, 1963. Also in *The Works of John Flavel*, 4:336–497. Edinburgh: Banner of Truth, 1982.

Frame, John M. *The Doctrine of God*, 274–88. Phillipsburg, NJ: P&R, 2002.

Frame, John M. *Systematic Theology*, 141–83. Phillipsburg, NJ: P&R, 2013.

George, Timothy. *Amazing Grace: God's Pursuit, Our Response*, 35–55. Wheaton: Crossway, 2011.

Gerstner, John H. *The Rational Biblical Theology of Jonathan Edwards*, 2:285–302. Orlando: Ligonier Ministries, 1992.

Gill, John. *A Complete Body of Doctrinal and Practical Divinity*, 277–304. Paris, AR: Baptist Standard Bearer, 1984.

Grudem, Wayne. *Systematic Theology*, 315–54. Grand Rapids: Zondervan, 1994.

Helm, Paul. *Calvin at the Centre*, 132–62. Oxford: Oxford University Press, 2010.

Helm, Paul. *The Providence of God*. Downers Grove, IL: IVP, 1994.

Helseth, Paul Kjoss. "God Causes All Things." In Paul Kjoss Helseth, et al, *Four Views on Divine Providence*, 25–62. Grand Rapids: Zondervan, 2011.

Heppe, Heinrich. *Reformed Dogmatics*, 251–80. Grand Rapids: Baker Book House, 1978.

Hodge, A. A. *Evangelical Theology*, 29–46. Edinburgh: Banner of Truth, 1990.

Hodge, A. A. *Outlines of Theology*, 258–79. Grand Rapids: Zondervan, 1973.

Hodge, Charles. *Systematic Theology*, 1:575–616. Grand Rapids: Eerdmans, 1979.

Hoeksema, Herman. *Reformed Dogmatics*, 1:322–47. 2nd ed. Grandville: Reformed Free Publishing Association, 2004.

Hopkins, Ezekiel. *The Works of Ezekiel Hopkins*, 3:368–88. Morgan, PA: Soli Deo Gloria, 1997.

Horton, Michael. *The Christian Faith*, 350–72. Grand Rapids: Zondervan, 2011.

Lloyd-Jones, D. Martyn. *Great Doctrines of the Bible*, 1:140–52. Wheaton: Crossway, 2003.

MacArthur, John and Richard Mayhue, eds. *Biblical Doctrine*, 218–21. Wheaton: Crossway, 2017.

Matthews, John. *The Divine Purpose*. Birmingham: Solid Ground Christian Books, 2009.

Morecraft, Joseph C., III. *Authentic Christianity*, 1:585–605. Powder Springs, GA: Minkoff Family Publishing and American Vision Press, 2009.

Moulin, Peter (Pierre Du). *The Anatomy of Arminianisme*, 6–20. Norwood: Walter J. Johnson, 1976.

Muller, Richard A. *Dictionary of Latin and Greek Theological Terms, Drawn Principally from Protestant Scholastic Theology*, 73–74, 298–99, 397, 402. 2nd ed. Grand Rapids: Baker Academic, 2017.

Murray, John. *The Collected Writings of John Murray*, 3:161–67. Edinburgh: Banner of Truth, 1976.

Niesel, Wilhelm. *The Theology of Calvin*, 70–79. Philadelphia: Westminster Press,1956.

Olevianus, Caspar. *An Exposition of the Apostles' Creed*, 43–50. Grand Rapids: Reformation Heritage Books, 2009.

Olevianus, Caspar. *A Firm Foundation*, 24–33. Grand Rapids: Baker Books, 1995.

Owen, John. *The Works of John Owen*, 10:30–43. Edinburgh: Banner of Truth, 1976.

Partee, Charles B. "Calvin on Universal and Particular Providence." In Donald K. McKim, ed. *Readings in Calvin's Theology*, 69–88. Grand Rapids: Baker Book House, 1984.

Pink, Arthur W. *The Sovereignty of God*, 41–58. Grand Rapids: Baker Book House, 1973.

Plumer, William S. *Jehovah-Jireh: A Treatise on Providence*. Harrisonburg, VA: Sprinkle Publications, 1993.

Polhill, Edwards. *The Works of Edward Polhill*, 40–52, 138–43. Morgan, PA: Soli Deo Gloria, 1998.

Reardon, P. H. "Calvin on Providence: The Development of an Insight." In Richard C. Gamble, ed. *Articles on Calvin and Calvinism*, 8:333–49. New York: Garland, 1992.

Roberts, Maurice. *The Thought of God*, 30–47. Edinburgh: Banner of Truth, 1992.

Schreiner, Susan E. *The Theater of His Glory: Nature and the Natural Order in the Thought of John Calvin*. Durham: Labyrinth Press, 1991.

Sedgwick, Obadiah. *Providence Handled Practically*. Grand Rapids: Reformation Heritage Books, 2007.

Selderhuis, Herman J., ed. *The Calvin Handbook*, 267–75. Grand Rapids: Eerdmans, 2009.

Shaw, Robert. *The Reformed Faith*, 107–14. Fearn: Christian Heritage, 2008.

Sibbes, Richard. *The Works of Richard Sibbes*, 5:35–54, 249–85. Edinburgh: Banner of Truth, 1978.

Smith, Morton H. *Systematic Theology*, 1:207–24. Greenville, SC: Greenville Seminary Press, 1994.

Spiegel, James S. *The Benefits of Providence*. Wheaton: Crossway, 2005.

Sproul, R. C. *The Invisible Hand*. Dallas: Word Publishing, 1996.

Spurgeon, Charles Haddon. *Metropolitan Tabernacle Pulpit*, 20:613–24, 54:493–503. Pasadena, TX: Pilgrim Publications, 1981.

Spurgeon, Charles Haddon. *New Park Street Pulpit*, 4:177–84. Pasadena, TX: Pilgrim Publications, 1981.

Spurgeon, Charles Haddon. *Sermons on Sovereignty*, 229–56. Pasadena, TX; Pilgrim Publications, 1990.

Talbert, Layton. *Not By Chance*. Greenville: BJU Press, 2001.

te Velde, Dolf, ed. *Synopsis Purioris Theologiae: Synopsis of a Purer Theology*, 1:260–83. Leiden: Brill, 2015.

Thomas, Derek W. H. *What is Providence?* Phillipsburg, NJ: P&R. 2008.

Turretin, Francis. *Institutes of Elenctic Theology*, 1:489–538. Phillipsburg, NJ: P&R, 1992.

Ursinus, Zacharias. *The Commentary of Dr. Zacharias Ursinus on the Heidelberg Catechism*, 148–64. Phillipsburg, NJ: P&R, n.d.

Ussher, James. *A Body of Divinity*, 95–102. Birmingham: Solid Ground Christian Books, 2007.

Van Dixhoorn, Chad. *Confessing the Faith*, 67–82. Edinburgh: Banner of Truth, 2014.

van Genderen, J. and W. H. Velema. *Concise Reformed Dogmatics*, 283–313. Phillipsburg, NJ: P&R, 2008.

VanderGroe, Theodorus. *The Christian's Only Comfort in Life and Death*, 1:151–76. Edited by Bartel Elshout and Joel R. Beeke. Grand Rapids: Reformation Heritage Books, 2016.

Vermigli, Peter Martyr. *The Peter Martyr*

Library, 4:171–96, 328–32. Kirksville, MO: Sixteenth Century Journal Publishers, 1996.

Vos, Geerhardus. *Reformed Dogmatics*, 1:183–202. Bellingham: Lexham Press, 2012.

Walsham, Alexandra. *Providence in Early Modern England*. New York: Oxford University Press, 2007.

Ware, Bruce A. *God's Greater Glory*, 15–32. Wheaton: Crossway, 2004.

Warfield, Benjamin B. *Selected Shorter Writings*, 1:110–15. Phillipsburg, NJ: Presbyterian and Reformed, 1970.

Watson, Thomas. *A Body of Divinity*, 119–27. Edinburgh: Banner of Truth, 1974.

Webster, John. "Providence." In Michael Allen and Scott R. Swain, eds. *Christian Dogmatics*, 148–64. Grand Rapids: Baker Academic, 2016.

Wendel, Francois. *Calvin: The Origins and Development of His Religious Thought*, 177–84. London: Collins, 1963.

Zwingli, Ulrich. *On Providence and Other Essays*. Durham: Labyrinth Press, 1983.

The Will of God

à Brakel, Wilhelmus. *The Christian's Reasonable Service*, 1:112–21. Ligonier, PA: Soli Deo Gloria, 1992.

Bac, J. Martin. *Perfect Will Theology: Divine Agency in Reformed Scholasticism as Against Suarez, Episcopius, Descartes, and Spinoza*. Leiden: Brill, 2010.

Bavinck, Herman. *Reformed Dogmatics*, 2:242–45. Grand Rapids: Baker Academic, 2003.

Berkhof, Louis. *Systematic Theology*, 76–79. Grand Rapids: Eerdmans, 1988.

Boyce, James Petigru. *Abstract of Systematic Theology*, 106–14. Cape Coral, FL: Founders Press, 2007.

Calvin, John. *Sermons on the Epistle to the Ephesians*, 50–65. London: Banner of Truth, 1973.

Christensen, Scott. *What About Free Will?*, 75–92, 203–04. Phillipsburg, NJ: P&R, 2016.

Crisp, Oliver B. *Jonathan Edwards and the Metaphysics of Sin*, 79–95. Aldershot: Ashgate, 2005.

Cunningham, William. *Historical Theology*, 2:451–59. London: Banner of Truth, 1969.

Dabney, Robert Lewis. *Discussions*, 1:282–313. Harrisonburg, VA: Sprinkle Publications, 1982.

Dabney, Robert Lewis. *Systematic Theology*, 161–64. Edinburgh: Banner of Truth, 1985.

Edwards, Jonathan. *The Works of Jonathan Edwards*, 13:170–71, 208; 18:211. New Haven: Yale University Press, 2000.

Forster, Greg. *The Joy of Calvinism*, 183–85. Wheaton: Crossway, 2012.

Frame, John M. *The Doctrine of God*, 528–42. Phillipsburg, NJ: P&R, 2002.

Frame, John M. *Systematic Theology*, 345–56. Phillipsburg, NJ: P&R, 2013.

Gamble, Richard C. *The Whole Counsel of God*, 196–98, 660–63. Phillipsburg, NJ: P&R, 2009.

Gill, John. *A Complete Body of Doctrinal and Practical Divinity*, 70–78. Paris, AR: Baptist Standard Bearer, 1984.

Heppe, Heinrich. *Reformed Dogmatics*, 81–92. Grand Rapids: Baker Book House, 1978.

Hodge, Charles. *Systematic Theology*, 1:402–06. Grand Rapids: Eerdmans, 1979.

Horton, Michael. *The Christian Faith*, 362–64. Grand Rapids: Zondervan, 2011.

Hulse, Erroll. *Who Saves, God or Me?* Darlington: Evangelical Press, 2008.

MacArthur, John and Richard Mayhue, eds. *Biblical Doctrine*, 185–88. Wheaton: Crossway, 2017.

McMahon, C. Matthew. *The Two Wills of God*. New Lenox, IL: Puritan Publications, 2005.

Moulin, Peter (Pierre Du). *The Anatomy of*

Arminianisme, 20–41, 261–82. Norwood: Walter J. Johnson, 1976.

Muller, Richard A. *Dictionary of Latin and Greek Theological Terms, Drawn Principally from Protestant Scholastic Theology*, 2nd ed., 397–402. Grand Rapids: Baker Academic, 2017.

Muller, Richard A. *Divine Will and Human Choice: Freedom, Contingency, and Necessity in Early Modern Reformed Thought*. Grand Rapids: Baker Academic, 2017.

Muller, Richard A. *Post-Reformation Reformed Dogmatics*, 3:432–75. 2nd ed. Grand Rapids: Baker Academic, 2003.

Murray, Iain H. *The Cross: The Pulpit of God's Love*. Edinburgh: Banner of Truth, 2008.

Murray, John. *Collected Writings of John Murray*, 4:113–32. Edinburgh: Banner of Truth, 1982.

Oliphint, K. Scott. *God with Us*, 93–109. Wheaton: Crossway, 2012.

Pink, Arthur W. *The Sovereignty of God*, 297–302. Grand Rapids: Baker Book House, 1973.

Piper, John. "Are There Two Wills in God? Divine Election and God's Desire for All to Be Saved." In Thomas R. Schreiner and Bruce A. Ware, eds. *The Grace of God, The Bondage of the Will*, 1:107–31. Grand Rapids: Baker, 1995.

Piper, John. *Does God Desire All to Be Saved?* Wheaton: Crossway, 2013.

Piper, John. *A Godward Life: Book Two*, 133–35. Sisters, OR: Multnomah, 1999.

Piper, John. *The Pursuit of God's Glory in Salvation*, 139–49. Wheaton: Crossway, 2009.

Sproul, R. C. *Everyone's a Theologian*, 71–75. Orlando: Reformation Trust, 2014.

Spurgeon, Charles Haddon. *Metropolitan Tabernacle Pulpit*, 26:49–60. Pasadena, TX: Pilgrim Publications, 1980.

te Velde, Dolf. *The Doctrine of God in Reformed Orthodoxy, Karl Barth, and the Utrecht School*, 189–204. Leiden: Brill, 2013.

Turretin, Francis. *Institutes of Elenctic Theology*, 1:218–34, 395–417. Phillipsburg, NJ: P&R, 1992.

Vos, Geerhardus. *Reformed Dogmatics*, 1:20–25. Bellingham: Lexham Press, 2012.

Divine Sovereignty and Human Responsibility

Alexander, Archibald. *Sermons of the Log College*, 229–55. Ligonier, PA: Soli Deo Gloria, 1993.

Augustine. *Grace and Free Choice* in *The Works of Saint Augustine*, 1/26:70–106. Hyde Park: New City Press, 1999.

Berkouwer, G. C. *Man: The Image of God*, 310–48. Grand Rapids: Eerdmans, 1962.

Boettner, Loraine. *The Reformed Doctrine of Predestination*, 208–27. Philadelphia: Presbyterian and Reformed, 1932.

Brown, Craig R. *The Five Dilemmas of Calvinism*, 43–58. Orlando: Ligonier Ministries, 2007.

Calvin, John. *Calvin's Calvinism*. 2nd ed. Edited by Henry Cole and Russell Dykstra. Jennison: Reformed Free Publishing Association, 2009.

Carson, D. A. *Divine Sovereignty and Human Responsibility*. Atlanta: John Knox Press, 1981.

Christensen, Scott. *What About Free Will?* Phillipsburg, NJ: P&R, 2016.

Clark, Gordon H. *Predestination*, 110–44. Phillipsburg, NJ: Presbyterian and Reformed, 1987.

Conner, Alan. *The Foundation of Our Faith: God or Man*. Sevierville, Tenn.: Covenant House Books, 1992.

Crisp, Oliver D. *Saving Calvinism: Expanding the Reformed Tradition*, 67–86. Downers Grove, IL: IVP Academic, 2016.

Cunningham, William. *The Reformers and the Theology of the Reformation*, 471–524. Edinburgh: Banner of Truth, 1979.

Custance, Arthur C. *Time and Eternity and Other Biblical Studies, The Doorway Papers*, 6:163–74. Grand Rapids: Zondervan, 1977.

Dabney, Robert Lewis. *Systematic Theology*, 120–32. Edinburgh: Banner of Truth, 1985.

Edwards, Jonathan. "The Freedom of the Will." In *The Works of Jonathan Edwards, Volume 1*. New Haven: Yale University Press, 1957.

Feinberg, John S. "God Ordains All Things." In David and Randall Basinger, eds. *Predestination & Free Will*, 17–43. Downers Grove, IL: InterVarsity Press, 1986.

Feinberg, John S. *No One Like Him*, 677–776. Wheaton: Crossway, 2001.

Forster, Greg. *The Joy of Calvinism*, 171–80. Wheaton: Crossway, 2012.

Frame, John M. *The Doctrine of God*, 119–59. Phillipsburg, NJ: P&R, 2002.

Frame, John M. *Systematic Theology*, 823–42. Phillipsburg, NJ: P&R, 2013.

Gerstner, John H. *The Early Writings*, 1:255–74. Morgan, PA: Soli Deo Gloria, 1997.

Girardeau, John Lafeyette. *Calvinism and Evangelical Arminianism*, 394–412. Harrisonburg, VA: Sprinkle Publications, 1984.

Greenway, Leonard. "The Sovereignty of God and Human Responsibility." In Jacob T. Hoogstra, ed. *The Sovereignty of God*, 184–95. Vestavia Hills: Solid Ground Christian Books, n.d.

Helm, Paul. *Calvin at the Centre*, 227–72. Oxford: Oxford University Press, 2010.

Helm, Paul. *Eternal God*, 144–70. Oxford: Clarendon Press, 1988.

Helm, Paul. *The Providence of God*, 161–92. Downers Grove, IL: IVP, 1994.

Luther, Martin. *The Bondage of the Will*. Cambridge: James Clarke, 1957.

Machen, J. Gresham. *The Christian View of Man*, 35–45. London: Banner of Truth, 1965.

MacMillan, J. Douglas. *The God of All Grace*, 136–41. Fearn: Christian Focus, 1993.

Martin, Hugh. *Christ for Us*, 114–38. Edinburgh: Banner of Truth, 1998.

Matthews, John. *The Divine Purpose*, 40–57, 74–92. Vestavia Hills: Solid Ground Christian Books, 2009.

Muller, Richard A. *Divine Will and Human Choice: Freedom, Contingency, and Necessity in Early Modern Reformed Thought*. Grand Rapids: Baker, 2017.

Murray, Iain H. *Pentecost — Today? The Biblical Basis for Understanding Revival*, 54–79, 200–215. Edinburgh: Banner of Truth, 1998.

Packer, J. A. *Evangelism and the Sovereignty of God*. Downers Grove, IL: InterVarsity Press, 1961.

Perkins, William. *The Works of William Perkins*, 6:385–443. Grand Rapids: Reformation Heritage Books, 2018.

Peterson, Robert A. and Michael D. Williams. *Why I Am Not an Arminian*, 136–61. Downers Grove: IVP, 2004.

Pink, Arthur W. *The Sovereignty of God*, 157–202. Grand Rapids: Baker Book House, 1973.

Poythress, Vern S. *Chance and the Sovereignty of God*, 53–62. Wheaton: Crossway, 2014.

Reisinger, Ernest C. *God's Will, Man's Will and Free Will*, 35–46. N.p.: Frontline Ministries, n.d.

Reymond, Robert L. *A New Systematic Theology of the Christian Faith*, 346–72. Nashville: Thomas Nelson, 1998.

Rice, N. L. *God Sovereign and Man Free*. Harrisonburg, VA: Sprinkle Publications, 1985.

Sproul, R. C. *Chosen by God*, 49–76. Wheaton: Tyndale House, 1986.

Spurgeon, Charles Haddon. *Metropolitan Tabernacle Pulpit*, 8:181–92. Pasadena, TX: Pilgrim Publications, 1981.

Spurgeon, Charles Haddon. *New Park Street Pulpit*, 4:233–40, 337–44. Pasadena, TX: Pilgrim Publications, 1981.

van Asselt, Willem J., et al, eds. *Reformed Thought on Freedom: The Concept of Free Choice in Early Modern Reformed Theology*. Grand Rapids: Baker Academic, 2010.

Vass, Larry Ivan. *A Reformed View of the Sovereignty of God in a Postmodern World*, 143–55. Baltimore: PublishAmerica, 2008.

Venema, Cornelis P. *But for the Grace of God:*

An Exposition of the Canons of Dort, 101–11. Grandville: Reformed Fellowship, 2011.

Vermigli, Peter Martyr. *The Peter Martyr Library*, 8:68–82. Kirksville, MO: Truman State University Press, 2003.

Ware, Bruce A. "The Compatibility of Determinism and Human Freedom" in Matthew Barrett and Thomas J. Nettles,

eds. *Whomever He Wills*, 212–30. Cape Coral, FL: Founders Press, 2012.

Ware, Bruce A. *God's Greater Glory*, 61–160. Wheaton: Crossway, 2004.

Wright, R. K. McGregor. *No Place for Sovereignty*. Downers Grove, IL: IVP, 1996.

Prayer and the Sovereignty of God

Abendroth, Mike. *The Sovereignty and Supremacy of King Jesus*, 151–64. Leominster: Day One, 2011.

Beck, Peter. *The Voice of Faith: Jonathan Edwards's Theology of Prayer*. Dundas: Joshua Press, 2010.

Beeke, Joel R. "The Communion of Men with God." In Burk Parsons, ed. *John Calvin: A Heart for Devotion, Doctrine & Doxology*, 231–46. Orlando: Reformation Trust, 2008.

Brown, Craig R. *The Five Dilemmas of Calvinism*, 77–88. Orlando: Ligonier Ministries, 2007.

Calvin, John. *Institutes of the Christian Religion*, 3:20:1–52 (pp. 850–920). Philadelphia: Westminster Press, 1960.

Carson, D. A. *A Call to Spiritual Reformation: Priorities from Paul and His Prayers*. Grand Rapids: Baker, 1992.

Christensen, Scott. *What About Free Will?*, 124–27. Phillipsburg, NJ: P&R, 2016.

Crisp, Oliver D. "John Calvin and Petitioning God." In *Retrieving Doctrine: Essays in Reformed Theology*, 133–55. Downers Grove, IL: IVP, 2010.

Gale, Stanley D. *Why Do We Pray?* Phillipsburg, NJ: P&R, 2012.

Hannah, John D. "Prayer and the Sovereignty of God." In Roy B. Zuck, ed. *Vital Theological Issues*, 11–20. Grand Rapids: Kregel, 1994.

Helm, Paul. *The Providence of God*, 145–60. Downers Grove, IL: IVP, 1994.

Kelly, Douglas. *If God Already Knows, Why Pray?* Fearn: Christian Focus, 1995.

Lloyd-Jones, D. Martyn. *Saved in Eternity*, 23–38. Wheaton: Crossway, 1988.

Morecraft, Joseph C., III. *Authentic Christianity*, 5:487–572. Powder Springs, GA: Minkoff Family Publishing and American Vision Press, 2009.

Palmer, B. M. *Theology of Prayer as Viewed in the Religion of Nature and in the System of Grace*. Harrisonburg, VA: Sprinkle Publications, 1980.

Partee, Charles. "Prayer and the Practice of Predestination." In Richard C. Gamble, ed. *Articles on Calvin and Calvinism*, 8:357–68. New York: Garland, 1992.

Phillips, Richard D. *Chosen in Christ*, 229–41. Phillipsburg, NJ: P&R, 2004.

Pink, Arthur W. *The Sovereignty of God*, 203–20. Grand Rapids: Baker Book House, 1973.

Piper, John. *A Godward Life*, 144–46. Sisters, OR: Multnomah, 1997.

Piper, John. *The Pleasures of God*, 212–38. Portland: Multnomah, 1991.

Samson, John. *Twelve What Abouts: Answering Common Objections Concerning God's Sovereignty in Election*, 135–42. Birmingham.: Solid Ground Christian Books, 2012.

Sproul, R. C. "Prayer and God's Sovereignty." In James Montgomery Boice, ed. *Our Sovereign God*, 127–36. Grand Rapids: Baker Book House, 1977.

Sproul, R. C. *Does Prayer Change Things?* Orlando: Ligonier Ministries, 1999.

Sproul, R. C. *Now That's a Good Question*, 195–216. Wheaton: Tyndale House, 1996.

Sproul, R. C. *The Prayer of the Lord*, 113–24. Orlando: Reformation Trust, 2009.

Storms, C. Samuel. "Prayer and Evangelism under God's Sovereignty." In Thomas R. Schreiner and Bruce A. Ware, eds. *Still Sovereign*, 307–23. Grand Rapids: Baker Books, 2000.

Storms, C. Samuel. *Chosen for Life*, Rev. ed., 201–11. Wheaton: Crossway, 2007.

Talbert, Layton. *Not By Chance*, 213–31. Greenville, SC: BJU Press, 2001.

Tiessen, Terrance L. *Providence and Prayer.* Downers Grove, IL: InterVarsity Press, 2000.

Ware, Bruce A. "Prayer and the Sovereignty of God." In Sam Storms and Justin Taylor, eds. *For the Fame of God's Name: Essays in Honor of John Piper*, 126–43. Wheaton: Crossway, 2010.

Ware, Bruce A. *God's Greater Glory*, 181–94. Wheaton: Crossway, 2004.

Watson, Thomas. *The Lord's Prayer*, 151–93. Edinburgh: Banner of Truth, 1978.

The Glory of God

Beeke, Joel R. "Seeing God's Glory." In Joseph A. Pipa Jr. and J. Andrew Wortman, eds. *Reformed Spirituality: Communing with Our Glorious God*, 19–28. Taylors: Southern Presbyterian Press, 2003.

Belcher, Richard P. *A Journey in God's Glory*. Fort Mill: Richbarry Press, 2005.

Binning, Hugh. *The Works of the Rev. Hugh Binning*, 3–8. Ligonier, PA: Soli Deo Gloria, 1992.

Boston, Thomas. *The Complete Works of the Late Rev. Thomas Boston*, 1:9–18. Wheaton: Richard Owen Roberts, 1980.

Edwards, Jonathan. "Concerning the End for Which God Created the World." In *The Works of Jonathan Edwards*, 8:403–536. New Haven: Yale University Press, 1989.

Edwards, Jonathan. *The Glory and Honor of God*, 223–44. Nashville: Broadman & Holman, 2004.

Edwards, Jonathan. *Our Great and Glorious God*, 85–94. Morgan, PA: Soli Deo Gloria, 2004.

Edwards, Jonathan. *The Works of Jonathan Edwards*, 13:152–252, 256, 272–77, 358–61, 374, 410, 419–21, 492–96, 502–03; 18:97, 117; 20:462–67, 482–83, 516–17; 23:131–41, 150–53, 213; 25:111–26. New Haven: Yale University Press, 1994.

Hall, John. *The Chief End of Man*. Birmingham: Solid Ground Christian Books, 2005.

Hannah, John D. *How Do We Glorify God?* Phillipsburg, NJ: P&R, 2008.

Holmes, Stephen R. *God of Grace and God of Glory*. Edinburgh: T. and T. Clark, 2000.

Hopkins, Ezekiel. *The Works of Ezekiel Hopkins*, 2:590–708. Morgan, PA: Soli Deo Gloria, 1997.

Krisanto, Billy. *Soli Deo Gloria: The Glory of God in the Thought of John Calvin*. New York: Peter Lang, 2011.

Kuizenga, Henry. "The Relation of God's Grace to His Glory in John Calvin." In Richard C. Gamble, ed. *Articles on Calvin and Calvinism*, 9:73–85. New York: Garland, 1997.

Lawson, Steven J. *Made in Our Image*, 151–64. Sisters, OR: Multnomah, 2000.

Lloyd-Jones, D. Martyn. *God's Ultimate Purpose*, 128–36. Grand Rapids: Baker Book House, 1978.

MacArthur, John. *The Gospel According to Paul*, 165–71. Nashville: Nelson Books, 2017.

MacArthur, John. *Our Awesome God*, 135–44. Wheaton: Crossway, 1993.

Morgan, Christopher W. and Robert A. Peterson, eds. *The Glory of God*. Wheaton: Crossway, 2010.

Muller, Richard A. *Post-Reformation Reformed Dogmatics*, 3:540–51. 2nd ed. Grand Rapids: Baker Academic, 2003.

Packer, J. I. *Hot Tub Religion*, 19–45. Wheaton: Tyndale House, 1987.

Pipa, Joseph A., Jr. "The Glory and Beauty of God." In Joseph A. Pipa Jr. and J. Andrew Wortman, eds. *Reformed Spirituality: Communing with Our Glorious God*, 1–18. Taylors: Southern Presbyterian Press, 2003.

Piper, John. "Jesus Christ as Denouement in the Theater of Glory: Calvin and the Supremacy of Christ in All Things." In John Piper and David Mathis, eds. *With Calvin in the Theater of God*, 133–45. Wheaton: Crossway, 2010.

Piper, John. *Desiring God*. Portland: Multnomah, 1986.

Piper, John. *God's Passion for His Glory*. Wheaton: Crossway, 1998.

Ryrie, Charles C. *Transformed by His Glory*. Wheaton: Victor Books, 1990.

Schreiner, Thomas R. "A Biblical Theology of the Glory of God." In Sam Storms and Justin Taylor, eds. *For the Fame of God's Name*, 215–34. Wheaton: Crossway, 2010.

Shedd, William G. T. *Sermons to the Spiritual Man*, 99–115. London: Banner of Truth, 1972.

Spurgeon, Charles Haddon. *Metropolitan Tabernacle Pulpit*, 48:37–45; 54:565–74; 61:97–107. Pasadena, TX: Pilgrim Publications, 1981.

Storms, Sam. *One Thing: Developing a Passion for the Beauty of God*. Fearn: Christian Focus, 2004.

Strong, Augustus Hopkins. *Systematic Theology*, 397–402. Old Tappan: Fleming H. Revell, 1979.

VanDrunnen, David. *God's Glory Alone*. Grand Rapids: Zondervan, 2015.

Warfield, Benjamin B. *Selected Shorter Writings of Benjamin B. Warfield*, 1:130–35. Nutley: Presbyterian and Reformed, 1970.

The Origin of Sin

à Brakel, Wilhelmus. *The Christian's Reasonable Service*, 1:339–48. Ligonier, PA: Soli Deo Gloria, 1992.

Adams, Jay. *The Grand Demonstration: A Biblical Study of the So-Called Problem of Evil*. Santa Barbara: EastGate Publishers, 1991.

Alexander, David E. and Daniel M. Johnson, eds. *Calvinism and the Problem of Evil*. Eugene: Pickwick, 2016.

Augustine. "Divine Providence and the Problem of Evil." In *The Fathers of the Church*, 5:229–332. Washington, D.C.: Catholic University of America Press, 1948.

Augustine. *Confessions*, 7:3:4–5:7, 11:17–13:19. *The Works of Saint Augustine*, 1/1: 161–64, 174–75. Hyde Park: New City Press, 1997.

Bavinck, Herman. *Reformed Dogmatics*, 2:240–41, 3:25–74. Grand Rapids: Baker Academic, 2003.

Beeke, Joel R. *Debated Issues in Sovereign Predestination*. Göttingen: Vandenhoeck & Ruprecht, 2017.

Bellamy, Joseph. "The Wisdom of God in the Permission of Sin." In *The Works of Joseph Bellamy*, 2:3–155. New York: Garland, 1987.

Berkhof, Louis. *Systematic Theology*, 78, 174–75, 219–26. Grand Rapids: Eerdmans, 1988.

Berkouwer, G. C. *Sin*, 1–148. Grand Rapids: Eerdmans, 1971.

Boettner, Loraine. *The Reformed Doctrine of Predestination*, 228–53. Philadelphia: Presbyterian and Reformed, 1932.

Brown, Craig R. *The Five Dilemmas of Calvinism*, 89–102. Orlando: Ligonier Ministries, 2007.

Bullinger, Henry (Heinrich). *The Decades of Henry Bullinger*, 2:361–84. Grand Rapids: Reformation Heritage Books, 2004.

Byrne, Peter. "Helm's God and the Authorship of Sin." In M. W. F. Stone, ed. *Reason and History*, 193–204. Aldershot: Ashgate, 2008.

Charnock, Stephen. *The Existence and*

Attributes of God, 2:139–71. Grand Rapids: Baker Book House, 1983.

Clark, Gordon H. *God and Evil: The Problem Solved*. Unicoi: Trinity Foundation, 2004.

Clark, Gordon H. *Religion, Reason and Revelation*, 194–241. Jefferson: Trinity Foundation, 1986.

Crisp, Oliver B. *Jonathan Edward and the Metaphysics of Sin*, 54–78. Aldershot: Ashgate, 2005.

Custance, Arthur C. *The Flood: Local or Global?*, *The Doorway Papers*, 9:109–63. Grand Rapids: Zondervan, 1979.

Custance, Arthur C. *The Sovereignty of Grace*, 263–74. Phillipsburg, NJ: Presbyterian and Reformed, 1979.

Edwards, Jonathan. *Our Great and Glorious God*, 66–75. Morgan, PA: Soli Deo Gloria, 2004.

Edwards, Jonathan. *The Works of Jonathan Edwards*, 1:397–414; 13:382–83, 533–35; 18:408–09. New Haven: Yale University Press, 1957.

Evans, G. R. *Augustine on Evil*. Cambridge: Cambridge University Press, 1991.

Feinberg, John S. *The Many Faces of Evil*. Wheaton: Crossway, 2004.

Forster, Greg. *The Joy of Calvinism*, 180–83. Wheaton: Crossway, 2012.

Frame, John M. *The Doctrine of God*, 160–82. Phillipsburg, NJ: P&R, 2002.

Gamble, Richard C. *The Whole Counsel of God*, 187–201. Phillipsburg, NJ: P&R, 2009.

Gerstner, John H. *The Rational Biblical Theology of Jonathan Edwards*, 2:301–14. Orlando: Ligonier Ministries, 1992.

Helm, Paul. *The Providence of God*, 161–216. Downers Grove, IL: InterVarsity Press, 1994.

Hodge, Charles. *Systematic Theology*, 1:543–49. Grand Rapids: Eerdmans, 1979.

Hoekema, Anthony. *Created in God's Image*, 112–32. Grand Rapids: Eerdmans, 1986.

Hopkins, Samuel. *The Works of Samuel Hopkins*, 2:527–46. New York: Garland, 1987.

Hughes, Philip Edgcumb. *The True Image*, 73–111. Grand Rapids: Eerdmans, 1989.

Kersten, G. H. *Reformed Dogmatics*, 1:212–15. Sioux Center: Netherlands Reformed Book and Publishing Committee, 1980.

Lloyd-Jones, D. Martyn. *The Christian Warfare*, 66–78. Grand Rapids: Baker Book House, 1976.

Luther, Martin. *Luther's Works*, 25:160–66. St. Louis: Concordia Publishing House, 1972.

Lyford, William. *The Instructed Christian*, 102–10. Morgan, PA: Soli Deo Gloria, n.d.

Mathewes, Charles T. *Evil and the Augustinian Tradition*. Cambridge: Cambridge University Press, 2001.

McLemore, Paul D. *God's Sovereignty and the Law of Causation*, 119–60. N.p.: Xulon Press, 2014.

Morecraft, Joseph C., III. *Authentic Christianity*, 1:651–57, 681–83. Powder Springs, GA: Minkoff Family Publishing and American Vision Press, 2009.

Muller, Richard A. *Dictionary of Latin and Greek Theological Terms, Drawn Principally from Protestant Scholastic Theology*, 202–03. 2nd ed. Grand Rapids: Baker Academic, 2017.

Oliphint, K. Scott. *Reasons for Faith*, 259–77. Phillipsburg, NJ: P&R, 2006.

Plantinga, Alvin C. *God, Freedom, and Evil*. Grand Rapids: Eerdmans, 1974.

Plantinga, Alvin C. *The Nature of Necessity*. Oxford: Clarendon Press, 1974.

Rehnman, Sebastian. "An Edwardsean Theodicy." In Maarten Wisse, Marcel Sarot and Willemien Otten, eds. *Scholasticism Reformed*, 303–21. Leiden: Brill, 2010.

Reymond, Robert L. *A New Systematic Theology of the Christian Faith*, 372–78. Nashville: Thomas Nelson, 1998.

Shedd, William G. T. *Calvinism: Pure and Mixed*, 84–91. Edinburgh: Banner of Truth, 1986.

Shedd, William G. T. *Dogmatic Theology*, 318–22. 3rd ed. Phillipsburg, NJ: P&R, 2003.

Spurgeon, Charles Haddon. "God's

Foreknowledge of Man's Sin." In *Metropolitan Tabernacle Pulpit*, 13:613–24. Pasadena, TX: Pilgrim Publications, 1989.

Vermigli, Peter Martyr. *The Peter Martyr Library*, 4:215–70, 333–34. Kirksville, MO:

Sixteenth Century Journal Publishers, 1996.

Wright, R. K. McGregor. *No Place for Sovereignty*, 177–204. Downers Grove, IL: IVP, 1996.

The Problem of Evil

Adams, Jay. *The Grand Demonstration: A Biblical Study of the So-Called Problem of Evil*. Santa Barbara: EastGate, 1991.

Alexander, David E. and Daniel M. Johnson, eds. *Calvinism and the Problem of Evil*. Eugene: Pickwick, 2016.

Augustine. "Divine Providence and the Problem of Evil." In *The Fathers of the Church*, 5:229–332. Washington, D.C.: Catholic University of America Press, 1948.

Bahnsen, Greg L. *Always Ready*, 163–75. Atlanta: American Vision, 1996.

Berkouwer, G. C. *The Providence of God*, 251–94. Grand Rapids: Eerdmans, 1952.

Blanchard, John. *Does God Believe in Atheists?*, 517–54. Darlington: Evangelical Press, 2000.

Blanchard, John. *Where Was God on September 11?* Darlington: Evangelical Press, 2002.

Boston, Thomas. "The Crook in the Lot." In *The Complete Works of the Late Rev. Thomas Boston*, 3:495–590. Wheaton: Richard Owen Roberts, 1980.

Calvin, John. *Calvin: Theological Treatises*, 331–43. Philadelphia: Westminster Press, 1954.

Calvin, John. *Sermons on Job*. Edinburgh: Banner of Truth, 1993.

Calvin, John. *Suffering — Understanding the Love of God*. Edited by Joseph Hill. Darlington: Evangelical Press, 2005.

Calvin, John. *Treatises Against the Anabaptists and Against the Libertines*, 238–58. Grand Rapids: Baker Book House, 1982.

Carson, D. A. "How Can We Reconcile the Love and the Transcendent Sovereignty of God?" In Douglas S. Huffman and Eric L. Johnson, eds. *God Under Fire*, 279–312. Grand Rapids: Zondervan, 2002.

Carson, D. A. *How Long, O Lord?* 2nd ed. Grand Rapids: Baker Books, 2006.

Christensen, Scott. *What About Free Will?*, 61–72, 112–33. Phillipsburg, NJ: P&R, 2016.

Clark, D. Marion. *The Problem of Good*. Phillipsburg, NJ: P&R, 2014.

Clark, Gordon H. *God and Evil: The Problem Solved*. Unicoi: Trinity Foundation, 2004.

Clark, Gordon H. *Religion, Reason and Revelation*, 194–241. Jefferson: Trinity Foundation, 1986.

Clotfelter, David. *Sinners in the Hands of a Good God*. Chicago: Moody Press, 2004.

Cosby, Brian H. *Suffering and Sovereignty: John Flavel and the Puritans on Afflictive Providence*. Grand Rapids: Reformation Heritage Books, 2012.

Cunningham, William. *Historical Theology*, 1:625–39. London: Banner of Truth, 1967.

Currid, John. *Why Do I Suffer? Suffering and the Sovereignty of God*. Fearn: Christian Focus, 2004.

Custance, Arthur C. *The Flood: Local or Global* in *The Doorway Papers*, 9:109–63. Grand Rapids: Zondervan, 1979.

de Petris, Paolo. *Calvin's Theodicy and the Hiddenness of God: Calvin's Sermons on the Book of Job*. New York: Peter Lang, 2012.

Duncan, J. Ligon. *Does Grace Grow Best in Winter?* Phillipsburg, NJ: P&R, 2009.

Feinberg, John S. "God, Freedom and Evil in Calvinist Thinking." In Thomas R. Schreiner and Bruce A. Ware, eds. *The Grace of God, The Bondage of the Will*, 2:459–83. Grand Rapids: Baker Books, 1995.

Bruce A. Ware, eds. *The Many Faces of Evil*. Wheaton: Crossway, 2004.

Bruce A. Ware, eds. *No One Like Him*, 777–96. Wheaton: Crossway, 2001.

Bruce A. Ware, eds. *Theologies and Evil*. Washington, D.C.: University Press of America, 1979.

Frame, John M. *Systematic Theology*, 282–303. Phillipsburg, NJ: P&R, 2013.

Gerstner, John H. *The Problem of Pleasure*. Phillipsburg, NJ: Presbyterian and Reformed, 1983. Also in: *Primitive Theology*, 415–42. Morgan, PA: Soli Deo Gloria, 1996.

Gill, John. *A Complete Body of Doctrinal and Practical Divinity*, 300–304. Paris, AR: Baptist Standard Bearer, 1984.

Grudem, Wayne. *Systematic Theology*, 322–30. Grand Rapids: Zondervan, 1994.

Helm, Paul. *John Calvin's Ideas*, 93–120. Oxford: Oxford University Press, 2004.

Helm, Paul. *The Providence of God*, 193–216. Downers Grove, IL: IVP, 1994.

Hodge, Charles. *Systematic Theology*, 1:589–90. Grand Rapids: Eerdmans, 1979.

Leahy, Fredrick. *The Hand of God*. Edinburgh: Banner of Truth, 2006.

Lloyd-Jones, D. Martyn. *Faith on Trial*. London: InterVarsity Fellowship, 1965.

Lloyd-Jones, D. Martyn. *Why Does God Allow Suffering?* Wheaton: Crossway, 1994.

MacArthur, John and Richard Mayhue, eds. *Biblical Doctrine*, 221–26, 474–75, 491–93. Wheaton: Crossway, 2017.

Macleod, Donald. *Behold Your God*, 25–30. Fearn: Christian Focus, 1995.

McManis, Clifford B. *Biblical Apologetics*, 457–515. N.p.: XLibris, 2012.

Morgan, Christopher W. and Robert A. Peterson, eds. *Suffering and the Goodness of God*. Wheaton: Crossway, 2008.

Murray, John J. *Behind a Frowning Providence*. Edinburgh: Banner of Truth, 1990.

Pink, Arthur W. *Comfort for Christians*. Grand Rapids: Baker Book House, 1990.

Piper, John and Justin Taylor, eds. *Suffering and the Sovereignty of God*. Wheaton: Crossway, 2006.

Piper, John. *The Misery of Job and the Mercy of God*. Wheaton: Crossway, 2002.

Piper, John. *Spectacular Sins and Their Global Purpose in the Glory of Christ*. Wheaton: Crossway, 2008.

Piper, John. *A Sweet and Bitter Providence*. Wheaton: Crossway Books, 2010.

Plantinga, Theodore. *Learning to Live with Evil*. Burlington: G. R. Welch, 1982.

Plumer, William S. *Jehovah-Jireh: A Treatise on Providence*. Harrisonburg, VA: Sprinkle Publications, 1993.

Spiegel, James S. *The Benefits of Providence*, 183–212. Wheaton: Crossway Books, 2005.

Spinney, Robert G. *Why Do Bad Things Happen to Good People? Thinking Biblically About the Problem of Sin in Our World*. Hartsville: Tulip Books, 2006.

Sproul, R. C. *Chosen by God*, 28–39. Wheaton: Tyndale House, 1986.

Sproul, R. C. *The Invisible Hand*. Dallas: Word Publishing, 1996.

Sproul, R. C. *Surprised by Suffering: The Role of Pain and Death in the Christian Life*. Orlando: Reformation Trust, 2009.

Spurgeon, Charles Haddon. *The Suffering of Man and the Sovereignty of God*. Oswego: Fox River Press, 2001.

Talbot, Mark R. "Bad Actors on a Broken Stage: Sin and Suffering in Calvin's World and Ours." In John Piper and David Mathis, eds. *With Calvin in the Theater of God*, 53–81. Wheaton: Crossway, 2010.

Thomas, Derek. *Calvin's Teaching on Job*. Fearn: Mentor/Christian Focus, 2004.

Turretin, Francis. *Institutes of Elenctic Theology*, 1:515–38. Phillipsburg, NJ: P&R, 1992.

van Genderen, J. and W. H. Velema. *Concise Reformed Dogmatics*, 305–13. Phillipsburg, NJ: P&R, 2008.

Vincent, Thomas. *God's Terrible Voice in the City*. Morgan, PA: Soli Deo Gloria, 1997.

Ware, Bruce A. *God's Greater Glory*, 163–80. Wheaton: Crossway, 2004.

Watson, Thomas. *All Things for Good*. Edinburgh: Banner of Truth, 1986.

Wellum, Stephen J. "God's Sovereignty Over Evil." In Matthew Barrett and Thomas J. Nettles, eds. *Whomever He Wills*, 231–68. Cape Coral, FL: Founders Press, 2012.

Wright, R. K. McGregor. *No Place for Sovereignty*, 177–204. Downers Grove, IL: IVP, 1996.

Original Sin

à Brakel, Wilhelmus. *The Christian's Reasonable Service*, 1:381–405. Ligonier, PA: Soli Deo Gloria, 1992.

Alexander, Archibald. "Original Sin." In Charles Hodge, et al. *Princeton versus the New Divinity*, 90–114. Edinburgh: Banner of Truth, 2001.

Bavinck, Herman. *Reformed Dogmatics*, 3:75–125. Grand Rapids: Baker Academic, 2003.

Beatrice, Pier Franco. *The Transmission of Sin: Augustine and the Pre-Augustinian Sources.* Oxford: Oxford University Press, 2013.

Berkouwer, G. C. *The Providence of God*, 232–75. Grand Rapids: Eerdmans, 1980.

Berkouwer, G. C. *Sin*, 424–567. Grand Rapids: Eerdmans, 1971.

Blocher, Henri A. G. *Original Sin: Illuminating the Riddle.* Leicester: Apollos, 1997.

Boston, Thomas. *The Complete Works of the Late Rev. Thomas Boston*, 1:273–75, 11:233–50. Wheaton: Richard Owen Roberts, 1980.

Boyce, James Petigru. *Abstract of Systematic Theology*, 230–58. Cape Coral, FL: Founders Press, 2007.

Bucer, Martin. *Common Places of Martin Bucer*, 119–42. Edited by David F. Wright. Appleford: Sutton Courtenay, 1977.

Bullinger, Henry (Heinrich). *The Decades of Henry Bullinger*, 2:384–400. Grand Rapids: Reformation Heritage Books, 2004.

Clark, Gordon H. *The Biblical Doctrine of Man*, 45–71. Jefferson: Trinity Foundation, 1984.

Clarkson, David. *The Works of David Clarkson*, 1:3–15. Edinburgh: Banner of Truth, 1988.

Crisp, Oliver B. "Jonathan Edwards on the Imputation of Sin." In *Retrieving Doctrine: Essays in Reformed Theology*, 47–68. Downers Grove, IL: InterVarsity Press, 2010.

Crisp, Oliver B. *An American Augustinian: Sin and Salvation in the Dogmatic Theology of William G. T. Shedd*, 12–55. Milton Keynes: Paternoster, 2007.

Crisp, Oliver B. *Jonathan Edwards and the Metaphysics of Sin*, 25–53, 96–129. Aldershot: Ashgate, 2005.

Culver, Robert. *Systematic Theology*, 378–405. Fearn: Mentor, 2005.

Cunningham, William. *Historical Theology*, 1:496–567. London: Banner of Truth, 1969.

Cunningham, William. *The Reformers and the Theology of the Reformation*, 371–95. London: Banner of Truth, 1969.

Dabney, Robert Lewis. *Systematic Theology*, 306–51. Edinburgh: Banner of Truth, 1985.

Dickinson, Jonathan. *The True Scripture Doctrine Concerning Some Important Points of Christian Faith*, 70–136. Harrisonburg, VA: Sprinkle Publications, 1992.

Edwards, Jonathan. "Original Sin." In *The Works of Jonathan Edwards, Volume 3*. New Haven: Yale University Press, 1970.

Gamble, Richard C. *The Whole Counsel of God*, 199–217. Phillipsburg, NJ: P&R, 2009.

Gerstner, John H. *The Rational Biblical Theology of Jonathan Edwards*, 2:323–35. Orlando: Ligonier Ministries, 1992.

Gerstner, John H. *Theology in Dialogue*, 187–97, 251–70. Morgan, PA: Soli Deo Gloria, 1996.

Girardeau, John Lafayette. *Calvinism and Evangelical Arminianism*, 197–274. Harrisonburg, VA: Sprinkle Publications, 1984.

Goodwin, Thomas. *The Works of Thomas Goodwin, Volume 10*. Eureka, CA: Tanski, 1996.

Grudem, Wayne. *Systematic Theology*, 494–96. Grand Rapids: Zondervan, 1994.

Hodge, A.A. *Outlines of Theology*, 325–37, 348–66. Grand Rapids: Zondervan, 1973.

Hodge, Charles. *Systematic Theology*, 2:192–256. Grand Rapids: Eerdmans, 1979.

Hoekema, Anthony A. *Created in God's Image*, 132–67. Grand Rapids: Eerdmans, 1986.

Horton, Michael. *The Christian Faith*, 408–31. Grand Rapids: Zondervan, 2011.

Hutchinson, George P. *The Problem of Original Sin in American Presbyterian Theology*. Phillipsburg, NJ: Presbyterian and Reformed, 1972.

Lloyd-Jones, D. Martyn. *God's Way of Reconciliation*, 41–53. Grand Rapids: Baker Book House, 1979.

Lloyd-Jones, D. Martyn. *Great Doctrines of the Bible*, 1:189–99. Wheaton: Crossway, 2003.

Lyford, William. *The Instructed Christian*, 230–52. Morgan, PA: Soli Deo Gloria, n.d.

MacArthur, John and Richard Mayhue, eds. *Biblical Doctrine*, 457–68. Wheaton: Crossway, 2017.

Machen, J. Gresham. *The Christian View of Man*, 220–32. London: Banner of Truth, 1965.

Madueme, Hans and Michael Reeves, eds. *Adam, the Fall, and Original Sin*. Grand Rapids: Baker Academic, 2014.

Morecraft, Joseph C., III. *Authentic Christianity*, 6:717–954. Powder Springs, GA: Minkoff Family Publishing and American Vision Press, 2009.

Moulin, Peter (Pierre Du). *The Anatomy of Arminianisme*, 41–80. Norwood: Walter J. Johnson, 1976.

Murray, John. *The Imputation of Adam's Sin*. Phillipsburg, NJ: Presbyterian and Reformed, 1977.

Niesel, Wilhelm. *The Theology of Calvin*, 80–88. Philadelphia: Westminster, 1956.

Owen, John. *The Works of John Owen*, 10:68–82. Edinburgh: Banner of Truth, 1976.

Perkins, William. *A Golden Chaine*, 17–31. N.p.: Puritan Reprints, 2010.

Pink, Arthur W. *Gleanings from the Scriptures*, 14–80. Chicago: Moody Press, 1969.

Polhill, Edward. *The Works of Edward Polhill*, 52–61. Morgan, PA: Soli Deo Gloria, 1998.

Rigby, Paul. *Original Sin in Augustine's Confessions*. Ottawa: University of Ottawa Press, 1987.

Selderhuis, Herman J., ed. *The Calvin Handbook*, 276–78. Grand Rapids: Eerdmans, 2009.

Shedd, William G. T. *Dogmatic Theology*, 550–609. 3rd ed. Phillipsburg, NJ: P&R, 2003.

Shedd, William G. T. *Sermons to the Natural Man*, 267–84. Edinburgh: Banner of Truth, 1977.

Shedd, William G. T. *Theological Essays*, 211–64. Minneapolis: Klock & Klock, 1981.

Smith, H. Shelton. *Changing Conceptions of Original Sin: A Study in American Theology Since 1750*. New York: Scribner's, 1955.

Smith, Morton H. *Systematic Theology*, 1:311–21. Greenville: Greenville Seminary Press, 1994.

Sproul, R. C. *Everyone's a Theologian*, 108–19. Orlando: Reformation Trust, 2014.

Storms, C. Samuel. *Tragedy in Eden: Original Sin in the Theology of Jonathan Edwards*. Lanham: University Press of America, 1985.

te Velde, Dolf, ed. *Synopsis Purioris Theologiae: Synopsis of a Purer Theology*, 1:350–83. Leiden: Brill, 2015.

Thornwell, James Henley. *The Collected Writings of James Henley Thornwell*, 1:301–51, 515–68. Edinburgh: Banner of Truth, 1974.

Turretin, Francis. *Institutes of Elenctic Theology*, 1:613–43. Phillipsburg, NJ: P&R, 1992.

Ursinus, Zacharias. *The Commentary of Dr. Zacharias Ursinus on the Heidelberg Catechism*, 39–44. Phillipsburg, NJ: Presbyterian and Reformed, n.d.

van Gelderen J. and W. H. Velema. *Concise*

Reformed Dogmatics, 402–14. Phillipsburg, NJ: P&R, 2008.

Van Til, Cornelius. "Original Sin, Imputation, and Inability." In Carl F. H. Henry, ed., *Basic Christian Doctrines*, 110–16. New York: Holt, Rinehart and Winston, 1962.

Vinke, Peter. "Of Original Sin Inhering." In *Puritan Sermons 1659–1689*, 5:115–34. Wheaton: Richard Owen Roberts, 1981.

Vos, Geerhardus. *Reformed Dogmatics*, 2:30–57. Bellingham: Lexham Press, 2012.

Watson, Thomas. *A Body of Divinity*, 128–48. Edinburgh: Banner of Truth, 1974.

Total Depravity

à Brakel, Wilhelmus. *The Christian's Reasonable Service*, 1:407–25. Ligonier, PA: Soli Deo Gloria, 1992.

Alexander, Archibald. "The Inability of Sinners." In Charles Hodge et al, *Princeton versus the New Divinity*, 115–40. Edinburgh: Banner of Truth, 2001.

Augustine. "The Free Choice of the Will" and "Grace and Free Will." In *The Fathers of the Church*, 59:63–308. Washington, D.C: Catholic University of America Press, 1968.

Augustine. *The Works of Saint Augustine*, 1/26: 71–106. Hyde Park: New City Press, 1999.

Barrett, Matthew. "The Bondage and Liberation of the Will." In Matthew Barrett, ed. *Reformation Theology*, 451–510. Wheaton: Crossway Books, 2017.

Barrett, Michael. *Salvation by Grace*, 37–68. Phillipsburg, NJ: P&R, 2013.

Baschera, Luca. "Total Depravity? The Consequences of Original Sin in John Calvin and Later Reformed Theology." in Herman J. Selderhuis, ed. *Calvinus clarissimus theologus*, 37–58. Göttingen: Vandenhoeck & Ruprecht, 2012.

Beeke, Joel R. and Mark Jones. *A Puritan Theology*, 203–16. Grand Rapids: Reformation Heritage Books, 2012.

Berkouwer, G. C. *Man: The Image of God*, 119–93. Grand Rapids: Eerdmans, 1962.

Berkouwer, G. C. *Sin*. Grand Rapids: Eerdmans, 1971.

Best, W. E. *Free Grace vs. Free Will*. Grand Rapids: Baker Book House, 1977.

Boettner, Loraine. *The Reformed Doctrine of Predestination*, 61–82. Philadelphia: Presbyterian and Reformed, 1932.

Boice, James Montgomery and Philip Graham Ryken. *The Doctrines of Grace*, 69–89. Wheaton: Crossway, 2002.

Bonar, Andrew. *Memoir and Remains of Robert Murray M'Cheyne*, 437–42. Edinburgh: Banner of Truth, 1978.

Boston, Thomas. *The Complete Works of the Late Rev. Thomas Boston*, 1:276–300, 2:371–83, 8:124–37, 11:251–339. Wheaton: Richard Owen Roberts, 1980.

Boston, Thomas. *Human Nature in Its Fourfold State*. London: Banner of Truth, 1964.

Boyce, James Petigru. *Abstract of Systematic Theology*, 239–58. Cape Coral, FL: Founders Press, 2007.

Brine, John. *A Treatise on Various Subjects*, 26–47. Paris, AR: Baptist Standard Bearer, 1987.

Burgess, Anthony. *A Treatise of Sin: The Deceitfulness of the Heart Unmasked*. Ames, IA: International Outreach, 2012.

Burns, Lanier. "'From Ordered Soul to Corrupted Nature': Calvin's View of Sin." In Sung Wook Chung, ed. *John Calvin and Evangelical Theology*, 85–106. Louisville: Westminster John Knox Press, 2001.

Burroughs, Jeremiah. *The Evil of Evils*. Ligonier, PA: Soli Deo Gloria, 1992.

Calvin, John. *The Bondage and Liberation of the Will*. Grand Rapids: Baker Books, 1996.

Calvin, John. *Institutes of the Christian Religion*, 1:2:1–6 (pp. 241–348). Philadelphia: Westminster Press, 1960.

Calvin, John. *Sermons on Genesis, 1:1–11:4*, 555–72. Edinburgh: Banner of Truth, 2009.

Calvin, John. *Sermons on the Epistle to the Ephesians*, 127–54, 405–19. London: Banner of Truth, 1973.

Campbell, Iain D. *The Doctrine of Sin*. Fearn: Mentor, 1999.

Charnock, Stephen. *The Existence and Attributes of God*, 1:89–175. Grand Rapids: Baker Book House, 1979.

Charnock, Stephen. *The Works of Stephen Charnock*, 5:459–525. Edinburgh: Banner of Truth, 1997.

Christensen, Scott. *What About Free Will?*, 134–87. Phillipsburg, NJ: P&R, 2016.

Clark, Gordon H. *Predestination*, 110–44. Phillipsburg, NJ: Presbyterian and Reformed, 1987.

Clarkson, David. *The Works of David Clarkson*, 2:101–36. Edinburgh: Banner of Truth, 1988.

Culver, Robert. *Systematic Theology*, 406–17. Fearn: Mentor, 2005.

Cunningham, William. *Historical Theology*, 1:496–639. London: Banner of Truth, 1969.

Custance, Arthur C. *Man in Adam and In Christ* in *The Doorway Papers*, 3:14–50. Grand Rapids: Zondervan, 1975.

Custance, Arthur C. *The Sovereignty of Grace*, 91–130. Phillipsburg, NJ: Presbyterian and Reformed, 1979.

Custance, Arthur C. *Two Men Called Adam*, 153–60. Brockville: Doorway Publications, 1983.

DeVine, Mark. "Total Depravity: A Biblical and Theological Examination." In Matthew Barrett and Thomas J. Nettles, eds. *Whomever He Wills*, 16–36. Cape Coral, FL: Founders Press, 2012.

Edwards, Jonathan. *The Torments of Hell: Jonathan Edwards on Eternal Damnation*, 1–15. Ames, IA: International Outreach, 2006.

Edwards, Jonathan. *The Unpublished Sermons of Jonathan Edwards*, 303–13. Edited by Michael D. McMullen. Mountain Home: BorderStone Press, 2012.

Edwards, Jonathan. *The Works of Jonathan Edwards, Volumes 1 and 3*; 10:337–50; 13:238–40, 245–46; 17:175–83; 18:406; 19:515–36; 20:39–52; 23:553–65. New Haven: Yale University Press, 1957.

Emmons, Nathanael. *Selfishness: The Essence of Total Depravity*. Ames, IA: International Outreach, 2009.

Frame, John M. *Systematic Theology*, 815–71. Phillipsburg, NJ: P&R, 2013.

Fuller, Andrew. *The Complete Works of the Rev. Andrew Fuller*, 2:662–80. Harrisonburg, VA: Sprinkle Publications, 1988.

Gamble, Richard C. *The Whole Counsel of God*, 218–43. Phillipsburg, NJ: P&R, 2009.

Gerstner, John H. *Primitive Theology*, 221–60. Morgan, PA: Soli Deo Gloria, 1996.

Gill, John. *The Cause of God and Truth*, 122–31, 183–98, 266–86. Grand Rapids: Baker Book House, 1980.

Gill, John. *A Complete Body of Doctrinal and Practical Divinity*, 321–24. Paris, AR: Baptist Standard Bearer, 1984.

Girardeau, John Lafayette. *Calvinism and Evangelical Arminianism*, 334–49. Harrisonburg, VA: Sprinkle Publications, 1984.

Godfrey, W. Robert. *Saving the Reformation: The Pastoral Theology of the Synod of Dort*, 53–64, 127–52. Orlando, FL: Reformation Trust, 2019.

Good, Kenneth H. *God's Gracious Purpose as Seen in the Gospel of John*, 16–42. Grand Rapids: Baker Book House, 1979.

Goodwin, Thomas. *The Works of Thomas Goodwin, Volume 10*; 6:73–116, 231–61. Eureka: Tanski, 1996.

Gregory, Thomas. "The Presbyterian Doctrine of Total Depravity." In R. C. Sproul, ed. *Soli Deo Gloria: Essays in Reformed Theology*, 36–54. Phillipsburg, NJ: P&R, 1976.

Grudem, Wayne. *Systematic Theology*, 496–501. Grand Rapids: Zondervan, 1994.

Hanko, Herman, Homer C., and Gise Van Baren. *The Five Points of Calvinism*, 9–24.

Grand Rapids: Reformed Free Publishing Association, 1976.

Harrison, Simon. *Augustine's Way into the Will: The Theological and Philosophical Significance of the De Libero Arbitrio.* Oxford: Oxford University Press, 2006.

Helm, Paul. *Human Nature from Calvin to Edwards.* Grand Rapids: Reformation Heritage Books, 2018.

Helm, Paul. *John Calvin's Ideas*, 157–83. Oxford: Oxford University Press, 2004.

Heppe, Heinrich. *Reformed Dogmatics*, 320–70. Grand Rapids: Baker Book House, 1978.

Hodge, A. A. *Outlines of Theology*, 338–47. Grand Rapids: Zondervan, 1973.

Hodge, Charles. *Systematic Theology*, 2:280–309. Grand Rapids: Eerdmans. 1979.

Hoeksema, Homer C. *The Voice of Our Fathers*, 425–625. Grand Rapids: Reformed Free Publishing Association, 1980.

Hoitenga, Dewey J., Jr. *John Calvin on the Will.* Grand Rapids: Baker Books, 1996.

Horton, Michael S. *The Christian Faith*, 431–34. Grand Rapids: Zondervan, 2011.

Horton, Michael S. *For Calvinism*, 35–52. Grand Rapids; Zondervan, 2011.

Horton, Michael S. *Putting Amazing Back into Grace*, 47–68. Grand Rapids: Baker, 1994.

Hulse, Erroll. *Who Saves, God or Me?*, 27–31. Darlington: Evangelical Press, 2008.

Hunt, Dave and James White. *Debating Calvinism*, 63–90. Sisters, OR: Multnomah, 2004.

Kuyper, Abraham. *Particular Grace: A Defense of God's Sovereignty in Salvation*, 53–72. Grandville: Reformed Free Publishing Association, 2001.

Kuyper, Abraham. *The Work of the Holy Spirit*, 252–82. Grand Rapids: Eerdmans, 1969.

Lawson, Steven J. *A Long Line of Godly Men*, 1:53–59, 79–80, 85–86, 90–92, 94, 108–11, 126–28, 139–43, 154–59, 170–74, 190–94, 202–06, 219–21, 230–31, 244–50, 260–63, 273–77, 311–13, 316–18, 329–31, 349–50, 383–84, 394–95, 401–03, 413–16, 428–29, 447–40, 469–70,

479–82, 500–505, 509–14, 533–36, 544–47. Orlando: Reformation Trust, 2006.

Lems, Shane. *The Doctrines of Grace*, 21–32. Phillipsburg, NJ: P&R, 2013.

Lloyd-Jones, D. Martyn. *Darkness and Light*, 25–77. Grand Rapids: Baker Book House, 1982.

Lloyd-Jones, D. Martyn. *God's Way of Reconciliation*, 26–68. Grand Rapids: Baker Book House, 1979.

Lloyd-Jones, D. Martyn. *Great Doctrines of the Bible*, 1:200–211. Wheaton: Crossway, 2003.

Love, Christopher. *The Natural Man's Condition.* Orlando: Northampton Press, 2012.

Luther, Martin. *The Bondage of the Will.* Grand Rapids: Fleming H. Revell, 2005.

Lyford, William. *The Instructed Christian*, 284–309. Morgan, PA: Soli Deo Gloria, n.d.

MacArthur, John. "Man's Radical Corruption." In Burk Parsons, ed. *John Calvin: A Heart for Devotion, Doctrine & Doxology*, 129–40. Orlando: Reformation Trust, 2008.

Machen, J. Gresham. *The Christian View of Man*, 161–232. London: Banner of Truth, 1965.

Manton, Thomas. "Man's Impotency to Help Himself Out of that Misery." In *Puritan Sermons 1659–1689*, 5:157–67. Wheaton: Richard Owen Roberts, 1981.

Manton, Thomas. *The Works of Thomas Manton*, 5:473–84. Worthington, PA: Maranatha Publications, n.d.

McClarty, Jim. *By Grace Alone*, 23–36. Smyrna, GA: GCA Publishing, 2007.

Montgomery, Daniel and Timothy Paul Jones. *PROOF: Finding Freedom Through the Intoxicating Joy of Irresistible Grace*, 46–66. Grand Rapids: Zondervan, 2015.

Moore, Russell D. "Without One Plea: Human Depravity and the Christian Gospel." In Thomas K. Ascol and Nathan A. Finn, eds. *Ministry By His Grace and For His Glory: Essays in Honor of Thomas J.*

Nettles, 111–22. Cape Coral, FL: Founders Press, 2011.

Morecraft, Joseph C., III. *Authentic Christianity*, 5:55–69. Powder Springs, GA: Minkoff Family Publishing and American Vision Press, 2009.

Morgan, Christopher W. and Robert A. Peterson, eds., *Fallen: A Theology of Sin*. Wheaton: Crossway, 2013.

Morgan, Edward, ed. *John Elias: Life, Letters and Essays*, 362–67. Edinburgh: Banner of Truth, 2004.

Morony, Stephen K. *The Noetic Effects of Sin: A Historical and Contemporary Exploration of How Sin Affects Our Thinking*. Lanham: Lexington Books, 2000.

Moulin, Peter (Pierre Du). *The Anatomy of Arminianisme*, 282–344. Norwood: Walter J. Johnson, 1976.

Muller, Richard A. *Dictionary of Latin and Greek Theological Terms, Drawn Principally from Protestant Scholastic Theology*, 200–203, 233. 2nd ed. Grand Rapids: Baker Academic, 2017.

Murphy, Martin. "Total Depravity." In R. C. Sproul Jr., ed. *After Darkness, Light*, 13–29. Phillipsburg, NJ: P&R, 2003.

Murray, John. *Collected Writings of John Murray*, 2:60–66, 83–89. Edinburgh: Banner of Truth, 1976.

Ness, Christopher. *An Antidote Against Arminianism*, 85–101. Choteau, MT: Old Paths Gospel Press, n.d.

Nettles, Thomas J. *By His Grace and For His Glory*, 323–34. Rev. ed. Cape Coral, FL: Founders Press, 2006.

Nettleton, Asahel. *Sermons from the Second Great Awakening*, 394–98. Ames, IA: International Outreach, 1995.

Oliphant, James H. *Thoughts on the Will*. Streamwood, IL: Primitive Baptist Library, 1977 (1899).

Orrick, Jim Scott. *Mere Calvinism*, 27–56. Phillipsburg: P&R, 2019.

Owen, John. *The Works of John Owen*, 3:242–82; 10:114–29. London: Banner of Truth, 1967.

Palmer, Edwin H. *The Five Points of Calvinism*, 9–23. Rev. ed. Grand Rapids: Baker Book House, 1984.

Parks, William. *Sermons on the Five Points of Calvinism*, 1–24. Choteau, MT: Old Paths Gospel Press, n.d.

Peterson, Robert A. and Michael D. Williams. *Why I Am Not an Arminian*, 162–72. Downers Grove, IL: IVP, 2004.

Peterson, Robert A. *Election and Free Will*, 125–54. Phillipsburg, NJ: P&R, 2007.

Phillips, Richard D. *Saved by Grace*, 1–31. Phillipsburg, NJ: P&R, 2009.

Phillips, Richard D. *What's So Great About the Doctrines of Grace?*, 17–32. Orlando: Reformation Trust, 2008.

Pink, Arthur W. *Gleanings from the Scriptures: Man's Total Depravity*. Chicago: Moody Press, 1969.

Pink, Arthur W. *The Sovereignty of God*, 177–202. Grand Rapids: Baker Book House, 1973.

Piper, John. *Five Points*, 17–24. Fearn: Christian Focus, 2013.

Piper, John. *TULIP: The Pursuit of God's Glory in Salvation*, 58–94, 97–110. Wheaton: Crossway, 2009.

Polhill, Edward. *The Works of Edward Polhill*, 175–78. Morgan, PA: Soli Deo Gloria, 1998.

Reed, R. C. *The Gospel as Taught by Calvin*, 15–31. Edinburgh: Banner of Truth, 2009.

Reisinger, Ernest C. *God's Will, Man's Will and Free Will*. N.p.: Frontline Ministries, n.d.

Ryle, J. C. *The True Christian*, 1–14. Welwyn: Evangelical Press, 1978.

Schreiner, Thomas R. and Bruce A. Ware, eds. *The Grace of God, The Bondage of the Will*, 2:279–96. Grand Rapids: Baker Books, 1995.

Selderhuis, Herman J., ed. *The Calvin Handbook*, 278–82. Grand Rapids: Eerdmans, 2009.

Shedd, William G. T. *Dogmatic Theology*, 570–602, 606–09. 3rd ed. Phillipsburg, NJ: P&R, 2003.

Shedd, William G. T. *Sermons to the Natural Man*, 78–122, 202–30. Edinburgh: Banner of Truth, 1977.

Smith, Morton H. *Systematic Theology*, 1:301–09. Greenville, SC: Greenville Seminary Press, 1994.

Sproul, R. C. *Grace Unknown*, 117–37. Grand Rapids: Baker Books, 1997.

Sproul, R. C. *Willing to Believe: The Controversy over Free Will*. Grand Rapids: Baker Books, 1997.

Spurgeon, Charles Haddon. *Metropolitan Tabernacle Pulpit*, 11:97–109, 13:49–60, 14:289–300, 16:85–96, 22:637–48, 39:181–89. Pasadena, TX: Pilgrim Publications, 1981.

Spurgeon, Charles Haddon. *New Park Street Pulpit*, 1:395–402, 4:137–44. Pasadena, TX: Pilgrim Publications, 1981.

Spurgeon, Charles Haddon. *Sermons on Sovereignty*, 121–33. Pasadena, TX: Pilgrim Publications, 1990.

Steele, David N., Curtis C. Thomas, and S. Lance Quinn. *The Five Points of Calvinism*, 18–27. 2nd ed. Phillipsburg, NJ: P&R, 2004.

Stewart, Pat. "The Biblical Doctrine of Depravity." In Thomas J. Ascol, ed. *Reclaiming the Gospel and Reforming Churches*, 33–52. Cape Coral, FL: Founders Press, 2003.

Storms, C. Samuel. "The Will: Fettered Yet Free." In John Piper and Justin Taylor, eds. *A God Entranced Vision of All Things*. Wheaton: Crossway, 2004.

Storms, C. Samuel. *Chosen for Life*, 53–68. Rev. ed. Wheaton: Crossway, 2006.

te Velde, Dolf, ed. *Synopsis Purioris Theologiae: Synopsis of a Purer Theology*, 1:384–431. Leiden: Brill, 2015.

Thornwell, James Henley. *The Collected Writings of James Henley Thornwell*, 1:352–441. Edinburgh: Banner of Truth, 1974.

Turretin, Francis. *Institutes of Elenctic Theology*, 1:659–83. Phillipsburg, NJ: P&R, 1992.

Ursinus, Zacharias. *The Commentary of Dr. Zacharias Ursinus on the Heidelberg Catechism*, 54–67. Phillipsburg, NJ: Presbyterian and Reformed, n.d.

Ussher, James. *A Body of Divinity*, 125–37. Birmingham: Solid Ground Christian Books, 2007.

Ussher, James. *The Puritan Pulpit: The Irish Puritans*, 26–52, 69–96. Orlando: Soli Deo Gloria, 2006.

van Asselt, Willem J., J. Martin Bac, and Roelf T. te Velde, eds. *Reformed Thought on Freedom*. Grand Rapids: Baker Academic, 2010.

van Genderen, J. and W. H. Velema. *Concise Reformed Dogmatics*, 385–436. Phillipsburg, NJ: P&R, 2008.

Vass, Larry Ivan. *A Reformed View of the Sovereignty of God in a Postmodern World*, 156–74. Baltimore: PublishAmerica, 2008.

Venema, Cornelis P. *But for the Grace of God: An Exposition of the Canons of Dort*, 53–63. Grandville: Reformed Fellowship, 2011.

Venning, Ralph. *The Plague of Plagues*. London: Banner of Truth, 1965.

Vermigli, Peter Martyr. *The Peter Martyr Library*, 4:271–327. Kirksville, MO: Sixteenth Century Publishers, 1998.

Vickers, Douglas. *Divine Redemption and the Refuge of Faith*, 74–106. Grand Rapids: Reformation Heritage Books, 2005.

Vos, Geerhardus. *Reformed Dogmatics*, 2:21–75. Bellingham: Lexham Press, 2012.

Warburton, Ben A. *Calvinism*, 126–48. Grand Rapids: Eerdmans, 1955.

Warfield, Benjamin B. *Selected Shorter Writings of Benjamin B. Warfield*, 2:725–28. Nutley: Presbyterian and Reformed, 1973.

Watkins, Stephen. "The Misery of Man's Estate by Nature." In *Puritan Sermons 1659–1689*, 5:135–56. Wheaton: Richard Owen Roberts, 1981.

Watson, Thomas. *The Mischief of Sin*. Pittsburgh: Soli Deo Gloria, 1994.

Watson, Thomas. *The Puritan Pulpit*, 149–89. Morgan, PA: Soli Deo Gloria, 2004.

White, James R. *The Potter's Freedom*, 91–120. Amityville: Calvary Press Publishing, 2000.

White, James R. *The Sovereign Grace of God*, 47–64. Lindenhurst: Great Christian Books, 2003.

Unconditional Election

à Brakel, Wilhelmus. *The Christian's Reasonable Service*, 1:211–50. Ligonier, PA: Soli Deo Gloria, 1992.

Abendroth. Mike. *The Sovereignty and Supremacy of King Jesus*, 165–81. Leominster: Day One, 2011.

Alexander, Archibald, ed. *Sermons of the Log College*, 99–188. Ligonier, PA: Soli Deo Gloria, 1993.

Allison, Greg. *Historical Theology*, 453–73. Grand Rapids: Zondervan, 2011.

Ames, William. *The Marrow of Theology*, 152–57. Boston: Pilgrim Press, 1968.

Augustine. *The Predestination of the Saints* in *The Works of Saint Augustine*, 1/26:149–87. Hyde Park: New City Press, 1999.

Backus, Isaac. *The Doctrine of Sovereign Grace*. Birmingham: Solid Ground Christian Books, 2009.

Barro, Antonio Carlos. "Election, Predestination and the Mission of God." In Sung Wook Chung, ed. *John Calvin and Evangelical Theology*, 181–98. Louisville: Westminster John Knox Press, 2009.

Bavinck, Herman. *Reformed Dogmatics*, 2:337–405. Grand Rapids: Baker Academic, 2003.

Beeke, Joel R. *Debated Issues in Sovereign Predestination*. Göttingen: Vandenhoeck & Ruprecht, 2017.

Beeke, Joel R. "Calvin on Similarities and Differences on Election and Reprobation." In Joel R. Beeke, David W. Hall, and Michael A. G. Haykin, eds. *Theology Made Practical: New Studies on John Calvin and His Legacy*. Grand Rapids: Reformation Heritage Books, 2017.

Belcher, Richard B. *Arthur W. Pink: Predestination*. Columbia: Richbarry Press, 1994.

Belcher, Richard B. *A Journey in Predestination*. Fort Mill, SC: Richbarry Press, 2013

Berkouwer, G. C. *Divine Election*. Grand Rapids: Eerdmans, 1960.

Billings, J. Todd and I. John Hesselink, eds. *Calvin's Theology and Its Reception*, 97–139. Louisville: Westminster John Knox Press, 2012.

Binning, Hugh. *The Works of the Rev. Hugh Binning, M.A.*, 71–88. Ligonier, PA: Soli Deo Gloria, 1992.

Boettner, Loraine. *The Reformed Doctrine of Predestination*. Philadelphia: Presbyterian and Reformed, 1932.

Boice, James Montgomery and Philip Graham Ryken. *The Doctrines of Grace*, 91–112. Wheaton: Crossway, 2002.

Boston, Thomas. *The Complete Works of the Late Rev. Thomas Boston*, 1:301–13. Wheaton: Richard Owen Roberts, 1980.

Bradford, John. *The Writings of John Bradford*, 1:211–20, 307–30. Edinburgh: Banner of Truth, 1979.

Brand, Chad Owen, ed. *Perspectives on Election: Five Views*, 1–58, 150–94. Nashville: Broadman & Holman, 2006.

Buis, Harry. *Historic Protestantism and Predestination*. Philadelphia: Presbyterian and Reformed, 1958.

Burgess, Charles. *Unearthing Your Heavenly Election*. Bloomington: WestBow Press, 2014.

Calvin, John. *Calvin's Calvinism*. 2nd ed. Edited by Henry Cole and Russell Dykstra. Jennison: Reformed Free Publishing Association, 2009.

Calvin, John. *Institutes of the Christian Religion*, 3:21–24 (pp. 920–88). Philadelphia: Westminster Press, 1960.

Calvin, John. *Sermons on Election and Reprobation*. Audubon: Old Paths Publications, 1996.

Calvin, John. *Sermons on the Epistle to the Ephesians*, 22–49. London: Banner of Truth, 1973.

Carr, Marc A. *The Case for Election*. N.p.: Xulon Press, 2012.

Carson, D. A. "How Can We Reconcile the Love and the Transcendent Sovereignty of God?" In Douglas S. Huffman and Eric L. Johnson, eds. *God Under Fire*, 279–312. Grand Rapids: Zondervan, 2002.

Clark, Gordon H. *Predestination*, 66–84. Phillipsburg, NJ: Presbyterian and Reformed, 1987.

Clark, R. Scott. "Election and Predestination: The Sovereign Expression of God (3.21–24)." In David W. Hall and Peter A. Lillback, eds. *A Theological Guide to Calvin's Institutes*, 90–122. Phillipsburg, NJ: P&R, 2008.

Crisp, Oliver D. *Saving Calvinism: Expanding the Reformed Tradition*, 47–66. Downers Grove, IL: IVP Academic, 2016.

Custance, Arthur C. *The Sovereignty of Grace*, 131–48. Phillipsburg, NJ: Presbyterian and Reformed, 1979.

Dabney, Robert Lewis. *Systematic Theology*, 223–46. Edinburgh: Banner of Truth, 1985.

Davis, Andrew M. "Unconditional Election: A Biblical and God-Glorifying Doctrine." In Matthew Barrett and Thomas J. Nettles, eds. *Whomever He Wills*, 37–76. Cape Coral, FL: Founders Press, 2012.

Dennison, James T., Jr., ed. *Reformed Confessions of the 16th and 17th Centuries in English Translation*, 1:692–820. Grand Rapids: Reformation Heritage Books, 2008.

Dickinson, Jonathan. *The True Scripture Doctrine Concerning Some Important Points of Christian Faith*, 5–69. Harrisonburg, VA: Sprinkle Publications, 1992.

Edwards, Jonathan. *Our Great and Glorious God*, 54–66. Morgan, PA: Soli Deo Gloria, 2004.

Edwards, Jonathan. *The Works of Jonathan Edwards*, 13:233–35; 17:276–328; 19:475–90;

20:177–81. New Haven: Yale University Press, 1994.

Forster, Greg. *The Joy of Calvinism*, 69–90. Wheaton: Crossway, 2012.

Frame, John M. *The Doctrine of God*, 317–30. Phillipsburg, NJ: P&R, 2002.

Frame, John M. *Systematic Theology*, 206–21. Phillipsburg, NJ: P&R, 2013.

Gentry, Kenneth L., Jr. *Predestination Made Easy*. Draper: Apologetics Group Media, 2010.

Gill, John. *The Cause of God and Truth*, 78–98, 158–63, 220–41. Grand Rapids: Baker Book House, 1980.

Gill, John. *A Complete Body of Doctrinal and Practical Divinity*, 176–92. Paris, AR: Baptist Standard Bearer, 1984.

Gill, John. *Sermons and Tracts*, 3:1–62, 100–132. Streamwood, IL: Primitive Baptist Library, 1981.

Girardeau, John Lafayette. *Calvinism and Evangelical Arminianism*, 14–160, 178–393. Harrisonburg, VA: Sprinkle Publications, 1984.

Godfrey, W. Robert. *Saving the Reformation: The Pastoral Theology of the Synod of Dort*, 35–46, 85–112. Orlando, FL: Reformation Trust, 2019.

Godfrey, W. Robert. "Unconditional Election." In R. C. Sproul Jr., ed. *After Darkness, Light*, 53–72. Phillipsburg, NJ: P&R, 2003.

Good, Kenneth H. *God's Gracious Purpose as Seen in the Gospel of John*, 43–69. Grand Rapids: Baker Book House, 1979.

Goodwin, Thomas. *The Works of Thomas Goodwin, Volume 9*. Eureka, CA: Tanski, 1996.

Grudem, Wayne. *Systematic Theology*, 669–91. Grand Rapids: Zondervan, 1994.

Hanko, Herman, Homer C. Hoeksema, and Gise Van Baren. *The Five Points of Calvinism*, 27–42. Grand Rapids: Reformed Free Publishing Association, 1976.

Heppe, Heinrich. *Reformed Dogmatics*, 163–

78. Grand Rapids: Baker Book House, 1978.

Hill, Richard J. "Dick." *A Glimpse of the Chosen: Glimpses of God's Elective Grace.* Bloomington: WestBow Press, 2016.

Hodge, A. A. *Outlines of Theology*, 214–36. Grand Rapids: Zondervan, 1973.

Hodge, Charles. *Systematic Theology*, 2:313–53. Grand Rapids: Eerdmans, 1978.

Hoeksema, Herman. *Reformed Dogmatics*, 2:220–37. 2nd ed. Grandville: Reformed Free Publishing Association, 2004.

Horton, Michael S. *The Christian Faith*, 560–72. Grand Rapids: Zondervan, 2011.

Horton, Michael S. *For Calvinism*, 53–79. Grand Rapids: Zondervan, 2011.

Horton, Michael S. *Putting Amazing Back into Grace*, 69–85. Grand Rapids: Baker, 1994.

Hulse, Erroll. "God's Sovereign Election." In Thomas K. Ascol and Nathan A. Finn, eds. *Ministry by His Grace and For His Glory*, 123–41. Cape Coral, FL: Founders Press, 2011.

Hulse, Erroll. *Who Saves, God or Me?*, 31–33, 82–84. Darlington: Evangelical Press, 2008.

Hunt, Dave and James White. *Debating Calvinism*, 91–116. Sisters, OR: Multnomah, 2004.

James, Frank A., III. *Peter Martyr Vermigli and Predestination.* Oxford: Clarendon Press, 1998.

Jewett, Paul K. *Election and Predestination.* Grand Rapids: Eerdmans, 1985.

Johns, Kenneth D. *Election: Love Before Time.* Phillipsburg, NJ: Presbyterian and Reformed, 1976.

Kersten, G. H. *Reformed Dogmatics*, 1:119–36. Sioux Center, IA: Netherlands Reformed Book and Publishing Committee, 1980.

Klooster, Fred H. *Calvin's Doctrine of Predestination.* Grand Rapids: Baker Book House, 1977.

Knox, John. *The Works of John Knox*, 5:7–468. Edinburgh: Banner of Truth, 2014.

Kolb, Robert, and Carl R. Trueman. *Between Wittenburg and Geneva: Lutheran and Reformed Theology in Conversation*, 87–116. Grand Rapids: Baker Academic, 2017.

Krankendonk, David H. *Teaching Predestination: Elnathan Parr and Pastoral Ministry in Early Stuart England.* Grand Rapids: Reformation Heritage Books, 2011.

Lawson, Steven J. *A Long Line of Godly Men*, 1:7–19, 60–62, 80, 94–97, 120–21, 143–45, 174–76, 194–96, 221, 225–26, 232–34, 236–37, 250–52, 278–80, 313, 318–20, 332, 351–61, 385, 403, 416–19, 429–31, 450–52, 470–73, 505–06, 514–17, 536, 547–48. Orlando: Reformation Trust, 2006.

Lems, Shane. *The Doctrines of Grace*, 33–44. Phillipsburg, NJ: P&R, 2013.

Link, Christian. "Election and Predestination." In Martin Ernst Hirzel and Martin Sallmann, eds. *John Calvin's Impact on Church and Society, 1509–2009*, 105–21. Grand Rapids: Eerdmans, 2009.

Lloyd-Jones, D. Martyn. *God's Ultimate Purpose*, 81–105. Grand Rapids: Baker Book House, 1978.

Lloyd-Jones, D. Martyn. *Great Doctrines of the Bible*, 1:212–23. Wheaton: Crossway, 2003.

Love, Christopher. *Preacher of God's Word*, 145–78. Morgan, PA: Soli Deo Gloria, 2000.

Love, Christopher. *A Treatise of Effectual Calling and Election.* Morgan, PA: Soli Deo Gloria, 1998.

Lutzer, Erwin. *The Doctrines That Divide*, 153–223. Grand Rapids: Kregel, 1998.

Lyford, William. *The Instructed Christian*, 179–230. Morgan, PA: Soli Deo Gloria, n.d.

M'Cheyne, Robert Murray. *Sermons of Robert Murray M'Cheyne*, 138–42. Edinburgh: Banner of Truth, 1972.

MacArthur, John. *The Love of God*, 127–47. Dallas: Word Publishing, 1996.

MacArthur, John and Richard Mayhue, eds. *Biblical Doctrine*, 493–504. Wheaton: Crossway, 2017.

Machen, J. Gresham. *The Christian View of Man*, 46–78. London: Banner of Truth, 1965.

MacLeod, Donald. *Behold Your God*, 213–27. Fearn: Christian Focus, 1995.

McClarty, Jim. *By Grace Alone*, 37–62. Smyrna, GA: GCA Publishing, 2007.

McLemore, Paul D. *God's Sovereignty and the Law of Causality*, 220–304. N.p.: Xulon Press, 2014.

Morecraft, Joseph C., III. *Authentic Christianity*, 1:420–39. Powder Springs, GA: Minkoff Family Publishing and American Vision Press, 2009.

Moulin, Peter (Pierre Du). *The Anatomy of Arminianisme*, 80–209. Norwood: Walter J. Johnson, 1976.

Muller, Richard A. *Christ and the Decree: Christology and Predestination in Reformed Theology from Calvin to Perkins*. Durham: Labyrinth Press, 1986.

Muller, Richard A. *Dictionary of Latin and Greek Theological Terms, Drawn Principally from Protestant Scholastic Theology*, 104, 274–276. 2nd ed. Grand Rapids: Baker Academic, 2017.

Murray, John. *Collected Writings of John Murray*, 2:123–31. Edinburgh: Banner of Truth, 1976.

Murray, Iain H. "The Puritans and the Doctrine of Election." In David Martyn Lloyd-Jones, ed. *Puritan Papers, 1:1956–1959*, 3–16. Phillipsburg, NJ: P&R, 2000.

Murrell, Adam. *Predestined to Believe*. Eugene: Resource Publications, 2008.

Ness, Christopher. *An Antidote Against Arminianism*, 5–61. Choteau, MT: Old Paths Gospel Press, n.d.

Nettles, Thomas J. *By His Grace and For His Glory*, 305–22. Rev. ed. Cape Coral, FL: Founders Press, 2006.

Niesel, Wilhelm. *The Theology of Calvin*, 159–81. Philadelphia: Westminster Press, 1956.

Orrick, Jim Scott. *Mere Calvinism*, 57–82. Phillipsburg: P&R, 2019.

Palmer, Edwin. *The Five Points of Calvinism*, 24–40. Rev. ed. Grand Rapids: Baker Book House, 1984.

Parks, William. *Sermons on the Five Points of Calvinism*, 25–48. Choteau, MT: Old Paths Gospel Press, n.d.

Perkins, William. *The Works of William Perkins*, Volume 6. Grand Rapids: Reformation Heritage Books, 2018.

Peterson, Robert A. and Michael D. Williams. *Why I Am Not an Arminian*, 42–66. Downers Grove: IVP, 2006.

Peterson, Robert A. *Election and Free Will*. Phillipsburg, NJ: P&R, 2007.

Phillips, Richard D. "Election and Reprobation." In Burk Parsons, ed. *John Calvin: A Heart for Devotion, Doctrine & Doxology*, 141–55. Orlando: Reformation Trust, 2008.

Phillips, Richard D. *Chosen in Christ*. Phillipsburg, NJ: P&R, 2004.

Phillips, Richard D. *What Are Election and Predestination?* Phillipsburg, NJ: P&R, 2006.

Phillips, Richard D *What's So Great About the Doctrines of Grace?*, 33–50. Orlando: Reformation Trust, 2008.

Pink, Arthur W. *The Doctrines of Election and Justification*. Grand Rapids: Baker Book House, 1976.

Pink, Arthur W. *The Sovereignty of God*. Grand Rapids: Baker Book House, 1973.

Piper, John. *Five Points*, 53–61. Fearn: Christian Focus, 2013.

Piper, John. *The Pleasures of God*, 123–58. Portland: Multnomah, 1991.

Piper, John. *TULIP: The Pursuit of God's Glory in Salvation*, 85–96, 111–49. Wheaton: Crossway, 2009.

Polhill, Edward. *The Works of Edward Polhill*, 117–27. Morgan, PA: Soli Deo Gloria, 1998.

Reed, R. C. *The Gospel as Taught by Calvin*, 47–67. Edinburgh: Banner of Truth, 2009.

Reymond, Robert L. *A New Systematic Theology of the Christian Faith*, 461–502. Nashville: Thomas Nelson, 1998.

Rice, N. L. *God Sovereign and Man Free*,

119–211. Harrisonburg, VA: Sprinkle Publications, 1985.

Robertson, Norwell. *Church-Members' Handbook of Theology*, 171–207. Harrisonburg, VA: Gano Books, 1983.

Rouwendal, Pieter. "The Doctrine of Predestination in Reformed Orthodoxy." In Herman J. Selderhuis, ed. *A Companion to Reformed Orthodoxy*, 552–89. Leiden: Brill, 2013.

Ryle, J. C. *Old Paths*, 429–45. Edinburgh: Banner of Truth, 2013.

Samson, John. *Twelve What Abouts: Answering Common Objections Concerning God's Sovereignty in Election*. Birmingham: Solid Ground Christian Books, 2009.

Schreiner, Thomas R. and Bruce A. Ware, eds. *The Grace of God, The Bondage of the Will*, 1:47–106, 2:251–28. Grand Rapids: Baker, 1995.

Schreiner, Thomas R. and Bruce A. Ware, eds. *Still Sovereign*, 47–106. Grand Rapids: Baker Books, 2000.

Selderhuis, Herman J., ed. *The Calvin Handbook*, 312–23. Grand Rapids: Eerdmans, 2009.

Selph, Robert B. *Southern Baptists and the Doctrine of Election*. Harrisonburg, VA: Sprinkle Publications, 1988.

Shedd, William G. T. *Dogmatic Theology*, 326–33. 3rd ed. Phillipsburg, NJ: P&R. 2003.

Smith, Morton H. *Systematic Theology*, 1:163–73. Greenville, SC: Greenville Seminary Press, 1994.

Sproul, R. C. *Chosen by God*. Wheaton: Tyndale House, 1986.

Sproul, R. C. *Grace Unknown*, 139–61. Grand Rapids: Baker Books, 1997.

Sproul, R. C. *Loved by God*. Nashville: Word Publishing, 2001.

Spurgeon Charles Haddon. *Metropolitan Tabernacle Pulpit*, 10:73–84, 485–96, 11:373–84, 12:421–32; 16:601–12; 18:181–92; 29:481–92; 30:469–80; 34:361–72; 36:325–36; 51: 49–59. Pasadena, TX: Pilgrim Publications, 1981.

Spurgeon Charles Haddon. *New Park Street Pulpit*, 1:311–22; 2:289–96; 3:129–36; 5:65–72, 113–20; 6:133–10, 301–08, 325–32. Pasadena, TX: Pilgrim Publications, 1981.

Spurgeon Charles Haddon. *Sermons on Sovereignty*, 51–80. Pasadena, TX: Pilgrim Publications, 1990.

Steele, David N., Curtis C. Thomas, and S. Lance Quinn. *The Five Points of Calvinism*. 2nd ed. Phillipsburg, NJ: P&R, 2004.

Storms, Sam, *Chosen for Life*. Rev. ed. Wheaton: Crossway, 2007.

Thornwell, James Henley. *The Collected Writings of James Henley Thornwell*, 2:105–201. Edinburgh: Banner of Truth, 1974.

Thuesen, Peter J. *Predestination: The American Career of a Contentious Doctrine*. Oxford: Oxford University Press, 2009.

Turretin, Francis. *Institutes of Elenctic Theology*, 1:341–79. Phillipsburg, NJ: P&R, 1992.

Ursinus, Zacharias. *The Commentary of Dr. Zacharias Ursinus on the Heidelberg Catechism*, 293–303. Phillipsburg, NJ: Presbyterian and Reformed, n.d.

van den Belt, Henk, ed. *Synoposis Purioris Theologiae: Synopsis of a Purer Theology*, 2:22–65. Leiden: Brill, 2016.

van Genderen, J. and W. H. Velema. *Concise Reformed Dogmatics*, 208–45. Phillipsburg, NJ: P&R, 2008.

Venema, Cornelis P. "Predestination and Election." In Matthew Barrett ed. *Reformation Theology*, 241–82. Wheaton: Crossway Books, 2017

Venema, Cornelis P. *But for the Grace of God: An Exposition of the Canons of Dort*, 21–35. Grandville: Reformed Fellowship, 2011.

Venema, Cornelis P. *Chosen in Christ*. Fearn: Mentor, 2019.

Venema, Cornelis P. *Heinrich Bullinger and the Doctrine of Predestination*. Grand Rapids: Baker Academic, 2002.

Vermigli, Peter Martyr. *The Peter Martyr Library*, 8:3–84. Kirksville, MO: Truman State University Press, 2003.

Vos, Geerhardus. *Reformed Dogmatics*, 1:97–155. Bellingham: Lexham Press, 2012.

Warburton, Ben A. *Calvinism*, 80–106. Grand Rapids: Eerdmans, 1955.

Warfield, Benjamin B. *Biblical and Theological Studies*, 270–333. Philadelphia: Presbyterian and Reformed, 1968.

Warfield, Benjamin B. *Selected Shorter Writings of Benjamin B. Warfield*, 1:285–98. Nutley: Presbyterian and Reformed, 1970.

Warfield, Benjamin B. *The Works of Benjamin B. Warfield*, 2:3–67; 9:117–234. Grand Rapids: Baker Book House, 1981.

Welty, Greg. "Election and Calling: A Biblical Theological Study." In E. Ray Clendenen and Brad J. Waggoner, eds.

Calvinism: A Southern Baptist Dialogue, 216–43. Nashville: B &H Academic, 2008.

Wendel, Francois. *Calvin: The Origins and Development of His Religious Thought*, 263–84. London: Collins, 1963.

White, James R. *The Potter's Freedom*, 171–204. Amityville: Calvary Press Publishing, 2000.

White, James R. *The Sovereign Grace of God*, 65–84. Lindenhurst: Great Christian Books, 2003.

Witsius, Herman. *The Economy of the Covenants Between God and Man*, 1:324–43. Escondido: Den Dulk Christian Foundation; Phillipsburg, NJ: P&R, 1990.

Zaspel, Fred G. *The Theology of B. B. Warfield*, 198–210, 422–33. Wheaton: Crossway, 2010.

Election and Foreknowledge

Baugh, S. M. "The Meaning of Foreknowledge." In Thomas R. Schreiner and Bruce A. Ware, eds. *Still Sovereign*, 183–200. Grand Rapids: Baker Books, 2000.

Jewett, Paul K. *Election and Predestination*, 67–73. Grand Rapids: Eerdmans, 1985.

Owen, John. *The Works of John Owen*, 10:22–30. Edinburgh: Banner of Truth, 1976.

Piper, John. *TULIP: The Pursuit of God's*

Glory in Salvation, 127–38. Wheaton: Crossway, 2009.

Sproul, R. C. *Chosen by God*, 127–38. Wheaton: Tyndale House, 1986.

Turretin, Francis. *Institutes of Elenctic Theology*, 1:355–64. Phillipsburg, NJ: P&R, 1992.

White, James. *The Sovereign Grace of God*, 141–48. Lindenhurst: Great Christian Books, 2003.

Election in Christ

Ambrose, Isaac. *Looking Unto Jesus*, 49–88. Harrisonburg, VA: Sprinkle Publications, 1986.

Berkouwer, G. C. *Divine Election*, 132–71. Grand Rapids: Eerdmans, 1960.

Crisp, Oliver B. *God Incarnate: Explorations in Christology*, 34–55. London: T. and T. Clark, 2009.

Edwards, Jonathan. *The Works of Jonathan Edwards*, 18:415–48. New Haven: Yale University Press, 2000.

Ellis, Branno. "The Eternal Decree in the Incarnate Son: Robert Rollock on the Relationship Between Christ and

Election." In Aaron Clay Denlinger, ed. *Reformed Orthodoxy in Scotland*, 45–65. London: Bloomsbury, 2015.

Gill, John. *A Complete Body of Doctrinal and Practical Divinity*, 180–82. Paris, AR: Baptist Standard Bearer, 1984.

Heppe, Heinrich. *Reformed Dogmatics*, 168–12. Grand Rapids: Baker Book House, 1978.

Hughes, Philip Edgcumb. *The True Image*, 178–82. Grand Rapids: Eerdmans, 1989.

Muller, Richard A. *Christ and the Decree: Christology and Predestination in Reformed*

Theology from Calvin to Perkins. Durham: Labyrinth Press, 1986.

Perkins, William. *The Golden Chaine*, 33–37. N.p.: Puritan Reprints, 2010.

Selderhuis, Herman J., ed. *The Calvin Handbook*, 265–67. Grand Rapids: Eerdmans, 2009.

Storms, C. Samuel. *Chosen for Life*, Rev. ed., 109–10. Wheaton: Crossway, 2007.

Treier, Daniel J. and Walter A. Elwell, eds.

Evangelical Dictionary of Theology, 3rd ed., 267–69. Grand Rapids: Baker Academic, 2017.

Turretin, Francis. *Institutes of Elenctic Theology*, 1:350–55. Phillipsburg, NJ: P&R, 1991.

van den Belt, Henk, ed. *Synopsis Purioris Theologiae: Synopsis of a Purer Theology*, 2:39–41. Leiden: Brill, 2016.

The Covenant of Redemption

à Brakel, Wilhelmus. *The Christian's Reasonable Service*, 1:251–63. Ligonier, PA: Soli Deo Gloria, 1992.

Allred, Frank. *The Eclipse of the Gospel*, 57–70. London: Grace Publications Trust, 2011.

Ambrose, Isaac. *Looking Unto Jesus*, 49–88. Harrisonburg, VA: Sprinkle Publications, 1986.

Bavinck, Herman. *Reformed Dogmatics*, 3:212–16. Grand Rapids: Baker Academic, 2003.

Beeke, Joel R. and Mark Jones. *A Puritan Theology*, 237–58. Grand Rapids: Reformation Heritage Books, 2012.

Berkhof, Louis. *Systematic Theology*, 265–71. Grand Rapids: Eerdmans, 1988.

Berkouwer, G. C. *Divine Election*, 161–71. Grand Rapids: Eerdmans, 1960.

Biehl, Craig. *The Infinite Merit of Christ*, 55–85. Jackson, Miss.: Reformed Academic Press, 2009.

Bogue, Carl. *Jonathan Edwards and the Covenant of Grace*, 95–124. Cherry Hill: Mack, 1975.

Boston, Thomas. *The Complete Works of the Late Rev. Thomas Boston*, 1:314–75. Wheaton: Richard Owen Roberts, 1980.

Brooks, Thomas. *The Works of Thomas Brooks*, 5:286–403. Edinburgh: Banner of Truth, 1980.

Campbell, Iain D. "Re-Visiting the Covenant of Redemption." In Iain D. Campbell and Malcolm Maclean, eds. *The People's Theologian*, 173–94. Fearn: Mentor, 2011.

Clark, Gordon H. *The Atonement*, 11–17. Jefferson: Trinity Foundation, 1987.

Daniels, Richard. *The Christology of John Owen*. 153–73. Grand Rapids: Reformation Heritage Books, 2004.

Edwards, Jonathan. *The Works of Jonathan Edwards*, 18:148–51, 536–37; 20:167, 430–45, 475–79; 25:142–54. New Haven: Yale University Press, 2000.

Erskine, Ralph. *The Works of Ralph Erskine*, 6:111–79. Glasgow: Free Presbyterian Publications, 1991.

Fesko, J. V. *The Covenant of Redemption: Origins, Development, and Reception*. Göttingen: Vandenhoeck & Ruprecht, 2015.

Fesko, J. V. *The Theology of the Westminster Standards*, 163–66. Wheaton: Crossway, 2014.

Fesko, J. V. *The Trinity and the Covenant of Redemption*. Fearn: Mentor, 2016.

Flavel, John. *The Works of John Flavel*, 1:52–62. Edinburgh: Banner of Truth, 1982.

Frame, John M. *Systematic Theology*, 59–60. Phillipsburg, NJ: P&R, 2013.

Gill, John. *A Body of Doctrinal and Practical Divinity*, 209–50. Paris, AR: Baptist Standard Bearer, 1984.

Goodwin, Thomas. *The Works of Thomas Goodwin*, 5:3–33. Eureka, CA: Tanski, 1996.

Heppe, Heinrich. *Reformed Dogmatics*, 168–70, 373–82. Grand Rapids: Baker Book House, 1978.

Hodge, Charles. *Systematic Theology*, 2:359–62. Grand Rapids: Eerdmans, 1979.

Hoeksema, Herman. *Reformed Dogmatics*, 1:403–53. 2nd ed. Grandville: Reformed Free Publishing Association, 2004.

Jacombe, Thomas. "The Covenant of Redemption Opened." In *Puritan Sermons 1659–1689*, 5:168–81. Wheaton: Richard Owen Roberts, 1981.

Jeon, Jeong Koo. *Covenant Theology: John Murray's and Meredith G. Kline's Response to the Historical Doctrine of Covenant Theology in Reformed Thought*, 213–19. Lanham: University Press of America, 1999.

Jones, Mark. "Covenant Christology: Herman Bavinck and the Pactum Salutis." In John Bolt, ed. *Five Studies in the Thought of Herman Bavinck, A Creator of Modern Dutch Theology*, 129–52. Lewiston: NY: Edwin Mellen Press, 2011.

Jones, Mark. *Why Heaven Kissed Earth: The Christology of the Puritan Reformed Orthodox Theologian, Thomas Goodwin (1600–1680)*, 123–45. Göttingen: Vandenhoeck & Ruprecht, 2010.

Lloyd-Jones, D. Martyn. *God's Ultimate Purpose*, 46–56. Grand Rapids: Baker Book House, 1978.

Lloyd-Jones, D. Martyn. *Saved in Eternity*, 53–65. Wheaton: Crossway, 1988.

MacArthur, John and Richard Mayhue, eds. *Biblical Doctrine*, 512–16. Wheaton: Crossway, 2017.

McGraw, Ryan M. *Christ's Glory, Your Good*, 1–13. Grand Rapids: Reformation Heritage Books, 2013.

McMahon, C. Matthew. *A Simple Overview of Covenant Theology*, 19–27. Lenox: Puritan Publications, 2005.

Morecraft, Joseph C., III. *Authentic Christianity*, 1:707–26. Powder Springs, GA: Minkoff Family Publishing and American Vision Press, 2009.

Muller, Richard A. *Dictionary of Latin and Greek Theological Terms, Drawn Principally from Protestant Scholastic Theology*, 252–53.

2nd ed. Grand Rapids: Baker Academic, 2017.

Nichols, Greg. *Covenant Theology: A Reformed and Baptistic Perspective on God's Covenants*, 303–19. Birmingham: Solid Ground Christian Books, 2011.

Oliphint, K. Scott. *God With Us*, 106–09. Wheaton: Crossway, 2012.

Owen, John. *The Works of John Owen*, 12:496–508. Edinburgh: Banner of Truth, 1979.

Pauw, Amy Plantinga. *"The Supreme Harmony of All": The Trinitarian Theology of Jonathan Edwards*, 92–118. Grand Rapids: Eerdmans, 2002.

Pink, Arthur W. *The Divine Covenants*, 13–25. Grand Rapids: Baker Book House, 1973.

Pink, Arthur W. *Gleanings from the Scriptures*, 205–11. Chicago: Moody Press, 1969.

Richard, Guy M. *The Supremacy of God in the Theology of Samuel Rutherford*, 116–31. Eugene: Wipf and Stock, 2008.

Rutherford, Samuel. *The Covenant of Life Opened*, 401–36. New Lenox: Puritan Publications, 2005.

Spurgeon, Charles Haddon. *New Park Street Pulpit*, 5:417–24. Pasadena, TX: Pilgrim Publications, 1981.

Swain, Scott R. "Covenant of Redemption." In Michael Allen and Scott R. Swain, eds. *Christian Dogmatics*, 107–25. Grand Rapids: Baker Academic, 2016.

Trueman, Carl R. "Atonement and the Covenant of Redemption in John Owen on the Nature of Christ's Satisfaction." In David Gibson and Jonathan Gibson, eds. *From Heaven He Came and Sought Her: Definite Atonement in Historical, Biblical, Theological, and Pastoral Perspective*, 201–23. Wheaton: Crossway Books, 2013.

Trueman, Carl. R. "The Harvest of Reformation Mythology? Patrick Gillespie and the Covenant of Redemption." In Maarten Wisse, Marcel Sarot, and Willemien Otten, eds. *Scholasticism Reformed*, 196–214. Leiden: Brill, 2010.

Trueman, Carl R. *The Claims of Truth: John*

Owen's Trinitarian Theology, 129–48. Carlisle: Paternoster, 1998.

van Asselt, Willem J. "Covenant Theology as Relational Theology: The Contributions of Johannes Cocceius (1618–1683) to a Living Reformed Theology." In Kelly M. Kapic and Mark Jones, eds. *The Ashgate Companion to John Owen's Theology*, 65–84. Farnham: Ashgate, 2012.

van Asselt, Willem J. *The Federal Theology of Johannes Cocceius (1603–1669)*, 227–39. Leiden: Brill, 2001.

van Genderen, J. and W. H. Velema. *Concise Reformed Dogmatics*, 200–208. Phillipsburg, NJ: P&R, 2008.

VanDrunnen, David and R. Scott Clark. "The Covenant before the Covenants." In R. Scott Clark, ed. *Covenant, Justification, and Pastoral Ministry*, 167–96. Phillipsburg, NJ: P&R, 2007.

Watts, Isaac. *The Works of the Reverend and Learned Isaac Watts, D.D.*, 1:509–19. New York: AMS, 1971.

Witsius, Herman. *The Economy of the Covenants Between God and Man*, 1:165–92. Escondido: Den Dulk Foundation; and Phillipsburg, NJ: P&R, 1990.

Objections to Election

Boettner, Loraine. *The Reformed Doctrine of Predestination*, 205–96. Philadelphia: Presbyterian and Reformed, 1932.

Calvin, John. *Calvin's Calvinism*. 2nd ed. Edited by Henry Cole and Russell Dykstra. Jennison: Reformed Free Publishing Association, 2009.

Carson, D. A. "How Can We Reconcile the Love of God and the Transcendent Sovereignty of God?" In Douglas S. Huffman, ed. *God Under Fire?*, 279–312. Grand Rapids: Zondervan, 2002.

Girardeau, John Lafayette. *Calvinism and Evangelical Arminianism*, 178–412. Harrisonburg, VA: Sprinkle Publications, 1984.

Murrell, Adam. *Predestined to Believe: Common Objections to the Reformed Faith Answered*. Eugene: Resource Publications, 2008.

Perkins, William. *A Golden Chaine*, 246–58. N.p.: Puritan Reprints, 2010.

Peterson, Robert A. *Election and Free Will*, 173–83. Phillipsburg, NJ: P&R, 2007.

Pink, Arthur W. *The Sovereignty of God*, 237–60. Grand Rapids: Baker Book House, 1973.

Samson, John. *Twelve What Abouts: Answering Common Objections Concerning God's Sovereignty in Election*. Birmingham: Solid Ground Christian Books, 2012.

The Destiny of the Elect

à Brakel, Wilhelmus. *The Christian's Reasonable Service*, 4:357–70. Ligonier, PA: Soli Deo Gloria, 1992.

Alcorn, Randy. *We Shall See God: Charles Spurgeon's Classic Devotional Thoughts on Heaven*. Carol Stream: Tyndale House, 2011.

Barnes, Tom. *Living in the Hope of Future Glory*. Darlington: Evangelical Press, 2006.

Bates, William. *The Whole Works of the Rev. W. Bates, D.D.*, 3:3–114, 369–479. Harrisonburg, VA: Sprinkle Publications, 1990.

Bavinck, Herman. *Reformed Dogmatics*, 4:715–30. Grand Rapids: Baker Academic, 2008.

Baxter, Richard. "The Saints' Everlasting Rest." In *The Practical Works of Richard Baxter*, 3:1–354. Ligonier, PA: Soli Deo Gloria, 1990.

Beeke, Joel R. and Mark Jones. *A Puritan*

Theology, 819–40. Grand Rapids: Reformation Heritage Books, 2012.

Blanchard, John. *The Hitch-Hiker's Guide to Heaven*. Darlington: Evangelical Press, 2013.

Boettner, Loraine. *Immortality*. Phillipsburg, NJ: Presbyterian and Reformed, 1981.

Bolton, Robert. *The Four Last Things*, 93–120. Pittsburgh: Soli Deo Gloria, 1994.

Boston, Thomas. *Human Nature in Its Fourfold State*. Edinburgh: Banner of Truth, 1964. Also in: *The Complete Works of the Late Rev. Thomas Boston, Volume 8*. Wheaton: Richard Owen Roberts, 1980.

Brooks, Thomas. *The Works of Thomas Brooks*, 1:399–468. Edinburgh: Banner of Truth, 1980.

Bunyan, John. *The Works of John Bunyan*, 3:725–45. Edinburgh: Banner of Truth, 1991.

Caldwell, Robert W. *Communion in the Spirit: The Holy Spirit as the Bond of Union in the Theology of Jonathan Edwards*, 169–93. Eugene: Wipf and Stock, 2007.

Case, Thomas. *The Select Works of Thomas Case, Part 2*. Ligonier, PA: Soli Deo Gloria, 1993.

Custance, Arthur C. *Two Men Called Adam*, 223–36. Brockville: Doorway Publications, 1983.

Davies, Eryl. *Heaven is a Far Better Place*. Darlington: Evangelical Press, 1999.

Donnelly, Edwards. *Biblical Teaching on the Doctrines of Heaven and Hell*. Edinburgh: Banner of Truth, 2001.

Durham, James. *The Blessed Death of Those Who Die in the Lord*. Morgan, PA: Soli Deo Gloria, 2003.

Durham, James. *The Unsearchable Riches of Christ*, 341–58. Morgan, PA: Soli Deo Gloria, 2002.

Edwards, Jonathan. "Heaven Is a World of Love." In *The Works of Jonathan Edwards*, 8:366–97. New Haven: Yale University Press, 1989. Also in: *Charity and Its Fruits*, 323–68. London: Banner of Truth, 1969.

Edwards, Jonathan. *Our Great and Glorious God*, 198–212. Morgan, PA: Soli Deo Gloria, 2004.

Edwards, Jonathan. *The Works of Jonathan Edwards*, 13:201–02, 263, 265–68, 295–96, 303, 328–29, 331, 350–51, 369–70, 437–39, 444–45, 478, 481–84; 14:134–60; 17:57–86, 251–61; 18:71–73, 107–11, 335–39, 350–51, 366–83, 427–34, 526–28, 533–34; 19:609–27, 734–46; 20:210–22, 231–34, 455–56, 469–74; 25:222–56. New Haven: Yale University Press, 1994.

Ellsworth, Roger. *What the Bible Teaches About Heaven*. Darlington: Evangelical Press, 2007.

Fuller, Andrew. *The Complete Works of the Rev. Andrew Fuller*, 1:333–41; 3:725–44. Harrisonburg, VA: Sprinkle Publications, 1988.

Gearing, William. *The Glory of Heaven*. Orlando: Soli Deo Gloria, 2005.

Gerstner, John H. *Jonathan Edwards on Heaven and Hell*. Grand Rapids: Baker Book House, 1980.

Gerstner, John H. *The Rational Biblical Theology of Jonathan Edwards*, 3:541–604. Orlando: Ligonier Ministries, 1993.

Gill, John. *Sermons and Tracts*, 1:167–94. Streamwood: Primitive Baptist Library, 1981.

Goodwin, Thomas. *The Works of Thomas Goodwin*, 7:337–471. Eureka, CA: Tanski, 1996.

Griffin, Edward D. *The Life and Sermons of Edward D. Griffin*, 2:433–47. Edinburgh: Banner of Truth, 1987.

Grudem, Wayne. *Systematic Theology*, 1158–64. Grand Rapids: Zondervan, 1994.

Henry, Matthew. *The Covenant of Grace*, 305–92. Fearn: Christian Heritage, 2002.

Hoekema, Anthony A. *The Bible and the Future*, 274–88. Grand Rapids: Eerdmans, 1979.

Horton, Michael. *The Christian Faith*, 688–710, 906–17, 984–90. Grand Rapids: Zondervan, 2011.

Howe, John. *The Works of the Reverend John*

Howe, 2:1–260; 3:315–41. Ligonier, PA: Soli Deo Gloria, 1990.

Lawson, Steven J. *Heaven Help Us!* Colorado Springs: NavPress, 1995.

Love, Christopher. *The Works of Christopher Love*, 1:333–540. Morgan, PA: Soli Deo Gloria, 1995.

MacArthur, John. *The Glory of Heaven*. Wheaton: Crossway, 1996.

Morecraft, Joseph C., III. *Authentic Christianity*, 3:339–510. Powder Springs, GA: Minkoff Family Publishing and American Vision Press, 2009.

Murray, John. *Redemption Accomplished and Applied*, 217–24. Grand Rapids: Eerdmans, 1955.

Owen, John. *The Works of John Owen*, 2:591–604. London: Banner of Truth, 1972.

Payson, Edward. *The Complete Works of Edward Payson*, 1:574–86; 2:305–18, 600–608. Harrisonburg, VA: Sprinkle Publications, 1987.

Pemberton, Ebenezer. *The Puritan Pulpit*, 296–312. Orlando: Soli Deo Gloria, 2006.

Perkins, William. *A Golden Chaine*, 207–13. N.p.: Puritan Reprints, 2010.

Phillips, Richard D. and Gabriel N. E. Fisher, eds. *These Last Days: A Christian View of History*. Phillipsburg, NJ: P&R, 2011.

Roberts, Maurice. *The Happiness of Heaven*. Grand Rapids: Reformation Heritage Books, 2009.

Roberts, Maurice. *The Thought of God*, 189–230. Edinburgh: Banner of Truth, 1992.

Rogers, Michael Allen. *What Happens After I Die?* Wheaton: Crossway, 2013.

Shedd, William G. T. *Sermons to the Spiritual Man*, 68–81, 167–80. London: Banner of Truth, 1972.

Sproul, R. C. *Heaven, Hell, Angels and Demons*, 13–47. Fearn: Christian Focus, 2011.

Spurgeon, Charles Haddon. *C. H. Spurgeon's Sermons Beyond Volume 63*, 78–91. Leominster: Day One, 2009.

Spurgeon, Charles Haddon. *Metropolitan Tabernacle Pulpit*, 11:240–52, 325–36, 433–44; 14:433–44; 36:73–84; 39:85–93; 62:73–84. Pasadena, TX: Pilgrim Publications, 1981.

Spurgeon, Charles Haddon. *New Park Street Pulpit*, 1:301–10; 2:17–24, 57–69; 3:25–32, 209–16; 4:185–92. Pasadena, TX: Pilgrim Publications, 1981.

Spurgeon, Charles Haddon. *No Tears in Heaven*. Fearn: Christian Heritage, 2014.

Storms, Sam. "Living with One Foot Raised: Calvin on the Glory of the Final Resurrection and Heaven." In John Piper and David Mathis, eds. *With Calvin in the Theater of Glory*, 111–32. Wheaton: Crossway, 2010.

Turretin, Francis. *Institutes of Elenctic Theology*, 3:608–37. Phillipsburg, NJ: P&R, 1992.

Venema, Cornelis P. *The Promise of the Future*, 363–91, 454–88. Edinburgh: Banner of Truth, 2000.

Vincent, Thomas. *Christ's Sudden and Certain Appearance to Judgment*. Morgan, PA: Soli Deo Gloria, 1996.

Vos, Geerhardus. *Reformed Dogmatics*, 5:255–310. Bellingham: Lexham Press, 2016.

Watson, Thomas. *Discourses on Important and Interesting Subjects*, 2:3–22. Ligonier, PA: Soli Deo Gloria, 1990.

Watson, Thomas. *The Fight of Faith Crowned*. Morgan: Soli Deo Gloria, 1996.

Watts, Isaac. *The World to Come*. Orlando: Soli Deo Gloria, 2005.

Witsius, Herman. *The Economy of the Covenants Between God and Man*, 2:81–107. Econdido: Den Dulk Foundation; and Phillipsburg, NJ: P&R, 1990.

Wolfe, Paul D. *Setting Our Sights on Heaven*. Edinburgh: Banner of Truth, 2012.

Woodcock, Thomas. "Of Heaven." In *Puritan Sermons 1659–1689*, 5:492–516. Wheaton: Richard Owen Roberts, 1981.

Practical Implications of Election

à Brakel, Wilhelmus. *The Christian's Reasonable Service*, 1:243–50. Ligonier, PA: Soli Deo Gloria, 1992.

Adams, Thomas. *An Exposition upon the Second Epistle General of St. Peter*, 113–26. Ligonier, PA: Soli Deo Gloria, 1990.

Beeke, Joel R. *The Quest for Full Assurance*. Edinburgh: Banner of Truth, 1999.

Kranendonk, David H. *Teaching Predestination: Elnathan Parr and Pastoral Ministry in Early Stuart England*. Grand Rapids: Reformation Heritage Books, 2011.

Leith, John H. *John Calvin's Doctrine of the Christian Life*, 120–38. Louisville: Westminster John Knox Press, 1989.

Love, Christopher. *A Treatise of Effectual Calling and Election*. Morgan, PA: Soli Deo Gloria, 1998.

Morecraft, Joseph C., III. *Authentic Christianity*, 3:255–337. Powder Springs, GA: Minkoff Family Publishing and American Vision Press, 2009.

Owen, John. *The Works of John Owen*, 3:591–604. London: Banner of Truth, 1972.

Perkins, William. *A Golden Chaine*, 261–64. N.p.: Puritan Reprints, 2010.

Schreiner, Thomas R. and Bruce A. Ware, eds. *The Grace of God, The Bondage of the Will*, 2:383–412. Grand Rapids: Baker, 1995.

Spurgeon, Charles Haddon. "David Dancing Before the Ark Because of His Election." In *Metropolitan Tabernacle Pulpit*, 34:361–72. Pasadena, TX: Pilgrim Publications, 1988.

The Doctrine of Reprobation

à Brakel, Wilhelmus. *The Christian's Reasonable Service*, 1:211–50. Ligonier, PA: Soli Deo Gloria, 1992.

Arrowsmith, John. *Armilla Catechetica: A Chain of Principles*, 310–58. Grand Rapids: Reformation Heritage Books, 2011.

Bavinck, Herman. *Reformed Dogmatics*, 2:393–99. Grand Rapids: Baker Academic, 2003.

Beeke, Joel R. "Calvin on Similarities and Differences of Election and Reprobation." In Joel R. Beeke, David W. Hall, and Michael A. G. Haykin, eds. *Theology Made Practical: New Studies on John Calvin and His Legacy*, 49–62. Grand Rapids: Reformation Heritage Books, 2017.

Beeke, Joel R. *Debated Issues in Sovereign Predestination*. Göttingen: Vandenhoeck & Ruprecht, 2017.

Boettner, Loraine. *The Reformed Doctrine of Predestination*, 104–26. Philadelphia: Presbyterian and Reformed, 1932.

Boyce, James Petigru. *Abstract of Systematic Theology*, 356–67. Cape Coral, FL: Founders Press, 2007.

Breward, Ian, ed. *The Work of William Perkins*, 250–56. Appleford: Sutton Courtenay Press, 1970.

Bunyan, John. "Reprobation Asserted." In *The Works of John Bunyan*, 2:335–58. Edinburgh: Banner of Truth, 1991.

Calvin, John. *Calvin's Calvinism*. 2nd ed. Edited by Henry Cole and Russell Dykstra. Jennison: Reformed Free Publishing Association, 2009.

Calvin, John. *Institutes of the Christian Religion*, 3:21–24 (pp. 920–87). Philadelphia: Westminster Press, 1960.

Calvin, John. *Sermons on Election and Reprobation*. Audubon: Old Path Publications, 1996.

Dabney, Robert Lewis. *Systematic Theology*, 238–46. Edinburgh: Banner of Truth, 1985.

Edwards, Jonathan. *The True Gospel: Jonathan Edwards on Eternal Salvation*, 189–224, 246–91. Edited by William C. Nichols.

Ames, IA: International Outreach, Inc., 2018.

Emmons, Nathanael. *Selfishness: The Essence of Moral Depravity*, 182–96. Ames, IA: International Outreach, 2009.

Fesko, J. V. *The Theology of the Westminster Standards*, 119–22. Wheaton: Crossway, 2014.

Frame, John M. *The Doctrine of God*, 330–34. Phillipsburg, NJ: P&R, 2002.

Frame, John M. *Systematic Theology*, 221–24. Phillipsburg, NJ: P&R, 2013.

Gill, John. *A Body of Doctrinal and Practical Divinity*, 192–98. Paris, AR: Baptist Standard Bearer, 1984.

Gill, John. *The Cause of God and Truth*, 71–78, 149–58. Grand Rapids: Baker Book House, 1980.

Girardeau, John Lafayette. *Calvinism and Evangelical Arminianism*, 161–77. Harrisonburg, VA: Sprinkle Publications, 1984.

Goodwin, Thomas. *The Works of Thomas Goodwin*, 9:84–230. Eureka, CA: Tanski, 1996.

Grudem, Wayne. *Systematic Theology*, 684–86. Grand Rapids: Zondervan, 1994.

Heppe, Heinrich. *Reformed Dogmatics*, 178–89. Grand Rapids: Baker Book House, 1978.

Hodge, A. A. *Outlines of Theology*, 222–23. Grand Rapids: Zondervan, 1973.

Hoeksema, Herman. *Reformed Dogmatics*, 1:228–40. 2nd ed. Grandville: Reformed Free Publishing Association, 2004.

Kersten, G. H. *Reformed Dogmatics*, 1:136–43. Sioux Center: Netherlands Reformed Book and Publishing Committee, 1980.

Klooster, Fred H. *Calvin's Doctrine of Predestination*, 55–86. Grand Rapids: Baker Book House, 1977.

Kuyper, Abraham. *The Work of the Holy Spirit*, 580–607. Grand Rapids: Eerdmans, 1969.

Lawson, Steven J. *A Long Line of Godly Men*, 1:83–85, 98–99, 105–06, 113–15, 155–56, 181–83, 222–24, 258–59, 300–301, 371–75, 438–39,

540–41. Orlando: Reformation Trust, 2006.

Lloyd-Jones, D. Martyn. *Romans: An Exposition of Chapter 9, God's Sovereign Purpose.* Edinburgh: Banner of Truth, 1991.

Love, Christopher. *Preacher of God's Word*, 127–44. Morgan, PA: Soli Deo Gloria, 2000.

Love, Christopher. *A Treatise of Effectual Calling and Election*, 231–47. Morgan, PA: Soli Deo Gloria, 1998.

Luther, Martin. *The Bondage of the Will*, 190–238. Grand Rapids: Fleming H. Revell, 1978.

Lyford, William. *The Instructed Christian*, 179–230. Morgan, PA: Soli Deo Gloria, n.d.

M'Cheyne, Robert Murray. *Sermons of Robert Murray M'Cheyne*, 180–85. Edinburgh: Banner of Truth, 2000.

MacArthur, John and Richard Mayhue, eds. *Biblical Doctrine*, 504–11. Wheaton: Crossway, 2017.

MacLeod, John. "God's Sovereign Choice of the Younger Son." In Jacob T. Hoogstra, ed. *The Sovereignty of God*, 169–83. Birmingham: Solid Ground Christian Books, 2008.

Manton, Thomas. *The Complete Works of Thomas Manton, D.D.*, 11:221–40. Worthington, PA: Maranatha Publications, n.d.

Morecraft, Joseph C., III. *Authentic Christianity*, 1:439–62. Powder Springs, GA: Minkoff Family Publishing and American Vision Press, 2009.

Moulin, Peter (Pierre Du). *The Anatomy of Arminianisme*, 209–24. Norwood: Walter J. Johnson, 1976.

Muller, Richard A. *Dictionary of Latin and Greek Theological Terms, Drawn Principally from Protestant Scholastic Theology*, 285–86, 312–13. 2nd ed. Grand Rapids: Baker Academic, 2017.

Palmer, Edwin H. *The Five Points of Calvinism*, 95–116. Rev. ed. Grand Rapids: Baker Book House, 1984.

Perkins, William. *A Golden Chaine*, 240–46. N.p.: Puritan Reprints, 2010.

Phillips, Richard D. "Election and Reprobation." In Burk Parsons, ed. *John Calvin: A Heart for Devotion, Doctrine & Doxology*, 141–55. Orlando: Reformation Trust, 2008.

Pink, Arthur W. *The Sovereignty of God*, 99–133. Grand Rapids: Baker Book House, 1973.

Piper, John. *The Justification of God*. Grand Rapids: Baker Books, 1993.

Polhill, Edward. *The Works of Edward Polhill*, 127–36. Morgan, PA: Soli Deo Gloria, 1998.

Ryken, Philip Graham. *The Sovereignty of God's Mercy*. Greenville, SC: Reformed Academic Press, 2001.

Samson, John. *Twelve What Abouts: Answering Common Objections Concerning God's Sovereignty in Election*, 117–28. Birmingham: Solid Ground Christian Books, 2012.

Schreiner, Thomas R. and Bruce A. Ware, eds. *The Grace of God, The Bondage of the Will*, 1:89–106. Grand Rapids: Baker Books, 1995.

Shedd, William G. T. *Calvinism: Pure and Mixed*, 69–91. Edinburgh: Banner of Truth, 1986.

Shedd, William G. T. *Dogmatic Theology*, 333–65. 3rd ed. Phillipsburg, NJ: P&R, 2003.

Sinnema, Donald. "Calvin's View of Reprobation." In Joel R. Beeke, ed. *Calvin for Today*, 115–36. Grand Rapids: Reformation Heritage Books, 2009.

Sproul, R. C. "Double Predestination." In R. C. Sproul, ed. *Soli Deo Gloria: Essays in Reformed Theology*, 63–72. Phillipsburg, NJ: Presbyterian and Reformed, 1976.

Sproul, R. C. *Chosen by God*, 139–60. Wheaton: Tyndale House, 1986.

Sproul, R. C. *Grace Unknown*, 157–61. Grand Rapids: Baker Books, 1997.

Spurgeon, Charles Haddon. *New Park Street Pulpit*, 5:113–20. Pasadena, TX: Pilgrim Publications, 1981.

Storms, Sam. *Chosen for Life*, 115–44. 2nd ed. Wheaton: Crossway, 2007.

Thornwell, James Henley. *The Collected Writings of James Henley Thornwell*, 2:105–201. Edinburgh: Banner of Truth, 1974.

Turretin, Francis. *Institutes of Elenctic Theology*, 1:380–417. Phillipsburg, NJ: P&R, 1992.

van den Belt, Henk, ed. *Synopsis Purioris Theologiae: Synopsis of a Purer Theology*, 2:51–65. Leiden: Brill, 2016.

van Genderen, J. and W. H. Velema. *Concise Reformed Dogmatics*, 231–39. Phillipsburg, NJ: P&R, 2008.

Vos, Geerhardus. *Redemptive History and Biblical Interpretation*, 412–14. Phillipsburg, NJ: Presbyterian and Reformed, 1980.

Webb, Robert Alexander. *Christian Salvation*, 37–42. Harrisonburg, VA: Sprinkle Publications, 1985.

White, James R. *The Potter's Freedom*, 205–28. Amityville: Calvary Press Publishing, 2000.

Zanchius, Jerome. *The Doctrine of Absolute Predestination*. Grand Rapids: Baker Book House, 1977.

The Destiny of the Reprobate

Adams, Richard. "Of Hell." In *Puritan Sermons 1659–1689*, 5:471–91. Wheaton: Richard Owen Roberts, 1981.

Augustine. *The City of God*, 21:1–27. *The Fathers of the Church*, 24:339–413. Washington, D.C.: Catholic University of America Press, 1954.

Bates, William. *The Whole Works of the Rev. W. Bates, D.D.*, 3:481–507. Harrisonburg, VA: Sprinkle Publications, 1990.

Bavinck, Herman. *Reformed Dogmatics*, 4:698–714. Grand Rapids: Baker Academic, 2008.

Baxter, Richard. *The Practical Works of Richard*

Baxter, 3:125–45. Ligonier, PA: Soli Deo Gloria, 1990.

Beeke, Joel R. and Mark Jones. *A Puritan Theology*, 819–40. Grand Rapids: Reformation Heritage Books, 2012.

Benton, John. *How Can a God of Love Send People to Hell?* Welwyn: Evangelical Press, 1985.

Blanchard, John. *Whatever Happened to Hell?* Wheaton: Crossway, 1995.

Bolton, Robert. *The Four Last Things*, 82–92. Pittsburgh: Soli Deo Gloria, 1994.

Boston, Thomas. *The Complete Works of the Late Rev. Thomas Boston*, 8:347–75. Wheaton: Richard Owen Roberts, 1980.

Brooks, Thomas. *The Works of Thomas Brooks*, 5:113–45. Edinburgh: Banner of Truth, 1980.

Buis, Harry. *The Doctrine of Eternal Punishment*. Philadelphia: Presbyterian and Reformed, 1957.

Bunyan, John. *Sighs from Hell*. Orlando: Northampton Press, 2012. Also in: *The Works of John Bunyan*, 3:666–726. Edinburgh: Banner of Truth, 1991.

Carson, D. A. *The Gagging of God*, 515–36. Grand Rapids: Zondervan, 1996.

Cho, Dongsun. *St. Augustine's Doctrine of Eternal Punishment*. Lewiston: Edwin Mellen Press, 2010.

Clotfelter, David. *Sinners in the Hands of a Good God*. Chicago: Moody Press, 2004.

Dabney, Robert Lewis. *Discussions*, 1:132–42, 466–81, 654–69. Harrisonburg, VA: Sprinkle Publications, 1982.

Dabney, Robert Lewis. *Systematic Theology*, 852–62. Edinburgh: Banner of Truth, 1985.

Davies, Eryl. *An Angry God?* Bryntirion: Evangelical Movement of Wales, 1991.

Donnelly, Edward. *Biblical Teaching on the Doctrines of Heaven and Hell*. Edinburgh: Banner of Truth, 2001.

Doolittle, Thomas. *Rebukes for Sin by the Flames of Hell*. Ames, IA: International Outreach, 2011.

Edwards, Jonathan. *The Glory and Honor of God*, 365–87. Nashville: Broadman & Holman, 2004.

Edwards, Jonathan. *Grace and Truth*. Ed. by Don Kistler. Orlando: The Northampton Press, 2017.

Edwards, Jonathan. *A Just and Righteous God*, 1–36, 68–80, 100–115, 127–51, 179–99. Orlando: Soli Deo Gloria, 2006.

Edwards, Jonathan. *The Torments of Hell: Jonathan Edwards on Eternal Damnation*. Edited by William Nichols. Ames, IA: International Outreach, 2006.

Edwards, Jonathan. *The True Gospel: Jonathan Edwards on Eternal Salvation*, 29–79. Edited by William C. Nichols. Ames, IA: International Outreach, Inc., 2018.

Edwards, Jonathan. *Unless You Repent*. Orlando: Soli Deo Gloria, 2005.

Edwards, Jonathan. *The Works of Jonathan Edwards*, 13:225–26, 348–50, 353, 366–67, 376, 379–81, 469, 477, 479–80, 522–23, 535–37; 14:297–328, 509–41; 18:90–93, 101–02, 113–14, 125–29, 196–97; 19:336–76; 20:17–24, 92–94, 107, 157–58, 166–89, 391–411, 575–603; 22:400–435; 23:391–411, 575–603. New Haven: Yale University Press, 1994.

Edwards, Jonathan. *The Wrath of Almighty God*. Morgan, PA: Soli Deo Gloria, 2004.

Flavel, John. *The Works of John Flavel*, 3:129–53. London: Banner of Truth, 1968.

Gerstner, John H. *Jonathan Edwards on Heaven and Hell*. Grand Rapids: Baker Book House, 1980.

Gerstner, John H. *The Rational Biblical Theology of Jonathan Edwards*, 3:501–40. Orlando: Ligonier Ministries, 1993.

Gerstner, John H. *Repent or Perish*. Ligonier, PA: Soli Deo Gloria, 1990.

Goodwin, Thomas. *The Works of Thomas Goodwin*, 10:490–567. Eureka, CA: Tanski, 1996.

Hart, Matthew J. "Calvin and the Problem of Hell." In David E. Alexander and Daniel M. Johnson, eds. *Calvinism and the Problem of Evil*, 248–72. Eugene, OR: Pickwick Publications, 2016.

Helm, Paul. *The Last Things*, 108–28. Edinburgh: Banner of Truth, 1989.

Hodge, A. A. *Evangelical Theology*, 364–82. Edinburgh: Banner of Truth, 1976.

Hodge, Charles. *Systematic Theology*, 3:866–80. Grand Rapids: Eerdmans, 1979.

Hoekema, Anthony A. *The Bible and the Future*, 253–73. Grand Rapids: Eerdmans, 1979.

Holmes, Stephen R. *God of Grace and God of Glory*, 199–240. Edinburgh: T. and T. Clark, 2000.

Hopkins, Samuel. *The Works of Samuel Hopkins*, 2:367–492. New York: Garland 1987.

Horton, Michael. *The Christian Faith*, 973–84. Grand Rapids: Zondervan, 2011.

Johnson, Trevor Christian. *Seeing Hell: On the Knowledge and Sight of Hell by the Saints (and their response to it)*. Enumclaw: Pleasant Word, 2004.

Love, Christopher. *A Treatise on Hell's Terror*. Coconut Creek: Puritan Publications, 2012.

Love, Christopher. *The Works of Christopher Love*, 1:511–676. Morgan, PA: Soli Deo Gloria, 1995.

M'Cheyne, Robert Murray. *A Basket of Fragments*, 148–73. Inverness: Christian Focus, 1975.

M'Cheyne, Robert Murray. *Sermons of Robert Murray M'Cheyne*, 165–79. London: Banner of Truth, 1961.

MacLeod, Donald. *Behold Your God*, 117–35. Fearn: Christian Focus, 1995.

Morecraft, Joseph C., III. *Authentic Christianity*, 3:436–63. Powder Springs, GA: Minkoff Family Publishing and American Vision Press, 2009.

Morey, Robert. *Death and the Afterlife*. Minneapolis: Bethany House, 1984.

Morgan, Chris. *Jonathan Edwards & Hell*. Fearn: Mentor, 2004.

Morgan, Christopher and Robert Peterson. *What is Hell?* Phillipsburg, NJ: P&R, 2010.

Morgan, Christopher W. and Robert A. Peterson, eds. *Hell Under Fire*. Grand Rapids: Zondervan, 2004.

Morgan, Christopher W. and Robert A. Peterson, eds. *Is Hell for Real or Does Everyone Go to Heaven?* Grand Rapids: Zondervan, 2011.

Owen, John. "A Dissertation on Divine Justice." In *The Works of John Owen*, 10:482–624. Edinburgh: Banner of Truth, 1976.

Packer, J. I. *The J. I. Packer Collection*, 210–26. Edited by Alister McGrath. Downers Grove, IL: IVP, 1999.

Payson, Edward. *The Complete Works of Edward Payson*, 2:319–31. Harrisonburg, VA: Sprinkle Publications, 1987.

Perkins, William. *A Golden Chaine*, 258–61. N.p.: Puritan Reprints, 2010.

Peterson, Robert A. *Hell on Trial*. Phillipsburg, NJ: P&R, 1995.

Shedd, William G. T. *The Doctrine of Endless Punishment*. Edinburgh: Banner of Truth, 1986.

Shedd, William G. T. *Dogmatic Theology*, 884–939. 3rd ed. Phillipsburg, NJ: P&R, 2003.

Spurgeon, Charles Haddon. *Metropolitan Tabernacle Pulpit*, 9:445–56; 10:669–80; 12:169–80. Pasadena, TX: Pilgrim Publications, 1981.

Spurgeon, Charles Haddon. *New Park Street Pulpit*, 1:301–10; 2:417–23; 6:461–68. Pasadena, TX: Pilgrim Publications, 1981.

Stoddard, Solomon. *The Fear of Hell Restrains Men from Sin*. Morgan, PA: Soli Deo Gloria, 2003.

Strong, William. *The Eternity and Certainty of Hell's Torments*. Coconut Creek: Puritan Publications, 2012.

Turretin, Francis. *Institutes of Elenctic Theology*, 3:604–07. Phillipsburg, NJ: P&R, 1992.

Ussher, James. *The Puritan Pulpit: The Irish Puritans*, 97–114. Orlando: Soli Deo Gloria, 2006.

Venema, Cornelis P. *The Promise of the Future*, 420–53. Edinburgh: Banner of Truth, 2000.

Vincent, Thomas. *Christ's Sudden and Certain Appearance to Judgment.* Morgan, PA: Soli Deo Gloria, 1996.

Vincent, Thomas. *Fire and Brimstone.* Morgan, PA: Soli Deo Gloria, 1999.

Vincent, Thomas. *The Way to Escape the Horrible and Eternal Burnings of Hell.* Coconut Creek: Puritan Publications, 2012.

Vos, Geerhardus. *Reformed Dogmatics,* 5:255–310. Bellingham: Lexham Press, 2016.

Warfield, Benjamin B. *Studies in Theology,* 447–60. Edinburgh: Banner of Truth, 1988.

Watson, Thomas. *The Mischief of Sin,* 91–102. Pittsburgh: Soli Deo Gloria, 1994.

Whitefield, George. *The Sermons of George Whitefield,* 1:441–52. Edited by Lee Gatiss. Wheaton: Crossway, 2012.

The Relation of Election and Reprobation

Beeke, Joel R. *Debated Issues in Sovereign Predestination.* Göttingen: Vandenhoeck & Ruprecht, 2017.

Beeke, Joel R. "Calvin on the Similarities and Differences on Election and Reprobation." In Joel R. Beeke, David W. Hall, and Michael A. G. Haykins, eds. *Theology Made Practical: New Studies on John Calvin and His Legacy.* Grand Rapids: Reformation Heritage Books, 2017.

Burroughs, Jeremiah. *Gospel Remission,* 103–07. Morgan, PA: Soli Deo Gloria, 1995.

Edwards, Jonathan. *The Wrath of Almighty God,* 232–53. Morgan, PA: Soli Deo Gloria, 2004.

Gill, John. *The Cause of God and Truth,* 83. Grand Rapids: Baker Book House, 1980.

Helm, Paul. "Are There Few That Be Saved?" In Nigel M. de S. Cameron, ed. *Universalism and the Doctrine of Hell,* 255–81. Carlisle: Paternoster, 1992.

Hoeksema, Herman. *God's Eternal Good Pleasure,* 21. Grand Rapids: Reformed Free Publishing Association, 1979.

Love, Christopher. *The Works of Christopher Love,* 1:614–38. Morgan, PA: Soli Deo Gloria, 1995.

Ryle, J. C. *Old Paths,* 61–87. Edinburgh: Banner of Truth, 2013.

Scougal, Henry. *The Works of the Rev. Henry Scougal,* 143–63. Morgan, PA: Soli Deo Gloria, 2002.

Shedd, William G. T. *Calvinism: Pure and Mixed.* Edinburgh: Banner of Truth, 1986.

Van Til, Cornelius. *The Defense of the Faith,* 413–16. Philadelphia: Presbyterian and Reformed, 1955.

Warfield, Benjamin B. "Are There Few That Be Saved?" In *Biblical and Theological Studies,* 334–50. Philadelphia: Presbyterian and Reformed, 1968.

The Order of the Decrees

Barth, Karl. *Church Dogmatics, Vol. II, Part 2,* 127–45. Edinburgh: T. and T. Clark, 1957.

Bavinck, Herman. *Reformed Dogmatics,* 2:361–92. Grand Rapids: Baker Academic, 2003.

Beeke, Joel R. "Calvin on Similarities and Differences of Election and Reprobation." In Joel R. Beeke, David W. Hall, and Michael A. G. Haykin, eds. *Theology Made Practical: New Studies on John Calvin*

and His Legacy, 49–62. Grand Rapids: Reformation Heritage Books, 2017.

Beeke, Joel R. *Debated Issues in Sovereign Predestination.* Göttingen: Vandenhoeck & Ruprecht, 2017.

Beeke, Joel R. "The Order of the Divine Decrees and the Geneva Academy: From Bezan Supralapsarianism to Turretinian Infralapsarianism." In John B. Roney and Martin I. Klauber, eds. *The Identity of Geneva: The Christian Commonwealth,*

1564–1864, 57–75. Westport: Greenwood Press, 1998.

Beeke, Joel R., and Mark Jones. *A Puritan Theology*, 149–59. Grand Rapids: Reformation Heritage Books, 2012.

Berkhof, Louis. *Systematic Theology*, 118–25. Grand Rapids: Eerdmans, 1988.

Berkouwer, G. C. *Divine Election*, 254–77. Grand Rapids: Eerdmans, 1960.

Boettner, Loraine. *The Reformed Doctrine of Predestination*, 126–30. Philadelphia: Presbyterian and Reformed, 1932.

Boston, Thomas. *The Complete Works of the Late Rev. Thomas Boston*, 1:149–66. Wheaton: Richard Owen Roberts, 1980.

Brand, Chad Owen, ed. *Perspectives on Election: Five Views*, 1–69, 150–205. Nashville: Broadman & Holman, 2006.

Bromiley, Geoffrey W. "The Decrees of God." In Carl F. H. Henry, ed. *Basic Christian Doctrines*, 42–48. New York: Holt, Rinehart and Winston, 1962.

Cairns, Alan. *Dictionary of Theological Terms*, 128, 234–35. 3rd ed. Belfast: Ambassador Publications, 2002.

Clark, Gordon H. *Ephesians*, 107–14. Jefferson: Trinity Foundation, 1985.

Clark, Gordon H. *Predestination*, 7–30. Phillipsburg, NJ: Presbyterian and Reformed, 1987.

Crisp, Oliver D. *Saving Calvinism: Expanding the Reformed Tradition*, 53–58. Downers Grove, IL: IVP Academic, 2016.

Cunningham, William. *The Reformers and the Theology of the Reformation*, 358–71. Edinburgh: Banner of Truth, 1979.

Dabney, Robert Lewis. *Systematic Theology*, 232–34. Edinburgh: Banner of Truth, 1985.

Daniel, Curt D. "Hyper-Calvinism and John Gill," 173–217. PhD Diss., University of Edinburgh, 1983.

Edwards, Jonathan. *The Works of Jonathan Edwards*, 13:216–17, 233, 383–84; 18:282–83, 314–21. New Haven: Yale University Press, 1994.

Treier, Daniel J. and Walter A. Elwell, eds. *Evangelical Dictionary of Theology*, 3rd ed., 235, 255–56, 429, 848–49. Grand Rapids: Baker Academic, 2017.

Feinberg, John S. *No One Like Him*, 531–36. Wheaton: Crossway, 2001.

Fesko, J. V. "Lapsarian Diversity at the Synod of Dort." In Michael A.G. Haykin and Mark Jones, eds. *Drawn into Controverie: Reformed Theological Diversity and Debate within Seventeenth-Century British Puritanism*, 99–123. Göttingen: Vandenhoeck & Ruprecht, 2011.

Fesko, J. V. "The Westminster Confession and Lapsarianism: Calvin and the Divines." In J. Ligon Duncan, ed., *The Westminster Confession into the 21st Century*, 2:477–525. Fearn: Mentor, 2004.

Fesko, J. V. *Diversity Within the Reformed Tradition: Supra- and Infralapsarianism in Calvin, Dort, and Westminster*. Greenville, SC: Reformed Academic Press, 2001.

Fesko, J. V. *The Doctrine of God*, 334–39. Phillipsburg, NJ: P&R, 2002.

Fesko, J. V. *The Theology of the Westminster Standards*, 111–19. Wheaton: Crossway, 2014.

Frame, John M. *Systematic Theology*, 224–28. Phillipsburg, NJ: P&R, 2013.

Gerstner, John H. *The Rational Biblical Theology of Jonathan Edwards*, 2:142–88. Orlando: Ligonier Ministries, 1992.

Gill, John. *A Complete Body of Doctrinal and Practical Divinity*, 182–85. Paris, AR: Baptist Standard Bearer, 1984.

Gill, John. *Sermons and Tracts*, 3:403–63. Streamwood, IL: Primitive Baptist Library, 1981.

Girardeau, John Lafayette. *Calvinism and Evangelical Arminianism*, 30–45, 217–18. Harrisonburg, VA: Sprinkle Publications, 1984.

Goodwin, Thomas. *The Works of Thomas Goodwin*, 9:84–149. Eureka, CA: Tanski, 1996.

Heppe, Heinrich. *Reformed Dogmatics*, 133–89. Grand Rapids: Baker Book House, 1978.

Hodge, A. A. *Outlines of Theology*, 230–34. Grand Rapids: Zondervan, 1973.

Hodge, Charles. *Systematic Theology*, 2:313–53. Grand Rapids: Eerdmans, 1979.

Hoeksema, Herman. *Reformed Dogmatics*, 1:231–37. 2nd ed. Grandville: Reformed Free Publishing Association, 2004.

Hopkins, Samuel. *The Works of Samuel Hopkins*, 2:67–150. New York: Garland, 1987.

Horton, Michael. *The Christian Faith*, 315–23. Grand Rapids: Zondervan, 2011.

Jewett, Paul K. *Election and Predestination*, 83–97. Grand Rapids: Eerdmans, 1985.

Kersten, G. H. *Reformed Dogmatics*, 1:126–30. Sioux Center: Netherlands Reformed Book and Publishing Committee, 1980.

MacLeod, Donald. "Definite Atonement and the Divine Decree." In David Gibson and Jonathan Gibson, eds. *From Heaven He Came and Sought Her*, 401–36. Wheaton: Crossway, 2013.

Moulin, Peter (Pierre Du). *The Anatomy of Arminianisme*, 91–103. Norwood: Walter J. Johnson, 1976.

Mouw, Richard J. *He Shines in All That's Fair: Culture and Common Grace*, 53–74. Grand Rapids: Eerdmans, 2001.

Muller, Richard A. *Dictionary of Latin and Greek Theological Terms, Drawn Principally from Protestant Scholastic Theology*, 249–50, 348–52. 2nd ed. Grand Rapids: Baker Academic, 2017.

Nicole, Roger. *Our Sovereign Saviour*, 33–45. Fearn: Christian Focus, 2002.

Perkins, William. *The Works of William Perkins*, Volume 6. Grand Rapids: Reformation Heritage Books, 2018.

Plantinga, Alvin. "Supralapsarianism, or "O Felix Culpa."" In Peter van Inwagen, ed. *Christian Faith and the Problem of Evil*, 1–25. Grand Rapids: Eerdmans, 2004.

Polhill, Edward. *The Works of Edward Polhill*, 111–211. Morgan, PA: Soli Deo Gloria, 1998.

Pronk, Cornelius. *No Other Foundation*

than Jesus Christ, 185–92. Mitchell: Free Reformed Publications, 2008.

Reymond, Robert L. "A Consistent Supralapsarian Perspective on Election." In Chad Owen Brand, ed. *Perspectives on Election: Five Views*, 150–94. Nashville: B&H Academic, 2006.

Reymond, Robert L. *A New Systematic Theology of the Christian Faith*, 479–502. Nashville: Thomas Nelson, 1998.

Rohls, Jan. *Reformed Confessions: Theology from Zurich to Barmen*, 148–65. Louisville: Westminster John Knox Press, 1998.

Rouwendal, Pieter. "The Doctrine of Predestination in Reformed Orthodoxy." In Herman J. Selderhuis, ed. *A Companion to Reformed Orthodoxy*, 554–56. Leiden: Brill, 2013.

Shedd, William G. T. *Calvinism: Pure and Mixed*, 29–68. Edinburgh: Banner of Truth, 1986.

Sinnema, Donald. "God's Eternal Decree and Its Temporal Execution: The Role of the Distinction in Theodore Beza." In Mack P. Holt, ed. *Adaptations of Calvinism in Reformation Europe*, 55–78. Aldershot: Ashgate, 2007.

Smith, Morton H. *Systematic Theology*, 1:173–77, 323–28. Greenville, SC: Greenville Seminary Press, 1994.

Storms, Sam. *Chosen for Life*, 213–19. Rev. ed., Wheaton: Crossway, 2007.

Thomas, Derek W. H. "The Westminster Consensus on the Decree: The Infra/Supra Lapsarian Debate." In J. Ligon Duncan, ed. *The Westminster Confession into the 21st Century*, 3:267–89. Fearn: Mentor, 2009.

Thornwell, James Henley. *The Collected Writings of James Henley Thornwell*, 2:17–27. Edinburgh: Banner of Truth, 1974.

Tseng, Shao Kai. *Karl Barth's Infralapsarian Theology*, especially 41–61. Downers Grove, IL: IVP Academic, 2016.

Turretin, Francis. *Institutes of Elenctic Theology*, 1:341–50, 417–30. Phillipsburg, NJ: P&R, 1992.

van Genderen, J. and W. H. Velema. *Concise*

Reformed Dogmatics, 228–31. Phillipsburg, NJ: P&R, 2008.

Van Til, Cornelius. *The Theology of James Daane*, 59–94. Philadelphia: Presbyterian and Reformed, 1959.

Vos, Geerhardus. *Reformed Dogmatics*, 1:142–55. Bellingham: Lexham Press, 2012.

Warfield, Benjamin B. *The Plan of Salvation*, 20–31. Grand Rapids: Eerdmans, 1971.

Young, William. "Infra- and Supralapsarianism." In *Reformed Thought: Selected Writings of William Young*, 21–24. Edited by Joel R. Beeke and Ray Lanning. Grand Rapids: Reformation Heritage Books, 2011.

The Election of Angels

Adams, Jay. *The Grand Demonstration*, 93–100. Santa Barbara: EastGate, 1991.

Alleine, Richard. *Heaven Opened: The Riches of God's Covenant*, 70–77. Morgan, PA: Soli Deo Gloria, 2000.

Augustine. *The City of God, Books IX–XII*. In Philip Schaff, ed. *A Select Library of Nicene and Post-Nicene Fathers of the Christian Church*, First Series, 2:166–244. Grand Rapids: Eerdmans, 1979.

Berkhof, Louis. *Systematic Theology*, 113. Grand Rapids: Eerdmans, 1988.

Bonar, Andrew. *Memoir and Remains of Robert Murray M'Cheyne*, 391–92. Edinburgh: Banner of Truth, 1978.

Boston, Thomas. *The Complete Works of the Late Rev. Thomas Boston*, 1:154–55. Wheaton: Richard Owen Roberts, 1980.

Burroughs, Jeremiah. *Gospel Remission*, 100–102. Morgan, PA: Soli Deo Gloria, 2002.

Charnock, Stephen. *The Existence and Attributes of God*, 2:262–64. Grand Rapids: Baker Book House, 1979.

Dabney, Robert Lewis. *Systematic Theology*, 230–32. Edinburgh: Banner of Truth, 1985.

Edwards, Jonathan. *The Works of Jonathan Edwards*, 13:428, 490–91; 18:58–62, 97–100, 106, 124–25, 206–11, 239–43, 383–90; 20:195–201. New Haven: Yale University Press, 1994.

Gill, John. *A Complete Body of Doctrinal and Practical Theology*, 176–77, 192–93, 304–09. Paris, AR: Baptist Standard Bearer, 1984.

Girardeau, John Lafayette. *Calvinism and Evangelical Arminianism*, 279–85. Harrisonburg, VA: Sprinkle Publications, 1984.

Heppe, Heinrich. *Reformed Dogmatics*, 152–54, 207–08. Grand Rapids: Baker Book House, 1978.

Love, Christopher. *Preacher of God's Word*, 164–65. Morgan, PA: Soli Deo Gloria, 2000.

Shedd, William G. T. *Dogmatic Theology*, 326–27, 357–58. 3rd ed. Phillipsburg, NJ: P&R, 2003.

Spurgeon, Charles Haddon. "Men Chosen — Fallen Angels Rejected." In *New Park Street Pulpit*, 2:289–96; cf. 5:66; 6:135. Pasadena, TX: Pilgrim Publications, 1981.

Spurgeon, Charles Haddon. *Metropolitan Tabernacle Pulpit*, 10:486–87. Pasadena, TX: Pilgrim Publications, 1981.

Turretin, Francis. *Institutes of Elenctic Theology*, 1:335–41. Phillipsburg, NJ: P&R, 1992.

Vos, Geerhardus. *Reformed Dogmatics*, 1:138–42. Bellingham: Lexham Press, 2012.

The Election of Dying Infants

Baker, Keren. *Empty Arms*. Darlington: Evangelical Press, 2010.

Bavinck, Herman. *Reformed Dogmatics*,

4:725–27. Grand Rapids: Baker Academic, 2008.

Boettner, Loraine. *The Reformed Doctrine*

of Predestination, 143–48. Philadelphia: Presbyterian and Reformed, 1932.

Brown, Craig R. *The Five Dilemmas of Calvinism*, 103–21. Orlando: Ligonier Ministries, 2007.

Bruce, James W., III. *From Grief to Glory*. Edinburgh: Banner of Truth, 2008.

Buswell, J. Oliver. *A Systematic Theology of the Christian Faith*, 2:161–62. Grand Rapids: Zondervan, 1962.

Custance, Arthur C. *The Sovereignty of Grace*, 105–07. Phillipsburg, NJ: Presbyterian and Reformed, 1979.

Edwards, Jonathan. *The Works of Jonathan Edwards*, 3:206–19. New Haven: Yale University Press, 1970.

Erickson, Millard J. *How Shall They Be Saved? The Destiny of Those Who Do Not Hear the Gospel*, 234–54. Grand Rapids: Baker, 1996.

Hodge, Charles. *Systematic Theology*, 1:26–27. Grand Rapids: Eerdmans, 1979.

Lightner, Robert. *Heaven for Those Who Can't Believe*. Schaumburg: Regular Baptist Press, 1987.

MacArthur, John. *Safe in the Arms of God*. Nashville: Thomas Nelson, 2003.

Nash. Ronald H. *When a Baby Dies*. Grand Rapids: Zondervan, 1999.

Roberts, Maurice. *The Happiness of Heaven*, 42–56. Grand Rapids: Reformation Heritage Books. 2009.

Shedd, William G. T. *Calvinism: Pure and Mixed*, 62–68, 107–15. Edinburgh: Banner of Truth, 1986.

Spurgeon, Charles Haddon. *Infant Salvation*. Pasadena, TX: Pilgrim Publications, n.d. Also in: *Metropolitan Tabernacle Pulpit*, 7:505–12. Pasadena, TX: Pilgrim Publications, 1981.

Venema, Cornelis, ed. *Christ and Covenant Theology*, 214–55. Phillipsburg: P & R, 2017.

Warfield, Benjamin B. "The Development of the Doctrine of Infant Salvation." In *Studies in Theology*, 411–46. Edinburgh: Banner of Truth, 1988. Also in: *The Works of Benjamin B. Warfield*, 9:411–46. Grand Rapids: Baker Book House, 1981.

Watts, Isaac. *The Works of the Reverend and Learned Isaac Watts, D.D.*, 6:174–82. New York: AMS, 1971.

Webb, Robert Alexander. *The Theology of Infant Salvation*. Harrisonburg, VA: Sprinkle Publications, 1981.

The Destiny of the Unevangelized

Barnhouse, Donald Grey. *Expositions of Bible Doctrines*, 2:67–77; 7:86–95. Grand Rapids: Eerdmans, 1973.

Boettner, Loraine. *The Reformed Doctrine of Predestination*, 117–21. Philadelphia: Presbyterian and Reformed, 1932.

Carson, D. A. *The Gagging of God*, 253–314. Grand Rapids: Zondervan, 1996.

Culver, Robert. *Systematic Theology*, 780–97. Fearn: Mentor, 2006.

Erickson, Millard J. *How Shall They Be Saved? The Destiny of Those Who Do Not Hear of Jesus*. Grand Rapids: Baker, 1996.

Gill, John. *The Cause of God and Truth*, 209–20. Grand Rapids: Baker Book House, 1980.

Girardeau, John Lafayette. *Calvinism*

and Evangelical Arminianism, 287–98. Harrisonburg, VA: Sprinkle Publications, 1984.

Helm, Paul. "Are There Few That Be Saved?" In Nigel M. de S. Cameron, ed. *Universalism and the Doctrine of Hell*, 255–81. Carlisle: Paternoster, 1992.

Hodge, Charles. *Systematic Theology*, 2:646–49. Grand Rapids: Eerdmans, 1979.

Jones, Hywel R. *Only One Way*. Bromley: Day One, 1996.

MacArthur, John. "Solus Christus." In R. C. Sproul Jr., ed. *After Darkness, Light*, 151–71. Phillipsburg, NJ: P&R, 2003.

MacArthur, John. *Why One Way?* Nashville: W Publishing Group, 2002.

McGraw, Ryan M. *The Ark of Safety: Is There*

Salvation Outside of the Church? Grand Rapids: Reformation Heritage Books, 2018.

Morey, Robert A. *The Saving Work of Christ*, 239–56. Sterling: Grace Abounding Ministries, 1980.

Morgan, Christopher W. and Robert A. Peterson, eds. *Faith Comes by Hearing: A Response to Inclusivism*. Downers Grove, IL: IVP, 2011.

Nash, Ronald H. *Is Jesus the Only Savior?* Grand Rapids: Zondervan, 1994.

Nicole, Roger. *Standing Forth*, 477–89. Fearn: Christian Focus, 2002.

Owen, John. *The Works of John Owen*, 10:108–15. Edinburgh: Banner of Truth, 1976.

Packer, J. I. *The Collected Shorter Writings of J. I. Packer*, 1:45–60, 161–98. Carlisle: Paternoster, 1998.

Packer, J. I. *The J. I. Packer Collection*, 35–46, 81–93. Edited by Alister McGrath. Downers Grove, IL: IVP, 1999.

Packer, J. I. *Revelations of the Cross*, 41–54, 139–72. Peabody: Hendrickson, 2013.

Phillips, Richard D. and Michael L. Johnson, eds. *Only One Way*. Phillipsburg: P&R, 2018.

Piper, John. *Jesus, the Only Way to God*. Grand Rapids: Baker Books, 2010.

Reymond, Robert L. *A New Systematic Theology of the Christian Faith*, 1085–93. Nashville: Thomas Nelson, 1998.

Ryken, Philip Graham. *Is Jesus the Only Way?* Wheaton: Crossway, 1999.

Shedd, William G. T. *Calvinism: Pure and Mixed*, 116–31. Edinburgh: Banner of Truth, 1986.

Sproul, R. C. *Ultimate Issues*, 69–86. Phillipsburg, NJ: P&R, 2005.

Strange, Daniel. *The Possibility of Salvation Among the Unevangelized: An Analysis of Inclusivism in Recent Evangelical Thought*. Carlisle: Paternoster, 2002.

Tiessen, Terrance L. *Who Can Be Saved?* Downers Grove: InterVarsity Press, 2004.

Wellum, Stephen. *Christ Alone: The Uniqueness of Jesus as Savior*. Grand Rapids: Zondervan, 2017.

The Extent of the Atonement

à Brakel, Wilhelmus. *The Christian's Reasonable Service*, 1:598–610. Ligonier, PA: Soli Deo Gloria, 1992.

Armstrong, Brian. *Calvinism and the Amyraut Heresy*. Madison: University of Wisconsin Press, 1969.

Ascol, Thomas K. "Redemption Defined." In Burk Parsons, ed. *John Calvin: A Heart for Devotion, Doctrine & Doxology*, 157–68. Orlando: Reformation Trust, 2008.

Barnes, Tom. *Atonement Matters*. Darlington: Evangelical Press, 2008.

Bavinck, Herman. *Reformed Dogmatics*, 3:455–75. Grand Rapids, Baker Academic, 2003.

Berkhof, Louis. *Systematic Theology*, 393–99. Grand Rapids: Eerdmans, 1988.

Bird, Michael F. *Evangelical Theology*, 420–34. Grand Rapids: Zondervan, 2013.

Blacketer, Raymond A. "Definite Atonement in Historical Perspective." In Charles E. Hill and Frank A. James, III, eds. *The Glory of the Atonement*, 304–23. Downers Grove, IL: IVP, 2004.

Boersma, Hans. *Violence, Hospitality, and the Cross*, 53–73. Grand Rapids: Baker Academic, 2004.

Boettner, Loraine. *The Reformed Doctrine of Predestination*, 150–61. Philadelphia: Presbyterian and Reformed, 1932.

Boettner, Loraine. *Studies in Theology*, 270–351. Phillipsburg, NJ: Presbyterian and Reformed, 1973.

Boice, James Montgomery and Philip Graham Ryken. *The Doctrines of Grace*, 113–34. Wheaton: Crossway, 2002.

Boice, James Montgomery, ed. *Our Sovereign God: Man, Christ, and the Atonement*, 105–78. Grand Rapids: Baker Book House, 1980.

Boyce, James Petigru. *Abstract of Systematic Theology*, 295–340. Cape Coral, FL: Founders Press, 2007.

Bray, Gerald. *God Has Spoken*, 888–920. Wheaton: Crossway, 2014.

Brown, Archibald G. *The Face of Jesus Christ: The Person and Work of Our Lord*. Edinburgh: Banner of Truth, 2102.

Carson, D. A. *The Difficult Doctrine of the Love of God*, 73–79. Wheaton: Crossway, 2000.

Chafer, Lewis Sperry. *Systematic Theology*, 3:183–205. Dallas: Dallas Seminary Press, 1948.

Clark, Gordon H. *The Atonement*. Jefferson: Trinity Foundation, 1987.

Clifford, Alan C. *Atonement and Justification: English Evangelical Theology 1640–1790 — An Evaluation*, 69–166. Oxford: Clarendon Press, 1990.

Clifford, Alan C. *Calvinus, Authentic Calvinism. A Clarification*. Norwich: Charenton Reformed Publishing, 1996.

Crisp, Oliver D. *An American Augustinian: Sin and Salvation in the Dogmatic Theology of William G. T. Shedd*. 115–15. Milton Keynes: Paternoster, 2007.

Crisp, Oliver D. *Deviant Calvinism*, 175–233. Minneapolis: Fortress Press, 2014.

Crisp, Oliver D. *Saving Calvinism: Expanding the Reformed Tradition*, 129–19. Downers Grove, IL: IVP Academic, 2016.

Culver, Robert. *Systematic Theology*, 570–52. Fearn: Mentor, 2005.

Cunningham, William. *Historical Theology*, 2:237–371. London: Banner of Truth, 1969.

Cunningham, William. *The Reformers and the Theology of the Reformation*, 395–402. London: Banner of Truth, 1969.

Custance, Arthur C. *The Sovereignty of Grace*, 149–14. Phillipsburg, NJ: Presbyterian and Reformed, 1979.

Dabney, Robert Lewis. *Christ Our Substitute*. Harrisonburg, VA: Sprinkle Publications, 1978.

Dabney, Robert Lewis. *Discussions*, 1:282–313.

Harrisonburg, VA: Sprinkle Publications, 1982.

Dabney, Robert Lewis. *Systematic Theology*, 518–55. Edinburgh: Banner of Truth, 1985.

Daniel, Curt D. "Hyper-Calvinism and John Gill," 496–607, 777–828. PhD Diss., University of Edinburgh, 1983.

Davenant, John. *A Dissertation on the Death of Christ*. Weston Rhyn: Quinta Press, 2006.

Dever, Mark and Michael Lawrence. *It is Well: Expositions on Substitutionary Atonement*. Wheaton: Crossway, 2010.

Douty, Norman. *The Death of Christ*. Swengel: Reiner, 1972. Reprinted as *Did Christ Die Only for the Elect?* Eugene: Wipf and Stock, 1998. 2nd ed. with new pagination, Irving, TX: Williams and Watrous, 1978.

Driscoll, Mark and Gerry Breshears. *Death by Love: Letters from the Cross*. Wheaton: Crossway, IL, 2008.

Edwards, Jonathan. *The Works of Jonathan Edwards*, 10:595–604; 13:174, 211–12; 478; 14:440–57; 18:450–52; 19:491–514; 25:657–75. New Haven: Yale University Press, 1992.

Elwell, Walter A. "Extent of Atonement." In Treier, Daniel J. and Walter A. Elwell, eds. *Evangelical Dictionary of Theology*, 3rd ed., 100–101. Grand Rapids: Baker Academic, 2017.

Fesko, J. V. *The Theology of the Westminster Standards*, 187–205. Wheaton: Crossway, 2014.

Flucher, Gabriel N.E., ed. *Atonement*. Phillipsburg, NJ: P&R, 2010.

Forster, Greg. *The Joy of Calvinism*, 47–67, 169–71. Wheaton: Crossway, 2012.

Fuller, Andrew. *The Complete Works of the Rev. Andrew Fuller*, 2:543–60, 692–98. Harrisonburg, VA: Sprinkle Publications, 1988.

Gamble, Richard C. *The Whole Counsel of God*, 2:568–77. Phillipsburg: P&R, 2018.

Gathercole, Simon. *Defending Substitution: An Essay on Atonement in Paul*. Grand Rapids: Baker Academic, 2015.

Gatiss, Lee. *For Us and Our Salvation: 'Limited Atonement' in the Bible, Doctrine,*

History and Ministry. London: Latimer Trust, 2012.

Gay, David H. J. *Particular Redemption and the Free Offer*. Biggleswade: Brachus, 2008.

Genke, Victor and Francis X. Gumerlock, eds. *Gottschalk and a Medieval Predestinarian Controversy: Texts Translated from the Latin*. Milwaukee: Marquette University Press, 2010.

Gerstner, John H. *Primitive Theology*, 329–468. Morgan, PA: Soli Deo Gloria, 1996.

Gibson, David and Jonathan Gibson, eds. *From Heaven He Came and Sought Her: Definite Atonement in Historical, Biblical, Theological, and Pastoral Perspective*. Wheaton: Crossway, 2013.

Gill, John. *A Body of Doctrinal and Practical Divinity*, 390–406, 427–39, 454–93. Paris, AR: Baptist Standard Bearer, 1984.

Gill, John. *The Cause of God and Truth*, 98–104, 163–78, 241–66. Grand Rapids: Baker Book House, 1980.

Godfrey, W. Robert. *Saving the Reformation: The Pastoral Theology of the Synod of Dort*, 47–52, 113–126. Orlando, FL: Reformation Trust, 2019.

Good, Kenneth H. *God's Gracious Purpose as Seen in the Gospel of John*, 70–97. Grand Rapids: Baker Book House, 1979.

Goodwin, Thomas. *The Works of Thomas Goodwin*, 5:137–337, 465–521. Eureka, CA: Tanski, 1996.

Grudem, Wayne. *Systematic Theology*, 594–603. Grand Rapids: Zondervan, 1994.

Haldane, J. A. *The Doctrine of the Atonement*. Choteau: Old Paths Gospel Publishers, n.d.

Hanko, Herman, Homer C. Hoeksema, and Gise Van Baren. *The Five Points of Calvinism*, 45–66. Grand Rapids: Reformed Free Publishing Association, 1976.

Heppe, Heinrich. *Reformed Dogmatics*, 448–87. Grand Rapids: Baker Book House, 1978.

Hodge, A. A. *The Atonement*, 321–95. Grand Rapids: Baker Book House, 1974.

Hodge, A. A. *Outlines of Theology*, 416–21. Grand Rapids: Zondervan, 1973.

Hodge, Charles. *Systematic Theology*, 2:544–62. Grand Rapids: Eerdmans, 1979.

Hoeksema, Herman. *The Triple Knowledge*, 1:508–43, 631–72. Grand Rapids: Reformed Free Publishing Association, 1976.

Hoeksema, Homer C. *The Voice of Our Fathers*, 323–423. Grand Rapids: Reformed Free Publishing Association, 1980.

Horton, Michael S. *The Christian Faith*, 516–20. Grand Rapids: Zondervan, 2011.

Horton, Michael and Fred Sanders, eds. *Five Views of the Extent of the Atonement*. Grand Rapids: Zondervan, 2018.

Horton, Michael S. *For Calvinism*, 80–98. Grand Rapids: Zondervan, 2011.

Horton, Michael S. *Mission Accomplished*. Darlington: Evangelical Press, 1990.

Horton, Michael S. *Putting Amazing Back into Grace*, 121–45. Grand Rapids: Baker Book House, 1994.

Hulse, Erroll. *Who Saves, God or Me?*, 34–40. Darlington: Evangelical Press, 2008.

Hunt, Dave and James White. *Debating Calvinism*, 169–96. Sisters, OR: Multnomah, 2004.

Hurrion, John. *Particular Redemption*. Edinburgh: Banner of Truth, 2017.

Jeffrey, Steve, Michael Ovey, and Andrew Sach. *Pierced for Our Transgressions*, 271–78. Wheaton: Crossway, 2007.

Johnson, Jeffrey D. *He Died for Me: Limited Atonement and the Universal Gospel*. Conway, AR: Free Grace Press, 2017.

Johnson, Phil. "The Extent of the Atonement." In John MacArthur, ed. *The Shepherd as Theologian*, 123–44. Eugene: Harvest House, 2017.

Kennedy, Kevin Dixon. *Union with Christ and the Extent of the Atonement in Calvin*. New York: Peter Lang, 2002.

Kuiper, R. B. *For Whom Did Christ Die?* Grand Rapids: Eerdmans, 1959. Reprinted, Grand Rapids: Baker Book House, 1982; and Eugene, OR: Wipf and Stock, 2003.

Kuyper, Abraham. *Particular Grace: A Defense*

of God's Sovereignty in Salvation, 23–52, 91–99, 208–16, 253–301. Grandville: Reformed Free Publishing Association, 2001.

Lawson, Steven J. *A Long Line of Godly Men*, 1:62–65, 81–82, 86–89, 92–93, 176–79, 196–97, 252–53, 281–89, 320–23, 332–33, 361–67, 386–88, 395–98, 403–05, 419–22, 431–32, 452–56, 473, 483–86, 537–38, 548–51. Orlando: Reformation Trust, 2006.

Letham, Robert. *The Work of Christ*, 225–47. Downers Grove, IL: IVP, 1993.

Long, Gary. *Definite Atonement*. Phillipsburg, NJ: Presbyterian and Reformed, 1977.

Lyford, William. *The Instructed Christian*, 257–83. Morgan, PA: Soli Deo Gloria, n.d.

Lynch, J. E. Hazlett. *Lamb of God Saviour of the World: The Soteriology of Rev. Dr. David Martyn Lloyd-Jones*. Bloomington: WestBow Press, 2015.

MacArthur, John. *The Gospel According to Paul*, 75–94, 137–64. Nashville: Nelson Books, 2017.

MacArthur, John and Richard Mayhue, eds. *Biblical Doctrine*, 543–65. Wheaton: Crossway, 2017.

MacLeod, Donald. *Christ Crucified*, 116–29. Downers Grove, IL: IVP Academic, 2014.

Martin, Hugh. *The Atonement*. Greenville, SC: Reformed Academic Press, 1997.

McClarty, Jim. *By Grace Alone*, 63–90. Smyrna, GA: GCA Publishing, 2007.

Moore, Jonathan D. "The Extent of the Atonement: English Hypothetical Universalism versus Particular Redemption." In Michael A. G. Haykin and Mark Jones, eds. *Drawn into Controversie: Reformed Theological Diversity and Debates Within Seventeenth-Century British Puritanism*, 124–82. Göttingen: Vandenhoeck & Ruprecht, 2011.

Moore, Jonathan D. *English Hypothetical Universalism: John Preston and the Softening of Reformed Theology*. Grand Rapids: Eerdmans, 2007.

Morecraft, Joseph C, III. *Authentic Christianity*, 2:85–105. Powder Springs, GA: Minkoff Family Publishing and American Vision Press, 2009.

Morey, Robert. *The Saving Work of Christ*. Southbridge: Crowne Publications, n.d.

Moulin, Peter (Pierre Du). *The Anatomy of Arminianisme*, 224–59. Norwood: Walter J. Johnson, 1976.

Muller, Richard A. *Dictionary of Latin and Greek Theological Terms, Drawn Principally from Protestant Scholastic Theology*, 321–23. 2nd ed. Grand Rapids: Baker Academic, 2017.

Murray, John. *Collected Writings of John Murray*, 1:29–85; 2:142–50. Edinburgh: Banner of Truth, 1976.

Murray, John. *For Whom Did Christ Die? The Extent of the Atonement*. Birmingham: Solid Ground Christian Books, 2010.

Murray, John. *Redemption Accomplished and Applied*, 69–85. Grand Rapids: Eerdmans, 1955.

Naselli, Andrew David and Mark A. Snoeberger, eds. *Perspectives on the Extent of the Atonement: 3 Views*. Nashville: B & H, 2015.

Nettles, Thomas J. "John Calvin's Understanding of the Death of Christ." In Matthew Barrett and Thomas J. Nettles, eds. *Whomever He Wills: A Surprising Display of Sovereign Mercy*, 77–119. Cape Coral, FL: Founders Press, 2012.

Nettles, Thomas J. *By His Grace and For His Glory*, 335–59. Rev. ed. Cape Coral, FL: Founders Press, 2006.

Nettles, Thomas J. *Living by Revealed Truth: The Life and Pastoral Theology of Charles Haddon Spurgeon*, 227–41. Fearn: Mentor, 2013.

Nicole, Roger R. "The Atonement." In Thomas K. Ascol, ed. *Reclaiming the Gospel and Reforming Churches*, 53–94. Cape Coral, FL: Founders Press, 2003.

Nicole, Roger R. "Covenant, Universal Call, and Definite Atonement." In Howard Griffith and John R. Muether, eds. *Creator Redeemer Consummator: A Festschrift for*

Meredith G. Kline, 193–202. Jackson, Miss.: Reformed Academic Press, 2000.

Nicole, Roger R. *Our Sovereign Saviour*, 57–73. Fearn: Mentor, 2002.

Nicole, Roger R. *Standing Forth*, 244–385. Fearn: Mentor, 2002.

Orrick, Jim Scott. *Mere Calvinism*, 83–132. Phillipsburg: P&R, 2019.

Owen, John. *The Death of Death in the Death of Christ*. Edinburgh: Banner of Truth, 1959. Also in *The Works of John Owen*, 10:139–479. See also 2:419–54; 12:591–616. Edinburgh: Banner of Truth, 1976.

Packer, J. I. and Mark Dever. *In My Place Condemned He Stood*, 111–44. Wheaton: Crossway, 2007.

Packer, J. I. *The Collected Shorter Writings of J. I. Packer*, 1:85–136, 155–58. Carlisle: Paternoster, 1998.

Packer, J. I. *Introductory Essay to The Death of Death in the Death of Christ*. London: Banner of Truth, 1959. Also in *A Quest for Godliness: The Puritan Vision of the Christian Life*, 125–48. Wheaton: Crossway, 1990.

Packer, J. I. *Revelations of the Cross*, 77–118, 133–36. Peabody: Hendrickson, 1013.

Palmer, Edwin H. *The Five Points of Calvinism*, 41–55. Rev. ed. Grand Rapids: Baker Book House, 1984.

Parks, William. *Sermons on the Five Points of Calvinism*, 49–69. Choteau, MT: Old Paths Gospel Press, n.d.

Peterson, Robert A. and Michael D. Williams. *Why I Am Not an Arminian*, 192–215. Downers Grove, IL: IVP, 2004.

Peterson, Robert A. *Calvin's Doctrine of the Atonement*. Phillipsburg, NJ: P&R, 1983.

Peterson, Robert A. *Salvation Accomplished by the Son*, 566–75. Wheaton: Crossway, 2012.

Phillips, Richard D. *The Death of the Savior: Studies in John's Gospel*. Edinburgh: Banner of Truth, 2012.

Phillips, Richard D. *Precious Blood: The Atoning Work of Christ*, 145–62, 179–203. Wheaton: Crossway, 2009.

Phillips, Richard D. *What is Atonement?* Phillipsburg, NJ: P&R, 2010.

Phillips, Richard D. *What's So Great About the Doctrines of Grace?*, 51–68. Orlando: Reformation Trust, 2008.

Pink, Arthur W. *The Atonement*. Swengel: Reiner, n.d. (Also published as *The Satisfaction of Christ*.)

Pink, Arthur W. *The Life of Faith*, 9–24. Fearn: Christian Focus, 1993.

Pink, Arthur W. *The Sovereignty of God*, 72–86, 311–20. Grand Rapids: Baker Book House, 1973.

Piper, John. *A Godward Life: Book Two*, 352–54. Sisters, OR: Multnomah, 1999.

Piper, John. *TULIP: The Pursuit of God's Glory in Salvation*, 150–72. Wheaton: Crossway, 2009.

Polhill, Edward. *The Works of Edward Polhill*, 143–75. Morgan, PA: Soli Deo Gloria, 1998.

Rainbow, Jonathan H. *The Will of God and the Cross*. Allison Park: Pickwick Publishing, 1990.

Reed, R. C. *The Gospel as Taught by Calvin*, 69–82. Edinburgh: Banner of Truth, 2009.

Reisinger, Ernest C. and D. Matthew Allen. *Beyond Five Points*, 74–80, 105–30. Cape Coral, FL: Founders Press, 2002.

Reymond, Robert L. *A New Systematic Theology of the Christian Faith*, 473–75, 671–702. Nashville: Thomas Nelson, 1998.

Robertson, Norwell. *Church-Members' Hand-Book of Theology*, 208–328. Harrisonburg, VA: Gano Books, 1983.

Robertson, O. Palmer. "Definite Atonement." In R. C. Sproul Jr., ed. *After Darkness, Light*, 95–110. Phillipsburg, NJ: P&R, 2003.

Rushton, William. *A Defense of Particular Redemption*. Elon College: Primitive Publications, n.d.

Russell, S. "Extent of Atonement." In Martin Davie, et al, eds. *New Dictionary of Theology*, 80–81. 2nd ed. Downers Grove, IL: InterVarsity Press, 2016.

Rutherford, Samuel. *The Covenant of Life*

Opened, 39–44, 265–77, 345–69. New Lenox: Puritan Publications, 2005.

Ryle, J. C. *Expository Thoughts on the Gospels*, 1:57–63, 141–70, 367; 2:221, 428–29; 3:208–10. London: James Clarke, 1975.

Sangar, James Mortimer. *The Redeemed: Who Are They?* N.p.: The Parsons Page, 2016.

Schrock, David. "Jesus Saves, No Asterisk Needed: Why I Preach the Gospel as Good News Requires Definite Atonement." In Matthew Barrett and Thomas J. Nettles, eds. *Whomever He Will: A Surprising Display of Sovereign Mercy*, 77–119. Cape Coral, FL: Founders Press, 2012.

Shedd, William G. T. *Dogmatic Theology*, 690–760. 3rd ed. Phillipsburg, NJ: P&R, 2003.

Shedd, William G. T. *Theological Essays*, 265–318. Minneapolis: Klock & Klock, 1981.

Shultz, Gary L., Jr. *A Multi-Intentioned View of the Extent of the Atonement*. Eugene: Wipf and Stock, 2013.

Smeaton, George. *The Apostles' Doctrines of the Atonement*. Edinburgh: Banner of Truth, 1991.

Smeaton, George. *Christ's Doctrine of the Atonement*. Edinburgh: Banner of Truth, 1991.

Smith, Morton H. *Systematic Theology*, 395–402. Greenville, SC: Greenville Seminary Press, 1994.

Snoddy, Richard. *The Soteriology of James Ussher*, 40–92. Oxford: Oxford University Press, 2014.

Sproul, R. C. *Grace Unknown*, 163–77. Grand Rapids: Baker Books, 1997.

Sproul, R. C. *The Truth of the Cross*, 137–53. Orlando: Reformation Trust, 2007.

Sproul, R. C. *The Work of Christ*. Colorado Springs: David C. Cook, 2012.

Spurgeon, Charles Haddon. "General, and Yet Particular." In *Metropolitan Tabernacle Pulpit*, 10:229–40. Pasadena, TX: Pilgrim Publications, 1981. See also 7:201–08; 15:301–12; 16:205–16; 20:493–504; 21:157–63; 21:172–80; 33:373–84; 38:553–62; 42:445–53, 505–14; 46:1–8; 51:517–26; 52:216–28; 56:313–22; 61:301–10.

Spurgeon, Charles Haddon. *C. H. Spurgeon's Sermons Beyond Volume 63*, 606–19. Leominster: Day One, 2009.

Spurgeon, Charles Haddon. *New Park Street Pulpit*, 4:129–36, 312–20; 6:181–96. Pasadena, TX: Pilgrim Publications, 1981.

Steele, David N., Curtis C. Thomas, and S. Lance Quinn. *The Five Points of Calvinism*, 39–52. 2nd ed. Phillipsburg, NJ: P&R, 2004.

Strong, Augustus Hopkins. *Systematic Theology*, 771–73. Old Tappan: Fleming H. Revell, 1979.

Symington, William. *The Atonement and Intercession of Jesus Christ*. Grand Rapids: Reformation Heritage Books, 2006.

Thomas, G. Michael. *The Extent of the Atonement: A Dilemma for Reformed Theology from Calvin to the Consensus (1536–1675)*. Carlisle: Paternoster, 1997.

Thomas, Geoff. "Limited Atonement: A Short Defense." In Thomas K. Ascol and Nathan A. Finn, eds. *Ministry By His Grace and For His Glory*, 142–55. Cape Coral, FL: Founders Press, 2011.

Thomas, Geoff. "Redeemed by the Son." In Thomas K. Ascol, ed. *Reclaiming the Gospel and Reforming Churches*, 111–24. Cape Coral, FL: Founders Press, 2003.

Thomas, Owen. *The Atonement Controversy in Welsh Theological Literature and Debate, 1707–1841*. Edinburgh: Banner of Truth, 2002.

Thornwell, James Henley. *The Collected Writings of James Henley Thornwell*, 2:198–290. Edinburgh: Banner of Truth, 1974.

Turretin, Francis. *Institutes of Elenctic Theology*, 2:455–82. Phillipsburg, NJ: P&R, 1992.

Turretin, Francis. *The Atonement of Christ*. Grand Rapids: Baker Book House, 1978.

Ursinus, Zacharias. *The Commentary of Dr. Zacharias Ursinus on the Heidelberg Catechism*, 215, 221–25. Phillipsburg, NJ: Presbyterian and Reformed, n.d.

Van Dixhoorn, Chad, ed. *The Minutes and Papers of the Westminster Assembly, 1643–1652*, 4:692–701. Oxford: Oxford University Press, 2012.

van Genderen, J. and W. H. Velema. *Concise Reformed Dogmatics*, 526–31. Phillipsburg, NJ: P&R, 2001.

Venema, Cornelis P. *But for the Grace of God: An Exposition of the Canons of Dort*, 37–51. Grandville: Reformed Fellowship, 2011.

Vos, Geerhardus. *Reformed Dogmatics*, 3:136–52. Bellingham: Lexham Press, 2014.

Waldron, Sam. "The Biblical Confirmation of Particular Redemption." In E. Ray Clendenen and Brad J. Waggoner, eds. *Calvinism: A Southern Baptist Dialogue*, 139–52. Nashville: B & H Academic, 2008.

Warburton, Ben A. *Calvinism*, 107–25. Grand Rapids: Eerdmans, 1955.

Warfield, Benjamin B. *Selected Shorter Writings of Benjamin B. Warfield*, 1:167–77. Nutley: Presbyterian and Reformed, 1970.

Webb, Robert Alexander. *Christian Salvation*, 148–223. Harrisonburg, VA: Sprinkle Publications, 1985.

Wells, Paul. *Cross Words*, 236–46. Fearn: Christian Focus, 2006.

Wells, Tom. *Fresh Springs*, 37–50. Dundas: Joshua Press, 2003.

Wells, Tom. *A Price for a People*. Edinburgh: Banner of Truth, 1992.

White, James R. *The Potter's Freedom*, 229–82. Amityville: Calvary Press Publishing, 2000.

White, James R. *The Sovereign Grace of God*, 85–96. Lindenhurst: Great Christian Books, 2003.

Williams Jarvis J. *For Whom Did Christ Die? The Extent of the Atonement in Paul's Theology.* Milton Keynes: Paternoster, 2012.

Williamson, John. *L of the Tulip*. Baltimore: PublishAmerica, 2009.

Witsius, Herman. *The Economy of the Covenants Between God and Man*, 1:234–71. Escondido: Den Dulk Foundation; and Phillipsburg, NJ: P&R, 1990.

Wright, R. K. McGregor. *No Place for Sovereignty*, 143–54. Downers Grove, IL: IVP, 1996.

Irresistible Grace

à Brakel, Wilhelmus. *The Christian's Reasonable Service*, 2:191–232. Ligonier, PA: Soli Deo Gloria, 1993.

Barrett, Matthew. "The Scriptural Affirmation of Monergism." In Matthew Barrett and Thomas J. Nettles, eds. *Whomever He Wills*, 120–87. Cape Coral, FL: Founders Press, 1012.

Barrett, Matthew. *Salvation by Grace: The Case for Effectual Calling and Regeneration*, 69–124. Phillipsburg, NJ: P&R, 2013.

Bavinck, Herman. *Reformed Dogmatics*, 4:29–44, 80–84. Grand Rapids: Baker Academic, 200S.

Bavinck, Herman. *Saved by Grace*. Grand Rapids: Reformation Heritage Books, 2008.

Beardslee, John W., III, ed. *Reformed Dogmatics*, 157–61. New York: Oxford University Press, 1965.

Boettner, Loraine. *The Reformed Doctrine of Predestination*, 162–81. Philadelphia: Presbyterian and Reformed, 1932.

Boice, James Montgomery and Philip Graham Ryken. *The Doctrines of Grace*, 135–54. Wheaton: Crossway, 2002.

Boston, Thomas. *The Complete Works of the Late Rev. Thomas Boston*, 1:557–80, 4:11–21. Wheaton: Richard Owen Roberts, 1980.

Boyce, James Petigru. *Abstract of Systematic Theology*, 367–73. Cape Coral, FL: Founders Press, 2007.

Breward, Ian, ed. *The Work of William Perkins*, 225–31. Appleford: Sutton Courtenay Press, 1970.

Brown, John. *The Systematic Theology of John Brown*, 336–58. Fearn: Christian Focus;

and Grand Rapids: Reformation Heritage Books, 2002.

Burns, J. Patout. *The Development of Augustine's Doctrine of Operative Grace.* Paris: Etudes Augustiniennes, 1980.

Custance, Arthur C. *The Sovereignty of Grace*, 175–89. Phillipsburg, NJ: Presbyterian and Reformed, 1979.

Dabney, Robert Lewis. *Systematic Theology*, 553–79. Edinburgh: Banner of Truth, 1985.

Dickinson, Jonathan. *The True Scripture Doctrine Concerning Some Important Points of Christian Faith*, 137–78. Harrisonburg, VA: Sprinkle Publications, 1992.

Duncan, John. *'Just a Talker': The Sayings of Dr. John Duncan*, 217–22. Edinburgh: Banner of Truth, 1997

Edwards, Brian H. *Grace: Amazing Grace*, 129–46. Leominster: Day One, 2002.

Edwards, Jonathan. *The Works of Jonathan Edwards*, 13:170–71, 208; 14:374–436; 17:142–72; 18:211; 21:149–311. New Haven: Yale University Press, 1992.

Erskine, Ralph. *The Works of Ralph Erskine*, 6:441–79. Glasgow: Free Presbyterian Publications, 1991.

Flavel, John. *The Method of Grace.* Grand Rapids: Baker Book House, 1977. Also in *The Works of John Flavel*, 2:3–474. Edinburgh: Banner of Truth, 1982.

Forster, Greg. *The Joy of Calvinism*, 91–119. Wheaton: Crossway, 2012.

Frame, John M. *Systematic Theology*, 934–42. Phillipsburg, NJ: P&R, 2013.

Geldenhuys, J. Norval. "Effectual Calling." In Carl F. H. Henry, ed. *Basic Christian Doctrines*, 170–84. New York: Holt, Rinehart and Winston, 1962.

Gerstner, John H. "Augustine on Irresistible Grace." In Henry Vander Goot, ed. *Life is Religion*, 135–58. St. Catherine's: Paideia Press, 1981.

Gill, John. *The Cause of God and Truth.* 105–21, 178–82, 286–99. Grand Rapids: Baker Book House, 1980.

Good, Kenneth H. *God's Gracious Purpose as Seen in the Gospel of John*, 98–131. Grand Rapids: Baker Book House, 1979.

Goodwin, Thomas. *The Work of the Holy Spirit in Our Salvation.* Edinburgh: Banner of Truth, 1979. Also in: *The Works of Thomas Goodwin, Volume 6.* Eureka, CA: Tanski, 1996.

Grudem, Wayne. *Systematic Theology*, 692–98. Grand Rapids; Zondervan, 1994.

Hanko, Herman, Homer C. Hoeksema, and Gise Van Baren. *The Five Points of Calvinism*, 69–80. Grand Rapids: Reformed Free Publishing Association, 1976.

Hicks, Tom. "Understanding Effectual Calling." In Thomas K. Ascol and Nathan A. Finn, eds. *Ministry By His Grace and For His Glory*, 156–69. Cape Coral, FL: Founders Press, 2011.

Hodge, A. A. *Outlines of Theology*, 445–55. Grand Rapids: Zondervan, 1973.

Hodge, Charles. *Systematic Theology*, 2:675–710. Grand Rapids: Eerdmans, 1979.

Hoekema, Anthony A. *Saved by Grace*, 80–92. Grand Rapids: Eerdmans, 1989.

Hoglund, Jonathan. *Called by Triune Grace: Divine Rhetoric and the Effectual Call.* Downers Grove: IVP Academic, 2016.

Horton, Michael S. *The Christian Faith*, 560–75. Grand Rapids: Zondervan, 2011.

Horton, Michael S. *Covenantal Salvation*, 216–42. Louisville: Westminster John Knox Press, 2007.

Horton, Michael S. *For Calvinism*, 99–115. Grand Rapids: Zondervan, 2011.

Horton, Michael S. *Putting Amazing Back into Grace*, 147–63. Grand Rapids: Baker Book House, 1994.

Hulse, Erroll. *Who Saves, God or Me?* 40–45. Darlington: Evangelical Press, 2008.

Hunt, Dave and James White. *Debating Calvinism*, 197–224. Sisters, OR: Multnomah, 2004.

Kersten, G. H. *Reformed Dogmatics*, 2:364–75. Sioux Center: Netherlands Reformed Book and Publishing Committee, 1980.

Kuyper, Abraham. *Particular Grace: A*

Defense of God's Sovereignty in Salvation. Grandville: Reformed Free Publishing Association, 2001.

Kuyper, Abraham. *The Work of the Holy Spirit,* 203–17, 338–53. Grand Rapids: Eerdmans, 1969.

Lawson, Steven J. *A Long Line of Godly Men,* 1:65–66, 82–83, 97–98, 112–13, 121, 145–46, 179–81, 197–99, 222, 229–30, 235, 253–56, 263–65, 289–95, 313–315, 323–26, 333–36, 367–70, 388–92, 398–99, 405, 423–25, 432–34, 456–60, 474–78, 487–88, 506–07, 517–21, 523, 538–50, 551–52. Orlando: Reformation Trust, 2006.

Lems, Shane. *The Doctrines of Grace,* 57–70. Phillipsburg, NJ: P&R, 2013.

Lloyd-Jones, D. Martyn. *Great Doctrines of the Bible,* 2:64–73. Wheaton: Crossway, 2003.

Love, Christopher. *A Treatise of Effectual Calling and Election.* Morgan, PA: Soli Deo Gloria, 1998.

Mathison, Keith A. "Transforming Grace." In Burk Parsons, ed. *John Calvin: A Heart for Devotion, Doctrine & Doxology,* 169–77. Orlando: Reformation Trust, 2008.

McClarty, Jim. *By Grace Alone,* 91–112. Smyrna, GA: GCA Publishing, 2007.

Montgomery, Daniel and Timothy Paul Jones. *PROOF: Finding Freedom Through the Intoxicating Joy of Irresistible Grace.* Grand Rapids: Zondervan, 2015.

Morecraft, Joseph C., III. *Authentic Christianity,* 2:660–93. Powder Springs, GA: Minkoff Family Publishing and American Vision Press, 2009.

Moulin, Peter (Pierre Du). *The Anatomy of Arminianisme,* 345–504. Norwood: Walter J. Johnson, 1976.

Muller, Richard A. *Dictionary of Latin and Greek Theological Terms, Drawn Principally from Protestant Scholastic Theology,* 396–97. 2nd ed. Grand Rapids: Baker Academic, 2017.

Murray, John. "Irresistible Grace." In R. C. Sproul, ed. *Soli Deo Gloria: Essays in Reformed Theology,* 55–62. Phillipsburg, NJ: Presbyterian and Reformed, 1976.

Murray, John. *The Collected Writings of John Murray,* 2:161–66. Edinburgh: Banner of Truth, 1977.

Murray, John. *Redemption Accomplished and Applied,* 109–15. Grand Rapids: Eerdmans, 1955.

Nettles, Tom. "Preaching Irresistible Grace." In Thomas J. Ascol, ed. *Reclaiming the Gospel and Reforming Churches,* 383–404. Cape Coral, FL: Founders Press, 2003.

Orrick, Jim Scott. *Mere Calvinism,* 133–60. Phillipsburg: P&R, 2019.

Owen, John. *The Works of John Owen,* 3:207–366; 9:217–36; 10:43–53; 129–37. Edinburgh: Banner of Truth, 1976.

Palmer, Edwin H. *The Five Points of Calvinism,* 56–67. Rev. ed. Grand Rapids: Baker Book House, 1984.

Parks, William. *Sermons on the Five Points of Calvinism,* 70–87. Choteau, MT: Old Paths Gospel Press, n.d.

Pemberton, Ebenezer. *The Puritan Pulpit,* 35–54. Orlando: Soli Deo Gloria, 2006.

Perkins, William. *A Golden Chaine,* 168–77. N.p.: Puritan Reprints, 2010.

Peterson, Robert A. and Michael D. Williams. *Why I Am Not an Arminian,* 173–91. Downers Grove, IL: IVP, 2004.

Phillips, Richard D. *What's So Great About the Doctrines of Grace?* 69–82. Orlando: Reformation Trust, 2008.

Pink, Arthur W. *The Holy Spirit,* 79–84. Grand Rapids: Baker Book House, 1970.

Pink, Arthur W. *The Sovereignty of God,* 49–79. Grand Rapids: Baker Book House, 1973.

Piper, John. *Five Points,* 25–36. Fearn: Christian Focus, 2013.

Piper, John. *TULIP: The Pursuit of God's Glory in Salvation,* 31–57, 97–110. Wheaton: Crossway, 2009.

Polhill, Edward. *The Works of Edward Polhill,* 175–211. Morgan, PA: Soli Deo Gloria, 1998.

Reed, R. C. *The Gospel as Taught by Calvin*, 33–46. Edinburgh: Banner of Truth, 2009.

Reymond, Robert L. *A New Systematic Theology of the Christian Faith*, 712–18. Nashville: Thomas Nelson, 1998.

Rollock, Robert. *Select Works of Robert Rollock*, 1:29–273. Grand Rapids: Reformation Heritage Books, 2007.

Rushdoony, Rousas John. *Salvation and Godly Rule*, 259–63. Vallecito: Ross House Books, 1983.

Schreiner, Thomas R. and Bruce A. Ware, eds. *The Grace of God, The Bondage of the Will*, 2:339–82. Grand Rapids: Baker, 1995.

Schreiner, Thomas R. and Bruce A. Ware, eds. *Still Sovereign*, 203–46. Grand Rapids: Baker Books, 2000.

Selderhuis, Herman J., ed. *The Calvin Handbook*, 282–87. Grand Rapids: Eerdmans, 2009.

Shaw, Robert. *The Reformed Faith*, 165–71. Fearn: Christian Heritage, 2008.

Sproul, R. C. *Everyone's a Theologian*, 226–231. Orlando: Reformation Trust, 2014.

Sproul, R. C. *Grace Unknown*, 179–96. Grand Rapids: Faker Books, 1997.

Sproul, R. C. *Truths We Confess*, 2:13–34. Phillipsburg, NJ: P&R, 2007.

Spurgeon, Charles Haddon. *Metropolitan Tabernacle Pulpit*, 10:633–44; 11:111–20; 14:661–72; 32:433–44; 36:325–36; 40:529–38; 52:445–53. Pasadena, TX: Pilgrim Publications, 1981.

Spurgeon, Charles Haddon. *New Park Street Pulpit*, 2:153–60, 5:129–36. Pasadena, TX: Pilgrim Publications, 1981.

Spurgeon, Charles Haddon. *Sermons on Sovereignty*, 107–19, 136–46. Pasadena, TX: Pilgrim Publications, 1990.

Steele, David N., Custis C. Thomas, and S. Lance Quinn. *The Five Points of Calvinism*, 52–64. 2nd ed. Phillipsburg, NJ: P&R, 2004.

Treier, Daniel J. and Walter A. Elwell, eds. *Evangelical Dictionary of Theology*, 3rd ed., 266. Grand Rapids: Baker Academic, 2017.

Turretin, Francis. *Institutes of Elenctic Theology*, 2:510–58. Phillipsburg, NJ: P&R, 1992.

van den Belt, Henk, ed. *Synopsis Purioris Theologiae: Synopsis of a Purer Theology*, 2:209–27. Leiden: Brill, 2016.

Van Dixhoorn, Chad. *Confessing the Faith*, 145–58, Edinburgh: Banner of Truth, 2014.

Venema, Cornelis P. *But for the Grace of God: An Exposition of the Canons of Dort*, 60–70. Grandville: Reformed Fellowship, 1994.

Warburton, Ben A. *Calvinism*, 149–68. Grand Rapids: Eerdmans, 1955.

Watson, Thomas. *All Things for Good*, 104–18. Edinburgh: Banner of Truth, 2011.

Watson, Thomas. *A Body of Divinity*, 220–26. Edinburgh: Banner of Truth, 1974.

Wells, David F. *God the Evangelist: How the Holy Spirit Works to Bring Men and Women to Faith*. Grand Rapids: Eerdmans, 1987.

Wells, Tom. *Faith: The Gift of God*, 55–67. Edinburgh: Banner of Truth, 1983.

Weltby, Greg. "Election and Calling: A Biblical Theological Study." In E. Ray Clendenen and Brad J. Waggoner, eds. *Calvinism: A Southern Baptist Dialogue*, 216–43. Nashville: B & H Academic, 2008.

White, James R. *Drawn by the Father*. Southbridge: Crown Publications, 1991.

White, James R. *The Potter's Freedom*, 283–328. Amityville: Calvary Press Publishing, 2000.

White, James R. *The Sovereign Grace of God*, 97–107. Lindenhurst: Great Christian Books, 2003.

White, Thomas. "Of Effectual Calling." In *Puritan Sermons 1659–1689*, 5:269–83. Wheaton: Richard Owen Roberts, 1981.

Wilson, Douglas J. "Irresistible Grace." In R. C. Sproul Jr., ed. *After Darkness, Light*, 137–49. Phillipsburg, NJ: P&R, 2003.

Wilterdink, Garret. *Tyrant or Father: A Study in Calvin's Doctrine of God*, 89–133. Bristol: Wyndham Hall Press, 1985.

Winslow, Octavius. *The Work of the Holy Spirit*. London: Banner of Truth, 1961.

Witsius, Herman. *The Economy of the Covenants Between God and Man*, 1:344–

56. Escondido: Den Dulk Foundation; and Phillipsburg, NJ: P&R, 1990.

Zaspel, Fred G. *The Theology of B. B. Warfield*, 433–40. Wheaton: Crossway, 2010.

The New Birth

à Brakel, Wilhelmus. *The Christian's Reasonable Service*, 2:233–60. Ligonier, PA: Soli Deo Gloria, 1992.

Adams, James E. *Decisional Regeneration vs. Divine Regeneration*. Vestavia Hills: Solid Ground Christian Books, 2010.

Alexander, Archibald, ed. *Sermons of the Log College*, 189–206, 256–308. Ligonier, PA: Soli Deo Gloria, 1993.

Alexander, Archibald. *Thoughts on Religious Experience*, 21–78. Edinburgh: Banner of Truth, 1978.

Barrett, Matthew. *Salvation by Grace: The Case for Effectual Calling and Regeneration*. Phillipsburg, NJ: P&R, 2013.

Barrett, Matthew. *What is Regeneration?* Phillipsburg, NJ: P&R, 2013.

Bavinck, Herman. *Reformed Dogmatics*, 4:45–95. Grand Rapids: Baker Academic, 2008.

Bavinck, Herman. *Saved by Grace*. Grand Rapids: Reformation Heritage Books, 2008.

Beeke, Joel R. and Mark Jones. *A Puritan Theology*, 463–80. Grand Rapids: Reformation Heritage Books, 2012.

Berkhof, Louis. *Systematic Theology*, 465–79. Grand Rapids: Eerdmans, 1988.

Boston, Thomas. *The Complete Works of the Late Rev. Thomas Boston*, 1:529–81. Wheaton: Richard Owen Roberts, 1980.

Boyce, James Petigru. *Abstract of Systematic Theology*, 373–82. Cape Coral, FL: Founders Press, 2007.

Brady, Gary. *What the Bible Teaches About Being Born Again*. Darlington: Evangelical Press, 2008.

Bunyan, John. *The Works of John Bunyan*, 2:755–58. Edinburgh: Banner of Truth, 1991.

Charnock, Stephen. *The New Birth*. Grand Rapids: Baker Book House, 1980. Also in: *The Works of Stephen Charnock*, 3:7–335. Edinburgh: Banner of Truth, 1985.

Christensen, Scott. *What About Free Will?* 187–90, 198–200, 208–18. Phillipsburg, NJ: P&R, 2016.

Citron, Bernhard. *New Birth: A Study of the Evangelical Doctrine or Conversion in the Protestant Fathers*. Edinburgh: Edinburgh University Press, 1951.

Clark, Gordon H. *Predestination*, 85–109. Phillipsburg, NJ: P&R, 1987.

Clarkson, David. *The Works of David Clarkson*, 2:3–33. Edinburgh: Banner of Truth, 1988.

Culver, Robert. *Systematic Theology*, 689–99. Fearn: Mentor, 2006.

Custance, Arthur C. *Man in Adam and in Christ, The Doorway Papers*, 3:170–80. Grand Rapids: Zondervan, 1975.

Dabney, Robert Lewis. *Discussions*, 1:482–95. Harrisonburg, VA: Sprinkle Publications, 1982.

de Vries, Pieter. *John Bunyan on the Order of Salvation*, 123–45. New York: Peter Lang, 1994.

Edwards, Jonathan. *Sermons on the Lord's Supper*, 176–90. Orlando: The Northampton Press, 2007.

Edwards, Jonathan. *The Works of Jonathan Edwards*, 13:357–58; 17:184–95; 20:68–74. New Haven: Yale University Press, 1994.

Ferguson, Sinclair. *Children of the Living God*, 15–23. Edinburgh: Banner of Truth, 1989.

Frame, John. *Systematic Theology*, 944–51. Phillipsburg, NJ: P&R, 2013.

Fuller, Andrew. *The Complete Works of the Rev. Andrew Fuller*, 3:776–79. Harrisonburg, VA: Sprinkle Publications, 1988.

Gatiss, Lee, ed. *The Sermons of George Whitefield*, 2:275–87. Wheaton: Crossway, 2012.

Gerstner, John H. *The Rational Biblical*

Theology of Jonathan Edwards, 3:137–90. Orlando: Ligonier Ministries, 1993.

Gill, John. *A Complete Body of Doctrinal and Practical Divinity*, 528–38. Paris, AR: Baptist Standard Bearer, 1984.

Goodwin, Thomas. *The Works of Thomas Goodwin*, 6:73–94, 151–230, 359–458. Eureka, CA: Tanski, 1996.

Grudem, Wayne. *Systematic Theology*, 699–708. Grand Rapids: Zondervan, 1994.

Hamilton, Stephen James. *"Born Again": A Portrait and Analysis of the Doctrine of Regeneration Within Evangelical Protestantism*, 100–132. Göttingen: Vandenhoeck & Ruprecht, 2017.

Hodge, A. A. *Outlines of Theology*, 456–64. Grand Rapids: Zondervan, 1973.

Hodge, Charles. *Systematic Theology*, 3:3–40. Grand Rapids: Eerdmans, 1979.

Hoekema, Anthony A. *Saved by Grace*, 93–112. Grand Rapids: Eerdmans, 1989.

Hoeksema, Herman. *Reformed Dogmatics*, 2:25–41. 2nd ed. Grandville: Reformed Free Publishing Association, 2004.

Hopkins, Ezekiel. *The Works of Ezekiel Hopkins*, 2:221–410. Morgan, PA: Soli Deo Gloria, 1997.

Horton, Michael. *The Christian Faith*, 572–77. Grand Rapids: Zondervan, 2011.

Kersten, G. H. *Reformed Dogmatics*, 2:376–93. Sioux Center: Netherlands Reformed Book and Publishing Committee, 1980.

Kirkpatrick, Daniel. *Monergism or Synergism?*, 85–128. Eugene, OR: Pickwick Publications, 2018.

Knudsen, Robert D. "The Nature of Regeneration." In Carl F.H. Henry, ed. *Christian Faith and Modern Theology*, 305–21. New York: Channel Press, 1964.

Kuyper, Abraham. *The Work of the Holy Spirit*, 293–337. Grand Rapids: Eerdmans, 1969.

Lawson, Steven J. *A Long Line of Godly Men*, 1:187–89, 211–12, 525–26. Orlando: Reformation Trust, 2006.

Lloyd-Jones, D. Martyn. *Experiencing the New Birth*. Wheaton: Crossway, 2015.

Lloyd-Jones, D. Martyn. *Great Doctrines of the Bible*, 2:74–94. Wheaton: Crossway, 2003.

Lloyd-Jones, D. Martyn. *The Kingdom of God*, 189–204. Wheaton: Crossway, 1992.

MacArthur, John and Richard Mayhue, eds. *Biblical Doctrine*, 349–53, 576–89. Wheaton: Crossway, 2017.

Manton, Thomas. *The Complete Works of Thomas Manton, D.D.*, 21:299–336. Worthington, PA: Maranatha Publications, n.d.

McGowan, A. T. B. *The New Birth*. Fearn: Christian Focus, 1996.

Morecraft, Joseph C., III. *Authentic Christianity*, 2:261–706. Powder Springs, GA: Minkoff Family Publishing and American Vision Press, 2009.

Morey, Robert A. *The Saving Work of Christ*, 109–36. Sterling: Grace Abounding Ministries, 1980.

Murray, John. *The Collected Writings of John Murray*, 2:167–201. Edinburgh: Banner of Truth, 1976.

Murray, John. *Redemption Accomplished and Applied*, 119–29. Grand Rapids: Eerdmans, 1955.

Nettleton, Asahel. *Sermons from the Second Great Awakening*, 143–49, 426–31. Ames, IA: International Outreach, 1995.

Owen, John. *The Works of John Owen*, 3:297–337. Edinburgh: Banner of Truth, 1976.

Packer, J. I. "Regeneration." In Treier, Daniel J. and Walter A. Elwell, eds. *Evangelical Dictionary of Theology*, 3rd ed., 734–35. Grand Rapids: Baker Academic, 2017.

Palmer, Edwin H. *The Holy Spirit*, 77–86. Philadelphia; Presbyterian and Reformed, 1964.

Payson, Edward. *The Complete Works of Edward Payson*, 2:205–16. Harrisonburg, VA: Sprinkle Publications, 1987.

Phelps, Austin. *The New Birth*. Birmingham: Solid Ground Christian Books, 2015.

Phillips, Richard D. *Saved by Grace*, 47–60. Phillipsburg, NJ: P&R, 2009.

Pink, Arthur W. *The Doctrine of Salvation*,

9–42. Grand Rapids: Baker Book House, 1975.

Piper, John. *Finally Alive*. Fearn: Christian Focus, 2009.

Piper, John. *A Godward Life: Book Two*, 249–51. Sisters, OR: Multnomah, 1997.

Rice, N. L. *God Sovereign and Man Free*, 162–78. Harrisonburg, VA: Sprinkle Publications, 1985.

Ryle, J. C. *Knots Untied*, 87–129. London: James Clarke, 1964.

Ryle, J. C. *A New Birth*. Grand Rapids: Baker Book House, 1977.

Ryle, J. C. *The True Christian*, 15–56. Welwyn: Evangelical Press, 1978.

Ryle, J. C. *The Upper Room*, 350–64. Edinburgh: Banner of Truth, 1977.

Shedd, William G. T. *Dogmatic Theology*, 761–86. 3rd ed. Phillipsburg, NJ: P&R, 2003.

Sibbes, Richard. *The Works of Richard Sibbes*, 7:127–37. Edinburgh: Banner of Truth, 1973.

Smallman, Stephen. *Beginnings: Understanding How We Experience the New Birth*. Phillipsburg; P&R, 2015.

Smeaton, George. *The Doctrine of the Holy Spirit*, 175–220. Edinburgh: Banner of Truth: 1974.

Smith, Morton H. *Systematic Theology*, 2:431–39. Greenville, SC: Greenville Seminary Press, 1994.

Spinney, Robert G. and Justin Dillehay. *Not the Way I Used to Be: Practical Implications of the Bible's Large Doctrine of Regeneration*. Hartsville: Tulip Books, 2007.

Sproul, R. C. *Chosen by God*, 101–26. Wheaton: Tyndale House, 1986.

Sproul, R. C. *What Does It Mean to be Born Again?* Lake Mary: Reformation Trust, 2010.

Spurgeon, Charles Haddon. *Metropolitan Tabernacle Pulpit*, 15:397–408; 17:133–44; 37:181–92; 38:361–69; 44:49–60; 54:577–88. Pasadena, TX: Pilgrim Publications, 1981.

Spurgeon, Charles Haddon. *New Park Street Pulpit*, 3:161–68; 3:185–92. Pasadena, TX: Pilgrim Publications, 1981.

Spurgeon, Charles Haddon. *Sermons on Sovereignty*, 147–59. Pasadena, TX: Pilgrim Publications, 1990.

Swinnock. George. *The Works of George Swinnock*, 5:1–261. Edinburgh: Banner of Truth, 1992.

Toon, Peter. *Born Again*. Grand Rapids: Baker Book House, 1987.

van den Belt, Henk, ed. *Synoposis Purioris Theologiae: Synopsis of a Purer Theology*, 2:277–303. Leiden: Brill, 2016.

van Genderen, J. and W. H. Velema. *Concise Reformed Dogmatics*, 585–89. Phillipsburg, NJ: P&R, 2008.

van Mastricht, Peter. *A Treatise on Regeneration*. Morgan, PA: Soli Deo Gloria, 2002.

Vass, Larry Ivan. *A Reformed View of the Sovereignty of God in a Postmodern World*, 175–274. Baltimore: PublishAmerica, 2008.

Vickers, Douglas. *When God Converts a Sinner*, 71–92. Eugene: Wipf and Stock, 2008.

Vos, Geerhardus. *Reformed Dogmatics*, 4:29–57. Bellingham: Lexham Press, 2015.

Warfield, Benjamin B. *Selected Shorter Writings of Benjamin B. Warfield*, 1:267–77, 2:321–24. Nutley: Presbyterian and Reformed, 1970.

Warfield, Benjamin B. *The Works of Benjamin B. Warfield*, 2:439–63. Grand Rapids: Baker Book House, 1981.

Watson, Thomas. *A Plea for the Godly*, 268–92. Pittsburgh: Soli Deo Gloria, 1993.

Webb, Robert Alexander. *Christian Salvation*, 293–325. Harrisonburg, VA: Sprinkle Publications, 1985.

Wells, David F. *Turning to God*. Grand Rapids: Baker Books, 2012.

Wells, Tom. *Faith: The Gift of God*, 55–77. Edinburgh: Banner of Truth, 1983.

Witherspoon, John. "A Practical Treatise on Regeneration." In *The Works of the Rev. John Witherspoon*, 1:73–219. Harrisonburg: Sprinkle, 2001.

Witsius, Herman. *The Economy of the Covenants Between God and Man*, 1:356–72.

Escondido: Den Dulk Foundation; and Phillipsburg, NJ: P&R, 1990.

The Gift of Faith

à Brakel, Wilhelmus. *The Christian's Reasonable Service*, 2:261–306. Ligonier, PA: Soli Deo Gloria, 1992.

Augustine. *The Works of Saint Augustine*, 1/26:150–67, 182–85. Hyde Park: New City Press, 1999.

Bavinck, Herman. *Reformed Dogmatics*, 4:96–140. Grand Rapids: Baker Academic, 2008.

Burroughs, Jeremiah. *Faith*. Orlando: The Northampton Press, 2011.

Clark, Gordon H. *Faith and Saving Faith*. Jefferson: Trinity Foundation, 1983.

Clark, Gordon H. *Predestination*, 101–09. Phillipsburg, NJ: Presbyterian and Reformed, 1987.

Clarkson, David. *The Works of David Clarkson*, 1:63–175. Edinburgh: Banner of Truth, 1988.

Gill, John. *A Complete Body of Doctrinal and Practical Divinity*, 730–46. Paris, AR: Baptist Standard Bearer, 1984.

Goodwin, Thomas. *The Object and Acts of Justifying Faith*. Edinburgh: Banner of Truth, 1985. Also published as *The Works of Thomas Goodwin, Volume 8*. Eureka, CA: Tanski, 1996.

Hodge, Charles. *Systematic Theology*, 3:41–113. Grand Rapids: Eerdmans, 1979.

Hoekema, Anthony A. *Saved by Grace*, 132–51. Grand Rapids: Eerdmans, 1989.

Kuyper, Abraham. *The Work of the Holy Spirit*, 406–14. Grand Rapids: Eerdmans, 1969.

Machen, J. Gresham. *What is Faith?* Grand Rapids: Eerdmans, 1962.

Murray, John. *The Collected Writings of John Murray*, 2:235–63. Edinburgh: Banner of Truth, 1976.

Murray, John. *Redemption Accomplished and Applied*, 133–43. Grand Rapids: Eerdmans, 1955.

Pemberton, Ebenezer. *The Puritan Pulpit*, 228–39. Orlando: Soli Deo Gloria, 2006.

Pink, Arthur W. *The Holy Spirit*, 85–87. Grand Rapids: Baker Book House, 1970.

Pink, Arthur W. *Studies in Saving Faith*. Swengel, PA: Reiner, n.d.

Polhill, Edward. *The Works of Edward Polhill*, 213–325. Morgan, PA: Soli Deo Gloria, 1998.

Richard, Guy M. *What is Faith?* Phillipsburg, NJ: P&R, 2012.

Shepherd, Victor. *The Nature and Function of Faith in the Theology of John Calvin*. Macon, GA: Mercer University Press, 1983.

Spurgeon, Charles Haddon. *Metropolitan Tabernacle Pulpit*, 18:37–48; 45:241–49. Pasadena, TX: Pilgrim Publications, 1981.

Storms, Sam. *Chosen for Life*, 69–75. 2nd ed. Wheaton: Crossway, 2007.

van Genderen, J. and W. R. Velema. *Concise Reformed Dogmatics*, 589–606. Phillipsburg, NJ: P&R, 2008.

Vickers, Douglas. *When God Converts a Sinner*, 45–70. Eugene: Wipf and Stock, 2008.

Vos, Geerhardus. *Reformed Dogmatics*, 4:72–132. Bellingham: Lexham Press, 2015.

Warfield, Benjamin B. *Biblical and Theological Studies*, 404–44. Philadelphia: Presbyterian and Reformed, 1968.

Warfield, Benjamin B. *The Works of Benjamin B. Warfield*, 2:467–508. Grand Rapids: Baker Book House, 1981.

Webb, Robert Alexander. *Christian Salvation*, 330–58. Harrisonburg, VA: Sprinkle Publications, 1985.

Wells, Tom. *Faith, The Gift of God*. Edinburgh: Banner of Truth, 1983.

The Order of Salvation

Bavinck, Herman. *Reformed Dogmatics*, 3:522–35. Grand Rapids: Baker Academic, 2003.

Bavinck, Herman. *Saved by Grace*, 100–109. Grand Rapids: Reformation Heritage Books, 2008.

Berkhof, Louis. *Systematic Theology*, 415–22. Grand Rapids: Eerdmans, 1988.

Berkouwer, G. C. *Faith and Justification*, 25–36, 143–68. Grand Rapids: Eerdmans, 1979.

Calvin, John. *Institutes of the Christian Religion*, Book 2 (pp. 535–1008). Philadelphia: Westminster Press, 1960.

Cara, Robert J. *Cracking the Foundation of the New Perspective on Paul: Covenantal Monism Versus Reformed Covenantal Theology*. Fearn: Mentor, 2017.

Collins, G. N. M. "Order of Salvation." In Treier, Daniel J. and Walter A. Elwell, eds. *Evangelical Dictionary of Theology*, 3rd ed., 622. Grand Rapids: Baker Academic, 2017.

Dabney, Robert Lewis. *Systematic Theology*, 655–58. Edinburgh: Banner of Truth, 1985.

Engelsma, David J. *Gospel Truth of Justification*. Jenison: Reformed Free Publishing Association, 2017.

Evans, William B. *Imputation and Impartation: Union with Christ in American Reformed Theology*, 52–57. Milton Keynes: Paternoster, 2008.

Ferguson, Sinclair B. "Ordo Salutis." In Martin Davie et al, eds. *New Dictionary of Theology*, 633–34. 2nd ed. Downers Grove, IL: InterVarsity Press, 2016.

Fesko, J. V. *Beyond Calvin: Union with Christ and Justification in Early Modern Reformed Theology (1517–1700)*, 53–162. Göttingen: Vandenhoeck & Ruprecht, 2012.

Fesko, J.V. "The Ground of Religion: Justification in the Reformed Tradition." In Matthew Barrett, ed. *The Doctrine on Which the Church Stands or Falls*, 701–38. Wheaton, IL: Crossway, 2019.

Gaffin, Richard B., Jr. *By Faith, Not by Sight: Paul and the Order of Salvation*. Bletchley: Paternoster, 2006.

Helm, Paul. *The Beginnings: Word and Spirit in Conversion*. Edinburgh: Banner of Truth, 1986.

Hodge, A. A. *Outlines of Theology*, 515–19. Grand Rapids: Zondervan, 1973.

Hodge, Charles. *Justification by Faith Alone*. Hobbs: Trinity Foundation, 1995.

Hoekema, Anthony A. *Saved by Grace*, 11–27. Grand Rapids: Eerdmans, 1989.

Hoeksema, Herman. *Reformed Dogmatics*, 2:16–24. 2nd ed. Grandville: Reformed Free Publishing Association, 2004.

Kersten, G. H. *Reformed Dogmatics*, 2:361–63. Sioux Center: Netherlands Reformed Book and Publishing Committee, 1980.

Letham, Robert. *The Westminster Assembly*, 242–92. Phillipsburg, NJ: P&R, 2009.

Maas, Korey D. "Justification by Faith Alone." In Matthew Barrett, ed. *Reformation Theology*, 511–48. Wheaton: Crossway Books, 2017.

MacArthur, John and Richard Mayhue, eds. *Biblical Doctrine*, 567–71, 609–24. Wheaton: Crossway, 2017.

McGowan, A. T. B. "Justification in the ordo salutis." In Bruce L. McCormack, ed. *Justification in Perspective: Historical Developments and Contemporary Challenges*, 147–63. Grand Rapids: Baker Academic, 2006.

Morey, Robert A. *The Saving Work of Christ*, 81–86. Sterling: Grace Abounding Ministries, 1980.

Muller, Richard A. *Calvin and the Reformed Tradition*, 161–243. Grand Rapids: Baker Academic, 2012.

Muller, Richard A. *Dictionary of Latin and Greek Theological Terms, Drawn Principally from Protestant Scholastic Theology*, 250. 2nd ed. Grand Rapids: Baker Academic, 2017.

Murray, John. *Redemption Accomplished and Applied*, 97–105. Grand Rapids: Eerdmans, 1955.

Owen, John. *The Works of John Owen, Volume 5*. Edinburgh: Banner of Truth, 1976.

Perkins, William. *A Golden Chaine*, 213–40. N.p.: Puritan Reprints, 2010.

Poole, N. J. *Stages of Religious Faith in the Classical Reformation Tradition: The Covenant Approach to the Ordo Salutis*. Lewiston: Edwin Mellen Press, 1995.

Schreiner, Thomas. *Faith Alone: The Doctrine of Justification*. Grand Rapids: Zondervan, 2015.

Storms, Sam. *Chosen for Life*, 145–57. 2nd ed. Wheaton: Crossway, 2007.

van den Belt, Henk, ed. *Synopsis Purioris Theologiae: Synopsis of a Purer Theology*, 2:304–41. Leiden: Brill, 2016.

Venema, Cornelis P. "Union with Christ, the 'Twofold Grace of God,' and the 'Order of Salvation' in Calvin's Theology." In Joel R. Beeke, ed. *Calvin for Today*, 91–113. Grand Rapids: Reformation Heritage Books, 2009.

Vos, Geerhardus. *Reformed Dogmatics*, 4:1–28. Bellingham: Lexham Press, 2015.

Webb, Robert Alexander. *Christian Salvation*, 271–73, 293. Harrisonburg, VA: Sprinkle Publications, 1985.

Zemek, George J. *A Biblical Theology of the Doctrines of Sovereign Grace*, 273–74. Little Rock: BTDSG, 2002.

Common Grace

Beach, J. Mark. "The Idea of a 'General Grace of God' in Some Sixteenth-Century Reformed Theologians other than Calvin." In Jordan J. Ballor and Jason Zuidema, eds. *Church and School in Early Modern Protestantism*, 97–109. Leiden: Brill, 2013.

Bavinck, Herman. "Calvin and Common Grace." In William Park Armstrong, ed. *Calvin and the Reformation*, 99–130. Grand Rapids: Baker Book House. 1980.

Berkhof, Louis. *Systematic Theology*, 432–46. Grand Rapids: Eerdmans, 1988.

Berkouwer, G. C. *The Providence of God*, 50–89. Grand Rapids: Eerdmans, 1980.

Boice, James Montgomery. *Amazing Grace*, 17–28. Wheaton: Tyndale House, 1993.

Bratt, James D., ed. *Abraham Kuyper: A Centennial Reader*, 165–201, 441–90. Grand Rapids: Eerdmans. 1998.

Cairns, Alan. *Dictionary of Theological Terms*, 96–101. 3rd ed. Belfast: Ambassador Productions, 2002.

Carson, D. A. *The Difficult Doctrine of the Love of God*. Wheaton: Crossway, 2000.

Charnock, Stephen. *The Existence and Attributes of God*, 2:208–355, especially 244–58. Grand Rapids: Baker Book House, 1979.

Edwards, Brian H. *Grace: Amazing Grace*, 19–41. Leominster: Day One, 2003.

Engelsma, David J. *Common Grace Revisited*. Grandville: Reformed Free Publishing Association, 2003.

Frame, John M. *Systematic Theology*, 237–39. Phillipsburg, NJ: P&R, 2013.

Gamble, Richard C. *The Whole Counsel of God*, 1:233–40. Phillipsburg, NJ: P&R, 2009.

Grudem, Wayne. *Systematic Theology*, 657–68. Grand Rapids: Zondervan, 1994.

Helm, Paul. "Can God Love the World?" In Kevin J. Vanhoozer, ed. *Nothing Greater, Nothing Better*, 168–85. Grand Rapids: Eerdmans, 2001.

Helm, Paul. *Calvin at the Centre*, 308–39. Oxford: Oxford University Press, 2010.

Helm, Paul. *John Calvin's Ideas*, 347–88. Oxford: Oxford University Press, 2004.

Hodge, Charles. *Systematic Theology*, 2:654–75. Grand Rapids: Eerdmans, 1979.

Horton, Michael. *The Christian Faith*, 364–68. Grand Rapids: Zondervan, 2011.

Kuyper, Abraham. *Common Grace*. 3 vols. Bellingham: Lexham Press, 2016.

Kuyper, Abraham. *Lectures on Calvinism*. Grand Rapids: Eerdmans, 1931.

Kuyper, Abraham. *The Work of the Holy Spirit*, 283–92. Grand Rapids: Eerdmans. 1969.

Lloyd-Jones, D. Martyn. *Great Doctrines of the Bible*, 2:22–29. Wheaton: Crossway, 2003.

MacArthur, John, Jr. *The Love of God*, 99–124, 191–225. Dallas: Word Publishing, 1996. MacArthur, John F., Jr. "God's Love." In Robert L. Thomas, ed. *The Master's Perspective on Contemporary Issues*, 232–52. Grand Rapids: Kregel, 1998.

MacLeod, Donald. *Behold Your God*, 145–76. Fearn: Christian Focus, 1995.

McGowan, Andrew. "Providence and Common Grace." In Francesca Aran Murphy and Philip G. Ziegler, eds. *The Providence of God: Deus Habet Concilium*, 109–28. London: T. and T. Clark, 2009.

Meeter, H. Henry. *The Basic Ideas of Calvinism*, 50–56. 6th ed. Grand Rapids: Baker Book House, 1990.

Morecraft, Joseph C., III. *Authentic Christianity*, 2:707–16. Powder Springs, GA: Minkoff Family Publishing and American Vision Press, 2009.

Morgan, Christopher, ed. *The Love of God*. Wheaton: Crossway, 2016.

Mouw, Richard J. *He Shines in All That's Fair*. Grand Rapids: Eerdmans, 2001.

Murray, John. *The Collected Writings of John Murray*, 2:93–119. Edinburgh: Banner of Truth, 1976.

Needham, N. R. *Common Grace and the Work of the Christian Institute*. Newcastle upon Tyne: The Christian Institute, 2008.

North, Gary. *Dominion and Common Grace*. Tyler: Institute for Christian Economics, 1987.

Osterhaven, M. Eugene. "Common Grace." In Carl F. H. Henry, ed. *Basic Christian Doctrines*, 171–77. New York: Holt, Rinehart and Winston, 1962.

Palmer, Edwin H. *The Holy Spirit*, 29–39. Philadelphia: Presbyterian and Reformed, 1964.

Pratt, John H., ed. *The Thought of the Evangelical Leaders*, 196–98. Edinburgh: Banner of Truth, 1998.

Shedd, William G. T. *Calvinism: Pure and Mixed*, 92–106. Edinburgh: Banner of Truth, 1986.

Sproul, R. C. *Everyone's a Theologian*, 215–19. Orlando: Reformation Trust, 2014.

Spurgeon, Charles Haddon. *Metropolitan Tabernacle Pulpit*, 26:48–60. Pasadena, TX: Pilgrim Publications, 1981.

Treier, Daniel J. and Walter A. Elwell, eds. *Evangelical Dictionary of Theology*, 3rd ed., 197–98. Grand Rapids: Baker Academic, 2017.

Van Til, Cornelius. *Common Grace and the Gospel*. Phillipsburg, NJ: Presbyterian and Reformed, 1974.

Van Til, Cornelius. *The Defense of the Faith*, 168–98. 1st ed. Philadelphia: Presbyterian and Reformed, 1955.

The Preservation and Perseverance of the Saints

à Brakel, Wilhelmus. *The Christian's Reasonable Service*, 4:275–300. Ligonier, PA: Soli Deo Gloria, 1992.

Adams, Jay E. "A Certain Inheritance." In Burk Parsons, ed. *John Calvin: A Heart for Devotion, Doctrine & Doxology*, 179–90. Orlando: Reformation Trust, 2008.

Adams, Jay E. "Perseverance of the Saints." In R. C. Sproul Jr., ed. *After Darkness, Light*, 173–87. Phillipsburg, NJ: P&R, 2003.

Aldersen, Richard. *No Holiness, No Heaven! Antinomianism Today*. Edinburgh: Banner of Truth, 1986.

Allison, Gregg R. *Historical Theology*, 542–61. Grand Rapids: Zondervan, 2011.

Augustine. "The Gift of Perseverance." In *The Works of Saint Augustine*, I/26:191–240. Hyde Park: New City Press, 1999.

Bateman, Herbert W., IV, ed. *Four Views on the Warning Passages in Hebrews*. Grand Rapids: Kregel, 2007.

Bavinck, Herman. *Reformed Dogmatics*,

4:266–70. Grand Rapids: Baker Academic, 2008.

Beeke, Joel R. and Mark Jones. *A Puritan Theology*, 601–17. Grand Rapids: Reformation Heritage Books, 2012.

Berkhof, Louis. *Systematic Theology*, 545–49. Grand Rapids: Eerdmans, 1988.

Berkouwer, G. C. *Faith and Perseverance*. Grand Rapids: Eerdmans, 1958.

Boettner, Loraine. *The Reformed Doctrine of Predestination*, 182–201. Philadelphia: Presbyterian and Reformed, 1932.

Boice, James Montgomery and Philip Graham Ryken. *The Doctrines of Grace*, 155–76. Wheaton: Crossway, 2002.

Boston, Thomas. *The Complete Works of the Late Rev. Thomas Boston*, 2:32–36. Wheaton: Richard Owen Roberts, 1980.

Boyce, James Petigru. *Abstract of Systematic Theology*, 425–36. Cape Coral, FL: Founders Press, 2007.

Calvin, John. *Institutes of the Christian Religion*, 3:24:6–11 (pp. 971–78). Philadelphia: Westminster Press, 1960.

Chrisope, Terry. *Confessing Jesus as Lord*. Fearn: Christian Focus, 2012.

Clotfelter, David. *Sinners in the Hands of a Good God*, 161–85. Chicago: Moody Press, 2004.

Collier, Jay T. *Debating Perseverance: The Augustinian Heritage in Post-Reformation England*. Oxford: Oxford University Press, 2018.

Culver, Robert. *Systematic Theology*, 765–72. Fearn: Mentor, 2006.

Cunningham, William. *Historical Theology*, 2:490–501. London: Banner of Truth, 1969.

Custance, Arthur C. *The Sovereignty of Grace*, 191–224. Phillipsburg, NJ: Presbyterian and Reformed, 1979.

Dabney, Robert Lewis. *Systematic Theology*, 687–89. Edinburgh: Banner of Truth, 1985.

Dickinson, Jonathan. *The True Scripture Doctrine Concerning Some Important Points of Christian Faith*, 219–52. Harrisonburg, VA: Sprinkle Publications, 1992.

Edwards, Jonathan. *Sermons on the Lord's Supper*, 171–86. Orlando: The Northampton Press, 2007.

Edwards, Jonathan. *The Works of Jonathan Edwards*, 10:597–608; 13:474–75, 480, 508; 18:340–41, 353–57, 498–500, 534–35. New Haven: Yale University Press, 1994.

Ferguson, Sinclair B. *By Grace Alone*, 65–81. Orlando: Reformation Trust, 2010.

Forster, Greg. *The Joy of Calvinism*, 121–43. Wheaton: Crossway, 2012.

Frame, John M. *Systematic Theology*, 998–1003. Phillipsburg, NJ: P&R, 2013.

Gerstner, John H. *The Rational Biblical Theology of Jonathan Edwards*, 3:329–62. Orlando: Ligonier Ministries, 1993.

Gill, John. *The Cause of God and Truth*, 131–49, 198–202, 300–316. Grand Rapids: Baker Book House, 1980.

Gill, John. *A Complete Body of Doctrinal and Practical Divinity*, 559–89. Paris, AR: Baptist Standard Bearer, 1984.

Gill, John. *Sermons and Tracts*, 3:63–100. Streamwood: Primitive Baptist Library, 1981.

Godfrey, W. Robert. *Saving the Reformation: The Pastoral Theology of the Synod of Dort*, 65–74, 153–72. Orlando, FL: Reformation Trust, 2019.

Good, Kenneth H. *God's Gracious Purpose as Seen in the Gospel of John*, 132–61. Grand Rapids: Baker Book House, 1979.

Gromacki, Robert. *Salvation is Forever*. Schaumburg: Regular Baptist Press, 1989.

Grudem, Wayne. *Systematic Theology*, 788–809. Grand Rapids: Zondervan, 1994.

Hanko, Herman, Homer C. Hoeksema, and Gise Van Baren. *The Five Points of Calvinism*, 83–95. Grand Rapids: Reformed Free Publishing Association, 1976.

Heppe, Heinrich. *Reformed Dogmatics*, 581–89. Grand Rapids: Baker Book House, 1978.

Hodge, A. A. *Outlines of Theology*, 542–47. Grand Rapids: Zondervan, 1973.

Hoekema, Anthony A. *Saved by Grace*, 234–56. Grand Rapids: Eerdmans, 1989.

Hoeksema, Herman. *Reformed Dogmatics*, 2:157–76. 2nd ed. Grandville: Reformed Free Publishing Association, 2004.

Hoeksema, Herman. *The Voice of Our Fathers*, 629–843. Grand Rapids: Reformed Free Publishing Association, 1980.

Horton, Michael S. "A Classical Calvinist View." In J. Matthew Pinson, ed. *Four Views on Eternal Security*, 21–59. Grand Rapids: Zondervan, 2002.

Horton, Michael S. *The Christian Faith*, 680–87. Grand Rapids: Zondervan, 2011.

Horton, Michael S. *For Calvinism*, 115–23. Grand Rapids; Zondervan, 2011.

Horton, Michael S. *Putting Amazing Back into Grace*, 205–14. Grand Rapids: Baker Book House, 1994.

Hulse, Erroll. *Who Saves, God or Me?* 45–48, 117–31. Darlington: Evangelical Press, 2008.

Kersten, G. H. *Reformed Dogmatics*, 2:447–56. Sioux Center: Netherlands Reformed Book and Publishing Committee, 1980.

Kuiper, Herman. *By Grace Alone*, 138–47. Grand Rapids: Eerdmans, 1955.

Lawson, Steven J. *A Long Line of Godly Men*, 1:66–68, 83, 128–29, 146–50, 199–200, 202, 206–08, 256–58, 265–66, 295–300, 327–28, 335, 370–71, 393, 399–401, 425–27, 434–38, 460–63, 488–92, 507–08, 521–22, 524–25, 552–57. Orlando: Reformation Trust, 2006.

Lems, Shane. *The Doctrines of Grace*, 71–83. Phillipsburg, NJ: P&R, 2013.

Lloyd-Jones, D. Martyn. *The Final Perseverance of the Saints*. Edinburgh: Banner of Truth, 1975.

Lloyd-Jones, D. Martyn. *Saved in Eternity*, 173–87. Wheaton: Crossway, 1988.

Lutzer, Erwin. *The Doctrines that Divide*, 225–39. Grand Rapids: Kregel, 1998.

MacArthur, John. *The Gospel According to Jesus*. 2nd ed. Grand Rapids: Zondervan, 1988.

MacArthur, John. *The Love of God*, 151–69. Dallas: Word Publishing, 1996.

MacArthur, John, and Richard Mayhue,

eds. *Biblical Doctrine*, 644–53. Wheaton: Crossway, 2017.

Matthews, John. *The Divine Purpose*, 153–86. Vestavia Hills; Solid Ground Christian Books, 2009.

McClarty, Jim. *By Grace Alone*, 113–36. Smyrna, GA: GCA, 2007.

Milton, Michael A. *What is Perseverance of the Saints?* Phillipsburg, NJ: P&R, 2009.

Montgomery, Daniel, and Timothy Paul Jones. *PROOF: Finding Freedom through the Intoxicating Joy of Irresistible Grace*, 108–24. Grand Rapids: Zondervan, 2015.

Morecraft. Joseph C., III. *Authentic Christianity*, 3:205–53. Powder Springs, GA: Minkoff Family Publishing and American Vision Press, 2009.

Morey, Robert A. *The Saving Work of Christ*, 231–38. Sterling: Grace Abounding Ministries, 1980.

Muller, Richard A. *Dictionary of Latin and Greek Theological Terms, Drawn Principally from Protestant Scholastic Theology*, 260. 2nd ed. Grand Rapids: Baker Academic, 2017.

Murray, John. *Redemption Accomplished and Applied*, 189–98. Grand Rapids: Eerdmans, 1955.

Ness, Christopher. *An Antidote Against Arminianism*, 102–26. Choteau, MT: Old Paths Gospel Press, n.d.

Nettles, Thomas J. *By His Grace and For His Glory*, 360–85. Rev. ed. Cape Coral, FL: Founders Press, 2006.

Nettleton, Asahel. *Sermons from the Second Great Awakening*, 191–204. Ames, IA: International Outreach, 1995.

Newton, Phil. "Perseverance: The True Nature of Saving Faith." In Thomas K. Ascol and Nathan A. Finn, eds. *Ministry by His Grace and For His Glory*, 170–86. Cape Coral, FL: Founders Press, 2011.

Nicole, Roger. "Some Comments on Hebrews 6:4–6 and the Doctrine of the Perseverance of God with the Saints." In Gerald F. Hawthorne, ed. *Current Issues in Biblical and Patristic Interpretation*, 355–64. Grand Rapids: Eerdmans, 1975.

Nicole, Roger. *Standing Forth*, 437–52. Fearn: Mentor, 2002.

Orrick, Jim Scott. *Mere Calvinism*, 161–200. Phillipsburg: P&R, 2019.

Owen, John. "The Doctrine of the Saints' Perseverance Explained and Confirmed." In *The Works of John Owen, Volume 11*. Edinburgh: Banner of Truth, 1976.

Palmer, Edwin H. *The Five Points of Calvinism*, 68–80. Rev. ed. Grand Rapids: Baker Book House, 1984.

Parks, William. *Sermons on the Five Points of Calvinism*, 88–111, Choteau, MT: Old Paths Gospel Press, n.d.

Peterson, Robert A. and Michael D. Williams. *Why I Am Not an Arminian*, 67–91. Downers Grove, IL: IVP, 2004.

Peterson, Robert A. *Our Secure Salvation*. Phillipsburg, NJ: P&R, 2009.

Phillips, Richard D. *What's So Great About the Doctrines of Grace?*, 83–97. Orlando: Reformation Trust, 2008.

Pink, Arthur W. *Eternal Security*. Grand Rapids: Baker Book House, 1996.

Piper, John and Justin Taylor, eds. *Stand: A Call for the Endurance of the Saints*. Wheaton: Crossway, 2008.

Piper, John. *A Godward Life: Book Two*, 203–06, 248–50. Sisters, OR: Multnomah, 1999.

Piper, John. *Five Points*, 63–76. Fearn: Christian Focus, 2013.

Piper, John. *TULIP: The Pursuit of God's Glory in Salvation*, 173–99. Wheaton: Crossway, 2009.

Reed, R. C. *The Gospel as Taught by Calvin*, 83–98. Edinburgh: Banner of Truth, 2009.

Reisinger, Ernest C. *Lord and Christ*. Phillipsburg, NJ: P&R, 1994.

Robertson, Norwell. *Church-Members' Hand-Book of Theology*, 144–70. Harrisonburg, VA: Gano Books, 1983.

Ryle, J. C. *Holiness*. Edinburgh: Banner of Truth, 2014.

Ryle, J. C. *Never Perish*. Choteau, MT: Gospel Mission, n.d.

Ryle, J. C. *Old Paths*, 447–90. Edinburgh: Banner of Truth, 2013.

Schreiner, Thomas R. "Promises of Preservation and Exhortations to Perseverance." In Matthew Barrett and Thomas J. Nettles, eds. *Whomever He Wills*, 188–211. Cape Coral, FL: Founders Press, 2012

Schreiner, Thomas R. *Run to Win the Prize: Perseverance in the New Testament*. Wheaton: Crossway, 2010.

Schreiner, Thomas R., and Ardel B. Caneday. *The Race Set Before Us: A Biblical Theology of Perseverance and Assurance*. Downers Grove: Intervarsity Press, 2001.

Schreiner, Thomas R., and Bruce A. Ware, eds. *The Grace of God, The Bondage of the Will*, 1:133–82. Grand Rapids: Baker, 1995.

Shaw, Robert. *The Reformed Faith*, 229–39. Fearn: Christian Heritage, 2008.

Smith, Morton H. *Systematic Theology*, 2:499–506. Greenville, SC: Greenville Seminary Press, 1994.

Sproul, R. C. *Everyone's a Theologian*, 252–57. Orlando: Reformation Trust, 2014.

Sproul, R. C. *Grace Unknown*, 197–216. Grand Rapids: Baker Books, 1996.

Sproul, R. C. *Truths We Confess*, 2:197–216. Phillipsburg, NJ: P&R, 2007.

Spurgeon, Charles Haddon. *Metropolitan Tabernacle Pulpit*, 10:85–96, 11:325–36, 15:289–300, 16:1–12, 18:337–48, 23:361–72, 24:708–20. 29:445–56, 35:541–52, 685–96, 38:193–201, 61:457–65. Pasadena, TX: Pilgrim Publications, 1981.

Spurgeon, Charles Haddon. *New Park Street Pulpit*, 2:169–76; 3:429–36, 5:59–64. Pasadena, TX: Pilgrim Publications, 1981.

Spurgeon, Charles Haddon. *Sermons on Sovereignty*, 201–14. Pasadena, TX: Pilgrim Publications, 1990.

Steele, David N., Curtis C. Thomas, and S. Lance Quinn. *The Five Points of Calvinism*, 64–78, 147–56. 2nd ed. Phillipsburg, NJ: P&R, 2004.

Storms, Sam. *Kept for Jesus*. Wheaton: Crossway, 2015.

Swinnock, George. *The Fading of the Flesh*

and the Flourishing of Faith. Grand Rapids: Reformation Heritage Books, 2009.

Thomas, C. Adrian. *A Case for Mixed-Audience with Reference to the Warning Passages in the Book of Hebrews*. New York: Peter Lang, 2008.

Turretin, Francis. *Institutes of Elenctic Theology*, 2:593–616. Phillipsburg, NJ: P&R, 1992.

van den Belt, Henk, ed. *Synoposis Purioris Theologiae: Synopsis of a Purer Theology*, 2:263–75. Leiden: Brill, 2016.

Van Dixhoorn, Chad. *Confessing the Faith*, 217–24. Edinburgh: Banner of Truth, 2014.

van Genderen, J. and W. H. Velema. *Concise Reformed Dogmatics*, 667–74. Phillipsburg, NJ: P&R, 2008.

Venema, Cornelis P. *But for the Grace of God: An Exposition of the Canons of Dort*, 77–87. Grandville: Reformed Fellowship, 2011.

Venema, Cornelis P. *But for the Grace of God: An Exposition of the Canons of Dort*, 71–82.

Grand Rapids: Reformed Fellowship, 1994.

Volf, Judith M. Gundy. *Paul and Perseverance*. Louisville: Westminster John Knox, 1990.

Wallace, Ronald S. *Calvin's Doctrine of the Christian Life*, 333–38. Edinburgh: Oliver & Boyd, 1959.

Warburton, Ben A. *Calvinism*, 169–88. Grand Rapids: Eerdmans, 1955.

Watson, Thomas. *A Body of Divinity*, 279–89. Edinburgh: Banner of Truth, 1974.

White, James. *The Sovereign Grace of God*, 109–22. Lindenhurst: Great Christian Books, 2003.

Witsius, Herman. *The Economy of the Covenants Between God and Man*, 2:55–81. Escondido: Den Dulk Foundation; and Phillipsburg, NJ: P&R, 1990.

Wright, R. K. McGregor. *No Place for Sovereignty*, 127–42. Downers Grove, IL: IVP, 1996.

Holy Scripture

à Brakel, Wilhelmus. *The Christian's Reasonable Service*, 1:23–81. Ligonier, PA: Soli Deo Gloria, 1992.

Allison, Gregg R. *Historical Theology*, 37–184. Grand Rapids: Zondervan, 2011.

Backus, Irena Doruta. *The Reformed Roots of the English New Testament*. Philadelphia: Pickwick Press, 1980.

Barnes, Tom. *Every Word Counts: Inerrant, Infallible, Unchanging*. Darlington: Evangelical Press, 2010.

Barrett, Matthew. *God's Word Alone*. Grand Rapids: Zondervan, 2016.

Bavinck, Herman. *Reformed Dogmatics*, 1:323–494. Grand Rapids: Baker Academic, 2003.

Beeke, Joel R. and Paul M. Smalley. *Reformed Systematic Theology*, vol. 1. Wheaton: Crossway, 2019.

Berkhof, Louis. *Principles of Biblical Interpretation*. Grand Rapids: Baker Book House, 1973.

Bilkes, Jerry. "Calvin on the Word of God."

In Joel R. Beeke, ed. *Calvin for Today*, 15–32. Grand Rapids: Reformation Heritage Books, 2009.

Boettner, Loraine. *Studies in Theology*, 9–49. Philadelphia: Presbyterian and Reformed, 1973.

Boice, James Montgomery. *Does Inerrancy Matter?* Oakland: International Council on Biblical Inerrancy, 1979.

Boice, James Montgomery. *Standing on the Rock: Upholding Biblical Authority in a Secular Age*. Grand Rapids: Kregel, 1999.

Boice, James Montgomery, ed. *The Foundation of Biblical Authority*. Grand Rapids: Zondervan, 1978.

Boston, Thomas. *The Complete Works of the Late Rev. Thomas Boston*, 1:19–76. Wheaton: Richard Owen Roberts, 1980.

Brown, John. *The Systematic Theology of John Brown*, 39–98. Fearn: Christian Focus; and Grand Rapids: Reformation Heritage Books, 2002.

Bullinger, Henry (Heinrich). *The Decades of Henry Bullinger*, 1:36–80. Grand Rapids: Reformation Heritage Books, 2004.

Bush, L. Russ and Tom J. Nettles. *Baptists and the Bible*. Chicago: Moody Press, 1980.

Calvin, John. *Institutes of the Christian Religion*, 1:7 (pp. 74–81). Philadelphia: Westminster Press. 1960.

Carson, D. A., ed. *The Enduring Authority of the Christian Scriptures*. Grand Rapids: Eerdmans, 2016.

Clark, Gordon H. *God's Hammer: The Bible and Its Critics*. Jefferson: Trinity Foundation, 1987.

Conn, Harvie M., ed. *Inerrancy and Hermeneutic*. Grand Rapids: Baker Book House, 1988.

Crampton, W. Gary. *By Scripture Alone*. Unicoi: Trinity Foundation, 2002.

Dabney, Robert Lewis. *Discussions*, 1:115–31, 350–98. Harrisonburg, VA: Sprinkle Publications, 1982.

Davies, Samuel. *Sermons*, 1:71–108. Pittsburgh: Soli Deo Gloria, 1993.

DeYoung, Kevin. *Taking God at His Word*. Wheaton: Crossway, 2014.

Edwards, Brian H. *Nothing But the Truth*. Welwyn: Evangelical Press, 1978.

Feinberg, John S. *Light in a Dark Place*. Wheaton: Crossway, 2018.

Ferguson, Sinclair B. *From the Mouth of God*. Edinburgh: Banner of Truth, 2014.

Ferrari, Andrea. *John Diodati's Doctrine of Holy Scripture*. Grand Rapids: Reformation Heritage Books, 2006.

Fesko, J. V. "The Doctrine of Scripture in Reformed Orthodoxy." In Herman J. Selderhuis, ed. *A Companion to Reformed Orthodoxy*, 429–64. Leiden: Brill, 2013.

Fesko, J. V. *The Theology of the Westminster Standards*, 65–94. Wheaton: Crossway, 2014.

Fluhrer, Gabriel N. E., ed. *Solid Ground: The Inerrant Word of God in an Errant World*. Phillipsburg, NJ: P&R, 2012.

Forstman, H. Jackson. *Word and Spirit: Calvin's Doctrine of Biblical Authority*. Stanford: Stanford University Press, 1962.

Frame, John M. *The Doctrine of the Word of God*. Phillipsburg, NJ: P&R, 2010.

Frame, John M. *John Frame's Selected Shorter Writings*, 3:27–85, 169–82. Phillipsburg, NJ: P&R, 2016.

Frame, John M. *Systematic Theology*, 519–693. Phillipsburg, NJ: P&R, 2013.

Gaffin, Richard B. *God's Word in Servant Form: Abraham Kuyper and Herman Bavinck on the Doctrine of Scripture*. Jackson: Reformed Academic Press, 2008.

Gamble, Richard C., ed., *Articles on Calvin and Calvinism, Volume 6*. New York: Garland, 1992.

Garner, David B., ed. *Did God Really Say?* Phillipsburg, NJ: P&R, 2012.

Gaussen, Louis. *The Divine Inspiration of the Bible*. Grand Rapids: Kregel, 1979.

Gerstner, John H. "The Nature of Revelation." In Carl F. H. Henry, ed. *Christian Faith and Modern Theology*, 95–109. New York: Channel Press, 1964.

Grudem, Wayne. *Systematic Theology*, 47–138. Grand Rapids: Zondervan, 1994.

Haldane, Robert. *The Authenticity and Inspiration of the Holy Scriptures*. Minneapolis: Klock & Klock, 1985.

Hannah, John D., ed. *Inerrancy and the Church*. Chicago: Moody Press, 1984.

Harris, R. Laird. *Inspiration and Canonicty of the Bible*. Grand Rapids: Zondervan, 1957.

Heppe, Heinrich. *Reformed Dogmatics*, 12–41. Grand Rapids: Baker Book House, 1978.

Hills, Edward F. *The King James Version Defended*. Des Moines: Christian Research Press, 1984.

Hodge, A. A. *Outlines of Theology*, 63–81, 656–57. Grand Rapids: Zondervan, 1973.

Hodge, Charles. *Systematic Theology*, 1:151–88. Grand Rapids: Eerdmans, 1979.

Hoeksema, Homer C. *The Doctrine of Scripture*. Grand Rapids; Reformed Free Publishing Association, 1990.

Horton, Michael. *The Christian Faith*, 113–218. Grand Rapids: Zondervan, 2011.

Horton, Michael. "Knowing God: Calvin's Understanding of Revelation." In Sung Wook Chung, ed. *John Calvin and Evangelical Theology*, 1–31. Louisville: Westminster John Knox Press, 2004.

Jones, Hywel, Edgar H. Andrews, and Iain H. Murray. *The Bible Under Attack.* Welwyn: Evangelical Press, 1978.

Kistemaker, Simon, ed. *Interpreting God's Word Today.* Philadelphia: Presbyterian and Reformed, 1970.

Kistler, Don, ed. *Sola Scriptura!* Morgan, PA: Soli Deo Gloria, 1995.

Kuyper, Abraham. *Principles of Sacred Theology,* 341–563. Grand Rapids: Eerdmans, 1968.

Leslie, Andrew M. *The Light of Grace: John Owen on the Authority of Scripture and Christian Faith.* Göttingen: Vandenhoek & Ruprecht, 2015.

Lillback, Peter A. and Richard B. Gaffin Jr., eds. *Thy Word is Still Truth.* Phillipsburg, NJ: P&R, 2013.

Lloyd-Jones, D. Martyn. *Authority,* 30–61. Edinburgh: Banner of Truth, 1984.

Lyford, William. *The Instructed Christian,* 30–67. Morgan: Soli Deo Gloria, n.d.

MacArthur, John, ed. *The Scripture Cannot Be Broken.* Wheaton: Crossway, 2015.

MacArthur, John. *Why Believe the Bible?* Grand Rapids: Baker Books, 2015.

MacArthur, John and Richard Mayhue, eds. *Biblical Doctrine,* 69–142. Wheaton: Crossway, 2017.

Manly, Basil. *The Bible Doctrine of Inspiration.* Harrisonburg, VA: Gano Books, 1985.

Masters, Peter. *Not Like Any Other Book: Interpreting the Bible.* London: The Wakeman Trust, 2004.

Mathison, Keith A. *The Shape of Sola Scriptura.* Moscow: Canon Press, 2001.

McGowan, A. T. B. "John Calvin's Doctrine of Scripture." In David W. Hall, ed. *Tributes to John Calvin,* 356–80. Phillipsburg, NJ: P&R, 2010.

McKim, Donald K. "Calvin's View of Scripture." In Donald K. McKim, ed.

Readings in Calvin's Theology, 43–68. Grand Rapids: Baker Book House, 1984.

McKim, Donald K., ed. *Calvin and the Bible.* Cambridge: Cambridge University Press, 2006.

Mohler, R. Albert, Jr. "When the Bible Speaks, God Speaks: The Classic Doctrine of Biblical Inerrancy." In J. Merrick and Stephen M. Garrett, eds. *Five Views on Biblical Inerrancy,* 29–58. Grand Rapids: Zondervan, 2013.

Morecraft, Joeseph C., III. *Authentic Christianity,* 1:139–234, 5:153–222. Powder Springs, GA: Minkoff Family Publishing and American Vision Press, 2009.

Muller, Richard A. *Post-Reformation Reformed Dogmatics, Volume 2.* 2nd ed. Grand Rapids: Baker Academic, 2003.

Murray, John. *The Collected Writings of John Murray,* 4:158–290. Edinburgh: Banner of Truth, 1976.

Nichols, Steven J. and Eric T. Brandt, eds. *Ancient Word, Changing Worlds: The Doctrine of Scripture in a Modern Age.* Wheaton: Crossway, 2009.

Nicole, Roger. *Standing Forth,* 27–242. Fearn: Mentor, 2002.

Owen, John. *Biblical Theology,* 769–854. Pittsburgh: Soli Deo Gloria, 1994.

Owen, John. *The Works of John Owen,* 4:1–234; 8:495–543; 16:281–526. Edinburgh: Banner of Truth, 1976.

Packer, J. I. *Beyond the Battle for the Bible.* Westchester: Cornerstone Books, 1980.

Packer, J. I. *The Collected Shorter Writings of J. I. Packer,* 3:3–238; 4:165–204. Carlisle: Paternoster, 1999. Packer, J. I. *Freedom, Authority and Scripture.* Downers Grove, IL: IVP, 1982.

Packer, J. I. *'Fundamentalism' and the Word of God.* Grand Rapids: Eerdmans, 1958.

Packer, J. I. *God Has Spoken.* 2nd ed. Grand Rapids: Baker Book House, 1994.

Packer, J. I. *God Speaks to Man.* Philadelphia: Westminster Press, 1965.

Pink, Arthur W. *The Divine Inspiration of the*

Bible. Grand Rapids: Baker Book House, 1982.

Piper, John. *A Peculiar Glory: How the Christian Scriptures Reveal Their Complete Truthfulness*. Wheaton: Crossway, 2016.

Poythress, Vern Sheridan. *Inerrancy and the Gospels*. Wheaton: Crossway, 2012.

Poythress, Vern Sheridan. *Inerrancy and Worldview*. Wheaton: Crossway, 2012.

Reymond, Robert L. *A New Systematic Theology of the Christian Faith*, 3–126. Nashville: Thomas Nelson, 1998.

Ryle, J. C. *Is All Scripture Inspired?* Edinburgh: Banner of Truth, 2003.

Ryle, J. C. *Old Paths*, 1–39. Cambridge: James Clarke, 1977.

Selderhuis, Herman J., ed. *The Calvin Handbook*, 235–44. Grand Rapids: Eerdmans, 2009.

Shaw, Robert. *The Reformed Faith*, 35–58. Fearn: Christian Heritage, 2008.

Shedd, William G. T. *Dogmatic Theology*, 85–150. 3rd ed. Phillipsburg, NJ: P&R, 2003.

Sproul, R. C. *Can I Trust the Bible?* Lake Mary: Reformation Trust, 2009.

Sproul, R.C. "The Case for Inerrancy: A Methodological Analysis." In Adam S. Francisco; Korey D. Maas; and Steven P. Mueller, eds. *Theologia et Apologia: Essays in Reformation Theology and Its Defense Presented to Rod Rosenblatt*, 45–66. Eugene, OR: Wipf & Stock, 2007.

Sproul, R. C. *Explaining Inerrancy*. Orlando: Ligonier Ministries, 1996.

Sproul, R. C. *Knowing Scripture*. Downers Grove, IL: IVP, 1977.

Sproul, R. C. *Scripture Alone*. Phillipsburg, NJ: P&R, 2004.

te Velde, Dolf, ed. *Synopsis Purioris Theologiae: Synopsis of a Purer Theology*, 1:48–149. Leiden: Brill, 2015.

Thomas, Geoff. *The Sure Word of God*. Bridgend: Bryntirion Press, 2008.

Thompson, Mark D. "Sola Scriptura." In Matthew Barrett, ed. *Reformation Theology*, 145–88. Wheaton: Crossway Books, 2017.

Turretin, Francis. *The Doctrine of Scripture*. Grand Rapids: Baker Book House, 1981.

Turretin, Francis. *Institutes of Elenctic Theology*, 1:55–167. Phillipsburg, NJ: P&R, 1992.

Ussher, James. *A Body of Divinity*, 1–23. Birmingham: Solid Ground Christian Books, 2007.

Van Bruggen, Jakob. *The Ancient Text of the New Testament*. Winnipeg: Premier, 1976.

Van Bruggen, Jakob. *The Future of the Bible*. Nashville: Thomas Nelson, 1978.

Van den Belt, Henk. *The Authority of Scripture in Reformed Theology*. Leiden: Brill, 2008.

Van Dixhoorn, Chad. *Confessing the Faith*, 3–28. Edinburgh: Banner of Truth 2014.

van Genderen, J. and W. H. Velema. *Concise Reformed Dogmatics*, 58–116. Phillipsburg, NJ: P&R, 2008.

Vanhoozer, Kevin. "Holy Scripture." In Michael Allen and Scott R. Swain, eds. *Christian Dogmatics*, 30–56. Grand Rapids: Baker Academic, 2016.

Warfield, Benjamin B. *The Inspiration and Authority of the Bible*. Phillipsburg, NJ: Presbyterian and Reformed, 1970.

Warfield, Benjamin B. *Selected Shorter Writings of Benjamin B. Warfield*, 2:537–638. Nutley: Presbyterian and Reformed, 1970.

Warfield, Benjamin B. *The Works of Benjamin B. Warfield*, 1:3–456; 6:155–336. Grand Rapids: Baker Book House, 1981.

Watson, Thomas. *A Body of Divinity*, 26–38. Edinburgh: Banner of Truth, 1974.

Weeks, Noel. *The Sufficiency of Scripture*. Edinburgh: Banner of Truth, 1998.

White, James R. *Scripture Alone*. Minneapolis: Bethany House, 2004.

Williams, James B. and Randolph Shaylor, eds. *God's Word in Our Hands: The Bible Preserved for Us*. Greenville, SC: Ambassador Emerald International, 2003.

Woolley, Paul, ed. *The Infallible Word*. Phillipsburg, NJ: P&R, 2002.

Young, Edward J. *The God-Breathed Scripture*. Willow Grove: The Committee for the Historian of the Orthodox Presbyterian Church, 2007.

Young, Edward J. *Thy Word Is Truth.* Edinburgh: Banner of Truth, 1991.

Zaspel, Fred G. *The Theology of B. B. Warfield,* 111–75. Wheaton: Crossway, 2010.

The Two Natures of Christ

à Brakel, Wilhelmus. *The Christian's Reasonable Service,* 1:493–516. Ligonier, PA: Soli Deo Gloria, 1992.

Alexander, J. W. *God Is Love,* 57–86. Edinburgh: Banner of Truth, 1985.

Ambrose, Isaac. *Looking Unto Jesus,* 169–84. Harrisonburg, VA: Sprinkle Publications, 1986.

Beardslee, John W., III, ed. *Reformed Dogmatics,* 90–94. New York: Oxford University Press, 1965.

Beeke, Joel R. and Mark Jones. *A Puritan Theology,* 335–45. Grand Rapids: Reformation Heritage Books, 2012.

Berkhof, Louis. *Systematic Theology,* 321–30. Grand Rapids: Eerdmans, 1988.

Berkouwer, G. C. *The Person of Christ,* especially 21–56. Grand Rapids: Eerdmans, 1954.

Boettner, Loraine. *Studies in Theology,* 140–269. Phillipsburg, NJ: Presbyterian and Reformed, 1973.

Boston, Thomas. *The Complete Works of the Late Rev. Thomas Boston,* 1:389–403. Wheaton: Richard Owen Roberts, 1980.

Breward, Ian, ed. *The Work of William Perkins,* 197–202. Appleford: Sutton Courtenay Press, 1970.

Bromiley, Geoffrey W. "The Reformers and the Humanity of Christ." In Marguerite Shuster and Richard Muller, eds. *Perspectives on Christology,* 79–104. Grand Rapids: Eerdmans, 1991.

Brown, John. *The Systematic Theology of John Brown,* 256–79. Fearn: Christian Focus; and Grand Rapids: Reformation Heritage Books, 2002.

Bullinger, Henry (Heinrich). *The Decades of Henry Bullinger,* 3: 238–73. Grand Rapids: Reformation Heritage Books, 2004.

Calvin, John. *Institutes of the Christian Religion,* 2:13:1–8 (pp. 474–93). Philadelphia: Westminster Press, 1960.

Clark, Gordon H. *The Incarnation.* Jefferson: Trinity Foundation, 1988.

Crisp, Oliver D. *An American Augustinian: Sin and Salvation in the Dogmatic Theology of William G. T. Shedd,* 56–74. Milton Keynes: Paternoster, 2007.

Crisp, Oliver D. *Divinity and Humanity.* Cambridge: Cambridge University Press, 2007.

Dennison, James T., Jr., ed. *Reformed Confessions of the 16th and 17th Centuries in English Translation,* 3:462–71, 649–62, 773–79. Grand Rapids: Reformation Heritage Books, 2012.

Edwards, Jonathan. *The Works of Jonathan Edwards,* 13:340–41, 528–32; 18:411–18; 20:153–54, 411–29, 607–40. New Haven: Yale University Press, 1994.

Ellis, Brannon. *Calvin, Classical Trinitarianism, and the Aseity of the Son.* Oxford: Oxford University Press, 2012.

Erickson, Millard J. *The Word Became Flesh.* Grand Rapids: Baker Academic, 2003.

Fesko, J. V. *The Theology of the Westminster Standards,* 169–84. Wheaton: Crossway, 2014.

Flavel, John. *The Works of John Flavel,* 1:72–85. London: Banner of Truth, 1968.

Foxgrover, David. "The Humanity of Christ Within Proper Limits." In Robert V. Schnucker, ed. *Calviniana: Ideas and Influences of Jean Calvin,* 93–106. Kirksville, MO: Sixteenth Century Journal Publishers, 1988.

Frame, John M. *Systematic Theology,* 446–71, 877–93. Phillipsburg, NJ: P&R, 2013.

Gerstner, John H. *Primitive Theology,* 113–60. Morgan, PA: Soli Deo Gloria, 1996.

Gerstner, John H. *The Rational Biblical*

Theology of Jonathan Edwards, 2:368–423. Orlando: Ligonier Ministries, 1992.

Goodwin, Thomas. *The Works of Thomas Goodwin*, 5:34–68. Eureka, CA: Tanski, 1996.

Grudem, Wayne. *Systematic Theology*, 529–67. Grand Rapids: Zondervan, 1994.

Helm, Paul. *John Calvin's Ideas*, 58–92. Oxford: Oxford University Press, 2004.

Heppe, Heinrich. *Reformed Dogmatics*, 410–47, 500–509. Grand Rapids: Baker Book House, 1978.

Hodge, A. A. *Evangelical Theology*, 194–200. Edinburgh: Banner of Truth, 1990.

Hodge, Charles. *Systematic Theology*, 2:378–418. Grand Rapids: Eerdmans, 1979.

Hoeksema, Herman. *Reformed Dogmatics*, 1:505–19. 2nd ed. Grandville: Reformed Free Publishing Association, 2004.

Hoogland, Marvin P. *Calvin's Perspective on the Exaltation of Christ in Comparison with the Post-Reformation Doctrine of the Two States*. Kampen: J. H. Kok, 1966.

Horton, Michael. *The Christian Faith*, 458–82. Grand Rapids: Zondervan, 2011.

Hyde, Daniel R. *God with Us: Knowing the Mystery of Who Jesus Is*. Grand Rapids: Reformation Heritage Books, 2007.

Kelly, Douglas F. *Systematic Theology*, 2:183–260. Fearn: Mentor, 2014.

Kolb, Robert, and Carl R. Trueman. *Between Wittenburg and Geneva: Lutheran and Reformed Theology in Conversation*, 59–87. Grand Rapids: Baker Academic, 2017.

Lee, Daniel Y. K. *The Holy Spirit as Bond in Calvin's Thought: Its Functions in Connection with the extra Calvinisticum*. Bern: Peter Lang, 2011.

Letham, Robert. "The Person of Christ." In Matthew Barrett, ed. *Reformation Theology*, 313–46. Wheaton: Crossway Books, 2017.

Lindholm, Stephen. *Jerome Zanchi (1516–90) and the Analysis of Reformed Scholastic Christology*. Göttingen: Vandenhoeck & Ruprecht, 2016.

Lloyd-Jones, D. Martyn. *Great Doctrines of the Bible*, 1:244–88. Wheaton: Crossway, 2003.

Lyford, William. *The Instructed Christian*, 110–24. Morgan, PA: Soli Deo Gloria, n.d.

MacArthur, John and Richard Mayhue, eds. *Biblical Doctrine*, 202–04, 235–71. Wheaton: Crossway, 2017.

Machen, J. Gresham. *The Person of Christ*. Philadelphia: Westminster Seminary Press, 2017.

MacLeod, Donald. *The Person of Christ*, 193–99. Downers Grove, IL: IVP, 1998.

Manton, Thomas. *The Works of Thomas Manton, D.D.*, 1:413–504. Worthington, PA: Maranatha Publications, n.d.

McCormack, Bruce L. *For Us and Our Salvation: Incarnation and Atonement in the Reformed Tradition*. Princeton: Princeton Theological Seminary, 1993.

McGinnis, Andrew M. *The Son of God Beyond the Flesh: A Historical and Theological Study of the Extra Calvinisticum*. London: Bloomsbury, 2014.

Morecraft, Joseph C., III. *Authentic Christianity*, 2:1–46. Powder Springs, GA: Minkoff Family Publishing and American Vision Press, 2009.

Muller, Richard A. *Dictionary of Latin and Greek Theological Terms, Drawn Principally from Protestant Scholastic Theology*, 69–71, 116–17, 125–26, 205, 260–64, 281–83, 374. 2nd ed. Grand Rapids: Baker Academic, 2017.

Muller, Richard A. *Post-Reformation Reformed Dogmatics*, 2nd ed., 4:275–332. Grand Rapids: Baker Academic, 2003.

Murray, John. *The Collected Writings of John Murray*, 2:132–41. Edinburgh: Banner of Truth, 1976.

Nicole, Roger. "Jesus Christ, the Unique Son of God: The Relationship of His Deity and Humanity." In J. D. Douglas, ed. *Let the Earth Hear His Voice*, 1041–48. Minneapolis: World Wide Publications, 1975.

Niesel, Wilhelm. *The Theology of Calvin*, 110–19. Philadelphia: Westminster, 1956.

Oberman, Heiko A. *The Dawn of the*

Reformation, 234–58. Grand Rapids: Eerdmans, 1988.

Oberman, Heiko A. "The 'Extra' Dimension in the Theology of Calvin." In Richard C. Gamble, ed. *Articles on Calvin and Calvinism*, 8:160–84. New York: Garland, 1992.

Olevianus, Caspar. *A Firm Foundation*, 46–63, 75–78. Grand Rapids: Baker Books, 1995.

Oliphint, K. Scott. *God with Us*, 133–222. Wheaton: Crossway, 2012.

Olyott, Stuart. *Jesus Is Both God and Man*, especially 121–43. Darlington: Evangelical Press, 2000.

Owen, John. *The Works of John Owen*, 1:1–421, especially 223–35 and 309–22; 2:413–19. Edinburgh: Banner of Truth, 1976.

Perkins, William. *A Golden Chaine*, 37–53. N.p.: Puritan Reprints, 2010.

Reymond, Robert L. *Jesus, Divine Messiah*. Fearn: Mentor, 2003.

Reymond, Robert L. *A New Systematic Theology of the Christian Faith*, 211–316. Nashville: Thomas Nelson, 1998.

Rohls, Jan. *Reformed Confessions: Theology from Zurich to Barmen*, 102–17. Louisville: Westminster John Knox, 1998.

Selderhuis, Herman J., ed. *The Calvin Handbook*, 253–54, 257–65. Grand Rapids: Eerdmans, 2009.

Shedd, William G. T. *Dogmatic Theology*, 613–58, especially 650–58. 3rd ed. Phillipsburg, NJ: P&R, 2003.

Torrance, Thomas F. *Incarnation: The Person and Life of Christ*, 213–32. Downers Grove, IL: IVP, 2008.

Torrance, Thomas F. *Space, Time and Incarnation*, 30–37. London: Oxford University Press, 1969.

Turretin, Francis. *Institutes of Elenctic Theology*, 1:282–92, 2:299–332, especially 321–32. Phillipsburg, NJ: P&R, 1992.

Tylenda, Joseph N. "Calvin's Understanding of the Communication of Properties." In Richard C. Gamble, ed. *Articles on Calvin and Calvinism*, 8:148–59. New York: Garland, 1992.

Ursinus, Zacharias. *The Commentary of Dr. Zacharias Ursinus on the Heidelberg Catechism*, 181–211. Phillipsburg, NJ: P&R, n.d.

Ussher, James. *A Body of Divinity*, 142–48. Birmingham: Solid Ground Christian Books, 2007.

Van Buren, Paul. "The Incarnation: Christ's Union with Us." In Donald K. McKim, ed. *Readings in Calvin's Theology*, 123–41. Grand Rapids: Baker Book House, 1984.

van den Belt, Henk, ed. *Synoposis Purioris Theologiae: Synopsis of a Purer Theology*, 2:67–129, 173–77, 185, 193. Leiden: Brill, 2016.

van Genderen, J. and W. H. Velema. *Concise Reformed Dogmatics*, 449–62. Phillipsburg, NJ: P&R, 2008.

VanderGroe, Theodorus. *The Christian's Only Comfort in Life and Death*, 1:71–86, 265–78. Edited by Bartel Elshout and Joel R. Beeke. Grand Rapids: Reformation Heritage Books, 2016.

Vermigli, Peter Martyr. *The Peter Martyr Library, Volume 2*. Kirksville, MO: Sixteenth Century Journal Publishers, 1995.

Vos, Geerhardus. *Reformed Dogmatics*, 3:20–84. Bellingham: Lexham Press, 2014.

Warfield, Benjamin B. *The Lord of Glory*. Grand Rapids: Zondervan, n.d.

Warfield, Benjamin B. *The Person and Work of Christ*, 211–64. Phillipsburg, NJ: Presbyterian and Reformed, 1970.

Warfield, Benjamin B. *The Works of Benjamin B. Warfield*, 2:175–209; 3:149–77, 259–310. Grand Rapids: Baker Book House, 1981.

Wellum, Stephen. *Christ Alone*. Grand Rapids: Zondervan, 2016.

Wellum, Stephen. *God the Son Incarnate*, especially 324–38. Wheaton: Crossway, 2016.

Willis, E. David. *Calvin's Catholic Christology: The Function of the So-Called Extra Calvinisticum in Calvin's Theology*. Leiden: Brill, 1966.

Zaspel, Fred G. *The Theology of B. B. Warfield*, 213–85. Wheaton: Crossway, 2010.

The Active and Passive Obedience of Christ

(Anonymous, ed.). *God's Gospel of Grace*, 163–215. Pensacola: Chapel Library, n.d.

à Brakel, Wilhelmus. *The Christian's Reasonable Service*, 1:610–12. Ligonier, PA: Soli Deo Gloria, 1992.

Bavinck, Herman. *Reformed Dogmatics*, 3:337–81. Grand Rapids: Baker Academic, 2003.

Beardslee, John W., III, ed. *Reformed Dogmatics*, 98–110. New York: Oxford University Press, 1965.

Berkhof, Louis. *Systematic Theology*, 324–25, 379–82. Grand Rapids: Eerdmans, 1988.

Berkouwer, G. C. *The Work of Christ*, 314–27. Grand Rapids: Eerdmans, 1965.

Biehl, Craig. *The Infinite Merit of Christ: The Glory of Christ's Obedience in the Theology of Jonathan Edwards*. Jackson: Reformed Academic Press, 2009.

Boettner, Loraine. *Studies in Theology*, 299–306. Phillipsburg, NJ: Presbyterian and Reformed, 1973.

Bonar, Horatius. *The Everlasting Righteousness*. Hobbs: Trinity Foundation, 1994.

Brine, John. *Christ's Active Obedience Imputed to His People*. Ossett: Christian Bookshop, 1995.

Buchanan, James. *The Doctrine of Justification*. London: Banner of Truth, 1961.

Bunyan, John. *The Works of John Bunyan*, 1:300–334; 2:278–334. Edinburgh: Banner of Truth, 1991.

Calvin, John. *Institutes of the Christian Religion*, 2:16:5 (pp. 507–10). Philadelphia: Westminster Press, 1960.

Carson, D. A. "The Vindication of Imputation: On Fields of Discourses and Semantic Fields." In Mark Husbands and David J. Treier, eds. *Justification: What's at Stake in the Current Debates*, 46–78.

Downers Grove, IL: InterVarsity Press, 2004.

Clark, R. Scott. "The Benefits of Christ: Double Justification in Protestant Theology before the Westminster Assembly." In Anthony T. Selvaggio, ed. *The Faith Once Delivered*, 107–34. Phillipsburg, NJ: P&R, 2007.

Clark, R. Scott. "Do This and Live: Christ's Active Obedience as the Ground of Justification." In R. Scott Clark, ed. *Covenant, Justification, and Pastoral Ministry*, 229–66. Phillipsburg, NJ: P&R, 2007.

Clarkson, David. *The Works of David Clarkson*, 1:273–330. Edinburgh: Banner of Truth, 1988.

Cunningham, William. *Historical Theology*, 2:45–56. London: Banner of Truth, 1969.

de Campos, Heber Carlos, Jr. *Doctrine in Development: Johannes Piscator and Debates over Christ's Active Obedience*. Grand Rapids: Reformation Heritage Books, 2017.

Edwards, Jonathan. *The Works of Jonathan Edwards*, 9:304–18; 13:319, 368, 377–78, 402–03, 464–65; 14:47–66; 19:143–242; 20:57, 376–77, 488. New Haven: Yale University Press, 1994.

Engelsma, David J. *Gospel Truth of Justification*, 342–85. Jenison: Reformed Free Publishing Association, 2017.

Evans, William. *Imputation and Impartation: Union with Christ in American Reformed Theology*. Milton Keynes: Paternoster, 2008.

Eveson, Philip H. *The Great Exchange: Justification by Faith Alone*. Epsom: Day One Publications, 1996.

Fesko, J. V. *Death in Adam, Life in Christ: The Doctrine of Imputation*. Fearn: Mentor, 2016.

Fesko, J. V. *Justification: Understanding the Classic Reformed Doctrine.* Phillipsburg: P & R, 2008.

Fesko, J. V. *The Theology of the Westminster Standards,* 207–38. Wheaton: Crossway, 2014.

Gatiss, Lee, ed. *The Sermons of George Whitefield,* 1:262–80. Wheaton: Crossway, 2012.

Gay, David H. J. *Christ's Obedience Imputed.* N.p.: Brachus, 2018.

Gentry, Peter J. and Stephen J. Wellum. *Kingdom Through Covenant,* 663–70. Wheaton: Crossway, 2012.

Gill, John. *A Complete Body of Doctrinal and Practical Divinity,* 396–406. Paris, AR: Baptist Standard Bearer, 1984.

Gill, John. *Sermons and Tracts,* 2:455–508. Streamwood, IL: Primitive Baptist Library, 1981.

Goodwin, Thomas. *The Works of Thomas Goodwin,* 5:337–52. Eureka, CA: Tanski, 1996.

Grew, Obadiah. *The Lord Our Righteousness.* Morgan, PA: Soli Deo Gloria, 2005.

Grudem, Wayne. *Systematic Theology,* 570–71. Grand Rapids: Zondervan, 1994.

Heppe, Heinrich. *Reformed Dogmatics,* 458–65. Grand Rapids: Baker Book House, 1978.

Hodge, A. A. *The Atonement,* 230–45. Grand Rapids: Baker Book House, 1974.

Hodge, A. A. *Outlines of Theology,* 405, 500–502, 506–07. Grand Rapids: Zondervan, 1973.

Hodge, Charles. *Justification by Faith Alone.* Hobbs: Trinity Foundation, 1995.

Hodge, Charles. *Systematic Theology,* 2:612–13, 3:142–43, 182–85. Grand Rapids: Eerdmans, 1979.

Horton, Michael S. "Traditional Reformed View." In James K. Beilby and Paul Rhodes Eddy, eds. *Justification: Five Views,* 83–111. Downers Grove: IVP Academic, 2011.

Jue, Jeffrey K. "The Active Obedience of Christ and the Theology of the Westminster Standards: A Historical Investigation." In K. Scott Oliphint, ed. *Justified in Christ,* 99–130. Fearn: Mentor, 2007.

Kettler, Christian D. *The Vicarious Humanity of Christ and the Reality of Salvation.* Lanham: University Press of America, 1991.

Kistler, Don, ed. *Justification by Faith Alone.* Morgan, PA: Soli Deo Gloria, 1995.

Maas, Korey D. "Justification by Faith Alone." In Matthew Barrett, ed. *Reformation Theology,* 511–48. Wheaton: Crossway Books, 2017.

Machen, J. Gresham. *God Transcendent,* 187–96. Edinburgh: Banner of Truth, 1982.

McGrath, Alister E. *Iustitia Dei: A History of the Christian Doctrine of Justification,* 3rd ed., 272–75. Cambridge: Cambridge University Press, 2005.

Muller, Richard A. *Dictionary of Latin and Greek Theological Terms, Drawn Principally from Protestant Scholastic Theology,* 182–84, 216–17, 237–38. 2nd ed. Grand Rapids: Baker Academic, 2017.

Murray, John. *The Collected Writings of John Murray,* 2:151–57. Edinburgh: Banner of Truth, 1976.

Murray, John. *Redemption Accomplished and Applied,* 25–30. Grand Rapids: Eerdmans, 1955.

Owen, John. "The Doctrine of Justification by Faith." In *The Works of John Owen,* 5:1–400, especially 251–75. Edinburgh: Banner of Truth, 1976.

Phillips, Richard D. "Glorying in the Imputed Righteousness of Christ." In Joel R. Beeke, ed. *The Beauty and Glory of Christ,* 121–34. Grand Rapids: Reformation Heritage Books, 2011.

Pink, Arthur W. *The Doctrines of Election and Justification.* Grand Rapids: Baker Book House, 1975.

Piper, John. *Counted Righteous in Christ.* Wheaton: Crossway, 2002.

Piper, John. *The Future of Justification.* Wheaton: Crossway, 2007.

Polhill, Edward. *The Works of Edward Polhill,*

76–93, 149–52, 160–61. Morgan, PA: Soli Deo Gloria, 1998.

Robertson, O. Palmer. *The Current Justification Controversy*. Unicoi: Trinity Foundation, 2003.

Schreiner, Thomas. *Faith Alone: The Doctrine of Justification*. Grand Rapids: Zondervan, 2015.

Shedd, William G. T. *Dogmatic Theology*, 3rd ed., 720–22, 757–58. Phillipsburg, NJ: P&R, 2003.

Sproul R. C. *Faith Alone: The Evangelical Doctrine of Justification*, especially 95–113. Grand Rapids: Baker Books, 1995.

Sproul R. C. *Getting the Gospel Right*. Grand Rapids: Baker Books, 1999.

Sproul R. C. *The Priest with Dirty Clothes*. Orlando: Reformation Trust, 2011.

Stoddard, Solomon. *The Safety of Appearing at the Day of Judgment, in the Righteousness of Christ, Opened and Applied*. Morgan, PA: Soli Deo Gloria, 1995.

Strange, Alan D. The Imputation of the Active Obedience of Christ in the Westminster Standards. Grand Rapids: Reformation Heritage Books, 2019.

Strange, Alan D. "The Imputation of the Active Obedience of Christ at the Westminster Assembly." In Michael A. G. Haykin and Mark Jones, eds. *Drawn into Controversie: Reformed Theological Diversity and Debates Within Seventeenth-Century British Puritanism*, 31–51.

Göttingen: Vandenhoeck & Ruprecht, 2011.

Trueman, Carl R. "John Owen on Justification." In K. Scott Oliphint, ed. *Justified in Christ*, 81–98. Fearn: Mentor, 2007.

Turretin, Francis. *Institutes of Elenctic Theology*, 2:646–56. Phillipsburg, NJ: P&R, 1992.

Van Dixhoorn, Chad. *The Minutes and Papers of the Westminster Assembly 1643–1652*, 2:53–107, 130–39. New York: Oxford University Press, 2012.

VanDrunnen, David. "To Obey is Better than Sacrifice: A Defense of the Active Obedience of Christ in the Light of Recent Criticism." In Gary L. W. Johnson and Guy P. Waters, eds. *By Faith Alone*, 95–131. Wheaton: Crossway, 2006.

Vermigli, Peter Martyr. *The Peter Martyr Library, Volume 2*. Kirksville, MO: Sixteenth Century Journal Publisher, 1995.

Vickers, Brian. *Jesus' Blood and Righteousness: Paul's Theology of Imputation*. Wheaton: Crossway, 2006.

Vos, Geerhardus. *Reformed Dogmatics*, 3:127–36. Bellingham: Lexham Press, 2014.

Waldron, Samuel E. *Faith, Obedience, and Justification: Current Evangelical Departures from Sola Fide*. Palmdale: Reformed Baptist Academic Press, 2006.

White, James R. *The God Who Justifies*, 111–18. Minneapolis: Bethany House, 2011.

The Law

à Brakel, Wilhelmus. *The Christian's Reasonable Service*, 3:35–242. Ligonier, PA: Soli Deo Gloria, 1992.

Aldersen, Richard. *No Holiness, No Heaven! Antinomianism Today*. Edinburgh: Banner of Truth, 1986.

Bahnsen, Greg. *By This Standard*. Tyler: Institute for Christian Economics, 1985.

Bahnsen, Greg. *Theonomy in Christian Ethics*. Rev. ed. Phillipsburg, NJ: Presbyterian and Reformed, 1974.

Bahnsen, Greg L., ed. *Five Views on Law and Gospel*, 13–173. Grand Rapids: Zondervan, 1996.

Barcellos, Richard C. *In Defense of the Decalogue: A Critique of New Covenant Theology*. Enumclaw: WinePress Publishing, 2001.

Barker, William S. and W. Robert Godfrey, eds. *Theonomy: A Reformed Critique*. Grand Rapids; Zondervan, 1990.

Begg, Alistair. *Pathway to Freedom*. Chicago: Moody Publishers, 2003.

Beisner, E. Calvin, ed. *The Auburn Avenue Theology, Pros and Cons*. Fort Lauderdale: Knox Theological Seminary, 2004.

Bellamy, Joseph. *Sin, the Law, and the Glory of the Gospel*. Ames, IA: International Outreach, 2008.

Berkhof, Louis. *Systematic Theology*, 612–15. Grand Rapids: Eerdmans, 1988.

Bolton, Samuel. *The True Bounds of Christian Freedom*. London: Banner of Truth, 1964.

Boston, Thomas. *The Complete Works of the Late. Rev. Thomas Boston*, 2:51–373. Wheaton: Richard Owen Roberts, 1980.

Bozeman, Theodore Dwight. *The Precisionist Strain: Disciplinary Religion & Antinomian Backlash in Puritanism to 1638*. Chapel Hill: University of North Carolina Press, 2004.

Brown, John. *The Systematic Theology of John Brown*, 450–517. Fearn: Christian Focus; and Grand Rapids: Reformation Heritage Books, 2002.

Bullinger, Henry (Heinrich). *The Decades of Henry Bullinger*, 1:193–436, 2:17–300. Grand Rapids: Reformation Heritage Books, 2004.

Bunyan, John. *The Works of John Bunyan*, 1:492–575. Edinburgh: Banner of Truth, 1991.

Burgess, Anthony. *Vindiciae Legis: A Vindication of the Morall Law and the Covenants*. Grand Rapids: Reformation Heritage Books, 2011.

Calvin, John. *The Covenant Enforced: Sermons on Deuteronomy 21 and 28*. Tyler: Institute for Christian Economics, 1990.

Calvin, John. *Institutes of the Christian Religion*, 2:7–11 (pp. 348–464). Philadelphia: Westminster Press, 1960.

Calvin, John. *John Calvin's Sermons on the Ten Commandments*. Grand Rapids: Baker Book House, 1980.

Calvin, John. *Sermons on Deuteronomy*. Edinburgh: Banner of Truth, 1987.

Casselli, Stephen J. *Divine Rule Maintained: Anthony Burgess, Covenant Theology,* and the Place of the Law in Reformed Scholasticism. Grand Rapids: Reformation Heritage Books, 2014.

Catherwood, Frederick. *First Things First*. Downers Grove, IL: InterVarsity Press, 1979.

Chantry, Walter J. *God's Righteous Kingdom*. Edinburgh: Banner of Truth, 1980.

Chilton, David. *Productive Christians in an Age of Guilt Manipulators*. Tyler: Institute for Christian Economics, 1981.

Como, David R. *Blown by the Spirit: Puritanism and the Emergence of an Antinomian Undergrown in Pre-Civil War England*. Stanford: Stanford University Press, 2004.

Dabney, Robert Lewis. *Systematic Theology*, 351–429. Edinburgh: Banner of Truth, 1985

DeMar, Gary and Peter J. Leithart. *The Reduction of Christianity*. Ft. Worth: Dominion Press, 1988.

DeMar, Gary. *The Debate Over Christian Reconstruction*. Ft. Worth: Dominion Press, 1988.

DeMar, Gary. *God and Government*. 3 vols. Atlanta: American Vision, 1981.

Douma, J. *The Ten Commandments*. Phillipsburg, NJ: P&R, 1996.

Durham, James. *A Practical Exposition of the Ten Commandments*. Dallas: Naphtali Press, 2002.

Edwards, Brian H. *The Ten Commandments for Today*. Bromley: Day One, 1996.

Eire, Carlos M. N. *War Against the Idols: The Reformation and Worship from Erasmus to Calvin*. Cambridge: Cambridge University Press, 1986.

Fairbairn, Patrick. *The Revelation of Law in Scripture*. Edinburgh: Banner of Truth, 1996.

Fesko, J. V. *The Theology of the Westminster Standards*, 267–98. Wheaton: Crossway, 2014.

Fisher, Edward. *The Marrow of Modern Divinity*. Swengel: Reiner, 1978.

Flavel, John. *The Works of John Flavel*, 2:287–306. London: Banner of Truth, 1968.

Frame, John M. *The Doctrine of the Christian Life*, 385–850. Phillipsburg, NJ: P&R, 2008.

Gamble, Whitney G. *Christ and the Law: Antinomianism and the Westminster Assembly*. Grand Rapids: Reformation Heritage Books, 2018.

Gay, David H. J. *Christ is All. No Sanctification by the Law*. Bedford: Brachus, 2013.

Gay, David H. J. *New Covenant Articles*. Bedford: Brachus, 2014.

Gentry, Kenneth L., Jr. *He Shall Have Dominion*. Tyler: Institute for Christian Economics, 1992.

Gerstner, John H. *Reasons for Duty*. Morgan, PA: Soli Deo Gloria, 1995.

Gill, John. *A Complete Body of Doctrinal and Practical Divinity*, 367–77, 991–94. Paris, AR: Baptist Standard Bearer, 1984.

Hesselink, I. John. *John Calvin's Concept of the Law*. Allison Park: Pickwick Publications, 1992.

Hodge, Charles. *Systematic Theology*, 3:259–465. Grand Rapids: Eerdmans, 1979.

Hoeksema, Herman. *The Triple Knowledge*, 3:117–450. Grand Rapids: Reformed Free Publishing Association, 1976.

Hopkins, Ezekiel. *The Works of Ezekiel Hopkins*, 1:236–602. Morgan, PA: Soli Deo Gloria, 1995.

Horton, Michael S. *The Law of Perfect Freedom*. Chicago: Moody Press, 1993.

House, H. Wayne and Thomas Ice. *Dominion Theology: Blessing or Curse?* Portland: Multnomah, 1988.

Ingram, T. Robert. *The World Under God's Law*. Houston: St. Thomas Press, 1962.

Johnson, Gary and Guy Waters. *By Faith Alone*. Wheaton: Crossway, 2007.

Jones, Mark. *Antinomianism: Reformed Theology's Unwelcome Guest?* Phillipsburg, NJ: P&R, 2013.

Jordan, James B. *The Law and the Covenant*. Tyler: Institute for Christian Economics, 1984.

Jordan, James B. *The Sociology of the Church*. Tyler: Geneva Ministries, 1986.

Kevan, Ernest F. *The Grace of Law*. Ligonier, PA: Soli Deo Gloria, 1993.

Kevan, Ernest F. *The Moral Law*. Phillipsburg, NJ: P&R, 1991.

Kolb, Robert, and Carl R. Trueman. *Between Wittenburg and Geneva: Lutheran and Reformed Theology in Conversation*, 31–58. Grand Rapids: Baker Academic, 2017.

Lee, Francis Nigel. *God's Ten Commandments: Yesterday, Today, Forever*. Ventura, CA: Nordskog, 2007.

Lee, Francis. *The Covenantal Sabbath*. London: Lord's Day Observation Society, 1969.

Leiter, Charles. *The Law of Christ*. Hannibal: Granted Ministries Press, 2012.

Leithart, Peter. *Against Christianity*. Moscow: Canon Press, 2003.

Lloyd-Jones, D. Martyn. *Born of God: Sermons from John 1*, 34–137. Edinburgh: Banner of Truth, 2011.

Masters, Peter. *God's Rules for Holiness*. London: The Wakeman Trust, 2003.

McVicar, Michael J. *Christian Reconstruction: R. J. Rushdoony and American Religious Conservatism*. Chapel Hill: University of North Carolina Press, 2015.

Mohler, R. Albert, Jr. *Words from the Fire: Hearing the Voice of God in the 10 Commandments*. Chicago: Moody Publishers, 2009.

Morecraft, Joseph C., III. *Authentic Christianity*, 3:511–897, 4:1–973, 5:1–53. Powder Springs, GA: Minkoff Family Publishing and American Vision Press, 2009.

Muller, Richard A. *Dictionary of Latin and Greek Theological Terms, Drawn Principally from Protestant Scholastic Theology*, 194–98, 384–85. 2nd ed. Grand Rapids: Baker Academic, 2017.

Murray, John. *The Collected Writings of John Murray*, 1:193–204, 4:133–41. Edinburgh: Banner of Truth, 1976.

Newton, John. *The Works of John Newton*, 1:339–50, 2:516–28. Edinburgh: Banner of Truth, 1985.

Niesel, Wilhelm. *The Theology of Calvin*, 92–103. Philadelphia: Westminster, 1956.

North, Gary and Gary DeMar. *Christian Reconstruction*. Tyler: Institute for Christian Economics, 1991.

North, Gary, ed. *Theonomy: An Informed Response*. Tyler: Institute for Christian Economics, 1991.

North, Gary. *The Sinai Strategy*. Tyler: Institute for Christian Economics, 1986.

North, Gary. *Tools of Dominion: The Case Laws of Exodus*. Tyler: Institute for Christian Economics, 1990.

North, Gary. *Unconditional Surrender*. Tyler: Geneva Press, 1981.

North, Gary. *Westminster's Confession*. Tyler: Institute for Christian Economics, 1991.

Otis, John M. *Danger in the Camp: An Analysis and Refutation of the Heresies of the Federal Vision*. Corpus Christi: Triumphant Publications, 2005.

Packer, J. I. *I Want to Be a Christian*, 185–240. Wheaton: Tyndale House, 1977.

Packer, J. I. *Keeping the Ten Commandments*. Wheaton: Crossway, 2007.

Perkins. William. *A Golden Chaine*, 53–149. N.p.: Puritan Reprints, 2010.

Pink, Arthur W. *The Ten Commandments*. Swengel: Reiner, n.d.

Plumer, William S. *The Law of God*. Harrisonburg, VA: Sprinkle Publications, 1996.

Poythress, Vern Sheridan. *The Shadow of Christ in the Law of Moses*. Brentwood: Wolgemuth and Hyatt, 1991.

Reisinger, Ernest C. *The Law and the Gospel*. Phillipsburg, NJ: P&R, 1997.

Ridgley, Thomas. *Commentary on the Larger Catechism*, 2:298–423. Edmonton: Still Waters Revival Books, 1993.

Robbins, John and Sean Gerety. *Not Reformed at All*. Unicoi: Trinity Foundation, 2004.

Robbins, John W. *A Companion to the Current Justification Controversy*. Unicoi: Trinity Foundation, 2003.

Robertson, O. Palmer. *The Current Justification Controversy*. Unicoi: Trinity Foundation, 2003.

Ross, Philip S. *From the Finger of God: The Biblical and Theological Basis for the Threefold Division of the Law*. Fearn: Mentor, 2010.

Rushdoony, Rousas J. *The Institutes of Biblical Law*. Phillipsburg, NJ: Presbyterian and Reformed, 1973.

Rushdoony, Rousas J. *The Roots of Reconstruction*. Vallecito: Ross House Books, 1991.

Rushdoony, Rousas J. *Systematic Theology*. 2 vols. Vallecito: Ross House Books, 1994.

Ryken, Philip Graham. *Written in Stone: The Ten Commandments and Today's Moral Crisis*. Wheaton: Crossway, 2003.

Scavizzi, Giuseppe. *The Controversy on Images from Calvin to Baronius*. New York: Peter Lang, 1992.

Schreiner, Thomas R. *40 Questions About Christians and the Law*. Grand Rapids: Kregel, 2010.

Schwertley, Brian M. *Auburn Avenue Theology: A Biblical Analysis*. Saunderstown: American Presbyterian Press, 2005.

Shedd, William G. T. *Sermons to the Natural Man*, 161–80, 231–48. Edinburgh: Banner of Truth, 1977.

Shedd, William G. T. *Sermons to the Spiritual Man*, 194–224. London: Banner of Truth, 1972.

Shepherd, Norman. *The Call of Grace*. Phillipsburg, NJ: P&R, 2000.

Tow, Timothy. *The Law of Moses & of Jesus*. Singapore: Christian Life Publishers, 1986.

Turretin, Francis. *Institutes of Elenctic Theology*, 2:1–167. Phillipsburg, NJ: P&R, 1992.

Ursinus, Zacharias. *The Commentary of Dr. Zacharias Ursinus on the Heidelberg Catechism*, 489–618. Phillipsburg, NJ: P&R, n.d.

Ussher, James. *The Puritan Pulpit: The Irish Puritans*, 53–68. Orlando: Soli Deo Gloria, 2006.

Van Dixhoorn, Chad. *Confessing the Faith*, 239–58. Edinburgh: Banner of Truth, 2014.

VanderGroe, Theodorus. *The Christian's Only Comfort in Life and Death*, 2:123–418. Edited by Bartel Elshout and Joel R. Beeke. Grand Rapids: Reformation Heritage Books, 2016.

Waters, Guy Prentiss. *The Federal Vision and Covenant Theology*. Phillipsburg, NJ: P&R, 2006.

Watson, Thomas. *The Ten Commandments*. Edinburgh: Banner of Truth, 1976.

Wells, Tom and Fred Zaspel. *New Covenant Theology*. Frederick: New Covenant Media, 2002.

Wilkins, Steve and Duane Garner, eds. *The Federal Vision*. Monroe: Athanasius Press, 2004.

Wilson, Douglas. *"Reformed" is Not Enough*. Moscow: Canon Press, 2002.

Zanchi, Girolamo. *On the Law in General*. Grand Rapids: Christian's Library Press, 2012.

Covenant Theology

à Brakel, Wilhelmus. 4:373–535. *The Christian's Reasonable Service*, 1:355–80, 427–63. Ligonier, PA: Soli Deo Gloria, 1992.

Alleine, Richard. *Heaven Opened: The Riches of God's Covenant*. Morgan, PA: Soli Deo Gloria, 2000.

Allis, Oswald T. *Prophecy and the Church*. Phillipsburg, NJ: Presbyterian and Reformed, 1974.

Baker, J. Wayne. *Heinrich Bullinger and the Covenant*. Athens: Ohio University Press, 1980.

Barcellos, Richard C., ed. *Recovering a Covenantal Heritage: Essays in Baptist Covenant Theology*. Palmdale: RBAP, 2014.

Bavinck, Herman. *Reformed Dogmatics*, 3:193–232. Grand Rapids: Baker Academic, 2003.

Beach, J. Mark. *Christ and the Covenant: Francis Turretin's Federal Theology as a Defense of the Doctrine of Grace*. Göttingen: Vandenhoeck & Ruprecht, 2007.

Beeke, Joel R. and Mark Jones. *A Puritan Theology*, 217–318. Grand Rapids: Reformation Heritage Books, 2012.

Belcher, Richard. *A Comparison of Dispensationalism and Covenant Theology*. Columbia: Richbarry Press, 1986.

Berkhof, Louis. *Systematic Theology*, 211–18, 262–301. Grand Rapids: Eerdmans, 1988.

Bierma, Lyle D. *German Calvinism in the Confessional Age: The Covenant Theology of Caspar Olevianus*. Grand Rapids: Baker Books, 1996.

Blackburn, Earl M. "Covenant Theology." In Rob Ventura, ed. *Going Beyond Five Points: Pursuing a More Comprehensive Reformation*, 131–78. Self-published, CreateSpace, 2016.

Blackburn, Earl M., ed. *Covenant Theology: A Baptist Distinctive*. Birmingham: Solid Ground Christian Books, 2013.

Bogue, Carl W. *Jonathan Edwards and the Covenant of Grace*. Cherry Hill: Mack, 1975.

Boston, Thomas. *The Complete Works of the Late Rev. Thomas Boston*, 8:379–604, 11:178–232. Wheaton: Richard Owen Roberts, 1980.

Campbell, Roderick. *Israel and the New Covenant*. Philadelphia: Presbyterian and Reformed, 1954.

Chafer, Louis Sperry. *Systematic Theology*. 8 vols. Dallas: Dallas Seminary Press, 1980.

Clark, R. Scott. *Caspar Olevianus and the Substance of the Covenant*. Grand Rapids: Reformation Heritage Books, 2005.

Cocceius, Johannes. *The Doctrine of the Covenant and Testament of God*. Grand Rapids: Reformation Heritage Books, 2016.

Coxe, Nehemiah and John Owen. *Covenant Theology from Adam to Christ*. Palmdale: Reformed Baptist Academic Press, 2005.

Davies, Gwyn. *Covenanting with God.* Aberystwyth: Evangelical Library of Wales, 1994.

Denault, Pascal. *The Distinctives of Baptist Covenant Theology.* Birmingham: Solid Ground Christian Books, 2013.

Elazar, Daniel J. and John Kincaid, eds. *The Covenant Connection from Federal Theology to Modern Federalism.* Lanham: Lexington Books, 2000.

Fesko, J. V. *The Theology of the Westminster Standards,* 125–67. Wheaton: Crossway, 2014.

Gaffin, Richard B., Jr., ed. *Redemptive History and Biblical Interpretation: The Shorter Writings of Geerhardus Vos,* 234–70, 400–411. Phillipsburg, NJ: Presbyterian and Reformed, 1980.

Gamble, Richard C., ed. *Articles on Calvin and Calvinism,* 8:2–110. New York: Garland, 1992.

Gentry, Peter J. and Stephen J. Wellum. *Kingdom Through Covenant.* Wheaton: Crossway, 2012.

Gerstner, John H. *The Rational Biblical Theology of Jonathan Edwards,* 2:79–141. Orlando: Ligonier Ministries, 1992.

Gerstner, John H. *Wrongly Dividing the Word of Truth.* Morgan: Soli Deo Gloria, 2000.

Gill, John. *A Complete Body of Doctrinal and Practical Divinity,* 214–50, 345–77. Paris, AR: Baptist Standard Bearer, 1984.

Golding, Peter. *Covenant Theology.* Fearn: Christian Focus, 2004.

Griffith, Howard, and John R. Muether, eds. *Creator Redeemer Consummator: A Festschrift for Meredith G. Kline.* Jackson: Reformed Theological Seminary, 2000.

Grudem, Wayne. *Systematic Theology,* 515–22. Grand Rapids: Zondervan, 1994.

Hendriksen, William. *The Covenant of Grace.* Grand Rapids: Baker Book House, 1978.

Henry, Matthew. *The Covenant of Grace.* Fearn: Christian Heritage, 2002.

Heppe, Heinrich. *Reformed Dogmatics,* 282–447, 581–89. Grand Rapids: Baker Book House, 1978.

Holwerda, David. *Jesus and Israel: One Covenant or Two?* Grand Rapids: Eerdmans, 1995.

Horton, Michael S. *Covenant and Eschatology.* Louisville: Westminster John Knox Press, 200:

Horton, Michael S. *Covenant and Salvation.* Louisville: Westminster John Knox Press, 2007.

Horton, Michael S. *God of Promise: Introducing Covenant Theology.* Grand Rapids: Baker Books, 2006.

Horton, Michael S. *Lord and Servant: A Covenant Christology.* Louisville: Westminster John Knox Press, 2005.

Horton, Michael S. *People and Place: A Covenant Ecclesiology.* Louisville: Westminster John Knox Press, 2008.

Howell, R. B. C. *The Covenants.* Wilmington: Hampton House Books, 1991.

Jeon, Jeong Koo. *Biblical Theology: Covenants and the Kingdom of God in Redemptive History.* Eugene, OR: Wipf & Stock, 2017.

Jeon, Jeong Koo. *Covenant Theology.* Lanham: University Press of America, 1999.

Jewett, Paul K. *Infant Baptism and the Covenant of Grace.* Grand Rapids: Eerdmans, 1978.

Johnson, Jeffrey D. *The Kingdom of God: A Baptist Expression of Covenant and Biblical Theology.* Conway, AR: Free Grace Press, 2014.

Karlberg, Mark W. *Covenant Theology in Reformed Perspective.* Eugene: Wipf and Stock, 2000.

Kline, Meredith G. *By Oath Consigned.* Grand Rapids: Eerdmans, 1960.

Kline, Meredith G. *Images of the Spirit.* Eugene: Wipf and Stock, 1998.

Kline, Meredith G. *Kingdom Prologue.* Overland Park: Two Age Press, 2000.

Kline, Meredith G. *The Structure of Biblical Authority.* Grand Rapids: Eerdmans, 1977.

Kline, Meredith G. *Treaty of the Great King.* Grand Rapids: Eerdmans, 1963.

Lee, Brian J. *Johannes Cocceius and the Exegetical Roots of Federal Theology.*

Göttingen: Vandenhoeck & Ruprecht, 2009.

Lillback, Peter A. *The Binding of God: Calvin's Role in the Development of Covenant Theology*. Grand Rapids: Baker Academic, 2001.

Lloyd-Jones, D. Martyn. *Great Doctrines of the Bible*, 1:224–44. Wheaton: Crossway, 2003.

Mangum, R. Todd. *The Dispensational-Covenantal Rift: The Fissuring of American Evangelical Theology from 1936 to 1944*. Eugene, OR: Wipf & Stock, 2007.

McCoy, Charles S., and J. Wayne Baker. *Fountainhead of Federalism: Heinrich Bullinger and the Covenant Tradition*. Louisville: Westminster John Knox Press, 1991

McMahon, C. Matthew. *A Simple Overview of Covenant Theology*. New Lenox: Puritan Publications, 2005.

Miller, Ronald D., James M. Renihan, and Francisco Orozco, eds. *Covenant Theology from Adam to Christ*. Palmdale: Reformed Baptist Academic Press, 2005.

Morecraft, Joseph C., III. *Authentic Christianity*, 1:685–861. Powder Springs, GA: Minkoff Family Publishing and American Vision Press, 2009.

Muller, Richard A. *Dictionary of Latin and Greek Theological Terms, Drawn Principally from Protestant Scholastic Theology*, 126–32. 2nd ed. Grand Rapids: Baker Academic, 2017.

Murray, John. *The Collected Writings of John Murray*, 4:216–40. Edinburgh: Banner of Truth, 1976.

Murray, John. *The Covenant of Grace*. Phillipsburg, PA: Presbyterian and Reformed, 1988.

Neilands, David. *Studies in the Covenant of Grace*. Phillipsburg, PA: Presbyterian and Reformed, 1980.

Nichols, Greg. *Covenant Theology: A Reformed and Baptist Perspective on God's Covenants*. Birmingham: Solid Ground Christian Books, 2011.

Osterhaven, M. E. "Covenant Theology." In Treier, Daniel J. and Walter A. Elwell, eds. *Evangelical Dictionary of Theology*, 3rd ed., 215–16, 311–12. Grand Rapids: Baker Academic, 2017.

Packer, J. I. *The Collected Shorter Writings of J. I. Packer*, 1:9–22: Carlisle: Paternoster, 1998.

Packer, J. I. *Revelations of the Cross*, 9–22. Peabody: Hendrickson, 1998.

Pietsch, B. M. *Dispensational Modernism*. Oxford: Oxford University Press, 2015.

Pink, Arthur W. *The Divine Covenants*. Grand Rapids: Baker Book House, 1975.

Poole, David N. J. *Stages of Religious Faith in the Classical Reformation Tradition: The Covenant Approach to the Ordo Salutis*. Lewiston: Edwin Mellen, 1995.

Ramsey, D. Patrick, and Joel R. Beeke. *An Analysis of Herman Witsius's The Economy of the Covenants*. Grand Rapids: Reformation Heritage Books, 2002.

Rhodes, Jonty. *Covenants Made Simple*. Phillipsburg, NJ: P&R, 2015.

Robertson, O. Palmer. *The Christ of the Covenants*. Phillipsburg, NJ: Presbyterian and Reformed, 1980.

Rollock, Robert. *Some Questions and Answers about God's Covenant and the Sacrament That Is a Seal of God's Covenant*. Translated by Aaron Clay Denlinger. Eugene: Pickwick, 2017.

Rutherford, Samuel. *The Covenant of Life Opened*. New Lenox: Puritan Publications, 2005.

Schreiner, Thomas R. *Covenant and God's Purpose for the World*. Wheaton: Crossway, 2017.

Selvaggio, Anthony T. "Unity or Disunity? Covenant Theology from Calvin to Westminster." In Anthony T. Selvaggio, ed. *The Faith Once Delivered*, 217–46. Phillipsburg, NJ: P&R, 2007.

Smith, Ralph. *The Eternal Covenant: How the Trinity Reshapes Covenant Theology*. Moscow: Canon Press, 2003.

Stam, Clarence. *The Covenant of Love:*

Exploring Our Relationship with God. Winnipeg: Premier, 1999.

Stoever, William. *A Faire and Easie Way to Heaven: Covenant Theology and Antinomianism in Early Massachusettes.* Middletown: Wesleyan University Press, 1978.

Strehle, Stephen. *Calvinism, Federalism, and Scholasticism.* New York: Peter Lang, 1988.

Turretin, Francis. *Institutes of Elenctic Theology,* 1:574–78, 2:169–269. Phillipsburg, NJ: P&R, 1992.

Van Asselt, Willem J. *The Federal Theology of Johannes Cocceius (1603–1669).* Leiden: Brill, 2001.

Van der Waal, C. *The Covenantal Gospel.* Neerlandia: Inheritance Publications, 1990.

Van Genderen, J. *Covenant and Election.* Neerlandia: Inheritance Publications, 1995.

Van Rohr, John. *The Covenant of Grace in Puritan Thought.* Atlanta: Scholars Press, 1986.

Venema, Cornelis P. *Christ and Covenant Theology.* Phillipsburg: P & R, 2017.

Vos, Geerhardus. "The Doctrine of the Covenant in Reformed Theology." In *Redemptive History and Biblical Interpretation,* 234–67. Phillipsburg, NJ: Presbyterian and Reformed, 1980.

Vos, Geerhardus. *Reformed Dogmatics,* 2:76–137. Bellingham: Lexham Press, 2012.

Waldron, Samuel E., and Richard C. Barcellos. *A Reformed Baptist Manifesto: The New Covenant Constitution of the Church.* Palmdale: Reformed Baptist Academic Press, 2004.

Weir, D. A. *The Origins of the Federal Theology in Sixteenth-Century Reformation Thought.* Oxford: Clarendon Press, 1990.

Williams, Michael D. *Far as the Curse is Found: The Covenantal Story of Redemption.* Phillipsburg, PA: P&R, 2006.

Witsius, Herman. *The Economy of the Covenants Between God and Man.* 2 vols. Escondido: Den Dulk Foundation; and Phillipsburg, NJ: P&R, 1990.

Woolsey, Andrew. *Unity and Continuity in Covenantal Thought.* Grand Rapids: Reformation Heritage Books, 2012.

Zinkland, John M. *Covenants: God's Claims.* Sioux Center: Dordt College Press, 1984.

The Church

"The Directory for the Publick Worship of God" and "The Form of Presbyterian Church Government." In *The Confession of Faith: The Larger and Shorter Catechisms, with the Scripture-Proofs at Large.* Glasgow: Free Presbyterian Publications, 1988.

à Brakel, Wilhelmus. *The Christian's Reasonable Service,* 2:3–187. Ligonier, PA: Soli Deo Gloria, 1992.

Avis, Paul D. L. *The Church in the Theology of the Reformers.* Atlanta: John Knox Press, 1981.

Bannerman, Douglas. *The Scripture Doctrine of the Church.* Grand Rapids: Baker Book House, 1976.

Bannerman, James. *The Church of Christ.* 2 vols. Edinburgh: Banner of Truth, 1974.

Bavinck, Herman. *Reformed Dogmatics,* 4:271–440. Grand Rapids: Baker Academic, 2008.

Baxter, Richard. *The Practical Works of Richard Baxter,* 1:547–736, 922–48. Ligonier, PA: Soli Deo Gloria, 1990.

Beeke, Joel R., ed. *Calvin for Today,* 139–91. Grand Rapids: Reformation Heritage Books, 2009.

Beeke, Joel R., and Mark Jones. *A Puritan Theology,* 621–769. Grand Rapids: Reformation Heritage Books, 2012.

Berkhof, Louis. *Systematic Theology,* 555–603. Grand Rapids: Eerdmans, 1988.

Berkouwer, G. C. *The Church*. Grand Rapids: Eerdmans, 1976.

Bogue, Carl W. *The Scriptural Law of Worship*. Dallas: Presbyterian Heritage Publications, 1988.

Brown, John. *The Systematic Theology of John Brown*, 550–76. Fearn: Christian Focus; and Grand Rapids: Reformation Heritage Books, 2002.

Bucer, Martin. *Common Places of Martin Bucer*, 201–34. Edited by David F. Wright. Appleford: Sutton Courtenay Press, 1972.

Bullinger, Henry (Heinrich). *The Decades of Henry Bullinger*. 4:3–163. Grand Rapids: Reformation Heritage Books, 2004.

Calvin, John. *Institutes of the Christian Religion*, Book 4 (pp. 1009–521). Philadelphia: Westminster, 1960.

Calvin, John. *Selected Works of John Calvin*, 3 vols. Grand Rapids: Baker Book House, 1983.

Clowney, Edmund P. *The Church*. Downers Grove, IL: IVP, 1995.

Cunningham, William. *Historical Theology*, 2:514–87. London: Banner of Truth, 1969.

Dabney, Robert Lewis. *Discussions*, Volume 2. Harrisonburg, VA: Sprinkle Publications, 1982.

DeMar, Gary. *God and Government*. 3 vols. Bristol: Wolgemuth and Hyatt, 1989.

Dever, Mark. *The Church*. Nashville: B & H, 2012.

Eire, Carlos M. N. *War Against the Idols: The Reformation of Worship from Erasmus to Calvin*. Cambridge: Cambridge University Press, 1986.

Fesko, J. V. *The Theology of the Westminster Standards*, 299–334. Wheaton: Crossway, 2014.

Frame, John M. *Systematic Theology*, 1017–69. Phillipsburg, NJ: P&R, 2013.

Gamble, Richard C., ed. *Articles on Calvin and Calvinism*, Volumes 10 and 11. New York: Garland, 1992.

George, Timothy, ed. *John Calvin and the Church*. Louisville: Westminster John Knox Press, 1990.

Gerstner, John H. *The Rational Biblical Theology of Jonathan Edwards*, 3:363–428. Orlando: Ligonier Ministries, 1993.

Goodwin, Thomas. *The Works of Thomas Goodwin*, Volume 11. Eureka, CA: Tanski, 1996.

Grudem, Wayne. *Systematic Theology*, 855–949. Grand Rapids: Zondervan, 1994.

Heppe, Heinrich. *Reformed Dogmatics*, 657–94. Grand Rapids: Baker Book House, 1978.

Hoeksema, Herman. *Reformed Dogmatics*, 2:179–278. 2nd ed. Grandville: Reformed Free Publishing Association, 2004.

Horton, Michael. *The Christian Faith*, 711–903. Grand Rapids: Zondervan, 2011.

Kuiper, R. B. *The Glorious Body of Christ*. London: Banner of Truth, 1966.

MacArthur, John, and Richard Mayhue, eds. *Biblical Doctrine*, 739–826. Wheaton: Crossway, 2017.

Milner, Benjamin Charles, Jr. *Calvin's Doctrine of the Church*. Leiden: Brill, 1970.

Morecraft, Joseph C., III. *Authentic Christianity*, 2:301–633. Powder Springs, GA: Minkoff Family Publishers and American Vision Press, 2009.

Murray, John. *The Collected Writings of John Murray*, 1:231–87; 2:321–65. Edinburgh: Banner of Truth, 1976.

Murray, Iain H., ed. *The Reformation of the Church: A Collection of Reformed and Puritan Documents on Church Issues*. Edinburgh: Banner of Truth, 1987.

Niesel, Wilhelm. *The Theology of Calvin*, 182–210. Philadelphia: Westminster Press, 1956.

Owen, John. *The Works of John Owen*, 8:282–309; 13; 15, especially pp. 188–373, 445–530; 16:2–253. Edinburgh: Banner of Truth, 1976.

Reymond, Robert L. *A New Systematic Theology of the Christian Faith*, 805–910. Nashville: Thomas Nelson, 1998.

Ryken, Philip Graham, Derek W. H. Thomas, and J. Ligon Duncan, III, eds. *Give Praise to God: A Vision for Reforming Worship*. Phillipsburg, NJ: P&R, 2003.

Ryle, J. C. *Knots Untied*, 168–91. Cambridge: James Clarke, 1964.

Ryle, J. C. *Warnings to the Church*, 9–28. Edinburgh: Banner of Truth, 1992.

Selderhuis, Herman J., ed. *The Calvin Handbook*, 323–32. Grand Rapids: Eerdmans, 2009.

Smith, Frank J., and David C. Lachman, eds. *Worship in the Presence of God*. Greenville, SC: Greenville Seminary Press, 1992.

Smith, Morton H. *Systematic Theology*, 2:515–73. Greenville, SC: Greenville Seminary Press, 1994.

Sproul, R. C. *Everyone's a Theologian*, 261–92. Orlando: Reformation Trust, 2014.

Thornwell, James Henley. *The Collected Writings of James Henley Thornwell*. 4 vols. Edinburgh: Banner of Truth, 1974.

Turretin. Francis. *Institutes of Elenctic Theology*, 3:1–336. Phillipsburg, NJ: P&R, 1992.

Ursinus, Zacharias. *The Commentary of Dr. Zacharias Ursinus on the Heidelberg Catechism*, 286–93, 441–63, 571–75. Phillipsburg, NJ: Presbyterian and Reformed, n.d.

van den Belt, Henk, ed. *Synoposis Purioris Theologiae: Synopsis of a Purer Theology*, 2:558–659. Leiden: Brill, 2016.

Van Dixhoorn, Chad. *Confessing the Faith*, 335–424. Edinburgh: Banner of Truth, 2014.

van Genderen, J., and W. H. Velema. *Concise Reformed Dogmatics*, 677–752. Phillipsburg, NJ: P&R, 2008.

Vos, Geerhardus. *Reformed Dogmatics*, 5:1–74. Bellingham: Lexham Press, 2016.

Waldron, Sam. "The Regulative Principle." In Rob Ventura, ed. *Going Beyond Five Points: Pursuing a More Comprehensive Reformation*, 59–130. Self-published, CreateSpace, 2016.

Walker, G. S. M. "Calvin and the Church." In Donald K. McKim, ed. *Readings in Calvin's Theology*, 212–30. Grand Rapids: Baker Book House, 1984.

Watts, Malcolm. *What is a Reformed Church?* Phillipsburg, NJ: P&R, 2011.

Wendel, Francois. *Calvin: The Origins and Development of His Religious Thought*, 291–312. London: Collins, 1963.

The Sacraments

à Brakel, Wilhelmus. *The Christian's Reasonable Service*, 2:525–600. Ligonier, PA: Soli Deo Gloria, 1992.

Adams, Jay E. *The Meaning and Mode of Baptism*. Phillipsburg, NJ: Presbyterian and Reformed, 1976.

Alexander, James W. *God is Love: Communion Addresses*. Edinburgh: Banner of Truth, 1985.

Bannerman, James. *The Church of Christ*, 2:128–85. Edinburgh: Banner of Truth, 1974.

Barth, Karl. *The Teaching of the Church Regarding Baptism*. London: SCM Press, 1948.

Bavinck, Herman. *Reformed Dogmatics*, 4:461–95, 540–85. Grand Rapids: Baker Academic, 2008.

Baxter, Richard. *The Practical Works of Richard Baxter*, 1:493–502. Ligonier, PA: Soli Deo Gloria, 1990.

Beeke, Joel R., and Mark Jones. *A Puritan Theology*, 725–60. Grand Rapids: Reformation Heritage Books, 2012.

Beeke, Joel R., and Paul Smalley, eds. *Feasting with Christ: Meditations on the Lord's Supper*. Darlington: Evangelical Press, 2012.

Belcher, Richard P. *A Journey in Baptism*. Columbia: Richbarry Press, 2003.

Berkhof, Louis. *Systematic Theology*, 604–58. Grand Rapids: Eerdmans, 1988.

Berkouwer, G. C. *The Sacraments*. Grand Rapids: Eerdmans, 1969.

Beza, Theodore. *A Clear and Simple Treatise on the Lord's Supper*. Translated by David

C. Noe. Grand Rapids: Reformation Heritage Books, 2016.

Bierma, Lyle D. *The Doctrine of the Sacraments in the Heidelberg Catechism: Melanchthonian, Calvinist, or Zwinglian?* Princeton: Princeton Theological Seminary, 1999.

Billings, J. Todd, and I. John Hesselink, eds. *Calvin's Theology and Its Reception*, 143–89. Louisville: Westminster John Knox Press, 2012.

Booth, Robert R. *Children of Promise.* Phillipsburg, NJ: P&R, 1995.

Boston, Thomas. *The Complete Works of the Late Rev. Thomas Boston*, 2:460–65, 481–97; 3:5–493; 4:11–465; 6:125–220; 10:133–45; 12:461–63. Wheaton: Richard Owen Roberts, 1980.

Bridge, William. *The Works of the Reverend William Bridge*, 4:128–61. Beaver Falls: Soli Deo Gloria, 1989.

Bruce, Robert. *The Mystery of the Lord's Supper.* Richmond: John Knox Press, 1958.

Bucer, Martin. *The Common Places of Martin Bucer*, 313–400. Edited by David F. Wright. Appleford: Sutton Courtenay Press, 1972.

Bullinger, Henry (Heinrich). *The Decades of Henry Bullinger*, 4:226–478. Grand Rapids: Reformation Heritage Books, 2004.

Bunyan, John. *The Works of John Bunyan.* 2:591–657. Edinburgh: Banner of Truth, 1991.

Buswell, J. Oliver, Jr. *A Systematic Theology of the Christian Religion*, 2:226–80. Grand Rapids; Zondervan, 1962.

Calvin, John. *Calvin: Theological Treatises*, 140–77, 257–332. London: SCM Press, 1954.

Calvin, John. *Institutes of the Christian Religion*, 4:14 and 17–18 (pp. 1276–1303, 1359–1448). Philadelphia: Westminster Press, 1960.

Calvin, John. *Selected Works of John Calvin*, 2:114–26, 163–579. Grand Rapids: Baker Book House, 1983.

Charnock, Stephen. *The Works of Stephen Charnock*, 4:392–482. Edinburgh: Banner of Truth, 1985.

Conner, Alan. *Covenant Children Today: Physical or Spiritual?* Owensboro: RBAP, 2007.

Coppes, Leonard. *Daddy, May I Take Communion?* Thornton: By the Author, 1988.

Crampton, W. Gary. *From Paedobaptism to Credobaptism: A Study of the Westminster Standards and Infant Baptism.* Owensboro: RBAP, 2010.

Cunningham, William. *Historical Theology*, 2:121–54. London: Banner of Truth, 1969.

Cunningham, William. *The Reformers and the Theology of the Reformation*, 212–91. Edinburgh: Banner of Truth, 1979.

Dabney, Robert Lewis. *Systematic Theology*, 800–817. Edinburgh: Banner of Truth, 1985.

Davis, Thomas J. *The Clearest Promises of God: The Development of Calvin's Eucharistic Teaching.* New York: AMS, 1995.

Davis, Thomas J. *This is My Body: The Presence of Christ in Reformed Thought.* Grand Rapids: Baker Academic, 2008.

Doolittle, Thomas. *A Treatise Concerning the Lord's Supper.* Morgan, PA: Soli Deo Gloria, 1998.

Duncan, J. Ligon. "True Communion with Christ: Calvin, Westminster and the Nature of Christ's Sacramental Presence." In J. Ligon Duncan, ed. *The Westminster Confession into the 21st Century*, 2:429–75. Fearn: Mentor, 2004.

Durand, Greg L. *God's Covenant and the Community of Believers.* Aurora: Crown Rights Book Company, 1995.

Edwards, Jonathan. *Sermons on the Lord's Supper.* Orlando: Northampton Press, 2007.

Elwood, Christopher. *The Body Broken: The Calvinistic Doctrine of the Eucharist and the Symbolization of Power in Sixteenth-Century France.* New York: Oxford University Press, 199.

Fesko, J. V. *Water, Word and Spirit: A Reformed Perspective on Baptism.* Grand Rapids: Reformation Heritage Books, 2010.

Flavel, John. *The Works of John Flavel*, 1:259–70; 6:378–469. London: Banner of Truth, 1968.

Frame, John M. *Systematic Theology*, 1060–69. Phillipsburg, NJ: P&R, 2013.

Fuller, Andrew. *The Complete Works of the Rev. Andrew Fuller*, 3:339–523. Harrisonburg, VA: Sprinkle Publications, 1988.

Gamble, Richard C., ed. *Articles on Calvin and Calvinism*, 8:222–53, 9:153–240. New York: Garland, 1992.

Gerrish, Brian A. *Grace and Gratitude: The Eucharistic Theology of John Calvin*. Minneapolis: Fortress Press, 1993.

Gerstner, John H. *The Rational Biblical Theology of Jonathan Edwards*, 3:429–75. Orlando: Ligonier Ministries, 1993.

Gill, John. *A Complete Body of Doctrinal and Practical Divinity*, 896–924, 995–1023. Paris, AR: Baptist Standard Bearer, 1984.

Gill, John. *Gospel Baptism*. Paris, AR: Baptist Standard Bearer, 2006.

Grudem, Wayne. *Systematic Theology*, 966–1002. Grand Rapids: Zondervan, 1994.

Hanko, Herman. *We and Our Children*. Grand Rapids: Reformed Free Publishing Association, 1981.

Henry, Matthew. *The Complete Works of the Rev. Matthew Henry*, 1:284–412, 489–566. Grand Rapids: Baker Book House, 1979.

Heppe, Heinrich. *Reformed Dogmatics*, 590–656. Grand Rapids: Baker Book House, 1978.

Hodge, A.A. *Outlines of Theology*, 631–50. Grand Rapids: Zondervan, 1973.

Hodge, Charles. *Systematic Theology*, 3:485–525. Grand Rapids: Eerdmans, 1979.

Hoeksema, Herman. *Reformed Dogmatics*, 2:316–421. 2nd ed. Grandville: Reformed Free Publishing Association, 2004.

Holifield, E. Brooks. *The Covenant Sealed: The Development of Puritan Sacramental Theology in Old and New England, 1510–1720*. New Haven: Yale University Press, 1974.

Hopkins, Ezekiel. *The Works of Ezekiel Hopkins*, 2:301–59. Morgan, PA: Soli Deo Gloria, 1997.

Horton, Michael. *The Christian Faith*, 751–827. Grand Rapids: Zondervan, 2011.

Hulse, Erroll. *The Testimony of Baptism*. Haywards Heath: Carey Publications, 1982.

Jewett, Paul K. *Infant Baptism and the Covenant of Grace*. Grand Rapids: Eerdmans, 1978.

Johnson, Jeffrey D. *The Fatal Flaw of the Theology Behind Infant Baptism*. Conway, AR: Free Grace Press, 2010.

Kevan, Ernest F. *The Lord's Supper*. London: Evangelical Press, 1966.

Kingdon, David. *Children of Abraham: A Reformed Baptist View of Baptism, the Covenant, and Children*. Haywards Heath: Henry E. Walter and Carey Publications, 1973.

Kolb, Robert, and Carl R. Trueman. *Between Wittenburg and Geneva: Lutheran and Reformed Theology in Conversation*, 147–207. Grand Rapids: Baker Academic, 2017.

Lanning, Ray B. *Glorious Remembrance: The Sacrament of the Lord's Supper as Administered in the Liturgy of the Reformed Churches*. Grand Rapids: Reformation Heritage Books, 2017.

Letham, Robert. *The Lord's Supper: Eternal Word in Broken Bread*. Phillipsburg, NJ: P&R, 2001.

Lloyd-Jones, D. Martyn. *Great Doctrines of the Bible*, 3:25–58. Wheaton: Crossway, 2003.

MacArthur, John, and Richard Mayhue, eds. *Biblical Doctrine*, 782–89. Wheaton: Crossway, 2017.

Maclean, Malcolm. *The Lord's Supper*. Fearn: Christian Focus, 2011.

Malone, Fred. *The Baptism of Disciples Alone*. Cape Coral, FL: Founders Press, 2003.

Manton, Thomas. *The Works of Thomas Manton, D.D.*, 5:459–71; 15:329–68, 487–99; 18:326–36. Worthington, PA: Maranatha Publications, n.d.

Marcel, Pierre Charles. *The Biblical Doctrine of Infant Baptism*. London: James Clarke, 1953.

Mathison, Keith A. *Given for You: Reclaiming Calvin's Doctrine of the Lord's Supper.* Phillipsburg, NJ: P&R, 2002.

McDonnell, Kilian. *John Calvin, the Church and the Eucharist.* Princeton: Princeton University Press, 1967.

McKim, Donald K., ed. *Major Themes in the Reformed Tradition*, 217–70. Grand Rapids: Eerdmans, 1992.

McLelland, Joseph C. *The Visible Words of God: An Exposition of the Sacramental Theology of Peter Martyr Vermigli, 1500–1562.* Grand Rapids: Eerdmans, 1957.

Morecraft, Joseph C., III. *Authentic Christianity*, 5:225–486. Powder Springs, GA: Minkoff Publishing Family and American Vision Press, 2009.

Murray, John. *Christian Baptism.* Phillipsburg, NJ: Presbyterian and Reformed, 1980.

Murray, John. *The Collected Writings of John Murray*, 2:366–84; 3:275–88. Edinburgh: Banner of Truth, 1976.

Niesel, Wilhelm. "The Sacraments." In Donald K. McKim, ed. *Readings in Calvin's Theology*, 244–59. Grand Rapids: Baker Book House, 1984.

Niesel, Wilhelm. *The Theology of Calvin*, 211–28. Philadelphia: Westminster. 1956.

Old, Hughes Oliphant. *Holy Communion in the Piety of the Reformed Church.* Powder Springs, GA: Tolle Lege, 2013.

Old, Hughes Oliphant. *The Shaping of the Reformed Baptismal Rite.* Grand Rapids: Eerdmans, 1992.

Owen, John. *The Works of John Owen*, 9:517–622; 16:258–68, 527–31. Edinburgh: Banner of Truth, 1976.

Payne, Jon D. *John Owen on the Lord's Supper.* Edinburgh: Banner of Truth, 2004.

Peck, Thomas E. *Writings of Thomas E. Peck*, 1:158–94. Edinburgh: Banner of Truth, 1999.

Perkins, William. *A Golden Chaine*, 151–66. N.p.: Puritan Reprints, 2010.

Reymond, Robert L. *A New Systematic Theology of the Christian Faith.* 455–967. Nashville: Thomas Nelson, 1999.

Riggs, John W. *Baptism in the Reformed Tradition.* Louisville; Westminster John Knox Press, 2002.

Rutherford, Samuel. *Fourteen Communion Sermons.* Edinburgh: James A. Dickson, 1986.

Ryken, Philip Graham, Derek W.H. Thomas, and J. Ligon Duncan, III, eds. *Give Praise to God.* Phillipsburg, NJ: P&R, 2003.

Ryle, J. B. *Knots Untied*, 68–86, 130–69. London: James Clarke, 1964.

Ryle, J. B. *The Upper Room*, 426–55. Edinburgh: Banner of Truth, 1977.

Saldenus, Guilelmus, and Wilhelmus à Brakel. *In Remembrance of Him: Profiting from the Lord's Supper.* Grand Rapids: Reformation Heritage Books, 2012.

Sartelle, John P. *What Christian Parents Should Know About Infant Baptism.* Phillipsburg, NJ: P&R, 1985.

Schenck, Lewis Bevans. *The Presbyterian Doctrine of Children in the Covenant.* Phillipsburg, NJ: P&R, 2003.

Schreiner, Thomas R. and Shawn D. Wright, eds. *Believer's Baptism: Sign of the New Covenant Church.* Nashville: B & H Publishing Group, 2006.

Selderhuis, Herman J., ed. *The Calvin Handbook*, 308–11, 344–55. Grand Rapids: Eerdmans, 2009.

Shaw, Robert. *The Reformed Faith*, 355–85. Fearn: Christian Heritage, 2008.

Shedd, William G. T. *Dogmatic Theology*, 809–27. 3rd ed. Phillipsburg, NJ: P&R, 2003.

Sibbes, Richard. *The Works of Richard Sibbes*, 4:59–112. Edinburgh: Banner of Truth, 1973.

Smith, Morton H. *Systematic Theology*, 2:673–96. Greenville, SC: Greenville Seminary Press, 1994.

Spear, Wayne R. "Calvin and Westminster on the Lord's Supper: Exegetical and Theological Considerations." In J. Ligon Duncan, III, ed. *The Westminster Confession into the 21st Century*, 3:385–414. Fearn: Mentor, 2009.

Spear, Wayne R. "The Nature of the Lord's Supper According to Calvin and the Westminster Assembly." In J. Ligon Duncan, III, ed. *The Westminster Confession into the 21st Century*, 3:355–84. Fearn: Mentor, 2009.

Spencer, Duane Edward. *Holy Baptism: Word Keys Which Unlock the Covenant*. Tyler: Geneva Ministries, 1984.

Spierling, Karen E. *Infant Baptism in Reformation Geneva*. Louisville: Westminster John Knox Press, 2005.

Sproul, R. C. *What is Baptism?* Orlando: Reformation Trust, 2012.

Spurgeon, Charles Haddon. *Metropolitan Tabernacle Pulpit*, 10:313–28, 413–24. Pasadena, TX: Pilgrim Publications, 1981.

Spurgeon, Charles Haddon. *Sermons on the Lord's Supper*. Peabody: Hendrickson, 2014.

Strawbridge, Greg, ed. *The Case for Covenant Communion*. Monroe: Athanasius Press, 2006.

Thornwell, James Henley. *The Collected Writings of James Henley Thornwell*, 3:283–412. Edinburgh: Banner of Truth, 1974.

Turretin, Francis. *Institutes of Elenctic Theology*, 3:421–560. Phillipsburg, NJ: P&R, 1992.

Ursinus, Zacharias. *The Commentary of Dr. Zacharias Ursinus on the Heidelberg Catechism*, 377–437. Phillipsburg, NJ: Presbyterian and Reformed, no date.

Ussher, James. *A Body of Divinity*, 364–90. Birmingham: Solid Ground Christian Books, 2007.

Van Dixhoorn, Chad. *Confessing the Faith*, 357–400. Edinburgh: Banner of Truth, 2014.

Van Dorn, Douglas. *Waters of Creation: A Biblical-Theological Study on Baptism*. Erie: Waters of Creation Publishing, 2009.

van Genderen, J. and W. H. Velema. *Concise Reformed Dogmatics*, 779–818. Phillipsburg, NJ: P&R, 2008.

VanderGroe, Theodorus. *The Christian's Only Comfort in Life and Death*, 1:543–56; 2:1–64. Edited by Bartel Elshout and Joel R. Beeke. Grand Rapids: Reformation Heritage Books, 2016.

Venema, Cornelis P. *Children at the Lord's Table? Assessing the Case for Paedocommunion*. Grand Rapids: Reformation Heritage Books, 2009.

Venema, Cornelis P. *The Lord's Supper and the "Popish Mass": A Study of Heidelberg Catechism Q & A 80*. Grand Rapids: Reformation Heritage Books, 2015.

Vermigli, Peter Martyr. *The Peter Martyr Library*, Volume 7. Kirksville, MO: Truman State University Press, 2000.

Vos, Geerhardus. *Reformed Dogmatics*, 5:75–249. Bellingham: Lexham Press, 2016.

Waldron, Samuel E. *Biblical Baptism*. Grand Rapids: Truth for Eternity Ministries, 1998.

Wallace, Ronald A. *Calvin's Doctrine of the Word and Sacrament*. London: Oliver and Boyd, 1953.

Wandel, Lee Palmer. *A Companion to the Eucharist in the Reformation*. Leiden: Brill, 2014.

Wandel, Lee Palmer. *The Eucharist in the Reformation*. Cambridge: Cambridge University Press, 2006.

Warfield, Benjamin B. *Selected Shorter Writings of Benjamin B. Warfield*, 1:325–38, 2:329–69. Nutley: Presbyterian and Reformed, 1970.

Warfield, Benjamin B. *Studies in Theology*, 389–410. Edinburgh: Banner of Truth, 1988.

Warfield, Benjamin B. *The Works of Benjamin B. Warfield*, 9:389–408. Grand Rapids: Baker Book House, 1981.

Waters, Guy Prentiss. *The Lord's Supper as the Sign and Seal of the New Covenant*. Wheaton: Crossway, 2019.

Watson, T. E. *Should Babies Be Baptized?* London: Grace Publications Trust, 1995.

Watson, Thomas. *The Lord's Supper*. Edinburgh: Banner of Truth, 2004.

Watson, Thomas. *The Mischief of Sin*, 103–62. Pittsburgh: Soli Deo Gloria, 1994.

Wendel, Francois. *Calvin: The Origins and Development of His Religious Thought*, 312–18, 329–55. London: Collins, 1963.

Witsius, Herman. *The Economy of the Covenants Between God and Man*, 2:444–64. Escondido: Den Dulk Foundation; and Phillipsburg, NJ: P&R, 1990.

Wright, David F. "Baptism at the Westminster Assembly." In J. Ligon Duncan, ed. *The Westminster Confession into the 21st Century*, 1:161–85. Fearn: Mentor, 2003.

Wright, David F. *Infant Baptism in Historical Perspective*. Milton Keynes: Paternoster, 2007.

Calvinistic Apologetics

Ahvio, Juha. *Theological Epistemology of Contemporary American Confessional Reformed Apologetics*. Helsinki: Luther-Agricola-Society, 2005.

Bahnsen, Greg L. *Always Ready: Directions for Defending the Faith*. Edited by Robert R. Booth. Atlanta: American Vision, 1996.

Bahnsen, Greg L. *Presuppositional Apologetics*. Powder Springs, GA: American Vision Press, 2008.

Bahnsen, Greg L. *Van Til's Apologetics*. Phillipsburg, NJ: P&R, 1998.

Baucham, Voddie, Jr. *Expository Apologetics*. Wheaton: Crossway, 2015.

Blanchard, John. *Does God Believe in Atheists?* Darlington: Evangelical Press, 2000.

Bril, K. A., H. Hart, and J. Klapwijk, eds. *The Idea of a Christian Philosophy: Essays in Honour of D. H. Th. Vollenhoven*. Toronto: Wedge Publishing Foundation, 1977.

Buswell, James Oliver, Jr. *A Christian View of Being and Knowing*. Grand Rapids: Zondervan, 1960.

Buswell, James Oliver, Jr. *A New Systematic Theology of the Christian Religion*. 2 vols. Grand Rapids; Zondervan, 1962.

Chaplin, Jonathan. *Herman Dooyeweerd: Christian Philosopher of State and Civil Society*. Notre Dame: University of Notre Dame Press, 2011.

Clark, Gordon H. *A Christian View of Men and Things*. Grand Rapids: Baker Book House, 1981.

Clark, Gordon H. *An Introduction to Christian Philosophy*. Jefferson: Trinity Foundation, 1993.

Clark, Gordon H. *Religion, Reason, and Revelation*. Jefferson: Trinity Foundation, 1986.

Clark, Gordon H. *Thales to Dewey: A History of Philosophy*. Jefferson: Trinity Foundation, 2000.

Crampton, W. Gary. *The Scripturalism of Gordon H. Clark*. Unicoi: Trinity Foundation, 1999.

Daniel, Stephen H. *The Philosophy of Jonathan Edwards*. Bloomington: Indiana University Press, 1994.

Dennis, Lane T., ed. *Francis A. Schaeffer: Portraits of the Man and His Work*. Westchester: Crossway, 1986.

Dooyeweerd, Herman. *In the Twilight of Western Thought*. Nutley: The Craig Press, 1975.

Dooyeweerd, Herman. *A New Critique of Theoretical Thought*. 4 vols. Philadelphia: Presbyterian and Reformed, 1953.

Douma, Douglas J. *The Presbyterian Philosopher: The Authorized Biography of Gordon H. Clark*. Eugene, OR: Wipf and Stock, 2016.

Fesko, J. V. *Reforming Apologetics: Retrieving the Classic Reformed Approach to Defending the Faith*. Grand Rapids: Baker Academic, 2019.

Follis, Bryan A. *Truth with Love: The Apologetics of Francis Schaeffer*. Wheaton: Crossway, 2006.

Fortmann, W. F. de Gaay, et al, eds. *Philosophy and Christianity: Philosophical Essays Dedicated to Professor Dr. Herman Dooyeweerd*. Kampen: J. H. Kok, 1965.

Frame, John M. *Apologetics: A Justification of Christian Belief.* 2nd ed. Phillipsburg, NJ: P&R, 2015.

Frame, John M. *Cornelius Van Til: An Analysis of His Thought.* Phillipsburg, NJ: P&R, 1995.

Frame, John M. *The Doctrine of the Knowledge of God.* Phillipsburg, NJ: Presbyterian and Reformed, 1987.

Geehan, E. R., ed. *Jerusalem and Athens: Critical Discussions on the Theology and Apologetics of Cornelius Van Til.* Phillipsburg, NJ: Presbyterian and Reformed, 1971.

Gerstner, John H. "A Primer on Apologetics." In *Primitive Theology,* 1–51. Morgan, PA: Soli Deo Gloria, 1996.

Halsey, Jim S. *For Such a Time as This.* Phillipsburg, NJ: Presbyterian and Reformed, 1976.

Hart, Hendrik, et al. *Rationality in the Calvinian Tradition.* Lanham: University Press of America, 1983.

Helm, Paul. *Faith with Reason.* Oxford: Clarendon Press, 2000.

Hoeksema, Herman. *The Clark-Van Til Controversy.* Hobbs: Trinity Foundation, 1995.

Kok, John H. *Vollenhoven: His Early Development.* Sioux Center: Dordt College Press, 1992.

Kuyper, Abraham. *Principles of Sacred Theology.* Grand Rapids: Eerdmans, 1968.

Lee, Francis Nigel. *A Christian Introduction to the History of Philosophy.* Nutley: The Craig Press, 1978.

Lee, Sang Hyun. *The Philosophical Theology of Jonathan Edwards.* Princeton: Princeton University Press, 1988.

Little, Bruce, A. *Francis Schaeffer: A Mind and Heart for God.* Phillipsburg, NJ: P&R, 2010.

McManis, Clifford B. *Biblical Apologetics.* N.p.: XLibris Corporation, 2012; revised edition, *Apologetics by the Book.* Sunnyvale, CA: GBF Press, 2017.

Nash, Ronald H. *Dooyeweerd and the Amsterdam Philosophy.* Grand Rapids: Zondervan, 1962.

Nash, Ronald H., ed. *The Philosophy of Gordon H. Clark.* Philadelphia: Presbyterian and Reformed, 1968.

North, Gary, ed. *Foundations of Christian Scholarship: Essays in the Van Til Perspective.* Vallecito: Ross House Books, 1979.

Notaro, Thom. *Van Til and the Use of Evidence.* Phillipsburg, NJ: Presbyterian and Reformed. 1985.

Oliphint, K. Scott. *The Battle Belongs to the Lord.* Phillipsburg, NJ: P&R, 2003.

Oliphint, K. Scott. *Reasons for Faith: Philosophy in the Service of Theology.* Phillipsburg, NJ: P&R, 2006.

Oliphint, K. Scott, and Lane G. Tipton, eds. *Revelation and Reason: New Essays in Reformed Apologetics.* Phillipsburg, NJ: P&R, 2007.

Parkhurst, Louis Gifford, Jr. *Francis Schaeffer: The Man and His Message.* Wheaton: Tyndale House, 1985.

Plantinga, Alvin C. *God, Freedom, and Evil.* Grand Rapids: Eerdmans, 1974.

Plantinga, Alvin C. *Warrant and Proper Function.* New York: Oxford University Press, 1993.

Plantinga, Alvin C. *Warranted Christian Belief.* New York: Oxford University Press, 2000.

Plantinga, Alvin C. *Warrant: The Current Debate.* New York: Oxford University Press, 1993.

Pratt, Richard. *Every Thought Captive.* Phillipsburg, NJ: Presbyterian and Reformed, 1979.

Reymond, Robert L. *The Justification of Knowledge.* Phillipsburg, NJ: Presbyterian and Reformed, 1974.

Ruesegger, Ronald W., ed. *Reflections on Francis Schaeffer.* Grand Rapids: Academie Books/Zondervan, 1986.

Schaeffer, Edith. *The Tapestry.* Waco: Word Books, 1981.

Schaeffer, Francis. *The Complete Works of*

Francis Schaeffer. Wheaton: Crossway, 1982.

Spier, J. M. *An Introduction to Christian Philosophy*. Philadelphia: Presbyterian and Reformed, 1954.

Spier, J. M. *What is Calvinistic Philosophy?* Grand Rapids: Eerdmans, 1953.

Sproul, R. C. *Defending Your Faith*. Wheaton: Crossway, 2003.

Sproul, R. C., Arthur Lindsley, and John Gerstner. *Classical Apologetics*. Grand Rapids: Zondervan, 1984.

Van Riessen, H. *The Society of the Future*. Philadelphia: Presbyterian and Reformed, 1954.

Van Til, Cornelius. *The Case for Calvinism*. Philadelphia: Presbyterian and Reformed, 1964.

Van Til, Cornelius. *Christian Apologetics*. Edited by William Edgar. Phillipsburg, NJ: P&R, 2003.

Van Til, Cornelius. *A Christian Theory of Knowledge*. Grand Rapids: Baker Book House, 1969.

Van Til, Cornelius. *The Defense of the Faith*. Philadelphia: Presbyterian and Reformed, 1955.

Vander Stelt, John C. *Philosophy and Scripture: A Study in Old Princeton and Westminster Theology*. Marlton: Mack Publishing Co., 1978.

White, William, Jr. *Van Til: Defender of the Faith*. Nashville: Thomas Nelson, 1979.

Wolterdorff, Nicholas. *Divine Discourse*. Cambridge: Cambridge University Press, 1995.

Young, William. *Toward a Reformed Philosophy*. Grand Rapids: Piet Hein; and Franeker: T. Weaver, 1952.

Reformed Evangelism

Alleine, Joseph. *A Sure Guide to Heaven*. Edinburgh: Banner of Truth, 1964.

Ascol, Thomas J., ed. *Reclaiming the Gospel and Reforming Churches*, 197–333. Cape Coral, FL: Founders Press, 2003.

Baxter, Richard. "A Call to the Unconverted." In *The Practical Works of Richard Baxter*, 2:502–44. Ligonier, PA: Soli Deo Gloria, 1990.

Beeke, Joel R. "Evangelism Rooted in Scripture: The Puritan Example." In Gary L. W. Johnson and R. Fowler White, eds. *Whatever Happened to the Reformation?*, 229–51. Phillipsburg, NJ: P&R, 2001.

Beeke, Joel R. *Puritan Evangelism: A Biblical Approach*. Grand Rapids: Reformation Heritage Books, 1999.

Beeke, Joel R. *Puritan Reformed Spirituality*, 54–72, 143–69. Grand Rapids: Reformation Heritage Books, 2004.

Beeke, Joel R., and Mark Jones. *A Puritan Theology*, 761–69. Grand Rapids: Reformation Heritage Books, 2012.

Beeke, Joel R., and Paul M. Smalley. *Prepared by Grace, for Grace: The Puritans on God's Way of Leading Sinners to Christ*. Grand Rapids: Reformation Heritage Books, 2013.

Belcher, Richard P. *A Journey in Evangelism and Missions*. Fort Mill: Richbarry Press, 2007.

Benton, John. *Evangelistic Calvinism*. Edinburgh: Banner of Truth, 2006.

Blanchard, John. *Right with God*. London: Banner of Truth, 1971.

Bonar, Horatius. *Words to Winners of Souls*. Phillipsburg, NJ: P&R, 1995.

Boston, Thomas. *The Art of Man-Fishing*. Grand Rapids: Baker Book House, 1977. Also in: *The Complete Works of the Late Rev. Thomas Boston*, 5:4–43. Wheaton: Richard Owen Roberts, 1980.

Bredenhof, Wes. *To Win Our Neighbors to Christ: The Missiology of the Three Forms of Unity*. Grand Rapids: Reformation Heritage Books, 2015.

Chantry, Walter. *Today's Gospel: Authentic or Synthetic?* London: Banner of Truth, 1970.

Clark, Gordon H. *Today's Evangelism: Counterfeit or Genuine?* Jefferson: Trinity Foundation, 1990.

Custance, Arthur C. *The Sovereignty of Grace*, 278–309. Phillipsburg, NJ: Presbyterian and Reformed, 1979.

Dabney, Robert Lewis. "God's Indiscriminate Proposals of Mercy, as Related to His Power, Wisdom and Sincerity." In *Discussions*, 1:282–313. Harrisonburg, VA: Sprinkle Publications, 1982.

Dallimore, Arnold. *George Whitefield*. 2 vols. London: Banner of Truth, 1970.

Dever, Mark. *The Gospel and Personal Evangelism*. Wheaton: Crossway, 2007.

Dever, Mark. *Understanding the Great Commission*. Nashville: B & H, 2016.

Fuller, Andrew. "The Gospel Worthy of All Acceptation." In *The Complete Works of the Rev. Andrew Fuller*, 2:328–511. Harrisonburg, VA: Sprinkle Publications, 1988.

Gamble, Richard C., ed. *Articles on Calvin and Calvinism*, 3:279–333. New York: Garland, 1992.

George, Timothy. *Amazing Grace: God's Pursuit, Our Response*, 101–21. Wheaton: Crossway, 1011.

Gerstner, John H. *The Rational Biblical Theology of Jonathan Edwards*, 3:1–49. Orlando: Ligonier Ministries, 1993.

Gerstner, John H. *Steps to Salvation: The Evangelistic Message of Jonathan Edwards*. Philadelphia: Westminster Press, 1960.

Good, Kenneth. *Christ's Teaching on the Theology of Evangelism*. Rochester: Backus Books, 1988.

Haykin, Michael A.G. "'A Sacrifice Well Pleasing to God': John Calvin and the Missional Endeavor of the Church." In Joel R. Beeke, David W. Hall, and Michael A. G. Haykins, eds. *Theology Made Practical: New Studies on John Calvin and His Legacy*, 131–42. Grand Rapids: Reformation Heritage Books, 2017.

Haykin, Michael A. G., and C. Jeffrey Robinson, eds. *To the Ends of the Earth:*

Calvin's Missional Vision and Legacy. Wheaton: Crossway Books, 2014.

Horton, Michael. *For Calvinism*, 151–69. Grand Rapids: Zondervan, 2011.

Howe, John. "The Redeemer's Tears Wept Over Lost Souls." In *The Works of the Rev. John Howe, M.A.*, 2:316–427. Ligonier, PA: Soli Deo Gloria, 1990.

Hulse, Erroll. *The Great Invitation*. Darlington: Evangelical Press, 1986.

Keiper, Ralph L. "Witnessing and God's Sovereignty." In James Montgomery Boice, ed. *Our Sovereign God*, 137–46. Grand Rapids: Baker Book House, 1977 .

Kennedy, John, and Horatius Bonar. *Evangelism: A Reformed Debate*. Portdinorwic: James Begg Society, 1997.

Kuiper, R. B. *God-Centered Evangelism*. Edinburgh: Banner of Truth, 1978.

Lawson, Steven J. *The Gospel Focus of Charles Spurgeon*. Orlando: Reformation Trust, 2012.

Lloyd-Jones, D. Martyn. *Evangelistic Sermons at Aberavon*. Edinburgh: Banner of Truth, 1983.

MacArthur, John. *The Gospel According to Jesus*. Rev. ed. Grand Rapids: Zondervan, 2008.

MacMillan, J. Douglas. *The God of All Grace*, 215–40. Fearn: Christian Focus, 1997.

Metzger, Will. *Tell the Truth*. Rev. ed. Downers Grove, IL: IVP, 2002.

Murray, Iain H. *The Invitation System*. London: Banner of Truth, 1973.

Murray, John. *The Collected Writings of John Murray*, 1:119–62. Edinburgh: Banner of Truth, 1976

Murray, John. *The Free Offer of the Gospel*. Edinburgh: Banner of Truth, 2001.

Nettles, Thomas J. *By His Grace and For His Glory*, 421–63. Rev. ed. Cape Coral, FL: Founders Press, 2006.

Nettles, Thomas J. *Living by Revealed Truth: The Life and Pastoral Theology of Charles Haddon Spurgeon*, 279–338. Fearn: Mentor, 2013.

Nichols, William C., ed. *Seeking God:*

Jonathan Edwards' Evangelism Contrasted with Modern Methodologies. Ames, IA: International Outreach, 2001.

Nicole, Roger. *Our Sovereign Saviour*, 131–42. Fearn: Christian Focus, 2002.

Packer, J. I. "A Calvinist — and an Evangelist!" In *The Collected Shorter Writings of J. I. Packer*, 2:205–10. See also pp. 159–267. Carlisle: Paternoster, 1998.

Packer, J. I. *Evangelism and the Sovereignty of God.* Downers Grove, IL: InterVarsity Press, 1961.

Phillips, Richard. *Jesus the Evangelist.* Orlando: Reformation Trust, 2007.

Piper, John. *Let the Nations Be Glad! The Supremacy of God in Missions.* 3rd ed. Grand Rapids: Baker Academic, 2010.

Prill, Thorsten. *Luther, Calvin and the Mission of the Church: The Mission Theology and Practice of the Protestant Reformers.* Kampen: GRIN Publishing, 2017.

Reisinger, Ernest. *Today's Evangelism.* Edinburgh: Banner of Truth, 1982.

Robertson, George W. *What is Evangelism?* Phillipsburg, NJ: P&R, 2014.

Rooy, Sidney. *The Theology of Missions in the Puritan Tradition.* Grand Rapids: Eerdmans, 1965.

Samuel, Leith. *How to Share Your Faith.* Welwyn: Evangelical Press, 1985.

Schreiner, Thomas R. and Bruce A. Ware, eds. *The Grace of God, The Bondage of the Will*, 1:233–48; 2:323–36. Grand Rapids: Baker, 1995.

Shedd, William G. T. *Sermons to the Spiritual Man*, 400–421. London: Banner of Truth, 1971.

Sills, David. "Missions and the Doctrines of Grace." In Thomas K. Ascol and Nathan A. Finn, eds. *Ministry By His Grace and For His Glory*, 234–48. Cape Coral, FL: Founders Press, 2011.

Spurgeon, Charles Haddon. "Compel Them to Come In." In *New Park Street Chapel Pulpit*, 5:17–24. Pasadena, TX: Pilgrim Publications, 1981.

Spurgeon, Charles Haddon. "Election No Discouragement to Seeking Souls." In *Metropolitan Tabernacle Pulpit*, 10:73–84. See also 30:49–60. Pasadena, TX: Pilgrim Publications, 1981.

Spurgeon, Charles Haddon. *The Soul Winner.* Grand Rapids: Eerdmans, 1978.

Storms, C. Samuel. "Prayer and Evangelism under God's Sovereignty." In Thomas R. Schreiner and Bruce A. Ware, eds. *Still Sovereign*, 307–23. Grand Rapids: Baker Books, 2000.

Venema, Cornelis P. *But for the Grace of God: An Exposition of the Canons of Dort*, 83–93. Grandville: Reformed Fellowship, 1994.

Walker, Jeremy. *The Brokenhearted Evangelist.* Grand Rapids: Reformation Heritage Books, 2012.

Washer, Paul. *Gospel Assurance and Warnings.* Grand Rapids: Reformation Heritage Books, 2014.

Washer, Paul. *The Gospel Call and True Conversion.* Grand Rapids: Reformation Heritage Books, 2013.

Washer, Paul. *The Gospel's Power and Message.* Grand Rapids: Reformation Heritage Books, 2012.

Watts, Malcolm. *What is a Reformed Church?*, 108–32. Grand Rapids: Reformation Heritage Books, 2011.

Wells, Tom. *Come to Me! An Urgent Invitation to Turn to Christ.* Edinburgh: Banner of Truth, 1986.

Arminian and Anti-Calvinist Works

(See also "The Synod of Dort" section of Bibliography)

Allen, David L. *The Extent of the Atonement:* *A Historical and Critical Review.* Nashville: B & H Academic, 2016.

Allen, David L., Eric Hankins, and Adam Harwood, eds. *Anyone Can Be Saved: A*

Defense of "Traditional" Southern Baptist Soteriology. Eugene: Wipf and Stock, 2016.

Allen, David L., and Steve W. Lemke, eds. *Whosoever Will: A Biblical-Theological Critique of Five Point Calvinism*. Nashville: B & H, 2010.

Anderson, H. C. *What We Should Know About Calvinism*. Moline: Christian Service Foundation, 1960.

Andreae, Jakob, and Theodore Beza. *Lutheranism vs. Calvinism: The Classic Debate at the Colloquy of Montbéliard 1586*. Translated by Clinton J. Armstrong. Edited by Jeffrey Mallinson. St. Louis: Concordia Publishing House, 2017.

Badger, Anthony B. *Confronting Calvinism: A Free Grace Refutation and Biblical Resolution of Radical Reformed Soteriology*. Self-published, CreateSpace, 2013.

Billton, James F. *True Wisdom Has Two Sides: Calvinism — is it Biblical?* Edinburgh: Grace Mount Publishers, 2001.

Brents, T. W. *The Gospel Plan of Salvation*. Nashville: Gospel Advocate Company, 1973.

Bryson, George. *The Five Points of Calvinism Weighed and Found Wanting*. Costa Mesa: The Word for Today, 1996.

Campana, Stephen. *The Calvinist Universalist*. Eugene: Resource Publications, 2014.

Carter, Ben M. *The Depersonalization of God: A Consideration of the Soteriological Difficulties in High Calvinism*. Lanham: University Press of America, 1989.

Carter, Charles W., ed. *A Contemporary Wesleyan Theology*. 2 vols. Grand Rapids: Francis Asbury Press, 1983.

Cassady, David. *Unconditional Eternal Security: "Yea, hath God said?"* N.p.: Xulon Press, 2008.

Coate, Micah. *A Cultish Side of Calvinism*. N.p.: Innovo Publishing, 2011.

Connell, John S. *The TULIP in the Garden*. Bloomington: WestBow Press, 2015.

Cooper, Jordan. *The Great Divide: A Lutheran Evaluation of Reformed Theology*. Eugene, OR: Wipf & Stock, 2015.

Corner, Daniel D. *The Believer's Conditional Security*. Washington: Evangelical Outreach, 1997.

Cottrell, Jack. *What the Bible Says about God the Redeemer*. Eugene: Wipf and Stock, 2000.

Cottrell, Jack. *What the Bible Says about God the Ruler*. Eugene: Wipf and Stock, 2000.

Cowburn, John. *Free Will, Predestination and Determinism*. Milwaukee: Marquette University Press, 2008. (Roman Catholic)

Cox, Michael. *Not One Little Child: A Biblical Critique of Calvinism*. Bloomington: WestBow Press, 2016.

Craig, William Lane. *The Only Wise God*. Grand Rapids: Baker Book House, 1987.

Dake, Finis Jennings. *Dake's Annotated Reference Bible*. Atlanta: Dake Bible Sales, 1963.

Dake, Finis Jennings. *God's Plan for Man*. Lawrenceville: Dake Bible Sales, 1987.

de Silva, J. W. *Calvinism: "Bitter for Sweet."* Kilmarnock: John Ritchie, 2014.

Dunning, H. Ray. *Grace, Faith and Holiness: A Wesleyan Systematic Theology*. Kansas City: Beacon Hill Press of Kansas City, 1988.

Feenstra, C. A. *Calvinism in the Light of God's Word*. Sioux Center: No publisher, 1968.

Finger, Thomas N. *Christian Theology*. 2 vols. Scottsdale: Herald Press, 1985.

Finney, Charles G. *Finney's Lectures in Systematic Theology*. Grand Rapids: Eerdmans, 1953.

Fischer, Austin. *Young, Restless, No Longer Reformed*. Eugene: Cascade Books, 2014.

Fisk, Samuel. *Calvinistic Paths Retraced*. Murfreesboro: Biblical Evangelism Press, 1985.

Fisk, Samuel. *Divine Sovereignty and Human Freedom*. Neptune: Loizeaux Brothers, 1973. Also published as: *Election and Predestination*. Eugene: Wipf and Stock, 2002.

Fisk, Samuel. *Five-Pont Calvinism and the Inconsistency of a Four-Point Position*. Brownsburg: Biblical Evangelism Press, 1980.

Fitch, Alger. *Pick the Brighter Tulip: There is an Alternative to Calvinism.* Joplin: College Press, 1993.

Forlines, F. Leroy. *Classical Arminianism.* Nashville: Randall House, 2011.

Forster, Roger T., and V. Paul Marston. *God's Strategy in Human History.* Wheaton: Tyndale House, 1973.

Gambrell, Ernest. *T.U.L.I.P. Heresy (False Doctrine) of John Calvin.* Memphis: Fundamental Baptist World Press, 1990.

Geisler, Norman. *Chosen but Free.* 3rd ed. Minneapolis: Bethany House, 2010.

Geisler, Norman. *Systematic Theology.* 4 vols. Minneapolis: Bethany House, 2004.

Gray, Donald J. *Predestination Brought into Focus.* Columbus: Brentwood Christian Press, 1988.

Greene, Oliver B. *Elected to Heaven or Hell?* Greenville, SC: The Gospel Hour, n.d.

Hitchcock, Steven L. *Recanting Calvinism For a Dynamic Gospel.* Maitland, FL: Xulon, 2011.

Hunt, Dave. *A Calvinist's Honest Doubts Resolved by Reason and God's Amazing Grace.* Bend, OR: The Berean Call, 2005.

Hunt, Dave. *What Love is This?* 3rd ed. Bend, OR: The Berean Call. 2006.

Huss, Mark. *Four Implications of Calvinism.* Collingswood, NJ: The Bible for Today, n.d.

Hutson, Curtis. *Why I Disagree with All Five Points of Calvinism.* Murfreesboro: Sword of the Lord, n.d.

James, Richard H. *Does God Give Man a Chance? A Refutation of Calvinism.* Lansing: Calvary Publishing, 2010.

Keathley, Kenneth. *Salvation and Sovereignty: A Molinist Approach.* Nashville: B & H, 2010.

Keener, Forrest L. *Grace Not Calvinism.* Lawton: The Watchman Press, 1992.

Kelly, Kent. *Inside the Tulip Controversy.* Southern Pines: Calvary Press, 1986.

Klein, William W. *The New Chosen People.* Grand Rapids: Academic Books/ Zondervan, 1990.

Knox, John S. *Arminius Stands His Ground.* Eugene, OR: Wipf & Stock, 2018.

Krejan, J. G. *Reformed Theology Unmasked.* Maitland, FL: Xulon, 2012.

Lennox, John C. *Determined to Believe?* Grand Rapids: Zondervan, 2017.

Lewis, Gordon R., and Bruce A. Demarest. *Integrative Theology.* 3 vols. Grand Rapids: Zondervan, 1987.

Lumpkins, Peter. *What is Calvinism?* Carrolton: Free Church Press, 2013.

Marshall, I. Howard. *Kept by the Power of God.* Minneapolis: Bethany Fellowship, 1969.

McComas, Wm. K. *Divinely Dear or Devilish Dangerous Doctrines?* Shelbyville: Bible & Literature Missionary Foundation, 1975.

McKinley, O. Glenn. *Where Two Creeds Meet: A Biblical Evaluation of Calvinism and Arminianism.* Kansas City: Beacon Hill Press, 1959.

Metcalfe, John. *The Westminster Confession Exploded: Deliverance from the Law.* Penn: The Publishing Trust, 1992.

Miller, Terry Lee. *"Calvinism": The Trojan Horse Within.* Bloomington: Xulon Press, 2012.

Moody, Dale. *The Word of Truth.* Grand Rapids: Eerdmans, 1981.

Mullins, Edgar Young. *The Christian Religion in Its Doctrinal Expression.* Valley Forge: Judson Press, 1974.

Nicholson, Roy S. *The Arminian Emphasis.* N.p.: No publisher, n.d.

Oden, Thomas C. *Doctrinal Standards in the Wesleyan Tradition.* Grand Rapids: Francis Asbury Press, 1988.

Oden, Thomas C. *Systematic Theology.* 3 vols. San Francisco: Harper & Row, 1987.

Oden, Thomas C. *The Transforming Power of Grace.* Nashville: Abingdon Press, 1993.

Olson, C. Gordon. *Beyond Calvinism and Arminianism: An Inductive Mediate Theology of Salvation.* Cedar Knolls: Global Gospel Ministries, 2002.

Olson, C. Gordon. *Getting the Gospel Right.*

Cedar Knolls: Global Gospel Publications, 2005.

Olson, Roger E. *Against Calvinism*. Grand Rapids: Zondervan, 2011.

Olson, Roger E. *Arminian Theology*. Downers Grove, IL: IVP, 2006.

Olson, Roger E. *How to be Evangelical Without Being Conservative*. Grand Rapids: Zondervan, 2008.

Olson, Roger E. *Reformed and Always Reforming: The Postconservative Approach to Evangelical Theology*. Grand Rapids: Baker Academic, 2007.

Page, Frank S. *Trouble with the Tulip*. Canton: Riverstone Group, 2000.

Picirilli, Robert E. *Grace, Faith, Free Will*. Nashville: Randall House. 2002.

Pinnock, Clark H., ed. *The Grace of God, The Will of Man: A Case for Arminianism*. Grand Rapids: Academie Books/ Zondervan, 1989.

Pinnock, Clark H., and John D. Wagner, eds. *Grace for All: The Arminian Dynamics of Salvation*. Eugene: Pickwick, 2015.

Pinnock, Clark H., ed. *Grace Unlimited*. Minneapolis: Bethany House, 1975.

Pinson, J. Matthew. *Arminian and Baptist*. Nashville: Randall House, 2015.

Punt, Neal. *What's Good About the Good News?* Chicago: Northland Press, 1988.

Ramsey, Willie. *Debate Notes on Baptist Doctrines*. Somerset: Willie Ramsey, 2010.

Rice, John R. *Hyper-Calvinism: A False Doctrine*. Murfreesboro, Tenn.: Sword of the Lord. 1970.

Rice, John R. *Predestined for Hell? No!* Murfreesboro: Sword of the Lord Foundation, 1958/1977.

Richardson, Byron P. *God Forbid*. Self-published, 1943.

Robinson, Michael D. *The Storms of Providence: Navigating the Waters of Calvinism, Arminianism, and Open Theism*. Lanham: University Press of America, 2003.

Rogers, Ronnie W. *Reflections of a Disenchanted Calvinist*. Bloomington: WestBow Press, 2016.

Ruckman, Peter S. *Hyper-Calvinism*. Pensacola: Bible Baptist Bookstore, 1984.

Ruckman, Peter S. *Why I Am Not a Calvinist*. Pensacola: Bible Baptist Bookstore, 1997.

Salza, John. *The Mystery of Predestination*. Charlotte: TAN Books, 2010. (Roman Catholic).

Schonberg, David. *Is Calvinism "Good News"?* Maitland, FL: Xulon, 2012.

Shank, Robert. *Elect in the Son*. Springfield, MO: Westcott Publishers, 1970.

Shank, Robert. *Life in the Son*. 2nd ed. Springfield, MO: Westcott Publishers, 1972.

Slaatte, Howard A. *The Arminian Arm of Theology*. Washington, D.C.: University Press of America, 1977.

Smelley, Hutson. *Deconstructing Calvinism*. Rev. ed. N.p.: Xulon, 2011.

Stam, Cornelius R. *Divine Election and Human Responsibility*. Chicago: Berean Bible Society, 1994.

Stanglin Keith D., Mark G. Bilby, and Mark H. Mann, eds. *Reconsidering Arminianism*. Nashville: Kingswood Books, 2014.

Sumner, Robert L. *An Examination of Tulip*. Murfreesboro, Tenn.: Biblical Evangelism Press, 1972.

Telford, Matthew. *Subjects of Sovereignty*. Acworth: Harvest Time Ministries, 1980.

Thiessen, Henry C. *Lectures in Systematic Theology*. Grand Rapids: Eerdmans, 1949.

Thornhill, A. Chadwick. *The Chosen People: Election, Paul and Second Temple Judaism*. Downers Grove, IL: IVP Academic, 2015.

Thorsen, Don. *Calvin Vs. Wesley*. Nashville: Abingdon Press, 2013.

Vance, Laurence M. *The Other Side of Calvinism*. Rev. ed. Pensacola: Vance Publications, 1999.

Voss, William B. *Free Will in the Bible*. N.p.: Selah Publishing Group, 2001.

Walls, Jerry L. *Does God Love Everyone?* Eugene: Cascade Books: 2016.

Walls, Jerry L., and Joseph R. Dongell. *Why*

I Am Not a Calvinist. Downers Grove, IL: InterVarsity Press, 2004.

Walther, C. F. W. *Walther's Works: All Glory to God*. Saint Louis: Concordia Publishing House, 2016.

Ward, Dudley. *Programmed by God or Free to Choose?* Eugene: Resource Publications, 2008.

Welsey, John. *The Works of John Wesley*, 13:201–570. Edited by Paul Wesley Chilcote and Kenneth J. Collins. Nashville: Abingdon, 2013.

Wiley, H. Orton. *Christian Theology*. 3 vols. Kansas City: Beacon Hill Press of Kansas City, 1940.

Wilkinson, David B. *Election and Predestination: Bridal Blessings*. Fort St. James: David B. Wilkinson, 1983.

Wilson, Paul. *The Sovereignty of God and Man's Responsibility or Arminianism vs. Calvinism*. Oak Park, IL: Bible Truth Publishers, 1975.

Witherington, Ben, III. *The Problem with Evangelical Theology*. Waco: Baylor University Press, 2005.

Yates, Bruce. *Beyond Calvinism*. Ft. Bragg: By the Author, 1993.

Younce, Max D. *Not Chosen to Salvation*. Madison: By the Author, n.d.

Practical Applications of Calvinism

Adams, Jay. *Counselling and the Five Points of Calvinism*. Phillipsburg, NJ: Presbyterian and Reformed, 1981.

Adams, Jay. *Lectures on Counselling*, 59–72. Grand Rapids: Baker Book House, 1978.

Alexander, Archibald. *Thoughts on Religious Experience*. Edinburgh: Banner of Truth, 1978.

Beeke, Joel R., and Mark Jones. *A Puritan Theology*, 843–971. Grand Rapids: Reformation Heritage Books, 2012.

Boettner, Loraine. *The Reformed Doctrine of Predestination*, 327–62. Philadelphia: Presbyterian and Reformed, 1932.

Boice, James Montgomery, and Philip Graham Ryken. *The Doctrines of Grace*, 179–226. Wheaton: Crossway, 2002.

Calvin, John. *The Golden Booklet of the True Christian Life*. Grand Rapids: Baker Book House, 1953.

Cunningham, William. *The Reformers and the Theology of the Reformation*, 525–608. Edinburgh: Banner of Truth, 1979.

Custance, Arthur C. *The Sovereignty of Grace*, 227–74. Phillipsburg, NJ: Presbyterian and Reformed, 1979.

Dutcher, Greg. *Killing Calvinism: How to Destroy a Perfectly Good Theology from the Inside*. Adelphi: Cruciform Press, 2012.

Edwards, Jonathan. "A Treatise on Religious Affections." In *The Works of Jonathan Edwards, Volume 2*. New Haven: Yale University Press, 1959.

Forster, Greg. *The Joy of Calvinism*. Wheaton: Crossway, 2012.

Ferguson, Sinclair B. "Reformed Theology — Reformed Lifestyle." In *Some Pastors and Teachers*, 553–78. Edinburgh: Banner of Truth, 2017.

Hamilton, Ian. *What is Experiential Calvinism?* Grand Rapids: Reformation Heritage Books, 2015.

Horton, Michael S. *Calvin on the Christian Life*. Wheaton: Crossway, 2014.

Horton, Michael S. *For Calvinism*, 124–50. Grand Rapids: Zondervan, 2011.

Horton, Michael S. *Putting Amazing Back into Grace*, 87–107. Grand Rapids: Baker, 1994.

Johnson, Terry L. *When Grace Comes Home: The Practical Difference that Calvinism Makes*. Fearn: Christian Focus, 2000.

Kuyper, Abraham. *Lectures on Calvinism*. Grand Rapids: Eerdmans, 1931.

Leith, John H. *John Calvin's Doctrine of the Christian Life*. Louisville: Westminster John Knox Press, 1989.

Martin, Albert M. *The Practical Implications*

of Calvinism. Edinburgh: Banner of Truth, 1979.

Medders, J.A. *Humble Calvinism*. N.p.: The Good Book Company, 2019.

Nettles, Thomas J. *By His Grace and For His Glory*, 387–463. Rev. ed. Cape Coral, FL: Founders Press, 2006.

Packer, J. I. *A Quest for Godliness: The Puritan Vision of the Christian Life*. Westchester: Crossway, 1990.

Parsons, Burk, ed. *John Calvin: A Heart for Devotion, Doctrine & Doxology*. Orlando: Reformation Trust, 2008.

Pink, Arthur W. *The Sovereignty of God*, 221–36. Grand Rapids: Baker Book House, 1973.

Pipa, Joseph A., Jr., and J. Andrew Wortman, eds. *Reformed Spirituality: Communing with Our Glorious God*. Taylors: Southern Presbyterian Press, 2003.

Piper, John. *Desiring God*. Portland: Multnomah, 1986.

Piper, John. *Future Grace*. Sisters, OR: Multnomah, 1995.

Reed, R. C. *The Gospel as Taught by Calvin*, 123–46. Edinburgh: Banner of Truth, 2009.

Rice, N. L. *God Sovereign and Man Free*, 179–93, 212–25. Harrisonburg, VA: Sprinkle Publications, 1985.

Ryken, Philip Graham. *What is a True Calvinist?* Phillipsburg, NJ: P&R, 2003.

Schreiner, Thomas R., and Bruce A. Ware, eds. *The Grace of God, The Bondage of the Will*, 1:203–48. Grand Rapids: Baker, 1995.

Spurgeon, Charles Haddon. "Preaching the Doctrines of Grace." In *C. H. Spurgeon's Forgotten College Addresses*, 161–70. Edited by Terence Peter Crosby. Leominster: DayOne, 2016.

Storms, Sam. *One Thing: Developing a Passion for the Beauty of God*. Fearn: Christian Focus, 2004.

Storms, Sam. *Pleasures Evermore: The Life-Changing Power of Enjoying God*. Colorado Springs: NavPress, 2000.

Warburton, Ben A. *Calvinism*, 189–248. Grand Rapids: Eerdmans, 1955.

Reformed Confessions of Faith

Barth, Karl. *Theology of the Reformed Confessions*. Louisville: Westminster John Knox Press, 2002.

Beeke, Joel R., and Sinclair B. Ferguson, eds. *Reformed Confessions Harmonized*. Grand Rapids: Baker Books, 1999.

Bierma, Lyle D., et al. *An Introduction to the Heidelberg Catechism*. Grand Rapids: Baker Academic, 2005.

Book of Confessions: Study Edition. Louisville: Geneva Press, 1999.

Broadus, John A. *Baptist Confessions, Covenants, and Catechisms*. Nashville: Broadman and Holman, 1996.

Cochrane, Arthur C. *Reformed Confessions of the 16th Century*. Philadelphia: Westminster Press, 1966.

The Confession of Faith: The Confession of Faith, The Larger and Shorter Catechisms, The Directory for the Public Worship of God, With Associated Historical Documents. Edinburgh: Banner of Truth, 2018.

The Confession of Faith, The Larger and Shorter Catechisms with the Scripture-Proofs at Large, Together with The Sum of Saving Knowledge. Glasgow: Free Presbyterian Publications, 1973.

Dennison, James T., Jr., ed. *Reformed Confessions of the 16th and 17th Centuries in English Translation*. 4 vols. Grand Rapids: Reformation Heritage Books, 2010.

The Doctrinal Standards, Liturgy, and Church Order of the Netherlands Reformed Congregations. Sioux Center: Netherlands Reformed Book and Publishing Committee, 1991.

Duncan, J. Ligon, III, ed. *The Westminster Confession into the 21st Century*. 3 vols. Fearn: Mentor, 2003.

Ecumenical Creeds and Reformed Confessions. Grand Rapids: CRG Publications, 1988.

Hall, Peter, ed. *The Harmony of Protestant Confessions.* Edmonton: Still Waters Revival Books, n.d.

Leith, John H., ed. *Creeds of the Churches*, 127–323. Atlanta: John Knox Press, 1977.

Lumpkin, W. L. *Baptist Confessions of Faith.* Valley Forge: Judson Press, 1969.

Melton, J. Gordon, ed. *The Encyclopedia of American Religions: Religious Creeds*, 163–255. Detroit: Gale Research Company, 1988.

Muller, Richard A. "Reformed Confessions and Catechisms." In Trevor A. Hart, ed. *The Dictionary of Historical Theology*, 466–85. Grand Rapids: Eerdmans, 2000.

Niesel, Wilhelm. *Reformed Symbolics.* Edinburgh: Oliver and Boyd, 1962.

Nixon, Leroy, ed. *Reformed Standards of Unity.* Grand Rapids: Society for Reformed Publishing, 1952.

Noll, Mark A., ed. *Confessions and Catechisms of the Reformation.* Grand Rapids: Baker Book House, 1991.

Pelikan, Jaroslav and Valerie Hotchkiss, eds. *Creeds and Confessions of Faith in the Christian Tradition*, 2:205–662. New Haven: Yale University Press, 2003.

Pipa, Joseph A., Jr. *The Westminster Confession of Faith Study Book.* Fearn: Christian Focus, 2005.

Plantinga, Cornelius, Jr. *A Place to Stand: A Study in Ecumenical Creeds and Reformed Confessions.* Grand Rapids: Board of Publications of the Christian Reformed Church, 1981.

Renihan, James M., ed. *True Confessions: Baptist Documents in the Reformed Family.* Owensboro: RBAP, 2004.

Rogers, Jack. *Presbyterian Creeds: A Guide to the Book of Confessions.* Philadelphia: Westminster Press, 1985.

Rohls, Jan. *Reformed Confessions.* Louisville: Westminster John Knox Press, 1998.

Schaff, Philip. *The Creeds of Christendom.* 3 vols. Grand Rapids: Baker Book House, 1966.

Scott, Thomas. *The Articles of the Synod of Dort.* Harrisonburg, VA: Sprinkle Publications, 1993.

Shedd, William G. T. *A History of Christian Doctrine*, 2:485–91. Eugene: Wipf and Stock, 1998.

Skilton, John H., ed. *Scripture and Confession.* Phillipsburg, NJ: Presbyterian and Reformed, 1973.

Torrance, Thomas F., ed. *The School of Faith.* London: James Clarke, 1959.

Van Dixhoorn, Chad, ed. *The Minutes and Papers of the Westminster Assembly, 1643–1653.* 5 vols. Oxford: Oxford University Press, 2012.

Vischer, Lukas, ed. *Reformed Witness Today: A Collection of Confessions and Statements of Faith Issued by Reformed Churches.* Bern: Evangelische Arbeitsstelle Oekumene Schweig, 1982.

Scripture Index

Romans

1 **Corinthians**

Index of Names

A

Abbot, George, Archbishop of
  Canterbury   73, 77, 495
Abelard, Peter   40, 228, 503
Adams, Jay   129, 259, 263, 294, 395, 690
Adams, Thomas   78
Agricola, Johann   650
Ainsworth, Henry   81
Akagi, Yoshimitsu   178
Aldersen, Richard   607
Alexander, Archibald   126, 128
Alexander, Eric   169
Alexander, James W.   126–127
Alexander, Joseph Addison   127
Alexander, W. Lindsey   143
Alleine, Joseph   80, 391, 692
Alleine, Richard   80
Allen, David L.   371, 507, 707
Allis, Oswald T.   128, 129
Alsted, Johann Heinrich   67
Alston, William   687
Ambrose (Aurelius Ambrosius)   34,
  494, 700
Ambrose, Isaac   78
Ames, William   56, 64, 65, 67, 68, 77,
  199, 389, 405, 446, 496, 710
Amyraut, Moyse   79, 93–98, 162, 228,
  481, 493, 664
Anderson, James William   579
Anselm (of Canterbury)   40, 314, 464,
  503, 509
Anyabwile, Thabiti   164
Aquinas, Thomas   40, 67, 69, 216, 470,
  487, 533, 682, 684

Aretius, Benedict   67
Aristotle   67, 68, 69, 201, 217, 533
Arminius, Jacob   61, 61–62, 63,
  71, 149, 152, 243, 395, 507, 603, 700, 701,
  702, 703, 707, 709
Armstrong, Brian   74, 97
Armstrong, William Park   128
Arnauld, Antoine   72
Arrowsmith, John   89, 94, 493
Ascol, Thomas   161
Asselt, Willem van   172
Atherton, Henry   104, 167
Aubigne, J. H. Merle d'   138
Augustine (of Hippo)   19,
  25, 26, 27, 33, 34, 35, 36, 37, 38, 39, 40, 41,
  42, 43, 48, 52, 67, 72, 84, 153, 202, 204,
  205, 206, 240, 241, 242, 246, 247, 250,
  261, 262, 265, 266, 268, 272, 273, 279,
  284, 291, 295, 310, 316, 317, 318, 323, 324,
  329, 342, 355, 367, 375, 376, 383, 384, 395,
  398, 403, 410, 418, 423, 443, 449, 458,
  464, 467, 470, 471, 478, 492, 494, 540,
  553, 555, 556, 557, 558, 589, 592, 624, 629,
  632, 636, 698, 700, 703, 705, 706, 712,
  714, 719, 721, 723, 724, 725, 727
Aurelius Augustinus. *See* Augustine (of
  Hippo)

B

Babbage, Stuart Barton   177
Backus, Irena   175
Backus, Isaac   135
Bahnsen, Greg   158, 444, 651, 685
Baillie, Donald   150

C